D1260089

MAR   2011

THE SINEWS OF WAR
ARMY LOGISTICS
1775–1953

by
James A. Huston

Unversity Press of the Pacific
Honolulu, Hawaii

The Sinews of War:
Army Logistics, 1775 - 1953

by
James A. Huston

ISBN: 1-4102-1368-4

Reprinted from the 1966 edition

University Press of the Pacific
Honolulu, Hawaii
http://www.universitypressofthepacific.com

Foreword

The Sinews of War, the second volume published in THE ARMY HIS-
TORICAL SERIES, pioneers in a field long neglected. Logistics is a subject
which few people, including professional soldiers, have thoroughly understood.
Yet logistics must support both tactical operations and the day-to-day life of the
Army in the same way that a well-run household supports the people who
live in it.

Professor Huston, who has served in tactical units in wartime and has studied
logistics in both war and peace, as a military man and a civilian has prepared
a clear and comprehensive history of U.S. Army logistics from the time of the American Revolution through the Korean War. He shows the role of all aspects of
logistics—supply; transportation; evacuation and hospitalization; and service—
in peace and in war, and in systematic fashion traces the development of the
Army's logistical system.

The Sinews of War is offered to professional military men in all the armed
services, and to thoughtful students of problems of national defense, as an essential
contribution to their education.

Washington, D.C.
24 September 1965

HAL C. PATTISON
Brigadier General, USA
Chief of Military History

The Author

Dr. James A. Huston, professor of history at Purdue University, received A.B. and A.M. degrees from Indiana University, and the Ph.D. from New York University. He has done graduate work at Oxford University and at the University of Fribourg. He has been the Ernest J. King Professor of Maritime History at the Naval War College and a NATO Fellow. In the summer of 1965 Dr. Huston was Director for the National Defense Education Act History Institute held at Purdue University. For the academic year 1966–67 he was a member of the faculty at the National War College, Washington, D.C.

Dr. Huston served with the 134th Infantry in the European Theater of Operations during World War II as a rifle battalion operations officer and is now a colonel of Infantry in the Active Reserve. He is the author of *Combat History of the 134th Infantry, Biography of a Battalion,* and *Across the Face of France,* as well as numerous articles on military and international affairs.

Preface

This work is the result of a suggestion by Lt. Gen. Williston B. Palmer, formerly Deputy Chief of Staff for Logistics and subsequently Vice Chief of Staff, that there is a need for a general historical survey of U.S. Army logistics. It is intended to contribute a better understanding of the significance of logistics in the American military experience, and to an appreciation of some of the Army's logistical problems in its conduct of war from the Revolutionary War through the Korean War.

Logistics covers a vast range of subjects, and one could not hope to cover them all within the limits of space available here. The word logistics came into general military use shortly before World War I but has been popular only since shortly before World War II, although its substance has been of concern as long as there have been armies. In Army usage it has come to include four principal elements in the support of military operations: (1) supply, including determination of requirements, procurement, and distribution; (2) transportation; (3) evacuation and hospitalization; and (4) service.

A dictionary definition of logistics in the mid-1930's (substantially the same as a dictionary definition of 1916) was: "The branch of military science dealing with the moving, quartering, and provisioning of armies." *The Dictionary of United States Army Terms* in 1944 defined logistics as "the art of planning and carrying out military movement, evacuation and supply." From that point various people, like Humpty Dumpty, began making it mean whatever they wanted it to mean. The Navy tended to give it a broader application; headquarters and staff agencies defined it to correspond with their own functions. By 1950 it had reached the ultimate when it was given an official definition in the *Dictionary of United States Military Terms for Joint Usage* to include virtually all military activity other than strategy and tactics. By 1957 the term had returned more closely to the traditional Army usage:

In its most comprehensive sense, those aspects of military operations which deal with: (1) Design and development, acquisition, storage, movement, distribution, maintenance, evacuation and disposition of matériel; (2) movement, evacuation and hospitalization of personnel; (3) acquisition or construction, maintenance, operation, and disposition of facilities; and (4) acquisition or furnishing of services.

Finally the definition given in the Army's *Field Service Regulations* (1949) is useful: "Logistics is that branch of administration which embraces the management and provision of supply, evacuation and hospitalization, transportation, and service. It envisages getting the right people and the appropriate supplies to the right place at the right time and in the proper condition." [1]

In short, logistics is the application of time and space factors to war. It is the economics of warfare, and it comprises, in the broadest sense, the three big M's of warfare—*matériel, movement,* and *maintenance.* If international politics is the "art of the possible," and war is its instrument, logistics is the art of defining and extending the possible. It provides the substance that physically permits an army to "live and move and have its being."

Something of the broad application of logistics may be seen in a summary of the responsibilities and functions of the Assistant Chief of Staff, G–4, as of 1950: (1) *direction:* directed and controlled the Technical Services; (2) *plans:* planned for logistical support of the Army in time of war, for keeping the Army abreast of scientific advancement, and for procurement, supply and services; (3) *research:* supervised Technical Service activities in applied and basic research on problems affecting the Army; (4) *development:* prepared, or directed the preparation of, studies, designs and tests for the improvement of equipment and weapons; (5) *tripartite standardization:* supervised the Army program for standardization in military procedures, administration, and production and interchangeability of equipment and parts with Canada and Great Britain; (6) *procurement:* obtained the weapons, equipment, and supplies currently needed in the Army; (7) *standards:* prescribed and codified specifications of materials and supplies to insure uniformity both in manufacture and in quality; (8) *cataloging:* developed a uniform means of identifying, classifying, and listing for items provided and distributed by the Army; (9) *requirements: computed* and analyzed needs and apportioned goods according to funding programs, relative priorities of demands, availability and other limiting factors; (10) *foreign aid:* supervised the Army's part in national programs for providing miltary equipment and civilian supplies for friendly foreign countries; (11) *distribution:* supervised the storage and distribution of equipment and supplies; (12) *maintenance:* supervised the upkeep of equipment to prolong its usefulness as much as possible; (13) *installations:* supervised the acquisition, disposal, construction, and maintenance of Army command and supply installations; (14) *movements:* supervised the movement of troops as well as of supplies; (15) *services:* supervised other services such as medical care, communications, and food service.[2]

---

[1] For an interesting and thoughtful discussion of the evolution in usage of the term "logistics," see introductory essay, "Logistics—The Word and the Thing," in Richard M. Leighton and Robert W. Coakley, *Global Logistics and Strategy, 1940–1943,* UNITED STATES ARMY IN WORLD WAR II (Washington, 1955), pp. 3–17. One of the first to use the word "logistics" in a book in America was Henry B. Carrington in *Battles of the American Revolution, 1775–1781* (New York, 1876). See also George C. Dyer, *Naval Logistics* (Annapolis, 1960), pp. 3–14.

[2] Lt. Gen. Thomas B. Larkin, "The Logistics Division," *The Quartermaster Review,* XXIX (March–April, 1950), 2–3.

History sometimes yields lessons of direct applicability which too often go unrecognized and unheeded, and sometimes are deliberately ignored—presumably on the naive assumption that "this time everything is different." People who have studied the records, or who have actually participated in the industrial mobilization and procurement activities of World War I and World War II, for instance, never cease to be amazed at how the lessons of the first were ignored in the second, and how frequently the same mistakes were repeated. Apparently some people carry a conviction that too much attention to the past will somehow limit flexibility in dealing with the present. On the contrary, history provides perspective for the judgment of ideas, policies, and procedures. How can one tell if a new idea is a good one, or indeed even if it is new, if there is no basis for comparison? Actually, a much more important contribution of history than its direct lessons is the pool of vicarious experience which it provides—experience which is the raw material of imagination. Adaptability, innovation, improvisation, and bold schemes depend upon imagination. It is a function of military history to provide rich experience out of which imaginative leaders will create new methods to meet new situations. Today, as a basis for decisions of public policy and military action, civilians as well as the military require some experience in military logistics.

The purpose of this work is to provide an introduction to some of that experience. In developing perspective it is necessary to guard against the danger of substituting apparent logic for fact, and permitting time to sanctify hasty judgments. Furthermore, it is necessary to guard against permitting the spectacular to overshadow the essential. Perspective requires that important logistical implications be spelled out. Too often in military history one is disposed to follow in close detail the movements of corps and divisions and companies on the battlefield without inquiring how they got there. Great armies appear, full-blown, from nowhere, do battle, then disappear. If they are to be brought to life, we must see how they lived.

No attempt has been made to cover the whole range of logistical matters, or even to cover completely any single aspect of logistics. Rather, the method has been to include a number of details by way of examples chosen for their significance or relevance—though often limited by the nature of the source material—putting them in their proper setting, so that altogether one may get some comprehension of the whole. In studying logistical history our problem is to do what Matthew Arnold attributed to Sophocles: he ". . . saw life steadily, and saw it whole."

In the attempt we keep before us these words from a report of the Meade Committee in 1945: "In the future there will be no excuse for repeating the mistakes about which we learned through the painful process of experience." And these words of General Omar N. Bradley: "And the shadow of military conflict . . . constantly hangs over us and our friends. . . . As long as the Communist doctrine seeks world-wide domination, this conflict will continue unabated.

We Americans must face this fact realistically and in our plans and programs— economic and political, psychological and military—consider carefully the time and space factors in this long-range struggle."

Special acknowledgment is due in the first instance to General Palmer who suggested that a study of U.S. Army logistics be undertaken, and to those who greeted the suggestion with sufficient interest, imagination, and faith to agree that it should be attempted—Maj. Gen. Orlando Ward who then was Chief of Military History; Dr. Kent Roberts Greenfield, then Chief Historian; Brig. Gen. (then Colonel) George C. O'Connor who was Chief of the War Histories Division; and Cols. Carl D. McFerren and Leo J. Meyer who also were members of the staff of the Office of the Chief of Military History and participated in the initial planning. In the research and writing, I have been most indebted to the pointed suggestions and helpful guidance of Dr. Greenfield; of Dr. Stetson Conn, first as Deputy and later as Chief Historian; and to Dr. John Miller, jr., who as Deputy Chief Historian, had the most direct contact with the work. They have made this an exciting adventure in higher education. These efforts have been made possible through the continuing interest of the succession of Chiefs of Military History who followed General Ward: Maj. Gens. Albert C. Smith, John H. Stokes, Jr., and Richard W. Stephens, and Brig. Gens. James A. Norell, William H. Harris, and Hal C. Pattison.

Others who have given the benefit of their expert knowledge in reading all or parts of the manuscript and in offering invaluable suggestions include Professors Harold F. Underhill and Rocco M. Paone. Other Army historians whose counsel and knowledge guided final revisions include: Maj. C. J. Bernardo; Dr. Abe Bortz, Dr. Robert W. Coakley, Dr. Byron Fairchild, and Dr. Stanley L. Falk; Col. Seneca W. Foote; Dr. Richard M. Leighton, Dr. Louis Morton, and Dr. Erna Risch. Lt. Col. Frederick Woodward Hopkins, USMCR, made available a copy of a manuscript written by his grandfather, Brevet Major John Henry Woodward, 23d New York Volunteers, who served on the staff of the Army of the Potomac. I am especially grateful to Rear Adm. Henry E. Eccles, USN (Ret.) who read the entire manuscript, and to the late Professor Kenneth P. Williams who read the original drafts of the Civil War chapters.

I am grateful to Dr. W. L. Ayres, formerly Dean of the Purdue School of Science, Education and Humanities; to Dr. M. B. Ogle, jr., formerly head of the Department of History, Government and Philosophy, and now Dean of the School of Humanities, Social Science and Education; to Dr. Walter O. Forster, currently head of the Department; and to the officers and staff of the Purdue Research Foundation, whose encouragement and support have made possible such an undertaking on my part.

For unfailing co-operation and assistance beyond the call of duty in obtaining information and in providing study facilities I am indebted especially to Prof. John H. Moriarty, Director of the Purdue University Libraries, and to Professors Abraham Barnett, Sue Crown, Keith Dowden, Oliver Dunn, Jane Ganfield,

George Meluch, Esther Schlundt, and John Veenstra, members of his library staff. I also am indebted to Messrs. Israel Wice and Charles F. Romanus and their staff of the General Reference Branch of the Office of the Chief of Military History for their consistent helpfulness through the years. For assistance at various times I wish to thank the staffs of the Library of Congress; the National Archives; the Army Library; Yale University Library; Whitney Museum in New Haven, Conn.; Fort Ticonderoga Library and Museum; Saratoga National Battle Monument; Washington Headquarters Library and Museum at Morristown, N.J.; Library of the Naval War College at Newport, R.I.; and the U.S. Army Logistics Management Center at Fort Lee, Va.

For research, clerical, and typing assistance at various stages, special thanks are due Mrs. Enid Barnett, Mrs. Eleanor Brown Schmucker, Mrs. Genevieve Gist, Miss Nina Davidson, Miss Charlotte Peters, Mrs. Anita Elkin, Mrs. Ruth Bessmer, and Mrs. Eleanor Laishley.

I am also grateful to Mrs. Frances R. Burdette and Mrs. Loretto C. Stevens for their careful and conscientious attention to the manuscript during the editorial phases of publication; to Mr. Elliot Dunay for compiling the maps; and to Miss Ruth A. Phillips for selecting the illustrations. Mrs. Ruth Knight compiled the index.

Again, I would like to express appreciation for the faithful support of a patient family over the long haul—to Florence, Nita Diane, and Jimmie Jacques.

The advice, counsel, and assistance so generously given me have greatly aided in the preparation and completion of this book. Responsibility for all interpretations, and for any deficiencies, is entirely mine.

Lafayette, Indiana
24 September 1965

JAMES A. HUSTON

Contents

PART ONE

The Formative Period

PART TWO

Emergence of Modern Warfare

PART THREE

Warfare Overseas

PART FOUR

Logistics of Global Warfare

PART FIVE

The Shadow of Conflict

PART SIX

The Uses of Logistical Experience

Charts

Table

Maps

Illustrations

Illustrations in this book are from Department of Defense files with the following exceptions: the picture on page 20 was obtained from the Library of Congress; the National Archives furnished the pictures on pages 11, 41, 162, 171, 194, 196, 197, 205, 208, 212, 219, 226, 243, 287, 299, 301, and 306; and the Yale University Art Gallery furnished the picture on page 97.

PART ONE

THE FORMATIVE PERIOD

CHAPTER I

Administrative Organization For the Revolutionary War

Although the supply and transportation of military forces has never been a really simple matter, governmental administration of these activities was relatively simple during the centuries of premodern warfare when the local commander had to depend almost entirely on his own resourcefulness. Bands of mercenaries which grew up in the German states and elsewhere on the Continent from the fourteenth to the seventeenth centuries as little self-sufficient communities of men, women, and children set the pattern for military formations throughout much of Europe. Adding improvements and imperfections of their own, the British adapted the German formations to create an army for the conquest and defense of their overseas empire.

The British Example

The principal staff officer of a British field army in the eighteenth century was the quartermaster general. As a sort of chief of staff he was responsible for collecting information, for helping the commander plan his marches, for distributing march orders, and for assisting the officer designated as "major general of the day" with camp layouts and forage arrangements.

By the end of the Seven Years' War (1763), the status of the War Office in London was virtually that of a great executive department. With the assistance of the master general of ordnance, the paymaster general, and the treasurer of the Navy, the Secretary of War made up the Army estimates for submission to Parliament. Besides being responsible for troop movement orders and for proper quartering of troops, the Secretary had various duties related to supply, transportation, finances, and organization of military units.

Extreme decentralization has been both a great strength and a notable weakness of the British Government in the conduct of its Empire. The Colonial Wars in America point up the weakness rather than the strength of that policy. Colonial settlements in America were themselves "decentralized"—far removed from each other and without transportation or communications that would permit effective co-operation among them. They devoted themselves primarily to local problems and local security, and, for military defense, were disposed to go it alone. The government made no effort to draft colonists into its military forces, nor even to impose any general taxation on the colonies for the support of the common defense. In time of war the colonies were merely asked to furnish certain quotas of men and supplies, but the final decision was up to each colony. Response varied with the public conscience of the local assemblies, the capabilities of local leaders, and the proximity of the direct threat. In any case, it was assumed that the central government had no right to order colonial soldiers to fight beyond the borders of their own colonies.

At times the British Parliament reimbursed individual colonies for provisions and stores. Often the sums voted seemed calculated rather to stimulate the raising and supplying of troops than to reflect an accurate cost accounting of contributions made. During the French and Indian War the British Government undertook to supply most of the arms, ammunition, tents, and provisions for the colonial troops; the colonies were expected to raise the troops, clothe them, and pay them—for which they were reimbursed by generous grants voted by Parliament.

Possibly the most complex supply system of British troops in America was that of the Royal Regiment of Artillery, which maintained its headquarters at Boston and branch storehouses at various other places. Under the supervision of the Ordnance Board, the Royal Regiment of Artillery had to keep a complete staff—comptroller, storekeeper and paymaster, clerk of stores, and two armorers at headquarters, and assistant clerks at the branch storehouses—in America to handle all the paper work required to keep track of the artillery stores. Commanders or quartermasters of the various regiments submitted their requisitions for artillery stores to the commander in chief. If he approved, the commander in chief notified the comptroller, who in turn instructed the storekeeper to issue the required supplies and equipment. The storekeeper received a receipt from the person to whom he issued the articles which he entered on

duplicate forms and in a ledger. The large number of items included on ordnance lists involved a great deal of record-keeping to account for receipts and issues. In addition to such obvious things as powder and shot, ordnance supplies included tarpaulins, leather buckets, tallow candles, scales, copper nails, priming wires, scissors, dragropes, and other articles needed to keep weapons firing. It is estimated that 4,194 horses (including 571 for the guns) and 1,000 wagons would have been needed to move by land the artillery and ordnance train required for Lord Loudon's abortive expeditions against Louisburg in 1757.

Colonial Militia

As in England, the militia system in all the colonies was based on the principle of the assize of arms; accordingly, all men were required to have arms and ammunition. Men who were able to purchase them were supposed to do so; those unable to buy them received weapons from the town, the purchase price repayable to the town as soon as possible. In Maryland, if a hired servant was unable to provide his own arms when called for military service, his master was required either to furnish the necessary arms and equipment or to serve himself in place of the servant. Men who failed to arm themselves were subject to fines or other punishment. Money from fines went into military unit funds for the purchase of drums, flags, and other extras.

Infantry units of the early colonial period followed the European pattern of two-thirds musketeers and one-third pikemen. Each pikeman was required to have a pike, corselet, headpiece, sword, and knapsack. The musketeer had to have a good musket (at this time usually a matchlock), a priming wire, scourer and mould, rest, sword, bandoleers, one pound of powder, twenty bullets, and twelve feet of match—a cord soaked in saltpetre. In Maryland after 1668 each man had to provide himself with fire-arms, sword, two pounds of powder, six pounds of shot, and four flints, and every sixth man had to carry an axe for felling trees.

The equipping of cavalry troops called for greater expense; only the well-to-do could afford to enlist in the mounted units. Under a law of 1648, each trooper in Massachusetts had to have a horse, bridle and saddle, sword belt, a carbine in a belt, or a case of pistols with holsters, a pound of powder, and twenty bullets. In 1668 the Governor of New York, when authorizing the enlistment of a cavalry troop, agreed to supply horses and equipment for those men unable to provide their own.

Each militia company was under the direction of locally elected captains, lieutenants, sergeants, and ensigns. Cavalry troops had, in addition, a cornet and a quartermaster. A key official of each company of the militia system was the clerk of the band who kept the lists of men subject to military service. All males between the ages of sixteen and sixty, with certain exceptions, were required to present themselves properly armed and equipped for training or inspection at appointed times and places.

The semblance of a general staff officer for supply was to be found in early Massachusetts, designated at first the Surveyor of Ordnance, later the Surveyor General of Arms. It appears that the office was filled at different times by a civilian, by a military officer, and by a commission. The Surveyor General of Arms was responsible to the General Court of the colony for de-livering powder and ammunition to the towns, and for receiving from them any excess stocks. It was up to him to recover arms loaned to towns or individuals, or to obtain payment and buy other weapons to replace them. He made purchases in cooperation with the treasurer. The towns were required to report the quantities of powder they had in stock to the Surveyor General of Arms, who prepared reports on the status of supply to guide the General Court in authorizing further purchases or in seeking arms from England. The colonial government frequently appointed committees to inspect his records.

Neither in Massachusetts nor in any of the other colonies was there a permanent commissary general or quartermaster to look after supplies of food, camp equipment, clothing, and transportation. These officers were appointed only when necessary for a particular expedition or campaign. Two men appointed commissaries for a Massachusetts force of 200 men sent to the aid of the Mohegans against the Narragansett Indians in 1645 prepared a list of provisions that included bread, salted beef, fish, peas, oatmeal, flour, butter, oil, vinegar, sugar, rum, and beer. The Massachusetts General Court at that time adopted a rule that when it was not in session the assistants or magistrates were authorized to send out soldiers to impress food supplies, carriages, vessels, and other necessary supplies and equipment, and to send warrants to the treasurer for payment.

The colonial militia had no uniforms, so that was no problem. Some of the Virginia companies were provided with medieval suits of armor brought over from England—until they were seen to be completely impractical for chasing naked Indians through the forest. On the march the men seldom used tents, and the companies had only small baggage trains or none at all. For the ordinary short expeditions against hostile Indians, the colonials carried their own arms and ammunition, blankets, and some food, cooked or uncooked.

Central Administration:
The Board of War

When the American colonies took up arms against Great Britain, it was to be expected that the military systems they would employ, including arrangements for logistical support, would be patterned after those with which they had become familiar while supporting the mother country in the intercolonial and Indian wars. Thus the weaknesses in central control that had characterized British colonial military efforts continued to plague the colonists as they battled for independent existence.

General high-level administration in the country was handicapped from the outset by the lack of any central executive authority. Direction of the war effort fell to the Continental Congress and to the thirteen colonies and the Congress attempted to administer the Continental Army through committees and boards. Weeks or months of discussion and debate frequently produced only costly delays. When a decision was made, the Congress often lacked the power to act decisively. The situation was not so much due to the rascality or inefficiency of any individual or group as it was to the historical position of the colonies. Efforts at centralization of defense and enlistment of colonial support for the burden of defense was the rock against which the British Empire was breaking. It hardly was to be expected that the colonies would at once grant to a congress, even of their own rep-

resentatives, powers for regulating a common defense which they were determined to deny to Parliament even at the expense of war. As a result, fourteen logistical systems—one for each of the colonies to the extent that each participated, plus that of the Continental Congress—attempted to mount a war effort.

In November 1775 Congress appointed a committee to consult with General Washington as to how continued regulation and support of the Continental Army might best be accomplished. Then in January 1776 a Congressional committee took up the question of establishing a war office. After five months of deliberation it offered a plan in keeping with the policy of limited authority and Congressional supremacy which inspired the country's representatives of the times. The plan provided for establishment of a Board of War and Ordnance to act as the executive agent of Congress for military affairs. As first organized (less than a month before the Declaration of Independence) the board was made up of five members of the Continental Congress and a paid secretary and clerks. Its duties were: supervision of raising, equipping, and dispatching troops; accounting for arms, ammunition, and equipment; storage of equipment not in use; maintenance of personnel records; and transmission of funds and communications as directed by Congress.

With John Adams as its first president and Richard Peters as permanent secretary, the board customarily met every morning and evening. While the members probably were conscientious and hard-working, none was experienced in military administration, and all labored under the burden of the other legislative and political responsibilities which they carried as members of Congress.

The principle of civilian supremacy was so well established that it appeared at times that the military would not even be strong enough to field an army. In the political climate of revolution, when every precaution had to be taken lest one tyranny give way to another and greater, shortcomings that otherwise might have seemed obvious remained in the system until the errors of early trials pointed to the immediate prospect that without changes the war and hopes for independence might be lost.

When the Board of War and Ordnance quickly gave indications of its incapacity to carry out satisfactorily the duties assigned to it, the first step toward improvement seemed to be a reorganization so that its members would be military experts able to devote their full attention to its business. But first a Congressional committee had to study the matter. It deliberated from December 1776 to July 1777; then reached the obvious solution which Congress adopted in October 1777. The new Board of War was made up of three persons who were not members of Congress and a secretary and such clerks as were necessary. The powers and duties of the new board were expanded to some extent to make explicit the board's responsibility for accounting for all clothing, medicines, and provisions, as well as ordnance belonging to the United States, and for preparing for Congress estimates of required military supplies and equipment. It had the further responsibility of supervising the building and management of arsenals, foundries, magazines, barracks, laboratories, and other public buildings needed for military purposes. The way was opened to bring in men experienced in military affairs to direct the war effort of what had become the "United States." Although this arrangement had undoubted advantages over the previous Congressional committees, in operation it revealed some striking weaknesses of its own.

These weaknesses related first of all to its membership. Original appointees to the new board were Maj. Gen. Thomas Mifflin, Col. Timothy Pickering, and Col. Robert H. Harrison. Colonel Harrison declined to serve. The appointments were made on 6 November. Three weeks later Congress expanded the board to five members, and added Maj. Gen. Horatio Gates, who became president, Joseph Trumbull, and Richard Peters, secretary of the old board. The men chosen were able enough and experienced in the business, but they did not fit well into the scheme of things at the moment. Gates had served under Washington at Cambridge, and recently had become a national hero after the victory at Saratoga, but he had permitted himself to become the champion of groups hostile to the commander in chief. Mifflin had just resigned as Quartermaster General, and he had become highly critical of Washington. Trumbull had recently resigned as Commissary General, and was in such ill health that he was unable to serve. Pickering and Peters were not particularly friendly toward Washington. Perhaps the Board of War seemed a good place to assign officers who had become disgruntled or disappointed elsewhere. As an agency of the Congress its make-up was likely to represent the divisions and the compromises found in Congress itself. At any rate Washington could hardly count upon enthusiastic support from a board whose membership was so heavily weighted against him. When Congress, at the suggestion of Washington, resolved to send a committee to the camp at Valley Forge to consult on what steps might be taken to improve conditions, and appointed Gates, Mifflin, and Pickering to the committee, each found reasons why he could not go.

By 1778 it was becoming difficult to find men willing to serve on the Board of War. In October its character was modified somewhat to include two members of Congress and three commissioners not members of Congress, but it remained essentially the same until at last it was superseded in 1781 by a war office.

The Military Staff

In resolutions of June and July 1775 the Continental Congress provided for the rudiments of a staff to administer particular aspects of the military establishment. On 16 June it passed legislation authorizing an Adjutant General, a Commissary General of Stores and Provisions, Quartermaster General, Paymaster General, Commissary General of Musters, and Chief Engineer for the Army. In July the Congress established a "hospital" (medical department), provided for a Barrack Master, and authorized a Commissary of Artillery. By the end of 1777 a Commissary General of Military Stores, a Commissary of Forage (under the Quartermaster General), a Commissary of Hides, and a Clothier General had been added. Co-ordination over these offices remained loose, at least until 1779 when all in greater or lesser degree were brought under the supervisory control of the Board of War. Even so, the administrative structure remained decentralized along functional lines. No single senior officer was responsible for the co-ordination of the various chiefs and commissaries.

The Commissary Departments

The instructions Congress approved on 20 June 1775 for Washington's guidance as

commander in chief stated: "You are to victual at the continental expense all such volunteers as have joined or shall join the united Army." [1] Congress provided for a Commissary General of Stores and Provisions to carry out the detailed tasks of supplying the Army, but it did not specify what kind of organization his department should have. On Washington's initiative and with Congressional approval, Joseph Trumbull, who had been serving as commissary for Connecticut, became the first Commissary General. Aside from prescribing a temporary ration, Washington had no instructions for him. While Trumbull's principal job was to organize the procurement and distribution of food supplies, frequently he found it necessary to go into the matter of obtaining transportation—actually the duty of the Quartermaster General—in order to make deliveries. After further studies an investigating committee came in with a recommendation which Congress approved on 10 June 1777 to divide the Commissary Department into two departments: if the whole business of supplying provisions for the Army was too much for one man to supervise, then perhaps two could do it better. A Commissary General of Purchases with four deputies and a Commissary General of Issues with three deputies were to be chosen by the Congress. The deputies had authority to appoint assistants as needed. The principle of restricting each purchasing agent to a specified district was introduced. An assistant of the Issues Department was to be stationed at every fort, post, magazine, or other place where provisions might be stored.

It was the intention of Congress to have

[1] Worthington C Ford and others, eds., *Journals of the Continental Congress*, 34 vols (Washington, 1904–1937), II, 101.

Trumbull remain as Commissary General of Purchases. But Trumbull had no sympathy with a system which permitted Congress to choose his deputies. Declaring that *"an imperium in imperio"* was being created, within a few weeks he resigned. In spite of shortcomings and obstacles, Trumbull's two years of effective effort in getting a Commissary Department established merited the praises of Congress bestowed two years later, after his death, in its approval of a committee report commending his services and granting an allowance to the estate of the Commissary General.[2] His successor was William Buchanan, who in the spring of 1778 was succeeded by Col. Jeremiah Wadsworth. Charles Stewart became Commissary General of Issues.

In April 1778 Congress finally came around to Trumbull's view that the Commissary General of Purchases should control his department, and gave that officer full powers to appoint or remove any of his subordinates. At the same time a change in the system of remuneration for members of the purchasing department was made. Instead of a percentage of the expenditures an assistant purchasing commissary received a prescribed allowance, such as 6⅔ cents for each hundredweight of flour or meal purchased, 26⅔ cents for each hundredweight of salt pork, and 3⅓ cents for a gallon of West India rum. Moreover, as an incentive for saving money rather than for paying high prices, a buyer was allowed 10 percent of the amount saved by the purchase of good quality provisions at prices less than those fixed by the respective states.[3]

Reasonable as this arrangement may seem, it did not last a year. Earlier Trumbull had complained that he was being discriminated against, for he alone of his department was not paid on a commission basis. The new arrangement provided that all funds for the Purchasing Department should be distributed through the Commissary General and through the deputies to the purchasing commissaries in the various districts. The Commissary General was allowed .5 percent of all funds which he transferred to the deputy commissaries general, the deputies received a payment of .5 percent of all the funds which they transferred to the purchasing commissaries in their districts, and the purchasing commissaries received an allowance of 2 percent of all their expenditures in their respective districts.

Colonel Wadsworth tried to resign as Commissary General of Purchases in June 1779, but Congress prevailed upon him to remain until a less inexpedient time, for it was the beginning of a campaign season. Wadsworth remained until near the end of the year when Ephraim Blaine succeeded him. After his resignation, Wadsworth continued to serve in contracting supplies. In the reorganization of January 1780, the Commissary General was once more put on a regular salary, and he was to receive six rations a day and forage for six horses. The purchasing commissaries continued to receive 2 percent of their expenditures, based on a price scale twentyfold greater than the prices of 1774 to allow for the depreciated currency. In November the department underwent further reorganizations and changes in pay. Because of his reduced responsibilities the Commissary General's salary was commensurately reduced at this time. Then, by a resolution of 10 July 1781,

---

[2] *Ibid.*, 31 March 1779, XIII, 395–98.
[3] John B. Barriger, *Legislative History of the Subsistence Department of the United States Army from June 6, 1775, to August 15, 1876* (Washington, 1876), pp 18–20

the Superintendent of Finance was authorized "to procure on contract all necessary supplies for the use of the army or armies of the United States."[4] To the extent that funds would be made available, this permitted the Superintendent of Finance largely to supplant the Commissary General of Purchases, though the latter continued to function through the Yorktown campaign.

As conditions demanded, Congress created, consolidated, or abolished other offices and departments for administering the services of supply. At first the Commissary General of Stores and Provisions had general charge of procurement of subsistence, and the procurement of arms and ammunition came directly under the Board of War and Ordnance. Later Congress provided for a separate Commissary General of Military Stores who was the agent of the Board of War and Ordnance for procurement of munitions and for supervision of the work of Continental armorers in repairing weapons. The Commissary General of Military Stores also had the duties of receiving and issuing ordnance supplies and equipment, and of maintaining records of all Continental ordnance stores.

To further complicate administrative responsibilities in ordnance supplies, a commander of artillery later came into the picture as the officer responsible for directing all ordnance activities in the field. Ordinarily ordnance supplies could be drawn from fixed magazines only with the approval of the Board of War and Ordnance; however, if getting such approval seemed likely to cause serious delays, the artillery commander could draw supplies from those depositories on his own authority. The artillery commander was responsible for cal-

culating ordnance requirements for the commander in chief's approval and presentation to the Board of War. Still another complication came with the appointment of a field commissary of military stores independent of the Commissary General of Military Stores, and a Surveyor of Ordnance (chosen by the Board of War) charged with inspecting magazines, foundries, shops belonging to the ordnance department, and ordnance in the field.

The Quartermaster's Department

Paralleling the establishment and more or less frequent reorganizations of the commissary departments was the Quartermaster's Department. Perhaps the greatest responsibility of the Quartermaster General was to provide transportation, but he also had duties relating to the construction of troop quarters—exercised through a barrack master general—and certain duties relating to the procurement and distribution of supplies. Also, following the British example, his role was similar to that of a chief of staff.

In the original organization the Continental Congress provided for one quartermaster general for the Grand Army and one deputy under him for the separate army. The appointment was left to Washington, and he chose a young, promising member of his personal staff, Thomas Mifflin, who at thirty-one had been a highly successful merchant when Washington called him to be aide-de-camp. As Quartermater General, Mifflin received the rank of colonel, though it was not long before he was made brigadier general, and then major general.

Mifflin served with energy and considerable ability for about a year, but then resigned. Washington turned to another

---

[4] *Journals of the Continental Congress,* XX, 734.

member of his personal staff for a replacement, Col. Stephen Moylan. It took only a few months to convince Moylan that the job was too big for him, and on his resignation Congress reappointed Mifflin. But Mifflin had lost his enthusiasm. After his promotion in February 1777 to major general he was anxious for a command away from the frustrations of the quartermaster service. He became involved in intrigue, and in the summer of 1777 simply did nothing. He resigned in October for reasons of ill health, but Congress asked that he continue to act until a successor could be found. Actually, it seems that Mifflin did nothing on this score either, although he accepted appointment to the Board of War in January, and the Quartermaster Department was left in a bad state for supporting the Army during the winter of 1777–1778.

Finally in March 1778 Maj. Gen. Nathanael Greene was persuaded to take on the thankless job of Quartermaster General. Reluctant to leave his field command, he did so only at the urging of Washington. It was not long before Greene began to feel the helplessness and frustration that his predecessors had experienced and by April 1779 he decided that he had had enough. Moreover, he too nourished ambitions for an important field command. He hoped to get command of the Southern Army, but that assignment went to Maj. Gen. Benjamin Lincoln. Congress refused to accept Greene's resignation and he continued as Quartermaster General for a little more than another year. In July 1780 Congress adopted a plan for the reorganization of his department that he found unsatisfactory. Greene felt that he had not been given a large enough staff to do all the things expected of him and that the pay was too low. He also objected to the lack of a provision

GENERAL MIFFLIN

for the two principal assistants for whom special arrangement had been made at the time of his original appointment. Furthermore, he was displeased with the continuation of the rule by which Congress held him financially and morally responsible for the acts of his subordinates. Congress had expressed an intent to consider the facts in special cases when General Mifflin had raised a similar objection, but it could not adopt the principle that the payment of money to a deputy or assistant relieved the chief of all responsibility for its use. An exchange of correspondence on this point gained nothing for Greene. Congress was willing to relax the strict application of the rule to some extent, as it had done in agreeing that the Commissary General should not be held liable for the misapplication of funds by his subordinates if he had obtained bonds from his deputy and assistant.

This was not enough to satisfy General

Greene, and he again resigned. Not content with a simple statement of resignation, he sent a sharp letter that aroused the hostility of the congressmen. Possibly his innocent reference to Congress as "Administration"—a word which had become odious in a connotation associated with the British Government—antagonized Congress unduly. It seemed for a time that Greene's resignation might go far beyond what he had intended, for a movement developed to dismiss him from the Army entirely. Greene's objections probably were based as much upon concern about the trustworthiness of the men involved as upon the plans for reorganizing his department.

Washington was distressed at losing the services of General Greene, for, as usual, the resignation had come at a crucial time. The commander in chief wrote: "Unless effectual measures are immediately taken to induce General Greene and the other principal officers of the department to continue their services, there must of necessity be a total stagnation of military business. We not only must cease the preparations for the campaign; but shall in all probability be obliged to disperse, if not disband the army for want of subsistence." [5] To be sure, other factors than the administrative machinery were at work in this situation, but, with everything else, General Washington feared that a disruption in the Quartermaster General's Department just then would bring about a collapse of the whole supply system.

Washington supported his lieutenant vigorously, as did members of a committee Congress appointed to visit Washington's

headquarters and make recommendations for improvements. Congressional reprimands fell upon the committee as well as upon the Quartermaster General. Many congressmen criticized Greene for resigning at this particular time and some of his friends felt that he was too rigid in his demands. In the end, Congress accepted Greene's resignation without dismissing him from the Army. As the new Quartermaster General, Congress chose Col. Timothy Pickering, previously a member of the Board of War, and a man not known to be particularly friendly toward General Washington.

Corps of Engineers

Leaders of the Revolution were hard put to find people able to perform all the duties required of military engineers. With the exception of a few who had served at Louisbourg, Lake George, Ticonderoga, Crown Point, and Quebec during the Colonial Wars, almost no one was to be found in the American service who had had any practical experience in the construction of defenses, or in the attack of fortified places. [6] Still these jobs had to be done and engineer officers had to be found among those few experienced officers, among foreign volunteers, and among men able to learn on the job. During the first three years of the war engineers were not formally organized as a distinctive branch. Engineer officers simply were staff officers, as were quartermasters, and companies of artificers, local militia, companies of Negroes, civilian laborers, and soldiers of the line performed the work of engineer troops.

---

[5] Ltr, Washington to President of Congress, 30 July 1780, in John F. Fitzpatrick, ed., *The Writings of George Washington from the Original Manuscript Sources, 1745–1799*, 29 vols (Washington, 1931–1944), XIX, 280

[6] Material in this section is based on *Historical Papers Relating to the Corps of Engineers and to Engineer Troops in the United States Army* (Washington Barracks, D.C., 1904)

Among the many foreign officers attracted to America during the Revolution were a number of experienced engineer officers. One of these was Thaddeus Kosciuszko, who arrived in Philadelphia from Poland in the summer of 1776. In October Congress appointed Kosciuszko an engineer and commissioned him a colonel. He served Schuyler and Gates expertly and loyally during the Saratoga campaign, and continued to serve until the end of the conflict. Most of the foreign engineers were Frenchmen. In April 1777 Count de Vrecourt was commissioned a colonel, Louis de Fleury was appointed lieutenant colonel a month later, and in July Lewis Mons de la Radiere was appointed colonel and Jean Baptiste Mons de Gouvion, lieutenant colonel. Shortly after his arrival in this country in July 1777, Louis le Bégue Du Portail received a commission as colonel of engineers, and in November he became a brigadier general.

Although foreign officers brought indispensable skill and experience to the American Army, their presence caused rivalry and misunderstanding. Friction over rank developed among foreign officers, and between foreign officers and Americans. French officers (those joining the Continental Army as individuals, not those serving under French command) claimed precedence over all other engineer officers in the Continental Army whatever their rank. Indeed, they found a distinction in titles: the French officers were designated colonel, or major, of the engineers, while the others were styled as simply colonel, or major, engineer.

One outstanding group of colonial specialists and soldiers were the amphibian regiments. Although not designated as engineers, Col. John Glover's amphibian regiment from Marblehead, and Col. Israel Hutchinson's regiment from Salem were in a very real sense specialized combat engineers. Fishermen and sailors, all the men in these units put their civilian occupational specialities to direct use when called upon to man the boats for major river-crossing operations. When not being used for their specialty they were among the best combat troops in the Army.

The beginning of another special type of engineer service—topographical engineering—came with the authorization by Congress in July 1777 for Washington to appoint Robert Erskine, "or any other person that he may think proper," Geographer and Surveyor of the Roads. His job was to prepare sketches, and to obtain and supervise guides for the Army. Washington, as he usually did, accepted the suggestion of Congress and appointed Erskine. Congress designated Simeon De Witt to fill the post after the death of Erskine in 1780. A second geographer was appointed for the Southern Department. In 1781 both were designated "Geographer to the United States of America" to perform such duties as the commander in chief and the commander of the Southern Department might prescribe.

Actually, Washington had been authorized to organize a corps of engineers when Congress, in December 1776 voted him full powers to raise sixteen battalions of infantry and additional units of artillery and cavalry. A Congressional resolution of 27 May 1778 provided for three companies of engineers, each to include a captain, three lieutenants, four sergeants, four corporals, and sixty privates. These companies were to be trained in the construction of field works so that they could instruct fatigue parties in preparing works and maintaining them against enemy fire. The commissioned officers were required to be schooled in mathematics, and the noncommissioned officers were required to be able to write a good hand. Later the troop units of the Engineer Department were referred to as companies of sappers and miners. Congress did not enact the resolution giving statutory basis for the Corps of Engineers until 11 March 1779. Under this resolution Congress appointed the commandant of the corps, who received his orders from Congress and from the commander in chief, and who was accountable to the commander in chief and to the Board of War. General Du Portail, already serving as chief engineer, became the first Commandant of the Corps of Engineers. In November 1781 he was promoted to major general.

Medical Department

Organization of a medical department—or "hospital", as the whole medical establishment then was referred to—for the Continental Army came almost as an afterthought. It was only in the eighteenth century that the administration of military medicine became a common function of government. The French were maintaining hospitals under military regulations as early as 1718. The English adopted this practice in the last two years of the Seven Years' War, but they had been developing more or less systematized methods of evacuation of casualties since Marlborough's time, in the early years of the century. In the Battle of Fontenoy (1745) regimental surgeons treated the wounded near the front lines; seriously wounded men were assembled at ambulance stations for major operations, and were then transferred to general hospitals in nearby cities. In 1748 the

British had a system of mobile, fixed, and convalescent hospitals. The French had begun the medical examination of Army recruits during the half-century preceding the American Revolution, but this was a practice which the British had not yet adopted.

In its resolutions of June 1775 establishing administrative machinery for support of the Army, the Continental Congress failed to make any mention of surgeons or a hospital establishment. The troops that had assembled more or less spontaneously around Boston in April and May had their share of physicians and surgeons who had come, just as had the farmers, clerks, and mechanics, to join in the fight against the British. When medical services were needed these men were available, but many of them remained as active members of line units rather than join distinctive medical units.

On his arrival at Cambridge, Washington saw immediately the need for a medical organization, and asked Congress for action on the matter. As it happened, Congress had recognized the need almost at the same time, and had taken steps in that direction before Washington's request arrived. By a resolution of 27 July 1775 the Continental Congress provided for a medical establishment intended to be capable of supporting an army of 20,000 men. Headed by a Director General, who was to take orders from the commander in chief, the medical department was to include four surgeons, an apothecary, twenty surgeons' mates, a nurse for every ten patients under the supervision of a matron, a clerk, and two storekeepers. Congress chose the Director General, and he in turn chose the surgeons and other members of the department.

After a Congressional investigation of the

medical service which began in November 1776, Congress approved a plan for a thoroughgoing reorganization in April 1777. The jurisdiction of the Director General had been vague: it was not clear whether hospital organizations in separate departments were subject to his authority, and relations with regimental surgeons had been a continuing source of friction. With the reorganization, the Director General was made the real executive head of the department. A deputy director general was appointed for hospitals east of the Hudson, another for the Northern Department, and, when needed, another for the Southern Department. Each general hospital was placed under the supervision of an assistant director general. Following rather closely the system used in the British Army, the new organization provided for a commissary of hospitals in each district to procure, store, and issue food, forage, and other common supplies; an apothecary general for each district to receive, prepare, and deliver medicines; and, in addition, senior surgeons, second surgeons, surgeon's mates, storekeepers, stewards, matrons, and nurses. Moreover a physician general and a surgeon general were appointed for each district and army to give technical supervision to the unit medical officers. The Director General, as in the past, continued to be responsible for procuring supplies such as bedding and bandages until that duty was assigned to the deputy director general for the central area.

For a long while the precise military status of medical officers remained poorly defined. Although they were subject to military regulations and to courts-martial, in some respects they seem to have been more nearly civilian attachés to the military body than officers of the Military Establishment. Then Congress began to vote the rights and

privileges to medical officers that earlier had been extended to line officers in matters of pay, retirement pay, access to public clothiers, and other fringe benefits. For the purposes of authorizing grants of land, the resolution of 30 September 1780 recognized the director of military hospitals as having the equivalent (not actual) rank of brigadier general; the chief physicians and the purveyor, colonel; the physicians and surgeons and the apothecary, lieutenant colonel; the regimental surgeons, the assistant to the purveyor, and the assistant to the apothecary, major; and the hospital and regimental surgeons' mates, captain.

Administration and Command Relationships

Throughout the Revolution a certain amount of confusion persisted in the distinctions and responsibilities for the administration of military affairs for the country as a whole—the ministerial responsibilities—and the administration of the Army in the field. Washington was commander in chief of all the forces of the new United States, and he also was commander of the Grand Army. When Congress provided for a Commissary General, it was not always clear whether his responsibilities extended to all the forces or only to Washington's immediate command, or to both. As has been noted the Congress originally provided for a Commissary General of Stores and Provisions, who apparently was to serve for all military forces under Congress, and for a Quartermaster General for the Grand Army, with a deputy under him for the separate armies; it also provided for a chief engineer for the Army in a separate department. Each reorganization produced a different setup. At one time Washington asks that the heads of the supply and service departments remain in the field with him—and Congress agrees. At another time Congress asks department heads to be at the seat of government—and finally provides for the Deputy Quartermaster General to remain at the seat of government while his chief serves with Washington's army. A still later reorganization provides for a Quartermaster General and an assistant appointed by Congress, a Deputy Quartermaster General appointed by the Quartermaster General for the main Army, and a deputy for each separate army.

The inefficiency of administration sometimes apparent at the top was reflected in the lower echelons in the early years of the war. The number of leaders with military experience was pretty well exhausted in filling positions at the higher levels, so that in the regiment and the company of the early Continental Army the art of supply administration was practically unknown. Yet much depended on these officers. As Baron von Steuben observed, "'A captain who did not know the number of men in his company could not know the number of rations and other articles necessary for it." [7]

Washington's own position and the extent of his responsibilities were not always clearcut. As commander in chief his authority extended to the Northern Department, yet the commander and staff of that department were chosen by Congress, and reported as often to Congress as to Washington. The administration of logistics in Washington's immediate command frequently left a great deal to be desired. Although continuously handicapped by inefficient and disorganized services of supply, it appears that he never established his own separate staff to organize the logistics of his field army.

There is no escaping the fact that much of the time his army was poorly housed, miserably clothed, ill-equipped, and underfed. Whenever failures in supply and services are noted in other armies, commanders usually are charged at least with a considerable share of the responsibility therefor. Supply was as much a function of command in 1776 and 1777 as it was a century and a half later; yet explanations for such failures in Washington's army are nearly always sought elsewhere: members of the Continental Congress were untutored in military affairs, and at times they interfered, and at other times sat inert while troubles and failures accumulated; or the commander's staff was inadequate; or the agents of the commissaries were corrupt or inept; or local officials failed to co-operate.

Some truth may be found in all these contentions. But the first task of the Continental Congress was to develop something of a united war effort. Its chief function was the essential political role of engineering agreement among colonies widely separated in geography and interest. Any member of the Congress could have devised a well-designed scheme of organization and administration; the difficult task was to win its acceptance by men who earnestly held opposing views. As for staff positions and commissaries agents, able people were not always available—or refused to make the obvious personal sacrifices involved—and agents themselves were handicapped by the lack of dependable financial support.

Unquestionably Washington was aware of the problems. At times his letters became one long series of complaints about his supply shortages. But why did he not act

---

[7] Quoted in Rudolf Cronau, *The Army of the American Revolution and Its Organizer* (New York; privately published, 1923), p. 17.

more vigorously? Why was he content to sit in his headquarters and write letters to Congress and to his friends explaining all his difficulties? Why did he not get out and do something about them?

Looked at solely from the standpoint of military effectiveness in the more narrow and restricted sense, Washington probably would not rank high as a logistician. His greatness lies in his appreciation of his own position, and in his ability to see the long-range political implications as well as the immediate military problem. Through long dark years of struggle, when other commanders frequently resigned rather than try to carry on amidst the frustrations of the system, Washington steadfastly held on, and in doing so he held the Revolution together. At times he did resort to the impressment of supplies or of horses or wagons but always reluctantly and always observing due process, for he was aware that to win the Revolution by alienating the people would be not to win it at all, and that the immediate military advantage might be achieved at the expense of long-term military security if the hostility of the countryside were to be aroused. Surely the temptation to assume complete authority must have been great at times; indeed Congress on occasion indicated its willingness to abdicate its responsibilities altogether in favor of Washington's personal rule. But he would have none of it. As a result, although his Army often was badly supplied, the objectives of the Revolution were not compromised, and seldom has any army accomplished its basic mission more thoroughly.

There have been few revolutions that have not passed into dictatorship. Cromwell in England, Napoleon in France, Bolivar and San Martin in South America—all were great leaders, but not consistent devotees to popular government. Washington consistently deferred to civilian authority, and for their part the Continental Congress and the governments of the co-operating states generally insisted upon going about their Revolution in an orderly way with respect for due process of law.

In his relations with Congress, Washington followed strictly certain simple rules which have been summarized by Douglas Southall Freeman as follows:

1. Congress must receive prompt, concise reports on all questions that did not involve military secrets of immediate bearing.
2. In these reports and in everything else, the authority of Congress was always to be acknowledged with proper deference, and the Army must be represented as consistently subordinate to the civil arm of continental government.
3. Concerning matters that could not be discussed in papers transmitted officially to Congress, it was desirable to write personally to friendly Delegates who were to use their discretion in passing these letters to other members.
4. Congress must have repeated and indisputable assurance that its orders would be obeyed promptly and economically if this were possible; and, if not, members were to be told why delay or change seemed necessary.
5. There was to be no public criticism of Congress by Washington and no imputation of unworthy motive. On the contrary, Delegates always were to be credited with seeking the country's welfare and that only.[8]

[8] Douglas Southall Freeman, *George Washington, A Biography*, 6 vols (New York: Charles Scribner's Sons, 1948–1954), V, *Victory with the Help of France* (1952), 487–88

CHAPTER II

Revolutionary War Procurement

To have any success in a military contest against the leading commercial power of the world, the United States had to exploit every possible means of obtaining essential military stores and provisions. Congress and the states established foundries and factories for the direct manufacture of munitions, but the only way munitions shortages could be overcome quickly—apart from the fortunate capture of arms such as took place at Ticonderoga—was by overseas procurement. British fleets imperiled overseas trade, and even coastal shipping trade was so hazardous that large numbers of horses and wagons had to be found to move supplies along inland routes from one colony to another.

Overseas Procurement

Suspicious that many merchants were more interested in profits than in American independence, the Continental Congress for a time undertook to import war stores on its own account, and it encouraged the individual states to export agricultural products in return for imports of war supplies. As it turned out, state trading was not very successful, for Congress found itself in competition with the states, and they with each other. Unquestionably a number of merchants grew rich in the war trade, and profiteering was common, but the mechants did make themselves virtually indispensable by importing war supplies from overseas and by sending out privateers to prey upon British supply ships.

British mercantile policy, of course, had forbidden direct trade between the colonies and the non-British world. On 20 October 1774 the First Continental Congress approved an agreement, known as the Continental or American) Association, which set up a nonimport, nonexport, nonconsumption policy directed against Great Britain as a measure of peaceful coercion, and in order to avoid supplying British forces. For a time merchants operated under the handicap of association policies, but by a resolution of July 1775 Congress provided that ships importing ordnance could export materials equal in value; copies of this resolution were posted in the West Indies. The state governments were advised to export agricultural products in exchange for arms and ammunition, and shipmasters were given licenses to leave port on condition that they bring back munitions. The July resolution sanctioned the smuggling of military supplies from foreign countries, and American ships set sail for Europe, Africa, and the West Indies on missions of profit and liberty. The Continental Association policy became effective in December and remained in effect for four months, but it was soon evident that the issues would not be resolved by economic sanctions. In April 1776 Congress took the fateful step of opening trade with all parts of the world not under British dominion. This, in effect, was the real declaration of independence.

Anticipating coming events, in the spring of 1775 Benjamin Franklin had opened negotiations for the shipment of munitions to America with merchants in England, France, and Holland, some of whom later became actual sources of procurement. After April 1776 Congress sent agents to many other European countries in quest of loans and supplies. American credit in Europe appears to have been very good in 1776 and 1777; however, failure of the United States to meet obligations and the effectiveness of British cruisers in denying exports caused a drop in America's credit rating abroad.

The most important American overseas procurement source was France, whose government encouraged arrangements for making munitions available to the American states. A central figure in this business was Pierre Augustin Caron de Beaumarchais who, operating the front organization known as *Hortalez et Cie.*, arranged for the shipment of large quantities of French arms to the order of American agents. Silas Deane went to Europe in 1776 as commercial and political agent for the Secret Committee of Congress, and also with a contract from the Commercial Committee of Congress to buy 40,000 pounds worth of goods in France for which he was to receive a commission of 5 percent. Deane sent three ships from France at the end of that year; the British captured two of them, but the third arrived safely with a valuable cargo.

The focal point for a great deal of the foreign commerce essential to the Americans was St. Eustatius, one of the Leeward Islands in the West Indies. This seven-square-mile Dutch-owned island lay in the midst of French, English, Spanish, and Danish colonies—only a few miles northwest of the British colony of St. Christopher and south of French-owned St. Bartholomew. In that age of mercantilism, the Dutch maintained St. Eustatius as a free port, and in peacetime it was an important trading center. During the Revolution it became a great entrepôt for the clandestine exchange of American produce for European munitions. As a convenient avenue for bypassing embargoes and nonimportation restrictions the island attracted merchants in quest of fortunes, and in so doing it provided lifeblood for Washington's armies.

Thomas Willing and Robert Morris of Philadelphia established regular connections with St. Eustatius, finding it the best way to communicate with their correspondent in Rotterdam. The States General of the United Netherlands issued proclamations prohibiting the export of munitions of war to the new American states, but they were apparently loosely enforced. It was reported that in the first five months of 1776 eighteen Dutch ships sailed from Holland with arms and ammunition for the Americans. A favorite expedient was to load the ships for Africa, the powder disguised in tea chests, rice barrels, and other innocent-appearing containers, then sail instead to St. Eustatius where powder was bringing six times the price paid in Holland. While Holland was a principal source of the munitions arriving at St. Eustatius, and the Dutch—with the benefit of a treaty with Great Britain recognizing the doctrine of "free ships, free goods"—were the principal neutral carriers, supplies from France, and apparently even from Great Britain itself, found their way to America by way of St.

THE PORT OF ST. EUSTATIUS, WITH AN AMERICAN SHIP AT ANCHOR (*fourth from left*). *From an old manuscript in the Library of Congress.*

Eustatius. Later, when the British extended the war to include the Netherlands, St. Eustatius became one of their primary objectives. The British seized the island in February 1781, capturing a number of vessels in port, and found an estimated three million pounds sterling worth of military stores, tobacco, and sugar. Ironically, a French fleet intercepted the British convoy carrying the most valuable part of the captured goods, and only eight of the thirty-four merchant ships in the convoy arrived safely in England. The French recaptured St. Eustatius a few months later.

A large part of the munitions brought into the United States from abroad, and a large share of the profits of many of the most prosperous merchants were not the result of ordinary commercial transactions at all. They came from successful raids by American privateers on the high seas. No less than 365 vessels of Boston were commissioned as privateers during the war. Salem had about 180, and nearly all the New England ports had a part in privateering. Success was so immediate that insurance rates from the East Indies to England rose 23 percent in 1776. Indeed it can be said with much truth that the Americans carried on the first two years of the war largely at British expense. However, this was a game that the British could play as well, and they retaliated by issuing letters of marque to many Loyalists. British reprisals became especially effective in 1777, but later, with the support of the French Fleet, American privateers were able to recover much of their business.

Purchases in France, Spain, Holland, and Prussia, and in the French, Spanish, and Dutch West Indies soon brought in several thousand muskets of various kinds. Raids on British stores in Bermuda and in the Bahamas and on British ships added further important ordnance supplies. Capture of a royal ordnance brig in November 1775, for example, yielded 2,000 muskets, 100,000 flints, 30 tons of musket shot, 30,000 round shot, 11 mortar beds, and a 13-inch brass mortar.[1] A Continental ship arriving at Chester late in July, 1776, brought 1,000 muskets, complete with bayonets, a barrel of flints, 54 boxes of musket balls, 366 pigs of lead, and 193 barrels of flour.[2] During 1777 the French shipped some 30,000 muskets, most of which arrived at two ports— 12,000 at Portsmouth and 11,000 at Philadelphia.

Domestic Procurement

Competition that developed between Congress and the states and among the states in overseas procurement persisted in domestic procurement. Federal and state agents bid against each other as might be expected when the agents' remuneration was a percentage of total funds disbursed.

The manufacture of gunpowder in the Massachusetts Bay colony appears to have begun as early as 1639, when the General Court granted 500 acres of land to Edward Bowen for that purpose. A powder mill was built at Dorchester before 1680. It is recorded that cannon were being cast at Henry Leonard's foundary in Lynn, Massachusetts, as early as 1647, and at Bridgewater, Connecticut, by 1648. Probably one-third of the muskets and other small arms used by the colonists during the period between the Pequot War (1637) and King William's War (1689–97) were made in America.

Small Arms

Special efforts to develop the manufacture of arms locally began before the outbreak of hostilities. Almost immediately after the British act in 1774 prohibiting the export of firearms to the colonies, Massachusetts established a public arms factory and appointed Richard Falley, a well-known arms maker of Westfield, master armorer to supervise the factory. Virginia followed with a plant at Rappahannock Forge, near Fredericksburg, in 1775, and Pennsylvania established a gunlock factory at Cherry Street in Philadelphia in February 1776 which soon became a fully developed armory. Most of the states' committees of safety designated one member to look after manufacture or purchase of arms. Many agreed with the Maryland committee on arms that the public manufacture of arms would be too expensive, and they relied on contracts with gunsmiths and blacksmiths for procuring weapons. In Maryland only twelve gunsmiths could be found who were able to turn out as many as twenty muskets each in a month, but altogether some 200 men in the various colonies were engaged for this work. Some colonies offered bounties or subsidies to encourage arms manufacture. In addition to the efforts of the committees of safety in the individual colonies, the Continental Congress acted to establish armories in Pennsylvania and New Jersey, and the Board of War and Ordnance contracted with local arms makers for the manufacture of arms on the Continental account. In the winter of 1775–76 Pennsylvania arms makers manufactured more than 4,000 muskets, complete.

A few machine tools were to be found in the armories in the middle colonies, and there appears to have been some division of labor in the arms shops in the cities, but these features were almost entirely absent in New England. In Great Britain during

---

[1] Willard M. Wallace, *Appeal to Arms, A Military History of the American Revolution* (New York: Harper and Brothers, 1950), p. 55.

[2] Peter Force, ed, *American Archives . . . A Documentary History of . . The North American Colonies* (Washington, 1837), 5th Series, I, 691

this same period it was common for a master armorer to farm out the making of the major parts of a weapon among several journeymen, each of whom specialized in making a particular part in his own home; the master would then assemble the weapon in his shop. This of course did not imply interchangeability of parts, but it did mean specialization of skills. Ordinarily the American gunsmith, perhaps with the assistance of one or two apprentices, worked on all parts of a weapon. Most of the smaller shops simply were cabins equipped with a forge and bellows at the rear, with an anvil nearby, and perhaps with a water-powered grindstone.

In spite of all efforts to obtain munitions—overseas procurement, capture, domestic manufacture, and purchase of private weapons from individuals—the arms shortage in the Continental Army remained critical throughout most of the war. The principal reason appears to have been that soldiers continued to carry their arms away with them at the expiration of their enlistment, and the rapid turnover in personnel meant rapid losses of weapons. As one discipline, Steuben attempted, apparently with some success, to curb this loss by introducing a strict system of property accountability, but losses continued. In February 1777 Congress resolved that all arms and accouterments belonging to the United States should be stamped or marked *United States* in the hope that all arms so marked, found anywhere except in Continental service, would be turned in. Even so, in 1780 the Board of War reported that only 5,000 serviceable muskets were to be found in Continental stores, and 200 men in Washington's Army were reported unfit for duty because they had no arms.

Artillery

As with small arms, the United States turned both to overseas sources and to domestic industries for artillery pieces. American-made guns generally were not as good as those obtained in Europe, but when the latter could not be obtained, local products were much sought after. A committee of the Continental Congress was appointed in January 1776 to estimate artillery requirements, find out what size cannon could be cast in the colonies, and devise ways of procuring them. A month later Congress instructed a committee on ways and means of procuring cannon to purchase or contract for the making of 250 12-pounders, 60 9-pounders, and 62 4-pounders. In July 1777 all the contracts made by this committee were turned over to the Board of War and Ordnance which was empowered to make further purchases of military stores offered for sale in the various states. Philadelphia foundries were casting both bronze and iron guns by 1775, and foundries soon were established at Reading and Warwick, Pennsylvania; Bridgewater, Massachusetts; Westham, Virginia, and other places. Daniel Jay was able to turn out one 9-pounder a day at Reading. Sixty heavy cannon ordered by Rhode Island in 1775 were cast at the Hope Foundry. The Connecticut Committee of Safety spent 1,450 pounds to fit a furnace at Salisbury for casting cannon and shot; employing fifty-nine men, this plant turned out guns ranging in caliber from 4- to 32-pounders. Near Morristown, New Jersey, Charles and Joseph Hoff, managers of the Hibernia Furnace for Lord Stirling, who was serving as a brigadier general in the Continental Army, received an order in 1776 to make cannon and shot.

In March 1778 they applied directly to Brig. Gen. Henry Knox, Chief of Artillery, for a similar order for that year.

One of the serious problems that manufacturers faced was the shortage of labor. It was common for the states at various times to grant exemptions from military service to men employed in essential war industries, but when the pressure for men in military service became too great such exemptions were withheld. The shops did not offer sufficient inducement—other than exemption from military service—to attract men from other pursuits. As a result, by 1778 the Sudbury Furnace, which had been converted to casting cannon, had come almost to a standstill, and a Philadelphia foundry turning out brass cannon had to cease operations altogether.

In October 1777 the Continental Congress requested Connecticut to permit workmen at the Salisbury works to cast mortars as directed by General Knox. The Hoffs were worried for a time in 1777 that they would have to shut down the Hibernia Furnace when they learned that there was to be a draft of the Morris County militia from which there were to be no exemptions except by order of the governor himself. For the next year authority was granted for exemptions to twenty-five men—not enough men to cut wood and make other preparations to start the blast furnace by 1 May for a long season; if these exemptions should be revoked, they feared that the plant would have to be shut down. The Hoff brothers were sure that the draft exemptions were the principal inducement for their workers, for most of them were farmers who had left their land solely to avoid service in the militia.

Very closely related to the arms industry, of course, was the primitive iron industry. A number of pre-existing iron works were converted to cannon foundries, and others had to be assured a supply of iron for their muskets and bayonets. Arms makers of the Connecticut Valley depended mostly on the Salisbury region for their iron, and New Jersey and eastern Pennsylvania were important for the middle states. One of the reasons that Washington was anxious to make a stand on the Brandywine in September 1777 was to protect the iron works in the vicinity. In January 1778 the Continental Congress asked New Jersey to place a responsible person in charge of iron made at the Andover works, for this was the only readily available domestic iron suitable for steel.

Gunpowder

Probably the most critical single item for supply for American forces in the Revolution was gunpowder. It was one of the first questions that the Second Continental Congress took up, though its policy was to restrict itself mainly to co-ordination and encouragement of the efforts of the individual colonies with whom primary responsibilities along these lines remained. Before Washington arrived at Cambridge to take command of the Army, Congress called upon New Hampshire, Rhode Island, and Connecticut to furnish as much powder as they could spare. In addition, those states plus New York and eastern New Jersey were to collect all the saltpeter and brimstone (sulphur) possible, and send it to the New York Provincial Convention, which would arrange to have these materials manufactured into gunpowder in New York mills. Western

New Jersey, Pennsylvania, Delaware, and Maryland were to send their saltpeter and sulphur to Philadelphia for manufacture. Congress urged the tobacco colonies to process saltpeter and sulphur, and guaranteed a market. In addition, Congress brought two French experts over to instruct Americans in the manufacture of saltpeter and gunpowder. Individual states circulated instructions and offered subsidies for private manufacture, and established a number of public powder mills.

The amount of gunpowder made from domestically extracted saltpeter represented but a small fraction of the total used. Of the total of about 2,347,000 pounds of powder available for the Revolutionary armies before the Saratoga campaign, well over 90 percent came from overseas or was produced in the colonies from imported saltpeter. The 80,000 pounds on hand at the outbreak of hostilities, and the 115,000 pounds produced domestically from domestic salpeter made up the difference. Even this amount was far below requirements, and frequently military operations had to be modified, and potential operations had to be left undone, because of shortages of powder.[3]

Vital elements of ammunition other than powder also were frequently lacking. Lead for bullets was hard to find, flints were scarce, and the number of men who could shape them were few; even cartridge paper was a serious problem.

Clothing and Equipage

Although clothing supply does not have the immediate urgency for an army that

ammunition does, serious shortages of clothing over a period of time can be as demoralizing as enemy defeat. It cannot be said that the American Revolutionary armies were uniformly well clothed at any time during the whole war. Serious shortages were developing by 1776. A large part of Washington's Army lacked sufficient clothing for ordinary military service in the fall of 1777, and the situation grew worse with the winter. Even in the summer of 1778 over a fifth of the men lacked shoes, and many were wearing thread-bare and tattered shirts and breeches. Some improvement was noticeable later, but while one unit would appear well dressed, other units never were adequately dressed.

Seldom was a man below the rank of colonel to be found in anything other than work clothes. Washington favored the brown riflemen's dress for his men—hunting shirt (deerskin for winter, linen for summer), which hung loosely outside the trousers; long breeches held down by straps under the shoes; round, dark hat with brim turned up to give a three-corner effect; black stockings; white belt over left shoulder to support the cartridge pouch. Only a few units actually appeared in buff and blue. Many wore the red coats that had been handed down from the French and Indian War or captured from British supply ships— but probably most popular among Continental troops was the blue uniform with red facings.

The first real approach to anything like uniform dress for Washington's troops came with a large shipment of clothing from France in the fall of 1778. In this shipment the breeches and waistcoats were alike, but some of the coats were blue and others brown. They were assigned by lot to the states so that North Carolina, Maryland,

[3] Orlando W. Stephenson, "The Supply of Gunpowder in 1776," *The American Historical Review*, XXX (January, 1925) 281.

New Jersey, and New York drew the favored blue, while the brown went to Virginia, Delaware, Pennsylvania, Massachusetts, and New Hampshire. After the requirements for blue coats in the first four states had been met, a second drawing made the blues also available in Massachusetts, Virginia, and Delaware. From 1779 blue was the official military color of the United States.

Following the British custom of requiring soldiers to purchase their own clothing, the Continental Congress in the fall of 1775 appointed a committee to purchase clothing to be placed in the hands of the Quartermaster General for sale to the soldiers at prime cost and charges plus a 5 percent commission for the Quartermaster General's Department. Payment was to be made by a stoppage of $1⅔ a month from the soldiers' pay.

In June 1776 Congress asked each state to have made for each soldier enlisting a suit of clothes, a felt hat, two shirts, two pairs of hose, two pairs of shoes, and a blanket. In addition, a committee of Congress, made up of a delegate from each state, continued efforts to purchase cloth in the states to be made into clothing for distribution to the Continental Army. Modifying the requirement that soldiers pay for their own uniforms, Congress in October 1776 promised a suit of clothes each year for every man who would enlist for the duration of the war.

In 1777 the Congress appointed a Clothier General to receive all clothing purchased by the Board of War through its agents abroad or in the United States. State clothiers, appointed by the respective states, also purchased clothing on the Congressional account. Each state clothier received the share of clothing assigned for the troops of his state, together with additional clothing purchased by his state. A Commissary of Hides, also first appointed in 1777, obtained

hides and arranged for having shoes made, or traded hides for finished shoes.

With the timely arrival of cargoes of clothing from abroad, Congress in May 1778 suspended all further purchases of the Clothier General and his deputies and agents, and transferred responsibility for clothing procurement, pending reorganization of that department, directly to the Board of War. Under the reorganization completed in March 1779, there still was a Clothier General, but each state also had a clothier (appointed by the state, but subject to removal by the commander in chief) who was to reside near the troops from his state. State clothiers were to receive all clothing purchased by their own states at Continental expense and a fair share of that imported on Continental account, and issue it to regimental paymasters who acted as clothiers for their regiments. If the troops of any state lacked clothing, the state government was to be notified; if any state had a surplus, it was to be delivered to another state or to the order of the Clothier General. At the same time a system of employing several commissaries of hides, appointed in the areas where required, replaced the single commissaries, and the Board of War appointed five such officials.

The individual soldier's load of personal clothing and equipment in the Revolution (both British and American) was not a great deal different from what it had been before or has been since, except that chronic supply shortages made the American soldier's burden rather lighter than it was intended to be. Standard equipment for a British infantryman included a musket weighing 11 pounds, 7 ounces; a coat weighing 5 pounds, 2 ounces; a knapsack weighing 7 pounds, 10 ounces, with its contents of 2 shirts, 3 pairs of socks, 2 pairs of stockings, 1 pair of summer breeches, 1 pair of shoes, brushes, and six rations, weighing 39 pounds, 7 ounces—a grand total of 63 pounds 10 ounces. "Standard equipment" for the American infantrymen was predicated on its availability. At various times they were issued muskets, bayonets, scabbards, belts, espontoons, extra flints, musket locks, swords and belts, blankets, knapsacks, haversacks, canteens, and ammunition. In addition each group of six or seven men carried tents, kettles, and linen covers.[4]

Food

Procurement of food differed from procurement of munitions in several respects. Not the least of these differences was the almost continuous demand for food procurement. In the conditions of the eighteenth century it was difficult to store food for very long periods of time, and salt, the essential element for preserving meat, was itself critically short. Munitions were rather specialized items for war—not readily available commercially, and not to be found in private hands in any large quantity. Civilian food, on the other hand, was quite satisfactory for the soldier. One of the ironies of the situation was that food appeared to be plentiful in the country but lacking in the Army, a fact which made the problem both less and more difficult. Meat and grain and vegetables in the hands of local farmers was more easily accessible to the Army than such supplies as gunpowder which required special plants and skills for manufacture.

If farmers refused to sell at satisfactory prices, however, the question of impressment or seizure inevitably arose with all the unhappy consequences possible in creating hostility among the local populace.

In general, each of the states at the outset appointed commissaries to procure provisions for their troops—sometimes under a unified system for the colony as a whole, sometimes under a district system by which commissaries were appointed for the troops in designated areas. For its part, the Continental Congress tried to co-ordinate shipments of supplies so that there would be food for everyone. Attempts by the Congress to purchase supplies encountered trouble from a lack of funds, and from a lack of confidence on the part of farmers that further funds would be forthcoming. By September 1775 Trumbull thought that lack of food might make it necessary to disband the Army before spring.

One handicap under which the Commissary General of Stores and Provisions labored in determining his requirements was the lack of a standard definition of the ration—indeed, each state had its own definition. After consultation with Washington and his staff, Congress in November 1775 approved the standard ration to include the following: 1 pound of beef, or ¾ pound of pork, or 1 pound of salt fish; 1 pound of bread or flour; 1 pint of milk, or payment of 1/72 dollars, and 1 quart of cider or spruce beer; 3 pints of peas or beans per man per week, or payment for other vegetables at $1 for each bushel of peas or beans allowed; 1 pint of corn meal or ½ pint of rice per man per week; 9 gallons of molasses per company of 100 men per week if used in lieu of the beer or cider; 3 pounds of candles for each 100 men per week; and 24

---

[4] John W. Wright, "Some Notes on the Continental Army," *William and Mary College Quarterly Historical Magazine*, XI (April, July, 1931), 91

A CONTINENTAL ARMY RATION. *Quartermaster display, Washington, 1931.*

pounds of salt, or 8 pounds of hard soap for each 100 men per week.[5]

In December Washington appointed a board of officers which recommended some modifications in the ration component that were approved for local use. These included directions that corned beef or pork should be issued for four days of each week, salt fish for one day, and fresh beef for two days. During the winter when milk could not be obtained, each man was to receive 1½ pounds of beef or 1¼ pounds of pork each day. Later, in 1778, Congress concluded that available food supplies varied so much from time to time and from place to place that it should be left to the commander in chief and to the commanders of separate departments to fix the ration components.

The terrible winters at Valley Forge and Morristown were the worst times for food supply, but critical shortages often persisted through the spring and until fall. Production of cattle, grain, and vegetables was increasing on American farms but the food did not reach the Army, and starvation in the midst of plenty was too much to ask even of an Army of patriots. With the authorization—in fact, the urging—of Congress, Washington on occasion found no other recourse but to seize food supplies from the farms in the vicinity of his camps. When military necessity left little choice, it seemed even to Congress that Washington risked the loss of his Army by too great respect for civilian sensibilities. In 1777, both in April and September, Congress sought to combine a policy of local requisition with

[5] Victor L. Johnson, *The Administration of the American Commissariat During the Revolutionary War* (Philadelphia: University of Pennsylvania Press, 1941), p 40

a scorched earth policy in the face of impending invasion. Then in December it adopted a resolution sharply criticizing Washington for the expense and inefficiency of his efforts to obtain supplies at a distance from his troops when supposedly large quantities of grain and cattle were nearby which, if not used, might fall into the hands of the enemy. The resolution further criticized Washington for his reluctance to use his authority to impress provisions: "Congress, firmly persuaded of General Washington's zeal and attachment to the interest of these States, can only impute his forbearance in exercising the powers invested in him . . . to a delicacy in exerting military authority on the citizens of States—a delicacy which, though highly laudable in general, may on critical exigencies prove destructive to the Army and prejudicial to the general liberties of America." [6]

Congress made it clear that it expected Washington to procure food supplies from the districts exposed to invasion. He was to require farmers within a radius of seventy miles of his camp to thresh their wheat or have it seized and paid for as straw. Everything useful to the Army that was not absolutely essential to the owners was to be carried off or destroyed.

Washington remained firm, however, in his cautious use of military power, and his avoidance of any act that would increase suspicion of that power. Moreover, he replied to Congress that more supplies actually had been obtained than they supposed. A short time later, when the commander in chief did resort to seizure of a small quantity of food and other supplies, he reported that this "excited the greatest alarm and uneasiness even among our best and warm-

est friends." [7] In his local requisitioning Washington tried to adhere as much as possible to due process of law. He applied to local magistrates who engaged contractors or appointed Army quartermasters as such, and, when necessary, issued instructions for farmers to make grain or other supplies available at stated prices approved by the magistrates. [8]

An attempt to meet the crisis which developed during the winter of 1779–80 by adoption of a system of procurement of "specific supplies" of foodstuffs and forage through contributions in kind by the states proved no more effective than the earlier methods of procurement. Improvement had to await financial and administrative reform.

Salt was essential for curing meats so they could be stored and transported, and it was the first special item of food supply upon which the Continental Congress found it necessary to take action to control prices. Military demands and difficulties of trading almost at once created a critical shortage. In May 1776 Congress advised committees of observation and inspection to regulate the price of salt subject to regulations of the state legislatures; whereupon authorities not only regulated the price, but also offered bounties for its production.

Whether the services performed by sutlers who followed the Army outweighed the

---

[6] *Journals of the Continental Congress*, 10 December 1777, IX, 1013–1014

[7] Quoted in Louis C Hatch, *The Administration of the American Revolutionary Army* (New York: Longman's, 1904), p. 91.

[8] See, for example, Ltrs, Joseph Lewis, Quartermaster at Morristown, to Col. Azarish Dunham, 23 June 1780; Lewis to all Justices, 12 January 1780, Lewis to Magistrates, 13 August 1780; Lewis to Moore Furman, Deputy Quartermaster General, 27 January 1780; Lewis to Justice Brookfield, 22 March 1780 Photostatic copies in Washington Headquarters Collection, Morristown, N.J.

dissatisfaction they promoted is problematical. They probably helped to save the ill-supplied soldiers from starvation, and prevented desertions. On the other hand, the exorbitant prices they charged caused loud complaints, however willing the soldiers were to hand over all their pay for a little good food and drink. Sutlers could command high prices of their customers and so were willing to pay high prices for their merchandise; consequently, they often outbid Army agents for available food supplies. At times perhaps they were indispensable in keeping the Army together, but they grew rich on the soldiers' poverty, and their competitive buying helped to create the shortages which, in turn, made them indispensable.

Forage

A class of supply that required close attention and was akin to that of provisions for the troops was forage for animals. Availability of forage not only imposed strict limitations on cavalry operations, it was a critical factor in the movement of artillery, and in the transportation of all the other supplies essential to the maintenance of the Army. This last factor alone at times led to the scattering of troops so that horses could be fed. Unfilled needs for forage also at times necessitated impressment.

Summary

Given the inexperience of the Revolutionary War leaders in the management of logistics, the lack of a central executive authority or centralized governmental machinery, the rivalries among the colonies, and the jealousies of local prerogatives, logistical support for the American Army during the first six years of the Revolution had the strong points and deficiencies that might be expected. Sometimes forceful, able men achieved good results in spite of all the handicaps. At other times incompetence, inefficiency, and selfishness were such that no system could have been effective. On the whole, the balance more often than not tipped in the direction of the unsatisfactory. The commissary system broke down almost completely in 1777–78, and attempts at reorganization showed at best only temporary improvements.

Many different facets of a complex situation combined to produce these unsatisfactory results. Certainly the problem of personnel—not only at the top, but among the agents and clerks upon whom the procurement system depended—was basic, and the political situation of the times was important. Two other related factors stand out as among the most significant in the chronic shortages of services and supplies that troubled the Continental Army: one of these was the shortage of transportation; the other was the lack of financial resources and organization. Transportation shortages were due in part to lack of finances, in part to the inefficient use of facilities that were available, and in particular to British control of the sea that threw an excessive burden on land transportation. Financial deficiencies were due largely to the governmental structure and the lack of an effective political organization and taxing system—and, again, to mismanagement of available resources.

The British had their own logistical problems, but they controlled the coastal waters and tidewater streams, and had the resources of a well-regarded exchequer at their disposal. Thus they held the logistical advantage, even though they were operating far from the homeland in a more or less hostile country.

Logistical failures made it clear that it was imperative for the Americans to overhaul their finances and improve their machinery for administering supplies and services for the Army if they were to win. Improvement did not come until after six years of war, when war weariness threatened total collapse. On the other hand, credit must be given to a structure that persisted so long with enough effectiveness to turn a long succession of failures and disappointments into ultimate success.

CHAPTER III

Continental Supply and Services

Distribution and Storage

Systems of distribution and storage in the Revolutionary War depended upon customary ways of doing things, enemy threats, strategic plans, and procurement and transportation of supplies. Storage and distribution of munitions received the first attention of Congress and commanders and staff officers.

Washington's principal line of communications extended on a line, above the head of navigation of the major rivers, between the Hudson River and Head of Elk (at the head of Chesapeake Bay). Along this line supplies could be stored relatively safe from capture to support the camps or movements of the Main Army in eastern Pennsylvania, New Jersey, and New York. The Northern Army operated independently with the Hudson River as its main line of communication, and later the Southern Army operated with virtually no line of communication or supply bases at all. Washington wanted to keep his depots well to the rear, away from the seacoast and navigable rivers where British ships could reach them.[1]

In 1776 Henry Knox, then a colonel, recommended the establishment of a "capital laboratory" for the preparation and storage

of arms and ammunition. With the endorsement of Washington, Congress approved the recommendation, and the first of the new ordnance depots was established at Carlisle, Pennsylvania, where it was centrally located and sufficiently far inland to be reasonably safe from capture. (*Map 1*)

In December 1776 Washington directed the establishment of other depots in Pennsylvania: one at York with supplies for 10,000 men for four months; one at Lancaster with two months' supplies; and one at Mill Town with ten days' supplies. For the troops marching from the South, Washington ordered supplies to be stored along the routes between Winchester, Virginia, and Lancaster, Pennsylvania, and along the route from Alexandria, Virginia, to Head of Elk. He wanted supplies for 10,000 men for six weeks in the vicinity of Philadelphia. Smaller magazines were to be established at Trenton, New Jersey, and at other places as necessary to support the Army as it passed through.

In 1778 General Greene disposed grain depots along Washington's line of communications to include 200,000 bushels on the Schuylkill River; 200,000 bushels distributed along a line to the rear of this, from Reading on the Schuylkill through Lancaster to Wright's Ferry on the Susquehanna; and 100,000 bushels between the Delaware River and the Hudson. Washington was not altogether pleased with this

---

[1] Wright, "Some Notes on the Continental Army," *William and Mary College Quarterly Historical Magazine,* XI (April, July, 1931), 204–205

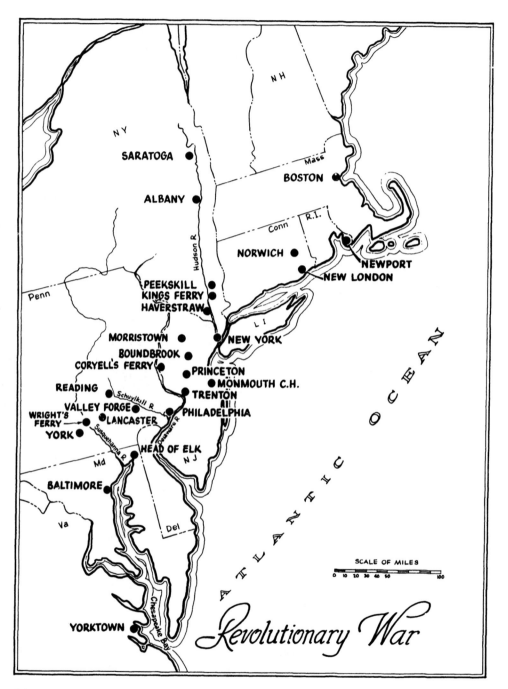

MAP 1

distribution, for he thought most of the places chosen were too much exposed to British attack.

With major operations in New England and New York another major depot convenient to these areas was needed. Knox urged Springfield, Massachusetts, as the site. The Continental Congress approved this in April 1777, with stipulations that the magazine should be large enough to contain 10,000 stand of arms and 200 tons of gunpowder, and that there should be a laboratory (shop) adjacent. Further specifications adopted in June provided that whenever any capital magazine was to be established, the commander in chief or the commander of the department should order storehouses and barracks for fifty men to be built within a stockade. Apparently the first work at Springfield was making and filling paper cartridges for muskets. Soon the Springfield Arsenal became, in effect, a general depot where not only ordnance stores, but food, fuel, clothing, tents and camp equipment, and horses and mules were stored. It developed into the most important arsenal in the United States, but apparently was not efficiently managed. At any rate, the Board of War in 1780 recommended that it be abandoned.

For troops on the march food supplies were stored along the route. A schedule worked out for the march of a battalion from central Pennsylvania to Philadelphia in 1777 provided that for the first division there should be six days' supplies for 200 men at Bedford by 28 March, three days' supplies for 200 men at Shippensburgh by 3 April, and six days' supplies at Carlisle by 6 April. A second division of 200 men was to pick up four days' supplies at Ligonier on 1 April, six days' at Bedford on 5 April, three days' at Shippensburgh on 10 April, and six days' at Carlisle on the 13th, while the third division, with 250 men, would be able to pick up the same number of days of supply at the same places on the 16th, 20th, 25th, and 28th, respectively. The intervals of seven to eight days and fifteen days between the divisions allowed time for replenishment of supplies along the route.[2]

Brigade and regimental quartermasters were general supply officers; through them supplies and equipment from all the supply departments funneled for distribution to the units. Regimental quartermasters commonly drew rations in bulk each week. More along the lines of what then were regarded as normal quartermaster functions, the regimental quartermaster also was charged with encamping or quartering the regiment, for moving baggage and conducting the pioneers when the regiment was on the march, and for receiving, storing, distributing, and recording all camp equipment.

Among the reforms which Steuben initiated after his appointment as Inspector General in February 1778 was a policy of strict supply discipline. His regulations of 1779 held regimental and company commanders answerable for the arms and ammunition in their units. If a soldier sold or carelessly lost a piece of equipment, he was subject to punishment and had to pay for the lost article through a stoppage of pay. Each soldier had to carry a personal account book in his knapsack, and at inspections he had to unstring his knapsack and spread every article of individual clothing and equipment on his blanket to be checked against the account book. Inspectors handled every musket, checked each car-

_____

[2] Memo, John Campbell to Brig Gen Edward Hand, 12 April 1777. MS, Morristown Headquarters Collection. The memorandum states 13 June, but this must be an error

tridge box, and counted all the flints and cartridges. Steuben declared that his system of accountability resulted in the saving of at least 800,000 French livres a year. Previously, when no company or individual property books were required, and when it was common for a soldier to take his musket with him when he left the service, General Knox had reported that before a campaign the military magazines always had to furnish 5,000 to 6,000 muskets to replace those that had been lost. Steuben maintained that that loss had been cut to less than twenty muskets in an entire campaign, a saving that was just as important as the work of procurement agents, in the states or abroad, in obtaining new arms.

Transportation

Although he was head of but one of several supply and service departments, the Quartermaster General functioned in effect as chief of staff and the chief supply officer of the Army. The principal reason for this ascendancy lay in his control of transportation: he had to arrange transportation for delivering or moving all supplies. To do so he had to overcome the handicaps of great distances and scattered settlements in the states, the barriers of forests and mountains and rivers cut or bridged by few improved roads, and the shortages of transportation facilities which could be used on the few routes that were open.

Undoubtedly the greatest advantage the British enjoyed in the Revolutionary War was control of the sea, not only because it enabled them to keep open their own communications with the homeland, but because of its special significance in a war against a country whose poorly developed internal transportation forced it to rely heavily on coasting vessels for transportation from one region to another. With the use of coastwise sea lanes denied the Americans much of the time, while open to the British, Northern and Southern states found mutual support generally impracticable. The supposed advantage of moving along interior lines lost all its significance in a situation where the enemy could move troops by ship around the periphery from one strategic location to another in one-fourth the time required for the Americans to move by slow and expensive overland transportation. Under favorable conditions, ships could run from Boston to Savannah in eight days. Troops could not expect to march that distance in less than thirty days—it often took that long for a courier to reach Washington from Greene's Southern Army. To the extent that state militia would report as each locality was threatened, the Americans were able to reduce their transportation needs; but successive local mobilizations were no real substitute for the rapid movement of organized units.

Inland waterways offered a number of advantages for the support of Continental forces, although except for the Hudson this means of transportation does not appear to have been fully exploited. Washington's movements more often were across the great rivers of the middle states than up or down them, but it seems that supply resources of the interior might have been used more effectively with a greater use of river transportation.

Late in the war General Greene did make some use of inland water transportation for the support of his Southern Army. As a former Quartermaster General, and as an accomplished field commander, Greene was fully alert to the transportation problem. Even while en route to take command in the

South he wrote Washington that one of his first moves would be to have the North Carolina rivers inspected in the hope that water routes might ease the transportation burden. He sent Brig. Gen. Edward Stevens to reconnoiter the Yadkin; Col. Edward Carrington, his quartermaster, to explore the Dan; and Col. Thaddeus Kosciuszko, his chief engineer, to inspect the Catawba. Throughout January 1781 Kosciuszko worked to get flat-bottomed boats built for use on the rivers. On 1 February Greene ordered as many of of the boats as were finished to follow his army when it moved out. Apparently, Cornwallis never permitted any regular system of resupply by water transportation to develop, but the boats did give Greene's forces some of the mobility which he employed so skillfully in his running engagements with the British.

Possibly the Susquehanna—where the ark, or "Susquehanna boat" was common—the Shenandoah, and other streams could have been used much more effectively to tap the resources of the hinterland for the support of military operations in the middle states. True, the rocky bed of the Susquehanna presented serious obstacles, but it is possible that smaller boats and a series of portages, as on the Hudson, would have been feasible and would have permitted more economical use of the limited land routes. But the western areas were sparsely settled, and the greatest need for supply movement was parallel to the seacoast. The secondary logistical problem of feeding the transport teams was greater than the primary logistical problem they would solve in transporting wheat, for instance, from south of Maryland to New Jersey. Overland shipment of flour from Annapolis to Boston was so expensive that General Greene suggested that it would be cheaper to send it in small boats—even if three of every four were captured.

When the commissaries general or their officers needed transportation, they were supposed to apply to the Quartermaster General for the necessary teams and wagons. Only in emergencies were they to hire horses and wagons on their own authority, and they were to pay no more than the amounts stipulated by Congress and the Quartermaster General. Under the Quartermaster General, a Wagon Master General and his assistants had direct charge of all horses, oxen, and wagons brought in. Congress had provided in 1776 for a Wagon Master and deputy, and a total of twenty conductors of wagons (a conductor for each ten wagons), and five conductors for the artillery. Again, the Wagon Master General and assistants were not to buy or hire any horses, cattle, or wagons without the direct order of the commander of the army or department with which they were serving, or of the Quartermaster General or one of his deputies. Horses sometimes were purchased specifically for the artillery, but more often they were transferred from one branch to another as needed.

Civilian drivers generally were hired for transportation service when possible, though frequently soldiers were detailed to that job. Even artillery horses ordinarily were driven by civilians, hired either by contract for a year or other term, or for a particular job. Congress discouraged the use of combat troops as drivers on the ground that it weakened the effectiveness of line units; moreover, soldiers themselves considered such work degrading. Control and discipline of the drivers sometimes presented a serious problem. In

March 1780 it was reported that a number of wagoners were delivering less flour at Morristown than they were picking up at Trenton, and at times they would just leave their loads at the roadside and go home without even reporting in at the Morristown magazine.[3]

To some extent American forces in the Revolution suffered a chronic shortage of supplies, but more often than not the real shortage was one of transportation. Lack of transportation not only was the reason that supplies available at one point did not reach troops at another point, but also the cause of a serious loss of supplies which, having been delivered at great cost, had to be abandoned or destroyed when withdrawal became necessary as happened with important quantities of stores at Fort Lee and New Brunswick. For the same reason food shortages were seriously aggravated. Large quantities of provisions had to be left to the British at Ticonderoga, and at one time in 1780 more than 2,000 barrels of salted meat were held up in Connecticut for want of transportation to Washington's camp because the Quartermaster General had no funds to hire necessary horses and wagons.

Actually, financial difficulties lay at the bottom of much of the transportation shortage. With no financial system adequate for obtaining either supplies or transportation, and with few farmers willing to donate goods or equipment, the alternative was seizure. As William Graham Sumner put it, "Impressment took the place of finance."[4] Reluctant as Washington was

to resort to impressment, it was an expedient adopted often by the state authorities throughout the war in all parts of the country, and was used most frequently to obtain transportation facilities.

The general system was to issue impressment warrants, presented by an officer or a local magistrate, under which the equipment seized was to be paid for at an established rate. The common rate for the hire of a wagon, horses, and driver in Pennsylvania in 1776 was fifteen shillings a day. In Rhode Island it was thirteen shillings for a wagon or cart drawn by one horse or one yoke of oxen, or by two yoke of oxen, and a driver. Military transportation in Rhode Island was on the basis of a schedule which called for four shillings for the first ton-mile, and one shilling and sixpence for each succeeding ton-mile.

As early as November 1775 Congress asked the New England legislatures to grant the generals authority to impress horses, wagons, and boats for transporting military supplies. In October 1776 the Connecticut legislature passed an act which provided that if a person refused to offer needed supplies or transportation facilties, a justice of the peace would issue an impress warrant authorizing a military officer to take the required items on payment of a fair price. Rhode Island had a policy of easy impressment until, apparently after some abuses, the legislature of that state passed an act in December 1778 to regulate the practice. Thereafter property could not be seized until after the owner had had a hearing; if the magistrate decided that the items could be spared, he would issue an impress warrant to the military officer. This procedure about ended effective impressment in Rhode Island.

The Pennsylvania Council of Safety in

---

[3] Ltr, Joe Gamble to Moore Furman, DQMG, 26 March 1780. MS, Morristown Headquarters Collection

[4] William Graham Sumner, *The Financier and the Finances of the American Revolution,* 2 vols. (New York: Dodd, Mead, and Co., 1892) I, 141.

November 1776 authorized a Pennsylvania colonel to impress horses to move cannon to Philadelphia. Impressment of horses and wagons was widespread in Pennsylvania in 1777 and 1778. After several instances of allotting wagon requisitions among the counties for impressment in November 1777, farmers of Lancaster County had to be given assurances that their wagons delivering provisions and fuel wood to Lancaster would not be seized; otherwise they would not even try to deliver the supplies. By 1780 the number of wagons reported in Lancaster County had been reduced from 1,620 to 370, and reductions in other counties were similar. Early in 1778 Pennsylvania adopted a systematic organization, with a state wagon master at its head, and a subordinate wagon master in each county. When the Continental Quartermaster General asked Pennsylvania to furnish 800 wagons in September 1778, and another 800 in October, the Executive Council protested to Congress against this heavy burden. A source of great dissatisfaction in Pennsylvania was reports of abuses in the whole system by the diversion to private use of vehicles impressed for public service. On one occasion it was charged that some wagons had been sent as far as Boston on private business. Another case was traced to Benedict Arnold, then commanding in Philadelphia, who had diverted wagons to move personal baggage. The Pennsylvania Assembly in April 1779 accused the Continental Quartermaster General of abusing the authority previously granted to him to requisition wagons, and adopted an act requiring that thereafter the state wagon master should comply with demands of the Quartermaster General only when ordered to do so by the Council of the State.

As in Pennsylvania, impressment of wagons had become so common in New Jersey in February and March of 1778 that the governor had to advertise that farmers need not fear the impressment of the horses, oxen, and wagons they used to deliver supplies to Trenton. Similar methods and objections were reported in the Southern states.

Just as Washington feared, local inhabitants considered impressment an obnoxious device, and many of those who were lukewarm toward the Revolution anyway were driven to the position of welcoming a British victory. But when it became a question of impress or perish, leaders of the Revolution had to accept the great risks of impressment against the greater risks of having no transportation or supplies for their military forces.

Engineer and Ordnance-Type Services

Although engineering services were imperfectly organized in the Continental Army, their essential functions were carried out under various auspices in a way generally advantageous to the Revolutionary cause. Broadly speaking, engineer officers performed three types of services—activities directly related to tactical operations, activities in support of transportation services, and construction, though in the latter two categories they were performing essentially quartermaster functions. Support of tactical operations included the selection and layout of defensive positions and supervision of the construction of fortifications and field works, and of opening the trenches and mines in siege operations. For the support of transportation they reconnoitered road routes and rivers and supervised the building and maintenance of roads and bridges and the building and operation of boats.

Construction work included barracks, magazines and depots, and other military facilities.

Col. Richard Gridley, chief engineer with the forces that collected around Boston, laid out a redoubt and breastworks with parapets six feet high on Breed's Hill for the defensive Battle of Bunker Hill. On Dorchester Heights Col. Rufus Putnam improved on camouflaged breastworks by packing the earth into barrels. The earth-packed barrels added to the appearance of the strength of the parapet, and had a double advantage in that they could be rolled down the slope onto the British as a sort of heavy missile. Very sturdy fortifications were developed at West Point under the supervision of Kosciuszko. Henry Knox, who as a colonel acted as Gridley's assistant engineer at Boston, directed the construction of fortifications and the placement of guns for the defense of New York, where 10,000 men worked during the spring and summer of 1776 to get well dug in before the British struck. Colonel Putnam, as chief engineer for the Grand Army, laid out a sizable pentagonal fort at Fort Washington, on the Hudson, though his lack of deep trenches, bombproofs, casemates, barracks or buildings other than a wooden magazine and headquarters, with no provision for fuel and water, made a strong and lengthy defense there most unlikely. A young French engineer, the Chevalier de Maudint du Plessis, improved an American fort on the Delaware River built for the purpose of interrupting British supply shipments. Chevaux de frize, an early version of underwater "hedgehogs" or rails designed to block navigation, were placed in the river to reinforce the measures against British shipping.

When General Gates went to take command of the Southern Army in the summer of 1780, Colonel Kosciuszko followed as chief engineer and he stayed on after General Greene relieved Gates as Southern commander in December of that year. As Greene's chief engineer, Kosciuszko had many and varied tasks to perform. One of the first was to reconnoiter the Catawba River, and to estimate its usefulness for navigation in the different seasons of the year by surveying the depths of the stream, the speeds of its current, and the locations of rocks, falls, and other hazards to navigation. Setting out by canoe, the Polish engineer accomplished that mission quickly and satisfactorily. In mid-December he was out selecting a campsite on the Pee Dee (Pedee) River where the Army would have access to supplies and transportation. In January 1781 he was gathering carpenters and tools and supervising the construction of boats to be used for carrying supplies on the rivers. Early in February he was hurrying to Boyd's Ferry on the Dan River to lay out and supervise the construction of defensive works. A few days later he was about eighty miles to the south, reconnoitering the area around Halifax on the Roanoke for the possible construction of defensive works. Some time during the next three months Kosciuszko probably advised Greene on the selection of battle positions, as at Guilford Court House and Hobkirk's Hill. In May he was supervising siege operations—the digging of parallels and towers—against the British at Ninety-Six. Then more reconnaissance work. In August he was in North Carolina at the request of the governor of that state to oversee the construction of a series of small posts dispersed through the state for the protection of military stores. Then as the trap for Cornwallis developed at Yorktown, he presumably directed his attention to the preparation of defenses to prevent the escape of the British.

Glover's and Hutchinson's amphibian regiments performed most useful services in river-crossing operations. Both regiments were withdrawn from the line to take charge of the boats when Washington's defeated Army evacuated Long Island on the night of 29–30 August 1776. For six hours the amphibian engineers rowed and sailed back and forth across the East River until by 0700 9,500 men with all their baggage, nearly all their artillery, stores, horses, and provisions had been landed safely on Manhattan Island. In Washington's celebrated predawn crossing of the Delaware for the attack on Trenton (26 December 1776), Glover's Marblehead amphibian engineers manned the Burham boats. The next fall this sturdy regiment served with distinction in Gate's Northern Army at Saratoga. In August 1778 the Marblehead amphibians again distinguished themselves when they ferried Maj. Gen. John Sullivan's army across Howland's Ferry to Tiverton, Rhode Island, another successful night crossing, and later on the recrossing to the mainland after Sullivan gave up the siege of Newport.

Sometimes companies of artificers and carpenters were raised whose functions combined those of both construction engineers and ordnance maintenance units. At the same time artificers identified with the artillery provided a more regular ordnance service. For both kinds of service, civilian workers were called in whenever necessary for particular tasks, causing a continuous source of difficulty. On the one hand, commanders were reluctant to take combat men out of the line to act as carpenters or artificers (the troops of course did a major part of the work in building their own field fortifications), and on the other hand the use of civilians led to charges of discrimination on the part of the regular Army artificers. A special report on the state of the regiment of artificers presented by the Board of War to Congress in May 1779 emphasized the disgruntled comments of the men of that regiment in contrasting their own wages with those paid to hired civilian artificers. In February 1780 the artillery artificers still were complaining about their low pay, and were particualrly unhappy about not receiving state rations as granted to other troops. After many appeals through the Board of War, the Pennsylvania government, from which state most of the men of this regiment came, finally agreed to allow state rations to the men from that state but not to the others. This, of course, did little for unit morale, and again, as was so often the case in the Continental Army, it was difficult to persuade men to re-enlist after the expiration of their three-year terms.[5]

Hospitalization and Medical Service

The first actual hospitals, in the sense of a facility for treating sick and wounded soldiers, were those which Massachusetts Bay established at Cambridge in several large private homes under the direction of Dr. John Warren, brother and pupil of the illustrious Maj. Gen. Joseph Warren who was killed at Bunker Hill. Soon additional hospitals were opened at Watertown and Roxbury, and on 27 June a special hospital for smallpox patients opened.

[5] L:r, Benjamin Flowers to Gen Washington, 25 February 1780   MS, Washington Papers, Library of Congress

Regulations adopted by the Continental Congress in October 1776 directed regimental surgeons to send to a general hospital the sick of their units who needed constant attention or nursing care. Regimental hospitals were forbidden to be set up in the vicinity of general hospitals. Steuben's regulations of 1779 provided for a morning sick call; when all sick were reported the surgeons visited them, and as necessary ordered them to the regimental or general hospital. Each regiment maintained two or three tents for those patients who could not be sent, or did not need to be sent, to the general hospital.

Conditions in civilian hospitals were far from attractive during the late eighteenth century, but with a few exceptions the military hospitals were intolerable even for people unused to sanitary and comfortable facilities. General Wayne called the hospital at Ticonderoga (December 1776) a "house of carnage" where the living mingled with the dead.[6] It seemed that hospitals nearly always lacked medicine, and even food. To make matters worse, they were centers of disease where men were crowded together so as to present the greatest possible obstacle to natural recovery. The arrival of open wagons carrying wretched soldiers groaning from the pain of wounds or disease often set off hostile protests from the local populace. An Army hospital in a community in those days met the same kind of opposition that the installation of an air base would meet a hundred and eighty years later. Dr. Benjamin Rush, signer of the Declaration of Independence and Surgeon General (later Physician General) of the hospitals of the Middle Department, de-

clared that the hospitals claimed more American lives than the enemy did.

Rush and others agreed with the contention of Dr. John Jones, professor of surgery at King's College and later a regimental surgeon in the Continental Army, that overcrowding and poor ventilation were major causes of the persistence of disease and high mortality in military hospitals. Observing the high mortality in the crowded hospitals of London and Paris, and noting that men treated in camp (in Europe as well as in America) seemed to recover more rapidly than those confined to hospitals, Jones advised that houses be avoided, and that churches, barns, and other buildings that were open to the rafters be used for hospitals.

The man who made Jones's idea the doctrine of the Continental Army in an age when the belief still prevailed that windows and doors should be kept shut tight against the night air was Dr. James Tilton. In charge of the general hospital at Trenton, Tilton introduced roughly built log huts, each accommodating five or six men, for hospital wards. For the winter encampment at Jockey Hollow (1779–80), Tilton designed an H-shaped, three-ward, log hospital. There were no connecting doors between wards. Outside doors and long windows on the south side of the building and vents in the roof permitted circulation of fresh air. Smoke from open fires placed near the center of each ward circulated through the wards for the purpose of combating infection, then passed outside through the openings in the roof. The center ward, with twelve beds, was for men suffering from fevers. The two wings, each with eight beds, were for men suffering from other diseases and from wounds. The isolation of the fever patients, the

---

[6] Force, ed., *American Archives*, 5th Series, III, 1359.

RECONSTRUCTION OF DR. TILTON'S HOSPITAL AT JOCKEY HOLLOW

maintenance of space between patients, and the provisions for ventilation undoubtedly did much to improve the prospects for recovery. In particular, Tilton was able to report a noticeable decrease in typhus, or "jail fever," and similar results were noticed wherever his system was adopted.[7]

Uncertainty about the causes of diseases and their spread limited the effectiveness of preventive measures. Luckily the strong ideas of Jones, Tilton, Rush, and others about ventilation and overcrowding did tend to reduce the spread of typhus

simply because exchange of disease-carrying lice was less likely when some distance was kept between patients.

Since victims of smallpox who recovered were generally immune from further attacks of the disease, it was one malady that lent itself to active preventive measures. Scars left by the disease advertised a man's immunity and pockmarked men were much sought after by recruiting officers. The idea of deliberately inducing a mild case of smallpox in order to immunize a person against the disease was introduced into England from Turkey in 1718. The practice of smallpox inoculation spread quickly to many parts of Europe. Cotton Mather introduced inoculation into the colonies at Boston in 1721, and stirred up a violent controversy which found most physicians in op-

[7] Harvey E. Brown, *Medical Department of the Army from 1775 to 1873* (Washington: Surgeon General's Office, 1873), pp. 52–53. A reconstruction of Tilton's hospital may be seen at Jockey Hollow, Morristown National Historical Park, Morristown, N.J.

position to him. Vaccination (the introduction of the cowpox virus, as distinct from inoculation with smallpox matter itself), first took place in England in 1774, but it was not proved until 1796, so that regular inoculation was the only preventive measure available during the Revolution. Because at best inoculation was dangerous and uncertain, several states adopted laws forbidding the practice. Many soldiers, however, feared inoculation much less than the terrible disease and resorted to self-inoculation, which probably encouraged the spread of epidemics more than it checked them. On the other hand, Washington himself was convinced that if men were given proper care and attention, inoculation would go far toward reducing serious smallpox cases in the Army. Dr. John Morgan, while Director General of the Hospital (Massachusetts Bay), introduced the practice of inoculation in the Continental Army, and published a book in 1776 recommending the procedure.

Inoculation had become common in the Continental Army by 1776, although it was not required by regulations. Then in February 1777 Washington ordered that all men of his command at Morristown be inoculated. Over strong protests he further directed that local citizens be inoculated. Martha Washington set the example. Inoculation ordinarily incapacitated a person for three or four weeks, and care was necessary so that the "mild" form of the disease would not develop into a severe case. Two churches were made available for use as inoculation hospitals, and troops designated for inoculation were quartered in small parties in private homes in Morristown and neighboring villages. As many as one-third of the men were ill at one time, but the whole program came off quite well. Epidemics continued to plague the camps, but successful inoculation did give protection, and proper timing could alleviate the possibility of smallpox weakening the Army at a critical moment.

Preventive measures against venereal diseases consisted of fines. On the recommendation of medical officers, Congress passed a resolution in 1778 which provided that $10 should be deducted from the pay of any officer and $4 from the pay of any enlisted man who entered a hospital for treatment of venereal disease. The act appears in part to have been a revenue-producing measure to finance the purchase of blankets and shirts for hospital patients. There is no evidence that the act had any important results either in reducing the incidence of venereal disease or in raising revenue.

For transportation—whether for patients or for equipment—the hospitals, as did the other elements of the Army, had to depend upon the quartermasters.

Making up and dispensing medicines was the duty of the Army apothecary. Favorite medicines and drugs then in use included such things as snakeroot, ginger, juniper berries, camomile flowers, rhubarb, and cinchona or Peruvian bark. The Apothecary General, Andrew Craigie, prepared and compounded most of the hospital drugs in his shop at Carlisle, Pennsylvania.

Although supply shortages were chronic, and conditions of terrible suffering and high mortality for sick and wounded men were common, the medical service of the Continental Army probably developed as well as other elements of the Revolutionary military organization. At times the imagination and resourcefulness of the medical leaders was remarkable, and their diligence and sense of duty—even though sometimes marred by personal rivalries and antagonisms, and by lack of medical knowledge—frequently overcame the handicaps of organizing from scratch an Army medical service under conditions of war and revolution, and with little experience in military medicine or any kind of medical practice at all.

CHAPTER IV

Logistics of the Saratoga Campaign

The supply system being developed under the auspices of the Continental Congress was parallelled by the supply systems organized in each of the states. Sometimes supplementing, sometimes ignoring, and sometimes working at cross-purposes with the agencies of the Continental Congress and the commander in chief, the committees and commissaries of the individual states were at once the bane and the fountainhead of Continental logistical support. Their first interest was to supply the troops from their own state and they were most to be relied upon when their own state was immediately threatened, but they also provided machinery for collecting supplies for general use requested by Congress.

The campaign in New York State during the summer and early fall of 1777 which ended with the surrender of Burgoyne's British force at Saratoga is worth considering for two reasons. First, it illustrates how state supply systems developed, and how state and national efforts supported one another for a successful outcome. Second, it serves to illustrate how the initial superiority of a force can be undermined by over-extended supply lines and overburdened transportation facilities.

Support in New York State

In New York, as in the other colonies, various committees sprang up in response to

the series of "repressive," "coercive," and "intolerable" acts of the British Parliament that preceded the outbreak of open revolt. After the commencement of hostilities popularly elected local and provincial committees took over control of state and local affairs to maintain law and order and to prosecute the war.

The Assembly of New York, dominated by conservative loyalists, at one time went so far as to petition the King and Parliament for a redress of grievances,[1] and appointed a committee of correspondence to keep touch with the other colonies, but war and independence were beyond its pale. After the colonial Assembly refused either to approve the actions of the First Continental Congress or to appoint delegates for the Second, it quickly lost its authority and met for the last time on 3 April 1775. On the initiative of the New York City Committee, a Provincial Convention met to choose delegates to the Continental Congress, and the New York City Committee furthermore urged county committees to elect representatives to the Provincial Congress. This extralegal legislature met in New York City on 22 May 1775, and, until the state constitution adopted in 1777 set up a bicameral legislature with an elected governor to manage the affairs of the state, it provided guidance for

---

[1] *Journal of the Votes and Proceedings of the Colony of New York, 1766–1776* (Albany, 1820), pp 109–17.

the county and city committees, and was the central authority for organizing New York's war effort. When the Congress was not in session the Committee of Safety carried on for it.[2]

At the outset of the Revolution New York, with a population of approximately 185,-000, ranked seventh among the thirteen colonies. In the first excitement of armed revolt New Yorkers moved energetically, taking upon themselves the task of equipping a sizable military force of 3,000 troops.

The county committees as well as the Provincial Congress moved swiftly to counter profiteering in the sale of military supplies. When the Congress discovered attempts to monopolize certain goods and raise prices, whether on blankets, lumber, cloth, or food supplies, it could seize the goods and pay only the standard price, or, if the goods were already purchased, it could force the seller to return the amount in excess of the standard price. The Albany County Committee fixed prices on tea, wheat, rye, oats, corn, and buckwheat.

As elsewhere one of the most difficult problems of supply for the New Yorkers was procurement of weapons and ammunition. As had long been the custom in the colonies, each man reporting for military service was expected to bring his own firearm, but many city dwellers and the younger sons of farmers had no arms of their own. New York officials sought to make up the shortage of arms and ammunition by purchase abroad and by purchase, seizure, and state manufacture at home, but the British blockade and financial problems strictly limited overseas purchases by the states as well as by the Continental Congress. Local committees

collected all the arms they could find in their counties, and seized muskets from Tories. Even the state clothier went to work collecting muskets. The Provincial Congress contracted with local gunsmiths to make as many muskets as practical, offered bounties and incentive payments for persons who would produce a given number of arms, and provided two-year, interest-free loans to anyone who would build a factory north of New York City to bore musket barrels. It also contracted for six-pounder brass cannon. In 1777 the state built an armory near Fishkill for the manufacture of arms. Men working in armaments industries were exempted from military service.

Efforts to buy powder in Europe and in the West Indies were only partially successful, and where local manufacture in this predominantly agricultural state had been meager, it had to be expanded. As for arms, so for the manufacture of powder and saltpeter: the state offered incentive payments and interest-free loans for the erection of new mills. Instructions on how to make powder and saltpeter were prepared and widely distributed. When early bounties failed to bring in the quantity of powder needed quickly enough, the state offered 100 percent profit on initial cost to anyone who would import it. It offered a bounty of a shilling a pound on powder made from saltpeter brought in from other states. Bullets were hardly less of a problem than powder. Inspection of the few old lead mines in the state proved them to be worthless, and other sources had to be found. Lead weights from fish nets and pewter dishes went into bullets—not to mention the statue of George III in New York City—but the most important source of lead was window weights from houses. Inhabitants of New York City alone contributed over 100 tons of lead from

[2] New York (St.) State Historian, *The American Revolution in New York: Its Political, Social, and Economic Significance* (Albany, 1926), pp. 27–103.

their windows. The state purchased cartridge paper by the ream, and hired minute men to make the cartridges. In addition to supplying its own forces, New York agreed to repay Connecticut the ammunition used by troops from that state in the capture of Fort Ticonderoga.

For supplying food to the military forces, New York was in a much better position. Basic food supplies in the state were not scarce, though poor transportation facilities and the reluctance of farmers to accept depreciated currency sometimes made them seem so. Nevertheless, New York officials were loath to see food supplies leave the state lest a real shortage develop. When it was reported that cattle and goods had been sent from Long Island to Connecticut a committee was appointed (January 1777) to recover them. In November 1777, after several months of consideration, the Committee of Safety put an embargo on wheat, meal, and grain, and a few weeks later extended it to flour. Shipments out of the state for general Continental use required special permits. If farmers refused to sell their products at the market price, the Provincial Congress authorized the commissary, the general, or the governor to seize the goods and pay only the market price, or a fair price as determined by three appraisers. In October 1776 the Provincial Congress ordered 8,000 bushels of wheat at a fixed price of 6 shillings 6 pence a bushel, which the mills at Peekskill and Croton ran day and night to turn into flour. As in the armories and powder mills, men working in the flour mills were exempted from military service. Coopers were brought in from the Army to make barrels.

Probably the most critical item on the food list, here as in other areas, was salt. Again the Provincial Congress offered loans and bounties to anyone who would erect a plant to obtain salt from sea water. Several companies were organized to take advantage of these offers, but they were unable to meet the demand created by cutting off importation by sea. The salt shortage became so acute that riots broke out among the civilian population. Finally, the state appealed to the Continental Congress for assistance, and was able to buy a quantity of salt stored at Plymouth, Massachusetts. In addition, a New Yorker living in Connecticut obtained permission from that state to manufacture salt to send to New York. When supplies came in, they were distributed to the civilian population through depots in each county where families had to present a ration card from the local committee in order to obtain their allowance.

For military clothing New York first turned to France, but with the disruption of sea communications the state bought cloth in Connecticut and Pennsylvania and farmed it out to country districts to be made up into garments. County committees collected shoes, stockings, blankets, and other items, paid for them, and delivered them to Albany for distribution to the troops. and the state reimbursed the counties. The committees collected hides, had them tanned, and employed local shoemakers to make and repair shoes. A commissary for the New York Line (New York's contingent in the Continental Army) bought clothing in Massachusetts for these troops in 1777. The state established a clothing storehouse where all kinds of clothing items and blankets were collected for distribution. To stimulate local production, the state called upon farmers to raise more flax and hemp (the state distributed large quantities of free hemp seed), and to improve the wool output of their sheep. People who sold or ate lambs and ewes were denounced as enemies of the country.

Preparations Against Invasion

When Maj. Gen. Phillip Schuyler of New York assumed command of the Northern Army in mid-1775, he had to start virtually from scratch to organize an effective military force and the logistical facilities to maintain it at a considerable distance from bases of supply. Made up mostly of New York, New Jersey, and Pennsylvania troops (of whom the Pennsylvanians were the best organized and equipped), the Northern Army was concentrated at Ticonderoga to hold the strategic fort which Ethan Allan and Benedict Arnold recently had taken from the British.

The critical element in supplying his army was transportation of supplies from the main supply base at Albany, 105 to 113 miles away. Schuyler developed a system during the next year which resembled the one Lord Loudon has used to support British and Colonial forces operating in the same area in the French and Indian War. It was the duty of the deputy quartermaster general of the Northern Department to receive supplies from the commissary general, and then get them from Albany to the troops. In November 1776 eleven bateaux, carrying 160 to 170 barrels, were being used for the transit of supplies from Albany to Half Moon. Each bateau was expected to make a trip a day. For the land movement from Half Moon to Stillwater, a minimum of thirty-four wagons were needed daily. From Stillwater to Saratoga Falls the supplies again went by water—seventeen bateaux, each of which had to make two trips every three days, were being used for this leg of the haul. Two wagons could carry them around Saratoga Falls; then four bateaux, each making three trips a day, moved them up the river to Fort Miller where again two wagons could carry them around the falls. The last leg of the river route to Fort Edward was accomplished in twelve bateaux. From Fort Edward to Ticonderoga either of two routes might be taken—to Fort George and then by way of Lake George, or to Fort Ann and then by way of Wood Creek and the southern arm of Lake Champlain. In either case seventy wagons were needed constantly for the land carriage to Fort George or Fort Ann where the troops picked up the supplies. From Fort George to Ticonderoga the route was by water to the north end of Lake George, then by land around the falls to the saw mills, then by water again on the connecting stream from Lake George, and so to the fort. To get supplies to Ticonderoga from Fort Ann, the soldiers stowed them in bateaux and rowed down Wood Creek until stopped by the falls near Skenesboro from where they rolled the barrels across a short portage to the south end of Lake Champlain, then continued on to the fort by boat.[3]

Whatever may have been General Schuyler's military capabilities and shortcomings, he did give close attention to logistical details, and in doing so he anticipated requirements months in advance, in a way not always matched by commanders in campaigns 175 years later. In the fall he was thinking ahead to the next spring; in the summer he

[3] Copy of Orders to Colonel Lewis, DQMG of the Northern Department, 9 November 1776, in Proceedings of a General Court Marital . . . for the Trial of Maj. Gen. Schuyler, October 1, 1778, published in *Collections of the New York Historical Society for 1879* (New York, 1880), XII, 39–40. (Hereafter referred to as Proceedings, Trial of Gen. Schuyler.)

was thinking of his needs for the coming winter. Like other commanders in similar situations, Schuyler wrote complaining letters to Congress about his lack of support, but he was not content to let it go at that: he did not wait idly for help to come—he did something about it himself.

Expecting an invasion from Canada in the winter or the following spring, in the fall of 1776 Schuyler sought to strengthen the key positions at Ticonderoga on the Lake Champlain route, and at Fort Stanwix on the Mohawk, which he thought the more likely invasion route. In November he urged the artillery commander, the chief engineer, the quartermaster general, and the commissary general to get in all necessary supplies before the campaign began. Specific measures he recommended at that time included: the building of 100 bateaux at Schenectady during February or March; the collection of lumber at Fort George; storing of materials for boat repairs at Fort George, Fort Ann, Skenesboro, and Schenectady; taking immediate steps to bring in rations for 5,000 men for eight months to Albany and to move them up to Fort Ann during the winter, and then to store a similar quantity of provisions at Albany to be held for shipment up the Mohawk if necessary; sending a train of light and heavy artillery to Albany, part of it to go to Ticonderoga and to Fort George during the winter when transportation over snow and frozen ground would be much easier than after the spring thaws; setting up a "laboratory" at Albany to prepare all necessary ammunition; and the raising of fifteen service companies (preferably civilians) for the quartermaster general's department to man the bateaux and keep the roads in repair, and four companies of carpenters for work on barracks and boats. He sug-

gested that some naval vessels should be built on Lake Champlain. He also wanted to get up bedding for the troops as soon as possible, glass for the barracks, and a quantity of woolen caps from Philadelphia. Noting the great expense and difficulty of transporting large quantities of food in the spring, Schuyler was anxious to lay in large stores of provisions at Fort George and Fort Ann during the winter. Since it was not likely that the Continental Commissary General could forward the desired quantities of meat to arrive before the river closed, Schuyler asked Trumbull that sufficient salt to cure 5,000 barrels of pork or beef be sent to the deputy commissary general for the Northern Department with orders for him to purchase the meat locally and salt it in Albany. He noted requirements for nails, steel, camp equipment, building materials, firewood, and all the items needed for quartering and feeding troops.

Ultimately the Continental Congress did approve of General Schuyler's defense plans and his requests for supplies and materials, but the approval was so long in coming that Schuyler on his own initiative did what he could to get things started. He appealed directly to the eastern states for artillery and ammunition, for building materials, and for carpenters. He sent his artillery commander to procure ordnance stores in the eastern states by purchase and from the Continental stores, and he authorized the artillery officer to engage a commissary of ordnance, a master of laboratory, and two conductors at the same pay as comparable officials received in the main army under Washington.

Attentive to the health of his troops, Schuyler ordered the post commanders at Ticonderoga to insist on personal cleanliness of their men and the cleanliness of their quarters, and to supervise closely the prep-

FORT TICONDEROGA, RESTORED

aration and cooking of food. He asked that an officer oversee the cooking in every company every day. He thought it best to have the food for a whole company cooked together, and ordered twenty large kettles for that purpose. He ordered the construction of a general hospital large enough for 600 patients at Mount Independence.

After the Continental Congress approved his plans for defensive works, Schuyler in February 1777 issued specific orders to his chief engineer for carrying them out. He instructed the engineer to sink caissons in the narrows on Lake George to obstruct navigation there, if it were found practical to do so, and to lay caissons and a boom across Lake Champlain between Ticonderoga and Mount Independence both to form a bridge for passing between the two points and to deny the entry of vessels into the south arm of the lake. The chief engineer

was also to collect materials and begin construction of fortifications and the general hospital at Mount Independence, and he was to send an engineer to Fort Stanwix to see what could be done about strengthening the defensive works on the Mohawk. In addition, at Mount Independence the chief engineer was to proceed with the repair of the provision storehouses, the construction of a bakery, and the construction of a house for the making of soap and candles. The general cautioned that carpenters required close supervision, and officers should be instructed to keep them at work. To the assistant engineer in charge of the work at Fort Stanwix (Fort Schuyler) he wrote: "Fortifications are at all times expensive; they become more so, when the artificers are suffered to while away their time. Your carpenters must therefore begin to work at day-light, and work until sun-set, allowing an hour for breakfast, and an hour and a half for dinner. No sitting down to smoke and drink at eleven o'clock, or at any other time, except that at meals. In very hot weather, two hours may be allowed at dinner." [4]

General Schuyler disliked to use soldiers for service chores. "It not only ruins soldiers to employ them in such business, and is more expensive," he said, "but also weakens the Army too much." [5] Nevertheless, soldiers had to be used if all the necessary construction work around Lake Champlain was to be completed before spring. The chief engineer, therefore, was instructed to get as many soldiers as he could to saw wood, and to pay them extra (by the foot) for their labor, as the cheapest way to get the most done.

Schuyler was disappointed with the results in the building of obstructions, defensive works, and facilities in the Ticonderoga area. The delays there he attributed to the late arrival of artificers, the late arrival of troop reinforcements—and these in too small numbers to garrison the place properly—and to a shortage of work cattle. With the arrival of additional stores ordered from the supply point at Bennington, and by resorting to impressment against local farmers, the shortage of food supplies was fairly well overcome by June 1777. Individual clothing and arms and equipment remained in a bad state, with many of the men in rags, and many without blankets.

In spite of all supply efforts, the Ticonderoga command was not ready when the at-

tack came. Undoubtedly two of the major causes of failure in this quarter were General Schuyler's personal unpopularity in New England—presumably owing in part to his position in the controversy relating to the "Hampshire Grants" (the area which ultimately broke away from New York to become Vermont)—and the deep-seated rivalry between Yankees and Yorkers. New Englanders united behind Maj. Gen. Horatio Gates of Virginia in efforts to have him replace Schuyler in command of the Northern Department. Gates had commanded Ticonderoga under Schuyler in the summer and fall of 1776. In March 1777 Congress gave the Northern command to Gates, but recalled General Schuyler late in May. Gates refused to resume his subordinate station at Ticonderoga, and Congress assigned Maj. Gen. Arthur St. Clair to command that post. During his brief tenure Gates, too, gave his attention to logistical problems. He redistributed the forces so that the line of communications from Albany would be better guarded, he ordered flour to be stored at Stillwater and at Fort Edward, and that the provisions be checked at Stillwater and Half Moon; however, little in the way of preparation and supply build-up was really accomplished during the two-month interim under Gates' command.

Local rivalries and jealousies among the individual states undoubtedly had far-reaching significance for the whole Continental war effort. They extended to the halls of Congress, the market places, and the Continental Army; but nowhere were their effects more evident than in the defense of New York against invasion. In a way, General Schuyler's greatest handicap was his New York citizenship. Gates, the Virginian, seemed far more successful in en-

---

[4] Copy of orders to Capt Marquisie, assistant engineer, 18 March 1777, in Proceedings, Trial of Gen. Schuyler, p. 87

[5] Extract, Ltr to Committee of Congress Appointed to Visit the Northern Department, 9 November 1776, in Proceedings, Trial of Gen. Schuyler, p. 37

ticing support from New England, just as Washington, the Virginian, won general support at the siege of Boston and later. Surely one of the reasons Washington superseded Artemus Ward, the Massachusetts general, in the command of the troops before Boston was the feeling of Massachusetts leaders that troops from the other colonies would be more likely to join the defense if an outsider were in command. New Yorkers, as the decisive days of 1777 approached, appear to have reasoned in the same way.

The Invasion and the Campaign

Peter Stuyvesant had observed over a century before, following the loss of Fort Orange to the English, "whosoever, by ship or ships, is master on the [Hudson] river, will in a short time be master of the fort." [6] The British had been in control of the mouth of the Hudson for some time, and it only remained for them to extend their control up the river to split the United States in two and to render mutual support between New England and the middle and southern states virtually impossible. But with the series of intervening falls and rapids along the way, more than ships alone were required for the task.

Preparations in Canada

While American preparations were going forward with varying degrees of success in and about New York, Lt. Gen. John Burgoyne was at work in Canada preparing his expedition for the march southward by way

of Lake Champlain and the Hudson. With the help of Lt. Col. Barry St. Leger's diversionary expedition down the Mohawk from Lake Ontario and a movement of British forces northward from New York City to meet him, Burgoyne hoped to gain complete British control of the Hudson valley, and thus open the way for an early conclusion of the war.

Sir Guy Carleton, governor of Quebec and commander of British forces in Canada, had received instructions to make the necessary logistical preparations for Burgoyne's expedition. Though doubtless disappointed at not receiving the command of so promising an enterprise himself, Carleton appears to have let no personal feelings interfere with his collection of supplies and equipment. Even so, he did little toward getting the transportation facilities essential for the expedition before Burgoyne's arrival. After his arrival on the scene Burgoyne waited for a month before doing anything to obtain the horses, carts, and drivers he would need, for he counted on having a large number of unarmed Canadian *corvées* formed into detachments to carry supplies across the portages. The use of carrying companies had worked well in other times and places, but in this case nothing could induce sufficient Canadian farm laborers to respond, thus making the acquisition of horses and carts and drivers even more important.

As it turned out, the contractors were unable to supply even the numbers of horses they had agreed to, and many of the drivers later deserted. Moreover, the British commander had hoped to have 2,000 Canadian militiamen with his army of something over 8,000 regulars (including over 3,000 German mercenaries) to serve as escorts and as pioneers to clear roads and build bridges,

---

[6] Quoted in Herbert L. Osgood, *The American Colonies in the 17th Century,* 3 vols. (New York: Macmillan Co., 1904–1907), II, 391.

but the total number of Canadians dwindled to about 150, and he had about half the 1,000 Indians he had anticipated. Despite difficulties with procuring transportation and with local recruiting, Burgoyne set out from Canada in the middle of June with a respectable force of about 9,500 men. He reached Ticonderoga on 1 July 1777, and seized the fort five days later.

Fall of Ticonderoga

By occupying Ticonderoga the Americans had imposed upon themselves the difficulties of carrying supplies between the Hudson (at Fort Edward) and the lakes. Moreover, the position of Ticonderoga at the northern tip of Lake George and just west of Lake Champlain permitted the British to sail with their heavy equipment, provisions, and heavily uniformed soldiers practically to the doorstep of the main American defense positions. The stretches of forest and hills that had to be cut through and climbed over, the rivers that had to be crossed, the falls that had to be bypassed between Fort Edward and Ticonderoga would have presented a critical barrier to the British advance had the Americans chosen to make their stand around Fort Edward. The enemy would have had to drag guns and supplies across rough country to arrive tired and disorganized before well-prepared defensive positions manned by a force still intact and well-supplied by the Hudson waterway. Instead, with scarcely one-third enough men to adequately garrison the Ticonderoga position, General St. Clair's force fell easy victim to Burgoyne's attack with serious losses of men and of large quantities of supplies. The British captured forty artillery pieces, large stocks of ammunition,

and 200 boats. Also left behind (mostly at Mount Independence) in the evacuation were 1,768 barrels of flour, 649 barrels of pork, 5 barrels of beef, 36 bushels of salt, 100 pounds of biscuit, 180 of peas, and 120 gallons of rum.

Ticonderoga was a kind of "Gibraltar" with such psychological importance that presumably an effort had to be made to hold it. In the aftermath of its fall members of the Continental Congress called for heads to roll, and the old New England–New York rivalry reasserted itself. Men from the eastern states denounced Schuyler as a villain and a traitor. Some maintained that he had traitorously sent too much food to Ticonderoga, so that it would be available for the British when they captured the place, while others insisted that he had prevented sufficient food from arriving for the men to hold the fort. A Congressional investigating committee was appointed to inquire into the matter, and it recommended court-martial.

Both General St. Clair and General Schuyler were tried. St. Clair was accused of treachery, cowardice, and incompetence for abandoning Ticonderoga and Mount Independence without a fight, and for losing many men and large quantities of supplies in so doing, but the court found him not guilty. Schuyler was charged with neglect of duty in being absent from Ticonderoga during the critical time, but he maintained that the commander of a whole department should not permit himself to be shut up in one fort under siege, that Congress had assigned General St. Clair to command at Ticonderoga, and that he, as department commander, could perform the greatest service by keeping the lines of communication open. He too was acquitted with the highest honor.

Tactics, Logistics, and Mobility

As he rode between Stillwater and Saratoga en route to Ticonderoga, General Schuyler had received the distressing news that the fort had fallen. Refusing to despair, he hastened to Fort Edward to do what he could to reorganize the fleeing American forces and stop Burgoyne. With his keen appreciation of logistical problems, Schuyler resorted to expedients to magnify those problems for the British as much as possible. He set brigades of axemen felling trees across the roads and into the navigable waters of Wood Creek. More important, he adopted a "scorched earth" policy for the whole area of the British advance. He had crops burned, bridges destroyed, and all possible horses, cattle, and wheeled vehicles moved out of Burgoyne's reach.[7] (*Map 2*)

Occupying Fort Edward without opposition, for Schuyler had withdrawn southward, Burgoyne gave his attention to bringing up his guns and heavy stores from Fort George. He was anxious to move forward, but not anxious enough to lighten his load. It was a frustrating, back-breaking task to move the supplies and equipment the sixteen to eighteen miles between Fort George and Fort Edward over the hilly, rough, often muddy road with only enough draft animals for a fraction of the tonnage. Carts continually broke down. Not over one-third of the horses contracted for in Canada had arrived by August, and the British were lucky to find fifty teams of oxen in the whole area.[8]

In the contest between weight and mobility, Burgoyne sacrificed mobility. He had more men than he could feed satisfactorily with his transportation. The British commander complained that a general in America must spend twenty hours considering how to feed his army for every one that he could give to thinking about how to fight it. He felt he needed extra men to garrison the forts at key points along his lengthening line of communication. He thought he needed all of his five or six thousand Regulars to accomplish his mission, but the very numbers made its accomplishment more difficult. Doubtless he had too much artillery: he insisted on dragging along first forty-six, then thirty-six guns—a greater number proportionate to his infantry than ordinarily would have been found in a British army even on favorable terrain. And each gun called for more ammunition; he carried nine tons of projectiles for his six and three pounders. He presumed he would have to use his guns against the series of forts in his path or against field works which the Americans were likely to prepare. But the delay in dragging up the cannon gave the Americans time to prepare their defenses—as a contemporary observed: "It was the very movement of that apparatus that created the necessity of employing it."[9] Burgoyne had too much baggage; his personal baggage alone required thirty carts.

---

[7] The material in this section is based primarily on· John Burgoyne, *A State of the Expedition from Canada, as laid before the House of Commons,* (London, 1780); *The Annual Register,* 1777; Hoffman Nickerson, *The Turning Point of the Revolution* (Boston: Houghton, 1928); Charles W. Snell, *Saratoga,* National Park Service Historical Handbook Series 4 (Washington, 1950).

[8] It is the conclusion of Charles W. Snell, formerly National Park Service historian at the Saratoga National Historical Park, and author of a detailed history of the Saratoga campaign, that Schuyler's action in removing horses, cattle, and vehicles from the area did more than anything else to halt Burgoyne's army.

[9] Quoted in Nickerson, *The Turning Point of the Revolution,* p. 165

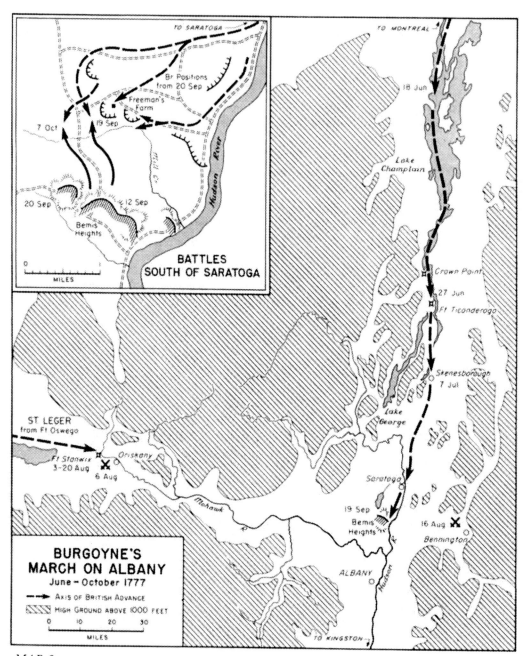

BATTLES
SOUTH OF SARATOGA

TO SARATOGA

Br Positions
from 20 Sep

Freeman's
Farm

7 Oct   19 Sep

20 Sep

12 Sep

Bemis
Heights

Hudson River

0
MILES

TO MONTREAL

18 Jun

Lake
Champlain

Crown Point

27 Jun

Ft Ticonderoga

Skenesborough
7 Jul

ST LEGER
from Ft Oswego

Lake
George

Ft Stanwix   Oriskany
3-20 Aug
6 Aug

Mohawk

Saratoga

19 Sep

Bemis
Heights

16 Aug

Bennington

ALBANY

Hudson

BURGOYNE'S
MARCH ON ALBANY
June – October 1777

Axis of British Advance

High Ground above 1000 feet

0   10   20   30
MILES

TO KINGSTON

MAP 2

The Bennington Raid

After fifteen days of heavy going, Burgoyne's men were able to move only ten boats and four days' food supplies to the Hudson River. The situation called for a bold gamble—and Burgoyne's gamble was to strike for supplies, not directly at the American force opposing him. His instructions to the commander of a detachment of German dragoons for a raid on Bennington, Vermont, were especially to get wagons and carriages with oxen to pull them, cattle, and (what almost persuaded the dragoon commander of the value of the expedition) horses for mounting his encumbered dragoons.

Things already had started to go badly for the British when St. Leger's force of about 1,600 Tories and Indians was checked by local militia at the bloody battle of Oriskany near Fort Stanwix on 6 August, but the real change in fortune came at Bennington. After an American force of New England militia under Brig. Gen. John Stark of New Hampshire administered a sound defeat to the detachment of German mercenaries (16 August 1777), Burgoyne had to give up the idea of supplying his troops from American stores until such time as he might reach Albany. The only advantage he gained from the Bennington raid was a reduction by about 800 in the number of men he had to feed, increasing seven days' supplies to eight. In his report to the House of Commons Burgoyne said:

> After the disappointment of the Bennington expedition, it was necessary to press forward a necessary supply of provision and other indispensable articles from Fort George. It is not uncommon for gentlemen, unacquainted with the peculiarities of the country to which I am alluding, to calculate the transport of magazines by measuring the distance upon a map, and then applying the resources of carriage, as practiced in other countries. I request permission to show their mistake.[10]

By this time a sizable American force had assembled to oppose the British invasion. Schuyler, refusing to get into a situation to be annihilated, had withdrawn first to Moses Hill, then had crossed the Hudson to Saratoga (later renamed Schuylerville), and on 3 August had halted near Stillwater to prepare defensive positions. After receiving word of St. Leger's arrival before Fort Stanwix, Schuyler dispatched an expedition to march under the command of Benedict Arnold to the relief of that fort, and withdrew the remainder of his force to the mouth of the Mohawk, twelve miles south of Stillwater and nine miles above Albany.

Surrender at Saratoga

Congress again shifted the command of the Northern Department, and once more Gates replaced Schuyler. Although appointed on 4 August, General Gates did not arrive at Albany to assume command until 19 August—just three days after the Bennington victory.

Freeman's Farm

In the weeks immediately after taking command, Gates was especially concerned about supply problems. Changes in personnel in the commissary departments had created confusion that had to be straightened out. His army was short of ammunition, and Gates kept appealing to the Springfield Armory to hasten the shipment of ordnance stores. The timely arrival of arms from France made badly needed muskets avail-

---

[10] Burgoyne, *State of the Expedition from Canada*, p. 20.

able for many of the units, and cannon, powder, clothing, and tents arrived from France when most needed to restore much of the goods lost at Ticonderoga. While Albany was considered the principal supply base, much of the activity of the commissaries supporting Gates's force centered around Peekskill where Maj. Gen. Israel Putnam, in command of the Highlands of the Hudson area, acted as something of a communications zone commander.

When Burgoyne reached Freeman's Farm on 19 September, about 9,800 Continental troops were available to Gates in the Northern Department, plus about 4,500 co-operating militia. Burgoyne had about 6,800 regulars and 870 auxiliaries.

Although the sharp action of 19 September involved only a part of the total forces, the Americans faced serious supply shortages afterward, especially of ammunition. Not only was it impossible to find bullets; not even materials to make bullets could be found. Through General Schuyler's help and the fortunate circumstance of an open line of communication the situation was eased. Though naturally disappointed at being relieved of command, Schuyler was not one to sulk in his tent and he offered to give what service he could in any capacity. Back in Albany he collected lead from the windows and roofs of the city to make the musket balls Gates' army so badly needed. At his own expense he also sent lumber to build a ponton bridge for retreat to the east side of the Hudson should that become necessary. General Gates sent to General Putnam for help in replenishing food stores. At this point Sir Henry Clinton was advancing toward the Highlands in a move which might yet bring relief to Burgoyne, and Putnam had to be looking after his own defenses; nevertheless he saw to it that 300

barrels of hard bread were rowed up the Hudson from Fishkill Landing, 300 more from Esopus (Kingston), and another 300 barrels sent from Sharon, Connecticut. Shortly thereafter he sent up 1,250 barrels of flour, which he swore would be the last, but a few days later he sent another 300 barrels of bread from Fishkill.

Bemis Heights: The Second Battle

For seventeen days after the engagement at Freeman's Farm the two armies sat facing each other. While Burgoyne vainly awaited the arrival of Clinton, regiment after regiment arrived to swell the ranks of Gates's Northern Army until it totaled more than 23,000 men—about half Continentals and half militia. After putting his troops on short rations on 3 October, Burgoyne had to decide quickly whether to attempt a retreat to the lakes or to attack. He still hoped that he could drive through the American positions and eventually meet Clinton. He determined first to order a reconnaissance in force. American counterattacks broke up the force and went on to take a British redoubt in the battle on 7 October for Bemis Heights. Burgoyne then decided to withdraw to Saratoga. The Americans were unable to pursue immediately because of the ration situation. The ration cycle for American troops was four days and the last issue had been on 3 October, so that another four days' supplies were due to be issued on the 7th. This was suspended during the battle, and no provision was made to echelon the ration supply points forward to follow the army. Consequently, units had to march back a mile and a half to camp to draw rations. It took the whole day of 9 October for the troops to draw and cook their rations. But Burgoyne still was not able to move swiftly enough to get away.

Hemmed in by Americans on every side and his supplies almost depleted with no hope of replenishment, Burgoyne at last surrendered on 17 October.

Evacuation and Hospitalization

Many of the most seriously wounded casualties of the Saratoga battles were evacuated to Albany. A week after the surrender a thousand wounded Americans, Britons, and Germans remained crowded in a Dutch church and several private houses that had been pressed into service as hospitals. Enemy soldiers received the same care as Americans, and English and German surgeons looked after them—though the greater skill of the English and the less sympathetic dispositions of the Germans were noticeable. Some thirty surgeons and surgeons' mates, altogether, were on constant duty. They worked throughout the long days trepanning fractured skulls, amputating limbs, dressing long-neglected wounds, treating with tincture of myrrh wounds that had become infested with maggots, and trying to comfort the wretched patients for whom little else could be done.

Summary

It would be difficult to find any campaign in which logistics played a more direct and decisive part than in this campaign of the Revolution. In the final analysis, it was the breakdown in Burgoyne's transportation—the failure of procurement in Canada, the failure of the *corvée* system, the failure of procurement or seizure en route—and the consequent delays which gave the Ameri-

cans time to reorganize, and ultimately led to Burgoyne's surrender. What he considered essential in numbers of men and artillery and baggage proved to be only a burden against success.

As has been noted, Britain's greatest logistical advantage during the Revolution was its command of the sea. When the British incautiously moved inland and transferred their dependence for supplies from direct support by the sea to long, difficult overland and inland waterway supply lines they abandoned that advantage—and met disaster. The British surrender at Saratoga had far-reaching results, for it brought France into the war on the side of the Americans, and France would ultimately neutralize British command of the sea sufficiently to bring about the final surrender of major British forces at Yorktown.

For their part, the Americans had developed a logistical system which, with all its specific failures and acute shortages, its cumbersome administration, and difficult interstate relations, probably worked at its best during the Saratoga campaign. Major lines of communication remained open throughout; resupply, though sometimes precarious, generally was adequate; and troops were sufficiently well re-equipped, particularly in the vastly superior firearm of Morgan's riflemen, to more than hold their own against the British and Germans.

Burgoyne allowed logistics to become his master instead of making logistics his servant. He was so concerned with getting everything up to meet all possible contingencies that he was too paralyzed to meet any contingency. In moving his heavy ordnance and stores he lost one of the most important elements in warfare—timing.

CHAPTER V

Deterioration and Revision

Crises in Supply and Transportation

Interspersed only by temporary periods of improvement, the supply and transportation systems of the Continental Army declined generally in effectiveness after the first year of the war. Logistical deficiencies became most pronounced during the winters, and Valley Forge and Morristown have become national symbols of the suffering and steadfastness of a little group of men who kept an army in the field and with it kept the flickering embers of the Revolution alive. The months in winter quarters, when simple existence and a little training were full-time occupations, were filled with greater hardship than most campaigns.

Beneath most of the obvious logistical difficulties lay a shortage of funds and an inadequate financial system. Financial deterioration continued until faith in Continental currency and in the public credit virtually disappeared. The failure of finance brought first an attempt to collect supplies from the states in kind, and at last the organization of a Treasury Department and appointment of a Superintendent of Finance who was assigned primary responsibility for Army procurement and who introduced the contract system. Centralization of administration finally included the appointment of a Secretary at War to oversee the military administration.

Valley Forge

In the week before Christmas 1777 the main army moved into the Valley Forge area. Streams and steep hills afforded defensive protection for the flanks and rear of the camp site, dense woods offered timber for shelter and fuel, and the Schuylkill River and Valley Creek provided a water supply. Washington of course wanted to avoid quartering his troops on the local inhabitants, and did not want to move into the towns farther west where the pressure of refugees already was creating problems. Some of his officers strongly opposed the Valley Forge site, but the commander in chief thought that the advantages of a fairly defensible location, that covered Reading and Lancaster from attack and protected the surrounding area from devastation while it denied the British access to provisions, outweighed the site's disadvantages.

Already wintry blasts were whistling through the hills, and the first order of business was shelter. Few buildings were to be found in the area, and, until they could build log huts, the men had to live in their thin, worn tents. As built to specifications, the cabins were sixteen feet long by fourteen feet wide with walls six and one-half feet high and high gabled roofs which were covered with saplings and straw or split boards. Windows were covered with oil

A Soldiers' Hut at Valley Forge, Restored

paper when it could be found. Inside, the cabins had bunks in three tiers built into each corner and a fireplace and chimney of clay-daubed wood at one end. General Washington offered a prize of $12.00 to the crew in each regiment that finished its hut in the quickest and most workmanlike manner, and Congress voted each man in the winning crew an extra month's pay. With these incentives, the men went to work— some felled trees, others trimmed and notched the logs, and still others dragged them to the site; some were put to preparing mud for caulking; then the huts were erected. The first party claimed its prize within two days, but, probably because of the lack of tools and nails, it was mid-January before all 9,000 men were housed. Even then many of the huts did not have enough straw for the roofs or for bedding or floor covering. Patients in the cabins set aside for hospitals had to lie on the bare poles of their bunks, for neither bed clothing nor straw was available for them. When the shortage became apparent, Congress authorized the Quartermaster General to seize straw, or if farmers refused to thresh their grain, seize the straw and the grain with it and pay only for the straw.

At least there was raw material with

SUPPLIES FOR VALLEY FORGE. *From an old woodcut.*

which to build shelter. Clothing supply was a more persistent problem. Some regiments had been destitute of clothes as early as October, partly because of the lax supply discipline of officers who did not make periodic inspections or report deficiencies. Hopes for early delivery of uniforms from France failed to materialize and efforts at local procurement were mostly ineffective. The Quartermaster General's transportation system virtually broke down. Even when items could be procured, poor co-ordination and lack of facilities held up delivery while thousands of men were without blankets and, because they had no decent shoes, sen-

tinals stood on their hats to protect their feet. At Christmas time more than one-third of the command was reported unfit for duty for want of clothing. A few states did well in providing clothing for their troops, which added to the discontent of the less fortunate. General Wayne applied 4,500 pounds of his own fortune toward clothing his men. Congress asked the states to adopt legislation for the appointment of agents who, in exchange for receipts or certificates, could seize for the Continental Army all woolen clothing, blankets, linens, shoes, stockings, hats—any articles suitable for the Army—from stocks that had been collected for sale, but not those for private use.

Actually, the winter of 1777–78 was relatively mild. Had huts been finished more promptly and had the supply of clothing and blankets been at all adequate, suffering from cold should have been negligible. In any event, the question soon came to be whether the main army would starve before it froze, for the food shortage was the worst of all.

Most of the winter the troops lived hand to mouth on scant provisions, and several times food stores were exhausted completely. When Washington learned, shortly before Christmas, that the meat supply was exhausted, that flour was reduced to twenty-five barrels, and that there were no prospects for additional supplies, he saw only three possibilities open for his army—starvation, dissolution, or dispersal so that the men might shift for themselves in finding food.

With the failure of the Clothier General's, Quartermaster General's, and Commissary General's departments, Congress intervened directly to procure wagons, clothing, meat, and flour. Washington's extraordinary powers were extended, and very reluctantly he resorted to impressment of supplies. Foraging and raiding parties had some success, and especially helpful were the raids of Allen McLane on British supply depots and farms holding supplies for the British. But conditions grew worse before they became better: in February the commissary had no provisions at all. General Washington's personal appeals to the governors of neighboring states received some response. He asked that the farmers set aside as many cattle as possible for army use, and that they bring in their produce for private sale at daily public markets he had organized at various places in the camp.

The shortage of transportation could cause all the other shortages. When private citizens were being paid 3 to 4 pounds a day for a wagon, team, and driver, Congress fixed a rate of 30 shillings for a wagon, four horses, and a driver, but few drivers could be found who would work for less than 40 to fifty shillings a day. Men who would drive for the Army's low pay ran the risk of being fined for absence if their militia units were called out while they were away. Many who did drive were unreliable and often abandoned the goods and left it to spoil. Even when wagons could be found, rain and snow had left the roads in such condition that they were impassable. Many draft horses belonging to the Army died of hunger at Valley Forge. Pork could not be brought from New Jersey, and flour had to be left on the wharves of the Susquehanna for want of transportation.

The sorry plight of the American soldiers at Valley Forge was in sharp contrast to the easy time the British were having in Philadelphia. Although he depended upon water communications with New York for most of his supplies, Maj. Gen. William Howe found the farmers of the surrounding counties quite willing to trade for British gold and he established markets around Philadelphia to encourage them. Trading with the British was not so much an expression of sympathy on the part of the farmers as it was a preference for hard money to Continental currency. In the contest of patriotism versus gold, gold had the advantage. Washington meted out severe punishment to soldiers found trading with the British, and he sent out patrols to stop supplies from reaching Philadelphia but with little success. Probably as demoralizing for the soldier at Valley Forge as his actual suffering were thoughts of the British living at ease in Philadelphia with the benefit of local food resources, and of civilians contentedly remaining by warm fires, eating well, reaping huge profits, and never exerting themselves for the relief of the miserable soldiers who were fighting their war.

After some revision in organization, and after the appointment of Nathanael Greene as Quartermaster General and Jeremiah Wadsworth as Commissary General of Purchases—and with the coming of spring—conditions began to improve. Attacking the transportation problem, Greene sent as far as New England and Virginia for wagons, sent engineers out to repair the roads and bridges between Valley Forge and Lancaster, had carts and boats constructed, established depots for grain all the way from the Hudson to Head of Elk, and persuaded the Pennsylvania legislature to relieve teamsters who were working for the Army from militia duty.

In the spring it was possible to issue a daily ration of one and a half pounds of bread, a pound of beef or fish or pork and beans, and a gill of whiskey. Soon fresh vegetables could be added to the ration, and the spring run of shad up the Schuylkill yielded thousands of fresh fish for daily consumption and hundreds of barrels of salted fish for future use.

With the benefit of Steuben's training program, Washington's army emerged from Valley Forge a better fighting organization. But how much justification there was for holding the main army in such a location amidst such suffering is open to some question. However desirable it may have been to keep an eye on the British at Philadelphia, or to hold a position for defending the surrounding region, Washington's first task was to keep an army in being. Weakened by exposure and near famine, the army at Val-

ley Forge hardly was in a position to do anything about the British in Philadelphia, or even to defend itself. Perhaps as much would have been gained by marching the whole army to the South where a more agreeable climate could have been found. Or, when transportation broke down, the army might have been marched to sources of supplies as Anthony Wayne had suggested in proposing an operation in New England when quantities of clothing that had been imported could not be moved from Portsmouth. "We shall," announced Wayne, "like Mahomet and the mountain, go to the clothing if the clothing won't come to us." [1] Marching the men up and down the countryside, from one state to another, surely would have harassed the British as much as did the enfeebled army at Valley Forge. Probably the greatest drawbacks to such a course as this were the political consequences of an apparent abandonment of the Philadelphia area, and the fact that the men did not have sufficient shoes and clothing to permit them to march. Still, the dispatch of whole regiments to act as carrying parties would seem to have been preferable to huddling around the fires at Valley Forge while starvation threatened.

Brief Respite

The energetic efforts of Greene and Wadsworth showed good results. During the whole period from early summer 1778 to November 1779 complaints about scarcity of food were relatively infrequent. Fortunately the winter of 1778–79 was mild, and the tactical situation was such that Washington believed he could avoid concentrating all of his army at one place.

[1] Quoted in Hatch, *The Administration of the Revolutionary Army*, p 99

With an eye to the availability of supplies in various localities, Washington divided his infantry among Danbury, Connecticut, West Point, New York, and Middlebrook, New Jersey, that winter. The cavalry was dispersed all the way from Durham, Connecticut, to Winchester, Virginia, in order to find forage.

In March 1779 Washington reported that his troops were better clothed than before, but he still pointed to irregularities and to inefficiency in the clothing department. He blamed mismanagement for the failure of large supplies of imported clothing to reach the troops and for the storage of other supplies far away from the troops and inaccessible to them. Even the new reorganizations failed to bring a satisfactory remedy, for there still was no centralized control.

Morristown

Although Valley Forge has come to be synonymous with winter suffering in popular American thinking, the winter of 1779–80 at Morristown and the neighboring camp at Jockey Hollow was much worse. Blizzards piled up several feet of snow, keeping the camp practically snowbound much of the time and adding immeasurably to the suffering of the ill-fed, ill-clothed men. As at Valley Forge, huts had to be built, but this time the weather was much colder and the delays just as long. Six hundred acres of woodland were cleared to build cabins for the 10,000 to 12,000 troops, many of whom were clothed in rags, and some whose only covering, day and night, was a single, worn blanket. Frequently the men were without bread for a week at a time, and issues of meat were limited to two pounds per man for ten days; sometimes there was

neither meat nor bread for periods of two and three days. Once more the soldiers were reduced to near starvation in the midst of plenty. Procurement was becoming increasingly difficult as farmers and merchants refused to accept the depreciated Continental or state currency. They either wanted hard money or scarce commodities, such as sugar and salt, which the Army needed but could not get for itself. At one time the Pennsylvania Government collected 5,000 cattle for the Army, but they could not be butchered because salt was not available to cure the meat. Short of waterpower, New York millers ground grain only for civilian consumption.

Heavy demands on the Army's limited funds developed early. While the camps were being constructed 400 to 600 civilian workers were employed. Inflation was such that wagoners had to be paid 20 pounds a day, and carpenters received $20 to $25 a day. Wood for fuel cost $6,000 to $7,000 a day; 100,000 bushels of coal, and quantities of iron were needed for the smiths; some 1,200,000 board feet of lumber were needed; and large sums were necessary for nails and other items, and to pay the foragers. At Christmas the Quartermaster General estimated that he needed a million dollars for these requirements. The Commissary General, too, was about out of funds by the end of December, and he requested $20,000. Having paid as high as 20 pounds a bushel for wheat, he said that he would husband the money as best he could, but that it should not be expected he would be able to purchase as much with that amount as with $100 seven years earlier.[2] Funds were not available in the amounts or

---

[2] Ltr, Lewis to Furman, DQMG, 25 December 1779 MS Morristown Headquarters Collection.

the currencies needed and once more Washington had to resort to other measures.

Working closely with local magistrates who were called in for a series of meetings with the Quartermaster General and commissary officers, Washington divided New Jersey into districts, and set a quota of provisions for each one to supply. Officers assigned to each district to collect the supplies were to apply to the local justice for a warrant authorizing seizure when necessary, whereupon a commissary officer and two magistrates would appraise the value of the goods, and a certificate would be given for payment, at the owner's option. Under this scheme Bergen County, for example, was to supply 600 bushels of grain and 200 cattle; Salem's quota was 750 bushels of grain and 200 cattle.[3] The New Jersey farmers responded so well that by 22 January it was optimistically reported: "Our troops are now very well supplied and our stores well filled with short forage"[4]

The adequacy of supplies after the response of the New Jersey farmers was temporary. By the end of January Joseph Lewis, quartermaster at Morristown, wrote to Moore Furman, the Deputy Quartermaster General: "I am under necessity of informing you that the loud clamours and complaints which monthly increase in arithmetical progression as the time elapses or the depreciation increases since the sup-

plies was given or service was done for the public—will oblige me also to withdraw my services, leave the post, and fly to you or some other place for refuge or protection."[5]

Since New Jersey resources already had been used in considerable quantity, Washington and the Board of War applied to other states for assistance in February and March. The governor of Maryland appointed commissioners to search and seize grain, but they raised as much hostility as provisions. The Commissary General found large quantities of beef cattle in Connecticut, but the prices were high, and he had no money. The difficulty was not only in a lack of funds with which to pay farmers and merchants, but the inability of the Commissary General of Purchases to find assistants who would work for Continental money.

Again, as at Valley Forge, the transportation problem was at the base of the supply problem, and questions of finance lay beneath it all. The Morristown post required never less than 100 teams, and frequently as many as 400 or 600 were used. There was some confusion in different rates (14, 15, or 20 pounds a day) paid by different officers, and in the practice of brigade and regimental quartermasters issuing certificates on their own authority for wagons and teams. In general the quartermaster appointed wagon masters to raise and conduct brigades of eight or ten four-horse teams to work with designated units. They were engaged to work until spring, but when neither cash nor forage was forthcoming many quit, and the troops suffered for it. Under their contracts, the wagoners were allowed one day in seven to repair equip-

---

[3] Christopher Ward, *The War of the Revolution,* 2 vols. (New York: The Macmillan Company, 1952), II, 613–14; Johnson, *The Administration of the American Commissariat,* p. 160; Hatch, *The Administration of the American Revolutionary Army,* p. 105; Ltr, William Henry, 2 January 1780, Library of Congress; Ltr, Lewis to Justice Stiles and copies to Stephen Day and Seth Babbit, 7 January 1780; Cir. Ltr, Lewis to All Justices, 21 Jan 1780. Last two in Morristown Headquarters Collection.

[4] Ltr, Lewis to Furman, 22 January 1780. Photostat in Morristown Headquarters Collection.

[5] Ltr, Lewis to Furman, 31 January 1780. Photostat in Morristown Headquarters Collection.

ment and collect forage, and one-half day each month for shoeing; any other time away from camp was not to be paid for. Many of the wagoners came a great distance from their farms each day, and arrived so late and left so early that the quartermaster insisted that they find quarters in camp. Then there was so much theft of horses and gear that some refused to stay at all; and others stayed only on condition that they be permitted to find quarters near the camp; however, so many officers and civilian carpenters, artificers, and other workers had taken quarters near the camp that the wagoners could find none closer than three or four miles distant.

Shortages reached the critical stage again in March. Quartermaster Lewis wrote, on the 22d: "We are now in the greatest distress for want of teams . . . what few we have left are on half allowance of grain, without hay. . . . The troops are likewise suffering for want of bread and unless some relief comes, we shall in three or four days feel the dreadful consequences attending the total want of bread and forage. . . . Good God . . . where are our resources fled—we are in the most pitiful situation and almost distracted with calls that are not in our power to answer." [6]

Instead of improving with spring that year Washington's supply situation continued to worsen. Creditors harassed the commissary agents for large sums owed for supplies already delivered and consumed, salt practically disappeared, and there was little prospect for any sufficiency of supplies. The Army had learned to expect to half starve during the winter but in 1780 it appeared that short rations would prevail most

of the summer as well. By 5 May 1780 provisions in the storehouses at Morristown had been reduced to seven days' supply of meat and thirteen days' supply of flour, with small chance for replenishment in sight. Charles Stuart, the commissary general of issues at Morristown, blamed local agents. In a letter to Moore Furman, Stuart wrote that it would be necessary to send some flour to West Point, "where they are suffering," and to American prisoners in New York. "For God's sake don't resign now," he pleaded. [7]

On 21 May 1780 the food supply failed completely, and four days later troops of the Connecticut Line mutinied and threatened to go into the country to find food for themselves. Quick-thinking officers were able to restore order, but only the arrival of supplies could restore confidence and morale. For Washington the Revolution had reached its darkest hour. On 28 May he wrote to Joseph Reed, president of the Executive Council of Pennsylvania:

All our departments, all our operations are at a stand, and unless a system very different from that which has for a long time prevailed be immediately adopted throughout the states our affairs must soon become desperate beyond the possibility of recovery. . . . Indeed I have almost ceased to hope. The country in general is in such a state of insensibility and indifference to its interests, that I dare not flatter myself with any change for the better. . . .

This is a decisive moment; one of the most, I will go further and say the most, important America has seen.

. . . .

The matter is reduced to a point. Either Pennsylvania must give us all the aid we ask of her, or we can undertake nothing. We

---

[6] Ltr, Lewis to Furman, 22 March 1780. Photostat in Headquarters Collection.

[7] Ltr, Stuart to Furman, 5 May 1780. Morristown Headquarters Collection.

must renounce every idea of cooperation, and must confess to our allies that we look wholly to them for our safety. This will be a state of humiliation and bitterness against which the feelings of every good American ought to revolt. . . . God grant we may be properly impressed with the consequences. . . .

The crisis in every point of view is extraordinary and extraordinary expedients are necessary. I am decided in this opinion.[8]

On the 29th the bitter news of the surrender of General Lincoln's entire force to Clinton at Charleston reached Washington. On the 31st he wrote to Joseph Jones, one of the Virginia delegates to the Continental Congress: "Certain I am that unless Congress speaks in a more decisive tone; unless they are vested with powers by the several States competent to the great purposes of War, or assume them as matter of right; and they, and the states respectively, act with more energy than they hitherto have done, that our cause is lost." [9]

On 12 August 1780 it was reported at Morristown that there were only twelve barrels of flour at the camp, and the army's daily requirement there was ninety-five barrels. By this time food supply actually was determining the movements of Washington's army. After a demonstration against New York, Washington returned to the New Jersey side of the Hudson in order not to consume supplies on the other side that might be needed later. When a force of Pennsylvania militia, estimated at 4,500 men, came to join him about 15 August, Washington had to turn them back, or find them a camp near food supplies, because he could not feed them. A few days later he marched to the vicinity of Fort Lee, on the

Hudson, to impress food supplies in that area.

Collapse and Reform in Finance and Procurement

Financial troubles for the United States began with the start of the Revolution, and supply officers almost continuously were harassed by a lack of funds. Having cast off the taxes of the British Government, colonial leaders hesitated to impose others—not only were the colonists opposed to taxation without representation, they were opposed to any taxes at all. A few states were able to maintain some system of tax collections, but those in which new Revolutionary governments replaced the old did not venture any taxation for two or three years. All the state tax systems were weak, and the Continental Congress relied for its support upon the states, who in turn relied upon the towns and counties, though with the issue of paper currency this order of dependence was reversed to a certain extent.

Inflation

In June 1775, Congress authorized an issue of bills not to exceed $2,000,000 in Spanish dollars. The issue was to be supported by tax quotas, payable in Continental bills or in gold or silver, set for each state to be paid in four annual installments beginning in 1779. In this way Congress had a way to make public expenditures without obtaining prior approval of the states in each case, and the states were bound to meet their expenditures by taxation. The money ideas of the members of Congress appeared to be generally sound, and they had no intention of issuing uncontrolled printing press money.

---

[8] Fitzpatrick, *The Writings of George Washington*, XVIII, 434–39.

[9] *Ibid.*, XVIII, 453.

But failure of the states to collect the required taxes, growing demands of an unexpectedly long war, and rising prices due to speculation and scarcity of goods led inevitably to that result. Once the process had begun it became a vicious circle with financial disaster at its vortex.

In the spring of 1780 the supply departments of the Army had neither money nor credit. The only thing left was barter and private credit. The Army might not have been able to survive had not a group of Philadelphia merchants, at the instigation of the French minister, formed a bank to extend credit for supplying it.

After the Council of Pennsylvania on 1 May 1781 quoted Continental currency at 175 to 1 against specie—and the public multiplied that by three to get a "realistic" rate of 525 to 1—Continental currency virtually disappeared, though it did continue to circulate to some extent in Virginia, North Carolina, and some other places for another year or so.

Specific Supplies

In the meantime the Army had to be fed, clothed, and equipped. With finances failing, Congress decided that the only thing to do was to obtain contributions from the states in kind.

In December 1779, when the treasury as well as the storehouses were depleted, Congress adopted a plan for the direct requisition of "specific supplies" on the states. Under the plan quotas of meat, flour, hay, fodder, salt, rum, tobacco, and other items were apportioned among the states according to their special resources. In this way each state could furnish directly the supplies which best suited it without the intervention of money, and the state could in turn collect taxes in kind from its inhabitants to meet the quotas. In effect, Congress recognized the complete inadequacy of the currency system and sanctioned barter. The system of specific supplies went into effect on 25 February 1780 with the approval by Congress of comprehensive quotas for all states (excepting Georgia), together with a price scale for comparing the relative value of commodities.[10]

While at first glance this system appeared to be a simple and ingenious solution to a difficult problem, it had grave weaknesses. Quartermaster General Greene saw them at once, and he drew up a long memorandum to impress his misgivings upon the commander in chief. He said in part:

The measure seems to be calculated more for the convenience of each state than for the accommodation of the service. The aggregate quantity ordered, tho' far short of the demands of the army, is proportioned on the states in such a manner that it would be difficult, if not impossible, to draw it into use; and this difficulty will increase as the scene of action may change from one extreme of the Continent to another.

Land Transportation is such a heavy and expensive branch of business, that more regard should be paid to this subject in the first purchase of all heavy articles than even to the prices of the articles themselves—for were such to be given in some states, and to be transported to the place of consumption, at the expence of the Continent, the public had better purchase them at double the price, nearer the place of consumption.

I do not mean to reject the plan altogether, but to improve upon it in some way, that the supplies of each state may be directed, like

---

[10] *Journals of the Continental Congress,* 25 February 1780. XVI, 196–97. Georgia at this time was still under British occupation and thus excepted from the quota.

little Rivulets, into one common channel for the support of the army at large.[11]

Attempts to collect the designated supplies demonstrated only too well General Greene's observations. States previously unable or unwilling to collect tax quotas voted by their own representatives did no better in making deliveries in kind. The administrative burden was nearly impossible. State representatives argued about fair apportionment of quotas. Furthermore, just as Greene anticipated, the transportation problem was an almost insurmountable barrier—when a state's supplies were deposited at a central depot, there was no way to move them.

Now the Army had to deal with thirteen state governments in order to gets its supplies. As James Madison observed, since Congress had given up the power of emitting money, it was as dependent upon the states as was the King on Parliament. Congress could not enlist, pay, nor feed a single soldier until the states first provided the means.[12]

Crisis of 1780–81

In the critical year of 1780 Congress and the commander in chief faced three momentous and immediate problems at once—feeding the troops then present, building an army for the next campaign, and, above all else, alleviating the financial chaos that threatened to undermine the whole military effort and to ruin the country.

Throughout the summer of 1780 the Army's supply situation was worse than it had been in previous years. Many of the quotas were unfilled, many that were filled were not moved, and many that were delivered contained foodstuffs of lowest quality. Specific supplies provided less than had the purchasing system. By October the Army again was reduced to living off the country.

When cold weather returned, the need for clothing again became critical. On New Year's Day 1781 the men of the Pennsylvania Line, disgruntled because of lack of pay and lack of clothing, staged an ugly mutiny at their Jockey Hollow camp, and began to march toward Philadelphia to impress their grievances upon Congress. They returned to camp only after negotiations at Princeton resulted in promises that they would be furnished certain items of clothing, that they would receive some of the pay due them, and that terms of enlistment would be clarified. A short time later when another mutiny broke out in the New Jersey Line at Pompton, swift and strict measures restored order.

Even with the advantage of less severe weather, conditions in the South were not much better. When General Greene took command of the Southern Army at Charlotte, North Carolina, in December 1780, he found that a force listed as having a strength of over 2,400 had less than 1,500 present for duty, and that not 800 of those present could be considered properly clothed and fed. Logistics in large part determined his first two actions—movement of the force to an area more agreeable for obtaining supplies locally, and risking the division of his army in the face of the superior forces of

[11] Remarks on the Resolution of Congress of the 25th February 1780 Requiring Each State to Furnish Certain Species of Supplies for the Support of the Army, Nathanael Greene to Washington. Washington Papers, Library of Congress (Some punctuation modified.)

[12] Letter from James Madison to Thomas Jefferson, 6 May 1780, in Edmund C. Burnett, ed., *Letters of Members of the Continental Congress*, 8 vols (Washington: Carnegie Institution of Washington, 1921–36), V, 128–29.

Cornwallis on the assumption that it would be easier for the two smaller contingents to live off the country.

When Benedict Arnold landed in Virginia with a British force of about 2,000 men at the beginning of January 1781, the only force on hand to oppose him was a detachment of 600 men under Steuben, which it was hoped would provide a nucleus for the mobilization of Virginia militia. Steuben was having a difficult enough time in supplying this small force; he reported that he had clothing for only 150 of his men. A British raid a few weeks earlier had shown the lack of preparedness in Virginia, and the legislature's call upon the counties for clothing, military stores, and wagons, and its order for the drafting of 3,000 men were unsuccessful. Thomas Jefferson, then governor of Virginia, was able to do little to raise troops or collect supplies, and those that were collected became the objectives of Arnold's raids. Almost at will he marched up and down the peninsula destroying stores, crops, and animals.

In March 1781 Washington sent Lafayette into Virginia with a force of about 1,500 men to try to put an end to Arnold's forays. It has been written of Lafayette's movement: "No operation of the war more clearly demonstrates the value of good logistics." [13] The expedition began auspiciously but quickly deteriorated as supplies ran out and plans for resupply failed. Thanks to drafts on the French treasury, Lafayette was able to distribute shoes and clothing to his men and to arrange for the force to draw rations every third day. At Head of Elk he collected arms, ammunition, medicine, and clothing to be shipped

down Chesapeake Bay. The French had agreed to send a fleet with a like number of troops to co-operate with Lafayette, but a British fleet countered that plan. Very soon Lafayette found it necessary to resort to impressment even for scant supplies—a step he took with great reluctance, but by April serious shortages were driving his men to desertion. The Virginia legislature had failed to adopt a bill for impressing supplies, and though Jefferson resorted to some requisitioning as the emergency grew, he apologized to local magistrates with the explanation that the legislature would have approved if in session. For the most part, however, the governor failed to act decisively or effectively. In May Governor Jefferson refused to recognize Lafayette's requisitions for horses, holding that taking stallions and mares would be tantamount to "killing the hen that laid the golden egg." [14] Shortly thereafter Cornwallis moved into Virginia from North Carolina, and on 20 May 1781 effected a junction with Arnold at Petersburg. Then the best Lafayette could do was keep out of Cornwallis' way until reinforcements arrived.

Superintendent of Finance

By this time Congress was ready to admit failure of the system of specific supplies. Finance had failed. Requisitions in kind had failed. The only thing left to do was the thing that must have seemed obvious, even if impolitic, all along—to centralize the management of the country's financial affairs in the hands of a person empowered to act decisively.

As early as February 1780 some leaders had suggested the appointment of a single

---

[13] Henry B. Harrington, *Battles of the American Revolution, 1775–1781* (New York, 1876), p. 591.

[14] James Brown Scott, *De Grasse à Yorktown* (Paris, 1931), p. 89.

financier to replace the boards and committees that had been attempting to run the Treasury Department, but another year of financial distress passed before Congress was able to come around to adopting the suggestion. An act of 6 February 1781 provided for three executive departments of treasury, marine, and war, each under an individual administrator responsible to Congress. Two weeks later Congress elected Robert Morris to head the Treasury Department with the title of Superintendent of Finance. At first reluctant to serve at such a thankless task when he was doing so well in business, Morris finally was persuaded by friends of the absolute necessity of his taking the office. On 13 March he wrote a conditional acceptance. His principal conditions were that he be permitted to retain his private business connections, and that he be granted complete authority over the appointment and dismissal of his subordinates. At first Congress demurred for the possibilities of conflict between the public interest and Morris' private business interests were too evident, but Morris made it clear that he would not undertake the job otherwise, and Congress agreed to his terms. The matter of control over subordinates was the subject of prolonged negotiations which resulted in Congress retaining the right to appoint certain of the subordinates, while Morris was given the right to suspend appointments made by Congress, and to remove for cause those persons appointed by himself. On 14 May 1781 he formally accepted, but he did not take the oath of office and enter upon his duties until 27 June. Gouverneur Morris of New York became his assistant. Robert Morris hoped that he would not be called upon to supply the Army until the following year, but he soon saw that conditions re-

quired immediate action, and he had set to work energetically and effectively before he took the oath of office. On 6 July Congress gave official sanction to the steps he had taken before being sworn in. In that summer of 1781 his work in getting supplies for the Yorktown campaign was invaluable.

Improvement in the financial condition of the country was almost immediate—Morris could not have taken office at a more opportune time. The collapse of Continental paper currency had become virtually complete in May. With the paper out of the way, specie began to circulate again, and Morris could carry on his current operations in specie, which he obtained by borrowing at home, by import transactions, and on his personal credit. Increased aid from France in 1781 included advances of specie enabling Morris and his associates to organize the Bank of North America, which was important in circulating notes, extending credit, and discounting notes which the Financier accepted for bills of exchange. With the changing monetary conditions Morris was also able to enforce reforms not heretofore practicable that resulted in reducing military expenditures. Fortunately, too, efforts at taxation at last began to yield some revenues. Finally, when the need was greatest, the improvement in American credit permitted the floating of a loan in Holland large enough to cover requirements to carry on the war successfully and bring it to an end.

The Superintendent of Finance soon became the central figure in Army procurement. He agreed with Washington and other leaders that the system of specific supplies was completely unsatisfactory, and returned to a cash basis as soon as possible.

Something of the key position which the

Superintendent of Finance occupied relative to Army logistics is indicated by the range of subjects that Morris took up with Washington in a series of conferences extending over a three-day period in August 1781. They included discussions of (1) the best means of forecasting troop strengths in order to determine requirements for rations, clothing, pay, and equipment; (2) how to conserve stores and provisions; (3) the manner of making up payrolls, and the possibility of deriving a recruiting fund from unexpended pay allowances resulting from desertions and casualties; (4) ways to reduce expenditures of clothing, and how to make officers of the clothing department accountable; (5) hospital economy; (6) retrenchment of the pay of the Army; (7) reducing the number of regiments and increasing the number of privates in each; (8) requiring officers to keep records of clothing and stopping soldier's pay to pay for replacement of clothing lost or sold; (9) allowances of rations and forage for dispatch carriers; (10) location of supply depots; (11) whether it would be preferable to negotiate subsistence contracts in terms of rations as a whole, or for certain food items separately; (12) the Quartermaster General's Department and forage supply; (13) the licensing of sutlers; (14) determination of the size of the Army for the next campaign; (15) appointment of a steward, and estimates for the general's table; (16) getting rid of Burgoyne's troops, still being held prisoner, by exchange or release; (17) treatment and exchange of prisoners generally; (18) use of water transportation for moving ordnance stores; (19) obtaining letters from the general to the French minister urging an extension of credit in France; (20) reactions of the French on proposals respecting the han-

dling of the exchange of funds and credit; (21) abolition of the postal franking privilege.[15]

Procurement by Contract

Convinced that the system of procurement by purchasing commissaries was inefficient and wasteful, Morris introduced a new system of private contracting as speedily as possible. He calculated that the support of commissary agents in the middle and eastern states was costing the equivalent of 5,000 rations. Private contracting had been the system used in European armies for a century and a half, but American leaders were too well aware of past records of profiteering to permit it in the early years of the Revolution. Suggestions for private contracting in 1776 were attributed to Tory influence, but by 1781 almost everyone was willing to try anything that promised improvement. Morris believed that private contracting with completely free, competitive trade was the way to get the best results. "In all countries engaged in war," he wrote, "experience has sooner or later pointed out contracts with private men of substance and talents equal to the understanding as the cheapest, most certain, and consequently the best mode of obtaining those articles, which are necessary for the subsistence, covering, clothing, and moving of any Army."[16]

Actually, competitive bidding for supply of the Army did not turn out to be all Morris had hoped. There appears to have been

[15] Min of Confs, Diary in Office of Finance, 21 August 1781. Robert Morris Papers, MS, Library of Congress.

[16] Quoted in Robert A. East, *Business Enterprise in the American Revolutionary Era* (New York: Columbia University Press, 1938), pp. 211–12.

a good deal of pooling of risks and profits among the competitors. Early in 1782 John Holker, who was the French consul and already involved in French contracts, obtained a one-third interest in William Duer's Northern Posts contract. In the same year Holker obtained an interest in the four shares that Duer had bought of Walter Livingston's $1\frac{3}{24}$ interest in Comfort Sand's Moving Army contract. Principal contractors got together to make joint demands upon Morris. A certain amount of collusion was evident among beef contractors who entered into private agreements with one another.

The main army, whether because of the contract system or in spite of it, was far better supplied than the Southern Army which was still on specific supplies. This led to some resentment in the South. Benjamin Harrison, who became governor of Virginia in November 1781, protested that Congress and its ministers had not extended measures taken in the North to Virginia and that the state was expected to carry the whole burden. Morris took the position that when Virginia imposed and collected the required taxes the army there would be supplied by contract. Morris did take steps to relieve General Greene's army in North Carolina. He sent a treasury officer to Greene with secret instructions to advance limited funds when absolutely necessary. In October 1782 John Banks offered to accept a contract to clothe the Southern Army if partial payment could be made in specie and the remainder in bills of the Financier. Greene persuaded the treasury agent to advance the $3,500 partial payment and Banks took the contract on which he delivered to the satisfaction of everyone. Later, Banks undertook a contract to provide rations

with less satisfactory performance—he became involved in speculation, could not meet the demands of his creditors, and General Greene had to give his personal guarantee in order to get the provisions.

The War Office

At the time it approved the organization of a Finance Department, Congress took the further significant step of providing for establishment of a War Office under a Secretary at War. No one was chosen to fill that position, however, until 30 October 1781 when Maj. Gen. Benjamin Lincoln was chosen to be Secretary at War. General Lincoln did not indicate his acceptance until 26 November; thus it was not until several weeks after Yorktown that a centralized administration was put in charge of the affairs of the Army.

At the beginning, the Secretary at War had no precise definition of his duties, but six years of war under committee and board direction had made it fairly clear what the duties ought to be. From time to time Congress added or defined certain specific duties. The Secretary was instructed to issue warrants to the head of each department for the pay and rations due the department, and departments were to send monthly reports of their accounts to the War Office for examination. On specific instructions regarding the Quartermaster's Department, the Secretary at War approved the Quartermaster General's appointments of assistants, and he reported to Congress officers employed in the Quartermaster's Department. In June 1782 Congress called upon the Secretary to investigate and report to Congress the reasons for delay in getting supplies to the Southern Army. The Secretary prescribed the uniform for the Army. He directed the building and management of magazines, barracks, and other public buildings approved by Congress. In general he had the functions of supervision, direction, and co-ordination which previously had been exercised by the Board of War.

Summary

Many phases of the Revolution were critical—failure at any one of the number of serious crises might have been disastrous. But, in a sense, the year 1781 was the really critical year of the war, for it was in that year that steps were at last taken toward financial reform and administrative improvement. The spirit of '76 thrived on buoyant enthusiasm for the daring step taken, and an excited people rallied to the cause. That first fine enthusiasm had worn off three years later, and it was the "spirit of '79 and '80"—the persevering resolution of a few hardy souls who were unwilling to admit that bankruptcy and supply failures could not be overcome—that culminated in the reforms instituted in '81 and carried the American Revolution through to its successful conclusion.

Finance was such a controlling limitation on American logistics during the Revolution that other deficiencies had little chance to become apparent. Supplies *per se* were not short so often as was transportation, and lack of financial resources more often than not lay beneath shortages of both. But it is not to be supposed that removal of the financial difficulties automatically would have dispelled all the logistical problems of the time. It will become evident that in later conflicts, when financial solvency is well established, logistical problems have a way of reappearing.

Still, the availability of hard cash explains much of the advantage British and French forces had during the Revolutionary War in procuring certain of their necessaries in America. Under the handicaps of poorly developed governmental organization and precarious financial support, administration of the Revolutionary Army was frustrating, but out of this very frustration may have grown the leadership which ultimately made such remarkable achievements possible.

As commander in chief, Washington cannot escape some of the responsibility for the poor supply of his army. It is true that the heads of supply departments were in somewhat anomalous positions with respect to Congress and the commander in chief, yet even when Congress granted him virtually unlimited authority, General Washington did little in a decisive, bold, and imaginative way to improve that situation. Much too large a burden of paper work rested on his own shoulders. His respect for civil authority and his courage and devotion to duty undoubtedly held the Revolution together during the long, dark years, and preserved its objectives. But his major contributions do not include a great deal of enterprise and ingenuity in administering his logistical arrangements until his direction of the Yorktown campaign, which is one of the greatest logistical achievements of the war.

In the commissariat Congress experimented with frequent changes in organization, sometimes with the effect of aggravating the conditions it sought to correct, and successive changes in Commissaries General caused uncertainty and confusion throughout the organization. Often commissary agents worked at cross-purposes, bidding against each other, and, as at Valley Forge, there was a lack of co-operation between the Quartermaster and Commissary Departments. Financial deterioration undermined whatever administration had accomplished. All of these ills might have been curbed by a stronger central government with executive authority adequate to the demands, but this was not politically feasible in the circumstances of the Revolution. Aside from the nature of the governmental machinery and the ability of its administrators, profiteering on the part of farmers and merchants and a good deal of graft and corruption among agents and employees of the supply departments contributed further to the difficulties of military supply, transportation, hospitalization, and service.

Attempts to substitute barter for finance by the system of specific supplies were not satisfactory. Private contracting was rather successful, but not altogether so. Whether a contract system of procurement was better for the Army than the earlier system of purchasing commissaries is difficult to say. Given adequate financial support and good administrative organization and procedures, it is quite likely that either system could have been satisfactory.

CHAPTER VI

Foreign Assistance and the Yorktown Campaign

French Assistance Before Saratoga

At the time of the American Revolution, modern conceptions of the legal rights and duties of neutral powers in time of war were only beginning to take form. The evolution of doctrine already extending back several centuries had not yet equated neutrality with impartiality, and during much of the preceding two hundred years assistance in provisions and money—and even in raising troops—had not been considered incompatible with neutrality. As rules of neutrality developed, a sharp distinction had to be drawn between the activities of neutral governments and of private merchants. A merchant of a neutral country might carry contraband of war to a belligerent country. In doing so he ran the risk of having his cargo searched and seized by naval forces of the opposing belligerent, but he thereby involved his own government in no violation of neutral obligations. For the neutral government itself to send munitions to a warring power, on the other hand, came to be regarded universally as an unfriendly and unneutral act.

The French were willing from the outset of the American Revolution to incur risks of both kinds to send munitions and other supplies to the Americans, and ultimately to go to war in their behalf. But in their assistance to the rebels the French were doing more than stretching the ill-defined canons of neutrality. Indeed, there could be no technical state of neutrality without a recognition of belligerency, and such a status the French were not yet willing to accord to the Americans. By persisting in aiding them, the French laid themselves open to charges of hostile intervention. Moreover, in trading with the new American states the French were running counter to the English Navigation Acts in an age when mercantilism was still the foundation of colonial empires.

Saratoga long has been regarded as a decisive campaign of the Revolution, not simply or even mainly because it resulted in the destruction of a British army and the elimination of a serious threat to the Northern states, but because it led directly to the alliance with France. It is also true that prior assistance from France made possible even that decisive American victory.

Scarcely had the Seven Years' War ended in the Peace of Paris (1763), by which France transferred to Great Britain all of Canada and virtually all French territory in America east of the Mississippi River, when the French began to seek and encourage dissension in Britain's American colonies. From 1764 on, secret agents of the French were in the colonies to report on possible needs for munitions and for engineers and artillerists. After hostilities actually broke out in 1775, all kinds of rumors swept through the colonies that foreign aid of various kinds was on the way. "The wiser a patriot was, the less he was confident of victory without foreign aid." [1] Serious leaders of the Continental Congress began to look to the possibilities of enlisting foreign aid. But the French were far ahead of them. In December 1775 Archard de Bonvouloir, a secret agent of the French ministry, arrived in Philadelphia with instructions to hint to members of Congress that French ports would be open to American trade. Meanwhile, the energetic and gifted Beaumarchais, in London on a secret mission for the French Government, had contacted Arthur Lee, agent of the colonies at the imperial capital. Largely on his own initiative, Lee arrived at understandings with Beaumarchais for encouraging French assistance. Then Beaumarchais turned all his persuasive powers on the French foreign minister, Charles Gravier de Vergennes, and on Louis XVI to win their approval for a policy of aid to the Americans.

Baron Anne Robert Jacques Turgot, French Controller General of Finance, warned that the treasury could not stand open war, and Vergennes was not unmindful that revolution in America might spread to less desirable areas. But clearly the American Revolution was an opportunity to strike a blow to weaken Britain by interrupting its colonial trade, and thus help restore the position of France as the first power of Europe. The principal French

ministers agreed that this might be accomplished without all the risk and financial burden of open war through the medium of secret aid to the American colonies.

For their part, the Americans had grave misgivings at first about accepting French aid. Nevertheless, in the interest of independence, they were able to overcome their feelings of enmity stemming from repeated conflicts in the colonial wars, the bitterness aroused by France's use of Indians against them in those wars, the repugnance of New England to French Catholic Canada, and the hesitation to associate in the name of freedom with the Bourbon despotism. They sent Silas Deane, in the guise of a merchant, to Paris in the spring of 1776 to seek permission to buy military supplies on credit. He arrived in July to find that the French Government already (in April) had agreed upon a policy of secret aid, and that Beaumarchais had set up his fictitious company, *Roderigue Hortalez et Cie.*, to make the policy effective. With the benefit of one million livres advanced from Louis XVI in May and another million from Charles III of Spain, Beaumarchais began to collect munitions—including arms directly from the French arsenals—and to ship them to the colonies by way of the West Indies. Legitimate merchants, too, were anxious to share in the illegitimate munitions trade with the American colonies.

While all of this was going on, French officials kept up appearances of technical friendship with the British and port authorities blinked at shipments passing through for the support of the revolution in America. On one occasion in 1777 part of a shipment of 200 brass cannon was routed through Dunkerque, where an English commissioner was in residence, from the

---

[1] C. H. Van Tyne, "French Aid Before the Alliance of 1778," *American Historical Review*, XXX (October, 1925), 33.

French arsenal at Douay to the Belgian port of Ostend for shipment to America. French officers entertained the English commissioner at dinner to keep him occupied while the guns were moved through Dunkerque. The British protested at various times, but the French only replied that it was difficult to stop all the illegal trade. When necessary, the French issued strict orders to prohibit unauthorized shipments, but in January 1778 government officials had to instruct port authorities at Le Havre and Nantes to stop asking embarrassing questions about cargoes bound for the West Indies. Unmindful of Deane's early successes, or indeed that French policy had anticipated his arrival, Congress sent Benjamin Franklin to join Deane and Arthur Lee in Paris with specific instructions to ask for 30,000 muskets and the loan of eight French warships. Altogether the French furnished probably 90 percent of the gunpowder as well as most of the muskets and a large part of the clothing that the Continental Army received prior to the Saratoga engagement.

French Alliance and Spanish Belligerency

With the conclusion of the formal alliance with France, General Washington and his army could look hopefully in the spring of 1778 for improvements in the fortunes of war. Valley Forge had dampened much of the rejoicing for Saratoga, but Saratoga by helping to bring about the French alliance bore rich fruit. Washington could plan for the campaigns ahead with some assurance that the arms, clothing, and financial support necessary for victory would be forthcoming. Perhaps most

important of all—the greatest advantage of France's entering the war openly rather than relying solely on secret aid—was the fact that French naval forces might now be available to neutralize British control of the seas. This could open the sea lanes and assure the arrival of greater quantities of supplies for the Americans, while at the same time it would interfere with British supply shipments and troop movements. In these optimistic developments Washington saw one possible danger—complacency. He feared that the Americans might assume that they had nothing further to do, but he was convinced that the Revolution would succeed only if the Americans could match foreign assistance with their own self-help.

In their quest for foreign assistance, American Revolutionary leaders did not confine their attention to France. Spain, bound to France by the Third Family Compact of the Bourbons, also offered some prospect of assistance. The contribution of one million livres by the Spanish court to the enterprise of Beaumarchais already has been noted. Some further Spanish aid reached the United States by way of Louisiana. Spain entered the war in June 1779, mainly in the hope of recovering Gibraltar, and as the ally only of France, not of the United States. Direct or indirect Spanish assistance to the American Revolution was never given with any particular enthusiasm for its success. In the beginning the Spanish were willing to give secret aid in order to foment discontent in the colonies and to weaken England, but not to encourage independence. Help from Spain almost ceased when, after the colonies declared their independence, that country became anxious lest the example of revolution and independence should spread to its own extensive colonies in America.

French Forces in America

The mechanics of foreign assistance were fairly simple. Although the French sent an expeditionary force of their own which made a distinct and essential contribution toward final victory, in general France limited logistical aid for the American forces to financial support, assistance in procurement, and water transportation. In their official relations the French conducted themselves as equals. There was no French advisory group to see that the Americans screened their requirements carefully, or used the supplies and equipment they received properly. A number of French and other foreign officers appeared in Washington's army, but they were subordinate to him and responsible to no outside authority. As has been noted earlier they created problems and, at times, ill-feeling by their demands for high rank and important assignments at the expense of ambitious Continental officers, but they represented officially no foreign government. Liaison officers served Washington and the Comte Jean Baptiste de Rochambeau, commander of the French forces in America, and the two commanders cooperated very closely, but Rochambeau never acted on any other assumption than that Washington was commander in chief of all the forces, and no French observers or advisers were assigned to American units to help them in their tactical and logistical problems. A general thoroughly schooled in the arts of war and a man of remarkable talents, Rochambeau never for a moment exhibited any doubt of Washing-

ton's authority, nor did he ever assert any superiority of the French knowledge of war. American officers always took precedence over French officers of equal rank. The French did, understandably, have doubts about the abilities of American officers, and they had secret instructions not to permit themselves to be sent out on a separate mission under any American general other than Washington. With these reservations, the veterans of Louis XVI's army accepted their status as allies and equals of the Revolutionary volunteers of America.

The French, thanks to more nearly adequate finances, generally were fairly well supplied, although they were disappointed that there was no offer of "reverse lend-lease." Rochambeau's chief commissary, Claude Blanchard, wrote of his problems in supplying the French troops on their march from Newport to the Hudson: "The Americans supplied us with nothing. We were obliged to purchase everything and provide ourselves with the merest trifles. It is said that it is better to make war in an enemy's country rather than among one's friends. If that is an axiom, it acquires more truth when war is made in a poor and exhausted country where the men are possessed of little knowledge, are selfish, and divided in their opinions." [2]

The Move to Virginia

Rochambeau's forces were ready to move on 18 June 1781 to join Washington on the Hudson. For the march Rochambeau

---

[2] Blanchard's Journal, as quoted in Stephen Bonsal, *When the French Were Here . . . the French Forces in America and Their Contribution to the Yorktown Campaign* (New York: Doubleday, Doran & Co., 1945), p. 87.

ordered food supplies and forage to be distributed through the column, and he directed the elements of the command to camp at separated places so that the troops would not become a burden on the local inhabitants. Blanchard preceded the column to buy and barter for provisions to supply the troops en route. An observer reported that the Duc de Lauzun's legion had a supply train of 810 wagons, each drawn by two yoke of oxen and a lead horse. Blanchard and the other supply officers complained about the lack of co-operation on the part of the civil population; nevertheless, supply generally seems to have been adequate and the column made good time, for Rochambeau reported: "We have made 220 miles in eleven days' march. There are not four provinces in the Kingdom of France where we could have travelled with as much order and economy, and without wanting for anything." [3]

Hoping to take immediate advantage of the French in the vicinity, Washington called for a two-pronged, night surprise attack against British forts on the north end of Manhattan Island. Everything seemed to go wrong, however, and the attack failed. Then during the period of 21–24 July 1781, the allies undertook a demonstration and reconnaissance in force with the result that the commanders agreed that they would be unable to carry the British positions. Now everything seemed to depend upon the arrival of the French fleet under the Comte de Grasse, which was supposed to be on the way from the West Indies.

On 14 August Admiral de Barras, commander of the French fleet that had reached Newport, informed Washington that De Grasse was on the way with twenty-nine warships and over 3,000 additional troops, but that he was coming to the Chesapeake rather than to New York and could remain in the area no later than 15 October. With just two months to concentrate forces in Virginia, 450 miles south of his present headquarters, and to conclude any operation with the support of the French fleet, Washington moved swiftly and decisively. In May he had sent General Wayne and the reorganized Pennsylvania Line southward from York, Pennsylvania, to Virginia to join Lafayette. On receiving the news of De Grasse's destination, he dropped plans for the seige of New York, and Rochambeau's whole army and as many Americans as could be spared from the Hudson prepared to move to Virginia as quickly as possible. Of his own main army, Washington ordered about half (2,500 men) to the south under the command of Maj. Gen. Benjamin Lincoln, while the remainder, under Maj. Gen. William Heath, stayed behind to guard the Hudson Valley and watch the British in New York. He sent his chief engineer to Virginia immediately to make advance preparations for the arrival of the infantry. The Northern states were asked for more recruits and militia to help in local defense. (*Map 3*)

The Americans crossed the Hudson on 20 and 21 August, while the French, held up by a shortage of transportation, did not complete their crossing until the 25th. Washington lost a whole day at Haverstraw because of a shortage of horses and oxen. Through northern New Jersey the allies moved in three columns—the French on the west through Pompton and Morristown to Middlebrook, part of the American troops on a route a short distance to the east of the French through Pompton and

[3] Quoted in Bonsal, *When the French Were Here*, p. 99.

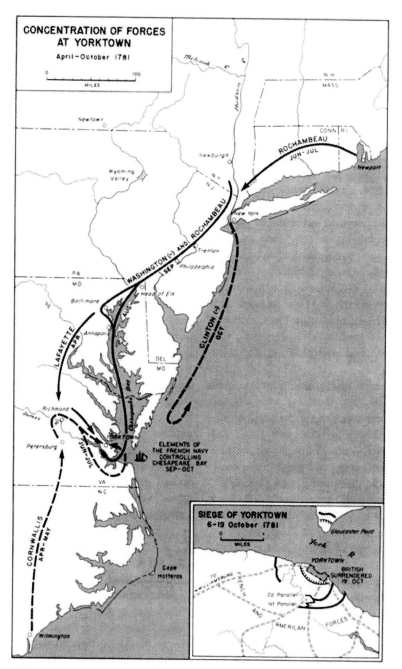

CONCENTRATION OF FORCES
AT YORKTOWN
April–October 1781

SIEGE OF YORKTOWN
6–19 October 1781

MAP 3

Chatham to Middlebrook where they joined the French, and the remainder of the Americans on a route still further to the east by way of Paramus and Brunswick to Princeton, where the forces converged to a single column. The plan was for the forces to rendezvous at Trenton where they would take boats down the Delaware River. On their arrival, however, only enough boats were available to carry the supplies and equipment and a few men. As the troops continued their march, supplies were obtained along the way. The French were impressed at how supplies were delivered to them, not always by farmers or hucksters, but at times by gayly dressed ladies driving well-groomed horses harnessed to their rustic wagons. The American force passed through Philadelphia on 2 September, and the French on the 3d and 4th. Covering the 200 miles from the New York base in fifteen days, the American troops arrived at Head of Elk on 6 September, and the French closed in two days later.

Washington and Rochambeau themselves left Trenton on 30 August for Philadelphia, where Washington set up his headquarters at the home of Robert Morris who had been energetically working to get the necessary logistical support for the campaign. On 28 August Morris had written to Washington:

I directed the Commissary-general immediately on my return from camp, to cause the deposit of three hundred barrels of flour, three hundred barrels of salt meat, and twelve hogshead of rum, to be made at the Head of Elk, and pointed out the means of obtaining them . . . I have written to the Quartermaster of Delaware and Maryland to exert himself in procuring the craft. . . . I have written to the Governor and several of the most eminent merchants in Baltimore to extend their assistance and influence in expediting this business. Foreseeing the necessity of supplies from Maryland and Delaware, I have written in the most pressing terms to the Governors and agents to have the specific supplies required of them by Congress in readiness for delivery to my order. . . . Still I fear you will be disappointed in some degree as to the shipping, and that I shall be compelled to make purchases of provisions, which, if it happens, must divert the money from those payments to the army that I wish to make. I have already advised your Excellency of the unhappy situation of money matters, and very much doubt if it will be possible to pay the detachment a month's pay, as you wish.[4]

As a matter of fact, Morris did, subsequently, contrive to raise funds to give Washington's troops a month's pay—with the first hard cash they had ever received. He was able to do it through the generosity of Rochambeau who, though his own war chest was running low, turned over half of what he had—equivalent to $20,000—as a one-month loan.

Morris further entered into the realm of interallied finance. First of all he thought some advantage for both sides could be gained by contracting for supplies for the French. One deal involved the sale to the French of flour received from Pennsylvania in 1781 as a part of its contribution of supplies in kind at $19,424, which made a profit of $6,883.[5] Moreover, Morris felt that if he were granted the management of the bills of exchange drawn by the French Army agents, as well as his own bills drawn on the Paris banks, he could lessen some of the losses

[4] Quoted in William Graham Sumner, *The Financier and Finances of the American Revolution*, 2 vols. (New York: Dodd, Mead, and Co., 1892), I, 302. For further statements of Morris's activities in regard to the Yorktown campaign, see Diary of the Office of Finance, 31 August, 1–5 September 1781. MS, Library of Congress.

[5] Sumner, *The Financier and Finances of the American Revolution*, I, 304.

in the exchange. The French preferred to do their purchasing with hard money, but when they did use bills of exchange, they permitted Morris to negotiate them.

In the capital city Washington had a chance to make a brief visit to Congress, to greet friends, and to relax briefly, but above all he concerned himself with logistical preparations for the further movement southward. He arranged for the use of militia to repair the roads which were to be used for the march to the south, and he wrote to many friends around Chester, Head of Elk, and the Eastern Shore asking the use of private shipping for the transportation of his army.

Washington and Rochambeau left Philadelphia on 5 September, after the French Army passed through. About three miles south of Chester a messenger brought Washington the news that De Grasse's fleet had arrived in Chesapeake Bay.

At Head of Elk enough shipping had been collected to transport only 2,000 men. Washington instructed General Lincoln, the troop commander, and General Pickering, the quartermaster general, to "combat load" those vessels at Head of Elk so that equipment first needed for land operations would be first available. He sent the troops for whom ships were not available at Head of Elk on to Baltimore in the hope of finding more transport there. Meanwhile Washington, Rochambeau, and their personal staffs, rode rapidly ahead. They paused for one day at Mount Vernon, and the commanders joined Lafayette at Williamsburg on 14 September. Washington found the supply and transportation situation in Virginia still poor. But the French reinforcements De Grasse had brought—3,000 men under the Marquis de Saint-Simon-Montblern—were on hand.

With no further word from De Grasse, nor from Admiral Barras, who was supposed to be sailing from Newport to join De Grasse, and with news that a British fleet was approaching, some doubt prevailed about control of the Chesapeake. The day after his rendezvous with Lafayette he received the welcome news that De Grasse had fought the British fleet to a standstill off the Virginia Capes, that Barras had joined him, and that the fleets were back in Chesapeake Bay. Washington immediately wrote to the French admiral asking that ships be sent up the Chesapeake to transport the remaining troops and supplies. But De Grasse and Barras had anticipated the request by dispatching all Barras' transports and some of the frigates to Baltimore. Advance troop elements with some stores embarked at Head of Elk, while the others embarked on frigates at Baltimore and Annapolis. Ships began arriving at the lower end of Chesapeake Bay on 19 September, but it was several days later when the vessels, making their way against unfavorable winds and through stormy weather, reached the landing sites at Jamestown Island, Burwell's Ferry, and College Landing near Williamsburg. Some contingents were as long as twelve and fourteen days—with some of the men in open boats all that time—en route from Head of Elk to the James River landings. All were ashore by 26 September.

Now concentrated at Williamsburg were Lafayette's small army, which had been operating since early spring against Cornwallis, Wayne's Pennsylvania Line, Saint-Simon's 3,000 French troops, the French troops who had remained on guard at Newport and had arrived with Barras, and Rochambeau's army and the American contingent under Lincoln. To make this remarkable concentration pay off it was necessary to get the supplies that would keep it together while it closed in on Cornwallis' defensive positions at Yorktown.

Fortunately, the supplies and the artillery that came by ship from the north arrived in good condition with little loss. Although Washington still was not assured of a steady supply of rations, the efforts of Virginia and Maryland, in spite of difficulties, were reducing deficiencies, and he was confident that greater exertion could overcome most of the shortages. Before starting siege operations he also wanted to build up a sizable reserve of artillery ammunition.

Arrival of the French fleets restored the financial resources of the war chests. Rochambeau's commissary general, Blanchard, wrote: "Our generals came and deposited with me 800,000 livres in piastres which M. de Grasse had brought for us." His immediate problem was to find a place to store such a quantity of gold and silver. He decided to keep it on the first floor of his quarters—a house with a cellar beneath it. "In the course of the night," the account continues, "the floor being weak broke under the weight of the coin and both the treasure and the sentinel guarding it were precipitated into the cellar, without, however, any loss of the first or injury to the latter." About his supply problems he complained: "I set to work, although without a piece of paper, or an employe or a bag of flour at my disposal. I was completely overwhelmed. I caused ovens to be constructed, but I was in want of tools and had to run about much and negotiate to obtain even a hammer." [6]

In the meantime, on 8 September General Greene had fought the last battle of his campaign in the Carolinas at Eutaw Springs,

whereupon he moved to Charleston. His army expanded to a force of over 6,000 men but it was fortunate that he was not called upon for further action against the enemy, for he never was able to escape the constant struggle for food, ammunition, and medicine.

Yorktown

Early on 28 September 1781 the allied army moved out from its camps near Williamsburg toward the British positions at Yorktown about twelve miles away. An advance guard of light dragoons, a brigade of the Virginia line, and riflemen of the Virginia militia led the way. For the first four or five miles the French and Americans formed a single column; then they divided. The combined force numbered about 16,600 men. Quartermaster General Pickering, following an example set by Benedict Arnold, used oxen to drag up the all-important siege guns.

If Cornwallis could have held out ten days longer the arrival of a British fleet of twenty-seven warships, with some 7,000 reinforcements from Clinton, might have changed matters. Instead he found himself hemmed in and bombarded, cut off from supplies and reinforcements somewhat as Burgoyne had been at Saratoga. At Saratoga the British had moved inland, out of reach of the logistical support of their fleet, and they had lost an army. At Yorktown they lost local naval superiority, and cut off from the logistical support of their fleet, again lost an army—and the war. French supplies had made possible the victory at Saratoga, and the victory at Saratoga had paved the way for the French alliance. Moreover, French supplies, financial support, a cooperating French army, and sup-

---

[6] Quoted in Bonsal, *When the French Were Here*, p. 140

port of a powerful French fleet made possible the victory at Yorktown. Possibility became reality by a remarkable logistical accomplishment in concentrating and supplying the allied forces.

Douglas Southall Freeman has written of the Yorktown campaign:

It is a textbook model in the relationship of allies and, above all, in concentration.

. . . .

How strange that these two aspects of the operations of August–October, 1781, have received so little attention! Thanks to Rochambeau the resources of the French engineering and artillery staffs were placed at Washington's disposal completely and unostentatiously. Few jealousies were aroused, while the French did brilliantly several things the inexperienced Americans scarcely would have been able to do at all.

This was particularly true of the running of the first and second "parallels," as the siege trenches were styled. Washington matched this with a concentration that ranks with the best Eighteenth-Century achievements of logistics, though Washington himself would not have understood what we mean by that overwhipped word. He heard on the fourteenth of August, 1781, when he was on the Hudson, that De Grasse's fleet was coming to Virginia. One month later, to the very day, Washington rode into Williamsburg in the knowledge that Barras' French squadron from Newport, the French garrison from that base, all their siege guns, the army of Rochambeau from the New York front, an American detachment of 2,000 men and the baggage of the Franco-American forces were moving toward him. Before the end of September, Washington had all these troops and most of this equipment in hand, and began his advance on the works of Cornwallis at Yorktown. He used every means of transportation he could find and he somehow was able to co-ordinate them. The Revolution produced nothing more remarkable.[7]

_____
[7] Douglas S. Freeman, "The Freeman Letters on George Washington," *American Heritage,* VII (February, 1956), 69.

In the same context Freeman wrote:

Perhaps the most interesting aspect—and certainly the least familiar—of the operations of the Revolutionary War proves to be the great concentration of the American and French forces on the Virginia Peninsula in the later summer and early autumn of 1781. Personally I was quite unprepared for so finished a military performance as this . . . proved to be. . . . When one reflects on the difficulties Washington had to overcome because of his financial distress, his feeble transportation, and his officers' lack of familiarity with French military practices, the concentration ranks with the Trenton-Princeton campaign as Washington's greatest success in arms. It may be more than that; so far as my limited knowledge runs, this was one of the most efficient concentrations of modern war.[8]

Summary

In effect the American Revolution finally was reduced to a contest for control of the marginal seas sufficient to permit logistical support by sea to the one side and deny it to the other. The assistance of France, first in furnishing supplies, and then in sending a fleet to gain local naval superiority at a critical time and place, was decisive. The British, too, had their problems, as they had to depend on England for most of their supplies. Yet, as long as they held control of the seas it appears to have been easier for the British to send supplies from England to New York than for the Americans to move supplies from New York to South Carolina. While Americans starved and froze at Valley Forge, the British in Philadelphia, with the benefit of local Pennsylvania resources, probably were the best supplied of any time during the war. In the spring of 1781, when the Americans were most desperate, the French expeditionary

_____
[8] *Ibid.,* VII. 70.

force and the French fleet arrived, specie began to circulate, and Robert Morris took energetic steps to reform the finances and improve Army procurement. By October, 1781 had turned from a year of desperation to a year of triumph.

The American effort, with all its shortcomings and times of crisis, ultimately was successful. French aid was indispensable, but with any less of an American contribution, all the French aid could not have brought about American independence. Ironically, assistance to a foreign revolution and the cost of the resultant European war very nearly bankrupted the treasury of the Bourbons, a factor in the domestic revolution that was to overthrow the French monarchy itself.

CHAPTER VII

Reduction and Reorganization

With independence at last assured, Congress set about liquidating the chief instrument of its attainment. Besides being looked upon as a heavy and unnecessary expense, an understandable fear existed that a standing army might be turned to the coercion of the states or become an instrument of despotism. The Congress hoped that the dangerous and objectionable features of a permanent military organization could be avoided by reliance on a "well-regulated and disciplined militia sufficiently armed and accoutered." [1]

The absolute nadir of authorized military strength for the United States was reached on 2 June 1784 when Congress, as an expedient, adopted a resolution which allowed for 25 privates to guard supplies at Fort Pitt and 55 more to guard stores at West Point "and other magazines." Officers for this miniscule force could be appointed in proportion to its size, but no officer could hold rank above captain. On the following day, however, Congress adopted another resolution (New Jersey and New York opposing) which recommended that Connecticut, New York, New Jersey, and Pennsylvania provide a total of 700 men from their militia for one year's service. These men were to be organized into one regiment of eight infantry companies and two artillery companies; they were to be armed by the United States, and would be "liable to all the rules and regulations formed for the government of the late army of the United States." Thus was formed the nucleus of what would become a regular standing army. In 1785 the terms of service were extended to three years, and in 1787 the men in service (less than 600) were offered another three-year term. On 29 September 1789, this force became the permanent Military Establishment under the newly adopted Constitution. Authorized strengths were increased to 1,216 men in 1790, and to 5,000 in 1792.

The office of the Quartermaster General was abolished in 1785, but its loss was hardly noticed so long as thinking was in terms of a small peace establishment with little consideration for emergency plans and preparations. Creation of the modern War Department, 7 August 1789 (with jurisdiction over Navy as well as Army affairs for the first nine years of its existence) was only a first step toward a logistics base. The President was authorized to entrust to the Secretary of War responsibility for military stores, but actual duties in this area remained vague.

Arms procurement was perhaps the most satisfactory aspect of logistics developments as the Army matured gradually with the nation during the fifty or sixty years following the Revolutionary War. Other aspects of logistics evolved more slowly. Nearly

---

[1] The material in this section is based on *Journals of the Continental Congress*, 2, 3 June 1784, XXVII, 519–40

twenty years passed before the administrative machinery for providing services and supplies reached the point where those activities could be facilitated rather than retarded under varying conditions.

Expeditions Against the Indians of the Northwest

In their baptism of fire against the Indians of the old Northwest Territory, the new Army and the "well-regulated militia" of the states seemed to forget all the logistical experience of the suffering and triumph of eight years of war for independence. Whatever the hopes for a reign of peace, here was a situation that had to be met boldly, for not only did Indian uprisings endanger the settlements and deny access to the West; the British persistently held a number of posts within territory recognized as belonging to the United States.

Harmar's Defeat

Charged with pacifying the Indians in the area, Maj. Gen. Arthur St. Clair, as Governor of the Northwest Territory and Superintendnt of the Northern Indian Department, in 1790 determined to send a military expedition against the Indians living in the upper Wabash and Maumee valleys. Col. Josiah Harmar was given command of the combined force of 320 regulars and 1,133 militiamen drawn from Pennsylvania and Kentucky.

Between July and October plans went forward swiftly for assembling the men and supplies at Fort Washington (Cincinnati). For subsistence supplies and for pack horses to transport them the force depended upon the firm of Elliott and Williams, who for the last two years had held the contract for provisioning troops on the frontier. By the first of October they reported to St. Clair that they had brought to Fort Washington 180,000 rations of flour and 200,000 rations of meat, together with 878 artillery and pack horses and about 150 men to handle them, thus fulfilling their agreement.[2] Meanwhile Secretary of War Henry Knox arranged for sending six tons of ammunition and made arrangements with the Treasury Department for the necessary funds.

Harmar received his first shock when the militiamen arrived without a large share of the arms, axes, and kettles he had expected them to have. His next shock came with the performance of his men in battle. After marching some 170 miles northward through the wilderness, and destroying a few abandoned Indian villages, the force was routed by Indians near the site of Fort Wayne, Indiana, where the St. Joseph and St. Mary Rivers join to form the Maumee. Much of the arms and equipment and rations were lost; 183 men were killed and 31 wounded. The loss of horses was far greater than it need have been for two reasons. First, owners were paid a daily rate for use of their animals and highly compensated if they were not returned; consequently, horsemasters and packhorse drivers found it to their advantage to allow the horses to be lost or stolen. Second, after frost destroyed the natural forage it was virtually impossible to maintain the pack train.

St. Clair's Expedition

Failure of logistical support undoubtedly had much to do with the failure of the next expedition, when St. Clair himself took the field against the Indians in 1791. Equip-

---

[2] Erna Risch, *Quartermaster Support of the Army: A History of the Corps, 1775–1939* (Washington, 1962), pp. 85–87.

ment left over from the earlier Indian campaign, and even from the Revolution, had to be restored to use. There was confusion between the Treasury and War Departments about the transfer of a supply contract from one contractor to another. Samuel Hodgdon, appointed quartermaster for the expedition in March 1791, remained in Philadelphia on the order of the Secretary of War until June; then, even though ordered by St. Clair to join the expedition without delay, he waited further at Fort Pitt on the orders of Maj. Gen. Richard Butler (second in command of the expedition) until August, and did not report to Fort Washington, where the army was encamped, until 10 September. Equipment was so deficient in quality and quantity that it took hours of work at Fort Washington to repair or make many essential items. Late deliveries of supplies and of boats delayed the arrival of reinforcements from Fort Pitt.

With all these setbacks it was September before St. Clair's forces were ready to move; nevertheless, bound by explicit instructions from the War Department, St. Clair pressed on—and was defeated before he ever reached his objective. Failure of the expedition can be attributed to: the length of time it took the War Department to furnish appropriation estimates and for the necessary authorizing act to be passed; troop inexperience and lack of discipline owing in part to shortness of time for training; mismanagement and negligence on the part of the supply contractor and the quartermaster; and lack of forage for the horses because, among other reasons, frost killed off the green forage upon which the expedition depended. For his own part, General St. Clair failed to provide the leadership and supervision to logistical preparations that might have assured success.

Wayne's Campaign

When Maj. Gen. Anthony Wayne set out to do in 1792 and 1793 what Harmar and St. Clair had been unable to do in 1790 and 1791, he had the advantage of a stronger, more neatly balanced force, the Legion of the United States.[3] He had more time for training, for obtaining supplies, and for improving the line of communication north of the Ohio. Even so, he faced many of the same logistical frustrations that had troubled St. Clair.

After trying in vain to get 270,000 rations stored at Ft. Greenville before the end of 1793 to support his future operations, Wayne was sure that some other way of supplying the Army than by private contract was essential. In this case the contractors, perhaps counting on a drop in prices, had been content to purchase only enough food to meet current needs, and had neither supplies nor transportation when Wayne called for immediate delivery of the provisions. Although the contractors lost seventy horses when Indians attacked their convoy, Wayne was not satisfied with their reason for nondelivery and he ordered the quartermaster to buy 250 packhorses and 40 pair of oxen or 60 wagon horses at the contractors' expense, and threatened to do much more. It seems, however, that Brig. Gen. James Wilkinson, Wayne's second in command, may have had a hand in reassuring the contractors and delaying the build-up of rations. But when Wayne amended his requirements to have 50,000 rations delivered

---

[3] In 1792 the armed forces were converted into the Legion of the United States. The Legion was composed of four elements known as sublegions; each sublegion was made up of the three combat branches—infantry, cavalry, and artillery This organization lasted until October 1796 when the sublegions became regiments. *Army Lineage*, II, 9–10

sixty to seventy miles north of Greenville, the contractors could not even move that number from Fort St. Clair, where they previously had been stored. After two years of preparation, Wayne still found it impossible to launch a campaign in the spring of 1794, and, like St. Clair, he faced the dangerous prospect of a fall campaign. Challenged by Indian attacks, he did move northward from Fort Greenville late in July, and gained his victory at Fallen Timbers in August. (*Map 4*)

Faulty Machinery

If there was anyone who should have appreciated the value of a Quartermaster General to military efficiency, it was President Washington, but he went along with the traditional assumption that a quartermaster was a staff officer necessary only in time of war, and he did not urge the appointment of a permanent supply officer until 1794. The post and grade of Quartermaster General was revived about a year later, and continued by acts of 1796 and 1797; however, the Quartermaster's duties related mainly to the delivery of supplies to troops garrisoned at frontier posts. It was not until after the War of 1812 that a permanent Quartermaster Bureau was established at the seat of the government.

Procurement remained a primary responsibility of the Treasury from 1784, when the Board of Treasury replaced the Superintendent of Finance, until 1798 when actual military purchasing, as well as determination of requirements, was placed under the direction of the chief officer of the War Department. In 1792 Alexander Hamilton persuaded Congress to assign responsibility for all military procurement to the Treasury Department because large-scale disbursements of public funds were involved, and because, in his view, government purchasing would be more efficient if centralized under one authority. In 1795 the task of buying military supplies was assigned specifically to the Purveyor of Public Supplies whose procurement activities continued to be under direct supervision of the Secretary of the Treasury.

The legislation of 1798 followed the "XYZ Affair" and the beginning of an undeclared naval war with France. In May of that year Congress authorized the President to raise a provisional three-year army of up to 10,000 men commanded by one lieutenant general and four major generals with a staff (if the President thought it expedient) of a Quartermaster General, an Inspector General, a Paymaster General, a Physician General, and their assistants. President Adams appointed Washington, then in retirement at Mount Vernon, to the post of lieutenant general. Alexander Hamilton became senior major general and directed most of the war preparations.

General Washington and General Hamilton urged the importance of a capable Quartermaster General, a post which was authorized by the act for the rank of lieutenant colonel. Supply responsibilities were divided between a Purveyor of Public Supplies for procurement and a Superintendent of Military Distribution—a division that worked no better than had the system used during the Revolution of a Commissary General of Purchases and a Commissary of Issues. In his new post, Hamilton blamed faulty organization, that is, the specific organization of agents, for much of his difficulty in obtaining supplies. His criticism did not extend to the division of the procurement and distribution functions which, six years earlier, he had recommended should

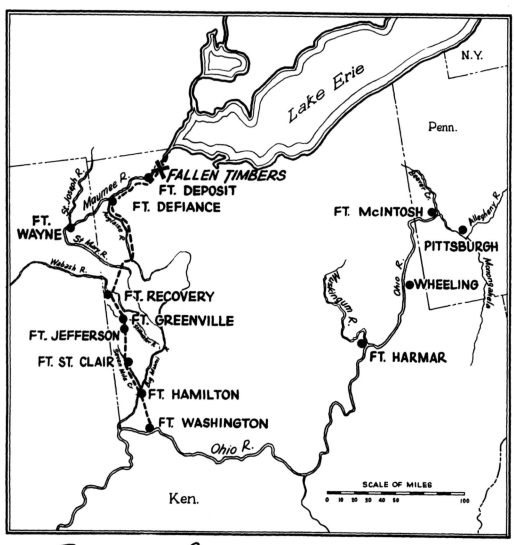

Indian Campaign of 1794

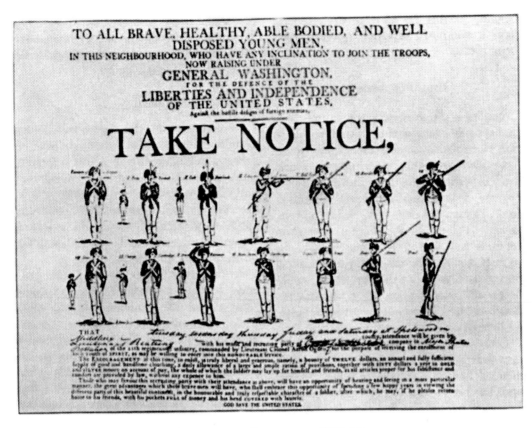

RECRUITING POSTER OF 1798–99

be even more pronounced. In any case, the expenditures and accounts of the Secretary of War for the purchase of military supplies were still subject to inspection and revision by the Secretary of the Treasury. This arrangement continued until 1812.

From 1802 to the outbreak of the War of 1812 a system of military agents and assistant agents superseded the Quartermaster's Department. The country was divided into three military departments and an agent appointed for each department. The military agents were civilian officials whose principal duties were the movement of sup-

plies and troops within their areas. At the different posts, lieutenants of the line were appointed assistant military agents in place of the former quartermasters. Assistant agents were accountable to the military agents of their departments, but control was loose and accountability could not be effectively enforced. At the same time, local commanders chafed under the restrictions, for, except in special cases, they had to apply to the Secretary of War before taking action on any repairs or local procurements of over fifty dollars. It was, altogether, an unsatisfactory arrangement—a measure of false economy costing far more in the long run than a complete, effective quartermaster organization.

Arms Procurement

Leaders of the American Revolution were under no illusion about the extent to which they owed their success to French assistance. They also knew that independence would itself be only an illusion if future national security was dependent upon assistance from France or from any other outside power. Before the Revolution, American colonists had looked to Great Britain for security against France. For the United States, as a sovereign power, there would be no advantage in having to turn to the Bourbons, on a more or less permanent basis, for defense against Great Britain.

Clearly one of the first steps toward military independence would be the development of domestic sources of arms. Some arms had been manufactured in the colonies for years before the Revolution, but the chief reliance had been on British weapons. Local armament makers had made a significant contribution to the Revolution—the rifle makers of Pennsylvania were without peers—but French arms had been essential to the victory.

Development of an armament base was a theme that immediately engaged the energetic attention of the brilliant young Alexander Hamilton, lately an aide-de-camp to the commander in chief, and one of the leading thinkers on national affairs and military policy of his time. It was an area, too, in which another brilliant young man, Eli Whitney, saw opportunity. These two men of genius—Hamilton, soldier, statesman, political theorist, and Whitney, inventor,

industrial pioneer, entrepreneur—were in the *avant-garde* of a group of imaginative men who set the course for the national arms policy of the United States.

Hamilton's Proposals

Scarcely had the Revolution ended when Hamilton, who had been elected to the Congress of the Confederation the preceding year, presented to Congress his views on a national arms system. In his report of 1783 on a military peace establishment Hamilton emphasized the need to establish, as soon as circumstances permitted, "public manufactories of arms, powder, etc." [4]

As Secretary of the Treasury eight years later, Hamilton presented his celebrated "Report on Manufactures" to Congress. This paper was, essentially, a case for economic nationalism. Hamilton proposed to use the taxing and import regulating powers of Congress, under the justification of the "general welfare" clause of the Constitution, to protect, subsidize, and foster manufacturing in the United States. Central to the whole program was the development of domestic industries for national security. In the preamble Hamilton stated that the report was being submitted in consequence of the attention he had given "to the subject of Manufactures, and particularly to the means of promoting such as will tend to render the United States independent of foreign nations for military and other essential supplies." [5]

After refuting general objections to the encouragement of manufactures in the body

---

[4] Henry Cabot Lodge, ed , *The Works of Alexander Hamilton*, Federal Edition, 12 vols. (New York: G. P. Putnam's Sons, 1904), VI, 467.

[5] *Ibid.*, IV, 70

of the report, Hamilton returned to the question of national defense:

Fire-arms and other military weapons may, it is conceived, be placed, without inconvenience, in the class of articles rated at fifteen per cent. There are already manufactories of these articles, which only require the stimulus of a certain demand to render them adequate to the supply of the United States.

It would also be a material aid to manufactures of this nature, as well as a means of public security, if provision should be made for an annual purchase of military weapons, of home manufacture, to a certain determinate extent, in order to encourage the formation of arsenals; and to replace, from time to time, such as should be drawn for use, so as always to have in store the quantity of each kind which should be deemed a competent supply.

But it may, thereafter, deserve legislative consideration, whether manufactories of all the necessary weapons of war ought not to be established on account of the government itself. Such establishments are agreeable to the usual practice of nations, and that practice seems founded on sufficient reason.

There appears to be an improvidence in leaving these essential implements of national defence to the casual speculations of individual adventure—a resource which can less be relied upon, in this case, than in most others; the articles in question not being objects of ordinary and indispensable private consumption or use. As a general rule, manufactories on the immediate account of government are to be avoided; but this seems to be one of the few exceptions which that rule admits, depending on very special reasons.[6]

Hamilton's "Report on Manufactures" so emphasized the role of the federal government in the national economy, under a very loose construction of the Constitution, and so offended the agrarian ideal of the Republicans, that a storm of protest rose against it. Thomas Jefferson and James Madison led an opposition which succeeded in pigeonholing the document—although a generation later Jefferson himself would write: "Experience has taught me that manufactures are now as necessary to our independence as to our comfort." [7] Nevertheless, in the next few years Hamilton saw the beginning—no doubt with some stimulus from the Whiskey Rebellion, Indian uprisings, threatened war with England, and, later, quasi war with France—of a national munitions system. In 1794 Congress authorized the construction of some national armories, and four years later authorized contracting for private manufacture of arms for the government.

Secretary of War Henry Knox echoed Hamilton's views in a message to the Senate in December 1793. He conceded that weapons manufactured in the United States might be more expensive than those imported from Europe, but he said this was of little significance "compared with the solid advantages which would result from extending and perfecting the means upon which our safety may ultimately depend." [8] Knox further urged, as had Hamilton, that arms be stockpiled. This time the response of Congress was prompt and decisive. Early in March 1794 a House committee reported in favor of appropriating funds for the purchase of 7,000 muskets and other munitions, and further recommended that two more arsenals should be established and that a national armory for the manufacture of arms should be erected. On 2 April Congress

____

[6] *Ibid.,* IV, 167–68. The "class of articles rated at fifteen per cent" were manufactured imports bearing the 15 percent tariff rate

[7] Philip S. Foner, ed , *Basic Writings of Thomas Jefferson* (Garden City, N Y.: 1950), p. 745. Reference is contained in a letter dated 9 January 1816 from Jefferson to Benjamin Austin.

[8] Report of the Secretary of War to the Senate, 16 December 1793, in *American State Papers, Military Affairs,* I, 44.

passed legislation authorizing three or four additional arsenals and magazines and the establishment of a national armory at each arsenal, more than doubling the amount recommended by the committee for the purchase of arms and ammunition.

The site chosen for the first national armory was Springfield, Massachusetts. A depot and a "laboratory" for cartridges had operated there during the Revolution, and it had continued to be one of the principal magazines and arsenals. It was, in fact, the only location that Secretary Knox thought was completely satisfactory; moreover, a number of gunsmiths, working individually on whatever state or federal jobs they could get, already had settled there. After engineer surveys of the Potomac River area and in North Carolina, President Washington chose Harper's Ferry, Virginia, as the site for the second national armory. A 435-acre site was purchased in 1794, and manufacture of arms began there in 1796. Some states established armories in the post-Revolution period, but the only one that lasted was the Virginia armory established at Richmond under a 1797 act of the legislature.

Even after the establishment of the national armories, government purchasing or contracting for munitions continued to be a major source of supply. Between 1792 and 1798 the government let domestic contracts, but the United States would never be able to free itself of dependence on foreign arms until a sufficiently continuous market offered American manufacturers encouragement to develop an adequate munitions industry.

Again in 1798 Alexander Hamilton, in a letter drafted for Washington to the Secretary of War, urged the stockpiling of a year's supply of arms and other military equipment for 50,000 men—a force strong enough to repel an invasion by the strongest European power.

Eli Whitney and Mass Production

It happened that Eli Whitney of New Haven, Connecticut, being desperately in need of capital, turned to the United States Government with a fantastic proposal to manufacture ten or fifteen thousand stand of arms at the very moment that the government could not afford to turn down any halfway realistic proposal for making arms. War with France threatened and, as he followed the debates in Congress on proposed appropriations for arms procurement, Whitney decided that here was the best possible opportunity to get a government contract. On 1 May 1798 he wrote to Oliver Wolcott, who had succeeded Hamilton as Secretary of the Treasury in 1795. Suggesting that the use of water-driven machinery would make possible the production of unheard-of numbers of weapons, Whitney simply asked for an opportunity to present his proposals. Wolcott answered immediately that he had already spoken to the Secretary of War of Whitney "as a person whose services might probably be rendered highly useful," and advised him to hasten to Philadelphia as soon as possible.[9] Whitney was in the capital by 24 May; a week later he submitted a draft contract, and on 14 June Secretary of the Treasury Wolcott signed a contract with him, based largely on the draft terms, for the manufacture of 10,000 muskets, complete with bayonets and ramrods, of which 4,000 were to be delivered by 30 September 1799, and the remaining 6,000 a year later. Besides the Whitney contract, the government

---

[9] Ltr, 16 May 1798, Eli Whitney Papers, Yale University.

signed agreements with twenty-six other contractors that year for a total of 40,200 muskets.

Whitney had decided that the only practical way to produce 10,000 satisfactory muskets in the United States, where there were few skilled armorers, was to reduce the complex steps of gunmaking to a series of more simple tasks, each of which could be done with less skilled hands; to design machines which would duplicate some of the armorer's skill; and that, for best results, it would be necessary to make parts precise enough to be interchangeable. These methods would permit the maximum division of labor, and would, moreover, make it possible to accomplish repairs simply by replacing parts. The making of interchangeable parts for muskets was really not a new idea. It had been tried in France as early as 1717, and as recently as 1785. Thomas Jefferson while minister to France had written of the latter effort to John Jay, Secretary of Foreign Affairs. The system had not caught on, for it had been assumed that parts could be made interchangeable only if every gunmaker were an expert, and this would make the cost prohibitive. Whitney's great contribution was to use the principle of interchangeability to reduce the cost by introducing machinery and jigs and fixtures to obtain the necessary precision without greater use of skilled artisans.

After posting the bond required for performance of his contract, Whitney received the promised $5,000 advance, and proceeded to build an arms plant at Mill Rock near New Haven. He encountered delays in getting the site he wanted; then an early and severe winter delayed the completion of a dam and buildings. He received a second advance early in January 1799, as soon as he reported expenditure of the first, but his factory was not completed until the middle of that month. In addition to the time lost in building the plant, he had trouble getting iron and getting teams to transport fuel; subcontractors failed him; he had trouble organizing the work; he could get no long-term credit to buy his materials.

Foreseeing that he would be unable to meet the contract schedule, he pleaded for more time. Since European sources of arms were being cut off, nearly everyone agreed that it was essential for the United States to develop a domestic arms industry—and in spite of his failure so far, Eli Whitney seemed the best prospect. Impressed by Whitney's explanation of the machinery he intended to use, Secretary of the Treasury Wolcott agreed to allow him more time, and offered to advance an additional $10,000 if Whitney would post greater security. Whitney got ten of the leading citizens of New Haven to go on a bond for him.

Another year of hard work brought Whitney little closer to his goal, and in November 1800 the assurances and understandings by which he had gained more time and financing virtually evaporated when Wolcott resigned as Secretary of the Treasury. Certain that pressure to show some results soon would be upon him again, Whitney decided that he had better go to Washington, where the government had just moved, to get new assurances from the new officials. Taking a bundle of musket parts and a letter of recommendation from Decius Wadsworth, an experienced ordnance man, Whitney set out for Washington.[10] There he made believers out of skeptics. He satisfied his friends' confidence in his method when he took his

[10] Ltr, Wadsworth to Secy Treasury, 24 Dec 1800. Eli Whitney Papers, Yale University.

musket parts before a meeting of high government officials, including Vice President Thomas Jefferson, and invited them to assemble locks by choosing various parts at random.

Alert to fresh approaches to weapons manufacture, Jefferson was immediately impressed with Whitney's demonstration.

When he became President, Jefferson transferred the administration of arms contracts from the Treasury to the War Department, where the emphasis would be less on meeting contractual obligations as such, and more on obtaining good muskets. His Secretary of War, Henry Dearborn—a veteran of Arnold's expedition to Quebec, of Valley Forge and Yorktown, and former Quartermaster General—was concerned about the delays in meeting delivery dates under the contracts of 1798, but he was patient and considerate.

The twenty-seven contractors of 1798 were to have delivered all their 40,200 muskets by 30 September 1800. At that time the government had received just 1,000. Only one or two ever completed their contracts. Whitney again and again had to ask for extensions of time but he held on, and finally delivered the last 500 muskets in 1809—nearly eleven years after signing the contract, and nine years behind schedule. But he had carried through his revolutionary system of manufacture, and he now had a plant available for further production.

Another outstanding arms maker of the time was Simeon North of Berlin, Connecticut, who in 1799 signed a contract to produce 500 pistols patterned on the French army pistol model of 1777. These were the first contract pistols made for the U.S. Army. In 1800 North signed a second contract for 1,500 more pistols. He, too, had to depend on advances of money by the

government, and he, too, pioneered in developing interchangeable parts.

The U.S. pistol model of 1805 made at Harper's Ferry and the model of 1807 made at Springfield were the first pistols to be manufactured in national armories. In addition, the Harper's Ferry armory made 4,000 model 1803 rifles.

Contracts of 1808 for Arming the Militia

One of the most important contributions to the development of a domestic arms industry was the enactment in 1808 of a bill which provided for the appropriation of an annual sum of $200,000 "for the purpose of providing arms and military equipment for the whole body of the militia of the United States, either by purchase or manufacture." [11]   The Purveyor of Public Supplies, Tench Coxe, advertised in the newspapers of leading cities for bids, and between 30 June and 9 November of that year Coxe let contracts to nineteen different firms for a total of 85,200 muskets. The delivery terms were for five years, with one-fifth of the total number, in most cases, due each year. Again the time schedule proved to be unrealistic and a number of the manufacturers unreliable: not a single contractor met the first year's schedule, and more than half of them made no deliveries at all the first year. By July 1813, when the contracts should have been nearly all completed, 34,477 muskets had been delivered. Some of the contractors proposed to deliver enough muskets to meet the financial advances the government had made, and then to terminate their contracts. Others pro-

---

[11] Quoted in Claud E. Fuller, *The Whitney Firearms* (Huntington, W. Va., Standard Publications, Inc., 1946) p 163.

ELI WHITNEY'S GUN FACTORY. *From a painting by William Giles Munson. Mabel Brady Garvan Collection, Yale University Art Gallery.*

posed to repay the monies. Callender Irvine, previously Superintendent of Military Stores, now Commissary General of Purchases and in charge of the contracts, thought it would be well to terminate them promptly. He said that the muskets had been patterned on poor models at a price for which it was impossible to make good muskets, and he suggested that many of them were worth nothing beyond their salvage value. Nevertheless, a precedent had been set for long-term arms contracts, and

the struggling industry had been given some stimulus just in time for war.

Some of the individual states also made efforts to procure arms for the militia. A contract offered by Governor Daniel Tompkins of New York, signed by Eli Whitney on 8 October 1808, allowed Whitney—with the benefit of a $13 price—to share sufficiently in the militia armament program to keep his armory alive. He completed this contract in two years—a year longer than he had reckoned, but still in less time than any other contractor—and then obtained additional orders for muskets from New York and Connecticut.

Artillery

Light field artillery, which came into prominence in the decades before the War of 1812, created new demands for the manufacture of artillery pieces. Artificers could make the carriages and other equipment needed, but only private foundries were able to cast the guns. In 1794 the Commissioner of Revenue contracted for cannon with the Hope Furnace in Rhode Island and with a furnace in Cecil County, Maryland. In 1796 the Secretary of the Treasury let another contract for cannon to the owners of the Maryland furnace. By 1798 privately owned foundries in nearly all the states were turning out cannon. Although Congress that year authorized the President to acquire a site for a national foundry, the expense of such a venture, together with the wholly satisfactory job being done by private industry, led him to forego such an establishment at that time.

In an attempt to assure a more reliable source of heavy guns, Secretary of War Dearborn attempted to persuade Henry Foxall of the Columbia Foundry to build a new foundry, at his own expense, on government land near Washington. This proposal did not attract Foxall. He felt that he would then be the one to bear the insecurity—the insecurity of relying on government policy for the operation of a plant that might be difficult to convert profitably to other uses. He suggested that, instead, the government should build its own foundry, which could, like the national armories for small arms, encourage uniformity of design and caliber, furnish data to help determine fair prices for private contractors, and constitute a source for extra production to meet emergencies. The government was not prepared to adopt this course. A Congressional committee reported in 1811 that 530 furnaces and forges were operating in the United States, and that the manufacture of cannon was adequate for emergencies. Foundries in Rhode Island, New Jersey, Pennsylvania, Maryland, and the District of Columbia had accepted government orders. Yet all these foundries were not able to meet the demands of war.

About 1801 Dearborn introduced a far-reaching change in American artillery weapons. On the grounds that the United States could free itself of dependence on foreign copper and tin while making guns of as good quality at a fraction of the cost, he ordered a change from bronze (then usually referred to as brass) to cast iron for field artillery pieces. Since the beginning of the Revolution bronze had been the favored metal for all American artillery weapons except the heaviest, which had been of cast iron. Although five or six times more expensive than iron, bronze was less brittle and less likely to burst. On the other hand, the bores of bronze weapons became worn more quickly. Secretary of War James McHenry had begun testing cast-iron field pieces during the flurry of preparations for possible war against France in 1798. Dearborn quickly followed up this work, and decided for the change in the face of contrary opinions throughout Europe and among many of the artillerists in America. In 1811 the first distinctive American-designed cannon to win wide recognition, the big Columbiad, was produced. Field service of the guns produced under Dearborn's direction seemed to justify his convictions, but the contest between bronze and cast iron would continue until the Civil War.

A development of no less significance was the adoption of a much-improved gun carriage system that facilitated maneuver and servicing of artillery in the field. In the old system ammunition was carried in separate wagons or two-wheeled tumbrels or carts, and there was no uniformity for wheels or other parts among the various carriages, wagons, limbers, and carts. Using a system designed by Jean Baptiste de Gribeauval, the French developed a uniform carriage system that included improvements in the carriages. Secretary Dearborn recognized many of the obvious advantages of the French innovations, but could not bring himself to copy a European system *in toto,* although he did introduce or approve, piecemeal, several changes from the old bracket-trail carriage. Wrought-iron axels replaced wood; carriages were reduced in weight by 30 percent; a center pole or tongue replaced the shafts with which horses previously had been hitched in single file, or tandem; and firing and traveling trunnions came into use for heavier caliber guns. Dearborn missed the main advantage of the Gribeauval system by passing over its feature of interchangeability of corresponding parts for all carriages and limbers.

On 12 April 1808 Congress authorized, among other units, a new regiment of light artillery which Dearborn hoped to equip completely with new gun carriages as well as new cast-iron guns, but he could find funds enough to equip only one company. A year later his successor as Secretary of War, William Eustis, accepted the Gribeauval system completely, and ordered the light artillery regiment equipped accord-ingly. This system was extended during the War of 1812.

Food, Clothing, and Medical Service

Many ordinary military supplies were obtained by the contract system, which operated much as it had in British and Colonial times—a contractor would undertake to furnish all necessary articles of supply for troops at a given post. There are arguments for either side of the question of whether procurement by contracting was preferable to direct purchase. The term contracting refers here to a system whereby the contractor had full responsibility for delivering stated supplies to a designated place. As Hamilton and Washington pointed out, the system of direct purchases by officers of the government put emphasis on satisfying the troops, on the quality of the supplies, and on assuring their delivery, but direct purchase was subject to the weaknesses of incompetent or unfaithful officials, and, since the buyers were little concerned with price, the system was likely to be less economical. Private contractors, on the other hand, were more interested in assuring their own profits than in delivering articles of good quality or making delivery at the times convenient to the purchaser. They were most concerned with prices; sometimes so much concerned that they postponed purchases and deliveries with a view to increased profits. There was a place for both systems. Magazines that had to be stocked in advance of possible operations might be supplied by contract, thought Hamilton and Washington, and military agents would then transport stock from the depots to posts and stations as needed. On contracts for provisions, as well as for weapons and other items requiring a large outlay of capital, it was customary to make advance payments to enable contractors to fulfil their commitments. The contract system, contracting for complete rations, remained the method of feeding the Army from the end of the Revolution to the end of the War of 1812, although it never did appear to be very successful. There was no subsistence department to superintend the supply of rations.

Clothing supply was often less reliable than ration supply during the decade and a half before the War of 1812, for this was the period of the Napoleonic Wars and consequent serious interruptions to American commerce, and European markets which furnished most of the clothing were shut off much of the time. On the other hand, American contractors frequently were unreliable even when cloth could be found in the domestic markets. They had to buy the cloth and engage needlewomen and tailors to make the uniforms, which were then delivered to the superintendent of military stores at Philadelphia. The paymaster issued the clothing—until 1792 charging it against the individual's pay, and afterward charging him only for extra items and for alterations.

Medical service after the Revolution was left entirely in the hands of the few regimental and post surgeons retained, again reflecting the thinking that no central staff organization was needed in peacetime. It, too, was paid for by deduction from the soldier's pay until the law of 1792 abolished such deductions. The war scare with France between 1798 and 1800 sparked a brief revival of the Medical Department with the appointment of Dr. James Craik, a neighbor of Washington's, as Physician General; but as soon as the crisis passed so did the Medical Department, to remain dormant until

another crisis arose in 1812. Although three Secretaries of War (McHenry, 1796–1800; Dearborn, 1801–1809; and Eustis, 1809–1813) had been medical directors, none did anything effective to improve the Medical Department organization. Medical supplies—the quinine bark, Turkish opium, flowers of sulphur, castor oil, mercurial ointment, brandy, sherry, and bedding—nevertheless, were fairly adequate during this whole period. The main difficulty was in the mechanics of finance and transportation.

Summary

Apprehensive of a potential threat to state rights and individual liberties by a powerful central government with a strong standing army at its command, members of Congress after the Revolution were determined to restrict both the government and its army and to put their chief reliance for national defense on the militia of the several states, depending for equipment as well as manpower upon state action. Such an attitude was not inconsistent with the purpose of the Revolution. In a sense, preservation of local autonomy against the encroachments of central authority was what the Revolution was all about. The country's policy makers were not prepared to substitute a new centralized government and new threats of tyranny for those from which they had just escaped.

But events forced their hand. They quickly discovered that threats to liberty and domestic tranquility would continue to arise from other sources than their own central government, and that truly effective common efforts were required to meet them. Impelled by such disturbances as Shays' Rebellion (1786), which for a time threatened the Springfield arsenal, the Whiskey Rebellion (1794) in western Pennsylvania, Indian hostilities in the Northwest Territory, and the danger of involvement in the Napoleonic Wars, the new nation gradually expanded its little standing army, and began to develop means to support it.

Logistical organization and effectiveness declined with the dissolution of the Continental Army. The contract system, effective as a last-ditch measure under Robert Morris in the victorious phase of the Revolution, left much to be desired in supplying the small garrisons and expeditionary forces during the next two decades. Normally, contracts could not be let until appropriations were made, and sometimes supplies could not be shipped from the East in time to use lake shipping, so that it was almost impossible to get supplies through during the winter months. But a promising beginning was made toward a national arms system based upon both government and private manufacture, and the steps undertaken to arm the militia provided a real basis for meeting wartime demands.

CHAPTER VIII

Thirty-five Years of Trial and Error

The War of 1812

By 1812 it might be expected that what apparently had been the greatest handicaps to effective logistical support during the Revolution had been removed. A central government, with executive authority and powers of taxation, had been functioning for nearly a quarter of a century. Financial solvency had been established. Administration of the Army had been vested in a War Department with a single Secretary of War. Nevertheless, when the United States again went to war with Great Britain the problems and deficiencies of logistical support reappeared.

As it existed early in 1812 the War Department was not much better for purposes of mobilizing an army and conducting a war than no department at all. With eight clerks, none of whom had had a year's experience, the Department of War hardly had enough staff to reorganize itself even when authorized to do so. Jefferson had wanted only a modest army, and had kept the size of the War Department proportionate to the three or four regiments maintained in the peace establishment rather than to the necessities of a possible emergency—the general philosophy being that without that possibility there really was no need for a War Department. Realistically, however, the problems that the Secretary had to handle did not necessarily correspond to the size of the forces being maintained.

Whether one or a dozen regiments were active, the Secretary of War, almost alone, had to perform the duties of Quartermaster General, Commissary General, and Master of Ordnance, as well as look after Indian affairs, military lands, and pensions.

Administrative Reorganization

As war with Great Britain approached in the spring of 1812, Congress began to take steps to revive the neglected supply and administrative departments. In March, April, and May 1812, Congress passed a series of bills that re-established the Quartermaster's Department under a Quartermaster General with a staff of deputies and assistants, and added a corps of artificers— masons, carpenters, blacksmiths, boat builders, harness makers, and laborers. The Ordnance Department was reorganized under a Commissary General of Ordnance, and the Corps of Engineers was augmented by a company of bombardiers, sappers, and miners. As was the case during the early years of the Revolution, this first round of legislation overlooked the Medical Department. It also was at this time that the final review of military purchasing was removed from the Treasury Department and made a responsibility of the Secretary of War, delegated to a Commissary General of Purchases.

A year later, on 3 March 1813, further legislation was enacted "for the better organization of the general staff of the army." As this law concerned the Quartermaster's Department, it, like the law of the previous year, reverted to the ambiguities of the Revolution. There were to be eight quartermasters general: one "attached to the main army" with brevet rank of brigadier general; the others with brevet rank of colonel. Most procurement functions continued under the Commissary General of Purchases. The greatest omission was that no provision was made for centralized responsibility for subsistence—food supply was to continue to be by the contract system which St. Clair and Wayne had found so unsatisfactory. Another act approved on the same day "the better to provide for the supplies of the United States [Army] . . ." authorized the position of Superintendent General of Military Supplies. This post was to be filled by a civilian to whom the Commissary General of Purchases, the quartermasters general, and other officers would be accountable, and who would be responsible for keeping "proper accounts of all military stores and supplies of every description purchased or distributed for use of the Army and for volunteers and militia in United States service," and apparently is about the nearest thing to an assistant chief of staff for logistics, or G–4, to be found at any time before creation of the Army General Staff.

Provisions for the Medical Department, neglected in the legislation of the previous year, were included in the reorganization act of 1813. Dr. James Tilton became Physician and Surgeon General of the newly revived department. A noted veteran of the Revolutionary War, Doctor Tilton had recently attracted attention with a book on military hospitals and the prevention and cure of diseases incident to an army, in which he stressed again the ideas on ventilation that he had so strongly advocated during the Revolution. Tilton preferred to make no hard and fast distinction between physicians and surgeons, but to use the available doctors as best suited the circumstances. Near the end of the war, in December 1814, a War Department general order for the first time gave a clear definition of the duties of the various medical officers, including the requisitioning and handling of medical supplies by surgeons, stewards, and apothecaries.

On the whole, the supply and service departments functioned rather better during the War of 1812 than anyone had a right to expect—considering the negligence of preceding years. But the delay necessarily involved in organizing the departments prolonged the series of initial military setbacks, and subsistence supply failed so completely that field commanders found it necessary to take local food procurement virtually into their own hands in order to keep their commands intact.

War Procurement

Abolition of the office of Purveyor of Public Supplies (28 March 1812) might have clarified to some extent the responsibilities for procurement, but the office of Commissary General of Purchases retained the functional division of labor in supply activities without eliminating overlapping duties. Aside from subsistence (still on the old contract system), the Purchasing Department was the principal agency of the War Department for outside procurement, while the Quartermaster and Ordnance Departments, in addition to certain service functions, were the principal issuing agencies. However, if purchasing commissaries were too far away in a given situation, quartermasters were authorized to make purchases, and if they incurred any losses in the delivery of clothing or subsistence, they could purchase supplies to make up the difference. The Secretary of War completed the confusing picture with a regulation making the Quartermaster General also responsible for insuring a supply of provisions for the troops.

Secretary of War William Eustis was disposed to concern himself personally with much of the detail of procurement, and as a result seemed to lose sight of the big picture. Early military defeats were bound to bring criticism on his head, and some of it centered on his preoccupation with detail. In the heat of dissatisfaction after the surrender of Detroit by Brig. Gen. William Hull (16 August 1812), Senator William H. Crawford declared:

A Secretary of War who, instead of forming general and comprehensive arrangements for the organization of his troops and for the successful prosecution of the campaign, consumes his time in reading advertisements of petty retailing merchants to find where he may purchase one hundred shoes or two hundred hats . . . cannot fail to bring disgrace upon himself, his immediate employers, and the nation.[1]

A decade of blockade, search and seizure, nonintercourse and embargo had put a severe strain on American commerce and on the national economy long before war preparation made itself felt. The nation's finances deteriorated rapidly with the misfortunes of war, and failed to recover even with reports of victory. For a time the ghastly inflation of the Revolution threatened to reappear, nullifying all improvements in organization and administration of the military departments. By 1814 the war effort was practically at a standstill. After the Capital City of Washington was burned in August of that year, the banks of Baltimore and Philadelphia suspended specie payments, and the banks of New York suspended specie payments a week later; thereafter no bank was to be found between New Orleans and Albany where payments were being made in anything but notes. James Monroe, who took over as Secretary of War (in addition to his duties as Secretary of State) in September 1814, found it necessary to add his personal guarantee to that of the government to obtain loans of depreciated bank notes from banks in Washington and Georgetown. The Treasury could not even meet the drafts drawn by Maj. Gen. Andrew Jackson during his operations around New Orleans in January 1815.

The irony of Revolutionary times reappeared when the British often found it easier to buy food supplies in the northern part of the country than did the Americans. Northern New York and Vermont are said to have furnished two-thirds of the fresh beef consumed by the British armies.

If the British were satisfied with American contractors, American commanders certainly were not. By March 1813 the breakdown of the contract system for Army subsistence supplies already had become so apparent that Congress authorized the President *either* to appoint temporarily a special commissary or commissaries *or* to authorize any Quartermaster Department officer to buy or to contract for and to issue any Army subsistence in cases of contractor's failure. This dictum alone suggests how

---

[1] Ltr, Crawford to Monroe, quoted in Henry Adams, *History of the United States of America During the First Administration of James Madison*, 2 vols (New York: Charles Scribner's Sons, 1921), II, 395.

completely inadequate the contract system was. It did contain the seeds of solutions that woud be adopted at future dates—first, a separate subsistence department; later, assignment of subsistence responsibilities to the Quartermaster's Department—but it did little good just then or immediately afterward. In 1815, for example, an individual contractor received a contract to supply rations at 19½ cents to all the forces from Niagara to Plattsburg, New York, for a period of six months; during the same period another firm agreed to supply troops in Louisiana and Mississippi at 15½ cents to 17½ cents a ration. Brig. Gen. Winfield Scott undoubtedly reflected the opinion of many field commanders when he wrote:

In time of war contractors may betray an army; they are not confidential and responsible agents appointed by the government. The principal only is known to the war office, and therefore may be supposed to be free from this objection; but his deputies and issuing agents are appointed without the concurrence or knowledge of the general or the government. The deputies or issuing agents are necessarily as well acquainted with the numerical strength of the army to which they are attached as the adjutant-general himself. For a bribe they may communicate this intelligence to the enemy, or fail to make issues at some critical moment, and thus defeat the best views and hopes of the commander in chief. The present mode of subsisting our armies puts the contractor above the general. If a contractor corresponds with the enemy, he can only be tried by the civil courts of the United States as in the case of other persons charged with treason (courts-martial having decided that contractors do not come within the meaning of the sixtieth article of the Rules and Articles of War); and if a contractor fails to make issues, he can only be punished by civil actions. I speak of cases arising within the limits of the United States. In the enemy's country I suppose a general who knows his

duty would not fail to hang a contractor who should, by guilty neglect or corruption, bring any serious disaster upon the army. . . .[2]

Brig. Gen. Edmund P. Gaines expressed his feelings about the system:

I have uniformly given the best attention in my power ever since the commencement of the war to the supply of rations and the conduct of contractors, and if I were called before heaven to answer whether we have not lost more men by the badness of the provisions than by the fire of the enemy, I should give it as my opinion that we had; and if asked what causes have tended most to retard our military operations and repress that high spirit of enterprise for which the American soldiers are preeminently distinguished, and the indulgence of which would not fail to veteranize our troops by the annoyance and destruction of the enemy, I should say the irregularity in the supply and badness of the rations have been the principal causes.[3]

Procurement of Small Arms

A few days after war was declared in June 1812 Eli Whitney offered again to accept a contract for the manufacture of muskets. His plant was in production on New York and Connecticut orders, and he was in a position to deliver muskets for the government with minimum delay. Whitney was thinking beyond the immediate war emergency, though the immediate crisis gave him his opportunity. He pointed out that the British Government, about 1796, had offered to take at a good price all the arms that all the manufacturers in Britain could make in fourteen years, and had then extended that time. The British, however, were hav-

---

[2] Ltr of Gen Scott, Incl with Ltr, Monroe to House Comm on Mil Affairs, 23 December 1814, *American State Papers, Military Affairs*, I, 600.

[3] *American State Papers, Military Affairs*, 600–601.

ing so much trouble with locks that 200,000 barrels awaited them. Whitney repeated that his objective was to substitute machinery for the skill of artisans. To assure a source of arms, he argued, the expensive machinery required should be employed constantly, and operations should be continuous for twenty years to justify the capital investment.

Secretary of War Eustis, within a month after receiving the offer, signed a contract with Whitney for 15,000 muskets at $13 each. Deliveries were to begin by 1 May 1813, and continue at the rate of 1,500 to 3,000 a year until all were completed—not later than the end of 1820. The model was to be the same as Whitney had been making for New York State.

The $500,000 remaining of appropriations of 1808 made it possible to hasten procurement of war needs. Eustis suggested in December 1812 that new agreements be made with those contractors still working on the 1808 contracts who were willing and able to carry on the work, and that the price be raised to $13 with the condition that the weapons conform closely to the approved pattern. The next month, however, Maj. Gen. John Armstrong replaced Eustis as Secretary of War, and when Armstrong transferred to the Commissary General of Purchases responsibility for administering the musket contracts, Irvine was in a position to insist on his favored model 1812 musket. Commissary General Irvine permitted the contractors of 1808 who had cleared their indebtedness to the United States, either by making enough muskets to cover the cash advances they had received or by repaying the cash, to obtain new contracts for muskets patterned on the 1812 model; they were, however, warned that

they could have no further advance payments.

Irvine exhibited a zeal for protecting the public interest which perhaps betrayed a private ambition as well as a personal stake in the musket model of 1812. The national armories and new contractors could be required to make the new musket, but Eli Whitney was working on a contract which specified the same model he had been making for New York which, to Irvine, was a completely unsatisfactory weapon. Directly he found Whitney's work unsatisfactory, and threatened to reject the muskets from Whitneyville. Whitney came out fighting. In personal interviews in Philadelphia and Washington and in an exchange of bitter letters, Whitney accused Irvine of trying to alter the terms of his contract by unilateral edict; Irvine, for his part, threatened to bring suit for nonfulfillment. Whitney carried his case to the President, and came away with the payment he was seeking and a promise that a man would be sent to inspect the muskets he had ready. Even so, he was not able to complete deliveries until 1822.[4]

Production of muskets at the national armories increased steadily from 1808 to 1811 and 1812. During 1811 and 1812 the Springfield Armory turned out 10,000 and 10,200 pieces, respectively; the Harper's Ferry Armory turned out 12,000 and 10,-140. Thereafter, production declined sharply—perhaps partly because of the introduction of the new Model 1812 musket designed by Inspector of Arms Marine T.

---

[4] Ltr, Irvine to Whitney, 26 October 1813, Ltr, Whitney to Irvine, 11 November 1813; Ltr, Irvine to Whitney, 17 November 1813; Ltr, Whitney to Irvine, 25 November 1813. All in Whitney Papers, Yale University. Jeanette Mirsky and Allan Nevins, *The World of Eli Whitney*, (New York: Macmillan Co., 1952), pp. 254–65.

Wickham—and throughout the War of 1812 never did recover prewar levels.

When it came to making pistols, Simeon North, now established at Middletown, Connecticut, still was in a class by himself, though he too had trouble meeting delivery schedules. In April 1813 North contracted to make 20,000 pistols. His contract, apparently the first to specify interchangeability, stated: "The component parts of the pistols are to correspond so exactly that one limb or part of one Pistol may be fitted to any other Pistol of the Twenty thousand." [5] North had been able to meet his schedules promptly for his 1799 contract, but he had to ask for more time to meet the new commitment. Although he had developed a system of interchangeability, his earlier promptness may have been possible because he gave greater attention to the actual making of pistols than to machinery needed for future mass production, and the present requirement introduced other problems besides the one of quantity alone. As was to be expected, Commissary General Irvine put pressure on him. North protested his ability to meet the schedule, but continued to fall behind. In January 1815 Irvine suggested that a partial explanation of North's tardiness might lie in reports that he (North) was selling fifty pistols a week privately in Boston, but North replied that the only pistols he sold privately were those failing to pass inspection.

Militia Supply

The War of 1812 is noted for its dependence on the militia system, which in itself involved special aspects of the problem of military supply—to insure that militiamen who reported for service came armed and equipped was only one part of the problem, and not a minor one. Earlier laws had established the principle that all militiamen were required to arm themselves; this, however, was not altogether practicable as there were not enough muskets and rifles in the country for everyone enrolled in the militia to buy his own. One of the laws passed before the declaration of war in 1812 authorized the President to require state governors to organize, arm, and equip their assigned portions of 100,000 militia.

While the militia system had serious drawbacks, there were advantages to having a military organization that was not tied to the traditional conservatism that the Regular forces evinced when confronted with new or different ideas and weapons. In his appeal for volunteers, the governor of Tennessee pronounced: "Those having no rifles of their own will be furnished by the state to the extent of the supply on hand. Each volunteer . . . is entitled to a dozen new short flints and lead enough to mold 100 bullets to fit that rifle. It is desired to avoid smoothbore muskets as much as possible. They may be good enough for Regular Soldiers but not the Citizen Volunteers of Tennessee." [6]

Support of Field Operations

Ambition and logistics determined the nature of the military campaigns in the War of 1812. The nation was, in effect, fighting a "three-front" war: the first over the traditional invasion routes to Canada by way of Lake Champlain and Niagara; the second in the area of Detroit and the

---

[5] Quoted in Fuller, *The Whitney Firearms,* p. 112.

[6] Quoted in Ellis C Lenz, *Muzzle Flashes* (Huntington, W. Va.: Standard Publications, Inc., 1944), p. 112.

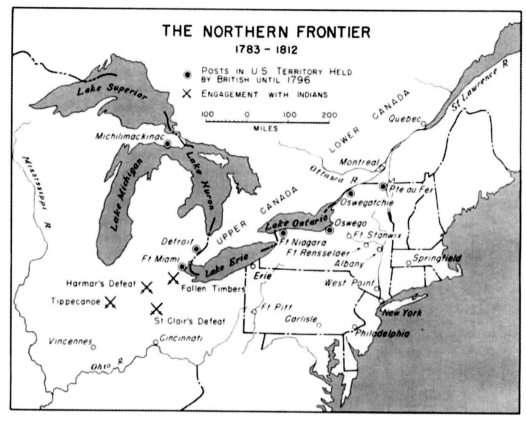

MAP 5

western shore of Lake Erie where settlement was far enough advanced to add it to the strategic avenues to Canada; the third in the South and on the Gulf Coast.

The Northwest—The area of some of the first action, the Northwest, was the most difficult to supply. Pittsburgh, the important depot area for the Indian campaigns of St. Clair and Wayne once again was the chief base for supplying the Northwest as well as for the movement of supplies down the rivers to New Orleans to avoid British vessels off the coast. It was a hard overland journey of 310 miles from Philadelphia to Pittsburgh. Beyond Pittsburgh supplies could be sent to the Northwest by boat on the Ohio River to Cincinnati, then north by the route of St. Clair and Wayne, or they could be carried on flatboats up the Wabash by the route Brig. Gen. William Henry Harrison had taken to Tippecanoe in 1811. The most direct communication between Pittsburgh and the Great Lakes was up the Allegheny River to Erie, the site of Fort Presque Isle. A more direct connection from the east, of course, was by way of the Mohawk valley to Buffalo. British control of the Great Lakes created a serious obstacle to northern invasion. (*Map 5*)

After General Hull's surrender, General

Harrison, hero of Tippecanoe, moved toward Detroit to recover lost ground and restore American prestige. Almost at once he ran into the same supply shortages that had hampered Hull when he started northward. It took a considerable time for needed supplies to be collected in the East and for them to be sent west by way of Pittsburgh. As Harrison remarked, his "troops marched from Kentucky in August to relieve General Hull, and the clothing for them left Philadelphia late in November." [7]

Secretary of War Eustis' personal direction of procurement activities for the Northwestern Department army did not avoid the pitfalls of unco-ordination, although General Harrison himself was responsible for some of the confusion. Convinced that rations could be obtained more economically in Ohio, Harrison cut back to 400,000 rations a purchase order Eustis had given to a contractor in the Pittsburgh area for 1,098,000 rations, including transportation. When Harrison's contractor in Ohio failed to deliver, Harrison had to restore the original order. Harrison also appointed a deputy commissary for his army, and directed him to purchase, when necessary, and store enough provisions at Fort Defiance, Urbana, and Wooster to support an army of 10,000 men. Frequently competing with each other for available resources, purchasing agents were not able in any case to meet Harrison's requirements, whereupon the commander ordered his officers to buy food supplies locally. Direction of supply activities other than subsistence were further confused when both the general (with War Department approval) and the Secretary of War appointed deputy quartermasters general to the Army. Eustis did take the initiative in alerting agents to forward such equipment as arms, ammunition, entrenching tools, tents, and camp equipage to the Northwestern Department army, and he gave Harrison a free hand in requisitioning supplies preparatory to moving against Detroit.

Harrison was not going to attempt any foolhardy expedition without supplies; neither was he, on the other hand, going to sit and wait until every waistcoat arrived before he acted. Indeed, he did not content himself with waiting until contractors and supply officers fulfilled their responsibilities. Cincinnati citizens responded to his request for homemade cartridges with 12,000 rounds forwarded by wagon train. He asked other towns for supplies of clothing. When his army bogged down in the winter rains, he set his troops for several days to salting down pork and to moving supplies up to the forts upon which his line of communication was based. When he reached Lake Erie in September 1813, Harrison waited until Commodore Oliver Perry had gained naval superiority, then moved his force (plus a herd of beef cattle) across the lake to the Canadian side. He caught up with the British at the Thames River on 5 October 1813 and won an important victory.

The Northeast—Transportation routes were somewhat easier for supporting the other fronts, but the supply situation was not much better. Contractors failed to deliver rations when they were needed most; there were no blankets when the weather was coldest; ammunition gave out at the most critical times.

In New England and New York, Maj. Gen. Henry Dearborn, appointed to command the Northern Department, acted as his own quartermaster general when he at-

---

[7] Quoted in Dorothy B Goebel, *William Henry Harrison* (Richmond, Va.: William B. Burford, 1941), pp 146–47

tempted to mount forces for invasions of Canada across the Niagara River and north from Lake Champlain. Brig. Gen. Morgan Lewis, appointed Quartermaster General to head the re-established Quartermaster's Department, arrived in Albany to supervise activities, but his efforts were of little assistance to Dearborn. Troops garrisoned at the northern frontier posts during the summer of 1812 were destitute of almost everything that mattered; nevertheless, amidst confusion and disorganization, supplies, though often in poor condition, gradually began to accumulate. Military agents at Philadelphia, Boston, and Albany—reappointed as deputy quartermasters general with the reorganization of the department—obtained tents, equipage and powder, and forwarded them through Albany. The Purveyor of Public Supplies and, later, the Commissary General of Purchases, contracted for clothing, mainly at Philadelphia, while deputy commissaries purchased more clothing in New York, Norwich, and Boston. An assistant deputy quartermaster general for the harbor of New York bought supplies in the New York area and expedited their transportation up the Hudson to Albany. Subsistence was obtained by contract, and was no more satisfactory than in the northwest. It was mid-October before the planned moves could begin; then both prongs of the invasion failed when militia refused to cross the boundary into foreign territory. There was nothing to do but go into winter quarters—but the quarters that had been ordered were not ready, and winter clothing had not arrived.

While Dearborn stayed at Albany, still performing quartermaster duties, crews of boatbuilders from New York City were at work at Sackets Harbor, constructing batteaux, designed to carry forty men and their

equipment, and naval vessels, and troops began to assemble for another invasion attempt. The batteaux proved to be unsafe, but the men boarded other vessels, and in April 1813 sailed with Commodore Isaac Chauncey's naval squadron for York (now Toronto). Following the capture of York, Dearborn's troops seized Fort George at the mouth of the Niagara. A September campaign against Montreal, under the personal supervision of the new Secretary of War, John Armstrong, operating with converging forces sailing down the St. Lawrence from Sackets Harbor and northward on Lake Champlain, got practically nowhere. And once again major logistical efforts turned from moving up campaign supplies to providing winter quarters.

In the next summer (July 1814) the army on the Niagara was able to give a better account of itself. A vigorous campaign under Maj. Gen. Jacob Brown resulted in the capture of Fort Erie, a sparkling victory at Chippewa, and a hard-fought battle resulting in a standoff at Lundy's Lane. But that was all. Active operations on the northern frontier ended in September with the repulse at Plattsburg of a British invasion attempt along the same route Burgoyne had taken in 1777.

Because he could not get the regulation blue for his brigade of regulars before the battle of Chippewa, Brig. Gen. Winfield Scott outfitted his well-drilled men in the gray of the New York militia. This created some confusion of identification among the enemy, but Scott's men established their identify by their performance, and the uniform set the precedent for the cadet gray of West Point. Again winter uniforms seldom reached the field before mid-winter, and when they did arrive in quantity, the quality was poor. Ration supply by the contract

GENERAL JACKSON AND HIS RIFLEMEN DURING THE DEFENSE OF NEW ORLEANS

system was no more effective than it had been in previous years.

The South—Even for the defense of Washington in July and August 1814, logistical organization did not function properly, and Brig. Gen. William H. Winder, hastily appointed commander of the newly created 10th Military District, found himself filling every role from commissary to messenger. As the British converged on the Capital he had no idea where to apply for guns, ammunition, tents, or other equipment needed by the troops gathering at Bladensburg.

Brig. Gen. Andrew Jackson was impa-tient with the details of logistics. During his campaigns in the Mississippi Territory that culminated in March 1814 with his decisive victory over the Creeks at Horse-shoe Bend, he had learned how difficult it was for an army to live off the country. In December of that same year, as he prepared for the defense of New Orleans, he found himself short of supplies, largely because of his own want of foresight in requisitioning or finding out what items were to be had in the New Orleans area. Local citizens furnished much of the clothing and bedding needed by militiamen who arrived without them.

The Kentucky rifle made the big difference in favor of United States forces in the battle of New Orleans, coupled with the deadly marksmanship of raw backwoods militiamen who were equipped with the new weapon. Army Regulars, meantime, still had to rely on the old, less accurate, musket.

Postwar Reorganization

Gains realized from the valuable and costly experience of the War of 1812 in staff reorganization were almost immediately thrown away as the staff again was reduced to match more closely the smaller size of the peacetime army. The Ordnance Department and the Purchasing Department were continued, but four brigade quartermasters replaced the Quartermaster's Department (actually, the President retained a Quartermaster General and two deputies provisionally to supervise demobilization) and only five surgeons and fifteen surgeon's mates—with no Physician and Surgeon General, but with the Apothecary General retained—remained in the Medical Department.

Then came two strong and imaginative Secretaries of War—imaginative enough to see the whole question of administrative organization in a different light, and strong enough to get something done about it. The first of these was William H. Crawford (1815–16). On the necessity of restoring the staff organization in peacetime he stated his position clearly and effectively in response to an inquiry from the House Military Affairs Committee:

The experience of the first two campaigns of the last war, which has furnished volumes of evidence upon this subject, had incontestably established not only the expediency, but the necessity of giving to the military establishment, in time of peace, the organization

which it must have to render it efficient in a state of war.

It is believed also to be demonstrable, that a complete organization of the staff will contribute as much to the economy of the establishment as to its efficiency.

The stationary staff of a military establishment should be substantially the same in peace as in war, without reference to the number or distribution of the troops of which it is composed.[8]

Secretary of War John C. Calhoun (1817–25), who shared Crawford's views, drafted a bill incorporating those ideas and saw it through Congress without essential change. It was undoubtedly the most significant single law affecting the supply and service organization of the Army enacted in the whole period between the Revolutionary War and the War with Mexico. This act, passed on 14 April 1818, provided for the organization of the Quartermaster, Subsistence and Medical Departments substantially in the form in which they remained for the next several decades.

Recent hostilities against the Seminoles in Florida had encouraged further consideration of military affairs, but even so Congress contemplated a further reduction in the Army. To its invitation for his thoughts on this and related subjects, Calhoun responded in December 1818 with a long and able paper. He saw clearly the limitations of what later would become known as the "division-slice" concept, and recognized that the size of the Army as such had little direct bearing on the necessary size and organization of the logistical staffs. Calhoun said, in part:

The staff, as organized by the act of last session, combines simplicity with efficiency, and is considered to be superior to that of the periods to which I have reference. In esti-

---

[8] *American State Papers, Military Affairs*, I, 636.

mating the expenses of the army, and particularly that of the staff, the two most expensive branches of it (the engineer and ordnance departments) ought not fairly to be included. Their duties are connected with the permanent preparation and defense of the country, and have so little reference to the existing military establishment, that if the army were reduced to a single regiment, no reduction could safely be made in either of them.

· · ·, · · · · · · · · · · · · ·

In fact, no part of our military organization requires more attention in peace than the general staff. It is in every service invariably the last in attaining perfection; and if neglected in peace, when there is leisure, it will be impossible, in the midst of the hurry and bustle of war, to bring it to perfection. It is in peace that it should receive a perfect organization, and that the officers should be trained to method and punctuality, so that, at the commencement of a war, instead of creating anew, nothing more should be necessary than to give to it the necessary enlargement. In this country particularly the staff cannot be neglected with impunity. Difficult as its operations are in actual service everywhere, it has here to encounter great and peculiar impediments, from the extent of the country, the badness and frequently the want of roads, and the sudden and unexpected calls which are often made on the militia. If it could be shown that the staff, in its present extent, was not necessary in peace, it would, with the view taken, be unwise to lop off any of its branches which would be necessary in actual service. With a defective staff, we must carry on our military operations under great disadvantages and be exposed, particularly at the commencement of a war, to great losses, embarrassments, and disasters.

· · · · · · · · · · · · · · · · ·

Our people, even the poorest, being accustomed to a plentiful mode of living, require, to preserve their health, a continuation, in a considerable degree, of the same habits of life in a camp; and sudden and great departure from it subjects them, as it is proved by experience, to great mortality. Our losses in the late and Revolutionary wars from this cause were probably much greater than from

the sword. However well qualified for the war in other respects, in the mere capacity of bearing privations, we are inferior to most nations. An American would starve on what a Tartar would live with comfort.

· · · · · · · · · · · · · · · · ·

The system [of supplying the Army with provisions] established at the last session will, in time of peace, be adequate to the cheap and certain supply of the army. The act provides for the appointment of a commissary-general, and as many assistants as the service may require, and authorizes the President to assign to them their duties in purchasing and issuing rations. It also directs that the ordinary supplies of the army should be made by contracts, to be made by the commissary-general, and to be delivered, on inspection, in the bulk, at such places as shall be stipulated in the contract.

· · · · · · · · · · · · · · · · ·

The defects of the mere contract system are so universally acknowledged by those who have experienced its operation in the late war, that it cannot be necessary to make many observations in relation to it. Nothing can appear more absurd than that the success of the most important military operations, on which the very fate of the country may depend, should ultimately rest on men who are subject to no military responsibility, and on whom there is no other hold than the penalty of a bond. When we add to this observation that it is often the interest of a contractor to fail at the most critical juncture, when the means of supply become the most expensive, it seems strange that the system should have been continued for a single campaign.[9]

The Ordnance Department was merged with the artillery in 1821, but the effect was more apparent than real. The result was a weakening of the ordnance service to the extent that it lost its commissioned officers (many of whom transferred to artillery), while ordnance enlisted men continued to perform their specialized duties. The department was restored as a separate bureau

---

[9] *Ibid.*, 780–82.

in 1832. Otherwise, the general organization of the War Department remained the same until the Mexican War.

Small Arms, 1816–46

Government Manufacture

Again going into the question of arming the militia, Congress in 1816 authorized the President to purchase sites for the construction of additional arsenals and armories. Five arsenals were added to the national system that year—the Bellona at Richmond, Virginia; the Pikesville at Pikesville, Maryland; the Washington in the District of Columbia; the Watertown at Watertown, Massachusetts, and the Frankford Arsenal at Philadelphia. Earlier, arsenals had been established at Rome, New York, in 1813, and at West Troy, New York (the Watervliet Arsenal), and at Pittsburgh (Allegheny Arsenal) in 1814. The arsenal at Augusta, Georgia, was established in 1817, and the one at Baton Rouge, Louisiana, in 1819. Some thought was given to locating a third national armory in the West, but the plan was never carried through.

Ordnance officers at the armories still resisted the adoption of interchangeability of parts on the ground that its value was strictly limited by the time and expense involved. They agreed that there was some value in making barrels, bayonets, and locks interchangeable, but not the parts of the locks.

Then came one of the most significant developments of this period—the introduction of the Hall breech-loading rifle in 1819. John Hall had obtained a patent for his rifle in 1811, but it had taken this long to perfect it and to persuade the Army to start producing it. After the weapon suc-

cessfully passed field testing with troops in 1816, Hall sold the idea to the Ordnance Department of producing it on the interchangeable system. Thus the Hall rifle not only became the first breechloader in the U.S. service; it also became the first weapon to be manufactured on the interchangeable parts system in a national armory. By signing an agreement to have the weapon produced in a national armory, Hall came out much better financially than did most of the gunmakers who tried to produce arms in their own plants. Under an agreement signed in 1819, the government acquired the right to produce the rifle on the basis of allowing Hall a royalty of $1.00 on each weapon and Hall joined the staff of the Harper's Ferry Armory, where the rifle was to be made, at a salary of $60 a month. In 1827 his salary was raised to $1,450 a year, and subsequently he received fees amounting to $9,000 for his invention of labor-saving machinery.

In the Army Board tests of 1818 and 1819, the Hall rifle demonstrated its superiority over the musket in every way—accuracy, rapidity of fire, reliability—nevertheless, the musket remained the standard infantry arm until after the Mexican War, and senior officers continued to insist on the superiority of muzzle-loaders. By the mid-1830's, Hall, by the use of die forging and machine cuts for essential fittings, had perfected the interchangeability of parts to the point where 100 rifles could be disassembled, the parts jumbled, and the rifles reassembled to new stocks with good fits in every case. Yet the national armories did not adopt the principle of interchangeable parts for other weapons until 1841. The cost was higher than the cost of muskets, but the cost of machinery installed at Harper's Ferry for making Hall's rifles amounted to only

$57,000 up to 31 January 1827, while the machinery for making muskets had cost $72,000. Originally, the average cost of making a Hall rifle, including patent rights and accessories, was figured at about $29.59; by 1835 the cost had been reduced to $14.50. But there still was no general adoption of the weapon for Regular infantry troops.

Although Joshua Shaw had developed the percussion cap before the War of 1812, and had received a patent on it in 1822, it did not come into general use until about the time of the Mexican War. The first percussion weapon accepted by the government was the 1833 model Hall breech-loading carbine manufactured by Simeon North, and Nicamor Kendall's percussion rifle had been used in Texas as early as 1835. National armories did not begin large-scale production of percussion arms until 1845 and 1846.

Natural distrust of new ideas and fear on the part of some officers that soldiers would be more likely to lose percussion caps than flints delayed acceptance; but there was also the element of cost involved in putting any new model into production. Every change made it necessary to distribute new patterns to private manufacturers, and the alteration of tools and machinery was so expensive that the armories resisted change. The superintendent of the Springfield Armory wrote to the Chief of Ordnance in 1817: "I have come to the conclusion that it is better to adhere to an uniform pattern than to be frequently changing; although the model may not be the most perfect." [10]

―――――――――

[10] Quoted in Felicia J. Deyrup, *Arms Makers of the Connecticut Valley: A Regional Study of the Economic Development of the Small Arms Industry, 1798–1870* (Northampton, Mass., Smith College, 1938), p. 57.

Some people considered the percussion cap the most important invention in firearms since the discovery of gunpowder, for it did much more than simply improve the system of ignition, as the flintlock had improved on the firelock. It also made practical the metallic cartridge case, which, in turn, assured the success of the breechloader.

A significant change in the direction of the national armories came in 1844 when the policy of using civilian superintendents gave way to the appointment of military commanders. Ordnance officers believed the reduction in costs during the next six years while improving the quality of weapons justified the change.

Private Manufacture

Simeon North, who continued to be the leading pistol maker in the country, branched out in 1823 when he signed a government contract to make Hall rifles then being made at the Harper's Ferry armory. Apparently North was the only private arms maker at the time who had sufficiently mastered the interchangeable parts system to meet the requirements of the rifle contractors. In 1828 and 1829 R. and J. D. Johnson signed a contract for 600 Hall rifles, Reuben Ellis agreed to make 500, Henry Deringer, long an accomplished rifle maker, contracted for 600, and North for another 1,200. Only North was able to deliver. Deringer and the Johnsons modified their contracts to make muskets instead. The Ellis contract, made under a special law of the State of New York, was canceled. North completed his contract, and continued to make rifles for many more years.

After 1830 the contract system for procuring small arms declined. Most of the old makes disappeared from the lists of manufacturers. Firms that depended too much upon one man died with the individual. Others, actually making less money than their accounting systems showed, were unable to finance themselves. Still others were able to operate as long as government patronage continued, but without it had to give up. Many lacked the flexibility and capital to keep up with the new arms being introduced. Only two armories in New England that had been established before 1830 survived until the Civil War: one was the government armory at Springfield; the other was Whitney's. For a time arms makers were kept in turmoil by doubts about the government's policy. With the introduction of the new model muskets in 1839 and 1840, the Ordnance Department had to promise long-term orders before the contractors would retool. No new contracts for muskets were let after 1840.

In the places of the old manufacturers a new group of highly competitive arms makers arose. With outside capital, they were able to free themselves of complete dependence upon government orders, and assumed the leadership in weapons design, machine tool development, and factory organization. One of the outstanding new firms was the Ames Manufacturing Company which began in the early 1830's to make swords and sabers on government contracts, but soon branched out into all kinds of other items for private as well as government markets. In the next few years the company accepted contracts for carbines and for bronze cannon. The Remington Company, too, got its start about this time with the purchase of machinery and an uncompleted carbine contract from Ames.

One of the most outstanding arms makers to appear in the period between 1830 and 1850 was Samuel Colt. Developing an idea that supposedly came to him as he watched the movements of a ship's wheel, Colt produced the revolver which he patented in 1836, and which almost immediately won wide popularity among Texas Rangers in the Texas War for Independence, and among soldiers in the Florida war. The Patent Arms Manufacturing Company, organized at Patterson, New Jersey, for the purpose, obtained the rights to manufacture Colt's pistol and the revolving rifles, carbines, and shotguns as well. But news of the success of Colt's revolvers in Florida and Texas spread slowly, the prices were high for citizens who had no real need for these repeaters in peacetime, and the Army was reluctant to accept too quickly such an apparently complicated—and obviously such an outstanding—weapon, and the Patent Arms Manufacturing Company went bankrupt in 1842. It remained for Captain Walker of the Texas Rangers at the time of the Mexican War to revive the Colt revolver. Colt then made arrangements with Whitney to manufacture the pistol for the government, and as a result accumulated the capital to open a plant in 1855 at Hartford, Connecticut, which was probably the most highly developed machine shop of its time.

Standards of arms manufacture had achieved new levels by the 1840's, but true interchangeability of parts, measured by close standards, was not yet the general rule.

Long-Term Contracting

Beginning with the funds appropriated for arming the militia, the government gradually hit upon a policy of providing orders to the most promising gun producing establishments on a long-term basis—six private armories enjoyed something of a special status, their contracts being renewed from time to time until late in the 1840's. These companies included Eli Whitney of Whitneyville, Connecticut, Lemuel Pomeroy of Pittsfield, Massachusetts, and Asa Waters of Sutton, Massachusetts, all of whom specialized in muskets; Henry Deringer of Philadelphia, who made rifles; Simeon North of Middletown, Connecticut, who specialized in pistols, and Nathan Starr, also of Middletown, who made swords. Secretary of War Calhoun accepted as governmental policy the principle of renewing contracts where former undertakings had been satisfactorily fulfilled, provided the terms were as low as any other bids. As Colonel George Bomford, the principal contracting officer for the Ordnance Department, put it:

> Without such inducements, contracts upon reasonable terms could not have been obtained; because the U States was the only customer the contractors could have, . . . In 1798, when the first attempt was made there were but few persons in the country acquainted with the business; and but one of these (Eli Whitney of Connecticut) who embarked in it succeeded; all the rest were either ruined by the attempt or found the business so unprofitable and hazardous as to induce them to relinquish it. In 1808, after the passage of the law making a permanent appropriation, a renewed attempt was made, and many of the contractors who were then engaged in the business have also failed. The steady support and patronage given by the Government since that time to the contractors whose skill, perseverance and capital saved them from early failure has resulted in the firm establishment of several manufactories of arms, and preserved to the country establishments of great importance to its security and defence.[11]

The government found a number of advantages in the long-term contracting system. Besides assuring an additional source of supply of arms, the system promoted a spirit of co-operation throughout the industry that was invaluable for arms procurement. However, a number of drawbacks also were evident. Ordnance officers generally considered the guns produced by private manufacturers inferior to those made in national armories. Moreover, not only was the average price of privately manufactured weapons somewhat higher than the average cost of those produced in the armories, but the government had to pay for inspection, which added to the cost. Contracts had to be renewed if the industry was to continue to be available, and this meant a continuous drain on government resources.

Contract renewal was a disadvantage from the viewpoint of the manufacturer as well, for he was at the mercy of government policy. The threat of complete nationalization of military weapons manufacture hung over him, and when a contract expired, if another was not available immediately, he had the expense of retaining his workers so as to be ready when the next order did come. At the same time, the existence of the private firms, in the spirit of co-operation that prevailed, appeared to benefit the national armories—if government inspection requirements and pressure upon the private armories to maintain high standards stimulated industrial technical progress, these manufacturers contributed to the national armories by sharing ideas and methods. It has been suggested that the principal reason for the pre-eminence of the Springfield Armory over Harper's Ferry was the latter's isolation from the industry and the former's close association with the arms makers of New England.

As to the advantages of public as against private manufacture of military weapons,

---

[11] Quoted in Mirsky and Nevins, *The World of Eli Whitney*, pp. 273-74

much is to be said on both sides. In the earlier period there was a great deal of sentiment in favor of depending on national armories altogether. After the Mexican War sentiment began to favor the procurement of all arms by contract. As Secretary of War (1853–57), Jefferson Davis thought both were needed for the best possible system of arms production. National armories were readily available and less expensive, and established price standards for private contractors. Private manufacturers seemed more likely to improve models and to experiment with new materials and new methods.

Artillery

Artillery, like small arms procurement, was on a rather more certain basis after the War of 1812. The West Point Foundry began to make cannon in 1816 under the direction of Gouverneur Kemble, and quickly became a leading supplier of heavy ordnance. This foundry and a number of others were established and maintained on the basis of assurances of continued support from the government. Like the small arms manufacturers, artillery manufacturers were at the mercy of government orders, but the government was completely dependent upon them for cannon. The arsenals at Washington, Pittsburgh and Watervliet constructed carriages, limbers, and caissons, and mounted the guns; but for the guns themselves they still were dependent on private foundries.

These were years of special significance for the artillery: a new carriage system was adopted, the contest between iron and bronze for cannon was renewed, and the whole spectrum of artillery matériel was systematized. Even as the United States was perfecting its adaptation of the French Gribeauval carriage system during the War of 1812, the British had developed a far superior system of their own. This superiority was not clearly demonstrated during the war, and its significance was lost upon almost everyone except one man—Col. Decius Wadsworth, who had been Chief of Ordnance since establishment of the department in 1812. In 1817 Wadsworth designed a stock-trail system based upon models captured from the British in 1814, but a board convened to consider the proposed change recommended retention of the Gribeauval system, and Secretary Calhoun accepted that recommendation. Meanwhile the French themselves, convinced of the superiority of the British system, added significant improvements of their own, and overcame strong national prejudice sufficiently for the stock-trail system to be adopted in 1827. The system's principal advantages were in ease and speed of limbering and unlimbering the guns, ability of limbered guns and caissons alike to turn about on a short radius, and convenience of the ammunition carriage and the mounting of the soldiers.

An officer sent to France in 1827 to make a study of the Gribeauval system returned with a report of the French adaptation of the stock-trail which immediately set off reconsideration in the United States. The Washington Arsenal built one of the new carriages in 1832 for trial, and a board recommended adoption in 1835. The new system was adopted in 1836; it gradually replaced the old system, vestiges of which remained until after the Civil War.

Meanwhile, the question of the most suitable metal for cannon had arisen again. Although cast-iron weapons had performed well during the War of 1812, they were bursting under the force of much-improved powder developed since the war. If full advantage was to be taken of the more powerful powder, stronger guns would have to be made.

A Board of Ordnance appointed in 1831 took up this question among others. Successive boards appointed in 1835, 1837, 1838, and 1839 all moved in the direction of returning to bronze for light artillery pieces. After another ten months of study and testing, a board appointed in 1839 unanimously concluded in February 1840 that bronze should be adopted. But Secretary of War Joel Poinsett remained unconvinced. He attached a great deal of weight to the desirability of independence from foreign materials for arms. Great quantities of iron were available domestically, but copper and tin would have to be imported. Poinsett felt that the greatest failure had been in the skill of the founders, and that the solution to the problem of improved guns lay in developing foundry skill rather than in adopting an expensive and scarce metal. Members of the Ordnance Board did not deny the cogency of Poinsett's argument, but they held that it would be unwise to delay procurement of new weapons until the necessary skills could be developed; that bronze weapons should be ordered immediately, and in the meantime steps be taken to improve iron foundry. Poinsett sensed no such urgency to go into a bronze procurement program. First he sent a mission composed of the three junior members of the Ordnance Board and William Wade, a former Army officer who now was an iron founder at Pittsburgh, to Europe to investigate cannon making there. Nearly everywhere they were impressed by the favor in which bronze was held, and they came home reinforced in their belief that the United States should change to that metal for its light artillery.

On the basis of their report, the Ordnance Board in January 1841 again voted a unanimous recommendation for the change, and this time Poinsett approved. The question would not come up again until American founders began making rifled cannon during the Civil War.

Another recommendation that the Ordnance Board made in its report of 1841 was for appointment of an agent or an officer of the Ordnance Department to oversee the manufacture of cannon at foundries where the government had contracts. Poinsett quickly approved, and appointed William Wade as "attending agent." Congress established the new position by law in 1842. The duty of this agent was to see that proper materials and methods were used, and he had authority to reject any weapons not made according to regulations. Again, there was a great deal of discussion in the War Department and in Congress about the advisability of establishing a national foundry or an Army gun factory, but the government continued to rely on four leading private foundries for its heavy ordnance. Under the new law, however, for the first time the Ordnance Department could prescribe specific rules for the selection and preparation of metals and for the steps in the fabrication of artillery pieces.

Earlier, in 1838, Poinsett had proposed the introduction of rockets and rocket units. The Board of Ordnance meeting that year approved this proposal, and the members of the mission to Europe in 1840 were much interested in what they saw of rocket-making in the different countries—by methods supposedly secret but apparently known to all. Thus the way was opened for the procurement and use of rockets in the Mexican War.

Another, and more significant at the

time, addition to artillery weapons came in 1844 with the adoption of the 8-inch and 10-inch Columbiads.

Finally, successive boards worked toward a more complete and precise definition of the whole artillery system. The first complete system was approved in 1819. After years of work in making improvements, approving the calibers and types of guns, howitzers, and mortars in the different categories (as light, siege, and seacoast), and preparing all the drawings and descriptions necessary to make it effective—a task assigned primarily to Maj. Alfred Mordecai— the new and complete system was ready for publication by the late 1840's.

The Seminole War

The most severe test for the Army in the period between the War of 1812 and the War with Mexico was the Second Seminole (Florida) War which dragged on for seven years (1836–42) of costly and exasperating operations. Ten generals, including Edmund P. Gaines, Winfield Scott, Thomas S. Jesup (the Quartermaster General), Zachary Taylor, William Eustis, Alexander Macomb, and other leading figures, all had a turn at commanding operations in Florida without any lasting results. Finally a measure of success came to the last commander, Col. William J. Worth. The impenetrable swamps and forests in the tropical heat were as great obstacles as the stubborn and skillful foe. Not counting battle casualties, no more than two-thirds of the men in a combat unit could be counted upon for action within thirty days after their arrival. The men had to work more than fight just to support themselves, although General Jesup complained that the southern militia

would not work for themselves, much less for the Army. Regulars had to perform duties not ordinarily assigned to them—drive wagons, work on roads and bridges, and other noncombat tasks. Transportation was so difficult that a week's rations had to be carried in haversacks. Sometimes canoes and boats could be used effectively, and a dredging machine was brought in to help open up channels. (*Map 6*)

For the first time steamboats came into extensive use in the support of United States military operations. Most of the troops and supplies used in Florida went by ship, usually chartered sailing vessels, from New York, Philadelphia, and Washington, or by steamboat from Charleston, Savannah, and New Orleans. About forty steamboats were in chartered service during 1836 and 1837. In the fall of 1840 five government-owned and six chartered steamboats were in regular service, mainly transporting forage for the 2,140 horses and mules in use in Florida. The principal depots were established at Palatka on the St. John's River, St. Augustine, Tampa Bay, and Cedar Key. All had extensive warehouses, repair shops, stables, quarters, and wharves. In the fall of 1840 more than one thousand civilians were employed at Florida depots and sub-depots.

For his campaign General Taylor established a series of garrisoned depots along his line of march. He was unable to carry out his whole plan, but in a six-weeks campaign he did succeed in penetrating 150 miles into hostile country, opening roads, building bridges and causeways, establishing two depots—and capturing 180 Indians and Negroes.

Medical officers had no rest. The sick

MAP 6

and wounded were evacuated on litters made of blankets and hides stretched on poles and carried on the backs of captured ponies. When post hospitals became overcrowded, patients were sent to general hospitals at Picolata and Cedar Key. In the period between 1 June 1841 and 28 February 1842, when the force in Florida numbered less than 5,000, the number of cases of sickness reported was 15,794.

In the final campaigns, Colonel Worth resorted to a series of summer offensives aimed at destroying the Indians' subsistence, so that the issue finally was settled by striking at enemy logistical resources.

Summary

Aside from the immediate issues and problems involved, the Florida War proved to be an invaluable training ground for the conduct of operations in Mexico four and five years later. Other advances which helped to prepare the Army for its triumphs in Mexico were: John C. Calhoun's reorga-

nization of the staff, the continuing program of small-arms procurement, and improvements in the system of artillery matériel.[12]

---

[12] For sources upon which Part I is based see Bibliography, pages 703–09.

PART TWO

EMERGENCE OF MODERN WARFARE

CHAPTER IX

War with Mexico: War Department Procurement and Supply

By the time of the War with Mexico, the War Department—or "Military Department" as it was commonly called—had become more or less set in its form of a central administrative office with a collection of autonomous bureaus. The "General Staff" in 1845 was no more than the several chiefs of the administrative and technical departments. War planning, general staff supervision, and effective co-ordination were alien to the whole system. But more than half a century of experience in war and peace, together with long continuity in office of the principal bureau chiefs, had given to the supply and service departments on the whole a competency never before known in the United States. Long service in office does not necessarily indicate special ability, but as long as flexibility and imagination are not sacrificed, experience must count for a great deal. At the outbreak of the Mexican War the General in Chief, Maj. Gen. Winfield Scott, had served almost five years as head of the Army, and his immediate predecessor, Maj. Gen. Alexander Macomb, had served for thirteen years. Col. Roger Jones had been Adjutant General for twenty-one years, Col. Thomas Lawson Surgeon General for nearly ten years, Col. Joseph G. Totten Chief Engineer for more than seven years, Col. George Bomford

Chief of Ordnance for fourteen years, and Brig. Gen. Thomas S. Jesup Quartermaster General for twenty-eight years.

As then organized, the War Department divided procurement, distribution, and service responsibilities among the independent bureaus according to the type of supplies or equipment or services involved. For a long time major responsibilities for procurement—particularly for contracting and purchasing on the open market—had been withheld from the military department. Until 1812, it will be recalled, the Treasury Department had this responsibility. Then the rather anomalous Purchasing Department performed this function until it was virtually abolished in 1842; afterward the bureau chiefs had complete charge of procurement, as well as storage and distribution of the supplies and equipment for which each was responsible. There is something to be said, perhaps, in favor of this arrangement, for it centralized procurement and so permitted development of uniform procedures. On the other hand, it did not work out altogether satisfactorily for the reason that division of responsibility for certain items of supply led to friction and the temptation for one office to blame another for supply failures. In the absence of general staff supervision and co-ordination, assignment of total responsibility for a given item of supply to a particular bureau had obvious advantages. Although trouble with Mexico had been brewing for months, the War Department and its bureaus had done little to anticipate the transportation, supply, and service requirements that war would bring.

Failure to take any effective measures in advance to prepare for war has been the subject of much criticism: against the War Department and the Army for failure to plan and anticipate, and against Congress for failure to appropriate the necessary funds. The fact is that much had been done to assure the country of a supply of arms, and equipment, with the possible exception of wagons that could be procured then about as rapidly as the Army could be organized to use them. In the circumstances of the 1840's what difference did it make, really, when mobilization of resources began? It is said that a great deal of time might have been saved had supply requirements been anticipated well before hostilities began. Perhaps the time between the opening and closing of formal hostilities would have been shortened, but that time would not necessarily have been more valuable than the time and effort released for other endeavors by refraining from extensive military preparations during the preceding months and years. In the 1845–46 situation, where the United States clearly held the initiative, and where the danger of invasion was remote, supply build-up could begin as well with the commencement of hostilities as at any other date. However likely war may appear to be, it is never absolutely certain until it begins, and in an age that permits of such deliberation, the greater total saving is likely to result from the postponement of all possible procurement and distribution of supplies until the actual be-

ginning of hostilities lends an element of certainty to the need for those activities.

The greatest deficiency in the War Department was the complete want of intelligence upon which to formulate practical logistical plans. Reliable information on elementary facts of topography, climate, and resources in Mexico had not been collected. General Scott, on the basis of some bit of misinformation that had come his way, announced there would be no advantage in attempting military operations before October, since the period from March to September was a rainy season in northern Mexico. Staff officers had no data on the navigability of the Rio Grande, on whether wagons could be used in Mexico, on the availability of mules in that country, or to what extent local resources might be depended upon for subsistence and forage.

Though uncertainty prevailed concerning the requirements that might develop, the War Department at least could move swiftly to expand the Army and undertake large-scale procurement of equipment once war had been declared. After conferences with President Polk on the preparation of his war message, members of the House Committee on Military Affairs quickly agreed to recommend an authorization of 50,000 volunteers and a sum of $10,000,000 for conducting the war. Congress accepted this recommendation in the war bill passed on 13 May 1846. Now that the emergency actually had come, Congress lost no time in approving appropriations and measures for expanding the Army which it never would have sanctioned on the mere assumption that war might come at some time in the future.

The act of 13 May also authorized calling of militia into service for six months; actually, however, militia were not used a great deal. Volunteers were to be placed on the same footing as Regular troops except as to clothing allowance. Volunteers were to receive an equivalent money payment in lieu of clothing, and were to furnish their own clothing. Volunteer cavalrymen were to furnish their own horses and special equipment. The United States would arm all volunteers mustered into federal service.

There seems to have been no kind of thoroughgoing analysis of requirements to support the estimates of 50,000 troops for twelve months and $10,000,000. On the contrary, President James K. Polk has been sharply criticized for making the assumption that a war in far-off Mexico could be successfully concluded within six to twelve months without any study of supply problems involved, and without reference to the nation's experience. But in this respect Polk's actions were not much different from those of his predecessors and successors when caught in a similar situation. Probably the estimates of the President and of Congress in this case were as close to actual requirements as were many of the appropriation bills of later years that were prepared after many man-hours of calculation, and then arbitrarily modified by higher authority or by Congress. Nor is Polk alone in swiftly adopting measures to meet an emergency without the benefit of detailed staff study. Polk had no staff study nor any general staff to make one. Even after the country had had many more decades of military experience, and a highly complex general staff had learned to prepare the most detailed studies and sound estimates of requirements, chief executives would meet new emergencies by making quick decisions without reference to staff studies. Except as an element in general experience and judgment, estimates of logistical feasibility

were out of place in such emergency decisions. The substance of the decision was not what could be done, but what had to be done.

President Polk permitted himself to hope that this war might be won without gunpowder and that Mexico might be overawed by the demonstrations of power that he contemplated rather than conquered by long-term, large-scale operations. His expressed hope that the war might be ended within twelve months was not so very far off the mark, although it seemed rash to some observers: actual hostilities lasted sixteen months from the time of Polk's war message in May 1846 to the surrender of Mexico City in September 1847.

General Scott lost no time in initiating action to move the necessary troops and supplies to the theater of war. Two days after passage of the war bill he notified the several "chiefs of the general staff" that an army of some 20,000 men, including the troops already in Texas, was to be directed, in several columns, against Mexico. The chiefs were to take steps to collect subsistence supplies in advance at rendezvous points designated for the Regular and volunteer troops, and along the lines of march that they were to follow. The General in Chief recommended a ration of hard bread and bacon for the marches. For the volunteer units it was necessary also to collect arms, accouterments, ammunition, camp equipage, and medical supplies at the rendezvous points except when routes of march passed depots or arsenals where the necessary equipment could be obtained. The Quartermaster General was to arrange for land and water transportation. The chiefs would be informed about rendezvous points and points of departure by the Adjutant General and by the calls for volunteers sent out by the Secretary of War to the state governors, but the general could say immediately that these places would include Cincinnati, Ohio; Madison or Jeffersonville, Indiana; Louisville and Smithland, Kentucky; Quincy or Alton, Illinois; Memphis and Nashville, Tennessee; Washington or Fulton on the Red River in Arkansas; and Natchez, Mississippi.

In the mobilization effort there was a chance for modern developments in transportation and communication to play a significant part. Probably the most important innovation was the steamboat. Railroads by this time had developed a fairly dense network in the northeastern states, but they had just begun to operate in the Mississippi Valley, and there were none west of the Mississippi. Indeed, it was not until ten years after the Mexican War that it was possible to travel the whole distance from the Atlantic coast to the Mississippi River by steam railway.

The telegraph by 1846 had revolutionized communications. Some 1,200 miles of telegraph lines linked Washington with New York, Philadelphia, and other cities, chiefly in the northeast. The telegraph still had not come to the southwest, and was not used tactically during the war, but it was important as an instrument for speeding the procurement of equipment in the northeastern states.

As the government's policies and strategic plans emerged in the summer of 1846, something of the logistical effort contemplated began to come clear. First of all, the Army of Observation under General Taylor—which had precipitated the action on the Rio Grande—was to take Monterrey, and head for the "heart of the country." Meanwhile, the Army of the West, which had marched from Fort Leavenworth on 5 June

under Col. Stephen W. Kearney, would be moving on New Mexico and California. In addition, an Army of the Center under Brig. Gen. John E. Wool was to march from San Antonio for Chihuahua. Soon it appeared that the best way to gain the Mexican capital would be by a march from Vera Cruz, and the general plan was modified to include an amphibious landing at Vera Cruz, and a march inland to the Valley of Mexico. These daring projects called for immediate steps for supply procurement on a large scale.

For arms and ammunition, the Army could turn to fairly well-stocked armories and arsenals, and to a group of private contractors who had been supplying the government for a number of years. Given time, the quartermaster depot at Philadelphia (Schuylkill Arsenal) could expand its production of clothing manyfold. For other items it was necessary to go to the open market, and to place contracts with private business firms for goods and services. Under laws and regulations that had been developing since 1798, and still remained in force, all contracts had to be by purchase in the open market, or by bids submitted according to previous advertisement. No advance of funds of any kind was permitted except to disbursing officers in order to permit them to make prompt payment. The old practice of paying contracting officers according to the amount of funds they disbursed had been abolished, and no officer whose pay was fixed by law was allowed to receive any additional allowance for the disbursement of public money. No member of Congress could share in any contract. All contracts for the Army were to be negotiated under the direction of the Secretary of War. An act of August 1846 required strict accounting of receipts and payments, prohibited the deposit, loan, or other use of public funds for private purposes, and established other safeguards against embezzlement. Perhaps more significant was the provision that after 1 April 1847 all payments were to be made in gold or silver coin, or, if the creditor agreed, in Treasury notes; no exchange of funds was to be made except for gold or silver.[1] This assurance of sound financial backing did much to ease the troubles that had plagued procurement officers in earlier days.

With the support of Congress and the general population that comes with a state of war, energetic procurement officers began to obtain equipment and to arrange for transportation for troops and supplies. By 30 June 1846 quartermasters, commissaries, paymasters, and other officers already had managed to spend over $3,000,000 of the $10,000,000 appropriation for "Mexican Hostilities."[2]

Arms and Ammunition

In many respects the volunteer soldiers of the Mexican War were regarded—especially by Regulars—as poorly trained, poorly disciplined, and frequently poorly equipped, but in one thing they had some claim to superiority, and that was in their firearms. The Regulars were still carrying flintlock muskets, for although percussion arms rapidly were coming into general use, General Scott objected to them on the ground that they had not yet been sufficiently tested for field use. But many volunteers, though entitled to arms from the government, preferred to rely on their personal Colt revolving pistols and rifles, Hall breech-loading rifles, Jencks carbines, and other percussion weapons. Jefferson Davis flatly refused to have his Mississippi volunteers armed with old flintlock muskets, and finally obtained Whitney rifles for them. There was no question of the superiority of rifles over muskets, except that it took much longer to reload the muzzle-loading rifles. Dragoons carried musketoons—light muskets on slings—or, in some cases, rifle carbines. Needless to say, the use of such a variety of infantry weapons complicated the problems of ammunition supply, maintenance, and repair parts supply.

The war started just as the transition to percussion arms in the U.S. Army began. The first limited adoption of a percussion weapon (the Hall) had occurred in 1833. The matter had been under continuous consideration since 1841, when in March 1845 the Ordnance Board recommended adoption of the Belgian method of converting flintlock muskets to percussion weapons. More than 14,300 percussion muskets were turned out in 1845. The first ones were issued to the West Point cadets, and they were slow reaching the Regular soldiers in Mexico, though in the course of the war the number of percussion caps issued was well over double the 400,000 flints issued.

At the same time the long contest went on for adoption of a breechloader. While the Hall rifle and the carbine had made good first impressions, they had not won general acceptance as basic weapons, and production of them had declined. There still was no breechloader that had overcome the handicap of serious gas leakage at the breech, which made for a variability in performance that tended to rob the weapons of

---

[1] Regulations for the Government of the Ordnance Department (Washington, 1852), app. 2, pp. 134–38.

[2] Account of Receipts and Expenditures of the Government for the Year Ending June 30, 1846, House Exec Doc 10, 29th Cong., 2d sess., pp. 174–75.

their accuracy. Moreover, after prolonged use, paper, cloth, and powder would foul the parts, and the rifling would fill with powder causing the piece to develop such a "kick" that it could not be fired from the shoulder. Until the development of the metallic cartridge case, more strict attention to cleaning, of course, was the answer to the latter problem, but this was difficult to manage in combat, and could lead to delays at critical times.

The fact that no foreign army had as yet adopted a breechloader for general use seemed to give added weight to the arguments of those opposed to adopting it in this country. The Prussians had produced their breech-loading "needle gun" in 1842, but it had made a poor showing. Another argument of opponents was more specious: they held that use of the breechloader, which could be fired so much more rapidly than the muzzle-loader, would put too much strain on the ammunition supply. Here a weapon was being criticized because it produced too much fire power! The answer surely would have been to give more attention to ammunition supply—even if half the soldiers had to be assigned as ammunition carriers—if the result produced more fire power against the enemy. In any case, the general service breechloader was at least another war away.

In December 1846 William Hale of England offered to the United States Government a new type of rocket in which he had replaced the cumbersome stick of the Congreve rocket. Hale's rocket was fitted with a rotary propelling mechanism, and an auxiliary firing chamber gave the rocket a pinwheel effect, thereby "spin stabilizing" it on its course. Trials by a joint Army-Navy board gave such a satisfactory result that the government purchased the right to

use Hale's invention, and quickly began producing the rockets. By November 1847, one arsenal had turned out 2,000 Hale rockets of $2\frac{1}{4}$-inch and $3\frac{1}{4}$-inch caliber.[3]

The Ordnance Department depended upon open purchases or private contracts for a great deal of its artillery, ammunition, and accouterments. Payment for an artillery piece was according to the weight of its projectile—a 12-pounder bronze howitzer cost 75 cents a pound; an 18-pounder garrison gun, 6 cents a pound; a 24-pounder siege gun, $133 a ton. Eight-inch shells for Columbiads were 5 cents a pound. Among the several contractors who furnished ordnance supplies and equipment, some of the principal firms making artillery, mortars, and carriages were C. Alger and Company, who made deliveries to Watertown, Massachusetts; N. P. Ames, who delivered to Springfield; and the West Point Foundry Association, which made deliveries to New York. H. A. Dingee, Robert Dingee, and J. J. Pittman all delivered infantry accouterments to New York, and J. Boyd and Sons delivered the same kind of equipment to Watertown. E. I. Dupont de Nemours & Company made gunpowder for delivery to the Frankford Arsenal, and Loomis, Swift and Masters delivered powder to Watervliet. Principal manufacturers of artillery shells and cannon balls included Chollar, Jones, and Company and the West Point Foundry Association who delivered to New York, and J. S. Wellford who delivered those items to Fort Monroe, Virginia.

National armories continued their sizable output of small arms and other equipment. During the year ending 30 June 1847 the Springfield Armory turned out 14,300 mus-

---

[3] Rpt, Ordnance Dept, 20 November 1847 (No 20), House Exec Doc 8, 30th Cong., 1st sess., p. 697.

kets complete, spare parts equal to 1,000 muskets, tools, and other items. The Harper's Ferry Armory at the same time, among other things, turned out 12,000 muskets, and completed from items on hand in various stages of manufacture some 1,590 assorted components of percussion muskets, 2,117 rifle components, and 20,979 components for muskets of the models of 1822 and 1840 for issue to arsenals and field armies for use in making repairs.[4] The twenty-two arsenals were engaged primarily in manufacturing accouterments and small arms and artillery ammunition in addition to repairing and maintaining arms and equipment.

On the whole, ordnance procurement and supply during the Mexican War was rapid and effective. It is true that a great many obsolete weapons went to Mexico, but they were not inferior to most of those in use by the Mexicans. In spite of the great distances, new equipment reached the fighting fronts quickly. Soon after the capture of Vera Cruz, forty-nine 10-inch mortars and close to 50,000 shells arrived for General Scott's army. They had been ordered just before he left Washington, and in the four-month interval had been manufactured, moved to the seacoast, put on board ships, transported to Vera Cruz, and landed.

Quartermaster Supplies and Transportation

In the early months of the war the Quartermaster's Department, no less than the Ordnance Department, worked under the pressures engendered by the need for immediate action in large-scale procurement. Between 15 August 1845 and the end of

1846, the Quartermaster's Department let 424 contracts. Most of them were for transportation—for the purchase or charter of vessels, or contracts for the transportation of specified troops or supplies between given points. Other contracts were for the purchase of wagons, or the hire of horses and wagons and pack mules. Still others were for fuel, building materials, repairs, troop quarters, iron camp kettles and mess pans, and other housekeeping needs. In addition, this was the first war in which the Quartermaster's Department was responsible for clothing.

To transport troops and supplies from points in the United States to Mexico, it was now possible to put chief reliance on the steamboat. Since steamboats were found to be the best means of supporting operations along the Rio Grande, the Quartermaster's Department procured a number of light-draft steamers and scows and barges for that purpose. For transportation along the Atlantic coast, in the Gulf of Mexico, and on the inland rivers, the Quartermaster's Department bought some vessels, chartered others, and for specific missions hired transportation for a particular service.

For additional land transportation in Mexico, quartermaster officers hired horses and wagons and drivers at $4 to $5 a day, purchased as many pack mules and saddles as possible all the way from Kentucky to Louisiana, and hired Mexican mules and muleteers at 55 cents a day. For wagon maintenance work, a number of civilians were hired. A master mechanic and six assistants contracted to go to Texas or Mexico from Washington, D.C., for $2.50 and $1.50 a day, respectively, and round-trip passage.

After the virtual abolition of the Purchasing Department in 1842, the Quarter-

[4] *Ibid.*, pp. 690–707.

master Department had complete responsibility for procurement of clothing, as well as for its storage, distribution, and accounting.

The Quartermaster General continued the system of clothing procurement and production that Callender Irvine had developed as Commissary General of Purchases. This activity centered on the Schuylkill Arsenal at Philadelphia. Quartermaster purchasing agents bought the required cloth from manufacturers for delivery to the arsenal where it was cut by government-employed cutters according to prescribed patterns. The work was farmed out to tailors and seamstresses who made the finished garments, which were then returned to the arsenal for inspection and acceptance. Reduction of appropriations in the years immediately preceding the war had only permitted enough operation at Schuylkill to supply the small peacetime Army, and to accumulate a reserve amounting to about a half-year's peacetime allowance. War brought rapid expansion to the arsenal. Soon ten times the 400 tailors and seamstresses who had been working on government orders were at work on new uniforms, and before the end of the war more than 85,000 garments of various kinds were being delivered to the depot each month. A branch clothing depot established at New York late in 1846 developed a capacity that could be expanded to meet any foreseeable emergency.

Regular troops in Mexico generally were well supplied with the blue uniform of short jacket, trousers, and cap with high, loose crown that was usual for the American soldier of the period. Volunteers, although authorized to wear similar uniforms, were, in fact, not so well off. It will be recalled that under the war bill volunteers had to furnish their own clothing, but they were entitled to a commutation in money. The War Department interpreted this to authorize a payment in advance of one year's clothing allowance, $42, to each volunteer, which seemed a simple enough arrangement, but serious disadvantages soon appeared.

Unfortunately many volunteers failed to apply their allowance to the purpose intended. Others tried to save some of the money by buying inferior clothing; some received inferior goods from unscrupulous sellers. When they arrived in Mexico their situation worsened. The Quartermaster's Department was able to furnish uniforms to the volunteers, but the approval of Congress was necessary. In his annual report of December 1846, Secretary of War Marcy recommended that the government issue clothing to volunteers. No action followed, and he made the same proposal a year later. Then some of the state legislatures began to pass resolutions asking that Congress increase the volunteers' clothing allowance. Early in 1848, after the war was over, and after the damage had been done, Congress approved an act to provide clothing for volunteers on the same basis as for Regulars.

Probably the most serious problem for quartermaster service throughout the Mexican War was manpower. The field armies did not generally have strength enough to spare men for quartermaster labor, and, since there was no corps of quartermaster troops, the only recourse was to hire, at high wages and at heavy expense in transportation, the mechanics, teamsters, and laborers—at times several thousand men—needed to perform quartermaster jobs. Few of the men thus hired were willing to engage for a period of more than six months, and even fewer were willing to renew their contracts. General Jesup, with the support of the Secretary of War, strongly urged the formation of a corps of workers, subject to the laws of the Army and having all the advantages of troops of the line. Enlistment of men in such a corps for the duration of war, he insisted, would reduce the cost of labor by a third and would more than double the efficiency of the Quartermaster's Department. Moreover, he saw no other way to remedy the evils that had become so obvious during the war.[5] Jesup's recommendations got nowhere with Congress.

Subsistence

Food supply remained the responsibility of a separate Subsistence Department. Temporarily expanded for the war by the addition of a number of volunteer officers, the bureau continued in much the same pattern as established in 1818 and 1821, and expanded in 1838.

The official ration for the Army had not changed materially since 1832 when the grog allowance had been dropped temporarily in favor of coffee, and 1838 when, for each one hundred rations, the coffee allowance was increased from four to six pounds and sugar from eight to twelve pounds, and whiskey was dropped permanently.

With the exception of some of the expeditions operating at great distances from bases or local sources of supply, most troops seemed to be generally well supplied with food. Commissary officers purchased food on the open market as needed, mainly at the big market centers in New York, Baltimore, New Orleans, and St. Louis, thus avoiding

serious losses from storing excessive quantities or accepting inferior qualities. Losses from accidents in transportation were heavy. For the first six months of the war, until it was learned that substantial quantities of food could be obtained in Mexico, field forces relied on depots supplied from the United States. A volunteer regiment sailing from New York for California in September 1846 carried more than a twelve-months' supply of rations.

The feeding of recruits was done largely by contract, and these contracts comprised most of those let by the Subsistence Department in 1846. There were a number of contracts to furnish fresh beef at certain designated posts—usually for a term of a year—and several special contracts to supply pork, bacon, flour, and bread. Some units in the field also were provisioned by contract.

Engineer Department

Perhaps nowhere was the lack of prewar co-ordination and appropriations more evident than in the Engineer Department. Anticipating possible river-crossing operations, General Taylor in September 1845 sent a request to the War Department for a ponton bridge train. The requisition went first to the Quartermaster General's office where it was referred to the Engineer Department, the agency responsible for military bridges. Here the request came to an Engineer lieutenant who was unable to find any funds in his bureau to cover the building of ponton bridge equipment. He had a vague recollection that some ponton bridging had been used in the Florida War; he did not know from what appropriations that equipment had been constructed, but he thought it not unlikely that it had been

[5] Rpt, Quartermaster General, 24 November 1847, House Exec Doc 8, 30th Cong., 1st sess., p. 548; Rpt, Secretary of War, 2 December 1847, House Exec Doc 8, 30th Cong., 1st sess., pp. 64–65.

from the transportation fund. Since this request was for a portable bridge, which would belong to the train of an army, and since it was to be used as a means of transportation for crossing streams, he thought construction might well be charged to the transportation appropriation of the Quartermaster's Department. But Quartermaster officers could find no appropriate funds either, and the Secretary of War saw no alternative but to await an appropriation by Congress. When Congress authorized the war appropriations it then was possible to let the contract to a Boston rubber company for the equipment. The bridge train arrived in Mexico in October 1846—long after Taylor had any need for it.

In the matter of manpower, the Engineer Department faced a situation similar to that of the Quartermaster's Department, but with a better measure of success. On 15 May 1846 Congress authorized the organization of one company of 100 sappers, miners, and pontoniers, to be called "engineer soldiers." The company was to be officered by the Engineers, and the men were to be on the same footing as other United States troops. They were to assist in the instruction of the duties of sappers, miners, and pontoniers at West Point, and detachments might be sent out to oversee and assist laborers in the construction and maintenance of fortifications. This arrangement really did not get at the problem of engineer labor in the field, because engineers retained for the most part their supervisory status. Actually, the engineer company was not organized in time to participate in Taylor's campaign in Mexico, but it did join his army in October 1846, and participated most effectively in the siege of Vera Cruz and in Scott's expedition to Mexico City. The

Chief Engineer recommended activation of two or three more such companies.

The Corps of Topographical Engineers (headed by Col. William Turnbull), a separate bureau during this period as was the Quartermaster's Department, had no success in enlisting specialist workers. Though popularly associated with civil works, most topographical engineer officers saw duty with the armies in Mexico, where they were handicapped in making their surveys by lack of personnel. Commanders nearly always were reluctant to reduce their combat strength by releasing detachments of troops to help in this work. When men were made available, they were unfamiliar with and unskilled in the tasks of adapting wagons to carry the special tools and equipment, and of handling the necessary tools, maps, and documents. Again, it was necessary to go to the expense and trouble of finding and hiring suitable civilians. The Chief Engineer recommended the enlistment of 200 men to be trained for these jobs, but the recommendation came to nothing.

Medical Services and Supplies

Surgeon General Thomas Lawson urged the addition of twelve to fifteen officers to the medical staff for service at general hospitals, depots, and along the lines of communication. Congress approved this request in the act of 11 February 1847 which authorized the President to appoint, with the advice and consent of the Senate, two additional surgeons and twelve assistant surgeons in the Regular Army. This act also clarified the military status of medical officers, which had been more or less vague ever since the Revolution. Regulations of 1840 had denied the right of any medical staff officer to preside over a board of survey or council of administration, though such officers might be detailed to serve on such boards with junior line officers. In 1843 General Scott decided that surgeons, since they did not have the actual military rank of field officers, were not entitled to the salute prescribed for majors. The act of 11 February 1847 at last provided that medical officers should have rank upon the same basis that their pay and allowances were determined, though such rank still would give them no authority to command in the line or in other staff departments.

Even after the expansion provided for in 1847, the Medical Department did not have enough surgeons and assistants to staff all the hospitals and stations in the United States as well as to serve the forces in Mexico. The only alternative was to continue to contract with civilian physicians for medical service. Arrangements varied a great deal. A number of civilian doctors accepted contracts to provide medical care and medicine at the arsenals, forts, and other installations. During 1846 three civilian physicians, two at $100 a month, and one at $75 a month, engaged to provide medical attendance with Taylor's army in Mexico until they could be relieved by medical officers.

Medical supplies appear to have been ample most of the time. Large quantities shipped from New York and New Orleans under the personal direction of the Surgeon General went out promptly. The Surgeon General directed the establishment of a general hospital at New Orleans and, later, one at Baton Rouge for the treatment of the wounded and sick evacuated from Mexico. Local procurement in New Orleans provided a large share of medical and hospital supplies for these hospitals, for units passing through en route to the war theater, and for the resupply of depots in Mexico.

Summary

The expeditions to Canada during the Revolution had involved operations at great distances from bases of supply, and against almost insurmountable obstacles to transportation, but until the War with Mexico the United States never had attempted anything like the support of such operations as the campaigns south of the Rio Grande, the amphibious landing at Vera Cruz and the march to Mexico City, or the marches to Santa Fe, to Chihauhua, and to California.

When Mexico City fell, the number of troops in the U.S. Army—forces that had to be equipped, transported, and supplied—was approximately 43,000, about half Regulars and half volunteers. (The term of enlistment for most of the twelve months' volunteers had expired, so that only 2,000 remained; all others had enlisted for the duration of the war.) Of this total, 17,000 Regulars and 15,000 volunteers were in General Scott's army in central Mexico; about 2,900 Regulars and 2,700 volunteers were in the army of occupation in northern Mexico; about 3,000 men (all volunteers except 250) were at Santa Fe under Brig. Gen. Sterling Price; 1,000 men (including about 200 Regulars) were in California; and something over 450 volunteers were on the Oregon Trail. All together, some 104,-000 troops were engaged during the course of the Mexican War, including 31,000 Regulars, 12,600 militia, and 60,600 volunteers and rangers of various categories. After the discharge of solders enlisted for the war, the effective strength of the U.S. Army (30 June 1848), was approximately 7,500.

Total War Department expenditures during the Mexican War were at the rate of about $39,000,000 a year. Some $15,842,-000 of the Army expenditures for Fiscal Year 1846–47 came out of appropriations for Mexican hostilities, but certainly a great part of the War Department's regular appropriations went for support of the war effort. Among these the largest single items were expenditures by the Quartermaster's Department of $3,960,000 for "transportation and supplies," and $3,183,250 for "transportation of the Army." Ordnance expenditures in that fiscal year included $558,600 for ordnance stores and supplies, and $366,000 for the national armories. Regular subsistence expenditures amounted to $1,754,000.[6]

---

[6] Account of Receipts and Expenditures of the Government for Year Ending June 30, 1847, House Exec Doc 7, 30th Cong., 1st sess., pp. 123–214; Estimates of Appropriations, House Exec Doc 2, 30th Cong , 1st sess., pp. 4–5, 7–8.

CHAPTER X

Support of Operations in Mexico

Anticipating final acceptance by Texas of annexation to the United States, and on the strength of the assurances which President Polk and Secretary of State James Buchanan had given that Texas would be defended against Mexican invasion, Acting Secretary of War George Bancroft on 14 June 1845 instructed Brig. Gen. Zachary Taylor to move his forces from Fort Jesup, on the Louisiana frontier, to a point on the Gulf of Mexico from which they could leave at the proper time for the western frontier of Texas. Within four days after Taylor received these instructions on 29 June, the 4th Infantry was on its way to New Orleans, and while the dragoons prepared horses and a train of sixty wagons for a long overland march to San Antonio, the 3d Infantry followed the 4th four days later. Taylor left for New Orleans on 9 July.

Taylor in Northern Mexico

On the strength of word from Andrew J. Donelson, American chargé d'affaires in Texas, that final ratification of annexation at a convention on 4 July was certain, and that invasion by Mexico was probable, Taylor prepared to move as quickly as possible to Corpus Christi at the mouth of the Nueces River. Commissary and quartermaster officers already were busy at New Orleans collecting supplies and chartering vessels when Taylor arrived on 15 July. Within another

week he was ready to embark for Texas. Shortly before midnight on 22 July eight companies of the 3d Infantry, joined by Taylor and his staff on the levee, marched up the gangplank to the steamer *Alabama*.

The ship weighed anchor at 0300, entered the Gulf about noon, and headed westward toward the coast of Texas. The 4th Infantry and Lt. Braxton Bragg's company of the 3d Artillery followed in sailing ships, while dragoons marched overland by way of San Antonio. The *Alabama* arrived at the islands off Corpus Christi Bay within two days, and the troops made a temporary camp on St. Joseph's Island. But the landing of troops and supplies by lighter, fishing boat, and raft across the shallow waters was so slow and difficult that it was late August before all of Taylor's immediate command had arrived at its destination. Reinforcements arriving in September brought the total strength of Taylor's army up to 4,000 men—half of the U.S. Army—comprised of a regiment of dragoons, five regiments of infantry, and sixteen companies of artillery.

Corpus Christi, then a hamlet of 100 people, could offer little in the way of supplies or entertainment, but it was not long before crowds of energetic followers began moving into the town to sell merchandise, to offer professional skills, and to entertain, inform, amuse, skin, and corrupt the soldiers. For the Army, the biggest task during the seven

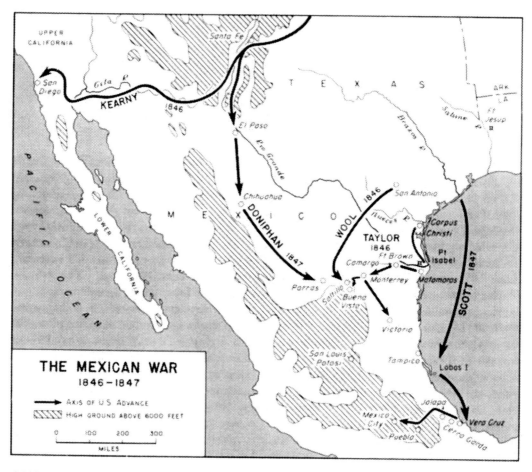

MAP 7

months of occupation at Corpus Christi was immediate supply for the troops and the build-up of stores and transportation facilities for the support of possible military operations.

On 13 January 1846, the day after he received a dispatch from the Minister to Mexico, John Slidell, announcing the Mexican Government's refusal to receive him as envoy, President Polk instructed General Taylor to move from Corpus Christi to the claimed southern boundary of Texas, the

Rio Grande. The President's instructions did not reach Taylor until 3 February. Then the general spent another month doing what he might have done during the preceding months—sending out topographical engineers to reconnoiter the country, and making other preparations. Finally, on 8 March Taylor's army began the movement southward that would bring the war to a head. (*Map 7*)

The destination was Point Isabel and the troops were in for a hike of nearly two hundred miles over sun-baked prairie. Even so early in the spring, the men suffered from sunburn and from thirst made overpowering by the distance between water holes, and aggravated by the choking ash of recently burned scrub rising in clouds from the marching feet.

The supply and escort ships arrived off Point Isabel (now Port Isabel) just a few hours after Taylor arrived, and work began almost at once to prepare the base and land supplies. Since it seemed likely that the Rio Grande itself would serve as the line of communication for future operations, a port and supply base at the mouth of that stream would have been preferable. Unfortunately, the Rio Grande had deposited a great bar of silt at its mouth which effectively blocked all navigation except for craft of the most shallow draft. The Brazos Santiago was so shallow that most equipment had to be landed by lighter; even so, it was more accessible than was the mouth of the river.

After the engagements at Palo Alto (8 May) and Resaca de la Palma (9 May), the way to the Rio Grande was open. Most of the Mexican forces, although in great disorder, escaped across the river, but when Taylor moved up to the river he stopped. He could not cross to Matamoros, he said, because he had no ponton bridge equipment, for which he blamed the Quartermaster's Department for having "ignored" his previous requests. The War Department blamed Congress for failing to appropriate funds that had been requested repeatedly in past years for this purpose. But recriminations would not get the army across the river. Taylor himself evidently had done nothing—such as build boats back at Point Isabel, or seize Mexican craft—to meet his need. At last he ordered lumber

from Point Isabel for building boats, and forays across the river netted some boats from the Mexicans. When on 18 May the Americans invaded Matamoros they discovered that the Mexican forces had withdrawn; whereupon most of Taylor's men simply crossed the river on the regular ferry.

Matamoros quickly took on all the aspects of an American-occupied town. American sutlers, merchants, tavern keepers, billiard parlor operators, gamblers, and others took over the stores on the plaza. Americans crowded in with Mexicans at the market where women sold milk, eggs, peaches, melons, vegetables, game, and even cooked short-order meals, while men bought and sold horses, cows, corn, hay, meat, bread, and sombreros. Anyone with provisions to sell was admitted to the American camp, and many Mexicans brought in bread, cakes, fruit, and sugar loaves. Riotous audiences of soldiers filled the theater. For months Matamoros was an American supply center, and army wagons crowded the streets.

The War Department advised Taylor that it might be wise, on the basis of health reports, to move as many of his troops as possible above Matamoros and to towns farther up the river before starting a fall campaign. The Secretary of War observed: "In taking these positions . . . the means of getting supplies, transporting munitions of war, as well as the ability to keep open the channels by which these supplies and munitions are to be furnished, are points to be well considered." [1]

Determined to attack Monterrey, Taylor decided to move his striking forces to Camargo on the San Juan River—about

---

[1] Ltr, Marcy to Taylor, 8 June 1846, House Exec Doc 119, 29th Cong., 2d sess., p. 49.

130 miles by land, or nearly twice that by water, up the Rio Grande from Matamoros—where he would establish his advance base. He planned to send most of the supplies by water; the army would march overland. Recent floods enabled steamboats recently arrived from New Orleans to carry some of the first infantry units, but there were not enough boats for everyone, and the rest marched to Camargo—it took seven good days—in the summer heat. Men marching along the "mountain road" (actually a desert road) suffered again from heat and thirst. The sun burned their faces and the hot ground burned their feet. The chaparral was too short to provide any shade and too thick to permit any breeze. Units that followed found some relief by resorting to night marches. From mid-July until the end of August, men and supplies continued to arrive at Camargo, and by late August about 25,000 American soldiers were encamped in a tent city extending three miles along the San Juan River. Still covered with mud from the recent flood, Camargo, a town of about 5,000 people, was perhaps the most unhealthy spot in the whole region; one-third to one-half of the men in the volunteer regiments were said to be sick. But on 19 August the first leg of the advance toward Monterrey began.

In the build-up of the army on the Rio Grande, troop reinforcements generally outran receipt of supplies. With the reflex action of a military commander facing an emergency, in April Taylor had appealed for more troops. The response was so great that he soon became "troop poor." The first to answer Taylor's call were militia units, limited to three months' service, from Louisiana and Texas. Arrivals of three-month militiamen soon stopped, but in the meantime the influx of twelve-month volun-

teers had begun and continued unabated. By 1 August General Taylor was crying "uncle." Men were arriving much faster than he could find any use for them, not only creating a supply burden in themselves, but impeding Taylor's "forward movement by engrossing all the resources of the Quartermaster's Department to land them and transport them to healthy conditions." [2]

As thousands of volunteers and shiploads of supplies arrived, depots grew around the port of debarkation at Point Isabel and a series of camps spread from Point Isabel to the Rio Grande, and on up the river. Dry ground and sea breeze made Point Isabel a favorite location, although the shallow harbor made unloading operations difficult. Quartermaster, commissary, and ordnance depots and shops were established. The main troop camp lay across the strait from Point Isabel on the north end of Brazos Island. About ten miles to the southwest was a smaller camp at the mouth of the Rio Grande where river steamer repair facilities were set up. Twenty-five to thirty miles up the river (or a third that distance by land) was another sizable camp at Burrita, and across the river and beyond a swamp lay Camp Belknap. Still further upstream, near Matamoros, were Camp Lomita, Camp Patterson, Camp Palo Alto, and Camp Lane.

It was a costly and time-consuming operation to transport supplies from the Gulf into the Rio Grande and to the advance depot at Camargo. Even ships drawing less than eight feet of water could not get closer than four miles to the mainland and Point Isabel, so that lighters had to bring in most of the supplies. Wagons then had to

---

[2] Ltr, Taylor to President Polk, 1 August 1846, House Exec Doc 119, 29th Cong, 2d sess, p 61

haul them overland and across a ford (later a bridge was erected) of the Boca Chica, then ten more miles overland to the mouth of the Rio Grande; alternately, light schooners could sail around Brazos Island and down to the river mouth, where here again the supplies had to be stored on the river bank, to await reloading onto river steamers. In the fall of 1845 General Jesup had suggested the construction of a railroad to connect the Brazos with the Rio Grande. This would have worked a local revolution in logistics. Unfortunately, neither the Quartermaster's Department nor the Topographical Engineers had an appropriation to cover such a project. As is so often the case, before the declaration of war there were no funds; after the declaration there was no time.

As General Taylor contemplated the situation from Matamoros, steamboats on the Rio Grande were indispensable for his operation, which in itself was revolutionary thinking. As he saw it, an army could not subsist on this country on the march to Monterrey. Vast numbers of pack mules would be needed for land transportation, and the river was the only practicable line of communication. For a time he was worried about the possibility of sailing boats up as far as Camargo on the shallow river, but spring rains raised his hopes, and quickly he became impatient for the light-draft steamers he needed. Not waiting for the Quartermaster General to act, Taylor sent four officers to New Orleans and northward to hire the necessary boats. With characteristic modesty, Taylor held his requirement to two boats, though the officers sent to New Orleans applied to the Quartermaster General for permission to double that number. His agents had to go as far afield as Louisville and Pittsburgh to find the light-draft boats; then storms delayed them while Taylor fumed, certain that someone must have given orders to suspend sending the boats to him. The boats began to arrive in July, and by the 23d twelve (four of which had been purchased and eight chartered) were chugging up and down the river carrying troops and supplies to Camargo. Experienced steamboat men from the United States served as captains, mates, and engineers, but most of the firemen and deck hands were Mexican nationals who were attracted by the pay and the novelty. The American commanders also relied on Mexican labor to unload and load the ships at the Brazos.

For a time after the heavy rains the land route to Camargo was practically impassable, and sole reliance had to be put on the steamboats. Later some troops, artillery, and wagons used the road. Movement from Camargo onward required more land transportation. As he had had to wait at Matamoros for boats, Taylor had to wait at Camargo for pack mules and wagons. In neither case is prior planning evident. For the earlier movements to Point Isabel and Matamoros, Taylor had relied on wagons for land transportation, but no one seems to have known whether wagons could be used southwest of the Rio Grande. Even in areas where they were being used, the system was not altogether satisfactory. Frequent breakdowns on the rough roads, and irresponsibility on the part of many of the hired drivers made wagon transportation unreliable or inadequate. Col. Trueman Cross, Taylor's chief quartermaster, had expressed the idea that all military wagons should be made uniformly with interchangeable parts, so that wrecks could be cannibalized to restore good wagons; furthermore, the colonel held that enlisted drivers should be used instead of hired teamsters who had proved so unsatisfactory.

Taylor's whole purpose in moving up to Camargo was to establish a depot to support his planned advance southwestward across the mountains to Monterrey and Saltillo. The only practicable artillery route appeared to be up the San Juan valley from Camargo. According to his information, he could not expect to find breadstuffs in any considerable quantity along this route short of Monterrey, possibly not before Saltillo. Beef, on the other hand, probably would be plentiful, and there might be some mutton. So, unless a hostile population drove away their cattle, meat rations for the invading force could be procured en route, but it probably would be necessary to depend for bread upon the Camargo depot all the way to Saltillo. From available transportation—particularly the pack mules that could be obtained in the area—Taylor figured that a force no larger than 6,000 men could be kept supplied with bread as far as Saltillo. This, then, would be the limit of the size of the attacking force. As for its make-up, the amount of forage available would be a limiting factor for the cavalry. Taylor doubted whether a large force could be maintained beyond Monterrey, although he did think that if it developed that as many as 10,000 men could be subsisted at Saltillo, it might then prove feasible to advance as far as San Luis Potosi which, he believed, would bring speedy proposals for peace. In any case, he felt sure that after his main column reached Saltillo, Brig. Gen. John E. Wool, marching from San Antonio, would have little trouble occupying Chihuahua, "ex-

cept that of procuring transportation and subsistence." [3]

Chafing at shortages of wagons, mules, horseshoes, medical supplies, and siege guns, General Taylor decided in August that the move toward Monterrey should be started anyway. Pack mules were the obvious solution to the wagon shortage, though Taylor began to obtain them only a short while before he planned to start out. Then quartermaster officers hired some 1,900 mules and big wooden pack saddles. Each mule could carry about 300 pounds. Reliance upon pack trains rather than upon wagons or boats for the main support of a major operation was a novel feature of this campaign. The commanders appointed regimental quartermasters—officers of the regiments rather than of the Quartermaster's Department—to organize and direct the new system. Besides directing the mule trains, regimental quartermasters were charged with buying forage, distributing clothing to the men, buying fresh food to supplement the ration, and keeping the regimental accounts.

On 19 August Brig. Gen. William J. Worth set out with his 2d Division of Regulars to establish a depot at Cerralva, about sixty miles from Camargo. His troops crossed the San Juan River over a bridge of steamboats, and then marched out across the rocky, sun-baked road, through Mier to Cerralvo, where they arrived on 25 August. Worth immediately set about collecting corn, beef, and forage, and sent out Lt. George Meade of the Topographical Engineers to reconnoiter routes toward Monterrey. Remaining units of Taylor's force followed from Camargo over the next two

---

[3] Ltr, Taylor to TAG, 15 August 1846, House Exec Doc 119, 29th Cong, 2d sess, p. 127.

DEFENDING A PACK TRAIN AGAINST A MEXICAN CAVALRY ATTACK

weeks. General Taylor left Camargo on 5 September.

By 12 September Taylor was ready to march again to cover the remaining sixty-five miles to Monterrey. With the 1,900 pack mules and about 180 wagons, the army's transportation required close attention throughout the marches. Each morning the muleteers, Mexican handlers who had been hired for $25 a month, tied tents, tentpoles, kettles, mess pans, axes, picks, coffee mills, ammunition chests, and all the other gear to the pack saddles. The loaded saddles had to be balanced and secured on the backs of the mules to withstand a day of jogging up and down hills and through thickets, and then unloaded in good time to make camp in the evening.

The American column reached the vicinity of Monterrey on 19 September. After five days of sharp battles the Mexican defenders evacuated the city.

Taylor had serious doubts about operations south of Monterrey. San Luis Potosi, a thriving city of some 60,000 inhabitants, beckoned, but a move to that city would mean doubling the length of his supply line from the Rio Grande, while the Mexicans would be shortening theirs. In the circumstances he thought that he would need 20,000 men—half of them Regulars—to accomplish such a mission, and limitations of supplies and transportation seemed to make the support of so large a force over that great distance altogether out of the question. "The task of beating the enemy is among the least difficult which we encounter," he wrote, "the great question of supplies necessarily controls all the operations in a country like this." [4] The people of Mexico presented to Taylor this dilemma: "If you come with few, we will overwhelm you; if you come with many, you will overwhelm yourselves." [5]

The only other major engagement for Taylor's army in northern Mexico was the battle of Buena Vista (22–23 February 1847)—notable as the first major action in history in which both sides were armed predominately with percussion weapons. Taylor's army by this time was made up mostly of volunteers who had been able to obtain percussion arms, and the Mexican Army had succeeded in obtaining foreign shipments of them. After the battle, Taylor was content to remain in the Monterrey-Saltillo area with detachments as far south as Agua Nueva and La Encarnación, while General Antonio López de Santa Anna and his army retreated all the way to San Luis Potosi.

The retreat of the Mexican Army to San Luis Potosi was a sad spectacle of men suffering from the exhaustion of heated battle and long marches as well as from hunger and thirst, for rations were short and water scarce. In defeat this army had great difficulty in procuring food supplies even from its own people. It should be noted that Santa Anna had succeeded in marching an army of some 20,000 men 250 miles—much of the distance across desert—to Buena Vista from San Luis Potosi in little more than three weeks. The same logistical obstacles that persuaded Taylor not to attempt the

march in the opposite direction, from Saltillo to San Luis, applied with hardly less force to Santa Anna, who nevertheless overcame them. Moreover, most of Santa Anna's army, though in disorder and suffering great hardship, survived the long desert trail back to San Luis Potosi.

General Taylor conducted local procurement on a strictly cash basis. Lt. Ulysses S. Grant, one of the regimental quartermasters, carried out Taylor's policy in this respect to such a degree that he even made full payment after he had to overcome forcibly the resistance and treachery of a local farmer. Thinking in the War Department was that Taylor perhaps showed too much leniency; that he was making the war so prosperous for local farmers that they never would want to sue for peace. Taylor was instructed, therefore, to obtain supplies by requiring them as contributions, neither paying for them or promising to pay for them. He was given leeway, however, if he felt he would not be able to get necessary supplies in this way. Taylor continued to insist that payment had to be made—sure that prompt cash payment had done much to overcome the hostility of the population and to facilitate his operations. Forced contributions, he felt, would have led owners to destroy that season's crops, and possibly to refuse to plant again the next year. Some units retained civilian contractors to buy food supplies locally.

One of Lieutenant Grant's most successful enterprises at Monterrey was his regimental bakery. He drew his regiment's bread ration in flour, then he rented ovens, bought fuel, and hired Mexican bakers. He not only provided fresh bread for his own regiment in this way, but sold it to other regiments at a good profit for his regimental

---

[4] Quoted in Roswell S. Ripley, *The War with Mexico*, 2 vols. (New York: Harper & Brothers, 1849), I, 335.

[5] *Ibid.*, II, 13.

fund—a fund used mostly for recreational facilities for the men.

Military operations in northern Mexico were almost uniformly successful for Taylor's army. Shortages of transportation had delayed Taylor for several weeks along the Rio Grande, but, generally speaking, logistical support based on the use of steamboats, with the Brazos serving as port of debarkation and the Rio Grande as line of communications, had been adequate for the occasion. Whenever inevitable deficiencies did appear, Taylor's first reaction seems to have been to hurl blame at the Quartermaster's Department. His criticism led to a near feud between himself and General Jesup, an old friend and comrade in the Florida War. The commander was not alone in his low opinion of the quartermasters—Lt. George B. McClellan wrote of them: "I have also come to the conclusion that the Quartermaster's Department is most woefully conducted—never trust anything to that Department which you can do for yourself." [6]

As he prepared to leave Camargo on the march to Monterrey, Taylor complained to the War Department that not enough transportation or supplies had accompanied the flood of volunteers sent upon him, that he had been delayed for weeks on the Rio Grande because steamboats had not been sent earlier, and that his lack of wagons would have made it impossible for him to move at all had he not been able to procure pack mules locally. He went on to list his supply shortages—camp equipage, horseshoes and horseshoe nails, and "many smaller deficiencies." The Secretary of War, William Marcy, referred the whole matter directly to the Quartermaster General. For his part, General Jesup earlier had protested that he was applying all the means and energies of his department to supporting General Taylor, not only out of a sense of duty, but out of a personal determination to reciprocate for Taylor's help in sustaining him in the Florida War.

Within a week after Marcy had sent him Taylor's bill of complaints, Jesup proposed setting up his office in New Orleans. He intended to direct the activities of his department from that port, and to inspect installations on the Rio Grande. He realized that there might be some embarrassment in the fact that his rank of major general would make him senior to every other officer in Mexico, including Taylor, but he was willing to waive that. He was ready to take orders from General Taylor, Maj. Gen. William O. Butler, Maj. Gen. Robert Patterson, or Brig. Gen. John E. Wool, "or any other officer whom the government or the accidents of services may place in command of the army, or any separate division of it." [7] He even offered to join Taylor's headquarters as a staff officer.

After a tour of inspection General Jesup admitted that the Quartermaster's Department was "far from being efficient," but this he attributed to not enough quartermaster officers. Major responsibility for shortages in transportation and supplies he returned to the door of General Taylor. The commander in the field had asked for only one steamboat early in May; late in May he had thought that four would suffice, and had sent his own agents to obtain them. He had made no requests for land transportation, and had not informed the War

[6] George B McClellan, *Mexican War Diary*, William Starr Myers, ed. (Princeton: Princeton University Press, 1917), p. 19.

[7] Ltr, Jesup to Marcy, 5 December 1846, House Exec Doc 119, 29th Cong., 2d sess., p. 264.

Department whether wagons could be used in Mexico. "In conducting a war, it is the duty of the government to designate the object to be accomplished; it is then the duty of the general who conducts the operations to call for the means required to accomplish that object. If he fail to do so, he is himself responsible for all the consequences of his omission." [8]

Compared with earlier Army experiences, logistical support for Taylor's army was exceptional. As for the deficiencies, something is to be said for several points of view. There had been no prior planning, no logistical estimates in the War Department. Before the war, Congress had not appropriated requested funds that would have permitted a better state of preparation. But as the situation actually worked out, General Taylor's failure to anticipate his requirements, his tardiness in making requisitions, and his failure to provide the War Department with timely information about the country in which he was to operate probably contributed most of all to the shortages of which he complained.

Long Marches

While Taylor's Army was winning control of the lower Rio Grande, and of Monterrey and Saltillo, expeditions moved west and south on some of the most remarkable marches in American military annals to claim the great Southwest for the United States and to threaten Mexico from other quarters. For each march, logistics far overshadowed tactics in gaining the objectives.

Brig. Gen. Stephen W. Kearney's Army of

the West set out from Fort Leavenworth for California in the last week in June 1846. The annual merchant's caravan, that year consisting of 414 wagons loaded with dry goods for markets in Santa Fe and Chihuahua, left from Independence, Missouri, to move with his expedition. When grass thinned out and water became scarce as the heat of summer became more intense, many of the horses weakened and faltered. When a mounted soldier lost his horse he would pay almost any price for another one; otherwise he had to walk or drive a wagon, though the fact is that the infantry moved quite as rapidly as the cavalry. Half rations were the best the men could expect most of the way, and they had to broil their meat and boil their coffee over a smoldering heap of ordure of buffalo, or "prairie fuel." After 800 miles and two months of exhausting travel, half rations, brackish water, buffalo gnats, and frayed nerves, the Army of the West entered Santa Fe.

Leaving Col. Alexander W. Doniphan in charge at Santa Fe, Kearney, with five companies of dragoons—mostly mounted on mules—two brass cannon on small wheels, and company supply wagons, set out for the Pacific coast on 25 September and on 12 December arrived at San Diego. Other forces were on the way to California, notably the Mormon Battalion which arrived six weeks later, and a regiment of New York volunteers (under Col. J. D. Stevenson), which had left New York by ship two weeks before Kearney's departure from Santa Fe and arrived in March, by which time the issue in California was settled. President Polk had indeed achieved one of his main objectives in less than twelve months, and with the expenditure of very little gunpowder.

Two other expeditions of independent

---

[8] Ltr, Jesup to Col H. Whiting, Asst QMG, 4 November 1846, House Exec Doc 119, 29th Cong., 2d sess, pp. 439–440.

commands were directed against Mexico proper as a part of the general scheme to force submission—General Wool's from San Antonio and Colonel Doniphan's from Santa Fe. Whatever the merits of Wool's expedition as a military maneuver, it did demonstrate what energy, determination, and resourcefulness could do in moving an effective force deep into enemy territory. Wool moved his army 900 miles, with full wagon trains, through country supposed to be unsuitable for wagons, and with no failure of rations in a country where food supplies often were scarce. General Jesup had thought it a great mistake to take wagons on such an expedition and had predicted that the trains would be lost and the operation would be a failure. Wool's men had not fired a shot in anger; they reached their destination equipped to fight, and were on hand for the battle of Buena Vista.

Meanwhile Doniphan's 1st Regiment of Missouri Volunteer Cavalry had been marching and fighting south from Santa Fe, expecting to meet Wool at Chihuahua, and completed a march without parallel—3,500 miles from Fort Leavenworth to Santa Fe, El Paso, Chihuahua, Saltillo, Monterrey, and Reynosa. From Reynosa they returned by water to New Orleans and a heroes' welcome, and then took river steamers for St. Louis where greater celebrations awaited them. Soon the expedition of Doniphan's Thousand was being compared with the march of Artaxerxes against Cyrus and the anabasis of the Ten Thousand Greeks under Xenophon.

Scott's Campaign

For some time consideration had been given in Washington to the possibility of operations aimed at the City of Mexico. General Taylor thought it impractical to attempt to keep open a line of communication extending 1,000 miles from the base camp at Camargo to the capital city. Despite the fact that the route south would approach both seacoasts, he felt that the topography of the country was such that no practical supply line could be opened and maintained either from Tampico or from the Pacific coast, and that if a decision was reached to send an expedition against the capital, the best route probably would be by way of Vera Cruz. Taylor's own recommendation simply to cut off the northern provinces and then hold a defensive line attracted a good deal of support, but as time went on it became more and more clear that the only way to bring the war to an end satisfactorily was to take Mexico City. The task was assigned to General Scott. On his shoulders rested the command of the Army's first major overseas expedition and amphibious assault.

As General in Chief, Scott was in a position to make his requirements clear to the supply bureaus and to set in motion the actions to fill them. In addition to the ordinary supplies needed for field operations of an army of 10,000 to 20,000 men, he wanted 140 surf boats to enable him to put ashore at one time about 5,000 men and eight pieces of artillery. He wanted a siege train of 8-inch howitzers and 24-pounders, and forty to fifty mortars—all with large stocks of ammunition. As for small arms, he of course preferred the flintlock muskets, but his men would be carrying all the Colt revolvers they could find. In the expectation that some unfordable streams might cross his path, he asked for a ponton train. Once the supply orders had been submitted, the Secretary of War allowed Scott little

THE VERA CRUZ LANDING. *Currier and Ives print.*

time to attend to such preparations personally—his place now, Secretary Marcy
thought, was in Mexico organizing his army.

Scott left Washington 24 November 1846
for New York, where he sailed for New
Orleans. After a brief stop at New Orleans he went on to the Brazos de Santiago
to direct the concentration of troops and
supplies. Quartermaster General Jesup
joined Scott at the Brazos complaining that
the Quartermaster's Department, besides its
own function, was having to do some of the
work of the Ordnance and other departments. Scott hoped to have his expedition

completed by mid-January, but he found it
necessary to go through an extra six weeks
of delays while he awaited the boats he
wanted, and while extra water casks were
made, filled, and delivered from New Orleans. Ice on the rivers, fog, windstorms,
and heavy rains interfered with shipping.
The first troop transports arrived near the
Brazos on 11 February. Embarkation proceeded both at the Brazos de Santiago and
at Tampico as rapidly as ships arrived. Scott
ordered all transports to carry food and water for men and horses for thirty days, except
that the last ships to embark might carry

only twenty days' water if necessary in order not to delay departure. Embarkation went smoothly. At Tampico, for instance, troops for the *Essex* marched through the town to the wharf, where surf boats took about sixty men at a time with their baggage to a steamboat, which in turn transferred them to the sailing ship. Sailors showed the men their berths and where to stow their baggage and arms. Leaving General Worth in charge of embarkation at the Brazos, Scott himself sailed aboard the steamship *Massachusetts* on 15 February. He touched briefly at Tampico to check on the embarkation of Maj. Gen. David E. Twiggs's and General Patterson's divisions, then proceeded to the rendezvous, the Lobos Islands, about sixty miles south of Tampico and nearly 200 miles from Vera Cruz, where protected anchorage—used by English smugglers for years—made an ideal concentration point. Each vessel left the Brazos and Tampico as soon as it was ready. By the end of February nearly 100 vessels and 10,000 troops had arrived at Lobos.

D-day was set for 8 March, but threatening storms forced postponement for a day. Early on the 9th about half of the 10,000 troops were crowded on the two frigates *Raritan* and *Potomac,* and the others on smaller naval vessels, and shortly after 1300 they arrived off Sacrificios. Immediately steamers towed the surf boats to their assigned positions, and the Regulars of Worth's division began scrambling into them—fifty to eighty men to a boat. Sailors manned the boats and attempted to bring them into line. A strong current threatened to scatter them until the steamer *Princeton,* anchored about 450 yards from the shore, put out hawsers and the boats were made fast in two long lines. On signal from the *Massachusetts,* about 1800, the boats cast off and pulled for the shore while gunboats anchored on the flanks covered the hills with fire. Worth's boat forged ahead, and when it struck bottom he leaped into the water and led his men ashore. With almost no hostile reaction, the boats made their return trips to land Patterson's volunteers, then Twiggs's division. By 2200 all 10,000 men and rations for two days were on the beach without the loss of a man or a boat.

For the next several days the landing of equipment and supplies and some reinforcements continued while Scott prepared to lay siege to Vera Cruz. A series of violent storms interrupted landing operations and swamped some of the boats, but persistence and hard work soon loaded the beaches with subsistence supplies, forage, ordnance wagons, horses, engineer equipment—all the equipment needed or wanted for an army bound for a long march into the interior of a hostile country. One day six siege guns, each weighing more than three tons, were landed, and about 200 seamen and volunteers had to drag them three miles through loose sand, and through a two-foot-deep lagoon. By 18 March sufficient supplies and equipment had been landed to begin operations, although Scott still had only a fraction of what he had requested.

After the capitulation of Vera Cruz on 29 March, Scott devoted his efforts to preparations for the march inland. He was delayed, however, by a lack of transportation. He had asked for at least 800 wagons. The first week in April the chief quartermaster at Vera Cruz reported that 180 wagons with teams were ready for the road, and 300 more wagons, without teams, still were on board ships. Many horses had been lost in the storms, and the number sent in the first place had been fewer than the general wanted.

Again Scott decided to move with what he had. He ordered that baggage be strictly limited—not more than three common tents, principally for arms and for the sick, to a company—and that all excess individual and unit baggage be packed, marked, and turned in to the quartermaster for storage. All wagons, carts, horses, and mules then with lower units or in private hands, including those that soldiers claimed to have captured or purchased from the Mexicans, were to be turned over to the quartermaster's department. Of the wagons for unit transportation, forty-five were assigned to the 2d Division and fifty-five to the volunteer division. One wagon was assigned to the medical director of each division for extra medicines and hospital stores. Ten wagons were turned over to the chief of ordnance for extra small arms ammunition (each infantryman was to carry forty rounds), and 100 wagons were assigned to the chief commissary for subsistence supplies. The chief quartermaster also was to send extra wagons with grain for the cavalry, artillery, and pack horses of each division. All wagons were to carry four days' supply of grain for their own teams. For additional supplies of food and forage the quartermasters and commissaries would have to make local purchases or send wagons back to the depot at Vera Cruz. Each infantryman was to carry four days' rations of hard bread and two days' rations of bacon or cooked pork; fresh beef would be issued on the march. Chiefs of the general staff assigned to each marching division an engineer, a topographical engineer, an ordnance officer, an assistant quartermaster, an assistant commissary, and a medical officer.

Capt. Abner R. Hetzel of the Quartermaster's Department remained in charge of the depot at Vera Cruz. The Tennessee Cavalry had to stay behind until the arrival of its horses, and a brigade of volunteers had to wait until more transportation was available.

For each of the divisions, the most difficult day of the whole march to Mexico City probably was the first. Twiggs's division led the way toward Jalapa on 8 April; Worth's followed three days later. The first ten miles strung out through deep sand, first along the beach, then over a narrow, sunken road. Even in April a burning sun bore down on tired men and animals. The path of the infantrymen could be followed by the coats, extra shoes, knapsacks, and bayonets they threw away to lighten their loads. The engineers found it necessary to partially unload their wagons for that first leg of the journey, and to shuttle their equipment forward by making second trips with the wagons. Teamsters lightened their loads simply by throwing away precious barrels of hard bread and salt pork. Unskilled drivers and unbroken mustangs damaged transportation equipment causing further loss of supplies. When horses and mules gave out, weary soldiers had to use ropes to drag animals and wagons through the sand. Soon the men, too, gave out and fell by the wayside. A few were put on the already heavily loaded wagons, others had to wait under guard beside the road until an empty wagon on its way back to pick up more supplies at Vera Cruz came along. Numbers of men died in the heat and toil of that first day's march. Happily, on the second day the American units reached a good hard-surfaced national road. Now only the Mexican

Army and supply shortages barred the way to Mexico City.

On 18 April the Americans met and overcame strong defenses organized by Santa Anna, who had come through the interior all the way from Buena Vista—first on El Telgrafo hill and then at Cerro Gordo. The next day Twiggs's division entered Jalapa. Here Scott had hoped to find local resources sufficiently plentiful to resupply his commissary, but he was disappointed. The situation was aggravated when Maj. Gen. John A. Quitman's brigade failed to bring up extra rations as expected, and when funds began to run low. Scott, however, already had taken steps to relieve the financial situation. Finding that foreign merchants in Vera Cruz would cash drafts on the United States, endorsed by himself, only at a 6 percent discount, he issued an order stating that United States forces would prohibit the shipment of any precious metals out of Vera Cruz without his consent, or without payment of an export duty equal to the discount rate. He had good reason to expect that this quickly would bring his drafts up to par.

With local procurement failing, General Scott redoubled efforts to move essential supplies to Jalapa from Vera Cruz before the yellow-fever season set in. He ordered each supply chief on his staff who accompanied him—ordnance, quartermaster, commissary, and medical—to send written requisitions to his own supply chief at the Vera Cruz depot. He himself sent instructions to Col. Henry Wilson, commander and governor of Vera Cruz, to see to it that these requisitions were filled promptly. He made a list of what he considered "indispensable" items—medicines and hospital stores, clothing, salt, ammunition, horseshoes, and coffee; and a second list, "almost equally so"—knapsacks,

blankets, hard bread, bacon, and camp kettles.[9] He still hoped to find sugar, flour, rice, fresh meat, beans, and forage in the country.

Worth's division and Quitman's brigade passed through to lead the advance out of Jalapa, through beautiful country to Puebla, a fine city of 80,000 inhabitants, approximately halfway between Jalapa and Mexico City. Worth entered Puebla without opposition on 15 May. Scott himself remained at Jalapa until a heavy wagon train arrived on the 20th. Twiggs's division departed two days later. Leaving garrisons at Jalapa and Perote, it arrived at Puebla on 29 May, one day after the general.

Scott's army stayed at Puebla until August waiting for supplies and reinforcements. Actually the army supplied itself very largely during this time by local procurement. The Mexican Government had forbidden the people to take anything into the city to sell, but the order was willingly and easily defied while the Americans were in occupation. This being so, it might be presumed that the army could have been provided on the march from local supplies as well as in Puebla. The trouble was that many items had to be brought in from some distance to the line of march, and thus would not have been readily available, and a few weeks were required to allow time for harvesting the new crops. More supplies continued to be brought forward from Vera Cruz. Scott wanted a sizable build-up before he went on, so that when the capital was captured it would not be necessary at once to scatter the army to fight for sup-

---

[9] Ltr, Scott to Wilson, Vera Cruz, 23 April 1847, House Exec Doc 60, 30th Cong, 1st sess., pp 946–47

plies. The want of reliable drivers and conductors, the serious shortage of wagons, the stretch of sandy road near the coast, and the threat of Mexican guerrillas all added to the difficulties and hazards of moving supplies over the long line of communication.

Immediately after the reinforcements arrived to replace 3,700 volunteers who had been sent back because their terms of enlistment were about to expire, Scott was ready to begin the march on Mexico City. Where caution had kept him in Puebla for weeks, audacity now led him virtually to cut his supply line with the coast altogether. The Jalapa garrison had joined his force. He did leave a small garrison at Puebla to protect his rear, but for supplies his army was to depend almost entirely upon the wagon trains that accompanied it and the country through which it passed. The divisions of General Twiggs, General Quitman, General Worth, and Brig. Gen. Gideon J. Pillow—totaling over 10,700 men—moved out one day apart. It must have pleased Scott to hear of remarks reported from abroad. The Duke of Wellington is reported to have said: "Scott is lost! He cannot capture the city and he cannot fall back upon his base." The London Morning Chronicle commented: "There is but one thing we know of that is more difficult than for the United States Army to get to Mexico, and that would be to get back again to Vera Cruz." [10]

Scott arrived at San Augustin on 18 August, only ten miles south of Mexico City, and established a depot and a general hospital.

The Mexican Army finally gave battle on 20 August at Contreras and Churubusco. Scott postponed an immediate march into Mexico City to permit preliminary peace negotiations. An armistice agreed to on 24 August lasted until 7 September, giving both sides time to recuperate. Under the terms of the armistice the Americans were allowed to go into the city for supplies. Long trips into the country were avoided because of the threat of Mexican cavalry who apparently did not recognize the armistice.

After two weeks of futile peace negotiations, General Scott decided it was time to move again. Two sharp battles at El Molino del Rey and at Chapultepec—where engineers again distinguished themselves in reconnaissance and preparation of routes, and where scaling ladders, carried all the way from Vera Cruz, finally were put to use—opened the way to Mexico City, and on 14 September 1847 General Quitman, marching with one shoe missing, led the American Army into Mexico City.

Santa Anna made one more effort. He attempted to cut off the American rear by taking Puebla, and kept the U.S. garrison there under siege. Brig. Gen. Joseph Lane, who had arrived at Vera Cruz with replacements after a difficult march with over 3,000 men, was halted at National Bridge by a fight which required him to send back for ammunition and supplies. He reached Puebla in October and relieved the garrison.

During nine months of occupation in Mexico City, supplies and services still had to be provided for Scott's army. In his disposition of troops Scott gave first attention to re-establishing and securing his line of communication to Vera Cruz. Subsistence could be obtained locally with little diffi-

---

[10] Quoted in Charles W. Elliott, *Winfield Scott, the Soldier and the Man* (New York: Macmillan, 1937), pp. 501–02.

culty. As at Monterrey, Lieutenant Grant, enterprising quartermaster and commissary of the 4th Infantry, again organized a bakery that provided bread for his own regiment and enough more to sell to the chief commissary for the rest of the army. Grant said he earned more for the regimental fund with his bakery in two months than he received in Army pay during the whole war.

The only serious shortage was clothing. At the end of October Scott dispatched a column of troops with a long train of empty wagons to Vera Cruz to bring up munitions and clothing. In the meantime, supply officers in Mexico City turned again to local resources. Capt. James R. Irwin, chief quartermaster, put 1,000 seamstresses to work making uniforms from local materials. Other items obtained in the city included horseshoes, spurs, and flagstaff spearheads forged by local blacksmiths from some 20,000 captured British-made muskets.

Medical problems were as great as ever. Approximately 1,250 Americans had been wounded in the battles before Mexico City, and many Mexican wounded had to be given some assistance. Disease mounted again until in December one-fourth of the command was sick. Hospitals were established in the best buildings available, but they were cold, damp, and poorly lighted and ventilated. As soon as practicable evacuation of casualties to the United States began—a long, tedious trip by wagon to Vera Cruz, then by ship to New Orleans. The general hospitals at New Orleans soon became overcrowded and another large hospital, Lawson Hospital, was constructed.

From Mexico City General Scott again sent to the Secretary of War bitter complaints of poor support for his campaign— and he carried his notion of conspiracies against him into his memoirs. He charged

that he had not been given half the troops promised him, and that the War Department had failed to provide adequate transportation or adequate supplies. But the real question is: what was adequate? If General Taylor erred on the side of anticipating too few requirements, General Scott may have erred on the side of demanding too much.

Summary

Who is a great logistician? Is it the commander who devotes most of his attention to supply and transport arrangements? Is it the supply chief who is able to deliver the immense tonnages? Either, perhaps may amount to greatness. But the evidence seems to point to the really great logistician as being the commander who has the judgment—indeed the genius—to take into account realistically all available resources, at home, in the theater, or wherever they are found, and to balance his requirements and his mission so that his objective may be gained in the least possible time with the least possible loss of men and supplies.

Neither Zachary Taylor nor Winfield Scott achieved that stature, but the General in Chief's prior planning—at least for his own campaign—his attention to detail, and his supervision of every phase paid off. On the other hand, he probably was delayed by his constant desire for more of everything than really was necessary—the vice of overestimating requirements. When carried too far, attempting to provide for every contingency can have consequences as unfortunate as those resulting from too little preparation. An army waiting for supplies it does not really need, or paralyzed by having to move more matériel than it does need, may be just as ineffective as an army that has completely outrun its supplies.

The final measure of achievement for logistics accomplishments must be the success with which men and matériel are delivered to the fighting front. American logistics during the Mexican War had many deficiencies, but relative to previous efforts and, more to the point, relative to the enemy's capability, logistics achievements of the campaigns in Mexico were outstanding. Most notable are the number of firsts: a line of communication maintained by steamboat, the first overseas expedition, "the first Army-Navy joint operation in an amphibious landing," a series of the longest marches undertaken in American military history up to that time. And all of these were attained with never a shortage of men or matériel that was serious enough to cost a major battle.

General Taylor and General Scott chafed at lack of transportation and at the delays in the arrival of supplies. But these irritations appeared quite differently to the Mexican commanders to whom it seemed that "the United States, rich and abundantly supplied with facilities for transportation, would now naturally take advantage of these circumstances. Unlike the Mexican Republic, which was embarrassed with obstacles, they could move their army with ease, from one end of their territory to the other." [11]

In many ways the United States enjoyed a position in relation to Mexico similar to that which Great Britain had held with the United States during the Revolutionary War. The United States, in addition to commanding greater industrial resources,

had complete control of the sea. The telling difference was that attempts by the Mexican Government to obtain direct and substantial foreign assistance were not successful. [12]

Postwar Developments

Demobilization

The greatest task of demobilization at the end of hostilities in Mexico was the return to the United States of the forces that had been dispersed over such great distances. More than one thousand officers, 26,000 enlisted men, and 5,000 civilian mechanics, laborers, and teamsters in central Mexico had to be evacuated from Vera Cruz; the men at Tampico and the Brazos brought the total to about 41,000. A fleet of government-owned ships was expanded three or four times by chartering additional ships—some on the Atlantic coast, but for the most part at New Orleans and ports in Mexico—to bring the men, animals, and wagons home. Returning vessels usually put in at New Orleans, because they could not be provisioned at the depots in Mexico for a longer voyage. Property, other than serviceable wagons, sound animals, and items in good condition that could be used at Santa Fe or other posts in New Mexico, was sold at auction in Mexico or at New Orleans.

Transportation to the New Frontier

Distance was a staggering problem for the Army after the Mexican War—as in-

---

[11] Ramon Alcaraz, *The Other Side; or Notes for the History of the War between Mexico and the United States*, translated and edited by Albert C. Ramsey (New York: John Wiley, 1850), p. 179.

[12] See George L. Rives, *The United States and Mexico, 1821–1848*, 2 vols. (New York: Charles Scribner's Sons, 1913), II, 81–104.

deed it had been during the war. Most of the small Army still on duty after demobilization was spread over the vast frontier regions between the Mississippi River and the Pacific Ocean. In 1850 only slightly more than 2,000 officers and men were stationed at 33 posts east of the Mississippi, while about 6,400 were stationed at 67 posts in the West. This trend continued through the next decade, so that by 1860 there were fewer than 1,000 officers and men stationed in the Department of the East, while over 13,000 were stationed in the Department of the West—Texas, New Mexico, Utah, Oregon, and California. Authorized Army strength in 1850 was about 50 percent more than that of 1844, but the cost of transportation in the six-year period had increased by 1,500 percent.

Most troops and supplies destined for Pacific coast stations went by ship from New York. The route most generally favored because less costly was the five-months' voyage around Cape Horn in chartered sailing vessels. The other route—to Panama and across the Isthmus by mule and canoe—took only one month but was more expensive and difficult than the voyage around the Horn. First class steamer passage was booked for troops going by way of Panama because of the likelihood of exposure to cholera during the delays common for sailing vessels in the Panama area. Until the completion of the railroad in 1855, the transfer of men and matériel across the Isthmus added to the cost and multiplied the difficulties of that route.

Convinced that it was more economical to charter vessels as needed than to maintain a fleet of ships, Quartermaster General Jesup quickly disposed of most of the vessels his department had acquired for support of operations in Mexico and for returning the troops afterward. He in fact anticipated the consolidation of sea transportation services under the Navy by a century in a proposal that the Navy assume responsibility for all ocean transportation for the Army as well as the Navy. Failing that, he nevertheless disposed of most of his ships by transfer to the Navy, to the Topographical Department, and to the Treasury, or sold them after inviting written bids. In 1849 the Quartermaster's Department had under its control four sailing ships on the Pacific coast, five steamers on the Florida coast, three schooners on the Gulf of Mexico, and three steamers operating on the Rio Grande.

Land transportation presented greater difficulties. Previously, most frontier posts had been fairly close to navigable water, but now long hauls overland were necessary to supply outposts on the western plains and in the mountain regions. The main frontier depot for supplying garrisons on the Santa Fe Trail and on the Oregon routes was at Fort Leavenworth, itself supplied by river boat from St. Louis. From Leavenworth wagons hauled supplies 310 miles to Fort Kearny, 637 miles to Fort Laramie, 728 miles to Fort Union, and 821 miles to Santa Fe. Supplies for posts in Texas were sent by ship 540 miles across the Gulf of Mexico from New Orleans to Indianola, then by wagon 420 miles to Fort Worth and 803 miles to El Paso.

As with ships, so with wagons: General Jesup decided it would be more economical to hire private transportation than to maintain government equipment. By May 1848 the system of contract freighting had been introduced to transport some supplies destined for Santa Fe, and two years later the system was in full operation at Fort Leavenworth. Private freight companies carried five times as much to posts on the Santa Fe

ARMY TOPOGRAPHICAL ENGINEERS EXPLORING THE COLORADO RIVER

and Oregon Trails as did the government. In 1850 contractors used 6,600 oxen and 780 men to carry 1,500 tons of supplies to those areas. Their wagons usually had a capacity of 2½ tons, and were drawn by ten to twelve animals. Later, huge wagons of five-ton capacity—the Murphy and the Espenshield made in St. Louis, and the Studebaker of South Bend, Indiana—became common.

The leading freight company was Russell, Majors and Waddell. On the basis of an offer to carry all necessary supplies in the area during all months of the year at a specified rate of so much per hundred pounds per hundred miles (varying accord-

ing to the country and the season), the firm was the sole carrier on the Santa Fe and Oregon Trails each year from 1855 through 1860, with the exception of 1859. In spite of an unfortunate involvement of the company and Secretary of War John B. Floyd in charges of favoritism and fraudulent transactions, the system worked reasonably well. It perhaps was more economical in the long run for the government not to have to maintain large numbers of its own wagons. Also, as long as Congress failed to accept the Quartermaster General's repeated recommendations for authorizing the recruitment of teamsters and other service troops so that it would not be necessary to hire civilian workers under unfavorable conditions, contract freighting seemed the only really practicable solution to the transportation problem.

A special experiment in overland transportation was undertaken in 1855 when an attempt was made to introduce camels as pack carriers in the southwest. Long interested in such a project, Secretary of War Jefferson Davis made arrangements as soon as Congress had appropriated $30,-000 to import 75 camels from North Africa to Texas. Put into service on a trial basis, they quickly demonstrated what everybody acquainted with the subject already knew—that they could carry heavy loads far greater distances per day than horses or mules, and required very little food and water while en route. But because the strange-looking creatures stampeded wagon and pack trains on the roads and unsympathetic soldiers and civilians turned against them, the experiment was a failure.

Weapons Development

Interest in developing an acceptable breech-loading rifle or musket quickened after the Mexican War. The Sharps rifle, patented in 1848, was an improvement over the Hall, but it still used paper cartridges, and a really satisfactory service breechloader was yet to be found. By way of encouragement Congress in 1854 appropriated $90,000 for testing and purchasing breechloaders, thereby causing a rash of new patents and proposals. A series of boards convened to examine and test new methods in the next four years, but found none which in the opinion of the officers consulted could replace the muzzle-loader for foot troops. They did agree that of the

weapons offered the Burnside carbine was most nearly satisfactory, presumably for mounted troops. Curiously, one of the board's chief objections to the Burnside was that it required a special metallic cartridge case. True, this would complicate problems of ammunition supply unless use became general, but the board was concerned mainly about expense—it pointed out that the cost of the metallic cartridge case alone was more than the cost of an entire round for the new U.S. rifle-musket. Actually, the metallic cartridge case was to prove to be the real secret of success for breech-loading rifles.

The first repeating rifle adopted, albeit for limited use, for the U.S. Army was the Colt revolving rifle Model 1855 (introduced in 1858). After the spectacular success of Colt revolvers (pistols) in the Mexican War, nothing seemed more reasonable than to expect that a repeating rifle operating on the same principle would have an enthusiastic reception. Indeed, its reception was enthusiastic, but the enthusiasm cooled when hands were injured by the accidental ignition of the cartridges in the cylinder (a situation avoided with the pistol since it was not necessary to hold it with one hand in front of the cylinder). If loaded carefully, so that the paper cartridges were not ruptured, Colt revolving rifles performed well enough, but such care was not practical for a military service weapon. The unfortunate experience with the Colt put a damper on the development of any repeating rifle: if the Colt, after the great success of the pistol, could not be made acceptable as a rifle, it was argued that all repeaters must be impractical.

The real missing link in the development of satisfactory repeating rifles was the metallic cartridge. With metallic cartridges it is quite likely that the Colt revolving rifle, or any of several other models, could have been made completely acceptable as military weapons. In 1857 Smith and Wesson began to manufacture the first really successful rim-fire cartridge for use in their .22-caliber revolver. The next year B. Tyler Henry introduced a .44-caliber rifle cartridge made on the same principle, and in 1860 he patented a fifteen-shot repeating rifle to use the new type of ammunition—a patent which he assigned to his employer, O. F. Winchester. Most important of all was George W. Morse's invention in 1858 of a metallic cartridge with center-fire primer and inside anvil. The Morse cartridge would open the way eventually for really successful repeating rifles.

Artillery was completely systematized. Building upon work begun by the Board of Ordnance in 1832—and in a way extending back to 1818—Major Mordecai was able to complete his draft of the artillery system of the United States for approval by the board and publication in 1849. The publication contained complete drawings and descriptions of the various guns, howitzers, and mortars, together with their carriages— some twenty-four weapons of various calibers falling into the general categories of field (including mountain), siege and garrison, and seacoast artillery. Calibers ranged from six-pounders to forty-two pounders and thirteen-inch mortars, and weights extended from the 164 pounds of the Coehorn mortar to the 15,260 pounds (unmounted) of the giant 10-inch Columbiad. Field artillery pieces and the lighter mortars still

were made of bronze. Carriages generally were of white oak reinforced with wrought iron until adoption of much-improved wrought-iron carriages in 1859. Probably the most significant change in artillery during the period prior to the Civil War was the adoption of the "Napoleon" gun in 1857. Introduced by Napoleon III in an effort to simplify his field artillery system with a single general purpose weapon that could perform the functions of howitzers as well as guns, and which, as a twelve-pounder, would be efficient enough and maneuverable enough to reduce the need for other calibers, this smoothbore bronze piece quickly demonstrated its effectiveness in the Crimean War. One of its chief advantages was simplification of the logistical problem of ammunition supply.

Artillery ammunition included solid shot, cannister, grape, explosive shell, spherical case, and carcass (an incendiary mortar shell). With improvement in spherical case ammunition and its importance for use against improved small arms, the number of these rounds carried in the ammunition chests of Napoleon guns and six-pounders was increased in 1858.

The decade of the fifties was a time of vast development in inland transportation—on the rivers and on the rapidly extending railways. Interest in weapons improvement begun in the 1830's and 1840's was intensified. The irony was that this added military potential would be mobilized not to repel a foreign invader, but to magnify the tragedy of internal strife.

CHAPTER XI

The Civil War: Organization for Logistics

Rarely in modern war has the side with logistical inferiority prevailed. However superior the generalship, or however brilliant the strategy and tactics, ultimate victory generally has gone to the side having the greater economic strength and thus the greater logistical potential. In the tremendous economic expansion of the United States between 1848 and 1860, the North greatly surpassed the South. Of more than thirty thousand miles of railways constructed by 1860, less than nine thousand miles lay within the states which seceded to form the Confederacy. Northern vessels dominated the inland waterways, and Yankee shipping on the high seas nearly equaled that of the British Empire. In manufacturing, mechanical improvements, finance, and even in food production, the North exceeded the Southern states. The North enjoyed a superiority in population of about 22,000,-000 in the states remaining with the Union against about 9,000,000, including 3,500,-000 slaves, in the seceding states.

The South had the one advantage of fighting a defensive war, and the supposed advantage of interior lines. The Confederate objective was independence. It could be accomplished by a successful defense against Northern invasion. If the best advantage is to be taken of fighting over interior lines, certainly a well-developed transportation net is essential; this the South had in only very limited degree. With con-

trol of the peripheral seas, a superior railway net, well-developed inland waterways, and vessels, the North could transfer troops and supplies more readily than could the Confederates. Southern leaders had to gamble that the North would lack the spirit to match its resources, and that the Confederacy would find friends and resources in Europe to help overcome Northern control of the seas and Northern economic superiority. Confederates liked to compare their situation with that of the states and Great Britain during the Revolutionary War, but in doing so they overlooked the decisive contribution France and Spain and Holland made, equalizing for the states the material superiority of the British. General Sherman had truth on his side when he wrote to a Southern friend: "In all history no nation of mere agriculturists ever made successful war against a nation of mechanics. . . . You are bound to fail." [1]

Major rivers, both as routes of communication and as defensive barriers, determined the direction of the principal attacks and campaigns of the war. Recognizing at least to some degree the logistical limitations and capabilities involved, Winfield Scott, still General in Chief of the U.S. Army at the outbreak of the Civil War, recom-

---

[1] Quoted in Bruce Catton, *Glory Road: The Bloody Route from Fredericksburg to Gettysburg* (New York: Doubleday, 1954), p. 261.

mended a tight naval blockade while a powerful offensive was sent down the Mississippi to New Orleans, but such a policy of constriction was too slow for those bent upon punishing the South and ending the war quickly. After Bull Run a more deliberate Northern strategy did unfold. The greatest campaigns continued to be directed against the Army of Northern Virginia. Careful watch had to be maintained against possible attacks on Washington. At the same time Union armies in the West fought to capture and hold Missouri, Kentucky, and Tennessee, and the main rivers leading into those states from the Ohio, while combined land and naval operations sought to open the Mississippi and detach the Southwest from the rest of the Confederacy. In the end, Grant's hammering campaign toward Richmond, combined with Sherman's march to the sea and the naval blockade, applied with a vengeance the "anaconda policy"—crushing the Confederacy with overwhelming manpower and resources. With such notable exceptions as Grant's Vicksburg campaign and Sherman's march through Georgia and the Carolinas, an army in a major operation required a well-developed base, with depots from which munitions, subsistence, field equipment, and medical supplies could be drawn, and connected by telegraph, roads, and railroads or waterways with the field army and with commercial centers of the country.

Seldom has a nation gone into a war as well prepared as it might have been. Ill prepared as the United States was for war in 1861, it certainly was far superior in present and potential strength to the Confederate States, which faced the problem of having to create a government as well as an army.

Mobilization

Federal Actions

Two days after the fall of Fort Sumter on 14 April 1861, President Lincoln began to mobilize the country for war—he issued his proclamation calling for 75,000 militia and called a special session of Congress to meet on July 4th.

How did Lincoln arrive at the figure 75,-000 for the number of troops to be called initially? Undoubtedly he plucked it out of the thin air, though he did it after consultation with his advisers, and two factors probably influenced his calculations. In the first place General Scott was thinking in terms of 85,000 men (25,000 Regular Army and 60,000 three-year volunteers) as being enough even for his proposed plan of constriction. With the present Army strength of approximately 16,000 men, Lincoln's call for 75,000 militia would bring his total force close to 92,000, greater by 7,000 men than Scott's estimate. Moreover, it seemed unlikely that a larger force could be organized and equipped satisfactorily within the three months to which militia services were limited. Lincoln's call for militia to serve for a period of three months suggested that he was anticipating a short war, but this limitation was not so much the result of his failure to appreciate the magnitude of the conflict into which he was heading as it was the reflection of restrictions imposed by the militia law of 1795 by which, for the moment, he considered himself bound.

As the situation worsened, the President's interpretation of legal restrictions became less restrained. Within a few days he directed the naval commandants at Boston, New York, and Philadelphia to purchase or charter ships for defense purposes; he empowered the governor of New York and certain New York citizens, from whom no security was required, to act for the Secretary of War and the Secretary of the Navy in making all necessary arrangements, for the time being, for the transportation of troops and munitions; he directed the Secretary of the Treasury to advance, without requiring security, and without a Congressional appropriation, $2,000,000 to a group of New York men to be used for the purchase of military supplies. Without consulting Congress, Lincoln in May decreed the expansion of the Regular Army by over 22,000 officers and men and the enlistment of 42,000 volunteers to serve for three years.

In mobilizing for war, popular thinking concentrated first on the raising of troops. Then, as frequently has been the case, troop mobilization so far outdistanced matériel mobilization as to impair the effectiveness of the whole undertaking. Little was to be gained by taking men away from farms, shops, and offices before supplies and equipment could be made available for them. General Taylor had been hard put to equip the numbers of volunteers sent to him during the Mexican War, and General McClellan, commanding in the West at the outbreak of the Civil War, soon found himself in the position of a commander "with nothing but men—no arms or supplies." The enthusiastic and insistent offers of troops following President Lincoln's requests for militia and volunteers seriously embarrassed the government; for the moment a major problem of the War Department was to hold the Army to a size that could be supplied and equipped. In his message to Congress on July 4th President Lincoln noted that "one of the greatest perplexities

of the government is to avoid receiving troops faster than it can provide for them." [2]

Militiamen and volunteers reported to appointed places of rendezvous in the states and moved by boat, railway train, and wagon to Washington—to take up quarters in public buildings or improvised barracks or in hastily constructed training camps—where they would be available for the defense of the capital or for a campaign against Richmond. Small camps, with facilities for one to four regiments, sprang up throughout the Northern states to serve as reception centers. From these, troops generally were sent through one of the larger camps: Benton Barracks at St. Louis, which housed about 40,000; the camps at Cairo, Illinois, with facilities for some 50,000 troops; Camp Dennison in Ohio, where over 12,000 troops were housed; or Camp Curtin, Pennsylvania, where over 20,000 men were concentrated at a time. As was customary, the first troops to arrive had to do most of the construction work on the barracks and other facilities; a Regular Army quartermaster brought in government lumber and laid out the camp, and the recruits then went to work. Many different types of barracks arose. Some had the appearance of elongated hog houses. More elaborate designs had upright walls beneath the gable roof. Ordinarily they were built to accommodate one company, sometimes two. A regimental camp, or a regimental area in a larger camp, would include officers' barracks fronting on the parade ground, a row of ten or twelve troop barracks spaced about

[2] A. Howard Meneely, *The War Department, 1861, A Study in Mobilization and Administration* (New York: Columbia University Press, 1928), pp 148–49.

A Winter Camp of the Civil War With Log Huts and Corduroy Walkway

twenty feet apart, with a cook shack behind each building and, if a cavalry unit, stables still further to the rear.

For the first eighty days of the war, until after Congress convened on July 4th, mobilization proceeded without any special federal legislation. Then the Congress quickly gave *ex post facto* approval to Lincoln's emergency war measures, and began consideration of a long list of bills intended to encourage the war effort and bring the conflict to a speedy conclusion. But the failure of federal forces at Bull Run on 21 July provided the real impetus for the most far-reaching legislation of the special session.

That unfortunate affair has been presented as the result of premature action to appease the cries of the multitude in the North for an immediate advance "Forward to Richmond." But Lincoln's order to advance was more the dictate of his own military judgment than a response to the popular clamor for action. Was it unreasonable to suppose that a government with an organized Military Establishment, however imperfect, at its command could mobilize more swiftly than could its adversary who had to organize both a government and an army? If, in the advantages of time, the years would lie with the North and its economic superiority, surely the weeks and months now passing would be on the side of the Confederacy, for it more than the Union required time to mobilize its available forces. Would the casualties be less or the victories easier when a finely trained, well-equipped Army of the Potomac later met a well-organized and trained Army of Northern Virginia? As Lincoln observed to Maj. Gen. Irvin McDowell, commander of the Union forces ordered to attack, "You are green, it is true; but they are green also; you are all green alike." [3] Unquestionably Bull Run had a sobering effect in the North, and served at once to stimulate war preparations; in the South it tended to justify overconfidence and to slow full mobilization.

Activities of the States

In the vigor and enthusiasm with which they pushed mobilization, the Northern states were far ahead of the federal government. State governors, with few exceptions, energetically took up the tasks of raising men and money, organizing units, and equipping and dispatching troops for war service. State legislatures co-operated zealously in authorizing funds and troops. The Wisconsin legislature, for instance, anticipated Lincoln's call for militia by passing an act appropriating $100,000 for raising troops a day before the news of the fall of Fort Sumter arrived; the New York legislature passed a similar act two days later, the day of Lincoln's proclamation, and other state legislatures then in session followed suit within the next few days or weeks. The greatest objection of the Northern governors to the President's call for troops was the small numbers asked. As Lincoln had done, some of the governors acted first and sought legislative approval afterward. On their

own responsibility they assembled troops, let contracts for feeding, clothing, equipping, and arming them, chartered steamers, and dispatched agents to Europe to procure arms.

Far from being a centralized program of the federal government, mobilization in 1861 was a collection of state programs with only a degree of federal co-ordination. Ironically, respect for states' rights, except the right to secede, was as strong in the North as in the South, and in military administration the central government of the Confederacy was able to assert supreme authority more swiftly than the Union. Carried beyond certain limits, this federal deference to state authority was bound to weaken the Northern war potential, but its indulgence was less the result of shortsightedness on the part of the statesmen concerned than of the political climate of the times. Few men at first recognized what a concerted effort would be required to overcome the "insurrection;" moreover, large standing armies and a highly centralized government still were regarded in all the states as threats to liberty.

In later coalition wars, it might be argued that it would be far more efficient for all the allies to integrate their efforts completely, with common recruiting of troops, common procurement of arms and supplies, and common administration as well as tactical direction of military forces, but national loyalties would make such procedures impracticable. To a certain extent, state loyalties and suspicion of centralized government made integration of the mobilization efforts for the Civil War impracticable until the seriousness of the situation made the necessity clear. At the same time, there were advantages in reliance upon the states for military mobilization in the circum-

---

[3] Thomas Harry Williams, *Lincoln and His Generals* (New York: Alfred A. Knopf, Inc., 1952), p. 21.

stances of 1861: at a time when the federal government was being seriously weakened by the defections of Southern sympathizers, and when the War Department was suffering from neglect and inefficiency, the states (aside from the border states) were for the most part united behind the war effort. They had the benefit of relatively efficient administrations, they commanded financial resources, and they could take the initiative in raising, organizing, and equipping military forces. The War Department had to leave it to the states to provide initial equipment, quarters, and transportation for the troops, although it was understood from the outset that they would be reimbursed for the expenses thus incurred. The cost of maintaining a soldier, including transportation from the place of rendezvous to the place of muster, became a charge upon the United States as soon as he was mustered into federal service. Since the federal government had neither the necessary supplies on hand nor the means of obtaining all that was needed quickly, Secretary of War Cameron asked the state governors to equip the troops and bill the United States.

Central Administration

Civilian

Division of authority and responsibility among the Secretary of War, the assistant secretaries, and the General in Chief never was clearly spelled out. During the early months of mobilization correspondence with state governors and other state officials who were contracting for arms and the direction of the activities of the various bureaus commanded most of the Secretary's attention. The first assistant secretary, Thomas A. Scott, was responsible mainly for matters pertaining to railroads and telegraph; he also had broad duties concerned with raising volunteer units, seeing that they received necessary supplies and equipment, and arranging for their movement. Charles A. Dana and Peter Watson were concerned primarily, though not exclusively, with procurement, including supervision of contracts, prosecution of fraud, and contact with field commanders on local procurement.

In the early part of the war, still further confusion in the administration of the war effort resulted from the intrusion of Cabinet officers outside their fields without the coordination of those directly responsible. In particular, Secretary of State William H. Seward frequently meddled in the affairs of the War Department. He appears to have considered himself Secretary of War as well as Secretary of State; at times he received military reports and gave military instructions without the knowledge either of the Secretary of War or of the General in Chief. When Edwin M. Stanton came into the Cabinet as Secretary of War, although he was a friend of Seward's, he soon changed that procedure.

Strangely, a good deal of the responsibility for directing the expansion of the Army fell to the Secretary of the Treasury, Salmon P. Chase. It was Chase, not Simon Cameron (Secretary of War from March 1861 to January 1862), who prepared the orders for organizing the Regular and volunteer troops called for in the President's May proclamation. For several months Chase functioned as a virtual special administrator for supplies and operations in the West, and kept up correspondence with many of the leading military commanders. Already occupied with political and administrative activities, Cameron offered little objection to

CIVIL WAR RECRUITING.   *A Frank Leslie illustration.*

this encroachment on the responsibilities of his department.

Paralyzed by the leadership of bureau chiefs rich in experience but poor in imagination, weakened by the departure of Southern sympathizers, demoralized by suspicions of disloyalty and by the discharge and appointment of employees for political purposes, the War Department did not overcome its inefficiency as long as Simon Cameron remained at its head. In January 1862 Lincoln seized an opportunity to send Cameron to Russia as American minister, and for his successor turned to the opposition party, selecting a Breckenridge Democrat, Edwin M. Stanton, who had served as Attorney General in the Buchanan Cabinet. From the day Stanton took over, changes in the War Department became evident. He immediately announced that the War Office would be closed on Tuesdays, Wednesdays, Thursdays, and Fridays to all business except that relating to active military operations in the field: Saturdays would be devoted to the business of members of Congress, and Mondays would be given to the business of the public. Benefiting from the experience gained by the greatly expanded War Department during the previous nine months, Stanton applied his energy, discipline, and administrative ability to remedy the loose handling of government contracts, to raise and transport troops, and to provide the munitions and supplies necessary for military success. He insisted on strict adherence to regulations, but he was able to cut through red tape. Above all, he insisted on getting things done.

Military

At the head of the Army itself, General Scott was in his twentieth year as General in Chief when the war began. Maj. Gen. George B. McClellan, a young man of thirty-five years, succeeded the veteran Scott on 1 November 1861. After Lincoln relieved McClellan as General in Chief on 11 March 1862, that office remained vacant until the arrival of Maj. Gen. Henry W. Halleck some four months later. In the interim the President and the Secretary of War acted as their own general in chief. For co-ordination of policies and for military advice, they set up the Army Board, which was made up of the chiefs of the War Department bureaus. Maj. Gen. Ethan A. Hitchcock, called to the War Department as special adviser, served as chairman of the board, and as such he filled some of the co-ordinating and advisory functions of a chief of staff. Halleck was General in Chief until Lt. Gen. Ulysses S. Grant received the command of all the Union armies in March 1864. Halleck then stayed on in Washington as Chief of Staff of the Army while Grant moved with the Army of the Potomac in the field.

At the onset of the War with Mexico, General in Chief Winfield Scott had acted promptly and decisively in issuing instruc-tions to the administrative bureau chiefs for the mobilization of men and supplies. At the outbreak of the Civil War Scott did little to stimulate activity in the bureaus. As a matter of fact, upon the inauguration of Franklin Pierce as President in 1853 he had moved his headquarters to New York, where he stayed until called back by President Buchanan in December 1860. He had thus virtually abdicated any control he might have had over the bureau chiefs. Most of his correspondence was with the field commanders and with state governors. When McClellan succeeded Scott, he assumed a position more akin to that which Scott had occupied during the Mexican War. He retained command of the principal army in the field, but established Headquarters of the Army in Washington and even asserted some direction over the bureaus. During his term as commander of the Army, War Department General Orders issued "by order of the Secretary of War" gave way almost entirely to a series of "General Orders, Headquarters of the Army," issued "by command of Major General McClellan" covering practically all subjects. After his relief from the supreme command, War Department General Orders resumed without any change in the number sequence.

Actually, the position of general in chief had no statutory basis. The President simply designated a senior officer to be "General in Chief," or "Commander of the Army," or "General of the Army." His duties depended upon instructions from the President, upon tradition, upon the Secretary of War, and upon his own personality. He was assumed to have command over all of the military geographical departments, but whether command of the Army included command over the administrative bureaus was not at all clear, For their part, the bureau chiefs liked to think of themselves as belonging to the Military Establishment, but not to the Army proper, and they considered themselves answerable only to the Secretary of War. The fact was that the laws and regulations nearly always stated that the duties of the respective chiefs were to be performed "under the direction of the Secretary of War." Presumably, the commanding general of the Army was responsible for drawing strategic plans, and these, of course, had important logistical implications. Scott did attempt to offer some tentative proposals, and to suggest what requirements—mainly of manpower—might be involved. But there was little in the way of co-ordinated planning, and little correlation between strategy and logistics—at least until Grant succeeded to the supreme command. Halleck as General in Chief never did really exercise command over all the armies.

During the last year of the war a distinctly modern arrangement in the high command appeared—if only for the moment. Unified command at the top was achieved when, by General Orders 98 of 12 March 1864, General Grant was assigned ". . . to the command of the Armies of the United States." The same orders specified that the Headquarters of the Army were to be in Washington and also with General Grant in the field. General Halleck, by these orders, was assigned ". . . to duty in Washington as Chief of Staff of the Army, under the direction of the Secretary of War and the Lieutenant General commanding."

It was reported that General Grant accepted the supreme command with the understanding that he would have command over the bureaus of the War Department, but he issued instructions to them rarely and then through General Halleck. In the field Grant retained his own "chief of staff to the Lieutenant General Commanding the Armies of the United States," a position which Congress authorized in March 1865. Although Grant maintained his headquarters with the Army of the Potomac, he insisted on keeping Maj. Gen. George G. Meade as army commander, for with Meade's capable handling of administrative details, the general could concentrate on the "big picture."

At Army Headquarters in Washington Halleck's position was not quite that of later chiefs of staff; nor did it really conform to the then current conception of a chief of staff as an officer responsible to the commander for co-ordinating the work of the administrative services. Nevertheless, besides performing in the extremely useful capacity of interpreter of civilian and military functions and reports, he was a valuable liaison officer between Grant and the President, the Secretary of War, and the department commanders.

Administrative chiefs of the War Department never actually acknowledged any change in their status, though their respect for Grant's wishes prevented serious conflict. They insisted that no commanding general, whatever his grade, could claim any administrative participation in the Secretary of War's paramount control over the bureaus. Consequently, for the most part the Secretary of War ran the War Department; the commanding general ran the armies in the field, and planned and carried out military operations. On the other hand General Hitchcock, who continued under the new organization as a special adviser to the Secretary of War, occasionally conducted general War Department business, thereby impinging the military on civilian prerogatives.

The Bureaus

In expanding to meet the first demands of mobilizing and supporting a great wartime army, the War Department quickly outgrew its modest four-story brick building immediately west of the White House. The office of the commanding general, as well as the Quartermaster's Department, Ordnance Department, and others moved across 17th Street to Winder's Building. Within three years the Quartermaster's Department found it necessary to move again, this time into a group of temporary buildings.

Perhaps the first to respond effectively to the new demands, and to maintain a high level of support throughout the war, was the Quartermaster's Department. Handicapped at first by the loss of its chief, Brig. Gen. Joseph E. Johnston, who resigned after ten months' service as Quartermaster General to take a Southern command in April 1861, this department showed the same deficiencies as the others in supplying newly mobilized troops, and in supporting the Bull Run campaign. But Brig. Gen. Montgomery C. Meigs, an engineer officer of distinction and a capable and dynamic administrator who succeeded Johnston as Quartermaster General, introduced efficient procedures which in subsequent years freed the department from complaints by governors and commanders about supply shortages. There were cases where untrustworthy contractors failed to deliver or tried to defraud the government, but most of these developed at local procurement levels.

Ordnance items, on the other hand, were more difficult to obtain quickly than food and clothing. Unfortunately, the administrative machinery of the Ordnance Department could not keep pace with the unprecedented demands for arms and ammunition, and shortages of munitions, confusion in distribution, and slowness in acceptance of new weapons continued to some extent through most of the war. Neither Col. Henry K. Craig, a veteran of ten years as Chief of Ordnance, nor Brig. Gen. James W. Ripley, who succeeded him in April 1861, displayed the drive and the imagination characteristic of the Quartermaster General.

Perhaps worst of all in the extent to which cumbersome organization and inefficiency impaired its ability to respond to the demands for large-scale mobilization was the Medical Department. Urged by the United States Sanitary Commissioner, who had the full support of General McClellan, Assistant Secretary of War Thomas Scott, and the President, Congress approved a reform bill in April 1862 which struck at the strict seniority system then in effect and permitted the introduction of a more effective system into the Medical Department. Probably of greater value in accomplishing the reform than the enactment of the law itself was the appointment of the youthful Col. William A. Hammond as Surgeon General to replace sixty-four-year-old Col. Clement A. Finley. Finley had been appointed Surgeon General just eleven months earlier upon the death of the veteran Col. Thomas Lawson who had been head of the Medical Department for twenty-five years.

Of the other supply and service bureaus, Col. George Gibson had been Commissary General of Subsistence for over forty-three years when he died in September 1861, to be replaced by Col. Joseph P. Taylor, a veteran of thirty-two years service in the department, who died in office at the age of

65 in 1864. Brig. Gen. Joseph G. Totten had served as Chief of Engineers more than twenty-five years when he died in 1864, and Col. John J. Abert had been Chief of Topographical Engineers twenty-seven years when he retired in 1861 at the age of 72, only to be succeeded by Col. Stephen H. Long who was four years older. In contrast, the newly formed Signal Corps had as its chief thirty-one-year-old Col. Albert J. Myer; when Myer was transferred in 1864, Col. Benjamin F. Fisher, age 29, succeeded him.

Responsibilities for Army procurement and distribution of supplies lay primarily with the Quartermaster's Department, the Subsistence Department, the Ordnance Department, and the Medical Department. The Quartermaster General was also charged with the transportation of the supplies of the other departments. For most items, procurement responsibility followed simple commodity lines: the Quartermaster's Department provided clothing; the Subsistence Department furnished rations. In some cases the using service procured certain of its own items; sometimes, as when Ordnance purchased horses for the light artillery, responsibility was decided according to the ultimate destination of the item or the use to which it was to be put.

The main functions of the Ordnance Department were to operate the arsenals and armories and to furnish all ordnance and ordnance stores, including cannon and artillery carriages, small arms and accouterments, horse equipment, ammunition, and tools and materials for the ordnance service.

The work of the Subsistence Department included procurement of two categories of supplies. The first and most important, of course, included all the items making up the ration. The second category, added after

1863, is another example of definition of responsibility according to the use of the item, or for the using service itself: it included articles needed for the preservation and issue of rations, such as tools, scales, measures, and stationery. The Quartermaster's Department still furnished storehouses, sheds, and paulins.

A quasi-independent adjunct of the Quartermaster's Department was the United States Military Railroads. After the appointment of Thomas A. Scott as Assistant Secretary of War to have general charge of railway transportation and telegraphs, Capt. R. N. Morley of the Quartermaster's Department was designated general manager of U.S. Military Railroads to superintend operations on government-controlled lines. On 11 February 1862, Daniel C. McCallum was commissioned a colonel and "appointed military director and superintendent of railroads in the United States.[4] In practice such control was limited generally to railroads in the combat zones.

Five additional bureaus completed the general staff structure in operation during the Civil War—the Adjutant General's Department, which had certain supply functions in connection with the recruiting service; the Provost Marshal General's Bureau, which was responsible for enrollment of forces for the draft and the enlistment of volunteers as well as the arrest of deserters; the Pay Department; the Inspector Gen-

---

[4] Rpt, Brig Gen D. C. McCallum, Director and General Manager, U S Military Railroads, to Maj Gen M. C. Meigs, QMG, 26 May 1866, in U.S Army (War Department) *The War of the Rebellion: A Compilation of The Official Records of the Union and Confederate Armies,* 4 series, 130 vols. (Washington, 1880–1901), ser. iii, V, 974. (Hereafter cited as *Official Records.*)

eral's Department; and the Judge Advocate General's Department.

Service Troops

A problem which had manifested itself in every war was more pronounced during the Civil War: that of finding men, either military or civilian, to perform the necessary service duties for the staff departments. There were some engineer troops and a few Ordnance and Signal Corps enlisted men who performed service duties. Other supply and service branches had some officers and noncommissioned officers assigned to them, but they had no special troops—teamsters, laborers, nurses, specialists, and the like were civilians hired for the purpose, or line soldiers temporarily detached from their regiments. Each chief quartermaster was responsible for hiring and supervising the employees under his command without any intervention by the Quartermaster General. Draft exemptions were sought for teamsters to encourage them to drive army wagons to western posts; however, teamsters were not only difficult to find, but very often proved to be recalcitrant employees, so that toward the end of the war the tendency was to replace civilian drivers with soldiers who could not resign or "swear back" with impunity—the need for reliable drivers overriding objections that combat units were thus diminished. Brig. Gen. Hermann Haupt, on the contrary, preferred civilians for the construction corps which he organized for the military railroads. At first Haupt's corps was made up of soldiers, but soldiers volunteering or detailed to this duty were found to be less satisfactory than skilled civilian mechanics and laborers. General Halleck favored using engineer troops for this work, to which Haupt would have ac-

ceded if an engineer regiment could have been assigned to him permanently for the purpose. Another construction corps later organized in the Military Division of the Mississippi remained civilian throughout the war, as did the U.S. Military Telegraph.

One of the principal sources of service personnel of all kinds was the increasing number of Negro "contrabands." At wages of forty to fifty cents a day and one ration, they served well as wagoners, ambulance drivers, hostlers, and laborers, and soon formed the major part of Haupt's construction corps. Negroes unloaded cargo for the Army of the Potomac on the Peninsula, dug entrenchments for Grant at Vicksburg, and repaired roads for Sherman on the march through Georgia. Not only did they relieve soldiers from such details, but often they performed the assigned tasks better.

The obvious solution to the problem of finding reliable, competent, service-type personnel, and one which the Quartermaster General had been urging for years, was to enlist and train men in units organized specifically for this kind of duty. A small beginning was made by the Corps of Engineers, but such a modest expansion could not begin to meet the need for field construction, bridging, and fortification work. Acts of Congress of August 1861 provided for the addition of three companies to the Corps of Engineers and one company to the Corps of Topographical Engineers (these two services were combined again in March 1863) to be organized in the same manner as the company of sappers, miners, and pontoniers authorized during the Mexican War. With one company already existing, these made a total of five official engineer companies that formed the Engineer Battalion of the Regular Army. This battalion of course was only the nucleus of the total engineers em-

A CONTR   CAMP, MANCHESTER, VIRGINIA

ployed; the bulk, as in other branches, came from the volunteers. Enlisted men in the Ordnance Department and the Signal Corps formed no distinctive units.

Requirements

Since there was no such thing as systematic war planning in the pre-Civil War Military Establishment, it could not be expected that there would be much logistical planning either. Still, years of experience were of some value in making estimates. Some kind of rudimentary planning based upon experience had to go into the various tables of supplies and equipment then in use. One of the best aids for planning support for the prewar frontier army was a compila-tion of the distances of all the western posts from supply depots and from navigable streams.

The most serious aspect of logistical planning was the calculation of requirements and budget estimates each year, for these were the basis for Congressional appropriations, which in turn governed the Army's activities. The Secretary of the Treasury was required by law to submit to Congress "estimates of appropriations," which amounted to requests for funds, for all the executive departments. The Secretary of War asked for estimates from the bureau chiefs to be submitted ordinarily by October for the fiscal year beginning the next 1 July. The Secretary reviewed the estimates, which at times he sent back for modification.

Sometimes he directed that a certain estimate be included for a particular purpose. The War Department submitted its total estimate to the Secretary of the Treasury in time for it to be transmitted to the Speaker of the House in November before Congress assembled in December.

Bureau estimates were based upon those submitted through the commanders of each geographical department to the Adjutant General. In making their estimates for appropriations the bureaus had to differentiate between figures based upon known facts and those based upon conjecture, and in their budget requests they had to make specific reference, by date, volume, and page to the authorizing legislation for their items. The Medical Department still referred to the act of 2 March 1799 for its basic authority, and the Ordnance Department to its basic law of 8 February 1815. By the spring of 1863, the Quartermaster General, in drawing up budgetary estimates, had to refer to eighteen prewar laws (dating from 1812 to 1856), and to twenty-five laws passed since the beginning of hostilities in 1861.

Bureau chiefs actually had little control over their estimates for fund requests. They did not decide the numbers and disposition of troops, although they had to base their requests on these figures. Army Regulations prescribed allowances for normal supplies and equipment. Sometimes items such as repair of barracks, would be postponed in the interest of economy but would turn up later—bigger than before. To review estimates submitted from the field, or to make over-all estimates for additional appropriations, was simply a question of applying authorized allowances against the troop basis, and making allowance for experience factors and special conditions. A basic problem throughout the war was finding a reliable troop basis. On 27 May 1861 Secretary of War Cameron sent a letter to the bureau chiefs asking them to make estimates of additional appropriation requirements for Fiscal Years 1861 and 1862. The estimates were submitted between 20 and 29 June. On 29 June Cameron sent an officer with oral instructions to ask for revised figures using an amended troop basis. The Quartermaster General and Paymaster General had used the figures for eleven additional Regular Army regiments, 207 regiments of three-year volunteers, and 80,000 three-month militia. The Commissary General of Subsistence had the same units figured, and had calculated that this would make 238,249 men for a year, plus 80,000 for 31 days, plus 8,770 women with the companies, and 20,000 civilian employees entitled to rations. The Surgeon General had figured on a force of 232,500 men. In preparing estimates for Fiscal Year 1865 (in the autumn of 1863) the Commissary General of Subsistence assumed a force of an average strength of 927,706, including employees. The Quartermaster General assumed optimistically that the force would be reduced before the beginning of the next fiscal year (July 1864), but the Surgeon General sent in a budget based on an aggregate force of 1,239,273 soldiers. Stanton returned this last one with instructions to cut it by 40 percent, which was done simply by reducing the size of the assumed force to 753,564 soldiers and 300,000 "contrabands." [5]

The Ordnance Department made a considerable effort to arrive at realistic replacement factors for weapons. Reports for three consecutive years indicated a longevity of about five years for cavalry carbines,

---

[5] Meneely, *The War Department*, p. 125.

four years for cavalry pistols, and seven years for infantry muskets. Computed a little more precisely, this gave replacement factors of 20 percent a year for the carbines, 26 percent for pistols, and 13 percent for muskets.

Field Organization

Administration of the Army in the field was by geographical departments and armies. Major departments were further subdivided into military districts; on the other hand, several departments might be grouped together in a geographical division. Generally speaking, the mobile forces of a major department were designated an army, (or an army corps) and the commander of the department was also commander of the army. Grant's successive commands, for example, were: Subdistrict of Mexico, Missouri; Military District of Southeast Missouri, later designated Military District of Cairo; District and Army of West Tennessee; Department and Army of the Tennessee; Military Division of the Mississippi; Armies of the United States. As commander of the Military Division of the Mississippi, Grant (and Maj. Gen. William T. Sherman after him) was theater commander over the Departments of the Ohio, the Cumberland, and the Tennessee; and, in effect, army group commander over the armies bearing the same respective names. Changes in boundaries and designations were frequent. For example, the Department of the Cumberland was formed in August 1861 to include Kentucky east of the Cumberland River and Tennessee. In March 1862 this department was merged into the Department of the Mississippi, but its army retained its organization and designation as the Army of the Ohio until

October 1862, when the Department of the Cumberland was re-established to include Tennessee east of the Tennessee River and such parts of Georgia and Alabama as might be occupied by federal troops. The Department of the Ohio was reconstituted in August 1862, but from August until October its army was the Army of Kentucky, and in this case army and department commanders were different officers.

Distinctions between the functions and responsibilities of an army commander and of a department commander were not always clear. Where command was in the same hands, as was usually the case, the distinction was not very important, but if a mobile army moved into the territory of another department, differences over jurisdiction and functions could be serious. When General McClellan took command of forces around Washington, he insisted that they be organized and designated an army rather than a geographical division. Winfield Scott, still General in Chief at the time, insisted, on the contrary, that the retention of the system of geographical divisions and departments was absolutely necessary. Unable to persuade Scott to change his views, McClellan proceeded on his own authority to redesignate the Division of the Potomac, the Army of the Potomac, and it continued to be known by that name throughout the war.

The movement of the main body of the Army of the Potomac to the Peninsula in March 1862 brought McClellan within the territorial bounds of the Department of Virginia, which was under the command of Maj. Gen. John E. Wool with headquarters at Fort Monroe. Normally an army controlled its own supply base and there was no intervening organization between the supply bureaus of the War Department and the geographic departments and armies. In this case Fort Monroe and all of Wool's 15,000 men were assigned to McClellan's command, but within ten days Fort Monroe and the troops previously assigned to the Department of Virginia were restored to the independent command of General Wool. The result was something of a precursor of what later developed into the communications zone: in effect, and in a limited way, by supporting the army to the front, General Wool was acting as a communications zone commander, an arrangement that seems to have been satisfactory to both commanders.

There was, of course, no general staff corps, but commanders did have the rudiments of a general staff in the aides-de-camp which they were authorized. Aides were appointed by the President, with the advice and consent of the Senate, on the recommendation of the commander, and they could remain with the commander when he was transferred. The heads of the War Department bureaus designated the adjutant general, quartermaster, commissary of subsistence, and inspector general for each army corps. These officers remained attached to their respective corps without regard to the movements of the corps commanders. Armies, corps, divisions, and brigades all had officers assigned from each of the supply departments to act for the unit as quartermaster, commissary, chief ordnance officer, and chief surgeon. Each regiment had a single supply officer—the regimental quartermaster, a lieutenant nominated by the regimental commander for appointment by the Secretary of War— whose duty it was to obtain all supplies other than ordnance for the regiment. An ordnance sergeant in each regiment was responsible for obtaining arms and ammunition and for keeping arms in repair. Commis-

saries were later appointed for regiments.

The question of control over major logistical installations—whether they should be under the direct command of the bureau chief in Washington, or whether they should be under the commander of the department in which they were located—sometimes was a troublesome problem during the Civil War as it has been at times throughout the Army's history. General depots were directly under War Department bureaus, but Army commanders had authority to establish certain depots in the field as needed.

For operations in the field an army ordinarily established a base, a grand depot at a location accessible to transportation to both front and rear, and remote enough from the battle areas to be relatively secure from hostile action. During offensive operations advance depots were established from which the army could draw supplies without having to go all the way back to its base for them. Supporting the grand depots of the armies were the major depots of the Quartermaster's and Subsistence Departments at such cities as New York, Boston, Philadelphia, Baltimore, Washington, Cincinnati, Louisville, St. Louis, Chicago, and New Orleans; the twenty-eight arsenals and armories of the Ordnance Department; and the central depot for medical supplies at Philadelphia, with storehouses in various parts of the country. The Quartermaster General sent supplies of clothing and equipage from the general depots to quartermaster officers stationed with the troops. Company commanders drew these items from the quartermasters on requisitions approved by the regimental commanders. In peacetime ordnance was issued from the armories and arsenals only by authority of the Chief of Ordnance in Washington, but during war any general or field officer commanding an army, garrison, or detachment could give an order for ordnance to supply his troops. Staff officers were expected to keep their immediate commanders, as well as their bureau chiefs, informed about their activities and the status of supply, and to pass on to the commander information received from the bureaus.

The organization of a major depot was hardly less complex than that of its parent bureau. The big quartermaster depot at Washington was organized into twelve branches to carry out assigned operations: wagon transportation, ocean and river transportation, charter of vessels, contracts for victualing chartered transports, railroad transportation, transportation of ordnance and ordnance stores at the Washington Arsenal, purchase and issue of miscellaneous quartermaster supplies and interment of deceased soldiers, receipt and issue of forage, provision of meals and quarters for transient soldiers and those in rest camp, construction and repairs, receipt and issue of clothing and equipage, and operation of the branch depot at Alexandria.

Summary

It is easy to find serious flaws in the Army's administrative structure during the Civil War, and to point to the confusion and red tape which seemed prevalent. Yet it should be remembered that organization is more often the product of tradition and policies and diplomacy and leadership than of clear-cut logic. Nor should it be forgotten that in spite of its obvious shortcomings the War Department in the 1860's administered what was in some respects the most rapid mobilization and the greatest war effort in American history. Without the benefit of an existing mobilized force such as the National Guard in 1917, or both National Guard and prewar draft in 1940, the Union Army strength expanded sixty-two times— from 16,000 men in 1861 to over 1,000,000 in 1865. No other expansion in the Army's history has come close to this figure. Total mobilization in proportion to population was the greatest of any period excepting World War II. Casualties were greater in proportion to population for the U.S. Army than in any other war.

The increase in expenditures of funds was even more spectacular. War Department expenditures leaped from $22,981,000 in Fiscal Year 1861 to $1,031,323,000 in Fiscal Year 1865—an increase of forty-five times! There was a tenfold increase in War Department expenditures between 1811 and 1814; they increased twenty-six times from 1916 to 1918, and seventeen times between 1941 and 1945.[6] It is not at all certain that the much improved administrative machinery of the two world wars really accomplished more logistically, in any truly relative comparison, than did the cumbersome machine which served Mr. Lincoln.

---

[6] U.S. Bureau of the Census, *Historical Statistics of the United States, 1789–1945* (Washington, 1949), pp. 299–301. (Table: Federal Government Finances—Treasury Expenditures: 1789 to 1945.)

CHAPTER XII

Industrial Mobilization and Procurement

Industrial mobilization for the Civil War was not the result of any farsighted advance planning. It was, rather, the result of economic pressures coming with recovery from four years of depression and from the demands for military supplies. At the outset, few could visualize the magnitude of the sustained effort that would be required to crush the rebellion. Nowhere was the failure to appreciate the extent of the conflict of greater consequence than in estimates of resources needed to wage it. Procurement programs, which in other times might have been more than adequate, soon showed themselves as only half-measures, and steps for financial support appeared "penny-wise and pound foolish."

Industrial Expansion and Government Enterprise

Under the stress of wartime dislocation and uncertainty, economic depression continued during the first several months of the war. Then, with the encouragement of rising protective tariffs, easy money, and the pent-up demands of the depression years, business began to boom. It is possible that these factors alone would have been sufficient to restore prosperity, but the actual stimulus to the economy came from the anticipation of profitable government contracts. Lacking plan or direction, the nation's war business quickly became a chaos of fierce competition, profiteering, and fraud. At the same time, the possibilities of handsome profits precipitated expansion and conversion of industry, and boosted to unprecedented heights the production of goods needed for the war effort.

Philadelphia probably was the largest manufacturing center in the country. Energetic industrialists built fifty-eight new factories in that city in 1862, another fifty-seven in 1863, and sixty-five more—most of them very large ones—in 1864. Cotton mills—forced to virtually suspend operations when Southern cotton was cut off—and carpet mills were converted to woolen mills; machine shops became arms factories; saw factories turned to making sabers; jewelry factories turned out brass buttons. No less significant than the expansion and conversion of old manufacturing industries was the extension of the factory system into clothing and shoe manufacture and the growth of the meat-packing industry. One of the basic war industries was the iron industry, which expanded greatly in the states of New York, New Jersey, and Pennsylvania. Six large iron mills were erected in Pittsburgh in one year. The total output of anthracite pig iron rose from approximately 524,500 tons to 684,300 tons a year between 1860 and 1864, and 80 percent of this production was in Pennsylvania. Rolling mills multiplied in all parts of the country, and much of the rolled iron previously imported was now produced at home. Steel manufacture never made much headway during the war. Though the advantages of steel for rails and for weapons were clear, and attempts to establish a steel industry had been made during the previous thirty years, Bessemer steel did not become available in the United States on a large scale until after the war.

Actually, the woolen mills led the way to prosperity. Civilian and military demands for woolen cloth to replace cotton, rapidly becoming unavailable, soon had the woolen mills booming. The industry could not begin to meet the military requirements in the first winter of the war, yet when the War Department made oversea purchases it strongly protested that the government should patronize home industries. But it was not long before the domestic industry was able to meet all the demands. With the benefit of the Morrill Tariff Act of March 1861 and the promise of Army contracts, old mills reopened and expanded, and hundreds of new mills were built, especially in the western states. Many of them worked nights and Sundays to keep up with orders. From a peacetime production of 85,000,000 pounds a year, the output of Northern woolen mills at the height of the war rose to 75,000,000 pounds for the armed forces and 138,000,000 pounds for the civilian economy.

Closely related to the growth of the woolen industry in supplying the Army was the development of the ready-made clothing industry. This had begun slowly in the 1830's, and had developed rapidly after the marketing of Elias Howe's sewing machine in 1849 and the subsequent large-scale manufacture of sewing machines by Singer & Company, Grover & Baker, and Wheeler & Wilson. Shirts that had required 14 hours

and 20 minutes to make by hand could be made by machine in 1 hour and 16 minutes. Concentrated largely in New York, Boston, Philadelphia, and Cincinnati, the ready-made clothing industry was ready when the war orders came. For the first time the United States could supply uniforms to its Army from domestic sources, which furnished most of the raw wool, manufactured the cloth, and made the uniforms.

Domestic industry supplied shoes as well as uniforms for the Army. Here, too, the sewing machine brought a revolution—without it the job never could have been done. The McKay sewing machine, put on the market in 1862, increased the speed of sewing uppers to soles a hundredfold, and within a year the production of shoes doubled.

Another important wartime expansion occurred in the meat-packing industry. With the closing of the Mississippi River, the packing of pork centered in Chicago. Where 270,000 hogs had been slaughtered in 1860, soon more than 900,000 were being packed in that city, and what previously had been for the most part a home industry, became a large-scale factory operation. The Union Stock Yards, with pens for 100,000 hogs and 10,000 cattle, were established at this time. Beef packing developed to some extent in Chicago and Milwaukee, but on a relatively small scale, and most communities throughout the country continued to depend on local slaughterhouses for their beef.

No less important for wartime food supply was the remarkable increase in wheat and flour production that followed the introduction of the reaper and the improvement of transportation. Even during the war years a growing surplus of wheat and flour continued to be available for export, and in the long-run Northern wheat proved to be superior to Southern cotton in the stakes of European diplomacy.

The government did not rely entirely on private entrepreneurs, reacting to the attraction of higher profits, for mobilization of industrial resources, but went into business on a rather large scale in areas where it appeared that private manufacturers would not suffice. The manufacture of small arms for the Army had been a national venture for a long time. Although the Harper's Ferry Armory had been destroyed to prevent its falling into the hands of the enemy, the Springfield Armory employed 3,000 men and production was expanded to 350,000 rifles a year at a cost per weapon of less than half the $20 paid to private manufacturers. The Springfield Armory turned out about one-third of the Army rifles manufactured in the United States during the war. The government also went into other types of business. It operated a clothing factory at Cincinnati as well as the one at Philadelphia, and laboratories for drugs and medicines at New York, Philadelphia, and St. Louis; later it operated meat-packing houses at Knoxville, Tennessee, and at Louisville and other towns in Kentucky.

The contrast between North and South in the capacity for economic mobilization became more marked as the years passed. By 1863 Northern industry was reaching peak production, and supplies for the most part were at last becoming plentiful. In the Confederate States shortages were increasing. Almost every material resource needed for war, except for the cotton which had failed to bring other necessities in sufficient quantity from Europe, was at a premium. Bread riots in the spring of 1863 emphasized the suffering that already had appeared in some places, and the great battles of that year warned of worse days to come. If it was a tactical and logistical disadvantage to the Union forces to have to do most of the fighting and to maintain long lines of communication in hostile territory, even more serious strategic and logistical disadvantages fell to the lot of the Confederacy. No matter how the battles went, Southern railways, factories, and farms suffered, and the problems of supplying the Confederate armies multiplied.

Foreign Procurement

Despite expansion of private industry and government facilities, it soon became apparent that domestic resources could not begin to meet the immediate demands for full-scale war, and the confusion of the New York market place spread to Europe. Five agents were reported to have arrived in Europe on one ship, there to bid against each other for arms—some good, some obsolescent, some unserviceable—for the Union forces.

Acting on his own authority, Maj. Gen. John C. Frémont sent his agents to buy rifles, cannon, and shells in England and France for the use of troops in his Department of the West, and the American ministers at London and Paris gave their approval to these transactions. In the European as in the domestic market, the Ordnance Department was slow to begin purchasing. After Congress authorized the enlistment of 500,000 volunteers, however, the shortage of arms became so critical that the War Department went into foreign procurement on a large scale. After October 1861 American ministers at European capitals became primary purchasing agents for the Federal Government.

During the first fifteen months of the war

arms purchases by the Federal Government in Europe alone included about 738,000 muskets, rifles, and carbines, more than ten times the quantity purchased from American manufacturers during that period. Even American private contractors subcontracted for a large share of their parts in Europe. These parts as well as arms purchased directly by the government were subject to inspection in Europe by ordnance officers sent for the purpose. British Enfield rifles and the official French army rifles were the most sought after weapons, but since the number available did not approach the quantities needed, other weapons of all types and descriptions were accepted. With the recent adoption of the needle gun or other improved models, many European states took this opportunity to rid themselves of obsolete weapons at high prices.

For clothing and individual equipment as well as munitions, federal and state agents turned to European sources, but total expenditures for textiles and blankets purchased abroad did not exceed $380,000. Although it clearly would have been impossible to arm and clothe Union armies during the first year and a half of war without European goods, the whole foreign procurement program was up against strong protectionist sentiments in the United States which demanded that American money be kept at home to help American industry. An ardent protectionist when he had been a member of the Senate, Secretary of War Cameron was reluctant to go into foreign markets at all until forced by the circumstances. Shortly after entering upon his duties, Secretary of War Edwin Stanton in January 1862 issued an order that no further contracts should be made for any article of foreign manufacture that could be pro-

duced in the United States, and all outstanding orders for purchases in foreign countries were revoked. Further foreign purchases did have to be allowed during the ensuing year, but all foreign procurement virtually came to an end by 1863. Indeed the Quartermaster General found it necessary to apologize in his report of 1862 for buying a lot of excellent uniforms and equipment in Europe at prices no greater than those being paid for American shoddy.

As frequently is the case, the Army found that its procurement policies could not be governed by military considerations alone. Inevitably the fiscal byproducts of public expenditures sometimes overshadowed the purpose of the expenditures themselves. As a result, the War Department was not able always to follow the general rule of obtaining the best quality at the lowest prices. There was another disadvantage to the policy of shunning foreign supplies: federal officials seemed to lose sight completely of the value of preclusive buying. Federal and state officials were not only competing with each other in Europe but also with Confederate agents. While the Northern agents rushed in to buy up most of the available surplus supplies, including obsolete weapons, Confederate agents cannily contracted for the output of some of the best factories in London and Birmingham. If Northern agents had contracted for existing stocks and future production of all the best weapons, the Confederacy would have suffered accordingly.

Army Contracting Policies

Profiteering and fraud always had accompanied earlier programs of war procurement, but never on such a vast scale as that which flourished during the early years of the Civil War. Profiteers and unscrupulous traders lost no opportunity to take advantage of the loose enforcement of rules and regulations under the pressure of large-scale purchasing and contracting and the haste of rapid mobilization to turn government requirements into private fortunes. War Department officials, Army officers, and state governors were interested first of all in results. They were more anxious to overcome delay than to assure themselves of fair prices; more anxious to arm and clothe their troops than to satisfy regulations. On the other hand, the first interest of too many contractors was to make a profit rather than to get on with the war. The lack of central co-ordination and the confusion among agents of the War Department, Army commanders, and state governors attracted profiteers, but corruption developed in private negotiations between government representatives and contractors even where there was no such competition. In some cases manufacturers received excessive prices for goods sold to the government. Middlemen having nothing to offer but promises and connections made fortunes by obtaining government contracts and then subletting them at a much lower figure to a manufacturer—or even to another middleman.

Lincoln himself, of course, had taken liberties with the law in the interests of mobilization, and he had backed Secretary of War Cameron when the latter was called to question for some of his extra-legal actions, but the President was very sensitive about any appearance of improper conduct. When the officer in charge of the abattoir in Washington adopted the policy of sending to the White House each day for the President's breakfast the choicest beefsteak cut from the 80 to 90 head of cattle slaugh-

tered daily for the Army of Potomac, Lincoln noticed the exceptional quality. On discovering that he was the subject of special consideration he asked that it be discontinued. The officer said that of course it would be discontinued if the President wished, but it seemed to him a very small matter. Lincoln replied, "That is true, but my observation is that frequently the most insignificant matter is the foundation for the worst scandal." [1]

Was all of the waste and fraud to be accepted as an inevitable, if unfortunate, accompaniment of large-scale war procurement? Certain members of Congress did not think so, and neither did Secretary of War Edwin Stanton.

When Congress assembled for the special session early in July 1861, its members already were suspicious about waste and corruption in military procurement, and one of the first actions of the House of Representatives was to establish a select committee to inquire into government contracts. Under the chairmanship of Charles H. Van Wyck of New York, for more than a year the committee investigated such things as the procurement of arms, horses, blankets, and food, the chartering of vessels, the activities of sutlers, and the handling of merchandise in the New York Custom House. The committee's procedure was to call witnesses, by subpoena if necessary, to give testimony in secret, then to submit the transcript to the witnesses for comment and correction before publishing the testimony with its report. Revelation of fraud brought de-

---

[1] John Henry Woodward, Bvt. Major, Army of the Potomac, A Narrative of the Family and Civil War Experience and Events of His Life, p. 14 MS in possession of Lt Col Frederick Woodward Hopkins, Santa Rosa, Calif

mands for action to curb it by strengthening the laws. Congress already had passed one act in 1861 to regulate the making of contracts, but almost immediately it went to work on more severe legislation to prevent fraud.

Fear of fraud has always been one of the major causes of government red tape. In tightened procurement regulations Quartermaster General Meigs saw the prospect that the whole war effort might be stifled with antifraud red tape. In a letter to Senator Henry Wilson the Quartermaster General said:

I know the responsibility attaching to any Government officer who ventures to argue against a bill whose object is stated as the prevention of frauds, but it is my duty to say to you that if the conditions in regard to contracts imposed by this bill become law the country may as well at once yield to the Southern rebels all they ask.

. . . .

Just such regulations as this bill imposes starved the British army with cold and hunger, while shiploads of stores and of provisions lay till they perished in Balaklava Bay.

Every purchase, every order to purchase or deliver, if accepted, is a contract. These orders are sent by telegraph. Contracts are thus made with persons a thousand miles away. If we are to trammel every purchase with new conditions of writing, of record, of affidavit, no human brain will be capable of conducting the business of the great supply departments of the Army.

. . . .

As a protection against fraud, he who will steal will not hesitate to shield himself from detection by violating an oath made as common as a customhouse oath.

. . . .

The greater the fraud the more perfect the papers. The law of 1861, chapter 84, section 10, in regard to making contracts, contains all that is really needed to secure the public.

More legislation will merely embarrass and delay the public service.[2]

For his part Secretary of War Stanton needed no new laws. As soon as he took office in January 1862 he acted vigorously against graft and profiteering. His order of 29 January which suspended foreign procurement also required all persons claiming to have any kind of contract or order from the War Department to give a written notice of such contract, together with a statement of what had been done under it, within fifteen days. "It is seldom that any necessity can prevent a contract from being reduced to writing," the order said, "and even when made by telegraph its terms can be speedily written and signed; and every claim founded on any pretended contract, agreement or license now outstanding, of which notice and a copy is not filed in accordance with this order, shall be deemed fraudulent and void."[3]

Fraud, profiteering, and extravagance most often appeared when officials failed to follow prescribed procedures. An act of 1860 provided that all purchases and contracts for supplies or services in any department of the government should be by advertising. An exception was made, however, when immediate delivery was necessary, in which case needed supplies or services might be obtained by open purchase or contract in the same manner as between individuals. This rule stayed in force throughout the war, when immediate deliveries frequently were necessary, and there was no time to advertise for bids. Unfortunately it was too easy to

_____

[2] Ltr, Meigs to Wilson, 2 August 1861, *Official Records*, ser. iii, I, 378–79.

[3] Quoted in Fletcher Pratt, *Stanton, Lincoln's Secretary of War* (New York, W. W Norton & Co., 1953), pp. 150–52.

abuse the privilege of direct purchase and to make every case an exception to the rule. Another rule not always observed was one that required ordnance stores to be contracted for through the senior ordnance officer. It is difficult to see how a commander in the field could always follow this rule and still accomplish his mission in an emergency situation. Yet the same emergency that allowed exceptions to procurement by competitive bids, and that justified the field commander in ignoring ordnance procedures, also opened the door to the profiteer and the grafter.

Actual contracting was little different from that of earlier periods, except for the use of the telegraph. Sometimes orders were transmitted in the form of telegrams, sometimes by letter, and sometimes by formal contract. A series of orders for arms from Colt's Patent Fire-arms Manufacturing Company in 1861, for example, included all these forms. A telegraph message from the Chief of Ordnance to Samuel Colt in May said simply, "Deliver the five hundred pistols to Major Thornton at New York Arsenal. For further orders, wait mail." [4] In June the Chief of Ordnance sent a letter order to Colt saying, "Please furnish this department, as soon as possible, with five thousand Colt's revolver pistols, of the latest pattern. The pistols are to undergo inspection, and the price will be the same as allowed for the same kind of pistols recently furnished by you." [5] In July, when it came to an order for 25,000 muskets, General Ripley signed a formal contract with Colt specifying that the arms were to be of the exact Springfield pattern, with interchangeable parts; they were to be delivered according to a strict time schedule; appendages were to be furnished and they were to be packed twenty to the box. The contract set the terms of payment, $20 for each stand of arms, payable on receipt in Washington of certificates of inspection and evidences of delivery of at least 1,000 muskets with appendages; finally the legal statement was included that no member of Congress would benefit from this contract. [6]

Financial Support

As in previous wars supply officers very early found themselves in financial embarrassment as they attempted to meet the costs of initial supply for a rapidly expanding army. Although he recognized the injustice of delayed payment General Meigs noted that this was one of the least of the injustices of a great war and he insisted that quartermaster purchasing agents continue to make every effort to obtain essential supplies as long as merchants, manufacturers, or capitalists could be found who were willing to take the risk.

When, in December 1861, the New York banks suspended specie payment, and the country went on a paper basis, it appeared that once again the government was headed toward that paralysis of inflation which had so weakened the war effort in the Revolution and the War of 1812. The Legal Tender Act of February 1862, authorizing the printing of United States notes as legal tender, added one more type of currency to the several thousands of kinds and denom-

[4] Msg, Ripley to Colt, 4 May 1861, Exec Doc, 40th Cong., 2d sess., vol. 12, Ordnance Dept, p. 100.

[5] Ltr, Ordnance Office to Colt, 12 June 1861, Exec Doc 40th Cong., 2d sess., vol. 12, Ordnance Dept, p. 100.

[6] Contract made by Chief of Ordnance with Colt's Arms Co., Exec Doc 40th Cong., 2d sess., vol. 12, Ordnance Dept, 100–101.

inations of state banknotes, not counting counterfeit bills, then in general circulation.

Neither the Administration nor Congress moved decisively to develop a tax program commensurate with financial requirements. A direct tax apportioned among the states and a modest income tax added something to the national revenue, but this income covered only a small fraction of the expenditures which by early 1863 had reached the rate of $2,500,000 a day. The only recourse was to make up the deficit by borrowing in the form of government bonds, or what amounted to forced loans of irredeemable notes. To dispose of the bonds, Secretary of the Treasury Chase turned to banker Jay Cooke who developed a high-pressure advertising program to sell the securities. The national banking acts of 1863 and 1864 helped to restabilize the banking system, and as a means of forced sale of government bonds and the source of still another form of currency, "national banknotes," which at least curbed to some extent the wildcat currency then in circulation, contributed substantially to Civil War finance.

During the first year of the war Army expenditures alone jumped from $22,981,-000 to $394,368,000, while total federal revenues rose only from $41,345,000 to $51,935,000. Army expenditures passed the one billion dollar mark in a single year for the first time in 1864–65. The national debt that year leaped to $2,682,592,000.[7]

Although Civil War finance left much to be desired and for a time the dearth of financial resources threatened the procurement effort, inflation did not get completely out of control, and the nation's financial structure did not collapse. The fact is that procurement hardly could have been greater, given the complexities of such a sudden and large-scale mobilization and the economic conditions and resources available at the time. Quartermaster General Meigs was not far wrong when he wrote, "No nation probably ever so quickly and so thoroughly organized and equipped so large an army and so nearly paid its way as we have done."[8]

Clothing and Equipage

Clothing is in immediate demand with every expansion of the Army, and it is difficult to improvise. Food of some kind may be found in local areas near encampments; arms and ammunition are urgent, but at least some requirements can be postponed until engagement with the enemy approaches. Clothing is needed immediately by every soldier mustered into the service. When the Civil War broke out clothing on hand in military warehouses was adequate enough for the continuous supply of the 16,000 men then in the Regular Army, but the enlistment of mass armies soon changed the whole picture. Contracting for uniforms in the summer of 1861 was based on the War Department's estimate of 300,000 men, but when Congress authorized the expansion of the Army to 500,000 volunteers, the nearly four million yards of blue cloth needed to provide just one uniform for each man was nowhere in sight.

The Quartermaster's Department had

---

[7] Albert B. Hart, *Salmon Portland Chase* (Boston: Houghton, Mifflin & Co., 1899), app. A, pp. 436–38 *passim*; see also Davis R. Dewey, *Financial History of the United States* (New York: Longmans, Green & Co., 1918), pp. 329–30.

[8] Ltr, Gen Meigs to Gov Morgan, 3 October 1861. *Official Records,* ser. iii, I, 559–60.

only one depot for clothing and equipage then in operation—the Schuylkill Arsenal at Philadelphia. The practice had been to purchase cloth on contract from manufacturers, and then to make it up into uniforms at this depot. The urgent demands of mobilization led to rapid enlargement of activities at Schuylkill, to the establishment of new depots at New York in 1861 and Cincinnati early in 1862, to direct procurement of ready-made clothing, and to dependence upon the co-operation of state authorities in outfitting their troops. The Philadelphia depot employed 8,000 to 10,000 people to make clothing and equipage. Merchants imported large quantities of cloth from abroad, and state governments and the Quartermaster's Department purchased it and then contracted for the manufacture of uniforms or made them up in government establishments. When regular sources of supply failed, the principal United States quartermaster in or near each state was authorized to go into the market to purchase needed items. In letting contracts to meet rapidly growing requirements, General Meigs recognized the danger that too great an immediate impact might drive prices skyward and might permit a few capitalists to gain control of the market. He therefore invited bids with the understanding that after ten days all bids received up to that time would be opened and contracts awarded. However, the advertisement was published as a standing invitation to manufacturers, and additional contracts were to be given from time to time to the lowest bidders who appeared and gave security for the fulfillment of their engagements. This procedure may seem to have been an open invitation to collusive bidding and its attendant abuses, but the worst feature of the clothing program appeared in the poor quality of the product procured in the early months of the war rather than in the contracting methods.

The quartermaster depots at Philadelphia, New York, and Cincinnati were the principal centers for clothing and equipage procurement. Quartermaster officers at Philadelphia purchased over 948,000 uniform coats and 591,000 jackets in addition to 2,219,000 yards of woolen cloth for coats during the war. Procurement of these items at New York and Cincinnati was on a somewhat smaller scale but the total for the three centers included over 2,985,000 coats and jackets and nearly 3,500,000 yards of cloth for coats. Other items included over 7,700,000 trousers, 5,900,000 woolen blankets, 1,890,000 rubber and painted blankets, 1,596,000 rubber and painted ponchos, and 10,860,000 boots and shoes, as well as hundreds of thousands of tents, camp kettles, mess pans, and scores of other items of clothing and equipment.[9]

Food

Food procurement had its ups and downs as the war ran its course. Rapid mobilization created administrative snarls in the Subsistence Department as it did in the other departments, but it did not produce the acute shortages common to such items as clothing and munitions. On the contrary, the fervor of mobilization throughout the North brought all kinds of contributions of food on the part of local communities and organizations, so that for a time many of the soldiers were eating better than they ever had. The procurement of food became a

_____

[9] Statement showing number of principal articles of clothing and equipage purchased at the depots of Philadelphia, New York, and Cincinnati. *Official Records*, ser. iii, V, 283–86.

problem after the excitement of mobilization had worn off. In this field, too, profiteers and dishonest merchants sought personal advantages, particularly in supplying beef, but munitions and clothing offered so much greater attractions that the supply of food was not dangerously impaired. Indeed, few general shortages of food owing to procurement deficiencies were to develop, and aside from various occasions when tactical operations or the movements of troops interrupted supply in the field, Northern soldiers generally were well fed throughout the war. At times some units went for too long on an unsavory diet of salt beef or pork and hardtack, but state governments and private organizations took it upon themselves to forward such things as potatoes, onions, beets, tomatoes, poultry, eggs, and canned fruit to give some variety to the diet and to help ward off scurvy. For the most part soldiers had better fare than the salt meat and hardtack that traditionally had been associated with the army ration. Canned and dehydrated foods, introduced in 1857, were used to some extent, but in the forms and small quantities then available they did little to add to the health-giving qualities of the ration. Even in 1861 the Commissary General assured the Secretary of War that never before in history had an army been so well provisioned. In bulk and calories, at least, this probably was true. The ration of the Union Army was nearly double that of the French, more than double the Prussian, Austrian, and Russian, and 20 percent above the British. Variety, however, often left much to be desired, and cooking frequently ruined whatever taste there was in the food. The most serious result of deficiencies in food supply, of course, was the impairment of the health of the troops. The addition of potatoes to the ration in 1862, and the supply of fresh vegetables, fruit, and other supplements obtained by foraging or by various forms of local procurement, and individual purchases from the stocks of sutlers added further essential elements to the diet.

Except for flour and fresh beef, the Army obtained most of its food supplies by advertising for bids in the cities of Boston, New York, Philadelphia, Baltimore, Cincinnati, Louisville, and St. Louis, then choosing the lowest bid for suitable items according to requirements of troops in the section of the country best served from a particular city or cities. Flour generally was procured in the same manner but at places closer to the field armies. Procurement of beef by the block or on the hoof was generally by contract, that is by negotiation. The Commissary Department was able to save a considerable sum of money by the sale of hides, tallow, and other byproducts of its meat industry. The depots at Washington and Alexandria alone recovered $1,370,000 in this way during the four years of the war.

New York was a major center for the procurement of nonperishable foods for troops all along the eastern and southeastern coast. During 1863 the Quartermaster's Department, in charge of food transportation, shipped from the port of New York an average of 7,000 packages of food a day for each working day of the year, and during 1864 the average was only slightly less.

Arms and Ammunition

In munitions procurement, problems appeared at the outset of the war and continued, with variations, until the end. First the munitions program was under pressure to arm as fast as possible the large number of men called into service; later, it had to keep up with the rapid expansion of the

Army and with the larger turnover of men as terms expired, casualties mounted, and new recruits appeared; and finally, it was under pressure to replace absolescent weapons with improved models. These same pressures brought on the conditions previously noted that, without strict supervision, led to fraudulent contracts, profiteering, middlemen, and the competitive purchasing which to a considerable extent characterized arms procurement during the first part of the war.

Variety, made necessary by the shortage of arms, aggravated the weapons supply problem. The regulation infantry weapon was supposed to be the caliber .58 Springfield muzzle-loading rifled musket, but the number of foreign muzzle-loading rifles brought into service was two-thirds as great as the number of Springfield weapons. There were also in the inventory several hundred thousand smoothbore muskets, about as many breech-loading carbines, and some breech-loading and repeating rifles. The foreign models, in addition to the British Enfields and the French army rifles, included many different kinds of Austrian, German, Belgian, and other weapons. This disparity of types added immensely to the task of the arsenals in keeping weapons in repair, to the burden of the Springfield Armory in supplying spare parts, and to problems of ammunition supply generally.

The biggest single munitions contractor during the war was Robert P. Parrott (West Point Iron and Cannon Foundry), famed for the big rifled gun which bore his name, who was awarded 2,332 contracts having a total value of $4,733,059. Close behind was Colt's Patent Fire Arms Company at Hartford, Connecticut, which held 267 contracts for a total value of $4,687,031. No

less than fifteen companies—including such names as J. T. Ames, Herman Boker and Company, Alfred Jenks and Son, Naylor and Company, E. Remington and Sons, Sharpe's Rifle Manufacturing Company, Starr Arms Company, and Spencer Arms Company—had contracts amounting to at least one million dollars each. The old firm of Eli Whitney of Whitneyville still was in the picture, but only to the extent of $353,647.[10]

Private industry was the source for all the artillery (although carriages and caissons were made at the arsenals), all the gunpowder, and a large share of the small arms procured during the Civil War. The Springfield Armory turned out about 802,000 rifled muskets (with the use of parts manufactured by private industry in a number of cases). Private arms makers produced 670,600 of these Springfield weapons. Other purchases, from domestic industry and from abroad, included nearly 1,225,000 muskets and rifles, over 400,000 carbines, and 372,800 revolvers.[11]

Summary

The military procurement program during the Civil War was enough in itself to put the United States into the rank of first-class powers. Despite the inefficiency of competitive purchasing and faulty supervision of contracts in the early months of the war and the swarms of profiteers and unscrupulous contractors who sought to increase their profits by offering inferior materials—

[10] Exec. Doc. 40th Cong., 2d sess., vol. 12, Ordnance Dept., 698–996.

[11] Rpt of Chief of Ordnance, 23 October 1866, House Exec Doc 1, 39th Cong., 2d sess., pp. 658–67.

despite all the imperfections of a procurement system which permitted these conditions to grow—the final achievement compares favorably with the best efforts of the major military powers of the world at that time. Emphasis upon domestic procurement delayed some efforts to get necessary supplies and equipment and tended to leave foreign sources open to the Confederacy, but in the end the United States had freed itself of dependence on foreign sources for military clothing and weapons even under conditions of virtually total mobilization. This newfound independence inspired confidence that, with the country's potential to meet any conceivable future wartime demands, it would not find itself at a serious disadvantage relative to any possible enemy.

CHAPTER XIII

New Weapons and Equipment

Several factors militated against the ready acceptance of new or improved weapons and equipment. Not the least of these were the dispositions and predispositions of the officers responsible, in particular the Chief of Ordnance, General Ripley. Undoubtedly a certain natural conservatism persisted in the Army where change was costly, and where officers were satisfied to retain weapons that had proved reliable over a period of years rather than risk untried models in a time of great emergency. But General Ripley during his service as Chief of Ordnance (April 1861–September 1863) was more than conservative; perhaps because of his responsibilities in arming a massive army so precipitately organized, he was actively hostile to most suggestions for weapons improvements. As long as the responsibility for procurement as well as the responsibility for acceptance of new equipment rested with the same agency, it could be expected that one function would suffer, and while General Ripley ruled the Ordnance Department there was no doubt as to which function that would be.

Although Ripley's attitude generally prevailed among the military, there were exceptions. His immediate successors in the Ordnance Department, Brig. Gen. George D. Ramsay and Brig. Gen. Alexander B. Dyer who became Chief of Ordnance in September 1864 were more receptive to new ideas, as was the inspector at the West

Point Foundry for much of the war, Capt. Stephen V. Benet. General Ripley took the position of "positively refusing to answer any requisitions for, or propositions to sell, new and untried arms." [1] On the other hand, General Dyer in a letter of 22 October 1864 to Secretary Stanton stated as his opinion "these inventions and improvements should not be disregarded, as they may result in important benefits to the public service. It will not do to stand still and rest content with what we have already attained." [2]

One of the really basic issues, and one which involved much more than personalities, was the advisability of putting new items into wartime production. Standardization for production presented the dilemma of timing which has characterized all modern wars, and which has become more pronounced with each technological advance: if standardization of weapons is established too soon, it may lead to production of obsolescent and inferior models; if it is established too late, the weapons may be superior but there will not be enough of them. When a new model is offered in the course of a major war, the advantages, even when fully demonstrated, must be weighed very care-

---

[1] Notes on the Subject of Contracting for Small Arms, 11 June 1861, House Exec Doc 67, 40th Cong., 2d sess., vol. V, 31.

[2] *Official Records,* ser iii, IV, 208.

fully against the general loss of production involved, problems in production of the new model, problems of spare parts and maintenance, and problems of ammunition supply and other indirect requirements that would result from its adoption. In other words, the usefulness of a new weapon or piece of equipment must be considered in its ratio to the practicability of its wartime production.

Secondary supply and maintenance problems particularly must be taken into account in adopting new items. Variety may be the spice of life, but it is poison to ordnance officers. The use of different kinds of weapons in a military unit multiply the problems of production, of replacement supply, and of spare parts. If the introduction of a new weapon also poses the need for a new and different kind of ammunition, clearly supply problems are further complicated. And herein lay the principal objection of General Ripley; here was the principal basis for his opposition to the acceptance of new weapons. He was sure that the Army already had too many different kinds of weapons in service; moreover, since almost everyone including the President anticipated a short war, Ripley was further convinced that manufacturers seeking contracts for new types of weapons would not be able to deliver before the demand stopped.

Still another consideration was that at the time of the Civil War the Army as yet could see no necessity for an organization whose purpose would be to seek out or encourage useful inventions. On the contrary, under a policy outlined in an 1852 regulation, the War Department required a hopeful inventor first to explain the nature and advantages of his device; then, if the Chief of Ordnance, where appropriate, was convinced that a test would be worthwhile, the

inventor had to furnish the test model. To be granted a hearing at all the inventor had to follow certain set procedures which might cost as much effort as he had put into his design. The entire burden of proof was upon the inventor, and in the end his success depended as much on his personality or connections as upon his technical proficiency. The attitude of the War Department seems to have been that the death of an idea was chiefly the inventor's loss. Screening procedures were more calculated to discourage crackpots than to stimulate any search for improvements. It seems never to have occurred to anyone that requirements might be developed for a specific need and scientists or inventors requested to submit proposals that would fulfill the requirements.

Undoubtedly a part of the difficulty in accepting new weapons and equipment was the very wealth of ideas, good and bad, being offered. Among the hundreds of proposals it was most difficult to know which of them would work out best in the long run, or even would work at all under battle conditions, and also be practicable in wartime production. To ask two or three expert gunmakers, for example, which was the best of several rifles was likely to result in two or three different answers, for what one weapon would gain in simplicity and lightness it might lose in accuracy and range, and preference for one over another depended on what weight each expert might assign to the various desirable characteristics of an ideal weapon. This dilemma emphasized only more strongly the shortcomings of War Department and technical service officers who failed to set up a proper system for considering, testing, and evaluating proposals for new matériel. Worse still, responsible ordnance experts, who did nothing themselves, resented it when someone else—including the President of the United States—took it upon himself to sponsor experiments or tests. Thus did they, after the manner of experts, tyrannize over progress.

Finally, other oblique policies affected the stand-pat-or-draw situation. For example, War Department policy encouraged the manufacture of American iron in order to become independent of foreign sources. As a consequence, the use of steel (the domestic supply of which was small) for making guns was discouraged.

Breechloaders and Repeaters

Probably the greatest controversy concerning weapons that raged during the Civil War (and one that has continued since then) had to do with the failure to use breechloaders, repeating rifles, and carbines more extensively. It has been claimed that Spencer seven-shooters used by Union soldiers during the last year of the war shortened the conflict by months, and that if this weapon, or one similar to it, had been adopted in the beginning the whole course of the war might have been changed.

Congress and various ordnance boards had been seeking a good breechloader for years, but at the outbreak of the war no really satisfactory model was on hand. In the year before the war George W. Morse had begun work at the Harper's Ferry Armory to convert muzzle-loaders to breechloaders, but Morse's defection to the South and the Confederate seizure of the Armory ended that project. Faced with immediate hostilities, the Ordnance Department had no choice but to issue whatever weapons it could find to meet the mobilization requirements of 1861; and few of those weapons were breechloaders. Once the fighting had

begun with muzzle-loaders, General Ripley was cool to any change that might disrupt or complicate problems of production, maintenance, and ammunition supply during the crisis.

Scores of models of breechloaders had been offered to the government for acceptance, but, although many would work well for a time, they were often too complicated and fragile for extensive field use. Moreover, two basic problems had not been solved: fouling of exposed working parts by paper, cloth, and powder, and gas leakage at the breech that not only made the gun dangerous to use but detracted from its fire power. Metallic cartridges, which increased the range and accuracy of the gun as well as its efficiency, and better construction of the gun itself were the answers to most of the difficulties, but when arms makers came up with these answers, critics then turned the very advantages of breech-loading repeaters into disadvantages. First they insisted that in the long run breech-loading actually saved little time. Later, when the breech-loader's rapid-fire superiority had been clearly demonstrated, they objected that the soldier would be tempted to load and fire as rapidly as possible and would thus waste most of his shot and create problems of ammunition supply. The claim that muzzle-loaders were ammunition savers was hardly valid, for in the heat of battle soldiers were given to multiple loading. Of 24,000 loaded muskets and rifles found on the battlefield of Gettysburg, 12,000 had double loads and 6,000 had from three to ten loads each.

Nevertheless, breech-loading repeaters were bound to make an appearance. General Frémont became involved in controversy when he repurchased a lot of Hall carbines for his troops in Missouri at a price over six times as great as that at which the Ordnance Department had disposed of them only a few weeks before the war, but these obsolete breechloaders apparently gave fairly satisfactory service during the first months of the war. The Sharps rifle, already in use for some eight years, showed up well in loading and in firing speed and accuracy during Marine Corps tests in February 1860, even though it still used paper cartridges. With mobilization it was in immediate demand; indeed, members of Col. Hiram Berdan's United States Sharpshooters threatened mutiny when the Ordnance Department delayed an order for them. A series of other breechloaders appeared—the Greene, the Gallagher, the Joslyn, the Ballard. The Ballard, using copper cartridges, was one of the most promising of all. But none of these was widely used.

Samuel W. Marsh developed a method for converting Springfield rifles to breechloaders which so impressed Benet, President Lincoln, and others that in October 1861 Marsh obtained an order for 25,000 of them—over the objections of General Ripley. This was the largest single order for breech-loading rifles during the war, but delays in the War Department when Stanton took over and the threat of a suit for patent infringement by the Joslyn Arms Company were fatal to the precarious financial backing of Marsh's Union Firearms Company, and he never was able to deliver. B. Tyler Henry went into production with his new fifteen-shot repeating rifle, using his .44-caliber rim-fire cartridge, under an inside contracting arrangement with the New Haven Arms Company (predecessor of the Winchester Repeating Arms Company). He was unable to get a sizable government order, but purchases by states and individuals brought perhaps 10,000 Henry repeaters into Civil War service.

The man who at last combined a forceful personality, salesmanship, and official connections with an excellent new weapon in the way essential to success was Christopher Spencer. He put enough seven-shot repeating rifles and carbines—the "seven-forked lightning"—into the hands of Union soldiers to make a deep imprint on the war. Many agreed that his were the finest rifles and carbines used during the war, though certainly other good weapons were offered. It was as important that he was also the best arms salesman then in business. Even if the Spencer was the best weapon available, it probably would have been no more significant in the war than any of a dozen others if Spencer had not first of all persevered at selling it until he won acceptance, and secondly, if he had not been able to deliver on the orders. Anything less would have been to no avail under the conditions in the War Department in the 1860's. Spencer had obtained a patent for his rifle a few months before Henry's patent was granted. Like the Henry, the Spencer used a special rim-fire metallic cartridge, though of larger caliber (.52). While the Henry magazine lay beneath the barrel, the magazine of the Spencer was concealed in the stock. The Spencer gun proved to be rather more dependable than the Henry for field service, and regiments equipped with Spencer seven-shot repeating carbines and rifles were important elements in Union successes in the Wilderness and in the dramatic victories of Sheridan's cavalry.

Spencer was ready to produce his repeating rifles when the Civil War began, but he was in for a long struggle to overcome the resistance of the Army Ordnance Department. His associate, Charles Cheney, was a friend of Secretary of the Navy Gideon Welles. This, together with the fact that the Navy as a whole was more receptive to new ideas than was the Army, and furthermore did not have the same worry about ammunition supply as did ground forces, led to the Navy's placing the first order for 700 Spencer rifles and carbines in June 1861, and eventually to the organization of the Spencer Rifle Manufacturing Company. At first Spencer was unable even to arrange for tests with Army Ordnance. In time, through the combined influence of Secretary Welles and James G. Blaine—then Speaker of the Maine House of Representatives, but already acquiring influence in national politics—plus a direct appeal to President Lincoln, the Spencer company in December 1861 obtained an order from the War Department for 10,000 repeaters. Even so, this was only a temporary victory, won at a time when weapons of almost every description were being purchased.

Early in 1863 Spencer set out on a long trip to demonstrate his weapon to the Army of the Cumberland and the Army of the West. Nearly everywhere he went officers and men were enthusiastic; but they were frustrated by the Ordnance Department. In August 1863 Spencer was able to arrange a meeting with Lincoln during which the President himself tested the repeater and was greatly impressed with it. At last, with battle testing and Presidential testing confirming the advantage of the Spencer repeater, and with the appointment of General Ramsay to succeed General Ripley as Chief of Ordnance, orders for the Spencer firearms began to increase. Most of the orders were for carbines for the cavalry which even General Ripley had conceded might be of value; there still was no general

move to arm the infantry with repeating rifles until 1864. During the war the Federal Government purchased something over 12,400 Spencer rifles, about 94,200 Spencer carbines (mostly during the last year of the war) and 58,238,000 Spencer cartridges from the Spencer company. In addition, 30,000 Spencers were made by the Burnside Rifle Company. Direct sales to soldiers, private organizations, and the states brought the total number of Spencer seven-shooters used in the war to about 200,000.

The Spencer seven-shooter probably was the greatest advantage in weapons that the North had over the South, for the Confederates never were able to develop a really satisfactory repeater and were unable to provide the special ammunition needed for the few that they captured. In fact, because of the lack of special ammunition Confederate soldiers were forbidden by general order to exchange their own muskets for Yankee repeaters when the latter were found on the battlefield.

After the initial impact of mobilization, and after General Ripley had left the Ordnance Department, the Army gave a little more attention to the development of improved weapons. By the end of 1864 General Dyer, then Chief of Ordnance, was convinced that the experience of the war had demonstrated the superiority of breechloaders for infantry as well as cavalry. A board made up of ordnance, cavalry, and infantry officers met at Springfield Armory in January 1865 to determine the best breechloaders and repeaters for general adoption. The board was willing to consider any type of breech-loading weapon whatever its caliber and weight. With the conclusion of the war, however, the President recommended that the old Springfield rifle muskets be converted to breechloaders and that no new weapon be adopted until further experience had demonstrated conclusively which was the best. The Army as a whole was not supplied with breechloaders until 1869, when the cavalry was issued Spencer and Sharps carbines, and the infantry and other troops converted Springfields.

Machine Guns

Proposals for machine guns represented even bolder advances than those for repeating rifles, and encountered much the same kind of opposition in the Ordnance Department. However, the machine gun did have some points in its favor toward obtaining a hearing. First of all, the machine gun was offered as a supplementary, not a replacement, weapon. That is to say, no tried and proved weapon had to be given up in order to adopt it. Furthermore, ammunition could be transported on the carriage with the gun so that the supply problem was not quite the same as that for the weapon of the individual soldier.

In 1861 Ezra Ripley patented a lightweight, breech-loading, multibarrel machine gun that incorporated such features as rate-of-fire control and safety factor in that the weapon could not be fired before the breech was locked. The Ripley gun fell victim to the resistance to change in the Ordnance Department and was not manufactured. Another machine gun, invented by Wilson Ager, was cautiously considered for purchase by the War Department in 1861. Known as the "coffee mill" gun, it was a crank-operated, single barrel, revolver-type weapon deriving its nickname from the hopper feed on its top.

The Gatling gun, most successful and most noted of the Civil War machine guns, worked on the long-known principle of revolving barrels, and combined the crank-operated, gravity feed mechanism of the coffee mill gun and the multibarrel arrangement of the Ripley gun. Dr. Richard J. Gatling demonstrated a working model before thousands of spectators at Indianapolis in 1862. Governor Oliver P. Morton of Indiana was quick to see some of the possibilities of the Gatling gun, and he urged the War Department to test it. Gatling made arrangements for the manufacture of his gun in Cincinnati; unfortunately, however, the factory burned, and it was some time before another Cincinnati firm was able to turn out twelve of his early models. The first Gatlings used paper cartridges, but the inventor very soon modified his 1862 model to take copper-cased rim-fire ammunition. As might be expected, General Ripley refused even to consider the new weapon. The Gatling gun did have a battle test, however, thanks to the one officer who always seemed willing to try anything new— Maj. Gen. Benjamin F. Butler. Not knowing of Ripley's earlier reaction, Butler ordered twelve guns and 12,000 cartridges at a total cost of $12,000; some of these guns saw service at the siege of Petersburg. This weapon was good enough for adoption by the Navy, but again the Army was more cautious.

Gatling continued to improve upon his machine gun until in 1865 he produced a model in which the objectionable features of earlier models had been virtually eliminated. After another year of testing, the Army at last officially adopted the gun in August 1866. By that time what possibly had been an additional obstacle to accepting the Gatling—the suspicion of disloyalty to the Union on the part of the southern-

GATLING GUN

born inventor—had been removed, and since the machine gun no longer was needed for combat, there was no serious objection to adopting it. But even the advocates of the weapon had failed so far to recognize its potential as an infantry weapon; they still looked upon it as an auxiliary to artillery or simply as a weapon for the defense of bridges, and even though adopted, the machine gun had little actual use in the American Army for several decades. With machine guns as with other weapons, Americans would gain credit for the invention, but other nations would take advantage of their use. While Germany would gain a reputation for building tomorrow's weapons today, the United States frequently would be content to build yesterday's weapons tomorrow.

Cannon

Just as private industry was responsible for developing most of the significant improvements in small arms during the Civil War period, so it was with heavy ordnance, for the Army depended entirely on private foundries for its artillery. Having little to fear from competition, and with little urging from the Chief of Ordnance, the West Point Foundry, principal producer of heavy ordnance for the Union, took the lead in two notable improvements. First, it applied the process devised by Maj. Thomas J. Rodman for casting guns on a hollow core and then cooling from the inside. This process added considerable strength to the Dahlgren gun, and in 1860 and 1861 guns of this type were being set up for coastal defense. Then came the Parrott rifle, developed by the director of the West Point Foundry. Parrott found that it was possible to add great strength to the breech of the gun—and so to its power and range—by encasing it with coiled wrought-iron hoops mounted red hot and then shrunk to a tight fit by cooling. Some of these guns were of tremendous size and strength—the "Swamp Angel" was a Parrott that hurled 200-pound shells 7,000 yards into Charleston; one 4.2-inch (30-pounder) Parrott fired 4,605 rounds before it burst. The United States impressed the world with the size of the guns it made—the cast-iron Rodman and Parrott guns probably were as good as any cast-iron cannon to be found anywhere—but little progress had been made with wrought iron or steel. The Ames Company did make some wrought-iron guns; when well made, they were stronger than the Rodman cast-iron guns, but they were far more expensive, and their quality varied so much as to make them unreliable. A number of breech-loading cannon were made, but they did not come into general use. Rodman also began a fundamental improvement in artillery ammunition by compressing powder into perforated discs, fitting the bore of the gun, for slower, progressive burning.

The Telegraph

By the time the Civil War began, the electric telegraph already had been amply demonstrated as an effective instrument for instantaneous communication over long distances, but its development had been almost entirely commercial. The telegraph had been used as long ago as the Mexican War to place orders for equipment and supplies and for the mobilization of forces. But as yet it had not significantly affected tactical operations in the field. General McClellan used it first in his campaign in western Virginia in June 1861. The Signal Corps developed standard sets of portable equipment which included twenty miles of insulated wire on reels that could be laid as fast as a man could walk. For more permanent lines, signal officers designed standard twelve-foot ashen poles fitted with insulators; 400 of these poles, together with ten miles of wire and batteries, were carried on each telegraph wagon. It was believed that ten miles of this wire could be strung, overhead, in four hours. The telegraph operators, often boys in their teens, were in the United States Military Telegraph, which, for all practical purposes, was under the Secretary of War. One year after McClellan's first use of the military telegraph, over 3,500 miles of land and submarine military lines were in operation. These lines increased by another 1,755 miles in the next year, and messages, varying in length from 10 to 1,000 words, were being sent at the rate of 3,300 a day. By the end of the war, some 15,000 miles of military lines had been constructed and were in operation.

The Observation Balloon

Another expedient whose potential value had been much increased by the development of the telegraph was the observation balloon. In June 1861 Thaddeus Lowe demonstrated to the satisfaction of Joseph Henry, superintendent of the Smithsonian Institution, a practical observation balloon. Henry was so impressed that he took Lowe directly to President Lincoln who, after seeing the device demonstrated, took the young aeronaut directly to General Scott to insist that something be done. A rival of Lowe's, John La Mountain, managed to be the first to make a really successful aerial observation with American forces on 31 July 1861 near Fortress Monroe. Ascending to an altitude of about 1,400 feet, La Mountain was able to see for about thirty miles around; he introduced the method of estimating the size of enemy forces by counting their tents and huts from the air. Lowe, however, won out as Chief Aeronaut of the Army of the Potomac, and with the support of McClellan improved and expanded his service. In 1862 he had six silk balloons, with portable gas-generating apparatus (depending on sulphuric acid and iron) capable of inflating a balloon in three hours sufficiently to lift two men to an altitude of 1,000 feet. Even so, aviation really did not catch on during the war, and its use was confined almost entirely to the Army of the Potomac. General McClellan sent balloon units to the Departments of the South and the Missouri, but both commanders were quite indifferent. Officers willing to send regiments after a piece of high ground that afforded good observation were unimpressed by a contrivance that put at their command an observation post on almost permanent call. After McClellan's departure, interest declined even in the

A RODMAN GUN OF BATTERY RODGERS, *emplaced on a bank of the Potomac River near Alexandria, Virginia, to prevent the Confederate fleet from approaching Washington.*

Army of the Potomac. Want of support to provide the equipment he needed, the uncertain organization of his corps, and the lack of trained observers caused Lowe to quit his post in 1863. Much to the surprise and relief of the Confederates, aerial observation was abandoned altogether shortly thereafter.

Summary

Although weapons improvements introduced during the Civil War were notable, the number rejected or never put to full use was depressing to men of imagination.

It may be that success in the Mexican War had made officers reluctant to give up weapons which had brought victory; at any rate, the conservatism of the Army was greater than that of the Navy. More important in the limited use made of inventions was the unsatisfactory machinery for screening—or encouraging—new ideas, and the difficulty of ferreting out the valuable discoveries from among the hundreds of fantastic ideas continually being offered. Most important of all, perhaps, were production problems and the secondary logistical problems created by adoption of new weapons

A TELEGRAPH FIELD STATION

and equipment—the loss of production at a critical time involved in changing a model during wartime, the difficulties of supplying spare parts and maintaining many different models, the problem of supplying special kinds of ammunition. All these difficulties suggested the need for a well-ordered peacetime research and development program so that improvements could be encouraged, and production models changed where indicated before a crisis intervened. But that would not be for yet another generation. The old saying that an army enters one war with the weapons with which it finished the last would be very nearly true for American forces for most of the next century. Still, new weapons and new equipment made a significant impact on Civil War operations. Certainly the use of the Spencer repeating rifles and carbines, improved artillery, and the military telegraph all redounded to the considerable advantage of the North.

CHAPTER XIV

Railroads and Inland Waterways

Railroads and rivers alike favored the North, so that the transportation system completed the pattern of general logistical advantages that the North enjoyed over the South throughout the Civil War. More often than not transportation is at the very heart of logistical efforts. Occasions when industrial capacity, or the procurement program, or the availability of raw materials determines the extent of the total logistical effort probably are less common than those when transportation is the limiting factor. In the Civil War, all these factors limited rather strictly what the South could do, but the logistical limitations of the South were nowhere more evident than in the transportation system. In the rapid expansion of railways during the decade preceding the war, the South had fallen far behind in the development of the facilities which went so far to make the Civil War truly the first modern war. Never had railroads played such a significant role in the conduct of war. That role was significant in the South as well as in the North, but the disparity between the sections was great enough to more than counterbalance whatever advantage the Confederacy might have had of moving on interior lines. Indeed it might be said that superior transportation actually gave to the North the advantage of interior lines— important not simply for shifting forces, but for mobilizing and supporting superior forces of all kinds. Total railway mileage in the Confederate States at the outbreak of the war was less than half that in the states of the Union; moreover, most of that mileage linked port cities with cotton-producing areas, running generally north and south in the western states, and providing no adequate connections in the east between Virginia and the Deep South. Northern railroads, on the contrary, accommodated traffic in practically all directions. One of the best-equipped and best-operated lines in the country—the Baltimore and Ohio— lay entirely within slave territory and would have been of immense value to the South, but it remained, except for some slight local interruptions, in the service of the North throughout the war.

Railroad Transportation

Secretary of War Cameron's first actions in arranging for the mobilization of troops called for in Lincoln's proclamation of 15 April 1861 assumed the use of railroads to concentrate and move men to Washington and other areas where needed. Cameron saw at once the necessity of government coordination, and he turned to railroad men to do this job for the government. But, possibly influenced by personal interests, the Secretary of War tended always to favor the Pennsylvania Railroad over its great competitor in east-west traffic, the Baltimore and Ohio. As his personal representative in co-ordinating rail transportation of troops and supplies to Washington, Cameron called in the capable president of the Pennsylvania, J. Edgar Thomson. He then appointed Thomas A. Scott, vice president of the Pennsylvania, to co-ordinate the transfer of men and supplies between the Pennsylvania and the Northern Central at Harrisburg, Pennsylvania. As assistant to Thomson he appointed Samuel M. Felton, president of the Philadelphia, Wilmington and Baltimore. No one questioned the abilities of these men, nor the logic of their choice, but notably absent from the circle of advisers was John W. Garrett, the president of the Baltimore and Ohio. Garrett's co-operation was essential, because all traffic for Washington funneled through Baltimore and was dependent upon the Washington branch of the B&O for moving from Baltimore to the capital. After Stanton became Secretary of War he established cordial relations with Garrett, and thereafter the great advantages of access to the lines of the B&O were put to better use. Scott's authority was considerably broadened when he was appointed on 23 May 1862 to be in charge of all government railways and telegraphs, or those that might be appropriated for government use. All instructions regarding railway transportation were to come from Scott's office, making him virtually an assistant secretary of war (in August his appointment to that status was made official).

A special transportation and telegraph office, established at the urging of Scott, foreshadowed the later separate and autonomous transportation corps. During the Civil War general direction of transportation remained with the Quartermaster General, but separate bureaus, still under his jurisdiction, were established for railway transportation and for telegraphs.

Railroad Rates

The official policy (after January 1862) was that no railroads were to charge the government more than was charged private individuals for the same purposes. Early in the war the Illinois Central offered the use of its roadway free of charge and the use of its rolling stock at rates to be adjusted in the future, and as a result the government made an arrangement for rates one-third less than those usually charged. But this kind of altruistic sentiment did not become general. A schedule of rates issued by the War Department in July 1861 allowed unnecessarily high rates. Paying local rates for long haul, the government was paying one-third more than private parties. The point was reached where regimental officers were able to play off one company against another, and to make arrangements for moving their units with the company that offered the biggest "kickback."

Excessive profits made by the railroad companies under Scott's ill-advised 1861 rate schedule incurred strong protests from congressmen and government officials, and early in 1862 Secretary of War Stanton called a convention of railroad managers to meet in Washington. A result of the convention was the recommendation that supplies be divided into four classes for the purpose of establishing transportation rates. New rates on this basis went into effect on 3 March 1862. As adopted by the Quartermaster General the first class of supplies included such items as drums, haversacks, camp kettles and mess pans, furniture, clothing, and powder in barrels or secure packages; the second class included small arms, wagons, mounted guns and caissons, medicines, coffee, tea, harness, and horses, cattle, and mules; the third class included fixed ammunition, Sibley stoves, and tools; the fourth class was comprised of such things as unmounted artillery, cannon balls and shells, horseshoes, lumber, nuts, bolts, washers, nails, spikes, wire, rope, and rations and forage. Rates for short hauls varied from five cents per ton-mile for first class supplies to four cents per ton-mile for fourth class supplies; for longer hauls they ranged from three cents per ton-mile for first class to one and three-fourths cents per ton-mile for fourth class. The regulations stipulated that the military tariff should be ten percent below the printed freight tariffs of the various companies in force at the time of the service except that no charge exceeding the stated maximum limits would be allowed.[1]

Government Control

As a means of persuading reluctant railroad owners to carry government business, and to clarify the authority of the President (if needed), in January 1862 Congress passed an act authorizing the President to seize any or all of the railroad lines in the United States and to make them and their officers, agents, and employees a part of the Military Establishment of the United States. On 11 February Daniel C. McCallum was commissioned a colonel and "appointed military director and superintendent of railroads in the United States, with authority to enter upon, take possession of, hold, and use all railroads, engines, cars, locomotives, equipments, appendages, and appurtenances that may be required for the transport of troops, arms, ammunition, and military supplies of the United States, and to do and perform all acts and things that may be necessary and proper to be done for the safe and speedy transport aforesaid." [2]

On 25 May 1862 Lincoln formally took military possession of all railroads in the United States; the main substance of the order lay in its injunction to railroad companies to hold themselves ready to transport troops and ammunition, to the exclusion of all other business. Actual operation remained in the hands of the company. Government seizure was implemented in the North only for the operation of short lines near Gettysburg at the time of the campaign in that area; for the operation of the Philadelphia and Reading Railroad during a strike of miners employed by that company; and for the operation of lines participating in the transfer of Eleventh and Twelfth Corps to the Chattanooga area. Otherwise lines operated by United States Military Railroads were confined to those captured or constructed in the war zones and put to use in support of the field armies. It was very largely the Military Railroads, with the benefit of the initiative and leadership of McCallum, that brought to the Civil War the first significant use of railroads on a large scale to supply armies in the field. With an organization that reached a total of nearly 25,000 men at one time (trainmen, dispatchers, and superintendents were civilian employees of the government), United

---

[1] *Official Records,* ser. iii, II, 838–41. Material in this paragraph is contained in items 9, 10, and 11 of papers accompanying the report of the Quartermaster General to the Secretary of War dated 18 November 1862. Item 9 (letter from Scott to Sibley, 12 July 1861) appears in tabular format in *Official Records,* ser. iii, I, 325–26. Item 10, Report of the Committee, sets forth classifications of matériel. Item 11 states the regulations as adopted on recommendation of the convention. This classification of supplies evidently was the forerunner of the supply classification system later adopted in the Army.

[2] Rpt, Brig Gen D. C. McCallum to Maj Gen M. C Meigs, QMG, 26 May 1866, *Official Records,* ser. iii, V, 974–1005.

States Military Railroads by the end of the war had operated over 2,100 miles of railways with a total of 419 engines and 6,330 cars. It laid or relaid 641 miles of track, built or rebuilt 137,418 feet of bridges, and showed total expenditures of approximately $42,462,000 and receipts of about $12,624,000.[3] (*Map 8*)

Construction

One of the keys to the successful operation of the Military Railroads was the rapid laying of track and construction of bridges. Yankee builders had demonstrated something of their aptitude for railroad construction in the restoration of the Annapolis and Baltimore lines, which had been destroyed in April 1861 to prevent hostile troop movements. But the real miracles of construction awaited the arrival of Hermann Haupt, an engineering genius who had graduated from West Point, had been professor of mathematics and engineering at Gettysburg, had later served as general superintendent and chief engineer of the Pennsylvania Railroad, and since 1856 had been engaged in constructing the Hoosac Tunnel in Massachusetts. Appointed aide-de-camp on the staff of General McDowell with the rank of colonel in April 1862, Haupt immediately faced a task which to a lesser man would have appeared patently impossible—reconstruction of the Richmond, Fredericksburg and Potomac Railroad, including major bridges over Ackakeek Creek and Potomac Creek, for the support of the Army of the Rappahannock. Less than a month after his first talk with General McDowell, Haupt had the job done. Working through rain and mud and darkness, crews of untrained soldiers restored the roadbed and laid the first three miles of track in three days. In fifteen hours they built a bridge 150 feet long and 30 feet high across Ackakeek Creek. Then came the most formidable part of the task—the bridging of the 400-foot chasm of Potomac Creek. For this job Haupt organized his workers into seventeen squads, varying in size from eight to fifty-seven men according to their missions, and assigned specific duties to each squad—cutting timbers, loading trucks, clearing roads, driving ox teams, framing and carrying timber to the bank, putting trestles together, moving out sliding beams and putting ties in place, and all the other tasks that had to be done. It had taken a year to build the permanent bridge now destroyed. Haupt and his men cut the equivalent of about 2.5 million board feet of timber, built log cribbing for foundations and erected thereon three stories of trestles rising to 80 feet above the water, and had the bridge finished in twelve days. Meanwhile Daniel Stone, a civilian engineer, supervised the construction of a 600-foot bridge across the Rappahannock. All was finished in time to support the movement of the army, although by then the military situation had changed to make the planned advance against Richmond impractical. For his achievement, on 28 May Haupt was formally appointed Chief of Construction and Transportation in the Department of the Rappahannock. On 5 September he became a brigadier general.

For transporting supplies on the military railroads in Virginia, General Haupt established these priorities: (1) subsistence for men in the field; (2) forage for horses; (3) ammunition; and (4) hospital supplies. If these were taken care of, then infantry regiments might be transported.

---

[3] *Ibid.*, pp. 1003–1005.

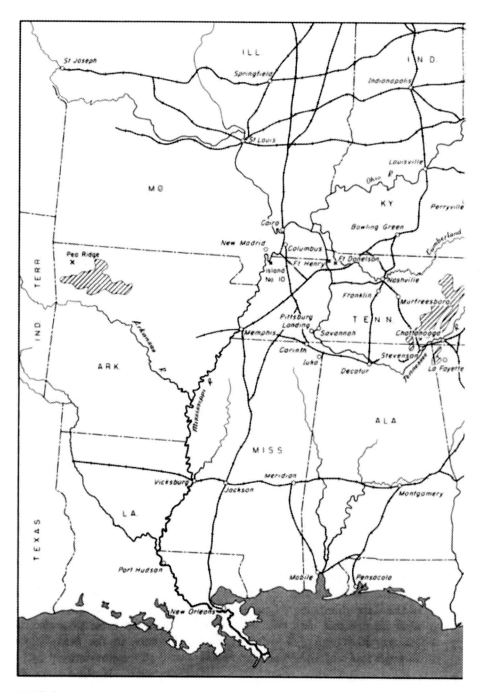

MAP 8

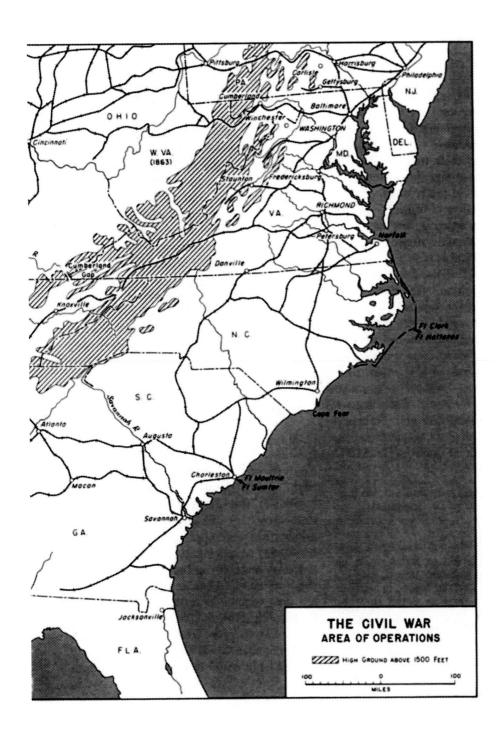

THE CIVIL WAR
AREA OF OPERATIONS

///// High Ground above 1500 Feet

100   0   100
MILES

Operation

Haupt insisted on running trains on schedule. Under the pressure of business and the demand of impatient military officers, railroads being used for military purposes frequently abandoned their schedules and resorted to exclusive use of telegraph orders for running their trains, which, of course, invited chaos any time telegraphic communications were interrupted. Other abuses delayed the flow of supplies. When supplies were forwarded to an advanced terminus before they were needed, the cars were not unloaded and so blocked the track; moreover, the supplies stood in danger of capture in case of retreat. The worst abuse of all perhaps was the failure to get cars unloaded and returned promptly. Frequently trains would be unloaded a car at a time when a sufficient crew should have been provided to unload the whole train at once. Moreover, forward units sometimes retained cars for weeks as storehouses.

As Chief of Construction and Transportation in the Division of the Rappahannock, Haupt issued a general order in June 1862 stating:

No officer, no surgeon or assistant, no paymaster, quartermaster, or commissary, no person, civil or military, whatever his rank or position, shall have the right to detain a train or order it to run in advance of schedule time. If cars are not unloaded or trains made up when the hour of starting arrives, engines must proceed with parts of trains, or without trains, and all the facts in detail must be reported in writing by the conductor, to be laid before the chief of transportation or the commanding general of the department.[4]

Quartermaster General Meigs backed up this order in October with a general circular saying: "Trains should not on any account be detained beyond their regular time of starting. It is better to furnish extra trains should the exigencies of the service demand them, rather than cause delay to the regular scheduled trains."[5] The Quartermaster General also inveighed against forwarding supplies to advanced terminals until they were really needed and against the detention of cars for use as storehouses. It had become clear to General Meigs that the surest way to create congestion at the front and shortages of cars at the rear was to let cars stand unloaded and to put freight in cars that could not be promptly unloaded. Yet that lesson seemed to be difficult to put across, for the Quartermaster General found it necessary to repeat the order several times, and in 1864 Secretary Stanton himself issued such an order twice.

Rail Support at Antietam

Antietam provided an early opportunity for a demonstration of the usefulness of railroads in emergency supply. When on the night of that great battle (16–17 September 1862), the Chief of Ordnance received urgent messages from General McClellan asking that a resupply of ammunition be forwarded as quickly as possible for the expected renewal of combat the next morning, the reaction was swift and decisive. Assistant Secretary of War Watson telegraphed the president of the Baltimore and Ohio asking him to make arrangements for a special train that "must be run as fast as any express train could be run." At midnight

---

[4] GO, Military Railroads, Division of the Rappahannock, 2 June 1862, *Official Records,* ser. iii, II. 102–03.

[5] Cir, 1 October 1862, *Official Records,* ser. iii, II. 625.

THE POTOMAC CREEK BRIDGE

Watson wired Scott, who had left the War Department on 1 June 1862 to return to his post with the Pennsylvania Railroad at Harrisburg, asking him to give personal attention to expediting the passage of the special train, and Secretary Stanton himself sent a telegram "To the officers, or any of them, of the Northern Central Railroad, Pennsylvania Central Railroad, and Cumberland Valley Railroad, at Harrisburg," urging all possible speed in getting the train through. Arriving at Baltimore at 0657, the ammunition train traveled over the Northern Central tracks to Harrisburg where it was delivered to the Cumberland Valley at 1020 and rushed on to Hagerstown, Maryland.

A second, duplicating, train then went directly to Frederick, Maryland, via the Baltimore and Ohio. Neither army was prepared to renew the attack on the 18th, but the ammunition was there for the Army of the Potomac if it had been needed. By this time congestion on both lines serving McClellan's army was strangling supply deliveries. General Haupt arrived at Hagerstown on 19 September, where he immediately set to work untangling a traffic jam of five or six trains. Then he rode over to Frederick where he found some 200 loaded cars standing on the B&O sidings at Monocacy, some of which had been there nearly a week; to get them unloaded and the cars returned, Haupt asked General Wool, then commanding the Middle Department, to assign one of his staff officers to supervise the job. This would suggest that with a little better organization McClellan could have had the means at hand to renew the attack for a decisive victory.[6]

Gettysburg

The Union victory in the Gettysburg campaign can, in great part, be ascribed to the effective use of the railroads to bring up supplies and men. In all the discussions of reasons for the Confederate failure in that decisive engagement, far too little attention has been given to the logistical advantage which federal forces enjoyed by virtue of rail supply. At the end of the three-day battle (1–3 July 1863), Confederate units were seriously short of ammunition as well as other supplies, and they did not have transportation available for rapid and continuous replenishment. Levels of supply in the Army of the Potomac, on the other hand, would have permitted a continuation of the battle for days longer. Even if the Confederate Army had been able to avoid the tactical errors attributed to it, and somehow had gained the victory at Gettysburg, it is very unlikely that it would have been able to sustain the campaign necessary for a really decisive vic-

tory over the Union Army. Certainly the efforts of General Haupt and his assistants in getting the railroads into operation to serve the Gettysburg battle area were as dramatic and as significant as, for instance, the race for little Round Top, or any of the other oft-related tactical episodes of the battle.

Arriving in Baltimore on the evening of 1 July, General Haupt had quickly set about organizing railway transportation to support the Army of the Potomac. Since Confederate cavalry had burned bridges on the Northern Central and the Hanover Railroad between Baltimore and Gettysburg and Littletown, Pennsylvania, and since the wagon haul from Frederick would be too great to make use of the Baltimore and Ohio practical, Haupt determined to use the nearest rail approach then open—the twenty-nine-mile-long line of the Western Maryland from Baltimore to Westminster, Maryland, about ten miles south of Littletown. This poorly kept single-track road had no telegraph, no water stations, no sidings or turntables, and had wood enough for only three or four trains a day. Haupt decided, however, that the road would have to be made to do for thirty trains a day. He sent for Adna Anderson, chief of construction, to come from Alexandria with a crew of 400 railroad men and a train of split wood, lanterns, buckets, and other essential items. Other trains brought in iron and more men, and rolling stock began to assemble in the Baltimore yards where quartermaster crews began loading supply trains.

To overcome the handicap of having no telegraph, and no sidings where trains might pass, Haupt set up a system to run trains in convoys of five each at intervals of eight hours. Brig. Gen. Rufus Ingalls, quarter-

[6] Ltr, Stanton to Officers of Railroads, 17 September 1862; Ltr, P. H. Watson to T. A. Scott, 17 September 1862, Official Records, ser. i, XIX, pt. II, 313–14; Kenneth P Williams, Lincoln Finds A General, A Military Study of the Civil War, 3 vols. (New York: The Macmillan Co., 1952), II, 458–60, 467–68; George E. Turner, Victory Rode the Rails; The Strategic Place of the Railroads in the Civil War (Indianapolis, Ind: Bobbs-Merrill Co., 1953), pp. 210–14; Ltr, Haupt to Halleck, 27 September 1862, in Hermann Haupt, Reminiscences of General Hermann Haupt . . . (Milwaukee, Wis.: Wright & Joys Co., 1901), pp. 139–43.

master of the Army of the Potomac, was to see that all cars were unloaded promptly at the railhead at Westminster—unloading time was the limiting factor on the quantity of supplies that could be delivered. For the return to Baltimore the trains ran backward. As soon as one convoy cleared the track, the next left. Crews filled the water tanks from streams along the way with the buckets brought from Alexandria for the purpose. By 3 July supplies were arriving at the Westminster railhead at the rate of 15,000 tons a day, and the returning trains were evacuating from 2,000 to 4,000 casualties daily to Baltimore. Meanwhile Haupt had lost no time in putting other crews to work to open the Northern Central to Hanover Junction and the Hanover Railroad from that point toward Gettysburg. By the afternoon of 4 July bridges and tracks had been restored to open this route as far as Littletown, and trains were bringing out additional thousands of casualties from that point. That night construction men worked through darkness and rain to complete the last bridge on the road to Gettysburg. The Army of the Potomac had more supplies than it could carry when it prepared to move. Under Haupt and Anderson the U.S. Military Railroads were able to support the Army of the Potomac by the inadequate Western Maryland Railroad in a way that the Confederacy had never been able to support Lee's Army over the Richmond, Fredericksburg and Potomac during the months Lee's army spent near Fredericksburg.

Support of Sherman's Atlanta Campaign

Probably the greatest achievement in supplying armies in the field by railroad during the war was the support of Sherman's Atlanta campaign in 1864. Recognizing fully his complete dependence on rail transportation, Sherman issued an order that trains on his supply lines would be used only for moving military personnel and supplies. When violent protests by sutlers, merchants, newspaper men, and Tennessee loyalists led President Lincoln to suggest that the order be modified, Sherman stood firm. From Nashville southward trains operated in convoys of four ten-car trains running at speeds of about ten miles an hour. Four such convoys each day provided a capacity of 1,600 tons, enough to allow for frequent accidents and still meet the army's requirements. General Sherman himself explained:

That single stem of railroad, four hundred and seventy-three miles long, supplied an army of one hundred thousand men and thirty-five thousand animals for the period of one hundred and ninety-six days, viz., from May 1 to November 12, 1864. To have delivered regularly that amount of food and forage by ordinary wagons would have required thirty-six thousand eight hundred wagons of six mules each, allowing each wagon to have hauled two tons twenty miles each day, a simple impossibility in roads such as then existed in that region of country. Therefore, I reiterate that the Atlanta campaign was an impossibility without these railroads.[7]

Troop Movements by Rail

Rail transportation of troops was a different problem. Administrative moves were common from the outset; indeed, for a time this seems to have been assumed to be the principal use of railroads during the war. It was in troop mobilization—the unprece-

---

[7] William Tecumseh Sherman, *Memoirs of William T. Sherman*, 2 vols., 4th ed. (New York: Webster and Co., 1891), II, 399.

A MILITARY TRAIN WITH A MORTAR MOUNTED ON A FLATCAR

dented and rapid concentration of large forces at Washington and at other centers—that the railroads made their first great impact on the war. It was possible to travel all the way from Indianapolis to Philadelphia at that time without changing cars, but in travel between most distant points several changes were necessary from a railroad of one gauge to another company's line of a different gauge. A fortunate unit might find passenger cars assigned to it; however, cattle cars were commonly used for troop travel. Boxcars of the United States Military Railroads had a rated capacity of "10 tons or 40 men."[8] The ordinary rate paid for the transportation of troop units was two cents per man per mile, with a baggage allowance of eighty pounds for each man. A general order of October 1861 required an agreement in transportation contracts stating that trains passing through disaffected parts of the country must stop at bridges to permit troops to alight and pass over on foot.

---

[8] Thomas Weber, *The Northern Railroads in the Civil War, 1861–1865* (New York: King's Crown Press, 1952), p. 285n.

Transfer of Eleventh and Twelfth Corps to Chattanooga

Undoubtedly the most dramatic troop movement by rail of the war was the transfer of the Eleventh and Twelfth Army Corps, under Maj. Gen. Joseph Hooker, from the Army of the Potomac in Virginia to the Army of the Cumberland at Chattanooga in the autumn of 1863.

The staff work and direction of the movement were left largely in civilian rather than military hands, but in the execution there was close co-operation all the way between civilian railroad men and military officers. It was agreed that McCallum should have charge of the original loadings and transportation to Washington. Garrett, with the assistance of William Smith, would supervise the movement from Washington to Jeffersonville, Indiana. Scott, now back at his duties as vice president of the Pennsylvania, with the assistance of John B. Anderson at Louisville, Frank Thomson at Nashville, and Quartermaster General Meigs at Chattanooga, would take charge of the transport south of the Ohio to its final destination. President Lincoln authorized General Hooker to take military possession of any railroads and equipment necessary for the operation, and General Meade was ordered to have the troops ready to leave promptly as soon as cars were available. Each man was to carry five days' cooked rations. Artillery units were to carry 200 rounds of ammunition; infantry units were to carry forty rounds of ammunition per man. Camp equipment and medical supplies would be held to a minimum. Cars loaded with five days' forage for artillery horses were to join trains at Alexandria. The B&O furnished most of the rolling stock for the first leg of

the move; the Northern Central, the Philadelphia, Wilmington, and Baltimore, and the U.S. Military Railroads in Virginia provided additional cars.

By the afternoon of 25 September the first trains carrying elements of the Eleventh Corps were passing through Washington. Others followed in an almost continuous stream for seventy-two hours. The first train arrived at Benwood on the West Virginia bank of the Ohio River at 1100 on 27 September. Garrett had seen that low water would make use of the ferry steamer impractical, and had ordered the construction of a ponton bridge (built in less than two days). By 28 September, when the last trains were loaded in Virginia, the first trains were passing beyond Columbus, Ohio. Something of a bottleneck developed at Indianapolis where troops were marched about a mile to the Soldier's Home to be fed, and then marched over to the tracks of the Indianapolis and Jeffersonville Railroad. From Jeffersonville the men crossed the Ohio River by ferry steamer to Louisville, Kentucky, where Scott and his assistants had concentrated locomotives and cars of five-foot gauge for the last leg of the move. It took about one and one-half hours at Louisville for the men to draw rations and load their trains. Late in the evening of 30 September the first four trains arrived at Bridgeport, Alabama, just five days after entraining at Culpeper Courthouse. Most of Hooker's force arrived within nine days after the departure of the first train. Although original plans and preparations had anticipated the movement of 15,000 men, the total actually turned out to be 23,300. By 8 October, less than two weeks after the midnight conference where the plan was first agreed upon, the troop movement was complete. Another stream of trains then brought up the impedimenta. At Indianapolis new track was laid to permit the transfer of loads directly between cars. Transfer of unit wagons, animals, and other supplies and equipment took about one week.

The transfer of the Eleventh and Twelfth Corps from the Rappahannock to the Tennessee reoriented military thinking on the use of the railroads. The Confederates already had transferred Longstreet's corps by rail from the Army of Northern Virginia to join Bragg's Army of Tennessee in time to play a significant part in the Battle of Chickamauga. Moving twice as many men considerably farther in less time, the Yankees demonstrated decisively the advantage of Northern transportation over Southern interior lines. However valiant their efforts, the ingenuity of the Confederates could not make up for their overtaxed and war-torn railways.

Movement of Twenty-third Corps

The only other comparable troop movement of the war was the transfer early in 1865 of Maj. Gen. John M. Schofield's Twenty-third Corps (15,000 men) from Clifton in southwestern Tennessee to the Cape Fear area of North Carolina on the Atlantic coast. The corps moved by river boats up the Tennessee River to the Ohio River, then up the Ohio to Cincinnati, by railroad to Washington, and in coastal vessels down the Potomac River and the Chesapeake Bay to North Carolina. Again the troops were to carry five days' cooked rations on the trains, and hot coffee was to be supplied at hundred-mile intervals. About three times as many cars were required for horses, artillery, and baggage as for men.

Thirty-eight trains were used to move the corps from Cincinnati to Bellaire where it was necessary to take the ferry to Benwood for the transfer to the Baltimore and Ohio. Cold weather contributed to a number of breakdowns en route, but in spite of all delays the entire corps was encamped along the banks of the Potomac eleven days after it had left Clifton, 1,400 miles away. The day after the last elements arrived on the Potomac, the first division sailed for North Carolina (4 February), and by 9 February, the corps was ready to begin the attack toward Wilmington.

Demobilization

The most extensive troop movements of all were accomplished after the end of the war when the armies dispersed from Washington after the grand review. In forty days (27 May to 6 July), 233,200 men, 12,838 horses, and 4,300,850 pounds of baggage left Washington on the Washington Branch Railroad, and then went on by connecting routes to Parkersburg, West Virginia, for river steamers down the Ohio, or to other rail points in the northeast or northwest from which the troops could reach towns near their homes.

Comparative Advantages

Neither the facilities nor the organization were at hand to maintain long-range support of Confederate armies on a scale to match that of the Union armies. There was no Lincoln to put the full authority of the government behind railroad operations, no Stanton to demand noninterference with military traffic, no Haupt to direct reconstruction and to demand that cars be unloaded and returned promptly, no McCallum to organize government-controlled railroads supporting armies in the field, no pool of experienced railroad executives like Thomson, Scott, Garrett, Smith, and Felton willing to assume responsibilities in coordinating railway transportation for the movement of troops and supplies.

That the railroads were one of the most vital factors in the logistics of the Civil War is undeniable, for it was then that the pattern was set that would be followed in future wars. For this reason some study of their first use in war on a large scale becomes most instructive. The suggestion has been made that if Southern secession had come a decade sooner—before the North had become bound together with iron tracks—it might have succeeded. It is more likely that the South would have been even worse off a decade earlier, for Northern control of the seas and major rivers during the war made the South relatively more dependent on railroads. Railways were new in warfare; they were the way of the future, and for this reason perhaps they merit more attention. All of which makes it easy to exaggerate the actual importance of the railroads in the war. But the new and dramatic should not be allowed to overshadow altogether other equally important, if more commonplace means of transportation. The fact is that steamboats and barges were just as important for military transportation during the Civil War as were the railroads. It is true that many military operations were directed against rail lines; it is equally true that campaigns were launched to gain control of the major rivers. In waterways and in vessels the advantage was again overwhelmingly on the side of the North.

River Transportation

Col. Lewis B. Parsons, then chief quartermaster of Western River Transportation at St. Louis, reported that in the transportation of troops during 1863 the number moved by rail was 193,023, and that moved by river boat 135,909. Of subsistence, ordnance, quartermaster, and medical stores, railroads transported 153,102,100 pounds, while river boats carried more than twice that amount, 337,912,363 pounds.[9]

The cargo capacity of western steamboats varied all the way from the 250 tons of the *Factor* to the 1,700 tons of the big *Sultana,* and the total available capacity was tremendous. An Army supply officer calculated that an ordinary Ohio River steamboat of 500 tons could carry enough supplies on one trip to subsist an army of 40,000 men and 18,000 horses for nearly two days.[10] This was equal to five 10-car freight trains. Steamboats individually were somewhat slower than railroad trains, of course, but the actual difference in speed was not appreciable. The running time of freight trains for the 339 railroad miles between Cincinnati and St. Louis was 30 hours (passenger trains made the run in 16 hours), while steamboats required 70 hours to traverse the 702 river miles between the two cities. On a tonnage basis, one steamboat could move 500 tons of freight from Cincinnati to St. Louis much more rapidly than could one or two trains shuttling back and forth.

Co-ordination of river transportation presented quite a different problem from that of dealing with the railroads, for there were

---

[9] Louis C. Hunter, *Steamboats on the Western Rivers* (Cambridge: Harvard University Press, 1949), p. 553n.

[10] *Ibid.*, pp. 555, 652.

TRANSPORTS ON THE TENNESSEE RIVER

no large-scale steamboat companies with which working agreements could be made. The existing civilian organization that proved to be so effective in providing railroad transportation had no counterpart on the rivers where one was likely to find as many owners as there were steamboats. The organization needed to handle the intricate problems of military transportation had to be provided by the Quartermaster's Department of the Army.

Transfer of Forces

Some of the feats of steamboat transportation in shifting forces and carrying supplies were as dramatic as the most spectacular rail movements. The 15,000 men that Grant led against Fort Henry in northern Tennessee traveled by steam transports from Cairo up the Ohio and the Tennessee, and when that fort had fallen, part of the force moved 110 miles by water to Fort Donelson on the Cumberland. A few weeks later a great fleet of 153 steamboats moved up to Pittsburgh Landing the forces that would fight under Grant at Shiloh. In December 1862 Colonel Parsons, on seven days' notice, commandeered 70 to 80 steamers at Cairo, St. Louis, and other ports and assembled them at Memphis to move a force of 40,000 men under General Sherman for the attack on Vicksburg. After participating in a two-day battle there, these troops re-embarked, went 300 miles on the Mississippi, the White, and the Arkansas Rivers, and, after capturing a fortification on the Arkansas, returned by boat to join in the siege of Vicksburg.

The role of steamboats in the transfer of Schofield's Twenty-third Corps from Tennessee to the east already has been noted. About the same time the Sixteenth Corps, under Maj. Gen. Andrew J. Smith was transferred from the Tennessee to New Orleans entirely by steamboat. Comprised of 17,314 men with 1,038 horses, 2,371 mules, 351 wagons, and 83 ambulances, the whole force embarked on a fleet of forty steamboats assembled at Eastport, on the Tennessee River below Muscle Shoals, between 5 and 8 February 1865. Sailing on 9 February, the steamers moved the 1,330 miles via the Tennessee, the Ohio, and the Mississippi to New Orleans in thirteen days. As with the railroads, some of the outstanding accomplishments in troop transportation came with demobilization. From the Parkersburg terminus of the Baltimore and Ohio Railroad, Ohio River steamers in a period of twenty-eight days carried 96,796 troops and 9,896 horses to ports below—about 7,000 of the men went to St. Louis, over 78,000 to Louisville, and the remainder to Lawrenceburg, Indiana, to Camp Dennison, and to Cincinnati, Ohio.[11]

Significance of River Transportation

The fact that the waterways carried such a large share of the troops and supplies transported during the war made it possible for the railroads generally to be adequate. Indeed water transportation was such an important factor in the war that it could be said that the railroads remained complementary to the older form of transportation. Unhappily for the Confederacy, river boats could do little to relieve the pressure on the inadequate railway system in the South. When rivers were open and when tonnage was available, the inland waterways offered a number of advantages. Northern armies following the Ohio, Mississippi, Cumberland, Tennessee, and other rivers into the heart of the enemy country assured themselves of a line of communication easy to defend and easy to keep open. Variations in water level, and ice in winter in some cases, presented obstacles, but these were minor as compared to the problems of defending a rail line against enemy raiders, reconstructing railroads and bridges, and keeping tracks and equipment in repair. General Sherman wrote, "We are much obliged to the Tennessee which has favored us most opportunely, for I am never easy with a railroad which takes a whole army to guard, each foot of rail being essential to the whole; whereas they can't stop the Tennessee, and each boat can make its own game." [12] The Count of Paris, accompanying the Union armies as an observer, was convinced that the military value of the western rivers was greater than that of the railroads. "We shall always find, therefore, that whenever the Federals were supported by a river," he wrote, "their progress was certain and their conquests decisive; whilst the successes they obtained by following a single line of railways were always precarious, new dangers springing up in their rear in proportion as they advanced." [13]

---

[11] Annual Rpt of the QMG for Fiscal Year 1865, *Official Records,* ser. iii, V, 231–32.

[12] Ltr, Sherman to Admiral Porter, quoted in Hunter, *Steamboats on the Western Rivers,* p. 555.
[13] Quoted in Hunter, *Steamboats on the Western Rivers,* pp. 559–60.

Summary

River transportation, then, had certain advantages over the railroads in its great capacity, flexibility, relative security against attack or obstruction, and low cost. The railroads, on the other hand, had a superior organization, they could be used with almost equal facility in all seasons, they connected major inland cities not accessible to steamboats, and tracks could be laid wherever needed for local operations. In the circumstances of the Civil War both railroad and water transportation were essential. Neither could have performed in so satisfactory a manner in sustaining such a long war on such a grand scale without the other. Without steamboats and railroads the character of the Civil War would have been wholly different.

CHAPTER XV

Services of Supply for Armies in the Field

The logistical system for the support of the field armies in the Civil War was substantially the same, though expanded and refined, as that in effect during the War with Mexico. On the whole, logistical missions were effectively accomplished. If European observers disagreed with some of the strategy of Federal commanders, they were impressed with the organization and support that made it possible to maintain and move the great armies.

Distribution System

During offensive operations advance depots were established from which an army could draw supplies without having to go all the way back to its base for them. For extended offensives, an advance depot might be expanded to a secondary base with sufficient supplies to provide against a temporary interruption in the line of communication. Temporary depots functioned as distributing points in the vicinity of the using units. As a rule an army tried to keep within two days' march from its advance depot. Frequently an army would shift its advance depot, and proceed toward the new one, located on a different railway or different river. Wagons were thus freed from an extra trip to bring up supplies, and the number of days that the army could operate in enemy country was doubled.

Field Transportation

Perhaps the most critical link in the supply chain was the transportation from an army's forward base to its units. Ordinarily the division was the unit of organization for the general supply trains, and they moved under the control of the division quartermasters, although on occasion they were decentralized to brigades. Sometimes all the trains of an army were massed together under the command of the senior corps quartermaster, with the other corps quartermasters and division and brigade quartermasters remaining in command of their sections.

Daily supply requirements amounted to about four pounds per man—three pounds for rations and one pound for ammunition and other items. In addition, it took about twenty-six pounds of forage to maintain each horse and twenty-three pounds for each mule. Thus, not only the number of wagons available, but the secondary logistical requirements of providing forage for the animals being used to haul the supplies limited the distance from its base at which an army could be supplied effectively. General Sherman stated that an army could not operate at a distance greater than one hundred miles from the supply source, for beyond that limit the teams coming and returning would consume the whole contents of their wagons.[1]

The Count of Paris explained how this supply multiplier operated as an army moved away from its base:

The American wagon, drawn by six mules, carries a load of 2000 pounds, sufficient, therefore, to supply 500 men, provided it can make the trip daily, going and returning, between the army and its depots. If the distance to be traveled is such as to require a whole day's march, one day being lost in returning empty, it will only be able to supply 500 men every other day, or 250 daily. To go a distance of two days' march from its base of operations is a very small matter for an army that is manoeuvring in front of the enemy, and yet, according to this computation, it will require four wagons to supply 500 men with provisions, or eight for 1000, and consequently 800 for 100,000 men. If this army of 100,000 men has 16,000 cavalry and artillery horses, a small number comparatively speaking, 200 more wagons will be required to carry their daily forage, and therefore, 800 to transport it to a distance of two days' march. These 1600 wagons are, in their turn, drawn by 9600 mules, which, also consuming twenty-five pounds during each of the three days out of four they are away from the depot, require 360 wagons more to carry their forage; these 360 wagons are drawn by 2400 animals, and in order to transport the food required by the latter, 92 additional wagons are necessary. Adding twenty wagons more, for general purposes, we shall find that 2000 wagons, drawn by 12,000 animals, are strictly necessary to victual an army of 100,000 men and 16,000 horses at only two days' march from its base of operations. In the same proportion, if this army finds itself separated from its base of operations by three days' march, 3760 wagons, drawn by 22,000 animals, will be found indispensable for that service.[2]

Allowances of transportation for armies in the field were the subject of much discussion during the war. An almost continuous battle went on against the tendency of commanders to increase the size of their trains. In September 1862 General Halleck issued a general order calling the attention of all officers "to the absolute necessity of reducing the baggage trains of troops in the field. The mobility of our armies is destroyed by the vast trains which attend them, and which they are required to guard. This evil requires a prompt remedy."[3] Quartermaster General Meigs thought it impractical to regulate the number of wagons in the general supply trains, for their need would increase with the distance of the army from its supply depot. But he did think that the headquarters and regimental trains carrying the baggage and supplies that always accompanied the units could be regulated. In 1862 the allowance for baggage trains was set at four wagons for the headquarters of an army corps, three for the headquarters of divisions and brigades, six for a full regiment of infantry, and three for a squadron of cavalry or a battery of light artillery. In 1864 Grant reduced Meigs's allowances for brigade headquarters and for infantry or cavalry regiments and artillery battalions to two wagons, and one wagon for an artillery battery in the armies operating against Richmond. At the same time he established allowances for the general supply trains. These allowances included seven wagons for each one thousand men to carry subsistence and forage; fifty wagons for each cavalry division to carry forage exclusively;

---

[1] William Tecumseh Sherman, "The Grand Strategy of the War of the Rebellion," *Century Magazine* (February, 1888), pp. 595–96

[2] Louis Philippe Albert d'Orleans, Comte de Paris, *History of the Civil War in America*, 4 vols.

(Philadelphia: Porter & Coates, 1875–1888), I, 212–13.

[3] WD GO 130, 14 September 1862, *Official Records*, ser. ii, II, 544.

four wagons for each battery of artillery to carry subsistence and forage; five forage and subsistence wagons for every twenty-five wagons of the artillery ammunition train; three wagons for each brigade to carry hospital supplies; subsistence and forage wagons for corps, division, and brigade headquarters at the rate of three, two, and one; and one wagon for each brigade to carry commissary stores for sales to officers. Ammunition trains were to carry nothing but ammunition, including an artillery ammunition reserve of twenty rounds for each gun; two wagons were allowed for fuzes, powder, and primers, and three for small arms ammunition for every one thousand men. The Army of the Potomac on the Peninsula, in the Antietam campaign, and in moving from Harper's Ferry to Washington used from twenty-five to twenty-nine wagons for each one thousand men. The ratio was somewhat less at the end of the war, but it never approached the ideal recommended by Napoleon in an earlier period—500 wagons for an army of 40,000 men.

Lincoln was sure that demands for more supplies and baggage than necessary were delaying the Federal armies. When a commander insisted on accumulating high levels of supplies, he had to get more wagons and animals to haul them and so required more forage and more extraduty men to handle the supplies and look after the animals.

When the Army of the Potomac made an eight-day march during the Chancellorsville campaign in May 1863 without wagons except for those carrying artillery ammunition and a few carrying forage, the Quartermaster General commented that this precedent had "changed the whole character of the war." The march had been accomplished by having the men carry three days' cooked rations, five days' hard bread, sugar, coffee, and salt; by taking along five days' fresh beef on the hoof; and by using pack mules for ammunition.

Food Supply

An important innovation in the regular ration of the Civil War was the provision that "desiccated" potatoes or mixed vegetables might be substituted for the prescribed beans, peas, rice, hominy, or fresh potatoes. (In his *Memoirs* Sherman notes that the men were notably unenthusiastic about the innovations in food, referring to them as "desecrated vegetables" and "consecrated milk.") Hermetically sealed cans and refrigeration for preserving food also were just coming into use at the time of the Civil War, and held great promise for military supply. Canning and refrigeration had not become general by the end of the war; yet the use of canned and frozen foods by the armies was not insignificant. Shipments from the depot at Louisville between 1 January and 31 August 1864, for example, included 110 gallons of canned cabbage, 34,860 cans of tomatoes, 26,856 cans of peaches, 23,112 cans of assorted fruit, 18,192 cans of oysters, 25,440 cans of condensed milk, and 5,820 cans of jelly. Meat packers in the Chicago area frequently froze their meat for shipment to Army depots, but difficulties arose when meat was shipped south since there were no facilities for maintaining refrigeration.

Distribution to companies and to individuals, of course, depended upon the situation. When an army was not moving, rations were issued for four days at a time. An officer from each regiment had charge of a special detail to receive the rations and issue them to the companies. When the regimental quartermaster drew his rations of fresh meat, he had to take his turn for the preferred cuts—one time the ration would be a hindquarter, and next time a forequarter. The men jealously watched the apportionment of their individual rations, with an especially anxious eye to see that they got their full share of coffee and sugar. In some units when the regimental quartermaster received a bag of coffee he carefully divided it for the ten companies. Then the orderly sergeant of each company had to divide his portion among all his men. A favored method was to spread two rubber blankets on the ground; on one the coffee would be poured in equal piles; at the same time the sugar ration would be divided in like fashion on the other blanket. Then everyone would march by and pick up one pile of each. Many men liked to mix the coffee and sugar to simplify the problem of carrying it, and to fortify themselves against the temptation of eating all the sugar at once.

The final step in food supply—the cooking—was pretty much of a haphazard affair throughout the war. In the beginning it was fairly common for regimental commissaries to issue each man his ration as the food came from the barrels and boxes, make kettles and skillets available, and then suggest that the men form groups of six to ten for the cooking. In each group the men took their turns at the cooking chores. It soon became apparent that some had greater talents along these lines than others, and eventually company cooks were appointed. Those companies fared best who found a professional chef in their ranks. Sometimes a company would find a Negro "contraband" with experience in a household kitchen who would act as company cook. In any case, plenty of men were willing to try,

for while on the cooking detail they were excused from all other duties. Cooks drew the company rations from the regimental commissary, prepared the meal, and served it in tin plates and cups to the men as they filed by the kitchen shack. The men then went off to their quarters to eat.

Favorite meals were baked beans with salt pork or beef, and vegetable stew when the ingredients were available. On the march, when units were separated from the wagon trains, cooking continued to be done by small groups or individuals. The prescribed march ration included 1 pound of hardtack, ¾ pound of salt pork or ¼ pound of fresh meat, coffee, sugar, and salt. With effort, the hardtack could be eaten quite agreeably—if not too old—as taken from the haversack. The men sometimes would soak and then fry this hard cracker in pork fat; sometimes they would crumble it in their coffee and eat it with a spoon. It could also be toasted on the end of a stick; besides improving the taste, toasting had the further advantage of driving the weevils out of the more aged crackers. For meat, the men always preferred salt pork to salt beef; the latter was likely to be so impregnated with salt that it could not be eaten until soaked overnight in running water, or so tough or so spoiled that it could not be eaten at all. Frequently the men ate their salt pork raw on hardtack, for this saved time, effort, and the trouble of carrying and washing utensils with no significant sacrifice in the flavor of the meat. Regular issues of fresh beef, maintained by driving along herds of cattle with the marching armies, provided a welcome change from the salt meats, but the fresh meat was not especially good. The flavor of beef from cattle marched long distances on short forage and then slaughtered and distributed the same

COOKING IN CAMP

day was not particularly appealing, and inevitably the cooks were accused of keeping the best cuts for themselves. When a company was lucky enough to draw steaks, the company cooks handed them out raw to the men who then broiled them on sticks.

For tonnage and bulk the item of daily supply that was even more important than food for the men was food for the animals. The prescribed forage ration per horse was fourteen pounds of hay and twelve pounds of oats, corn, or barley, or a total of twenty-six pounds. As organized by the third year of the war, armies in the field generally had for cavalry, artillery, and the wagon trains half as many horses and mules as soldiers. Thus daily forage requirements were three times as great, in tonnage, as subsistence requirements.

Ammunition Supply

During combat the highest priority had to be given to the supply of ammunition. The soldier armed with the standard rifle-musket usually carried into battle sixty rounds of ammunition—forty rounds in the leather cartridge box on his belt and twenty in his pockets or knapsack. When a battery or regiment needed to replenish its ammunition, the commander (through the ordnance sergeant) sent for a wagon to come up from the trains. The wagon moved up as near as cover and concealment would allow, and men carried the ammunition forward. When possible, ammunition as well as subsistence wagons came up at night to distribute supplies for the next day. Higher commanders soon learned the value of the principle that the impetus of supply is from the rear.

The Army of the Potomac

General McClellan set the pattern for the organization and administration of field armies when he took over command of the Army of the Potomac after Bull Run. In view of the complete lack of experience in the country in handling and supplying large bodies of troops, he was singularly successful in finding able officers to staff the supply departments. In nearly every case chiefs or key assistants appointed by McClellan remained with the Army of the Potomac through later campaigns, and several stayed throughout the war. Col. Henry F. Clark served as the Army of the Potomac's chief commissariat for more than two years. Brig. Gen. Rufus Ingalls served as principal assistant to the chief quartermaster, Brig. Gen. Stewart Van Vliet, until July 1862, when he became chief quartermaster. He held that position until he became chief quartermaster for the group of armies operating against Richmond under General Grant. Surgeon Jonathan Letterman, after succeeding Charles S. Tripler, gave especially valuable service as medical director.

Maj. Gen. John G. Barnard was on the staff as chief engineer until he became chief engineer of the combined armies. The remarkable transformation in the Army of the Potomac in the six months preceding its embarkation for the Peninsula, as well as the reputation it earned for well-ordered administration, was in no small measure attributable to the staff McClellan brought together. To co-ordinate their work, McClellan created the position of chief of staff, and always maintained personal interest in the effective execution of administrative details. If many questioned McClellan's tactics, or his tact, or his moral courage, few questioned his contributions as the organizer of an army.

The Peninsular Campaign

When, after months of reorganization, training, and other preparations, McClellan at last was ready to set out on a campaign against the enemy in the spring of 1862, the expedition involved logistical complexities never dreamed of by officers whose most demanding previous experiences had been moving and supplying elements of Scott's and Taylor's small armies in Mexico. Intending to move his army to the peninsula formed by the York and James Rivers, McClellan determined to strike at Richmond from the southeast, and thus to turn the major streams into logistical allies rather than tactical obstacles. Embarkation at Alexandria began on 17 March 1862, and the last troops of the expeditionary forces landed on the Peninsula on 6 April. In the interim some 400 steamers and sailing vessels transported approximately 110,000 men, more than 14,500 animals, and 44 batteries of artillery, together with the supply wagons, ambulances, ponton trains, and other supplies and equipment needed for such an army. The only losses were nine stranded lighters and eight drowned mules. The major base depots for supporting the Army of the Potomac were at Alexandria, Baltimore, and Annapolis. The first advance base was at Fort Monroe (which was temporarily part of the Army of the Potomac but reverted to the control of General Wool's Department of Virginia). As it advanced upon the Peninsula, the army opened depots at Cheeseman's Landing and Brick House on the York River; the main base was established on the Pamunkey River at White House which was connected by rail with an advance depot at Savage Station. The base at White House was later shifted to Harrison's Landing on the James River.

The difficulty in moving up supplies undoubtedly delayed the advance of the Federal Army up the Peninsula toward Richmond. Most of the trouble was in the local distribution of supplies to a large army (nearly 100,000 men) on the move with limited routes. Although the advance generally was by brigade with brigade trains following each brigade when possible, often the road net made this impractical and trains were then massed under army control. Lack of system and organization in the early phase of the advance made support unsatisfactory. Congestion on the single road from Yorktown to Williamsburg became so bad that it was impossible to bring up rations until a temporary depot could be opened at Queens Creek where it was possible to make further use of water transportation. As the Army of the Potomac moved into the vicinity of Richmond, it required more and more wagons for its supply. Because of the nature of the facilities and the distribution of the forces

before the capital of the Confederacy, only a small part of the command could be supplied from the railhead at Savage Station, which was less than ten miles east of Richmond, and connected by a direct rail line with the main base at White House, about fifteen miles to the northeast. Most of the roads were corduroyed, but so rough that the wear and tear on wagons became a major problem in the whole supply operation. When prolonged rains made the roads almost impassable, loads had to be lightened, and this added still more to the requirements for wagons. Nevertheless the Federal Army was well supplied when it met and drove back the first major Confederate counterthrust at Seven Pines (Fair Oaks), just seven miles from Richmond, at the end of May.

During the next month of relatively light activity on the fighting front, the supply build-up continued. Then Stonewall Jackson's forces joined Lee's and the Confederates struck back in a series of battles known as the Seven Days (25 June–1 July). In the face of these attacks McClellan carried through one of his more remarkable achievements on the Peninsula in his change of bases from White House to Harrison's Landing, some thirty-five miles to the south, on the James River. He thus avoided the evident Confederate threat against his line of communication; the army, however, had to carry its own supplies during the interval, which impeded its movements at a time when it was fighting for its life against a vigorous foe. By a series of delaying engagements, the Federal forces succeeded in holding their ground and arrived at their destination intact. In preparation for the move entire trains of supplies were burned and tons of ammunition were dumped into the rivers so that supplies that could not be carried would not fall into the hands of the Confederates. While the soldiers carried two to three days' cooked rations, the wagons carried another three days', and a herd of over 2,500 cattle went along. In addition, the trains included five days' forage for 40,000 animals, as well as 350 artillery pieces, and ammunition. With 5,000 wagons and 25,000 horses and mules, the army carried 25,000 tons of essential supplies. Daily requirements for the army during the Seven Days amounted to about 600 tons of ammunition, rations, forage, and medical supplies.

After sharp local engagements at Mechanicsburg (about eight miles north-north-east of Richmond) on 26 June and a setback at Gaines's Mill on 27 June, McClellan continued his retirement to the south while Lee waited to see whether he (McClellan) in fact was moving to the James, or whether he was going to retreat eastward down the Peninsula whence he had come. By the 29th the direction was clear, but it was too late for Lee to intercede effectively. The Federals held firmly at Savage Station (29 June) to protect their crossing of the Chickahominy, and at Glendale and Frayser's Farm (30 June) to protect the difficult crossing of White Oak Swamp where the engineer battalion labored long and hard to keep the roadway passable for the long columns of wagons. At Malvern Hill, near the banks of the James, McClellan prepared excellent defensive positions, and on 1 July repulsed the Confederates with heavy losses in the greatest battle of the Seven Days. Resumption of an offensive toward Richmond did not now seem feasible to McClellan, mainly because of the necessity of resupplying his units. He retreated another seven miles down the James, through a downpour of rain, to Harrison's Landing where Federal supply ships as well as gunboats were on hand for support. The new base, on an excellent waterway, was almost exactly the same distance to the southeast of Richmond that White House was to the northeast (about fifteen miles); but the Army of the Potomac, too, was that far away, instead of six to eight miles as at Mechanicsburg and Fair Oaks. The army still had 3,100 wagons, 350 ambulances, 17,000 horses (including cavalry and artillery horses), and 8,000 mules.

As McClellan prepared for movement against Richmond by way of Petersburg, thus anticipating Grant's scheme of 1864–65, he received orders to remove his army from the Peninsula to Aquia Creek on the Potomac. While the army, with the wagon trains, began on 14 August the march toward Fort Monroe where there were better facilities for embarkation, all the matériel the wagons could not carry, together with 12,000 sick, some artillery and cavalry units, and one infantry division were embarking at Harrison's Landing. Under the protection of Federal gunboats, engineers put a bridge across the Chickahominy near where it flowed into the James. The last soldier marched back across the Chickahominy on 18 August, and by the 20th the army was distributed among Newport News, Yorktown, and Fort Monroe, ready to embark as rapidly as available transport permitted.

The Maryland Campaign

For the Maryland campaign in September 1862, the Army of the Potomac first drew its supplies directly from the base at Alexandria by means of its own wagon trains. After the recapture of Frederick, Maryland, supplies went from the base at Baltimore over the Baltimore and Ohio

Railroad, though for a time a temporary depot had to be maintained on the east bank of the Monocacy River while a bridge was rebuilt across the stream. Following the battle of South Mountain supplies went over the Cumberland Valley Railroad to a depot at Hagerstown. After the great battle of Antietam, supplies came from Alexandria, Baltimore, Philadelphia, and New York to an advance depot at Harper's Ferry, and later to a depot at Berlin. When the army eventually recrossed the Potomac, it again drew most of its supplies from Alexandria—by the Manassas Gap Railroad to Salem. Throughout the campaign supplies seem to have been abundant, yet a great deal of confusion attended the whole logistical effort. A good part of the confusion could be attributed to the absorption into the Army of the Potomac of demoralized and disorganized units which had shared the defeat at Second Bull Run (29–30 August) in the Army of Virginia under Maj. Gen. John Pope. About a week before the battle of Antietam, Quartermaster General Meigs complained to McClellan that the depot quartermaster had received his requisitions but had no transportation to send the supplies to the front as requested; that anyway the job was one for the army's own supply trains; and, in addition, the chief quartermaster of the Army of the Potomac was supposed to turn surplus wagons over to the depot quartermaster and he had not done so. Meigs suggested that it might be a good idea to empower the chief quartermaster to correct the apparent confusion. Ingalls' immediate reaction was, "It is true there exists much confusion in the trains belonging to the Army of Virginia, but none in the Army of the Potomac. . . . It does not appear that the commander of the Army of Virginia

ever knew how many wagons there were, nor what quartermasters were on duty." [4] Still all reasonable requirements were met. When McClellan telegraphed for emergency shipments of ammunition to be delivered the day after the battle, a convoy of 414 wagons loaded with ammunition went toward Frederick by road, while two special trains went to Frederick and Hagerstown.

In subsequent weeks McClellan's command seemed to grow progressively worse in supply discipline; furthermore the commander indicated all kinds of exaggerated requirements for supplies—uniforms, shoes, hospital tents, small arms, horses. Much was wasted, and much was left behind when the army moved. It never really appeared to be in serious want of anything. As Ingalls observed, "An army will never move if it waits until all the different commanders report that they are ready and want no more supplies." [5]

For the ill-fated Fredericksburg campaign which Maj. Gen. Ambrose E. Burnside undertook shortly after succeeding McClellan in command of the Army of the Potomac, advance depots at Aquia and Belle Plain forwarded supplies by the short Aquia and Fredericksburg Railroad to Falmouth and other temporary depots along the line.

Hooker's Reorganization

General Burnside served as commander of the Army of the Potomac for only two months. In January 1863 Maj. Gen. Joseph Hooker was called upon to reorganize the Army of the Potomac after its disastrous defeat at Fredericksburg in Decem-

---

[4] Ltr, Ingalls to Williams, 10 September 1862, *Official Records*, ser. i, XIX, pt. 2, 235.
[5] Quoted in Williams, *Lincoln Finds a General*, II, 467.

ber 1862 while under Burnside's command. Though known as "Fighting Joe," General Hooker probably performed his greatest service for the Army of the Potomac in the early months of his command by introducing much-needed administrative reforms.

Upon taking command he found that commissary officers had taken to enriching themselves by selling fresh and desiccated vegetables for private profit while they continued to issue only salt pork, hardtack, and coffee to the troops, and he proceeded to remedy that situation immediately. One of his first orders required that flour or soft bread be issued to the troops at least four times a week, fresh potatoes or onions twice a week, and desiccated mixed vegetables or potatoes once a week. The order further required any commissary who did not issue provisions according to the schedule to get from the officer in charge of the depot from which he drew his supplies a certificate stating that the foods were not on hand. He also ordered all regimental commanders to see that regular company cooks prepared the food while the army was in camp.

Another reform he insisted upon was that ordnance requisitions be submitted correctly and that ammunition reserves be kept at designated levels. Regimental commanders were required to sign requisitions and forward them in duplicate to the acting division ordance officer, who made a consolidated requisition that had to be signed by the division commander (by the corps commander in the case of cavalry) and presented to the chief ordnance officer at army headquarters. Copies of the original requisitions were enclosed with the consolidated form and forwarded to Washington. Artillery ammunition requisitions echeloned from battery commander to corps chief of artillery, to the army chief of artillery, to the chief ordnance officer. If forms were not properly filled out, or were changed in any way, they were returned. On the 15th of each month division ordnance officers were required to submit an ammunition status report through their division and corps commanders to the chief ordnance officer. General Hooker also insisted on improvement of camp sanitation and renovation of the hospitals. By continuous personal inspections he assured himself that his instructions were being carried out. Like McClellan, he did not measure up to the requirements of a great field commander, but by his attention to the welfare of his men and his insistence on systematic supply procedures he recreated the Army of the Potomac into a fighting force capable of great victories.

Through the Wilderness

Mostly inactive since Gettysburg (1–3 July 1863), the Army of the Potomac from December 1863 until May 1864 occupied its old positions in Virginia along the Rapidan River in the vicinity of Culpeper, with depots at Brandy Station and other points along the Orange and Alexandria Railroad. On 4 May when Grant launched his great campaign across the Rapidan through the Wilderness, the depots were broken up and all surplus supplies sent back to Alexandria. Once more the Aquia Creek Railroad had to be repaired and the bridge over Potomac Creek rebuilt (this time in forty hours); depots again were established at Aquia, Belle Plain, and Fredericksburg. On 21 May these depots were closed out and a new depot was opened at Port Royal. Ten days later an advance depot was established at White House on the Pamunkey, where an advance depot had supported the Army of the Potomac in the Peninsular campaign two years previously. The advantage of maintaining depots within reach of the waterways was a major factor in Grant's decision to cross the Rapidan below rather than above Lee's army.

Grant's forces crossing the Rapidan included the Army of the Potomac under Meade and the Ninth Corps under Burnside (which operated as a separate command until incorporated into the Army of the Potomac on 25 May), and numbered all together about 125,000 men. The troops were ordered to carry fifty rounds of ammunition and three days' rations, while three days' beef on the hoof (8,000 to 10,-000 cattle) accompanied the army, and the supply trains carried ten days' subsistence and forage. The number of horses and mules for cavalry, artillery, officers' mounts, and trains totaled more than 56,000. It took 20,000 men to handle the 4,300 wagons and 835 ambulances making up the trains. Trains of such magnitude undoubtedly embarrassed Grant's movements, but he saw no way of avoiding that difficulty. The inevitable delays in the advance allowed the Confederates to give battle in the dense thickets of the Wilderness and to exact a high price for each foot of ground given. Supply continued generally good. The confusion in the wagon trains two years earlier had been eliminated. Grant declared that there never was a better organized corps than the quartermaster corps of the Army of the Potomac in 1864.

General Ingalls had unit identification markings painted on all the wagons—corps insignia, division color, and brigade number. Other stripes or markings indicated the contents of the wagon—cavalry or infantry ammunition, grain or hay, bread, pork, beans,

or coffee, and so on. When a wagon was unloaded, it went back immediately to the depot to be reloaded with exactly the same type of article. During the battle of the Wilderness the wagon trains were kept up within five miles of the front.

Problems of supply and evacuation had never been greater than in the six weeks of almost continuous fighting during which the Army of the Potomac made its way from the Rapidan to the James. There had been long, hand-fought battles before, but usually a period of rest and reorganization had followed. Grant's policy was to hammer constantly at the enemy and it left no time to the contenders on either side for extensive rehabilitation. Heavy fighting meant that quantities of ammunition as well as the forage and subsistence necessary in that country for a large, slowly moving army had to be brought up continuously. It also meant that casualties in unprecedented numbers (almost 55,000) had to be evacuated. The same wagons that carried supplies to the front brought the wounded to the rear. Some 7,000 seriously wounded men were carried from the Wilderness to an evacuation hospital at Fredericksburg, and after preliminary treatment there were sent by rail and river transportation to Washington.

The James River Crossing

One of the outstanding logistical feats of the war for the Army of the Potomac was undertaken at this point—its transfer from Cold Harbor in the Wilderness area to the south bank of the James River for the drive on Petersburg. Maj. James C. Duane, chief engineer of the Army of the Potomac, supervised the digging of intrenchments for the army's protection while it withdrew from the active front. The task

SUPPLY WAGONS AND PONTON WHARF AT CITY POINT

of bridging the first major river barrier, the Chickahominy, fell to the 50th New York Engineers. Using canvas as well as wooden pontons, the New York Engineers put in bridges at Long Bridge for the crossing of the Second and Fifth Corps, at Jones's Bridge for the Sixth and Ninth Corps, and one at Cole's Ferry, where the river reached a width of over 1,200 feet, for the supply trains. The Cole's Ferry site required long corduroy approaches and piers plus all the pontons in the regiment, and the bridge could not be completed until the units upstream had crossed and the bridges had been dismantled so those pontons could be reused at Cole's Ferry.

In the meantime work proceeded on the longest ponton bridge of them all—the bridge across the James River. The site chosen was at Douthart's house, a point on a north-south neck of the river about midway between Wilcox's Landing and Wyanoke Landing, and the bridge would hit the opposite shore between Windmill Point and Fort Powhatan. (A better site in the vicinity of Malvern Hill and Bermuda Hundred would have given the Army of the Potomac a route to Petersburg ten to fifteen miles shorter, but would have put the crossing under the observation, and probably the guns, of Lee's Army.) By nightfall on 13 June a detail of 150 axmen had cut and trimmed about 1,200 feet of timber, and some 3,000 feet of timber had been brought down to the creek above Fort Powhatan ready to be rafted across to the northeast

STORAGE AREA *for guns and ammunition, City Point.*

shore. Engineers, reinforced by details from the Second Corps, worked late that night and early the next morning completing the approaches on both sides of the river, including a 150-foot pier over a soft marsh on the northeast bank. At 1400 on 14 June the United States Engineer Battalion began laying the bridge. Two companies worked from each end to emplace the pontons. Built on 101 wooden pontons, the bridge was 2,200 feet long—probably the longest ponton bridge in the history of warfare.[6]

By 2300 the bridge was complete except for a 100-foot passageway left open for vessels to move through. While the trains crossed over (beginning at 0200 on 15 June) this passageway was filled in by a

mid-section held in place against the current by three schooners anchored in the channel. The long bridge held up well under the heavy traffic, and within forty-eight hours the army was across. Perhaps half of the infantry crossed by steamboat ferries operating between Wilcox's Landing and Windmill Point where the New York Engineers had repaired the old wharf and built a new one. Elements crossing on the bridge included a train of wagons and artillery 35 miles long, a herd of 3,500 beef cattle, about half of the infantry of Meade's command, and 4,000 cavalry.

City Point

During the months of stabilized trench warfare around Petersburg, the depot established at City Point, at the confluence of the Appomattox and James Rivers, grew into the greatest advance army base of the war. Separate wharves and storage areas were assigned for each class of supply—subsistence, forage, clothing, camp equipment, railway equipment, medical supplies, ammunition, and horses and mules. More than 1,800 men were employed on the wharves and in the warehouses, repair shops, blacksmith shops, and bakery, and the Railroad Construction Corps employed another two to three thousand. During the year over 3,600 carriages and 2,400 ambulances were repaired, and over 50,000 horses and mules were shod. Twenty large ovens could turn out 11,000 bread rations a day. Five corps hospitals were brought together to form a huge base, or evacuation, hospital that was well equipped to care for 6,000 patients, and was capable of caring for 10,000 evacuees in an emergency. Completely in tents at first, the hospital eventually was housed in ninety pavillions and 324 hospital tents. Two

---

[6] The longest floating bridge built by the U.S. Army in World War II was across the Rhine and was 1,260 feet long. It took engineers about fifty-two hours to construct.

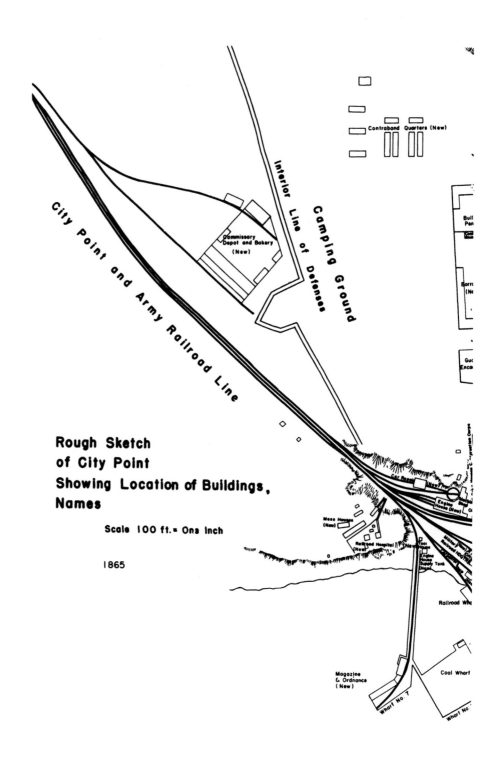

Contraband Quarters (New)

Camping Ground

Interior Line of Defenses

City Point and Army Railroad Line

Commissary Depot and Bakery (New)

Rough Sketch
of City Point
Showing Location of Buildings,
Names

Scale 100 ft. = One Inch

1865

Car Repair (New)

Engine House (New)

Mess House (New)

Railroad Hospital (New)

Engine House (New)

Supply Tank (New)

New Tool

Railroad Wharf

Magazine & Ordnance (New)

Coal Wharf

Wharf No. 1

Wharf No.

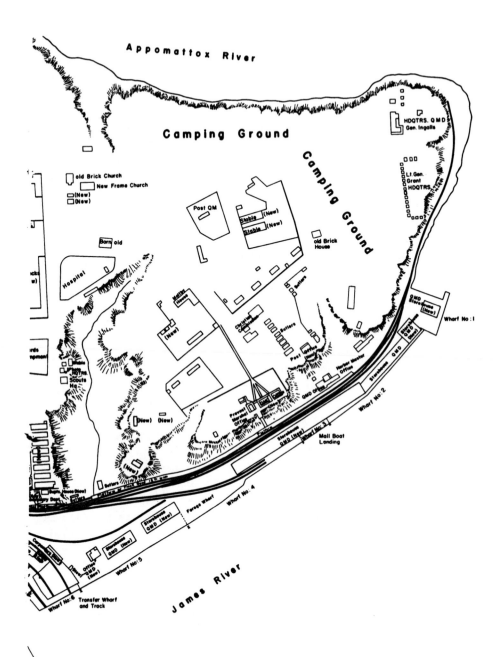

Appomattox River

Camping Ground

Camping Ground

HDQTRS. QMD
Gen. Ingalls

Lt. Gen.
Grant
HDQTRS.

old Brick Church

New Frame Church

(New)

(New)

Post QM

Stable (New)

Stable (New)

old Brick
House

Barn old

Hospital

Settlers

Mattie
House

(New)

Christian
Commission

QMD
Store
House
(New)

Wharf No: 1

Settlers

Post Office

Harbor Master
Office

Stable
QMD
(Old)

Stable QMD

Stable
QMD
(New)

(New)

HDQTRS
Scouts
Hq.

QMD Office

Wharf No: 2

Provost
Marshal
Office

(New)   (New)

Storehouse
QMD (New)

Wharf No: 3

Mail Boat
Landing

(New)

Settlers

(New)

Wharf No: 4

Forage Wharf

(Supt. House (New))

Storehouse
QMD (New)

Office
QMD
(New)

Wharf No: 5

Wharf No: 6 Transfer Wharf
and Track

James River

steam pumps provided water, and a steam laundry could handle 6,000 pieces a week. Only the open latrines detracted from the otherwise excellent arrangement of the hospital and camp. (*Map 9*)

With almost no local procurement possible, practically all supplies had to be shipped in. At any given time an average of 40 steamboats and tugs, 75 sailing ships, and 100 barges were in service (at eastern ports, en route, or at City Point) bringing stores to the base. In the spring of 1865, 390 chartered and government-owned vessels (190 steamers, 60 tugs, 40 sailing vessels, and 100 barges) were in service supplying the armies before Richmond at a daily expense of $48,000. Shipments of forage during the winter months averaged $1,000,000 a month. Several shipments daily arrived for the sutlers, who provided extra fruit, vegetables, and other foods and articles for sale to the soldiers, and the Sanitary Commission brought in such commodities as canned tomatoes and pickles.

Distribution of supplies to troops in the front lines was made by railroad and wagon. After completion of a military railroad extending from City Point for twenty miles over the bed of the old City Point Railroad and along the line of trenches, forward units could be supplied in all weather with little difficulty. By the fall of 1864 eighteen trains a day were delivering supplies to stations in rear of the positions and evacuating casualties to the City Point hospital.

The Western Theater

Meanwhile the armies in the west had been winning their share of successes, and they, too, had been adding new dimensions to logistics. The use of inland waterways had been an outstanding feature of military operations since the early days of the war. The Atlanta campaign was based upon an extraordinarily long railway line of communication, and Grant's Vicksburg campaign and Sherman's march from Atlanta to the sea involved large-scale maneuvers through enemy country without any lines of communication at all.

Vicksburg

Grant's attempt against Vicksburg in December 1862 first went awry when General Sherman and Admiral David D. Porter found the intended route by way of the Yazoo River and Chickasaw Bayou completely impossible. Then Confederate cavalry destroyed Grant's depot and a million dollars' worth of ordnance, subsistence, and quartermaster supplies at Holley Springs, and cut the railroad between Columbus, Kentucky, and Jackson, Tennessee, leaving Grant's army to subsist for more than two weeks without regular issues of rations and forage. After another ill-fated attempt by Sherman and Porter to overcome the bayous in January and February 1863, Grant decided that the only thing to do was to cross the Mississippi, bypassing the Confederate stronghold, and recross the river south of Vicksburg and make another attempt from the rear. With the failure of efforts to open a waterway through the bayous or to complete a canal across the narrow neck of land opposite Vicksburg so that the Confederate batteries could be avoided, Grant and Porter decided that the Union gunboats, together with the transports that were needed for the supplies (the flooded land on the west side was barely passable for troops, much less for wagons), as well as for use as ferries to put the troops back on the east shore of the river below Vicksburg, would have to run the batteries. When most of the civilian crews on the river transports balked at such a hazardous undertaking, Grant called for volunteers from the troops, and enough came forward to man 100 steamers had they been needed. On the night of 16 April, seven transports convoyed by eight gunboats made the first attempt. All except one transport got through. Immediately Grant ordered six more transports, each loaded with 100,000 rations, to be made ready to run the batteries by the 22d. Actually seven transports, towing twelve barges, made that attempt, and again six got through, although six of the twelve barges were disabled. (*Map 10*)

It was then possible to ferry the troops back across the river. They landed at Bruinsburg, sixty miles south of Vicksburg and took the town on 3 May. An advance depot established at Bruinsburg soon afterward was moved upstream to Grand Gulf. So that steamboats bringing in additional supplies would not have to run the Confederate batteries again, Grant ordered the commander of the military district to build a road, as soon as the water fell sufficiently, from above Vicksburg at Young's Point to a landing site eight miles below Vicksburg opposite Warrenton. To Sherman, whose corps was bringing up the rear, Grant sent instructions to collect 120 wagons and send them to Grand Gulf to pick up 100,000 pounds of bacon, hard bread, coffee, sugar, and salt. He planned for ammunition and hard bread to be the only items that would have to be resupplied in any amount on the march, and for the country to provide forage and most of the subsistence. Grant in-

structed the commissary at Grand Gulf to load all wagons coming for supplies promptly regardless of requisitions or reports: red tape was not to interfere with rapid action.

While Sherman worried about the congestion that would result from trying to supply an army of 50,000 men by a single road from Grand Gulf, Grant made plans to strike into the interior without any base at all. Starting out with no trains, and an average of two days' rations in haversacks, Grant's army collected wagons as well as food and forage in the country. Each night wagons heavily loaded with impressed supplies rolled into camp. In the twenty days that the army marched 200 miles, fought five successful battles, seized the state capital at Jackson, destroyed railroads in the vicinity, and took up positions to the rear of Vicksburg, only five days' rations were issued, and no shortage of supplies was noticed. By freeing himself of a long line of communication, Grant saved the manpower needed to protect that line, and he could move swiftly, which, in turn, made living off the country more feasible. With the Federals in position to begin the investment of Vicksburg on 19 May, the Confederates evacuated Haynes' Bluff, on the Yazoo, and it became the Union supply depot; first supply trains for Haynes' Bluff reached Grant's army with rations on 21 May. By 14 June reinforcements swelled the ranks of the Vicksburg besiegers to 71,000 men; by 20 June 220 guns were in position. All could be supplied easily. The Confederates defending Vicksburg were completely cut off, and it was only a matter of time until they capitulated on 4 July. Many still consider the Vicksburg campaign Grant's greatest achievement.

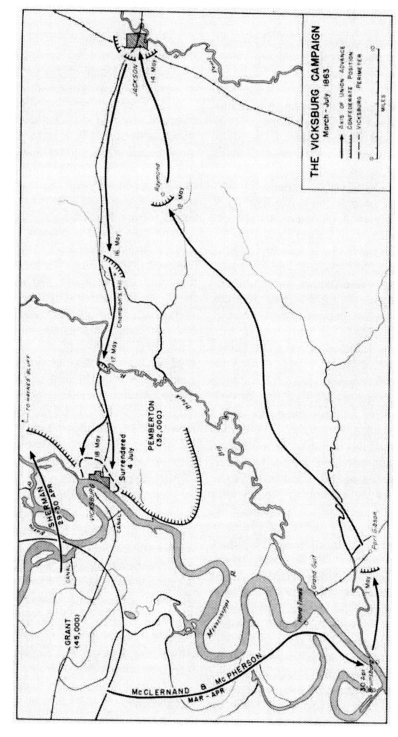

THE VICKSBURG CAMPAIGN
March – July 1863

AXIS OF UNION ADVANCE
CONFEDERATE POSITION
VICKSBURG PERIMETER

MILES

JACKSON
14 May
Raymond
12 May
16 May
Champion's Hill
17 May
PEMBERTON
(32,000)
TO HAINES BLUFF
18 May
Surrendered
4 July
SHERMAN
29-30 APR
VICKSBURG
CANAL
CANAL
GRANT
(45,000)
Mississippi
Port Gibson
Grand Gulf
1 May
McCLERNAND & McPHERSON
MAR – APR
30 Apr
Bruinsburg

MAP 10

Chattanooga

Later that year Maj. Gen. William S. Rosecrans found himself holding Chattanooga with no effective line of communication, and the result was very nearly disastrous. Rosecrans had begun the campaign against Chattanooga, an important military communications center, with perhaps 80,000 men, 60,000 horses and mules, and 4,800 wagons and ambulances, though the number penned up in the city after the battle of Chickamauga (18–20 September) was not much over half that. With the enemy holding the rail line upon which Rosecrans had depended, the only way to bring supplies in to Chattanooga was by a difficult mountain road sixty miles to a point from which the railroad was open to Nashville. Traffic and bad weather soon made this route impractical, and Confederate cavalry threatened trains that did venture out. Only half of the normal supply of ammunition was on hand—perhaps enough for one battle. All troops were reduced to half rations; blankets and coats had been left behind at Chickamauga; 3,000 wounded soldiers lay in hospitals and camps without proper medical supplies, and with no means of evacuation; 10,000 horses and mules died for want of forage. At the end of September the two corps transferred from the Army of the Potomac with General Hooker commanding began to arrive. Grant, elevated to the supreme command in the west in mid-October, began to concentrate his forces in the area. By the end of October Hooker's force had opened the "Cracker Line," and small steamboats could bring rations up on the lower Tennessee. In November the decisive battles of Missionary Ridge and Lookout Mountain established Chattanooga firmly in Union hands.

Grant's "Mobile Plan"

After the Chattanooga campaign, Grant revived a proposal he had offered first at the time of the fall of Vicksburg and repeated several times since—a campaign against Mobile, Alabama. Considering that supply and transportation limitations during the winter months would make impossible any effective campaign southward from Chattanooga before spring, and that inaction would only give the enemy opportunity to recover from his recent defeats, Grant insisted that a telling blow could be struck in the Deep South. Now that the Mississippi was open, and troops and supplies could be easily transported to New Orleans and to Mobile, he estimated that he could take Mobile by the end of January. If the garrison put up a stubborn defense, he proposed to lay siege with a large enough force to contain it, then to launch a campaign into the interior of Alabama and possibly Georgia. He felt sure that the result would be to secure the entire states of Alabama and Mississippi, and much of Georgia—or at least to force Lee to abandon Virginia and North Carolina.

Grant persuaded Assistant Secretary of War Dana, then accompanying him in the field, of the soundness of his plan, and Dana returned to Washington to urge it upon Lincoln, Stanton, and Halleck. Dana's reply to Grant made it appear that all had accepted the proposal, but Halleck quickly dispelled any real hope for carrying it out by insisting that a series of nonessential tasks take priority. Grant was anticipating by a year the sort of conclusion to the war that he ultimately would be able to effect. Had the Mobile Plan materialized, it would have made good use of Northern logistical capabilities in a way that undoubtedly would have seriously weakened the war-making capacity of the South, and conceivably could have shortened the war by months.

Atlanta Campaign

When at last Federal armies did set out for the Southern heartland under General Sherman, they did so with the full support of the General in Chief as a part of his grand strategical plan. The principal change in the situation between the one year and the next was the elevation of General Grant to the position of over-all command. Sherman spent March and April 1964 supervising the administrative details involved in reorganizing his forces, building up supplies, and co-ordinating with Grant for the opening of the campaign against Atlanta. The three participating armies, the Armies of the Cumberland, the Tennessee, and the Ohio, were in the vicinity of Chattanooga, where they drew their supplies by rail from the depot at Nashville, which in turn received its supplies by rail and by river steamer from the base at Louisville. Brig. Gen. George H. Thomas, commander of the Department of the Cumberland, had jurisdiction over the Nashville and Chattanooga Railroad, inevitably causing suspicion in the other two armies that they were not getting their fair share of the supplies until Sherman took over direct control of the railroads.

To maintain as much mobility as possible for the advance, Sherman ordered each man to carry food and clothing for five days. Each regiment was limited to one wagon and one ambulance, and the officers of each company could have one pack animal for their baggage. Tents were forbidden except for hospital purposes, though General Thomas insisted on taking along his headquarters tents as well as the big wagon he used for a mobile office. The combined armies had a strength of about 100,000 men, and by 1 July they had 5,180 wagons and 860 ambulances, and over 60,000 horses and mules. Sherman maintained a rear headquarters at Nashville where a clerical staff, linked by telegraph to the advance headquarters, relieved him of much paper work. To improve mobility further, he had a topographer appointed in each division who collected information on the terrain for use on new maps which were duplicated by a photographic process and distributed periodically. Louisville continued to be the primary base for the whole campaign, while the advance depots at Nashville and Chattanooga expanded into secondary bases. Other advance depots at Knoxville and Johnsonville, Tennessee, also supported Sherman's armies, and temporary depots at Allatoona and Big Shanty supplied the immediate needs of troops in the vicinity of those places. Later a depot was established at Atlanta. Ultimately the depot of Chattanooga had a thirty-day supply of rations for 100,000 men, and clothing for six months.

The supply problem was uppermost in Sherman's mind, and he insisted upon moving reserves forward. He tried to keep on hand, in the wagon trains, twenty days' food supply. He was dependant upon a long, precarious rail connection for all of his supplies. When the water was low supplies from Louisville had to come 185 miles by rail to Nashville, then another 150 miles from Nashville to Chattanooga, and finally approximately another 150 miles by single track from Chattanooga to Atlanta. To provide a cushion against possible interruption of communications, Sherman calculated that he needed a railroad capacity of 130 carloads a day. After his unpopular order closing the railroads to civilian passengers and freight, he still was unable to get deliveries of more than about ninety carloads a day, because rolling stock was just not available for any more than that. He met the need with an order that all trains arriving at Nashville from Louisville be detained for use on the Chattanooga line. When this brought a protest from the Louisville and Nashville Railroad, he advised it to make a similar forced loan on trains arriving at Jeffersonville, Indiana. As a result, cars from all parts of the North soon were appearing on the military railroad in Georgia. Reconstruction of the railroad southward from Chattanooga went forward with the armies, and at no time were the trains more than five days behind General Sherman. A civilian superintendent of bridge construction, E. C. Smeed, performed miracles of construction in replacing the bridge over the Etowah River (625 feet long, 75 feet high, built in six days by 600 men of the Construction Corps) and over the Chattahoochee River (740 feet long and 90 feet high, built in four and one-half days). Maj. Gen. Grenville M. Dodge personally directed a pioneer corps of 1,500 men in rebuilding railroads and bridges; perhaps his most notable achievement was the building of a bridge 1,400 feet long at Roswell, Georgia, in less than four days.

Once opened, this long supply line had to be kept open. Strong detachments occupied fortified posts at Chattanooga, and through Georgia at Ringgold, Dalton, Resaca, Rome, Kingston, the Etowah bridge, Allatoona, Kennesaw, and Marietta. Solidly built blockhouses protected each bridge. But the real secret to the success of maintaining the supply line was not protection—no force could protect every foot of the way against active enemy raiders. Rather, the secret lay in the rapid repair of damage to facilities. Detachments of the Construction Corps were stationed at critical points with trainloads of rails, ties, and timbers, ready to move out on short notice to repair damaged track. (A Confederate story had it that Sherman carried along duplicate tunnels.) Once, in October 1864, after Maj. Gen. John B. Hood's Confederate troops had torn up nine miles of track, 10,000 men turned out to restore the roadbed and put in 35,000 ties, while the regular construction crew went to work re-laying rails, and finished the job within a week. On one occasion a Northern train got through a damaged area before the Confederate cavalry leader could get back and report to his commander the success of his raid.

In preparing for and supporting the Atlanta campaign, the commissary of subsistence at the primary base at Louisville expanded operations a hundredfold. During 1864, while he was purchasing, receiving, and forwarding 300,000 rations a day, he also was running a cracker bakery that used 400 barrels of flour a day, and a bread bakery that used 150 barrels of flour a day; he furnished one to five thousand meals a day for a rest camp; supplied rations for twenty-one hospitals with about 20,000 patients; packed about 1,000 hogs a day at three pork houses; put up 6,000 gallons of pickles a day; and received about 1,000 head of cattle a day. To be able to supply all of Sherman's needs he leased new storage facilities at Jeffersonville, and built up a stock of 10,000,000 rations. The depot at

Chattanooga forwarded an average of 412,000 rations a day from 1 May to 12 August for the 105,000 soldiers and 30,000 civilian employees traveling with Sherman's armies. Some additional supplies were shipped from Cincinnati and St. Louis to Nashville. Supplies from Louisville were sent forward both by water and railroad. When cars were available, beef cattle went by rail; otherwise they were driven in herds of 500, and the commissary arranged for feeding stations along the way to Nashville.

In his own appraisal of the campaign, made while it still was in progress, Sherman took greatest pride in the fact that "for one hundred days not a man or horse has been without ample food, or a musket or gun without adequate ammunition." [7] His first and last concern was supply.

Sherman's March to the Sea

If the Atlanta campaign was notable for maintenance of its long line of communication and adequate supply, the march to the sea that followed was notable for the lack of bases and supply lines to support it. The march through Georgia to Savannah was, first of all, a shift of bases. On a vaster scale, it was in this respect similar to the shift the Army of the Potomac accomplished from the Pamunkey to the James in 1862 or to the James in 1864, or Grant's march from the Mississippi to the Yazoo in the Vicksburg campaign of 1863. In all those cases the armies concerned were marching *toward* new supply bases. In the march to the sea Sherman saw his role primarily as one of joining forces with Grant

to overwhelm Lee, and to do this it was necessary to reach the seacoast for a new supply depot. At the same time he saw this as the best way to nullify Hood's threat to his line of communications.

Sherman detached a part of his force under Thomas to continue to watch Hood, and to defend Tennessee; but while Hood moved to cut the long line of communication that Sherman had maintained with such care, Sherman determined to turn his back on the enemy with the major part of his command and march for the coast. Breaks in the railway line were repaired to permit the necessary supplies to be collected at Atlanta, and for all the matériel no longer wanted to be sent back to Chattanooga and Nashville. Each soldier received a complete set of clothing and shoes, wagons were loaded with rations, forage, ammunition, and other supplies, and torn canvas wagon covers were replaced. Then Sherman's own men tore up the track as far back as Allatoona and the Etowah bridge. Between 10 and 15 November the four corps making up the expedition set out for Savannah, 300 miles away. The force numbered about 62,000 men, not counting civilian attendants, and took with it about 14,700 horses (including cavalry), 19,400 mules, about 2,500 wagons each drawn by six mules, and about 600 ambulances each one drawn by two horses. Eight horses were assigned to each of the sixty-five artillery pieces, the caissons, and the forges. The wagons, with about 2,500 pounds each, carried rations for twenty days, forage for five days, and 200 rounds of ammunition for each man and each artillery piece. Each soldier carried with him forty rounds of ammunition and three days' rations. About 3,400 beef cattle accompanied the army. Baggage was held to a minimum. Tents still were prohibited; each man car-

---

[7] Ltr, W. T. Sherman to his wife, c. 11 August 1864, quoted in B. H. Liddell Hart, *Sherman: Soldier, Realist, American* (New York: Dodd, Mead & Co., 1930), p. 294.

ried little more than a single blanket for himself. A coffee pot and a stewing pan sufficed for each group of messmates. The four corps marched by four parallel routes when possible. On an ordinary day, each corps was supposed to start at 0700 and march fifteen miles before making camp for the night. There was no army supply train, but each corps commander controlled his own trains.

For resupply of subsistence and forage, Sherman turned frankly and systematically to foraging on the country. The country was too sparsely settled and the distances were too great to allow orderly requisitioning through local magistrates. Sherman authorized brigade commanders to detail foraging parties of about fifty men. After being oriented on the day's route of march and the next intended stopping place, the parties would strike out before daylight. Going five or six miles to the flank of the column, they would visit every farm and plantation within range. They gathered all the bacon, corn meal, turkeys, chickens, ducks, geese, hogs, grain, and other food for men and animals that they could carry in the light wagons or carriages they picked up, then returned to the main road where, if early enough, they awaited the arrival of the empty wagons in the trains and turned over their supplies to the brigade commissaries. Captured cattle and sheep were driven along until needed. Enough horses, mules, and beef cattle were commandeered for the army to have more of all these animals when it reached Savannah than it had when it left Atlanta.

While reports of disaster to the Yankees appeared in the Confederate press, the War Department proceeded confidently with preparations to resupply Sherman's army when it reached the coast. On the chance that Lee might abandon his position in Virginia and turn against Sherman, the Quartermaster General sent a few supply ships to Pensacola, in case it should become necessary for Sherman to turn south before reaching his goal, but the main supply fleet waited at Port Royal, South Carolina. As soon as Fort McAllister (near Savannah) had fallen, wrecking crews arrived to begin clearing the channels of obstacles, and light steamers relayed from the transports to landings up the Ogeechee and Savannah Rivers all the clothing, shoes, shelter tents, forage, rations, wagons and wagon parts, harness, tools, hospital supplies, and other items that imaginative supply officers had anticipated an army so long out of contact with a base would need.

As far as Sherman was concerned, he had demonstrated that armies were not tied down to bases. But three important factors made possible his living off the country in this instance. First, his army was continuously on the move. No army could have remained stationary in that country for any period of time and found enough subsistence and forage in the immediate vicinity to sustain it. Second, Sherman's march was feasible because the Georgia fields were no longer devoted almost exclusively to cotton, as they had been previously. Third, there was almost no fighting, and thus no drain on the ammunition supply; ammunition was a critical item which could not be found growing on trees.

Through the Carolinas

Sherman's march northward through the Carolinas, begun on 1 February 1865, was conducted in much the same way as the march through Georgia, but it was longer, more difficult, more violent, and even more rapid. Heavy rains and cold weather added hardships to the march, but the force of over 60,000 men, with trains about the same size as before, marched 425 miles to Goldsboro, North Carolina, in fifty days. Again it marched without a base and without lines of communication, living off the country and destroying enemy resources and installations as it went. Two divisions of the Construction Corps that had been transferred by railroad from Nashville to Baltimore, and thence by ocean steamer to Savannah, re-embarked when it developed that Sherman was going to continue wrecking railroads instead of repairing them, and went to Wilmington and Morehead City to work with the additional forces under Maj. Gen. John M. Schofield and Maj. Gen. Alfred H. Terry. From those two North Carolina coastal cities they restored the railway lines to Goldsboro, and ultimately northward to Wilson and northwestward beyond Raleigh. When the right wing of Sherman's force arrived at Goldsboro on 22 March, it found Schofield's Twenty-third Corps (which had been transferred from the Tennessee in January) in occupation, and communications with the seacoast open. Trains with three days' rations were waiting. The Twenty-third Corps and Terry's Tenth Corps were then reconstituted the Army of the Ohio and joined to Sherman's command, the other elements of which were reorganized as the Army of the Tennessee and the Army of Georgia.

All together the Construction Corps reopened nearly 300 miles of railroads in North Carolina, and built a wharf covering 54,000 square feet at the ocean terminus of the Atlantic and North Carolina Railroad near Morehead City. A number of canal boats and barges went up the Neuse River

to New Berne to relieve some of the pressure on the railroads. While the armies prepared and then moved out for the final showdown with General Joseph E. Johnston's Confederate forces, depots were established at Sister's Ferry, Fayetteville, and Raleigh, as well as at Morehead City, New Berne, and Goldsboro. Vessels supplying the armies during this period included 73 steamers, 8 tugs, 15 sailing vessels, and 2 pilot boats, as well as a number of barges. Subsistence supplies sent from Boston, New York, Alexandria, Fort Monroe, and Norfolk to Savannah, King's Bridge, Hilton Head, and Morehead City for Sherman's forces during the period from December 1864 to May 1865 included 9,852,000 pounds of meats, 22,848,000 pounds of breadstuffs, 1,173,000 pounds of vegetables, 1,652,000 pounds of coffee, 2,734,000 pounds of sugar, and proportionate amounts of other elements of the ration.

Wilson's Cavalry Raid

Meanwhile Maj. Gen. James H. Wilson had set out on one of the greatest cavalry raids of the war to administer the *coup de grâce* to Alabama. With an independent cavalry corps of 10,000 horsemen, 3,000 infantry, and 20 horse-drawn artillery pieces, Wilson crossed the Tennessee River from Gravelly Springs on 22 March 1865 to strike rapidly and heavily against remaining railroads, factories, mills, and stockpiles in the area between the Alabama and the Chattahoochie Rivers which might yet serve a desperate Confederate stand. Each man carried five days' rations in his haversack; each horseman also carried two days' forage in his saddlebags. Fifty special wagons carried ponton bridge equipment, and another 150 wagons brought up ammunition and other supplies. While resting and preparing at Gravelly Springs, Wilson had been hard put to find forage for all of his horses, but once he was moving rapidly, that problem became simpler. After routing the Confederate force commanded by Lt. Gen. Nathan B. Forrest at Ebenezer Church, Wilson took Selma; then, destroying resources on the way, he entered Montgomery, and moved on across Alabama to cross the Chattahoochee and attack Columbus, Georgia—the only significant arsenal and supply base remaining in the area—and West Point, Georgia. Wilson's corps was in Macon, in central Georgia, when hostilities ended. Aiming directly at the remaining logistical capabilities of Georgia and Alabama, Wilson played a significant part in numbering the last days of the Confederacy.

CHAPTER XVI

Evacuation and Hospitalization

One aspect of logistical support for the armies in the field deserves special mention—the evacuation and hospitalization of the sick and wounded. The general system of collecting and transporting wounded soldiers from the battlefield to field hospitals and general hospitals that was developed during the Civil War became the standard in the Army for the next century.

Army medical service fell far short of providing needed support in the early battles, but after reorganization and infusion of new policies, a medical service subsequently evolved that won the commendation of the world:

After the organization . . . was perfected, the medical service in the field was based upon an independent hospital and ambulance establishment for each division of three brigades. The *personnel* of the division hospital consisted of a Surgeon in charge, with an Assistant Surgeon as executive officer and a second Assistant Surgeon as recorder, an operating staff of three Surgeons aided by three Assistant Surgeons, and the requisite number of nurses and attendants.

The division ambulance train was commanded by a First Lieutenant of the line, assisted by a Second Lieutenant for each brigade. The enlisted men detailed for ambulance duty were a sergeant for each regiment, three privates for each ambulance, and one private for each wagon. The ambulance train consisted of from one to three ambulances for each regiment, squadron, or battery, a medicine wagon for each brigade, and two or more supply wagons. The hospital and ambulance train were under the control of the Surgeon-in-Chief of the Division. The division hospitals were usually located just out of the range of artillery fire. Sometimes three or more division hospitals were consolidated under the orders of a Corps Medical Director who was assisted by his Medical Inspector, Quartermaster, Commissary, and chief ambulance officer.

The medical officers not employed at field hospitals accompanied their regiments and established temporary depots as near as practicable to the line of battle.

As soon as possible after every engagement the wounded were transferred from the division or corps hospitals to the base or general hospitals, which at one time numbered 205; these were under the charge and command of the Regular or Volunteer Staff, assisted by Acting Assistant Surgeons, Medical Cadets, and officers of the 2nd Battalion of the Veteran Reserve Corps.[1]

Evacuation

Widespread suffering of neglected sick and wounded was common during the months of war that preceded the introduction of well-ordered ambulance and field hospital systems. Many men wounded at the first battle of Bull Run had to walk twenty miles back to Washington before they could find medical treatment. At Ball's Bluff and Belmont many wounded

---

[1] *Medical and Surgical History of the War of the Rebellion (1861–65): Prepared in accordance with Acts of Congress under Direction of Surgeon General Barnes, U.S. Army* (Washington, 1875–1888), II, pt. 3, 902.

were left to die on the field because there were no facilities to evacuate them. Thirteen thousand Union casualties at Shiloh completely swamped the undermanned medical staffs and meager hospital facilities of the Army of the Tennessee and the Army of the Ohio, and shortages of medical supplies and of transportation for evacuation revealed with new emphasis the shortcomings of a Medical Department which, in view of the unexpectedly high casualty rate, would have been inadequate in any case. More supplies and transportation were available for the Army of the Potomac on the Peninsula, but the lack of a systematic evacuation system allowed a re-enactment of unattended suffering at Seven Pines and Fair Oaks and during the Seven Days Battle. This had other unfortunate consequences: when no one else was there to help, soldiers quickly fell out of line to help wounded comrades to the rear, and as a result, whole companies tended to melt away after suffering a few casualties. Further lack of co-ordination was in evidence at Second Bull Run, when even the available transportation could not be put to good use because irresponsible ambulance drivers refused to help put the wounded in their ambulances or to give other assistance, and even turned to plundering the commissary and hospital supplies.

The Letterman System

The autumn of 1862 brought a change of fortune in field medical service. With Surgeon General Hammond's reforms taking effect at the top, Jonathan Letterman, who became medical director of the Army of the Potomac in July 1862, provided the counterpart in the field. The ambulance system, field hospital system, and medical supply system that Letterman introduced ultimately became standard throughout the armies of the United States.

Initial removal of the wounded from the battlefield usually was by hand litters. Over 50,000 hand stretchers of various types were purchased and issued during the war. Probably the most common of these was the Halstead, made of unbleached canvas on ash poles, with legs, iron braces, and shoulder straps, and slightly lighter and more compact than the Satterlee which it superseded. Field expedients included hurdles, gates, window shutters, and ladders, covered with hay or brush. Sometimes horse or mule litters, cacolets—chairlike affairs swung on either side of a mule's back— were used for longer hauls through country where wheeled vehicles could not readily go.

The greatest weakness in the evacuation chain at first was in the removal of casualties from regimental first aid stations or collecting points to hospital facilities in the rear. Surgeons had to depend on the Quartermaster's Department for ambulance transportation, and upon details of men from nonmedical units for assistance. These arrangements were most difficult to make in units heavily engaged, and thus most in need of evacuation assistance.

Almost from the beginning of the war various private citizens urged the establishment of a separate ambulance corps under the control of the Medical Department. In April 1862 Surgeon Charles S. Tripler, then medical director of the Army of the Potomac, urged that an experienced quartermaster and an assistant commissary of subsistence be attached to the staff of the chief medical officer of a field army so that he would not have to negotiate with the Quartermaster's and Commissary Departments through third parties for the supplies and transportation he needed. When Letterman succeeded Tripler as medical director of the Army of the Potomac, he quickly saw the necessity of an ambulance service, independent of Quartermaster control and having its own officers, which would free surgeons, busy with other duties when ambulances were most needed, of immediate responsibility. Surgeon General Hammond shared Letterman's views, but his efforts to get general approval for a separate ambulance corps under control of the Medical Department aroused the opposition of the Quartermaster General and got nowhere with General in Chief Halleck and the Secretary of War. Quartermaster General Meigs protested that it would be as reasonable to make the ordnance, infantry, artillery, and all the other branches of the Army independent of the Quartermaster's Department, and let each obtain its own vehicles, animals, and forage. He ridiculed the idea that physicians and surgeons would be more competent to purchase and contract for the transportation needed to move the sick and wounded than would Quartermaster officers trained and experienced in procuring all kinds of transportation. But the fact remained that evacuation was less than satisfactory.

If Hammond found little support for his proposals in the War Department, at least he could give his own blessing to Letterman's efforts, and with the added support of General McClellan, the medical director of the Army of the Potomac proceeded to set up a new ambulance system in that army. The system somewhat resembled the "Flying Ambulance Legion" attached to Napoleon's Imperial Guard. Letterman's plan was to appoint certain officers to have direct charge of ambulances, together with the horses, harness, and other equipment needed to operate them, and to put them on call by medical officers as required. Under a special order issued on 2 August 1862 the ambulance corps was organized on the basis of an allowance of one 4-horse and two 2-horse ambulances, and one transport cart for each regiment, with three soldiers assigned as drivers and attendants for each ambulance, and one soldier as driver for each transport cart. The regimental ambulance corps was under the command of a sergeant; all of these detachments for a brigade were under a second lieutenant. A captain was commandant of the ambulance corps for each army corps. He received his instructions for the distribution of ambulances and the points to which casualties were to be transported from the medical director of the army corps. He was required to make a personal inspection each week, and to forward a report through the army corps medical director to the medical director of the army on whether any ambulances had been used for any other purpose than the transportation of the sick and wounded or of medical supplies. In camp the ambulance trains ordinarily were parked with the brigades, and when needed to evacuate sick or wounded men, regimental medical officers requisitioned them from the commander of the brigade ambulance corps. On the march the ambulance train of each division moved ahead of the wagon trains. Later ambulances in camp also were parked by division. It was specifically ordered that no persons except members of the ambulance corps would be permitted to evacuate any casualty from the battlefield.

The advantages of Letterman's system became apparent even before there had been time to organize it completely, and the idea spread rapidly. In spite of the very heavy casualties, evacuation for the right wing of

EVACUATING CASUALTIES BY AMBULANCE

the army (where the system had been organized) at Antietam was rapid and efficient in comparison with previous efforts. The system first was in full operation at the battle of Fredericksburg (13 December 1862), and the improvement in battlefield evacuation was remarkable. After an ambulance corps was started in Sherman's army corps, medical inspector Edward P. Vollum persuaded General Grant to establish the system throughout the Army of the Tennessee in March 1863. Meanwhile agitation had grown in the U.S. Sanitary Commission and other civilian circles for a statutory ambulance corps for the entire United States Army. Dr. Henry I. Browditch, whose wounded son had died through neglect on the battlefield, took it upon himself to lead the movement for ambulance service reform. Rebuffed by the opposition or indif-

ference of General in Chief Halleck, he turned to Congress. A bill providing for an ambulance corps passed the House of Representatives in February 1863, but died in Senate committee. A year later a bill incorporating the Letterman system for all armies passed both houses, and received Presidential approval on 11 March 1864.

Ambulances

The Civil War was the first conflict in which armies of the United States used specially designed ambulance wagons for the evacuation of the wounded. A board of medical officers in 1859 had approved two types of two-wheeled ambulances (one designed by Surgeon Clement A. Finley and the other by Assistant Surgeon Richard H. Coolidge), and a heavy four-wheeled ambulance wagon designed by Surgeon Tripler. Medical officers recommended use of the two-wheeled ambulance for transporting dangerously sick or wounded men, but experience soon proved these vehicles to be impractical—they jolted so badly that wounded men begged to be let out of them. The Tripler four-wheeled ambulance, though heavy and cumbersome, quickly supplanted the two-wheeled models. Then a lighter four-wheeled model designed by General Rosecrans and known as the Wheeling came into fairly general use. Many other designs were offered and of these probably the most serviceable one, used in the last years of the war, was a heavier wagon designed by Brig. Gen. Daniel H. Rucker in which were installed hinged cots that could be folded into seats along the sides of the van.

Evacuation to Base and General Hospitals

For evacuation beyond the field hospitals to base and general hospitals, medical officers depended upon both water and rail transportation. The assumption that the recovery of sick men would be hastened if they were removed to climates to which they were better accustomed made it especially desirable to develop long lines of evacuation.

Evacuation by steamboat in the western theater where the great rivers served the combat areas should have been a simple matter. But no hospital transport service had been organized in advance, and division of authority between the Medical Department and the Quartermaster's Department again imposed serious administrative obstacles. The first steamboat used for large-scale evacuation on the western rivers

was the *City of Memphis,* ordered by Grant from Cairo to Fort Henry in February 1862. (Agents of the U.S. Sanitary Commission arrived with a boat from Cincinnati to assist.) After being used for ten days as a receiving boat to transfer sick and wounded from Fort Henry to other boats, the *City of Memphis* left Fort Henry on 18 February with 475 casualties for Paducah, Kentucky. During the next five months the *Memphis* carried some 7,000 casualties to hospitals at Memphis, St. Louis, and Keokuk, Iowa, on the Mississippi; at Mound City, Illinois, Evansville, Indiana, Louisville, and Cincinnati on the Ohio; and at Savannah, Tennessee, on the Tennessee. Then, after several months out of action, the *Memphis* returned to service during the Vicksburg campaign. One of the most noted of the hospital steamers in the West was the *D. A. January,* a 450-ton side-wheeler that carried more than 23,000 patients in the period from April 1862 to August 1865.

The transfer of operations to the Virginia Peninsula in the spring of 1862 presented further opportunities for evacuation by water routes in the eastern theater. Again the Medical Department was not prepared, and the attempt by the Quartermaster's Department to use the same vessels for all purposes complicated the evacuation system. Many vessels were used temporarily for evacuating the sick and wounded, but few were fitted as regular hospital transports. The first vessel assigned (April 1862) to evacuating casualties from the Peninsula appears to have been the *Daniel Webster.* The initiative in developing this service had come largely from the U.S. Sanitary Commission, and it fell to the commission to find the necessary bedding, medicines, and surgical appliances to outfit the vessel, and to look after the patients on the voyage from the

York River to New York. A short time later the Sanitary Commission outfitted the *Ocean Queen*, a large vessel capable of carrying 1,000 patients, but after a single voyage to New York with 900 patients this ship was withdrawn from the hospital service and sent with troops to the Gulf of Mexico. The want of organization, control, and co-ordination left much to be desired in the evacuation from the Peninsula. Intended to serve as an auxiliary, the Sanitary Commission found itself burdened with almost the whole task. It had to rely on the co-operation of medical officers, which was not always forthcoming, on the Quartermaster's Department for boats that were not always available, on civilian volunteer surgeons and nurses who were not always dependable, and upon crews who were not under military discipline.

Not only in Virginia but in other areas as well, it frequently occurred that vessels assigned for the evacuation of casualties would be claimed by the Quartermaster's Department for some other use after only a few trips. Protests of medical officers finally brought about a change in this situation. When in November 1863 the commanding general of the Department of the South ordered the return of a hospital steamer to the Quartermaster's Department, the Surgeon General obtained an order from the Secretary of War to restore the vessel to hospital service. A further incident involving the same steamer at last caused the War Department to issue a general order in February 1865 to the effect that hospital transports would be exclusively under the control of the Medical Department and would not be diverted by orders of local or department commanders or of officers of other staff departments.

The use of railways for the evacuation of casualties began very early in the war when a train of ordinary boxcars, loaded with badly wounded survivors of the battle of Wilson's Creek, pulled out of Rolla, Missouri, for St. Louis in August 1861. Returning supply trains were used for the evacuation of casualties throughout the war, but these cars were not satisfactory for the long distances to the general hospitals. Once more the U.S. Sanitary Commission was instrumental in bringing about improvement. Dr. Elisha Harris of the commission designed a special hospital car and urged that special trains be operated under systematic procedures. Quartermaster General Meigs approved the plan and put some government-owned railway cars at the disposal of Harris. Eastern railway companies cooperated by furnishing additional equipment, and the Sanitary Commission purchased its own locomotive so that the hospital train would not be delayed by other calls for the locomotive on which it must depend. In the fall of 1862 daily hospital train service began between Washington and New York, and continued until the end of the war.

When the experiment had proved successful, the Sanitary Commission turned over to the Medical Department the management of hospital cars and trains, and, with the benefit of the earlier experience, the government fitted out improved hospital cars. A typical hospital train serving the Army of the Cumberland, for instance, was made up of ten cars as follows: one boxcar fitted as baggage and commissary car; one kitchen car divided into three compartments, dining room, storeroom, and kitchen proper; one ordinary passenger car for men not confined to their beds; five cars with beds—first-class passenger cars transformed into hospital wards; a surgeon's car, converted from an ordinary passenger car by removing seats and adding partitions and fixtures, and a conductor's car for the train crew. In the Army of the Potomac the complete hospital train included ten cars for the sick and wounded, one for the kitchen and dispensary, and one for the surgeon in charge. The surgeon in charge was the commander of a hospital train, and the civilian train crew employed by the Quartermaster's Department operated under his orders. On a hospital steamboat the chief medical officer had to act as an assistant quartermaster and commissary of subsistence, but the surgeon in charge of a hospital train drew his rations as he would at a general hospital. His staff ordinarily included one medical assistant and one hospital steward with enlisted men detailed as cooks, nurses, and hospital attendants. All together hospital trains carried about 225,-000 patients during the war.

As ultimately worked out, then, battlefield evacuation was organized by army corps. It will be recalled that officers and men were detailed from each corps for service in its own ambulance corps. In the evacuation of casualties litter bearers brought the wounded to temporary hospitals or collecting stations in the rear of which ambulances were stationed. Surgeons not needed in the field hospitals organized these collecting stations and there gave what first aid they could before the patients were loaded onto the ambulance wagons. The ambulances carried the patients about three miles to the rear to the field hospital. The field hospital of each corps was made up of sections corresponding to the divisions in the corps and under the charge of the division medical officers. Further evacuation was done by ambulance wagon, hospi-

tal train, freight train, or boat to the base hospital located at the army main supply base, and finally by railway or steamboat to the general hospitals in various parts of the country.

Hospitalization

Field Hospitals

Hospitals set up for the support of the early operations in northern Virginia included the regimental tent hospitals and general hospitals in Alexandria and Washington and those improvised in old hotels and other buildings. Field hospitals gradually evolved toward larger units. While medical director of the Army of the Potomac, Tripler at first resisted efforts to establish brigade hospitals as having no authority in Army Regulations. Finally he permitted some brigade hospitals during the Peninsula campaign, but he was careful to conduct them as aggregations of regimental hospitals. Generally they were assigned temporary quarters in available buildings. The first tent field hospital of any size seems to have been one organized during the battle of Shiloh (6 April 1862) by medical inspector Bernard J. D. Irwin of the 4th Division, Army of the Ohio. Using tents from the recaptured camp of a division of troops who had been made prisoners the preceding day, Irwin set up accommodations for 300 patients. Large field hospitals supported the western armies at the siege of Corinth, Mississippi, and in later campaigns. In the fall of 1862 Letterman made the division hospital the rule in the Army of the Potomac, abolishing regimental hospitals (though they lingered until 1864). Letterman's field hospital system had certain defects— it was an *ad hoc* arrangement put into effect only for an engagement, personnel and equipment still came largely from the brigades, and the hospitals and ambulance corps were weakened by calls for personnel and equipment for service in the rear areas. Surgeon Thomas A. McParlin, who succeeded Letterman as medical director of the Army of the Potomac, subsequently was able to overcome most of these deficiencies. By 1863 the usual procedure was to cluster division hospitals together to form corps hospitals.

The regulation hospital tent was a wall tent 14 feet long, 14 feet 6 inches in breadth, and 11 feet high in the middle with walls 4 feet 6 inches high. A fly covered each tent. One tent would accommodate eight patients, and, if desired, two or more tents could be joined together to form a single larger ward. In addition to three hospital tents each regiment received one tepeelike Sibley tent and one wedge tent, but these were not often used for hospital purposes. Wood-burning stoves frequently were used to heat hospital tents, but a favorite method of heating was the so-called California plan by which a fire pit was dug outside the door and connected by a trench passing through the tent to a chimney in the rear. Covered with sheet-iron plates, this trench allowed the heat to pass through the whole length of the tent and kept it comfortably warm even in the coldest weather.

Base and General Hospitals

There was no well-defined evacuation policy, and the criteria for evacuating men beyond the field hospitals to base or general hospitals were the subject of long argument among the medical officers concerned. Sometimes surgeons at base hospitals refused to accept patients sent to them, and returned them to their camps. In the West the reputation that base hospitals acquired as being charnel houses did not result simply from unsanitary conditions in those hospitals, but from the fact that surgeons at field hospitals adopted the policy of sending only the dying to the rear. Tripler thought the sick did much better in regimental than in general hospitals; he regarded the latter as nuisances "to be tolerated only because there are occasions when they are absolutely necessary—as, for instance, when the army is put in motion and cannot transport its sick." [2]

During Sherman's Atlanta campaign the sick and wounded were evacuated from large "hospital depots" at Atlanta, Marietta, Kingston, and Rome, Georgia, to general hospitals at Chattanooga, Nashville, and Louisville. Three connecting hospital trains covered the 470 miles between Atlanta and Louisville on regular schedules. Some patients went directly to Louisville. Usually, however, patients remained at Nashville or Chattanooga until they had partially recovered, and were then moved to Louisville to make space for other casualties being brought from the depots below. The Army of the Cumberland had a large "traveling general hospital" which was in effect an evacuation hospital. It had 100 large tents with facilities for 1,000 patients. As the army advanced through northern Georgia the hospital displaced forward to successive locations at Ringold, Resaca, Big Shanty, Marietta, Vining's Station, and Atlanta. It received 58,500 casualties, including 15,500 wounded, of which 31,300 returned to their units, 26,000 were evacuated to general hospitals farther north, and 1,200 died.

---

[2] Quoted in Louis C. Duncan, "Evolution of the Ambulance Corps and Field Hospital," *Military Surgeon,* XXXII (March, 1913), 225.

AN ARMY HOSPITAL NEAR WASHINGTON

The largest hospital in the Army at the outbreak of the Civil War was the 40-bed post hospital at Fort Leavenworth. There were no general hospitals. When it became obvious that this war would entail large-scale combat operations, it also became obvious that crises lay ahead in providing hospital accommodations. Nevertheless, the Quartermaster's Department hesitated to embark upon a construction program to meet the need until the clamor raised by the U.S. Sanitary Commission became too loud to be ignored. Hospitals improvised in hotels, schools, and other buildings of the cities did not have the sanitary facilities required, their construction was not suitable for hospital activities, and they could not meet the demands for ventilation in an era when fresh air was a passion. Sanitary Commission agents urged that pavilion-type hospitals of the kind developed by the British in the

Crimea be built. In these hospitals each ward was in a separate building or pavilion sometimes joined together by a corridor or covered walk. At the suggestion of Assistant Surgeon Hammond, made long before he became Surgeon General, Assistant Surgeon Letterman, then medical director of the Department of West Virginia, ordered the construction of the first pavilion-type hospital for the U.S. Army at Parkersburg early in 1862—a wooden shed featuring ridge ventilation. A modest hospital construction program undertaken in 1862 could only begin to meet the demands for space. The movement of the Army of the Potomac to the Peninsula filled the hospitals of Washington with sick men who had to be left behind, but it also made available a number of barracks which were put to use as hospitals. Casualties evacuated from Fortress Monroe during the Peninsula campaign quickly filled the 6,000 beds that had been provided at Washington, Philadelphia, and Baltimore; additional beds were set up in the Capitol and in Georgetown prison, and convalescents were placed in private homes. During the summer additional barracks were taken over, hospital tents set up, and older hospitals expanded so that 20,000 beds were available in the area when the wounded arrived from Antietam. Washington hospitals were practically cleared when Grant opened his campaign in 1864, but casualties from the Wilderness and Spottsylvania quickly overtaxed them again.

In the West the principal general hospitals were at Memphis, Nashville, Chattanooga, and on the Ohio River. The largest hospital was the Jefferson General Hospital at Jeffersonville, Indiana. Built in the winter of 1863–64 at a cost of $250,000, it had twenty-four pavilions radiating from a circular corridor nearly half a mile in circumference. Offices, surgeon's rooms, bakery, and laundry were inside the circle, easily accessible to all the wards. Its original capacity of 2,000 beds was later expanded to 2,600; it was to have been further enlarged to 5,000 beds—which would have made it the largest hospital in the world—when the war ended.

Actually the pavilion buildings of these large general hospitals were cheaper to construct than were tents. The costly part was providing facilities for heating, cooking, laundry, and water supply. Many were heated by steam, and most of them had steam machinery for washing and for pumping water. At just one hospital the daily consumption of water at times exceeded 100,000 gallons. After a slow start, the construction program gained such momentum that total capacity almost doubled each year from 1862 to 1864. In the last

year of the war 204 general hospitals with a total capacity of 136,894 beds were serving the Federal armies.

Administration of a general hospital was entrusted to a surgeon in charge who had complete military command. In the larger hospitals the surgeon in charge had an executive officer who was responsible for the office and records, supervised the admission of patients, and prepared the required reports. Ward physicians were responsible for the medical and surgical treatment of the patients and for the care of the ward. One of the ward physicians was detailed as medical officer of the day to inspect all the wards, prescribe in case of emergency in the absence of the ward physician, and admit patients in the absence of the executive officer. Each ward had a wardmaster who, in the absence of the physician, supervised the nurses, the care of the patients, and was responsible for cleanliness and discipline. Hospital stewards had charge of the dispensary and property. Sometimes medical cadets served as clerks and dressers under the immediate supervision of the ward physician. Most large hospitals had a chaplain who had supervision over the postal service, reading room, library, and cemetery. Convalescents and limited-duty men frequently served as nurses and attendants. Other employees were hired from civilian ranks. A hospital of 1,000 beds could be expected to have twenty wardmasters, forty to one hundred nurses, five or six cooks and eight or ten cooks' assistants, three or four bakers, four or five launderers, ten to fifteen men in the blacksmith, painter, and carpenter shops, and stables, and another ten to fifteen in the dispensary and the storerooms, three or four for cemetery duties, three orderlies for officers' quarters and mess rooms, and about ten clerks and messengers in the head-quarters office and library. Many medical officers were convinced that this staff of 120 to 200 employees could have been substantially reduced if a regularly enlisted medical corps made up of able-bodied men had been available.

Nurses

An important innovation in Civil War hospitals was the common use of women nurses. With the example of Florence Nightingale in the Crimea before them, women from all parts of the country volunteered for nursing service with the Army. The leader of this movement was Dorothea Dix. Already renowned for her work in reforming the care of the insane, and familiar with the work of the British Sanitary Commission and with the hospitals on the Black Sea, she reported to the Secretary of War to offer her services just four days after Lincoln's call for 75,000 militia. Her offer was accepted almost at once, and for several weeks she worked to provide nurses for hospitals in the Washington area. In June 1861 she was made "Superintendent of Female Nurses," and she served in this capacity without pay throughout the remainder of the war. In August Congress legally authorized the use of women nurses in the general or permanent hospitals when the Surgeon General or the surgeon in charge deemed it desirable. Their pay and allowances amounted to 40 cents a day and one ration. Absence of clear-cut lines of authority, the almost complete lack of nurses' training, the strict notions Miss Dix held about the proper qualifications for nurses, her obstinate sense of duty, and the prejudice against the use of women as nurses caused a great deal of friction between Miss

Dix and her nurses, and the medical officers. Specific objections arose when doctors learned that some of the women were disposed to ignore dietary instructions for the patients, and would substitute favorite home remedies of their own for the doctors' prescriptions. At first Miss Dix asserted virtually complete control over the selection of nurses. Candidates were required to be between the ages of thirty and fifty, and plain in appearance and dress. The inclination of surgeons to bypass Miss Dix in appointing nurses or to discharge her appointees without cause led to much controversy until a general order of October 1863 settled the matter. This order required the surgeon in charge to give specific reasons for discharging a nurse, and provided that no women nurses should be carried on the rolls except those appointed by Miss Dix—unless they were especially appointed by the Surgeon General. But it became evident that this proviso had opened the gate when Acting Surgeon General Joseph K. Barnes let it be known that he would appoint any woman requested by the surgeon in charge of a hospital "irrespective of age, size, or looks." Eventually a number of the nurses went through short training courses—sometimes under the auspices of the U.S. Sanitary Commission—before joining the staff of an Army hospital. Elizabeth Blackwell, probably the first modern woman to receive a medical degree, trained nurses for the Woman's Central Association of Relief in New York. At several hospitals, private organizations—notably religious orders such as the Sisters of Charity—provided nurses. Actually, the major nursing duties remained with male nurses. At West's Building in Baltimore, twenty of seventy nurses at one time were women, while at the hospital on Bedloe's Island in New York Harbor ten out of seventy were women. On the average the ratio of women nurses to men was about one to four or five. Perhaps as many as 3,200 women served as nurses at some time during the war; even these oftentimes were not assigned to actual nursing duties. At the end of the war medical officers generally testified that women nurses gave their best service in connection with preparing extra diets, in the linen room, and in the laundry, while male help usually was preferred in the wards.

Sanitation

To a generation accustomed to antiseptic surgery and antibiotic medicine as matters of course, treatment given the sick and wounded soldiers of the Civil War would seem crude indeed. Yet medical practice in the Civil War showed considerable advances over that of previous wars. Probably the greatest advance was in the improvement in camp and hospital sanitation in the later years of the war. Even so, disease claimed twice as many lives as did battle wounds. During the great battles surgery sometimes seemed little more than butchery, and infection of wounds was considered normal. Nevertheless experience led surgeons to suspect airborne virus or poisoned air of spreading infection from one patient to another, and they became sufficiently aware of the transmission of infection by direct contact to apply antiseptics to open cuts in their hands before touching a wound infected with "hospital gangrene." Many kinds of antiseptics and disinfectants were used, though frequently not in the right way nor at the right times, and there seems to have been a kind of blind spot when it came to sterilization of surgical instruments. In these circumstances the introduction of

anesthetics, primarily chloroform and ether, was not an unmixed blessing, for with them surgeons were encouraged to undertake operations that would have been unthinkable without them, and thus to spread further the dangerous infections occasioned by their septic instuments. The great discoveries in bacteriology were occurring during this period—too late to be put to use in wartime surgical and medical treatment, although war experience brought American surgeons remarkably close to some of the procedures which would be indicated by those discoveries. It was only in 1858 that Louis Pasteur had demonstrated the connection between bacteria and fermentation, and the susceptibility of bacteria to sterilization; it was 1864 when Joseph Lister, having reached the conclusion that microorganisms caused suppuration in wounds, demonstrated in the Glasgow Infirmary how infection could be prevented by strict cleanliness and the use of antiseptics; and it was not until 1876 that Robert Koch, in Berlin, and Pasteur, in Paris, showed that specific bacteria caused specific diseases.

In the meantime, the experience of American Civil War medical officers was being recorded in thousands of case histories, drawings, general observations, and statistical reports to become a storehouse of information for medical instruction. These records may have lacked the scientific explanations of cause and effect insofar as bacteria were concerned, but they indicated what could be expected to happen in certain conditions and suggested effective steps to avoid undesirable consequences. The record of American surgeons in the Civil War compares favorably with that of other armies of the same general period. For instance, French Army surgeons during the Franco-Prussian War (twelve years after

Pasteur's demonstration, and six after Lister's) performed 13,000 amputations of which 10,000 proved fatal; of 29,980 amputations officially recorded by Union surgeons during the Civil War, only 7,459 proved fatal (results of 1,719 cases were not finally reported).

For the whole period of the war, from 1861 to 1 July 1865, the general hospitals treated 1,057,423 cases among white troops. The mortality rate among them was 8 percent.

Summary

On the whole, the medical record of the Civil War was good. Sick and wounded soldiers had better care than ever before. Seemingly barbaric in many ways to later generations, it was as humane as could be expected in the light of knowledge available at the time. The improvement in the organization and administration of the Medical Department between 1861 and 1865 was notable. By the end of 1864 both Hammond and Letterman had left the Army, but the large, smoothly functioning organization they had built continued working efficiently, without change, to the end of the war. Their systems of evacuation, hospitalization, and medical supply by that time were undoubtedly the most effective that the world had seen, and they were continued as a permanent feature of Army organization. What had begun as a confused system of regimental hospitals and ambulance units had evolved into the integrated division and corps field hospitals supported by corps ambulance organizations. Well-ordered evacuation and convalescent hospitals had appeared; and the great pavilion general hospitals, where at last rules of sanitation were enforced, were one of the wonders of the age. Hospital boats and hospital trains moved patients, in at least relative comfort, over long distances. Civilian agencies such as the U.S. Sanitary Commission had learned much and taught much in rendering a real service on their own part and in insisting upon reform in the Medical Department.

In methods of evacuation and hospitalization, as in other respects, the Civil War was indeed the "first modern war." Mobilization on such a vast scale, introduction of new weapons and equipment, use of railroads in moving troops and supplies—in all of these ways the Civil War can be called the first modern American war. Still, it must be remembered that more muzzle-loaders than repeaters were used, that steamboats were as important as railroads, and that antiseptic surgery and bacteriology were just about to usher in truly modern medical practice. After the war the Army would be demobilized and what remained would be scattered mostly among western outposts. The surge toward modernization stimulated by war once again would decline to a slough of indifference, to be disturbed only now and then by the demands of Indian warfare and by a few imaginative officers seeking steady improvement, until a new national emergency should once more call forth the waves of progress.

CHAPTER XVII

The "Old Army" and the West

After the Civil War the Army experienced a decade of responsibility in the military occupation of the "conquered provinces" of the South, but its major concern was a return to the service which always had been its major responsibility during the interwar periods—defense on the frontiers. Indian conflicts had continued as a side show during the War for Southern Independence; after the war they once more became the main event, reaching an enormity without precedent since the Seminole Wars. For a quarter of a century after its reorganization in 1866 the Army was occupied largely in what was referred to at the time as the "battle of civilization." As transcontinental railroads pushed their way westward the Army escorted the surveying expeditions, occupied the mountain passes, and protected the working parties. Whenever hostile Indians threatened, miners, ranchers, merchants, and settlers called upon the Army for action. By the beginning of 1891 the powerful Indian tribes had been subjugated, disarmed, and pacified. The winning of the West by the "old Army" was virtually complete.[1]

---

[1] Rpt, Brig Gen Nelson A. Miles, Comdr Div of the Pacific, in *Report of the Major-General Commanding the Army to the Secretary of War, 1889* (Washington, 1889), pp. 114–15.

Administration and Control

Territorial administration of the Army followed generally the pattern that had evolved during the war. As reorganized in June 1865 the territory of the United States was divided into nineteen departments grouped under five military divisions. Alterations in this arrangement were frequent; the Department of the Platte, with headquarters in Omaha, was created in March 1866 for the purpose of facilitating protection and assistance for the Union Pacific Railroad; the Department of Dakota was established soon afterwards, with headquarters at St. Paul, to serve a similar purpose for the Northern Pacific Railroad. Later the divisions were abolished, and the departments were extended in area and reduced in number.

As far as command of the administrative bureaus—and the general control of Army logistics which this entailed—was concerned, the Secretary of War and the bureau chiefs again eclipsed the General of the Army. The *modus vivendi* by which Grant had retained a measure of *de facto* control over the bureaus as commander of all the armies ceased. Grant had expressed his views on the subject upon assuming the supreme command during the war, and had reiterated them in a long letter to Secretary Stanton in 1866, and again to Sherman privately after the election of 1868. It was, therefore, reasonable to expect that when Grant became President he would insist upon a definition of responsibilities in the War Department that would clearly spell out the subordination of the staff departments to the general commanding. In fact this at first appeared to be the case. The order announcing the appointment of General Sherman to command the Army, issued through Secretary of War John M. Schofield the very day after Grant's inauguration (4 March 1869), stated: "The chiefs of staff corps, departments, and bureaus will report to and act under the immediate orders of the General commanding the army." [2] In his general orders upon assuming command, Sherman named all the heads of staff departments and bureaus as members of his staff, conforming to Grant's stated opinion that the bureau chiefs should bear the same relationship to the General in Chief as the heads of the various staff departments serving a field army bore to the commanding general. The reaction to his orders was both swift and bitter. Sherman soon became "aware that the heads of several of the staff corps were restive under this new order of things, for by long usage they had grown to believe themselves not officers of the army in the technical sense, but a part of the War Department, the civil branch of the Government which connects the army with the President and Congress." [3]

Within three weeks the order was rescinded, and an incredulous General Sherman went to Grant for an explanation. Instead of reaffirming his stated views, President Grant went along with opinions ex-pressed in Congress that putting the bureau chiefs directly under the General of the Army probably was contrary to the laws establishing the bureaus. Sherman felt helpless to deal with the Indian troubles effectively as long as he was denied control over arrangements for providing the horses, wagons, ammunition, and food essential for any kind of military operations. He found it simpler to get the information he needed for preparing orders from the distant division or department commanders than from the bureaus in Washington.

Conditions went from bad to worse after William W. Belknap succeeded John A. Rawlins, Grant's old chief of staff, as Secretary of War. In November 1871 Sherman left for a tour of Europe, and he found no improvement when he returned ten months later. He then protested that orders were issued by the Secretary of War without the knowledge of the General of the Army, that he often had to rely on the newspapers for information, and that he felt that he was not master in his own house. Finally, he concluded that it would be best to get completely away from Washington and in October 1874 he moved the Headquarters of the Army to St. Louis where, despite severe criticism from some political leaders, he stayed until after Belknap resigned under a cloud of scandal in 1876. The new Secretary of War, Alphonso Taft of Cincinnati, called the Army chief back to Washington, and did maintain a more co-operative attitude, although the general policy continued.

Peacetime Progress

Ordnance

With the end of the Civil War, ordnance officers had time to consider carefully and

---

[2] Quoted in Sherman, *Memoirs*, II, 441.
[3] *Ibid.*

deliberately various proposals for improving United States arms. They deliberated so well that soldiers still were carrying single-shot Springfield breechloaders twenty-five years later. The Winchester model of 1873 became famous throughout the West, and was used by everyone except the Army. A board of officers did approve a Hotchkiss rifle (made by Winchester) that was tested in 1878 and, after a second series of trials in 1881, accepted for field test an improved Hotchkiss, a Lee (made by Remington), and a Chaffee-Reese (made at the Springfield Armory). Even when field tests had extended for over a year, the Chief of Ordnance, Maj. Gen. Stephen V. Benet, still was unwilling to replace the single-shot Springfield. Ironically, the Winchester Company was so discouraged by government policies that it did not even enter the competition in 1890 when at last a repeating rifle—the Krag-Jorgenson—was adopted. On the other hand, the government had officially adopted the Gatling machine gun in 1866, and several of these weapons were on the table of allowances for each detachment in the field.

Improvements in heavy ordnance, while having little effect on operations against the Indians, were of some significance. In particular, heavier, rifled guns replaced the smoothbores, and steel replaced cast iron. A board of officers considering proposed improvements throughout a year, 1881–82, recommended for trial some twenty-four suggestions, while rejecting eighty-one proposals for such things as revolving cannon, glass bombshells, breech shells, and various gun mechanisms. About 1885 the Army began making its own artillery tubes at the Watervliet Arsenal. It was reported in 1889 that the Japanese had developed a superior smokeless powder, but were keeping it a closely guarded secret.

Medical Service

Peacetime progress was slow, too, in medical service. But here the inertia or backwardness of the whole population rather than the Army alone could be blamed. If the use of antiseptics, as such, still was not common in the Army in the early 1880's, it should be remembered that Lister still was being ridiculed in London at that time. One need that successive surgeons general agreed upon as most important for the improvement of evacuation and hospitalization services was the enlistment of a regular hospital corps. Recommendations for such a corps during the war had come to nothing. For some time, the Secretary of War had been authorized to appoint hospital stewards, but there was no permanently established corps to include privates as well as stewards until 1887. Women might still be employed as nurses, but there was no regular nurses' corps until the Spanish-American War. In the 1870's the large general hospitals had disappeared, and the Army had only post hospitals—all barrack or temporary structures big enough for twelve to twenty-five beds. Hospitals were built to last only ten years, for the general belief was that in ten years the building would become so saturated with hospital poisons that it should be abandoned. Two special hospitals, one at the Soldiers' Home in Washington and one at West Point, were built during this period. In January 1887 the Army and Navy General Hospital at Hot Springs—the only general hospital in use between the Civil War and the Spanish-American War—opened with capacity for sixteen officers and sixty-four enlisted men.

Transportation and Supply

Supplying the troops in the West, few as they were, still posed problems. Major quantities of supplies were obtained by contract in the East or Middle West and shipped by rail and river boat to the accessible Army post nearest the forts or troops to be supplied. From the post supplies were carried forward by wagon trains or pack animals. Extension of the trans-Mississippi railroads eased the transportation problem in particular areas. In some cases whole wagon trains, completely loaded, could be moved by rail with wagons lashed to flatcars and mules in closed cars. At times, however, it seemed that the use of railroads created more problems than it solved. In the 1870's all money earned by the Union Pacific, the Central Pacific, and the Kansas Pacific had to be paid to the Secretary of the Treasury as assignee for those railroads pending litigation in the courts. Payment for any transportation on the land-grant railroads was prohibited by law, which caused embarrassment to officers, and resulted in legal proceedings when differences arose on conditions for such transportation. Further negotiations and compromises were necessary with various railroads indebted to the United States. For water transportation, the Quartermaster's Department retained only a few vessels for service in harbors and along the seacoast. Privately owned vessels handled all water transportation on the western rivers. By far the most expensive method of transportation was by wagon. Regular express lines such as Wells Fargo, wagon trains engaged by private contractors, and Army wagons driven by civilian teamsters all moved military supplies in the West. Total expenditures for hired wagons, teamsters, purchase

and repair of wagons, and stage transportation exceeded those for rail and water transportation combined.

Probably the least satisfactory element of supply in the western outposts was food supply. Buffalo, beef cattle, and local garden produce could make up deficiencies a part of the time, but the official ration, even when of fair quality was none too palatable without these supplements. Unfortunately, some unscrupulous contractors supplied inferior foods—or sometimes no food at all. Maj. Gen. George A. Custer reported an instance when unbroken packages of provisions shipped from the main depot were found to contain huge stones. Boxes of bread that had been baked in 1861 were shipped and issued to western troops in 1867. The inevitable results of poor food were ill health and dissatisfaction, and a consequent rate of desertion which, in such a small Army, became at times alarming.

Frontier Posts

Army logistics during this period was more of a throwback to pre-Civil War days than a continuation of developments that had marked wartime progress. Logistical problems once again were: to support small detachments scattered over thousands of miles of plains and mountains; to maintain widely separated posts on the frontier; and, now and then, to bring together supplies and forces for a major campaign—major, that is, in terms of the relative size of the Army as a whole and that of garrisons ordinarily maintained in frontier forts, but actually little more than a raid or reconnaissance in force when compared with the great armies and campaigns of the recent war. The basic problems were complicated by the rugged terrain and the nonexistence

MAP 11

of communications facilities in some areas. Moreover, troops were being constantly moved to meet a threat first here, then there (one cavalry troop, for instance, changed stations nine times in eleven months), and even for small detachments the single factor of distance in the West imposed logistical difficulties unlike anything encountered in other parts of the country. (*Map 11*)

After the war a chain of forts, more or less integrated, formed a general line of defense on the frontier from Mexico to Canada. Beyond the frontier additional forts guarded key points farther west. But the extension of the railroads and establishment of permanent settlements altered the pattern of Army posts as the frontier pushed westward. By the time the location of a proposed new line of forts farther west was decided upon, the frontier had moved beyond any proposed line, and the new forts were never built.

The southwestern line of defense was made up of an inner chain of forts built immediately after the War with Mexico, and an outer chain built about ten years later. During the few years that both lines were occupied they were to have constituted a co-ordinated, flexible defense system, with infantry garrisoned on the outer line and cavalry kept in support on the inner line. Posts on the outer chain were to be supplied from posts on the second line; then storehouses on the outer chain would supply a force of up to 200 men and horses for a march of 100 or 200 miles into Indian country where an advance base would be established. While one company brought up supplies, one or two others could move farther forward for operations. The system had much to recommend it, but communications and available forces never reached a level that could support really effective operations at great distance across the plains. Postwar improvements included building additional forts to form a new line of defense, linking the posts by telegraph, and joining them with roads.

One of the first postwar forts to be built in Texas was Fort Griffin. Permanent stone structures were planned, but pending their completion temporary wooden houses and huts served the garrison and two buildings were brought in from deserted ranches to become a "prefabricated" commissary building and a hospital. The depot quartermaster at San Antonio brought in steam saw mills, tools, building equipment, and mechanics to hasten construction of the temporary quarters, but it was impossible to erect the number of buildings needed at the time. Six men were crowded into each of the 8- by 14-foot huts. Officers, whose billets were single small huts containing one room and a kitchen, were accused of using soldiers to build comfortable officers' quarters instead of to fight Indians.

In the Northwest one of the more important base posts was Fort Laramie in Wyoming. At this time it was not a fortress of blockhouses and walls but a sprawling collection of all kinds of adobe and wooden structures, including barracks for six companies. Water was easily obtained from the nearby Laramie River, but wood for fuel had to be hauled fifteen miles. The nearest supply depot was almost ninety miles away at Cheyenne, and the vicissitudes of the trail made it advisable to keep six months' supplies on hand. (*Map 12*)

The line of posts northwest of Fort Laramie included Fort Reno and Fort Phil Kearney on the short-lived Bozeman Trail to the Montana mining country. The post at Fort Phil Kearney extended for 1,600 feet along the Big Piney River; the fort proper was built at the northwest end of the post in an area measuring 800 by 600 feet. Despite repeated Indian raids, construction at Fort Phil Kearney had proceeded during the summer and fall of 1866. Seventy-five to one hundred men cut timber and hauled logs from the woods almost seven miles from the post, while other details operated saw mills and put up the stockade and buildings. By October the forty-two buildings of the fort proper had been erected, stables and corrals were completed, and the stockade and blockhouses were raised.

The purchase of Alaska in 1867 cata-

GUARDING THE OVERLAND MAIL

pulted the nation's frontier to its northwest limit, and the Army's responsibilities as defender of the frontier multiplied as did its logistics problems. In December 1867 a small force of 250 infantrymen and artillerymen moved into headquarters established at Sitka. The detachment was soon involved in Indian unrest, but its most continuous and arduous battle was against weather and terrain. The problems of transportation increased in the next year when reinforcements arrived at Kodiak Island and Cook Inlet.

Indian Wars

Out on the plains General Sherman, first as commander of the Military Division of the Missouri and later as General of the Army, felt a sense of frustration in attempt-ing to police that vast area with the small resources at his command. Little could be done against Indian hit-and-run raids on scattered frontier settlements or emigrants and travelers on the trails. Attempts to pursue these bands were almost futile. One contemporary observer estimated that from the spring of 1866 to 1868 there were as many skirmishes along the Bozeman Trail, around Forts Reno, Phil Kearney, and C. F. Smith, as there were days in the year. During the last six months of 1867, posts in Texas sent out twenty-six expeditions against the Indians. New Mexico had little protection, and as far as Sherman was concerned it deserved little—he thought the best idea would be to give it all back to the Mexicans. He estimated that a cavalry force of about 2,500 would be needed to police the territory and that food and forage,

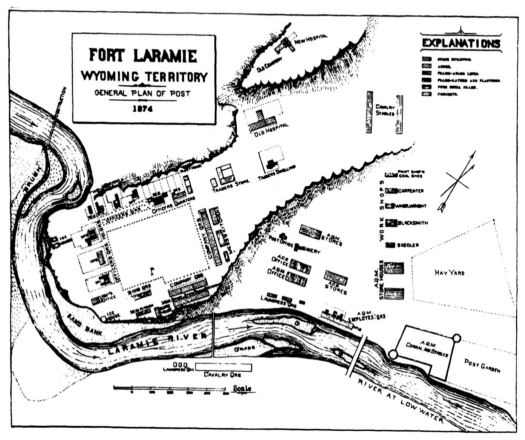

MAP 12

which would have to be hauled one thousand miles, would cost $1,000 a year for each soldier supported. Sherman's view was that cavalry expeditions would have to be sent out to patrol the principal western routes during the travel season. The small Army posts, he thought, would serve principally as forage depots for the cavalry expeditions. But on the High Plains, soldiers were kept busy simply gathering hay, cutting fuel, repairing barracks, and doing other tasks in order to defend themselves against the severe winters. Further complications arose from the efforts of civilian traders to prosper at the expense of the Army, controversies with the Department of the Interior about jurisdiction over Indian affairs, and requests for the Army to feed certain of the tribes.

Connor's Powder River Expedition

For his Powder River expedition in 1865, aimed at pacifying hostile tribes in northern Wyoming and northeastern Montana, Brig. Gen. Patrick E. Connor found it necessary

FORT PHIL KEARNEY, DAKOTA TERRITORY, 1867

to press into service privately owned wagons at Fort Laramie when the needed Army wagons failed to arrive. Trains belonging to two traders and sutlers who planned to accompany the expedition anyway and those belonging to a man who was there to put up a telegraph line were commandeered. All together 200 wagons moved out with Connor's western division on what was to be a three-pronged expedition. Forage and some other items were in short supply and the first leg of the march was to find grassland where the horses and mules could feed. While the command rested at the designated depot camp early in July the teamsters employed by A. C. Leighton, who owned 130 of the 200 wagons, demanded higher wages. Leighton refused and most of the drivers quit; whereupon General

Connor ordered soldiers to take over the wagons. The dissident teamsters built a raft and started to float it down the Laramie River, but an Indian attack a short distance downstream persuaded them to return to their wagons. The expedition moved on at the end of July, leaving behind a thousand sacks of corn forage at the camp for want of transportation. About 170 miles northwest of Laramie the soldiers built Fort Connor (later renamed Fort Reno). After a series of skirmishes with the Arapahoes and the Sioux, but before he was able to deliver his intended knockout blow, Connor received orders to cease operations and return to Laramie. The Fort Laramie post hospital was crowded with patients, and when the post commander learned of the planned departure of Leighton's wagon train for

Fort Leavenworth, he put ninety patients—most of them suffering from scurvy—aboard, and issued Spencer rifles and plenty of ammunition to everyone. As it turned out, the sick and wounded soldiers had to fight for their lives when strong Indian attacks struck at the wagons as they moved along the trail between Julesberg and Alkali Station.

Sheridan's Winter Campaign of 1868

Continued Indian raids and unrest after the conclusion of treaties early in 1868 by which the Cheyennes, Arapahoes, Kiowas, and Comanches had ageed to settle peaceably on reservations in the Indian Territory convinced Maj. Gen. Philip H. Sheridan, commanding the Division of the Missouri, that a general uprising was imminent. He concluded that the only way to meet the threat was to launch a winter campaign, striking at the hostile tribes when their ponies would be weak from lack of food, and when cold weather and snow would hamper all efforts to escape. Moving his headquarters from Leavenworth to Fort Hays at the terminus of the Kansas Pacific Railroad, which offered a good site for a supply depot and from which the long preparations for such a campaign could be supervised, Sheridan arranged for supplies, wagon transportation, and guides. He obtained the promise of reinforcements to the extent of five troops of the 5th Cavalry and a Kansas volunteer cavalry regiment to add to the 7th and 10th Cavalry and the 3d, 5th, and part of the 38th Infantry with which he had to garrison the posts and protect the settlements, trails, and railroad working parties in his department, as well as the mobile columns for his expeditionary forces. Sher-

idan ordered the commander of the military district to assemble the troops designated for the main column and to establish a supply depot about one hundred miles south of Fort Dodge. The depot was established at the confluence of Beaver and Wolf Creeks, and was named Camp Supply.

At the end of October adequate supply reserves for the main columns had been accumulated at Fort Dodge and Fort Lyon, and Sheridan ordered an additional three months' supply of subsistence and forage sent to Fort Gibson for final delivery at Fort Arbuckle. Sheridan arrived at Camp Supply on 21 November to take personal command. The plan called for a co-operating force of 500 men to move up from Fort Bascom, New Mexico, establish a supply depot at Monument Creek, and operate along the Canadian River; a second column was to move up from the Arkansas to establish a depot on the North Canadian, and operate toward the Antelope Hills; and the main column would strike at the Indian villages on the upper Washita. Cold rains, and then severe blizzards and heavy snows descended on the makeshift camps. Awaiting the delayed arrival of the Kansas Volunteers, Sheridan sent Custer and the 7th Cavalry to launch a preliminary attack on Black Kettle's village of Cheyennes on the Washita.

At dawn on 23 November Custer's troopers moved out through a blinding snow storm. Observation was so restricted that the commander had to "navigate" by compass. Trails had to be broken and bridges improvised for the wagons, and man and beast alike suffered from the freezing wind and the exhausting effort to get through deep snow. To the leaders this kind of weather was welcome, for the purpose of the winter campaign was to take advantage of weather when the Army could move and the Indians could not. Three days of this difficult marching brought the 7th Cavalry to the vicinity of the Cheyenne village. Leaving the wagon train in the rear under the guard of an officer and eighty cavalrymen, the troops moved up to attacking positions. Although the gray morning was cold, the men dropped their overcoats and the haversacks containing their extra rations and left them under the guard of one man from each company. Before Custer's men could jump off, the Indians attacked. Surrounding the cavalry troops momentarily, the Cheyennes made off with the stacked overcoats and haversacks, so that the troopers were compelled to endure the bitter cold without overcoats or rations. Nevertheless a dawn attack on the Indians was successful. Then a strong Indian counterattack developed, threatening the whole force when ammunition began to run low. Thanks to a regimental quartermaster who brought up an ammunition wagon and drove it through the midst of the attackers to his own lines, the cavalrymen were able to repulse the Indians and to destroy their village. A detachment of one officer and nineteen men that had been sent on reconnaissance became isolated during the battle and all twenty were massacred. Otherwise casualties were light.

After this success Custer marched back through continuing snow storms to rejoin Sheridan at Camp Supply. By this time the Kansas regiment had arrived, and on 7 December Sheridan moved his whole main column down the Washita valley. Retracing Custer's route, Sheridan was able to launch his main attack on 16 December when word came to him that the tribes had agreed to settle peaceably on their reserva-

tions. With the hostile tribes rounded up, Indian attacks gave no further serious troubles in this area. But other hostile Indians remained in the Southwest and the North.

Stanley's Yellowstone Expedition

Steamboats as well as wagons played an important part in the logistical support of Brig. Gen. David S. Stanley's Yellowstone expedition in 1873. Sent westward from Fort Rice and Fort Lincoln (near Bismarck) the expedition was to provide escort for the preliminary surveying party of the Northern Pacific Railroad. (*Map 13*) Including the 7th Cavalry under Custer, twenty infantry companies, and a detachment of Indian scouts, the force numbered over 1,500 officers and men. As soon as the expedition left Fort Rice, three steamboats—the *Peninah, Far West,* and *Key West*—started up the Missouri River for the Yellowstone River and the mouth of the Glendive Creek where a supply depot was to be established. An infantry escort was taken aboard at Fort Buford. A large wagon train meanwhile accompanied the rest of the troops on their more direct overland march. By the time the column had covered half the distance to Glendive Creek, many of the wagons had been emptied and returned to Fort Lincoln for additional supplies. While heavy rains hindered the wagon train, the boats reached Glendive well ahead of the column, and the men on board at once began building a stockade and unloading supplies. Two boats returned to the lower river, but the *Key West* stayed on to serve as transport and patrol boat for the expedition. When Custer arrived with his advance guard some twelve days later and decided to move the camp and depot sev-

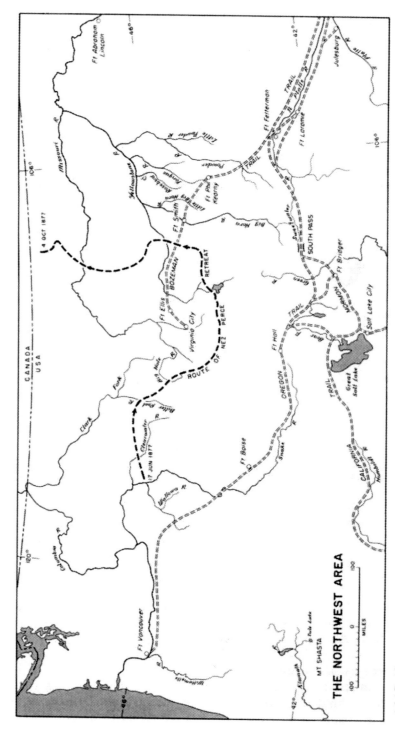

THE NORTHWEST AREA

MAP 13

eral miles upstream, it fell to the *Key West* to transfer the supplies to the new site, known as Stanley's Stockade. It helped ferry the men across the river and then remained on call at the depot until shortly afterward, when it was replaced by a new boat, the *Josephine,* belonging to the same company. When the expedition returned to the supply depot from its long foray to the Big Horn River, the few wounded men who had made the tortuous journey back were evacuated on board the *Josephine* to Fort Lincoln.

Campaigns Against the Sioux, 1876

Disturbed by warlike preparations by the Sioux under Sitting Bull and Crazy Horse, General Sheridan ordered another winter campaign early in 1876. He was to discover that winter on the northern plains could be far more severe even than the blizzards he had experienced farther south in his successful winter operation of 1868. Authority for the campaign did not come from Washington until March. Brig. Gen. George Crook, commanding the Department of the Platte, then sent Col. Joseph J. Reynolds from Fort Fetterman to destroy a village of Cheyenne and Sioux on the Little Powder River, after which a severe blizzard made further campaigning at that time impossible. Later Sheridan directed Crook and Brig. Gen. Alfred H. Terry, commanding the Department of Dakota, to undertake a concerted effort against the Sioux. Leaving Fort Fetterman on 29 May, Crook encountered a large party of well-armed Sioux on 17 June near the headwaters of the Rosebud River, and there fought a desperate battle which prevented his effecting a planned junction with Terry's forces near the Little Big Horn.

Meanwhile Terry led his main column, including Custer's 7th Cavalry and parts of the 6th and 17th Infantry, from Fort Lincoln westward to the confluence of the Powder and Yellowstone Rivers. From here Terry sent Maj. Marcus A. Reno and six troops of the 7th Cavalry, with ten days' rations carried on pack mules, to reconnoiter the country south of the Yellowstone from the Tongue to the Powder and Rosebud Rivers. Continuing up the Yellowstone to the mouth of the Rosebud, the main column met another force of twelve companies of infantry and cavalry which had advanced from Fort Ellis, Montana, under Col. John Gibbon.

The steamboat *Far West* was again put in service to transport supplies. At Fort Lincoln it had taken on 200 tons of forage, subsistence, quartermaster's equipment, medical supplies, and small arms ammunition. Picking up an infantry company at Fort Buford again to act as escort, the *Far West* had met Gibbon's force at Stanley's Stockade and had sailed on to the mouth of the Powder River where Terry came up a little later. The *Far West* again had the task of transferring a supply depot, this time from Stanley's Stockade to the mouth of the Powder River.

At the mouth of the Rosebud, Terry ordered Custer and his 600 cavalry to move up that stream until he came to an Indian trail, which Major Reno had reported, and to follow the trail to the camp of the hostile Sioux presumed to be along the Little Big Horn. Here he was to get into position to prevent the escape of the Indians as Terry with the remainder of his force came up the Little Big Horn from the north.

Early on the morning of 22 June the 7th Cavalry drew supplies for fifteen days from the *Far West*—stacked on the bank before sunrise by the boat's thirty deckhands—and the civilian packers loaded the mule trains (mules were drafted for this service from the wagon trains). Extra issue of salt suggested that the troopers might be living on mule or horse meat before they returned. After making about fourteen miles the first day, Custer's men rode hard the next two days, covering over thirty miles a day, until on the 25th they came to the vicinity of the Indian camps. Discovered by Indian scouts, Custer apparently thought that the only thing he could do was attack at once and not await the arrival of Terry and Gibbon. In any case, he divided his command into three battalions, delegating one troop to stay behind as rear guard with the pack train which, with the civilian packers, composed a fourth element of about 130 men. The battalions went their separate ways to locate the Indians. Custer, with the five troops remaining under his direct command, rode to his fateful "last stand."

Meanwhile Terry's force and Gibbon's column continued up opposite sides of the Yellowstone and the Big Horn, and the steamboat *Far West,* going along with reserve supplies, served as headquarters for the commanders and as communications boat between the two columns. With the help of soldiers who dragged the boat over some of the rapids by long cables, the *Far West* pushed its way up the tortuous channel of the Big Horn to the mouth of the Little Big Horn, farther than any steamboat had navigated those streams.

When Terry arrived at the site of the battle, on 27 June, the Indians had withdrawn. Immediately he prepared to have the wounded survivors—members of Major Reno's battalion who had not been with Custer himself—taken to the supply

steamer for evacuation. By hand and mule litters fifty-two wounded men were brought over the rough trail to the boat. Comanche, the injured horse of one of Custer's captains, and the sole living thing found on the Custer field two days after the battle, was also taken on board the boat for evacuation. Although it was essential to get the seriously wounded men to a hospital speedily, the *Far West* had to await the return of Gibbon's troops to ferry them to the north bank of the Yellowstone and to issue supplies for their return journey. By the time the *Far West* sailed, fourteen of the wounded were sufficiently recovered to remain at General Terry's camp. The *Josephine* was on the way with additional supplies for these troops. For its part, the *Far West* set a record for the trip back to Fort Lincoln, averaging over 13 miles an hour for the entire 710-mile journey.

In the inevitable sequel to the disaster on the Little Big Horn, General Sheridan acted swiftly to send every available man to reinforce Terry and Crook for the renewal of their punitive campaign against the Sioux. In the north Terry moved his supply depot from the Powder River to a site opposite the mouth of the Rosebud, and here concentrated his troops and stored the supplies being brought in by steamboats. Reinforcements arrived by boat also, so that by the end of July Terry and Crook each had a force of 2,000 men. They effected a junction on the Rosebud on 10 August, but failed to trap the Indians and for weeks pursued the Sioux across the rough country. One of Crook's companies captured a small village in September. In October, after a band of Sioux had attacked a wagon train bound for the Tongue River, Col. Nelson A. Miles led a force in pursuit and captured a village of 3,000 Indians. Soon afterward some bands came into the agencies and were disarmed. Sitting Bull finally retired to Canada with his group of die-hards; Crazy Horse and his 2,000 followers did not surrender until May.

There were other outbreaks of violence in the next few years. Among the most notable of these conflicts was the war against Chief Joseph's small band of Nez Percés in 1877. When Joseph finally surrendered to Colonel Miles, Sheridan ordered all the Nez Percés to be sent to Fort Lincoln where it would be cheaper to feed them. A fleet of fourteen flatboats was used to transport some 200 wounded braves and women and children from Fort Keogh, while the remaining 240 traveled overland with the 7th Cavalry. The army commissary issued rations of dried pork, brown sugar, hardtack, coffee, rice, beans, flour, and baking powder to each boat. Game shot along the way provided fresh meat. After a cold trip of 600 miles, the boats arrived at Fort Lincoln on 17 November, and the overland column came in a few days later.

Except for a brief outbreak with the Utes in Colorado in September 1879 and some counterraids in the Southwest by General Crook against the Chiricahuas Apaches under such leaders as Geronimo, Indian hostilities appeared to be at an end.

End of Indian Hostilities

During the 1880's Army leaders looked forward confidently to continuing Indian peace. Then in 1890 the Sioux made their final great effort. Growing restive because of further restrictions and broken pledges, and driven to fanaticism by the preaching of a new messiah who promised restoration of their hunting grounds, the Indians threatened a general uprising.

The situation had become so tense by November 1890 that the Commissioner for Indian Affairs called upon the War Department for help. The immediate problem was to protect the extensive settlements surrounding the Sioux reservation in the Bad Lands of South Dakota. For this purpose reinforcements from nearly all parts of the trans-Mississippi West were rushed to the command of Maj. Gen. Nelson A. Miles (now commanding the Department of the Missouri) until his forces concentrated at the reservation included nearly one-half the infantry and cavalry of the entire Army. The only serious conflict to disturb the disarming and peaceful resettlement of the hostile warriors was an unfortunate outbreak on 29 December at Wounded Knee Creek involving the 7th Cavalry and a band of Indians under Big Foot, a conflict that resulted in the death of thirty soldiers and 200 Indians, including men, women, and children.

Logistical efforts, once again handicapped by cold winter weather, followed the same general pattern as in earlier expeditions. One significant development, however, was the first experience in battle of the recently organized Hospital Corps. The medical organization at Pine Ridge Agency, South Dakota, consisted of a division field hospital with two medical officers, two noncommissioned officers, and ten privates of the Hospital Corps. It had facilities, under canvas, for sixty patients. Two ambulances, two surgeons, one hospital steward, and four privates of the Medical Corps accompanied the two battalions of the 7th Cavalry. After the battle at Wounded Knee two wounded officers and twenty-nine enlisted men, as well as twenty-eight wounded Indians, were evacuated to the field hospital. In its first test in battle, the Hospital Corps was reported to have met all expectations.

A few other skirmishes with Indians occurred—one as late as September 1898 at Leech Lake, Minnesota—but it may be said that 1891 marked the end of the Indian Wars in the United States.

Summary

In the quarter of a century after the post-Civil War reorganization of the Army, there was little change, actually, in Army logistics. Other than adapting himself to think in terms of smaller forces and greater distances, and sometimes colder weather, a commissary or quartermaster should have had little difficulty in adjusting to the conditions at any time during this period. A supply officer in the West in 1866 would have been quite familiar with his duties and procedures if reassigned to a similar post in 1891.

There was no improvement in the prescribed ration for years. Although a number of officers contended that soldiers eating only the issued ration would be very likely to get scurvy, and urged that fresh vegetables be added to the garrison ration, others insisted that the ration was most generous and that a soldier should "be a man and eat beans," and had their way until vegetables were added in 1890. The best way for a company to avoid scurvy and to maintain troop morale still was to find an ingenious sergeant with a flare for trading what soldiers would not eat for fresh foods that they would eat, and to cultivate company gardens and keep company hogs and cattle. For years, too, the Commissary General of Subsistence had been vainly urging

Congressional authorization for the enlistment of a qualified cook for each troop, company, and battery. In the early 1890's, common mess halls replaced company messes at several of the larger posts, but special training for cooks and bakers did not begin until 1905.

Generally, the supply situation in the Army appeared to be quite satisfactory. The Quartermaster's Department had little difficulty in meeting demands either for supplies or transportation, though some fault was found with the general policy that required purchasing to be done by public advertising for competitive bids. At times this appeared to defeat the very purpose it was meant to serve for on various occasions purchasing officers found that they could often get much better prices by private negotiation than by public advertisement. Actually, public advertisement seemed to result in compelling the government to pay the highest quotable price rather than the lowest acceptable price because public advertisement simply notified other firms of any disposition on the part of one to sell below the price for standardized articles agreed to by the leading dealers.

In 1889 the Army, with a total strength of 25,000 officers and men, occupied some 134 posts scattered across the country, the largest garrison consisting of 700 men. But improved communications made it feasible to follow a policy of concentrating troops at fewer but somewhat larger posts. Even as this post concentration was taking place, the termination of major Indian hostilities brought hasty action to cut back field transportation in the interest of economy. Army trains were broken up in 1895. The Indian wars had served to keep alive to some extent the well-arranged and well-equipped system of field transportation developed during the Civil War; retrenchment threatened its dissolution. Much has been made of personnel limitations on the Army in peacetime, but cuts in transportation and other logistical services can hardly have been less significant.

In the next quarter of a century the change in Army logistics would be more remarkable than had the lack of change in the preceding twenty-five years. It would become clear that the Civil War was just barely the beginning of modern warfare. In many respects the changes in weapons and equipment, transportation, medical service, and general administrative organization for logistical support between 1892 and 1918 would exceed all the changes that had come about in all the years from 1775 to the 1890's. And they would be only the beginning of the big change.[4]

[4] For sources upon which Part II is based see Bibliography, pages 709–16.

PART THREE

WARFARE OVERSEAS

CHAPTER XVIII

The War With Spain

Industrial Growth and Military Change

For the position of the United States in world affairs, 1890 was highly significant. That year the United States surpassed Great Britain in the production of both pig iron and steel. Already ahead of France, Germany, and Russia in output of pig iron by 1870, and in output of steel by 1875, American industrial production showed remarkable increases during the period between the Civil War and World War I. Steel production may be said to have begun in the United States in 1867 when about 20,000 tons were produced. It rose to 1.4 million tons in 1880, reached world leadership with 4.3 million tons in 1890, and more than doubled that output by 1898. Rapid increases continued in the following decades. German production expanded rapidly to 18.9 million tons in 1913, but American production had increased to 31.8 million tons by that year, and in 1918 the American production of 45.2 million tons represented nearly 58 percent of total world output of steel.

In the decade of the 1890's coal production in the United States also surpassed that of Great Britain, and by 1914 was greater than British production by 163 million tons, and greater than the German by 178 million tons. In the years between 1885 and 1913 total American industrial production

was increasing at an annual rate of 5.2 percent, that of Germany was increasing at 4.5 percent, and that of Great Britain at 2.11 percent, while that of Russia, on a lower base, was developing at a rate of 5.72 percent. The American share in world manufactures jumped from less than 20 percent in 1880 to more than 35 percent in 1913. In 1870 American production was about 10 percent greater than German; in 1900 it was over 100 percent greater, and in 1913 it was 150 percent greater.

The arms industry to a greater extent could be adjudged for its economic by-products—maintaining industrial profits, relieving unemployment—as well as for the immediate requirement of providing arms for the military and the longer range necessity of stockpiling reserves and maintaining capacity to meet future emergency requirements. In the 1890's these considerations applied more to naval programs than to the modest requirements of the Army; nevertheless, they would enter into national policy calculations in a way that eventually would have important consequences for Army procurement.

More and more, mobilization would be gauged by the response of industry. There was a hard-won lesson in the realization that repetition of past miscalculations in granting priority to manpower over industrial mobilization could only more seriously delay the war effort unless equipment deficits could be made up from outside sources.

A characteristic of war after 1898 having special emphasis for Americans would be the support of war overseas. For the first time since the landing and support of Scott's expedition to central Mexico in 1847, major units of the U.S. Army would embark for an overseas campaign in 1898. Expeditions to Cuba and Puerto Rico would be followed by landings halfway around the world in the Philippine Islands. And these efforts would be only a prelude to the "bridge of ships to France" in 1917 and 1918, and the landing of more than 2,000,000 American soldiers and 7,452,000 tons of Army supplies for U.S. participation in total war in Europe.

In military, as in other affairs, success often is the greatest enemy of progress. It is difficult to abandon weapons or organization or procedures closely identified with a great victory—and much of what had been good enough to "win the war" in the 1860's was stolidly intact at the end of the century.

Progress in weapons came before significant changes in administration. The most notable improvements in Army ordnance were the acquisition of modern seacoast guns (though their installation was behind the schedule set by the Endicott Board in 1885) and the adoption of the Danish-designed Krag-Jorgenson magazine rifle. Although several improvements had been accepted and different models approved, chief reliance of the Army for a shoulder weapon had been upon the .45-caliber, single-shot model of 1873, which still fired black powder. Behind European powers in finding a suitable formula for smokeless powder, the United States Army had none of the weapons which used the newer ammunition until it adopted the Krag. The War Department approved the Krag-Jorgensen in 1892,

but a nationalistic upsurge in Congress delayed production for two years to give American designers a further chance to come up with a better gun. Tests of fourteen American models failed to reveal a superior weapon and the manufacture and issue of the Krag-Jorgensen began in 1894. By 1897 all of the small Regular Army had been equipped with it; the National Guard still had to be content with the obsolete 1873's. From this time the availability and the effectiveness of smokeless powder continued to be controversial questions right through World War II and the Korean War.

If the Army was slow in changing its weapons, it was even slower in changing its administrative machinery and staff. The striking successes of the Prussian Army in 1864, 1866, and 1870–71 attracted the attention of the world to the Prussian General Staff. In a real sense the disasters of Jena and Auerstedt in 1806 had paved the way for creation of the Prussian General Staff. A further administrative improvement in the German system was the ultimate subordination of the supply and transportation services to the military commander. The Germans, too, had introduced refinements into supply distribution which would prevail in major armies in the years ahead— the system of continuous resupply from the rear through a chain of depots and distributing points. The United States Army could look to the great achievements of its administrative staff in the Civil War with little inclination to accept the Prussian model. Proposals for changes in its administrative machinery in the 1870's were mainly in the direction of consolidation of certain existing bureaus and toward the rotation of officers between staff and line assignments. There were as yet no serious moves to adopt a formal general staff, nor to effect clear-cut military command over administrative bureaus. Proposed consolidation of the Quartermaster's, Commissary's, Pay, and administrative branch of the Ordnance Department into a single supply department failed to come about, the argument against it being that wartime expansion would still make it necessary to assign these functions to different officers, so that, in effect if not in name, the old division of responsibility would reappear. On the other hand, this argument ignored the advantage there might be in a unified command over the logistical structure.

Mobilization of Men and Matériel

To say that the Army was unprepared for war in 1898 is to say nothing new nor anything really meaningful. Preparedness always is relative, never absolute. Estimates of preparedness have meaning only in relation to the capabilities of a potential enemy, and in relation to the time and place of anticipated operations. If the Grand Army of 1865 had been allowed to dwindle to a token force of 25,000 men in 1898, it was because there had been no compelling reason to have it otherwise. There had been no threat of foreign invasion since 1815, and no foreign war since 1847. Moreover, the country had demonstrated a tremendous capacity for mobilization in the Civil War. In these circumstances it hardly was to be expected that a large Military Establishment would be maintained. Even the increasing prospect of war with Spain following the insurrection in Cuba in 1895 brought about no increase in outlays for the War Department. Expenditures for maintenance of the Military Establishment continued to be not a great deal more than they were for rivers and harbors. The 25,000-man ceiling established in 1870—while the Ten Years' War was going on in Cuba—remained in effect until 1898.

Criticisms about unpreparedness generally have been leveled at the small size of the standing Army and the lack of well-trained reserves. But these criticisms fail to recognize the significance of the rapidly increasing industrial potential of the United States in the 1890's. This potential alone was making of the United States a nation better able to wage war, although neither government nor military leaders recognized its significance and so did not take full advantage of it in developing matériel reserves and industrial mobilization plans. Actually, mobilized manpower alone may at times be a source of weakness rather than of strength. Indeed it seems clear that a serious handicap of the Spanish in Cuba was the extravagant size of the army they attempted to maintain there.

Before the War with Spain began in April 1898 the War Department had been able to do practically nothing to anticipate it. Even the destruction of the battleship *Maine*, 15 February 1898, hardly disturbed the peacetime routine of the War Department, when in the opinion of many people war had become inevitable. Six weeks before the declaration of war Congress did appropriate $50,000,000 for national defense, but President William McKinley applied such a strict interpretation of the term "national defense," that he permitted none of these funds to be used for any other purpose than the improvement of coast defenses and fortifications. This appropriation did permit a hastening of the coast defense program, which had been in progress for some thirteen years, but the War Department had no reserve supplies on hand and could not purchase or even contract for any of the items that would be needed for mobilizing an army. The stepped-up program for coast defense did have one advantage beyond the purely defensive one of emplacing guns: it gave to the Ordnance, Engineer, and Signal Departments an opportunity to expand their activities and improve their organizations. On the other hand, the Quartermasters Department and the Subsistence and Medical Departments did not even have that advantage. Up to 23 April they were permitted to do nothing outside their ordinary routine; they could order nothing in the way of additional supplies.

The machinery for the administration of logistics had not changed much since the Civil War, or since the War of 1812, for that matter. Its efficiency had, if anything, declined. The division of authority between the Secretary of War and the General of the Army frequently had led to friction, a situation that still prevailed in 1898. There never had been any statutory definition of the functions of the commanding general, but Army Regulations prescribed that matters pertaining to discipline and military control should be under his orders, while fiscal affairs were to be conducted by the Secretary of War through the several staff departments. Such a policy led to a continued violation of the integrity of administration and military command whose importance had been so clearly demonstrated in the Franco-Prussian War. It meant, too, that the Secretary of War had to be his own chief of staff in co-ordinating the activities of the bureaus—to the extent that they did not fall under the military control of the commanding general.

Generally it is assumed that in undertaking a war effort a government must be on guard against two extremes in the public attitude: complacency or panic. But there is a third attitude that may be almost as dangerous: overenthusiasm. This last was the condition during the War with Spain when an enthusiastic populace made all kinds of impossible offers and impossible demands to hasten the winning of the war and to enhance individual roles therein.

When, after thirty-three years of peace during the greater part of which the Army did not exceed 26,000 men, it suddenly became necessary to move, arm, clothe, feed, and equip more than a quarter of a million men, confusion and chaos should not have been altogether unexpected. Given the existing situation, it may even be said that the War Department in many ways did a remarkable job of meeting the enormous task suddenly thrust upon it.

In the absence of any real external threat, it is understandable that the country was unwilling to maintain a large military establishment. Less excusable was the failure to keep even the modest forces of the Regular Army and National Guard well equipped. In modern war (and this was true in the 1890's) troops without arms and equipment are little better than no troops at all. Curiously, the country insisted on keeping certain minimum forces in peacetime, but not on maintaining the equipment that would keep them ready to meet the purpose for which they existed. As to major war preparedness, it might have been better to maintain sizable stockpiles of modern arms and equipment and no troops at all than the other way around. The declaration of war magnified the disparity. There seems to be some psychological compulsion about a formal declaration of war that demands immediate and large-scale mobilization of manpower. It led in 1898, as in previous wars, to placing an unwarranted priority on assembling men, with the result that thousands were accepted into the Army long before there was the slightest possibility of furnishing them with proper arms and equipment. When the war call sounds, it always seems patriotically more tangible for men to respond to the colors: there is nothing especially dramatic about unlocking a storehouse of equipment.

The numerous catalogues of errors of the War with Spain generally have failed to emphasize what probably was the most serious error of all—the undue priority of manpower mobilization over matériel mobilization. There was much to support the recommendations of General Miles (then Major General Commanding the Army) shortly before the declaration of war that 50,000 volunteers be accepted, and that an additional auxiliary force of 40,000 men be organized to man coast defenses and constitute a reserve. With the expansion of the Regular Army to 62,600, and the enlistment of 10,000 men immune to tropical diseases, this would have made a total force of 162,600 men. In the view of General Miles, it was "of the first importance to equip such a force rather than to partly equip a much larger number." [1] Instead, the Army multiplied to a total of 274,700 men by August—less than one-fifth of whom saw any kind of campaign service. As Theodore Roosevelt later observed, it would have been as easy, so far as finding the men was concerned, to raise a volunteer brigade or a division as a regiment, but "the difficulty lay in arming, equipping, mounting, and disciplining the men we selected." [2]

There was not even enough equipment on hand to outfit the expanded Regular Army. The only immediate demand that the War Department could meet was in the supply of Krag-Jorgensen rifles and carbines for the Regulars. The volunteers had to be content with the old .45-caliber Springfields—and no smokeless-powder ammunition. Regulars and volunteers alike were short of wagons, harness, tents, camp equipment, and medical supplies. All Regulars had to wear winter uniforms to the tropics. Some 5,000 canvas khaki uniforms sent to Tampa proved to be just as hot as the woolens and without their protection.

The policy of depending upon the states to provide initial equipment for volunteer units had proved to be unfortunate. The supposition that state troops were fully armed and equipped, or that their equipment had been kept in good condition, was unfounded. Dependence upon the states did nothing to hasten mobilization, and led to confusion when regiments entered the service with arms and equipment that almost immediately had to be condemned and replaced. Further, it led to difficulty in the settlement of accounts between the states and the Federal Government. This whole deficiency in arms goes back in part to the lack of adequate funds. An increase in Congressional appropriations in 1887 from $200,000 to $400,000 still was only $3.75 per man. If a small Regular establishment could be justified, that made all the more important a well-armed militia.

One volunteer regiment was more favorably situated to get equipment than the others—the 1st U.S. Volunteer Cavalry, the celebrated "Rough Riders" of Leonard Wood and Theodore Roosevelt. Colonel Wood made full use of his own knowledge of Army procedures and of Roosevelt's political influence in Washington to outfit the

---

[1] *Annual Report of the Major-General Commanding the Army to the Secretary of War, 1898,* pp. 18–22.
[2] Theodore Roosevelt, "The Rough Riders," *Scribner's Magazine,* XXV (January, 1899), 7.

regiment promptly. Roosevelt described their industry in attending to these matters:

It was evident that the ordnance and quartermaster's bureaus could not meet, for some time to come, one-tenth of the demands that would be made upon them; and it was all important to get in first with our demands. Thanks to his [Wood's] knowledge of the situation and promptness, we immediately put in our requisitions for the articles indispensable for the equipment of the regiment; and then, by ceaseless worrying of excellent bureaucrats, who had no idea how to do things quickly or how to meet an emergency, we succeeded in getting our rifles, cartridges, revolvers, clothing, shelter-tents, and horse gear just in time to enable us to go on the Santiago expedition.[3]

A special triumph was their success in obtaining Krag-Jorgensen carbines. When armed as Regulars the prospect improved of the regiment's being brigaded with Regular units, and thus the likelihood of early action.

Determination of total requirements was a matter of making inventories of equipment furnished to units by their states, calculating needs on the basis of lists of individual and unit equipment, taking into account additional needs for reserve supplies for training and for oversea expeditions, and calculating rations and other expendable supplies on the basis of total numbers and individual allowances prescribed by law and by regulation.

The factor most difficult to weigh accurately in determining total requirements for supplies and equipment was the effect of campaign plans. This always is most difficult, but plans for operations against the Spanish were so imprecise, so subject to change, and so little related to questions of logistical feasibility, that there was created a sizable blindspot in the whole logistical

program. It was assumed that no major operations would be undertaken in Cuba during the rainy season, which was due to start within a month after the declaration of war, thus giving the nation some five months' grace in which to organize, equip, and train the volunteer army. In the meantime there might be reconnaissance and harassing expeditions, and there would be a series of expeditions during May and June to take supplies and equipment to Cuban insurgents, adding still another demand to the total requirements. Then almost immediately came the demand for an expeditionary force to the Philippines.

On the basis of estimates which could be prepared fairly accurately in terms of initial equipment and replenishment supplies for the number of troops mobilized, but which could be made only roughly to allow for the support of military operations, Congress responded generously to requests for funds. Here was another aspect of the psychological magic of the declaration of war. Funds previously unavailable for military preparedness now were lavished upon the Army. The Quartermaster General had had appropriations of $7,700,000 for the regular service of his department during Fiscal Year 1898. From the special national defense appropriation of $50,000,000, approved 9 March 1898, the Quartermaster's Department received $1,500,000, but one-third of this was earmarked for transporting ordnance to seacoast fortifications, and the remainder was not made available for another six weeks. By 4 May, the Quartermaster General found three times the amount of his last annual appropriation heaped upon him, and two months later another $103,-200,000 was added to that. All together expenditures of the War Department from extraordinary appropriations to the end of

---

[3] Roosevelt, "The Rough Riders," *op. cit.*

1898 amounted to $244,392,856. This amount was in addition to the expenditures of $62,534,784 from ordinary appropriations for Fiscal Year 1898, and ordinary appropriations for 1899. Special appropriations of $500,000 for the expeditionary force to Cuba were put under the direction of the Major General Commanding the Army, who returned over half of this amount to the Treasury.

Procurement of clothing and equipment rose from practically nothing to hundreds of thousands of items within a few weeks after the declaration of war. After no purchases of shirts or trousers in the whole period from 1 July 1897 to 30 April 1898 the Quartermaster's Department contracted for or purchased more than half a million of each in three and one-half months (1 May to 15 August 1898). Contracts for and purchases of shoes, amounting to 27,950 pairs in the preceding year, covered 782,303 pairs in these three and one-half months.

Before the declaration of war the Subsistence Department acted to assure that at each post sufficient travel rations were on hand for the full garrison in case of movement orders, and commissary officers compiled lists of sources for the purchase of ration components on short notice. At or near each major camp, the Commissary General established a depot, and instructed purchasing and depot commissaries at New York, Baltimore, Chicago, St. Louis, Kansas City, New Orleans, and San Francisco to purchase and ship to the depots enough subsistence supplies to meet all current demands and to maintain 60 days' supply on hand. Regulars moving to camps at first carried 30 days' rations with them in order to save the food from deterioration, but late in May this action was suspended because there were more rations on hand

than could be cared for. Anticipating future operations, the Secretary of War had stored at Tampa 90 days' rations for 70,000 men.

As had always been the case in times of rapid mobilization, charges of corruption in war contracts were forthcoming, but many were never substantiated. On the whole, the situation seems to have been much better than during the early months of the Civil War. Undoubtedly the most sensational charge was one leveled against the Subsistence Department by General Miles— that harmful "embalmed" beef was being sent to the troops. Curiously, General Miles made his accusation in testimony before the Dodge Commission during its investigation of the conduct of the war in December 1898, which (if his accusation was true) meant that he had remained silent for several weeks knowing that shipments of such meat were being made. The commission inspected the camps, sent for samples of beef from the commissaries in Cuba and Puerto Rico for analysis by Department of Agriculture chemists, took testimony from witnesses, and could find no evidence that any meat had been treated with chemicals to preserve it. Large shipments were made both of refrigerated and of canned beef, and it could hardly be denied that frequently they arrived in an unsavory condition. In particular the canned beef, which had been a part of the travel ration since 1878, was intended only for use in the travel ration, and for serving only after further cooking with vegetables and seasoning. The controversy over the alleged shipments of "embalmed" beef—in part, perhaps, a result of personal feelings between the Major General Commanding and the Commissary General—probably created a greater disturbance in the War Department than did the arrival of the meat in the field.

The great task of the Ordnance Department after the declaration of war was to find arms for the new levies of troops. The question was whether to delay arming until the Krag-Jorgensen rifles could be provided for all, or to use the .45-caliber Springfields, with which the National Guard still was armed, for all forces; or whether to retain the Krag-Jorgensen for the Regular units who already had it, and supply the Springfield .45 for the volunteers. The last solution was the one adopted. Within a week after war formally began General Miles recommended that the manufacture of Krag-Jorgensens be cut back, or suspended. Something may be said for this action in the interest of uniformity, but necessary retooling and change in methods at the armories would have caused intolerable delays; therefore, instead the Ordnance Department increased the output of the newer rifles and carbines at the Springfield and Rock Island armories. Still, the increased production was of little actual consequence: less than 1,000 of the 26,728 Krag-Jorgensen rifles produced between 1 April and 1 September were issued, though by 8 December another 56,400 had been issued. There were on hand more than enough .45-caliber Springfields for the total force mobilized.

Fraught with confusion, wasted motion, and lack of co-ordination as it was, the mobilization of men and matériel was little short of remarkable. Starting almost from scratch the Army had under arms more than a quarter of a million men within four months. Less than five weeks after the first call for troops an expeditionary force sailed from San Francisco for the Philippines, and less than two weeks later a force set out for the invasion of Cuba. It should be recalled that at the beginning of the Civil War, after the President's call for militia on 15 April and the call for volunteers on 3 May 1861, only 16,161 enlisted men had been mustered into service by the end of May; in 1898, with the first call for volunteers on 23 April and the second on 25 May, 163,626 enlisted men had been mustered into service by the end of May. The total strength of 274,717 officers and men that the Army reached in August 1898 was not attained in the Civil War until November.

The Santiago Campaign

Concentration and Embarkation at Tampa

The confusion of the Santiago campaign began with the movement of troops and supplies to Tampa, Florida. Many Regular Army units had begun the move to Tampa a week before the declaration of war, while other units were moved to mobilization points at New Orleans, Mobile, and Chickamauga Park, Georgia. In the next several weeks each change in plans brought additional units and supplies streaming toward Tampa. Plans which at first called for assembling 5,000 troops there gave way to plans calling for 12,000, then 25,000. And the confusion seemed to multiply as the number of troops increased.

It was the old story of "Hurry up and wait." Units were rushed to Tampa, and then sat for weeks while quartermasters and commissaries tried to sort the thousands of tons of supplies pouring in, while the War Department modified strategic plans, and while the Navy tried to determine the whereabouts of the Spanish Fleet.

The two railroads serving the Tampa area soon were clogged with freight cars. Facili-

TRANSPORTS CROWD THE DOCKS AT TAMPA, 1898

ties and wagons were lacking for rapid unloading, and many cars arrived without
invoices or bills of lading, so that their contents could be determined only by personal
inspection. Within a few weeks a thousand
cars were backed up on sidings as far away
as Columbia, South Carolina, and only five
Government wagons and twelve hired civilian wagons were on hand for unloading.
When additional wagons did begin to arrive, they came knocked down and had to
be assembled. Quartermaster officers
blamed the railroad companies, and the
fiercely competing railroad companies (the

Plant Line and the Florida Central) blamed
each other and the quartermasters. The
real problem was unloading. If warehousing could be found, and if the cars could be
unloaded rapidly and the supplies stored in
an orderly manner, then it really would not
have mattered much that they arrived ahead
of their bills of lading. After the Commissary General issued peremptory orders to
unload cars promptly, and authorized commissary officers to hire additional warehousing when necessary, the situation eased
somewhat with respect to subsistence stores.
Aggravating though it was, the railway

blockage was no disaster. The concentration of troops and supplies at Tampa was far from being a smooth operation. It was chaotic and inefficient, and would have injured the sensibilities of any orderly administrator. But this is not to say that it was ineffective, for the needed troops and supplies were there, and that was most important.

At the outbreak of war the Army had neither an ocean-going vessel nor experience in operating transports. To assemble a fleet for the anticipated movement to Cuba, the Quartermaster's Department considered every vessel of American registry on the Gulf and Atlantic coasts. The fleet grew slowly: only three or four ships had been chartered by the end of April, about thirty by 26 May. All had been freighters, and none had the ventilation or accommodations prescribed for troops, so that considerable work was necessary to install bunks, extra water tanks, and additional ventilators to make them usable at all. An unfortunate miscalculation in the carrying capacity of the ships added to the already confused situation at the time of embarkation. With no experience of their own, and no vessels with which to work, Quartermaster officers, not unnaturally, used the British standard for calculating the troopship requirements, which was figured at one man for each ton and a half of capacity. Estimates based on this ratio proved to be greatly excessive when applied to the converted freighters. Instead of the capacity for 25,000 troops that officers at Tampa reported to the Quartermaster General, the ships assembled could not carry 17,000.

Carpenters had begun fitting the vessels with bunks and stalls while en route. The work of loading ordnance stores and other bulky items began simultaneously with loading coal and water, as soon as the ships started to arrive at the port. When this was completed at the end of May, the loading of rations, arms, ammunition, forage, wagons, and medical supplies could begin. The animals were to go on board just before the embarkation of troops. Maj. Gen. William R. Shafter, commander of the expeditionary force, had hoped to complete loading supplies and animals in three days, but it took a week of round-the-clock labor to get it finished. Because of poor wharf facilities stevedores had to carry or truck most of the supplies over improvised platforms across the fifty feet from the railroad siding to the vessels in the channel. Efforts to combat load the vessels at least to the extent of keeping units intact and their baggage and supplies with them, added to the complexities of loading, and were made especially difficult by the manner in which the supplies arrived over the congested railroad. Full cargoes were not on hand, and it was necessary to pull ships out into the harbor, and return them to the pier to complete loading. Shafter ordered rations and ammunition put on board each ship so that it could act separately if it became detached.

Orders to the chief commissary of the expedition were to load six months' rations for 20,000 men. In the interest of haste this amount was reduced to two months' rations. Then the chief quartermaster designated several vessels on each of which 100,000 rations were to be placed so that all would be assured of a reserve in case of separation. This amounted to some 5,000 tons of food, and much of it had to be handled several times. The stevedores became so exhausted that they would fall asleep wherever they happened to be whenever they were relieved. Similarly, artillery pieces and carriages and ammunition arrived at different times from different arsenals. The decision of the commanders that guns should be mounted on carriages before being loaded further delayed the operation, though it may have preserved the utility of the guns on the other side.

Cavalry horses had to be left behind, but some 2,300 draft and pack animals went along. Transportation accompanying the expedition for use in Cuba was hardly adequate; it included 114 army wagons (six-mule), 81 escort wagons, and 7 ambulances, together with another 84 wagons shipped from Mobile.

Loading of supplies and animals was finally completed at 1100 on 6 June, and Shafter ordered the embarkation of troops to begin at noon. However, the first troop train could not get through until 0230 the next morning. Then began the final mad rush. Chief quartermaster Col. Charles F. Humphrey attempted to assign regiments to ships according to their strength as they arrived. Soon all semblance of orderly assignment to vessels and punctual marching of units to their assigned places disappeared, and it seemed to be a case of every unit for itself. One of General Shafter's aides later wrote: "The frantic efforts for places on the transport were only equalled by similar efforts to get back to the United States after the expedition had been in Cuba a short time."[4] With the War Department applying pressure for haste, General Shafter on the afternoon of 7 June notified all commanders that units not on board the next

morning would be left behind. That did it. By 2200 the railroad had become so congested that the entire operation ground to a halt. No one else reached the pier until daylight.

The clearest lesson in the whole episode was the unsuitability of the Tampa area for staging and embarking an overseas expedition of this kind. Why, then, was it chosen? Apparently because of its proximity to Cuba (306 nautical miles from Havana) and the assumption that a force of not more than 5,000 men would be shipped at that time for a reconnaissance in force. If, as some of the thinking indicates, the expedition was to be one of opportunity, there was reason for staging it at the nearest port, prepared to move on short notice. As soon as the project went beyond this conception, and as soon as the objective was shifted to Santiago rather than Havana, Tampa lost its advantage even on the score of proximity to the goal. Undoubtedly the expedition could have been embarked more cheaply, as well as far more efficiently, from a major east coast port such as New York or Norfolk. The distance from New York to Santiago was little more than 400 miles greater than from Tampa to Santiago. Any loss of time in covering that distance surely would have been more than made up by the efficiency of embarkation, and would, in addition, have saved a significant part of the long and relatively costly rail hauls of troops and supplies from the northeast to Florida. If east coast ports were avoided because of the supposed threat of the Spanish Fleet, at least New Orleans—about 600 miles from Havana—would have offered obvious advantages over Tampa.

That lack of facilities and undue haste rather than want of experience and plan-

---

[4] J. D. Miley, *In Cuba with Shafter* (New York: Charles Scribner's Sons, 1899), pp. 27–28.

ning were the chief difficulties at Tampa is suggested by the relatively smooth embarkations of the forces for Puerto Rico and for the Philippines. With little difficulty, between 20 and 28 July, forces numbering 3,571 officers and men departed from Charleston, 2,896 from Tampa, and 5,317 from Newport News, Virginia, to join the force of 3,415 officers and men leaving Guantanamo with General Miles on 21 July for the invasion of Puerto Rico. Once the necessary ships could be found, embarkations for the Philippines at San Francisco proceeded smoothly enough. The first contingent of 2,500 officers and men left three weeks before the Santiago expedition left Tampa; the second, of about 3,500 officers and men, left on 15 June; and the third, 4,800, left on 27 and 29 June. A fourth contingent of nearly 5,000 left late in July.

Debarkation

After a naval bombardment against an imaginary enemy, the landings at Daiquiri in Cuba commenced in heavy seas on the morning of 22 June. A number of the merchant captains refused to bring their vessels close in to shore, which lengthened the stretch of water to be negotiated by the small boats. Steam launches and boats from the accompanying naval ships joined the boats of the transports to carry the troops ashore. The most effective system was for the steam launches to tow strings of boats tied together. By sunset about 6,000 men had been landed with the loss of two soldiers drowned. Debarkation continued at Daiquiri the next day until 1600, when the sea became too rough. Shafter meanwhile had shifted the landing of remaining units to Siboney, where most of the troops went ashore directly on the beach while an engineer company built a temporary pier upon which to off-load supplies. Some landings continued after darkness with the benefit of Navy searchlights. By evening of the fourth day the debarkation of the troops, plus the landing of an additional 3,500 of General Garcia's Cuban insurgents, was virtually complete, the first stage of the first oversea landing operation since the landing of Scott's considerably smaller army at Vera Cruz in 1847. (*Map 14*)

For the discharge of supplies and equipment the Army was left to its own resources. To get the animals ashore the simple expedient was to open the side hatches, push them into the water, and let them swim for it. Fifty out of 450 mules were lost when they turned the wrong way and swam out to sea, or swam around to the wrong side of the cove and drowned under the rocks. The wagons, siege guns, and light artillery were put ashore at Daiquiri. The chief commissary labored to carry out his instructions to put ashore 200,000 rations each at Daiquiri and Siboney, but it was all he could do to keep a day or two ahead of daily requirements. Although it had taken a week to load the transports at Tampa, General Shafter was surprised that it should take a week to disembark the command and essential supplies. After Shafter's decision to establish his supply base at Siboney, all reinforcements and additional supplies were landed at that point. It took still another week and a half to get ashore three days' reserve supplies.

Under rather more favorable circumstances, the landings in Puerto Rico in July went smoothly. At Guanica engineers used a ponton bridge train to make a floating wharf over which more than 1,000 ani-

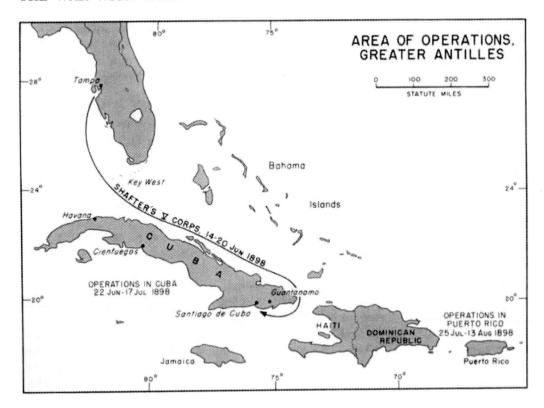

AREA OF OPERATIONS,
GREATER ANTILLES

MAP 14

mals and most of the heavy matériel were landed without accident.

Inland Supply

With little thought for the morrow, the first units ashore in Cuba rushed off headlong in search of the enemy, not waiting for supplies to be landed. With each step forward in the stifling heat the burden on the soldier's back became greater. Some units took the precaution of dropping their packs and stacking them under guard, but in other units the men simply threw away each item as it seemed to lose its importance under the hot sun. Many discarded all of

their three days' rations as well as entrenching tools and other items. Even posting guards proved to be of no avail, for they were pressed into service to help move the wounded to the rear and had to leave their supplies for anyone who found them.

In the beginning, the competition of unit-controlled transportation for passage over a single, narrow, muddy road led to such confusion and delay that before long it gave way to a more systematic and centralized control. When not on the road, all the wagons stayed at the forward supply depot near field headquarters. Telephone lines connected the headquarters with the depots and with the divisions. Each morning all wagons not needed for hauling supplies forward to the units went back to the main depots at Siboney and Daiquiri for resupply. Those going to Siboney would return the same day, while those for Daiquiri returned the next day. According to this arrangement all empty wagons were moving to the rear in the morning, and toward the front in the afternoon. This probably would have worked well enough, but a shortage of transportation, the poor roads, swollen streams, and illness among the teamsters inevitably led to supply shortages. For some time it was possible to bring up only the bread, meat, coffee and sugar of the ration; the vegetables and other items could be delivered only occasionally. Some units actually had to go without food for a day or two, but they usually were the ones that had failed to follow instructions for each soldier to carry three days' rations. Ammunition was given high priority on pack trains, and generally was plentiful. Clothing, tentage, utensils—all were in short supply. Perhaps the most serious shortage for six weeks after the landings was in medical supplies. Again the principal difficulty was not failure to ship the supplies, but the failure to unload them promptly, plus the serious shortage of transportation to move them forward.

Expeditions to the Philippines

While the Army was struggling to rush troops and supplies to Cuba and Puerto Rico, and then to rush them home again, it was adding to its store of experience in oversea expeditions by sending men and matériel to the other side of the world. In prompt response to Commodore George Dewey's call for 5,000 men to help him take and hold Manila and control the Philippines, the Army sent seven expeditions, with a total of 16,000 officers and men and supplies for six months, out of San Francisco and across the Pacific during the late spring and summer of 1898.

Although organized to support about 3,000 men under peacetime conditions, the San Francisco quartermaster's depot expanded its activities to meet quickly the requirements for over 30,000 troops preparing for overseas movement. For the convoys to the Philippines the Subsistence Department brought in food supplies constituting rations for six months. For resupply, the Commissary General, through the United States consul general at Melbourne, Australia, contracted for refrigerated beef and fresh vegetables to be shipped to Manila from Australia.

The most serious problem in connection with launching the Pacific expeditions was to find the necessary shipping. Only by threatened seizures, and finally by transferring some vessels from the Atlantic was it possible to obtain the vessels needed. But even if all vessels flying the American flag had been chartered or purchased the total would not really have been enough, and it was necessary to ask Congress to grant American registry to foreign ships available for charter. Another real problem, however, presented itself in the great distances over which the ships were scattered. Ultimately twenty vessels on the Pacific were obtained—eighteen by charter and two by purchase—to transport troops and supplies to the Philippines.

Protected by Dewey's squadron, the Army forces had little to fear from Spanish guns when they landed near Manila. The first contingent landed in fair weather at Cavite; the second and third landed at Tambo, six miles down the beach, and set up Camp

TROOPS EMBARKING AT MANILA

Dewey in a long, narrow peanut field just beyond the beach and within range of Spanish artillery. Men and supplies went ashore on Philippine lighters known as cascos, towed by captured Spanish tugboats. Each lighter could carry about two hundred men with their shelter tents, packs, and ten days' rations. In bad weather landing operations at Tambo had to be suspended for days, and on occasion the beach was strewn with supplies washed up from swamped boats. Later supplies were landed near a protected river mouth at Paranaque.

To move supplies from the shore to the camps it was necessary to use ponies and carabaos, or water buffaloes, drawing native two-wheeled carts, until sufficient mules arrived from the United States. In addition, Chinese hand carriers were used to great advantage. For a time four coolies were attached to each company, and they provided valuable service in such duties as bringing up ammunition and food, and carrying the dead or wounded to the rear. After active operations against Manila had been concluded, the commander discharged these coolies lest the troops become "spoiled" from having the Chinese do all the dirty work.

Summary

In popular thinking the War with Spain always has been something of a farce, and certainly there are examples of error and in-efficiency to give support to such a view. But the United States never has been noted for the efficiency and smoothness of its military activities in the opening phase of any war. The great difference in the War with Spain was that there was little oppor-tunity—or need—for later improvements to overshadow earlier deficiences. Indeed, the reputation of the Army suffered by its very success. Objectives were so quickly won, and hostilities were so soon terminated that the War really never progressed beyond the opening phase. By 17 July, eighty-three days after the declaration of war, the Santiago campaign had ended. By 13 August, 110 days after the declaration of war, the campaigns in Puerto Rico and in the Philippines had been brought to success-ful conclusions. If the Civil War had ended 110 days after it began, ten days after the Battle of Bull Run, would the Federal Army and the War Department now be remem-bered for a great war effort? If World War I had ended by 17 July 1917, 110 days after the entry of the United States, when Ameri-can forces had as yet made no contact with the enemy, when only the 1st Division had arrived in France, and when there were fewer men overseas than in the summer of 1898, would the contribution of the United States Army be highly regarded, and would its efficiency and organization now be praised? If World War II had ended 110 days after the attack on Pearl Harbor, that is by 27 March 1942, when U.S. forces on the Bataan Peninsula were fighting the last weeks of their losing battle, when only 5,000 men had arrived in Australia, and only two divisions had arrived in the United King-dom (in spite of the advantage of the opera-tion of selective service for a year and a

half before Pearl Harbor), would the American war effort then have been some-thing to marvel at?

Several writers have entered eloquent pleas for a larger standing Army with the argument of economy—that it would have been far less costly if a relatively larger army had been maintained throughout the period from 1865 to 1898, and a significant part of the waste resulting from the hasty mobili-zation thus could have been avoided.[5] As a matter of fact, the cost of maintaining the Army during the War with Spain (about $322 million for the Fiscal Year 1898) was not proportionately greater than it had been to maintain the peacetime Army (an aver-age of about $45 million a year from 1870 to 1897 for an army of about 26,000 men) during the preceding years. It seems doubt-ful, then, that the additional cost of larger forces during those years would have been offset by appreciably lower costs during the war. Moreover, the plea for a larger peace-time Army ignores the lack of any external threat that would have justified it in the eyes of Congress and the voters. Conceivably a larger standing army would have resulted in more and better equipment, but that was hardly an argument to sway public opinion.

No one claims that the country was in a satisfactory state of preparedness when the War with Spain came. The Dodge Com-mission, appointed to investigate the con-duct of the war, heard testimony that led to

---

[5] See for example: Herbert H. Sargent, *The Campaign of Santiago de Cuba* (Chicago: A. C. McClurg & Co., 1914), III, 126–40; Frederic L. Huidekoper, *The Military Unpreparedness of the United States* (New York: Macmillan Co., 1916), pp 274–78; Maj. Theodore Schwan, *Report on the Organization of the German Army* (Washing-ton, 1894), p. 13.

a conclusion that perhaps for the first time in American military history recognized in an official way the priority of matériel preparedness over manpower preparedness. The commission reported: "large supplies of all material not liable to deterioration should be kept on hand, to be continuously issued and renewed, so that in any emergency they might be available." [6] Specifically, the commission recommended that the Quartermaster's Department keep on hand sufficient equipment for at least four months for any army of 100,000 men of all articles of clothing, camp and garrison equipage, and other quartermaster supplies that would not deteriorate in storage or could not be obtained quickly on the open market. It further recommended that sufficient medical supplies for a year for an army of at least four times current actual strength be stocked in medical depots.

The Chief of Ordnance, Brig. Gen. Stephen V. Benet, fully agreed. He recommended that field and siege artillery, with carriages and harness, for an army of 500,000 men be kept on hand to provide a cushion for the six-months' preparation needed to turn out these items in quantity if required for large-scale mobilization. He stated that for the same reason three months' supply of ammunition for all guns should be stocked. The ordnance chief recognized the dilemma of keeping on hand a large number of small arms, and yet having the latest models. As a solution he suggested that whenever there was a change of model in a rifle 100,000 should be procured as

soon as possible, and machinery be installed at the arsenals as quickly as possible to give them a capacity for turning out 2,500 a day. In peacetime 35,000 rifles a year would be manufactured—the arsenals always retaining the capacity for rapid expansion. Even then it was recognized that many of the reserve arms probably would have to be older models, and that it was likely they would have to be issued temporarily in case of a large-scale mobilization. This was one of the first difficulties the Inspector General recognized, as he recommended that the National Guard be armed with the same kind of rifles as the Regular Army—a most important solution logistically in that it permitted the use of the same ammunition. The problem never really became acute during the War with Spain, because in the limited campaigns most of the troops involved could be armed with the Krag-Jorgensen. Actually the Santiago Campaign was the first in which armies of both sides were armed with small-caliber magazine rifles. Other significant recommendations of the Inspector General's Department on the basis of War with Spain experience included: establishment of reserve depots where the quota from each state could be equipped when called; organization of a "strategic staff"; periodic encampments, maneuvers, and practice mobilizations; organization of a sea transportation service, possibly under control of the Navy; and development of a corps of trained civilian teamsters and packers for an effectively organized pack-train service.

Perhaps the most glaring failure of the Army in the War with Spain, by present standards, was in troop health. At least ten times as many men died from disease as from battle wounds. In 1898 the death

_____

[6] The Dodge Commission, *Report of the Commission Appointed by the President to Investigate the Conduct of the War Department in the War with Spain,* 8 vols. (Washington, 1900), I, 114.

rate from other than battle causes was 27.01 per thousand among volunteers, and 23.61 among men of the Regular Army, while the rate for the previous year, 1897, was 5.11 from all causes. This situation can be attributed to two conditions. The first was ignorance; however, when knowledge became available it was put to immediate use. For example, one month after Ronald Ross published his findings that malaria was transmitted by anopheline mosquitoes (July 1898), the knowledge was being applied in the Philippines. The most prevalent disease was typhoid fever. Though sanitary conditions improved quickly in the camps, no one guessed that the most probable factor in causing the epidemics was the presence of carriers in the kitchens. The second condition contributing to the high disease rate was overmobilization. Bringing together in camps thousands more men than were needed added unnecessarily to the likelihood of disease.

Apparently the mobilization of American forces was based purely upon a numerical calculation of manpower—the United States needed so many men because Spain had so many—and ignored the critical questions of status of arms and equipment and means of supply. Actually, Spain sent to Cuba more troops than it could support effectively, and thus weakened its strength. The more complex logistical support for armies becomes, the less satisfactory it is to calculate relative effectiveness in terms of numbers of men alone, and the more important it becomes to emphasize matériel mobilization.

The influence tending most toward conservatism in an army is victory. The unassailable, "We won the war, didn't we?" has glossed over thousands of errors. In 1898, however, despite short campaigns and a brilliant victory, there was public dissatisfaction with the War Department—a feeling that it should have done better. Since the war did not last long enough for the War Department, the Administration, and the Congress to overcome many of the most obvious shortcomings, the criticisms remained in full force: the time had come for administrative reorganization, a complete overhaul of the Army's administrative system was overdue. Some thought that at least the Subsistence Department, and possibly others, should be merged with the Quartermaster's Department to form one big supply department; others would go even further and proposed separation—particularly of the transportation service from the Quartermaster's Department—rather than consolidation. The die-hards insisted that the trouble was not in the system, that there was no need for fundamental reorganization of a system that had worked so well for Grant, Sherman, and Sheridan.

When it was pointed out later how smoothly and efficiently the Japanese conducted their disembarkation at Chemulpo in 1904, and how the American disembarkation at Daiquiri suffered by comparison, it could also be pointed out how smoothly and efficiently the Americans executed their embarkation at San Francisco and disembarkation at Manila. Deficiencies perhaps were more the result of a lack of leadership over the years that had permitted neglect of planning and preparation even with the small resources available, rather than of inherent weaknesses in the organizational structure.

Allowing for all these things, perhaps there has been some exaggeration in the statements of waste and inefficiency during the war. Sometimes waste of materials and time and effort in an orderly fashion is less obvious than when it is accompanied by disorder and confusion; but the waste—the cost in total man-hours and materials—is not necessarily less. In military affairs results must be preferred to efficiency, and orderly procedure can never be allowed to interfere with winning an objective. The chaotic conditions under which Shafter's expedition was moved to Cuba, though they seem inexcusable, stemmed from poor intelligence and rapidly changing plans in response to supposedly changing situations. With all its inefficiency, the results of the expedition were remarkable.

CHAPTER XIX

The Interwar Years, 1899–1917

In spite of the exhilaration resulting from the victory in the War with Spain, a major impression remained that the war had been conducted inefficiently. Even though the restoration of peace revived much of the popular complacency on military affairs, the report of the Dodge Commission on the conduct of the war, and continuing demands for the support of operations in the Philippines to put down the insurrection fed the uneasy feeling that something was wrong with the Army's structure. The war had not lasted long enough to force needed changes, but the evidences of inefficiency and poor co-ordination were such that those hoping for reform became convinced that the time had come to act.

Organizational Reform

There is something to be said for Secretary of War Russell A. Alger's observation that in the year following the end of hostilities with Spain the supply bureaus had been called upon to perform larger tasks, and had done so without public criticism. An army four times the size of Shafter's force that went to Cuba had been transported twelve times that distance with little of the confusion and inefficiency characterizing the earlier efforts. Adequate supplies, including the same kind of canned beef, were being received in the Philippines without serious complaint. Earlier impressions of

near failure, however, could not be so easily overcome. A future situation might present more immediate threats, when there would be less opportunity to demonstrate procedures improved by recent experience. Clearly all had not been well in the War Department, and a good deal of the trouble had been in the co-ordination and administration of logistics.

When Secretary Alger resigned in the summer of 1899, President McKinley called upon Elihu Root, a New York lawyer, to be Secretary of War. When Root protested that he knew nothing about war or the Army, McKinley indicated that the major concern at the moment would be the administration of the islands recently detached from Spain. But soon after Root moved into the War office on 1 August he discovered that some reorganization was going to be necessary if he were to accomplish anything in the way he hoped, even in the administration of the Spanish islands.

In spite of his unfamiliarity with military affairs—or perhaps in part because of it— Root began with great energy and effectiveness to bring about the needed reforms. These pertained mainly to creating a general staff, replacing the commanding general of the army with a chief of staff, introducing a system of detail to staff assignments for short terms instead of the permanent tenure system then prevailing in the bureaus, and developing the Army's educational system, with a war college at the top. The new secretary brought to this task a remarkable perception. He saw clearly where predecessors had seen through a glass darkly. Through inquiry and investigation and study he grasped what the role of a general staff ought to be, and he was able to convince the political leaders of the time as well as to instruct the Army itself. He went straight to the heart of the matter in his first annual report:

The real object of having an army is to provide for war. . . .

Yet the precise contrary is really the theory upon which the entire treatment of our army proceeded for the thirty-three years between the Civil War and the War with Spain. . . . The result was an elaborate system admirably adapted to secure pecuniary accountability and economy of expenditure in time of peace.[1]

Root saw the preparation of an army for war as involving at least four major elements: (1) preparation of war plans; (2) preparation of war matériel, including the development of new weapons and equipment; (3) selection and promotion of officers according to merit; and (4) training of officers and men in the maneuvers of large bodies of troops. He then went on to recommend the establishment of a war college, and appointment to staff assignments for fixed terms.

Aside from the organization of a general staff, the proper functions of a commanding general of the Army had been a matter of concern and dispute for years. The practice had been to divide responsibilities between the Secretary of War and the commanding general. The latter was charged with training, discipline, inspections, and the general administration of the Army in the field. But the Secretary of War retained control of all financial, and so most logistical matters, and the chiefs of the supply bureaus generally reported to him directly. The assigned activities of the commanding general in peacetime were not always essential, and in trying to make a role for himself he frequently made trouble. On the other hand the bureau chiefs, each secure in his own empire, tended to ignore the commanding general and the other departments.

Root proceeded adroitly to win support. He knew that he could count on backing from most of the line officers, from younger officers in the bureaus, from some powerful friends in Congress, and, above all, from President Roosevelt. The annual reports of the Secretary of War were distributed widely to explain the needs for reorganization. Root attempted no "railroading" operation, but went patiently about the task of informing the public and Congress, and lining up support in the Military Affairs Committees. While his assistant, Maj. William H. Carter, was anxious to rush ahead with a general staff bill in 1901, Root was content to accept that year a bill enlarging the Regular Army and, incidentally, abolishing the permanent tenure system in favor of four-year details in the bureaus. Opposition to this latter provision was minimized by making it apply only to future assignments; those already in the bureaus would retain their tenure. Meanwhile, with the benefit of appropriations for the purpose in 1900 and 1901 he proceeded to establish the Army War College by general order in November 1901; in practice the college would function as an embryonic general staff.

---

[1] Report of the Secretary of War, *Annual Reports of the War Department for the Fiscal Year Ended June 30, 1899*, 3 vols. (Washington, 1899), I, 45–46.

A general staff bill was offered early in 1902, but was withdrawn and reworked. It was presented again at the next session of Congress in December, and passed, essentially intact, in February 1903. The law stated that the General Staff Corps should be charged with the preparation of defense and mobilization plans, with investigation and reporting on all questions affecting the Army's efficiency, and with acting as agents of the Secretary of War and respective commanders in providing information and in co-ordinating action.

Establishment of the General Staff was only the beginning of the battle to develop an effective organization. Even though the decision had been made, many of those who had opposed the idea refused to accept it, and for a time there was some doubt as to whether there really would be any improvement in co-ordination at all. In getting his program through Congress, Secretary Root had exhibited the same knowledge, patience, and deference which had characterized Washington's relations with the Continental Congress during the dark days of the Revolution. More would be needed to win general acceptance in the Army itself.

Senior officers in the bureaus began to agitate for abolition of the short detail system, and some of the bureau chiefs never were able to subordinate themselves to the General Staff. The very basis for this independent attitude was in part the old system of permanent tenure. It was difficult for bureau chiefs who had been at their jobs for five to ten years, and whose whole careers were within the bureaus, to accept the direction of young, temporary staff officers. Moreover, long tenure in Washington permitted the development of strong personal ties with members of Congress that worked as an independent source of power.

Beneath the surface of routine and paper work, a struggle for power developed within the War Department. It broke out into the open after Maj. Gen. Leonard Wood had become Chief of Staff in 1910 and Henry L. Stimson had become Secretary of War in 1911. Maj. Gen. Fred C. Ainsworth, The Adjutant General, allowed his opposition to the general staff system and his concern for the prerogatives of his own office to grow into hostility toward his old friend, General Wood, who now was his chief. For his part, General Wood was no less strong-willed and ambitious. In the battle for the survival of the General Staff and the primacy of the Chief of Staff as originally conceived, the antagonists were the two senior generals of the Army (both of whom had been medical officers). Behind General Ainsworth lay a century of tradition and powerful supporters in Congress. Behind General Wood were the law, the Secretary of War, and President William Howard Taft.

The showdown came when The Adjutant General responded to a proposal for abolishing the requirement that bimonthly muster rolls be furnished by all Army units. He submitted a belated memorandum couched in language that invited charges of insubordination. When Secretary Stimson read the memorandum, he at once relieved Ainsworth of his duties as Adjutant General, and prepared for a court-martial. This move Ainsworth forestalled by requesting retirement from the Army.

The supremacy of the Chief of Staff had been upheld, but Stimson found that he had leaped from the frying pan of internal conflict into the fire of Congressional displeasure. The House Committee on Military Affairs demanded all the papers on the Ainsworth affair, which Stimson supplied, although he insisted that he did so as a matter of courtesy and not as a legal requirement. Moreover, Congress attached a rider to the Army appropriation bill incorporating a whole series of provisions—included were abolition of the detail system, long-term enlistments, and others that Wood had opposed and Ainsworth had supported; a provision that would fix all Army posts subject to change only by action of a board of five retired officers and two members of each house of Congress; and even a set of qualifications for the Chief of Staff that would have made Wood ineligible. The bill, of course presented President Taft with the dilemma of having to accept all the obnoxious provisions, or of having to veto the bill, thus stopping all pay and allowances for the whole Army.

The situation was fraught with political overtones, and could not have come at a more inopportune time. Not only did President Taft face a politically divided Congress, but division threatened his own party, and he faced a fight for his own renomination in an election year. To send a veto message was likely to lose further support in Congress and at the national convention, and would give support to General Wood, a close friend of Theodore Roosevelt who was opposing Taft for the nomination. To Stimson the issue was clear, and he prepared a veto message which fitted Taft's own ideas; in spite of the political risk, Taft saw it as his duty to save the General Staff from Congressional domination, and he vetoed the bill. The outcome was that Congress provided for continuing appropriations by joint resolution until a new appropriation bill could be passed without the rider. In the showdown, the President had stood with the General Staff system. The system would be challenged again on the eve of World War I, and would not really come into its own until it had gone through the crucible of war.

As for the supply services themselves, Root had hoped for a consolidation of the Quartermaster's, Subsistence, and Paymaster's Departments into a single Department of Supply, but he was unable to get this plan through Congress. Taft, Root's successor as Secretary of War, had strongly recommended the formation of a general service corps to replace civilian employees and soldiers detailed from line units for duty as wagon masters, engineers, firemen, overseers, teamsters, packers, carpenters, blacksmiths, clerks, and laborers, but this recommendation, too, failed to win approval. Then the Army Appropriation Act as finally approved in August 1912 provided for both the Root and Taft recommendations. The original bill, as it passed each house in different form, provided that the Quartermaster, Pay, and Subsistence Departments should be combined into a new Supply Corps. The assumption was, at least on the part of some advocates, that the new corps would be responsible for procurement and distribution of all common use items, that is, items used by more than one bureau, and it might have developed into something like the Navy Supply Corps. But in conference committee the name Supply Corps was changed to Quartermaster Corps, which led to the assumption that an expansion to obtain higher rank for The Quartermaster General was behind the proposal. The bill also authorized a general service corps of 6,000 men to be permanently attached to the Quartermaster Corps without counting against the regular allotment of enlisted men as already provided.

Elihu Root has been criticized for his contention that "with our 80 millions of people there never will be the slightest difficulty in raising an army of any size which it is possible to put into the field.   Our trouble never will be in raising soldiers; our trouble will always be the limit of possibility in transporting, clothing, arming, feeding and caring for our soldiers, and that requires organization." [2]   Criticism might be justified if it were based on the assumption that Root believed that volunteer armies alone could be relied on for the protection of the nation.   The second part of his statement, however, makes it clear that Root realized that the secret of mobilization is not in raising troops, but in marshaling transportation, supplies, and services—that in organization and planning, matériel mobilization should take precedence over manpower mobilization—and in this observation he was seeing the realities as few others did.

New Developments in Weapons and Equipment

One of Root's main hopes in establishing the General Staff was that it would provide a means for "keeping pace with the progress of military science" [3] and for adapting matériel to the anticipated conditions of future war.   But in the decade and a half that followed there was little evidence that personality, special interest, tradition, inertia, and ambition were any less significant than before.   And even if War Department reorganization had been more successful in co-ordinating and encouraging research and

development on new weapons and equipment, it alone could not have significantly reduced those factors in Congress when it came to making appropriations.

The principal agency for this kind of responsibility, the Board of Ordnance and Fortification, continued to function as it had before, under an act of 1888.   Successor to the ordnance boards which had been convened at various times since the 1830's, it was charged with making "all needful and proper purchases, experiments, and tests to ascertain . . . the most effective guns, small arms, cartridges, projectiles, fuzes, explosives, torpedoes, armor plates, and other implements and engines of war. . . ." [4]   The Board always had a series of tests before it, and as early as 1907 and 1908 automatic and semiautomatic cannon showed much promise as potentially effective weapons.   By 1913 and 1914, as a result of designs developed in the Ordnance Department and the encouragement of private arms makers, it appeared that a practical semiautomatic rifle might be within reach.   The Springfield rifle, Model 1903, it generally was agreed, took second place to none in shoulder weapons, particularly after a new type of ammunition had been developed in 1906.   When the American team won the Olympic rifle shoot in 1908 with the 1903 Springfield and 1906 ammunition, the claim to superiority seemed to be well established.   Actually, the new rifle was issued to troops beginning in 1905, and by 1908 the entire Army and the National Guard (except in two states) had been equipped with it.

The 3-inch artillery pieces adopted in

---

[2] Walter Millis, *Arms and Men; A Study in American Military History* (New York: Putnam, 1956), p. 180.

[3] Elihu Root. *The Military and Colonial Policy of the United States* (Cambridge: Harvard University Press, 1916), p. 354.

[4] Report of Board of Ordnance and Fortification, *Annual Reports of the War Department . . . 1907* (Washington, 1907), II, 221.

1902 and improved in subsequent years were about as good as any. In 1905 the Army went into the gunpowder business with the construction of a plant for smokeless powder at the Picatinny Arsenal, Dover, New Jersey.

Still, in matériel that would matter most in the future—machine guns, motor vehicles, airplanes, armored vehicles—the old negative attitude most often prevailed. As had been the case over the decades, personalities and individual interests too often seemed more important than the merits of an idea and the national interest. Unquestionably it was difficult to screen out from the mass of schemes continually forwarded to the War Department those ideas that had some merit. In part this was a failure of organization, but there was also a deficiency in attitude. Although efforts were made to encourage the development of improved weapons, the whole approach generally was one of testing and screening ideas that came to the attention of the Army, rather than one of pushing a vigorous pursuit of ideas. If an inventor brought in a new weapon, it still was up to him to prove his case, and the kind of hearing he got might depend as much on who he happened to be and what his attitude was as upon the ingenuity and practicability of his device.

Hiram Maxim, the American inventor who went to England and there developed the first practical automatic machine gun (publicly demonstrated in 1885), found a market for his deadly weapon among most of the European powers, but not in the United States. John M. Browning developed his recoil-operated machine gun in 1900, but found so little interest shown in it that he turned to weapons of greater interest to sportsmen until 1910, and the Army did not adopt this "best of all machine guns" until 1917. The Russo-Japanese War in 1904 and 1905 impressed all observers in Manchuria with the effectiveness of automatic machine guns, but the United States did nothing to replace its Gatling guns until 1909 when it adopted the mediocre light Benet-Mercie machine gun. Boards approved Vickers (Maxim) guns tested in 1913 and 1914, but nothing came of their recommendations.

About the same time the Lewis light machine gun was tested and turned down. Later, its rejection became the subject of controversy in the War Department, in Congress, and in the press when the Lewis gun came into prominent use in the British Army after the outbreak of the European War in 1914. It was difficult to understand why a gun invented by an American officer could become the favorite light machine gun of British troops in battle, and yet not be acceptable to the American Ordnance Department. Dissatisfied with the Ordnance Department's tests, General Wood, then commanding the Eastern Department, set up a series of tests of his own at Plattsburgh, and came away completely sold on the Lewis. One explanation of the rejection was that the inventor had not brought his weapon directly to the Army, but had taken it to a private company which now offered it for sale. Too, there may have been some personal antagonism in the Ordnance Department, where there was an expression of impatience about the failure of the manufacturer to make test models available. But here again the initiative had been left to the parties offering the gun; there was no question of the War Department's searching out the best possible weapons. When congressmen inquired why the Lewis gun had not been adopted, the reply was that the Vickers had shown up better in the tests of 1913. But then the question became: why had not the Vickers been adopted? Apparently the War Department was waiting for the best, confronted by the eternal dilemma of whether to standardize production or wait for a better model. In this case it waited, and the Army probably had the best machine guns and automatic rifles in the world—after World War I was over.

The automobile was beginning to capture the imagination of the country, but it made little imprint for a time on the Army. When Quartermaster General Charles F. Humphrey in 1906 bought six automobiles for use in California, Washington, D.C., and Cuba, the Treasury ruled that he had exceeded his authority under the appropriations and charged them to his personal account. In 1906–07 the Quartermaster's Department was able to purchase twelve automobiles, but tests indicated that their degree of usefulness and the cost of maintenance argued against "their substitution for any of the standard means of army transportation." [5] Finding "existing types" of automobiles unsatisfactory for military use, the department was content to let it go at that, making no effort to find new types that would be satisfactory. During the next several years the Army bought from one to four automobiles a year at a cost of a little over $3,000 apiece. Then in 1911 the Inspector General, if not the Quartermaster General, became convinced that the time had come to develop military motor trucks. The use of one truck and two motorcycles during three months' maneu-

vers of a provisional brigade in southern California convincingly demonstrated their usefulness. About the same time, the Inspector General of the Department of the Lakes came to the conclusion that the Army should undertake some experimentation to develop a motor truck "to replace the field wagon to the greatest possible extent." [6] Whereupon the Quartermaster Department began a developmental and testing program to produce a suitable Army truck, but funds were so restricted that the program could accomplish very little. A test run in 1912 of two Army trucks and a privately owned company truck from Washington, D.C. to Fort Benjamin Harrison at Indianapolis, covering 1,524 miles in forty-eight days, did not give wholly satisfactory results but did show the trucks had some promise. Motor trucks already were beginning to replace horses and wagons at the supply depots, and by 1913 the Quartermaster Corps had adopted general specifications for a 1½-ton truck.

The Army first used motor vehicles significantly in the supply columns of Pershing's expedition to Mexico in 1916. Trucks used in the supply columns were commercial types, and were regarded more as a substitute for railroads than for horses and wagons. Armored cars also made their appearance in the field at this time, proving their worth and the quick response the motor industry was capable of. Within twenty-two hours after receiving a telephone order for twenty-seven armored cars, the Packard Motor Car Company had the cars on their way by special train with a driver and mechanic for each car shipped.

[5] Report of the Quartermaster General, *Annual Reports of the War Department for the Fiscal Year Ended June 30, 1907* (Washington, 1907), *II*, 36–37.

[6] Report of the Inspector General, *War Department Annual Reports, 1911*, 4 vols, (Washington, 1912), I, 274.

TRUCK CONVOY WITH THE PERSHING EXPEDITION TO MEXICO

Fifty-one hours after leaving Detroit, the vehicles arrived on the Mexican border. This example and impressive reports from Europe on the use of armored vehicles prompted some congressmen to urge an increase in the appropriation for armored vehicles from $150,000 to $300,000 or $500,000, but without success.

With aviation it was the same old story— a mechanism invented by Americans, but first put to general use abroad. In 1914 while congressmen were congratulating themselves on not being carried away by extravagant claims for combat aviation, and while the chief of the Signal Corps himself was waiting for the airplane to be "proved" before lending any enthusiasm to its development, Great Britain already had established an Experimental Branch in its Royal Flying Corps. Undoubtedly the disappointing failure of Samuel P. Langley's

"aerodrome" in 1903 shook the faith of military leaders as well as of Congress, and even though the Wright brothers successfully met Army specifications in a test at Fort Myer, Virginia, in 1908, the death of Lt. Thomas Selfridge and the injury of Orville Wright when the successful plane crashed a few days later added to the discouragement with the project. In June 1912 unofficial experiments at College Park, Maryland, that demonstrated the feasibility of firing machine guns from aircraft excited widespread public interest, but the Army took no official notice.

While the Germans already had flown a plane twenty-four hours nonstop, the Russians had built a four-engine plane, and the British had mounted cannon on aircraft, American military planes had progressed little since 1908. At a time when France already had 260 airplanes, Russia 100, and

Germany, Britain, and Italy 46, 29, and 26, respectively, the United States was content with six. The appropriation of $125,000 for Army aviation for Fiscal Year 1913 was as much as had been appropriated all together during the preceding five years, but it was only a small fraction of the millions being appropriated by all the major European powers, and less even than the $400,000 appropriated by Mexico. The Signal Corps did go so far as to organize a small aviation center at San Diego, California, and in 1914 and 1915 it conducted competitive tests for improved airplanes and engines. But it was not until 1916, with the demonstrations of two years of war in Europe as convincing evidence, that the United States seriously stepped up efforts to develop an air arm, and even those efforts were timid. A squadron of eight aircraft supported Pershing's 1916 expedition in Mexico, but even in the absence of opposition all were wrecked within six weeks.

Perhaps all the experimentation and attempts to develop new weapons and equipment in the United States during this period were bound to be of little avail in any case. Would the position of the United States really have been any different if better machine guns had been adopted, if motor trucks and airplanes and armored cars had been perfected? The critical question was not the development of new ideas, but getting the new weapons in sufficient quantity to be effective. The Springfield M1903 probably was the best military rifle in the world, but even though the entire Army and National Guard had been equipped with it, this number was such a small part of the total needed that when war came it was necessary to adapt the British Enfield in the interest of mass production. The United States 3-inch gun was not so inferior to the French 75 as to be unusable, but so few were available that it was necessary to rely on the French artillery weapons for American units in France. It is not likely that the story would have been very different with other items that the Army might have developed but did not.

Aside from the direct impact, actual and potential, of new weapons and means of transportation in battle, and the direct logistical problems involved in their development, their secondary logistical significance would be hardly less important once they came into use. Adoption of machine guns complicated the ammunition supply, for not only did their use mean a tremendous increase in requirements for small arms ammunition, but the use of foreign models necessitated supplying two kinds of ammunition until the guns could be rechambered for American ammunition. Increased use of motor vehicles would substitute requirements of gasoline and oil for hay and oats, and in turn would affect the structure of the supply system itself. All of these complications waited over the horizon while the United States approached involvement in a world war, relatively innocent of the changes rapidly taking place.

Expeditions Abroad

Meanwhile, the Army was broadening its experience in handling the logistical problems involved in moving and supporting forces overseas for active military operations, an area in which American achievement would prove comparable to the best.

The Philippine Insurrection

Although politically and tactically the Philippine Insurrection was quite a different

ORVILLE WRIGHT DEMONSTRATING HIS PLANE AT FORT MYER

operation from the War with Spain, logistically both should be considered as a unit. In a way the insurrection provided a setting for that second phase of logistical support, after the initial confusion of entering into a war had been overcome, which the shortness of the War with Spain had denied. It also afforded an opportunity for refurbishing reputations for logistical support that had been tarnished in 1898. But most important, it marked the beginning of a new era for the Army, when support of overseas forces would become a permanent responsi-

bility, and fighting brush-fire wars abroad would become a common occurrence.

Less than a month after the outbreak of the insurrection, Congress passed an act authorizing the Regular Army to be maintained at a strength of 65,000 men, and a volunteer force of 35,000 men to be raised not from the states individually but from the country at large. The increase in forces was to be but for two years and four months, until 1 July 1901. With little of the confusion accompanying the expedition to Cuba a year earlier, troop transports by the early summer of 1899 were leaving New York for Manila by way of the Suez Canal, and from San Francisco by way of Honolulu. The transports carried twenty-three new regiments of volunteers. Another regiment of infantry and one of cavalry were formed from state volunteers who were already in the islands and who were induced to stay. To carry out these movements the Army had acquired some twenty-three ocean-going ships, and the total number of owned and chartered vessels of all kinds reached 125—not counting 200 small craft used for interisland service in the Phillippines—operated by the recently formed Army Transport Service. Eventually the total forces used to put down the insurrection included over 75,000 regulars and 50,000 volunteers.

Throughout the operations in the Philippines the greatest obstacles to effective logistical support were the climate and the lack of land transportation facilities. Extensive operations were almost impossible during the rainy season when, as in the spring of 1899, as much as forty-six inches of rain fell in a single month. The dry season was almost as bad, when the tropical sun sapped the energy of the troops. Sickness again claimed more casualties than did battle. Supplies of all kinds deteriorated rapidly in that climate, and a great deal of loss resulted from the lack of co-ordination between the movements of troops and the movements of supplies, so that at times supplies accumulated at points where they were no longer needed. When units moved back to the United States, accumulated supplies either had to be shipped back to the United States, or be disposed of locally at a considerable loss. It would have been difficult enough to keep up with the needs under the best of conditions. The garrisoning of

hundreds of posts and the expeditions conducted at widely separated places and at great distances from the main centers of supply presented problems similar in a way to those attending the Indian Wars.

The China Relief Expedition

While the Philippine Insurrection was at its height, the presence of American forces in the Philippines made it possible for the United States to participate in the expedition to relieve the beleaguered legations in Peking during the Boxer Rebellion in 1900. In this action, for the first time since the Revolutionary War, American soldiers joined in a coalition effort with forces from other nations.

All together the American forces ordered from the Philippines, from the United States, and from Cuba, to take part in the China Relief Expedition numbered nearly 15,500 officers and men, of whom about 10,000 were infantry; 3,000, cavalry; 1,000, artillery; and 800 marines; and 875 service troops. Between 5,000 and 6,000 men arrived in China before the capture of Peking. The 9th Infantry was in China just nineteen days after receiving its initial order at Luzon in the Philippines.

Manila and Pacific ports of the United States served in effect as primary bases, funneling men and materials through the Japanese port of Nagasaki. The advance base was established at Taku on the Gulf of Chihli, about forty miles from Tientsin. Since ice in that region ordinarily blocks navigation after about 1 December, it was necessary to arrange for delivery by mid-November of six months' supplies of ammunition, food, heavy winter clothing, fuel, lumber for quarters, stoves, medical supplies, and other items.

Tientsin was captured on 13 July. On 4 August a force of about 2,500 Americans, in the company of larger Japanese, Russian, and British contingents and a smaller French contingent, began the advance from Tientsin on Peking. As soon as their horses could be brought ashore at the stormy Gulf of Chihli, a troop of the 6th Cavalry joined the advance, while the other American forces remained behind to guard the line of communication. Only a fraction of the unit transportation had arrived and, although some wagons brought up ammunition and rations and mule pack trains arrived just in time to help, chief reliance for supplies was on a fleet of junks on the Pei Ho and on large carrying parties of Chinese coolies. Each junk carried from six to twelve tons of reserve ammunition or other supplies, and with the benefit of favorable winds and the pulling of coolies, the craft moved up the stream at about the speed that the troops marched although because of the meandering course of the river, the troops often were separated from their supplies by several miles. On the march each man carried 100 rounds of ammunition, one days' ration, a mess kit, shelter half, and sometimes a blanket. A Signal Corps detachment building a telegraph line kept pace with the march.

After overcoming scattered opposition en route, the international column arrived before Peking on 14 August. Men of the 14th Infantry scaled the walls, and relieved the legations that afternoon. Two days later the expedition occupied the inner Imperial City, and on the 28th troops of all the co-operating powers paraded in the Forbidden City.

The big question then became whether the troops would remain in occupation until winter. Although the greatest complaint at the moment was the excessive heat, Maj. Gen. Adna R. Chaffee, commander of the American force, was most concerned about cold weather. He recognized that if his troops were to stay in Peking for the winter, the railroad would have to be repaired or he would have to move his supplies from Taku before the river froze. His own observation was that the presence of the troops was complicating the supply situation for the civilian population, and he recommended that his men be withdrawn as soon as possible. Weeks passed without a decision, until finally Chaffee decided he could wait no longer. He assembled a fleet of junks and brought up the supplies ahead of the ice—a fortunate move, for he did remain through the winter. In February he was informed that U.S. forces were to be reduced to a legation guard of about two companies, and as soon as he could he began transferring surplus stores to the coast. Mounted units moved out first, in April, to help ease the demand for forage. Chaffee and the 9th Infantry left Peking on 23 May 1901.

Mexican Crises

What threatened to be a far more serious involvement was the situation that developed in Mexico. When rioting broke out in the City of Mexico in November 1910, challenging the thirty-year rule of the "Iron Dictator," Porfirio Diaz, United States Cavalry forces near the border were augmented until they patrolled the entire border from Brownsville, Texas, to San Diego, California. Hoping to avoid intervention, but persuaded that a show of force might help stabilize the situation, in mid-February 1911 President Taft ordered the mobilization of a "maneuver division" at San

Antonio under the command of Maj. Gen. William H. Carter, Assistant Chief of Staff. At the same time a force composed of provisional regiments of the Coast Artillery Corps concentrated at Galveston, Texas, as the 1st Separate Brigade, and two infantry regiments mobilized at San Diego. All together, over 23,000 officers and men from all parts of the United States were involved in this movement. It was an impressive concentration in some ways, but it revealed deficiencies in mobilization planning and co-ordination. Local units were ready on time in most cases, but there were delays in arranging for rail transportation and in getting the necessary cars where they were needed promptly. In part these delays arose because there had been no time for warning orders, and probably it was too much to expect better results under those circumstances. By the end of March (twenty-five days after Taft's order was issued), nearly 15,000 men had arrived at their destinations. But the maneuver division did not reach its maximum strength until the end of May. During the summer most of the units returned to their home stations.

A second mobilization in February 1913 at Galveston and Texas City was accomplished somewhat more rapidly and effectively, but the 11,000 officers and men collected there as the 2d Division hardly comprised a combat division ready to take the field against a major enemy. Without the well-organized ammunition and supply trains and the transportation needed to make a division an effective fighting force, this organization could be little more than a token force. Still, it provided one more bit of experience for mobilizing larger forces.

About the same time it appeared that another overseas expedition might be in the making. After reports that the American Embassy in Mexico City had been fired upon, President Taft asked Secretary of War Stimson how long it would take to organize a relief expedition if that became necessary. Stimson's response was that a single telegram would clear the way for loading transports on standby at Newport News. The next morning the New England Brigade received a warning order, and awaited orders to move, but the crisis passed.

A year later an expedition did sail from Galveston to relieve naval forces occupying Vera Cruz—an instance of the rapid movement of an expeditionary force sent overseas under prospective combat conditions. As the Vera Cruz crisis developed, Brig. Gen. Frederick Funston was instructed to have the 5th Brigade, 2d Division, ready to sail on short notice from Galveston. On 23 April 1914, the day after a landing party of sailors and marines had seized the Mexican port, orders came to move at once with as much of the Army force as could be carried in the four Army transports sent to Galveston. The very next day approximately 3,200 officers and men shipped out of Galveston, followed two days later by a battalion of field artillery that left from Texas City aboard a chartered ship. Landing at Vera Cruz on 28 April, Funston took command of the Marine detachment already there, and with his combined force occupied the city out through the suburbs, extending his lines to include the source of the city's water supply nine miles away.

All of the elements of Funston's brigade did not sail, lest this apparent reinforcement upset the delicate negotiations then taking place. Some of the transports were converted to other uses. The *McClellan,* for example, after debarking its troops at Vera Cruz returned to Galveston, was sent from there to New Orleans to be converted to a refrigerated storage ship, and then went to New York to take on a cargo of beef for the Vera Cruz garrison. In anticipation of possible reinforcement, the Transport Service in May chartered eight additional ships and had them refitted at New York to carry troops or animals.

Supply operated according to a plan approved by the Secretary of War in March 1913. Units of the 2d Division were supplied from the base depot at Galveston upon requisition through division headquarters. For replenishment of supplies the Galveston depot drew upon the general depot at St. Louis. Quartermaster items not available at St. Louis were obtained from New York, Philadelphia, or Jeffersonville. Food supplies generally were procured locally, except that evaporated milk came from St. Louis, bacon and canned meats from Chicago, and fresh beef from Houston and Fort Worth. Accountability for expendable items and subsistence stores terminated with their transfer from the Galveston depot to the local units, while nonexpendable items were issued to organizations on memorandum receipt. For troops stationed along the border from Texas to Arizona, the same system applied, the depot at El Paso serving as the point of supply.

Galveston became the main supply point for the occupation garrison at Vera Cruz, and ordinary supplies were forwarded automatically. For a time shipments were irregularly scheduled, but in June the transport *San Marcos* was put on regular schedule, leaving Galveston on the 1st and 15th of

each month until the withdrawal of the forces from Vera Cruz in November. Funston had to manage without most of his organizational transportation; for local movement of men and supplies he took over the four railroads entering Vera Cruz, and operated them with American conductors and engineers and Mexican firemen and brakemen.

The next chapter in Mexican affairs involved mobilization on a large scale and actual invasion of Mexican territory. In 1916 most of the Regular Army and nearly all of the National Guard were mobilized in the vicinity of the Mexican border, and Brig. Gen. John J. Pershing led a punitive expedition into Mexico in pursuit of Pancho Villa. The real significance to the United States of operations in Mexico was that they served as rehearsal and preparation—within less than a year the United States was called upon to undertake the greatest overseas expedition in history to help turn the tide in the World War then raging in Europe.

Summary

The Army that was called upon to meet the challenge of world war was quite a different Army from the one the United States had known twenty years earlier. In the eighteen years since 1898 it had become the Army of a world power. A military organization that had been bound to the soil of the United States since 1848, which had operated for a century and a half with a supply system governed by a permanent unco-ordinated bureaucracy at the top, and which had given little attention to war planning, by 1916 was a "new" army in which all this had changed. Where previously

GENERAL PERSHING *and men fording a river during the expedition to Mexico.*

there had been no experience in organizing or maintaining expeditionary forces, now such forces had been mobilized and dispatched at various times to Cuba, Puerto Rico, the Philippines, China, and Mexico. Where it had been uncommon for even regiments to be assembled together, divisions and corps had been organized, transported, and supplied at numerous times and places. Where planning and co-ordination frequently had been wanting, now a General Staff had been organized and at least had made a beginning in the overall direction required for effective military operations.

But what probably was the Army's greatest deficiency—its matériel preparation for war—had not changed. In spite of the recognition after the War with Spain that the

key to rapid military mobilization was matériel preparation; i.e., stockpiling supplies and equipment and industrial mobilization planning, very little had in fact been accomplished along those lines during the period of transformation.

Army planning and procurement had not kept up with new developments in the full military use of advances in machine guns, motor trucks, armored vehicles, and aircraft. Even more serious were the insufficient quantities of supplies and equipment in the inventory to support a major mobilization in a war situation. Some steps were taken in 1911 to establish central depots for general reserve supplies, but the problem of adequately stocking them remained, with field artillery equipment and ammunition in shortest supply.

Serious shortages in the National Guard of animals, wagons, artillery, ammunition, clothing, ambulances, and other matériel made it clear that the organized militia could not be counted upon as an early mobilization force for war. And as long as it continued to be common belief that military mobilization was a matter of raising men before arms, this unsatisfactory state of affairs would persist.

CHAPTER XX

World War I: Industrial Mobilization and Procurement

A country as divided in its attitudes toward military preparedness as it was toward the definition of American interests in the conflict raging in Europe during 1915 and 1916 approached hesitantly the complete involvement that would at last resolve all doubts about a need for full mobilization and decisive action. In their place other doubts arose concerning what the nature of the American contribution should be—whether a large army should be sent overseas, or whether matériel assistance for the Allies might be enough—and how best to mobilize and put to use the great resources of the United States in support of whatever programs might be required.

Plans and Preparations

After prolonged hearings before the military affairs committees of both houses, Congress passed the National Defense Act which the President approved on 3 June 1916. It provided for a modest increase in the Regular Army, for a National Guard subject to call into federal service, and for an Officers Reserve Corps whose members would be recruited from graduates of courses of military instruction in the colleges and from volunteer officers' training camps modeled after the one General Wood had organized at Plattsburg. Although an important section of the National Defense Act recognized the importance of industrial mobilization and granted to the President broad powers to effect it in time of war, the legislation, as had most of the public discussion preceding it, emphasized preparation and mobilization of manpower, at least so far as the Army was concerned.

Henry Breckenridge, Assistant Secretary of War to Lindley M. Garrison who resigned in February 1916, turned in his resignation shortly after his chief's and wrote a book, *Preparedness,* to explain his position. Breckenridge devoted his book to the necessity for improving manpower preparedness by having a larger Regular Army and a large body of trained reserves; he did not even raise the critical question of matériel preparedness. The General Staff went further. A study on Personnel Versus Matériel in Plans for National Defense, published by the Army War College in November 1915, not only maintained the *idée fixe* that national security required universal military service and a large army of trained men; it also warned that there had been a tendency on the part of some people to exaggerate the importance of matériel in modern war and to underrate the importance of personnel. The study pointed out that the increasing complexity of modern arms and equipment made the thorough training of men more important than ever, and concluded that the side with the largest body of trained men would be successful. Whether, for the individual soldier, the firing of a modern rifle was more complicated than firing the old muzzle-loader, or the driving of a motor truck was much more complicated than harnessing horses and driving a wagon, or the operation of modern artillery was much more difficult than operating the old, was at least debatable. The War College pamphlet ignored the really basic question: Which takes longer to develop—trained manpower for a large army, or the matériel it will use?

Noting that ". . . twentieth-century warfare demands that the blood of the soldiers must be mingled with from three to five parts of the sweat of the men in the factories, mills, mines, and fields of the nation in arms," [1] one of the members of the Naval Consulting Board, Howard E. Coffin, an automotive engineer, took the initiative in setting up a Committee on Industrial Preparedness to make a survey of industry. It operated through five-man subcommittees organized in each state. The task of listing and analyzing industrial plants in terms of their actual capacities for the production of military supplies and munitions fell to Walter S. Gifford, a statistician of the American Telephone and Telegraph Company. A number of people, in different contexts, began to discuss the advisability of organizing some kind of machinery within the government to co-ordinate the work of industrial preparedness.

President Woodrow Wilson was impressed with the importance of this activity, and as early as December 1915 he called upon Congress for the "creation of the right instrumentalities by which to mobilize our economic resources in any time of national necessity." [2] As a result, a rider to the Army Appropriation Act, approved on 29 August 1916, created the Council of National Defense "for the co-ordination of industries and resources for the national security and welfare." The council itself was made up of six members of the President's Cabinet—the Secretaries of War, Navy, Interior, Agriculture, Commerce, and Labor—but it functioned principally through its Advisory Commission composed of seven dollar-a-year men chosen for their expert knowledge in special fields, and a permanent director and staff. The council's function was planning and co-ordination, not administration. The organization in March 1917 of the Munitions Standards Board, under the Council of National Defense, with Frank A. Scott as chairman, and its absorption early in April by the General Munitions Board, also under the chairmanship of Scott, completed the organization of a kind of "general staff" for war industry, the forerunner of the War Industries Board.

In spite of meager appropriations and negative attitudes toward such steps as were taken for industrial preparedness, and in addition to the activities of the Council of National Defense and its agencies, two factors did operate in the prewar years to prepare for industrial mobilization to a far greater extent than otherwise would have been the case. The first was the acceptance by American industries of large munitions

[1] Josephus Daniels, *The Wilson Era, Years of Peace, 1910–1917* (Chapel Hill, University of North Carolina Press, 1944), p. 493.

[2] Ray S. Baker, *Woodrow Wilson, Life and Letters*, 8 vols. (New York: Doubleday, Doran & Co., Inc., 1937), VI, 308.

orders for the Allies. The second was the mobilization of forces on the Mexican border.

After a short period of depression following the outbreak of war in Europe in 1914, American industry, thanks in part to orders from the Allies, revived and started to expand. American companies shipped explosives, firearms, and a small quantity of airplanes and parts valued at over $806,-000,000 to the Allied Powers between August 1914 and March 1917. If shipments of other iron and steel manufacture; copper, brass, and aluminum and their respective manufactures; and acids are included, the total value was $2,188,000,000.

As has been noted, the Mexican crisis fortunately passed without war, but the consequent mobilization proved invaluable as a dress rehearsal and readiness test for what lay ahead. It afforded experience in large-scale troop movements by rail. It gave an opportunity to introduce the Army to problems of procuring and maintaining and repairing motor vehicles, and to the use of motor transportation for supply in the field. It also uncovered serious supply shortages and weaknesses in the supply system, but purchases then of reserve stocks of quartermaster supplies made it possible after the declaration of war to equip (except for clothing, tentage, and animals) all units called into service.

The regular staff studies of the War College Division had little to contribute to realistic logistical planning for war. The division's work seemed to lack insight and imagination, and part of this was due to the attitude of the government, which sought to maintain the appearance of strict neutrality. Just as McKinley in 1898 had interpreted "national defense" so strictly as to hamper the expenditure of funds even for

normal preparedness, now Wilson, for the time being, seemed to apply restrictions even to the formulation of plans. While war raged in Europe, and while the likelihood of American involvement became more and more real, the War College had to content itself with making plans for repelling invasion on the coast of the United States. Even aside from this the General Staff showed little imagination. A study on Strategic Location of Military Depots, Arsenals, and Manufacturing Plants in the United States turned out to be no more than a plea to move all such installations out of any area west of the Sierra Nevada or Cascade Mountains, east of the Appalachians, or within 200 miles of the Canadian or Mexican borders; this would have ruled out the maintenance of any facilities in the vicinity of New York, Boston, Springfield, Philadelphia, Washington, Chicago, San Antonio, or San Francisco. A Study on Places of Origin and Ability to Procure Supplies Needed in Vast Quantities in Time of War was a seven-page summary of what had not been done and what needed to be done; it did carry a recommendation that enough matériel reserves be stored, over an eight-year period, to equip a force of 1,000,000 men. This step would have been commendable in 1906, but it was hardly suited to the situation in 1915 and 1916; moreover, the problem of winning appropriations to support even so modest a plan remained just as difficult. Rather less in touch with reality was the General Staff study mentioned above, Personnel Versus Matériel in Plans for National Defense. In spite of the fact that in each of its wars the United States had given personnel mobilization priority over matériel mobilization, often with unfortunate results, this study suggested that the influence of matériel on the issue of war usually had been much over-emphasized. It suggested, too, that the experience on the Western Front in Europe should not weigh too heavily on American military policy, but that lessons should be sought in the lesser theaters of the war where operations approximated more closely what would happen in case of an attack on the United States!

Determination of Requirements

The nearest attempt to deal with the questions of matériel requirements and industrial capacity was the appointment of a board of officers (November 1916) under Col. Francis J. Kernan to investigate the desirability of government manufacture of arms and equipment. In its inquiries the board surveyed the status of supply in the technical services and the capabilities of manufacturing establishments in the country for production of military goods, but it arrived at no complete estimates of capacity, other than estimates on the part of the bureau chiefs as to how long it would take to procure equipment of various kinds for an army of 500,000 men, 1,000,000 men, or 2,000,000 men.

It was easy enough to calculate requirements for initial equipment by multiplying the allowances given in the tables of organization and tables of fundamental allowances by the number and kinds of units to be called into service, but this left unanswered the question as to whether the allowances were realistic, and the even more difficult question as to the accuracy of estimates of probable expenditures and requirements for replacement supplies. The information was available in the experience of European armies that had been at war for over two years; yet the General Staff had done almost nothing to collate, to bring up to date, or to analyze this information in order to develop experience factors and requirements upon which to base a procurement program. The Kernan Board in November and December 1916 was still relying on rough estimates prepared a year earlier—before the great battle of Verdun, where attacks and counterattacks went on almost continuously for ten months, and cost the French 460,000 casualties; before the Somme offensive where British losses were nearly as great; and before the introduction of the tank in the Somme and the beginning of large-scale gas warfare.

The tentative troop program adopted at the beginning of the war contemplated sending to France as quickly as possible one tactical division "to show the flag," mainly for the morale effect upon both the Allies and the enemy, and following this division with a large enough expeditionary force to make an effective contribution. The size of the tactical division was not determined precisely, as it would depend largely on the shipping available, but in a general way it was assumed that the capacity of sixteen National Guard camps and sixteen National Army cantonments would be used to train a force of one million men which could be in France by the end of 1918. A number of people at this time thought that the United States' contribution would be limited to a token force and matériel assistance—and the Aviation Section of the Signal Corps accepted a French suggestion that it should include 4,500 aviators.

In July 1917 General Pershing submitted his proposals for an American Expeditionary Force (AEF) of thirty divisions, and followed up these proposals with recommendations for supporting service troops and for priorities of shipments. Pershing's recommendations provided the basis for the program the War Department adopted on 7 October, scheduling the shipment of troops so as to put thirty divisions (ten of which would be training and replacement divisions), together with necessary corps, army, and services of supply troops—a total of 1,370,000 men—in France by 31 December 1918. In the spring of 1918 it became clear that this number would not be adequate. The serious defeat of the Italians at Caporetto, and the elimination of Russia from the war the preceding fall had allowed the Germans to transfer troops to the Western Front for their series of massive assaults aimed at forcing a decision before American reinforcements could become decisive. It also was becoming clear by this time that unrestricted submarine warfare was failing the Germans. Thus both the necessity for and the possibility of shipping American troops to France in far greater numbers became apparent about the same time. In July 1918 both Secretary of War Newton D. Baker and General Peyton C. March, now Chief of Staff, concluded that 80 American divisions (although Pershing was insisting upon 100) could and must be shipped to France by 30 June 1919. The 80 divisions, together with the additional supporting troops, plus 18 divisions to be retained in the United States, became the official program and continued in effect until the armistice. It provided that 2,350,000 men, rather than 1,370,000, should be in France by the end of 1918, and that 3,360,000 should be there by 30 June 1919. In September an extension of this program was approved and sent to the chiefs of the supply departments to form the basis for their estimates of requirements for the next fiscal year. The extended

program provided for an Army of 100 divisions (4,260,000 men) in France and twelve divisions (1,290,000 men) in the United States, a total of 5,550,000 men by 30 June 1920.

A most significant influence on the determination of requirements and upon the whole procurement program—one that had been present in no previous war effort of the United States—was the agreed division of labor with the Allies. Thus light, medium, and heavy artillery for American units in France would be supplied by French and British gun factories, while the United States would concentrate on the production of propellants, high explosives, and heavy artillery shells. For many other items of equipment, too, the Americans would rely upon the French and British so that precious shipping might be saved for American food and raw materials and for American troops. Still another important consideration in determining requirements was the need to maintain sizable reserve stocks and large quantities in the supply pipeline in order to assure continuous resupply.

One of the important elements in scheduling was the time required to manufacture and ship items of supplies and equipment. It took one year, for instance, to produce a finished light artillery shell and put it on board ship, so for items of this kind requirements had to be anticipated a year in advance—an almost impossible task. Another element of timing was in correlation of mobilization of troops with the availability of equipment. Perhaps in this case there was some justification for allowing troop mobilization to get ahead of matériel procurement for much of the equipment could be obtained from the Allies overseas. But this means of procurement could not be used to satisfy immediate needs for shelter, clothing, and training equipment, and Secretary of War Baker received some criticism from members of Congress for calling troops before facilities were ready for them. Actually some of the contingents of draftees scheduled to be called late in 1917 were not called up until several weeks later because of shortages of supplies and equipment. Even so, the total strength of all components of the Army had reached 1,500,000 men within nine months after the declaration of war. The Secretary of War was under great pressure from the Allies—a situation which could not be publicized at the time—for a quick build-up of American forces. He had relied upon contractors' estimates of production that proved to be unduly optimistic, but he realized the urgency of swift action. He did not accept the 80-division program until the required industrial and shipping capacities had been surveyed, and the War Industries Board and the Chief of Staff had attested to its logistical feasibility.

Finance

Once again war caught the War Department in a state of acute financial embarrassment. The Congress had reached the constitutional limit of its session on 4 March 1917 without passing either the deficiency bill to pay for the punitive expedition into Mexico and the mobilization of the National Guard along the border, or the Regular Army appropriation bill for Fiscal Year 1917. No more inopportune time for such failures could have been found. A special session was called 1 April because of the war emergency, and the deficiency bill as finally approved on 17 April carried an additional appropriation of $100 million for "National Security and Defense." In the meantime the War Department was bringing together the estimates of the bureaus for equipping one million men, and shortly after the declaration of war Secretary Baker went before the House Appropriations Committee to request a shocking $3 billion. He hoped to get this emergency appropriation as a lump sum so that funds might be transferred from one purpose to another as requirements changed, or to take care of items that in the haste might have been overlooked. Congress, however, was not willing to grant any such blank check. The committee called the bureau chiefs to explain in detail the purposes of their requests, and required an itemized breakdown that would freeze all funds to the specific purpose for which they were granted. All this took weeks, and the appropriation was not approved until 15 June.

The total funds Congress appropriated for the War Department for Fiscal Year 1918 finally amounted to more than $7.5 billion—nearly fifty times the department's appropriations for the normal year of 1915, and ten times the 1915 appropriations for all activities of the government. Appropriations for the Ordnance Department for the year ($3.2 billion) were equal to more than three times the value of all products of the iron and steel industries in the United States in 1914, and the Quartermaster Corps appropriations of over $3 billion were four times as great as appropriations for all governmental purposes in 1915. Together, Ordnance and Quartermaster appropriations for 1918 equaled one-fourth the gross value of all products of all industries of the United States in 1914.

War Department Reorganization

As for the General Staff, it had failed to mature in the way hoped for by its creators. To some of the bureau chiefs it seemed to be just one more layer of red tape and its main result the further delay of urgent business. By design or by oversight the National Defense Act of 1916 appeared to have opened the way to a restoration of the independence of the bureaus. In the opinion of the Judge Advocate General the section stating that the General Staff "should be exclusively employed . . . on other duties not of an administrative nature" meant that the supervisory function of the General Staff had been eliminated, leaving only its advisory function. Secretary Baker ruled, however, that the wording did not change the intent of the original General Staff Act, and that the function of supervising and co-ordinating bureau activities would continue. Nevertheless, more than the preservation of formal legal authority would be needed to save the General Staff system, and under the impact of the great mobilization the whole structure of the War Department soon was near collapse.

The National Defense Act of 1916 had limited the number of officers who could be assigned to the General Staff to fifty-five, and, apparently reflecting fears of some kind of military junta, forbade more than half of the General Staff officers to be stationed in Washington. Actually the strength of the General Staff was nineteen officers in Washington and twenty-two elsewhere. Acts approved in May 1917 removed these restrictions and subsequently the General Staff grew to comprise 1,222 officers.

On 28 December 1917 a series of steps began for the complete reorganization of the General Staff to include a revamping of logistical control. By 9 February 1918 the General Staff had assumed the form of five divisions each of which was under an Assistant Chief of Staff. One of these was given the title of Director of Purchases and Supplies, and another, Director of Storage and Traffic. These two divisions were merged formally on 16 April 1918 into the Purchase, Storage and Traffic Division, with Maj. Gen. George W. Goethals, previously Director of Storage and Traffic, as the head of the combined division. At the same time Goethals retained his post as Acting Quartermaster General. In addition, there was a gradual consolidation of procurement of all except technical items in the Quartermaster Corps. Passage of the Overman Act in May 1918 gave the President a free hand to reorganize agencies and reassign functions, and thus permitted completion of the War Department's reorganization, which was announced formally on 26 August. In the meantime direction of the Army's logistical activities had become almost completely centralized under the Director of Purchase, Storage and Traffic. (*Chart 1*) Authority for the new logistics organization stated:

At the head of the organization is a Director of Purchase, Storage and Traffic, whose function is executive and not supervisory. He receives the Army program from another division of the General Staff, and his is the responsibility for the computation of requirements to meet that program and the filling of these requirements. He is in command of the supply organization and relieves the Chief of Staff from all detail of and responsibility for supply.

The fundamental idea of this reorganization is first, the consolidation in one department of the purchase of all standard articles of merchandise, leaving in the bureaus the purchase, production, and inspection of highly technical

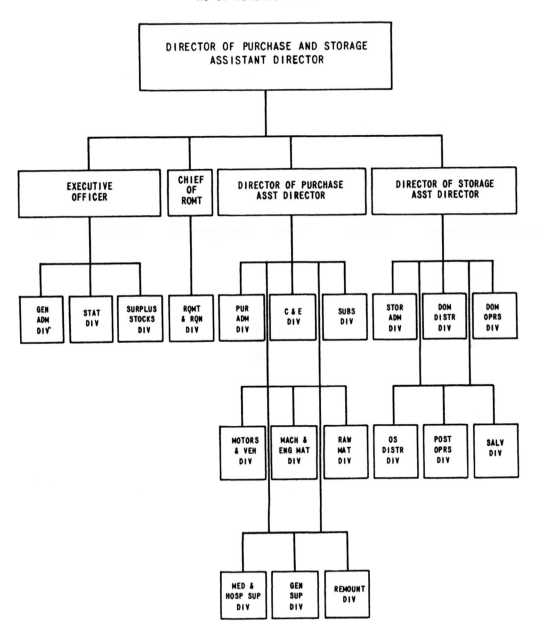

CHART 1

ORGANIZATION OF OFFICE DIRECTOR PURCHASE AND STORAGE
AS OF NOVEMBER 1918

DIRECTOR OF PURCHASE AND STORAGE
ASSISTANT DIRECTOR

EXECUTIVE OFFICER

CHIEF OF ROMT

DIRECTOR OF PURCHASE
ASST DIRECTOR

DIRECTOR OF STORAGE
ASST DIRECTOR

GEN ADM DIV

STAT DIV

SURPLUS STOCKS DIV

RQMT & RQN DIV

PUR ADM DIV

C & E DIV

SUBS DIV

STOR ADM DIV

DOM DISTR DIV

DOM OPRS DIV

MOTORS & VEH DIV

MACH & ENG MAT DIV

RAW MAT DIV

OS DISTR DIV

POST OPRS DIV

SALV DIV

MED & HOSP SUP DIV

GEN SUP DIV

REMOUNT DIV

material, such as ordnance, aircraft, etc., and second, the storage, distribution, and issue within the United States, and their storage prior to shipment abroad, of all War Department supplies, whether standard or special (including those excepted from procurement.)[3]

There remained the ever-present question of civilian versus military supervision and control of Army procurement. By training and experience an Army officer usually was less fitted to the tasks of contracting and production than was a man from business whose career had been concerned with those matters. On the other hand, military people thought that the using service should buy the material it needed— even though in actual practice the procurement agency (for example, the Ordnance Department) might be no more the actual user (the infantry or artillery) than would have been a civilian agency. Yet co-ordination between user and buyer was essential, and would be removed one step further by assigning it to an agency outside the Army. Some members of Congress urged a separate ministry of munitions along the lines of the one the British had set up to have charge of all procurement, but President Wilson opposed this solution. He noted that almost every step of co-ordination resulted in a certain amount of delay and a certain demoralization in the agencies involved; he thought that a new department would seriously hamper the activities of the Navy, which by this time were well under way, and would offer no advantages to the Army, then in the process of reorganizing its procurement structure. On the other hand, there was an extension of civilian supervision within the War Department,

following somewhat the example of the Navy Department.

In November 1917 Secretary Baker called Benedict Crowell, a man whose training and experience had been in industry, to be Assistant Secretary of War and to take over administration of the War Department's industrial activities. Subsequently Crowell received the additional title, Director of Munitions. He conceived of his role as the co-ordinator of the bureaus in procurement activities, and he looked to the Purchase, Storage and Traffic Division as the agency through which his decisions were given effect and through which he exercised control. His control thus was more real than apparent, because before passage of the Overman Act it had been necessary to make use of the General Staff machinery for the legal authority to develop the kind of organization desired; otherwise the whole organization might have been completely civilian, with no mention at all of the General Staff. Although the Purchase, Storage and Traffic Division was a part of the General Staff, the Chief of Staff did not in fact exercise supervision over its procurement functions. As Crowell described it, the Chief of Staff was the Secretary of War's military adviser, while the Assistant Secretary was the Secretary's industrial adviser. This meant that General Goethals had two immediate chiefs; on military matters he reported to the Chief of Staff; on industrial matters, to the Assistant Secretary, and the latter was the contact with outside agencies of the government and with industry.

Procurement

Controls

Never had American industry been organized and controlled in the way it was under

---

[3] Report of the Chief of Staff. *Annual Reports of the War Department,* 1919, I, 416.

the War Industries Board. The "vitals" of the War Industries Board were its fifty-seven (as of 11 November 1918) commodity sections. Made up of experts experienced in a particular industry, together with members from the Army, Navy and other interested procurement agencies, each commodity section functioned as a kind of miniature War Industries Board for a particular commodity. The Purchase, Storage and Traffic Division of the General Staff set up a series of Army commodity committes, made up of representatives from the interested supply bureaus, to parallel the commodity sections of the War Industries Board. The chairman of each of these Army committees served as a member of the corresponding commodity section of the War Industries Board, where he represented the Army as a whole.

Probably no aspect of the co-ordination of procurement and the control of the war economy was more important than the development of a system of priorities. The early competition among the Army's supply departments for materials, supplies, facilities, fuel, labor, and transportation led to chaos in the market place. Within three months after the declaration of war, the Army had placed more than 60,000 orders. A significant task of the later Purchase, Storage, and Traffic Division was to develop a priorities system within the Army, and to represent the interests of the Army in the higher priorities agencies.

Thus a system evolved which included graded priority certificates for work of different degrees of importance; a classification of industry, and even of certain plants within an industry, according to their relative importance in the war effort; and, finally, a scheme of automatic classifications under which certain classes of orders required no priority certificates. As the system eventually worked out for the Army, a priorities committee within each supply bureau settled questions of preference within the bureau, then the requests went to the Army priorities officer in the Purchase, Traffic and Storage Division for resolution of conflicts among bureaus, after which the requests went to the Priorities Committee of the War Industries Board. By the end of the war almost all the industries concerned were operating under priority schedules closely correlated with the total Army program.

Contract Principles

In placing orders of all kinds for goods and services during the war the War Department entered into some 30,000 contracts involving obligations of more than $7.5 billion. Strict legal rules governed government contract procedures. Rules in effect at the start of the war provided that in nearly all cases it was necessary to advertise for competitive bids, giving complete specifications, and to award the contract to the best bid so long as the bidder was responsible and known to be able to fulfill the terms. There were, however, certain exceptions. A contract already properly made might be increased without opening it to further competitive bids, and, if previous advertising had brought forth no bids, it was permissible to negotiate directly with a manufacturer who was the sole source of supply. Several other legal safeguards, some dating back to legislation passed during the Civil War, were intended to protect the interests of the government. All contracts were supposed to be in writing. The contracting officer had to attach a sworn statement that the contract had been made without any benefit or advantage to himself, or any corrupt advantage to the contractor or to any other person. At the behest of the Attorney General all departments inserted a clause in their contracts which required the contractor to disclaim the employment of any third party for a fee in obtaining the contract, for, just as they had during the Civil War, the "five-percenters" descended upon Washington to interpose themselves between departments and the market. The War Department also adopted the policy that purchases through jobbers should be made only in exceptional circumstances. Probably the most common irregularities in the drawing of contracts under the pressure of war business were the more or less common uses of the informal procurement order and having a subordinate officer sign contracts for the authorized contracting officer.

A further important exception to the rule requiring advertising for bids, was a provision in the law that advertising might be suspended in the event of a national emergency. Moreover, the National Defense Act of 1916 empowered the President, through the Secretary of War or other department head, in time of actual or imminent war, to place an order with a firm at prices fixed by the department; if the producer refused this arrangement, his plant might be commandeered and operated through the Ordnance Department, with payment of just compensation. Within a week after the declaration of war Secretary of War Baker issued an order finding a national emergency to exist within the meaning of the law, and authorizing the negotiation of contracts without resort to formal advertising.

The normal form of contract in peacetime was the lump-sum, or fixed-price con-tract, and this continued to be used throughout the war for most purchases by the Quartermaster Corps, the Engineer Corps, and the Medical Corps, but for major projects or new products involving unknown costs, frequent changes in specifications, and other conditions this type of contract had serious disadvantages.

In the spring of 1917 some two hundred builders and contractors came to Washington to consult with the General Munitions Board on the gigantic task of constructing new camps and cantonments. In conference they concluded that the best way to get the job done would be on the basis of contracts allowing for payment of costs plus a percentage of costs as profit. Such contracts were known in private industry and the Navy had used them at times before the war but never on such a vast scale as was now proposed. After careful study the General Munitions Board accepted the principle and recommended approval, which was given in turn by the Advisory Commission, the full Council of National Defense, and the President.

While the cost-plus principle overcame the disadvantages of the lump-sum contract, no one was blind to the inherent serious possibilities for waste and extravagance. In its simple form the cost-plus contract encouraged carelessness, and even the padding of costs, for the higher the costs the higher the profits. The Construction Division never used any cost-plus-percentage contracts without a maximum fee. Throughout the war it used an emergency form contract, first drafted by the Emergency Construction Committee of the Council of National Defense and modified slightly several times, which provided for cost plus a sliding scale fee for all the construction work in building the camps, cantonments, depots, and other facilities. After this form of contract had been in use for construction work for several months the War Department called a committee of leading engineers, architects, contractors, and business men to study the various types of contracts and to recommend the one best suited to the conditions. The committee returned a unanimous recommendation for continuation of the cost-plus-with-limited-fee principle.   Changes could be made without revising this kind of contract, materials could be substituted wherever desirable, the government could furnish materials when expedient to do so, partial payments could be made promptly to cover the contractors' costs, the government automatically acquired all surplus materials, and the government could reserve the right to pay transportation charges on materials and thus take advantage of land-grant and bond credits. None of these was possible under the ordinary lump-sum contract. Aside from essential considerations of speed and flexibility, it is doubtful that the cost was greater than it would have been under competitive bidding and lump-sum contracts under those wartime conditions. A further refinement in some cost-plus contracts was a provision which allowed a bonus to the contractor for reducing his costs. Frequently this arrangement had good results and, in some cases, savings resulting from lower costs than had been estimated were divided three ways—among the contractor, the laboring force, and the government.

Another type of contract closely related to the cost-plus was the agency contract whereby a reliable firm acted as agent for the government in the construction and, or, the operation of a plant. The government paid all the bills, and the agent received a fee for its service, either a percentage of the costs or a fixed fee.

A major problem in all contracting was controlling the costs. In the construction contracts referred to above the Army representative had complete control of the expenditures of the contractor. Firms accepting ordnance contracts were expected to keep a completely separate set of records pertaining to their government work, including daily time reports on each workman, and to give Army inspectors and auditors access at all times to all places where materials were received, stored, used, processed, and shipped, and to all records pertaining to them. An attempt in June 1917 to apply price redetermination, however, resulted in serious delays for ordnance. In the face of soaring steel prices, the Secretary of War directed that no further contracts for steel be entered into without a provision that the price should be adjusted to the price which later would be agreed upon by government officials. The manufacturers refused to accept orders under these conditions. As a consequence ordnance work was delayed until September when, after a stormy session, the War Industries Board and representatives of the steel industry arrived at an agreeable fixed price.

Facilities

With the coming of war it was necessary to find every possible facility, government or private, that could be put to use. This included not only expansion of the government's arsenals and manufactories but also contruction of vast new government-owned or government-financed plants. All together the government built or financed sixteen of the ninety-two plants ultimately engaged in the manufacture of powder and high explosives, about as many other plants for loading shells, bombs, grenades, boosters, fuzes, and propellants, five of eighteen new gun factories of various kinds, four nitrate plants, and eight plants for the manufacture of toxic gas, gas masks, and for loading gas shells.

Although industrial conversion began as soon as the war, it was a hit-and-miss affair for several months. Army procurement officers, or ambitious industrialists, or others, would take the initiative in making a contract for a plant to turn out some new product for the Army, and then hope that it could be done. Not until late 1917 did the War Industries Board set up machinery to regulate these procedures by creating a regional organization covering the country and a Resources and Conversion Section in Washington. The Ordnance Department and the Quartermaster Corps also had regional organizations, and they co-operated with regional War Industries Board advisers on problems of industrial conversion. The real problem was not in persuading the manufacturer to change over his plant on short notice, but to keep him from making the wrong changes.

The selection of sites delayed the construction of camp and cantonment facilities. Secretary Baker relied on the recommendations of the departmental commanders, but pressure came from all parts of the country to have camps located in particular communities, so that two months passed before all the sites had been chosen. Recommendations of Army officers that National Guard camps, at which tents were to be used for shelter, be located mainly in the South brought political accusations that the Democratic administration was favoring the Solid South. The cantonments were to consist almost entirely of wooden buildings—there

was already a shortage of canvas, so that they were no more expensive than additional tent cities would have been—and were to be located mostly in the north and east. Each cantonment was to accommodate from 40,000 to 60,000 troops and 10,000 animals, and was to have streets, lights, sewerage, water, kitchens, and hospitals commensurate with a city of that size. Problems of clearing sites, excavating, grading, drainage, bringing in materials, and labor varied a great deal from one location to another, even though the buildings and, in some cases the layouts, were of uniform design. It was intended that the camps and cantonments should be built to correspond to the Army's organization: a company was to be housed as a unit in one barrack building; one or more whole divisions would be quartered in a single cantonment. It did not take much longer to build the camps and cantonments than it did to choose the sites. By 4 September 1917 accommodations were ready for 430,000 men, and in 1918 the total capacity of forts, camps, cantonments, and special camps, reached nearly 1,800,000.

Arms and Ammunition

Rifles—Certainly no less important than housing the troops was arming them. The ordnance problem (which by the time of World War I meant the procurement of 100,000 different items of equipment, a large share of which were noncommercial) was, in the first instance, mainly one of providing small arms. Thanks largely to Allied orders, small arms manufacturers already had reached a substantial capacity, but they were producing foreign models. This raised a fundamental question: should their facilities be converted to produce the

Springfield, or, in the interest of saving time, should the United States adopt the British Enfield rifle for its own forces, and make use of facilities already available? A third possibility was to adapt the Enfield to American ammunition. In a meeting with the chairman of the Small Arms Subcommittee of the Munitions Standards Board the manufacturers estimated that it would take eighteen months for any of them to get ready to make the Springfield, and they recommended that the United States adopt the Enfield, either using British ammunition or modifying the Enfield to take American ammunition, as the Army preferred. Modification would entail a delay of approximately thirty days. It was decided to use the Springfield to equip the Regular Army and first units of the National Guard and to keep it in production at the armories, but to adopt the Enfield, modified for American ammunition, for the remainder of the forces. The decision to modify the Enfield was criticized as delaying production unnecessarily; however, the Chief of Ordnance and other officers wanted to avoid having two kinds of rifle ammunition for American units, and they felt certain that the Enfield would work much better with the American ammunition.

Machine Guns—The machine gun question was more complicated. Even though the machine gun had become the master of the battlefield in Europe, Americans had failed to recognize this development fully. Belated efforts in 1916 to improve the machine gun situation in the Army had had little effect before the declaration of war. The British-developed Vickers heavy machine gun had been adopted, but only 125 had been ordered until December 1916 when the War Department placed an order for 4,000 with the Colt

company. None were on hand at the beginning of the war. The total machine gun armament then consisted of 670 of the older Benet-Mercie machine rifles, 282 Maxim machine guns of the 1904 model, 353 Lewis machine guns built for British ammunition, and 148 of the Colt 1895 model.

On 1 February 1917, the day that Germany resumed unrestricted submarine warfare, the chief of the Navy's Bureau of Ordnance wired the Marlin-Rockwell Corporation to inquire how soon it could make machine guns for the Navy. He had no funds, nor any idea how many might be ordered; nevertheless he requested that the company, then working on a Russian order, make preparations. With nothing more to go on the company ordered materials for 5,000 machine guns; in May the Navy placed an order for 2,500. Meanwhile the vice president of the company inquired of the Army Ordnance Department about interest there, but found none. Actually the Marlin gun was obsolete, and Army Ordnance officers were not satisfied with it, although there was something to be said for the contention that several thousand Marlin guns would be better than no machine guns at all. Later the Marlin gun was adapted for use on aircraft, synchronized to fire between the propeller blades, and for that purpose proved to be one of the best machine guns available.

For reasons even now not wholly clear the Army did not take advantage of another more modern machine gun that had been tested in combat in Europe and was then in production in the United States for the British and Canadian Governments—the Lewis machine gun. In a test conducted by a machine gun board in 1916 the Lewis gun was held not to be satisfactory, and further competitive tests were scheduled for May 1917. As has been noted, General Wood, who had been impressed with the Lewis gun as early as 1912, conducted a series of tests at Plattsburg in which the gun was completely satisfactory. In the fall of 1916 Wood urged immediate and careful consideration of the Lewis gun in view of the experience of the British with it in two years of war. Even after the declaration of war the War Department did not move up tests scheduled for May, but the Navy and Marine Corps asked for seperate tests. Conducted on 15 April with guns made to take American ammunition, the tests were so satisfactory that the Navy quickly ordered 3,500 Lewis guns, and they became standard equipment for the Marine Corps. On the strength of the Navy tests the Army also ordered 1,300 of this model, and after the gun showed up well in the May tests, the Army in June and July ordered 18,400. Then it found that the Lewis was admirably suited for use as a flexible gun (that is, one that could be mounted on a pivot to fire in all directions) on aircraft, and in September the War Department ordered some aircraft models; a little later it changed all the older orders to call for the aircraft guns. These guns never were adopted for ground troops.

Much to their dismay, marines arriving in France with the Lewis guns with which they had trained were required to turn in their American guns for inferior Chauchat machine rifles; yet the Marine Corps continued to use them for several years after the war. Even Colonel Lewis' disclaimer of any royalties for Lewis guns purchased by the United States—in all he returned to the government royalties amounting to more than a million dollars—became a question of controversy. Defense of the Ordnance Department's policy at times has taken the form of criticism of the attitude or activities of Colonel Lewis, the implication being that he deserved no further consideration. This suggests something of the same attitude that prevailed at times during the Civil War— that the treatment accorded new weapons was related to the personality or the deserving character of the inventor rather than the real issue—the merits of the weapon.

Meanwhile the War Department had found a superior light automatic rifle and a heavy machine gun. It accepted the Browning automatic rifle after a popular demonstration held in February 1917. Tests for Browning's heavy water-cooled machine gun were held in May 1917 at Springfield where one gun fired 20,000 rounds without a malfunction or broken part and then fired another 20,000 rounds without the failure of any part. A second gun fired a single burst lasting over forty-eight minutes. The test results aroused the enthusiasm of witnesses, and two officers rushed to Washington to urge quick acceptance of the gun before the formal reports arrived. But the Ordnance Department would not be hurried into placing orders for the better model gun it had presumably been waiting for while refusing to order machine guns already in production. The department did not move to procure Browning machine guns until July; however, once started, machine gun production was phenomenal. Production of all models, both for ground use and for aircraft, totaled 226,500 by the end of 1918. Of the ground use models, 56,600 were Browning heavies, nearly 70,000 Browning automatic rifles, and 12,000 Vickers; most numerous of the aircraft guns were 39,200 Lewis and 38,000 Marlin. Yet, because the War Department refused to order the Vickers and the Lewis early enough, and because it delayed in plac-

LEWIS MACHINE GUN MOUNTED ON A SALMSON AIRPLANE. *A crewman is servicing
one of the guns. France, 1918.*

ing orders for the Browning, American forces in France fought almost the entire war with French Hotchkiss machine guns and Chauchat automatic rifles. Browning machine guns were first used in combat on 26 September 1918, just a month and a half before the armistice, but very few ever reached the fighting fronts.

Artillery—If anything had been more impressive on the battlefields of Europe from 1914 to 1917 than the importance of the machine gun, it was the extravagant use of artillery. The favorite field artillery piece was the French 75, which new American plants were built to produce. Manufacture of the highly regarded French recoil mechanism presented perhaps the most difficult aspect of the industrial problem, but the United States adopted the French

recuperators for the 75-mm. gun, the 155-mm. gun, the 155-mm. howitzer, and the 240-mm. howitzer, and proceeded to manufacture them. This was a feat that even the Germans had been unable to duplicate, and that several Americans averred could never be done by mass-production methods. The only French recuperator in actual production before the armistice was the one for the 155-mm. howitzer for which a special Dodge Brothers plant completed the machining and assembling of 743 from forgings made by the West Machine Company and the Watertown Arsenal. It took several months to get complete drawings from the French, which then had to be translated from the metric system. If American production of field artillery was small before the armistice (only 1,642 complete units) it had reached the stage for much greater production in what was expected to be the big year of 1919. By April 1919 more than 3,000 complete units of artillery had been produced—as much as the total purchased abroad from the French and British. The only American-made artillery pieces to reach the battle front were 109 75-mm. guns, and 24 8-inch howitzers, plus 8 14-inch naval guns set up on railway mounts and operated by units of the U.S. Navy.

Ammunition—The ammunition program involved the construction of three bag-loading plants; the production of TNT, amatol, and picric acid, for which the government built six big plants; the adoption of French and British shell designs, and the development of a huge shell-making industry; and, finally, the development of facilities for shell-loading. All these, plus the huge quantities of powder and components shipped to the Allies, resulted in production through November 1918 of over 15,000,000 rounds of artillery ammunition for the guns of the AEF. Ammunition manufacture also included production of over 3.5 billion rounds of small arms ammunition, of which 1.8 billion rounds were shipped overseas.

The Impact of the Gasoline Engine

Vehicles—The revolution in warfare, leaving its imprint on World War I, and in turn hastened by it, extended to transportation as well as to firepower, and of fundamental importance to both was the gasoline engine. Introduced hesitatingly, especially on the Allied side, and by improvisation in the early months of the war, motor vehicles had become basic necessities in all the armies by the end of the war. As in other aspects of this war, Americans at first could see, but

could not believe; then, once they believed, they performed unbelievable feats.

In this greatest of all motor-vehicle-producing countries, the use of motor cars and trucks in war had received little more consideration than the use of caterpillar tractors—until 1916. The Quartermaster Corps was the agency responsible for procurement of virtually all Army transportation, but during the Mexican crisis of 1916 each bureau had begun to purchase motor vehicles to fit its own special needs. In 1917, therefore, each using service was buying its own vehicles, a practice that resulted inevitably in competition, duplication, and complete lack of standardization, all of which complicated the problems of providing replacement vehicles and spare parts. At one time the Army was using 294 different makes and body types of vehicles. In April 1918 all the motor sections of the various bureaus were brought together under the Quartermaster General to form the Motor Transport Service, which was to have charge of all motor procurement. A separate Motor Transport Corps, formed in August 1918, had the procurement function for a few weeks but it then became only a service organization, and procurement of all vehicles (except tanks) was assigned to a division under the Purchase, Storage and Traffic Division of the General Staff.

The most notable achievement in standardization and production was in the Standard B truck. Under the direction of the Quartermaster General, a committee of fifty engineers met with Army officers in Washington to choose the best of several types of parts and assemblies for use in the new 3-ton cargo truck. They chose designs that had been proved, would suit the purpose, and would not infringe on patent

BROWNING MACHINE GUN *with ammu-nition box attached.*

rights. A smaller group of manufacturers then organized the production program. They selected twenty leading truck factories as assembly plants and let contracts for parts to some 150 other manufacturers. As production started more contracts were let until orders called for nearly 43,000 of the standard truck chassis. About 10,000 were produced before the armistice, and 8,000 were shipped overseas.

Tanks—For direct combat, the gasoline engine made its entry in the tank and the airplane. Although the tank depended upon the American-invented caterpillar traction system, no one in the United States appears to have applied the idea to a war machine. That application was born of the necessity created by the machine gun and barbed wire on the Western Front.

Under development both in France and in Britain, the tank finally came into existence largely through the efforts of the British Admiralty. It was not revealed—and then perhaps prematurely—until 15 September 1916 in the Somme, and achieved its first striking success (although forfeited for lack of reserves and insufficient numbers) at Cambrai on 19 November 1917. Thus there was little time to initiate any U.S. tank program, and though the effort was made the program never got off the ground. Total U.S. tank production up to 11 November 1918 amounted to 76, but 22,400 had been ordered, and all the work done in that connection, while it had no effect on World War I, provided valuable experience for the future. By a co-operative arrangement with France and Great Britain the United States undertook the production of a light tank modeled after the French 6-ton Renault, and entered into a treaty with Great Britain for the co-operative production of a heavy tank to be assembled in France from armored hulls and guns supplied by the British, and with engines, traction mechanisms and electrical equipment from the United States. The latter, known as the Anglo-American Mark VIII, was a great success, but only one was completed before the armistice.

Aircraft—Probably the most ambitious, disappointing, dramatic, and controversial production story of World War I was that of aircraft. Once again Americans had neglected an American invention in its development for either war or peaceful purposes. To be sure, Congress in 1915 had established the National Advisory Committee for Aeronautics, and the Council of National Defense had given some attention to aviation. But when the United States entered the war, the Army had fifty-five serv-

BRITISH TANK CARRYING U.S. SIGNAL CORPS PHOTOGRAPHERS TO THE FRONT, *France, 1918.*

iceable airplanes—all out of date— and only sixty-five people who could fly an airplane. Another 350 planes were on order, but as soon as information on Allied planes was available it became obvious that they, too, were antiquated, and the contractors asked to be released. The aircraft industry in the United States consisted of the Curtiss Company and a dozen or so small manufacturers, not over six of whom had ever made as many as ten airplanes. The industry had produced about 800 training planes during the preceding years for the Allies.

The complications of aircraft production, little realized when the ambitious programs were accepted, soon became evident. Aside from all the difficulties of finding aeronautical engineers, building additional factory facilities, solving design problems (particularly for using American engines), and production, serious problems in obtaining raw materials arose. These involved the development of a long-staple cotton cloth, used for covering the airplanes, to replace the linen which was not available in the quantities needed; development of a new dope for applying to the cloth to give a smooth, waterproof surface; cultivation of castor beans to supply the necessary lubricants until a mineral oil could be developed for the purpose; and, above all, the problem of obtaining spruce, the principal wood used

in making airframes. In spite of all difficulties, 11,700 planes, of which about half
were training planes, had been produced in
the United States by the time of the armistice, and the DeHavilland–4 was being
produced at the rate of over 1,100 a month.

The brightest spot in the aircraft story,
and one of the outstanding American industrial achievements of the war, was the production of the Liberty engine. In May
1917 Col. E. A. Deeds of the Signal Corps
made the bold decision to proceed with the
design and production of a standard aviation engine. As in the case of the Standard
B truck, this engine was to incorporate all
the best features of known engines in a way
suited to American mass-production methods. On 29 May J. G. Vincent and E. J.
Hall (of the Packard Motor Car Company
and the Hall-Scott Motor Car Company,
respectively) began drawing plans for an
8-cylinder and a 12-cylinder model. Less
than six weeks later the first working model
of the 8-cylinder engine, to be known as the
Liberty, was delivered in Washington, and
within another six weeks the first 12-cylinder
engine had successfully completed its 50-
hour test. Production engineers of the leading automobile companies as well as men
experienced with aircraft engines had been
consulted in the designing and, once production began, no major changes in design
were necessary, though the horsepower of
the 12-cylinder model was stepped up from
330 to over 400. In August 1917 the Aircraft Production Board placed contracts
for 10,000 8-cylinder engines with the Ford
Motor Company, and contracts for a total
of 22,500 12-cylinder Liberties with the
Packard Motor Car Company, where much
of the development work had been done,
and with Lincoln, Ford, General Motors
(Buick and Cadillac), Nordyke & Marman,

and the Trego Motors Corporation. Then
word from a commission of observers in
France that production ought to be concentrated on the 12-cylinder engines interrupted production with cancellation of
Ford's big contract for the 8-cylinder. Later
the increased popularity of single-seater
planes led to a request from the AEF to
have production of the 8-cylinder models
resumed. So successful were the Liberty
engines that the Allied governments quickly
placed large orders for them for use in their
own planes. Orders with the original manufacturers were increased, and large facilities of the Willys-Overland and Olds Companies were added. Total orders amounted
to 56,100 for 12-cylinder Liberties, and
8,000 for the 8-cylinder type. Actual production to the date of the armistice
amounted to 13,500, of which 4,400 were
shipped overseas to the AEF and 1,000 to
the Allies.

Food, Clothing, and Medicine

Procurement of the ordinary necessities
of food and clothing and equipage in World
War I differed little from earlier experience,
except that food procurement had become
a responsibility of the Subsistence Division
of the Quartermaster Corps, and a Food
Purchase Board co-ordinated the purchases
of the Army, the Navy, and the Allies.
Nearly everyone was obsessed with a determination to avoid another "embalmed beef"
scandal, and this time no such controversy
developed.

As for clothing, there were the inevitable
shortages during the early months, and the
surfeit at the end. The most serious problem was that of obtaining wool, and to
assure a supply the government itself went
into the wool business, the Quartermaster

Clothing and Equipage Division taking over the entire wool trade of the United States. The division bought all the raw wool at fixed prices—the Army's wool administrator purchased some 722,000,000 pounds—and sold it to clothing contractors. In turn, the lack of a well-developed dye industry posed further problems.

To procure supplies for field, hospital, and veterinary use the Medical Department—with the co-ordination of the General Medical Board of the Council of National Defense—had to develop domestic sources for the many surgical instruments and medicines which before 1914 had been imported from Germany.

Summary

American industry had never been so completely mobilized, nor so fully integrated, nor so rapidly expanded, nor so strictly controlled by the government, as it was during those war years. The number of American soldiers engaged in combat operations was less than the number of Union soldiers in the Civil War, and the pace of mobilization was no greater than that of the Civil War or the War with Spain, but in the magnitude of the procurement program and the industrial undertaking, there was no comparison. Production figures do not give the full picture, for in many areas maximum production was only beginning when the war ended. Had the program planned and begun for 1919 been carried through, the results would have been the marvel of the world. Faulty organization, lack of planning, and complicated problems inherent in converting and expanding industry and in building new industries delayed procurement and production programs seriously, but once those obstacles had been overcome, results were rapid and gratifying. It should be remembered, too, that some current production was sacrificed in favor of the greater production planned for 1919 and 1920.

In assessing World War I industrial mobilization and procurement as a whole, four general observations stand out for emphasis. The first is the importance of Allied orders, before the United States entered into the war in stimulating the expansion and preparedness of the munitions industry of the United States. The second is the importance of the mobilization of forces on the Mexican border in advancing the logistical readiness of the Army for the bigger undertakings it would face a year later. The third is the importance of the availability of industrial capacity in France and Great Britain for the initial equipment of American forces overseas which was able to make up for the failure of the United States to maintain adequate matériel reserves, and also the decision not to continue integration of U.S. and Allied industry in this way, but for the United States to develop a balanced program of its own. Finally, all efforts pointed to 1919 as the big year, the year of decision. If the military objective was won earlier than expected, that should be no cause for disparagement of a procurement and production program which, fortunately, was not needed.

CHAPTER XXI

Interallied Co-ordination

Coalition warfare, the conduct of war in close association with allies, which was to characterize warfare for the United States in the twentieth century, was virtually unknown to the country in 1917–18, and in some ways the experience in international co-operation was one of the most significant aspects of American participation in World War I. Not since the Revolution had the United States been in a war alongside an ally. Indeed, national feeling had become so deeply ingrained against "entangling alliances" that the President in 1917 was careful to draw a distinction in defining the relationship of the United States to the Entente Powers as one of an "associate" rather than an "ally". Yet no participant was more firm in urging co-ordination of effort and the organization of machinery for control even while insisting on the maintenance of the national identity of its Army. Actually, the European Allies themselves were little practiced in real co-ordination of effort.

Allied Purchases in the United States

While the entry of the United States into the war encouraged an increase in the procurement activities of the Allies in the United States, it also complicated the picture by introducing bureaus of the United States Government as competitors for some of the same supplies. Previously, the firm of J. P. Morgan and Company, through an office organized under Edward R. Stettinius, had acted as purchasing agent for the British and French Governments, and thus had curtailed to a degree competition between them. But with the active involvement of the United States in the war, Morgan considered it both better and more proper for these activities to be transferred to an official agency. Stettinius accordingly closed his special office, but the British did nothing immediately to replace it, so that at the same time that the Army and the Navy supply departments were entering the market to meet their mobilization requirements—frequently in competition with each other—the Allies also were competing in the same market.

Secretary of the Treasury William Gibbs McAdoo insisted that some kind of organization be formed to co-ordinate Allied requirements and their financial and purchasing activities. Otherwise he did not see how it would be possible to justify advancing the huge credits for which they were asking. While the Allies delayed further in setting up a clearing house in Europe, President Wilson and McAdoo took steps at least to co-ordinate Allied purchases in the United States. On 24 August the Secretary of the Treasury signed an agreement with representatives of Great Britain, France, Italy, and Russia for the creation of a Purchasing Commission for the Allies with headquarters in Washington. The members of the commission, Bernard M. Baruch, Robert S. Lovett, and Robert S. Brookings, also were members of the newly created War Industries Board, which helped to make co-ordination more effective. The commission met daily at first then twice weekly with Allied representatives to agree on requirements and priorities; the Allied agents, just as the Army procurement officers, did the actual purchasing. Although limited to an advisory capacity and without other authority than persuasion, the commission nevertheless improved the situation for all concerned. It became a division of the reorganized War Industries Board in March 1918, with the advantage of all the power of that body. Machinery for United States–Allied co-ordination, of which the Purchasing Commission was a beginning, was essential in order that the American people could have some assurance as to the application of funds being loaned to the Allies; the Allies could have some protection on prices in their commercial negotiations; Allied purchases would not disrupt the American economy; and orders of the United States and the Allies could be met without interference from each other.

Commodity and Shipping Controls

During negotiations with the British in August 1917 on commercial policy and raw materials, the French Ministry of Commerce developed the concept that the Allies, through their purchases, their own resources, and control of the seas, were in fact masters of the world markets in basic raw materials, and that what was needed was an interallied executive, patterned after one organized earlier for wheat, for each raw material. About the same time Her-

bert Hoover, United States Food Administrator, was urging that the Allies unify their purchases of food. A further step in this direction was the organization in September 1917 of the Interallied Meats and Fats Executive. Like the Interallied Wheat Executive, it had a British, a French and an Italian member, and its headquarters was in London. It made its purchases in the United States through the Allied Provisions Export Commission, sitting in New York. Made up of representatives of the same three governments, this commission had a role with respect to meats and fats comparable to that of the Wheat Export Company with respect to cereals. It had to clear its purchases with the Division of Co-ordination of Purchase (organized in October) of the U.S. Food Administration, which allotted available supplies and fixed prices, and then notify the Packers' Committee which distributed orders among the packing houses. As for sugar, the British Royal Commission on Sugar Supply already had been purchasing sugar for the other Allies, and in September 1917 an International Sugar Committee was organized in New York to centralize the whole procedure of buying and allocating Cuban and American sugar. In October negotiations began for the pooling of Allied buying of nitrates, but the organization of the first executive to control such industrial raw materials was not completed until January 1918.

While negotiations for closer economic co-operation dragged on slowly but surely during the summer and early autumn of 1917, a new disaster was brewing in northern Italy that would drive the Allies to closer collaboration. This was the breakthrough of the Austro-German armies at Caporetto in October–November 1917. A week after the first major Italian retreat, as

British and French divisions hurried to help reinforce the new positions, the Prime Ministers of Great Britain, France, and Italy met at Rapallo and formed the Supreme War Council, made up of the premiers together with a second representative from each government, and with a permanent military representative from each power to co-ordinate political and military policy in the conduct of the war. Headquarters for the Council was to be at Versailles.

From this point, steps toward logistical co-ordination quickened. The French Minister of Commerce proposed to go to the United States with a detailed report showing the world shipping situation, the anticipated reduction in imports for 1918, means to increase tonnage, the labor situation, the munitions shortage, and estimates of shipping needed to transport and supply an American army of 1,000,000 men. Then President Wilson accepted a British suggestion that he send a mission headed by his adviser, Edward M. House (Colonel House), to a general Allied conference to discuss these questions with British and French leaders. Maj. Gen. Tasker H. Bliss, Chief of Staff, accompanied House to Europe as military adviser. Other members of the mission included the Chief of Naval Operations, the Assistant Secretary of the Treasury, and the chairman of the War Trade Board, along with representatives from the War Industries Board, the Food Administration, and the U.S. Shipping Board.

The mission arrived in London at the time of the Caporetto disaster and the overthrow of the Kerensky regime in Russia; it visited briefly with British leaders, then went to Paris for preliminary conversations prior to the Interallied Conference, which con-

vened on 29 November. Prime ministers, foreign secretaries, ambassadors, special representatives, and military and economic experts, representing eighteen Allied nations, assembled for the opening plenary session of the conference at the French Foreign Office. It lasted eight minutes. France's Premier Clemenceau, presiding, limited his opening address to six sentences, the last two were: "The order of the day is work. Let us get to work." [1] This was the signal for the conference to resolve itself into committees which immediately went into executive session where the experts could work out plans for furthering economic and military co-ordination. Concurrently, Colonel House and General Bliss participated in a meeting of the Supreme War Council to discuss proposals for establishing some kind of unity of command and to make general plans for the military effort of 1918 when it was expected that German divisions released from the Russian front would be thrown into the battles in the West.

Allied prospects seemed dark in April 1917 because of the losses of shipping, and the recent events in Italy and Russia had not brightened them. Driven by necessity, and by the insistence of the U.S. representatives, the Allies moved to perfect their machinery for co-operation. Results of the work begun at the Interallied Conference were so far-reaching in achievements in cooperation that the conference may be regarded as a turning point in the war. The conference committees proposed that an extensive system of executives and committees be set up to cover the whole range of essential foods and raw materials, and that organizations be established to co-ordinate

---

[1] Report of Colonel House, State Department, *Foreign Relations,* 1917, Supplement 2, I, 443.

Allied activities in finance, transportation, and munitions.

Immediately after the Paris conference the organization to collate Allied requests for loans upon which Secretary of the Treasury McAdoo had been insisting finally came into being in the Interallied Council on War Purchases and Finance which sat in London and Paris under the chairmanship of the American representative, Oscar T. Crosby. By the time this council was formed its purpose had become less urgent, for the limiting factor on Allied purchases was then recognized to be not credit, but rather the availability of materials and shipping. This realization gave added importance to the organizations set up to deal with those matters. Foremost among them was the Allied Maritime Transport Council organized in February and March 1918. The council was made up of ministerial representatives from each of the principal European Allies and delegates from the United States. It held but four formal meetings, while an executive, made up of one representative from each participant and an international secretariat working under it, carried on the daily business of correlating shipping requirements and making allocations. Anxious to have representatives from the various supply departments themselves resolve their competing demands, the Maritime Transport Council urged the further formation of program committees covering all essential goods, as had been proposed at the Paris conference. The Council on War Purchases and Finance joined in this recommendation.

The Nitrate of Soda Executive had been formed in December 1917, and in a short time it gained control of the entire nitrate production of Chile. A little later, and with

somewhat greater difficulty, the Interallied Tin Executive was formed. The War Industries Board sent a foreign mission headed by Leland L. Summers to Europe to negotiate for the creation of other committees and to see that American resources were put to the best use in the war effort and that American purchasing agents in Europe received the same benefits in price and conditions as did agents of the local governments.

Although the Allied Maritime Transport Council did not have a status superior to the other councils, it gradually came to assume a leading position by virtue of its control of shipping. Actually, the Maritime Transport Council had no direct executive power except over the pool of neutral shipping assigned to it, and depended upon the consent of the governments concerned and upon the governments' execution of policies the council developed. But the make-up of its membership—the minister responsible for shipping in each country (except for the American delegate)—assured the carrying out of agreements arrived at in the council. The fact that Great Britain was the only member that had tonnage beyond its own requirements gave that nation a decisive voice in the council's proceedings.

After prolonged deliberations on the subject, in the spring of 1918 the Allies were driven once more by the threat of disaster to agree on another step which everyone already knew was necessary—unified command over the armies in the field. Recognizing the peril resulting from the lack of reserves under central control when the great German offensive of 21 March broke through the British positions in the Arras sector near the point of juncture with the French, the Supreme War Council in

April 1918 called upon Marshal Ferdinand Foch to be in fact, though not actually in name, Allied Commander in Chief.

Division of Labor and Co-ordination of Requirements

After the United States entered the war, some Americans would have been pleased to follow an "America first" policy in arming and equipping troops, even though at the outset many did not anticipate sending a large American army to Europe. But neither the War Department nor the War Industries Board was disposed to follow any policy that would weaken the forces already in action by diverting resources to equip an army that could not be at the front in strength for months to come. Indeed, the President in his war message said that the equipment of American forces should be accomplished with as little interference as possible with the duty of supplying the armies already at war with Germany. Actually the British and French were getting from their own industries most of the equipment they needed, but they had to have raw materials. Thus a division of labor between the United States and the European Allies could be effected, permitting American units to be equipped much more rapidly than otherwise would have been possible and without interfering seriously with the flow of materials from the United States to Allied countries. Both the British and French missions in Washington pointed out these possibilities and the advantages of such arrangements.

The French mission in the United States worked out a scale of raw materials needed for each major item to be manufactured in French factories. Thus for each 75-mm. gun the United States would supply six tons of steel, for each 155-mm. howitzer, forty tons of steel, and for each 155-mm. gun, sixty tons of steel. Most of the artillery, artillery ammunition, aircraft, and tanks, and a large share of the automatic weapons for the AEF came from France.[2] (*Table 1*) The British-American agreement of January 1918 for the provision of certain parts for tanks to be assembled jointly in France already has been mentioned. The United States obtained trench mortars and some artillery and aircraft from Britain. The Allies furnished thousands of smaller items to each other every day. All together these measures of international reciprocal supply not only saved much time in getting American forces into action, but permitted a maximum effort on the part of the Allied armies, and, perhaps of greatest importance, they saved a great deal of ocean tonnage.

The advantages of relying on French and British armament for American troops in Europe were self-evident. France alone had demonstrated a capacity to provide all of the artillery and probably all of the ammunition for all the American forces that could be landed. Nevertheless, the United States assumed that French and British armament should be supplied to only the first 2 million Americans to arrive in Europe, and that in the meantime United States industrial conversion and expansion would proceed at a rate that would make the United States independent of Allied arms by 1919. Conversion and expansion with a view toward a self-contained national arms industry, however, proved to be costly

---

[2] Marcel Vigneras, *Rearming the French,* UNITED STATES ARMY IN WORLD WAR II (Washington, 1957), p. 4.

TABLE 1—EQUIPMENT FURNISHED AMERICAN EXPEDITIONARY FORCES IN WORLD WAR I,
BY TYPE AND SUPPLYING COUNTRY: 6 APRIL 1917–11 NOVEMBER 1918

Type	Total	From France	From Great Britain	From United States
Artillery [a]	4,194	3,532	160	502
Howitzer, 9.2-inch	40	0	40	0
Howitzer, 8-inch	208	0	120	88
Howitzer, 155-mm.	798	796	0	2
Gun, 10-inch, sea coast	15	0	0	15
Gun, 8-inch, sea coast	6	0	0	6
Gun, 6-inch, sea coast	74	0	0	74
Gun, 155-mm. (GPF)	233	233	0	0
Gun, 5-inch, sea coast	26	0	0	26
Gun, 4.7-inch	71	0	0	71
Gun, 75-mm.	2,022	1,862	0	160
Gun, 37-mm.	701	641	0	60
Railroad artillery [a]	158	[b] 140	0	18
Howitzer, 400-mm.	4	4	0	0
Gun, 14-inch	84	66	0	18
Gun, 340-mm.	2	2	0	0
Gun, 32-cm.	12	12	0	0
Gun, 24-cm.	24	24	0	0
Gun, 19-cm.	32	32	0	0
Caissons	9,023	2,658	0	6,365
Howitzer, 155-mm.	1,994	796	0	1,198
Gun, 4.7-inch	219	0	0	219
Gun, 75-mm.	6,810	1,862	0	4,948

See footnotes at end of table.

in two ways: first, a tremendous increase in expenditures, and second, an actual reduction in total supplies available.

Had the war production of the United States been integrated with that of the Allies on a continuing basis, the expense of converting much of American industry and building new facilities could have been avoided, as could the disruption of production and resultant reduction of output. If the United States had concentrated its efforts on items such as rifles, machine guns, aircraft engines, gunpowder, raw materials, and semifinished goods, as well as items already produced commercially, it could have contributed larger quantities of all supplies to the Allied nations, and at much less cost. As it was, the United States spent $7 billion for ordnance alone, and tied up the services of thousands of officers, enlisted men, and civilian workers to create virtually a new industry; yet, aside from small arms and about two-thirds of its machine guns, fought the war with French and British ordnance.

TABLE 1—EQUIPMENT FURNISHED AMERICAN EXPEDITIONARY FORCES IN WORLD WAR I, BY TYPE AND SUPPLYING COUNTRY: 6 APRIL 1917–11 NOVEMBER 1918—Continued

Type	Total	From France	From Great Britain	From United States
Trench mortars	2,555	237	1,427	891
Mortar, 240-mm.	101	101	0	0
Mortar, 8-inch, Stokes	1,757	0	914	843
Mortar, 6-inch, Newton	561	0	513	48
Mortar, 58-mm.	136	136	0	0
Automatic weapons	124,352	40,484	0	83,868
Browning machine gun	30,089	0	0	30,089
Vickers machine gun	10,411	0	0	10,411
Hotchkiss machine gun	5,255	5,255	0	0
Browning rifle	43,368	0	0	43,368
Chauchat machine rifle				
8-mm.	15,988	15,988	0	0
.30-caliber	19,241	19,241	0	0
Tanks	289	227	26	36
Renault	237	227	0	10
Mark IV	24	0	12	12
Mark V and Mark VI	28	0	14	14
Airplanes	ᶜ 6,345	4,874	258	1,213
Balloons	295	20	0	275
Horses	225,598	136,114	21,759	67,725

ᵃ Nearly all artillery ammunition used up to 11 November 1918, approximately 10 million rounds, was of French manufacture.
ᵇ Loaned by France.
ᶜ Excludes 19 airplanes furnished by Italy.
Source Marcel Vigneras, *Rearming the French*, UNITED STATES ARMY IN WORLD WAR II (Washington, 1957), p. 4

Perhaps a concentration of effort in a few areas of production would not have been politically expedient at the time, but that is not to say that it would not have been the wiser course to follow. On the other hand, a fear that German success in France might eliminate the French war industry as a source of Allied supply probably supported the decision, for in that eventuality it would have been essential for the United States to have an independent capability.

In any event, the long-range benefits of the policy were realized in the postwar international position of the United States: the pursuit of a policy to build a national war industry that would be capable of supplying American soldiers and would be independent of outside sources provided the basis and experience for the war industry to which, not twenty-five years later, France and Great Britain would look for their very survival.

Movement of U.S. Forces to Europe

In some ways the most serious problem requiring co-ordination among the Allies was that of sending American troops to France—the numbers and the types of troops to be sent, and the shipping arrangements to get them there. Many problems of logistical co-ordination, including the supply of American forces, hinged on these decisions. After the German breakthrough in March 1918 the Military Representatives of the Supreme War Council called for the immediate use, temporarily, of American units in French and British corps and divisions, and asked that further shipments of American troops be entirely of infantry and machine gun units until otherwise directed. Secretary of War Baker was in Europe at the time, and after conferring with Pershing and Bliss he recommended to the President approval of this policy with the understanding that as soon as possible any American units attached to Allied armies would be returned to American control for the formation of an independent American army. An agreement with the British on a six-division plan was modified to give priority to riflemen and machine gunners, and it was agreed that additional troops to be brought over on American transports would train and be employed with the French.

Sensitive to any action that might threaten the formation of a distinct U.S. army to fight under its own flag, Pershing hoped that the scheduled shipments of balanced forces could be resumed quickly. Another German breakthrough in April, however, made the situation still more critical, and added to the pressure for American infantry replacements. Most of the tremendous British and French casualties were among their infantry. They still had enough artillery and service troops to support all the divisions they planned to maintain, and it seemed an inefficient use of shipping to bring over American artillery and service units when there was such a critical shortage of infantry replacements. Consequently, the British and French asked that the priority on infantry shipments continue. But there were sharp differences: The British, who would have to furnish the additional ships needed to bring more American troops, wanted some assurance that the troops would be used in a way best to support their efforts. The French wanted some assurance that a fair proportion of American troops would be assigned to their sections. General Pershing wanted assurances that American units would be returned to his control at the earliest possible moment for the formation of a separate American army. All these views came out in an urgent conference of the Supreme War Council and the military chiefs at Abbeville on 1–2 May, where the principle was agreed to specifically that an American army should be formed as soon as possible, but that during the current emergency priority should continue to be given to riflemen and machine gunners and that American troops would be brought to France as rapidly as Allied transportation would permit.

The priority given to the shipment of rifle and machine gun units upset the whole schedule of American training and troop movements, and seriously handicapped the Services of Supply in France where more troops and supplies were arriving without corresponding increases in the units to receive and look after them. French and British services had to provide service support for units assigned to their sectors, and their service units, too, were becoming so overtaxed that they sought relief. Moreover, the priority already given to the transportation of infantry units had nearly exhausted the troops of that category in the United States who had even partial training, and Pershing still was anxious to bring over the troops that would enable him to form corps and armies with adequate services of supply. When the War Department notified General Pershing in September that it would not be possible to change the priority of troop movements already under way when he asked that no more infantry be sent, he decided to break up the next five combat divisions to arrive and to use the men as service troops and replacements for the support of the newly formed American First Army in its first offensive against the Saint Mihiel salient.

Co-ordination of Support for the Armies

As soon as American troops began to arrive in France liaison officers were assigned at all levels where French and American officials came into contact to solve the day-to-day problems of co-ordination with local authorities for the use of transportation and facilities. In time, as the number of U.S. troops in France multiplied and the consequent problems grew more complex, supply officers began to visualize a more regularized machinery for closer co-ordination of the supply activities of all the Allies in support of their armies at the front. The acceptance of unity of command for the armies made unified supply support even more desirable. In March 1918 Col. Charles G. Dawes, whose duties as general purchasing agent for the AEF brought him into almost daily contact with Allied officials, proposed to General Pershing that an Allied board be

formed to co-ordinate transportation and storage in the rear of the Allied armies.

Pershing quickly adopted the proposal and in May obtained an agreement from Clemenceau accepting the principle of pooling supplies, storage facilities, and transportation for the common support of the Allied armies, and concurring in the organization of a board to effect this co-ordination. The board, whose decisions required unanimous consent, would be made up of a representative from each Allied Army. Subsequently Italy, Great Britain, and Belgium adhered to the agreement, and on 28 June 1918 the Military Board of Allied Supply held its first meeting in Paris. Colonel Dawes was the representative for the United States, and Colonel Charles Payot, French assistant chief of staff in charge of the services of the rear, was elected permanent chairman.

Marshal Foch came to place a great deal of reliance on the Military Board of Allied Supply, and he later proposed the complete integration of all Allied supply activity under a single commander. Ironically, it was for Pershing, who had been the principal mover for co-ordinating supply and a leading advocate of unity of command, to oppose it. Pershing pointed out that as long as each national commander retained tactical control of his own troops, even though they were under the strategic direction of Foch, each commander also would insist on control over his own supplies. In the circumstances he thought it best simply to extend the authority of the existing board as far as was consistent with present policy.

In the few months during which it functioned the Military Board of Allied Supply clearly demonstrated the advantages of co-ordination. Each member had a staff assigned to the board, and by the time of the armistice it was beginning to function as a true interallied staff. As one of its early tasks, the staff studied the question of storage facilities and developed the first comprehensive picture of storage facilities in France. In a July board meeting the French and Americans agreed to pool artillery ammunition, a decision which greatly facilitated the supply of ammunition to the units of one army operating in the vicinity of another, and provided a reserve supply that could be made available where needed most.

The board also took steps to organize an interallied motor transport reserve, and to standardize regulations for the organization of traffic circulation, the transportation of troops, and the transportation of matériel. It organized at Rozoy an interallied center for the instruction of officers in the regulations governing motor transportation. As to the reserve pool of motor trucks, the commanders agreed to everything except to making the necessary trucks available until finally, in November, the respective commanders announced they would make available for the pool—simply to be on call to Marshal Foch, not physically pulled back—7,000 trucks from the French Army, 3,165 from the American, 100 from the Belgian, and approximately 1,000 from the British.

In order to save on the use of railway cars the Board of Allied Supply reached agreement on a standard ration of oats and hay for horses and studied the question of rations for men. Although the Interallied Transportation Committee, a consulting organization established earlier in Paris, was considering the question of the use of railway facilities, officers concerned also sought the co-operation of the Board of Allied Supply. The study sought to determine the minimum needs for the armies, to establish priorities for delivery of supplies and rules

for loading and unloading by troops, and tried to reduce to a minimum the practice of holding reserve supplies on railway cars.

Other activities that the board promoted included regulation of the gasoline supply and pooling of gasoline cans, improved coordination in the use of narrow-gauge railway materials, construction of a telephone and telegraph system to link the headquarters of Marshal Foch with those of the Allied commanders, and encouragement of an agreement between the French and Americans on the use of wood. Its staff work also included preparation of a statistical statement reflecting all troops, supplies, and means of transportation in the Allied armies in France as of 31 October 1918, and the collection of data on and a comparative study of the supply systems of each of the Allied armies for the benefit of future military study.

Summary

By the fall of 1918 machinery for Allied logistical co-operation was operating effectively. By 1918 necessity—first the danger of imminent defeat, then the prospect of ultimate victory—drove the Allies to a coordination of effort and only then brought together the weight of superior resources as well as numbers against the common enemy. In the United States the government resisted temptation to arm "America first" at the expense of keeping needed materials moving to the Allies. Although the decision to develop a completely independent war industry for the support of American troops in 1919 was costly, it was possibly a wise move in the long run for the fortunes of the immediate war might have turned for the worse, and in any case it served the later security of the United States. When they had to, the French and the British made available vast resources to arm and transport American troops.

As Allied efforts grew, the necessity for co-ordination became more clear—to eliminate competition in purchasing which only resulted in inefficient procurement and unduly high prices; to allocate among the Allies certain scarce commodities; to organize supplies and shipping so as to make the best possible use of available ships; and, finally to make available certain supplies, transportation, and storage facilities in France for best use at critical times and places on the fighting fronts. Moreover, all this had to be done with consideration for national sensibilities.

Maj. Gen. James G. Harbord, Commanding General, American Services of Supply, noted of the French: "They are the most delightful, exasperating, unreliable, trustworthy, sensitive, unsanitary, cleanly, dirty, artistic, clever, and stupid people that the writer has ever known. Intensely academic and theoretical yet splendidly practical at times, it will be a wonder if we do not feel as much like fighting them as we do the Germans before the war is over, for our alliance tries human patience—American patience—almost to the limit." [3] Maj. Gen. Fox Conner, chief of operations on the staff of General Headquarters, AEF, observed that dealing with the enemy was simple and straightforward compared with securing co-operation with an ally.

---

[3] J. G. Harbord, *Leaves From a War Diary* (New York: Dodd, Mead, 1925), p. 299.

CHAPTER XXII

The Road to France

Transportation Within the United States

Organization

Thanks to early planning and organization stimulated by threatening developments in Mexico and the outbreak of war in Europe, the railroads were able to meet the demands for troop movement in 1917 without serious dislocation. Organization for the co-ordination of transportation then expanded with the growing conception of the magnitude of the war and in response to the absolute necessity of the moment.

As early as May 1914, at the time of the Vera Cruz incident, the American Railway Association sent a representative to Washington to discuss ways of co-operation between the railroads and the government in matters relating to the movement of troops and military supplies. Over a year later, after the sinking of the *Lusitania* had raised the prospect of American involvement in the European war, the Secretary of War suggested that the Railway Association name a special committee on co-operation with military authorities. After nearly a year of conferences a committee had, by June 1916, worked out a scheme for unified operations in handling military traffic—just in time for its first big test, mobilization of National Guard units on the Mexican border. Previously, arrangements for the movement of troops by rail had been made by the depot

quartermaster at the place of origin with the railway company on the basis of competitive bids wherever feasible. The new system centralized rail movements of troops with an executive designated by the railroad committee in Washington who dispatched all trains. An agreement reached between the Quartermaster General and railroad representatives on 1 January 1917 completely did away with the former contract system.

With the declaration of war the Railway Association's committees in Washington expanded considerably. Daniel Willard, chairman of the Advisory Commission of the Council of National Defense and president of the Baltimore and Ohio, called a meeting of railway executives in Washington for 11 April. This meeting resulted in adoption of a statement pledging co-ordination of operations in a "continental railway system . . . to produce a maximum of national transportation efficiency." [1] The Railway Association at the same time expanded its special committee on national defense and formed an executive committee which came to be known as the "Railroads' War Board." As assistant to the chairman of a smaller general committee set up to supervise operations, George Hodges—the

---

[1] Walker D. Hines, *War History of American Railroads* (New Haven· Yale University Press, 1928), p. 11.

man who had been in charge of moving troops to the Mexican border—became the effective operating director through a troop-movement office. This office, an agency of the Railway Association rather than of the government, maintained a field service throughout the United States. It assigned a general transportation agent at the headquarters of each of the Army's six geographic departments, and at each camp or post where troops were moving in or out it assigned an agent. All wore "A.R.A." brassards. Each major railroad designated an officer to be in charge of troop transportation in co-operation with the general agent at Army department headquarters. The Transportation Division of the Quartermaster Corps continued as the Army's co-ordinating agency for the time being.

Organization of the Embarkation Service on 4 August 1917 to control the movement of all troops and supplies destined for overseas did not materially affect the system of troop transportation under the co-ordination of the Railroads' War Board. Later, when the government took over the railroads (December 1917), the troop-movement office remained intact as an agency of the United States Railroad Administration. After the Division of Inland Transportation of the Storage and Traffic Division of the General Staff (later designated the Inland Traffic Service, as a division of the Purchase, Traffic, and Storage Division) absorbed the transportation functions of the Quartermaster Corps, it continued to operate through the troop-movement office of the Railway Association. (Consolidation of the Embarkation Service and the Inland Traffic Service to form a single Transportation Service did not take place until March 1919.)

Troop Movement

Movement of troops within the United States had five phases. The first was the movement of units of the Regular Army to various camps, mostly from stations near the Mexican border. Involving about 25,500 officers and men—including the movement of units assigned to the 1st Division to Hoboken—this operation was completed by early June 1917. Then the movement of over 343,000 National Guard troops to their training camps extended over an eleven-week period beginning 4 August. A month after the beginning of the mobilization of the National Guard the most complicated phase of all began—the movement of selective service men from their homes to the cantonments. So that transportation facilities would not be overtaxed, the original draft calls were kept small and the men traveled on regular trains, but by 19 September the Selective Service System was moving into high gear, and special trains hauling men to camp became common all over the country. From 4,581 entraining points the drafted men left at first for one of the sixteen National Army cantonments, but later they went to practically every camp, post, and station in the United States. Transportation of selective service men by rail rose to peaks of 50,000 in a day and over 400,000 in a month, and included nearly all of the 2,800,000 men inducted through the Selective Service System. Departure of a train with newly inducted men became the occasion for a local patriotic holiday: stores closed, bands played, speeches and cheers filled the air, and great crowds filled the station platform. Until liquor finally was banned for men boarding troop trains, it often formed a central feature of the departure celebrations, and in some cases contributed to an air of considerable informality. It was recorded that cowboys and miners riding on a train out of Arizona had been able to bring large stocks of liquor aboard. With this encouragement they insisted on riding on the roofs of cars, turning the aisles into gambling dens, and practicing with their lariats to rope with equal facility strange animals and innocent bystanders on station platforms. When they had exhausted their liquor supply, they looted a saloon in Colorado.

By August 1917 it already was becoming necessary to shift troops about from one camp to another, and the necessity increased as mobilization advanced. These movements included those of regiments and special units to make up divisions, of Negro units from the South in accordance with the policy of assigning a proportion of Negro troops to the divisions, the transfer of drafted men from the cantonments to fill new National Guard and Regular Army divisions, and movements of units to southern camps when possible for the first winter. As the practice evolved of developing a certain division of labor among the various training sites it added to the requirement for intercamp travel. In fact this phase accounted for half of the troop travel in the United States between October 1917 and January 1918. The final phase of the troop movement program was, of course, the movement of units to ports of embarkation—2,175,000 men from 1 May 1917 to 11 November 1918, of whom aver 80 percent went to the New York area.

Near the end of the war the 8th Division, 18,800 strong (less its artillery brigade), was able to move from Camp Frémont, California, to Camp Mills, Long Island, in forty-two trains that covered an average distance of 3,444 miles in an average time of 7 days and 3 hours. Six trains departed daily at one and one-half hour intervals from 0900 on each of seven successive days beginning on 18 October. Thus the first train was approaching its destination in New York as the last was departing in California. Routed over different lines, the trains avoided serious congestion, although there was some delay caused by the need to transfer men stricken with influenza to hospitals along the way.

Movement of Supplies

If the movement of troops by rail proceeded fairly efficiently from the early weeks of the war, such was not the case in the rather greater task of moving supplies and equipment. Neither the Army nor the railroads had organized and planned in a way to cope successfully with the tremendous freight movements demanded by the war.

By 1915 inefficiencies in the handling of commercial freight cars had reached a point where shortages of cars to haul grain crops in the fall and coal in the winter had become an annual expectation, and generally in times of good business it was difficult to get satisfactory railroad service in many parts of the country. This situation was not the result of an actual shortage of rolling stock, but of the chaotic method of handling cars, including the practice of some companies to hoard cars not belonging to them, the overtaxing of facilities in certain areas, and to some extent, federal and state restrictions. With the outbreak of war in Europe, purchases of the belligerent governments in the United States led to unprecedented demands on transportation. December 1916 witnessed the worst freight car congestion in the history of American railroads up to that time—and the United States was not as yet in the war. In some areas lack of freight cars forced mills to shut down, food products spoiled, and prices soared; at the same time there were so many cars in other areas that almost nothing could move. The port of New York was almost completely choked. The situation had improved only slightly when the declaration of war in April 1917 threw on the railroads the additional burden of hauling building materials to the sites of the new cantonments, building materials and raw materials to the sites of the new munition plants, and munitions from new plants to ports, as well as supplies and equipment for the build-up and support of an expeditionary force in Europe.

The Army's own system of handling its requests for railroad service did nothing to alleviate the situation. Initially, each supply bureau or other agency made its own transportation arrangements, except that the Quartermaster Corps handled certain general matters. Each bureau had its own machinery for arranging for transportation of supplies for which it was responsible, and this was its only concern with transport. Thus the competition among the bureaus in procurement noted earlier persisted in transportation. As each bureau emphasized speed in getting its supplies to the ports, with no co-ordination among them, the inevitable result was to add to the congestion. After the formation of the Embarkation Service in August 1917, the supply bureaus were required to obtain a transportation release before shipping any material to a port. At first the commanding general of the port granted these releases, but after October 1917 the function was centralized in the headquarters of the Embarkation Service in Washington. This was the first major step toward establishing effective control to relieve the freight traffic congestion, but for a time the Embarkation Service did not have the authority to back up its rulings and frequently they were disregarded.

A further handicap to the handling of freight grew out of an unco-ordinated priority system. Not only the War Department, but the Navy Department and the Shipping Board as well, resorted to priorities to gain preference in transportation. All three agencies entered into an arrangement with the Railroads' War Board for a system of tags to mark government freight for expedited handling. But soon government agents in all parts of the country were tagging their shipments, so that practically all government freight was shipped on priority —and when all were granted priority, none had priority. Indeed, tagging made matters worse, for cars had to be rearranged so that those with prior markings would precede later ones, and items were rushed forward without regard to real timeliness.

By December 1917 the tag system had all but collapsed. The chaotic conditions of a year earlier had reproduced and multiplied, and were further complicated by weeks of cold, stormy weather. With the armies in Europe clamoring for supplies and German submarine warfare claiming a serious toll of Allied shipping, the port at New York was virtually paralyzed. Two hundred ships lay in New York harbor awaiting cargoes and fuel while 44,320 carloads of freight (nearly two million tons) backed up along the Atlantic seaboard and as far west as Buffalo and Pittsburgh. No matter how the goods were tagged for priority, it was next to impossible even to find the items that were to make up particular cargoes.

Under the circumstances there appeared to be nothing left except for the government to step in. On 26 December 1917 President Wilson issued a proclamation taking possession and control of the railroads through the Secretary of War (according to the legal arrangement of the Army Appropriation Act of 1916), to be effective two days later. He designated Secretary of the Treasury McAdoo Director General of Railroads. Wilson had followed formally the precedent of Lincoln, but in actuality he had gone much further than Lincoln. In an explanatory statement accompanying his proclamation the President said:

This is a war of resources no less than of men, perhaps even more than of men, and it is necessary for the complete mobilization of our resources that the transportation systems of the country should be organized and employed under a single authority and a simplified method of coordination which have not proved possible under private management and control.[2]

The government's assumption of control over the railroads did not change radically either the organizational structure or the personnel under which they operated. The new United States Railroad Administration took over most of the co-ordinating machinery that the Railroads' War Board had developed, and added to it the authority of federal law to enforce its regulations and thus to achieve by direction the national consolidation that had not been achieved voluntarily.

Hardly less important than government control of the railroads in relieving railroad

traffic congestion and developing a system which in the next several months would carry a volume of freight to the ports four or five times greater than that at any time in 1917, was the Army's own action to centralize its transportation activities. The Inland Traffic Division, organized on 10 January 1918 and redesignated the Inland Traffic Service on 22 April, provided the strict co-ordination of military shipments that had been missing. For a field staff the new agency at first relied on the extensive organization the Ordnance Department had developed. In April the Traffic Service took over the Ordnance organization, and in the next few months broadened it to put freight agents at every important Army station. Meanwhile the War Department took the final step toward consolidation which should have been obvious all along— it abolished the separate transportation units that had grown up in the various supply bureaus, and transferred their activities to the Inland Traffic Service.

The key to control was an embargo on all Army freight—at first placed on the areas around the principal Atlantic ports, and later extended to include all important shipping points throughout the country—and the requirement of a War Department transportation order for the shipment of Army freight into the embargoed areas. No War Department bureau or government contractor could load any freight (except for less-than-carload lots) for those areas without presenting a transportation order and without having an assigned serial number on all bills of lading and waybills. The Railway Administration required the railroads to observe this rule. Application for transportation orders had to be made to the Inland Traffic Service in Washington, and before granting an order for a shipment des-

---

[2] Quoted in Hines, *War History of American Railroads,* p. 248

tined for overseas, a release had to be obtained from the Embarkation Service.

Still, whatever action the Army took could not be wholly effective so long as it remained in competition with other agencies. To solve this problem of competition among agencies the Director General of Railroads set up a committee for government-wide co-ordination which included the chief of the Inland Traffic Service and corresponding managers from the Navy, the Food Administration, the Fuel Administration, the United States Shipping Board, and the War Industries Board. At weekly meetings this group determined the priorities for virtually all government shipments. Through a system of shipping permits the Railroad Administration in addition imposed much the same kind of restrictions on commercial shipments. For less-than-car-load lots it adopted a "sailing-day plan" by which full trains were scheduled to leave at specified times between major eastern points.

All together, these efforts at co-ordination, and the steps taken to correct abuses such as mishandling cars, diverting shipments, unscrupulous uses of transportation orders, and other practices that inevitably occurred, had rapid effect. Shipments of matériel to the posts, for instance, after declining from 177,904 tons in December 1917 to 118,752 in January 1918, went up to 233,317 tons in February. Thereafter the tonnage moving to the ports went up every month (with the exception of June when it was only slightly less than in May), until it reached a peak of 809,774 tons in November 1918. This is not to say that all transportation problems were solved—transportation continued to be the bottleneck of production throughout the war. Even during the height of the war effort in 1918, the transportation of 75-mm.

artillery shells took twice as much time as did their manufacture.

Oversea Movements

Ports of Embarkation

Although War Department planning had envisaged the organization of ports of embarkation under single commanders, several weeks passed in 1917 before any steps were taken in that direction. Field service regulations already spelled out the duties of a port commander. Essentially they were: command over all administrative agencies assigned to the port, arrangements for camps in the vicinity, arrangements for supplies, scheduling embarkation of troops, and control of traffic incident to operations. Apparently, however, it was not clear at first that the extent of American participation in the war in Europe was going to be sufficiently great to require a central organization. The first units to go overseas moved under the control of the Water Transportation Branch of the Quartermaster Corps, acting through the general superintendent of the Army Transport Service at New York. Then early in June Maj. Gen. J. Franklin Bell, commanding general of the Eastern Department, whose headquarters were on Governor's Island, was instructed to perform the functions of commander of the New York Port of Embarkation until a line officer could be designated to take command. A port commander was assigned on 7 July, and on the 27th of that month headquarters of the New York Port of Embarkation were established formally at Hoboken, New Jersey, where the government had seized the piers of the North-German Lloyd and Hamburg-American steamship companies. All officers commanding local activities of the supply bureaus became members of the staff of the commanding general. On the same day a second primary port of embarkation was established at Newport News, Virginia. Ports at Baltimore, Philadelphia, and Boston in the United States and Montreal, Halifax, and St. Johns in Canada, operated at various times as secondary ports (for cargo) and as subports of the New York Port of Embarkation. Detachments were not maintained permanently at those points, but were sent as needed.

With the organization of the Embarkation Service in early August 1917, the ports of embarkation came under its supervision and control. This arrangement continued during most of the war, until 27 September 1918 when the ports were separated and made co-ordinate agencies directly under the Purchase, Storage, and Traffic Division of the General Staff.

From a small beginning at Hoboken, the New York Port of Embarkation expanded throughout the area. Maj. Gen. David C. Shanks, when he arrived on 1 August 1917 to take command, had 77 officers under him; by the end of the war officers in his staff and operating activities numbered 2,500. Facilities ultimately included piers, warehouses, embarkation camps, and hospitals. There were 12 piers at Hoboken, 8 in Brooklyn (6 of these commandeered from the Bush Terminal Company), and 3 on the North River in Manhattan. At Hoboken there were 7 warehouses; in Brooklyn 120 Bush Company warehouses and 2 belonging to the Army supply base covered 57 acres of land. The New York Engineer Depot at Kearney, New Jersey, became another Army supply base, and at Port Newark $15 million went into facilities built on reclaimed swampland to establish a base

that finally had 9 warehouses and covered 133 acres of land, but was never satisfactory for live storage. General Shanks also had within his command 3 embarkation camps: Camp Merritt with capacity for 38,000 transients, Camp Mills with capacity for 40,000, and part of Camp Upton with capacity for 18,000. (Camp Dix, New Jersey, although used as an embarkation camp, remained under the direct jurisdiction of the War Department.) There was, besides, a nurses' mobilization station. Of hospitals the command counted 4 embarkation hospitals, 5 debarkation hospitals, a general hospital, an auxiliary hospital, and 2 base hospitals.

One of the biggest headaches for troop commanders was the shipment of organizational equipment and animals. In honor of the old Army rule that an organization's equipment must accompany it wherever it might go, units spent hours packing and marking equipment before leaving their home stations, sent it to different ports according to its nature, followed it through the port of embarkation, and, with good luck, picked it up on the other side. To make the best use of shipping space with all the nondescript equipment of a division sent in this way was clearly impossible. At last the War Department came around to the obvious but revolutionary solution: all units moving overseas would turn in their organizational equipment and draw new equipment on the other side. The commander and his men were thus relieved of the burden of packing and marking and shipping, and of the trying duty of tracing and searching for baggage. This simple solution also made possible the shipment of divisional materials in bulk.

Major supply activities for replacement of unserviceable individual clothing and equipment remained at the embarkation camps. Broad definitions of unserviceability gave the soldiers almost complete new outfits when they went overseas. This in itself was a measure of shipping conservation for it eliminated much of the need to find shipping space for replacement items. Movement orders specified exactly what equipment each soldier was to have, and each soldier presumably would arrive at the port fully and properly equipped. In practice, however, this really was not expected to be so. Shortages of equipment in outlying camps and depots were too common, and changes in specifications from the AEF were too frequent for any organization to be ready to sail on arrival at the port. The best that could be done was to make a good beginning and thus relieve some of the last minute pressure.

Troop Embarkation

Most units moved to the piers and boarded the transports within two or three days of arrival at an embarkation camp. From Camp Merritt most of the troops moved to the piers by ferry. "Normally" they were scheduled to be on the piers to begin boarding at 0800 when the pier inspectors and checkers came on duty. It was over an hour's march from the camp to Alpine Landing, where contingents of 2,000 to 3,000 men—a number equal to the capacity of one ferryboat—would march out at half-hour intervals between 0100 and 0400 or 0430 hours. It would take about half an hour to load a ferryboat, and then two hours to reach the piers. The contingents would ordinarily be made up of platoons or detachments from several regiments or other units so that each ferryboat would discharge a share of its passengers at each pier being used that day. In this way work could proceed at the same time on all the piers with a minimum of congestion, and unit integrity would be restored at the piers while several transports were being loaded simultaneously. Sometimes there would be a second embarkation in the afternoon. On the same day other units would be moving by the Long Island Railroad from Camp Mills and Camp Upton to ferryboats at Long Island City.

After some experience, embarkation proceeded rapidly. The *Leviathan* could take aboard 10,000 troops in two hours. The record day for embarkation was 31 August 1918 when over 51,000 troops boarded seventeen vessels at the New York port, said to be the largest number of passengers ever to have sailed from any port in a single day up to that time.

Planning for troop embarkations was detailed and complete. Near the end of each month the Operations Division of the General Staff in Washington held a meeting to determine what troops would sail and in what order and from what points during the next month. The chief of embarkation reviewed the port facilities that would be available; the embarkation director of the British Ministry of Shipping presented a schedule, by name and capacity, of the British ships that would be available during the period; a representative of the U.S. Navy presented a list of American ships that would be available during the first ten days of the month and promised additional forecasts at ten-day intervals; a representative of the troop-movement office of the Railroad Administration was present to co-ordinate the use of the railroads in getting troops to the ports. The Operations Division then could apply this information to the AEF shipping schedule, which showed the units designated for movement overseas, their state of readiness, and the priority for movement. In spite of all these preparations, actual sailings never went as planned. Ships were lost or damaged as the result of enemy action or storms or would be diverted to other uses; fuel would not be available at the moment; labor disputes would delay sailings; machinery would break down. The dispatch office at the port of embarkation was in almost constant turmoil attempting to match troops with capacity so as to avoid all possible delays and make full use of all facilities.

All together, 88 percent of troops embarking for overseas went through the New York Port of Embarkation. By the time of the armistice this amounted to a total of about 1,656,000 from New York Harbor, and 142,000 from the subports attached to the New York organization. Another 288,-000 troops embarked (from October 1917 to December 1918) through the other primary port of embarkation at Newport News.[3]

Supply Shipments

As with procurement and inland transportation the consistent trend in organization and control of shipments of supplies overseas was toward centralization. The Embarkation Service continued to be responsible for the loading and operation of all Army cargo vessels until February 1918 when the Shipping Control Committee, organized by agreement between the Secretary of War and the chairman of the U.S. Shipping Board, took over the duties of the War Board for the Port of New York and also those of the Embarkation Service relating to the loading and operation of ships. Indeed, the Shipping Control Committee was organized to operate all the pooled shipping available to the United States as a single system.

The whole shipping program had to be geared to critical points along the lines that might become bottlenecks. It was futile to rush supplies to the ports faster than they could be loaded; ships had to be made available to take advantage of the facilities, but ships could not be sent across the Atlantic in too large numbers at any one time lest the French ports be congested. So far as scheduling of supply shipments was concerned at the weekly shipping meetings, results were rather more satisfactory than in the movement of troops, for, once the organization had been developed, the Shipping Control Committee never failed to provide the cargo tonnage that had been promised for any month.

Shipments of supplies to the AEF were based upon an automatic supply system. This was a step toward reducing the vast complexities of resupplying an army of several hundred thousand men overseas that became obvious fairly early. After several conferences among the supply chiefs in Europe and several exchanges of cables between the AEF and the War Department, the system went into effect in September 1917. On the basis of authorized issues where they had been established as regular, and on the basis of French and British consumption experience during the war for other items, shipments from the United States would be made insofar as possible according to the total strength of the Expeditionary Forces, plus troops actually en route,

[3] Benedict Crowell and Robert Forrest Wilson, *The Road to France I, The Transportation of Troops and Military Supplies, 1917–1918*, in the series "How America Went to War," 6 vols. (New Haven· Yale University Press, 1921), 298

as of the first of each month. As a guide to planning, the chiefs of the AEF supply services prepared lists of the quantities of items required for each 25,000 men. In addition to the automatic shipments further shipments had to be made to build up reserve stocks in Europe, hopefully, to ninety-day levels. The idea was to ship four months' supplies with each troop movement to stock a 90-day reserve besides the 30-days' supplies for consumption and emergency. In this way, cables and requisitions were needed only to meet exceptions and special needs not covered in the automatic supply tables. Changing conditions in the military situation, in transportation, production, and availability for local purchase in Europe required frequent changes in requisitions. In effect, the governor of supply was more often the availability of shipping than the requirements as calculated according to various tables and anticipated needs. There was almost never enough shipping to meet the requirements as calculated, and shipments of initial supplies and equipment as well as of automatic replenishment frequently had to be curtailed.

In practice each of the supply services in France received an allotment of tonnage based on what the Shipping Control Committee announced would be available for the month. They then made up requests, arranging items in order of their urgency, for supplies previously reported as being at the ports in the United States. The G–1 of the Services of Supply in France eliminated items obtainable in Europe, then consolidated all the requests into a priority cable for transmission to the War Department. As a further aid to planning for supplies not on the automatic lists, the AEF submitted with the priority cable a courier cable showing estimated needs for the next two succeeding months. Each month, then, the priority cable automatically canceled the tentative courier cables and it became the basis for the monthly shipping program. If an emergency arose necessitating the shipment of items not listed in the priority cable, the service concerned had to cancel by cable the equivalent tonnage of other supplies.

It was never possible to build up the hoped-for ninety-day reserve in Europe, and finally in 1918 the AEF staffs, facing the realities of the situation, accepted a forty-five day reserve as a more realistic policy. Even the more modest goal was substantial in view of the rapid build-up of troops and the shortage of shipping. From small beginnings averaging less than 16,000 short tons a month in June, July, and August, 1917, monthly shipments of Army cargo grew to over a half million tons in July 1918, reached 750,000 tons in October, and in November hit the peak of 829,000 tons. From the entry into the war to the signing of the armistice the Army shipped 5,130,000 tons of cargo across the Atlantic. Another 2,320,000 tons were added to that between 11 November and 30 April 1919.[4]

---

[4] James G. Harbord, *The American Army in France, 1917–1919* (Boston: Little, Brown, 1936), p. 120; Rpt, Secretary of War, *Annual Reports of the War Department, 1918*, I, 32; Crowell and Wilson, *The Road to France II. The Transportation of Troops and Military Supplies, 1917–1918* (How America Went to War), 549–50; Rpt, Chief of Transportation, *Annual Reports of the War Department, 1919*, 4930–53, *passim*; War Department, *Order of Battle of Land Forces, Zone of the Interior* (Washington, 1949), p. 507; Leonard P. Ayres, *The War With Germany, a Statistical Summary* (Washington, 1919), pp. 44–46; Maj Paul A. Larned, A Resume of the Shipment of Locomotives in World War I (Army War College, 1942).

Ocean Transportation

Whatever the problems of troop mobilization and railroad transportation, however great were the problems of production, the primary limiting factor on an effective American effort throughout most of the war was the availability of ocean shipping. Estimates in December 1917 indicated that 1,920,000 gross registered tons in troop transports, and 1,589,000 gross tons in cargo shipping would be needed to put and maintain 1,000,000 men in France by the end of June 1918. Nowhere near this amount of shipping was in sight. Indeed, shipping actually available to the Army at that time was little more than one-fourth of the indicated requirement. When the war in Europe broke out in 1914, no less than 90 percent of United States foreign trade was being carried by foreign-owned ships. Then Great Britain and France diverted their merchant fleets to war needs, vessels belonging to Germany and Austria were bottled up in neutral ports, the submarine menace restricted the use of shipping by neutral countries which, as a consequence, could exact high rates. The limitations thus imposed by the war on ocean shipping presented a grave problem for the United States just to meet its ordinary commercial needs, and as the prospect of involvement in the war increased, the nation's precarious maritime position became more apparent. Even so, President Wilson's pleas for Congressional action went unheeded, except for an act of August 1914 which admitted shipbuilding materials duty free and allowed ships purchased abroad to be given American registry until September 1916 when Congress passed legislation authorizing organization of the United States Shipping Board. Within a week after the declaration of war, the Ship-ping Board formed the Emergency Fleet Corporation—the first government-owned corporation since the Second Bank of the United States and the Panama Railroad—to be its agency for building and operating ships. Maj. Gen. George W. Goethals was named general manager of the corporation.

The most obvious and immediate source for additional tonnage was the German shipping that had been lying in American ports since 1914 and included the great new *Vaterland* (54,000 gross tons), *George Washington* (26,000 tons), *Amerika* (23,-000 tons), *Kronprinzessin Cecile* (25,000 tons), *President Lincoln* (19,000 tons), *President Grant* (18,000 tons), and fourteen other passenger vessels and eighty-four cargo ships aggregating nearly 300,000 tons. Alerted Army units boarded the ships immediately on receiving word that the President had signed the war resolution. The crews made no concerted try to scuttle the ships, but the machinery had been wrecked in nearly all of them. After some electric welding and patching of broken cylinders by the Navy, and some time in drydock for scraping and conversion, all the ships entered the American service. The only adequate drydocking facilities that could be found for the *Vaterland* were in England at the Liverpool shipyards, where it was converted to a troopship with a capacity of 12,000 officers and men. Rechristened the *Leviathan,* this ship, by the spring of 1918, was delivering to Europe the equivalent of a German division a month. In addition to the ships seized in American harbors, the Shipping Board obtained German and Austrian ships seized in the harbors of other countries when those nations followed the United States in declaring war. All together, the converted German passenger ships carried half a million men to fight against the Fatherland. At the same time the Army seized Austro-Hungarian ships in the United States, even though technically Austria-Hungary still was at peace with the United States.

The high rate of losses from submarines (nearly 870,000 gross tons of Allied and neutral shipping in April 1917) made it clear that the construction of ships would have to be redoubled if the Allies were to continue in the war very long. The U.S. Shipping Board and its Emergency Fleet Corporation quickly and energetically attacked the problem, but for a time their quickness and energy were no match for the obstacles encountered. Differences in policy, arising in part from the question of preference for steel as against wooden ships and in part from conflicts of authority between the head of the Shipping Board and the head of the Emergency Fleet Corporation, led eventually to the resignation of both men. Edward N. Hurley succeeded to the chairmanship of the Shipping Board, with more direct authority over the Fleet Corporation of which, after an interval, Charles Piez became directing head, to be succeeded in April 1918 by Charles M. Schwab. Hurley pushed forward on all fronts. He decided that there would be ships of steel, of wood, and of concrete.

The largest part of the program was carried out at Hog Island, near Philadelphia, where steel ships were constructed according to standard design and mass production techniques. Here 30,000 men worked at fifty shipways, and by November 1918 they were laying six keels a week; yet not a single ship from Hog Island was delivered in time to carry a war cargo. All the tonnage from wholly new construction that did get into service by the end of the war was approximately 650,000 gross tons, or about 10 per-

cent of the American-operated merchant fleet. As in other sectors of the war effort, 1919 was to have been a big year. Contracts had been drawn for construction of 2,249 passenger, cargo, refrigerator, and tanker ships, with an aggregate gross tonnage of approximately 8,500,000, equal to one-fourth the total merchant tonnage of all the Allies and the United States in 1914.

As it became apparent that new construction was not going to be available in time to meet the imperative needs of 1918, the Shipping Board looked for other, as yet untapped, sources. One expedient was to bring ships from the Great Lakes to east coast ports by way of Lake Erie and Lake Ontario. In order to negotiate the Welland Canal some of these ships had to be cut in two. In any event, no such expedient could ease the general shortage of ready shipping. Neutral shipping that was not being fully used on the Atlantic was the other major possibility. With the use of economic pressure in the form of forbidding American exports to the countries concerned unless they were willing to charter a substantial part of their merchant fleet, the United States acquired substantial tonnage from Norway, Sweden, Denmark, and Japan. The Netherlands, however, resisted all such pressures, and in March 1918 the United States resorted to the old law of angary (though later more often referred to as the general right of requisition), according to which under certain conditions a belligerent may seize neutral property within its jurisdiction, to seize the 87 Dutch vessels, approximately 332,000 gross tons, lying in American harbors.

In the crisis of 1918 British shipping made up most of the deficit in troop transports, but cargo tonnage never did meet the requirements imposed by the 80-division program. Resurveys of all available shipping and diversion of American ships from various Allied services, and from the nitrate, chrome, manganese, sulphur, phosphate, New England coal, and other trades yielded additional ships; but arrangements for 200,-000 dead-weight tons of Allied shipping for loading in September and October 1918 still left a deficit of some 900,000 tons for those months. Cargo actually shipped, in short tons, fell about 250,000 tons below stated requirements during each of those months. Had the war continued, it is likely that transportation of troops would have had to be cut back in order to ease the pressure for cargo tonnage to support them. Here, again, the prospects for a surplus of tonnage by March 1919 were good.

With shipping at such a premium throughout the war, and with so many competing demands that had to be met at least to some degree if the total war effort was to be effective, co-ordination and control of the facilities available was a vital matter. The Army was up against stiff competition in bidding for tonnage—Bernard Baruch of the War Industries Board demanded tonnage for critical raw materials imports. Herbert Hoover of the Food Administration insisted on ships for food stores, not to mention the Navy's need to supply its forces. Each agency was pretty much on its own until August 1917 when the Shipping Board took over control of all American-flag vessels; thereafter each claimant had to appeal to the board for ships. The Army commissioned a shipping expert and stationed him at the Shipping Board to insure that all possible vessels suitable for Army service were so assigned. Army ships had to go through the delay of having guns mounted to satisfy a Navy requirement for ships entering the war zone.

To operate its ships, the Army had had to depend on civilian crews, whether the ships were Army-owned or chartered. The Quartermaster General, for at least two years before the United States entered the war, had attempted to obtain militarization of the Army Transport Service so that Army vessels would be operated by commissioned officers and enlisted crews, but because of objections in the General Staff to commissioning such officers in the Army nothing had been accomplished. Trouble arose with the civilian crews almost coincident with the beginning of wartime operations. Seamen left Army ships to take higher paying jobs on other vessels; at critical times they sometimes refused to sail until they were granted a wage increase. A further difficulty existed in that civilian crews tended to be less exact in their discipline. Moreover, civilian-operated ships in convoy might be more likely to disclose their presence to the enemy, and to be less precise in following the rules for maneuvering ships in close formation. In these circumstances, in the summer of 1917 the Army gave up its prerogative of operating its own troop transports to the Navy's Cruiser and Transport Force, which then not only organized, conducted, and commanded the troop convoys, but also provided officers and crews for the ships. For the first time, too, the Army entrusted the feeding of its men to another agency, with the Navy providing supplies and provisions for the voyages.

For a time the Army continued to operate its own cargo ships with civilian crews. Then in September 1917 no crew could be found for a ship that was loaded and scheduled to join a convoy, and the Navy produced a crew from its ranks. After this happened several more times during the next weeks, in December the Army entered into an agreement with the Navy which provided

CONVOY OF TROOPSHIPS

that the Navy would furnish crews for cargo and animals ships as well as for troop transports. In January 1918 the Bureau of Operations established the Naval Overseas Transportation Service (NOTS) to operate cargo vessels and to recruit and train crews for them. Besides transporting supplies to the AEF, NOTS was charged with transporting fuel and mines for American naval forces in European waters and with transporting food and other cargoes for the U.S. Shipping Board. Actually, the Army continued to operate about one-third of the ships in the AEF supply service, including a number secured through the Shipping Board on time-form charters which implied that the ships would be operated by the private owners with civilian crews. Satisfactory as Navy operation of the Army's transports was, the Chief of Transportation and the Quartermaster General still warned

against regarding it as a "normal" situation. They felt that, while the transport service should be militarized, the Army should control it so that reliance would not be completely on the Navy should other demands require all the Navy's resources.

The Convoy System

The British rendered a great service in the safe passage of troop and cargo ships in the organization and command of convoys. Urged by Prime Minister David Lloyd George and by President Wilson and Admiral William S. Sims of the United States and going counter to the views of high-ranking British and American naval officers as well as merchant seamen, the British Admiralty inaugurated the convoy system in June 1917 when losses to submarines had become intolerable. It proved its effectiveness almost immediately. Cargo losses were reduced subsequently by nearly 90 percent, and the U.S. Army crossed the Atlantic without loss.

American naval units provided a sizable share of the destroyer escorts for the convoys, but the protection of cargo ships was mainly a British operation. In command of all escort ships assigned to the cargo convoy service was the British commander in chief of the American and West Indian Naval Station organized for the purpose; he maintained his headquarters aboard a converted yacht in the Potomac River during the principal period of operations. The U.S. Navy ordinarily organized and controlled convoys carrying American troops when they were made up of American ships, while the British Navy usually escorted the British liners.

Summary

In World War 1, as in most wars, the chief logistical limitation on the military effort was transportation. Never before had any nation attempted to transport and supply so large a force at such a great distance from its home bases. Initial congestion and confusion on the railways and at the ports ultimately gave way to planning, organization, and control effective enough to accomplish the unprecedented tasks that had been undertaken. The convoy system and the acquisition of ships finally overcame the submarine menace after it threatened to paralyze the entire war effort of the Allies.

In nineteen months, May 1917 through November 1918, more than two million American soldiers and nearly six million short tons of supplies and equipment for them were transported to France—half a million men and two million tons of supplies in the first thirteen months, and a million and a half men and four million tons of supplies in the last six months—and probably both figures could have been doubled in the next year. But these impressive accomplishments and the great victory of November 1918 obscured some real deficiencies. The shipping shortage never had been overcome and, in terms of requirements for the approved 80-division program, there was no prospect that it could be overcome before March 1919. The more emphasis that was put on transporting troops, as was the case after the big German drives of the spring of 1918, the greater was the strain on transportation for supplies, for every man sent to France added immediately to the daily requirements for maintenance and to the quantities needed to maintain reserves even at a constant level in terms of days of supply. If somehow the deficiency of ocean tonnage could have been overcome quickly, there is still no assurance that the supply program and the inland transportation system in the United States—not to mention the port and transportation systems in France—could have kept pace. The supply bureaus in the United States had not been able to build up reserves at ports in the United States; congestion, yes, but reserves, no. Ships had not been delayed for want of available cargo, but had there been enough ships to meet all requirements, it probably would not have been possible to avoid such delays. Indications were strong in November 1918 that there would have to be a slowing down of troop movements overseas shortly in order to allow supply shipments to catch up.

It was not only a matter of tonnage; it was a matter of balance as well. With no immediate and sizable addition to the cargo fleet to match the additional British shipping assigned to troop transportation, there was danger that the line of communications and supplies in France would not be able to support the growing numbers of troops. If the United States actually had put into France the 100 divisions Foch and Pershing wanted, they might have become paralyzed for want of supplies before they could have made their full weight felt. Already there was a tendency in the shipping programs, as there always had been in mobilization, to emphasize personnel ahead of matériel, when a little more emphasis on construction and supply build-up might actually have hastened the effective participation of larger forces. Reliance upon Great Britain for such a large share of the troop carrying capacity subjected the United States to strong pressures for sending troops in the way the British desired. When Foch and the Allied governments called for riflemen and machine gunners, and the British agreed to provide the ships for these categories, it was difficult to resist. In this situation the British even were tempted to insist on how the troops were to be employed regardless of Allied or American plans, as when Lloyd George at one point threatened to cut British tonnage if the American forces were to be used east of Verdun.

Perhaps the pouring of American men into France in 1918 with little regard about how they were to be supplied made that year decisive. Winston Churchill, then Minister of Munitions, later described it thus:

Henceforward the main effort of the United States was to send men to France up to the fullest limit of ocean transport. In large formations or in small, trained or half-trained, without regard to armament, equipment or supplies, American manhood was to proceed to the war. The use to be made of all these great numbers of men, their organization, their training, their ammunition, their food and clothing—all were questions to be solved later on. This was an act of faith of the highest merit. No one who did not possess that intense form of power which comes from expressing the will of a free people could have dared to decree a policy in appearance so improvident and even reckless. A hundred valid arguments existed against it, but all were relegated to a lower plane. From this moment the United States poured men into France, and by this action more than any other which it was in their power to take helped to bring the war to a speedy termination.[5]

It was not quite fair to say that the great increase in the shipment of men to France was done without regard to their supplies and equipment. Even the modest diversion of additional British cargo tonnage to support the growing American force in France was done with the knowledge that it would mean cutting 2,000,000 tons of European imports of food and munitions from calculated minimum requirements for the winter of 1918–19.

The risk involved shortages for everyone concerned—in food supply for the Allied populations, in munitions for their armies, and in supplies for the AEF. Then victory came in November 1918. That victory, arriving as it did before the risk potential had to be realized and negating the grandiose plans for 1919, might have been the greatest danger for the future, for with it the "hundred valid arguments" against taking such a risk were obscured, and since then have been glossed over. Yet, daring is never to be despised in war, and risk is relative: If the Allies faced serious supply shortages in that winter, what of the enemy whose commerce had been swept from the seas?

---

[5] Winston S. Churchill, *The World Crisis, 1916–1918*, 4 vols. (New York: Scribners, 1927), II, 197.

CHAPTER XXIII

Services of Supply in France

More on the basis of the Prussian example in the war of 1870–71 then of the American experience in the Civil War and in the War with Spain (with which the officers concerned were less familiar), the General Staff before the outbreak of World War I had included in the Field Service Regulations an outline of a line of communication organization for the support of armies in the field. A concept of a line of communication had, of course, existed in the United States Army from the earliest times. Nathanael Greene, it will be recalled, as Quartermaster General during the Revolutionary War had set up a string of supply depots which he referred to as a "line of communication." The earlier ideal had been self-containment; that is, an army should carry with it, in the hands of the troops and in its baggage trains, the military supplies essential for a campaign, and rely upon the resources of the country through which it operated for the remainder. Then—and this was true for the most part in the Civil War—it came to be the practice for armies to tie themselves to sizable bases, and the army, in effect, dragged its supplies from the rear.

It remained for the Prussians to develop fully the principle of continuous replenishment from the rear through a system of staging. They demonstrated the effectiveness of the new supply system in the short war with Austria in 1866, and showed an expanded and improved version in the Franco-Prussian War. The impetus of sup-

ply was from the rear, through a system of depots that stretched out behind an advancing army like the extensions of a telescope, with continuous shuttling from the rearward depot to the next one forward.

Even the elaborate system of the Germans, however, had broken down by 1914 when supplies were unable to keep up with the armies sweeping toward Paris. By this time the French had developed a supply system equal to that of the Germans, and perhaps surpassing it in flexibility. When the war on the Western Front settled down to stabilized trench warfare, it became in some respects a "logistician's dream": regular supply lines and schedules could be set up, depots and even forward railheads could be organized on a semipermanent basis, and requirements could be calculated in fairly accurate terms.

In setting up its own supply system the United States had the advantage of nearly three years of Allied experience, even though it was clear that a peculiar set of circumstances would have to be met in maintaining a sizable army across 3,000 miles of ocean. Yet, in spite of all the earlier planning and experience, the American line of communication in France "grew like Topsy".

Organization and Administration

When General Pershing and his staff arrived in Liverpool on 8 June 1917, the

American military mission which previously had been established in Paris had a preliminary report ready for him on prospective locations for American forces and the use of French ports and railways. A few days later the general sent a board of officers ahead to visit various ports and make more specific recommendations. Circumstances and the desires of the French largely dictated the choices. Considerations of avoiding the Channel ports which already were overtaxed with British shipping, using railroads not already congested with traffic in support of French and British forces, avoiding cutting across British and French supply lines in so far as possible, and respecting the desire of the French to have their own forces interposed between the enemy and Paris, all pointed to an eastern sector for American forces. At the suggestion of the French, the 1st Division was to go to the area of Gondrecourt for training. This indicated a probable line of communication of about 500 miles across France from the ports, a distance which, together with the need for flexibility in meeting enemy attacks as well as in building up for Allied attacks at various points, made it desirable to develop a system of base, intermediate, and advanced storage for supplies.

Saint-Nazaire at the mouth of the Loire River, was designated Base Port No. 1 by oral orders of General Pershing on 21 June 1917, and became the starting point for the line of communication. To serve the anticipated American forces, it would have to extend in the direction of Gondrecourt, and the intermediate and advance storage depots would have to be along this line. The choice for the principal intermediate storage fell to Gièvres, on the main railroad line from Saint-Nazaire through Tours and toward Dijon. For advance storage in the vicinity of the designated training area for American troops, Is-sur-Tille, where the French already had a regulating station in operation, was chosen as the principal location. Work hardly had begun on facilities at Gièvres when the growing conception of the role American forces should play in the war made it evident that additional port facilities would be needed as well as another intermediate depot. The Gironde River area was then developed, with facilities at Bordeaux, Bassens, and Talmont; this area was destined to become more important than the Loire for landing American troops and supplies. This development, as well as the desirability of dispersing supplies to some extent, led to establishment of a second major intermediate depot at Montierchaume, near Châteauroux, on the main railroad connecting Bordeaux with the Saint-Nazaire–Is-sur-Tille line.

Later, other ports came into use. Brest was the only French port which could accommodate some of the deep-draft German passenger ships that the United States took over, and it became the principal port for troop debarkation. During the crisis in the spring of 1918, when American infantrymen were being rushed to France in British ships, many by way of England, the Channel ports, primarily Le Havre, Cherbourg, and Boulogne, were used for debarkation. Later that year the Mediterranean port of Marseille became an important port of entry for heavy cargo. (*Map 15*)

Meanwhile the organization for co-ordinating the activities of the ports and depots was taking shape. In July 1917 the Line of Communications was organized with headquarters in Paris, but the Advance Section, organized about the same time to exercise control over logistical activities in the divisional training areas with a rear limit

A SERVICES OF SUPPLY AREA IN FRANCE

corresponding to the French Zone of the Armies, remained directly under General Headquarters, AEF. By a general order issued on 13 August, the Advance Section became a definite part of the Line of Communications organization, an Intermediate Section was established with headquarters at Nevers, the former site of Advance Section headquarters, and the previously established base ports became the nuclei for new base sections. Presently the whole coast of France and adjacent *departements* for some distance inland were included in the base section organization. At first Base Section No. 3 included activities in England as well as in the French Channel ports, but it was later divided and its headquarters moved to London, whereupon, Base Section No. 4 was organized with headquarters at Le

Havre. The District of Paris, comprising the *departements* of the Seine and Seine-et-Oise, and later the *arrondissement* of Tours, remained directly under the Commanding General, Line of Communications, exempt from control of the Intermediate Section. Commanders of base and intermediate sections were designated Assistant Chiefs of Staff, Line of Communications. Another major element of the Line of Communications, although it operated independently, was the Service of Military Railways.

The system as it operated at the end of 1917 divided responsibility for supply into three phases: procurement, care and storage, and transportation. Procurement was the responsibility of the chiefs of the supply departments at General Headquarters, Chaumont (with European purchases co-

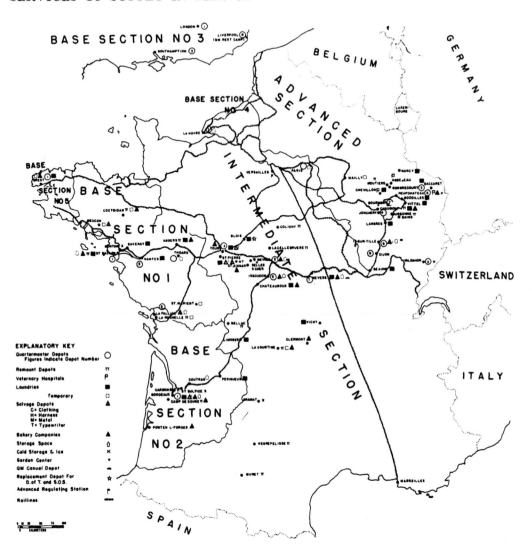

MAP OF FRANCE SHOWING QMC AEF ACTIVITIES
Prepared in Office Chief QM, AEF, May 27, 1918

MAP 15

ordinated through the General Purchasing Agent); care and storage was the responsibility of the Commanding General, Line of Communications; the Director General of Transportation was responsible for unloading troops and freight at the ports and for transporting them by rail to stations, depots, and regulating stations. Co-ordination of all these activities was a function of the General Staff at GHQ, usually through the Coordination Section. On the surface this arrangement seemed logical enough, but as the AEF expanded, structural weaknesses became more and more evident. The chief difficulties arose from the lack of specific definitions of jurisdiction and the overlapping of functions.

Sensitive to the growing deficiencies in organizational structure, General Pershing invited the chiefs of the staff sections and departments, and the division and brigade commanders as well, to make recommendations for changes. Early in February 1918 he asked Col. Johnson Hagood to head a board of officers to study the replies and to make recommendations for reorganization of the headquarters, general staff, and supply services of the AEF. Recommendations extended from those that would have more or less preserved the *status quo* through those in favor of centralizing all responsibility for supply under a single officer, to some advocating demilitarization of the whole rear logistical organization in favor of reorganization under civilian leaders along business lines.

After seven days in continuous session the Hagood Board came up with a far-reaching proposal for centralization of the AEF's supply organization. The board considered that the most important question before it was the necessity for providing a single and direct line of responsibility for all matters of supply while making the fullest use of the knowledge and experience of the chiefs of administrative and technical services already on the staff of the Commander in Chief. General Pershing approved the recommendations almost completely, and, with a few exceptions, they went into effect in February and March with Maj. Gen. Francis J. Kernan as commanding general.

While retaining their titles and authority as members of the staff of the Commander in Chief, the chiefs of the administrative and technical services thereafter were to exercise all their functions in matters of procurement, transportation, and supply under the direction of the Commanding General, Services of Supply (SOS), as the Line of Communications was redesignated after a brief designation as Service of the Rear. Chiefs of all of the services, with the exception of the Adjutant General, Inspector General, Judge Advocate, and chief of the Tank Corps, moved from Chaumont to Tours. Each service chief appointed an officer to represent him on the General Staff at Chaumont. In addition, a Service of Utilities was established under the Commanding General, SOS, to include the Transportation Department, Motor Transport Service, Construction and Forestry Service, and Division of Light Railways and Roads. The General Purchasing Agent also came under the SOS although his headquarters remained in Paris.

At the same time the heads of the various sections of the General Staff at Chaumont were made assistant chiefs of staff, and designated respectively G–1, G–2, G–3, G–4, and G–5.[1] A similar staff organization was provided for the Commanding General, Services of Supply.

The intention of the Hagood Board had been to make the Commanding General, SOS, a kind of chief of staff for supply, with

---

[1] At that time Staff designations denoted the following functions: G–1, Administration; G–2, Intelligence, G–3, Operations; G–4, Supply, G–5, Training.

territorial jurisdiction extending right down to the receiving units, and with the major elements of G–1 and G–4 to be transferred from Chaumont to Tours along with the administrative and technical service chiefs. Somehow this part of the recommendations never went into effect, and there continued to be doubts about the responsibilities and authority of G–4 at Chaumont with respect to the Commanding General, SOS. The latter was supposed to co-ordinate all the supply activities of the technical services, but the matter of jurisdiction in the Advance Section and over the regulating stations continued to be obscure. In practice, G–4 at General Headquarters retained control of the regulating station at Is-sur-Tille, and since this also was the site of the principal advance storage, the Advance Section, SOS, was left with little authority.

In April, Headquarters, SOS, moved from the crowded quarters of the Hotel Metropole in Tours to the more commodious Barracks 66 and Rannes Barracks in the same city. Departments that had been seriously cramped in the hotel now occupied only 15 percent of their assigned office space, although with the rapid expansion of activities in the next few months, these quarters, too, would soon become overcrowded.

As Chief of Staff, Services of Supply, Hagood, now a brigadier general, laid down rules for staff procedure which carried a ring of relevance a generation later. He described his rules as follows:

General Staff procedure:

The training at West Point for mathematical precision, the temptation to work out puzzles, the long-established custom of our finance department to look for lost pennies, the habit of passing up for decision of higher authority all interesting or knotty problems, no matter how inconsequential, all indicated that certain fundamental principles must be firmly established for the government of myself and my General Staff assistants if we were to find time in each twenty-four hours to handle the big problems and let the little ones go. These principles were:

First: Rank and authority should not be confused with knowledge. . . . If after a full discussion I could not agree with a bureau chief . . . upon a matter lying wholly within his department, I yielded my judgment to his and let him do it his own way.

Second: When intelligent men differed on matters of minor importance, a minor official had to decide between them.

Third: No subordinate officer should make a final unfavorable decision on any matter which a bureau chief or section commander considered vital to his interests. . . .

Fourth: No order, memorandum, instructions, or plan could be changed and issued by the General Staff without first submitting it in final form to the man who originated it. . . .

Fifth: The bureau chiefs were required to see that there was no unnecessary delay in getting General Staff approval of their projects. . . .

Sixth: Complete responsibility was placed upon the bureau chiefs and section commanders for the initiation and prosecution of all that was needful within their respective spheres unless they were specifically told otherwise. . . . That is, all powers not specifically reserved for higher authority were delegated to subordinates. No bureau chief or section commander could stand around wondering if THEY were to look after this or that. If he had heard nothing to the contrary, he was "THEY".[2]

Early in July 1918 there was a serious proposal afoot in Washington, confirming rumors which already had reached General

_____

[2] Johnson Hagood, *The Services of Supply* (Boston: Houghton Mifflin Company, 1927), pp. 163–64.

Pershing's headquarters, for detaching the Services of Supply from AEF control, placing it directly under the War Department, and sending General Goethals to France to take command of supply operations there. Pershing learned officially of the proposal from a letter Secretary of War Baker sent to him inviting his comments.

The Secretary could not have known Pershing very well if he really did not know what the reply would be to this proposal. Indeed, it would have been rare ever to find any military commander assenting without protest to any division of his command. Nothing could have stirred Pershing to quicker action. On 26 July, almost immediately after receiving Secretary Baker's letter, he sent for Maj. Gen. James G. Harbord, then at Nanteuil-le-Haudouin in command of the 2d Division, to come at once to Chaumont. After a five-hour motor trip, Harbord arrived at Pershing's quarters, in a château in the Val des Escoliers, about 2100 hours. The Commander in Chief said that he and his staff had for some time been considering changes in the Services of Supply, and had agreed that Harbord, with the advantage of his experience as chief of staff at General Headquarters and his recently won reputation as a field commander, together with the confidence everyone had in his ability and judgment, made him the logical choice to take command of the SOS. He added that now the arrival of a letter from Secretary Baker made it necessary to make some changes immediately, and suggested that Harbord think about it until morning. Though he was disappointed at having to relinquish his division, and his ambition of perhaps one day commanding a corps or even an army, Harbord could give only one reply; the next day he returned to his head-

quarters and prepared to leave for Tours.

Pershing reached for the pad on his desk, wrote across the top, "RUSH, RUSH, RUSH, RUSH," [3] and drafted a cable to Secretary Baker:

. . . I very much appreciate your desire to relieve me of every burden that might interfere with the direction of military operations. However, there appears to be an exaggerated view concerning the personal attention required in handling the details of administration of this command. Our organization here is fulfilling its functions as planned. Since your visit, the greater part of the details have been shifted to the general staff and an increasing amount to the services of supply. When it becomes necessary for me to be constantly at the front I shall retain general control through the general staff.

. . . the system includes transportation up to the trenches and is intimately interwoven with our whole organization. The whole must remain absolutely under one head. Any division of responsibility or coordinate control in any sense would be fatal. The man who fights the armies must control their supply through subordinates responsible to him alone. The responsibility is then fixed and the possibility of conflicting authority avoided. This military principle is vital and cannot be violated without inviting failure. It is the very principle which we all urged upon the Allies when we got a supreme commander. It is applied in the British Army in France and as far as possible in the French army. As in those armies the general in charge of the services of supply and lines of communication of our forces must be subordinate to the Commander-in-Chief. I very earnestly urge upon you Mr. Secretary that no variations of this principle be permitted.[4]

---

[3] Frederick Palmer, *John J. Pershing, General of the Armies* (Harrisburg, Pa.: The Military Service Publishing Co., 1948), p. 256.

[4] Cable, Pershing to Secy. War, 27 Jul 18, Extract in *United States Army in the World War 1917–1919* (Washington 1948), II, 553.

The next day General Pershing expanded on this theme and other matters in a long letter to the Secretary:

> I do not wish to appear unappreciative of any suggestion from you because I know that it is your desire to do the best possible to help, and have satisfied myself by a knowledge of this fact. I do think, however, that General Harbord can handle it as well as, or better than, any one I know; besides, I have every confidence in General Harbord and know that he is going to pull in the team. I should have put Harbord in some time ago but his division was in the line. Now it goes to a quiet sector and his services can be spared.[5]

The next morning Pershing went to Tours to preside over the change in command, then left with Harbord on an inspection tour of the ports.

Actually the proposal to place the Services of Supply directly under the War Department—in effect, to extend the "zone of the interior" across the Atlantic and up to the advance zone—was not so far-fetched as Pershing represented it to be. To say that the man who fights armies must control their supplies does not say how far back that control should extend. Certainly Pershing was dependent upon the War Department for shipments from the United States though he did not control activities at New York or Philadelphia. It could as reasonably be argued that all major supply activities in France as well as in the United States should be under single authority. In fact, the French commander in chief did not control French supply activities in the zone of the interior, in the rear of the Zone of the Armies, which coincided in territorial extent

GENERAL HARBORD

with the base and intermediate sections of the U.S. Services of Supply. He had to rely on the Ministry of War, the Ministry of Transportation, and other agencies. French military commanders, under the commander in chief, did control the lines of communication in the Zone of the Rear and the *Zone des Étapes* which were subdivisions of the *Zone des Armées*. The commander of the Zone of the Rear was directly under the commander in chief, as was the American SOS commander, while the *Zone des Étapes* was subdivided into areas under directors (general officers) responsible to commanders of armies or groups of armies, and the *Zone de L'Avant* comprised the army areas directly under the army commanders. The French commander in chief never had to concern himself with

---

[5] John J. Pershing, *My Experiences in the World War* (New York: Frederick A. Stokes Co., 1931), II. 191.

questions relating to the procurement of supplies in the interior of the country or from abroad, and the Minister of Transportation was responsible for transporting supplies down to the regulating stations. The British commander in chief did have control over his lines of communication to the French coast, but actually these were relatively small areas, and most of the type of activity carried on in the American base and intermediate sections the British accomplished in England under the direction of the War Office.

The origin of the plan to extend direct War Department control over the Services of Supply still is not clear. Doubtless it was a result in part of the criticism in Washington of the congestion in the French ports and of the slow turnaround time for ships. As early as 3 June 1918 Colonel House had suggested to the President that Edward Stettinius be sent over in his capacity as Assistant Secretary of War to take charge of supply services in the rear areas, and a few days later, when Wilson asked Secretary Baker for his opinion, the latter agreed with House, but suggested that General Goethals, a military commander, be sent rather than Stettinius. General March later wrote that he first heard about the proposal early in July, and understood that it emanated from the White House. General Harbord found evidence in a series of letters from Goethals to his son indicating that March was in touch with Goethals on the matter early in June, the implication being that March saw here a chance to find an appropriate overseas billet for Goethals.[6]

In any case, the incident was a turning point in the history of the Army's system for the control of logistics. Pershing's reaction and Baker's acceptance of his view set the precedent for allowing oversea commanders to control their lines of communication.

Pershing considered that his real answer to the War Department proposal was the assignment of Harbord to command the SOS. At the same time he strengthened the hand of the new commander by adding to his authority. No longer was it necessary for the SOS to clear its communications with the War Department through GHQ at Chaumont; on all matters of supply not involving questions of policy, the Commanding General, SOS, could speak with the same authority of the commander in chief as could the GHQ General Staff. Already the promptness of action and vigor of support in the War Department had improved, so that now the organization and control on both sides of the Atlantic appeared to be equal to the task. For a time it had seemed that the tradition for independence and red tape in the War Department's supply bureaus might nullify much of the action being taken in France. Evidently moved by principles contrary to those General Hagood spelled out for the SOS staff, staff officers in Washington had seemed impelled to substitute their own judgment for that of Pershing and his staff

[6] Ray Stannard Baker, *Woodrow Wilson, Life and Letters* (New York: Doubleday, Doran & Co., 1935–39), VIII, 186–87, 197, 258; Frederick Palmer, *Newton D. Baker, America at War*, 2 vols. (New York: Dodd Mead & Co., 1931), II, 331–35;

Palmer, *John J. Pershing*, pp. 255–59; Pershing, *My Experiences in the World War*, II, 180–91, James G. Harbord, *The American Army in France, 1917–1919* (Boston: Little, Brown and Company, 1936), pp. 347–56; James G. Harbord, *Leaves From a War Diary* (New York: Dodd, Mead & Co., 1925), pp. 339–40; Peyton C. March, *The Nation at War* (Garden City, N.Y.: Doubleday, Doran & Co., 1932), pp. 193–96; Hagood, *The Services of Supply*, pp. 260–61; Frederick L. Paxson, *America at War, 1917–1918*, 2 vols. (Boston: Houghton Mifflin Company, 1939), II, 351–52.

as to his real needs. In some instances, it was reported, staff officers in Washington sought the opinion of Allied officers there about AEF requirements, and sometimes the latter were known to make inquiries of French authorities in Paris, who in turn sought the information from Pershing! To officers in the AEF it was not at all clear why their requests, based on their own studies, should be reviewed and screened by officers in Washington who had access to no other information.

In contrast to his predecessor who had made relatively few inspection trips (and then nearly always by motor car), and who had not been given to making corrections and issuing orders on the ground, Harbord determined to spend most of his time on inspection tours, to travel by rail so that he could travel at night and, moreover, could maintain communications with headquarters and be prepared to issue orders on the ground whenever needed. He was convinced that only in this way could such a loose-knit organization with such widely separated units as the SOS be built into an effective team with the *esprit de corps* necessary to get the job done. As he put it, he was taking a leaf from the book of experience of the ancient oriental rulers who appeared frequently among their subjects to personally redress grievances, distribute praise and blame as needed, and thus to demonstrate interest in their people and what they were doing.

Throughout its operations probably no single problem was more serious for the SOS than the acquisition and employment of service troops. After several weeks of study in the summer of 1917, Pershing's staff prepared a Service of the Rear Project showing by category the number of service troops considered necessary: a total of 329,653 for an army of 1,328,448 men, or not quite 25 percent. In the circumstances this proportion appeared to be a minimum, but it never was attained. Accurate anticipation of the need for service troops in large-scale operations is always difficult, and to apply any set formula is almost impossible. The number of service troops needed will depend upon such variable factors as the length of the lines of communication, the nature of the combat operations, the nature of the country, the availability of local resources, the support given to or received from allied units, the availability of local labor, and enemy action. As it turned out, the requirements for service troops that Pershing submitted to the War Department in September 1917 were not far wrong. The requirements never were met, and there always was a more or less serious shortage of personnel in the SOS.

It was possible to rely on civilian labor for many of the tasks of construction, depot operations, and communications in the SOS, but this created further problems of administration and control. The Labor Bureau, organized under the General Purchasing Agent in Paris, made arrangements with the French Government on conditions of employment and the recruitment of civilian workers. Later the Labor Bureau moved to Tours, and reported to G–4, SOS, although an office in Paris continued to work through the General Purchasing Agent on labor relations with the French authorities.

As might be expected morale posed a special problem for troops assigned to the SOS. Although a soldier might be glad to have an assignment beyond the range of enemy fire, he still was likely to be troubled by constant reminders that his role was one of secondary importance. He was called upon to work for long hours at hard tasks without the compensating reward of the glamour popularly attaching to the combat man. A popular army song in France said, "Mother, take down your service flag, your son's in the S.O.S." [7] The feeling that he had been passed by, that he was not making an important contribution probably was most serious among officers, and the very problems of leadership this created, particularly at the lower levels, only added to the general attitude of discontent. Officers considered unfit for combat duty were sent back to a reclassification depot at Blois, and most of them were reassigned to the SOS. Sometimes these men worked out satisfactorily, but often it meant that the less capable officers were assigned to SOS units.

Transportation

Undoubtedly one of the biggest headaches for the SOS was the organization and control of transportation. Strongly opposing points of view had to be reconciled. Engineer and Quartermaster officers looked with dissatisfaction on the transfer of their responsibilities for certain aspects of transportation to a new organization. Railroad men assigned to operate the Transportation Department in France wanted to run the railroads like commercial lines in the United States, outside strict military control, while military commanders responsible for supply insisted on militarizing the Transportation Service and making it subordinate to the military commander. In the rear areas there was conflict of authority between the

transportation officers and the base section commanders in regard to the unloading of ships, and in the forward areas there was confusion of jurisdiction as between GHQ and SOS over the Transportation Department.

Reception of Troops

Troop debarkations began at Saint-Nazaire, and then Brest became the principal port for the landing of troops, though Le Havre was a close second. Fully half of the American soldiers going to France—usually those carried in British transports—landed at Liverpool, Glasgow, or other ports in the United Kingdom, and after a few days in rest camps moved across the Channel to Le Havre, Cherbourg, Calais, or one of the other Channel ports. This made more work for Base Section No. 3 in England, but it permitted the big British transports to turn around quickly, and to use the shortest routes across the Atlantic. Seldom did all of the elements of a division arrive at a single port—units of the 3d, 29th, and 36th Divisions, for instance, landed at Saint-Nazaire, Bordeaux, and Brest, as well as at English ports from which they moved to Le Havre.

Facilities for the reception of troops varied a great deal, and never were altogether satisfactory. For a time, reception at Brest consisted of marching the new arrivals out to an open field. Later it was possible to set up a large tent camp, with good messing facilities staffed by French cooks, at Pontanezen near Brest. The initial survey had indicated that Brest might handle 18,000 troops a month, but when the big rush began in the spring of 1918, and the base section commander, Brig. Gen. George H. Harries, was asked how many troops he could re-

---

[7] Frederick Palmer, *Our Greatest Battle* (New York: Dodd, Mead & Co., 1919), p. 393; Elmer W. Sherwood, *The Diary of a Rainbow Veteran* (Terre Haute, Ind.: Moore-Langen Co., 1929), p. 100.

ceive there, he replied that he could handle all that they could send. He was put to the test near the end of May when a convoy arrived carrying 42,000 troops. The chief transport officer commandeered everything that would float to use as lighters and to make a bridge of ships to bring the troops to land. The whole debarkation was completed in twenty-four hours. On another occasion, some time later, a convoy of fourteen ships, with 46,000 men on board, arrived at Brest; over 35,000 of them were lightered ashore that same afternoon and marched to the reception camp, while another 18,000 men from a previous convoy marched out of the camp to the railroad station to take trains for forward areas.

Discharge of Cargo

The problem of discharging cargo to support this army was rather more difficult. Shortages of equipment and facilities together with shortages of personnel able to do the various tasks efficiently, handicapped operations. Congestion around the docks became commonplace. There was no point in making all kinds of extraordinary efforts to get more shipping and to hasten the departure of convoys from New York if they could not be promptly unloaded in France. Each day's delay in the turnaround of a ship was said to mean the loss of the equivalent of $10,000. Early in 1918 the wharves at Saint-Nazaire had reached a state of general confusion. While stevedores rested, or even slept in the warehouses, piles of supplies waited to be sorted and put into some kind of orderly arrangement. This was during the period of divided authority, when the base commander was responsible for quartering and feeding the stevedore troops, but they worked under the supervision of trans-

portation officers who were independent of the local SOS organization.

During his tour of the ports with Harbord, Pershing had spoken to the stevedore battalions about the importance of their work, and he promised that if they did well, later they might get their turn at the front. Their frank response was that they would rather go home than any nearer the fighting. Now Harbord hit upon the idea of exploiting this homesickness. Early in September he and his aides worked out a scheme of competition among the ports which they called "The Race to Berlin," using as the incentive the promise that the winning company would be the first to go home at the end of the war. Performance for each port was calculated on the basis of its average performance during the preceding eight weeks, so that ratio of improvement over its own past record was the basis for comparison. Standings were telegraphed to all headquarters each week, and published in *The Stars and Stripes,* the AEF newspaper. In addition to the prize of first to go home, leading companies at each port were awarded leave to the Mediterranean area, and the commander of the leading port for the month flew a pennant from his headquarters.

The competition produced spectacular results. Discharge of cargo increased by about 20 percent during the period of the race, and the average detention time for transatlantic cargo vessels dropped from 14 days for 84 vessels in July to 11.04 days for 138 ships in November. Total cargo discharged at all French ports for the AEF through 11 November 1918, including that arriving from Great Britain and other foreign sources as well as that shipped from the United States, amounted to 5,960,000 tons. The figure grew to 9,577,000 tons by the end of May 1919. Nevertheless, all this would not have been enough to meet the requirements for continuing the war through 1919 with the size force contemplated. Cargo landed during the month preceding the armistice was equal to only 65 percent of current requirements for 2,000,000 men, and it would have been necessary to triple the average daily rate of discharge of cargo to meet the needs for the planned army of 3,500,000 in July 1919, not to mention the need to make up the accumulating shortages. By using gantry cranes to the fullest extent possible, by working around the clock at all ports, by completing the additional facilities under construction, by making maximum use of dolphins and lighters for offshore discharge, and by other expedients, perhaps the job could have been done, but it is doubtful. Granting that possibility it is doubtful whether arrivals from the United States would have been able to keep up, and more doubtful still whether such quantities could have been moved inland even if they could have been loaded, brought to port, and discharged.

Railway Transportation

As the weeks of intense activity during 1918 passed, it became more and more evident that the real supply bottlenecks were evacuation from the ports and movement to forward areas. In June Secretary of War Baker expressed his concern to Pershing: "Our tables seem to show that the evacuations from the ports from month to month are less than the cargo discharges there, so that there seems to be a constant increase in accumulated and unevacuated cargo at the ports which we use; and I am fearful

that if we secured additional cargo ships we would simply add to the congestion of the ports, rather than add to your supplies." [8]

At first glance the American transportation problem in France must have seemed virtually impossible. The strain of three and four years of war alone, with all manpower mobilized as fully as possible to support the war effort, left enough problems in the maintenance of railways and highways to make doubly difficult the additional burdens on the system.

At first it was necessary for the Americans to rely for their needs entirely upon French trains and French crews, co-ordinated through American liaison officers. Later, American crews and trains were able to take over a part of the task. But there were further difficulties in language, plus differences in equipment and methods to interpose delays and inefficiencies.

The French maintained standard troop trains referred to as T.U. (*type unique*), made up of 30 boxcars (40 men or eight horses), 17 flatcars, a coach, and two cabooses for the train crew, intended to carry a battalion of infantry or a battery of artillery, with all organic transportation and equipment. If a unit did not fill a train completely, the extra cars remained empty; this was deemed quicker than making up special trains to fit every unit. When the Americans adopted the practice of sending troops overseas without organizational equipment, the French made up a standard T.A. (*type américain*) train, with capacity for 1,600 officers and men, to move the American units inland from the ports. To move an American division with its equipment, 50 to 58 T.U. trains were required.

---

[8] Quoted in Palmer, *Newton D. Baker*, II, 331.

Motor Transportation

By the time of World War I the use of motor transportation had become significant, but it was more of a supplement to horses and wagons for local transportation than a substitute for railroads for long hauls. Truck convoys did carry supplies from the ports to forward areas, but usually in connection with the delivery of the vehicles to forward units. A fixed percentage, at first 25 percent but later reduced to 10 percent, of all vehicles arriving at the ports went to the SOS, while the remainder were distributed by G–4, GHQ. The AEF never did have more than half the vehicles called for in tables of organization and other estimates, and no one knew how accurately these represented true needs.

Control of motor transportation was at first a responsibility of the Quartermaster Corps. After the use of motor trucks in Pershing's Punitive Expedition in Mexico, some steps had been taken to extend their use, and four truck companies and a repair unit arrived in France in June 1917. In December 1917 a Motor Transport Service, within the Quartermaster Corps, was formed in the AEF. It was transferred to the Service of Utilities, SOS, in February 1918, and in July became a separate service, designated the Motor Transport Corps. At first the Motor Transport Service had only technical supervision, but later it was made responsible for operating the vehicles in the SOS. All vehicles, passenger cars as well as trucks, were pooled under district commanders in each section to be assigned to particular tasks as needed. Operational responsibility included the make-up and routing of truck convoys for delivery to units.

Inland Waterways

In spite of the historical reliance of American armies on river transportation, AEF planners initially gave almost no thought to the possible use of French rivers and canals for the support of American forces. Distances seemed too great in any case to rely to any marked extent on slow-moving barges. But when it became evident how hard-pressed the railroads were going to be to handle the necessary traffic, any means of relieving them even slightly was welcomed. Arrangements were made for the loan of tugs and barges from the British, and for taking over a number of French barges that were unserviceable but could be reconditioned; however, chief reliance had to be on individually owned French barges chartered through the co-operation of the French Government. All these sources had put thirteen tugs and 307 barges at the disposal of the American service by the time of the armistice. (Tugs ordinarily were used on the rivers, while horses usually towed the barges on the canals.) Tonnages shipped by inland waterway were minor—monthly totals reached 47,000 tons in October—but especially for shipment of coal and wood even this amount represented a considerable relief to local railroad congestion. Most of the river traffic was on the Seine River, from Le Havre and Rouen to below Paris, though some barge traffic went to Dijon, Gimouville Saint-Satur, and Montargis. The canal system was well-disposed to serve the American front, and, given earlier planning and more equipment, it could have had far greater logistical significance. Plans being put into effect when the armistice was signed would have tripled the volume of supplies transported on the inland waterways—to about 150,000 tons a month, or some 5 percent of the total AEF tonnage passing through the French ports—had the war continued. The British for some time had been shipping 250,000 tons a month on the rivers and canals in their sector.

Supply

The two principal sources of supply for the AEF were, of course, shipments from the United States and purchases in Europe. Then a sort of "in between" source became important for certain items—cultivation and manufacture by the Army or under Army supervision in France.

Local Procurement

In the interest of saving time as well as precious ocean tonnage, not to mention the fact that many items simply were not available in the United States, first emphasis was upon local procurement.[9]

As had been the case in the United States until General Staff control had become effective, U.S. supply departments in France and England at once began to compete with each other and even with the Allied armies in bidding for supplies. In August 1917 General Pershing moved to co-ordinate these purchases. Overruling the recommendations of a staff study, he established at Paris a General Purchasing Board, made up of the purchasing officers of each of the supply services plus representatives from the Red Cross and the Young Men's Christian Association (YMCA), and he called upon Charles G. Dawes, a prominent banker and

a long-time friend, then a lieutenant colonel with an engineer regiment in France, to be chairman of the board and General Purchasing Agent. Dawes, who subsequently achieved the rank of brigadier general, entered upon his new assignment with gusto.

The new arrangement centralized supervision, but not procurement operations. Although he was called the General Purchasing Agent, Dawes actually did no purchasing himself—each service continued to do its own purchasing. The General Purchasing Board provided a forum for co-ordinating activity, and Dawes held a veto over purchases. He, in effect, made the policies. Soon after taking up his duties as Purchasing Agent, Dawes was able to have changed the policy that had required all requisitions for purchases from the French Government to go through the chief of staff at GHQ, and he was then the final authority on all such requests. With the organization of the broadened SOS, the General Purchasing Agent was made a member of the staff of the commanding general; but he continued to have close contact with Pershing, and he maintained a fairly independent, though co-operative, operation. It was up to Dawes to negotiate agreements with the governments concerned covering procurement policies and to search out and develop all possible sources of supply in neutral as well as in Allied countries. Responding to conditions as they arose, he organized a Labor Bureau, a Board of Contracts and Adjustments, a Technical Board to co-ordinate electrical power, and a Bureau of Reciprocal Supply, and the administrative machinery necessary for such a vast enterprise.

Procurement in Europe reached substantial proportions. How important it was in saving ocean tonnage may be seen in the fact that the AEF actually obtained a greater

---

[9] See above, Chapter XXI, for a discussion of ordnance and other supplies furnished by Great Britain and France.

REPAIRING CLOTHING AT THE SALVAGE DEPOT, TOURS

tonnage of supplies from European sources than through all of the efforts of the War Department in making shipments from the United States. Through December 1918 the AEF received 7,675,000 ship tons of supplies from the United States, while it received the equivalent of over 10,000,000 ship tons from European procurement.

In the process of carrying out his duties, Dawes developed strong convictions that the type of co-ordinating agency Pershing had set up was the correct one. He soon rejected the idea that Army procurement should be conducted as a business, with complete centralization. He took time to prepare a memorandum for the historical record in February and March 1918 which gains weight from the fact that he himself was a business man, and is making no plea that he should have had more authority. He said in part:

The argument of the business man is that if all purchasing and supply activities were centralized in one distinct army department, created to supply all other branches of the service, there would be obviated competition among the various departments, piecemeal and wasteful purchases, loose methods, insufficient estimation of forward collective needs, and many other objections now incident to some extent to the present system. . . . It was with this belief that I took up my duties as General Purchasing Agent of the American Expeditionary Force, under a new system of central control devised personally by General Pershing against the advice of a reporting army board to whom the subject had been first referred.

. . . .

My idea, as that of many other business men, had been that the law of the United States, which so jealously guarded the independent right of purchase and supply in departments of the service, was on our statute books as a result of a lack of business knowledge and foresight on the part of legislators, instead of its being, as it is, the logical, legitimate, and necessary evolution of thousands of years of actual military experience.

. . . .

The statement is frequently made that the business organization of an army is the same in its purpose as the business organization of any great corporation. This is misleading. . . . The prime consideration, in the establishment in normal business organization of central control of purchase, is the surrounding of purchasing activity with checks and balances compelling due consideration of every purchase from the standpoint of its relation to a prospective profit. . . . The first purpose of the army business organization in time of war is the securing of necessary military supplies irrespective of any question of financial profit, yet as cheaply and expeditiously as possible without prejudice to military effectiveness.[10]

A special source of supply in Europe was production by the U.S. Army itself. This often called for local procurement of facilities, construction materials, raw materials, and labor. It was most important, perhaps, in food supply. A quartermaster major, Otto H. Goldstein, who had been a wholesale grocer in Chicago, built a plant near Paris for roasting and grinding coffee which in September 1918 was turning out

90,000 pounds a day; three similar plants were added, and by 1919 they would have been able to provide the entire coffee requirement for the AEF. Major Goldstein also arranged to rent idle chocolate-making machinery from the French owners, and soon he had nearly a dozen factories turning out 4,000,000 pounds of chocolate a month for the ration component, and another 1,000,000 pounds made into candies for sale to the soldiers. Next Goldstein was called upon to produce hard bread, and he reached a production of 9,000,000 pounds a month. He also devised a mechanical process that turned out 1,500,000 pounds of macaroni a month. A string of Quartermaster bakeries extending from the ports to the armies turned out the pound of bread for each man each day that the AEF required. Vegetable gardens cultivated by individual units provided important ration supplements, and a Garden Service was organized with plans to cultivate gardens on a large scale in 1919. In the fall of 1918 over 10,000 men were at work cutting fuel wood for the AEF.

A related source of supply was in the operation of the big salvage depots where all kinds of clothing and equipment were reconditioned, and materials saved and made into useful products. Salvage Depot No. 1, near Tours, alone was turning out nearly $3.4 million worth of reconditioned clothing a month by August 1918; it was but one of nearly twenty salvage depots, having nearly one million square feet of working space, then in operation. This was the first systematic salvage operation in war.

Supply Policies and Distribution

The automatic supply system worked out even better than most supply officers had

---

[10] Charles G. Dawes, *A Journal of the Great War*, 2 vols. (Boston: Houghton Mifflin Co., 1921), I, 76n.

dared hope, though the big problem of finding enough shipping to meet requirements persisted until the end of the war. What made the situation seem especially critical in the fall of 1918, of course, was the spectacular rise in troop shipments in July and August. Even though increasing tonnages were being shipped, they could not keep pace with the rapidly growing requirements in terms of increasing troop strength. A cable to the War Department on 28 October stated: "On account of failure to receive the supplies called for in past months our reserves are so depleted that the reduction in number of troops shipped during October cannot reduce our requirements for supplies to be shipped during that month. The shipments for October are falling so far short of what we need that prospects are extremely alarming." [11] If all shipments had been made as requested, it is doubtful whether they could have been moved away from the ports; still, there would have been some satisfaction simply in having them on the near side of the ocean, where they might be counted as a part of the reserves. The AEF's established supply policy of maintaining a 90-day stock of supplies—45 days at the base depots, 30 days at the intermediate depots, and 15 days in the Advance Section—was more or less arbitrary. In spite of the studies which preceded this decision, the figure was one that, in effect, had to be taken out of the air. There was nothing to indicate that that quantity of reserve supplies was absolutely essential. The British plan originally had been to maintain 30 days' supplies at the base depots and another 8 days' forward, but the total

reserves actually maintained at the ports never exceeded 22 days. Of course the British were close to their home bases, and the American dread of interruption of the ocean supply line dictated a conservative figure. As it developed, the submarine menace was overcome, and there was no serious threat of interruption. This, together with the more important fact that the projected 90-day level for most supplies never had been possible to approach, finally led to the change in favor of a 45-day level.

Reserves are, in any case, psychological as well as physical phenomena. It may be reassuring to know that enough supplies are on hand to withstand a three-month interruption of overseas communications, but if that figure has been taken as representing a minimum requirement, and stocks never reach more than half that level, then a feeling of uneasiness over a situation where reserves are "half depleted" may develop. By arbitrarily halving the reserve requirements, AEF stocks immediately were seen as approaching the required levels. After March 1918 the supply of rations on hand never fell below the 45-day level (it fluctuated between 72 days in June and 48 days in September), so that what had seemed a serious shortage appeared as an adequate supply; and, in the circumstances, it was adequate.

Ammunition was divided among the sections according to the same ratio, but Ordnance officers concluded that all ammunition not stored at base depots, or necessary to have an emergency reserve in case of loss, or for temporary storage to relieve congestion at the ports, should be shipped directly to advance depots located where rapid shipments could be made to army depots.

Mainly as an aid to distribution, supplies in the AEF (from December 1917), were

[11] Report, CG SOS, AEF, *U.S. Army in the World War*, XV, 12–13.

divided into four classes. Class 1 comprised all items of daily automatic supply, including rations, fuel, gasoline, and oil. Daily automatic supply depended upon the actual troop strength and number of animals in an organization. This information went from the division G–1 (corps G–1 for corps troops) to army G–4 who telegraphed it to the regulating officer at least once a week. The regulating officer might call upon the depot (normally the advance depot) to ship items marked for specific divisions, or might have them shipped in bulk; under this arrangement, shipments of forage or fuel, for example, would be in carload lots so that overissues and underissues would have to be averaged out over a period of days.

Class 2 supplies, including mainly personal clothing and bedding, were shipped on requisitions submitted by company commanders, consolidated and approved by regimental commanders, and forwarded through division (or corps) G–1 (army G–4 for army troops) directly to the advance depot. In this case the regulating officer entered the picture only if necessary to indicate order of priority if there was a shortage of railway cars and to record shipments passing through his station.

Requisitions for Class 3 supplies, comprising all other authorized equipment provided for in the tables, including weapons, vehicles, and rolling kitchens, were handled in the same way as those for Class 2, except that they were to be filled insofar as possible by the division supply officer and from army dumps or parks before being sent to the advance depot for the remainder.

Class 4 supplies included ammunition, construction materials, special equipment, and items which by orders from time to time might be excepted from Classes 2 and 3.

Requisitions for this class were handled in the same way as those for Class 3 except that that part sent to depots to be filled had to pass through G–4 at GHQ where it would be considered in the light of contemplated operations and the needs of other units. Credits for certain quantities might be established at the depots upon which army could draw without reference to GHQ.

Units in rear of the Advance Section obtained their Class 1, 2, and 3 supplies on requisitions made direct to the depots. Requisitions for their Class 4 supplies had to be submitted to the chief of the supply service concerned who, on approval, sent them to the proper depot to be filled.

The depots, in turn, obtained their supplies automatically to the extent practicable, and for the rest submitted requisitions to the chief of service. A controlled stores policy, adopted in the summer of 1918, centralized accountability of stocks and enabled supply service chiefs to equalize stocks according to current supply policies among the depots. This, in effect, extended further the system of automatic supply, for the chief of service concerned had essential items shipped to a depot as soon as his status reports showed that a shortage of those items was developing at that place, and no special action by the depot staff was necessary. (*Chart 2*)

Of all the developments and innovations of World War I, American logistics officers seemed to think that the finest was the institution of the regulating station and the regulating officer adopted from the French, who considered it to be about the only innovation developed in their long years of study preceding the war that could be retained with little change when the war came. The

CHART 2

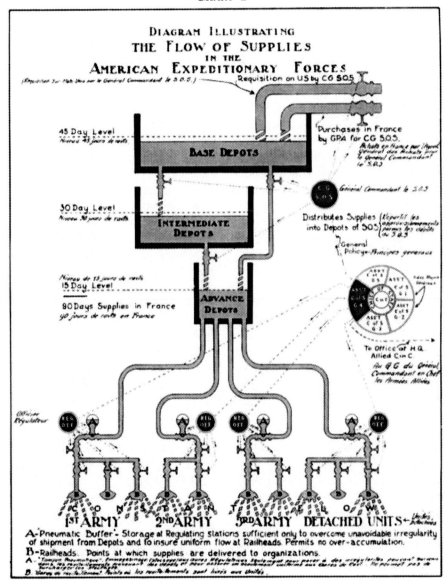

main trouble for the Americans was in deciding who should regulate the regulating officer.

A regulating station was a large railroad yard where cars from the depots and other installations in the rear were received and made up into trains or *rames*.[12]   The use of division *rames* permitted the greatest flexi-

[12] A *rame* is a string of cars for a division or other unit, so that if a single train were to carry supplies for more than one unit it would be made up of one *rame* for each unit.

bility in the redirection of supplies to keep up with rapid changes in the location of the divisions.

At the regulating station control of supplies passed from the SOS to GHQ for delivery to the armies. The regulating officer was designated officially as a member of the G–4 Section of GHQ, but he also belonged to the headquarters of the army which he served. General Harbord thought the regulating officer should belong to the G–4 Section of SOS, and be directly under the supervision of the commander of the Advance Section in whose area he operated. As Harbord saw it, "the Regulating Officer was thus the bridge over which [G–4, GHQ] continued to travel from Supervision to Operation, and to divide and overlap the authority of the Commanding General of the Services of Supply." [13] Actually, Col. Milosh R. Hilgard, the regulating officer at Is-sur-Tille went about his task with an independent determination to get results to which the formal arrangement of the hierarchy over him made little practical difference.

The AEF constructed two regulating stations, the one at Is-sur-Tille, the principal station for supplying American forces during much of the time, and a second at Liffol-le-Grand. For other parts of the front it was possible to use facilities that the French already had organized. These included regulating stations at Saint-Dizier, Gray, Le Bourget, Noisy-le-Sec, Mantes, and Creil. The regulating station at Is-sur-Tille had the advantages and disadvantages of being located adjacent to the principal advance depot, which facilitated co-ordination, but led to a constant threat of congestion on the

railroads. For a regulating station this could be fatal.

A daily supply train, with cars carrying rations, mail, express, replacement troops, and whatever else might be going to the units, went from the regulating station to the railroad. The equivalent of 25 French railway cars was needed for the daily supplies of a division. Ideally there was a railhead for each division, and a train for each division, but often these had to be shared. At the more or less permanent railheads such as those serving the Saint-Mihiel and Meuse-Argonne sectors, there was some storage of emergency supplies. At the more temporary railheads, supplies were unloaded directly from the railway cars to division transportation. Ordinarily, a one-day supply of rations was kept on hand at the railhead or at the refilling point (the refilling point sometimes coincided with the railhead, sometimes was located a short distance away) so that division trains could pick up their rations immediately on arrival without having to wait for that day's supply train.

Near the end of the war a system of army depots, particularly for ordnance, was developing. This permitted shipments in trainload lots to the army depots, and prompt delivery to the units. The shortage of cars often made it impossible to get small shipments of Class 3 supplies from the SOS depot to the unit quickly. Supply officers anticipated that the greatest drawback of the army depot system would be that, with supplies so easy to obtain, units might become careless and wasteful.

The pay-off of the whole complex supply system was in the delivery of needed supplies on time to the troops on the line whether they were in stabilized or in rapidly changing situations. A parallel aspect of

[13] Harbord, James G., *The American Army in France, 1917–1919*, p. 364.

logistics was the timely movement of the troops themselves to a threatened point to meet an enemy attack, or to an assembly area and a line of departure for an attack of their own. Here logistics, strategy, and tactics merged for the ultimate decision.

From the railheads supplies went forward by narrow-gauge railroad, motor trucks, mule-drawn and horse-drawn wagon, pack train, and by hand. The individual soldier went into battle carrying equipment which, though it had not become lighter since the Civil War, had become more complex. If the 50 to 70 pounds that he carried seemed a burden, perhaps he could gain some satisfaction in knowing that it was less heavy than in the other armies.

A railhead or refilling point might be practically adjacent to a division dump, or it might be as far as twenty-five miles to the rear. For longer hauls, two companies of the division supply train, operating under the direction of the division quartermaster, might be stationed at the railhead to bring up rations, forage, and other supplies each day in convoys of 3-ton trucks. Sometimes narrow-gauge railroads relieved the motor transportation. Units in the rear with transportation would pick up their supplies at the railheads. For the forward units convoys of some fourteen trucks took the supplies up at night; rations would be divided and loaded according to units, with issue slips prepared to reduce confusion in the night distribution. The greatest difficulty occurred when the troops were on the move. Then trucks might be on the road forty-eight hours before they could get back to the dump, and sometimes they could not find the units at all. Mule-drawn wagons sometimes carried the rations up to the kitchen areas. Whenever conditions permitted, the kitchens prepared hot meals,

and troops not on the firing line could come to the rear to eat. For the others hot food was carried to the trenches in marmite cans. Gas attacks frequently rendered food supplies useless, and then a call would go back for immediate resupply or the emergency rations kept in the trenches in gas-proof containers would be used. In offensive operations, the emergency rations frequently were used anyway—packed twenty-five rations in a galvanized iron box, they were easy to handle and required no elaborate cooking facilities.

Division ammunition trains set up ammunition dumps, and during active operations the trucks of their motor battalion and the wagons of their horse battalion were in almost constant use. Often they were pressed into service to haul rations and other supplies as well as ammunition. When roads became impassable, some units found it expedient to obtain burros and to send both ammunition and rations up by pack trains.

Ordnance resupply was ordinarily through the division mobile ordnance repair shops, where weapons were turned in for repair or replacement. When it was not possible to set up a complete shop near the combat units, a forward section might be set up within walking distance of the companies, with the machine shop some distance in the rear. A truck would bring up parts to the forward section daily and pick up weapons that could not be repaired there. Some commanders insisted on frequent inspection of weapons by Ordnance sergeants; if possible, the Ordnance sergeant detailed to each artillery regiment inspected all the guns of the regiment each day, and had all possible repairs made at the positions.

Clothing and other supplies as needed ordinarily went up with the rations if there was sufficient transportation. Emergency supplies of clothing had to be sent up after a heavy gas attack, but reissues of clothing generally were reserved for a time when troops could be brought back for baths and delousing. Intervals between those opportunities varied from a few days to several weeks.

An essential item that could not be overlooked in operations involving big armies was water supply—water for men and water for animals. Provisional engineer organizations had the responsibility of finding sources of water, operating purification facilities, piping water and storing it, and sending it up in tank trucks or tank cars on the narrow-gauge railroads to be distributed to water wagons or tanks for the units.

Battlefield Logistics

Of all the problems of logistics, the most serious at the battlefield as in the rear was transportation. Shortages of vehicles, shortages of horses, and bad road conditions militated against Pershing's determination to return to open warfare. The obstacles, however, were not so great that they could not be overcome, at least at critical times and places; and if the AEF never had but half the motor vehicles considered necessary, nonetheless, it was the truck and the key role it played which, more than any other single thing, characterized battlefield logistics of World War I in contrast to previous wars. At one time ambulances would be called in to deliver rations, and at another trucks would have to evacuate casualties. The long hours that vehicles had to be kept in operation meant hard work for maintenance men as well as for drivers.

The shortage of horses made the shortage of motor trucks more serious. In fact, the motorization of additional units, particularly field artillery, was stepped up in order to help overcome the shortage of horses, but it was hard to find either horses or trucks.

Even when trucks and horses were available, they could not always operate, for under heavy traffic, especially in bad weather, roads soon gave way, and trucks and wagons frequently bogged down. Offensive operations were likely to move over battlefields completely impassable for vehicles, which meant that road details had to be ready at critical points to keep roads in repair and to build new ones as they were needed. Had the entire Army been set to building roads, an adequate network could not have been built as fast as needed across some of the no man's lands; however, engineer units did manage to keep enough roads open to get supplies forward most of the time. In November 1918 some 28,000 men were at work on the roads in the army areas, and five engineer battalions were operating quarries to provide crushed stone. Across country torn by shell holes, plank roads sometimes were laid because they were quicker, even though more expensive and less permanent than stone fill.

The narrow-gauge railroad offered the best alternative to the truck and the road. A system of 60-cm. lines developed during the period of stabilized warfare proved invaluable in serving the forward areas when offensive operations started. By laying connections across no man's land to the enemy's system, the advancing Allied troops could be kept up with easily. Track could be made up in sections of ties and rails in advance and laid very rapidly. It was estimated that it took a detail of 60 men ten hours to build a quarter-mile of plank road (four meters wide), whereas as much as three miles of light railroad track was laid by 135 men in five hours. During their spring offensives in 1918, the Germans laid 60-cm. track alongside practically every important highway, and actually used the light railways to carry most of their supplies. Of the 1,400 kilometers of light railroads the AEF was operating at the time of the armistice, over half had been taken from the Germans. Powered with over 100 steam and 60 gasoline locomotives, these lines during October 1918 carried an average of 8,100 tons of supplies a day. Local units frequently put down light track (usually 40-cm.) to serve artillery positions, machine gun positions, and strongpoints. In these cases men or animals would move the small cars. All together the light railways did the work of several thousand motor trucks; more important, they could operate at times when the roads became impassable under heavy truck traffic and trucks could not be used at all.

Battlefield evacuation of the wounded, patterned after the system developed during the Civil War, had very different problems of application in the varying types of combat in France. Each division sanitary train had a field hospital section and an ambulance section which was authorized (but seldom issued in full) twelve mule-drawn ambulances and thirty-six motor ambulances. During the period of stabilized trench warfare, there were no serious problems: evacuation hospitals could be established in huts or buildings on a more or less permanent basis, and the relatively few casualties did not overtax facilities. In some cases the French handed over complete hospitals, with full equipment, to the American units relieving them. But when the great German offensives in the spring of 1918 pushed Allied positions back, and the Allied counteroffensive beginning in July kept moving

in the opposite direction, it became a different story. There were not enough hospitals or hospital trains, or ambulances, and rough rides to the rear and long waiting all too often then were the lot of the wounded man.

Salvage of matériel from the battlefield, using wagons and trucks from the division ammunition train or from wherever they could be obtained, turned out to be a major supply effort. Special details were pressed into this work after a battle had subsided. They would collect equipment and send it to the rear on returning ration trucks. After the battle of 14–18 July 1918 on the Marne, a detail of 600 replacements collected nearly 300 truckloads of equipment to be turned over to the salvage squad at the railhead at Chailly Boissy.

Saint-Mihiel

With the counteroffensive in the Aisne-Marne sector successfully under way, in the summer of 1918 Pershing returned to his project for forming a separate American army. Foch ultimately agreed to his proposal to make a limited attack with an American army against the Saint-Mihiel salient—on condition that the Americans would be ready to launch another offensive in the Meuse-Argonne sector by 25 September. While there was a concentration of American divisions in the Aisne-Marne region, American units in August 1918 were scattered all along the front from the Swiss border to the Channel. To assemble them into a single army north of Toul posed one of the great logistical undertaking of the war. On 11 August American divisions began moving by rail, by truck, by the motor busses that earlier had been pressed into service from the streets of Paris and London, and on foot to the area of the

SUPPLIES ON A CONGESTED ROAD IN FRANCE

newly formed American First Army.
Three divisions came from the British front,
four from the Vesle River front (Aisne-
Marne sector), two from the Vosges in the
extreme east, and three from training areas
in the vicinity of Chaumont; four already
were in the Saint-Mihiel region. On 12
September the First Army, with nine American divisions and four French divisions in
the line and three American divisions in
army reserve, attacked both sides and point
of the Saint-Mihiel salient.

Supply again could be based on the advance depot and regulating station at Is-
sur-Tille, though it still was a considerable
distance from the fighting front. Work on
a forward regulating station at Liffol-le-
Grand had been delayed during the weeks
of uncertainty as to exactly where the American front would be. For army service
units, air service and tank units, corps and
army artillery, and divisions moving up
in preparation for the Meuse-Argonne offensive; a regulating station was established
at Saint-Dizier, and to serve it, the intermediate depot at Gièvres once more was
designated an advance depot. When the
threat of German attack was no longer a
menace, supplies could be built up farther
forward to support the advance.

MULE HAULING FOOD TO THE FRONT ON A NARROW-GAUGE RAILROAD

Rains falling over the Saint-Mihiel battlefield added to the inevitable complication of supply. Mud on roads that would have been congested under the best of conditions held truck wheels firmly in grip, and lines of supplies backed up waiting for an engineer breakthrough. Engineers began laying railroad as soon as the attack began, and they widened a French one-meter line that had been laid in 1914, then left unused for four years. German light railways were taken over and roads built across the seas of mud. Since this was a limited objective attack, concluded within four days, the obstacles to supply did not become critical.

The Meuse-Argonne

Far more serious was the build-up and support of the Meuse-Argonne offensive. With his eyes open, Pershing accepted a commitment to launch within twenty-three days two great offensives in areas forty miles apart. Starting ten days before the Saint-Mihiel battle began, he had to concentrate 600,000 men, 2,700 guns, and 1,000,000 tons of supplies to launch a still greater operation thirteen days after the Saint-Mihiel attack. Logistical problems would have been a little simpler if the second American offensive could have been launched farther to the east, but the decision that it should be in the area forty miles west of Saint-Mihiel, between the Argonne Forest and the Meuse River, required a reorientation of supply lines. The Meuse-Argonne offensive was to be a part of a co-ordinated attack with the French Fourth Army on the left, aiming at Mézières and Sedan. Time and distance obviated the possibility of the divisions in the attack at Saint-Mihiel participating in the initial phase of the Meuse-Argonne.

Except for one division, actual movements of troops did not begin until the Saint-Mihiel attack was under way, and then every precaution had to be taken to preserve secrecy. Nine divisions were to be in the assault, but fifteen, including seven transferred from the Saint-Mihiel sector, were to be concentrated. A single division with its trains occupied nineteen miles of road space, and in this area where roads were few, where French divisions had to be relieved at the front and in reserve, where the French had to move up forces and supplies for their co-ordinated attack, and where movement had to be restricted to darkness, the logistical complications were unequaled. Still, all forces were in position at the appointed time, though all were grateful for one-day's postponement in the time for the attack. With the greatest artillery barrage Americans had ever fired they jumped off at dawn on 26 September against positions the enemy had held with little variation for nearly four years.

A railroad from Sainte-Menehould to Verdun paralleled the front and was the main route of supply. Railheads for all the forward divisions were established along this line; others were established on the lines running to the rear. All together, there were nineteen railheads served principally through the regulating station at Saint-Dizier. Only two standard-gauge railroads ran forward in the direction of the advance, one of them in the French zone, the other under enemy fire. This meant that the First Army had to rely on the narrow-gauge railroads running in the direction of Montfaucon and in the Argonne Forest which could be tied into the German system as the advance continued, and on the three roads which ran as far as the front lines. Across no man's land, roads would have to be built and tracks laid if the advance was to continue.

The 40,000 tons of artillery ammunition in place when the battle began had to be replenished by 12 to 14 daily trainloads. Between 26 September and 11 November, American artillery fired 4,214,000 rounds of ammunition. Divisions had to be brought out of the line and new ones sent in; materials for roads and railroads had to be brought up without interfering with regular supplies. In contrast to the army general depot that had been established at Lieusaint during the Château-Thierry operations, in the Meuse-Argonne each service established several depots and kept them well forward—24 ammunition depots, 12 ordnance, 9 quartermaster, 9 gasoline and oil, 8 water points, 7 chemical warfare, plus depots for medical, motor, tank, and signal supplies, and 34 evacuation hospitals, were set up. In the area 3,500 motor trucks and 93,000 animals, as well as 215 miles of light railways, ultimately were in operation.

Following the advance closely, engineers built a standard-gauge line from Aubréville through the Argonne to connect to a line at Apremont which ran northeastward to Grand Pré and they repaired sections of the Verdun-Sedan line as quickly as they were cleared of enemy fire. When new railheads were opened as far north as Dun-sur-Meuse and Châtel-Chéhéry, those to the rear served the reserve divisions.

Delivering supplies to the units on the battlefield was, aside from the actual fighting, the most difficult aspect of the whole Meuse-Argonne operation. The thousands of trucks and animals in use were but a fraction of what was thought to be needed. Pershing stripped the SOS of its trucks and animals—thus crippling operations at the ports and at construction projects—and he called men out of the SOS to run depots, repair vehicles, and build roads in the army area. The fact that he could do this was one of his justifications for keeping the SOS under his command.

Even if all the vehicles and animals called for had been available, it is difficult to see how many more of them could have moved across the morass of the battle zone. The whole area of no man's land was covered with interlocking shell holes and piles of debris. Infantrymen of the 4th Division in their initial attack carried boards from their trenches on which to cross the mud of the valley of Forges Creek. Pioneer units and engineers went to work building roads. They put in a plank road from Avocourt to Montfaucon. In many places they used sandbags and gravel—on one road alone they used 40,000 sandbags. It took three to five trains a day to bring in road-building materials, not to mention the six or seven trains a day for railway construction materials. The diarist of the 42d Division reported, "The condition of the roads is wretched. The orders are, 'guns up first, then ammunition for the guns, coffee and food later.' " [14]

Great activity went on in darkness. On every road behind the lines, a tangle of trucks and wagons would be trying to move forward with supplies. Ambulances carrying wounded to the rear had to wait for guns and ammunition to pass. Labor battalions were at work continuously trying to keep the roads passable, and ammunition companies were put to road building as well. Energetic officers fresh to the experience would hurry forward to break the traffic jam in front of them, disrupt even the semblance of a system, and assure the development of a half-dozen more tie-ups.

In the first phase of the offensive, many men went hungry. After consuming the two days of iron rations they carried, they were frequently without resupply. Rolling kitchens followed as closely as they could, but it was not possible very often to send hot meals forward to the fighting units. Details could go back to the ration dumps and pick up more iron rations, but then sometimes were unable to find their units when they returned. Hungry men in the advance searched dead comrades and enemy soldiers for rations.

As casualties mounted, the medical units were hard pressed to care for them. Sometimes it took six tired and weakened litter bearers to carry a man. Ambulances under heavy shellfire carried the wounded from aid stations to hospitals. Ten hospital trains a day evacuated wounded and sick men further to the rear.

On 10 October the American Second Army became operational, and on the 12th it took over a sector on the right of the First Army. On the same day the new regulating station at Liffol-le-Grand opened to serve it.

---

[14] Sherwood, *The Diary of a Rainbow Veteran,* p. 175.

ROLLING KITCHEN SET UP FOR MESS

Facilities

In terms of the Army's previous experience, the facilities and activities of the SOS in France were immense. In terms of requirements, many thought they were not nearly enough. At each of no less than 130 cities, towns and villages in nearly all parts of France from one to a dozen major activities for the support of the AEF were in operation.

Sites were chosen, presumably, according to the best places from which to support operations at the front, but often compromises had to be made. Dijon, for instance, could not be used as extensively as desired because the movement of troops through there to and from Italy created too much congestion.

Buildings were leased or requisitioned through arrangements with the French, or they were constructed. Negotiations with French authorities for use of the sites at first were long and tedious; however, the organization of periodic conferences later eased this situation. For construction projects it was necessary not only to get permission to use the land and to detail the terms of its lease, but also to have the whole construction plan approved, including arrangements for labor and materials.

Major construction completed before the

armistice included over 15,000 barracks whose combined length would be 285 miles; hospitals for nearly 146,000 beds, equivalent to 146 miles of wards; covered storage space amounting to nearly 22,000,000 square feet, or 500 acres; 947 miles of standard-gauge railroads, all of it in yards except for a six-mile double-track cutoff around Nevers which included a bridge 2,190 feet long across the Loire River; the pier, warehousing and switching facilities to accomodate the docking of ten vessels at Bassens; a 750-foot pier, 84 lighters, and 7 derrick barges at Saint-Loubès; large municipal water supply developments at such places as Brest, Saint-Nazaire, and in the Bordeaux region; storage tanks along the seacoast for 150,000 barrels of gasoline and oil; remount space for 30,000 animals and veterinary hospital space for 23,000 animals. Most of the lumber for this construction had to come from France, whose foresters carefully marked the trees for cutting. By October 1918, 91 sawmills were in operation, and by December they had produced nearly 190,000,000 board-feet of lumber, over 3,000,000 railroad ties, and more than 1,170,000 poles and pit props, not to mention 375 miles of cord wood for fuel.[15]

---

[15] Final Report, ACofS, G–4, GHQ, AEF *U.S. Army in the World War*, XIV, 70–71, 147–48, 223–25; *U.S. Army in the World War*, XV (Washington, 1948), 75–79; Report of the Military Board of Allied Supply, 2 vols. (Washington, 1924, 1925) II, 868–82, 910–21; Jacques Aldebert De Pineton, Comte de Chambrun, *The American Army in the European Conflict* (New York: The Macmillan Company, 1919), pp. 92–115, 342–50; Hagood, *The Services of Supply*, pp. 160–62, 340–42; Isaac Marcosson, *S.O.S., America's Miracle in France* (New York: John Lane Co., 1918), pp. 220–36, 289–92; William J. Wilgus, *Transporting the A.E.F. in Western Europe* (New York: Columbia University Press, 1931), pp. 290–302.

Summary

On 31 October 1918 the AEF had a strength of 81,800 officers, with 1,037,000 men in the zone of the armies, and 855,600 men in the rear (including combat replacements as well as service troops), together with 47,700 civilian workers, and 35,000 prisoners of war being used as laborers. It had 20,000 saddle horses, 94,000 draft animals, and 2,500 pack animals in the zone of the armies, and 25,000 saddle horses, 21,500 draft animals, and 87 pack animals in the rear. It had on hand 70,000,000 rations, including 15,500,000 in the zone of the armies, for the men, and 4,500,000 rations of forage for the animals. It had a total of nearly 30,000 trucks, 7,800 motor cars, and 13,700 motorcycles. The AEF was operating, partially, 6,000 miles of standard-gauge and 1,400 miles of narrow-gauge railroads; it had in operation 1,380 locomotives and 14,000 cars for standard-gauge, and 450 locomotives and 3,300 cars for narrow-gauge railroads. Its weapons included 1,400 pieces of heavy artillery, 1,890 pieces of field artillery, 1,362,000 rifles, 68,000 machine guns and automatic rifles, 1,000 trench mortars, and 240 tanks, and it had 868 airplanes and 79 balloons in the zone of the armies and 1,092 airplanes and 140 balloons in the depots and rear areas. Its ammunition supply included, in the zone of the armies, 122,400 rounds for heavy artillery, 2,500,000 rounds for field artillery, and 166,000,000 rounds for rifles and machine guns; in the rear areas, 310,800 rounds for heavy artillery, 6,470,000 rounds for field artillery, and 716,000,000 rounds of small arms ammunition. Hospitals at that time included 153 in the zone of the armies, with beds for 48,520 patients of which 30,241 were occupied; hospitals in the rear areas had a capacity of 224,330 beds of which 133,526 were occupied.[16]

Was all of this enough? Surely for some military leaders there is no such thing as enough. With millions of tons of supplies descending upon them, threatening to smother them, the cry always is for more. In World War I commanders feared that the armies, just freed from the immobility of trench warfare, were threatened by the weight of their supplies and, conditioned to a vast administrative structure and highly organized railway facilities, had become subject to further immobilization as soon as they ventured away from their previously developed communications.

In spite of the real or imagined shortages of most items, the logistical efforts of the AEF and of the Allies did prove to be sufficient to accomplish the task at hand. If men at the front sometimes went hungry, if ammunition sometimes ran low, if evacuation of the wounded sometimes was less than satisfactory, it more than likely was not the result of any general shortage of supplies in the area or even of transportation, but the result of enemy action and the inherent difficulties of getting supplies forward and casualties rearward during intensive combat. On a visit to the 1st, 2d, 3d, 4th, and 28th Divisions a week after the launching of the Aisne-Marne counteroffensive, General Hagood found all the division commanders satisfied with the logistical support they were receiving from the SOS.

Nevertheless, the success of battle seems to have concealed some serious deficiencies. Yes, supplies and facilities proved to be sufficient for the task at hand; but what if the war had continued several months more?

Then this is not so sure. A few more weeks or months of combat as extensive as that in the Meuse-Argonne—and plans were afoot for the Second Army to launch another offensive in mid-November—might have threatened the entire system. It is unlikely that available transportation was enough to continue for long the delivery of supplies to the front at the rate they were being consumed, and even had that been possible, reserves might have been near depletion before new shortages of ocean shipping could have been overcome. Many more weeks of casualties at the rate they were suffered in the Meuse-Argonne (in six weeks the United States had 120,000 killed and wounded, or nearly 50 percent of its battle casualties for the whole war) would have overwhelmed the U.S. evacuation and hospitalization system, which in turn would have further complicated the movement of men and supplies.

Even the organization for logistics had not been completely settled at the time of the armistice. Pershing had been able to hold to his position that the Services of Supply should be under his command and not under a co-ordinate commander under the War Department though logic was not necessarily altogether on his side on this point. Relations between GHQ and SOS continued to be vague. There was a certain rivalry between the commanding general at Tours and the G–4 at Chaumont, and control of activities in the Advance Section was always divided. It would have helped if an army rear boundary had been drawn to mark off the army area from the Advance Section. It might have helped more if the suggestion had been taken to move G–4 and G–1 completely to Tours. As it was, a certain "layering" of headquarters existed, particularly during the period before field armies were organized.

---

[16] Report of Military Board of Allied Supply, I, 48–62.

In the general picture transportation remained the key. At first the critical item was ocean shipping. Then it was the unloading of ships. Then it was inland transportation—mostly a lack of equipment, but, again, the organization for co-ordination and control was unsatisfactory much of the time. Contributing to the difficulty was the lack of service personnel that resulted largely from the emergency shipment overseas of infantry troops during the spring of 1918 to help meet the threat of the great German offensives.

In a way, all aspects of logistics in the AEF were interrelated. Many of the shortcomings could be attributed to lack of experience and to a corresponding lack of advance planning, and to a certain multiplier factor which caused a deficiency in one area or activity to run through many other areas and activities, magnifying existing deficiencies or creating new ones. But experience of the kind required was experience that neither the AEF nor any other army had, for the support of such a force at such a distance from its homeland and from its base ports was a pioneer effort in 1917 and 1918.

CHAPTER XXIV

Demobilization

When the armistice of 11 November 1918 at last stilled the guns all along the Western Front, the first thought of Americans on both sides of the Atlantic was to "get the boys home by Christmas." The gigantic industrial and military machine of the United States, only beginning to run in high gear, suddenly had to be thrown into reverse. For months the cry had been for more of everything; suddenly the cry was to stop everything—except the ships and trains to bring the men home.

To the Rhineland

The immediate logistical problem for the AEF after the armistice was the movement and supply of the American forces designated for occupation to their assigned area around Coblenz.

After allowing German troops six days to evacuate the immediate front, Allied forces on 17 November began a co-ordinated advance all along the line from the Channel to the Swiss border. In the American zone, the newly formed Third Army, designated the American Army of Occupation, controlled the advance. Marching two corps abreast, the divisions moving on parallel roads when possible, the Third Army advanced across Lorraine and across Luxembourg to reach the German frontier on 23 November. While on this move, men marched an average of about twelve miles a day.

On 9 December, cavalry patrols reached the Rhine at Remagen, and on the 13th units began crossing the Rhine. On the 19th the American forces, now numbering nearly 240,000 officers and men, completed the occupation of their assigned sector of the Coblenz bridgehead.

The opening of railroads followed immediately upon the advance of the troops, and as soon as railheads could be opened near the division zones of advance, the supply problem eased. During the march, divisions drew supplies from as many as nine successive railheads. Trucks hauled rations in bulk from the railheads to refilling points where ration details unloaded them and broke them down for issue to the units.

Expeditions to Russia

Another area of activity involving American participation after the armistice was the intervention in Russia. The forces involved were small, but some of the logistical problems were unique in American experience.

Archangel

After a small Allied detachment of British, French, and Serbians had landed at Murmansk in the spring of 1918 for the stated purpose of facilitating the evacuation of Czechs (liberated prisoners in Russia) reported moving across Russia, President Wilson yielded to Allied pressure for American participation in a somewhat larger expedition to Archangel. In the meantime an Allied force, including fifty American sailors, sailed from Murmansk to Archangel, where it seized that city and overthrew the local Soviet.

On 27 August an expedition made up of an infantry regiment, a battalion of engineers, a field hospital company, and an ambulance company, all drawn from the newly arrived 85th Division, sailed from Newcastle-on-Tyne, England, for Archangel. Reinforcements of 500 officers and men sailed a month later. The Czechs had been turned back from their northward march in June, but there was still the danger that military supplies stored at Murmansk and Archangel might fall into German hands and that those northern ports might be used as submarine bases. The fighting that broke out, however, was against bolshevist forces seeking to re-establish control over the area.

The American contingent arrived at Archangel on 4 September and became a part of the Allied forces under British command. The whole operation was commanded by the British; American forces were British equipped, clothed, and fed. U.S. troops were scattered along a 450-mile front, from Onega on the southwest arm of the White Sea to Ust Padenga to the south, and Pinega to the east, with some outposts as far as 200 miles from the base at Archangel. Although the port at Murmansk was open the year round, the port of Archangel was ice-bound from October to May. The single railroad running south from Archangel was of only limited use in bringing up supplies. Long nights, heavy snows, and severe cold added incalculable complications. During the winter, supplies went to

the outposts by convoys of one-horse *travois* or sleds.

Siberia

Meanwhile a rather larger American force was participating in the Allied intervention in eastern Siberia. After much soul-searching during the summer of 1918, President Wilson finally agreed to co-operate with the Japanese in this venture. Earlier the Western Allies had been interested in the project mainly with a view to supporting Czechs and friendly Russians in restoring a second front against Germany. But this seemed out of the question since the Bolsheviki in western Russia had adopted a hostile attitude toward any such scheme, and the Czechs were moving eastward across Siberia. What finally brought the matter to a head was the capture of Vladivostok by one group of Czechs, while another group still was making its way eastward from central Siberia. The United States had so identified itself with the new Czechoslovak Republic that ties of sentiment alone were enough to recommend support for the Czechs then trying to complete their anabasis across Siberia. Indeed, General March said that there was nothing but sentiment to support such an operation; on the grounds of logistical difficulties, the inadvisability of diverting men and resources from Western Europe and the lack of any prospect for military decisiveness, he opposed the whole thing from the start but was overruled.

On 3 August 1918 Secretary of War Baker met Maj. Gen. William S. Graves, then commanding the 8th Division at Camp Frémont, California, at Kansas City to give him his instructions as commander of the American Expeditionary Force, Siberia.

The purpose was to aid the Czechoslovaks, guard military stores at Vladivostok, and to help the Russians, if they desired, in their efforts at self-government and self-defense —and to do this without intervening or taking sides in Russian politics. All Allied forces in Siberia were under Japanese command, but General Graves never would permit any action on the part of American forces that might be construed as being in violation of his instructions.

Actually, the problems of cold-weather logistics proved to be less difficult than had been imagined. American forces were stationed mainly along the Trans-Siberian Railroad east of Lake Baikal, on the southern extension of the railroad from Khabarovsk, and at Vladivostok. Although the temperature at Vladivostok fell to as low as 34° below zero (F.) and reached 46° below at Chita where the mean temperature for January was 18° below zero, the air generally was clear and dry and the sensible temperature was rather higher. The snow was light enough that wheeled vehicles could operate throughout the winter. The American soldiers came well supplied with winter clothing, they found good shelter, and they generally had good food; hence they suffered little because of the weather.

There was no special difficulty in shipping supplies from Manila to Vladivostok, which was kept open all winter with the aid of ice-breakers, and then by rail to the various troop locations. Early in 1919 the Russian Railway Service Corps, made up of American railroad men who had been in the area for over a year assisting Russian railroad operations, began to supervise railroad activities on the Trans-Siberian and Chinese-Eastern Railroads within the zone of Allied operations.

A major concern of American logistics was the delivery of munitions, supplies and food to the czarist provisional government of Admiral Aleksandr V. Kolchak, then taking its turn at trying to overthrow the Bolsheviks. As far as General Graves could see, the original reasons given for the intervention had evaporated. The only real purpose seemed to be to oppose the spread of bolshevism, yet Graves had serious misgivings on this score since it seemed a violation of his instructions not to take sides in Russian politics.

Clashes with armed partisans along the railroads resulted in some thirty-six battle deaths in the Siberian area for American soldiers after the armistice had been signed in Europe. Remaining longer than the Archangel expedition, this force saw two Siberian winters. American units withdrew, and sailed for Manila between 17 January and 20 April 1920.

Return of the AEF

Although Secretary Baker at first favored troop demobilization according to occupational specialty in order to ease the shock on the national economy, the War Department finally adopted a plan for demobilization by units—divisions overseas preferably would be returned in order of departure from the United States. The unit demobilization plan was adopted as the one best calculated to preserve the units needed for the Army's continuing missions, including the supply and maintenance of the forces overseas and the logistical activities necessary to bring all the men home, but even these units had been considerably altered by the time they reached their home stations.

In France, after a few days of hesitation, Pershing released all troops not needed for the Army of Occupation or its support. This meant that something over half of the AEF could return to the United States as soon as transportation could be found. It took about a month to get facilities and shipping ready so that embarkation could begin. The chief quartermaster, charged with the task of preparing facilities and organizing embarkation, designated Brest, Saint-Nazaire, and Bordeaux as the principal ports of embarkation; of these Brest turned out to be by far the most important.

At or near the ports, small rest camps for arriving troops had to be turned into huge embarkation camps for departing troops. Camp Pontanezen at Brest had served Napoleon's troops with barracks for 1,500 men. The reception and rest camps set up there during World War I could accommodate about 50,000 men. For embarkation the camp was expanded to take 80,000 men. Use of Pontanezen and the other camps did not await completion, and as construction went on during the rainy winter months of 1918–19, so did embarkation. Many returning soldiers carried away a lasting impression of Pontanezen as a sea of mud in which they were stuck while waiting for their ships. By spring when most of the construction was completed—and when shelter was less needed—the camps, long rows of tar-papered, rough, board buildings connected by boardwalks, had become more livable.

The biggest camp of all was the embarkation center built on the site of the AEF's classification and replacement camp at Le Mans, where the capacity of the old camp—about 120,000 troops—was nearly doubled after the armistice, and the troop population never fell below 100,000 men until the late spring of 1919. The camp was used as a divisional center, and most of the combat divisions stopped there for reorganization and processing before going to Brest or Saint-Nazaire to board ships.

Even before the armistice, American leaders had anticipated the problem of finding ships to bring the AEF home. Some expressed concern that British ships would be withdrawn from American service, and that while American ships were taxed with bringing troops home the British would recapture commercial routes and markets. Aside from the long-range considerations of commercial competition, England faced immediate tasks of returning British colonial and dominion troops to their homelands and of importing foodstuffs and other essential goods for the civilian population. As expected, England withdrew its shipping almost at once, as did France and Italy. Brig. Gen. Frank T. Hines, chief of the Embarkation Service (in December combined with the Inland Traffic Service to form the Transportation Service under the leadership of Hines) moved just as promptly to make up the difference.

Troopships left at the disposal of the Army (American-flag vessels) after the armistice had a single-lift capacity of 112,-000 men. Under war conditions they had been able to transport about 100,000 men a month across the Atlantic. Now that the convoy system could be abandoned, this monthly rate could be increased by perhaps 50 percent, but even at that rate it would have taken over a year to return the AEF.

With no further demands for large shipments of guns and ammunition, animals, vehicles, and other war materials, the obvious solution was to convert as many as possible of the large fleet of American cargo ships to troop carriers. Conversion required a large outlay of money and time, but in the long run it saved both. Shipyards congested with the construction of new vessels on order by the Emergency Fleet Corporation, were soon freed for the task of conversion. Averaging forty-one days per ship, fifty-eight of the fastest and largest cargo ships were fitted with the necessary bunks, galleys, messing areas, and sanitation facilities, and put into service as troop passenger ships. This project alone more than doubled the capacity of the troop-carrying fleet.

The Navy installed bunks and other facilities on 14 battleships and 10 cruisers, giving a total capacity of 28,600 troops, and diverted them to the transatlantic ferry. Ten large German vessels, idle for nearly five years at their German berths, were turned over to the United States, and after quick repairs were put into service. With the aid of passage obtained on British commercial liners and available American transports, some 70,000 American soldiers stationed in Great Britain landed in the United States within six weeks after the signing of the armistice. Finally, General Hines managed to charter 33 passenger ships from Italian, French, Spanish, and Dutch owners. By 23 June 1919 the United States' troop-carrying fleet was bigger by 40 ships than the entire fleet of American and Allied troopships available to the United States before the armistice. With a total of 174 vessels having single-lift capacity of 419,000 troops, embarkations from France reached a peak of 368,000 for the month of June 1919— 60,000 more than ever embarked from the United States in a single month.

Industrial Demobilization

An even more complex matter than the return of the troops was that of the concurrent industrial demobilization. When the armistice was signed, there were outstand-ing some 30,000 War Department contracts and agreements which, on completion, would involve an expenditure of about $7.5 billion. Contracts containing a termination clause presented no special problem. Most of them could be terminated and settled quickly on the basis, generally, of allowing payment for all finished articles and reimbursement for expenditures on work in progress, plus up to 10 percent of these costs for the use of capital and services, but without allowance for prospective profits, as provided in the contracts themselves. These contracts, however, were just the beginning, for only since 7 September had there been a requirement to include a standard termination clause in all contracts; therefore a great number of outstanding contracts contained no such provision.

The problem, then, was to negotiate termination agreements that would be accepted as amendments to contracts having no termination provisions.

Conceivably, the War Department could have simply canceled all contracts, but this would have worked obvious hardships not only on the individual producers but on the economy as a whole, not to mention the unmanageable number of claims that would have gone to the claims court. Instead, contractors were asked to suspend production pending preparation of termination schedules and negotiation of termination agreements. When worked out, the schedules and agreements frequently permitted resumption of some production so that there would be a more or less gradual tapering off. The bases of settlement generally followed the policies previously established in the standard termination clauses.

Further serious problems of settlement arose when the Comptroller of the Treasury issued a ruling shortly after the armistice

AEF TROOPS, HOMEWARD BOUND

which forbade payment for unfinished work under agreements that had not been reduced to writing in proper legal form. This meant that for two broad categories of contractors no settlement was possible at all. The first included those who held written contracts that were considered invalid because of some technical deficiency. The most important of this group were the "proxy contracts," which had been signed on behalf of the government by officers who had been appointed by contracting officers to act as their deputies, and so had not received the necessary delegation of authority from the Secretary of War himself. The second category comprised those for whom no formal contract had been drawn. In the interest of cutting red tape and getting

production started as quickly as possible without waiting for the formal document, a number of officers had made out direct purchase orders; many others had allowed letters of intent, or even oral agreements, to stand as binding agreements pending the drawing of a formal contract. Accepting these on good faith, businessmen had often hurried forward their production without further delay. Then the armistice and the Treasury's ruling caught them.

Some obvious injustices were so numerous that Congress finally came to the rescue with an act known as the Dent Law, approved 2 March 1919, which authorized the Secretary of War to settle all contracts, informal as well as formal, which could be shown to have been entered into in good faith—with the proviso that no payment could be made for prospective profits. Anticipating passage of the Dent Law, the War Department already had negotiated a large number of settlements that only awaited the approval of the act for signature and execution. The three to four months' delay undoubtedly created hardship for many contractors, but thereafter settlements proceeded at a reasonable pace.

In order to settle the invalid contracts under the Dent Law, they were divided into two classes. The first was composed of those for which there was written evidence, whether a faulty formal contract or some kind of correspondence or memoranda. These went through the regular procedure for final approval by the War Claims Board. The second class consisted of those agreements which were at least in part oral. Because they required the taking of testimony, these cases went to the Board of Contract Adjustment. When the terms of an agreement had been established, the Board of Contract Adjustment either referred the contract to the proper district board for settlement, or itself determined the amount due and issued an award. Some 7,000 claims were filed under the terms of the Dent Law.

In the process of reconverting war industry to a peacetime status, the main considerations were: the impact on the domestic economy; the additional production, if any, desirable to contribute to adequate reserves; and to what extent and in what ways facilities and machinery should be retained for an industrial reserve. The general policy was to allow completion of most items on which work had begun, to permit a tapering-off process in most plants, and to retain some of the facilities in reserve.

Surplus Property Disposal

With the abrupt termination of hostilities, the Army found itself with vast quantities of supplies on hand for which there was no foreseeable use, and leaders in Europe as well as in America faced the problem of what should be saved and what should be disposed of. For the Army the problem was chiefly one of comparing maintenance costs and obsolescence with possible future requirements. Any really accurate answers could be found only with the benefit of omniscient planners who might have precise information on the future. As timing is one of the most difficult problems of industrial mobilization—when to standardize certain models, and when to go into full production on certain items—so it is in demobilization. In each case it is not a simple problem of obsolescence versus quantity; it is more complex than that. Whether obsolete or not it may actually cost a great deal more to hold a given piece of equipment in storage and to keep it in good repair than to sell or even abandon that equipment and to buy a replacement several years later. The question, and it was an unanswerable one, was: how long will this equipment have to be stored and maintained before it is needed again?

If the property was held in storage, the cost might add up to more than the cost of buying new equipment later; if sold at nominal rates, it would tend to depress the market, which would bring criticism from affected merchants. If the property was destroyed, abandoned, or allowed to deteriorate, government officials would be blamed for waste. As it turned out, some equipment did accrue storage costs exceeding its value; some did depress markets in various places; some did waste away; and some became involved in fraudulent transactions.

Liquidation of Property Overseas

Initially the question was one of retaining sufficient supplies for the AEF, and of allowing for a possible resumption of hostilities. The policy adopted, then, was to maintain no war reserves of supplies that could be obtained on the open market within thirty days; to maintain a sufficient reserve of those supplies which required more than thirty days but less than six months for procurement for expansion of the peace army into a war army with complete initial equipment; to retain a six-months' supply for the war army of supplies requiring more than six months but less than a year for procurement, and a year's supply for support of the war army for those items requiring over a year to obtain. This definition of reserve requirements also provided the definition of surplus. All above the quantities needed for those reserves and current maintenance were to be sold.

When hostilities ceased, Edward R. Stettinius already had been in Europe for several months as special representative of the Secretary of War in making contract adjustments. He continued this work immediately after the signing of the armistice, and he became a member, with General Dawes and Col. John A. Hull, of the Advisory Liquidation Board which General Harbord appointed near the end of November. Harbord also appointed a General Sales Agent, Brig. Gen. Charles R. Krauthoff, to begin arranging for the sale of surplus property. In February 1919 the War Department established the United States Liquidation Commission under the chairmanship of Edwin B. Parker, with Dawes of the AEF continuing as a member, to supervise the settlement of all contracts and other claims and property sales in Europe. Congress passed supporting legislation in March.

An inventory of AEF installations indicated that surplus property with a value of some $1.5 billion (the Army never depreciated property, no matter how old) was on hand. The lack of shipping, when all available ships were being used for returning the men, and the lack of any need for most of the property in the United States made it desirable to dispose of the greater part of it in Europe. About 850,000 tons of equipment—mostly artillery and road-making machinery—was shipped to the United States. All the rest went up for sale in Europe.

Since most of the property was located in France, the problem of disposal centered there. Numerous complications developed in French claims for port dues for the use of the ports and charges for the use of French railroads, which had to be balanced against the use of American rolling stock and train crews. Furthermore, the French insisted that import duties that had been waived on all goods destined for use by the AEF would have to be paid on any goods now sold to private purchasers. Moreover, goods sold outside France could hardly be moved on the badly deteriorated railroads. Obviously, the best solution was to negotiate a bulk sale of all remaining property to the French Government at the earliest possible moment. This was done during the summer of 1919, and the bulk sale was concluded on 1 August by which various claims were canceled and the French Government agreed to pay $400 million in 10-year, interest-bearing bonds for all fixed and designated movable property remaining in France. A further general settlement of claims followed in November, covering transactions on both sides of the Atlantic, which resulted in a small net balance in favor of the United States.

Sale of Surplus Property in the United States

The sale of surplus property in the United States was rather more complicated than were sales abroad, principally because there was no other government to whom a bulk sale in place could be made as had been done in France. Moreover, the amount to be sold in the United States was greater. According to rough estimates, surplus war supplies in the Army inventory in the United States on 11 November 1918 had a procurement value of about $2 billion—about $700 million more than that in the inventory of the AEF. The tapering off of industry in the next several weeks added several hundred million dollars worth to the total, and all this does not take into account real estate and facilities to be disposed of.

Actual sale of surplus property continued to be the responsibility of the respective supply bureau that had procured it, but all sales activities were under the supervision of the newly established Sales Branch of the Division of Purchase, Storage, and Traffic. With the exception of some sales made to foreign companies and governments, the Sales Branch did no direct selling.

After the threat to the domestic market had eased somewhat, Congress on 29 July 1919 authorized the War Department to enter into retail sales of food, clothing, and household supplies. The first attempt was made by mail, through the post offices. Local postmasters were to receive orders and payment and to send in consolidated requi-

sitions, but this was beyond the experience of most of the postmasters, and the system broke down. A couple of months later the War Department set up a system whereby stores in various parts of the country (25 at first, finally 77) could sell surplus goods over the counter. Prices were set at 80 percent of the prevailing price. The stores did fairly well, but people were not willing to go to the inconvenience of seeking them out for the 20 percent savings on goods that might not turn out to be exactly what they wanted.

The Army took its greatest financial loss in the disposal of surplus buildings and grounds. The greatest value of the camps and cantonments was in the labor that had gone into their construction and in their utility for military purposes. The price obtained for materials salvaged from the sites could be but a small fraction of the construction cost. Further loss could be assumed from the fact that most of the sites had been leased rather than purchased, and what had been improvements for the Army's use now represented damages from the owner's point of view.

In view of the great loss to be taken, and in view of the need of such costly facilities in great haste in the event of another general mobilization, it might have been wise for the Army to have retained most of the major camps and cantonments on a standby basis. It is true that maintenance over the years would have been costly, but reconstruction under emergency conditions might have been more costly. However, the basic question was not simply one of maintenance versus reconstruction, it was the extent to which these facilities could contribute to rapid mobilization, and thus to general military preparedness.

The sixteen National Guard camps and a large number of special purpose camps had been tent camps, so that they had only a fraction of the buildings of a cantonment. In a number of instances storage buildings and hospitals were set aside. Otherwise all of the National Guard camps and most of the special purpose camps were condemned for salvage. Within a year 14 National Guard camps, 3 embarkation camps, 16 special and regular training camps, 4 flying fields, 4 hospitals, and various small buildings had been disposed of for about $4,215,-000, where the original cost of construction at the National Guard camps alone had been about six times that much. Camp Beauregard in Louisiana, which had cost $4,300,000 brought $43,000 in salvage recovery, and Camp Hancock in Georgia which cost $6,000,000 brought $75,000. The others realized only slightly better amounts. Yet, any price at all was net gain for the Army, for the facilities were completely useless; the investment had been made to provide training and other facilities for troops in the shortest possible time, not to realize a return on sales. The proper balance between immediate and long-range economic considerations, and between financial cost and the maintenance of mobilization readiness still had not been determined; however, the pattern that had come to characterize the American tradition was clear: short-term economies generally should prevail over hoped-for long-term economies, and economy in general should prevail over military readiness, and in demobilization speed should prevail over all.[1]

Summary

In their own contemporary appraisals of their total effort in World War I, Americans frequently were given to an extreme self-consciousness and a certain sentimentality which perhaps betrays a sense of inferiority in their determination to show how well all elements of the AEF did in comparison with their Allies, and how the Americans were more than a match for the best troops of Imperial Germany. It was "American manhood" that was being spent, and writers were at almost as much pains to establish the equality of American fighting men with the veterans of France and Great Britain as with "the best that the Kaiser could send against them." In the same way, American industry was held up for comparison, and victory was seen as being as much a triumph of Yankee industrial ingenuity as it was of the bravery of the righteous on the battlefield.

In those protestations there was much truth, and if they carried a ring of exaggerated sentiment calculated to overcome responses of incredulity perhaps it was because the accomplishments themselves were almost beyond belief for even the most experienced observers. A German staff estimate shortly after the United States entered the war told the world that the United States could not equip and transport to Europe within a year an army of over 500,-000 men. In December 1917 a War Department estimate concluded that no more than 1,030,000 men could be landed in France by October 1918, and even as late as March 1918 this estimate had been increased only to 1,088,000 men, while studies at Pershing's headquarters indicated that a more realistic figure would be 771,000 men by 1 September. But on 1 July the War Department could announce that the first million men had sailed; and a second million would land within the next four months. No such movement of troops, in

---

[1] Crowell and Wilson, "How America Went to War," *Demobilization . . . 1918–1920*, pp. 256–68.

size of force transported over so great a distance in so short a time, had ever before been accomplished. Forty-two over-size divisions moved to France; 28 engaged in battle; and the equivalent of another 22 divisions manned the bases and lines of communication of the Services of Supply. On 1 April 1918, the Germans held a rifle superiority of 300,000. Thanks to the expeditious arrival of the Americans, by November the Allies had a superiority of over 600,000.

Still, it is not quite accurate to suggest that the United States had equipped and transported an army of 2,000,000 men to Europe in less than nineteen months. That army could not have been moved without the heavy contribution of Allied (mostly British) shipping and it could not have been made effective in time without the ordnance Great Britain and France made available.

The major factors limiting the American war effort were: (1) availability of ocean shipping for troops as well as for cargo, (2) production of artillery, and (3) commitments of U.S. industry to supply both finished products and raw materials for the Allied countries.

The rate of manpower mobilization for the initial phase of World War I actually was less than that for the Civil War or even, so far as it went, for the Spanish-American War. Once more there was the belated recognition that manpower was not the primary element in speedy mobilization for modern war. Assistant Secretary of War Crowell noted: "The war taught us that America can organize, train, and transport troops of a superior sort at a rate which leaves far behind any practicable program for the manufacture of munitions. It upset the previous opinion that adequate military preparedness is largely a question of trained man power." [2]

The total outlay of the War Department during the war amounted to some $16 billion, and allowing for the value of real assets acquired, recovery from the sale of surplus, and other returns, direct costs for the Army were at least $8 billion. The cost of ordnance alone to equip what was to be the first 5,000,000 men brought into the Army was equal to half the total funds the nation appropriated from the First Continental Congress to the declaration of war in April 1917. The list of standard items in the Army's supply system grew from 20,000 items in 1917 to 120,000 in 1919. [3]

The tremendous upsurge in the expenditure of artillery ammunition is an indication not only of the improvement in guns, but also a testimony to industrial production and to the improved methods of supply in the field. Although the artillery ammunition expenditure of the Union Army was by far the greatest up to that time, and required an unprecedented industrial mobilization, the 1,950,000 rounds that Union forces fired in the year ending 30 June 1864 is to be compared with the 8,100,000 rounds the American forces fired in the year ending 10 November 1918—and the British and French forces each fired nearly ten times that amount. Union forces at Gettysburg fired 32,700 rounds of artillery ammunition in three days; in four days at Saint-Mihiel the AEF fired 1,093,200 rounds.

---

[2] Crowell and Wilson, "How America Went to War," *The Armies of Industry I,* p. xxii.

[3] Crowell and Wilson, "How America Went to War," *Demobilization,* pp. 315–21; *Armies of Industry I,* pp. 32–33; *Armies of Industry II,* p. 661.

At the time of the armistice the strength of the American force in France exceeded that of the British, and it is likely that if the war had continued another year the American forces would have been larger than the French. At the beginning of 1918 the AEF held but 1 percent of the battle line of the Western Front; by November it held 21 percent. In war production the major contribution of the United States was in rifles, which exceeded the production of either France or Great Britain; machine guns and automatic rifles, in which American production exceeded the British; smokeless powder, which exceeded the combined production of the principal Allied powers; rifle and machine gun ammunition, whose production was almost as great as the French; and high explosives, in which American production was about half that of the British and the French.

The full impact of the American war effort is to be guaged in terms of what "would have been" had the war continued through 1919. If that had been the case, and if the anticipated shipping and supply shortages of the winter of 1919 could have been overcome without serious setback, then by late 1919 the AEF in France would have numbered 4,000,000 men supplied almost wholly, with the exception of artillery, from American sources delivered by American-built ships, and having adequate motor and animal transportation. Surely this prospect as well as the grim battles of 1918 weighed heavily in the German decision to end the war in 1918.

The American potential to make war far from home perhaps was the most important revelation of World War I. For the future, the big question would be whether American planning would reflect the war experience by emphasizing the importance to military preparedness of maintaining matériel reserves and industrial mobilization plans. Whether the clear trend toward increased motorization and mechanization would relieve or complicate the logistical problems remained to be seen. Consumption of supplies during the war had been beyond anything previously imagined, but the stabilization of the front had permitted the organization of a supply system which made that rate of consumption possible. For all the modern advances, the horse rather than the gasoline engine still dominated the supply lines. As was later pointed out, the greatest single class of supplies shipped by the British to France was hay and oats—5,439,000 tons, as compared to 759,000 tons of gasoline and oil. It was argued that complete motorization of local transportation and the widespread use of combat vehicles would restore mobility to the battlefield, and that requirements for hay and oats and harness and veterinary stores, and for moving the animals themselves, would be relieved. But motorized mobility would bring with it demands for other supplies, and for new ways to keep up with those demands. Whatever the trend of war in the future, the United States had assured itself a measure of involvement that would be almost unavoidable, for it had revealed the greatest war-making capacity that the world had ever seen.[4]

---

[4] For sources upon which Part III is based see Bibliography, pages 717–23.

PART FOUR

LOGISTICS OF GLOBAL WARFARE

CHAPTER XXV

Logistical Organization and Planning, 1920–1945

Postwar and Prewar Reorganization

The form the General Staff and the War Department assumed after World War I bore the unmistakable imprint of the Pershing organization of the American Expeditionary Force, but was adapted to the wartime organization of the War Department itself, and grafted onto the bureau system. Still another element in postwar reorganization was Assistant Secretary of War Benedict Crowell's conception of the proper division of civilian and military authority in supply activities.

Crowell believed that the General Staff had no business in the procurement and production of military supplies. The General Staff, he thought, should restrict its interest in production matters to the military aspects, and the Assistant Secretary should control the industrial aspects without reference to the General Staff. He considered that the staff's function in this area was to determine the Army's requirements and to supervise distribution of finished items; but that the purchase, the production, the contacts with industry should be left to civilian officials schooled in the language and methods of industry. The wartime arrangement by which the Assistant Secretary had worked through the Purchase, Storage, and Traffic Division had been one of only legal expediency, and Crowell feared that continuation of that system in the permanent establishment might lead to General Staff control over the production of supplies, and might in time of emergency lead to conditions as chaotic as the independent bureau system had been. Secretary of War Baker, while sympathetic to the idea of civilian control over procurement, opposed the idea of assigning this responsibility by law to the Assistant Secretary. He would have preferred that it be assigned to the Secretary who then might retain it himself, or delegate it to one of his assistants. Nevertheless, Crowell's opinion prevailed pretty largely in the National Defense Act of 1920, which charged the Assistant Secretary of War with "supervision of the procurement of all military supplies and other business of the War Department pertaining thereto." The law did not provide for a Munitions Department under the Assistant Secretary as Crowell had hoped it would, but it did assign to the Assistant Secretary responsibility for economic mobilization planning.

Three new branches—Air Service, Chemical Warfare Service, and Finance—were established. Infantry, Cavalry, and Field Artillery chiefs were given status equal to that of bureau chiefs (the chief of the Coast Artillery had had this status since 1908).

A reorganization of the General Staff in 1921 under General Pershing as Chief of Staff and General Harbord (who recently had headed a board of officers to study War Department organization) as his deputy, brought it into conformity with the staff organization Pershing had found so successful in the American Expeditionary Force. It divided the General Staff into five major divisions, each under an assistant chief of staff: Personnel (G–1), Military Intelligence (G–2), Operations and Training (G–3), Supply (G–4), and War Plans Division (WPD). The War Plans Division was to prepare war plans, and in time of war provide the nucleus for a GHQ to take the field, presumably with the Chief of Staff as commander. The new organization further strengthened the position of the Assistant Secretary of War. Whereas the War Department orders of the previous year had implied that he would operate through the General Staff, it now appeared that he was to exercise an independent supervisory authority. Thereafter the supply bureaus would report directly to the Assistant Secretary on matters of procurement and economic mobilization, although they would continue to report to the General Staff (G–4) on other supply matters. Curiously enough, though General Harbord had been commanding general of the Services of Supply in France, he made no recommendation for a comparable organization in the War Department.

The 1921 organization of the War Department and the General Staff remained essentially unchanged until World War II. In July 1940 a General Headquarters was activated to supervise training of field forces, and potentially to serve as the staff of the field commander (the Chief of Staff) in the event of war operations. Contrary to earlier assumptions, the War Plans Division remained intact as a major division of the General Staff. In 1941 the War Department created the Army Air Forces as an independent command on a level with GHQ. In the meantime, Secretary of War Henry L. Stimson had obtained a change in the National Defense Act to assign procurement responsibility to the Secretary with authority to delegate it to any of his assistants. Stimson also obtained authorization to appoint an Under Secretary of War. He elevated Assistant Secretary Robert P. Patterson to the new post in July 1940, and delegated to him the duties of supervising procurement. As Assistant Secretary in 1939, Louis Johnson had maintained a staff of about 50 officers, and a year later the total of officers and civilians in his office was but 181. Under Secretary Patterson went directly into operations, and soon he had a staff of 1,200 officers and civilians working for him, while the total number in the office of the Assistant Chief of Staff, G–4, was approximately 280.

Under the procedures prevailing at the time, G–4 set up the types and numbers of items needed, added the time element, and sent this "shipping list" to the Under Secretary. The Under Secretary broke down the requirements and sent them to the chiefs of the appropriate supply services for procurement. The Technical Services placed the contracts, followed production, and made inspections under the direction of the Under Secretary. When supplies were ready for delivery, G–4 took up the duty of supervising their distribution by the services. Procurement policy and industrial mobilization were the sphere of the Under Secretary; determination of requirements and distribution were the tasks of G–4. Actual execution under both lines of authority remained with the supply services, which was as Benedict Crowell had indicated it should be; however, there was no direct command authority over the supply services, and no machinery for the close co-ordination of the entire logistics area at any level below the Secretary of War himself.

Strategic and Logistical Planning

Measured against the planning accomplished during the formative years of the General Staff from 1903 to 1917, planning in the years between the world wars was impressive indeed. Even so, in the emergency situation of 1940 and 1941, plans to meet such a situation appear to have been desultory and too incomplete to be translated rapidly into action. Some advances had been made toward high-level co-ordination but they had fallen short of that common understanding and comprehensiveness upon which effectiveness depends. Troop mobilization depended on the availability of supplies and equipment and transportation, and matériel requirements depended upon troop mobilization. Mobilization of the civilian economy depended upon the extent of military mobilization, and the scale of mobilization depended upon its feasibility in relation to industrial capacity and availability of raw materials. Planning had not been sufficiently informed, realistic, and continuous, to bring all elements into proper balance. On the other hand, it had served to educate the officers involved to some extent; it had revealed certain possibilities to be further explored and certain blind alleys to be avoided; and it had developed some machinery that would be needed and useful when mobilization did in fact begin.

Planning Responsibilities

Charged with the development of strategic plans, the War Plans Division calculated what forces would be necessary to achieve objectives in possible theaters of operations. Matters requiring Navy co-operation were referred to the Joint Army and Navy Board, formally reconstituted after World War I to include the Army Chief of Staff, the Chief of Naval Operations, and the principal plans and operations officers. The Joint Board met irregularly as needed, and functioned mainly through the Joint Planning Committee made up of the war plans chiefs and their first assistants from both services. After May 1941 the Planning Committee set up a Joint Strategical Committee to make more detailed studies. The Joint Board was only an advisory body, but it performed a useful and necessary service until it was superseded in 1942 by the Joint Chiefs of Staff.

The Assistant Secretary of War had statutory responsibility for economic mobilization planning, which was centered in the Planning Branch of the Procurement Division of the Office of the Assistant Secretary of War. From the Planning Branch came the initiative for co-ordination of industrial mobilization planning with the Navy, for creation of the Army Industrial College, for development of procurement planning in the supply bureaus, and, finally, for the formulation of the Industrial Mobilization Plan.

Under the law the Assistant Secretary of War actually had authority to direct economic mobilization planning throughout the government, but it was clear that in wartime the Navy would be a competing claimant for resources, and some degree of joint planning for economic mobilization was indicated. Accordingly the Army and Navy Munitions Board was established by joint action of the Secretaries of War and the Navy in June 1922, with the Assistant Secretary of War and the Assistant Secretary of the Navy constituting its membership. Operations began through a series of committees made up of representatives drawn from the two departments. Officers were not assigned to full-time duty with the board until the 1930's when a permanent executive committee was set up to give some full-time direction to its activities. The board then became the sponsor of the Industrial Mobilization Plan, wherein it was assumed that the Army and Navy Munitions Board would act as the central control authority for economic mobilization in time of national emergency until such time as an appropriate civilian agency, presumably along the lines of the War Industries Board, should be set up to assume that responsibility.

Preparation of detailed procurement plans was left to the supply arms and services that would have actual procurement responsibility. Each of these bureaus had established a procurement planning section in its headquarters in May 1921, which, following the general plans and policies laid down by the Assistant Secretary of War, developed and revised procurement plans that became the basis for contract placements in 1940 and 1941.

A particularly far-sighted step in preparing for economic mobilization was the establishment of the Army Industrial College, which opened in 1924 under the direct supervision of the Assistant Secretary of War. Army officers (Navy and Marine Corps officers were admitted in 1925) assigned to the college as students had an opportunity for a year's full-time study in the basic economic, political, industrial, administrative, and legal aspects of economic mobilization for war. In addition, faculty members and students prepared studies and participated in consultations contributing to the preparation of the Industrial Mobilization Plan.

War Plans

Most of the war plans emanating from the War Plans Division during the 1920's and 1930's contemplated only minor emergency actions. Aimed in the direction of providing a plan for all possible contingencies, the plans showed a fine impartiality in the choice of nations as potential enemies without reference to the current international situation. On the other hand, all suffered from the same unrealistic limitation that had prevailed in pre-World War I planning and that apparently was accepted as a matter of national policy: all plans should be for the defense of the United States, by the United States alone, against any or all combinations of foreign powers. The much more likely prospect of participation in coalition warfare overseas was for the most part ignored.

The most significant of a series of war plans assigned color code names to correspond generally to the supposed enemy in each case was the ORANGE plan, which visualized war against Japan in the Pacific. As of 1935 this plan assumed that such a war would result in the early loss of the Philippines, and would then require a progressive movement through the Marshall and Caroline Islands to secure a line of communication to the Western Pacific. Army planners doubted that execution of the plan would be worth the cost, and in the passage of the Philippine Independence Act in 1934 they saw an opportunity to curtail the over-commitment of the United States in that area. But the Navy insisted that the fleet should be prepared to take the offensive in the Western Pacific should war break out with Japan. A revision of the plan in 1938 represented a compromise calculated to ob-scure the differences between the services, but it remained clear that the U.S. Army units in the Philippines, which retained the basic mission of denying Manila Bay to Japanese forces, would have little hope of reinforcement in case of war.

By 1938 and 1939 the international situa-tion had deteriorated to the point that mili-tary planners were called upon to prepare plans that assumed co-operation with Great Britain and France in projecting forces to South America, to the Pacific, or to Europe and Africa to defeat Japan, Germany, and Italy, singly or in combination. The new plans appeared as the RAINBOW series. By far the most important of this series was RAINBOW 5, which combined the hemis-phere defense mission of RAINBOW 1 with an assumption that American forces should be sent to the Eastern Atlantic and to Africa and/or Europe to join in concerted action with the British and French for the decisive defeat of Germany and Italy. The fall of France and the growing danger of war with Japan in 1940 forced planners to look more directly at the prospect of involvment. On the whole they were far more pessimistic than was President Franklin D. Roosevelt. Contrary to Roosevelt's views, plans officers assumed that Great Britain would not be able to hold out for six months after the surrender of France, and they were anxious to avoid any commitment that would in-volve the United States in its current condi-tion of unpreparedness. Then, as hopes grew with continued British resistance, RAINBOW 5 was attuned to the new situa-tion, and defense of the British Isles and de-feat of the Axis Powers in Europe remained primary aims. RAINBOW 5 was integrated with Navy plans and was in accord with U.S.-British staff conversations of early 1941; in June 1941 it emerged as a joint war plan with the approval of the Secretaries of War and the Navy. In August the Army Chief of Staff approved revised Army RAIN-BOW 5 plans based on the joint plan.

Although G–4 and the supply services were directly concerned with the logistical implications of the war plans, the War Plans Division found it necessary to take these im-plications into account when drawing its plans. As chief of the division during 1941, Brig. Gen. Leonard T. Gerow wanted logis-tical requirements to be drawn logically from the types, numbers, and missions of forces contemplated in the strategic plans. This was reasonable and "realistic," but it was impracticable, for the plans themselves generally were too far from reality—particu-larly so long as the potential enemies held the initiative. About the best that could be done was to anticipate the total forces that might be available to oppose the enemy, guess what their most likely makeup would be, and try to get as much as possible of the best possible equipment to make them most effective.

Industrial Mobilization Plans

Planning for procurement and industrial mobilization during the 1920's and 1930's about kept pace with war planning. With little to go on other than World War I ex-perience, and faced with small annual budgets that put the Army back on a peace footing, plus some return to the attitude which regarded peace as normal for the Army, successive Assistant Secretaries of War and the planning branches of the supply services went about the task of formulating plans for the procurement of all major items, and undertook to develop policies and procedures and proposed organizational machinery for a wartime procurement program. Procurement planning involved assessment of the types of supplies and equipment that would be needed to meet given emergencies, calculation of quantities that would be needed at stated intervals after an assumed M-day (general mobilization day), parceling out the procurement load amongst the procurement and manufacturing districts in the United States, and selecting and preparing facilities to produce the needed items. Revisions of the General Mobilization Plan reflected too few studies of feasibility, and attempted to establish a rate of troop mobilization that was beyond the capacity of industrial facilities to support adequately in the earlier stages. In an effort to correlate troop and matériel mobilization more closely, the General Staff from 1936 replaced the general mobilization plans with a Protective Mobilization Plan for rapidly mobilizing a well-equipped emergency force made up essentially of the Regular Army and the National Guard and then expanding at a more deliberate pace in order to allow for the slower mobilization of industry. The Protective Mobilization Plan was the basis for procurement requirements when large-scale rearmament began in 1940.

Surveys of some 25,000 industrial plants indicated that about 10,000 would be capable of some kind of military production, and all 10,000 were assigned certain items or categories of items they should be prepared to produce; many plants were given "educational orders" to familiarize them with their war production assignments. The Ordnance Department's arsenals satisfied the Army's peacetime requirements for arms and ammunition, but it was estimated that they could supply no more than 10 percent of wartime needs. A one-million-man Army could be supplied, it was thought, by the idle capacity in the industrial system in the late 1930's; but support for a four-million-man Army, for instance, would necessitate extensive conversion of industry from civilian to military production.

Beyond procurement planning it was necessary to look to plans for broader industrial mobilization, with all the implications in conversion of industry and expansion of facilities, controls over raw materials, labor relations, and co-ordination of other elements of the economy to assure fulfillment of procurement plans without disruption of the civilian economy. These broader aspects, too, were the responsibility of the Assistant Secretary of War, and, while the major planning had to be done in the War Department and in co-operation with the Navy under the Army and Navy Munitions Board, the assumption always existed that the actual administration of an industrial mobilization program would be under a civilian "superagency" (comparable to the World War I War Industries Board) appointed directly by the President. In a way this assumption complicated and weakened the planning process, for plans were being made that, presumably, would be carried out by an outside agency.

After several attempts to prepare plans relating to certain areas of activity, the Office of the Assistant Secretary of War in 1930 completed a comprehensive Industrial Mobilization Plan, of which revised editions, prepared under the aegis of the Army and Navy Munitions Board, appeared in 1933, 1936, and 1939. In its final form (1939) the Industrial Mobilization Plan envisaged a War Resources Administration as the central control agency over War Finance, War Trade, War Labor, and Price Control organizations, with separate selective service and public relations agencies reporting directly to the President. The plan provided for commodity committees, dear to the heart of Bernard Baruch, and prescribed policies for the stockpiling and control of strategic and critical materials. In order to counter criticisms that civilian leaders had had no significant part in drawing up the plan, in the summer of 1939 the War Department invited a group of prominent business men to act as a review committee on the educational order program. Chairman of the committee was Benedict Crowell.

Efforts to have Congress pass legislation that would make it possible to put the Industrial Mobilization Plan into effect immediately upon declaration of an emergency were uniformly unsuccessful. Nevertheless, when war in Europe appeared imminent in August 1939, President Roosevelt appointed a War Resources Board under the chairmanship of Edward R. Stettinius, Jr., which clearly was intended (by Assistant Secretary Johnson if not by the President) to become the War Resources Administration of the Industrial Mobilization Plan if the plan were put into effect. Meanwhile the board was to advise the Army and Navy Munitions Board on policies pertaining to economic mobilization. It surveyed materials and facilities, made plans for price controls, and studied such special problems as synthetic rubber. It reviewed the Indus-

trial Mobilization Plan and gave its approval. Public opinion, still impressed by the Senate investigations of the munitions industry of 1934–36 and divided between isolation and participation in the critical world events of the times, appeared unreceptive to strong economic controls or central direction of an industrial mobilization effort. Moreover, criticism had developed over the make-up of the War Resources Board. For these and other reasons the President rejected the Industrial Mobilization Plan, and asked Bernard Baruch and John Hancock, former Secretary of the Navy, to prepare a modified plan. They came in with a plan that had a greater degree of flexibility in that it got away from the strict M-day concept of the Army plan, and recognized a planning, transition, and war stage in mobilization; it also moved away from the superagency idea in favor of several agencies under the President and away from concentrating emergency powers in the War Department. The Baruch recommendations were embodied in a report of the War Resources Board which the President promptly suppressed and kept secret until the end of the war. By November 1939 the War Resources Board evidently had outlived its usefulness and it went out of existence.

The turn of events in Europe in the spring of 1940 sparked new demands for putting the Industrial Mobilization Plan into effect, but White House advisers, barely acquainted with the contents of the plan or how it was prepared and holding that World War I experience which had had such influence on the plan no longer was valid, discouraged its acceptance. President Roosevelt feared the plan would remove the direction of industrial mobilization too far from his own control; and Secretary of War Harry H. Woodring himself was lukewarm toward it and openly critical of Assistant Secretary Louis Johnson's efforts in favor of rearmament. As a result the Industrial Mobilization Plan never was formally put into effect; however, its provisions were in fact used in many instances to meet situations which demonstrated their necessity and essential soundness in a way that mere appeal to the experiences of another war never could have done. Probably the greatest deficiency in the plan itself was one not mentioned at the time—its lack of a really effective means to control the allocation of basic materials such as steel, copper, and aluminum.

Steps Toward Rearmament

On 28 May 1940 President Roosevelt, relying on existing law, revived the old Advisory Commission to the Council of National Defense, and so set the stage for a painful repetition of the experience of World War I what would become an extensive rearmament program. After months and years of hesitating, faltering steps in that direction, mobilization was about to begin. It would proceed gradually, however, urged on by the shock of events in the European war, and contrary to the immediate all-out effort contemplated by the M-day concept in the Industrial Mobilization Plan. Actually, there was not very much difference between a gradual build-up and an immediate all-out effort once firm decisions on eventual goals were made, for in the existing state of preparedness no urgency could have attained mobilization much more swiftly than it was accomplished once rearmament was undertaken in earnest. The conversion, expansion, and contruction of industrial facilities

would have been a necessary first measure in any case.

Until 1940, world events had little noticeable effect on Army budgets. Japanese occupation of Manchuria in 1931, while regrettable, was thought to be too remote to affect the security of the United States. The Marco Polo Bridge incident in 1937, when the Japanese moved into China proper, in a way was the first step on the path to Pearl Harbor, but not even the economic recession of that year was enough to persuade Congress to accept a War Department recommendation for the expenditure of a modest sum for industrial preparation for the production of modern weapons. No less startling events on the other side of the world had any greater impact on the United States. The German occupation of Austria in the spring of 1938 had no more discernible effect on Army procurement than had the Italian invasion of Ethiopia in 1935, the German reoccupation of the Rhineland in 1936, or the Spanish Civil War from 1936 to 1939, and requests for funds to build up a small reserve of modern arms and special equipment were unavailing.

Congress seemed to be reflecting the mood of a people determined to stay out of war at almost any cost, and President Roosevelt, perhaps smarting from the unenthusiastic response to his speech in 1937 calling for a "quarantine of aggressors," was not yet prepared to recommend otherwise. Almost the only interruption to the ordinary course of limited annual Army budgets was an act which Congress passed in June 1938 authorizing the expenditure of $2 million during each of the next five fiscal years for educational orders as a means of preparing industry for possible mobilization tasks. Then the Czechoslovakian crisis, culminating in the Munich conference on

29–30 September 1938, and confidential reports from American ambassadors in Europe testifying to German war preparations convinced Roosevelt of the necessity for quick action. He was especially anxious for a build-up of air power, a position he made clear in a conference with military and political leaders on 14 November. The Army took advantage of the opening to attempt to get a balanced build-up, and everyone rushed in to try to make up for deficiencies that had been accumulating for years. After repeated revisions, the President in January 1939, laid before Congress a proposed $575 million arms program—of which $110 million were for new equipment for ground forces. German absorption of the remainder of a Czechoslovakia left vulnerable by the loss of its frontier lines as a result of the Munich agreement added impetus to Congressional approval of this program, in separate acts, in the spring of 1939. The procurement of new weapons was to be spread over a period of three years, with deliveries commencing in September 1940.

The outbreak of war in Europe with the invasion of Poland in September 1939 had less effect than might be supposed upon the Army's rearmament program. Actual appropriations already approved for the War Department for Fiscal Year 1940 were more than double those approved for the previous year. But the war in Europe, after the blitzkrieg in Poland, settled into the period of inactivity commentators referred to as the "sitzkrieg," and "phony war;" and Congress, whose constituents quickly lapsed into a false sense of security fostered by "quiet on the Western Front" and wishful thinking, considered the addition in February of $100 million to the current year's appropriations as ample. Indeed,

the total funds of $1.1 billion for the fiscal year did seem substantial when compared to War Department appropriations that had averaged less than $252 million a year during the preceding twenty-one years, and which for Fiscal Year 1939 had totaled approximately $496 million. It took the Nazi blitzkrieg in the west and the fall of France in the spring of 1940 to shock the American people into decisive action. The Army Chief of Staff, General George C. Marshall, had a cool reception from Congress when he appeared before the House Committee on Appropriations in February 1940 to defend the Army's request for $853 million for the next fiscal year—calculated to obtain essential and critical items for the currently authorized strength of the Regular Army (227,000 men) and the National Guard (235,000 men) and to stock certain critical items for the remainder of the planned Initial Protective Force. Ten days after the Germans moved into Norway (9 April 1940), G–4 asked the supply services to submit by the next day estimates to cover critical items omitted from the earlier request.

Members of Congress at last began to inquire into the nation's preparedness status. They were shocked to learn that there were not enough effective antiaircraft guns to defend a single major American city; that some coast defense guns had not been fired for twenty years, and nearly all were vulnerable to air attack; that the field artillery still relied almost entirely on the 5,000 French 75's left over from World War I, and that it would be another fourteen to sixteen months before the forty-eight 105-mm. howitzers for which funds had been provided could be delivered. Congress learned that the Army had virtually no tanks or tank-type vehicles other than about 400 light infantry tanks and similar cavalry combat cars which now seemed pitifully inadequate in the face of the impressive showing of the German panzer forces. The ammunition supply was equally discouraging. There was little comfort to be derived from the President's reassurances in a nationwide radio address that there were "on hand or on order" 792 tanks, 744 antitank guns, 741 modernized 75-mm. guns, and 2,000 antiaircraft guns, for only a small part of these were on hand, and of that part most of the tanks were light and half of the antiaircraft guns were .50-caliber machine guns.

Revival of the Advisory Commission to the Council for National Defense in May 1940 set in motion the machinery for economic mobilization, and the rearmament program began in June inaugurated the "defense period" of war preparation—a time somewhat akin to the preparedness period of 1916. Nevertheless, rearmament efforts were considerably less than all-out, and President Roosevelt resisted the urging of military leaders for total mobilization.

By the end of June, Congress had provided $2.75 billion for Army procurement, and with the air blitz raging on Britain, it added another $4 billion in August, and $1.4 billion more in October. With the grant of $4.8 billion to the War Department under the Lend-Lease Act of March 1941, the total War Department funds for Fiscal Year 1941 came to about $13 billion. The regular appropriation for the next fiscal year, passed eight days after the German invasion of Russia in June 1941, was nearly $10.6 billion. After the announcement of the Atlantic Charter in August, another $4.25 billion were added, and before Pearl Harbor another $7.4 billion. Thus the total funds made available to the War Department from June 1940 to December 1941 was nearly $36 billion—more than the combined expenditures of the Army and the Navy during World War I.

Undoubtedly the supply programs received their greatest impetus from the adoption in August 1940 of a resolution which authorized calling the National Guard into federal service and the enactment in September of the first peacetime draft law in American history. By December 1940 the Army's strength was over 600,000 officers and men; six months later it was over 1,460,000. Here was a substantial force already short of equipment as soon as it came into being: once more troops were being mobilized before they could be equipped. That strange popular psychology of matériel mobilization again was at work—all the intellectual conviction of the reasonableness and the necessity of maintaining matériel reserves was of little avail; it seemed to be necessary to have unarmed or ill-equipped men for all to see before it was possible to get equipment for them. As the year for which the National Guard and the original selective service men had been called neared expiration, Congress extended the law by a very narrow margin of time and the Army, just beginning to become effective, was preserved. The eighteen months of rearmament during the defense period from June 1940 to Pearl Harbor probably were crucial for the American war effort. Although some have complained of a lost year during 1939–40 while mobilization machinery was being developed in a rather ineffective and incomplete way, it is possible that as much was done during the defense period toward that total mobilization and war production record which soon was to amaze the world as could have been done even if the United States actually had been involved in the war eighteen months earlier. Certainly if the contributions of the United States during the critical years of 1942–45 had been delayed another eighteen months, the cost would have been much higher, for by then there might have been no strong allies left to share the burden.

Another bit of emotional response that may have had considerable effect on plans and mobilization was the emphasis given to defense of the Western Hemisphere. Although the Caribbean long had been acknowledged as an area of vital interest to the United States, the extension of concern throughout the hemisphere was based less on immediate threats and interests than upon general sentiment which, like the Monroe Doctrine, perhaps developed as a corollary to the hope of noninvolvement in Europe. For some reason a German lodgement in the Rio de la Plata area would have been viewed with greater alarm, although it was 6,000 miles away, than would a German arrival at Cherbourg, only 3,000 miles distant. The RAINBOW plans, General Marshall's staff conferences, the President's messages to Congress, all referred repeatedly to the problem of hemisphere defense. Indeed, the proviso in the draft legislation and the National Guard resolution that draftees and guardsmen should not be available for service "beyond the limits of the Western Hemisphere" except in territories and possessions of the United States, suggested that there would be less objection to an expedition to Patagonia or the Andes than to the reinforcement of Great Britain.

Emergency Expedition Plans

While rearmament and mobilization were only beginning, the Army also during 1940 and 1941 made plans for organizing and equipping forces to meet possible emergency calls and for sending troops and supplies to garrison newly acquired bases in the Atlantic and to strengthen positions in the Pacific. All these efforts seem meager in retrospect, but worst of all at the time was the embarrassmant attending the effort of even moving a small expeditionary force. Caught in the dilemma of having to provide cadres for expanding its forces and providing equipment for training as well as preparing for emergency operations, the Army discovered that it could hardly move a force overseas. Staffs were unfamiliar with the logistical problems involved, troops had had little training in such operations, equipment was short, and, even if all other problems were overcome, transportation was lacking. Forces preparing for possible "protective occupation" of French islands in the West Indies should there be a threat of a German take-over were only half the size considered necessary; they needed double the five and ten days desired for them to be ready to move out to reinforce Navy and Marine assault forces, and transports could not have been made available for several days or weeks more. Conditions had improved little in the spring of 1941 when the Army was called upon to provide some 25,000 men for a possible expedition, under Navy command, to the Azores. This expedition was canceled, but an Army force of about 6,000 men was sent to Iceland in August to reinforce marines who had landed there a month earlier. Meanwhile, small garrisons were sent to occupy the Atlantic bases leased from Great Britain in the destroyers-for-bases deal of the summer of 1940; reinforcements were sent to Alaska, where construction of facilities for an air base and for garrisoning troops was being rushed; and (in something of a reversal of the General Staff's previous atti-tude) men and supplies were dispatched to the Philippines.

Even so, on 1 December 1941 only about 10 percent of the Army was deployed out-side the continental United States. By far the largest single oversea establishment was in Hawaii where nearly 43,000 men were stationed. Nineteen thousand men, to-gether with 12,000 Philippine Scouts, were in the Philippines backing up the recently mobilized 100,000-man Philippine Army. The Alaska garrisons had been increased to a strength of about 24,000 officers and men. Another 66,000 were in the Caribbean De-fense Command, which included the Pan-ama Canal Zone, Puerto Rico, the Bahamas, Antigua, Santa Lucia, Trinidad, and British Guiana. Troops stationed in the North Atlantic included 1,200 in Bermuda, 2,383 in Newfoundland, and 687 in Green-land, as well as nearly 6,000 in Iceland.

Army combat forces in the continental United States had been organized into 27 infantry divisions, five new armored divi-sions, two cavalry divisions, and about 200 incomplete air squadrons. Only seven of these divisions could have been equipped for combat duty, and lack of shipping would have made it impossible to transport most of the troops overseas even if they had been fully equipped.

The Army Service Forces

Lack of effective top level co-ordination, and the dispersion of procurement and supply activities among the supply services again threatened to delay the service and supply of the Army as mobilization meas-ures quickened after Pearl Harbor. As had been the case in 1917, the demands of war revealed serious weaknesses in the organi-zational machinery. There was, in fact, no machinery for the close co-ordination of the whole logistics area anywhere below the Secretary of War himself. This situation, together with a restless desire for greater autonomy on the part of the Air Forces, led to another far-reaching reorganization of the War Department which became effec-tive on 9 March 1942. The new arrange-ment set up a command structure between the General Staff and the arms and services. The Army Ground Forces (AGF), Army Air Forces (AAF), and Army Service Forces shared command responsibility equally under the War Department.[1] The offices of the chiefs of the combat arms—Infantry, Cavalry, Field Artillery, Coast Ar-tillery—were abolished, and their functions transferred to Headquarters, Army Ground Forces. Chiefs of administrative and tech-nical services were retained but became sub-ordinate to the commanding general of the Army Service Forces. The organization for supply operations filled the gap left open in the Pershing reorganization of 1921, for it set up a supply services organization an-alogous to Pershing's in the AEF. Maj. Gen. Brehon B. Somervell who was ap-pointed Commanding General, Army Serv-ice Forces, held a position similar in many respects to that of the Director of Purchase, Storage, and Traffic in World War I. The new organization did not solve the weakness of divided authority: on procurement mat-ters the commanding general of ASF re-ported directly to the Under Secretary of

---

[1] General Orders 14, 12 March 1943, changed the name of Services of Supply (SOS) to Army Service Forces (ASF). Army Service Forces is used for the remainder of the volume when referring to the Washington command. Theaters continued to use the Services of Supply designation, a distinction honored in the text.

War; on other matters he reported to the Chief of Staff. (*Chart 3*)

Although establishment of the Army Service Forces set authoritative direction over the supply services, the organization for logistics in the War Department became, if anything, more confusing. First of all, the supply services continued to act under a division of responsibility based upon particular commodities rather than upon distinct functions. That is, the Quartermaster Corps and the Ordnance Department, for instance, each performed all the functions of procurement, storage, distribution, and maintenance for the particular types of equipment and supplies charged to them. Co-ordination was thus made both more difficult and more necessary, and this was where the Army Service Forces came into the picture. Furthermore, the supply services, even though they had been "unified" under the ASF, maintained individual distinctions and continued to perform the function of command over troops as well as that of technical staffs in the War Department. Headquarters Army Service Forces, absorbed most of the staffs of the Under Secretary of War and of G–4, though both of those agencies retained their supervisory roles. While the ASF staff charged with logistic planning and supervision grew, G–4 shrank to a minor agency of twelve officers and twenty-six civilian employees. By July 1944 the strength of G–4 had climbed back to thirty-seven officers, and a little later to forty-five, but the Director of Plans and Operations in Headquarters, Army Service Forces, had a staff of 232 officers and 369 civilians, the Control Office had another 190 people, and similar accretions of strength had appeared in the offices of the Director of Matériel and the Director of Supply.

GENERAL SOMERVELL

In the meantime another staff agency for high-level logistic planning and co-ordinating logistics with strategy had risen to a position of central importance; it was the Logistics Group of Operations Division (as the War Plans Division was redesignated in May 1943), War Department General Staff. The functions left to G–4 after Army Service Forces began operations were more or less taken over by the Operations Division, and it was that agency rather than G–4 which, together with ASF, furnished the Army's representation on the Joint Logistics Committee serving the Joint Chiefs of Staff. If this were not complicated enough, the Army Air Forces had its own logistical staff (A–4), its own Matériel Command, which functioned as another supply or technical service, and very soon began to develop some duplicating services opposed to Army Service Forces. In addition to all these conflicts

CHART 3—THE REORGANIZED ARMY: SEPTEMBER 1942

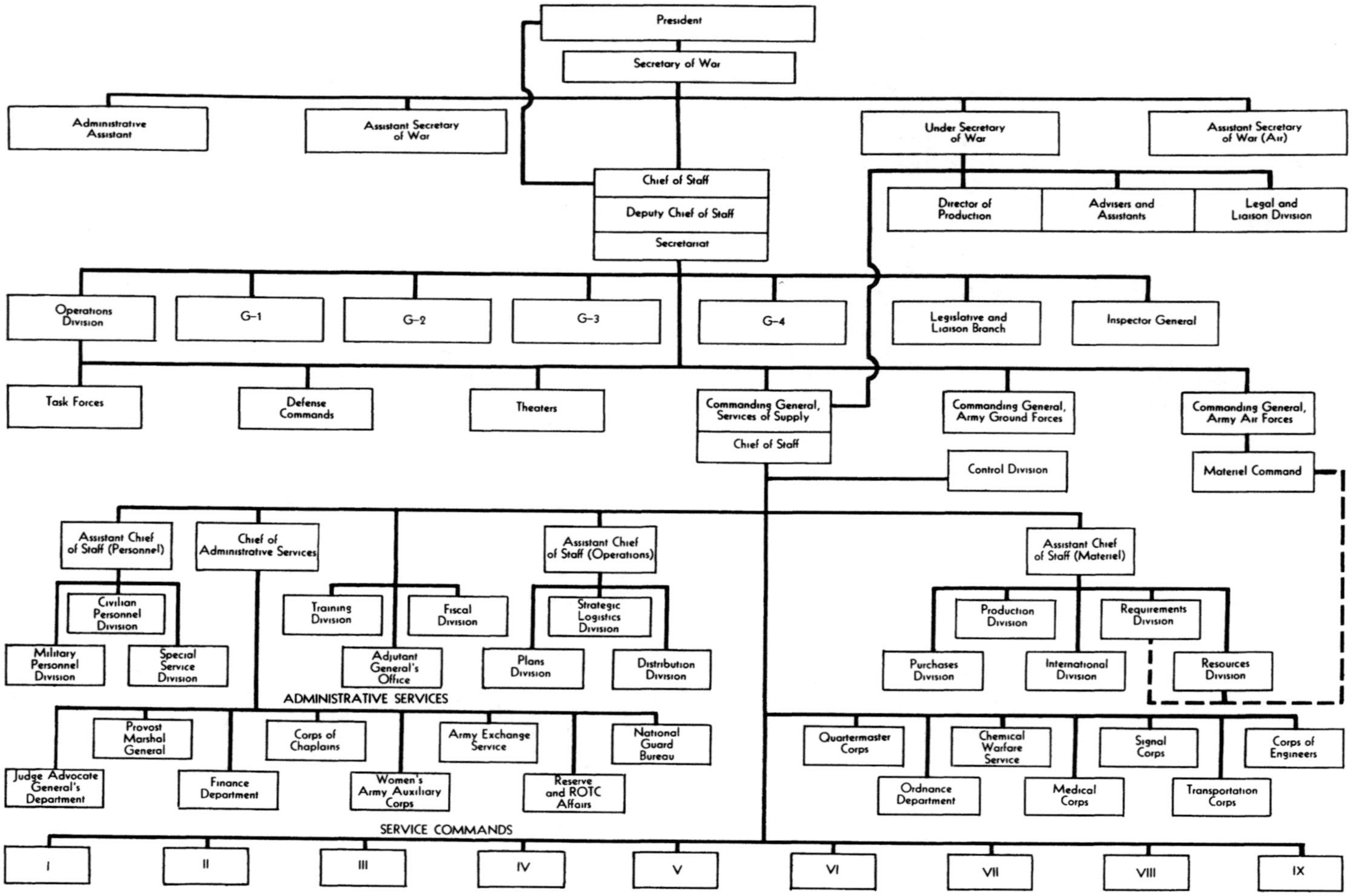

CHART 4—ORGANIZATION OF THE ARMY SERVICE FORCES: 15 AUGUST 1944

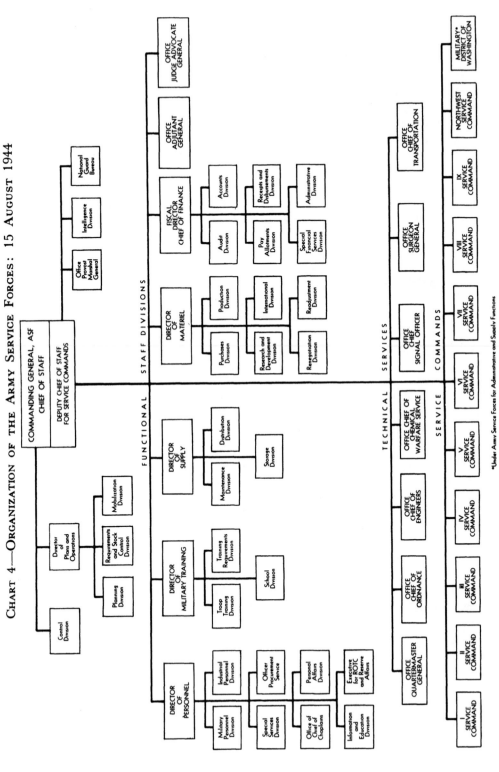

*Under Army Service Forces for Administrative and Supply Functions

the Army Service Forces organization had the responsibility of command over such administrative bureaus as the offices of The Adjutant General, the Judge Advocate General, and the Chief of Chaplains. ASF was something of a catch-all for the assignment of all offices which logically could go nowhere else. All together it at one time commanded eight administrative services, nine service commands (formerly known as corps areas) whose chief function was to supervise the operation of the posts, camps and stations within their respective areas, six ports of embarkation, and nine general depots, all of which previously had reported directly to the Chief of Staff. It was an unwieldy organization that only a strong personality could have pulled together, and that personality it had in General Somervell. (*Chart 4*)

Such a drastic reorganization, amid the pressures of wartime mobilization, was bound to leave lines of authority and definitions of responsibility obscure in a number of instances where points of friction were bound to arise. Differences between Army Service Forces and Army Ground Forces developed, particularly with regard to the assignment of personnel, as a result of the system of classifying and assigning men according to their civilian occupation specialties. Since the duties of men in the Army Service Forces frequently corresponded to civilian occupations, while no such relevance existed for such duties as machine gunner, rifleman, or artilleryman, there was basis for the feeling in Army Ground Forces that it was being slighted in the assignment of the best soldier material. The fact that Army Service Forces had charge of personnel did not help that situation. Ultimately, over the protest of ASF,

a physical profile system, which gave greater weight to physical qualifications, was adopted. On the whole, however, these differences were minor compared to the disputes over jurisdiction and policy that developed with the Army Air Forces and with the Operations Division of the General Staff.

Air Forces officers, anxious to limit any restrictions on their newly won autonomy and alive to any opportunity to move in the direction of a completely independent air force, were sensitive to almost any appearance of subjection to Army Service Forces. The Air Forces had been given responsibility for procurement of all equipment "peculiar to the Army Air Forces," but General Somervell thought that procurement policies and procedures should be uniform throughout the Army. He was able to accomplish a measure of general supervision by the device of insisting that staff officers of ASF should be designated as representatives of the Under Secretary of War when dealing with AAF. There were almost continuous disputes about what equipment should be regarded as "peculiar to the Army Air Forces." The most bitter controversies of all concerned the management of Army air bases and the operation of services attached to them. All camps, posts, and stations operated for units of Army Ground Forces were under the command of ASF through the service commands, but air bases came under the jurisdiction of AAF. Still, it had been indicated that services insofar as practicable should be provided by ASF. In practice, the Air Forces tended to develop its own system, including the operation of station hospitals, signal communications, stock control system, and the management of repairs and utilities. All of these became sore points between the two major commands, each one anxious to perform its assigned duties well, and each one concerned for its own prestige.

Jurisdictional controversies of a different kind developed between ASF and the Operations Division. Operations was the only division of the General Staff that remained essentially intact after the reorganization of 1942. Indeed, its staff of more than three hundred officers and civilians was more than double the combined strength of G–1, G–2, G–3, and G–4. Charged with preparing plans and strategic direction of forces in the theaters of war, it was, in effect, a complete general staff in itself. One basic question was the relationship between strategy and logistics. General Somervell insisted that he must be informed of strategic plans well in advance in order to allow for logistic planning on the part of ASF; on the other hand, he was not unwilling to offer his own recommendations for future military operations on the basis of his estimates of logistic capabilities. Somervell felt that his headquarters should not only contribute technical advice in the matter of logistical data, but that it should participate in the strategic decisions. He resented the fact that Operations Division furnished most of the representation on the joint planning committees, and ASF was for the most part frozen out of strategic planning. Irritations multiplied when Operations Division interfered with some logistic activity of ASF relating to oversea support, or when ASF took the initiative in some matter affecting a theater of war.

The new War Department organization was scarcely more than a year old when General Somevell offered a series of proposals for further drastic reorganization. His first move was to recommend the absorption of G–1, G–4, and the Logistics Group of the Operations Division into ASF headquarters. This proposal received no encouragement from General Marshall, and got nowhere. About the same time Somervell proposed a reorganization of the internal structure of Army Service Forces along functional lines which met with General Marshall's approval, for he hoped to accomplish such a revision while the problems of war still recommended it, and before the expected postwar rush for recovery of bureaucratic position should have a chance to set in. The plan would have eliminated the technical services as technical staff and operating agencies of Army Service Forces, and would have substituted a staff including The Surgeon General minus his procurement and supply functions, and directors of utilities, communications, transportation, procurement, supply, personnel administration, and fiscal affairs. A leak to the press brought outcries that the War Department was to be turned into a "New Deal" agency staffed with "political generals." Cries of dictatorship sprang from those who themselves seemed more anxious to preserve their lesser domains than to exchange hope of return to cherished prerogatives for promises of logistical efficiency. Secretary of War Stimson, recalling the controversies of 1911 and 1912 involving The Adjutant General and the General Staff and fearing just such a reaction as had developed, remained cool to the plan. Congressmen, alert to political opportunity as well as to any threat to favored bureaus, contributed so much to the clamor of opposition that President Roosevelt, though he was sympathetic toward the plan, felt constrained to drop it.

Perhaps if it had been presented with more political finesse, perhaps if even the traditional titles of Chief of Engineers, Chief of Ordnance, and Quartermaster General had been retained for the new directorates, the plan could have been put across. Whether or not the hoped-for efficiencies would have developed cannot be said. Failure to have it adopted probably strengthened the notion that the War Department would retain one organization for wartime emergencies and another, more familiar if less efficient, for the "permanent" peacetime establishment. Actually Somervell's proposals anticipated by twenty years the kind of functional reorganization which one day would in fact be adopted.

During the closing months of the war, the War Department yielded to a demand of The Surgeon General for direct access to the General Staff on policy matters independent of Army Service Forces control. Somewhat later the other chiefs of technical services received similar authority. Thus the stage was set for abolition of Army Service Forces and a return for the time to the "normalcy" of the prewar General Staff and supply bureaus. Still, the new organization of 1946 reflected the wartime experience and Somervell's recommendation to consolidate the logsitics staff of ASF and the Logistics Group of Operations Division with G–4; however, the consolidation took place at General Staff level under a director of Service, Supply and Procurement with the understanding that the new staff directors would "operate" as well as plan and supervise.

Joint and Combined Staffs

The need for joint strategic and logistic planning had been recognized earlier in the establishment of the Joint Army and Navy Board and the Joint Army and Navy Munitions Board, but the actual machinery for joint logistical co-ordination remained rudimentary. With the growing emergency after the outbreak of World War II in Europe it quickly became evident that improved joint (Army and Navy) planning, and combined (international) planning as well, would be necessary if the United States became involved in global conflict. Much in the way of Army requirements for material and transportation was the result of such high-level planning, and logistical considerations, at the same time, played an important part in determining the nature of those plans.

The Joint Chiefs of Staff (JCS) structure had its origin as an almost automatic result of the arrival of the British military chiefs in Washington for discussions soon after the United States entered the war. To prepare themselves for these international conversations, and subsequently to participate satisfactorily in the U.S.–U.K. Combined Chiefs of Staff (CCS), the American chiefs—the Chief of Staff of the Army, the Chief of Naval Operations, the Commanding General, Army Air Forces, and, a little later, the Chief of Staff to the Commander in Chief—found it desirable to co-ordinate policies among themselves before meeting with their British counterparts. As a result, the Joint Chiefs of Staff grew into the principal top military co-ordinating agency for the armed forces of the United States, and eventually it took over the functions of the old Joint Army and Navy Board. Although the Joint Chiefs had no standing either by statute or by executive order and did not even have a charter defining its functions, from the time of the first formal meetings in February 1942 the effective authority of the Joint Chiefs of Staff grew steadily and remained unchallenged throughout the war.

Both the Army and Navy paid lip service to the principle of unity of command, and as the war progressed the principle was put into practice in the oversea theaters to bring forces of the Army and Navy under a single commander, but it never was achieved on the home front. In the summer of 1941 the General Board of the Navy proposed the appointment of a supreme commander, responsible to the President, with a joint general staff. The Army had come around with a similar proposal shortly after Pearl Harbor, but by that time the Navy had grown cool to the idea and it was dropped. The Joint Chiefs of Staff, then, was as close to a high command as was developed. It operated as a committee, and stood at the apex of a system of committees engaged in co-ordination of activities and joint planning. The Joint Staff Planners was the principal planning agency serving the Joint Chiefs, and initially the main working committee under the Joint Staff Planners was the Joint U.S. Strategic Committee. The Joint Staff planners, associated with their British colleagues, served as the Combined Staff Planners for the Combined Chiefs of Staff. At first there was no separate joint agency for logistical planning as such, although the Joint Military Transportation Committee and the corresponding Combined Military Transportation Committee served this function insofar as it pertained to transportation, the Army-Navy Petroleum Board co-ordinated the supply of petroleum products, and the U.S. representatives on the Munitions Assignments Board helped to co-ordinate requirements and allocations of munitions. Much of the work of the Joint and Combined Chiefs themselves had to do with logistics in the formulation of general requirements and the allocation of shipping and equipment to support their strategic plans, but the Joint Staff Planners and Joint U.S. Strategic Committee included no logistics experts in their membership.

The North Africa operation in 1942 revealed such weaknesses in joint logistical co-ordination that some overhauling of the joint committee system took place. Most important from the viewpoint of logistics planning was the formation of the Joint Administrative Committee, which in October 1943 became the Joint Logistics Committee. This committee filled an obvious need, but members of the Joint Staff Planners feared that it might have too much influence in strategic planning—that the logistic tail might wag the strategic dog. They argued that imaginative strategic planning could not be tied down by the restrictive judgment of logistical experts about what could or could not be done: that logistics experts should not, in effect, be given a veto over strategic plans. Some strategic planners seemed to have an idea that an imperfect organization could somehow reduce the importance of logistics itself. The Joint Staff Planners were able to enforce a procedure requiring that logistical plans be forwarded through themselves to the Joint Chiefs. They also had their way in insisting that membership on the Joint Logistics Committee be made up of one representative each from Army Air Forces, Army Service Forces, and Operations Division, rather than the two members from Army Service Forces that General Somervell had urged. On the other hand, they finally accepted the formation of a working committee, the Joint Logistics Plans Committee, to serve the Joint Logistics Committee in a way that the Joint War Plans Committee (successor to the Joint U.S. Strategic Committee) served the Joint Staff Planners.

Made up of six permanent members drawn from the same sources as its parent committee, the Joint Logistics Plans Committee worked through a system of associate members in developing its detailed planning data. These officers, serving the joint staff in addition to their other duties, often found the demands made upon them too much for effective performance. Quickly their number grew to more than a hundred and fifty. Then in April 1944 permanent associate members were appointed, nine from the Navy, and ten from the Army of whom three each came from Air Forces, Service Forces, and the Operations Division, and one from the G–4 office. These full-time assignments permitted much more effective planning.

The Joint Logistics Committee took over some of the duties assigned the U.S. representatives of the Munitions Assignments Board. The latter body was, in the fall of 1943, renamed the Joint Munitions Allocation Committee with responsibility for allocating finished munitions between the Army and Navy and for developing joint policy on questions of international allocations which came before the Combined Munitions Assignments Board.

Largely as a result of pressure from James F. Byrnes, Director of the Office of War Mobilization, the Joint Chiefs of Staff in September 1943 had set up the Joint Production Survey Committee as a logistical counterpart of the committee of high-ranking elder statesmen that had been organized earlier to look at the big picture in strategic plans—the Joint Strategic Survey Committee. More specifically the Joint Production Survey Committee was to step in where other agencies such as the Army and Navy Munitions Board and the Munitions Assignments Board had failed to provide liaison between the civilian mobilization agencies and the Joint Chiefs of Staff in determining the logistical feasibility of strategic plans and relating military requirements to production possibilities.

Finally, on the logistics side of the Joint Production Survey Committee, the Joint Logistics Committee and the Joint Logistics Plans Committee could be said to parallel the Joint Strategic Survey Committee, the Joint Staff Planners, and the Joint War Plans Committee on the strategic planning side. They were not co-ordinate structures, for the strategic planners continued to have the upper hand. The Joint Staff Planners brought together strategy and logistics but that committee included no logistics experts as such. Army Service Forces representatives on the logistics committees never ceased to complain about this arrangement, for they felt that logistical considerations were not given sufficient weight in strategic planning and that strategic plans were not communicated in a way to permit most effective logistical planning to support them.

Apart from the joint logistics planning under the Joint Chiefs of Staff, Army-Navy collaboration developed in various areas of procurement. The Joint Army and Navy Munitions Board virtually went out of existence after formation of the War Production Board in 1942, though some of its nominal subcommittees continued to function. A Joint Specifications Board worked at developing common specifications for supply items of common interest. There were joint arrangements for the procurement of textiles, food, and petroleum, as well as frequent exchanges of data between the Army technical services and the Navy bureaus, and co-ordination of policies for contract termination.

Summary

In the entire area of World War II logistical planning and organization the most striking feaure is the extent to which revision was necessary after the war started. Planning, while useful in many ways, was not attuned to the times, and the peacetime organization could not meet the strain of war emergency. This situation was not new in the American experience. Indeed, in comparison with meeting the demands of earlier wars, the preparation for World War II was rather notable. The Army structure did not have the flexibility that would permit it to exist in drought and flourish in flood without major changes when crisis struck. Still, it did have the flexibility to change when necessity demanded that it do so, even in the face of enemy action.

CHAPTER XXVI

World War II Strategy and Logistics

Everybody likes to talk about and analyze strategy, for there is about it the attractive quality of intellectual contest. Logistics, on the other hand, is the more pedestrian application to war of the factors of time and space: it does not determine the course of action to be taken; it does set the stage for the action and its limits, and often will indicate a preferred course of action. War frequently is likened to a game of chess, but chess is no strategic game, for there is no logistics.

To the question of whether there can be a strategic decision distinct from a logistical decision the answer must be no, for virtually all considerations entering into the major decisions of war are logistical. Logic would suggest—and military planners would prefer to believe—that logistic plans stem from strategic plans; that first there must be strategic decisions and plans, with logistic plans drawn as a consequence of them to provide support at the right place and the right time. World War II turned out to be somewhat the reverse of this logical sequence of events. There were certain obvious strategic moves; there were certain choices; but more often than not the chosen strategy hinged on logistical factors and their implications, particularly for high-level procurement planning. At the level of specific planning for specific operations, logistic plans were based on strategic decisions. On the other hand, high-level strategic decisions generally were based on logistical limitations more than on any other consideration.

Throughout the war, logistic planners had to operate without strategic plans sufficiently explicit and approved far enough in advance to provide a firm basis for production programs. And it could hardly have been otherwise, for production lead time of eighteen months to two years for major items was too great to allow for such specific assumptions as long as the enemy held the initiative. Instead, the American production effort was geared to a determination to out-produce the enemy. Economic mobilization was based, not on strategic plans, but on building up an arsenal of material to equip divisions and squadrons which then would be available to implement future strategic plans. This was the thinking behind the munitions program of 1940, and behind President Roosevelt's call to make the nation an "arsenal of democracy" in providing assistance to the Allies under the lend-lease program. The greatest influences on the character of the "Victory Program" of 1941 were a memorandum of Under Secretary of War Robert P. Patterson to the effect that the total amount of production was of greater immediate importance than the ultimate use to which it might be put and the directive of the President calling for an estimate of the equipment needed "to exceed by an appropriate amount that available to our potential enemies." [1] Although this kind of thinking caused some protest from the War Plans Division, it still was paramount in the munitions programs of 1942 and 1943. Subsequent strategic decisions might modify the munitions program but they could not determine it, because time would not wait for them. The best that Army Service Forces could do was to anticipate as closely as possible what the strategic plans would be, and then attempt to govern the qualitative aspects of its program accordingly.

By the end of 7 December 1941 there was no question that the United States was up against formidable opposition. Japan, considered by most military observers to be incapable of striking in more than one place, on the same day attacked Pearl Harbor; Kota Bharu in British Malaya; Singora and Pattani, in Thailand; Singapore; Guam; Hong Kong; Wake; and the Philippine Islands. Japanese forces spread swiftly throughout the Western Pacific, supported by a war economy that had begun orientation toward war production as early as 1928 and whose heavy industry had increased from that time to 1940 by 500 percent and whose total output had increased by 85 percent. Aircraft, aluminum, machine tool, automotive, and tank industries had been built from almost nothing. Acquisitions in Manchuria and China had helped relieve Japan of shortages of coking coal, iron ore, salt, and food; expansion through Malaya and the East Indies would augment sources of both critical raw materials and food. Nevertheless, Japan was in no position to wage a long war, for Japanese industry was at the mercy of its sea communications—no country could have been less self-sufficient. The industrial potential of Japan was no more than 10 percent of that of the United States, but because Japan had expanded its industrial capacity so rapidly and was already geared to war production, many people tended to underrate its current strength.

The tenuous naval superiority in the Western Pacific that Japan gained by the devastation of the U.S. fleet at Pearl Harbor and its two to one numerical superiority over Allied air forces in the area were eventually negated by the United States' capacity to restore and greatly increase its naval strength while building up ground and air forces which gave to the United States a clear logistical advantage in a long war.

The swift Japanese expansion in the Pacific and Southeast Asia could be pushed back only by overcoming tremendous logistical problems, for this would be a war of magnificent distances. The thousands of miles separating one base or strategic area from another were nautical miles, however, which meant that the economic distance, that is, the distance in terms of the cost of transportation, was but a fraction of what it would have been over land. If the sea lanes could be kept open for the United States and its allies and closed for the enemy, the logistic advantage was likely to be decisive. Moreover, the Japanese advanced so rapidly that they neglected to go to all-out economic mobilization until reversals of fortune demanded it, and it was they who, in the end, had too little too late.

Germany was the world's second industrial power. By December 1941 it had added the resources of most of the rest of Europe to its own, and its armies were driving to the gates of Moscow. A highly de-

---

[1] Ltr, President to Secy of War, 9 July 1941, quoted in R. Elberton Smith, *The Army and Economic Mobilization,* UNITED STATES ARMY IN WORLD WAR II (Washington, 1959), p 135.

veloped railway network and a modern system of military highways facilitated the movement of troops and supplies from one part of the country to another. German submarines, more menacing than ever, threatened to sever Atlantic communications between America and Britain. German scientists and engineers had made incredible strides in developing new machinery and methods of production, besides a wide range of synthetics in motor fuel, rubber, and other products to lessen the dependence of the Reich on overseas imports. Nevertheless, German war production remained surprisingly low for the first three years of the war. It was low in relation to what outside observers thought; it was low in relation to later German production; it was low in relation to that of Great Britain. Actually in 1940, 1941, and 1942 British production of aircraft, trucks, tanks, self-propelled guns, and several other types of armament exceeded Germany's. The world, amazed at the German blitzkrieg across Poland, into Scandinavia, through the Low Countries, France, and Yugoslavia, easily overestimated the current production of the German armaments industry. One result of this inaccuracy probably was an inflation of American requirements in terms of what had to be done to surpass the supposed production of the enemy. At the same time, the Germans themselves were so impressed with their own accomplishments that they did not undertake full-scale industrial mobilization until after the United States had entered the war, after their failure before Moscow, and after their defeat at Stalingrad in February 1943. Then, in the face of heavy bombing attacks, German industrial production climbed until the spring of 1944. As in World War I, Germany again enjoyed the supposed advan-

tage of interior lines, but again control of the peripheral seas proved to be more important. Shorter lines of communication were an advantage in lessening total requirements, but made little difference once American industry began to fill the pipelines of oversea supply.

Germany and Japan alike were led by early successes to overconfidence, which actually delayed their achievement of full economic mobilization. This handicap the United States was able to avoid, though there was a tendency for a time to overrate the swiftness with which Japan could be brought to terms.

For the United States there was no question from the moment of the attack on Pearl Harbor but that this war would require an all-out effort to defeat Germany, Italy, and Japan.

Even the American war potential, however, could not be expected to overwhelm all three enemies simultaneously. Here was a question of logistical limitation, and it provided the basis for the first and fundamental strategic decision for waging global war—that the main effort should be aimed first at defeating the Axis Powers in Europe while fighting a holding campaign against Japan. Army and Navy staff officers had been considering for several years the prospect of having to fight a two-ocean war, and in November 1940 Admiral Harold R. Stark, Chief of Naval Operations, presented a memorandum proposing the "Germany first" strategy should the United States become involved in war with both Germany and Japan at the same time. General Marshall, Army Chief of Staff, agreed with the proposal, and the Joint Board accepted it in January 1941. It was confirmed in secret conversations with British staff officers in the ensuing weeks, and became a part of war plan RAINBOW 5, which was approved by the Secretaries of War and the Navy in May and June.

The Japanese attack on Pearl Harbor created some sentiment in the United States for going after the Japanese first, but the Germany-first decision was reconfirmed in conversations with the British a few weeks after the attack, and in spite of various pressures for a change it remained firm to the end of hostilities.

The logistical factor of limited resources recommended concentration against one enemy at a time. Other logistical factors, mainly the shorter distance across the Atlantic, which would make assistance to the Allies more immediate, and the danger to Atlantic communications posed by German submarines and raiders, indicated Germany and Italy as the first targets. Conditions of late 1941, when it appeared that Great Britain and the Soviet Union were in danger of succumbing if major assistance were not forthcoming, reinforced the earlier decision.

Nevertheless, circumstances forced the first moves of American strategic deployment to be in the direction of the Pacific. First it was necessary to close a ring around the Japanese before any holding action could be effective. Japanese advances in the Philippines, down the Malay Peninsula, through the East Indies, and into the South Pacific required a shift in emphasis, for the time being, away from the planned build-up of land and air power in the Atlantic in favor of concentrating on building a great base in Australia and securing lines of communication to it so that the Japanese might be checked before it was too late. The British at this time were hoping for an early occupation of French North Africa, with American co-operation, but they also were concerned about the Japanese threat to

Australia and New Zealand. The decision to send U.S. troops and supplies to Australia meant a diversion of troopships and, more important, of cargo ships that would be needed to send any sizable forces across the Atlantic, and would thus delay North African operations at least until May 1942. Actually, the Navy program for a two-ocean fleet and its continued interest in the Pacific considerably influenced the conduct of the war throughout. In spite of emphasis on Germany first, the Pacific war soon grew into much more than a holding operation. The resultant scattering of forces around the world had grave logistical implications.

There seemed to be no enduring answers to the basic questions of deployment. Continuing pressures made it necessary to iterate again and again decisions already taken; sometimes to modify them. While troops and supplies were on the way to Australia, questions came up about reinforcing Hawaii and which islands of the Pacific should be garrisoned, and always in the background loomed the urgency and the futility of trying in some way to save the Phillipines. In the other direction there were again questions about how many troops should be sent to occupy bases in the Atlantic and Caribbean, whether an early occupation of North Africa should be undertaken and whether American forces should be concentrated in the British Isles preparatory to an invasion of the Continent. Events in North Africa, including a new counteroffensive by the German *Afrika Korps* against the British Eighth Army, and the unco-operative attitude of the Vichy government of France led to the abandonment by early March of plans for an invasion of that area. The Joint Chiefs of Staff shortly thereafter decided to restrict the allocation of forces to the Pacific to the number already committed and to begin to build up forces in the United Kingdom.

In April 1942 President Roosevelt sent General Marshall and Harry Hopkins to London to present to Prime Minister Winston S. Churchill and his military staff a plan to prepare and launch an invasion across the English Channel. Briefly, the plan called for: (1) immediate co-ordination of procurement priorities, allocations of matériel, and movements of troops and equipment; (2) preparations for launching a possible emergency landing on the Continent should an imminent collapse of the Soviet Union or a possible deterioration of German strength call for such action; and (3) a cross-Channel invasion with 48 divisions and some 5,800 aircraft (of which 30 divisions, with a million men all together, and 3,250 aircraft would be American) with a target date of 1 April 1943. The British accepted the U.S. proposal, but not without qualifications—such as maintaining strong forces in the Middle East and Indian Ocean area—and reservations.

Basic differences in British and American views on the strategy to be adopted in the war against Germany arose repeatedly. In general, the British favored a peripheral strategy, closing a ring around German power with sea and air forces, and striking at the Continent in a series of limited actions with mobile ground forces; for major operations they preferred the Mediterranean, the "soft under belly" of Europe as the Prime Minister termed it. The Americans, on the other hand, insisted on a great offensive, to be mounted from Great Britain, across the Channel. The British were influenced by recollections of the frightfully costly warfare in northern France during four years of World War I, by a desire to do something early with the forces available, and by

doubts about the logistical feasibility of mounting a massive invasion. The American view also reflected logistics considerations—the longer and more difficult supply lines necessary for supporting large-scale operations in the Mediterranean, the difficulty of supporting forces across the mountains of southern Europe, and a conviction that the quickest way to complete victory lay in a strike at the industrial heartland of Germany. Differences between British and American views were more a matter of emphasis than of substance, and represented differences in views of particular leaders rather than rigid national positions. As the situation unfolded, the British indicated that they were quite willing to accept a cross-Channel invasion, but they wanted it to be really massive, with a really good prospect of success; the Americans following the lead of the President, were willing to go along with expanded operations in the Mediterranean as complementary to operations in northwestern France. Hardly less significant were recurring differences among American leaders on emphasizing Europe or the Pacific in deployment of forces and in strategic plans.

Adoption of the plan for the build-up of forces in the United Kingdom (referred to by the code name, BOLERO), and invasion of the Continent in 1943 (ROUNDUP) entailed no basic change in the pre-Pearl Harbor Victory Program, except that the President and the Joint Chiefs of Staff urged an increase in the production of aircraft, ships, tanks, guns, and amphibious equipment. The real limiting factor for the concentration in the British Isles would be cargo ships, and already it was evident that the most critical item for the invasion was landing craft. The idea of using specially designed ships and small craft for direct discharge of vehicles and supplies as well as men on the beaches was a new one, but their use was essential for operations contemplated in the Pacific as well as in the Atlantic and Mediterranean. The Army had to depend upon the Navy for procurement of these vessels, and the Navy was disposed to give priority to its regular shipbuilding programs. Moreover, American requirements had been drawn in terms of small landing craft until the British were able to persuade the President and his advisers of the need for larger, ocean-going landing ships in May 1942. The new program began at once, and for a short time during the next summer construction of landing craft had priority over all other shipbuilding.

The BOLERO plan could not be carried through without reckoning with prior claims for limited resources and with new demands in the various theaters. When questions arose in April and again in May 1942 about sending additional forces to the Pacific, reinforcing the Middle East, stepping up aid to China, and increasing lend-lease to the Soviet Union—all at the expense of BOLERO—President Roosevelt in each case decided in favor of continuing the build-up in the British Isles.

By the end of August 1942 some 170,000 American troops had arrived in or were en route to the United Kingdom, and about 1.3 million ship tons of Army cargo had moved to that area during June, July, and August. While a sizable achievement, this was but a fraction of what would be needed to mount such an invasion as was hoped for in April 1943. It is doubtful if enough shipping could have been found to carry through the program in that time, and it is even more doubtful that British ports and inland transportation could have handled it. With the need for commitment of additional forces in the Middle East and increased aid to Russia, the prospect of a continental invasion in the spring of 1943 grew more remote, and plans for a possible emergency landing in 1942 practically were given up.

But President Roosevelt was anxious for a significant operation against Germany in 1942—General Marshall later observed that in war it was necessary for the politicians to do something big every year. It took little convincing on the part of Churchill, who had long cherished a desire for an invasion of North Africa, to persuade President Roosevelt, over the protests of his military advisers, to accept that arena for action in 1942. American leaders recognized the value of heading off German occupation of northwest Africa, of securing the British line of communication through the Mediterranean, and of acquiring a base for possible future land and air operations in the Mediterranean and southern Europe, but they feared that such a diversion of resources must lead to a postponement of what they always considered the main event—a massive attack against western Europe—and they were correct. It soon was evident to all that the planned cross-Channel attack could not be launched in 1943. Again it was a matter of logistics. Certainly there was no strategic reason why North Africa and western Europe should not be invaded simultaneously—any more than there was any strategic objection to simultaneous all-out efforts against Germany and Japan— but the resources were not there in the face of stepping up deployment in the Pacific. The weakening of the BOLERO program and the tacit postponement of an invasion of Europe also made it possible to give more attention to demands for sending reinforcements to the Pacific. Shortly after the naval victory over the Japanese Fleet at

Midway in June 1942, approval was given for going over to a limited offensive. In August 1942 a Marine amphibious force could land on Guadalcanal, and Army reinforcements could go in two months later. By the end of December 1942 the strength of Army forces arrayed against Japan had reached 464,000 men—some 200,000 more than had been contemplated in plans approved the previous spring—while those deployed against Germany and Italy, about 378,000, were about 50,000 fewer than had been planned. From this point the Army found itself committed to a policy of "scatterization," which its leaders had hoped to avoid.

The campaign in North Africa was launched in November 1942. When the North Africa operation seemed to be proceeding to a successful conclusion, Allied leaders had to face demands from every side as to what the next step should be. There still was the American concern for returning to a build-up for a cross-Channel attack as soon as possible; the British wanted to expand operations in the Mediterranean; Air Forces commanders wanted a chance to knock out Germany by strategic bombardment; General Douglas MacArthur, Supreme Commander, Southwest Pacific Area, wanted to step up offensive operations in the Southwest Pacific; Admiral Chester W. Nimitz, Commander in Chief, Pacific Ocean Area, wanted reinforcements for the South and Central Pacific; more needed to be done in Southeast Asia; the Soviet Union wanted more lend-lease material as well as an Allied second front in Europe.

In January 1943 Roosevelt and Churchill and their military chiefs met at Casablanca to attempt to resolve these conflicting demands. The result was a compromise that attempted to satisfy about everybody at the expense of concentrating on any place. Since an invasion of Western Europe that year was out of the question anyway, it was agreed that the build-up in the British Isles should be resumed, but only after mounting an invasion of Sicily, a massive air bombardment of Germany, a stepped-up offensive against the submarine, preparation for an offensive in Burma, closing the ring against the main Japanese base in the Southwest Pacific, Rabaul; and a push against Japanese-held islands in the Central Pacific. Plans for Europe and the Mediterranean were a triumph for the British preference for peripheral strategy and attrition; they also satisfied the need to do something in 1943. Offensive plans for Asia and the Pacific satisfied certain American demands for more emphasis on those areas. The all-important invasion of Western Europe could be expected to have priority for 1944.

Even without the build-up for invasion as the immediate project, the program outlined for 1943 spread logistical resources so thin that it threatened to bog down before getting fairly started. As the North Africa campaign dragged on through spring, it continued to drain supplies and shipping, and the decisions reached in January at Casablanca had been based upon apparently unrealistic assumptions about the amount of shipping available and necessary to meet those worldwide commitments. A more serious crisis developed in British imports in March 1943. While the Joint Chiefs of Staff were warning the President that reductions in American shipping allocations to the British import program as well as drastic curtailment of civilian commitments would be necessary if the Casablanca decisions were to be carried out, Foreign Secretary

Anthony Eden of Great Britain, Lewis Douglas, deputy administrator of the United States War Shipping Administration, and Harry Hopkins were urging upon the President the necessity of fulfilling commitments to provide American shipping for British imports. Agreeing with the view of these men that the whole Allied war effort would be jeopardized by a failure in the British import program, and that shipping probably could be found sufficient for the Casablanca programs as well, Roosevelt in another one of the few instances where he overruled clear recommendations of the military chiefs, decided that ships must be allocated to Britain. In the end, it was possible to meet most of the requirements, which suggested that perhaps Lewis Douglas had some justification for his contention that military planners habitually inflated their shipping requirements. Thanks mainly to a sharp decline in shipping losses to submarine action, plus the continuing increase in ship construction, the great deficits in shipping that the military planners had foreseen had largely disappeared by August 1943.

At that time things were looking better all around. Most important was the firm decision, agreed to by American and British leaders at a two-week conference in Washington in May, to launch a cross-Channel invasion in the spring of 1944. The old British-American debate, the Mediterranean versus the cross-Channel operation came up again, and again it was largely a question of logistics in general and of landing craft in particular. The Americans were not unwilling to support further operations in the Mediterranean aimed at knocking Italy out of the war, if it could be done without draining men and equipment needed for the invasion of western France; the British were willing to accept a firm target date and force size for the invasion if operations could proceed in the Mediterranean, which might, in fact, substantially improve the chance of success of that invasion. The two nations' agreement was that a cross-Channel attack should be launched with a target date of 1 May 1944, on the basis of twenty-nine American and British divisions to be in the United Kingdom by that time, and with sufficient landing craft (estimated at 4,504) to lift five divisions—three in assault and two in immediate follow-up—simultaneously. American fears that the Mediterranean might become a continuous drain on resources that might weaken the main effort in western France were eased by an agreement which established a ceiling of twenty-seven divisions in all for the Mediterranean (quite a sizable diversion at that from original plans for concentrating in the British Isles), and a commitment for the transfer, beginning 1 November, of four American and three British divisions from the Mediterranean to Great Britain.

If the Americans had reservations about British enthusiasm for the cross-Channel operation, the British were suspicious of an American pull to the Pacific to the neglect of what was supposed to be the main strategic effort against the European Axis. Nevertheless, the Washington conference also agreed to a more specific implementation of the Casablanca plans for stepping up the offensive in the Southwest and Central Pacific areas as well as for expelling the Japanese from the Aleutians. Ground operations in the China-Burma-India (CBI) theater were relegated to a secondary role in favor of increased emphasis on improving air transportation to China over the

Hump, and building up air forces in that area.

Logistic problems and limitations assured a continuation of the strategic debate. Decisions made "firm" still remained open to question. Although during the summer of 1943 Lt. Gen. Sir Frederick Morgan, appointed Chief of Staff to the Supreme Allied Commander (designate), and his combined staff in London were able to draft a plan for Operation OVERLORD, as the cross-Channel operation now was designated, this did not arrest demands for increasing commitments in the Mediterranean and in the Far East. General Marshall was most anxious to come to a final agreement on the plan and then adhere to it, for, he observed, every shift in plans resulted in logistical dislocations such as had happened in the BOLERO program when the North Africa operation was undertaken, and the implications for production, loading of convoys, and other such matters extended throughout the American mobilization effort. At the first Quebec Conference in August 1943 the British and American heads of government and military chiefs reaffirmed their commitment to the western European invasion, made their plans more concrete for a concentration of forces and equipment in Great Britain, and in a more precise way established operations in the Mediterranean as subsidiary to the OVERLORD plan. The conferees even went so far as to choose an optimistic target date—October 1944—for ending the war in Europe as an aid to planning future operations in Japan which, they surmised, might be concluded twelve months after victory in Europe. The momentum of offensives against the Japanese in the meantime was to be maintained, though there still was no agreement about

what form the operations for the final defeat of Japan should take.

There was concern at the Quebec Conference about the logistical feasibility of maintaining such widespread offensive operations. The Combined Planning Staff considered that generally speaking the status of equipment of Allied forces was at this time remarkably satisfactory. To be sure, some critical items, such as radar and radio equipment, still were in short supply, more cargo-handling equipment was needed, and a shortage of aviation gasoline was potentially serious, but none of these was of the nature to affect strategic plans. The shortages that threatened to limit the offensive strategy as agreed to at Quebec were those relating to mobility—merchant shipping, assault shipping, and transport aircraft—an area of the greatest difficulty in arriving at satisfactory estimates of needs and resources. Large deficits in shipping, after further debate and calculation, would turn into surpluses, and pessimism would turn into optimism more quickly as a result of a re-examination of resources than of revised strategic plans. Nonetheless, the problems were real and continuing.

Not until the conferences at Cairo and Tehran in November and December 1943 could there be assurances that the cross-Channel operation was to go on as scheduled. Once again Churchill urged an expansion of activities in the Mediterranean, including an attack on Rhodes in the Aegean Sea with a view to opening the Dardanelles if Turkey could be persuaded to enter the war. Churchill thought it a mistake to hold rigidly to the 1 May date for the invasion of western France at the expense of keeping an active theater going and of taking full advantage of further opportunities in the active theater to weaken the enemy's hold. American military leaders feared above all else that the Russians, anxious to establish a direct trade route through the Black Sea and seeking relief for the pressure on their forces in the Ukraine, would welcome the British suggestions for the eastern Mediterranean, but this concern probably overlooked the political implications the Russians attached to the military occupation of eastern European countries. Churchill insisted that the plans to invade France would be strengthened by the Mediterranean operations, and the gain might be worth postponing D-day for a couple of months. As President Roosevelt put it: "The problem before them [was] essentially one of logistics—whether OVERLORD could be retained 'in all its integrity' and, at the same time, the Mediterranean be kept 'ablaze.' "[2] It came somewhat as a surprise that Stalin threw his full weight in favor of the western front in France as scheduled. If the other operations suggested for the Mediterranean, including a landing in southern France, further operations in Italy, and proposals for the Aegean were subsidiary to that project, Stalin said, then they should be governed by it, and not vice versa. As a further step toward making OVERLORD plans definite, Stalin urged the immediate appointment of an Allied commander for the operation. President Roosevelt announced the appointment of General Dwight D. Eisenhower to that post on 6 December 1943.

The military chiefs did agree to, and the President and Prime Minister accepted the decision, that the assault shipping presently in the Mediterranean (mainly sixty-eight

LST's (landing ships, tank)) should be retained there until mid-January as Eisenhower had requested to support the Italian campaign; although this probably would mean the postponement of D-day to about 1 June, it still would be interpreted as "May" in the conversations with the Russians. Agreement that a landing also should be effected against southern France simultaneously with OVERLORD or shortly thereafter meant that even more landing craft would have to be found. And this meant the cancellation of a proposed amphibious operation off Burma and the transfer of landing craft from the Southeast Asia Command, as well as diversion to Europe of other craft earmarked for the Pacific.

In view of the forces already being supported in the Mediterranean, it cannot be maintained that the proposed operations in the Aegean Sea and possibly above the Adriatic were necessarily not logistically feasible; however, it is clear that, in terms of landing craft if nothing else, all these operations could not have been carried out without further postponing the landings in France. The British appeared to have far less confidence than their American counterparts in the American industrial potential to deliver the weight needed for decisive results in a direct attack. But with the advantage of the relatively short distance across the North Atlantic and the availability of Great Britain as a base for staging a great amphibious assault, American leaders were sure that this was where they could be most effective. It could be argued that there would have been political advantages to operations in eastern Europe, but logistics pointed to the west, and logistics and the west prevailed.

Logistical considerations continued to play a dominant role in the development of further plans and preparations for OVER-

[2] Maurice Matloff, *Strategic Planning for Coalition Warfare, 1943–1944*, UNITED STATES ARMY IN WORLD WAR II (Washington, 1959), p 352.

LORD itself. Port capacities were a continuing factor in the choice of the lodgment area, and availability of shipping was the constant concern in the size of the build-up.

General Eisenhower arrived in London on 14 January to oversee detailed planning to accomplish the mission defined for him a month later in a directive from the Combined Chiefs of Staff:

You will enter the continent of Europe and, in conjunction with the other United Nations, undertake operations aimed at the heart of Germany and the destruction of her armed forces. The date for entering the Continent is the month of May, 1944. After adequate Channel ports have been secured, exploitation will be directed towards securing an area that will facilitate both ground and air operations against the enemy.[3]

Already General Sir Bernard L. Montgomery, British commander designated to command the Allied ground forces in the assault, had examined the OVERLORD plan, and had recommended that it be expanded by extending the planned invasion front from twenty-five miles to about forty-five miles and by increasing the size of the assault force from three to five divisions (plus three airborne divisions instead of two as planned), retaining two divisions preloaded in assault craft for immediate follow-up. These views reflected those of General Eisenhower, and they were able to win acceptance of them, which immediately raised the problem that always had limited amphibious operations plans—the availability of landing craft. Eisenhower had hoped to be able to hold to the early May date for launching the attack, but the need to wait for another month's production of landing craft led to definite postponement to the end of that month. When it developed that even this time would not yield enough boats, a lengthy debate went on about canceling or postponing the planned invasion of southern France scheduled to go simultaneously with OVERLORD in order to transfer to Britain the landing craft being held for that operation. Curiously enough, at this point it was the British who urged cancellation of the Mediterranean project while the Americans insisted on carrying it out. At first plans for the southern France operation were scaled down in order to reduce requirements for landing craft. Then, when stalemate developed in Italy, tying down forces there, the operation was postponed. (If the landing craft sent to the Pacific had been sent to Europe, the shortages for OVERLORD and southern France might have been averted.) In a telegram to General Marshall during these discussions (April 1944) Churchill said:

The whole of this difficult question only arises out of the absurd shortage of L. S. T. s. How it is that the plans of two great empires like Britain and the United States should be so much hamstrung and limited by a hundred or two of these particular vessels will never be understood by history. I am deeply concerned at the strong disinclination of the American Government even to keep the manufacture of L. S. T. s. at its full height so as to have a sufficient number to give us to help you in the war against Japan. The absence of these special vessels may limit our whole war effort on your left flank, and I fear we shall be accused unjustly of not doing our best, as we are resolved to do.[4]

---

[3] Quoted in *Report by the Supreme Allied Commander to the Combined Chiefs of Staff on the Operations in Europe of the Allied Expeditionary Force 6 June 1944 to 8 May 1945* (Washington, 1945), p. vi.

[4] Winston S. Churchill, *Closing the Ring*, (Boston: The Houghton Mifflin Company, 1951), p. 514.

Meanwhile the build-up of U.S. troops and supplies in the United Kingdom had been growing since the autumn of 1943. In the first five months of 1944 the number of men and the tonnage of supplies in Great Britain had nearly doubled. With the arrival of 1,527,000 American troops by May 1944 the goal set by the Combined Chiefs of Staff at the Quebec Conference in August 1943 had been exceeded. In addition, some 5,000,000 long tons of American military cargo had been landed in Britain by that time.

The vast scale of the Normandy invasion left no doubt about the primacy of that effort over the Mediterranean, nor about making effective the basic decision to beat Germany first. But the contest for resources between Europe and the Far East would continue.

One reason for what appeared as excessive commitments to the Pacific was the competition between the Army and the Navy and the acceptance of supporting simultaneously offensives in the Southwest Pacific and the Central Pacific. Central direction of the war was not characterized by hard decisions. On the contrary, the commitee procedures of the Joint Chiefs of Staff resulted in a strategy of opportunism where it was easier to agree upon specific operations as opportunity presented than it was to agree upon a consistent grand design. Compromise among various demands and recommended courses of action betrayed a desire to avoid altogether harsh choices— or simply reflected an inability to obtain interservice agreement on decisions when the interests of one service would suffer without compensating by some kind of concession elsewhere. Faced with dilemmas growing out of limitations of resources, when no de-

cision could have satisfied everybody but when a clear-cut decision on priorities indicating major and secondary efforts might have seemed desirable from the broad point of view, the Joint Chiefs at times had a tendency to fight the problem, such as accepting overoptimistic assumptions about the availability of shipping rather than make a firm choice.

Even as plans for the Normandy invasion were being completed, Nimitz was taking a giant stride in the Central Pacific. Offensive action being mounted in the Marshalls, aiming at the Marianas and the isolation of Truk and the Carolines, would involve amphibious forces almost as large as those invading Normandy. MacArthur, too, was stepping up his campaign to return to the Philippines. His forces had advanced along the northern coast of New Guinea as far as Biak Island, and had leapfrogged into the Admiralities. A hundred thousand Japanese preparing a warm reception at Rabaul had been bypassed and left to wither on the vine. While the build-up for OVERLORD reached its climax, reinforcements to the extent of seven Army divisions were going to the Pacific, making a total of twenty all together. The transfer of six divisions from the South Pacific and three from the Central Pacific brought the Army strength of the Southwest Pacific to fourteen divisions by June 1944, while the arrival of four additional divisions increased the net Army strength in the Central Pacific to six divisions. But each arrival or transfer of a new division brought with it added problems of shipping and service support. MacArthur was especially concerned about the lack of service troops. "The great problem of warfare in the Pacific is to move forces into contact and maintain them," he stated. "Victory is dependent upon the solution of the logistic problem." [5]   Postponement of the planned invasion of southern France made it possible to meet immediate shipping requirements in the Pacific, though the Joint Chiefs of Staff warned: "The shortage in shipping during the coming months may affect the strategy of the war in both Europe and the Pacific, unless all concerned exercise the most rigid economy and adopt all possible expedients to conserve both personnel and cargo shipping." [6]   No relief could be expected for the shortage of landing craft until after the Normandy invasion.

In the face of continuing rivalry between the Southwest Pacific and the Central Pacific for a major share of limited resources the Joint Chiefs of Staff held to the flexible strategy of a double-pronged attack, west across the Central Pacific, and northwest by MacArthur's command, converging on the general area of the Philippines and Formosa (Taiwan).   Priorities and objectives might be changed as the situation developed.

Meanwhile the other major theater of the war against Japan, the China-Burma-India theater, fell into decline with the transfer of landing craft to Europe and decisions that no major land offensive should be planned for the Asiatic Continent.   Operations did continue in North Burma, but the main activity concerned getting enough supplies over the Hump to keep the Chinese war effort alive.   Basing B–29 bombers at airfields in China to threaten the Japanese home islands sparked some additional interest for support in the theater, but it also set off a Japanese offensive to eliminate the airfields.   Plans already were under way to shift the B–29's to the Marianas where lo-

gistics support would be less difficult.   Like the garrisons on many of the Pacific Islands, Japanese forces in Southeast Asia could be bypassed.

With the successful launching of OVERLORD, the British-American debate on operations in the Mediterranean erupted once more.   American leaders moved for a revival of the plan for invasion of southern France, or possibly a modification of objectives in southern France, while the British proposal supported a landing in the Bay of Biscay area; all, however, were aimed at providing additional port facilities to strengthen the OVERLORD effort.   Churchill argued with great persuasiveness for keeping troops needed for such an operation in Italy for offensive action across the Adriatic to the Istrian Peninsula and through the Lubljana Gap of Yugoslavia to southern Hungary.   He was thinking of political as well as logistical advantages—making the best use of forces and shipping already in the Mediterranean, and the American commander in Italy, Lt. Gen. Mark W. Clark, agreed with him.   But American military leaders generally were impatient with political considerations, sometimes losing sight of the fact, perhaps, that the very purpose of a war is political, not military.   Above all they wanted all efforts aimed directly at the objective: the earliest possible defeat of Germany.   Roosevelt firmly backed the thinking of his military chiefs.   His expressed doubts about whether logistical limitations would permit putting more than six divisions into the fighting beyond the Lubljana Gap may have been a rationalization.   Surely, if the Russians could maintain large forces through this area with long land lines of communication, the British and American Allies could have done so

---

[5] Quoted in Matloff, *Strategic Planning for Coalition Warfare, 1943–44,* p. 461.

[6] Quoted in *ibid.,* p. 463.

with their sea communications through the Adriatic. In any case, when Roosevelt refused to permit the use of U.S. troops in the venture, a reluctant Churchill had little choice but to go along with the invasion of southern France, finally agreed to for 15 August 1944. Thus at last, the long debate came to an end, and the Mediterranean, like the CBI, became a holding theater.

Meanwhile a debate between the Army and Navy went on all summer over objectives in the war in the Pacific. Mainly this debate concerned whether Luzon or Formosa should be the major target, and whether one or the other might be bypassed. MacArthur was insisting on direct liberation of the Philippines as a political and moral responsibility as well as a military necessity for preparing further operations against Japan. Admiral Ernest J. King, Chief of Naval Operations, on the other hand, was pressing his colleagues on the Joint Chiefs of Staff to accept Formosa as the major objective, in which case Admiral Nimitz' forces in the Central Pacific would make the attack. Differences between Army and Navy staffs on this point reflected different assumptions about logistical support which were growing out of MacArthur's and Nimitz' operations. An officer of Army Service Forces planning staff stated the objections to the Central Pacific approach in these terms:

Bases from which supplies will have to be transported to support the landings are so far distant that movement will be slow and supplies will have to be transported in freighters and transferred at sea to small craft to be put ashore instead of being moved directly in small craft from a close-in base. . . . The line of communication will be much more exposed to raider, air and submarine attack than would the line of communication from SWPA. . . . The easy access that has been enjoyed against the Gilberts and Marshalls is an outpost action which does not adequately justify any assumption that landing operations closer in to the Japanese inner zone can be executed with equal facility. . . .[7]

In addition to concern about the great distances over open sea involved, Army planners had serious misgivings about the adequacy of the Marianas and Palaus for providing the bases needed to mount the kind of massive assaults needed against the Japanese inner defenses. But Navy logistics officers saw the situation quite differently. While the Army held to its belief in large land bases and while operations in the Southwest Pacific had been over relatively short water distances (frequently shore-to-shore, requiring only landing craft), in the Central Pacific long approaches over wide expanses of open ocean had become the rule. The Navy was developing elaborate techniques for floating base support, using combat loaders and fleet auxiliaries, and relied upon carrier-based air support. Admiral King would not rely on bases in the Marianas for more than a small fraction of the build-up for a major offensive against Formosa (or the Philippines), but would mount it from such widely separated points as Hawaii, Manus, Milne Bay, New Caledonia, Guadalcanal, and Espíritu Santo, and, would rely upon direct shipments from the United States, by way of the Marianas, for follow-up support. Such procedures had been followed with success in mounting the North African invasion as well as in the Guadalcanal and Gilberts operations.

---

[7] Memo, Wood for Somervell, 20 Feb 44, quoted in Robert W. Coakley and Richard M. Leighton, Global Logistics and Strategy, 1934–1945, a forthcoming volume in UNITED STATES ARMY IN WORLD WAR II. See draft MS, OCMH, ch. XVI, p. 35.

In the end the decision, like so many others, hinged on immediate logistic resources. Means were available for the Luzon operation, but not for Formosa, and could not be counted upon until resources, particularly cargo shipping and service troops, could be spared from the war in Europe. On the other hand, MacArthur held that logistic limitations would not permit a speed-up in the schedule of his advance. Later he did revise his schedule to call for landings on Morotai on 15 September, the Talauds on 15 October, Saragani and Mindanao on 15 November, and Leyte in the central Philippines on 20 December. On this basis MacArthur hoped to be able to land on Luzon in the Lingayen Gulf region on 20 February. Then, while the second Quebec Conference was in session, in September 1944 the Joint Chiefs of Staff received a message from Admiral Nimitz forwarding a recommendation of Admiral William F. Halsey, given after his carrier planes had attacked the central Philippines, that the proposed operations against the Talauds and Mindanao, as well as plans for Central Pacific forces to take Yap, be canceled in favor of a direct thrust to Leyte. Nimitz offered to put forces scheduled for Yap at the disposal of MacArthur for the invasion, and a query to MacArthur brought a quick reply that he was prepared to land on Leyte on 20 October. It then was possible to make firm plans for taking Luzon, and the landings there could be moved up to early January.

At the same time the projected operation against Formosa came up for review. Now it appeared that more could be accomplished at less cost by moving directly to the Ryukyus and Bonins, approaching the home islands of Japan. All agreed that Formosa would require a major undertaking. Admiral King favored the Formosa attack, but he conceded that it probably would not be feasible until after the defeat of Germany, when additional resources could be made available from Europe. Admiral Nimitz, therefore, was directed to undertake a landing on Iwo Jima in the Bonins on 20 January, and in the Ryukyus by 1 March 1945.

The German counteroffensive in the Ardennes in December 1944 complicated plans for redeployment of resources to the Pacific, but already means had been found to support the campaign in the Philippines, and operations there went very much according to schedule.

The question still remained whether Japan finally could be defeated by air and naval power alone, as far as the home islands were concerned, or whether an invasion would be necessary. The Army took the pessimistic view. At the Yalta Conference in January 1945 General Marshall and Admiral King reported that plans had been prepared for an invasion of the home islands of Kyushu and Honshu in 1945, though it was recognized that these plans would depend upon redeployment from Europe, which would take four to six months after the surrender of Germany. For planning purposes it was assumed that the defeat of Germany could be accomplished by 1 July, and that it would take about eighteen months after that date to end the war against Japan.

Plans for redeployment involved the most ambitious logistical operations of the war—or of any war—for the American forces. They called for the movement of 1.2 million men from Europe (800,000 by way of the United States, and 400,000 directly) to the Pacific, the transfer of 5 million tons of supplies and equipment from Europe to the Pacific, and the return of another 5 million tons to the United States. The Eighth Air Force swiftly redeployed after V–E Day, and the redeployment of ground forces began. The build-up in the Philippines and on Okinawa for the planned invasion of the Japanese home islands proceeded rapidly. Logistic factors very largely determined the choice of target dates and the size of forces. Plans called for two major operations. The first, scheduled tentatively for 1 November 1945, was to be a three-pronged attack by Sixth Army on the southern Japanese island of Kyushu. The second, scheduled for 1 March 1946 with a force of nine infantry divisions, two armored divisions, and three Marine Corps divisions, under Eighth Army and Tenth Army, followed by First Army, to be redeployed from Europe with ten infantry and one airborne divisions, was to be aimed initially at the Konto plain east of Tokyo.

Then came the rapid turn of events in August 1945: the atomic bomb on Hiroshima on the 6th; USSR entry into the war against Japan on the 8th, and the swift moves of the Red Army across Manchuria, into Korea and into the southern half of Sakhalin; the second atomic bomb, on Nagasaki, on the 9th; and finally, the Japanese request for peace terms on the 10th. The machinery of redeployment for invasion was abruptly reversed.

By V–J Day all of the eighty-nine divisions that the Army had mobilized (one other had been mobilized but inactivated in North Africa) had been deployed overseas, and all but two had seen combat. At that time Army forces in the Pacific still had only the twenty-one divisions with which they had stepped up their operations in 1944.

What really was the effect of the Europe-first decision? Actually, it probably made very little difference to the progress of the war in the Pacific, where the limiting factor on operations was not ground forces nor even supplies for their support, but rather shipping and the availability of sea-based and land-based air cover, which, in turn depended upon the recovery of the U.S. Pacific Fleet and the building of airfields within range of objectives. Once the new *Essex*-class carriers and the floating repair and supply system were available, long-range offensive operations could begin. Until they were available little more could be done no matter how many troops and supplies might have beeen available. On the other hand, it is quite likely that a contrary decision in favor of the Pacific first would have caused serious delays to the successful conclusion of the war in Europe. Divisions and shipping diverted to the Pacific would have made the Normandy invasion impossible until some redeployment could have taken place, and prolonged delay might have resulted in a dangerous strengthening of the German position relative to that of the British and Russian.

Indeed, there have been numerous contentions that the Pacific war was an undue drag on the main effort in Europe. Was there in fact a pull to the Pacific? First of all, it must be granted that in practice if not officially the Pacific did enjoy a priority in deployment of American forces during the early months of the war, but this was more a matter of necessity than of design. Then it was a question of getting enough forces out there to secure a supply line to

Australia and to contain the Japanese expansion. Furthermore, the delays in getting firm commitments firmly held for the OVERLORD operation permitted sending more men and resources to the Pacific than otherwise would have been the case, so that about the maximum usable strength was on hand for the conditions of the time. It must be granted, too, that Admiral King's strong influence consistently leaned to the Pacific—the area of greatest naval concentration—and MacArthur never did reconcile himself to the Europe-first decision and never ceased his attempts to get it reversed. The CBI had to give up most of its landing craft for the European landings, and much additional landing craft for the Pacific had to be held up until after the Normandy invasion. Two divisions en route to the west coast for shipment to the Pacific in February 1945 were halted and rushed back across the country and onto fast ships to reinforce European armies weakened in the Ardennes battles. By this time the ratio of divisions in Europe to those in the Pacific was 3.5 to 1, without taking into account the six Marine divisions in the Pacific. In a way the American chiefs of staff learned to use the demands of the Pacific as a bargaining instrument when their British colleagues brought up the question of stepping up operations in the Mediterranean: if there was to be a diversion from the main effort in Western Europe, they maintained it ought to go to the Pacific.

A number of uncertainties contributed to difficulties in planning throughout World War II. The fact that the enemy held the initiative for several months in the beginning made long-range plans difficult; the changing fortunes of war frequently made it necessary to modify plans, which nearly always entailed delay; the submarine campaign and civilian and other competing requirements made it difficult to anticipate shipping; uncertainties about the effectiveness of amphibious landings on well-defended coasts when that kind of warfare was necessary in all major theaters multiplied planning problems. Finally, the continuing debates over priorities as between the war in Europe and the war against Japan, and over the peripheral strategy and the direct-attack strategy for Europe, and competition between the Southwest and Central Pacific Areas against Japan all made it virtually impossible to arrive at firm, long-range logistic plans.

The major strategic decisions of the war were in the main based on logistical considerations, and were themselves essentially logistical decisions. As far as high policy was concerned, strategic decisions did not govern industrial mobilization and procurement, but only modified details of those programs. Even deployment did not at first reflect major strategic decisions, though of course in the end the deployment of forces did correspond to those decisions in a general way.

CHAPTER XXVII

Lend-Lease

Direct involvement of the United States in World War II may be said to have begun with the passage of the Lend-Lease Act in March 1941, which committed the United States to an Allied victory at least to the extent that matériel support could help bring it about. The Lend-Lease Act was not a sudden or an isolated step, but the culmination of a long series of steps taken in the direction of co-operation with the Allies as the threat of war became greater.

Origins and Inception

As early as 1937 informal conversations between American and British naval leaders had anticipated certain measures of co-operation in the event of a war involving both powers against a common enemy. Within a month after the German take-over of Austria in March 1938 a British purchasing mission had arrived in the United States to survey the aircraft industry. In the first, tentative moves toward rearmament following hard upon the Munich conference in the fall of 1938, President Roosevelt had emphasized the building of aircraft for France and Britain as well as for the United States. A French survey mission headed by the dynamic industrialist, Jean Monnet, had prepared the way for French purchase orders early in 1939 that laid the groundwork for the expansion of production. But the Neutrality Acts, a group of laws passed between 1935 and 1937 aimed less at preserving traditional neutral rights and duties than at staying out of war on the basis of a superficial analysis of the cause for American entry into World War I, posed an ironic obstacle. So long as peace was maintained, French and British orders could be filled without question, but if these countries became involved in war, the Neutrality Acts required an embargo on the shipment of arms to them. When war became a fact in September 1939, shipments had to be suspended until the "cash and carry" amendment to the Neutrality Acts was adopted. Within a few days of the declaration of war, a British Purchasing Commisison, headed by Arthur B. Purvis, a leading Canadian Industrialist, was formally established. An Anglo-French Co-ordinating Commission then began operations in London under the direction of Jean Monnet, and an Anglo-French Purchasing Board, under Purvis, in Washington. By mid-1939 British and French orders reached such proportions as to raise questions of priority in American industry for meeting the needs of the United States as against those of the Allies, and the President assigned to the Army and Navy Munitions Board the task of co-ordinating those purchases. In December of that year he set up a committee made up of representatives from the Army, the Navy, and the Treasury Department Procurement Division, under the chairmanship of Secretary of the Treasury Henry Morgenthau, Jr., to act as liaison with foreign governments on matters of procurement. The choice of Morgenthau for this role can be attributed, apparently, to a feeling that he could be expected to take a less parochial view than either the Army or Navy and that he would zealously follow through on national armaments policies.

These activities had given impetus to the expansion of facilities for the production of aircraft, machine tools, weapons, and ammunition, but before production could become effective Allied defenses on the European Continent collapsed. After Dunkerque the British, desperate but determined to fight on, called for an urgent shipment of arms to replace those left on the beaches of France. Roosevelt responded with an emergency shipment of World War I Enfield rifles, 75-mm. guns, machine guns, and ammunition by resorting to the device of having the Army declare them surplus (with the expectation that they would be replaced by new items), and selling them to a private corporation for resale to Great Britain. In September 1940 the transfer of fifty World War I destroyers to Britain in return for leases of Atlantic bases was effected. A Joint Aircraft Committee, made up of British and American air officers, was formed in the autumn of 1940 to work toward aircraft standardization and the allocation of finished planes. Although no set formula was ever adopted, Roosevelt by this time had committed himself to an even-stephen division with the British of aircraft, tanks, and other major items from current U.S. production.

Increasing reliance of the British on new weapons and equipment from the United States brought to a head a basic question on standardization. In World War I the United States had used an adaptation of a British-model rifle rather than its own

Springfield because the arms factories already had been tooled and were producing British models under earlier orders. The question then had been whether British types of rifles, artillery pieces, and ammunition should be produced when requirements for rearming the U.S. forces had to be met concurrently. This time the War Department refused to allow orders for British types, so that the British had to work out ways for arming certain of their units with American types without at the same time jeopardizing their own production effort or unduly complicating their supply system.

The most serious problem for the British in the fall of 1940 was the impending depletion of their dollar resources. All dollar reserves, including those resulting from the British Government's expropriation of dollar investments held by British subjects, were nearly exhausted. The British outlay in purchases and in building new factories in the United States amounted to nearly $4.5 billion. But there could be no more. Something drastic had to be done if Britain was to hold out.

After meditating on a long and detailed letter from Winston Churchill during a Caribbean cruise, Roosevelt on 17 December 1940 called a news conference at the White House. Having explained the situation and various ways of dealing with it, the President went on to say:

Now, what I am trying to do is eliminate the dollar sign. That is something brand new in the thoughts of everybody in this room, I think—get rid of the silly, foolish old dollar sign.

Well, let me give you an illustration. Suppose my neighbor's home catches fire, and I have a length of garden hose four or five hundred feet away. If he can take my garden hose and connect it up with his hydrant, I may help him to put out the fire. Now what do I do? I don't say to him before that operation, "Neighbor, my garden hose cost me $15; you have to pay me $15 for it." What is the transaction that goes on? I don't want $15— I want my garden hose back after the fire is over.[1]

Three months of vigorous debate followed. Many Americans argued, with Roosevelt, that effective aid to Great Britain was the best means for the United States to avoid war; they found hope in Churchill's appeal, "give us the tools, and we'll finish the job." [2] Others warned that that position was a clear abandonment of neutrality, and would lead directly to war; many felt that in the circumstances of 1941 the security of the United States was bound with the security of Britain, whatever one might think about getting into war.

Conceived as an instrument to provide effective matériel assistance in a common war effort, without provoking the irritating aftermath incident to equating a war measure with a commercial loan such as troubled international relations after World War I, lend-lease aid was granted with no assumption of full repayment. The act provided that the President might "sell, transfer title to, exchange, lease, lend, or otherwise dispose of . . . any defense article" to any country whose defense the President deemed "vital to the defense of the United States." Transfers from current stocks and from production under earlier appropriations were limited to $1.3 billion in total value, and such transfers had to have the approval of the Army Chief of Staff or the Chief of Naval Operations—thus giving to the military chiefs a veto over their own commander in chief—but new procurement, whether from manufacture in government arsenals or by private contractors, was limited only by the amounts of appropriations available. Urgency for immediate deliveries gave special importance to the provision for transfer from current productions. Unless sooner terminated by concurrent resolution of Congress, authority to enter into lend-lease arrangements would end on 30 June 1943, and authority to carry out contracts or agreements made with foreign governments before that date would continue until 1 July 1946. Congress subsequently made three one-year extensions of the act, so that the final date set for making lend-lease commitments was 30 June 1946, with authority to carry them out until 1 July 1949.

Administration

The President at first kept the direction of the lend-lease program largely in his own hands, but called upon his close adviser, Harry L. Hopkins, to act for him as a kind of unofficial administrator. To handle the details of co-ordination and reporting, in May he set up the Division of Defense Aid Reports with Maj. Gen. James H. Burns, executive assistant to the Under Secretary of War, as executive officer. Although the President was authorized to exercise his powers through any departments or agencies that he might choose, many decisions needing immediate attention were his alone to make: which countries should receive aid, what terms ought to govern such aid, to what extent foreign aid should be granted priority over the needs of the U.S. Army and Navy.

---

[1] Samuel I. Rosenman, comp., "The Public Papers and Addresses of Franklin D. Roosevelt," 1940 Volume: *War—and Aid to Democracies* (New York: The Macmillan Company, 1941), p. 607.

[2] Quoted in Robert E. Sherwood, *Roosevelt and Hopkins, An Intimate History* (New York: Harper & Brothers, 1948), p. 261.

After a few months of this informal organization, during which the President personally signed all allocation orders and transfer letters, he set up the Office of Lend-Lease Administration under Edward R. Stettinius, Jr., son of one of the assistant secretaries of war during World War I, and formerly chairman of the board of the United States Steel Corporation. This organization continued until the autumn of 1943 when the Office of Lend-Lease Administration, together with a dozen other agencies and activities in the field of international economic relations, was consolidated in the new Foreign Economic Administration under Leo T. Crowley. All of these agencies were concerned mainly with co-ordination and record-keeping.

The business of procurement and supply of military matériel for foreign governments remained with the military bureaus. Within the Army the division of responsibility among the procurement and supply agencies, and the necessity, until after Pearl Harbor, of developing separate supply programs to correspond to separate appropriations, further complicated the administrative machinery. Later, when Congress appropriated funds for military lend-lease supplies directly to the War Department, the Army could develop a single supply program for its own and Allied needs. The organizational structure began to improve when Col. Henry S. Aurand was named Defense Aid Director of the War Department on 1 October 1941. Though he remained responsible to four or five different supervisors, including the Under Secretary and the two Assistant Secretaries of War, each one having a separate responsibility in the program, as well as to his chiefs on the General Staff, Colonel Aurand was able to bring together most of

the committees and staff sections engaged in lend-lease activities. After the War Department reorganization of 1942 his office became the International Division of Army Service Forces.

The lend-lease program got off to a fast start with an appropriation of $7 billion in March 1941, and another for $5.985 billion in October. Approximately $6.4 billion of the total amount was for Army procurement. This was about as much as was appropriated for the Army's own procurement for Fiscal Year 1941, and almost exactly equal to the total War Department appropriations for all purposes for the preceding nineteen fiscal years. Some saw in this program a serious competitor for matériel that the U.S. Army would be needing. It probably would be more fair to recognize that lend-lease provided the impetus for a gain of six months to a year in the conversion and expansion of American industry so that it could meet the Army's needs as well as those of the Navy and the Allies in the years ahead. This made it especially important to insist that weapons and equipment produced under the program should be American types.

The General Staff adopted an 80–20 formula as the basis for preparing lists of available equipment. This represented something of a compromise with earlier insistence in the War Department that requirements for the Army's own forces as contemplated under the Protective Mobilization Plan should be met first. The 80–20 formula provided that 20 percent of current production might go for foreign assistance until requirements for the protective mobilization force were met, plus one month's maintenance reserve; then the ratio might be reversed so that 80 percent could be transferred to other countries. Military leaders began to see a successful lend-lease program as a way to expand American military production that would later be available for U.S. needs if necessary. In practice, the President continued to play it by ear as emergency demands of Great Britain for the Middle East, minor concessions to the Netherlands East Indies and to China, and major demands of the Soviet Union were met at the expense of the Army's own projects. In spite of the pull of competing demands and crises, it was possible to adhere fairly closely to the 80–20 formula, even though the President never did accept it as a commitment.

The Programs

Great Britain

British and American leaders meeting in Washington in the weeks following Pearl Harbor were aware of the necessity for logistic as well as for strategic co-ordination. Machinery intended to move in this direction had been evolving with the relatively slow munitions build-up of the preceding year. With the impetus of Pearl Harbor, and taking full advantage of the preparatory work, the conference very early reached agreement on a more complete organization for international collaboration. Inevitably the experiences of war brought additions and modifications, but basically the pattern for the operation of probably the closest military alliance in history—accomplished without any treaty of alliance—was set by January 1942.

In the interest of clarification and simplicity of terminology, it was agreed that the word "joint" would be reserved for reference to interservice operations or activities within one nation (although it continued to be used in connection with some U.S.-Canadian boards and with some agencies formed with Latin-American nations), while "combined" would be used with reference to agencies and activities of international, specifically British-American, scope. At the pinnacle of the military organization, subject only to the President and the Prime Minister, was the Combined Chiefs of Staff (CCS). But CCS really was not a separate and distinct entity; rather it was a combination of the chiefs of staff of each nation who continued their own work separately. The Combined Chiefs met in formal session only at the series of international conferences where the major strategic decisions of the war were taken. Between conferences, the Joint Staff Mission in Washington, representing the British chiefs, held weekly meetings with the United States Joint Chiefs of Staff, and, together with a combined secretariat and a combined planning staff (which actually did less planning than did the regular national staffs), provided continuity for the Combined Chiefs.

Leaders at the Washington Conference accepted the principle that "the entire munitions resources of Great Britain and the United States will be deemed to be in a common pool" from which assignments should be made according to strategic needs. The Munitions Assignments Board (MAB) was established at the same time to operate under the Combined Chiefs of Staff in effecting the co-ordination of combined action in logistics with combined strategy. MAB worked through a Washington committee made up of military representatives but with a civilian chairman, Harry Hopkins, and through a similar London committee under a British chairman, Lord Beaverbrook. Two other agencies that also emerged from the Washington Conference were to deal with particular problems demanding immediate international attention—the Combined Shipping Adjustment Board and the Combined Raw Materials Board. Five months later the establishment of the Combined Production and Resources Board and the Combined Food Board completed the pattern of earlier British proposals to correspond to the analysis by the British Supply Council (which became the body for co-ordination of the British missions and participants on the combined boards in the United States) of the steps of international logistics: (1) determination of strategic concept and its expression in military requirements; (2) translation into raw materials necessary for production; (3) production itself; (4) assignment of finished weapons; (5) shipping.

Reluctantly following the British lead, the Americans agreed informally to a division of labor between the Washington and London Munitions Assignments Boards whereby members of the British Empire and the European Allies would apply to London, while the Latin American republics and China would apply to Washington. Each would satisfy requirements to the extent possible from stocks within the respective country, and turn to its transatlantic counterpart for the remainder. In practice this meant that a large share of the requests ultimately came to Washington, but allocations from Washington for the Allied governments-in-exile generally were made in bulk to England and the London Assignments Board made the suballocations. Both boards did most of their work through committees for ground, naval, and air forces. Allocations were supposed to be based upon strategic plans and agreed priorities for the theaters, but logistic plans often could not await precise strategic planning, and had to

be based more upon assumptions and hopes than upon well-defined strategy.

The other combined boards generally consisted of two-man teams—one British and one American member—surrounded by a system of committees. In some ways they resembled the international committees and councils that had co-ordinated purchases and controlled raw materials and shipping during World War I. At the same time, for example, the boards did not have the power of decision as had the Allied Maritime Transport Executive of World War I, or the current Munitions Assignments Board, for that matter. Yet, the team and the committee recommendations were important in bringing into phase the separate national programs toward a common purpose.

The machinery for Allied co-operation during World War II was rather less formalized and less complete than that which ultimately developed in 1917–18. No Supreme War Council sat as the over-all directing authority. The President of the United States and the Prime Minister of Great Britain performed that function at their international meetings and through direct communications. This left out the other members of the United Nations coalition in the making of policy, which was as the British and American leaders intended it should be. Only China objected to the arrangement, but was persuaded to go along with it by being recognized as a theater outside the scope of the Combined Chiefs of Staff, while participating in their plans in Southeast Asia. Canada, holding a peculiar position between Great Britain and the United States, participated on separate boards with each nation, and finally won distinct membership on the Combined Production and Resources Board and the Combined Food Board. Other British Commonwealth countries, notably Australia and New Zealand, maintained sizable supply missions in Washington, and their members contributed important advice to the several committees but never as full members of the combined boards. Heads of the Commonwealth and Empire missions in Washington formed a Principal Commonwealth Supply Committee for their own co-ordination.

If the pooling of munitions had been complete there would appear to have been little reason for continuation of the Lend-Lease Administration (except for civilian goods), but this was less an allocation agency than a co-ordinator of requirements, appropriations, and procurement. The practice generally came to be for lend-lease to be programmed to the "British Empire" as an entity, and to allow the Commonwealth members to handle the suballocations, though they made cash purchases in the United States directly.

When British forces were actively engaged on several fronts, before the Americans had begun to fight, and when British war production was greater than the American, the idea of pooling the munitions resources of the two nations seemed reasonable and practical enough to American leaders. But as American participation grew in all theaters, and as American war production in mid-1942 pulled ahead of the British and a year later exceeded it by four times, pressure mounted in the United States for control over its own resources. The protégé arrangement for division of authority between the London and Washington Munitions Assignments Boards never did work out fully, and the center of gravity for the whole program became more and more clearly established in Washington. British hopes for a truly integrated international munitions program, one administered by the Combined Production and Resources Board on the basis of combined requirements as determined by the Combined Chiefs of Staff, never materialized. Early in the war the British had urged strategic necessity as the criterion for the allocation of munitions; later, when the American strategic requirements had grown far greater, the United States adopted this position to the disadvantage of Great Britain. Gradually lend-lease came to be regarded less as a means for pooling resources than as an instrument of the national policy of the United States—which, of course, it had been proclaimed to be at the outset. Nevertheless, British-American co-operation probably was the closest ever among allies, and all together the British Empire received about one-fourth of all its munitions through American lend-lease.

For about a year the International Supply Committee continued to co-ordinate lend-lease requirements for ground forces equipment under lend-lease and the Joint Aircraft Committee to co-ordinate air equipment requirements, but after a few months none of the international agencies had much influence on the determination of American military requirements. Agencies of the Army Service Forces in general drew up the various parts of the Army Supply Program, including its lend-lease aspects. Co-ordination of lend-lease functions within Army Services Forces fell to the International Division which furnished the chairman and secretariat for the Munitions Assignments Committee (Ground), liaison with foreign governments participating in lend-lease, and staff for correlating lend-lease and U.S. Army requirements. On the other hand, the Operations Division of the General Staff had the major role in determining assignments policy.

During 1943, with abolition of the International Supply Committee, administration of military lend-lease was left almost exclusively in the hands of Army Service Forces. Requests from foreign governments no longer went to the Munitions Assignments Board, but to General Somervell, and War Department Conference Groups, without British representation, replaced the combined subcommittees of the Munitions Assignments Committee (Ground).

Soviet Union

The German invasion of the Soviet Union in June 1941 raised hope for a great new weight against the German war machine and at the same time aroused fears that the invasion would succeed in integrating Russian resources with those of Central Europe, thus adding new strength to the Axis. Churchill immediately offered all possible British aid to the USSR. Against the doubts of his military advisers, Roosevelt too decided that aid should go to the Soviet Union—to get matériel to forces already deployed in battle. At first American aid was in the form of cash purchases. Then, after a series of U.S.–U.K. conferences the United States joined in negotiations in Moscow which resulted in a tripartite protocol (signed 1 October 1941) committing both the United States and Great Britain to deliver to the USSR stated amounts of military equipment. A few weeks later the President put the whole program of U.S. aid to the Soviet Union under lend-lease with an allocation of $1 billion.

Much as the British favored aid to USSR, they feared that the U.S. commitments would mean a cut in the share of matériel for themselves; they had hoped to combine the Russian program with their own, and to retain the right of suballocating for Soviet requirements.. At the same time, U.S. military leaders were cool toward another substantial drain on American equipment when they were having a difficult enough time equipping their own forces—and, in view of an expected early Russian collapse, to no apparent purpose. The highly critical attitude that Russian representatives revealed did nothing toward alleviating this coolness. Then Pearl Harbor, coinciding as it did with the German drive on Moscow, magnified feelings that supplies could not be spared now that American forces would have to be mobilized, and that aid to the USSR would be futile.

Nevertheless, Roosevelt held firmly to his policy of all possible aid for Russia. The limits of possibility were set not so much by the availability of supplies—a decision that U.S. units in training should have only 50 percent of their authorized equipment helped to stretch available quantities—as by the means of delivery to the Soviet Union. The northern route to Archangel and Murmansk was terribly difficult in winter, and German submarines soon made it almost impossible at any time. The route across the Pacific came too close to Japan, and Vladivostok was too far from the fighting fronts to be very useful. The Mediterranean was closed to most Allied shipping. The approach through the Persian Gulf and Iran was left as a possibility.

With an eye to the potential usefulness of transportation connections across Iran the British and Russians had agreed on a joint occupation of that country in August 1941, but in the next year did little to develop facilities while they turned their attention to other tasks, and relied on the northern route for delivery of supplies. In May 1942 losses to submarines became so serious that Churchill decided at first that northern convoys would have to be drastically reduced, and then that they would have to be canceled altogether. The decision in July for the invasion of North Africa made it necessary to concentrate shipping for that purpose, and, as Russian aid was being nearly cut off, Stalin had to be told that the second front for which he had been clamoring would have to be postponed in favor of a second front in North Africa. If Russian resistance were to be maintained, the only recourse was to open a large-scale line of communication through Iran. Churchill and Roosevelt quickly agreed that this must be done, though it took their staffs several weeks to work out the details. General Somervell's staff actually worked out the basic plan, calling for operation of the ports, railroad, and truck routes by the U.S. Army, and the Combined Chiefs of Staff approved it with minor modifications on 22 September 1942. A long period of transition followed in which Americans gradually took over facilities from the British, military construction units replaced civilian contractors, and the capacities of the ports and the railroad gradually expanded. Curiously, matériel earmarked for the Soviet Union had been granted almost the highest possible priority, but the materials needed for developing the facilities to make effective delivery had been among the lowest. Once development of communications facilities in the Persian Corridor had been decided upon, that project enjoyed higher priority than the build-up in the United Kingdom. In addition, the North Pacific became an important route for delivering civilian-type goods to the Soviet Union. U.S. ships turned over to the USSR were able to proceed past Hokkaido without Japanese interference. After about three months' delay while Russia repaired port facilities and negotiated a new agreement with the United States, shipments by way of the Black Sea, principally to Odessa, began in January 1945, and this route quickly replaced the Persian Gulf for access from the southwest.

American programs for aid to the Soviet Union under the first two protocols (1941 to 1943) fell about 25 percent short, but deliveries for Fiscal Year 1944 were 30 percent above commitments, and those for 1944–45 already were 95 percent complete when V–E Day allowed a revision in schedules nearly two months before the end of the fiscal year. About 40,000 long tons of supplies reached the Soviet Union by way of the Persian Corridor in September 1942. In September 1943 (the same month that the Persian Gulf Command as a separate command reporting directly to the War Department superseded the former Persian Gulf Service Command under U.S. Army Forces in the Middle East at Cairo) deliveries to the Soviet Union by this route reached over 200,000 tons. The Third Protocol (Fiscal Year 1944) alone comprised a program for shipping 5,100,000 tons—2,700,000 by the Pacific route, and 2,400,000 tons by the Atlantic. Difficulties in the North Pacific made it necessary to shift considerable quantities to the Atlantic, and northern convoys, with British escort, were resumed in November 1944. Military items under the Third Protocol program included, among other things, approximately 5,000 aircraft, 20,000 jeeps, 3,000 artillery prime movers, 2,000 medium tanks, 132,000 trucks, 10,000 railroad flatcars, 500 locomotives, and 100,000 field telephones.

China

The only other major recipient of lend-lease aid before Pearl Harbor was China. Greece and Yugoslavia were included in the original program, but the Nazis reached Athens and Belgrade before the aid could arrive. Although British requirements had been almost the whole concern of the framers of the Lend-Lease Act, a request for a billion-dollar program for China was promptly presented. It was the work of China Defense Supplies, Inc., a corporation formed under the laws of Delaware with T. V. Soong, brother-in-law of Chiang Kai-shek, at its head, and staffed largely by American business men. In May the President declared China eligible for lend-lease aid, but serious obstacles were in the way. Virtually all available surplus stocks already had been released to the British, and the allocation of appropriated funds had been based entirely on aid to Great Britain. The Chinese program represented a serious competitor for limited supplies and for available shipping. Nevertheless, it was the policy of the United States to use all possible means to prop up China as an effective power against Japan, and by making adjustments here and there some $200 million worth of equipment was earmarked for China. Chinese requests were included along with the British in the second lend-lease appropriation in October 1941.

Most serious of all was the problem of access to China. The only approach open was by way of Burma, and extensive improvement to that line of communication was necessary before any sizable shipments of supplies could be delivered. While Pearl Harbor added to the desirability of aid to China, increased Japanese activity in Southeast Asia also made access even more difficult. Projects for equipment for the Chinese Army allowed for thirty divisions in 1941 and 1942, then sixty divisions; in 1943 they reverted to the original thirty divisions plus 10 percent for thirty additional divisions for training purposes. Actually supplies, for the most part, when they did materialize, had to be stored in depots in India until the Assam line of communication could be improved and until the Stilwell Road could be opened, although some essential supplies were delivered by air over the Hump. Supplies to U.S.-sponsored Chinese divisions in India and Burma gained by drawing supplies from U.S. depots just as American units did. While initial equipment still had to be cleared by the Munitions Assignments Board, the War Department late in 1944 permitted direct requisitioning on the Los Angeles Port of Embarkation for maintenance supplies for Chinese units in India and Burma.

France

A rather different kind of problem presented itself with proposals for rearming the French. It seemed a strange, unreal, situation that France, the source of major assistance for American forces in the Revolution and again in World War I, now should lay prostrate, almost entirely dependent upon American matériel for any recovery of military strength. Although the British had been supplying Free French Forces under General Charles de Gaulle, American leaders, perhaps underestimating the support for de Gaulle within France, had turned down his pleas for assistance. Then the invasion of North Africa in the fall of

FRENCH TROOPS WITH LEND-LEASE TANKS, *parading through Algiers on Bastille Day, 1943.*

1942 brought to a head the question of providing equipment for the sizable French forces there which so far had remained loyal to the Vichy government. The Americans sponsored General Henri Giraud, lately escaped from a German prison camp, for commander in chief of French forces in North Africa, and at Casablanca he obtained what he considered to be firm commitments for the rearmament of the French forces. The British had some qualms about American plans for rearming the French both on the grounds of another competing claimant for limited resources, and of sponsorship of a French military regime in competition with de Gaulle. Nevertheless, all agreed with the views of General Marshall and President Roosevelt, stated at Casablanca, that rearmament of French units so that they might become effective fighting forces would be an economical addition to Allied strength; rearmed French troops could save just that much in personnel shipping from the United States. General Eisenhower, as theater commander, had been granted a large measure of authority over French rearmament. In December 1942 he had set up a Joint Rearmament Committee as a staff section of his Allied Force Headquarters to review French requests and develop a long-range program. Equipment for the French went through U.S. supply channels. The Munitions Assignments Board confirmed the allocations only after the transfers had been made, and all supplies thus turned over were charged to the French lend-lease account.

In the Tunisian campaign French troops, demonstrating their loyalty and determination, qualified for further assistance. In Italy the French corps under General Alphonse Juin proved its effectiveness in a way that gave impetus to plans for completing the rearmament program, and in France and Germany the 1st French Army under General Jean de Lattre de Tassigny carried its full weight in the climactic campaigns of the war, while Maj. Gen. Jacques Leclerc's 2d French Armored Division demonstrated effective use of American equipment with American forces in the race across France.

This was a novel experience: rearming the entire army of a major nation. All together the United States furnished full initial equipment and complete maintenance for 250,000 men organized in eight divisions and 300 supporting units raised in North Africa, together with about one-third of the initial equipment and complete maintenance for another 50,000 men in three divisions and forty supporting units activated in Metropolitan France. It also equipped nineteen air squadrons and sixty supporting units. Another 200,000 men in local Territorial forces in Africa received partial supplies from the United States, and about 260,000 men in the French forces depended almost entirely upon American rations.[3] Probably the greatest weakness in this program was the lack of sufficient service troops to make it fully effective.

De Gaulle quickly had gained the ascendancy over Giraud in North Africa, and made

himself the effective ruler of Free France, although the Allies did not recognize his French Provisional Government until October 1944. De Gaulle's sensitivity over exclusion from Allied councils and full participation in plans for the liberation of his own country was a constant source of embarrassment. He agreed to place French units under the operational control of Supreme Allied Headquarters even though he had no representation on its staff, but he insisted on retaining a measure of control for French national purposes.

Political and logistical controversy went together. When Strasbourg was left in an exposed salient as a result of German counterattacks around Colmar at the same time as the Ardennes counteroffensive in December 1944, Eisenhower ordered the 1st French Army, through 6th Army Group, to withdraw from Strasbourg in favor of a better defensive position. But de Gaulle, insisting that the psychological impact of giving up Strasbourg would be a serious blow to the morale of the French nation, countermanded the order, and went to see Eisenhower to insist on his position. The Supreme Commander suggested that he could no longer permit American supplies to go to the French forces if they did not obey the order. But when De Gaulle pointed out that American supply lines ran all the way across France, and that he could take no responsibility for their security if a withdrawal led to dissatisfaction among the French, Eisenhower was able to see the soundness of the French position. In April 1945 when the French refused to evacuate Stuttgart as ordered by Lt. Gen. Jacob L. Devers to permit the U.S. Seventh Army to establish lines of communication through the town, which lay in its zone of operations, Eisenhower suspended further deliveries of equip-

---

[3] Marcel Vigneras, *Rearming the French*, UNITED STATES ARMY IN WORLD WAR II (Washington, 1957), pp. 401–02.

ment under the program or rearming units raised in Metropolitan France. A few weeks later refusal of other French forces to withdraw from Italian territory when so ordered incurred further suspensions of supply deliveries. By then V–E Day had come, and the rearmament program (except for preparation of a French expeditionary corps for the Far East) had ended. Throughout, the United States insisted that France develop its own supply system so that with the end of hostilities a revived French Army could then stand on its own feet and contribute to French postwar recovery of national strength.

Latin America and Other Programs

Countries of potential value in supporting the Allies or providing logistical facilities, but who were not actively engaged in military operations, had to be content with lower priorities in lend-lease assistance. Liberated countries came in for shares of lend-lease aid as they rejoined the war effort. British-sponsored plans for aid to Turkey did not amount to very much until late in the war.

After modest sales programs to Latin American countries under various terms in 1940, they were brought into the lend-lease program the next year. Differences over requirements for weapons and equipment, both as to types and quantities, complicated relations throughout the war, and the Latin American programs all together never amounted to more than 1 percent of all lend-lease aid. Still, the part that 1 percent played in encouraging economic co-operation, in making some return for the willingness of sixteen Latin American nations to permit the development of U.S. air and naval bases on their territory, and in present-

ing a solid front against the Axis, is not to be ignored. Brazil, which provided important bases for approaches to the Caribbean and for the South Atlantic air route, and which sent an expeditionary force to Italy, received more than 70 percent of lend-lease aid to Latin America.

The War Department's policy was that insofar as possible theater commanders should control lend-lease in their areas, including the screening of requests, determining priorities for shipping, and distribution, though allocations had to come from Washington. The extent to which this worked out in practice depended upon the extent to which American control was dominant. Control by the theater commander was almost complete in the Southwest Pacific, the South Pacific, China, and North Africa, but the British would not agree to it in the Middle East, and not until 1944 in India and Southeast Asia.

Reverse Lend-Lease

An aspect of Allied co-operation which grew in importance as American operations overseas expanded was reverse lend-lease, which permitted theater commanders to arrange for the use of local facilities and for local procurement of supplies without involving cash transactions. General Purchasing Boards organized in Australia and in the United Kingdom in 1942 became the models for organizations for local procurement in other theaters. Nearly everywhere that American soldiers went, reverse lend-lease helped to support them. American forces deployed to Australia and New Zealand were able to obtain most of their food and a good deal of their clothing locally under reciprocal aid arrangements. Reverse lend-lease provided a convenient mechanism for obtaining housing, transportation, and training facilities. It never could approach the total volume of lend-lease itself, but it provided a means for a two-way pooling of all available resources at tremendous savings in shipping, handling, and time. The total value of reverse lend-lease, over $7.8 billion, was almost one-sixth the value of total lend-lease aid. Most of this came from the British Commonwealth.

Summary

By 1945 lend-lease goods and services of all kinds being furnished to allies of the United States had reached an annual rate of $15 billion. Total lend-lease furnished from March 1941 to December 1945 amounted to more than $48 billion. This included aircraft and parts (to the extent of $8.2 billion), tanks and other combat vehicles and parts ($3.9 billion), trucks and parts ($2.5 billion), weapons ($3 billion), ammunition ($1.5 billion), military clothing, signal equipment, chemical warfare items, and other military equipment and supplies, as well as ships, industrial equipment, raw materials, food, and other goods and services. About $31.6 billion worth went to the countries of the British Empire, $11 billion to the USSR, over $3.23 billion to France, and about $1.6 billion to China.[4]

The magnitude of the lend-lease program gave to the United States an effective means for influencing Allied policy. It was especially effective at times in persuading China and France and sometimes Great Britain to go along with United States views. It might have been put to more effective use with respect to Russia. It was a part of the American disposition, however, to avoid political issues and implications. Eisenhower was impatient with proposals that seemed to be based upon political considerations. Somervell and others were very sensitive to anything that might tend to give to the British some postwar advantage, or that might contribute to the postwar rebuilding of France or China. But surely the purpose of the war was not to be found in the war itself, but precisely in the kind of postwar world that would emerge.

---

[4] Twenty-second Report to Congress on Lend-Lease Operations, House Doc 663, 79th Cong., 2d sess. Jun 14, 1946, pp. 17–18.

CHAPTER XXVIII

Industrial Mobilization and Procurement

From the moment the United States became actively involved in World War II it was clear that the country must mobilize for total war. To the question "how much?" the answer already was evident: "as much as possible of everything." But this still left crucial questions to be answered. How much was possible? What was the proper "mix?" Should facilities and resources be devoted to motor trucks or airplanes? Should there be more small arms or more artillery? Were landing craft more essential than railway cars? What possible basis was there for knowing what would be needed one to two years hence when current production plans would be in terms of military hardware?

Planners and responsible leaders during World War II took small advantage of the example and experience of the country's mobilization for World War I, but went about making many of the same mistakes and suffering the same frustrations as had their predecessors. They reassured themselves that "this war is different," and excused their mistakes and frustrations with the observation that no one could foretell what form the war would take. Indeed, no one could foresee the future in any detail; but neither could the future be left to chance and the enemy. The war could, at least to a degree, be shaped to a desired form, depending on the decisions made for conducting it, which, in their turn, must depend on prevailing strategic concepts, estimates of relative capabilities, enemy actions, and, above all, imagination.

Perhaps the greatest failure of all was the failure of Germany to read the lessons of 1918 and 1919 on the capacity of the United States to produce. Early in 1942, when war production was just beginning its expansion, General Somervell said:

The road ahead is dim with the dust of battles still unfought. How long that road is, no one can know. But it is shorter than it would have been had not our enemies misjudged us and themselves. For, when Hitler put his war on wheels he ran it straight down our alley. When he hitched his chariot to an internal combustion engine, he opened up a new battle front—a front that we know well. It's called Detroit.[1]

Industrial Expansion

Following its practice in all wars, the United States on the eve of World War II mobilized troops before weapons and equipment could possibly be available for them. Although in the spring of 1940 the United States was the leading industrial power of the world with tremendous potential for expansion, it was far down the scale when it came to facilities for turning out munitions of war. There was neither the powder on hand nor the facilities to produce it to provide one day's supply for the

---

[1] Quoted in Automobile Manufacturers Association, *Freedom's Arsenal* (Detroit: American Automobile Manufacturers Association, 1950), p. v.

force the United States would have overseas within three years. Soldiers on maneuvers in 1940 and 1941 often had to be content to use trucks to simulate tanks, and to carry sticks to represent guns and mortars. Lack of production facilities for military equipment made evident by orders from the Western Allies, lend-lease requirements, and the needs of partial mobilization, became critical with Pearl Harbor and total mobilization when more emphasis came to be placed where it probably should have been placed at first: on industrial mobilization as the key to rapid military mobilization. It became clear that facilities would have to be expanded in every possible way—by conversion of existing civilian plants to war production, by expansion of the government's own arsenals, by construction of new facilities, and by encouraging expansion and new construction on the part of private industry and by combinations of private and government undertakings.

The greatest boon to privately financed expansion of facilities for the production of essential war goods was the tax amortization law which permitted a deduction from taxable income of 20 percent a year of the cost of building or acquiring facilities for national defense purposes. This was in lieu of the normal depreciation allowance of 5 to 10 percent a year. Thus complete amortization of new facilities could be accomplished in five years, and if the national emergency or the need for the plant should end before that time, complete amortization would be allowed for the shorter period. Coupled with higher rates on corporate income taxes and an excess profits tax adopted about the same time, the amortization law proved to be a powerful incentive for expansion, but could not alone possibly provide all the facilities that would be needed.

More direct government action was necessary.

The first approach to government financing of industrial expansion took the form of Emergency Plant Facilities (EPF) contracts. In general these provided for government reimbursement, by monthly payments over a five-year period, of the costs of conversion or construction. Companies arranged for financing through banks or other private sources and made their own construction contracts. The contractor held title to the facility until full reimbursement had been received, when it reverted to the government, but he held an option to buy at cost less depreciation. Difficulties in satisfying the banks, the expense to the War Department to hold funds equal to the whole amount due on these facilities and still pay interest of 2½ to 4 percent, and problems of arriving at depreciation and meeting tax requirements led to the early obsolescence of this type of contract. More favorable arrangements soon were available under Defense Plant Corporation contracts. Set up by the Reconstruction Finance Corporation in August 1940, the Defense Plant Corporation, after a determination of need by the Army or other agency, would enter into a contract with the private firm to provide it with the funds needed for site acquisition and construction. The Defense Plant Corporation retained title to the property, and construction contracts of the lessee remained subject to its approval. The lessee paid a nominal rental (perhaps a dollar a year), depreciation rental, or full rental, depending on the nature of the items produced. At the end of the emergency the lessee had the option to buy the facility at cost less rental payments, or cost less depreciation, whichever was higher. Interest on the loan was at the rate of 1½ percent. Over 80 percent of the $3 billion which the Defense Plant Corporation advanced went for expanding facilities for the production of aircraft and related items.

Most important were the facilities constructed with the War Department's own funds. There was some expansion at the arsenals and depots operated by the War Department, but for the most part the new War Department-owned facilities were built by private construction companies under cost-plus-a-fixed-fee contracts, and operated by private contractors for a management fee. Generally referred to as government-owned, contractor-operated plants, they were mostly ordnance facilities for the production of powder, bombs, shells, and chemicals. The largest, the Sunflower Ordnance Works at Lawrence, Kansas, represented a capital outlay of more than $180,000,000. This program also began with rearmament in 1940, gained impetus with the passage of the Lend-Lease Act in March 1941, and was redoubled after Pearl Harbor. The total investment in new War Department facilities through September 1945 was over $4.3 billion. These were mostly facilities having little or no use for commercial production, and, since they remained in the hands of the War Department, they could be retained in reserve after the war.

Production and Materials Controls

The rearmament program of 1940 hardly was under way before strains began to appear in the American economy, ill-prepared as it was for the support of war. Where only a few years before the market had been glutted with products of all kinds, now serious shortages quickly began to develop in

cotton, flannel and linen cloth; cotton duck and webbing; aluminum, and various alloy steels. With additional military orders, other shortages at all levels of production appeared. Most serious of all was the shortage of machine tools, the root cause of many of the other shortages along the line. Clearly special governmental organization and controls would be necessary to channel materials and production efforts into the places where they were most needed, and to effect a mobilization of the economy sufficient to support the defense effort. The problem was to apply just the right amount of direction and control to eliminate waste and inefficiency without discouraging all-out efforts, and so obtain the greatest possible output. Hesitantly at first, the government went through essentially the same steps, repeating most of the same errors, and with about the same results as had been the case in the industrial mobilization for World War I. Ultimately the total effort and accomplishment, after more than a year of defense preparation and four years of war, far overshadowed the two-year mobilization effort of World War I, but the trials were about the same—once again experience, unfortunately, proved little help in avoiding the early problems and delays of organization and control. Although Bernard Baruch, chairman of the War Industries Board during World War I, was called in to give the benefit of his experience, his recommendations on organizing industry committees, priorities, and price controls for the most part were ignored until later conditions forced their acceptance. Similarly, studies of the Army Industrial College, organized in 1924 for the very purpose of preparing for industrial mobilization, received little attention. At the beginning it was largely a matter of opinion as to what the requirements were going to be. In 1940 and 1941, as in 1916, there were sharp differences as to whether the United States actually would be drawn into war. Until these doubts were resolved, half-measures often had to be accepted, though by 1941 the American economy was becoming more and more geared for war. Even so, it took some drastic changes in organization and control to meet the impact of war.

Shortly after his call for 50,000 aircraft and a billion-dollar supplementary appropriation for defense in May 1940, President Roosevelt set up the Office of Emergency Management to function within the Executive Office of the President as a kind of overseer for various special defense agencies as they appeared. Then he revived the Advisory Commission to the Council of National Defense which had been provided for in 1916. With the fall of France, the Joint Army and Navy Munitions Board again organized a Priorities Committee. The National Defense Advisory Commission had only advisory powers, and it had no chairman, but able men such as William S. Knudsen, president of General Motors, who headed the Commission's Industrial Division; Edward R. Stettinius, Jr., chairman of the board of the United States Steel Corporation, in charge of the Materials Division, and Ralph Budd, president of the Burlington Railroad, who headed the Transportation Division, laid the groundwork for the industrial mobilization which followed. However, it soon became evident that a directing agency with more authority was needed. Before the end of 1940, the Office of Production Management (OPM), with Knudsen as director general, and Sidney Hillman, a leader of organized labor, as associate director general, superseded the Advisory Commission. Some divisions,

such as Prices and Transportation, spun off to become separate agencies.

Meanwhile passage of the first peacetime selective service law in United States history hastened the whole mobilization effort. The Selective Service and Training Act, passed on 16 September 1940, provided not only for the drafting of men, but authorized obligatory orders on industry, and empowered the government to seize and operate plants if necessary. Moreover, President Roosevelt's campaign for a third term strengthened the hand of the government in that direction, for, despite considerable opposition, leaders of both parties supported mobilization measures and aid to Britain. Even so, the political climate did not seem appropriate for a full-scale effort, and the Office of Production Management, suffering from the same weaknesses in authority and direction as its predecessor, soon went the same way.

The Office of Price Administration (OPA), first established as the Office of Price Administration and Civilian Supply in April 1941, combined two divisions of the National Defense Advisory Commission under the leadership of Leon Henderson. Friction between Henderson's agency and the OPM led President Roosevelt to fall back on his favorite device to overcome organizational failures—setting up a new agency without abolishing the old. In August 1941 he appointed the Supply Priorities and Allocations Board to bring together representatives of the military service and the principal mobilization agencies. Presided over by Vice President Henry Wallace, as chairman of the Economic Defense Board, and with Donald Nelson, a former executive of Sears, Roebuck and Company who had been head of the OPM Purchases Division, as its executive director,

SPAB was a policy-making body without any staff of its own. In some ways it confused even further the lines of authority for direction of industrial mobilization and settled no basic differences on requirements and priorities. In January 1942 SPAB gave way to the War Production Board (WPB), with Nelson as its Chairman.[2]

With doubts about the national purpose resolved by Pearl Harbor, and with authority to enforce compliance through the granting of priorities and allocations, the new organization began to demonstrate its effectiveness almost at once. Still, the Office of Price Administration, the Office of Defense Transportation, the War Manpower Commission, the War Food Administration, and other agencies remained or were established as separate agencies, and the Army and Navy retained control over their own procurements. In October 1942 Roosevelt called James F. Byrnes from the Supreme Court to become Director of Economic Stabilization as an over-all co-ordinator. Seven months later Byrnes became director of the Office of War Mobilization with broad powers for managing the war agencies; in this position he came to be known as the "Assistant President."

With the establishment of the War Production Board the principle of civilian direction of economic mobilization was set. But military procurement was still a military function. Contacts between the WPB and Army Service Forces frequently were at points of friction, and suspicions persisted that each was attempting to take over the functions of the other. With the examples before them of Great Britain and Canada, where civilian ministries of supply had appeared to be quite successful in military procurement, a good many business and political leaders were convinced that this would be a good system for the United States. Let the military people prepare their shopping lists, so the argument ran, and then turn them over to a civilian agency manned by people familiar with business and industry to get the orders filled. This position had a familiar ring to those familiar with World War I mobilization, but it could not be lightly dismissed. On the other hand, there were those who held that the Army (and the Navy) not only should develop requirements, but should also exercise sufficient control over production and resources to insure that their orders would be filled. In the system that developed, responsibility for military procurement did remain with the military, but the War Production Board controlled priorities, and struck the balance between military and essential civilian requirements. Although the President had assigned to the chairman of the War Production Board broad powers over war procurement, WPB influence over military procurement declined after the spring of 1942, and the services assumed increasing responsibility in procurement policy.

Some people, in WPB, in Congress, and elsewhere, saw in each increment of Army authority an attempt to take over the national economy. Vigorously denying any such ambition, Secretary Stimson, Under Secretary Patterson, and General Somervell all protested their respect for civilian control, but they continued to insist that procure-

---

[2] Knudsen was commissioned a lieutenant general in January 1942, and assigned to the Office of the Under Secretary of War as Director of Production. This move at last centralized authority, coming around approximately to the kind of organization found successful in the War Industries Board of World War I and recommended in the Industrial Mobilization Plan.

ment was a part of military logistics which could not be separated from the other aspects of logistics, and that an Army responsible for developing strategy and conducting war must have control of its logistics to make these plans and operations effective. If the chairman of the War Production Board were given complete authority to determine what materials the armed forces might receive, the Army asserted, this in effect made him a commander in chief who could determine what kind of war was to be fought. Here is where co-ordination with the Joint Chiefs of Staff was necessary if that body was in fact to carry on supreme military direction of the war.

Although it was clear almost from the outset of the defense build-up that a system of priorities would be necessary if military production orders were to be filled as needed, the process went through several painful steps between 1940 and late 1942. The Joint Army and Navy Munitions Board Priorities Committee developed a system of priority classification which was extended under OPM's Defense Supplies Rating Plan. Weaknesses appeared quickly and compounded rapidly in a system that depended at first upon voluntary compliance, and was based only on a vertical approach by which ratings were granted according to end items and then filtered down. Even the introduction of mandatory preference for defense orders in December 1940 did little to overcome basic deficiencies. A tendency to grant high priorities to everything, to give "out-of-line" ratings to meet special problems, the granting of blanket ratings to companies for all their contracts rather than according to individual orders, and the practice of "lifting" materials or facilities already designated for one use by obtaining a preference rating for another, all contributed to an

unending inflation in priority ratings. In these circumstances it was impossible to guarantee tools or materials even though priorities were granted, and the whole system broke down. One corrective measure attacked the problem from the other end of the scale by allocating specific quantities of machine tools or raw materials for certain purposes. With only the Quartermaster Corps approving among the Army's procurement agencies, the War Production Board in mid-1942 put into effect the Production Requirements Plan whereby allocations of materials were made directly by WPB to the various firms. This system bypassed the services, and gave them little leeway in shifting requirements to make up deficiencies in their own programs. It did have the advantage of attempting to balance in a systematic way total requirements and materials resources. It paved the way for the highly successful system adopted in November 1942—the Controlled Materials Plan, based largely on British experience.

The Controlled Materials Plan (CMP) went into effect at what probably was the darkest hour for the war production effort. It was a vertical system working somewhat like the shipping allocation system. While other materials remained under the previous priorities system or the Production Requirements Plan, the new Controlled Materials Plan applied to steel, copper, and aluminum. The War Department and the other claimant agencies such as the Navy, Lend-Lease Administration, Maritime Commission, and Office of Civilian Supply of WPB submitted their requirements for these materials, based on their procurement plans, a quarter in advance, to the WPB Requirements Committee, upon which each agency was represented. On the basis of supply data furnished by the appropriate material division of WPB and on the total requirements submitted, the committee made allocations of the materials to the respective claimants who in turn made allocations to their contractors. Direction of the Controlled Materials Plan within the Army was centralized in the CMP Control Branch, Production Division of Army Service Forces, though allotments to contractors were made through the technical services responsible for procurement. Although complexities of calculating requirements, and particularly of relating them to lead time, and of resolving conflicting claims for scarce materials continued, the Controlled Materials Plan provided the best means for handling steel, copper, and aluminum allocations. For a time there was continued controversy over retention of a so-called "B list" of materials still subject to horizontal controls by which WPB received statements of requirements in terms of dollar value or units of end items, then made allocations directly to the firms; by 1944 this procedure was virtually abandoned for military items.

Aside from the control of basic materials and tools, other control measures were necessary to assure efficient production of military supplies. First of all, the matter of realistic production schedules had to be considered, and special procedures were adopted to deal with bottlenecks whenever they threatened to delay production. It was as important to schedule the production of components needed in the production of major items as to allocate raw materials or to schedule production of the finished items. In addition, systematic programs for conserving scarce materials, procedures for the government to furnish materials and equipment in certain cases, importation and stockpiling of strategic and critical materials, and export controls, all contributed to the general purpose of expediting production.

With the prodding and probing of the Truman Committee and other interested committees of Congress anxious to be helpful in their revelations of waste or inefficiency or corruption, with the most immediate problems of industrial conversion, manpower and labor relations, and allocation of materials in some way resolved, and pressured by military operations and strategic decisions, war production in the United States in 1943 was in high gear. At last it appeared to most military leaders that all the troops that could be raised could be equipped and transported and resupplied, and the whole nation took confidence that now victory was just a matter of time. The rapid advance of the armies across France in the summer of 1944 turned confidence into overconfidence, and production slow-downs threatened serious consequences for the supply of such items as ammunition when it became necessary to meet strong counterattacks at the end of the year when the Germans struck back through the Ardennes.

Determination of Requirements

However difficult to apply all the factors that had to be taken into account, some kind of a program other than simply "more of everything" was necessary both to coordinate the industrial effort with strategic plans and to give some guidance for strategic as well as logistic planning.

The same elements were at work in the calculation of requirements for World War II that had been present in all the previous wars, although now the complexities could be defined a little more sharply. In assessing requirements generally it was useful to think of supplies and equipment according to various types of categories. There was a distinction between "critical" items, those difficult to produce or having long lead time (a year or more), and "essential" items which might be important, but could be more readily produced. A distinction could be drawn along items of regular or standard issue whose quantity depended mainly on the size of the Army, expendable items depending largely on the nature and intensity of combat (such as ammunition), and special equipment depending mainly on particular strategic plans or special projects (such as landing craft and construction materials). Further, a distinction had to be made simply between more or less durable equipment and expendable supplies, those ordinarily consumed in a single use.

In arriving at the requirements for any item of equipment, the first step was to determine the need for initial supply. This in turn depended upon three basic factors each of which in itself was the result of estimates, guesses, predictions, compromises. These factors were the troop basis, a calculation developed by G–3 and the Operations Division of the General Staff showing the expected strength of the Army in terms of total number of men and according to numbers and types of divisions and other units for the next one to two years; unit allowances, as expressed in tables of allowances and tables of basic allowances, and later in tables of organization and equipment and tables of individual clothing and equipment; and special equipment such as might be needed in jungle, desert, amphibious or other specialized warfare, or needed for a particular operation at hand.

The second step in determining equipment requirements for troops was to estimate the need for replacing equipment as it became damaged or worn out. This de-

pended on experience factors. At first tables developed from World War I experience, figured in terms of the percentage of each item lost in a month of various types of operations, had to be used. Later the tables could be revised on the basis of more immediate experience.

Finally, requirements had to allow for quantities in the distribution system—stocks needed (or estimated) for reserve in the theaters, near the ports of embarkation, and at distribution points in the United States; quantities in transit (a variable depending on the length of the supply lines and the methods and efficiency of transportation); losses in transit due to enemy action or other causes; and, for items of individual clothing, additional allowances for size tariffs, depending on the item and the size of the unit being served.

As for expendable supplies, of which the principal items were subsistence, ammunition and fuel, initial issue was of no consideration apart from consumption and distribution requirements. These requirements were expressed in terms of days of supply. An ammunition day of supply was the number of rounds used on the average per gun in the theater; a thirty-days' supply for the theater, then, would represent that average figure times the number of guns times thirty. A ration, as always, was food for one man for one day. Gasoline, too, was given in days of supply for each type of vehicle, and, again, it was necessary to allow for reserves and for quantities in transit or lost in the distribution system.

Basic assumptions underlying the supply effort—that supply should be adequate, and that it was better to have too much than too little; and that supply in so far as possible should be automatic—that is, that it should be sent forward to the theaters and units without requisitioning—added significantly to the total requirements. Presently those assumptions had to be modified somewhat by greater consideration for feasibility and balance.

In the continuing debate between logistics and strategy, it would seem logical that a basic element in the determination of requirements should have been the strategic plans. Often logisticians complained that their plans were uncertain and vague because they had no strategic plans from the Joint Chiefs of Staff to guide them, but it hardly could have been otherwise. Strategy had to follow politics and the fortunes of war and firm plans for strategic undertakings eighteen months to two years in advance, in time to influence major procurement in a significantly continuing way, could not be expected. It was necessary, then, to guess what the force requirements would be, and, in turn, what the matériel requirements would be. Logic also might have suggested that requirements for industrial facilities, raw materials and labor would have depended upon the calculation of military requirements; however, in an all-out effort, it was, once again, more likely to be the other way around. Military requirements had to be geared to strategic plans not yet formed, and gauged to national resources not yet measured.

President Roosevelt took a different approach to the determination of requirements: for him it was not a matter of carefully calculating quantities called for by a series of tables based on abstract plans, nor even a matter of going to the limits of assumed feasibility, but simply a matter of doing what had to be done in relation to the enemy threat. In May 1940, as the Western Front in Europe was collapsing under the Nazi blitzkrieg, the War Department, under prodding, finally was moved to call for an increase in its current aircraft program of 5,500 planes to 19,000. The President dramatically set a goal of 50,000 aircraft a year for the Army and Navy. Where did he get such a figure? Apparently from the same kind of intuition and thin air that prompted Polk's call for 50,000 volunteers and Lincoln's call for 75,000 militia. If Lord Beaverbrook, Secretary of State Cordell Hull, and other political advisers influenced Roosevelt's bold program, General Staff studies of the time certainly did not.

With the President's example before them, the General Staff set about revising its estimates to accord more closely with the requirements of waging global war should that become necessary. Major impetus in this direction came from the British and, again, from the President. Near the end of 1940 and in early 1941, the British, following a device developed by the French production representative, Jean Monnet, prepared a balance sheet showing in parallel columns estimates of British and Empire production, estimates of requirements, and the deficiencies, and indicating that the differences could be made up only from the United States. This produced something of a shock for American planners, and it also probably produced a bigger initial appropriation under lend-lease. A rearmament program, geared to arming the "protective mobilization force" was under way, but still long-range, co-ordinated plans were lacking.

Two weeks after Germany invaded Russia on 22 June 1941, Roosevelt asked the Secretaries of War and the Navy to prepare a report on the munitions and equipment that would be required to exceed by a fair margin that available to potential enemies. Some staff officers were afraid that this request implied an assumption that Germany could be defeated by superior matériel production alone. On the other hand—manpower and strategy aside—it would not be very safe to assume victory on less production than that of which the enemy was capable. Although Brig. Gen. Leonard T. Gerow, chief of the War Plans Division, was anxious to follow the logical sequence of deriving manpower requirements from strategic plans, and thus arriving at matériel requirements, Maj. Albert C. Wedemeyer, who drew the immediate assignment, went about it backwards. He arrived at a manpower figure, not from any analysis of strategic plans, but from figures showing what manpower could be expected to be available for the Army after requirements of industry, agriculture, and the Navy had been met. Adding a certain safety factor, he came up with a figure of 8,795,-658 which, in spite of various internal errors, came within a half million of the actual peak strength of the Army in May 1945. Major Wedemeyer proceeded to break this total down into numbers and types of divisions and other units (these forecasts did not hold up so well), and this became the troop basis for the Victory Program, with July 1943 set as the target date for realization. The supply services determined the quantities of major items of equipment needed on this basis, and the whole went to the Joint Army and Navy Board to be joined with the Navy report and forwarded to the President in September. A separate report carried estimates of Axis production. Meanwhile Prime Minister Winston Churchill had called for a combined British-American program for victory. A new balance sheet, this one made up with one column for the United States and the other column for the United States and the other for the United Kingdom and Canada, showed stocks on hand and realistic production forecasts for a long list of major items based on programs then in effect, and revealed how far behind American production really was.

As it was, the Victory Program represented far higher goals than anything previously considered, though it was only a paper plan to be used in the event of all-out war. In assuming maximum mobilization, the Victory Program did reflect an apparent strategic concept of sending massed armies against the Germans on the European continent. The Air Corps program, prepared separately, assumed a prominent role for strategic bombing. Newspaper disclosure of much of the contents of the secret document on 4 December 1941 set the stage for a storm of political controversy until the attack on Pearl Harbor three days later laid it to rest.

Now that the country was at war it was both necessary and possible to put a long-range program into effect. While military staffs worked feverishly to develop more detailed statements of requirements, Roosevelt again came up with a program of his own. In December at a White House conference with Churchill and Lord Beaverbrook, the British Minister of Supply, the President, using as a basis figures which Donald Nelson of the War Production Board had furnished, prepared a "Must" Program for unheard-of quantities of planes, tanks, ships, and guns. After arbitrarily revising some of his figures upward the night before, he went before Congress on 6 January 1942 to give his State of the Union message, and in it to indicate a part of his Victory Program for production. Where current plans called for the production of 28,600 aircraft during 1942, he now called for 60,000, and for 125,000 during 1943;

the goal for tank production went up from 20,400 for 1942 to 45,000, and to 75,000 for the next year; for antiaircraft guns, from 6,300 to 20,000, and then 35,000; during the current year he called for doubling the planned output of 7,000 antitank guns, raising the production of machine guns from 168,000 to 500,000, and the tonnage of bombs from 84,000 to 720,000. Military and civilian leaders alike gasped at these figures, and some opined that the President had "gone in for the numbers racket." But he let it be known that he was in dead earnest. No, his figures again were not the result of careful calculations, but they were a challenge to "think big" all along the line.

Attempts to meet the President's goals raised very serious problems. Many secondary requirements sprang from them. Airplanes had to have hangars and gasoline and maintenance facilities, not to mention pilots, if they were to be operational; guns, to be useful, had to have prime movers and ammunition; tanks had to have fuel and ammunition. And all the men to operate and maintain all this equipment had to be housed, clothed, fed, provided with individual weapons and ammunition, trained, and transported.

The Army's War Munitions Program, growing out of its revisions of the Victory Program and the President's requests, the Navy's increased requirements, the need for facilities not yet programed, and the requirements for stepped-up lend-lease shipments to Britain and to the Soviet Union, not to mention plans for the deployment of troops to the Pacific and to the United Kingdom, when placed alongside the needs of civilian economy added up to a total which the War Production Board estimated to be far above the capacity of American industry to produce in any reasonable time. A bitter controversy over the feasibility of the procurement program between the Army and the War Production Board ensued over the next several months. In the end Under Secretary of War Patterson agreed that the Production Board's basic position was correct, but the solution of the problem was not to be found in creating a super board to sit over the Army, Navy, and Maritime Commission to reconcile strategy with production feasibility, as the WPB report had recommended; rather it was for the Joint Chiefs of Staff to recast their strategic and logistic plans to conform to the production limit as set by WPB. The Joint Chiefs thereupon reduced their combined military program for 1943 from $93 billion to $80 billion. The Army's share of the $13 billion reduction was $9 billion, the greatest single reduction in its program during the war.

Meanwhile the Army General Staff had been developing a more comprehensive and useful statement of its over-all requirements. The computation of requirements in the War Munitions Program adopted early in 1942 made no allowance for distribution requirements, included no analysis of stocks on hand, did not cover expendable supplies, and made no provision for construction, lend-lease, and certain Navy items for the procurement of which the Army was responsible. For an ordered procurement program it was necessary to fill these gaps, and this General Somervell, first as G–4 and later as commanding general of the Army Service Forces, undertook to do by developing a comprehensive supply program that would be a thorough and authoritative statement of requirements. As defined in the publication titled Army Supply Program, which began in March 1942, the new program took into account virtually all the factors which the previous program had left out. Revised semiannually, the Army Supply Program stated the procurement objectives for the next two to three calendar years, and became the basic statement of requirements and the basic procurement directive. It continued until the last few months of the war when the more comprehensive and detailed Supply Control System replaced it. Based on elaborate supply and demand studies of up to 1,900 principal items and 900,000 secondary items, Supply Control System reports came out monthly with revisions in estimates of requirements and other supply data.

The difficulties of relating long-range requirements to strategy probably were inherent in the kind of total war into which World War II developed. For a limited war, the nature of the objective and the strategy might indeed set the limits for matériel requirements, time permitting; but for total war the limit was total productive capacity. Recognition of this limiting factor, and even determining what the actual limits were, did little to further the computation of specific requirements for specific numbers and types of forces. Probably the greatest variable in this connection turned out to be the one which had to be at the very foundation of the requirements problem—the troop basis. While Major Wedemeyer's Victory Program troop basis retained validity as a total figure, the make-up of units went through drastic and frequent changes. Official revisions of the troop basis, as the war progressed, were issued monthly. The War Department troop basis approved in November 1942 envisaged (and in fact authorized), so far as ground forces were concerned, an Army of 100 divisions (62 infantry, 2 cavalry, 20 armored, 10 motorized, and 6 airborne) by the end of 1943. In response to economic

feasibility, availability of shipping, and other limitations when the Army had to cut back its supply program, the troop basis was revised in mid–1943 to provide for 90 divisions, and reductions in various tables of organization and equipment further reduced the attending supply requirements. On the other hand, the practice of scattering forces around the world in widely separated theaters, and the opening of such commands as the Persian Gulf and the China-Burma-India where most of the activity was in fact logistical, continuously added to the pressure for service troops. Though many revisions followed, particularly in nondivisonal units, the 90-division target remained, and at the end of the war the Army comprised 89 divisions—66 infantry, 1 cavalry (dismounted), 16 armored, 5 airborne, and 1 mountain, all of them overseas.

Industrial capacity and reductions in troop bases were not the only factors leading to reductions in the Army Supply Program. Pressure from the newly established Office of War Mobilization in the summer of 1943 led to the appointment of a War Department Procurement Review Board which, after a thoroughgoing study, recommended some sharp reductions in Army requirements. The board found that rigid adherence to certain supply policies, assumed consumption factors, and tables of equipment, with little regard to variables in local conditions, was contributing to the setting of unrealistic requirements and consequent waste of resources. In view of the nation's food-producing capacity and highly developed transportation system, the board found the ninety-day reserve of nonperishable food established by the Quartermaster Corps in the United States too high. It sharply criticized an unrealistic application of the "day of supply" concept in determining ammunition requirements, for reserve stocks of ammunition were exceeding all reasonable needs. The Review Board pointed out that failure to discriminate among theaters on the basis of local conditions was resulting in much waste; vehicles and items of heavy equipment, for instance, were being shipped alike to Pacific islands where there were no roads and to North Africa, on the basis of common tables of allowances. As in World War I, soldiers were overburdened with individual clothing and equipment, inevitably resulting in serious waste. Moreover, there seemed to be no way of stopping a program once it had started even though the original need no longer existed as, for instance, the completion of camps in the Caribbean that never would be used, and the continuation of an ambitious program of seacoast artillery long after the apparent threat to U.S. coasts had disappeared.

Even before the Procurement Review Board had submitted its report the Army had taken steps to put into effect many of its recommendations. As a follow-up, the Deputy Chief of Staff in September 1943 appointed a Special Committee for the Re-Study of Reserves, with Brig. Gen. George J. Richards as chairman. Its duty was to survey and make recommendations on five areas of requirements determination: (1) the strategic reserve; (2) theater reserves; (3) stockpiles in the United States; (4) the day of supply; and (5) maintenance, distribution, and shipping loss factors. Again the general result was a broad reduction in Army requirements.

Aside from the more or less formal bases for calculating requirements, the progress of the war itself, as anticipated needs became satisfied, led to thoughts about cutbacks of procurement programs. Civilian agencies were far more anxious for action on this score than were the military, though by early 1944 it appeared that the battle of production had been won, and months before the Normandy landings, Secretary Stimson announced far-reaching reductions in procurement.

Research and Development

Aside from the calculation of total quantities of supplies and equipment needed, the question of quality—the introduction of improved models, new types, and entirely new items—added complications to logistics problems throughout the war.

Improvements in weapons and equipment had come slowly for the Army during the interwar period, and to a considerable degree it had to follow the familiar pattern of entering one war with the weapons of the last. Even after the outbreak of war, some of the old inertia, some of the old narrowness, still prevailed. Concern about who would control a new device loomed larger in some minds than how effective it might be for the national purpose; sometimes pride in a particular service dominated pride in the U.S. service. Sometimes, as in early attitudes toward the pneumatic-float treadway bridge developed in Germany, and the Bailey bridge developed in Great Britain, some officers betrayed a coolness toward devices "not invented here." Soon, however, the trend took an entirely opposite direction, and under the pressure of war an enthusiasm for research and development in military weapons and equipment grew on an unprecedented scale. Thanks to the initiative of a group of civilian scientists and engineers headed by Vannevar Bush, James B. Conant, and Karl Compton, modest military programs were transformed into urgent matters of national teamwork. The organization developed under the National Defense Research Committee, the Office of Scientific Research and Development, together with the National Inventors' Council set up in the Department of Commerce, the Office of Production Research and Development, and the older, respected, National Advisory Committee for Aeronautics and the National Academy of Sciences. It provided a structure far beyond any previously seen along these lines in the United States and far surpassing any to be found for the purpose in Germany or Japan. Perhaps the fact that research and development now encompassed more than any supply service or, indeed, the War Department itself, had something to do with the spectacular results achieved, but the spirit had caught on throughout most of the Army. Instead of calling for the tried and the true, everyone now wanted something new and revolutionary.

The introduction of such things as radar, improved tanks, new kinds of aircraft and bombs, rockets, amphibious vehicles, landing craft, and proximity-fuzed artillery shells, in the process of revolutionizing warfare also introduced new logistical problems. It was a long process to bring a completely new device into operation against the enemy—beyond the primary research there were production engineering and the whole process of production. Attempts to short-circuit these stages usually led to trouble.

The dilemma became not only one of when to standardize, but also when to slow production in order to modify. Changes in aircraft design came so swiftly that a continuing tug of war went on between leaders and production people anxious to obtain large quantities, and engineers insisting on adding improvements. Often the changes were the result of requests from command-

ers in the field. The incorporation of any changes not only slowed production, but complicated the field logistical picture by adding difficulties to the maintenance of so many varying models of equipment.

Procurement Policies

Except as the most common denominator for expressing calls upon manpower and resources, financial problems were secondary for wartime procurement. While more elaborate accounting procedures were neccassary to keep track of the huge sums involved in the fourteenfold increase in Army expenditures during the war, Army budgets now were targets rather than ceilings. In fact, $60 billion (for all agencies) of unused appropriations remained on the books at the end of the war. Nevertheless, firmer central control over Army finances came with the appointment of a fiscal director in the Army Service Forces, and control of funds became a principal means for controlling and co-ordinating policies of the Army services.

Contracts and Pricing

Government contracting and purchasing policies always have been subject to a good deal of red tape not only in protecting public expenditures, but also in supporting certain special interests or secondary economic policies. In addition to legislation of long standing that required formal advertising for competitive bids and awards to the lowest responsible bidder, other laws in effect at the time of Pearl Harbor included those which required the use of only domestically produced materials, prohibited payroll deductions, forbade the employment of women under eighteen years of age on government orders, limited workers under government contracts to an eight-hour day, prohibited advance payments to government contractors, and established various labor standards. Whether calculated to protect the public purse or to protect special interests, these laws and regulations set up such an imposing bundle of red tape that many firms preferred to avoid all government contracts rather than attempt to modify their policies and organizations to conform to government restrictions. The result was unfortunate even in peacetime. In wartime it was intolerable. After delaying the rearmament program during the 1940–41 defense period to a considerable extent, most of these restrictions were swept away shortly after Pearl Harbor, though Army procurement agencies never were permitted to lose sight of the desirability of economy in all their transactions.

The pressure for speed which came with full involvement in the war brought a growing preference for contracting by negotiation rather than through formal advertising, until early in 1942 when the War Production Board abandoned the latter method altogether. For a time the new freedom in contracting imposed new restrictions as headquarters and agencies at various levels introduced their own restrictions to insure themselves against charges of favoritism, collusion, or improper awards of contracts. Insofar as practical, the principle of competition remained in the practice of soliciting informal bids from as many responsible and qualified suppliers as possible, and then making awards to the lowest bidders. But speed and capacity to perform were essential. In the interest of effecting as efficient an industrial mobilization as possible, the policy was to place contracts involving difficult problems with those firms best

equipped to handle them. In these cases invitations to bid went to firms needing to add the least machinery and equipment in order to fill the orders. Less complicated tasks were reserved where possible for smaller concerns.

There was a strong trend toward decentralization of procurement responsibilities and actual negotiation of contracts. Chiefs of the technical services were authorized to award contracts involving expenditures of up to $5 million without reference to higher authority, and they in turn could further delegate this authority. This they did in varying degrees. The Quartermaster General, for instance, went all the way, and extended full authority to Quartermaster field procurement officers to enter into agreements up to the $5 million limit. The Chief of Transportation, on the other hand, centered all responsibility for negotiating contracts for major items in his procurement division, while supply officers in the transportation zones and at the ports of embarkation purchased secondary items and administered all the contracts placed in their respective areas.

Depending upon the nature of the items and the circumstances, contracts during World War II generally were either of the cost-plus-a-fixed-fee type or the fixed-price—whether lump sum or unit price—type. The cost-plus-a-percentage-of-cost contract that had been the subject of much investigation and criticism after World War I was outlawed from the beginning. Soon committees of both houses of Congress were reporting widespread abuses under the cost-plus-a-fixed-fee contracts, and were recommending that they too be abolished.

The outlawing of the cost-plus-a-percentage-of-cost contract may have been an instance where apparent logic triumphed over facts. There had indeed been extravagance and abuse of these contracts during World War I, but because at first glance it seemed logical that nothing else could be expected under an arrangement where a contractor's profit went up in proportion to his costs, the relative disadvantages of other forms of contracts tended to be overlooked. The form of cost-plus contract in most general use during World War I carried a sliding scale and a maximum fee. Now, by outlawing this type of contract in favor of the cost-plus-a-fixed-fee, the maximum fee was likely to become the fixed fee, without the benefit of a lower sliding scale based upon percentage of cost.

Again, logic favored a fixed-price agreement over any kind of a cost reimbursable arrangement, for only then was it possible to be sure what the ultimate cost to the government was going to be. But this too had serious drawbacks. Bidders felt it necessary to allow for every possible contingency in addition to a high profit in arriving at a fixed-price proposal. Actually, the ratio of profit to cost was far greater in the fixed-price than in the cost-plus-a-fixed-fee contracts; moreover, the costs were not necessarily less. In arriving at his price the bidder had to allow for all conceivable costs, and then he was tempted to use inferior materials and less-qualified workers, and to take undesirable shortcuts in filling the contract. When it came to research and development contracts, or the manufacture of new items for which there was no production experience, bidders were unlikely to accept at all unless there was some guarantee for covering costs which no one at the moment could forecast accurately. But by 1945 Under Secretary of War Patterson felt that there had been enough cost experience to permit converting all cost-plus contracts

to fixed-price types. Hostilities ended before this program could be completed, but it represented the ultimate in a trend which had been operating from the early months of the war.

Probably the most difficult general problem in procurement was arriving at accurate cost estimates and settling on reasonable prices. Convinced that it could not be done satisfactorily in advance, the War Department in March 1942 issued regulations providing for the redetermination of prices according to a formula and ceiling applied after preliminary and trial runs of production and for revision of prices, either upward or downward, after 20 to 40 percent of a contract had been completed. The next month Congress passed the Renegotiation Act. As amended in October of that year, the act made it mandatory to include a renegotiation clause in all contracts with firms having renegotiable sales of over $100,000 in a fiscal year, and excepting contracts in the primary extracting industries such as mining and timber. The Secretary had discretionary power to exempt certain other contracts, and to rule that renegotiation would not apply to portions of certain contracts during certain periods of time. This allowed a measure of flexibility in offering incentives by sharing cost-savings with contractors, and by assuring them, after renegotiation, of firm forward prices not subject to further renegotiation. The Renegotiation Act of 1943 (approved in February 1944) extended the blanket exemption to $500,000.

At first the assumption had been that renegotiation would apply only to fixed-price contracts, but soon it became clear that excessive profits also were being made on cost-plus-a-fixed-fee contracts, and they too came under the scrutiny of the War Department Price Adjustment Board. Renegotiation did not apply so much to construction contracts as to supply contracts. For the latter a procedure had evolved whereby cost-plus-a-fixed-fee was set on a unit basis, so that while the margin of profit might be small per unit, large volume and the reduction in costs with production experience frequently led to an accumulation of profits that were high indeed. Yet recovery of excessive payments made under this type of contract was small compared to the amounts under fixed-price contracts. All together the War Department recaptured nearly $7.5 billion through the renegotiation of contracts, and the Navy and other government agencies recaptured about $3.5 billion. While not insignificant, these amounts are not very large in comparison with the total military procurement outlay of $300 billion for the war; in any event, excess profits taxes would have returned $7 billion to $8 billion of the total recovered. The real purpose of the renegotiation policy was not so much to recover excess profits as to prevent them. To the extent that it resulted in closer pricing and inflation control, the policy promoted efficiency in the use of resources, and, together with other measures taken for those purposes, renegotiation had a high degree of success in its main purpose.

The greatest weaknesses in the renegotiation laws undoubtedly were in the exemptions of raw materials and agricultural products and of construction contracts based on competitive bidding, as well as the blanket exemption of all firms having less than $500,000 in renegotiable sales in a year and certain permissive exemptions. All these exemptions opened the way for special consideration for special interests, while it was doubtful whether any of the general exemptions were justified either on moral or economic grounds. Far from relieving the administrative burden, they added to it.

One of the most significant developments in procurement pricing during World War II came with the adoption of a policy of progressive pricing. Although public emphasis tended to center on excess profits as the main object of concern, these profits represented but a small fraction of the total prices. Reduction in costs represented more efficient use of resources. This was the main object of the Army's consistent philosophy of "close pricing." The trouble was that even when original prices could be set close to cost, the results of experience as evidenced in increased efficiency and added volume could widen the gap between cost and profit—or costs as calculated might remain close to the price when they could have been reduced by more careful management. This actually amounted to a hidden inflation. In adopting progressive pricing, Army procurement agencies gave up the idea that there was a single ideal price for any particular contract, and adopted the idea of reviewing prices from time to time while a contract was in effect. On the basis of experience or the appearance of unforeseen developments, prices then might be adjusted either upward or downward, so that three or four different prices might be in effect during the term of the contract. It was assumed, too, that the contractor might retain a higher profit margin when he reduced his costs, and he might be guaranteed retention of this gain by exemption from negotiation. Both contractors and contracting officers were hesitant about using progressive pricing for some time, the former because they wanted to retain the higher prices as protection against all contingencies, and the latter because they feared that the higher margins of profit that were likely to be granted might appear unreasonable, or the result of collusion, to some future investigating committee. By 1944, however, the practice had come into fairly general use, and it probably made a real contribution to reduction in costs and increased efficiency.

A further consideration in price redetermination and renegotiation was the over-all position of the firm in question. It soon became evident that in cases of companies having a large number of war contracts, a far more accurate picture of costs and profits could be seen if all the company's government business were examined together rather than individually, contract by contract. As developed by the summer of 1944, the company pricing program involved the appointment of pricing teams to examine the situation of selected companies and to analyze the extent and causes of high prices, high costs, and excessive profits. This made it possible to give special attention to common costs among several contracts, differentials in civilian and military business, total volume, and subcontract prices. Earlier, subcontract prices had had little scrutiny, and unduly high prices for components simply were passed on, usually with a mark-up, to the government. Some of the most notable examples of extravagant profits were likely to be here. When subcontract prices were found to be a major factor in a prime contractor's price position, the War Department entered into direct negotiations with the company's subcontractors with a view to recovering excessive profits and reducing prices; these savings would be passed to the prime contractor who in turn would be persuaded to pass the savings along to the government. The effectiveness of the company-pricing program for the eighteen

months it was in effect is difficult to assess. In particular cases it demonstrated great merit, and the fact that 100 major contractors held two-thirds of the War Department's contracts as well as a large number of subcontracts indicates the coverage that the selection of this number of companies for price review could mean.

The Civilian Economy

Further problems for Army procurement agencies rose out of efforts to control inflation and hold the price line in the civilian economy. As contemplated in the Industrial Mobilization Plan, the Office of Price Administration (OPA) was established for this purpose. Immediately the question had to be met as to the extent the regulations of this agency would extend to military goods. Both the Secretary of the Navy and the Secretary of War appealed to Congress as well as to the President to permit the military services to make their own determination as to when exemptions from OPA price ceilings should be granted. The request was refused. The Secretaries then turned to negotiations with OPA, and subsequently arrived at an agreement whereby strictly military goods—comprising about two-thirds of military procurements—should be exempted from OPA regulations. There remained an important area of overlap, particularly in items of food and clothing, where military procurement had to be based on OPA price ceilings. As for rationed items, the OPA generally agreed to allow the Army unlimited rationing accounts in return for the Quartermaster General's undertaking to establish limits for their use. In many cases Army posts set up their own boards for issuing coupons to soldiers for the purchase of gasoline, tires, and other items for their private use.

Some points of controversy developed when OPA on occasion sought to extend its authority over strictly military items, and the red tape and delays involved in attempts to obtain relief from price ceilings on items the Army considered essential were irritating; however, close liaison between the War Department and OPA, and a general appreciation of the problems each faced, helped to maintain a healthy attitude of co-operation. On the whole OPA's remarkable success in resisting the heavy inflationary pressures of wartime was of great benefit to Army procurement. The stabilization of prices not only permitted vast savings, but encouraged conditions for negotiation of firm prices in military procurement. The success of the Army's own battle against high prices was suggested by the publication of quarterly indexes which showed a continuous decline in unit prices, for all except quartermaster items which were largely civilian-type goods, from 1942 to the end of the war.

Small Business

In the natural course of attempting to mobilize rapidly, and of placing orders where there was greatest confidence in obtaining large-scale production quickly, Army contracts tended to be concentrated with a relatively few large firms. In the early stages of mobilization it hardly could have been otherwise. But this brought the inevitable complaints from smaller firms which, without war contracts, found it increasingly difficult to obtain raw materials, and thus to remain in business at all. Actually, the picture of distress was exaggerated, for a large number of small plants already were busy with government contracts, subcontracts, or essential civilian orders. Nevertheless, there was a general feeling that at a time when all available resources were needed in the war effort small business should not be allowed to decline. If the main purpose of Congress in passing the Small Business Act in 1942 was relief for small firms, it paralleled a purpose of the Army to broaden the industrial production base. The act assigned various duties to the chairman of the War Production Board which he in turn delegated to a Smaller War Plants Division. This division worked closely with the Smaller War Plants Corporation which was established to make loans or advances to small concerns; to acquire and lease land, equipment, and materials; and to act as a prime contractor for war goods which then would be filled by subcontracting. The Smaller War Plants Division of the War Production Board was to survey production capabilities among small plants, and it might even certify certain small companies to be capable of filling certain contracts, in which case it was incumbent upon the procurement agency to award the contract to the company so designated. While the general pressure for mobilizing smaller plants probably benefited the economic mobilization, some of the specific measures were frought with dangers. In practice the Smaller War Plants Division preferred to "designate" rather than "certify" plants, and then leave it to the discretion of the Army as to whether a plant could perform on a contract. As for the provision that the Smaller War Plants Corporation could act as prime contractor in organizing pools of subcontractors, this practice quickly fell into disuse and was of little significance, although its framers had considered it to be the heart of the act. On the whole, mobilization of small plants—those having fewer than 500 employees—probably could not have been accomplished much sooner even had the Small Business Act been passed sooner, though the extent to which such facilities finally were used in military production probably was considerably greater than it would have been without the act. From 1943 to 1945 the share of the dollar value of War Department contracts going to small business rose from 12.6 percent to 27.4 percent. In addition, these firms received a growing share of subcontracts under the prime contracts of larger companies.

Procurement in Action

Inevitably special problems arose in connection with the procurement and production of almost all of the hundreds of types of weapons, equipment and supplies needed for the World War II forces. Sometimes items had to be substituted, and sometimes plans had to be changed, but on the whole production went far beyond what most people had dreamed possible in earlier years. Still, it should be noted that in some ways production did fall short of early hopes and expectations, and actually was never really stretched to its limits.

Arms and Ammunition

The transfer to Great Britain of a large share of the Army's reserve of small arms after the Dunkerque evacuation in 1940 stirred the Ordnance Department and Congress to action in procurement of new arms. Although the 1903 Springfield rifle was a favorite target weapon for more than half a century, it never did enjoy the distinction of being the standard rifle in a war. In World War I it had to give way to the En-

field in the interest of rapid production; in World War II it was superseded by the semiautomatic M1, or Garand, though Springfields in the hundreds of thousands were used until the new Garand became available, and even then a model was retained for use as a sniper's rifle. Actually, the Garand had been adopted in the mid-1930's with the first production models coming off the lines of the Springfield Armory in 1937. "Bugs" appeared in the production model, however, and in 1940 strong sentiment developed in Congress and in the press in favor of a rival semiautomatic rifle which Capt. Melvin M. Johnson, Jr., of the Marine Corps Reserve had designed. The ensuing controversy ended only after the Marine Corps itself finally adopted the Garand. No one claimed that the Garand was more accurate or more reliable than the old Springfield, but it was a semiautomatic weapon that could fire several times more rapidly than any hand-operated bolt-action weapon, and its lighter recoil and ease of operation made it a desirable weapon for troops in combat. On the other hand, difficulties arose in production, particularly in maintaining the fine tolerances necessary for interchangeability, and the high rate of production needed was not reached until the end of 1943. The Springfield Armory was turning out 1,000 M1 rifles a day in the autumn of 1941, but later this had to be raised to 3,000, and the Winchester company raised its output from 100 to 750 a day. Total M1 production between 1940 and 1945 amounted to over 4,000,000.

In the meantime the Remington Arms Company, beginning production of the Springfield 1903 for the British in 1941 with machinery from the Rock Island Arsenal, and the L. C. Smith-Corona Typewriter Corporation by early 1944 turned out over 1,300,000 Springfields, modified to facilitate production rather than to improve the weapon. The Browning automatic rifle, introduced near the end of World War I, found unexpected favor with infantrymen of World War II, and 188,000 of these were produced largely by the New England Small Arms Corporation, an organization formed by six New England firms. In addition, various firms produced another million rifles, Lee-Enfields, for the British. The biggest small arms production story of the war was in the carbine, a light, short-barreled rifle intended to replace the automatic pistols and rifles carried by troops serving crew-served weapons, by service troops, and by most officers. Just fourteen days after being invited to enter competitive tests for such a weapon, Winchester submitted a model which passed preliminary tests; then, with only thirty-four days in which to perfect the design, won the competition. Winchester and the Inland Manufacturing Division of General Motors, joined later by several other companies most of which had been engaged in making hardware, juke boxes, and typewriters, proceeded to turn out over 6,100,000 of these carbines by 1945.

For machine guns the United States relied on improved models of the Browning that had been adopted during or immediately after World War I. An improved version of the .50-caliber, adopted in 1933, in different forms became standard for aircraft, antiaircraft, and tank use. By the time of Pearl Harbor ten plants, including the Rock Island Arsenal, the Colt Company (mostly British orders), the Savage Arms Company, and several divisions of General Motors were producing machine guns at a rate of about 27,600 .30-caliber and 50,000 .50-caliber guns a year. In the next year total produc-

SOLDIER EXPLAINING HIS BAZOOKA *to an aged Tennessean.*

tion increased tenfold, and in spite of production stoppages and bottlenecks at different times, production kept up with requirements nearly the whole time. Machine gun production was one of the most successful aspects of the whole Ordnance program.

The most unusual infantry weapon to appear during World War II was the 2.36-inch rocket launcher, quickly dubbed the "bazooka" by reason of its similarity in appearance to the homemade musical instrument made famous by radio comedian Bob Burns. Firing by electrical impulse a rocket carrying a shaped charge, the bazooka at last provided the foot soldier with a means for knocking out a tank (though in practice it turned out to be more useful against machine gun emplacements, pillboxes, and buildings). Perhaps most unusual of all was the fact that here, in 1942, was a new weapon that was simpler rather than more complex. The General Electric Company was given but thirty days in which to deliver the first order of 5,000. Then, using over one hundred subcontractors, the company met production schedules for 60,000 more in 1942, about 100,000 in 1943, and 200,000 in 1944, even though many improvements were added on the basis of battlefield experience. The only other major producer of bazookas was the Cheney Bigelow Wire Works of Springfield, Massachusetts, which turned out about 40,000 of a modified version during the winter of 1944–45.

Recoilless rifles, the 57-mm. and 75-mm. artillery pieces that could be carried by hand or fired from a machine gun mount on a jeep, showed great promise in demonstrations in Europe and in action on Okinawa, but they appeared too late to make an important contribution to the war.

When it came to bigger guns, the Army's position on the eve of war was rather less satisfactory than in small arms. For the most part it still relied on the French 75-mm. guns of World War I fame. The 105-mm. howitzer which was to become the artillery workhorse had been under development throughout the interwar period, but was not adopted in its final form until 1940.

As World War II approached, planners tended to pass by any concerted effort for artillery production, presumably on the assumption that aerial bombing would take over much of the work of artillery in future warfare. The Army had relied on its own arsenals, mainly Watervliet and Watertown, for production of the few guns and howitzers it obtained between the wars, so that no private manufacturers were in any position to enter the field quickly. When the rearmament program started, the gunmakers

who had kept the art alive at the arsenals were nearly swamped, not only in expanding their own facilities but in providing instructions and assistance for private companies accepting contracts. Low priorities for artillery made the machine tool bottleneck especially acute, and delayed production during the early months of the war. Meanwhile plant facilities were being expanded rapidly, and output increased sharply in 1942.

A 155-mm. howitzer took its place as companion piece of the 105 in division artillery. Development of a 240-mm. howitzer and an 8-inch gun had begun immediately after World War I, but lack of appropriations forced a fifteen-year interruption until World War II. Two mortars which became standard in the infantry, the 60-mm. and the 81-mm., had been obtained in the 1930's from a French firm, and presented no serious production problems once the program was launched—except for an unexpected shortage of the 60-mm. growing out of suddenly increased requirements in the European theater in 1944. Tank guns and antitank guns, aircraft guns and antiaircraft guns, and self-propelled guns and howitzers comprised by far the greatest share of all artillery weapons. Of highest priority were the antiaircraft guns where the chief emphasis and the major problems were with the new 90-mm. Production fell considerably behind the President's "Must" Program, until ultimately he was convinced that so many guns (5,400 for 1942) were not needed, and the requirements were cut in half. Production of tank guns lagged far behind production of tanks during the first half of 1942; when it did catch up, the 75-mm. gun carried on American tanks was no match for the German 88 which the tanks frequently encountered. Production of aircraft cannon, on the other hand, was able to keep pace with aircraft production practically from the beginning.

In the early part of the war emphasis in artillery production, as was true for many other items, was on all-out production all along the line, with no effective program for scheduling and balancing components until the end of 1942.

Modifications in the design of weapons probably was caused as often by the necessity to speed production or conserve scarce materials as to improve performance. It was a happy combination when an improved production method resulted also in a superior product. Such was the case of two major techniques for making gun tubes that had been developed about the time of World War I, but were applied during World War II for the first time on a large scale. The first was cold-working, or "autofettage," based upon earlier French practice which, by the application of hydraulic pressure within the bore, accomplished the same kind of strengthening as had been achieved during the Civil War by shrinking hoops on the outside of the barrel. The other was centrifugal casting, whereby molten steel was poured into a revolving mold, and was shaped by the centrifugal force. The result was simplified and speedier production, economy of materials, and greater uniformity of strength than could be achieved by forging.

Over $3 billion went into the expansion program for government-owned, contractor-operated facilities engaged in the manufacture of ammunition. In the biggest program of its kind undertaken during the war, these facilities eventually included twelve plants for maufacturing the chemical components of explosives, twenty-one plants for making high explosives and smokeless powder, and twenty-five for loading shells and bombs. All together these plants produced over a billion rounds of artillery ammunition and about 4.5 million tons of several types of bombs. Even this output was not enough to keep up with an appetite that seemed to grow with eating. Each new campaign brought a higher statement of requirements than had been forecast, though in most cases there were no actual shortages in the theaters. Only the end of the war curtailed further expansion of ammunition facilities. Besides plants for producing artillery ammunition and bombs, a dozen government-owned, contractor-operated plants were built to augment production of small arms ammunition that had been centered at the Frankford Arsenal in Philadelphia. Total capacity reached 71 million rounds a day, and total production of small arms ammunition from 1940 to 1945 amounted to over 41 billion rounds, mostly .30- and .50-caliber. Although production of small arms ammunition did not involve the complications of producing fuzes or manufacturing and loading high explosives, it nevertheless had its share of difficulties. One problem common to making both small arms and light and medium artillery ammunition was the serious shortage of copper needed for the brass cartridge cases. Attempts to develop satisfactory steel cartridge cases to replace copper casings were not successful during the war, but the necessity for a substitute diminished as the Controlled Materials Plan eased the copper shortage.

Vehicles

Undoubtedly the most revolutionary change in the American ground forces of World War II was their almost complete motorization. With the exception of certain special cases, such as the mountain warfare in Italy, animals had disappeared from the service areas as well as the combat units in the United States Army, and, almost as needed, troops and supplies could be moved by motor truck, while combat vehicles appeared by the thousands to restore to warfare the mobility that had been so slightly employed in World War I.

After the German blitzkrieg in Poland and through the Low Countries and France, it was generally agreed that tanks had become an essential element of warfare, but great disagreement continued about types needed and how they should be used. U.S. military doctrine had emphasized the light tank, insisting that the role of the medium tank was to secure the breakthrough of the light tank, and in the latter category the United States had kept fairly close to the pace of other military powers. Then emphasis shifted to the medium tank, and leaders of the Armored Force and of Army Ground Forces throughout most of the war held to the view that the war should be fought with the medium M4, General Sherman. Ordnance experts recommended almost from the beginning the development of heavier tanks with more powerful guns. Even though the Germans rushed into production the heavy Tiger and Panther, the fact that they out-gunned the U.S. models and had better armor protection had little immediate consequence in American tank development, for according to U.S. Army doctrine tanks were not intended to fight tanks, and furthermore Army Regulations forbade tanks heavier than thirty tons— both of which rules Hitler ignored.

The launching of a big tank production program in the United States coincided with the fall of France in 1940 and the arrival of a British tank commission anxious to obtain thousands of tanks as quickly as possible. The greatest step forward was the signing of a contract to build and operate a completely new tank plant—the Detroit Tank Arsenal—by the Chrysler Corporation. The greatest drawback was the lack of a satisfactory design for a medium tank. In the interest of speed, the M3, General Grant, despite its high silhouette, riveted construction, and the position of its 75-mm. gun at the "right shoulder," first went into production until the improved Sherman, without rivets, and with its gun mounted in a fully traversing turret, could be perfected. It then became the standard medium tank. The Ordnance Corps had been at work on a heavy tank, carrying a 90-mm. gun, which eventually appeared as the T26, General Pershing, but it was delayed so long by Ground Forces insistence that there was no need for it that it arrived too late to have much influence in battle. While officers of the Armored Force kept insisting that tanks were not supposed to fight tanks, doughboys observed bitterly that when they were ordered to attack they were told "you cannot fight tanks with tanks, and you cannot use tank destroyers for attack," so the infantryman must advance in his "armored O.D. shirt" against German Tigers and Panthers.

Aside from basic differences on doctrine and the design of tanks, other differences came up repeatedly. One of these was the matter of whether diesel or gasoline engines should be used. The early assumption was that diesel engines should be used in the interest of economy of fuel and durability, plus a supposed greater measure of safety from fire. Later, however, U.S. planners were less in favor of diesel engines, largely because of other logistical considerations. One of these was the complication of having

SHERMAN TANKS, MOUNTING 75-MM. GUNS, IN ACTION IN FRANCE

to maintain a separate supply line for diesel fuel when most Army vehicles used gasoline. Furthermore, it was argued, the supposed savings resulting from the use of diesel fuel would be to some extent a false economy because of the fact that to obtain such vast quantities of diesel fuel, gasoline or other products would be given off in the refining process which might just as well be used to power gasoline engines. On the other side of the argument it was pointed out that with a greater use of diesel fuel a better balance of petroleum products would be achieved, and thus a more complete and economical use of potential fuels. Although diesel-powered tanks, amounting at the time to twice the number being produced for American forces, continued to go to the British and the Russians, production for American

use went almost wholly over to the gasoline engines in 1942. Development of the Ford GAA engine, tested at Aberdeen Proving Ground by Chrysler and General Motors engineers, added to the general acceptability of gasoline power.

Over 25 percent of the more than 88,000 tanks produced between 1940 and 1945 were produced at the Detroit Tank Arsenal. Other plants, operated mostly by automobile or railway equipment manufacturers, produced the remainder. Hundreds of plants produced tank components.

Although motor trucks were much more closely akin to commercial models than were combat vehicles, special military specifications were such as to make commercial experience only partially applicable. Moreover, during peacetime, the requirements for competitive bidding made it most difficult to develop satisfactory military vehicles, for it was held that the preparation of detailed specifications or standardization by the Army would eliminate competition. As an officer observed in 1936, "vehicle types and models that fully meet military requirements are not practicable of production in quantity in time of war nor legally procurable in time of peace.[3]

So far as motor transportation during World War II was concerned, the 2½-ton 6x6 (actually the truck had ten tires, for the rear four wheels were dual) was the workhorse. Fully loaded, the versatile 2½-ton could climb a 65-percent grade from a standing start, move along the face of a hill without losing its balance, and was equally at home running down a smooth highway or over wet fields, or through thickets of 2½-inch trees. Soon after production began in January 1941 demand increased so much that it became the most serious production problem in the truck program. The Yellow Truck and Coach Company (taken over in 1943 by General Motors) continued to be the chief producer throughout the war, although Studebaker, Reo, and International Harvester later participated, mostly for lend-lease requirements.

The other favorite motor vehicle of World War II was the little 4x4 which came to be known as the jeep. The original model was developed in 1940 by the American Bantam Car Company of Butler, Pennsylvania. When it came to placing production orders, the Quartermaster Corps, over the protests of Bantam, brought in Willys-Overland and Ford for equal shares, on the ground that it was desirable to have more than one com-

pany ready to produce in case of war. All three companies improved upon their designs, and after competitive tests, the Willys model was standardized. Then, for a contract to produce 16,000 jeeps, competitive bids were invited on an all-or-none basis. Willys submitted the low bid. The Quartermaster Corps made the award to Ford as being a larger and more dependable producer. However, the Office of Production Management overruled the Quartermaster decision, and the contract went to Willys. This time the order was not divided, on the ground that it was desirable to be sure that all jeeps were identical. As demand increased additional orders went to Ford (but not to Bantam) to produce jeeps according to Willys blueprints.

Early delays in motor truck production were attributable mainly to the difficulty of obtaining three components—constant velocity joints, transfer cases, and bogie rear axles—needed for the all-wheel drive used in most Army vehicles. Other parts and components were in more general use in commercial trucks. The supply of spare parts to keep the vehicles serviceable posed a related problem, and one made vastly more complicated by the continued use of large numbers of different models. Some 330 different types of vehicles, as compared to 216 during World War I, were in service in World War II. Fortunately, the 2½-ton truck and the jeep constituted well over half of the nearly 2.4 million motor vehicles produced between 1940 and 1945, so that problems of maintenance and spare parts were eased accordingly. Prewar standardization would have contributed much more in this direction.

In the matter of responsibility for motor vehicles procurement, the Quartermaster Corps still had this function during the early

---

[3] Quoted in Smith, *The Army and Economic Mobilization*, p. 253.

part of the war, but, largely for the advantage of centering maintenance of both combat and transport vehicles in the same authority, some sentiment developed for reviving a separate Motor Transport Corps such as had been created during World War I to have responsibility for procurement as well as maintenance (but not operation of transportation) of all motor vehicles. Both the Quartermaster Corps and the Ordnance Corps objected to this notion, as most organizations object to any loss of function, and both indicated willingness to take on the whole job. It went to Ordnance in August 1942.

Aircraft

One of the great production stories of the war is that related to aircraft. West Coast aviation companies, eastern aircraft manufacturers, and automobile companies and their suppliers, all of whom before had been fiercely competitive, organized and integrated their activities in expansion, conversion, and new facilities until the President's "fantastic" call in 1940 for 50,000 aircraft came to be a rather unimaginative request. In this field shortages of materials and machine tools were most critical, but the production record proves how well the industry surmounted all problems. Working together in committees and subcommittees, contractors and the Air Corps ironed out problems of design, engineering, and production.

In 1939 the entire aircraft industry of the United States produced 5,865 planes. It hardly had produced 50,000 planes together since the Wright brothers' first flight at Kitty Hawk in 1903. By 1942 what had been essentially a handcraft industry had been converted to mass production, and in 1944 it attained a peak production of 96,318 aircraft. The total produced from 1940 through 1945 was over 303,300, of which about three-fourths were procured by the Army Air Forces. This feat had to be accomplished along with improvements in quality as well as quantity. Young lads who had been collecting box-top photographs of the sleek P–39 Airacobra were amazed to learn that it was no match for the Japanese Zero or the German Messerschmidt and that the other standard fighter of 1940, the P–40 Warhawk, though able to hold its own a little better, also was obsolete. Fortunately, improved designs of fighters as well as bombers were on the way. The twin-engine, twin-fuselage P–38 Lightning had been designed in 1937, but only sixty-nine were on hand at the time of Pearl Harbor. Two other superior fighters, designed in 1940, did not get into combat until 1943. These were Republic's P–47 Thunderbolt, and North American's P–51 Mustang, a plane which proved to be the finest bomber escort in the war, but which the U.S. Army Air Forces largely ignored until after the British had been impressed with its qualities.

One reason for the lag in fighter plane production early in the war doubtless was the assumption of bomber superiority in the AAF. First priority in design and production went to the heavy bombers, the Boeing B–17 Flying Fortress, designed in 1933, and the Consolidated B–24 Liberator, designed in 1939. The Boeing B–29 Superfortress was designed in 1940. Contracts for its production were let even before it had been flight tested. Deliveries began in August 1943, and within the next two years over 3,700 had been accepted, of which over one thousand were based in the Marianas, engaging in long-range attacks against Japan.

JEEP ON A HILLSIDE IN ITALY

At the beginning of the war, two companies, Wright Aeronautical Corporation and Pratt and Whitney dominated the field in the production of aircraft engines, while a third, the Allison Division of General Motors, was coming into the picture as a producer of liquid-cooled, in-line engines. These companies continued to be the leading producers, though major automobile companies, as licensees, were contributing 60 percent of the horsepower output by 1944. Similarly, the old-line aircraft companies, converted to basic mass-production techniques, produced most of the airframes used during the war.

The most notable newcomer to the group was the Ford Motor Company. In 1940 Ford offered to undertake the mass produc-

tion of airplanes at the rate of one an hour—an offer having dramatic appeal in the dark days when France was falling before the German onslaught, but considered to be impracticable of realization. The War Department was not prepared to freeze design as would be necessary, and a statement of the Assistant Secretary of War in 1938 to the effect that combat aircraft were not adaptable to mass-production techniques remained the official policy. It was the old logistical dilemma of quality versus quantity. Ford showed little interest in manufacturing aircraft parts—the attitude was that complete airplanes should be turned out. Early in 1941 the company was persuaded to join with other automobile makers in parts production, but was not satisfied with this arrangement for a moment, and on its own initiative proceeded to build one of the largest industrial facilities in the world at Willow Run near Detroit to turn out B-24 heavy bombers. The main building at Willow Run was nearly a mile long, and into it went 1,600 machine tools, 7,500 jigs and fixtures, and an overhead conveyor system with cranes having a capacity of 19 tons. All this activity was regularized with a production contract signed in October 1941. Then complete redrawing, and in many cases redesigning of parts, of the aircraft was necessary so that it could be put on the production line; next came the big job of tooling and retooling before the production model was made firm. Eleven months after ground had been broken for the new plant B-24's began coming off the line at Willow Run, but the rate of output was low for another twelve months. Difficulties in adapting the use of dies and presses to working with aluminum, and almost continual changes in Air Forces requirements never did permit the Willow Run plant to run at full capacity. Given the cost and time necessary for complete tooling, and given the continuous design changes which characterized war production it was not clear at the conclusion of the war whether the Ford system actually was superior to that of the older aircraft companies in final results, but the experience did point the way to possible future improvement.

Clothing and Equipment

The problems of design, industrial co-ordination, expansion of capacity, scheduling, and materials common to the procurement of munitions, vehicles, and aircraft also appeared in varying degrees in the procurement of other supplies and equipment. In 1941 the Army, used to peacetime garrison soldiering in the United States, was ill-prepared to clothe and equip troops for global conflict in all climates. Neither satisfactory jungle uniforms nor winter combat clothing were on hand. Efforts to overcome these deficiencies while stepping up procurement of all standard items at once developed shortages in textiles, and added production delays.

A satisfactory jungle uniform did not go into production until near the end of the war. There was better luck in the addition of several items of winter wear, such as woolen jackets, sweaters, and headgear, though development of a good combat boot and of a shoepac that would protect against trench foot in operations over cold, wet terrain came late. Special equipment had to be developed, too, for a new type of fighting man in this war—the airborne soldier. Paratroopers and glidermen had to have parachutes (for which nylon had to be substituted for silk), jump boots, special packs,

and other specialized items of unit and personal equipment. A new steel helmet provided better protection than the shallow "tin hat" of World War I. One of the worst shortages developed in cotton duck. Requirements of that fabric for tents, vehicle covers, ammunition bags, and other items far exceeded all previous demands, and only by conversion of a part of the textile industry could they be met. Many items of Quartermaster equipment had to be redesigned to substitute other materials for much of the rubber, copper, tin, and nylon which had been previously used.

Rations

The Subsistence Division of the Quartermaster Corps, lineal descendant of the formerly independent Subsistence Department, continued to supervise food procurement; however, the peacetime practice of decentralized purchasing gave way to a nationally co-ordinated system in which three Quartermaster depots did the buying of nonperishable items, while a chain of thirty-five Quartermaster Market Centers, operating under the administrative supervision of the Chicago Market Center, handled the buying of perishable foods.

During wartime virtually all troops were issued field rations, the menus more or less standardized depending on season, location, and transportation, instead of relying on the peacetime garrison ration system under which an organization could obtain food pretty much according to its own tastes. Field ration A approximated the garrison ration, and the diet of soldiers stationed in the continental United States contained approximately 70 percent fresh foods. Field ration B was the same except for the substitution of nonperishables, so that troops

A Day's Supply of K Rations

stationed overseas received a large share of canned meats, fruits, and vegetables, besides quantities of such items as dehydrated potatoes and dehydrated eggs. As refrigerator space became available on cargo ships, more fresh foods were shipped overseas.

The combat soldier learned to rely on a family of combat rations. Two of these, the C ration and the D ration, had been developed just before the war. The first, replacing the reserve ration of World War I, consisted of meat components (usually hash or stew), biscuits, beverage powder, and sweets, packed in two cylindrical cans for each meal. Modifications during the war permitted the inclusion of a variety of ten different meat components by 1945. The D ration meal was a highly concentrated bar of cocoa, oat flour, and skim milk powder, weighing four ounces and containing 600 calories, for emergency use in place of the World War I emergency iron ration.

The K ration, developed during the war originally for parachute troops, became most familiar to men in front-line combat. One meal, packed in a cardboard box 6½ inches long, it quickly came into general use in combat areas, appreciated more for its convenience than for its palatability. More attractive were the five-in-one and ten-in-one rations designed for the group feeding of tank or gun crews or detachments isolated from kitchens. These, too, came into general use in combat areas.

Food shortages at times plagued procurement officers and frequently produced an imbalance of components that led to the monotony of diet which planners constantly sought to eliminate. Most serious was the difficulty of procuring canned meats when the producers, having to sell under OPA price ceilings while buying meat without controlled prices, refused to bid on Army contracts. This caused a crisis in 1942 until the OPA granted an exemption for finished meat products, at first temporarily, and then indefinitely. The importation of beef from South America helped to ease the general shortage.

Engineer Equipment and Construction

At first glance it may seem that in any competition for materials and facilities, tanks and other combat matériel must have priority, and so they did at first. But tanks cannot operate without bases, and aircraft cannot operate without airfields. The logistical importance of such engineer items as tractors, earthmovers, cranes, and shovels mounted rapidly until in 1944 requirements were fully met, and it was possible to cut back production after January 1945. In mobile warfare, bridging was as necessary for the uninterrupted advance of the attacking forces as were guns and vehicles. The main problem in supplying the popular floating treadway bridges was the shortage of canvas and rubber needed for the pneumatic floats; again deliveries had just begun to meet demand by the end of 1944. Procurement of Bailey bridges, on the other hand, was more than enough to meet demand in 1944, but unfortunately practically none could be used in the European theater because the parts proved to be not interchangeable with the British-made Baileys already in use there.

The first impact of military mobilization was on military installations for housing, training, and supplying the troops. Camps constructed during World War II were much more elaborate, and on a larger scale than those built during World War I. Again speed was the watchword, and builders—sometimes single firms, at other times several companies working on parallel contracts on a big site—mobilized workers and materials to meet the demand. Contracts generally were of the cost-plus-a-fixed-fee type. Sometimes tracts of land as large as three million acres were leased for maneuver areas. At the beginning the Quartermaster Corps was charged with construction within the United States, but in December 1941 this responsibility was transferred to the Corps of Engineers, which previously had been responsible only for construction overseas and for civil projects for improvement of rivers and harbors within the United States. Total cost of all the Army camps, hospitals, airfields, arsenals, depots, and storage, port, transportation, and other facilities—sufficient for 5.3 million troops in the United States at one time—was $7.2 billion for installations built within the zone of the interior, and $1.8 billion for those built overseas.

Transportation Equipment

The Army Transportation Corps procured vessels used by the Army other than landing craft for which the Navy (except for a short period) had procurement responsibility. Mainly because of the failure to anticipate requirements, landing craft procurement became one of the real strategic bottlenecks. Vessels obtained by the Transportation Corps included all kinds of tugboats, lighters, ferries, motor launches, and miscellaneous small craft.

The Transportation Corps built, operated, and maintained railroads in many parts of the world. It contracted for all sorts of railway equipment—steam, diesel, and gasoline locomotives; freight, passenger, and hospital cars; and the heavy maintenance equipment, thousands of miles of track, and other material necessary to keep the railroads running.

Chemical Equipment

Although toxic gases were not used during World War II, a good deal of effort went into the production of some 146,000 tons (nearly twice the production of Germany) of these agents in the United States, and into the production of over 30 million gas masks of various types, as well as ointments, protective clothing, and decontamination equipment. In addition, the Chemical Warfare Service manufactured or contracted for a number of special items that were widely used, such as 4.2-inch mortars, flame throwers, and smoke-generating equipment; incendiary and smoke bombs, shells, and grenades; and napalm.

Communications

Radio and telephone communications added a new dimension to warfare in greatly

simplifying its control, while at the same time they immeasurably complicated procurement for its support. "Handy-talkies" and "walkie-talkie" radios and sound-powered telephones extended communications down to the rifle platoons. Sets were improved to meet the need of tanks, aircraft, and higher headquarters. Radar detection was an exciting new development of World War II, and presented its own problems in procurement of the highly specialized equipment.

The Atomic Bomb

The largest and most complex single project of World War II had no effect, other than the diversion of critical materials from other programs of highest priority, until the final few weeks of the war in the Pacific. That was the atomic bomb project. Placed under the direction of the "Manhattan District" of the Corps of Engineers when turned over to the Army from the Office of Scientific Research and Development in the summer of 1942, it became a $2.2 billion undertaking, and involved the co-ordinated efforts of scientists and engineers and laborers, of universities, and of industrial corporations. Secretary of War Stimson called the production of the atomic bomb "the greatest achievement of the combined efforts of science industry, and the military in all history." [4]

With several avenues possible for the production of fission material (uranium 235, or plutonium) but with none as yet proved, Brig. Gen. Leslie R. Groves, commander of the Manhattan District, determined to press along all fronts simultaneously. In Septem-

---

[4] Quoted in James P. Baxter, 3d, *Scientists Against Time* (Boston: Little, Brown and Co., 1946), p. 438.

ber 1942 Groves chose the site for the construction of production plants—the Clinton Engineer Works—and town for the workers at what soon would become known as Oak Ridge, Tennessee, about twenty miles from Knoxville. There facilities would be built for the separation of uranium 235 isotopes from the more common uranium 238 by each of three processes, as well as a laboratory and pilot plant for the production of plutonium.

On the basis largely of research being done at Columbia University, the Kellex Company, a company formed for the purpose by the M. W. Kellogg Company, which had been working with the Columbia scientists on design for a pilot plant, accepted a contract to proceed directly to the construction of a full-size gaseous diffusion plant without waiting for a pilot plant. The Carbide and Carbon Chemicals Corporation, operating subsidiary of the Union Carbide and Carbon Corporation, agreed to operate the plant. About the same time, Stone & Webster, general contractors for the construction of the town, also accepted a contract to build a plant for recovering uranium 235 by the electromagnetic process, based on research being done at the University of California. The Tennessee Eastman Corporation, primarily an operating unit of the Eastman Kodak Company, which had built the Holston Ordnance Works near Kingsport, Tennessee, served as consultants and operators of the plant. Within nine months Stone & Webster had 10,000 people on their payroll, and Tennessee Eastman had 4,800 people at work. As a kind of backstop for the other two processes, the Manhattan District contracted with the H. K. Ferguson Company of Cleveland for construction of a thermal diffusion plant, based on a process developed at the

Naval Research Laboratories. Much of the work in all cases was done by subcontractors.

In the meantime a group of scientists at the University of Chicago working with Enrico Fermi had achieved the first self-sustaining chain reaction in their laboratory in a squash court under the stands at Stagg Field. Later this pile was moved to the Argonne National Laboratories near Chicago. This work provided the basis for the plutonium process. For cost plus a fixed fee of $1.00, the Du Pont Company agreed to build a pilot plant for plutonium at Oak Ridge, to be operated by the Metallurgical Laboratory (the University of Chicago group), and to engineer, design, construct, and operate a huge plant for the production of plutonium at Hanford, Washington, where the quantities of water needed for cooling the reactor piles were available from the Columbia River. Before long some 25,000 workers were on the job at Hanford. A third major installation was needed for the work of actually making a bomb from the fissionable materials produced at Oak Ridge and Hanford. This was developed in the establishment in New Mexico of the Los Alamos Scientific Laboratory near the end of 1942, under the direction of J. Robert Oppenheimer.

The extent the project reached in a few months is summed up in the following:

By 1943, the project had grown so rapidly in so many directions that no one individual could follow it. As the year began, earth-movers were already carving huge excavations out of the narrow Tennessee valleys for three plants and a new American city. Across the country a network of university laboratories and private contractors were designing and fabricating components to specifications unprecedented in mass-production efforts. Now, to follow the fortunes of the bomb, one had to observe physicists assembling vacuum tanks and high-voltage equipment at the University

ENLISTED MEN'S BARRACKS AND MESS HALL, CAMP DETRICK, MARYLAND

of California Radiation Laboratory, engineers laying precision-machined blocks of graphite within a concrete cube in Tennessee, chemists testing fragile pieces of porous metal in corrosive gases at Columbia University, scientists exploring the fundamentals of the fission process in New Mexico, and Army officers planning the transformation of a desert into an industrial city in the Pacific Northwest.[5]

All the problems and frustrations of any such gigantic undertaking were com-

pounded by the battles with the unknown. The pressure of haste, the bypassing of pilot plants in the processes for uranium 235, the problems involved in assembling thousands of workers in isolated areas, not to mention the battles for priorities to obtain processing equipment and scarce materials surely would have discouraged any men had not the stakes been so high.

Before the end of 1944 success appeared to be in sight. Engineers at Oak Ridge had devised a scheme to operate separation plants as a unit so as to make best use of the advantages of each process. Results at

[5] Richard G. Hewlett and Oscar E. Anderson, Jr, "The New World, 1939/1946," vol. I, *A History of the United States Atomic Energy Commission* (University Park, Pa.: Pennsylvania State University Press, 1962), p 6.

PRODUCTION PLANT AT THE OAK RIDGE ATOMIC ENERGY COMPLEX

Hanford as well as Oak Ridge were encouraging, and in the late spring of 1945 significant quantities of both uranium 235 and plutonium were reaching the laboratory at Los Alamos. On 16 July 1945 the Manhattan District detonated the first atomic bomb at Alamogordo Air Base in New Mexico. A uranium 235 device, its force proved to be the equivalent of 20,000 tons of TNT—four times greater than its developers had expected. On 6 August an American B–29 dropped a uranium bomb on Hiroshima. Three days later Nagasaki was hit by a plutonium bomb.

Summary

Several outstanding features contributed to a total productive achievement during World War II that could not have been imagined previously. Industrial mobilization and procurement were marked by swift conversion of industry to a wartime basis and expansion of both government and private facilities for wartime production, as well as by the fearless acceptance of requirements to accomplish what had to be done. The policy of close-pricing in procurement contracts helped to reduce costs and increase efficiency. Controls, such as the Controlled Materials Plan, inaugurated to reduce competition for materials and facilities and thus eliminate bottlenecks in machine tool production and critical raw materials, greatly expedited both industrial mobilization and military procurement.

During the war years American industry produced, for the Navy as well as the Army, 40 percent of the world production of munitions, a fact that figured greatly in the Allied victory. Total War Department ex-penditures for the period from 1 July 1940 to 31 August 1945 were $167.4 billion, or 55 percent of all national defense expenditures, and almost 50 percent of the total federal budget for that period. Great as the achievement was, it might have been greater, and the job might have been done more swiftly if better use had been made of previous experience. Whether it would be surpassed in the future would depend on necessity and on the extent to which this experience might be applied.

CHAPTER XXIX

Global Distribution and Transportation

For logistics, as with strategy and tactics, the battle is the pay-off. Beyond the procurement of military supplies and equipment there remain the closely related activities of storage, distribution, and transportation to get matériel into the hands of the troops, and all to the battle areas. World War II put the whole distribution process into a new dimension, the dimension of global warfare, when active theaters a world apart had to be supported simultaneously.

Organization for Supply Services

From the fountainhead of the War Department in Washington logistical authority and responsibility flowed down three diverging but concurrent streams—through the chiefs of the technical services to Class IV installations; through the service commands to posts, camps, and stations in the United States; through oversea theater commanders to communications zones and operational armies. The good fortune of the United States in two world wars in keeping combat operations distant from its own shores gave to it a military organization structure considerably different from those of a land power such as Germany or the Soviet Union where internal military districts had to be closely related to the operational organization.

Within the zone of interior—which included all the continental United States—installations were classified in four categories according to the degree or nature of control exercised by the service commands. Class I installations were directly under the command of the service commands and included reception centers, repair shops, Army Service Forces training centers, and all named general hospitals except Walter Reed. Class II installations were those at which Army Ground Forces units were stationed for training; here the service commands appointed the post commanders and were responsible for all housekeeping duties, but had no command over the troops or training of Ground Forces. Class III were Air Forces installations where the ASF service commands had limited housekeeping duties. Class IV installations and activities were "exempted" from service command control, and remained under the command of the head of an administrative or technical service, though the service commands performed some limited housekeeping functions. Class IV installations, such as depots and ports of embarkation, performed functions relating directly to nationwide programs that needed centralized control for effectiveness. General depots handling supplies of more than one technical service came under the command and management of The Quartermaster General, though the sections remained under the supervision and control of their respective technical service chiefs.

Oversea commanders, benefiting from the precedent of World War I when General

Pershing maintained virtually complete independence from the Chief of Staff in Washington, enjoyed an autonomy far greater than any to be found in the continental United States. The kind of organization established in a theater of operations for logistic support stemmed mainly from World War I experience, although local variations reflected widely differing conditions. In general, the assumption was that a theater of operations would be divided into a combat zone and a communications zone. The dividing line between the two zones, established by the theater commander, generally coincided with the rear boundaries of the field armies occupying the combat zone. Army administrative and service units, possibly brought together in an Army Service Command in special situations such as amphibious operations, performed their service and supply functions mostly within the Army service area—the territory between the corps rear boundary and the combat zone rear boundary—though they might be located anywhere in the combat zone. Similarly, corps and divisions had rear boundaries that defined their territorial responsibility and provided rear areas in which service troops could function.

The communications zone was a territorial organization extending from the combat zone rear boundary to the theater boundary as fixed by the Joint Chiefs of Staff. Its purpose was to relieve combat commanders of logistical and territorial responsibility not immediately affected by the conduct of operations. The organization of the communications zone depended on the size and nature of the theater and the type of operations being conducted. In a large land theater the communications zone might be

divided into subordinate commands, including one or more base sections (adjacent to the coastal areas), intermediate sections, and advance sections (adjacent to the combat zone). Responsibility was delegated to the section commanders for logistic support through their areas. Some services, such as railway service, pipe lines, truck service, inland waterways, and major construction might then be held out as intersectional services and administered directly from communications zone headquarters, though in World War II the practice too often was to permit divided command. In other cases the communications zone might not be divided at all, but its commander could assign specific tasks to districts (usually confined to limited administration and territorial responsibility, but not charged with the support of combat forces), bases (for support of a force), or areas. Districts, bases, or areas operated directly under communications zone headquarters even when sections had been organized to handle most functions, or they operated as subordinate elements of sections.

U.S. Army theaters of operations usually corresponded to Allied theaters, but not always. The U.S. Army established the European Theater of Operations (ETO) under General Eisenhower in 1942, and by agreement with the Navy it served as a joint command. Later its area was redefined to correspond with that coming under the combined British-American Allied Expeditionary Force. In North Africa, Eisenhower was a U.S. Army theater commander as well as an Allied commander, an arrangement that continued when the theater was redesignated and expanded under a British commander as the Mediterranean Theater of Operations (MTO). In the Pacific, General MacArthur's Southwest Pacific Area (SWPA) was an Allied and a joint command, and it also comprised a U.S. Army theater. The Pacific Ocean Area (POA) under Admiral Nimitz also was recognized as an Allied command, though actually it functioned as a U.S. joint theater; the South Pacific Area had a separate organization, but was subordinate to Nimitz, while he commanded directly the Central Pacific and the North Pacific subdivisions.

In Southeast Asia the structure was much more complicated. There the China-Burma-India theater was a U.S. Army theater that had grown up without any official designation as such from the War Department, but where Lt. Gen. Joseph W. Stilwell was recognized as theater commander. It extended over the area of the China Theater, which was an Allied theater under the command of Generalissimo Chiang Kai-shek with Stilwell as chief of staff, independent of the Combined Chiefs of Staff; over Burma which was within the area of another Allied command, the Southeast Asia Command (after August 1943), under Admiral Lord Louis Mountbatten with Stilwell acting as deputy commander; and over India which comprised a separate British command responsible to the Government of India. In October 1944 the U.S. command was divided into separate China and India-Burma Theaters.

The Supply System

Different kinds of supplies were frequently designated according to the responsible service, that is, Quartermaster, Ordnance, and so forth; but for planning and distribution purposes classification according to handling and use continued. In the interwar period supplies had been placed in five categories as a modification and refinement of the four-class system of World War I. Class I consisted of supplies generally consumed at a uniform rate regardless of conditions, principally food. Class II supplies included clothing, weapons, and other items for which there were specific allowances for units or for individuals on tables of organization and equipment, tables of basic allowances, tables of allowances, and other lists. Class III consisted of gasoline, lubricating oil, and other fuels and lubricants, commonly referred to as POL (aviation fuels and lubricants were classified III–A). Class IV was a miscellaneous category for items such as construction and fortification materials needed for special purposes or not otherwise classified. Class V was ammunition, explosives, and c h e m i c a l agents.

Before World War II most supplies for distribution, other than ammunition, were stored at five general depots where, through the corps area commander, a station could place its requisitions with the appropriate technical service section at the general depot in its area. The upsurge of activity in wartime made this arrangement impractical. It no longer was feasible to store all items even of a single technical service at one place, much less all of the items of most of the services. Therefore depots began to specialize in certain major items—one in artillery, for instance, another in tanks, another in clothing. Frequently several depots had to specialize in the same commodity. These came to be known as key depots. Others, known as distribution depots continued to handle a broad group of commodities, but for units within a limited area. Both kinds of depots were assigned "satellites," or reserve depots, to handle overflow. Storage systems developed independently by each of the technical services were brought under centralized control in ASF so that space could be transferred from one service to another, and a measure of balance could be maintained between supply and demand among the different areas. By the end of 1942 the additional depot facilities needed had been completed or were under construction. A Quartermaster depot generally covered one hundred to eight hundred acres of land while the Ordnance Department had six depots with over 20,000 acres each. At the peak of war activity 125 large installations were active in the continental United States where 2,000,000 people handled over 4,000,000 tons of supplies a month. Special effort went into packaging and packing supplies so that they could withstand long shipments protected against the effects of moisture, insects, and fungus.

Newly activated units received their authorized allowances of initial equipment automatically since the technical services shipped it directly, on the basis of approved tables, without requisitions from depots or manufacturers to post supply officers. For replenishment supplies, after January 1942, units in the United States placed requisitions with post supply officers who filled them from station stocks or forwarded them directly to the depot concerned without having to go through any higher headquarters. Certain items, listed as controlled items or otherwise as critical items, were subject to strict distribution controls, and requisitions for such items as tanks, heavy artillery, certain ammunition, mortars, flame throwers, tires and tubes, dry batteries, X-ray film, heavy tentage, field wire, and various radio and radar sets had to have the approval of

the appropriate chief of technical service before being filled. During their initial training, divisional units received half of their equipment allowances, and nondivisional units received 20 percent.

Perhaps the most significant control measure was the stock control system adopted in 1943. This system provided for a prescribed stock level for each post, and post supply officers had to make periodic physical inventories to assure conformity to the prescribed levels. A reporting system had to be developed to keep track of the items on hand at the depots, on requisition, on procurement, in transit, and so on, and the technical services soon began moving the duties involved out of Washington to stock control points in various parts of the country. Gradually, the services also began delegating the computation of requirements for all but a few major items to inventory control points, which often were located at the same place as the stock control points.

Total quantities of items—levels of supply—which oversea theaters were to keep on hand were determined by the War Department on the basis of JCS operational and planning directives and recommendations of the theater commander. These were prescribed in terms of days of supply, that is, the supplies estimated to be necessary for one day for the conditions of the operation and for the force stated. The minimum level of supply was the quantity needed to support operations during any reasonably anticipated interruption of supply lines, and it was considered a reserve to be used when reshipments were delayed or the operating level was temporarily insufficient. The operating level of supply was the quantity needed to support operations during the interval between resupply shipments. The maximum level of supply was the minimum level plus the operating level; it was the total authorized for the theater to have on hand under War Department directives.

Sometimes unimaginative or arbitrary use of the day of supply concept led to difficulties in the accumulation of disproportionately large reserves. At the same time theater levels were subject to revision as a result of changes in operational needs, the general availability or supplies and transportation, and the competing requirements of other theaters. Requirements of the different theaters varied according to local conditions, but on the whole, and as a general average, it took 1,600 tons daily—1,100 tons of dry cargo of all classes, 475 tons of bulk petroleum products, and 25 tons of vehicles—to maintain a division slice (a division at full strength plus a proportionate share of all supporting and service troops, calculated at a total of 40,000 men), plus two air wing slices (5,000 men each), in combat. Of this amount, 595 tons went to the combat zone for ground forces, and 65 tons for the air forces units, and 365 tons went up to the division area. In terms of pounds per man per day, there was a good deal of variation between the European and Pacific theaters in various classes of supply, but the total came to nearly the same—66.8 pounds per man per day in the European theater, and 67.4 in the Pacific. In Europe it took 7.17 pounds of rations per man per day, as compared to 6.71 pounds in the Pacific. While it took 1 pound of clothing and equipage, 11.9 pounds of construction materials, and 5.14 pounds of ammunition per man per day in the Pacific, the requirements for the European theater for those supplies were .426, 7.28, and 3.64 pounds, respectively. Air Forces ammunition amounted to an additional equivalent of 4.4 pounds per man per day in Europe, and 3.5

pounds in the Pacific.[1] As had been noted in World War I, there again was a noticeable tendency to overequip the soldier. This not only added to the burden the individual soldier had to carry, but it taxed transportation and, moreover, put unnecessarily heavy demands on the whole supply system.

For supplying oversea theaters from the United States, the ports of embarkation became, in effect, supply regulating points. In order to localize responsibility, port commanders were charged with handling the flow of supplies into and out of their ports in accordance with the theaters' needs. At the ports, Oversea Supply Divisions functioned in a way as Army Service Forces staff divisions to supervise all matters pertaining to the supply of the oversea commands and bases which were the responsibility of the respective ports. This responsibility was divided according to areas in order to clarify functions and simplify procedures. Thus the New York Port of Embarkation was responsible for supplying the European and Mediterranean theaters; Boston for the North Atlantic; Charleston for the Bahamas, Central Africa, and the Middle East; New Orleans for Latin America and the Caribbean and South Atlantic bases; San Francisco for the Pacific; Los Angeles for China-Burma-India; Seattle, for Alaska. Other ports might be used as outports of the major ports, but they always operated under the direction of the port commander having responsibility for the particular area. Port and oversea commands exchanged liaison officers, and the port commanders issued monthly policy charts listing such things as directives in force, levels of supply, and troop

---

[1] FM 101–10, Organization, Technical and Logistical Data, August 1949, pp. 223–88, 303–04, 490.

strength, so that close co-ordination could be maintained. An oversea command then would requisition supplies from its supplying port, the Oversea Supply Division would edit the requisitions, and forward extracts to the depots furnishing the types of goods called for. Requisitions for controlled or special items went to the headquarters of the technical service concerned or to Army Service Forces headquarters. (*Chart 5*)

During the first months of operations in a new theater, the expectation was that supply from the continental United States would be on an automatic basis. For a time a system of preshipment, without regard to current troop movements, was used to build up supplies in the British Isles for planned future operations. Units moving into a new theater carried with them their initial equipment and supplies together with enough replacement and maintenance supplies to keep them going for a short while. The technical services then shipped supplies periodically without requisitions according to prearranged schedules. Some supplies, such as rations and gasoline, that were consumed at a fairly uniform rate, remained on automatic supply; others came under the requisition method. Neither method served satisfactorily in situations where there was a shortage of required items, or, as frequently happened, where information was incomplete.

Overseas commanders were supposed to keep the ports informed about shortages and excesses in subsistence supplies and fuel, the extent of local procurement of supplies in the theater, storage space, priorities desired in the shipment of supplies, and ports of entry to be used. But information often was slow in coming, or did not come at all. The greatest difficulty in meeting requirements for automatic supply was in determining the strength and composition of the forces in the theater being supplied. The Operations Division of the General Staff was supposed to furnish the ports a troop basis, revised quarterly, together with monthly troop lists showing troops present and en route to the various theaters, but these figures were not furnished regularly, and usually were many weeks out of date. A port could record its own troop movements, but in the early part of the war had no way of finding out what troops had moved through other ports or had arrived from other areas in the theater for which it had major responsibility. Reports from the overseas commands were hardly more reliable than the others, and the practice of basing requisitions on projected rather than actual troop strength often led to duplication.

The emphasis on automatic supply, which continued through most of 1942 while minimum theater levels were being established, began to shift as it became evident that unbalanced stocks and large reserves were accumulating in several theaters. Clearly, if control, and supply itself, were to be made effective, some way had to be found to get better information. Already, in March 1942, the War Department had instituted a Materiel Status Report listing on-hand quantities, as well as quantities authorized, of selected scarce items, including ammunition, to be submitted monthly to the department by overseas commanders. Originally the G–4 staff had intended that this report should serve as a requisition; however, because of expected difficulties in eliminating overlapping reports of shortages and the difficulties of correlating successive reports as they were affected by shipments and by changes in troop bases, this feature was dropped for the time being leading to further confusion when commanders used it as a requisition. Moreover, the report covered only a fraction of the items supplied.

In the spring of 1943 the War Department moved to systematize the reporting system. The new system required port commanders to prepare three major reports for the theaters they served on the basis of data provided by theater commanders as well as from their own records. These reports were a revised Monthly Materiel Status Report for selected Class II and Class IV items, a monthly Automatic Supply Report for subsistence and fuel (replaced a little later by a Selected Items Report on certain Class I and III items) and an Ammunition Supply Report to be submitted every ten days. The system required Operations Division of the General Staff to furnish Army Service Forces with an official troop basis for each oversea theater within eight days after the end of each month. Copies went simultaneously to Army Service Forces headquarters and to theater commanders. Showing quantities en route as well as theater stocks and theater allowances, the reports soon came to serve as requisitions for the items covered.

About the same time the practice was confirmed whereby Air Forces technical supplies were requisitioned directly from the Air Service Command, an organization already functioning autonomously so far as Army Service Forces was concerned, at Patterson Field, Ohio. In this case the port of embarkation was bypassed completely in the requisitioning channel, though Army Air Forces still was supposed to provide periodic information on the movement of cargo under its control.

On the basis of experience up to the autumn of 1943 the War Department adopted an assumption that overseas supply operations might be expected to develop in three successive phases with the opening of a new theater. During the first phase all supply would be automatic. This would continue until the second phase—considered the normal phase—when procedures would become semiautomatic, with the supply of controlled items and ammunition based upon status reports, and other supplies depending on requisitions. In the third phase, expected to occur considerably later, supply would be by requisition only. Curiously, it was expected that it would be possible to go over completely to the system of requisitioning only when a theater had become stabilized. Yet it was precisely in the stabilized theater—as had been true in a relative sense in World War I—that automatic supply should have worked best, for then information should be most complete and abrupt changes in status less frequent. On the other hand, when automatic supply was most difficult, at the beginning of an operation or the opening of a new theater, was precisely when automatic supply was most necessary.

The system of semiautomatic supply remained in effect substantially as developed by fall of 1943 until the end of the war, but familiar problems continued to reappear. Serious discrepancies between port records and figures supplied by the theaters were still common, theater inventories seldom were adequate, and time lag still made the status reports out of date before supply action could be taken on them. In fact, one study by Army Service Forces headquarters concluded that the use of the Materiel Status Report actually was slowing down rather than speeding up delivery of supplies to the theaters. Among the constant efforts to make the system work,

CHART 5—

ZONE OF INTERIOR

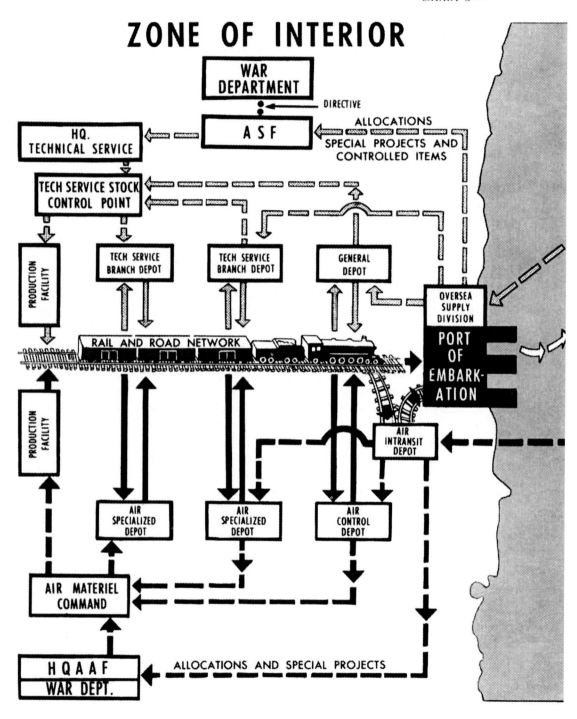

OVERSEA THEATER·

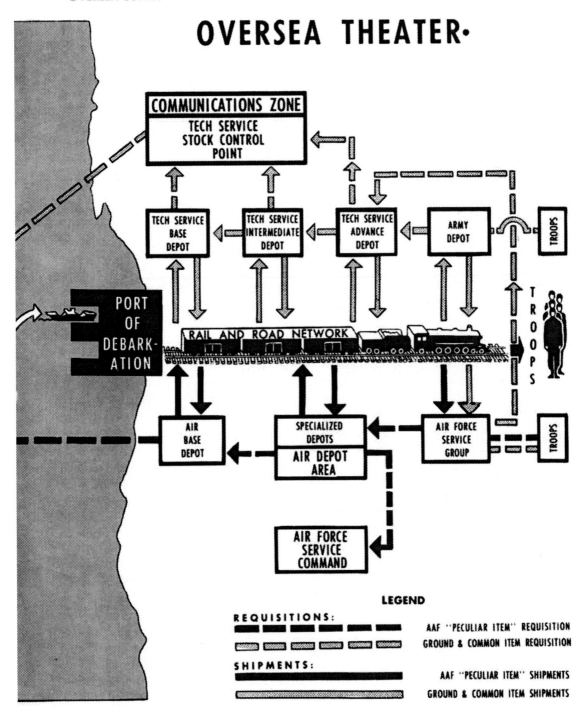

a major improvement required the port commander to keep a "perpetual inventory" for each overseas command for which he had responsibility. This was to be based upon a firm inventory which the overseas theater commander was to furnish at a mutually agreeable date, and kept up to date by notification of arrival of vessels in the theater and reports from the theater on items lost, expended, or transferred. For his part the theater commander also was to keep a perpetual inventory which would be adjusted from time to time with the one kept at the port. In 1944 the whole system of supply on the basis of status reports was called into question. Then the trend became to extend the stock control system in effect in the zone of interior—based on central records of depot stocks and issues upon which both production and distribution requirements were calculated—to the oversea commands insofar as practicable.

A new system went into effect only a week before the end of hostilities in Europe. It continued the perpetual inventory at the ports, but a Critical Items Report, no longer itself to serve as a requisition, replaced the Materiel Status Report. All theaters were placed on requisition supply, but requisitions for critical items were to go directly to the chiefs of the technical services rather than to the ports. The technical services tried to anticipate demands by preparing distribution plans for the allocation of items expected to be in short supply during the next three months. While the new system never was fully tested, the conclusion at Army Service Forces headquarters was that stock control and requisitioning was the best system of supply, and should replace automatic supply as soon as practicable in any oversea theater. Automatic supply never did seem to be as satisfactory during World War II as it had been in supplying the AEF in World War I—no doubt because of the different conditions of a multiple-theater war and failure to make distinctions for authorized equipment needs according to areas.

So long as there were not enough supplies and equipment to satisfy all demands, some system of priorities in supply distribution was necessary. Priorities were co-ordinated in the General Staff. The Operations Division Logistics Group and G–3 determined them, while the technical services prepared lists of the controlled items (consolidated and edited in Army Service Forces headquarters and forwarded to G–4 for approval), subject to basic priorities. The number of listed controlled items varied from a high of 776 in the spring of 1943 to 130 in June 1945. Items not actually on the controlled lists were in fact handled in much the same way when in short supply. In the first part of the war the main problem was to determine priorities as between overseas theaters and training in the United States. In general the system allowed 100 percent of authorized equipment to units in category A, comprising units overseas and those alerted or subject to early movement overseas, units of the defense commands, and school and testing units; 50 percent of most items to units in category B (those in training for some time, but not earmarked for overseas movement); and 20 percent equipment for the remainder, category C, mostly newly activated units. In the latter half of the war, the major priorities problem was determination of the order among overseas theaters themselves. The general rule was to grant highest priority to operations in progress or planned for the immediate future, with preference to requirements for the war against Germany as against those for the war against Japan. Thus in 1944 first priority went to the European theater, while the Mediterranean held the second, the principal Pacific theaters, third, and China-Burma-India, fourth. After V–E Day, the Pacific theater held first priority, China and India-Burma, second, the European theater, third, and the Mediterranean, fourth. In practice, however, the Operations Division frequently determined priorities for specific items on an *ad hoc* basis as among the theaters, and often different projects or operations within the same theater were assigned different priorities. In distributing supplies under the priorities system, the general practice was to provide all table of organization and equipment supplies in order of priority, to provide maintenance and operational supplies to each claimant in order, and, finally, to provide stocks needed for maximum authorized levels of supply in each case.

It was difficult enough to maintain effective supply of regularly authorized items of supplies and equipment, but more difficult by far was the supply of special purpose items not covered by the different tables of equipment and tables of allowances. These included all Class IV supplies of which the most important were Engineer construction materials and Transportation Corps equipment, and all major Class II items (individual and organizational clothing and equipment) over and above those authorized in the tables. One way in which these additional supplies and equipment could be obtained was through special lists of equipment submitted for War Department approval for particular units. These usually were concerned with noncritical items, and usually presented no great difficulty. Less satisfactory was the practice of simply submitting requisitions for

additional supplies and equipment on short notice. Even though justification of the additional requirements could be found, hasty attempts to meet them in this manner were bound to lead to confusion and waste.

Special needs to meet special conditions were so frequent that some kind of routine procedure was needed to meet them. By the end of 1943, therefore, an "operational project system" was developed whereby the theater commander prepared a "project" to cover special needs for an anticipated operation in connection with his mission, assigned it a key number, and submitted it directly to the War Department Operations Division. With the project the theater included either a detailed bill of materials, or sufficiently detailed information of requirements to permit the War Department to compute one, and indicated what materials could be obtained locally in the theater. When it had been reviewed by the technical services concerned and approved by Army Service Forces and Operations Division, the bill of materials became an approved requirement against which requisitions submitted to the ports would be honored. As an additional aid to timely procurement, after early 1944 theaters were required to file quarterly estimates for Engineer construction materials and Transportation Corps equipment needed for keyed projects three to five quarters in advance. As might have been expected, timing was the greatest trouble. Often requisitions followed so closely upon the submission of projects that little time was gained in preparing for them, but, again, this was a result of frequent changes in the strategic picture and in tactical decisions. As in the broader case of general procurement it was difficult to maintain the logic of basing logistic requirements on strategic and tactical decisions when those decisions allowed so little time for adjustment of procurement and shipping schedules. Again it was for the War Department to try to anticipate needs. During 1944 the practice began for the Planning Division of Army Service Forces itself to prepare projects which served as the main guide for the theaters in preparing their own requirements for operational supplies, and to an extent alerted the technical services on what to expect. The theaters still had to submit their projects before supply action could begin. (*Chart 6*)

Responsibility for supply extended down the chain of command from the theater commander to the smallest unit commander; each was responsible for the supply of troops within his own command. The communications zone commander was responsible for the bulk supply of all items to the armies and theater and communications zone troops. When a theater communications zone was divided into sections, supply operations became the direct responsibility of the section commanders, but the control of theater supply remained the responsibility of the communications zone commander, under the theater commander. The army group was principally a tactical and not an administrative headquarters, but an army group commander was responsible for supply policies affecting the armies in his group and the determination of priorities and the allocation of service troops among them. The field army did have full administrative as well as tactical functions. The normal procedure was for the communications zone to deliver supplies to army depots, or, at times, to army supply points where they could be issued directly to subordinate units. The army was responsible for receiving, storing, and distributing the supplies. Again, the corps ordinarily was not

a link in the chain of supply; however, the corps commander supervised the use of ammunition or items in short supply considered to have direct tactical significance. When operating independently of an army, the corps then, of course, had to assume responsibility for its own supply. The division ordinarily got its supplies directly from army depots or supply points, and it operated distributing points for rations and fuel. Service elements of the division carried small stocks of Class II and Class IV supplies. The supply of ammunition was based upon a system of keeping on hand in the using units a determined basic load (established by the War Department, and expressed in the number of rounds by type that could be carried by a unit in its organic transportation) which was replenished as used.

Distribution of supplies followed two general methods. The first was unit distribution, by which the higher unit, in its own transportation, delivered supplies to the using unit's bivouac, dump, or distributing point. The second was supply point distribution, by which the using unit picked up its supplies at the supply point (depot, railhead, airhead or other point). The normal procedure was for the communications zone in delivering supplies to armies to use unit distribution, and for armies and divisions to use supply point distribution. It was the rule in theaters of operations for depots to ship supplies to supported depots or supply points, and to make all arrangements for transportation to do so.

In a war given to mechanization and the use of motor transportation on a scale never before approached, and in which new kinds of equipment were being introduced at every turn, the ever-present problem of the maintenance of equipment took on new significance. Efforts to standardize shop pro-

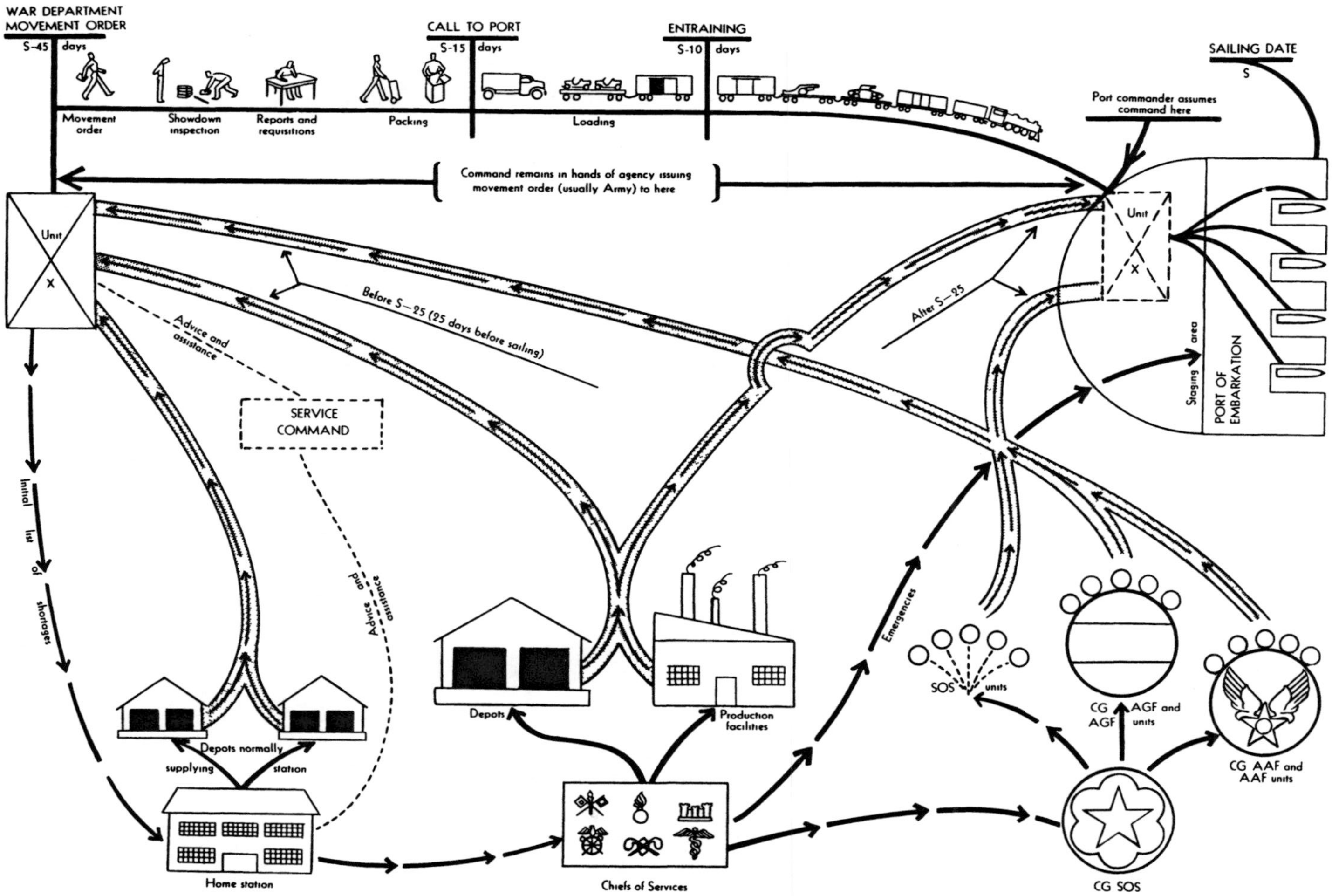

CHART 6—PROCEDURE FOR EQUIPPING A TYPICAL AGF UNIT FOR OVERSEAS MOVEMENT (POM): FEBRUARY 1943

cedures, reduce the number of models in use, and promote preventive maintenance all helped to ease the problem. Throughout the war spare parts supply presented the most difficult maintenance problem. A system of determining requirements for spare parts by shops and units on the basis of experience factors and stocking parts at maintenance shops cut down on delays, but the greatest difficulties lay in anticipating requirements sufficiently in advance to have parts in the distribution system at all, and then controlling them so that they were available where most needed. As the newspaper correspondent Ernie Pyle wrote, "This is not a war of ammunition, tanks, guns, and trucks alone. It is as much a war of replenishing spare parts to keep them in combat as it is a war of major equipment." [2] By the mid-war period shipments of ordnance spare parts alone were at the rate of more than one hundred million pieces a month.

Inland Transportation

Undoubtedly the key to the logistics of World War II was transportation. More often than not this had been the limiting factor to past logistical efforts, but now, to meet the demands of the world's greatest industrial power in conducting a war spread all over the globe, it was more prominent than ever.

Railroads in the United States

An immediate question was whether the railroads would fare any better than they

had during World War I when the system so nearly collapsed that the government took over their operation. Thanks to better organizations, in particular to the Car Service Division of the Association of American Railroads, to the emergency powers exercised by the Interstate Commerce Commission and the Office of Defense Transportation, and to improvements in railway facilities to the extent of $8 billion in capital expenditures since the last war, while highways, waterways and pipelines were able to carry a greater share of the traffic, the railroads were able to continue throughout the war under private management. Actually the total freight car loadings at the peak of World War II were less than they had been in 1918, but the total ton-miles carried in 1944 was 80 percent greater. As for Army freight, the 105 million tons moved during 1944 was nearly ten times that for Fiscal Year 1919.

Anxious to avoid the kind of port congestion that had paralyzed oversea shipments in 1917, the Office of The Quartermaster General and later the Transportation Corps (after March 1942) worked closely with the Association of American Railroads to develop a system of holding and reconsignment points to regulate arrivals at the ports. Seldom were freight cars held up at the ports for longer than ten days. The Office of Defense Transportation waged a continuous campaign against light loading and using cars for storage and so delaying their movement. The average speed of cars moving on the roads and through terminals increased from 43.9 miles a day in 1941 to 51.7 miles a day in 1944. A further measure toward the efficient use of cars was the Army's inauguration of the consolidated car service which established consolidation stations where less-than-carload lots could be

---

[2] Quoted in Harry C. Thomson and Lida Mayo, *The Ordnance Department: Procurement and Supply,* UNITED STATES ARMY IN WORLD WAR II (Washington, 1960), p. 300.

brought together to be shipped in full cars. The Navy, Marine Corps, and Coast Guard joined in this service.

In moving troops the railroads did better with less equipment than they had during World War I. Again, better organization and planning on the part of the railroads themselves as well as in the Army produced good results. It took 63 trains, comprised of 442 tourist sleeping cars, 48 standard sleepers, 89 baggage cars, 90 kitchen cars, 1,124 flatcars, and 89 boxcars, to move an infantry division with its equipment in 1942. It took 69 trains, with a total of 2,221 cars to move an armored division. During 1943 an average of 28,815 passenger and freight cars a month were used in special troop trains or as special cars attached to regular trains. Joint agreements worked out each year between regional passenger associations and the armed forces governed the movement of military passengers. From 1943 the Army put into service, by arrangement with the Pullman Company, a series of newly designed government-owned troop sleepers and troop kitchen cars. In general, the routing of Army troop movements was centralized in the Traffic Control Division of the Office of the Chief of Transportation. For small groups (generally less than forty people and requiring no more than one car) Army transportation officers at the station of departure made arrangements directly with local railroad representatives.

Other Transportation in the Zone of Interior

Other means of transportation carried a relatively small share, probably not over 10 percent, of the Army's traffic, but this was enough to provide significant relief for the overburdened railroads. Highway motor carriers were especially useful for short hauls, barges on the rivers and canals provided welcome relief in the movement of nonurgent bulk goods, and airlines were valuable for small emergency shipments.

Perhaps even more significant for military operations were the oil pipelines. A wartime construction program increased the capacity for pipeline delivery of petroleum products to the east coast from 50,000 barrels a day at the beginning of the war to 754,000 barrels a day. One line known as Big Inch alone had a capacity equal to 30,000 tank cars or 60 to 75 ships. A second line, Little Big Inch, paralleling the other most of the way, delivered 235,000 barrels of gasoline and fuel oil a day—72 percent of it for military supplies.

Ocean Transportation

Ports of Embarkation

The regulation of oversea traffic focused in the port of embarkation where policies and activities relating both to supply and transportation came together, and sometimes worked at cross purposes. The result was a jurisdictional contest for control of the ports. During World War I, it will be recalled, the ports began operations under divided authority, later were brought under a single commander responsible to the Embarkation Service, and finally, near the end of the war, were consolidated directly under the Purchase, Storage, and Traffic Division of the General Staff. In World War II port jurisdiction was originally under the Army Transport Service of the Office of The Quartermaster General, and there were no supply functions as such involved. Shortly after Pearl Harbor the Transportation Branch of G-4, War Department General

Staff, was given jurisdiction. In March 1942 ports were assigned to the newly created Transportation Corps, by which time they also had been assigned the mission of co-ordinating supply for designated oversea theaters. This assignment seemed to give to the Chief of Transportation undue ascendancy over the chiefs of the other technical services and an undue independence of Army Service Forces headquarters. Without any formal reorganization, the Oversea Supply Divisions that had been organized at the ports came more directly under the supervision of the Assistant Chief of Staff for Operations, Army Service Forces. In a contest between the proper distribution of supplies according to determined priorities and the most efficient use of transportation, supply was the first consideration. (*Map 16*)

With improved efficiency resulting from longer experience, the ports of embarkation operated essentially as they had during World War I. They were responsible for regulating the arrival of outbound cargo according to the shipping assigned, and for loading the vessels and dispatching them on schedule. They had to devise special methods for handling heavy and bulky items, and they had to exercise special care in the transshipment of large quantities of explosives. It was up to them to process tanks, trucks, guns, and other equipment to assure their arrival in the oversea theaters in good condition.

Throughout the war the greatest problems in port operations occurred at the Pacific ports. The greater distances from sources of supply, the greater distances to destinations, the use of undeveloped island bases, uncertainties of shipping, and rapidly changing requirements, made reliable scheduling difficult. With the shifting emphasis

on shipments to the Pacific late in the war there was some danger that the railroads serving San Francisco might be overtaxed.

Port commanders similarly controlled troop movements overseas from home station to staging area, carried out final inspections and processing both of troops and equipment, prepared billeting plans for the transports, loaded the equipment, and embarked the troops according to planned schedules. There were some early complaints from the theaters regarding information on troop movements, but with experience, greater resources, and better organization, the exchange of information between ports and theaters improved. It was up to the Operations Division of the General Staff to keep theater commanders informed about action on their requests for troops, but the port commanders provided information about actual movements. About a week to ten days before a scheduled sailing, the port commander concerned would send a loading cable to the theater giving the units to be loaded on what ships and their tentative time of departure. A sailing cable brought this information up to date, and gave the actual time of departure as soon as possible after a ship or convoy had sailed. Changes in priorities, changes in availability of ships, shortages of equipment, failure of units to meet inspection requirements, and other matters caused frequent changes in schedules but all that was a part of war. No such force had ever before been sent overseas. It was more than three and one-half times as great as the AEF of World War I.

Preparation for Overseas Movement

Staging troops for overseas movement was done in much the same way that it had

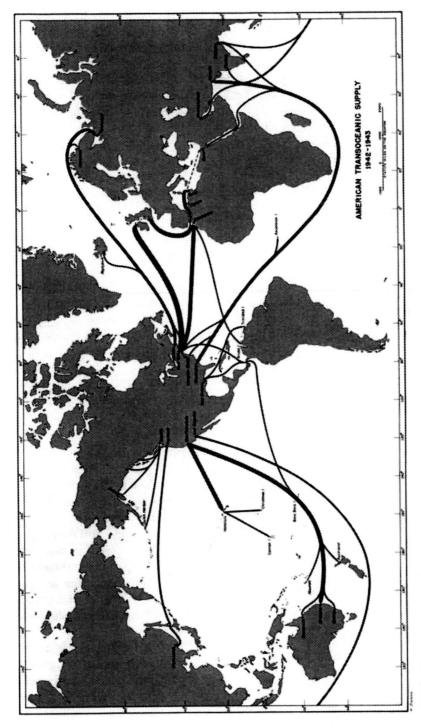

AMERICAN TRANSOCEANIC SUPPLY
1942 - 1943

MAP 16

been done during World War I. For a time there was some sentiment for doing away with staging areas, and moving troops directly from home stations to shipside, but soon that was seen to be as impractical in 1942 as it had been in 1917. New York, which handled by far the greatest traffic of any of the ports, had the two largest staging area camps—Camp Kilmer, New Jersey, with capacity for over 37,500 men, and Camp Shanks, New York, with capacity for over 34,600; in addition Fort Hamilton, with capacity for 5,700 troops, was used as a staging area as needed. Camp Miles Standish, near Boston, had a capacity of 23,400, and Camp Patrick Henry, Virginia, serving Hampton Roads, had a capacity of 24,100. On the west coast, the principal staging area for San Francisco was Camp Stoneman, with facilities for 30,600 men. Units were supposed to complete all training, fill troop strength, and draw complete personal and organizational equipment in accordance with War Department instructions codified in a manual called Preparation for Overseas Movement (POM), but almost all arrived at the ports with some deficiencies, usually in equipment, to be made up. In many cases authorized equipment had not been made available to alerted units in time for them to obtain it at their home stations; sometimes priorities were changed, and movement dates were moved up; sometimes inspections were inadequate, or requirements had not been anticipated far enough in advance. Often new equipment was authorized too late to be issued at the home station, as for instance the new type of gas masks which many troops received at the staging areas. These camps also had to maintain training facilities so that troops receiving new types of equipment could become familiar with it, or individuals who

had not completed their weapons training could do so. The length of stay at the staging areas varied from a few days to two weeks or longer, depending on the deficiencies that had to be overcome and on the availability of ships. Usually it took units less than two weeks to pass through the ports.

Movements Overseas

As during World War I, a great problem in the overseas movement of troops was the shipment of organizational equipment. The solution found in 1917–18—for units to turn in their equipment before leaving, then draw new equipment on the other side, thus permitting bulk shipment of equipment without the delays and difficulties of marking it and keeping track of it at every turn—was applied only to a limited degree in World War II. The preshipment of equipment to the United Kingdom, when shipping was available and conditions permitted, was the most effective application of this method. At other times it could not be done because, it was said, sufficient shipping was not available, though bulk shipments actually took less tonnage than any other; or there was not enough time, though it took less time to draw new equipment from central depots than to search for equipment marked for particular units arriving at various times and at different ports; or certain items of equipment were not available in sufficient quantities, though in the long run it should have taken less equipment if shipped in bulk to central points than if it was stored at various destinations awaiting claimants.

The main difficulties in maintaining an effective preshipment program appear to have been the wide scattering of forces and the absence of well-defined strategic decisions. When supplies were short, it might have been a serious handicap to flexibility to have had large quantities stored at a few places. In the Pacific, particularly, where distances were so great between areas of actual and potential operations, and where the basic strategy was one of opportunism, it would have been most difficult to find a place where equipment could be stored and issued in bulk. Still, this did not necessarily make impractical the bulk shipment of authorized equipment to destinations to which units already were ordered. Bulk shipment, moreover, eliminated the necessity for units to mark and keep track of all their own particular items. But even this assumes a great deal for the accuracy of records in overseas theaters when often equipment could not be found by item even when it was known to have arrived. Moreover, Army Ground Forces applied constant pressure to retain as much equipment as possible for troop training in the United States.

Special loading or handling of organizational equipment was necessary when units were designated for early entry into combat. Commanders nearly always preferred unit loading, that is, loading a unit's equipment in the same ships with its men. This had the obvious advantage of assuring the arrival of the unit and its equipment at the same time and at the same port, but it usually made inefficient use of space, and frequently was not practical at all, for cargo space and troop space was not likely to be in balance. The great British liners, the *Queen Mary* and the *Queen Elizabeth,* could each carry up to 15,000 troops, but only 500 tons of cargo. In convoy loading the men and their unit's equipment went in different ships, but in the same convoy. This made more efficient use of space, but had only limited application, for convoys seldom were used in the Pacific, and in the Atlantic the slower cargo ships usually sailed in separate convoys from troop transports. The fast ships, such as the *Queens,* did not even travel in convoy.

Combat loading was a special kind of unit loading used for landings on hostile shores whereby troops and equipment were loaded so that debarkation would take place in the order needed as the unit went into battle. Combat loading was necessary for all of the scores of amphibious operations undertaken during the war. Usually such operations were mounted from forward bases, but Maj. Gen. George S. Patton, Jr.'s, Western Task Force was combat-loaded at Hampton Roads in October 1942 for the invasion of North Africa. Considerable confusion accompanied that effort, but the combat loading of the task force under Maj. Gen. Troy H. Middleton for the invasion of Sicily at Hampton Roads in June 1943 went much more smoothly. Other forces for the attacks against Attu, Kiska, and Adak in the Aleutians combat-loaded at west coast ports in April and July 1943.

Plans for the reinforcement of troops in Europe after the Normandy landings in the spring of 1944 called for all units arriving from the United States after D plus 90 to be landed directly on the Continent, and to be ready to fight within fifteen days after landing. To meet the requirement all available fast cargo ships had to be assigned for convoy loading with the units. The Transportation Corps organized the Northeast Equipment Staging Area at the Elmira Holding and Reconsignment Point, Elmira, New York, to serve both the New York and Boston Ports of Embarkation by receiving all organizational equipment that could not reach home stations by stated deadlines, and then forwarding it to the ports in time to be loaded for the unit's convoy. At times, as in September 1944, troop movements were too heavy for equipment to keep pace and some had to go in later convoys, but on the whole it worked out well. In particular, the equipment staging area provided that measure of flexibility necessary for response to frequent changes in sailing dates. Assembling a mixed convoy, loading equipment, embarking troops, arranging for naval escort, and moving to arrive at the desired port at the proper time was one of the most complex logistical tasks of the war. The confusion, the delays, the mistakes were remarkably small in relation to the total accomplishment. (*Map 17*)

Early in 1944 the War Department devised a new system of exchanging organizational equipment in order to save shipping in the Pacific. The 38th Division, for instance, when it moved from California to Hawaii to replace the 6th which was moving from Hawaii to the Southwest Pacific, left its equipment on the ships for the 6th which moved in the same vessels, and the 38th took over the equipment the 6th left in Hawaii.

For the early supply replenishment of troops in combat a system of block loading was adopted in the Pacific in late 1943. Under this procedure blocks of supplies expected to be needed early in an invasion were loaded in such a way that they could be discharged at different times and places as needed. The supplies could be called for simply by block number. A similar system, referred to as prestowage was used to support the Normandy invasion, and later became common in the Pacific. After the Normandy landings, a large number of ships were commodity-loaded for support of the operations there. This meant that an entire ship was loaded with a single type or class of

supplies so that they could be found and unloaded quickly as needed. In all these cases ships were used for storage, contrary to longstanding transportation doctrine that neither railway cars nor ships should be put to such use; however, in the absence of facilities ashore, and because the uncertainties in the situations made flexibility a necessity, it probably was a more effective use of the ships than to have them bring up more supplies that could not be stored ashore so as to be readily accessible. This was a view which the Navy tacitly accepted, but the War Shipping Administration as well as the Army continued to insist it was a wasteful use of shipping that could be overcome by proper scheduling.

Ocean Shipping

The most important limitations on the oversea movement of troops and supplies undoubtedly were the capacities of ports and the local transportation facilities at destinations. There was a limit to how much could be landed at British ports within a given time. In western France there were no ports at all for several weeks after the Normandy landings, and over-the-beach landings were common on the Pacific islands. Sometimes port facilities in the United States were taxed to maintain the high level of outshipments called for. But these elements did not receive most attention from Allied planners for whom the matter of greatest concern was the same as that of World War I—ocean shipping. These matters were, of course, not unrelated. Long discharge time in ports with poor facilities, waiting for make-up of convoys, and the use of ships for storage in the absence of facilities near the battle areas, all added to the problem of finding enough ships.

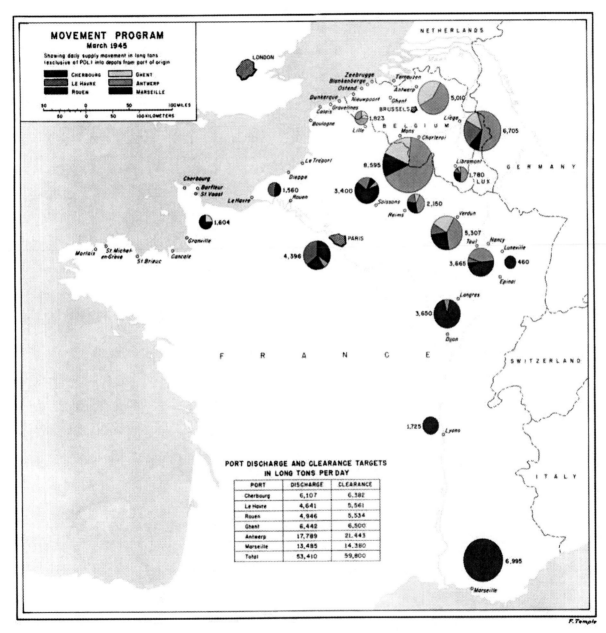

MOVEMENT PROGRAM
March 1945

Showing daily supply movement in long tons
(exclusive of POL) into depots from port of origin

CHERBOURG		GHENT	
LE HAVRE		ANTWERP	
ROUEN		MARSEILLE	

PORT DISCHARGE AND CLEARANCE TARGETS
IN LONG TONS PER DAY

PORT	DISCHARGE	CLEARANCE
Cherbourg	6,107	6,382
Le Havre	4,641	5,561
Rouen	4,946	5,534
Ghent	6,442	6,500
Antwerp	17,789	21,443
Marseille	13,485	14,380
Total	53,410	59,800

F. Temple

MAP 17

Enemy aviation, surface raiders, and especially submarines, continued to menace shipping throughout the war, although the threat was neutralized by about May 1943. In November 1942 losses of Allied and neutral shipping reached a peak of over 900,000 gross tons for the month, exceeding even the worst month of World War I, April 1917. For the whole war period, from September 1939 through August 1945 the total losses of nearly 24,000,000 gross tons were nearly double those of World War I, with about two-thirds of them the result of German submarine action. By the summer of 1942 losses had exceeded new construction by 10,000,000 gross tons; then new construction began to exceed losses, and, with the decisive victory over the submarine in the spring of 1943 and the upsurge in American shipbuilding, the cumulative deficit was eliminated by October. Nevertheless, the need to move in convoys and to take special precautions against submarines continued to add to the shipping requirements, particularly in the Atlantic.

It never was an easy matter to estimate the shipping that would be needed during a given period, nor to anticipate what would be available. The central problem was finding a desirable balance between personnel and equipment, and shipping. It can be said that there was a real crisis in shipping until the spring of 1943, and the British economy as well as Allied military operations were in jeopardy, but serious concern continued long after that because no one was willing to assume that sinkings would not continue at a high rate. Americans consistently tended to overestimate their shipping requirements, and the British exhibited an habitual anxiety about the adequacy of their stocks. When American and British planners came to the Washington Confer-

ence in May 1943 with figures showing a combined deficit of 2¼ to 3¼ million deadweight tons for the second half of that year, it appeared that Allied strategic plans might have to be modified if additional shipping could not be found. Within a few days this shortage had been reduced by about two million tons. Had there been a sudden increase in shipbuilding? A sudden reduction in losses? No. The planners had recalculated their figures, and thus had added more ships in a few hours than the shipyards could have turned out in weeks or months. By the time of the Quebec Conference in August 1943, the United States, for the first time, could show a surplus in shipping, and the Combined Chiefs could conclude with satisfaction that all essential commitments could be met. Yet, in November gloom returned with the prospect of further shortages, though there had been no change in strategic plans, no increase in losses at sea, and new construction was running ahead of schedule. Again at Cairo the Combined Staff Planners took another look at their figures and, after considerable debate, were able to turn a deficit into a surplus.

In the mass production of ships the United States took up where it had left off in World War I. It took 244 days to build the first Liberty ship, a slow freighter adapted from a British design; steady improvements in the use of prefabricated parts and assembly line methods reduced the average construction time to 39.2 days in December 1943. Half of the merchant ships produced in the United States during the war were Libertys. The faster Victory ship appeared in 1944, but was not produced in such large quantities. Many of both types were converted to troop transports and other uses. The shipbuilding program, carried out under the Maritime Commission, included the construction of 5,570 vessels, with a total of over 55 million dead-weight tons, during the period 1941–45. The Army, entering the war with six ships in its Transport Service, was the principal user of this tonnage throughout the war.

As in World War I, shipping was pooled, and came under centralized control. Attempts to accomplish this by allocating shipping by agreement of the Army, the Navy, and Maritime Commission through their representatives on a Strategic Shipping Board were not satisfactory, and the responsibility was assigned to the War Shipping Administration established by the President in February 1942. The Army had some misgivings over entrusting such a significant aspect of its logistics to an outside agency, but the arrangement worked out fairly well. The Army retained control over its own vessels, though the Shipping Administration had to be kept informed about Army movements, and might assign return cargoes. Actually, of a total of 1,706 vessels in Army service in July 1945, only 186 were operated by the Army. It was up to the War Shipping Administration to make allocations among the various claimants—lend-lease, civilian needs, foreign control, and Army and Navy. At the height of operations, military representatives met daily with officials of the War Shipping Administration to work out fluctuations in needs and resources. The War Shipping Administration was the control agency for the pool of British and American ships assigned to it, while a second Allied pool operated from London under British control. The Combined Chiefs of Staff and the Joint Chiefs of Staff, usually working through the Combined Military Transportation Committee

and the Joint Military Transportation Committee, further allocated the vessels made available for military use.

Before the war the Army and the Navy had agreed that in case of hostilities the World War I procedure in which the Navy manned and operated the Army's ships should be revived, and when war came, the Navy did provide crews for the Army's transports for a time. Attempts, largely on the initiative of the Army, to form a unified Army and Navy ocean transportation service were unsuccessful. In the end, the War Shipping Administration operated most of the ships with civilian crews.

The whole transportation program was one requiring international as well as interagency co-operation. It was to be expected that in both areas petty concern for prestige or personal advantage and an eye to the implications for postwar position would interfere with the task at hand, but somehow the larger issues usually took precedence and missions were accomplished in a way previously thought impossible.

Air Transportation

Air transportation had just begun to come into its own and the special problems it presented had no solutions in previous experience. In terms of total tonnage carried, air transportation seems almost insignificant, but the speed with which small groups of men and small quantities of high-priority cargo could be carried great distances, often to places otherwise virtually inaccessible, added a new dimension to warfare with tremendous implications for the future. In fact, probably more significant than the actual tonnage carried during World War II was the accumulation of experience for the future.

PREPARING FOR A FLIGHT OVER THE HUMP. *A C–46 cargo plane takes on supplies while it is being serviced, Assam, India.*

Organized in June 1942 from the Air Corps Ferrying Command which had been established a year earlier to fly lend-lease aircraft to the Allies, the Air Transport Command of the Army Air Forces became the headquarters for a world-wide air transportation system whose main mission was to fly passengers and supplies to the oversea theaters. (Air transportation within the theaters was the responsibility of troop carrier units assigned to them.) Relying mostly on twin-engine C–47 (DC–3) and four-engine C–54 (DC–4) aircraft, the Air Transport Command flew regular routes across the South Atlantic to Dakar and other points in Africa; across the Middle Atlantic

by way of Labrador, Newfoundland, Greenland, and Iceland; and over a northwest route to Alaska, and via Hawaii to the Southwest Pacific. A long line, carrying supplies brought in by ship and air, extended across Africa to Karachi and Calcutta, picked up the route from Bengal to Assam, then crossed the Hump to Kumming in China. The long and often seemingly futile effort to fly supplies into China received more public attention than any other Air Transport Command operation. Air delivery of gasoline, munitions, and other supplies to China reached a peak of 71,000 tons during the month of July 1945. The total for the war was 650,000 tons. Two convoys of thirty-five Liberty ships each could have carried that amount. To what extent the strategic results justified the logistical effort remains open to question, but it is a clear demonstration of what could be done in an emergency situation.

Evacuation and Hospitalization

A major task of returning aircraft as well as troopships was the evacuation of sick and wounded men from oversea theaters to the United States, for hospital ships were not available for that purpose. During the period from January 1942 through August 1945 more than 518,000 patients debarked at Army ports, and another 121,400 arrived by air. Admissions to Army hospitals during that time totaled approximately 5,100,000 in the oversea theaters, and about 8,900,000 in the United States. The highest number on the hospital registers at any one time was 266,500 in the theaters of operations at the end of January 1945, and over 318,000 in the United States at the end of June 1945. In May 1945 over 57,000 patients were evacuated from the theaters to the United States.

The chief surgeon of a theater prepared the general plan for evacuation and hospitalization of the sick and wounded in accordance with the theater commander's policies; the major subordinate commands carried it out. The evacuation and hospitalization system was based on the principle that it was the responsibility of rearward units to relieve forward units of their casualties in accordance with the evacuation policy. This policy, established by the War Department after consultation with the theater commanders, laid down the maximum number of days that patients should be held in the theater for treatment; a patient whose

illness or wound required treatment for a longer period than that number of days would be evacuated to the United States. Because of the lack of hospital facilities a 90-day policy was approved for the Southwest Pacific, South Pacific, and North Africa; in August 1943 a 180-day policy was established for Europe and the CBI, while all other theaters were ordered to go to a 120-day policy as soon as possible.

Evacuation within a combat zone was by litter, by jeeps, and by ambulances. Air evacuation within a combat zone might be made by liaison planes or light transport aircraft. Surface evacuation from the combat zone, whether by motor vehicle, by ship, or by rail, was solely the responsibility of the communications zone commander; air evacuation within the theater was the responsibility of the theater commander, requiring the co-operation of air force and communications zone commanders and of the army surgeon. Air evacuation to the United States was the responsibility of the Air Transport Command, but the communications zone had to arrange for the patients' arrival at the airfields and for their care until they boarded the planes.

The type of hospitals ordinarily assigned to the armies included evacuation, convalescent, and portable surgical hospitals. Those assigned to the communications zone included field, convalescent, station, and general hospitals. Evacuation hospitals constituted "the neck of the funnel" through which all casualties (less those evacuated by airplane) had to pass in their transit from the combat zone to hospitals in the communications zone. Evacuation hospitals were located when possible twelve to thirty or more miles from the battle front, on good roads and near airfields, railroads, or waterways. Portable surgical hospitals, 25-bed

The 2d Evacuation Hospital in France

units first developed in the Southwest Pacific in 1942, were mobile units used to reinforce division clearing stations by providing surgical treatment for patients in too serious condition for further immediate movement to the rear. Convalescents and other patients showing prospect of early return to combat effectiveness remained at convalescent hospitals in the army area.

Field hospitals were mobile hospitals capable of giving station hospital type of service in the field where there was a temporary concentration of troops, or while a fixed hospital was being constructed. Station hospitals were fixed units which served only a limited assigned area where there was a large enough concentration of

service troops to require local hospitalization; they usually did not receive patients from the combat zone. General hospitals were fixed units of 1,000, 1,500, or 2,000-bed capacity, equipped to give complete treatment for all cases in the theater. Most of their patients could be expected to come from the combat zone.

Summary

In spite of glaring examples of overages and shortages in some theaters, and problems of distribution and transportation that never entirely disappeared, theaters for the most part received the supplies and equipment

they needed at the times and places necessary for their operations. No operation,
once definitely scheduled by the Combined
Chiefs or the Joint Chiefs of Staff, ever was
held up because of failure of the supply
system. The system depended upon the
accumulation of generous reserve and
back-up supplies all the way along the supply
lines so that difficulties or failures at one
point would not hold up deliveries to the
battle areas when needed. Build-up of
large oversea reserves was made necessary
by the threat of enemy aviation and submarines, and made possible by the absence
after early 1943 of appreciable enemy submarine and air action. It never was possible to anticipate requirements accurately,
but by planning for the widest possible range
of contingencies plus a good deal of imaginative improvisation, the Army distribution
system, matching its procurement effort,
achieved unparalleled results. At the same
time, world-wide evacuation of casualties
for the best possible medical care provided
that one extra link of essential encouragement for undertakings so great.

CHAPTER XXX

Battle Support

Logistical considerations and limitations were as prominent in the strategy of campaigns and the tactics of battle as in the higher strategy of global war. The ultimate aim of all logistics is to get the proper combat elements to the right place at the right time, properly equipped to fight, and with the means at hand to maintain them in the accomplishment of their missions.

In far-reaching reorganization of tactical units during the period 1940–42 the big square division that had persisted since World War I, an organization based on four infantry regiments organized under two brigades, gave way to a triangular division based on three regiments having no brigade structure. The new streamlined infantry division, intended to be more suitable for open warfare, had a total strength of approximately 15,500 officers and men. All horse transportation was eliminated in contrast to the German division which still relied on mixed horse and motor transport, and service elements were minimized on the assumption that the division ordinarily would operate as a part of a corps and army to which additional supporting units would be attached. These changes had been urged by General Pershing as early as 1920, had been tentatively approved by the War Department in 1935, and field tested in 1937 and 1939. But it was not until after the fall of France in 1940 that the new table of organization and equipment was adopted. It was applied to divisions of the Regular

Army almost immediately; National Guard divisions were not reorganized until after Pearl Harbor. Newly mobilized divisions followed the triangular organization from the start. The airborne division was organized as a miniature infantry division around two glider regiments and one parachute regiment. Other special variants of the infantry division, in vogue only to a limited extent or for a short while, were the mountain division, the jungle division, and the light division. Armored divisions were also provided for. Their organization, as finally worked out in 1943, permitted a greater degree of flexibility by abandoning the regimental organization altogether, and providing for two combat commands and a reserve command to which might be attached varying numbers of the division's three tank battalions, three armored infantry battalions, and three armored artillery battalions. (Two of the armored divisions continued to operate with the old regimental organization.) One cavalry division remained, but it fought dismounted as an infantry division throughout the war.

In general the triangular pattern appeared throughout the tactical organization. At each level in the infantry structure three units, plus supporting elements, comprised the next higher organization. Thus three rifle squads went into the rifle platoon. Three rifle platoons, plus a weapons platoon and plus a headquarters including a supply sergeant, mess sergeant, and cooks made up the rifle company. Three rifle companies, together with a heavy weapons company (81-mm. mortars and .30-caliber machine guns) and a headquarters company including an ammunition and pioneer platoon, an antitank platoon, and a communications section made up the infantry battalion. Three battalions together with a cannon company, antitank company, and headquarters elements comprised the infantry regiment. Three regiments, together with division artillery consisting of a headquarters and three light (105-mm. howitzer) and one medium (155-mm. howitzer) battalions, and a reconnaissance troop (armored cavalry), military police platoon, ordnance company, quartermaster company, signal company, medical battalion, engineer battalion, and headquarters and band comprised the infantry division. Ordinarily in Europe a medium tank battalion and tank destroyer battalion were attached to the infantry division. Battalions of the Armored Force, separate units as well as those organic to armored divisions, were organized as self-contained units, each with its own service company to bring up supplies.

North Africa and the Mediterranean

The invasion of North Africa in November 1942 was a graduate school in logistics when too many officers had not yet completed even elementary school in that subject, but on the whole the officers learned their lessons well. The short time—little more than three months—between the decision and the execution would have made logistical preparations difficult under the most favorable conditions. Not only the first ground offensive undertaken by Americans against the European Axis, it was also the greatest overseas expeditionary assault

ever undertaken up to that time. Moreover, it was launched, not from a nearby base, but by forces mounted simultaneously in the United States and the United Kingdom, thousands of miles from each other and from the landing sites. Further, the fact that this was the first major combined British-American operation added to the problems of coordination. The greatest enemy of orderly procedure was change. Changes in tactical plans, changes in shipping plans, shortages of supplies, a determination to provide American troops with the latest equipment for their first engagement against the Germans, differing desires of troop commanders, and planning on both sides of the Atlantic which was not always in phase led to almost innumerable changes in logistical requirements and timing. After strenuous efforts had been made to bring units up to authorized equipment levels, it was decided to cut their allowance by 50 percent. Planners in Washington preparing for the Western Task Force that was to sail from Hampton Roads, Virginia, had to adjust to no less than fifty-seven changes during a seventeen-day period in September.

A situation as shocking to the War Department as it was embarrassing to the Services of Supply in the European theater developed when it became necessary to reorder large quantities of Class II and IV supplies that were known to be already in the United Kingdom, but which, because of faulty marking and lack of proper records, could not be found in time to equip the forces preparing to sail from Britain. It hardly helped matters when requisitions arrived without proper identification, and when timely status of supply reports were lacking. In addition to shipments from the United States, shortages in Great Britain were made up by borrowing from the British and by emergency local procurement, including emergency production in British factories. Again, it was not always clear how real the shortages were, for the addition of all kinds of matériel for the comfort and convenience of the soldier and ambitions for stocking large reserves added considerably to what really were immediately essential supplies.

Availability of combat loaders (vessels especially rigged and designed to carry assault forces and cargo to the vicinity of the projected landing together with the landing craft and lighters necessary to put the forces ashore) limited the size of the assault forces to some extent, but the main limitation both on the size of the assault and on its later support was the size of convoys that naval leaders considered within the limits of reasonable safety for escort.

All the preceding delays and changes made of the loading a chaotic scramble characterized more by haste and improvisation than by well-developed plans and procedures. Things continued to go wrong right up to the time of departure, but somehow most of the ships got away on time. With great good fortune, all three task forces, the Western, sailing from the United States to the Casablanca area, the Central, a U.S. force sailing from the United Kingdom to Oran, and the Eastern, a primarily British force with a few American troops, sailing to Algiers, made their landings on schedule, and within forty-eight hours seized their objectives. A parachute battalion made the 1,500-mile trip from England in C–47 transports in twelve hours, marking the first American airborne operation of the war. All together, the invasion task forces comprised about 107,000 men.

The approved supply plan for support of forces in North Africa put into effect the new procedures for centralizing responsibilities at a port of embarkation—in this instance, New York. The plan was not announced until nearly a month after the landings and it would take some time for the new procedures involved to become routine. It set a ninety days' level for reserve supplies in North Africa, and thirty days of Class I and II in the United Kingdom, though it recognized that such reserves would have to be built up slowly. Actually, by early 1943 a number of shortages had turned into excesses. In April 1943 automatic supply was suspended in favor of supply based on requisitions and status of supply reports. To get supplies up to the fighting fronts, it was necessary to haul them overland by rail and by truck, some 1,400 miles from Casablanca, or about half that distance from Oran. The British operated the port of Algiers. Later in the campaign the use of several British-controlled ports east of Algiers eased considerably the burden on land transportation. (*Map 18*)

The North Africa operation impressed upon everyone a fact they already knew but did not always feel inclined to recognize: the necessity for close co-ordination between tactical and logistical planning. It was, moreover, a pioneering effort and suffered from all the shortcomings inherent in being the first-of-a-kind. The invasion of North Africa served as a proving ground for developing data for supply replenishment, for service troops, for troop replacements, for casualty estimates, and for amphibious assault planning and support. All would be put to use in coming operations in Sicily, Italy, and France.

The invasion of Sicily (July 1943) had the benefit of better planning and preparation as well as the advantage of being staged mostly from the relatively near North African shore. For the first time a naval

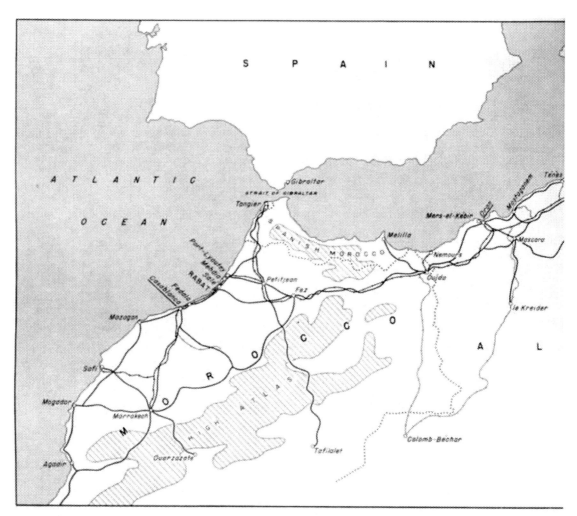

MAP 18

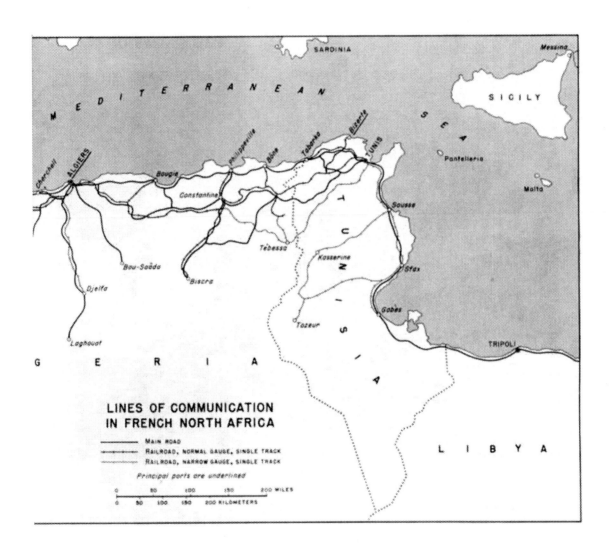

LINES OF COMMUNICATION
IN FRENCH NORTH AFRICA

———————— Main road
⊢—⊢—⊢—⊢ Railroad, normal gauge, single track
——————— Railroad, narrow gauge, single track

Principal ports are underlined

0	50	100	150	200 MILES
0	50	100	150	200 KILOMETERS

DUKW MOUNTING A 105-MM. HOWITZER *on a beach during maneuvers in Italy.*

beach battalion co-ordinated the landing of supplies, and an engineer amphibian brigade organized the beaches. The Dukw, the versatile 2½-ton amphibian truck, made its combat support debut, and promptly proved itself completely indispensable to over-the-beach operations. The engineer amphibian brigade, having demonstrated its value in unloading supplies on the beaches, was pushed beyond its capabilities when called upon to forward them to the front. Without a base section of the Services of Supply to support it, Seventh Army had to organize its own rear, and it pressed the engineer brigade into operating depots. Failure here was the greatest threat to the

rapid movement of the Seventh Army around Sicily. As one observer pointed out, the faster an army moved and the harder it struck, the bigger must be its administrative tail.

Landings at Salerno (September 1943) and Anzio (January 1944) provided more experience in pointing to the feasibility of extended over-the-beach supply and of how the capacity of a minor port might be stepped up to support major operations.

On the Italian mainland it was possible to develop a fairly complete communications zone organization and to get railways and highways into operation for large-scale support, but in the slow slugging match up the peninsula against determined German opposition the most memorable aspects of that campaign probably could be summed up in "mud, mountains, and mules." The Seventh Army had already discovered the usefulness of pack animals while crossing the rough terrain of Sicily, where some 4,000 mules, horses, and donkeys had been used to bring up ammunition, signal equipment, rations, and water. For the advance north of Naples the Fifth Army organized Italian pack train companies, and Peninsular Base Section sought mules wherever they could be found in the theater. By December 1943 Fifth Army was using over 2,250 pack animals, and the number was growing as rapidly as additional animals could be found. The use of animals added secondary logistical problems. Forage became so short that it was necessary to establish a Joint Purchasing Forage Board. The arrival of the 10th Mountain Division late in 1944 with mules from the United States added further complications by necessitating the shipment of grain and hay from the United States. Nine mule ships were withdrawn from the Burma-India run to bring in the 7,000 mules the mountain division required, but hostilities ended before the project was finished.

The European Theater of Operations

Normandy

Logistics was a constant and overriding factor in the conception, planning, and execution of the Normandy invasion in June 1944. It will be recalled that the question of logistics was greatly responsible for the preference of American military chiefs for a cross-Channel attack for the main effort as opposed to a Mediterranean or other approach on the Continent. In development of the plans for the great invasion, logistics dominated the definition of objectives, the choice of landing sites, the size of the assault force, and plans for building up the initial forces and pushing inland. Availability of shipping, including landing craft, coasters, troop transports, cargo ships, tankers, and lighters, and capacity for discharge on the Continent were the most common items for planning and worrying sessions in the crowded weeks of preparation preceding D–day.

The supply plan for the support of the invasion forces provided for the prestowage of supplies (90,000 tons for First Army alone) in coasters, landing craft, and motor transport ships (adapted Liberty's) sufficient for the first eight days. Then, after a thirteen-day transition period during which prestowage would end, more use would be made of commodity-loaded Liberty ships until after D plus 41 when the major burden would be on deep-draft ships from the United States, supplemented by a smaller number of coasters from the United Kingdom. Arrangements for special delivery of small quantities of urgently needed items by reserved shipping and by air, and for the substitution of ammunition and certain other items for scheduled Class IV items when requested for any particular day lent some flexibility to an otherwise rigid plan. As the time drew near, the G–4 at Supreme Allied Headquarters surmised that the operation could be supported if everything went according to plan, for there was no margin of safety. In a way, perhaps military supply is like private income in that a requirement develops for everything known to be available.

In preparing and maintaining the mar-

MULES OF THE 601ST FIELD ARTILLERY BATTALION (MOUNTAIN) ON AN LST

shaling areas for the U.S. troops, Southern Base Section of the Communications Zone used 54,000 men. It trained 4,500 new cooks in three months to prepare the necessary meals, and it operated 3,800 trucks to haul men and supplies.

After a twenty-four hour postponement because of bad weather—some convoys already under way had to turn back—the largest fleet ever assembled, comprising some 5,000 vessels (some estimates, counting "everything that would float" put the number as high as 7,000), carried British, Canadian, and American divisions to five designated beaches on the Normandy coast. Nearly 2,400 troop carrier aircraft and over 860 gliders carried one British and two U.S. airborne divisions to drop zones behind the beaches four to five hours before H-hour. The American forces alone numbered 130,000 men in the assault, initial follow-up, and preloaded build-up waves. In the next ninety days that force would grow to 1,330,000 men.

Orderly plans for organization of the beaches melted away under a heavy surf and, especially at the eastern American beach, designated OMAHA, fierce enemy

PACK MULES IN MOUNTAINS OF ITALY

lifted previous objections, and permitted the beaching of landing ships during low tide, when their cargoes could be discharged directly on the beaches without the need for boats, floating piers, or ponton causeways. Even coasters were beached and discharged in this way after 20 June. Artificial harbors, the components for which had been laboriously towed across the channel, gave some promise of value, but the one in the American sector, known as MULBERRY A, just after it went into operation at OMAHA beach, was swamped in the severe storm which struck on 19 June. The breakwater still protected the Dukws and small craft there, but how valuable the harbor as such might have been remains open to question. The surprise came in the quantity of goods that could be landed over the beaches, and this type of unloading continued as a major activity far beyond the time originally planned. Some of the greatest handicaps arose in keeping track of what cargoes were being carried by what vessels, and in trying to hold to a system of unloading according to priority. When the Navy insisted on unloading everything regardless of priority, the rate of discharge became much greater; after this "system" had transferred the confusion from the sea to the shore sufficiently, a degree of priority discharge had to be reinstituted. In the confusion of precarious moments, chaos seemed to rule supreme, and all of the plans of this best-planned operation seemed to be going awry. But in broad outline the plans held up well.

The Race Across France

After initial successes, the attacks in Normandy quickly fell behind schedule. Allied planners had hoped for the fall of Cherbourg by D plus 8; it did not come

resistance. Soldiers burdened with at least sixty-eight pounds of equipment provided to meet any contingency except carrying it ashore under fire found themselves hardly able to move for hours. Gradually overcoming the difficulties resulting from wreckage along the shore and poorly co-ordinated ship-to-shore operations, engineer special brigades soon were able to begin building up supplies on the beaches. Six steel barges beached near the end of D-day served as ready-made ammunition distributing points. Amphibian trucks and small craft busily brought in additional supplies, but the greatest impetus came when the Navy

SUPPLIES COMING ASHORE ON A NORMANDY BEACHHEAD, D-DAY

until D plus 21 (27 June). The V Corps was to have taken St. Lô by D plus 9, but it was not occupied until D plus 48 (18 July). Then, after the breakout in late July, the armies not only made up for lost time, but plunged far ahead of all schedules. The plan had assumed a halt at the Seine of about a month which would permit a more or less orderly build-up before the next phase. The advancing columns reached the Seine only eleven days ahead of schedule, but in the preceding thirty days they had covered a distance expected to take seventy. By D plus 90 when it was planned that they should close to the Seine, spearheads of the Third Army were 200 miles

beyond. Such an eruption was bound to throw logistical machinery out of gear. What had been the battle of unloading at the beaches now was eclipsed by the battle of transportation to keep pace with the racing armies.

French railroads and rolling stock had been so badly damaged by bombing that they could bear only a fraction of the necessary burden. Chief reliance then had to be on motor trucks. This resulted in the establishment in late August of the Red Ball Express, operating on a one-way return loop highway system in which the roads were reserved for its traffic. By 29 August it reached a peak strength of 132 truck com-

GASOLINE TANK TRUCKS OF THE RED BALL EXPRESS

panies, with 5,958 vehicles, and on that day hauled a record of 12,342 tons of supplies. Within the next two weeks the route was extended until it reached all the way from St. Lô to Versailles, where it forked, the northern branch going on to Soissons for support of the First Army, and the southern branch to Sommesous for support of the Third. Whatever trucks could be spared were pressed into service for this mission. Most of them were 2½-ton cargo carriers. A remarkable record of achievement in delivering supplies might have been even more remarkable if advance planning at all levels had anticipated the need for such a great dependence on motor transportation

to supply two armies engaged in rapid pursuit. Heavy duty, 10-ton semitrailer and truck-tractor combinations sufficient to permit a shuttle system might have made all the difference, but pleas of the theater transportation officer had been ignored, and, anyway, such a procurement requirement had not been anticipated in the War Department sufficiently far in advance to make it realizable. In weighing demands for trucks against other demands no less urgently pressed, planners apparently had assumed greater usefulness for French railroads than previous Allied bombing strikes would justify. Curiously enough, most of the heavy trucks sent to Europe at this time had been produced as a result of strategic-logistic plans drawn in headquarters of Army Service Forces on the assumption that they would be needed in the CBI when the Burma Road should be reopened.

Other defects in the Red Ball Express sapped some of its effectiveness. There were not enough military police for policing the route and controlling traffic. Division of control with section commanders through whose areas the routes passed led to abuses and lack of co-ordination. Almost continuous use of vehicles for long hours in an effort to meet emergency goals made it virtually impossible for the inadequate repair facilities available to keep the trucks rolling. Exhausted drivers, many of them without training, frequently became careless about preventive maintenance. Fatigue drove some of the drivers to malingering and even sabotage, and some took advantage of loose supervision and yielded to the temptation to sell their cargoes on the lucrative French black market. The great accomplishment of hauling 412,193 tons of supplies in eighty-one days of operation in spite of all the deficiencies made the more bitter the realization of what might have been done.

With the benefit of the Red Ball experience, other motor express routes operated in other areas at various times.

It had been expected that airlift would provide a valuable supplementary means of delivering supplies to meet emergency demands, but air delivery never did meet its full potential during the time when it was most needed to support the pursuit across France. Requests both for scheduled and emergency supply by air were submitted to the Combined Air Transport Operations Room, organized originally under Supreme Headquarters, and later under the control of the First Allied Airborne Army after the

formation of that headquarters. But the determination of priorities remained with a Priorities Board at Supreme Headquarters, and usually took the form of a compromise among various claimants, including 21 Army Group (British), the U.S. 12th Army Group, civil relief of Paris, and demands of the Allied Airborne Army for withholding troop carriers to prepare for planned airborne operations.

Poor planning and co-ordination often reduced the full use even of the aviation resources that were available. Requests often were duplicated. Delays arose when supplies were found to be located in depots far from airfields, or a supply agency would arrange for supplies and aircraft but fail to arrange for trucks. Bad weather delayed planned missions. The First and Third Armies received as much as 1,200 tons of supplies by air in a day, but the average from mid-August to mid-September was less than 500 tons a day for the two armies. Troop carriers resupplied the airborne divisions by airdrop during the period before link-up with the beachhead, but that was a difficult and costly procedure. For reliable, large-scale supply operations it was necessary to have airfields for landing as near as possible to where the supplies were needed. The lack of these fields was a principal factor in limiting the whole effort. When a forward field could be developed quickly for supply operations, as the one at Orléans for supporting the Third Army, air combat units soon moved in and pre-empted it for the use of bombers and fighters. The other principal hindrance to maximum air delivery was the competing demand of the First Allied Airborne Army. In the summer of 1944 the ground armies were moving more swiftly than the airborne army could plan; a whole series of operations had to be canceled as the ground forces raced past the planned objectives before the airborne operation could be mounted. But the preparation for these operations meant that supplies had to be built up for their support, and transport planes of the Troop Carrier Command had to be diverted to be ready to carry both men and supplies.

Undoubtedly the most critical single item in the pursuit was gasoline. Petroleum products accounted for one-fourth of the tonnage moved to the Continent all together, but in this situation its lack or availability determined whether the advance would continue or halt. With the bulk discharge of tankers by ship-to-shore pipelines beginning by 3 July, fuel supply in Normandy had been adequate. But bad weather and other difficulties delayed completion of a planned system of underwater pipelines across the Channel until late August. More significantly, laying the pipeline system for bulk delivery of fuel toward the front could not keep pace with the rapid advances. In late September three lines were in operation, but the most advanced of them still was twenty miles short of the Seine. Railway tank cars and tank trucks made up most of the difference, but deliveries to the using units were in 5-gallon cans, hauled by truck and sometimes by air, and at times the shortage of gasoline at the front resulted from a shortage of cans rather than a shortage of the fuel itself.

By September the supply lines were about played out. Each additional mile of advance multiplied the difficulties of bringing up supplies to sustain it. With all transportation already overtaxed, something had to give. In the midst of rapid advances at the end of August and the beginning of September, some units of the Third Army had to content themselves with ten or twelve days

in bivouac at basic training and care and cleaning of equipment, for there was not enough gasoline to move ahead. Perhaps the time could have been better used in walking to the Moselle where the enemy, glad for the respite, had a chance to prepare a defense line. General Patton was pleading for a chance to rush on through the heart of Germany with his Third Army: Lt. Gen. Omar N. Bradley favored a major thrust by the 12th Army Group. Most emphatically of all, Field Marshal Montgomery had been urging "one powerful full-blooded thrust across the Rhine and into the heart of Germany, backed by the whole of the resources of the Allied Armies."[1] But Eisenhower felt that "any pencillike thrust into the heart of Germany such as [Montgomery] proposed would meet nothing but certain destruction," and he "would not consider it."[2] Instead, the Supreme Commander decided in favor of a "broad front" strategy by which all the Allied armies would close to the Rhine, build up their supplies, and then make multiple crossings of the river. This would allow a chance for the supply lines to catch up. It also would give the enemy a chance to make some preparations of his own.

The rationale against the single thrust generally has been on the basis of the logistical limitations. But it was precisely the logistical limitations that led Montgomery and the others to want to concentrate all available resources behind a single, decisive blow rather than attempt to spread them thinly across the whole broad front. Actually, Eisenhower did authorize a main

---

[1] Field Marshal the Viscount Montgomery of Alamein, *Normandy to the Baltic* (Boston: Houghton Mifflin Company, 1948), p 193.

[2] Dwight D. Eisenhower, *Crusade in Europe* (New York: Doubleday & Company, Inc., 1948), p 306.

effort in the north for the attempt to secure a crossing of the lower Rhine at Arnhem, but this was to be a limited offensive. Just enough supplies were diverted from the Third Army and part of the First Army to immobilize them, but not enough to 21 Army Group to make its action decisive.

Another logistical consideration led to Eisenhower's decision to make a main, if limited, effort in the north: to clear the access to the port of Antwerp so that it could be used in building up supplies for the offensive across the Rhine.

Logisticians had been embarrassed by success. A breakthrough, the aim of all offensive operations, was the one contingency against which they were unable to prepare. Since 1942 they had been planning an emergency operation (SLEDGEHAMMER) for a hasty invasion of the Continent in case of an imminent German collapse; when that collapse appeared imminent, they could mount no such offensive. Requirements calculated for the weeks ahead were multiplied by the continuing arrival of more divisions, when those already in action could not be fully supported. Possibly those calculations were further inflated by unrealistic factors. Requirements were based upon an assumed daily need of about 650 tons of supplies for each division, but experience showed the average daily requirement of an armored division in pursuit and exploitation to be 328 tons, and for an infantry division 296 tons. It is interesting to speculate on what might have been the result if the Germans had offered stiff resistance at the Seine, and if a month's delay had been necessary there with daily requirements for the divisions attacking strongly defended positions nearly twice the tonnage (mostly ammunition) needed in pursuit; or if they had forced the Americans into a defensive

situation with (for infantry divisions) an even greater tonnage requirement.

Meanwhile the landing in southern France on 15 August brought another U.S. Army and co-operating French forces into the battle. In less than a month they advanced over 300 miles to link up with the Third Army. The limitation on the size and the timing of that operation was logistical—mainly the availability of landing craft. That it could be done at all, and in the south of France rather than somewhere else, was because of the logistical fact that troops and resources already were in the Mediterranean. The principal reason for the landing also was by then logistical, to secure another major port (Marseille was taken on 28 August) and open a second line of communication to support the campaigns in Europe. Gaining Marseille also promised to make up for some of the loss resulting from the unexpectedly slow clearance of Channel and North Sea ports.

Communications Zone

Though it had to cover a vastly greater area and operate on a much larger scale, the organization of the Communications Zone followed in a general way the one the Services of Supply had developed during World War I and the pattern which ultimately had emerged in North Africa and the Mediterranean. Although in this case the theater staff also served as the Communications Zone staff, the vague definition of authority of those two organizations, such as had persisted between SOS and Pershing's GHQ, reappeared. Further, the existence of Supreme Headquarters, Allied Expeditionary Force (SHAEF) added a new complication, as the American section of that headquarters tended more and more to act as a theater staff, since General Eisenhower was theater commander as well as Allied commander. Ill-defined lines of authority and responsibility bred chronic problems of coordination throughout the war in Europe. Appointment of Lt. Gen. John C. H. Lee to be Deputy Theater Commander for Administration as well as Commanding General, Communications Zone, appeared for a time to give a certain integration to the structure; but this was deceptive, for field commanders resisted the arrangement and General Eisenhower finally rescinded it. The result was an anomalous situation in whch theater and Communications Zone staffs overlapped (where the chiefs of technical services had theaterwide responsibilities) but the Communications Zone commander had no theaterwide responsibility as such. It was a confusion between theater and Communications Zone organization—indeed, a confusion in conception—which would not end with World War II. (*Map 19*)

Again, as in World War I, jurisdictional conflict between area commands and functional commands and between "command" and "technical control" was a problem at various times. More serious for the effective operation of the logistical support system was the tendency (again as in World War I), to reassign officers found unfit for combat duty to positions of responsibility in this "rear area" where training and competence were hardly less in demand.

Communications Zone came in for special criticism when it moved its headquarters to Paris in September 1944. In the first place, Eisenhower thought that Paris should have been avoided altogether for this purpose, though he did concede finally that Paris was the logical center for logistical control on the Continent. Worse was the timing of the move, necessitating the diversion of precious motor and air transportation, and causing disruption of headquarters activity at the very time that supply shortages forced the armies to halt in their race across France. In mid-August a sizable forward echelon of Communications Zone headquarters moved from England to an area near Valognes where engineers had put up tented quarters for 11,000 persons and had built about 560,000 square feet of hutted office space. Only a few days later this whole group, together with other elements that had remained in England, moved to Paris. The operation took about two weeks. By mid-October Americans had taken over about 90 percent of the hotel space of the city. Communications Zone headquarters occupied 167 hotels, and the Seine Base Section another 129. Supreme Headquarters and other organizations were using about 25 more.

Developing its structure logically according to the progress of the armies, Communications Zone developed a territorial organization which ultimately comprised three base sections, two intermediate sections, and two advance sections. The Southern Line of Communications, based on Marseille following the invasion of southern France and the organization of the 6th Army Group, operated until February 1945 as a separate though subordinate headquarters under the command of Maj. Gen. Thomas B. Larkin, who also was named deputy commander of the Communications Zone.

Distribution

Port operations, assumed from the beginning to be the key to success, really began to achieve large proportions only as the pursuit ended, and the armies settled down for a

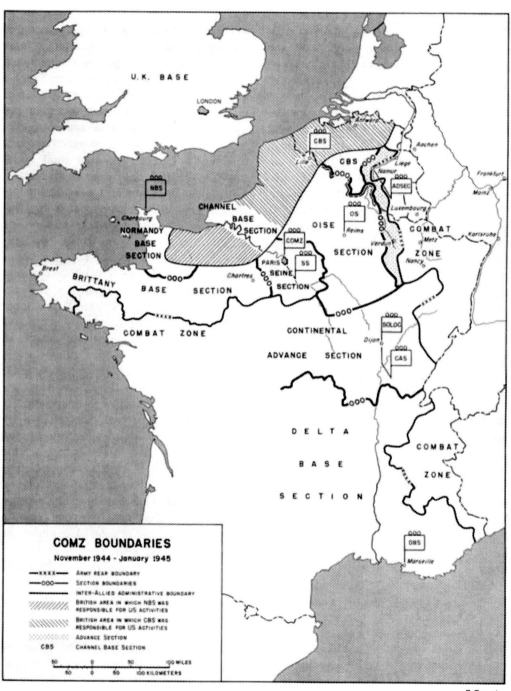

COMZ BOUNDARIES

November 1944 - January 1945

xxxx	ARMY REAR BOUNDARY
ooo	SECTION BOUNDARIES
	INTER-ALLIED ADMINISTRATIVE BOUNDARY
	BRITISH AREA IN WHICH NBS WAS RESPONSIBLE FOR US ACTIVITIES
	BRITISH AREA IN WHICH CBS WAS RESPONSIBLE FOR US ACTIVITIES
	ADVANCE SECTION
CBS	CHANNEL BASE SECTION

50   0   50   100 MILES

50   0   50   100 KILOMETERS

U.K. BASE

LONDON

CBS

CBS

ADSEC

Aachen

Frankfurt

Namur

Liege

Luxembourg

Mons

NBS

Cherbourg

CHANNEL

BASE

SECTION

OS

Reims

Verdun

Metz

Karlsruhe

COMBAT

ZONE

Nancy

NORMANDY

BASE

SECTION

OISE

SECTION

COMZ

PARIS

SS

SEINE

SECTION

Brest

BRITTANY

BASE

SECTION

Chartres

COMBAT   ZONE

CONTINENTAL

ADVANCE   SECTION

SOLOC

Dijon

CAS

DELTA

BASE

SECTION

COMBAT

ZONE

DBS

Marseille

F. Temple

MAP 19

long winter campaign. Cherbourg, a prime target for the Normandy invasion itself, was so badly damaged that it could not begin operations until 16 July, and then at a rate of only about 2,000 tons a day. But until late August it remained the most important port, and by then it was able to discharge 12,000 or more tons of cargo a day. The ports of Le Havre and Rouen handled rather less. When the southern French ports were opened, particularly Marseille, they were able to receive cargo more quickly than expected. Actually, Marseille discharged more American cargo than any other European port during the war. By reason of its facilities as well as its proximity to the front, the port of Antwerp, which was captured intact, became the most important of all the European ports after the enemy had been cleared from the Schelde estuary approaches to it. This port remained under British command, but its facilities were divided between the British and Americans with the expectation that it would be possible for the British to move 17,500 tons a day to their forward depots, while the Americans could move 22,500 tons to their depots, both exclusive of bulk gasoline and oil. In April 1945 Antwerp reached a peak monthly discharge rate of 628,217 long tons.

One of the most serious shortcomings of the distribution system in Europe was the lack of an adequate system of depots properly echeloned in depth. In this regard the logistic structure probably was inferior to that devised during World War I. Base depots were not sufficiently developed to keep the ports cleared and to permit selective forwarding of supplies. There was no adequate system of intermediate depots for storing the bulk of supplies to take the pres-

sure off the bases and to provide closer support to the front. There was no satisfactory system of inventory and supply control. As had happened in the United Kingdom before the invasion of North Africa, stocks at Antwerp were unloaded and stored so hastily that supply officers lost track of them, and when units ordered certain items known to be on hand, it was easier at times to place a new order in the United States than to search the Antwerp warehouses. The reason for all this was not so much a disregard for proper organization and control or lack of planning as it was the nature of fast-moving warfare which allowed no time for organization of the logistical tail. The stabilized warfare during the time when the World War I depots were set up was a far different situation from that of 1944 and 1945.

For normal resupply, most front-line infantry companies depended upon the arrival of jeeps and trailers each evening, enemy and terrain permitting, usually under cover of darkness when in contact, with rations, water, radio batteries, and dry socks. A resupply of ammunition was likely to go up at the same time, though the battalion ammunition and pioneer platoon maintained an ammunition distributing point where a detail could be sent to pick up ammunition when needed. Whenever possible most commanders liked to send up hot meals, in marmite cans, and platoons or squads would go back successively for their food. But more and more frequently units came to rely on a daily distribution of K rations or 10-in-1 rations which, being cold, could be eaten almost any time. Men would try to find some shelter where they could make a fire of the ration containers to heat water for instant coffee or chocolate. At times, when jeeps were unable to get close to the front-line positions, headquarters platoons and reserve companies would be pressed into service to hand-carry the supplies.

The Ardennes

The German Ardennes counteroffensive upset supply operations; some of the depots in Belgium were threatened, and even activities at Antwerp had to be suspended for a few days.

Called upon to give up its offensive in the Saar in order to shift its weight 50 to 75 miles to the north against the flank of the Bulge, the Third Army had two divisions in the counterattack within two days. Some 133,000 tanks and trucks rolled day and night over the icy roads. The switch of the bulk of Third Army forces, with supplies and equipment, to the new front within the week was one of the remarkable moves of the war.

Although the 101st Airborne Division moved overland when it was called up from reserve to help stem the German tide, the fact that it was an airborne division contributed substantially to its survival at Bastogne, for when it was surrounded it had to depend on emergency air supply. The 101st had had training and experience in working with the IX Troop Carrier Command on resupply by air. It had a rear base organization outside the encircled area which could help co-ordinate resupply missions. It had its own pathfinder teams, experienced in working with the division and with the troop carriers, which were able to drop in the vicinity of Bastogne and set up radar aids to assure the arrival of the supply planes. Its staff and its men were trained and experienced in recovering supplies dropped by parachute and landed by glider.

One of the serious consequences for U.S. forces of the Ardennes operation was the loss of equipment, including some 684 medium tanks, 2,600 trucks (2½-ton), 280 heavy guns, 4,000 machine guns, 10,000 rifles, 70,000 bayonets, 24,000 rocket launchers, 21,000 radio sets, and 11,000 telephones. Six complete hospitals were lost.

East of the Rhine

For the crossing of the Rhine the Allied build-up resembled that for the Channel crossing. But this time plans were deliberately laid for the support of a rapid and sustained advance across Germany. By February 1945 deliveries were being made by rail well forward into army service areas. For high priority freight a special train, known as the Toot Sweet Express, had begun operating in September 1944 to make daily deliveries all the way from Cherbourg and Paris to forward depots in the Advance Section; this service continued until after V–E Day. Another special delivery service, called the Meat Ball Express began in March to deliver perishables on alternate days from Namur to the First and Ninth Armies.

The greatest problem in maintaining railway transportation to support the armies beyond the Rhine was bridging the river. To meet it, engineers again rose to miracles of construction. On the basis of planning begun early in October 1944, they were able to arrange for the necessary naval craft, steel beams, and other materials. As soon as bridgeheads had been secured they went to work. The 1056th Port Construction and Repair Group completed the first railway bridge across the Rhine at Wesel in ten days. This was a structure of twenty-three spans over a total length of 1,753 feet; more-

TRAIN CROSSING THE RHINE ON THE WESEL BRIDGE

over, the site chosen made it necessary to build a second bridge over the Lippe tributary, a six-span structure of 463 feet. Starting a few days later (4 April 1945) Engineer Group B completed another railway bridge at Mainz in ten days—making use of an old bridge site, this involved 2,100 feet of new construction to make an over-all length of 3,445 feet. Farther south engineer units of the Seventh Army built two bridges under the direction of the 1st Military Railway Service, one at Mannheim and the other at Karlsruhe. A fifth railway bridge, built by units of Engineer Group B at Duisburg in the Ruhr area but completed too late for use before V–E Day, was a thirty-eight span, 2,815-foot structure completed in the record time of six and one-half days.

With completion of the bridges, the railroads quickly became the chief means for long-distance hauling across the Rhine. The main bridges, being single-track structures, became serious bottlenecks in the absence at first of effective traffic control, and the demands put upon them were beyond their capacities. The bridge at Wesel had a capacity estimated at 7,000 to 8,000 tons a day, but actually carried traffic averaging over 10,000 tons a day during the week before V–E Day. More serious was the perennial problem of getting freight cars unloaded and returned rapidly. Everywhere there was a tendency to hold supplies in railway cars as mobile reserves. In some cases, especially in Third Army, only cars carrying most urgent supplies were forwarded, while the others were sidetracked. By the end of April some 2,000 loaded cars still were at former army railheads west of the Rhine, and 12,-000 more cars had been sent east of the Rhine than had been returned. Pressure for rolling stock continued to mount as supply lines lengthened and civilian demands increased. The 250,000 cars and the 11,500 locomotives in use at the end of April would have been far from adequate had military operations continued much longer.

If there had been doubts and lack of planning and improvisation in the use of highway transportation in the drive across France in the summer of 1944, the situation was far different in the drive across Germany in the spring of 1945. Thoroughgoing planning for an elaborate system of motor transportation—later referred to as the XYZ Operation—began early in February, and steps had been taken to obtain the necessary vehicles. Chief reliance for long-distance hauling, in contrast to the situation in 1944, was to be put on 10-ton tractor-trailer combinations, with a number of 10-ton heavy duty diesel units and 2½-ton units available for local and feeder operations. The Motor Transport Service set up a marshaling yard type of operations on the main routes to handle the trailers in the same way that the Military Railway Service handled freight cars. Organization and control measures reflected earlier experience gained from the Red Ball and other motor hauls. Within a week after starting operations on 25 March the XYZ Operation was delivering 12,000 tons a day to the four advancing U.S. armies. By the end of April fully three-fourths of all motor transportation in the Communications Zone had

been mobilized for this operation, and deliveries were averaging 15,000 tons a day. Constant changes in loading and delivery points resulted from the rapid advances of the armies, and also from the rapid advances of the railways which made it possible to shift railheads forward so that distances for the truck hauls ordinarily were much shorter than they had been for the Red Ball Express. (*Map 20*)

Air transportation also evidenced improvement over the previous summer. One reason contributing to the more effective airlift was better co-ordination of supply requests. Another reason was that tactical aviation did not now present competition to supply operations, for enough forward airfields were available. Moreover, after the great airborne operation in connection with the Rhine crossings, no airborne plans were sufficiently advanced to cause diversion of aircraft from supply delivery tasks as they had been in 1944. The improvement in air transportation was most important for units of General Patton's Third Army as they pushed into Austria and Czechoslovakia. Some 22 percent (22,500 tons, or six million gallons) of all the gasoline going to the Third Army between 30 March and 8 May went by air, and it received 11 percent of its total issues of rations by air.

Inevitably maintenance of vehicles and supply of spare parts was the greatest obstacle to maximum performance even though planning also had taken this problem into account. With the concentration of so much transportation in one effort, other operations were bound to suffer, a fact that became most apparent in port clearance. In the short run there is no doubt that the highest movement priority had to go to forward deliveries, but though

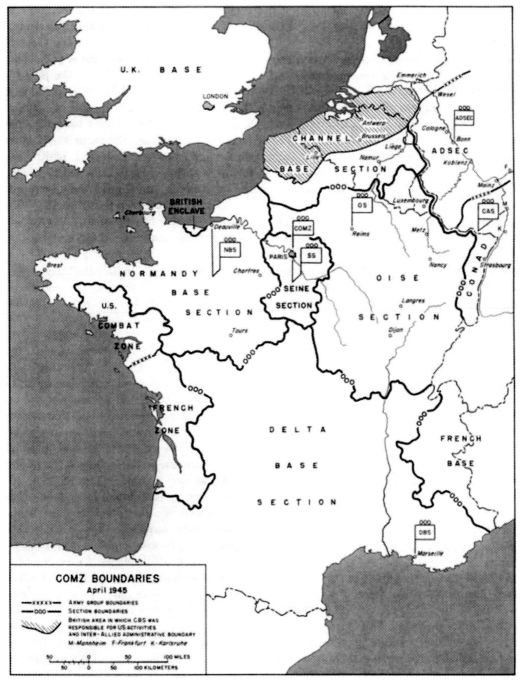

MAP 20

effective at the time, indications are that it could not have been kept up over a very long period of time.

If operations in Germany had been prolonged, it is likely that the same stresses and strains that had limited the advance in 1944 would have reappeared. With the benefit of earlier experience in organization and control, the advantage of far greater resources in transportation, and the gain from thorough plans and preparations, the contrast with earlier efforts was striking. Here was a case where the logisticians were not surprised or embarrassed by the success of breakthrough operations; they anticipated it. This time the armies could keep moving, right up to the Elbe River and beyond until firm contact was established with the Russians, and the war in Europe was finished.

The Pacific and the Far East

The war in the Pacific presented a sharp contrast in the means of logistical support with those found in Europe. In the Pacific emphasis always had to be on water transportation and on development of port and storage facilities to make effective use of shipping. Operations thousands of miles apart, supported from one island base to another, had to be maintained simultaneously. (*Map 21*)

The Fall of the Philippines

Logistics predominated in the Army's first, heartbreaking action of the war—the defense of the Philippines. The ORANGE and RAINBOW plans had assumed that strength could not be built up sufficiently in the Philippines to permit their retention against a full-scale attack, and consequently there had been no build-up of supplies to-

ward that end, though the expectation had been that Bataan could be held for a minimum of six months. Doubtless General MacArthur's decision to fight it out on the beaches instead of adhering to the plan for an immediate and orderly withdrawal into the peninsula hastened the loss of Bataan, for supplies sent forward for the beach defense had to be abandoned in many cases during the hasty withdrawal which followed. Then, when the few efforts to run the tightening Japanese blockade were unavailing, supplies began to run short. Lack of food probably more than any other single factor forced the end of resistance on Bataan.

Joint Logistics and Special Problems

As the war spread across the vast reaches of the western Pacific throughout east Asia and back again, the sheer exertion required to exist often overshadowed the special skills of artillery adjustment or rifle marksmanship. The environment of tropical seas and islands cast logistics in a wholly different light from that found in the more familiar surroundings of Europe. Railway networks and finished highway systems were foreign to most of the combat areas. Logistical organization, allowances of equipment, and standard operating procedures developed for continental warfare were largely inappropriate. Dispersal of forces and supplies over tremendous distances and reliance on water transportation to bring them together as needed were common throughout. Rapid deterioration of supplies in the hot, wet climate characteristic of much of the area complicated the factors of supply storage and distribution. The incidence of malaria added to the problems of medical care. Lack of maps and terrain data, and lack of ports

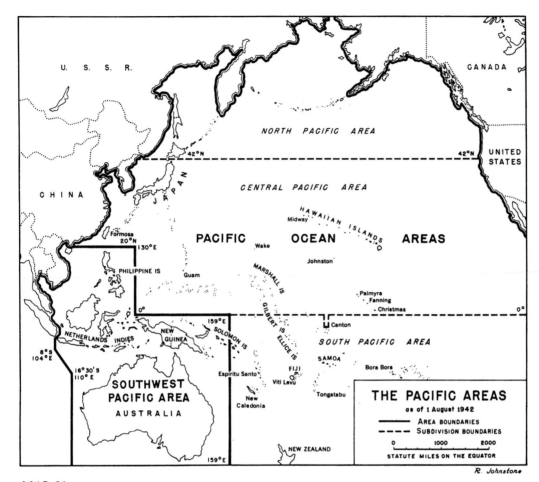

MAP 21

and other facilities of all kinds hampered nearly all operations. Jungle often limited every effort at inland movement and construction of airfields and base facilities.

The long series of amphibious operations and reliance on oversea lines of communication, not only from the United States, but within the theaters, brought forces of the Army and Navy and Marine Corps into close and continuous contact throughout the war in the Pacific. The situation cried for the integration of logistics for the support of joint operations, but, as is usually the case, this was more evident to commanders on the scene than to planners in Washington. Recommendations made independently by Admiral Nimitz and Lt. Gen. Delos C. Emmons, Army commander in Hawaii, for a system of joint supply in the Pacific Ocean Area received a cool reception, largely because General Somervell lacked confidence in the Navy's logistical organization and feared that Army interests would suffer. Steps toward closer cooperation followed the course of battle. A Joint Logistical Plan approved (July 1942) for the South Pacific entrusted local pro-curement—a major activity in arranging for the use of local facilities and the pur-chase of food and other supplies—to a joint board, and assigned each of the services cer-tain logistical responsibilities for the sup-port of the other, while supply from the United States remained separate. Later, as offensive operations began with insuf-ficient regard for the logistical problems, Somervell could give his support for a far more comprehensive plan of logistical unity. Nimitz formed a joint staff according to which a Logistics Division, J–4, at last would give some central direction to logis-tics in the Pacific Ocean Area, but the full measure of integration which this kind of warfare seemed so clearly to call for at all levels never was forthcoming.

In general, Army-Navy co-ordination of logistics was slowly realized, and reflected different approaches to problems, different kinds of problems, and different experiences. Previously, the closest co-ordination re-quired had been in transporting and pro-tecting troops and supplies overseas, but in the theaters each service had to operate pretty much on its own. In the Pacific, Army and Navy elements were thrown into intimate contact at every level. Inevitably an officer's views reflected his own training and experience, and often these precluded a full appreciation of viewpoints in the other service resulting in an appearance of petty parochialism where, in fact, differences of conviction were very real. A difference in emphasis in the conduct of the war magni-fied other differences. Whatever the basic strategic decision to seek victory first in Europe, the primary Navy war was the Pa-cific war, and it was bound to receive pri-ority in Navy thinking, while the Army's biggest effort was in Europe, and it could

accept limitations in the Pacific unaccept-able to the Navy.

The very machinery of logistics varied greatly. The Army, geared for massive land campaigns, had developed a system of cen-tralized control and orderly distribution. The Navy, emphasizing the support of forces at sea, retained a high degree of decentrali-zation, concentrating its depots at the ports, relying on the supply bureaus to carry out their responsibilities without close over-all command, and granting much autonomy and flexibility to supply distribution in for-ward areas. By early 1942 the Navy had carried its flexibility in forward supply to unprecedented length with one of the great logistical innovations of the war: auxiliary units amounting to floating bases. With fuel, ammunition, provisions, and other sup-plies, as well as repair facilities, afloat, the fleets had the "long legs" needed to move and fight almost indefinitely without return-ing to any fixed advanced base. The Navy system might well have been more readily adaptable to the Army's island warfare needs than the closely organized communi-cations system that worked so well in Europe.

Widespread duplication of effort by Army and Navy agencies and the consequent waste of resources when everything seemed criti-cally short where most needed, plus the con-stant need for strategic and tactical co-ordi-nation, and, above all, the need to make the most efficient and economical use of available shipping where the great distances added a premium to every vessel, developed pressures for real logistical co-ordination. But other factors militated against it. Brig. Gen. LeRoy Lutes, Assistant Chief of Staff for Operations, Army Service Forces, who had been lukewarm toward the unification of logistics, on his return from a visit to the

MOBILE DRYDOCK, MANUS ISLAND

Pacific in October 1942 recommended a complete union of the overseas supply lines of the two services. Somervell, too, now was ready to back unification; but the Navy, possibly frightened away by the development of the Army Service Forces organization, reversed its earlier position favoring such a move, and decided that the Army must have been right in the first place. Finally, General Marshall and Admiral King, in their capacities as Army Chief of Staff and Chief of Naval Operations, attained a compromise that resulted in the Basic Logistical Plan for Command Areas Involving Joint Army and Navy Operations issued in March 1943. While avoiding any close-knit logistical integration at home, this document put the main burden for logistic co-ordination on the theater commanders. It urged the development of unified supply staffs and joint staff planning. The hope was that, with agreement upon supply policies and priorities in the theaters, submittals of identical copies of shipping priorities by Army and Navy to their respective agencies on the west coast of the United States would achieve a co-ordination that would extend back along the lines of communication. Although a good deal of joint procurement and service had been going on, still no general system of joint procurement, storage, or transportation existed in the United States, or any real unification of supply lines from the U.S. ports to the Pacific theaters. The main instrument for co-ordination of west coast shipping was the Joint Army-Navy War Shipping Administration Ship Operations Committee instituted informally in San Francisco early in 1943.

A serious shortage of shipping in 1943 made co-ordination more difficult than ever, and also made joint action more imperative. For a time in August and September the scramble for space left shipments against agreed joint priorities lists forty-five days behind schedule. After the situation had eased somewhat, more orderly procedures came into general use. By mid-1944 the system of allocating troop shipping according to joint personnel priority lists operated quite smoothly. Theater commanders proposed priority lists on the basis of troop availability lists furnished monthly by the War and Navy Departments. Matching the theater lists against a list of available shipping, a joint committee then prepared a single joint priority list, which then became the guide for the Joint Surface Personnel Transportation Committee in San Francisco (a subcommittee of the Ship Operations Committee) to work out the details of scheduling movements. The greatest difficulty in the system occurred from the lack of criteria for establishing priority between the Pacific Ocean Area and the Southwest Pacific Area.

A comparable joint priority list and procedure for shipping cargo was never achieved. To make any system work in the Pacific would have been difficult without a great deal of experience to base it on. As a comparison, a force of 40,000 U.S. personnel in Australia required almost as much shipping to move and maintain it as did a U.S. force of 100,000 men in the Brit-

ish Isles. With forces scattered over thousands of miles of ocean area, it was impractical to establish central reserve stocks and a systematic flow of supplies through a series of depots. Neither was it practical simply to make wholesale deliveries of supplies to the theaters and expect the theaters to make "local" deliveries to points extending over two or three thousand miles. On the contrary, standard procedure came to be for the theaters to determine requirements and forward requisitions, then for deliveries from the United States to be made directly to many individual bases. In 1944 Army shipments from the United States were going to some seventy different destinations in the Pacific.

To make direct shipments most effective, a way had to be found around the "normal" procedures of sorting, storage, and distribution. This came with the introduction of block-loading, which began in the Central Pacific in 1943. On the basis of its own experience factors, the theater determined a standard block made up according to the requirements for a given number of men for a given number of days. At first defined as supplies for one thousand men for 20 days, it later was extended to 30 days. Composition of the blocks followed two patterns. For supporting the early phase of an operation a block consisted of all types of supplies needed by the number of men for the number of days. For resupply it came to be the practice to depend upon solid block ships carrying only one class of supply, the load still made up on the basis of the quantity of a particular class of supply needed for 30 days. A group of ships then would be dispatched in a convoy or within a specified sailing period so that together they would provide all classes of supply.

Under the block-loading system, the theater could simply order so many standard blocks, or so many blocks of given classes, to be delivered to any designated advance base. The greatest difficulties in the system were in the determination of requirements and the frequent redefinition of blocks.

Special requirements beyond routine supply that could be precalculated had to be met in other ways, and although organization had become rather more systematized by the last several months of the war, improvisation characterized supply and transportation activities to the end. Conditions could never be precisely anticipated, though the War Department attempted to do so, largely at the insistence of the Operations Division, by the keyed "project system" according to which Class IV supplies for special purposes were supposed to be ordered months in advance for specific construction projects the nature of which could only be guessed at the time. Other kinds of special supplies had to be ordered to meet special conditions as they arose—canvas buckets, water cans, and extra canteens for an island where water was short; machetes for hacking through jungle growth; special tropical clothing; and materials for combating insects. Quartermaster units were able to step up their operations on some of the islands by the use of palletized loads. Front-line supplies at different times were air-dropped, hand-carried, or brought up in jeeps over freshly cut trails. Frequent and sudden changes in objectives and repeated advances in timing, growing out of and leading to further unanticipated success, created some of the same kinds of problems for Pacific supply officers as did the breakthrough in Europe. But in the Pacific embarrassment was less acute, for reliance on water transportation permitted a degree of flexibility impossible in Europe. Ships already under way for one island could be diverted to another without serious loss, and if at times the supply lines bent under the strain, they never broke. The momentum of the stepped-up offensives, once gained, never diminished.

Plagued by inadequate facilities for ship discharge and with insufficient service troops, harried port officers pressed into service combat troops, Navy and Marine units, and native labor to try to overcome the congestion of shipping that followed from one base to the next as the fighting moved forward in the Pacific theaters, and probably was the greatest continuing logistical problem in the Pacific. Congestion reached critical proportions at Nouméa, New Caledonia, in the autumn of 1942; the shipping tie-up had scarcely been overcome there when it reappeared at Guadalcanal as preparations mounted for further offensives in the northern Solomons, and later it moved to the Marianas. In the Southwest Pacific the critical congestion of shipping appeared later, for as long as supplies continued to go into the Australian base, the well-developed ports of Brisbane and Sydney were adequate. Moreover, the Southwest Pacific Area was able to rely to a greater extent on local procurement; indeed MacArthur's staff reported that in the last half of 1942 the Southwest Pacific received a smaller tonnage of supplies from the United States than the theater itself shipped out to the neighboring South Pacific. Then, as the Southwest Pacific offensives moved forward, serious congestion appeared at Milne Bay, and successively at Hollandia and, worst of all, Leyte. With Manila recaptured, a sizable, fairly modern port at last was at hand, but the

Japanese had damaged it so badly that all the shipping directed to it could not be handled. A related problem existed in the displacement forward of rear bases. Actually, it was easier to rely on regular shipment from the United States than to find shipping for supplies left on bases hundreds or thousands of miles to the rear. When supplies were moved forward, the burden of unloading them in forward areas negated any contribution of essential supplies, so that all efforts for efficient roll-up were only partially successful.

Southwest Pacific Area

The fact that the Southwest Pacific Area was an Allied as well as a joint command, with Australian forces and other smaller elements, actively participating, complicated the problem of logistical organization for General MacArthur. Actually he never did set up a combined or joint staff in any full sense. His General Headquarters remained essentially an Army staff throughout, with the addition of American and Australian naval officers and Australian Army officers as technical assistants at various levels. His approach to logistics was to leave supply lines of each of the national service components separate with firm coordination only at the top level. Having no general unified organization either for planning or operations with respect to supply, transportation, communication, construction, or administrative services at lower levels, and only limited arrangements for joint procurement or cross-servicing, GHQ exercised co-ordination through a system of priorities control over shipments of cargo into the theater. General Sir Thomas Blamey, Australian Army commander in chief, was named commander of Allied

Land Forces, but his headquarters actually controlled only training and a certain amount of common administration. For field operations, MacArthur maintained a task force organization known as the ALAMO Force, with the commander of the Sixth Army, Lt. Gen. Walter Kreuger, as commander, to which was attached the Sixth Army and Australian elements as required. There was a consolidation of forward Australian and American supply services for support of particular campaigns, as for the support of operations in New Guinea where GHQ in October 1942 established in Papua the Combined Operational Service Command to control all Allied lines of communication activities. Operating under the New Guinea Force, it had the deputy commander of the U.S. Army Services of Supply as its commander, and an officer of the Australian Staff Corps as his deputy.

The Army's Services of Supply in the Southwest Pacific had to bend conventional organization to adapt to conditions, but it also suffered from a lack of definition of responsibility to a greater degree than was the case in Europe, for its staff had to operate in the shadow of GHQ. As the situation developed, SOS organized six base sections in Australia and an advance section in New Guinea, but it did not operate in close support of combat units. Ordinarily, each task force commander improvised a service command to organize and operate his rear area until combat operations had been completed in the vicinity, when facilities would be turned over to SOS. For the Leyte operation, involving the support of over 200,000 men, a new command, the Army Service Command, was organized as a major command of Sixth Army for immediate logistical support.

China-Burma-India

In the China-Burma-India theater the central objective as well as the central problem was logistical. The major value of the campaign in Burma lay in re-establishing communications with China, and the greatest obstacle to successful completion of the campaign was the difficulty in getting up supplies to support the forces engaged. Pack animals and natives carried supplies to the fronts. For months long-range penetration columns, operating in the Japanese rear, depended on airdrops. But major operations and effective support of the Chinese depended upon expansion of the Assam line of communication. (*Map 22*)

Tremendous efforts went into improving the port of Calcutta, into providing operational and maintenance personnel for stepping up traffic on the Bengal and Assam Railway, into getting the fullest use out of the Brahmaputra barge line operated by several British companies, into constructing airfields in Assam, and into laying pipelines from Calcutta and Chittagong to Upper Assam. All this was necessary to complete the vital link in communications across the rugged, jungle-covered mountains and swampy valleys—the Ledo Road—to link up with the old Burma Road, as well as to bring up supplies for air delivery over the Hump, and to support current combat operations. In May 1943 scarcely 5,000 tons of supplies were brought in over the Assam line of communication; in October 1944 that figure had risen to nearly 125,000 tons. While operations against the Japanese continued, so did work on the road and pipelines. In January 1945 the Stilwell Road, over 1,000 miles long, opened, and six months later the pipeline was completed to Kunming.

Pacific Ocean Areas

In the Pacific Ocean Areas, where Army, Navy, and Marine forces were present in about equal numbers, and where they frequently were thrown into close contact in the course of operations, joint organization and procedures for logistics were far more advanced than in the CBI or the Southwest Pacific.

Steps toward a joint logistical system began very early in the South Pacific subtheater. Vice Adm. Robert L. Ghormley, commander under Admiral Nimitz of the South Pacific Area, set up a joint purchasing board in May 1942 to co-ordinate local procurement in New Zealand and on smaller islands in the area, with the Navy responsible for delivering supplies purchased there to both services. When Maj. Gen. Millard F. Harmon became commanding general of U.S. Army Forces in the South Pacific Area, he co-operated closely with Ghormley and naval forces on logistical support. Subsequently the Army assumed responsibility for obtaining provisions as necessary from the continental United States for all shore-based forces except those in Samoa, while the Navy supplied gasoline and oil for all forces. But no amount of co-operation could reduce very much the logistical problems arising out of the ratio of forces to distance. This command covered more than a million square miles, almost all of it ocean. Some bases were 3,000 miles apart. Only four ports with usable terminal installations existed in the entire area—Auckland and Wellington in New Zealand, Suva in the Fiji Islands, and Nouméa, New Caledonia. After the confusion (which might have been expected) of the first offensive operation of the war at Guadalcanal, and faced with the tremendous congestion de-

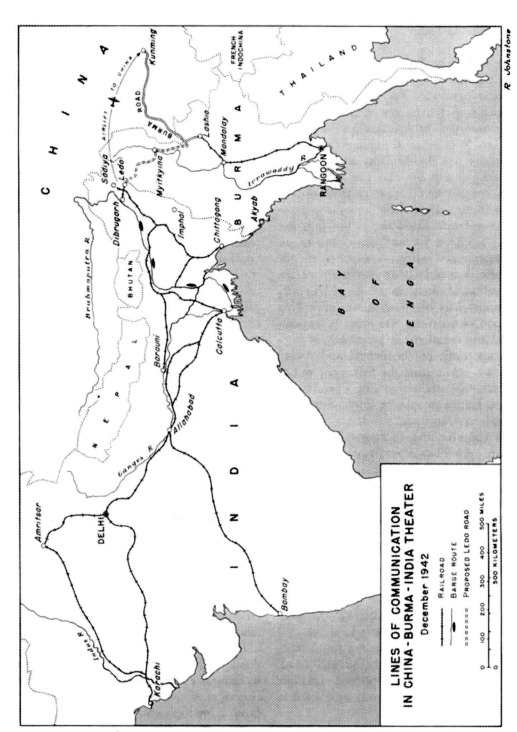

LINES OF COMMUNICATION
IN CHINA-BURMA-INDIA THEATER
December 1942

RAILROAD
BARGE ROUTE
PROPOSED LEDO ROAD

0 100 200 300 400 500 MILES
0 100 200 300 400 500 KILOMETERS

R. Johnstone

MAP 22

veloping at Nouméa, Admiral William F. Halsey, Jr., Ghormley's successor as commander of the area, moved for further joint arrangements to handle incoming shipments and to move supplies forward. Halsey gave Army commanders full responsibility for co-ordinating logistical support for Guadalcanal and for port operations at Nouméa. Neither Ghormley nor Halsey saw any need to set up a joint staff organization, and the Army commanders, too, were satisfied with the results obtained by informal conferences and close working relationships. After promulgation of the Basic Logistical Plan, however, Admiral Nimitz decreed in May 1943 that arrangements in the South Pacific should be given a more formal structure. Admiral Halsey thereupon established the Joint Logistics Board on which Army, Navy, and Marine service commanders were to do formally what they already had been doing informally. In early 1944 a joint logistical staff replaced the Joint Board, but it, too, was for the most part a paper organization. Most of the actual joint planning and logistical operations were done through a Joint Working Board made up of subordinates organized into various subcommittees as needed. The board never did work out satisfactory procedures for determining joint supply requirements to be filled from the United States, for making inventory control effective, or for planning base development.

The Army's logistical organization in the South Pacific gradually took form with a Services of Supply and service commands established on the islands of major activity. With eleven different bases and 400 separate organizations under its administrative control, but with never enough men to accomplish the tasks involved, Brig. Gen. Robert G. Breene, SOS commander, at no time was able to satisfy the demands from Washington for effective inventory control. Supply accounting became fairly accurate only after October 1944, when the South Pacific had become a rear base area.

The command and administrative machinery developed under Admiral Nimitz had special complications growing out of the fact that Nimitz was at the same time commander in chief of the Pacific Ocean Area, commander of the Central Pacific and North Pacific Areas, and commander in chief of the Pacific Fleet. Nevertheless, it was in Nimitz' commands that joint logistics reached its highest development. After a series of recommendations and studies, both in the Pacific and in Washington, Admiral Nimitz in September 1943 organized a joint staff for his headquarters at Pearl Harbor. It was the only truly functioning theater joint staff of the war, and even though it fell considerably short of many Army officers' hopes, it became the prototype for later unified command staffs. It comprised four staff sections, each one including Army, Navy, and Marine Corps officers. These sections were: J-1, Plans, under a naval officer; J-2, Intelligence, under an Army officer (there were also some British and Australian officers in this section); J-3, Operations, under a naval officer; and J-4, Logistics, under an Army officer (Brig. Gen. Edmond Leavey, drawn from Somervell's Army Service Forces staff). Later a fifth section, J-5, General Administration, was added under a naval officer.

The J-4 section had branches for transportation, fuel, supply, and advanced bases. Throughout, Leavey worked very closely with the commander of the Service Force, Pacific Fleet, but co-operation still did not go as far as Leavey and others would have desired; as for instance, bringing in representatives of the Army and Navy technical and supply services to form a sort of special staff including medical, signal, ordnance, engineer, quartermaster, transportation, and other sections. Neither did Nimitz agree to the recommendations of General Marshall and others that he turn over the command of the subordinate areas and the fleet to other officers, for he thought that this would lead to an unnecessary proliferation of headquarters and a loosening of control. Already, however, he had formed the Central Pacific Force, a separate joint task force under the command of Rear Adm. Raymond A. Spruance, for the invasion of the Gilbert Islands (November 1943) and this would be his approach for future operations.

Actually, the joint staff system in the Central Pacific worked relatively smoothly, and much of the reason for its successful operation was that Nimitz and the men he had chosen for his staff were determined to make it work. One veteran of this service described Nimitz' joint staff as "the smoothest, most competent group I ever worked with." [3] At times relations with Lt. Gen. Robert C. Richardson, Jr., who succeeded Emmons as commander of the Hawaiian Department and in August 1943 was named Commanding General, U.S. Army Forces, Central Pacific Area, were not so smooth. Although he had applauded the moves for a joint staff, Richardson was disposed to uphold traditional service prerogatives of the Army whenever questions of further centralization of supply and administration came up. There never was a unification of logistical systems in the area around Hawaii, and each service requisitioned most of its own requirements from the United States, but in the forward areas experience

and planning soon led to many instances of close logistical integration. As in other circumstances the control of shipping was the secret to logistical co-ordination, and judged by the relative lack of congestion and retention of ships, shipping control in the Central Pacific was superior to that in any other theater of the war. Under a system of joint theater planning and joint base commands, ships were echeloned according to detailed plans so that the supplies would arrive as needed and in proper order. Army engineers and Navy construction battalions (Seabees) accomplished wonders of construction in building air bases and support bases for amphibious operations in the offensive westward across the Pacific.

As for the Army's logistical structure in this area, the Army Port and Service Command, under Army Forces in the Central Pacific, succeeded the Hawaiian Department Service Forces. With the expansion of operations across the Central Pacific and the closing out of the South Pacific Area as a subtheater, the South Pacific Base Command superseded U.S. Army Forces in the South Pacific Area under the broadened U.S. Army Forces in the Pacific Ocean Areas, and the Army Port and Service Command was made subordinate to a newly established Central Pacific Base Command. Subsequently (April 1945) the Western Pacific Base Command was established for the logistical support of Army forces (and Navy and Marine forces as directed) in the Marianas, the western Carolines, and on Iwo Jima. Okinawa remained the responsibility of the Central Base Command.

Amphibious Warfare in the Pacific

Logistical procedures developed to mount and support the scores of amphibious opera-

[3] Memo, Rear Adm Henry E. Eccles for the author, 9 Jul 63.

tions in the Pacific, and based upon the experience of the great landings in North Africa, Sicily, Italy, Normandy, and southern France, constituted one of the major American contributions to the art of warfare.

The most significant innovation determining the special characteristics of these operations was the design and construction of special vessels for the purpose—combat loaders and landing craft of various types. Combat loaders were specially designed and rigged transports for carrying assault forces and cargo to the vicinity of hostile shores for landing by boats and lighters carried on board. Combat loaders were of three main types—the attack personnel transport (APA); the converted destroyer transport (APD), for carrying personnel and equipment; and the attack cargo transport (AKA), mainly for cargo. Although designs for special landing craft were being prepared in the United States, it was the Japanese who introduced these vessels into warfare in their invasions of the Philippines and Malaya, and the British had made some use of similar craft in their North African operations. The United States soon developed new types and produced them in great quantities. They quickly became so important that they were critical items of equipment throughout the war, and, as already noted, strategic decisions and the timing of major operations frequently hinged upon their availability.

The common characteristics of these vessels were a bow which could be opened to permit lowering a ramp, or a bow which itself could be lowered as a ramp so that troops, tanks, trucks and other vehicles could move out directly to the beaches under their own power; shallow draft; and controlled water ballast so that the vessel could be beached at low tide and floated off at high tide. The vessels fell into two general categories: landing ships, ocean-going ships especially useful for shore-to-shore operations, and landing craft, intended to be carried on board combat loaders or other ships or to be used across relatively narrow straits. Of the dozen or so types, the most important of the ships probably were the LST (landing ship, tank) which might carry, for example, 20 medium tanks on its tank deck with 11 2½-ton trucks on its main deck; the LSM (landing ship, medium); and the LSD (landing ship, dock), a floating drydock which carried landing craft and amphibious vehicles and launched them by flooding the hold. The most common of the landing craft were the LCI (landing craft, infantry) the large version of which could carry 200 men or 75 long tons of cargo; various models of the LCT (landing craft, tank); the LCM (landing craft, mechanized); and the LCVP (landing craft, vehicle, personnel), which could carry 36 men and one ¾-ton truck or 4 tons of cargo. In addition there were amphibious vehicles which could be launched from ships and proceed across water and up on the beaches under their own power such as the Alligator, an amphibous tractor used to carry troops and equipment ashore; the amphibious tank, for combat support; and the previously noted amphibious 2½-ton truck, the Dukw.

The shipping required for an amphibious assault force varied according to the length of the voyage, the mission, special equipment, and the proportion of landing craft and amphibious vehicles carried. For a short voyage, a force equivalent to a reinforced infantry division of some 22,300 men, with 3,600 vehicles, in a fairly typical case might take 9 APA's, 6 AKA's, 36 LST's, 12 LSM's, and 3 LSD's. In the choice of landing sites the main considerations had to do with the advantages or disadvantages of the beaches: their exits and their approaches in permitting logistical follow-up as well as the initial landings. It was desirable to avoid the reefs and shoals characteristic of Pacific atolls and islands, and if they could not be cleared by four feet at low tide, then it was necessary to go in at higher tide, even though that complicated beaching and floating of the craft. Beaches with too gentle a slope caused landing craft to ground at long distance from the shore line, while a too steep gradient made discharge of vessels difficult. In a surf running higher than four or five feet, amphibious vehicles operated at great hazard. The beaches themselves had to be firm enough for traction.

For amphibious operations over any extended distance in the Southwest Pacific, troops generally were transported in APD's and landed by landing craft carried on board. If the landing had to be made over coral reefs blocking the way to the beaches, amphibious tractors and Dukw's had to be used for the initial assault. As soon as a way was cleared, LCT's carrying tanks and shore party engineering equipment, were launched from the flooded well of an LSD, and then successive waves of infantry arrived in LCI's hopefully spaced and timed to avoid congestion. About an hour after the assault, several LST's would arrive with troops, vehicles, and supplies to be unloaded before nightfall. For the follow-up after a landing, any and all types of landing vessels might be used. Echelons usually would go in at three- to five-day intervals until Army Services of Supply could take over responsibility with its own merchant shipping.

For shore-to-shore operations, MacArthur relied on Army engineer special brigades to man fleets of landing craft, and this gave them special significance, for only in the Southwest Pacific Area did the Navy not man all the boats in such operations. After specialized training at the Engineer Amphibian Command on Cape Cod, the 2d Engineer Amphibian Brigade (later redesignated as the 2d Engineer Special Brigade) went to the Southwest Pacific in November 1942; a second brigade arrived in October 1943, and a third in May 1944. Like the brigades serving in the Mediterranean and in the Normandy landings, these brigades also had responsibility for organizing shore party teams to unload the assault ships and to set up supply dumps, and in the follow-up phase they provided local transportation and lighterage for supply build-up. Beach parties, as distinct from shore parties, were Navy units charged with co-ordinating the arrival of boats and ships on the beaches, seeing to the evacuation of casualties into waiting vessels, and getting vessels back off the beaches once they had been unloaded. In all of these duties they had to work very closely with the engineer shore parties. Ultimately the VII Amphibious Force, controlling the Navy beaching craft of MacArthur's command, organized and trained eight beach parties, each composed of three naval officers and eighteen men.

Return to the Philippines

Southwest Pacific forces got their first test in the ways of amphibious warfare in operations along the coast of New Guinea, perfected them in campaigns against islands from Biak and Noemfoor to Morotai, and reached their highest achievement in the return to the Philippines. Operations never went according to plan, but they came closer to it with experience, and results always were effective.

The October 1944 invasion of Leyte was the biggest operation in the Pacific up to that time, and required the closest kind of co-operation between area commanders. An invasion force of 150,000 men, larger than the American assault elements in the Normandy landings, was assembled off Leyte from points as widely distant as Hawaii in the Central Pacific Area and Hollandia, New Guinea, in the Southwest Pacific Area.

Originally marked for an invasion of Yap, XXIV Corps' two divisions embarked at Honolulu on 13 September aboard transports of the III Amphibious Force. With cancellation of the Yap plans XXIV Corps was shifted to the Leyte operation and proceeded to Manus Island for completion of staging. At Manus the assault troops transferred from AKA's to LST's for the last leg of the journey. Sixth Army units, including X Corps and Sixth Army Service Command, were staged at Hollandia. A month after XXIV Corps left Hawaii X Corps' 24th Infantry Division and the Sixth Army Service Command got under way from Hollandia in vessels of the VII Amphibious Force; two days later they joined with ships bringing another X Corps unit, the 1st Cavalry Division, from Manus. When the forces merged they formed a convoy of some 518 ocean-going troop and cargo ships of various types supported by about 180 warships. The convoy arrived off Leyte as scheduled for the landing on 20 October. (*Maps 23 and 24*)

Almost simultaneously at 1000 assault troops of X Corps, in amphibian tractors and LCI's led by a wave of amphibian tanks launched about 5,000 yards from the shore, hit the beaches (designated White and Red) in the San Pedro Bay area near Tacloban; about fourteen miles to the south XXIV Corps hit the beaches designated

LST Bound For Hollandia

Orange, Blue, Violet, and Yellow around Dulag. In a separate action a regiment of the 24th Infantry Division landed in the vicinity of Panaon Strait to hold the entrance to Sogod Bay. The XXIV Corps had retained the supplies and equipment provided for the Yap expedition, and carried ashore a 30-day supply of rations and medical supplies; twenty days of clothing, weapons, vehicles, fuels, and construction materials; and seven units of fire for all artillery weapons and five units for other weapons. The X Corps was to take ashore ten days of all supplies other than engineer, and thirty days of those, and two units of fire for all weapons; within ten days additional supplies were to be brought in to permit building up to thirty days for most categories, and fifteen days for motor fuel. Resupply stocks were being shipped from the United States and Australia, and were

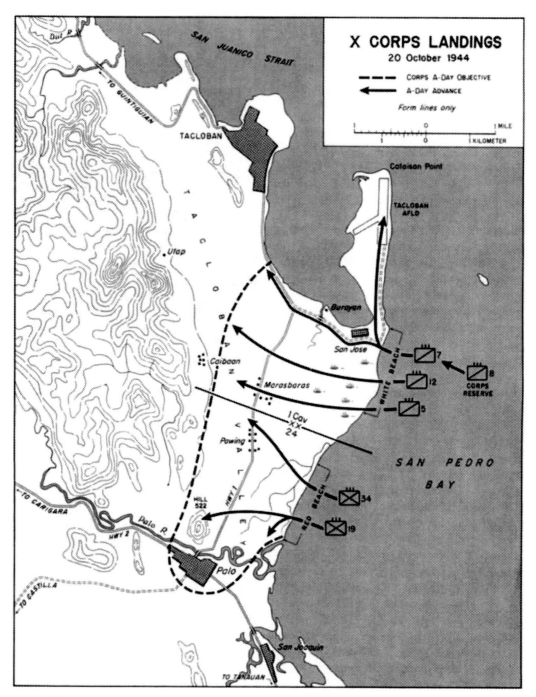

MAP 23

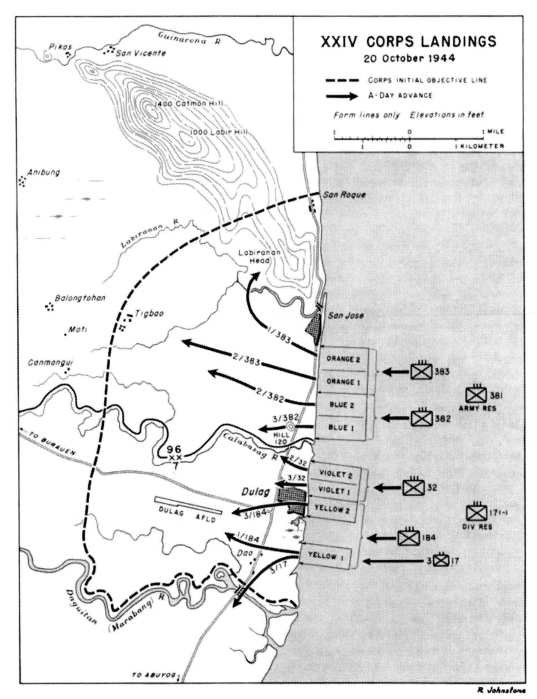

XXIV CORPS LANDINGS
20 October 1944

- - - CORPS INITIAL OBJECTIVE LINE
→ A-DAY ADVANCE

Form lines only. Elevations in feet.

MAP 24

on call at New Guinea. In addition, ten Liberty ships, eight at Hollandia and two in the Palaus, were to be held loaded in floating reserve.

In the main landings opposition was relatively light and the beaches were receptive to landing. But swampy, wooded terrain blocked most of the exits, and at one beach in the northern sector the approaches were too shallow for the LST's to come in and they had to withdraw under hostile fire. Within an hour after the landings supplies and equipment began to pour onto the beaches. Then the trouble began. Many of the ships had not been properly combat-loaded, so that supplies could not be unloaded in the order needed. Ship's crews and soldiers detailed to stay on board for the work did their best to get vehicles and supplies unloaded from the APA's, AKA's, and LST's, making good use of LSM's as lighters. On the northern beaches (X Corps) shore parties from two regiments of the 2d Engineer Special Brigade controlled the unloading on the beaches; in the XXIV Corps sector, the shore parties were drawn from two combat engineer groups because the Central Pacific Area from which this force came had no engineer special brigades.

Congestion soon appeared nearly everywhere. Some of the shore parties did not land early enough to develop proper organization before supplies began to arrive; plans had to be changed for handling supplies from some of the LST's when it became necessary to divert them to another beach; boats were carelessly loaded in many cases. Supplies were strewn over the beaches, or thrown onto vehicles with little order; beach parties brought in supplies faster than shore parties could handle them; swampy land restricted the usable area. The shore party supporting the 7th Division near Dulag probably had the smoothest organization and operation. During the early phases this shore party used what it called the "drugstore system" of delivering supplies by Dukws directly from LST's anchored off the shore to front-line units. Thus it could fill requests an hour after they were received without hampering concurrent orderly build-up of dumps. Six hours after the landings the shore party had sufficiently organized regimental dumps about 500 yards inland to fill requisitions there and to give up direct deliveries by amphibious truck. During the first day some 107,450 tons of equipment and supplies were discharged over the beaches of the Sixth Army. The first congestion on the beaches was quickly relieved, but was soon followed by a general congestion of almost unprecedented magnitude.

In the days that followed, both tactical and logistical operations became more difficult, and delays of the one delayed the other. The greatest problems resulted from the terrain and the weather. Construction of airfields fell far behind schedule, and in some cases had to be abandoned, delaying air support and permitting Japanese reinforcements. Suitable areas for supply bases, hospitals, and other installations were hard to find, for swamps and rice paddies during a period of heavy rain were good for no such purposes. Roads, old ones or new ones, laboriously cut through by engineers, quickly disintegrated. In the northern sector supplies gravitated to the Tacloban airstrip, and hundreds of vehicles and thousands of tons of ammunition, rations, and fuel, strewn about the area, made it impossible to commence work on the airstrip itself until they could be cleared away. During November the Sixth Army Service Command established its major base at

Tacloban, where two deepwater berths were found intact and additional docking facilities and several lighterage wharves were constructed. In addition, the service command established a sub-base at Dulag and a supply point at Carigara. But successive resupply convoys kept arriving before the preceding ones could be unloaded, and Japanese bombers kept attacking the ships.

Once supplies were ashore, the problem of moving them up to front-line troops was always a hard one. As the roads became virtually unusable, more and more reliance had to be placed upon water transportation. Naval vessels and amphibious vehicles carried supplies around as close as possible to the troops; then vehicles were used when possible, but often carrying parties had to be made up of soldiers and Filipino civilians. In many cases supplies were air-dropped to forces otherwise isolated. When the Japanese decided to make a decisive stand for Leyte, additional forces were brought in, and the landing of the 112th Cavalry Regimental Combat Team, the 11th Airborne Division, and elements of the 38th Infantry Division, as well as the 32d and 77th Infantry Divisions which had been in reserve added to the problems of logistic support. As forces joined on the west side of the island, and then drove northward, supply lines were stretched to the breaking point, and only the dispatch of additional amphibious vessels relieved the critical supply situation. By 26 December a general level of five to ten days' supply of all classes had been built up, and this was maintained for the rest of the operation. Nearly two and one-half months after the initial landings Leyte finally was secured.

In some ways over-the-beach supply operations in support of the landings in the Lingayen Gulf area of Luzon on 9 January 1945 showed improvements over the Leyte experience—thanks in part to the better terrain and the absence of resistance at most points, but also to better organization. Congestion on the beaches inevitably reappeared, however, and the perpetual shortage of labor for unloading was further aggravated by a tendency of men to disappear from their tasks in favor of fraternizing with the local Filipinos.

Joint procedures for logistic support of amphibious operations were most advanced in the Central Pacific Area where directives from Admiral Nimitz' headquarters ordinarily defined three phases for an operation. Control over logistics was in the hands of the commander in each phase—the first, the assault phase, came under the amphibious task force commander, usually Vice Adm. Richmond Kelly Turner; the second, the land operations phase, came under a ground forces commander, usually Lt. Gen. Holland M. Smith, Marine Corps, and the third, a garrison phase, came under a garrison or base commander of the service having major responsibility for base development. As Central Pacific campaigns moved westward, the Army was assigned major responsibility for base development on Makin in the Gilberts, Kwajalein in the Marshalls, Saipan in the Marianas, and Anguar in the Palaus. Joint staff planning sought to anticipate joint requirements for each operation, and there was a certain division of labor in supply and services even though each service continued to requisition through its own channels on rear bases and the United States. In planning for base materials, the Navy avoided the Army's keyed project system (in which each project was handled as a distinct unit) by making up standard units that could be called for in the amount needed for the development of any base. The Navy system, used in the Pacific Ocean Area for advance bases, in effect, extended block-loading and, to a degree, automatic supply to virtually all categories.

Okinawa

Four months before the Leyte operation, the Central Pacific Force already had launched an amphibious attack of comparable magnitude. Just nine days after the landings in Normandy, on the other side of the world a force of over 127,500 men—two-thirds of whom were marines—with a convoy of 535 transports and warships, arrived after a one-thousand-mile voyage from Eniwetok to the Marianas for successive assaults against Saipan, Tinian, and Guam. The operation, which began with the benefit of only three months of planning, was carried out 3,600 miles away from the main base in Hawaii.

By far the greatest battle against the Japanese was the last. An assault force of nearly 183,000 soldiers and marines with 747,100 measurement tons of cargo went into the invasion of Okinawa. Troops and supplies went aboard 430 assault transports and landing ships at ports on the American west coast, Hawaii, Espíritu Santo in New Caledonia, Guadalcanal, the Russell Islands, Saipan, and Leyte. They assembled at Eniwetok, Ulithi, Saipan, and Leyte. Additional ships brought follow-up forces and supplies for building up a base. The Navy commander of the task force, Admiral Turner, was responsible for delivering the troops and supplies to the beaches. The Army commander, Lt. Gen. Simon B. Buckner, Jr., commanding the Tenth Army, was responsible for landing the supplies and moving them to dumps. The Island Command Okinawa operated as an army service command for Tenth Army in providing immediate logistic support and in base development. The assault units carried a 30-day supply of rations, clothing, fuel, and other essential items, and five units of fire. Automatic resupply was scheduled in twenty-one shipments to leave the United States at 10-day intervals (beginning 20 February 1945) for regulating stations at Ulithi and Eniwetok to await call by General Buckner.

Careful planning and a surprising lack of enemy resistance made possible fast and effective organization of the beaches after the landings on 1 April 1945. Landing craft could cross the reef during four or five hours at flood tide, and were able to discharge cargo directly on the beach, while larger ships unloaded at the reef. General unloading began 3 April, and in the absence of the enemy, continued through the night under floodlights. Storms interrupted unloading, but on the whole cargo came in faster than it could be cleared. Control of the beaches passed successively up the chain of command until Tenth Army, acting through the 1st Engineer Special Brigade, a unit experienced in European landing operations, and the Island Command, assumed control on 9 April. Navy beachmasters directed the movements of incoming ships. At the end of May the Joint Freight Handling Facilities, under Navy command, relieved the 1st Engineer Special Brigade of all shore party operations, and Quartermaster service and truck companies previously assigned to the brigade were assigned to the 53d Medium Port, which in turn was attached to Joint Freight Handling Facilities. This arrangement continued until August when Army and Navy cargo operations were separated.

Japanese air attacks, incuding kamikazi

TANAPAG HARBOR, SAIPAN

suicide planes, first encountered at Leyte, were in greater force than ever before at Okinawa and disrupted supply activities. Failure to capture the port of Naha as had been planned made it necessary to depend on over-the-beach operations for supply, and resort to selective unloading caused further congestion. Installation of floating causeways and building of makeshift piers helped somewhat, but by the end of the campaign in June, unloading had fallen over 200,000 measurement tons behind schedule. The end of hostilities on Okinawa brought no slackening of logistical effort, for its capture was regarded as but a preparatory step for the invasion of the Japanese home islands. When improvement of port facilities became possible, discharge of cargo was stepped up from a rate of 20,000 measurement tons a day in June to over 37,700 measurement tons a day in July.

Preparations for the Invasion of Japan

The planned assault on Japan would have dwarfed even the Okinawa operation. When Japan surrendered, General MacArthur, to whose command the forces in the Ryukyus had been transferred on 31 July, was preparing his forces for the final blow. On Luzon the Sixth Army was regrouping

THE INVASION OF OKINAWA

for its assigned invasion of Kyushu, and the advance detachment of First Army had arrived from Europe to begin preparations for its part in the later invasion of Honshu. A maximum logistic effort was called for.

Although from the beginning there had been those who urged a single theater command structure for the entire Pacific, the Joint Chiefs of Staff never had been able to bring themselves to a firm choice between MacArthur and Nimitz, and they did not do so now. MacArthur was given command over the planned invasion of Japan, but Nimitz was to be a co-ordinate, not a subordinate, commander. Climax became anticlimax, not only because the last and biggest planned operation proved to be unnecessary, but also because the logistical organization machinery to carry it out was to be somewhat of a return to the prewar concept of separate Army and Navy commands, with co-operation depending upon agreement between the commanders concerned. General MacArthur's headquarters had not achieved the degree of interservice logistical integration that had evolved in the Pacific Ocean Area, and organizational arrangements for his broadened command reflected that experience. An Army-Navy Conference on Shipping and Supply in May and a conference at Guam in June between representatives of MacArthur and Nimitz developed joint arrangements for support of the Kyushu operation. Already Army Service Forces in Washington and the theater Army staff had prepared logistic plans for this final phase. While the initial assault would be mounted and supplied from Pacific bases, it was expected that resupply would be direct from the United States. The Army would maintain major distribution points in the Philippines, with air depots at Guam, Manila, and later on Okinawa. In the absence of a general agreement, the Army and Navy each would control the shipping for support of forces under its control, with the Army exercising major control over shipping to common ports in the operational area. Regulating stations would be operated at Ulithi and Okinawa. Detailed plans had been developed for the special loading of 482 ships for the Kyushu operation and some 700 for Honshu.

With the Japanese surrender it became necessary to put into effect only the recently developed plans for unopposed occupation. The 11th Airborne Division, the 27th Infantry Division, and elements of General Headquarters were airlifted from the Philippines by way of Okinawa to Tokyo. The remainder of the Sixth and Eighth Armies arrived by sea—135 of the vessels had been specially loaded for the invasion—to move into their assigned occupation zones in Japan. An Army service command was assigned to each army. The XXIV Corps, with a newly organized Army service command assigned to it, went to Korea. The greatest of all wars was at an end on all fronts.

Summary

In the days and the hours when Americans went ashore on the Normandy beaches on 6 June 1944, when they crossed the Elbe River in mid-April 1945, when other Americans went ashore on the beaches of Okinawa half a world away, the history of the Army's logistics reached its fulfillment. In putting ashore and maintaining forces of such great numbers of men, 3,000 to 6,000 miles from their own homeland and 12,000 miles from each other, with their own supplies and equipment piled behind them in their own boats and ships, the U.S. Army, in co-operation with the Navy, had done what no other army in history had ever done. Nothing could be compared with it.

In the period from December 1941 through August 1945 the Army had deployed some 6,902,000 officers and men overseas. About 4,300,000 of these went to Europe, Africa, and the Middle East; about 2,250,000 to the Pacific and the CBI, and about 350,000 to Alaska, Latin America and the Atlantic bases. Cargo shipments during the period totaled over 126,-700,000 measurement tons, in roughly the same proportions as the troops to oversea theaters. Total supplies sent to forces in the European Theater of Operations alone, including local procurement in France and Great Britain (about 13,300,000 tons) but excluding construction in the United Kingdom, amounted to more than 47,600,000 long tons—nearly six times the amount (including local procurement) sent to the AEF in World War I.[4]

---

[4] Chester Wardlow, *The Transportation Corps: Responsibilities, Organization, and Operations,* UNITED STATES ARMY IN WORLD WAR II (Washington, 1951), pp. 10–17; Logistics in World War II: Final Report of Army Service Forces, 1 July 1947, pp. 242–43; Lt. Col. Randolph Leigh, *48 Million Tons to Eisenhower* (Washington, The Infantry Journal Press, 1945), pp. 4–7.

CHAPTER XXXI

Demobilization Once More

Relief from the perils and tensions of all-out war which came with the end of combat operations in 1945 was accompanied by a belief that current major problems had been solved. In spite of disillusionments that followed World War I, for the moment bright hopes for a brave new world relegated continuing problems to the background. Logistical problems, for example, were, if anything, greater than before. The Army had been deployed over the globe during the course of four years. People demanded its return in a few months. Mountains of equipment that had piled up as war industry hit its peak in 1944 and 1945 had to be disposed of. The national economy, geared to full war production, had to be reversed for rapid reconversion to meet mounting shortages of civilian goods. Beyond the immediate problems of liquidating the war machinery and cleaning up the battle areas, it would become increasingly clear in the years ahead that problems assumed to be purely political would have their military facets. U.S. foreign policy commitments would be effective only to the extent that a military establishment was at hand to support them.

The ragged ending of World War II left without precise definition the beginning of the postwar period. The world-wide extent of the war, the apparent necessity of maintaining certain legal fictions in order to continue controls over the domestic economy, and the play of international politics re-sulted in a graduated termination of the conflict. For certain purposes—such as the beginning of limited demobilization and industrial reconversion, and suspension of lend-lease shipments to those Allies participating only in the European war—World War II ended on V–E Day, 8 May 1945. For certain other purposes—such as the cancellation of war contracts—the war ended with the Japanese acceptance of surrender terms on 14 August 1945. For some purposes—such as general demobilization and industrial reconversion, and termination of lend-lease—the war ended on 2 September 1945 with the signing of the instrument of surrender on the USS *Missouri* in Tokyo Bay. For still other purposes—such as the duration of the Surplus Property Act and other matters generally relating to domestic policy—the war ended with the President's proclamation of the cessation of hostilities, 31 December 1946. The war with Italy, Bulgaria, Hungary, Rumania, and Finland ended officially when peace treaties with those nations became effective on 15 September 1947. The war with Germany officially ended with the Joint Resolution of Congress approved on 19 October 1951. Finally, the war with Japan came to an official end on the date that the treaty of peace with Japan became effective on 28 April 1952.

The years between V–E Day and the Japanese peace treaty saw perhaps the greatest retrenchment program, and then the greatest peacetime build-up in history. Almost from the start new tensions replaced the old. Demands, first to husband resources, then to rebuild, soon overtook those for continued reduction. In his final report as Chief of Staff of the Army in 1948, General of the Army Dwight D. Eisenhower wrote:

In the fall of 1945 our military forces in Europe and the Orient were still formidable; our network of bases and depots was global in extent; vast stores of armament and supply were maintained across the world. Since then, the manpower of the wartime Army has been returned home to be replaced fractionally by postwar volunteers; all but critically important bases have been evacuated; surplus property has been turned over to appropriate government agencies for disposition. But the peace has not become the peace of which war's victims dreamed.[1]

Bringing the Boys Home

"With victory, a stampede for demobilization swept over the country."[2] Long-absent soldiers and anxious relatives and friends exerted understandable pressure on government officials for quick return of troops from overseas and their rapid discharge from the Army. Clinging to the civilian-soldier tradition of Cincinnatus and the Minute Men, Americans could not bring themselves to admit that a large postwar military force might be necessary. The only misgivings about immediate and rapid demobilization seemed to be the possibility of widespread unemployment during the period of readjustment, but even those ap-

prehensions soon dissipated. In the end, the rate of troop returns bore little relationship to considerations of changing foreign commitments and responsibilities or to continuing supply missions. The only real limitation during the months immediately after V–J Day was, once again, the availability of shipping.

Even as demobilization accelerated, signs appeared that raised serious doubts as to its wisdom. As early as 16 October 1945 Secretary of War Robert P. Patterson, Secretary of the Navy James V. Forrestal, and Secretary of State James F. Byrnes agreed upon the inadvisability of continuing the rapid demobilization, for, within six weeks of the final victory, Russian intransigence had made it clear that difficult times lay ahead. Yet the Secretary of State counseled against making public the details of the Soviet diplomacy on the ground that the Russians would thereby be given an excuse to claim that provocations had justified their actions.

Troop movements of unprecedented scope had been under way for more than three months when Japan capitulated. During that period redeployment of forces from Europe to the Pacific had first priority, but simultaneously demobilization began for troops not needed in operations planned against Japan. The unexpected swiftness of the surrender centered attention on demobilization. The five million men who had gone overseas during a period of four years were to be brought home within fourteen months. Target dates called for the return of all troops by the end of June 1946, with the exception of occupation and garrison forces (370,000 in Europe, 400,000 in the Pacific, and 100,000 in other areas). Over 550 ships, including battleships, aircraft carriers, hospital ships, transports, and cargo vessels—and the British liner *Queen*

---

[1] *Final Report of the Chief of Staff, United States Army, to the Secretary of the Army, 7 February 1948*, p. 1.

[2] *First Report of the Secretary of Defense, 1948*, p. 59.

Mary—served as troop carriers during this period. Foreign brides added to the Army's responsibilities for transporting people to the United States. Some 35,000 war brides and 15,000 children in the British Isles alone awaited transportation.

Repatriation of War Dead

In sharp contrast to activities that resulted generally in the happy reunion of soldiers and dependents was the Army's sensitive task of returning the war dead to the United States or arranging permanent burial abroad. Throughout the war teams had been at work recovering the bodies of dead soldiers, and long after the shooting war stopped search teams in Burma still had to defend themselves against local attacks. Expeditions into remote mountain areas, through jungles, and across deserts were necessary to find the victims of air crashes. Even in this task international politics interfered. The Russians halted American searches for war dead in the Soviet zone of Austria in September 1947. Teams got into Poland, but when the program was completed elsewhere by 30 June 1949, clearance had not yet been forthcoming for entry into Lithuania or into the Soviet Union.

Shortages of steel for the manufacture of caskets delayed the repatriation schedule, and it was not until 10 October 1947 that the first mortuary ship arrived at San Francisco. By the next May twelve Army ships were in this service, and within a year over 71,000 remains had been returned. Under the law setting up the program, the decision as to whether a soldier's body should be returned to the United States or whether it should be given permanent burial in an oversea cemetery was left to the next of kin.

Approximately two-thirds of those replying to the War Department's letters requested repatriation. By mid-1949, over 150,000 war dead had been returned.

Disposal of Surplus Property

Problems and Policies

The return of oversea troops to the United States and the movement and discharge of men though a gigantic logistical undertaking was perhaps less significant logistically than the effects of the rapid demobilization of personnel on the handling of the vast quantities of surplus matériel. The Army's point system, under which a soldier accumulated credit toward his discharge on the basis of length of service, overseas service, campaign stars, decorations, and dependent children, bore no relationship to the integrity of units and little to the needs of the Army. The infantry had taken a high percentage of casualties in combat, limiting the opportunities of many for winning campaign stars and decorations, and shortening their service overseas. The consequent rate of turnover in the infantry resulted in fewer accumulated points. As a result, service troops, who had a lower rate of turnover, found themselves with relatively higher point credits, which made them eligible for early discharge. This meant the loss of skilled technicians and the disintegration of essential service units at the very time the Army was facing what were, in some ways, its greatest logistical problems of the war. "Only those present in the units at the time will know the disastrous effect of the demobilization program on supply and maintenance activities. Before we were through officers were performing the duties of mechanics and everybody was doing what they could to save the situation." [3]

Japanese acceptance of United Nations surrender terms of 14 August 1945 caught the Army without systematic plans for types and quantities of matériel that should be returned to the United States. When the Chief of Staff, shortly after the capitulation, indicated an intention for more rapid demobilization than had been previously considered, Army Service Forces was just beginning a study of the problem of returning supplies and equipment. Theater commanders were left in a difficult position: if they shipped out supplies immediately, without further instructions, they were likely to tie up valuable shipping with cargo not needed in the United States; if they waited for completion of the ASF study, outloading activities in Europe would be practically suspended from about 15 September to some time in November, while troop strength (and thus the capability of handling the matériel) would be rapidly decreasing. Already troops were being moved out of the European and Mediterranean theaters faster than were supplies and equipment. As of August 1945 total stocks in the MTO amounted to an estimated five million tons, while those in the European theater came to another twenty-four million tons. About one million tons a month could be shipped from European ports. By the spring of 1946 ETO forces were down to occupation strength, but they were concentrated in Germany far from the major ports where outshipments could be handled.

In the Pacific an ambitious roll-up plan

to gather up supplies scattered over the Pacific islands and bring them in to bases near service units and close to civilian markets began in July 1945. Armed with lists of civilian-type goods most needed in the United States, teams set to work on Guadacanal and New Caledonia; and later moved to New Guinea, the Philippines, Okinawa, Iwo Jima, and finally Japan. During the first five months of 1946, 289 ships arrived at the San Francisco Port of Embarkation with cargoes of equipment (mostly ordnance) from the Pacific. But here, too, the depletion of units overtook the collection of matériel, and little could be done just then to salvage great quantities of goods left behind.

The quantities of equipment and supplies on hand when the shooting stopped were beyond imagination. Inventories showed Army Service Forces and Army Air Forces supplies having respective procurement costs of $14.6 billion and $3.9 billion in oversea theaters alone. Procurement value of the Army's world-wide stocks of personal property, exclusive of Air Force property, amounted to $31.464 billion. Ammunition, tanks, and gasoline drums; telephone wire, jeeps, machine tools, and bulldozers; canteens, shirts, shoes, coats, and tentage; airplanes, boats, and watches; and thousands of other items from the Elbe River to Calcutta and from Detroit to West Africa awaited disposition. Moreover, the Army had on its hands the fixed installations—airfields, seaports, storage facilities, railway equipment, camps, hospitals—that had been needed to carry out its world-wide activities. These included 2,871 installations, which had cost an estimated $3.4 billion, just in areas outside the continental United States.

It can be assumed that any sizable war will leave large quantities of surplus prop-

---

[3] Maj. Gen. James M. Gavin, quoted in DA Pamphlet 20–210, *History of Personnel Demobilization in the United States Army* (July, 1952), prepared by Maj. John C. Sparrow, p. 274.

erty to be disposed of when it ends. But certain factors and conditions operating in World War II contributed to an especially large amount of leftover stocks. The very magnitude of the mobilization made it clear that demobilization would be a tremendous task. To effectively supply an army that reached a strength of eight and one-third million men would in itself contribute to a substantial surplus upon the demobilization of that force. The build-up over a period of five years added considerably to that surplus. Additional surplus resulted from the fact that early in the war the Army had fallen heir to the property of such agencies as the Civilian Conservation Corps and the National Youth Administration when they were liquidated, and so found itself with certain property not suitable to military purposes once something better was available. A more important factor was the global extent of the conflict. Because supplies had to be stockpiled in widely separated theaters of operations, and carried over long supply routes, the pipelines had to be kept filled with several months' supplies. When hostilities ended—at a time that could not be calculated in advance—most of those quantities in the pipelines of the Army's worldwide supply system immediately became surplus. Other more or less unique sources of surplus were the unconsumed and returnable lend-lease goods that had been delivered to Allied governments and the great bulk of captured enemy matériel resulting from the complete collapse of Germany and Japan. Finally, the widespread tendency to overstock and oversupply was a real factor in the creation of unprecedented surpluses. American forces in Europe in 1944–45 had more surplus than the total supplies of the AEF in 1917–18. If the Army actually did not need as many as 123

million pairs of shoes (some 14.4 pairs per man figured on the basis of its peak strength of 8.3 million men) or if each soldier would not wear out something over nine herringbone jackets during the four years of war, then the supply of those items contributed to surplus from the very outset.

As after World War I, the disposal of surplus property posed a dilemma: to sell at nominal rates, which would tend to depress markets and bring criticism from affected merchants, or to destroy equipment or permit it to deteriorate and bring down accusations of waste. Again as with post-World War I property disposal, despite precautions some sales did depress markets, some matériel did go to waste, and some did get into the hands of fraudulent operators.

Another problem military commanders and government officials faced was that of deciding what should be saved and what should be disposed of. This, too, had been a problem after World War I, but was now multiplied by the inconceivably greater quantities of property. Moreover, once again, obsolescence and maintenance costs had to be balanced against future requirements that could not be foretold with any degree of accuracy.

The Surplus Property Act of 1944, which governed property disposals until 1949, laid down so many objectives that it was difficult for any agency to cover them all. Disposal was not a matter of simple business transactions, though officials received frequent counsel that they should adopt business methods in all their dealings. Disposal agencies were "to obtain for the Government, as nearly as possible, the fair value of surplus property" only after they had taken care to pursue these objectives: (1) make the most effective use of the property for war purposes; (2) aid the re-establishment of a peacetime economy of free, independent, private enterprise; (3) facilitate the transition from wartime to peacetime production; (4) discourage monopoly and strengthen small business; (5) foster family-type farming; (6) give returning veterans an opportunity to establish themselves in business, professions, and agriculture; (7) encourage postwar employment opportunities; (8) discourage sales to speculators; (9) develop foreign markets and mutually advantageous international economic relations; (10) make a wide distribution of commodities to consumers at fair prices; (11) insure a broad and equitable distribution of surplus property; (12) protect free markets from uncontrolled dumping; (13) use the normal channels of trade and commerce so far as possible in disposing of surplus property; (14) promote production, employment, and utilization of resources; (15) stimulate new independent enterprises; (16) prevent, "insofar as possible," unusual and excessive profits out of surplus property; (17) dispose of the property as promptly as feasible without fostering monopoly or unduly disturbing the economy; and (18) dispose of government-owned transportation facilities to promote adequate and economical transportation and of other major facilities for similarly advantageous uses. Which of these objectives were to have highest priorities was not clear.

The War Department on 14 September 1945 announced a policy to the effect that surplus would be that property on hand which exceeded the sum of the following requirements: (1) consumption during the demobilization periods; (2) the Peacetime Army Supply Program; (3) Western Hemisphere Defense Program; (4) approved supplies for the Philippine Army; (5) the War Department Reserve; and (6) other requirements currently approved. The

policy invited almost immediate differences of opinion. As expected, the argument became one of liberal declarations of surplus versus saving for future needs.

During the period of consideration of these policies, a note to the Chief of Staff pointed out with disarming simplicity that the whole complex problem might easily be approached from a completely different direction:

Present delays have resulted in no small degree from a lack of basic information within the War Department as to what is to be retained, and what declared surplus. There are rumors of a "Maxwell Study" and a "Hodges Board." Neither are necessary, because there are perfectly definite limitations on what can be retained. These limitations are the number and size of depots that can be maintained in the future, together with maintenance of their stocks, on appropriations which can be reasonably expected. Give a Chief of Supply Service the space he can have, and if he can't tell what should be put in it, no one else can.

This space allotment should be made by G–4 after getting a figure from the Budget Branch.[4]

How much of the total inventory of supplies in any theater might become surplus depended upon War Department policies and commitments for the postwar period. At first much of the emphasis was on the return of property to the United States. Officers facing the difficult problem of surplus disposal in the United States itself, however, soon came to doubt the wisdom of bringing back more property without first considering its future use. In general, the theater commander could determine what property was excess to the needs of the

_____

[4] Note received by CofS, 30 Dec 45, sub: Proposed Method of Disposing of Surplus Property, forwarded with Memo WDCSA 400.703 (30 Jan 46), G–4 400.703 (IV).

theater, and report that determination to the Army Service Forces, or, for property pertaining to aircraft, to Army Air Forces. Property previously classified obsolete by ASF or AAF could be declared surplus without further reference, and the same procedure would hold for perishable subsistence and for certain classes of items that the commanding generals of the ASF and AAF might list from time to time. Other instructions called for the immediate return to the United States of certain classes of supplies whenever they were found to be excess to theater needs.

Overseas Disposal

Largest of the foreign bulk sales was made to France by an agreement signed on 28 May 1946, which involved the sale of property having an estimated original cost of over $1.13 billion. A separate sale agreement signed with France in July 1946 disposed of all surplus ammunition remaining in France, plus 50,000 long tons to be shipped from Germany and 2,500 long tons in Belgium that had been declared surplus specifically for the purpose of balancing French rearmament requirements. These sales practically completed sales operations with the French Government.

A bulk sale to the United Kingdom, including Army surplus having an original cost of about $238 million was concluded on 6 December 1945. Similar sales followed to Belgium and Italy and, finally, to Germany.

General Joseph T. McNarney, Commanding General, United States Forces, European Theater (USFET), saw the possibility of transferring quantities of Army surplus goods to the German economy in order to meet serious shortages of food, clothing, medical supplies, and other essential items. Holding that the action was necessary in order to prevent the spread of disease and unrest, he found a precedent in the policies General MacArthur was at that time carrying out in Japan. General McNarney decided to transfer surplus goods to the German economy in return for quantitative receipts signed by the minister-presidents of the German States for which military government would record the value in dollars as a future obligation to the United States to be paid from profits of German exports whenever a favorable balance of trade might be restored. Both the Treasury and the State Department objected to this procedure. The Treasury Department maintained that such an arrangement was beyond the authority of the military commander, for, in effect, it amounted to the extension of a loan to Germany and to supplementing the Congressional appropriation for the occupation. The State Department said the Army was disposing of surplus in violation of the Surplus Property Act, which assigned this function to the Office of the Foreign Liquidation Commissioner (OFLC). Another objection was to a War Department decision that quantitative receipts did not constitute valid credit vouchers for relief from accountability for the property so transferred.

Ironically, these difficulties arose chiefly because General McNarney and Lt. Gen. Lucius D. Clay, the military governor under his command, sought to obtain some obligation for repayment to the United States for property being transferred to the Germans. Technically, they could have held that the property was not surplus at all—it was needed to carry out the occupation mission, it was not "property in excess of theater requirements." Actually, this was the position USFET assumed when Maj. Gen. Carter B. Magruder, G–4 of the European theater, notified the Central Field Commissioner of OFLC in Paris that the establishment of a self-supporting economy in Germany would be given priority over the declaration of surplus "under any circumstances."

Final close-out of Office of the Foreign Liquidation Commissioner in Paris came on 15 May 1949. Property still unsold that the Army had declared to OFLC went back to the Army as unsalable. The heads of the various military missions in Europe received instructions on handling any inquiries arising from OFLC operations. One major account remained open. An amendment signed 12 May 1949 extended the 1946 agreement with Belgium, under which that government accepted surplus property for resale on the basis of a 50 percent share of the proceeds, to 1 July 1951. By that time the principal interest of the United States would be not in the sale, but in the recovery of some of the huge stocks it had disposed of in Europe.

Although property left over after the battles in the Pacific and the Far East was less abundant than that in Europe, it was far more scattered, and much more difficult to get to. When V–J Day came, huge quantities of supplies and equipment had been stockpiled on Guam, Saipan, Iwo Jima, and in the Philippines to support the planned invasion of Japan. Other quantities lay in earlier battle and staging areas from Hawaii to Guadalcanal and from New Caledonia to Australia. Then came demobilization. Lack of experienced men was more serious in the Pacific than in Europe, for the battle against deterioration was more intense. Tens of thousands of trucks and thousands of artillery pieces, as well as tanks,

ammunition, accessories, and supplies simply had to be left behind. Jungle rot and curious natives soon set about patiently decimating the complicated machines they suddenly found at their complete disposal. Other quantities were declared to the Foreign Liquidation Commissioner (to the Surplus Property Division of the Department of the Interior in Hawaii and Alaska) and sold, some went into reserve stocks of the Far East Command, some went to relieve distress in both liberated and occupied areas, and some was returned to the United States. Stevedores shifted from one island to another in the South Pacific area to ship out property, and by July 1946 that area was being closed out. Then property from the outlying Hawaiian Islands, from the Gilberts, and from the Marshalls had to be brought in to Oahu.

While not always the most profitable, bulk sales certainly were the most convenient; and often, when time was short and personnel lacking, it was the only practicable method of selling large quantities of surplus property. The Office of the Foreign Liquidation Commissioner resorted to this expedient in negotiating major sales to India, China, and the Philippines as well as in smaller sales to Australia and other countries.

Conclusions

Disposition of surplus property was a continuing activity, both during war and during peacetime operations. But the magnitude of the problem falling to the Army after V–J Day brought about a number of changes in procedure. First was the decentralization of authority to act at local depots and stations. Further, the demand for speed reduced the earlier procedure of circulariz-

A Once Busy Dock and Warehouse Area of Finschhafen, New Guinea, *as it appeared late in 1946.*

ing other services to find out if they needed a particular item before it was declared to the disposal agency. This led to one of those obvious difficulties the Army dreaded most—the likelihood that one service would go out to buy items in the market while another service was disposing of the same types of items as surplus, and, even worse, the possibility of the Army's buying back some of its own surplus. Procurement regulations did lay down the rule that technical services must offer their excess property to other services and stipulated "care will be taken to avoid purchasing property obtainable through disposal agencies from commercial sources." Army Air Forces suggested that a clause should be inserted in procurement contracts that would require a cost breakdown to show any use of surplus property. The chief of the Readjustment Branch, Service, Supply and Procurement (SS&P), doubted the legal right to do this, but he thought it might be possible to demand a statement that any finished item obtained from a contractor was not one that the contractor had obtained from the government. He suggested that the only sure way to prevent such conditions would be to insist upon thorough screening of items before they were declared surplus, though it might help for the War Assets Administration to require all buyers to certify that what they bought would not be resold to a government agency.

On the face of it, these suggestions seemed to be examples of lessons a junior officer often learned early in his career—that sometimes in the Army the paper is more important than the deed, that some commanders are more anxious to protect themselves by requiring a bundle of certificates than they are to actually do what the certificates purport to testify. This was a case of committing a second error to cover up the first. It appeared to be more important to avoid criticism than to get equipment at the lowest price. If the same quality item could be had from a surplus property dealer at a lower price than from anyone else, why should it not have been preferable to buy the article from him? The answer, of course, was that these staff officers had learned the overriding importance of maintaining the confidence of the Congress and of the public. In order to keep ammunition from the hands of critics whose principal purpose in life seemed to be to undermine that confidence, whether or not justified, it sometimes was more important to avoid the appearance of extravagance than to avoid extravagance itself, even at the expense, at times, of what would actually have been greater economy.

Termination of War Contracts

When the fighting ended, war industries still were near peak production. As long as they continued in operation thereafter, they would be adding to the great quantities of surplus which immediately began to accumulate. To avoid that unnecessary production, to reduce military expenditures as

much as possible, to supply badly needed civilian goods, and to overcome threats of unemployment during the period of readjustment, it was necessary to settle war contracts as quickly and as expeditiously as possible and to get the plants back into civilian activities.

Within five minutes after the announcement of the surrender of Japan on the evening of 14 August 1945, the technical services released previously prepared telegrams directing the procurement districts to terminate war contracts. Two days later some 60,000 technical services contracts, involving commitments of $7.3 billion had been canceled. The addition of Air Forces contract cancellations to those of the technical services brought the total War Department cancellations for August to 70,848, with a total canceled commitment value of nearly $15 billion. The previous peak, following V–E Day in May, had been less than a third as much. By the end of September the War Department had on its hands a contract settlement job involving commitments of $24 billion. At that time the War Department had almost 22,000 persons working full time at the task, plus another 8,000 who worked on settlement assignments for short periods during August and September. A year later the job was virtually complete.

Termination of Lend-Lease

Liquidation of lend-lease operations presented problems hardly less complex than other major aspects of matériel demobilization. The understanding was that the recipient governments would, at the end of the war emergency, return only those articles the President should determine "to be useful in the defense of the United States of America or of the Western Hemisphere or to be otherwise of use to the United States of America." [5]   In commenting on the third extension of the Lend-Lease Act in April 1945, President Truman promised that lend-lease aid would be carried on "until the unconditional surrender or complete defeat of Germany and Japan." [6]   This statement seemed to be reassuring news to Allied nations depending upon that aid, for it was assumed that the war against Japan would probably continue for eighteen months after the surrender of Germany.   On the contrary, Truman's remark should have been taken as a warning against the time when lend-lease would cease.   As the end of hostilities appeared to be approaching, early termination of lend-lease had been hinted, but apparently the first positive statement to that effect was in the letters of 20 August 1945 from Leo Crowley, Director of the Foreign Economic Administration, to the heads of all foreign purchasing commissions in Washington, notifying them of President Truman's decision to terminate lend-lease operations.   In ordering its abrupt end, President Truman directed that all outstanding contracts be canceled, "except where Allied Governments agree to take them over, or where it is in the interest of the United States to complete them." [7]   Administration spokesmen hastened to explain that this did not mean the immediate cutting off of supplies; the only difference was

that after V–J Day recipient governments would have to pay cash or obtain credit for the goods and services they received.   The Allies were to be given an opportunity to buy the goods in the lend-lease pipeline, that is goods then on order and in the process of manufacture, on the basis of payment in thirty annual installments with interest at $2\frac{2}{3}$ percent.   This, however, was small comfort to the governments, particularly Great Britain, who were caught in the midst of redeploying forces to the Far East, and who were operating on the assumption that lend-lease would continue for another year and a half.

Protests against the abrupt cancellation of lend-lease quickly reached Washington, but President Truman held firm to his announced policy.   In a special message to Congress on 6 September, the President reiterated that policy, but, referring to the settlement of lend-lease accounts, he recognized that the Allies could not be expected to pay dollars "for the overwhelming portion of lend-lease obligations."   Administration spokesmen, unable to understand the surprise of lend-lease recipients at its termination as of V–J Day, referred to statements made by President Roosevelt in November 1944 and by Leo Crowley in February 1945, which made it clear that lend-lease would end when the war ended. At the same time President Truman was urging Congress "not to end the war status hastily." [8]   When the war ended, of course, depended upon the purpose in question.

In the consideration of settlements of lend-lease accounts, the Secretary of War

---

[5] British Master Agreement, 23 February 1942, printed in Appendix V, *Twenty-first Report to Congress on Lend-Lease Operations*, House Doc 432, 79th Cong., 2d sess., November 17, 1947.

[6] Statement of the President, released 17 Apr 45, "Public Papers of the President of the United States," *Harry S. Truman, April 12 to December 31, 1945* (Washington, 1961), p. 7.

[7] *The New York Times* (late city edition), August 22, 1945.

[8] Felix Belair, Jr., in *The New York Times* (late city edition), September 9, 1945; *The New York Times* (late city edition), August 22, 1945; *The New York Times* (late city edition), August 25, 1945.

indicated to the Foreign Economic Administrator that the interest of the War Department was limited to the physical return of those lend-lease items (1) needed for the Army's own supply requirements, (2) to be returned or destroyed for reasons of technical security, or (3) needed for reasons of "strategic security," presumably to keep them from being used to build up potential enemies. Later surveys by the Intelligence Division of Army Service Forces, and by Army Air Forces, indicated that the recovery of lend-lease articles in the interest of technical security or national security would not be warranted. Although the United States, in the lend-lease master agreements with the various Allied governments, reserved the right of recapture of items not "destroyed, lost, or consumed," policy generally was not to exercise that right. Recipient governments paid only for nonmilitary lend-lease having value for peacetime purposes. Lend-lease military equipment generally was included in the agreements covering disposal of surplus property.

Lend-lease settlements also involved the disposal of reverse lend-lease, or reciprocal aid—property foreign governments had provided for the United States. Title to such property was assumed to remain with the supplying government, and was not to be disposed of without first obtaining the consent and instructions of the supplying government. Oversea commanders had authority to determine any reverse lend-lease property in their commands to be surplus and to return it without any further reference. These properties included real estate and fixed installations, with the exception of airfields having an investment value of over $100,000 and radio facilities of the Army Command and Administrative Network, which were to be reported to the Chief of Engineers before disposal.

Transfers of surplus property and lend-lease goods made up but a part of the total United States aid to over fifty countries in the period between 1 July 1945 and 31 December 1946. That assistance—including cash loans, transfers of goods and services on terms of deferred payment, and grants in money and in kind—totaled $14.3 billion. Only $7.8 billion of that amount actually was spent in that time, but the commitment remained to be added to other assistance that would be granted in succeeding years.[9] Foreign military aid would continue to be a dominant consideration in the Army's logistical policies as it began reorganizing for the postwar period.[10]

---

[9] Brookings Institution, *Major Problems in United States Foreign Policy, 1947* (Washington: The Brookings Institution, 1947), pp. 165–66; *Annual Report of the Secretary of the Army, 1948* (Washington, 1949), p. 126.

[10] For sources upon which Part IV is based see Bibliography, pages 723–28.

PART FIVE

THE SHADOW OF CONFLICT

CHAPTER XXXII

Not Peace, Not War

After the successful conclusion of World War II, Old Army men could permit themselves to look forward with nostalgic yearning to the early exchange of shelter tents and foxholes for brick barracks, jungles and hedgerows for trim lawns, endless mud for smooth pavements, beachheads for swimming pools, and night combat patrols for Saturday morning inspections. They could look forward to a return to "normal peacetime functions" of housekeeping, paper work, care and cleaning of equipment, guard duty, and training. Sentimental attachments for certain features of the Old Army persisted outside the Army in such actions as that of Congress to prolong the quartermaster remount service for procuring horses even though no horse cavalry saw action in World War II and that arm had become wholly obsolete.

Housekeeping was, of course, no end in itself, but it consumed a great deal of both time and resources in the postwar military establishment. Rapid demobilization in itself created unprecedented problems in logistics, but while that went on other activities relating more directly to the maintenance of an army on a permanent footing could not be ignored. The decline in activities for the logistical support of the Army was not proportional to the decline in its troop strength. It was true that the logistical services would have but a fraction of the troops to support that they had had during the war, but it also was clear that the peacetime Army would be far larger than any the United States had previously maintained. This meant immediate demands for permanent quarters and facilities where temporary wartime structures were insufficient. At the same time, many logistical activities were not directly related to the troop strength of the moment, but more directly to a potential force to be mobilized in the event of another emergency. Indeed, the problem of storing and caring for weapons and equipment was much greater, rather than less, than it had been during full mobilization. As the Chief of Ordnance put it, "If the Army was reduced to ten men and a boy, the same amount of work we are doing now would be necessary." [1] With an Army of 10,000,000 men most of the equipment would be in the hands of the troops, and it would be their job to take care of it; reduced to a million men, the Army had to find ways of taking care of its equipment in huge lots.

Reorganizations

Army Reorganization of 1946

Although a military organization presumably should be geared for war at any time, the Army generally has found it necessary

---

[1] Maj. Gen. E. S. Hughes, Chief of Ordnance, Testimony Before the *Hearings of the House Subcommittee on Appropriations,* 14 March 1947, 80th Cong., 1st sess., p. 963.

to undertake a major reorganization upon entering a war, and again upon emerging into peacetime. This had reached the point where peacetime activities had been considered the "normal" state of affairs, while war, presumably the principal reason for the existence of a military establishment, seemed to be regarded as an unfortunate interruption of the normal way of doing things. It could be expected, then, that the Army, sheathing its sword after the battles of World War II, would have to effect a fundamental reorganization in order to return to its peacetime pursuits. But there was to be no settling down to an undisturbed routine of soldiering. It soon became evident that war had given way not to peace, but to "cold war," and in its inevitable postwar reorganization, the Army had to maintain the means to support worldwide policies. Such responsibilities had been increasing since 1898, but now for the first time they would be carried by the United States as the leading world power, confronting at once the major threat to its position and a direct threat to its own security.

As was the case after World War I, a board of officers, this time under Lt. Gen. Alexander M. Patch, was convened to study and make recommendations on the postwar organization of the War Department and the Army. Giving little consideration to the type of functional organization proposed in 1943, the board recommended an organization which in a number of ways returned to the structural arrangement of 1939. However, it agreed to a principle which repudiated the old concept that "a General Staff should be restricted to matters of high policy and planning and must not operate." Holding that such a concept led to the "devitalization of the General Staff during wartime," [2] the board frankly recommended that the heads of the major divisions of the General Staff be redesignated "directors" in place of the former title of Assistant Chiefs of Staff, with the understanding that they had to operate and direct so that orders and instructions would be issued and carried out as intended. This and most of the other recommendations of the Patch Board formed the basis for the reorganization, which went into effect 11 June 1946.

Most significant was the attempt to centralize logistical staff responsibilities. Army Service Forces was abolished, and its staff responsibilities in supply and service activities were transferred to the Director of Service, Supply and Procurement—the new division of the General Staff which replaced the old G–4. The functions of the Logistics Group of the Operations Division were also transferred to SS&P. The technical services retained their full identity and individual responsibilities as before, but reported on matters of service, supply, and procurement to the Director of Service, Supply and Procurement. For the most part, this arrangement was not much different from the one that had prevailed before the war, for the technical services again reported directly to the other divisions of the General Staff on matters falling within their areas of interest. But there was one important difference. The short-circuit to the Under Secretary was eliminated by the proviso that the services should go through SS&P on procurement matters. The Director of SS&P, however, as the commanding general of Army Service Forces had done before him, reported directly to the Under Secretary on procurement matters, and to

[2] Report of Board of Officers on Reorganization of the War Department, 18 October 1945, Tab B.

the Chief of Staff on other matters. The other divisions of the General Staff followed the new pattern.

Army Reorganization of 1950

For the Army, reorganization in 1946, and that of 1948 as well, represented but interim measures pending a more complete reorganization that would have its legal basis in a new act of Congress. The Army Organization Act of 1950 made permanent the Stimson procedure by which all authority was assigned to the Secretary with authority to redelegate to the Under Secretary or to either of the Assistant Secretaries.

Perhaps the greatest difficulty in establishing, and then maintaining and expanding, the General Staff to fill its role was the apparent fear of Congress that it might lead to military dictatorship. It seemed that most of the fears sprang from the name: the automatic response to the words *General Staff* seemed to be, *Prussian General Staff*. One congressman stated very frankly, "If you folks down there would just forget the word 'staff' and 'general' and call it something else, you wouldn't have anywhere near the trouble you are getting about staffing your people. . . . And my evidence to support that statement is that there is no limitation on the personnel in the Office of the Chief of Naval Operations." [3] Because of the legal restriction on the number of officers who could be assigned to the General Staff, it was necessary to resort to the subterfuge of detailing officers to "duty with" the General Staff. While the law allowed a General Staff of 102, at one time about 1,100 actually were serving with it.

Against suggestions that an organization similar to Army Service Forces was necessary to exercise command over the technical services or that the traditional services should be abolished in favor of a functionalized structure in which only one agency was responsible for procurement, another for supply storage and distribution, and another for research and development, Lt. Gen. Thomas B. Larkin believed that the technical services system, under a strong G–4 office, could be made to work satisfactorily. After a little over a year as Secretary of Defense, Robert A. Lovett was not so sure. Shortly before leaving office in January 1953, he stated:

Of these seven technical services, all are in one degree or another in the business of design, procurement, production, supply, distribution, warehousing, and issue. Their functions over-lap in a number of items, thus adding substantial complications to the difficult problem of administration and control.

It has always amazed me that the system worked at all and the fact that it works rather well is a tribute to the inborn capacity of team-work in the average American.

A reorganization of the technical services would be no more painful than backing into a buzz saw, but I believe that it is long overdue.[4]

Logistical Commands

The supply of oversea theaters from the United States continued to operate under the types of organization developed during World War II. When a communications zone section was needed, a headquarters would be formed at the last minute, under a table of distribution drawn for the immediate purpose, from people who happened to be thrown together on the job.

---

[3] *Hearings Before Subcommittee of the Committee on Armed Services*, HR 187, 1–20 March 1950, 81st Cong., 2d sess., pp. 6052–53.

[4] Ltr, Robert A. Lovett to the President (Truman), 18 Nov. 52, p. 11. Mimeo copy in OCMH.

The result was confusion and wasted effort. The procedure, moreover, led to temptations toward "empire building" since there were no permanent tables of organization.

In 1944 G–4 asked the Command and General Staff School at Fort Leavenworth to study the problem with a view to improving the situation. The response was a recommendation for the organization of a logistical division. Just as the infantry division was a basic unit of combined combat arms, the logistical division would be a basic unit of combined technical and administrative services. It would have organic service and administrative units numbering approximately 26,000 men to provide communications zone support for a reinforced corps. The proposals further envisaged a logistical corps with a strength of some 67,000 men for the support of a field army.

The staff study proposals were carried out, though the units were designated "logistical commands." They were to have as their principal mission the operation of a section (base, intermediate, or advance) of a communications zone. Under exceptional conditions it was contemplated that they might operate in a combat zone (perhaps as an army service command), or as an administration and rehabilitation unit in a stricken area where civil means had broken down.

Reserve Components

What amounted to a somewhat special aspect of building up reserve supplies for emergency use was logistic support for the National Guard, Organized Reserve Corps, and Reserve Officers' Training Corps. Equipment issued to National Guard and Reserve units would be in responsible hands for care and storage; and, to the extent that

it would fill their mobilization needs, it was a part of the mobilization reserve stocks.

The greater the reduction in the Regular Army after World War II, the greater was the presumed reliance on Reserve Components, and the results of logistical support for the Reserve program would be twofold: to the degree that peacetime training of Reserve units would save wartime training, there would be a concomitant accumulation of reserve equipment, and, upon emergency mobilization, there would be a reduction in training time for raw recruits and officer candidates. The Reserve program, then, was a kind of stockpiling of men and materials. For the units to be more than paper organizations and to have real significance for national defense they had to have some degree of mobilization readiness, and for this they had to have a complete and continuous training program and the equipment with which to train and to form a basis for rapid expansion and for emergency missions.

The likelihood of emergency was, indeed, the *raison d'être* of the Reserve Components, and their total logistical accumulations—equipment, space, and training time —added to the Army's capability of maintaining the national security. Moreover, the physical, current requirements of an existing organization were more easily justified to Congress and the public than equivalent stocks destined to be set aside in some vaguely defined stockpile for some vaguely defined emergency. Indirectly as well as directly, therefore, the Reserve program significantly affected matériel reserves.

Unification

The experience of World War II had brought into sharp focus demands for military reorganization far beyond the simple return to peacetime "normalcy." This experience had demonstrated, apparently to the satisfaction of most Americans who concerned themselves with the problems of military security, the need for unification of the armed forces. Several factors—some long antedating World War II, some growing out of that conflict, but all gaining impetus from it—influenced various segments of opinion toward support of that objective. Briefly, they can be summarized to include the following: (1) Pearl Harbor; (2) the wartime organization of the Joint Chiefs of Staff; (3) the generally successful unified commands in oversea theaters; (4) the increasing importance of the airplane in warfare and the growing desire of the Army Air Forces for independence; and (5) the apparent waste and inefficiency resulting from the duplicating activities of the separate logistical systems of the Army and the Navy.

Approved by the President on 26 July, the National Security Act of 1947 established machinery for co-ordinating military policy with other policies of the government affecting national security, and, while providing for a Department of the Army, Department of the Navy, and Department of the Air Force as separate executive departments, brought them together in a National Military Establishment under a Secretary of Defense.

Ironically, James Forrestal, who as Secretary of the Navy had opposed strong central authority over the National Military Establishment, became the first Secretary of Defense, and upon his shoulders fell the task of making work the defective machinery he had helped to create. He went about his job with determination, resourcefulness, and hard work, and it was not long before he was recommending changes. Rob-

ert P. Patterson as Secretary of War had insisted from the beginning on the necessity for even more effective central control. He had called for abolition of the National Military Establishment structure with its three executive departments in favor of a single executive department—a Department of Defense—under a Secretary of Defense with broad powers to manage and direct its activities. Furthermore, he had called for a Chief of Staff, with an armed forces general staff, responsible to the Secretary of Defense. After his resignation in July 1947, Patterson continued to carry great weight as a disinterested authority, and his recommendations together with those of Secretary of Defense Forrestal resulted in the National Security Act Amendments of 1949. These amendments converted the National Military Establishment into the Department of Defense, broadened the powers of the Secretary of Defense, modified the membership and functions of certain of the other organs of national security, provided for a chairman of the Joint Chiefs of Staff, and provided for setting up a performance budget and rules for uniform property and financial management. The military departments ceased to have separate cabinet status.

At the apex of the organization for national security was the National Security Council, which made up, for the first time, a kind of permanent war cabinet to co-ordinate matters affecting foreign policy, military policy, and national resources at the highest governmental level. Under the amended National Security Act, the National Security Council was composed of the President, the Vice President, the Secretary of State, the Secretary of Defense, and the Chairman of the National Security Resources Board.

The National Security Resources Board was an economic mobilization planning agency. It estimated the needs of war, appraising the resources that would be available for meeting those needs, measuring deficiencies in resources as against requirements, and determining measures necessary to overcome those deficiencies. The board's duty was to advise the President on the coordination of military, industrial, and civilian mobilization. It was not a part of the Department of Defense. As an advisory agency for the President, the National Security Resources Board had no operating functions, but it was anticipated that its Mobilization Planning Staff would become operational in the event of mobilization. Thus the Office of the Director of Production was designed to become an Office of War Production; the Office of the Director of Transportation and Storage was to be a nucleus for an Office of War Transportation; the Manpower Division of the Office of the Director of Human Resources was intended to be the nucleus for an Office of War Manpower; and under the Director of Economic Management, the Economic Stabilization Division was intended to grow into an Office of Economic Stabilization, and the Foreign Economics Division was to become an Office of Economic Warfare. Clearly World War II experience was being used as the basis for planning future economic mobilization, an important advance over both World War I and World War II when mobilization began with little such planning and when, by trial and error, the organizations of the economic mobilization agencies changed frequently even while attempting to get their activities started.

Under the Unification Act of 1947 the Munitions Board, composed of a chairman appointed from civilian life by the President and an under secretary or assistant secretary from each of the three military departments, superseded the Army-Navy Munitions Board. The new organization's functions in assisting the Secretary of Defense in the discharge of his responsibilities and in supporting strategic and logistic plans prepared by the Joint Chiefs of Staff remained essentially the same as those of the old board. Those duties were more sharply defined, however, and in some respects were broadened. In particular, the new board was to be concerned not only with military aspects of industrial mobilization, production, and procurement, but with supply distribution plans and policies as well.

The wartime Office of Scientific Research and Development and the Joint Committee on New Weapons and Equipment of the Joint Chiefs of Staff, both under the chairmanship of Vannevar Bush, were the direct antecedents of the postwar organization for scientific research for national security. The Research and Development Board, established as a result of the Unification Act, had no laboratories of its own and did not undertake research projects on its own. The Army, Navy, and Air Force each conducted its own research and development program with its own appropriations. The job of the Research and Development Board was to supervise and co-ordinate individual service programs into an integrated program. Under the authority of the Secretary of Defense, the board could direct a service to modify a program or to undertake new projects. By keeping in close touch with the projects of all the services, it was able to eliminate duplication and to speed up research in one service by making use of a discovery found in another. Its review of the research and development budgets of the military departments for the Secretary of Defense permitted close supervision of the whole program.

The Joint Chiefs of Staff organization was the nerve center of national defense unification. The general committee structure and the ways of operating that had grown up during the war generally persisted through the new organization. Perhaps the most significant change, aside from the addition of a chairman, was the creation of a Joint Staff to work full time under the Joint Chiefs. By the Act of 1947, the size of the Joint Staff was limited to 100 officers, but the amendments of 1949 permitted 210 officers.

Under the Director of the Joint Staff, who was executive officer of the JCS organization, the Joint Staff was divided into three groups—Joint Strategic Plans Group, Joint Intelligence Group, and Joint Logistics Plans Group. Each served as the full-time working staff for the corresponding committee. These particular committees each had four members—a deputy director of the Joint Staff and a representative from each of the military services. Thus the Joint Logistics Plans Committee included the Deputy Director of the Joint Staff for Logistics and logistic planning representatives from the staffs of the Army, Navy, and Air Force. This committee of part-time members had the responsibility of submitting logistics plans recommendations to the Joint Chiefs. They assigned the task of preparing papers and data to the full-time Joint Logistics Group of the Joint Staff which worked for them.

The growth of the committee system around the Joint Chiefs of Staff, which itself functioned as a committee, represented a fundamental difference between Army and Navy thinking. The Army generally had insisted upon single, clear-cut lines of authority and responsibility, with decisions resting upon one individual at each level who made that decision with the assistance of information and advice furnished by a competent staff. But perhaps resort to committees was the only practical way to bring together sincere and resolute men of different experience and contrary views.

"The creation of an efficient and clear-headed approach to the budget," wrote Secretary of Defense Forrestal to Hanson Baldwin in 1948, "is the greatest central problem of unification, and everything else, more or less, stems from it."[5] Here was where the Joint Chiefs of Staff would exercise a more and more important control over the armed services.

In accordance with recommendations of the Hoover Commission, the National Security Act amendments of 1949 provided that the military budgets should be converted from the agency budget to the cost-of-performance type of budget in which appropriations would be broken down not according to the particular individual agency handling a given matter, but according to functional programs and activities. To curb overdrafts and deficiencies during a fiscal year, appropriations for the year were to be available for commitment only after the Secretary of Defense had approved scheduled rates of obligation. The act authorized the establishment of working-capital funds for financing inventories of supplies and industrial or commercial types of activities providing common services within or among the departments and agencies of the Department of Defense. It set up management funds within each military department for the purpose of facilitating operations

---

[5] Walter Millis, ed., *The Forrestal Diaries* (New York: The Viking Press, 1951), p. 448.

financed by two or more appropriations where the costs could not be readily broken down according to the individual appropriations.

Unification did not imply any attempt to combine the supply services of the military departments, but the Secretary of Defense was interested in promoting uniformity in procedures where possible, and in improving co-operation between services in their supply and service activities. This co-operation included mainly the expansion of "common service" in which one department, out of its own budget, provided common services for either or both of the other departments, and of "cross-servicing" by which one department would provide service for another department under arrangements for payment out of appropriations of the receiving department. In November 1949 the Secretary of Defense directed the Munitions Board to develop, in keeping with the assignment of logistics responsibilities by the Joint Chiefs of Staff, a supply system for the Department of Defense. Each of the three military departments was to man and operate a supply system, but common policies, standards, and procedures would be followed where practicable.

Among the earliest and best known concrete examples of projects in unification occurred in the fields of transportation. In June 1948 the Air Force's Air Transport Command and the Naval Air Transport Service consolidated into the Military Air Transport Service to provide global air transportation for all the armed forces. Some time later the Army gave up its troop transport service in favor of the Navy's Military Sea Transportation Service, which would provide water transportation for all the military departments. Co-ordination of the use of private transportation facilities

in moving military personnel and supplies then came under another joint agency, the Military Traffic Service.

Division was, ironically, the first immediate consequence for the Army of national defense unification. The Army Air Forces had gained substantial operational autonomy during World War II, but the administrative and technical services supporting it had remained so intermeshed with those supporting the ground forces that major surgery was necessary to separate them. Thus, while one of the objectives of the National Security Act had been to reduce costs and increase efficiency by eliminating duplication, the immediate result, insofar as the Army and Air Force were concerned, was just the reverse. This "unified separation" meant, in fact, a tendency toward duplication of activities which previously had been consolidated. The Secretary of Defense was required to take steps to eliminate unnecessary duplication or overlapping in the fields of procurement, supply, transportation, storage, health, and research; at the same time he had to develop, by transfer, a third military department without disturbing the efficiency of either the Army or the Air Force.

Of activities in the field of logistics affected by Army-Air Force agreements, savings had been made as of 31 December 1948 in three items, while there had been an increase in costs for sixteen items. A report to the Secretary of Defense on elimination of overlapping and duplication of facilities and services for Fiscal Year 1949 estimated that savings resulting from those steps totalled $20 million for the year—of which $17 million would be recurring annual savings. Of this total, $9 million was attributed to adoption of a clothing credit system in both the Army and the Air Force

—which of course bore little relation to unification; on the contrary, the new Air Force uniform may later have added considerably to the total clothing costs. Moreover, nearly $1.7 million in savings was attributed to consolidation of services and facilities of local Army and Air Force activities—activities which need not have been separated in the first place. Actual savings that could be attributed to unification resulted from projects involving co-operation of the Navy with one or both of the other services.

The Air Force immediately wanted a distribution system of its own, and the Army, finding that its duties of cross and common service involved rather thankless tasks, did little to discourage that ambition. Secretary of Defense Louis Johnson signed a directive of 19 November 1949 which stated that each department was to "man and operate a supply system." The Army agreed to negotiate with the Air Force toward the Air Force's assumption of distribution functions from the Army technical services for its own needs. Congress was dismayed at what appeared to be a violation of the very principles of unification. As a result the Office of the Secretary of Defense issued a directive in July 1951, stating that there would be no more changes in the distribution systems without the specific approval of the Secretary of Defense.

U.S. European Command

Unification among the three armed forces as well as within the Army itself had existed on a rather complete basis in overseas organizations. Major areas came under unified commands as established by the Joint Chiefs of Staff and, while they operated under the strategic direction of the Joint Chiefs, one of the Chiefs of Staff was designated the executive agent for an area. In the 1950's major overseas unified commands included the Far East Command, Alaskan Command, Caribbean Command, Pacific Command, and European Command, all of them unified in a manner of speaking, but operating in a maze of military organization. Nowhere was the maze more perplexing than in the European area before formation of the U.S. European Command.

With separation of U.S. Forces, Austria, from the European Command in 1949, the latter became, for all practical purposes, a unified command for Western Germany only. No less than six independent commands were operating directly under the Joint Chiefs of Staff in the European area: European Command; U.S. Air Forces in Europe; Naval Forces, Eastern Atlantic and Mediterranean; U.S. Forces, Austria; Trieste United States Troops; and the Strategic Air Command. The logistics problems became intolerable when military activities expanded to meet what appeared to be growing threats of war following the outbreak of the Korean War in June 1950. The tactical structure of Supreme Headquarters, Allied Powers, Europe (SHAPE), set up under the North Atlantic Treaty Organization was superimposed on the existing structure for emergency war plans, giving some unity to tactical planning but solving no immediate logistical problems.

Attempts to deal with the unsolved problems in logistical co-ordination for the European area were bound to lead sooner or later to a realization of the need for a supreme military authority in Europe. At last, in July 1952, the Joint Chiefs of Staff took the inevitable step and set up a true unified command in Europe with General Matthew B. Ridgway (previously designated as Supreme Allied Commander to replace General

Eisenhower) as its commander in chief. Some semantic gymnastics were necessary in order to distinguish the new command from the old European Command. The new organization was designated the U.S. European Command, and subordinate to it were the three former Joint Chiefs of Staff "unified commands"—European Command, now redesignated as U.S. Army, Europe, with headquarters remaining at Heidelberg; U.S. Air Forces in Europe, with headquarters at Wiesbaden; and U.S. Naval Forces, Eastern Atlantic and Mediterranean, with headquarters in London. Headquarters for U.S. European Command were at Frankfort initially, and later were moved to the Paris area. General Thomas T. Handy, previously Commander in Chief, European Command, was named Deputy Commander in Chief of the new U.S. European Command with broad authority to exercise actual command on behalf of General Ridgway who still had to give much of his attention to the Allied organization in Europe for which he also was responsible.

What amounted to a built-in weakness of unified command in certain situations was the limitation retained on the commander's authority over logistics. Although success in carrying out missions depended as much on logistics as upon anything else, in this realm the unified commander's authority was most restricted. He had responsibility for co-ordinating the logistics support for the elements of his command, but he lacked command authority over the logistical elements of the services under his command. He could invite Air Force and Army units to negotiate on the joint use of facilities, but he could not, without appealing to the Joint Chiefs of Staff, order such joint use. He was expected to make comments and recommendations on all phases of logistics affecting

his command but they had to be approved by the Joint Chiefs of Staff before they could be put into effect. The service commanders of a unified command were supposed to operate under the broad policy direction of the commander in chief, but they also were to retain operating details of any logistic support system in accordance with instructions from their respective military departments in Washington. Generally the Army was more willing to grant broad authority to the unified commander than were the Navy and Air Force. Whenever a component commander disagreed with the unified commander on contemplated action in a logistical matter of importance, the Navy and Air Force proposed that the matter should be made the subject of correspondence among the three services, and then if not agreed upon should be submitted to the Joint Chiefs of Staff. The Army maintained that such a procedure would cause unwarranted delays that would be intolerable in wartime.

The vagueness of logistical authority and responsibility in unified commands overseas reflected the vagueness in the Department of Defense and among the service chiefs arising from an inability to resolve differences sufficiently to present clear-cut decisions. As a result, diplomacy had to replace military direction, and "muddling through" each difficulty in turn as it presented itself had to replace reliance on firm policies for logistical control.

All of the strategic and tactical skill in the world could not overcome fundamental failures in logistical co-ordination. The problems which had persuaded the Joint Chiefs of Staff to set up an over-all European Command were primarily logistical. But General Ridgway soon found that reorganization itself was not enough to resolve those problems unless authority went along with it. In October 1952 he wrote to the Joint Chiefs of Staff that the authority delegated to USCINCEUR was "inadequate to his logistical responsibilities." The European commander said further:

In short, his [USCINCEUR'S] authority in the logistical field does not provide "command authority" but merely authority to "coordinate." In JAAF (Joint Action Armed Forces) it is precisely stated what is meant by "coordination," which is essentially persuasion. If persuasion fails to produce agreement between the services, then by JAAF the matter must be referred to Washington for decision. I feel that this procedure is inefficient and that power of decision must rest with CINCEUR.[6]

The result was a far-reaching decision on the part of the Joint Chiefs of Staff to grant to the commander in chief in Europe directive authority in the field of logistics. This did not mean that logistic activities in Europe thereby would be consolidated. Individual service responsibilities would remain much the same as before, but in the event of disagreement between the services on matters of joint interest, the commander in chief himself could settle the matter. At the same time the Joint Chiefs of Staff, again following General Ridgway's recommendations, instructed the commander in chief in Europe that headquarters of U.S. European Command would perform directly the functions of a joint communications zone headquarters and not set up any intervening headquarters for those functions. One special joint agency would be established—a joint construction agency. In adopting these measures for strengthening the logistics position of the Commander in Chief, Eu-

rope, the Joint Chiefs of Staff made it clear that their recommendations were not necessarily applicable to unified commands in general. Similar problems in other areas would have to be handled specifically as they arose.

Response to International Crises

The likelihood of an emergency against which the Army had to maintain preparedness even as it went about its tasks of reorganization and retrenchment was rising in 1947 and 1948. A background of recurring international tension overshadowed continuing efforts at peacetime economy.

American reaction to threats of further expansion of Soviet areas of domination was swift, but in some ways it also was fickle. At times it seemed a part of the American character to rise to heights of miraculous achievement when meeting a crisis, and then to relax into a state of wishful complacency that would require new miracles to meet the next crisis. Demands for economy and sharp cuts in appropriations for current military functions after V-J Day made it necessary to keep all logistical activities not relating directly to liquidation of the war effort to a bare minimum. During this period of postwar economy, budgetary figures arrived at after long hours of consideration and revision in the offices of the chiefs of the technical services and in the office of G-4 bore little resemblance to the congressional appropriations with which the Army's logistical agencies had to work. Often estimates compiled after thousands of man-hours of calculations and deliberations fared little better than might have some figure plucked from the air without any thought at all. As an example, for Fiscal Year 1948 the Ordnance Department

---

[6] Ltr, Gen M. B. Ridgway to CofS USA for JCS, 18 Oct 52, sub: Establishment of a Joint Logistical Command in Europe.

estimated that, to cover procurement of essential ammunition and equipment, storage and distribution of ordnance matériel, maintenance of stand-by plants and arsenals, industrial mobilization planning, training, and research and development activities, it would need $750,000,000. The Bureau of the Budget cut this figure to $275,-000,000. Congress reduced the appropriation to $245,532,800 together with authorization to enter into contracts to the extent of another $2,000,000.

By the spring of 1948 critical international developments had impressed upon military and political leaders the importance of looking again to military preparedness.

American policy already had been put to the test in Greece when, on 24 February 1947, the British Ambassador in Washington notified the Secretary of State that because of serious financial difficulties at home the British Government would have to discontinue assistance to both Greece and Turkey at the end of March. A note from the Greek Government asking aid from the United States arrived about a week later. Appearing before a joint session of Congress on 12 March 1947, President Truman asked for $300 million for assistance to Greece and $100 million for Turkey. Half of the funds for Greece and all of those for Turkey were to go for military assistance. This was a case where military necessity took precedence over economic assistance, for no economic aid could be made effective until military stability had been established. Essentially the President's address was a plea for logistical support. It called for military supplies and equipment to the threatened countries, and it called for military, as well as economic, advisers to be sent to supervise the positive application of the assistance program.

During the last half of 1947 and early 1948 even the appearance of free choice disappeared from most countries behind the Iron Curtain. In a series of swift seizures of total authority, the Communists moved to consolidate their control. On 31 May 1947 Communists ousted Premier Ference Nagy of Hungary whose Smallholders Party had won an absolute majority in the election of 1945; shortly thereafter they broke up Nagy's party and drove him into exile. In October Stanislaw Mikolajczyk, vice premier of Poland and leader of the Peasant Party, had to flee for his life when the Communists moved in to take complete control. That same month Communist leaders met in Warsaw to organize their Communist Information Bureau (Cominform) as successor to the old Communist International (Comintern). In November 1947 the notorious Ana Pauker became foreign minister of Roumania, and her Communist regime dissolved the National Peasant Party, imprisoning its leader, Iuliu Maniu; King Michael went into exile in December. In Bulgaria the Agrarian Union Party was broken up and its leader, Nikola Petkov, was hanged; Bulgaria adopted a new Soviet-type constitution in December.

Then came the final blow. So far Czechoslovakia had been able to hold to something of its tradition of democracy, and its leaders still hoped that it might be a "bridge" between the East and the West. But in February 1948 that country too came under full Soviet sway. Foreign Minister Jan Masaryk fell to his death from a window. Shortly thereafter Eduard Benes, a sick and broken man, gave up the presidency.

Perhaps more than any other action up to that time, the *coup d'etat* in Czechoslovakia indicated the real danger posed by Soviet policies. "When Czechoslovakia, which had done everything possible to conciliate the Soviet Union, was seized by the communists in February 1948, little doubt remained in Western minds that the communist ambitions could be checked only through the evidence of superior power." [7]

Another major danger spot developed in Palestine. In November 1947 the General Assembly of the United Nations, with the support of the United States, adopted a plan for the partition of the country between Arabs and Jews, and for termination of the British mandate on 15 May 1948. In March 1948 the United States proposed that partition be delayed in favor of a temporary trusteeship arrangement, but this proposal got no action. With the termination of the British mandate, the Jewish Agency proclaimed the new state of Israel, and the United States immediately extended recognition. All these events precipitated the outbreak of war between Israel and the neighboring Arab states.

The new dominions of India and Pakistan were in conflict over the northern province of Kashmir, and in January 1948 the United Nations set up a commission to try to settle that question; in June Indian armed forces moved into Hyderabad to obtain the state's accession to the Indian Union. In the East Indies sporadic fighting between Dutch and Indonesian forces still flared.

Near the end of March 1948, General Lucius Clay, commander in chief of the European Command and military governor of Germany, received notice from the So-viet commander that under a new system of inspection being inaugurated on 1 April it would be necessary for Russian soldiers to board Allied military trains to inspect shipments going through the Soviet Zone. During the next several weeks Soviet needling tactics interfered with some highway traffic, attempted to regulate air traffic, slowed the clearance of trains. In the last week of June the Russians cut off all traffic between the Western Zones and Berlin.

In China the situation deteriorated rapidly, and in the fall of 1948 Chiang appealed for immediate and greatly increased aid, but the Government of the United States considered it was too late for effective aid. By the summer of 1949 Communist forces had won control of all north and central China, and on 5 August the State Department issued a "white paper" announcing that no further active support of the Nationalist Government was contemplated. In October the Communists announced the establishment of the Peoples' Republic of China with its capital at Peiping. By the end of the year, with Communist control of the Chinese mainland virtually complete, the Nationalist regime had taken refuge on the island of Formosa.

Meanwhile in the divided country of Korea, Communist-oriented North Korea continued to harass the democratically-oriented Republic of Korea south of the 38th parallel. Constant streams of propaganda backed up by armed raids sought to bring South Korea under Communist domination.

Because of the grave developments in the international situation, the President in March 1948 directed the Secretary of Defense to prepare supplementary budget estimates which, when added to the budget already submitted to Congress in January,

---

[7] The Brookings Institution, *Major Problems of the United States Foreign Policy, 1949–1950* (Washington: The Brookings Institution, 1949), p. 99.

would provide a balanced military force and would permit the beginning of modernization of weapons and equipment. Comparing the situation to that of 1914 and 1939, Secretary of Defense Forrestal recommended an expansion of the armed forces to include the addition of 240,000 men to the Army. Several leaders suggested the development of plans for reorganizing some kind of a War Production Board, and Bernard Baruch urged that a standby plan for full industrial mobilization be prepared. Lewis Douglas, U.S. Ambassador to Great Britain, warned Forrestal that it would be most dangerous for the country to get the impression that this was a temporary period of tension. "I think," said Douglas, "this will be with us for the next decade." [8]

On 17 March 1948 the President recommended that Congress pass a new selective service act. This call for a peacetime draft did indeed seem to be a re-enactment of 1940. But this time the opposition, while sometimes vigorous, was much weaker than it had been on the eve of World War II. The Senate passed the measure, after a brief filibuster, by a vote of 78 to 10 on 10 June; the House passed the bill soon thereafter, and it went to the White House on 19 June. The President signed it on 24 June (the day the Russians made their blockade of Berlin complete). At that time the Army numbered 538,000, as against a planned strength of 667,000. On 1 December it reached 660,000—the largest peacetime volunteer Army in history. The first draft call went out for 10,000 men in November, 15,000 in December, and 10,000 in January. Congress had authorized the Army to reach a strength of 900,000 (including 110,000 one-year trainees) by June 1949.[9]

Retrenchment

Even while the program for a build-up of the armed forces was under consideration, signs of let-down began to appear. Secretary of Defense Forrestal in May 1948 expressed concern "because of the changing tempo of the Congress and in the relaxation of tension." "On March 17," he noted, "we could have had Selective Service through both houses in three days. Today there is serious question about the passage of such a bill." [10] The expansion program would continue through about the first half of 1949, and then cut-backs would begin once more.

The defense budget for Fiscal Year 1950 dropped from the $17.5 billion figure which Secretary Forrestal suggested, to one of $16.9 billion which the military budget committee under General Joseph T. McNarney and the Joint Chiefs of Staff had agreed to, then to the $14.2 billion which the President included in his budget message in January 1949. After he succeeded Forrestal as Secretary of Defense on 28 March 1949, Louis A. Johnson lost little time in promising further cuts in military expenditures. In October he announced that orders cutting funds for Fiscal Year 1950 by $800 million would reduce funds for the Navy 9 percent, for the Army 8 percent, and for the Air Force 3½ percent. In December Johnson said that the economy

---

[8] Quoted in Millis, *The Forrestal Diaries*, p. 400.

[9] *First Report of the Secretary of Defense, 1948,* p. 39; *Annual Report of the Secretary of the Army, 1948,* pp. 6, 73–74; Millis, *The Forrestal Diaries,* pp. 400–401, 409–10, 428, 447.

[10] *Ibid.,* p. 444.

drive would keep defense expenditures for Fiscal Year 1950 down to $13 billion.[11]

It seemed that the President, the Secretary of Defense, and the Congress were trying to outdo each other in effecting economies in defense expenditures. Some leaders stood out against these cut-backs. Perhaps the most vocal was Representative Carl Vinson of Georgia, Chairman of the House Armed Services Committee. Even when Johnson was being honored at a dinner on the night of his entry into office as Secretary of Defense, Chief Justice Fred M. Vinson, addressing the gathering, recalled the days of complacency and smugness in 1940 "when our country was asleep at the switch." "We are in troublesome days," he said, "days perhaps analogous to those which preceded World War II." [12]

Instead of the 900,000 men planned for the end of Fiscal Year 1949, the Army had to cut its strength back to 677,000. Such a cutback coming in the midst of a program of expansion was bound to disrupt activities. "Much . . . time and energy had to be diverted to convulsive replanning and reallocation of men and materials to come within the new limits." [13]   Between 1 January and 1 June 1950 that strength had to be cut further to 630,000 in order to meet budgetary limits. In some ways the personnel cuts—extending to civilian as well as military personnel of the Department of the Army—were false economies, not only as they impaired aspects of defense preparedness, but as they interfered with programs such as

supply control studies that were designed to achieve economy.

In the spring of 1950 an important reduction in the Army's depot system was underway. Shipments for foreign military aid and disposal of remaining surplus stocks reduced space requirements. Demands of economy hastened plans for depot deactivations, contemplated to reduce the number of active depots from 70 to 53.

The impact of the rearmament program had been scarcely discernible on the Army's monthly obligations and expenditures. Total Army obligations, representing orders for goods and services, amounted to $1.162 billion for June 1947, to $697 million in June 1948, and $779 in June 1949. Then they dropped to the postwar low of $309 million in August 1949. Shipment of goods overseas was the one logistics area that responded sharply to international developments during this postwar period. These shipments leaped from 795,232 measurement tons in February 1947 to over 1,945,000 tons in July of that year. Then shipments dropped back to slightly over 1,000,000 tons in November, only to go up to more than 2,000,000 tons both in July and in August 1948. After another drop to less than 1,000,000 tons in November, shipments went back to 1,250,000 in December and remained well above the million-ton mark for the next several months, suggesting that supplies were being consumed considerably faster than they were being replaced.

Meanwhile the international situation remained tense, and commitments calling for American logistical support increased rather than decreased. To carry out all of its world-wide responsibilities the Army was authorized a total strength for all commands, as of 30 June 1950, of 630,201.

---

[11] Ibid., pp. 508–11, 535; The New York Times (late city editions), March 29, 1949; October 9, 1949; December 8, 1949.

[12] The New York Times (late city edition), March 29, 1949, p. 3.

[13] Annual Report of the Secretary of the Army, 1948, p. 85.

The actual assigned strength on 26 June was 591,100. Of this strength, 244,263 men were in overseas units scattered from Germany to Japan and from Alaska to Panama—with all the logistical support implications of such widespread troops distribution. By far the largest number in any oversea theater was the 108,550 men assigned to the Far East Command, though the command was nearly 10,000 under its authorized strength, and it included Army forces in the Philippines, the Ryukyus, the Marianas and Bonins, as well as those in Japan. U.S. Army Forces in Europe, located mainly in Germany, numbered 80,018, those in Austria 9,492, and Trieste United States Troops numbered 4,783. Slightly over 7,000 were assigned to the Pacific, and a similar number to Alaska (the number authorized for Alaska was 12,564), while 12,263 were in the Caribbean.

The National Guard had a strength ceiling of 350,000 (it had reached a strength of 355,000 before being forced to cut down),

and the Organized Reserve Corps a strength of 255,000. Students enrolled in the Reserve Officers' Training Corps totaled approximately 185,000 in some 375 educational institutions.[14]

In the everlasting contest between economy and preparedness that was the central theme of peacetime logistics, the greater consideration was on the side of economy. The consequences were evident in the closing of camps, depots, and industrial facilities, the substantial depletion and deterioration of matériel reserves, and the delays in production of new models and new types of equipment. The economy as well as military preparedness might have been better served by the maintenance of more standby installations, more effective preservation of reserve stocks, and a more active program of constant modernization.

---

[14] Weekly Estimate of Army Command Strength as of 26 June 1950, STW–1037, AGO Statistical and Accounting Br., 3 Jul 50, Pt I, p. 55.

CHAPTER XXXIII

Cold War Logistics

Certainly the support of the military occupation demanded the major part of overseas logistical commitments immediately after the war, but the irony in the situation was the changing orientation of security measures under which that logistical support continued. Initial occupation policy was aimed almost wholly against a possible resurgence of power on the part of Germany and Japan. This too was the tenor of the United Nations Charter, for the machinery of international peace enforcement had been designed to operate smoothly only when operating against the former enemies. That a recovery of power and the creation of a new threat to world security was possible had been demonstrated in the rise of Nazi Germany out of the defeat of World War I. But if anything at all was clear in world affairs in 1945, it was that Germany and Japan, prostrate under the heavy blows of aerial bombardment and complete defeat on land and sea, constituted no immediate threat to the security of the United States. Only one country in the world—whatever policy it might pursue—had the physical capacity to pose such an immediate threat to the United States, and that country was the Soviet Union. Neglect of the realities of power politics led to some disillusionment when threats to the national security began to appear from the actions of an erstwhile ally. But those actions led to an important change of emphasis in occupation policies.

More and more it became evident that U.S. forces were being kept in Germany, Austria, and Japan less to keep those countries down than to block possible aggression on the part of that former ally.

In one area after another the United States faced the challenge of Communist attack. In the Near East, in Europe, and in the Far East unprecedented measures were necessary to meet what were, for the United States, unprecedented threats. And each had to be met in a world-wide context of general and continuous peril.

Military Aid to Greece

The Communist guerrilla warfare in Greece, which became the object of immediate concern to the United States in 1947, was but a continuation of raids, sabotage, and civil strife that had been going on for some time. In December 1947 the Joint Chiefs of Staff established the Joint U.S. Military Advisory and Planning Group (JUSMAPG), under Maj. Gen. William G. Livesay, to give active assistance in operational and logistical advice to the Greek armed forces.

A peculiarity of the Greek military supply situation was that the Greek forces had been equipped largely with British equipment. In the interest of preserving operational continuity, it was desirable that replacement items and spare parts should be furnished from British sources, at least for the time being. In order to arrange for the procurement of these necessary British items, and to serve as financial agency in making payments to the British Government for supplies obtained from its stocks, the General Staff Liaison Group was established in London in May 1947, one week after the President approved the Greek-Turkish Aid Bill. The Liaison Group was an agency of the Logistics Division (later G–4), Army General Staff, and of the Materials, Supply and Procurement Division of the Air Staff, in co-ordinating, supervising, controlling, and making payments for supplies obtained from British depots for Greece and Turkey under the American aid program. For its part Great Britain continued to maintain a relatively large mission and several thousand British troops in Greece at the expense of the British Government.

Guerrilla forces in Greece were only about 20,000 strong, but that number of armed bandits loosed on the country could create a remarkable amount of havoc. Under a hard core of Communist leadership, people who found a life of brigandage satisfying or profitable and numbers of fugitives from justice made up much of the following. Many of the guerrillas were men who had been conscripted forcibly in raids on villages, and then had been held obedient through terror. Although sporadic guerrilla activity broke out in many parts of Greece, the most numerous and successful attacks took place throughout the rural sections of mountainous northern Greece—in Epirus, Macedonia, and Thrace.

In contrast with other military aid programs that would develop later, the largest category of supplies Greece obtained from the United States at this time was not ord-

nance, but quartermaster supplies, to the extent of over half of the total value. Surplus property made up much of the early shipments to Greece, and a number of items came from surplus stocks still in the European and Mediterranean areas. Additional equipment was obtained at no further cost to the United States by the recovery of lend-lease matériel from Great Britain. By the end of 1947 total shipments of military supplies to Greece from all sources reached 147,000 long tons, with an estimated transfer value of $40 million.

During the first weeks of supply operations under the aid program stocks of supplies and equipment were built up in the Greek military depots. Beginning in September the distribution of supplies to the troops proceeded rapidly. Within a few weeks delivery of hundreds of motor vehicles increased the mobility of Greek units immeasurably although serious shortages in vehicles remained. Other logistic deficiencies were in the supply of automatic weapons, mountain artillery, mortars, and ammunition for light antiaircraft guns and in the organization and functioning of supply services, maintenance system, and medical service. During the spring and summer of 1948 the U.S. Army Group, Greece (USAGG), helped to locate and build up supply installations for the support of military operations getting under way. Perhaps already Lt. Gen. James A. Van Fleet, commander of the U.S. Army group, had developed the enthusiasm for artillery fire for which he was to become noted in Korea. Unexpectedly heavy expenditures of artillery ammunition during the early phase of operations in the Grammos area of northwestern Greece immediately made necessary a strict rationing system until further supplies could be built up. By 30 June 1948, 69 ships had brought into Greece cargoes of military supplies totaling 382,000 measurement tons of trucks, weapons, ammunition, communications and fire control equipment, engineer equipment, rations, and other supplies. Tactical operations being undertaken were not being held back by shortages of supplies.

Sometimes it seemed that all the supply efforts and the tactical operations of the Greek forces were to no avail. They would train men, distribute equipment, make a successful attack, and a few weeks later would find themselves facing as many guerrillas as ever. President Truman shared the general disappointment with the results. He reported in December 1948: "The encouraging prospect for substantial elimination of the Greek guerrilla forces which existed at the time of the victory of the Greek National Army in the Grammos Mountains . . . has unfortunately not materialized. A military stalemate has ensued which has prolonged the struggle." [1]

But important developments outside Greece lent higher hopes for success to the greater efforts to be undertaken in the ensuing months. Tito's break with Moscow in June 1948, and the subsequent closing of the Yugoslav-Greek frontier denied the rebels their most important supply base and sanctuary .

Meanwhile the flow of supplies and programs for training and revitalizing the Greek armed forces continued. One special measure armed civilian groups so that they could have some means of protecting themselves against guerrilla raids. This measure went a long way toward persuading many refugees to return to their homes where they could resume much-needed agricultural production. It also involved bringing certain irregular military units under centralized control.

A change in supply procedures effective in August 1948 made the U.S. Army Group, Greece, responsible for deciding whether given supplies should be requisitioned from the United States or from the United Kingdom. Previously this decision had been the duty of the Director of Logistics in Washington, but the advisers in Greece were in a better position to place requisitions according to the types of equipment that required British or American parts, the extent of replacement of certain British equipment with American models, time factors, and other considerations upon which the decision had to be based. After the change, requisitions from USAGG went directly to the chiefs of the technical services (or to the London Logistics Group). In 1949 it was taking an average time of six to eight months after the request for supplies to be delivered in Greece from the United States, and from four to six months for delivery from the United Kingdom.

In January 1949 General Alexander Papagos, the man who had given Mussolini's legions such a rough time when they invaded Greece in 1940, accepted appointment as commander in chief of the Greek Armed Forces. Holding himself independent of political influences, the World War II hero enforced strict discipline in the senior ranks of the army, adopted many reforms which JUSMAPG had been recommending, and breathed new vigor into the whole Greek military effort. After six months of seemingly hopeless stalemate, victory came swiftly and, except for isolated outbreaks, completely.

---

[1] The President's letter of transmittal, *Fifth Report to Congress on Assistance to Greece and Turkey, for Period ending September 30, 1948.*

Aid for Turkey and the Middle East

Greece and Turkey were neighbors in the strategic Near East, and both received military assistance from the United States under the same legislation, but conditions in the two countries differed sharply. Turkey had been spared the devastation of World War II, and it was not the impoverished country that Greece was. Guerrilla bands and domestic violence did not dominate large areas of Turkish territory as was the case in Greece. The threat to Turkey was clear and direct: The Soviet Union coveted control of the Dardanelles and Bosporus and the annexation of provinces in northeastern Anatolia.

The same act of Congress which authorized the original $200,000,000 program of economic and military assistance for Greece also authorized a $100,000,000 program of military aid to Turkey. At the time Turkey had under arms a force of half a million men, though its army was, as Secretary of War Patterson put it, "what you might call a 1910 army." The aim was to increase Turkish military effectiveness by modernizing the weapons and equipment of the armed forces without adding appreciably to the national budget, and to permit the release of men from the armed forces so that they could return to productive civilian occupations. In this instance the immediate objective was not to build up the troop strength of the armed forces, but to reduce it.

Under the original Greek-Turkish Aid Program, military assistance provided for Turkey was about half of that granted to Greece. Under the later Mutual Defense Assistance Program (MDAP), the total matériel approved for Turkey for fiscal years 1950 through 1953 ($656.8 million, including $38.5 million worth of surplus stocks)

was greater than the Greek total by over $135 million. Most of the difference resulted from the amount provided for the air force, including air base construction.

The action of the Turkish Brigade in Korea—the largest force furnished by any United Nations member outside the United States and the United Kingdom—seemed to fully justify the confidence placed in the Turkish Army. Most important, Turkish integrity had been maintained without any sign of weakness in the face of Soviet attempts at intimidation.

Iran, too, got a head start on military assistance before the beginning of the general Mutual Defense Assistance Program. In 1948 the United States made an agreement with Iran for the sale of $10 million worth of surplus military equipment, under the terms of the Surplus Property Act of 1944, on a credit basis. The principal aim of American military aid to Iran, both under the surplus property program and under the later Mutual Defense Assistance Program was to strengthen the army and the gendarmerie so that they might maintain order within the country. The Iranian Government did not sign the required bilateral agreement for mutual defense assistance until 23 May 1950, and only after protracted negotiations. A military assistance advisory group, in addition to the two military missions already there, then went to Iran to supervise execution of the new program. MDAP shipments did not reach sizable proportions until early 1951, and even then, of course, they were on a much more modest scale than those to Greece and Turkey. The Mutual Security Act of 1951 required a further agreement or statement of guarantee on the part of recipient countries before they could be declared eligible for additional aid. The State and Defense Departments interpreted this strictly as a requirement for additional assurances even though bilateral agreements under the Mutual Defense Assistance Act already had been signed. Premier Mohammed Mossadegh refused to give any further assurances. At the end of the ninety-day period permitted by the Mutual Security Act for compliance, on 8 January 1952 military aid to Iran was suspended. After American officials gave notice that the program would be canceled and the funds reallocated, Mossadegh finally signed an innocuous statement, and shipments were resumed, effective 24 April.

American leaders hoped to promote further stability and security in the Middle East through a regional defense arrangement, presuming that the possibility of American assistance would encourage participation in a common defense organization. But almost insoluble diplomatic problems still present in mid-1953 made an early conclusion of an effective Middle East pact unlikely. Great Britain's differences with Iran over nationalization of oil holdings, the tense British-Egyptian dispute over the Suez Canal, the Israeli-Arab situation (and British and American relations involved), all blocked the way to military co-operation and assistance in the Middle East. The Baghdad Pact (later the Central Treaty Organization) was signed in 1955; the United States has co-operated as an associate.

The Berlin Airlift

The most critical situation of all in 1948 resulted from the Soviet renewal of the blockade of Berlin with the apparent purpose of ending the Western occupation. Already President Truman had made it clear to Secretary of Defense Forrestal that the policy would remain fixed: to stay in Berlin. A meeting of State Department and military officials at the Pentagon on Sunday afternoon, 27 June, upheld this view. On the same day Lt. Gen. Curtis E. LeMay, commander of the United States Air Forces in Europe, met with General Clay in Berlin to discuss plans for an airlift. The next day General LeMay announced that he was going to send airfreight to Berlin at maximum capacity, twenty-four hours a day, seven days a week, on a wartime basis with no holidays. Four squadrons of C–54 transport planes were on the way to Germany, and were due to arrive about 5 July.

The airlift for the supply of military forces in Berlin had already begun on 21 June, and the experience of the April airlift had permitted planning for rapid action. Tonnage jumped from 5.88 tons carried in three C–47 planes on the 21st, to 156.42 tons in sixty-four planes on 24 June. But the supply of the civilian population of West Berlin was something else and called for hasty planning and improvisation. Headquarters of the European Command first learned of such a project on 26 June, and the first civilian supplies went into Tempelhof Airfield, Berlin, on 28 June.

The maximum air effort needed to carry out these missions of civilian as well as military supply called for essential support from Army logistical agencies of the European Command. They had to furnish necessary trucks and keep them in repair, to provide quarters for aircrews, to expand air terminal facilities, to provide communications, and to bring in gasoline. They had to deliver to the airports the supplies destined for the military forces in Berlin, receive them at the Berlin end, and distribute them to the Berlin garrisons. In the beginning of the civil supply program, which became known as Operation VITTLES, the Army was responsible for finding the supplies and getting them to and from the airplanes. Later (28 July) the Bipartite Control Office took over responsibility for getting the German food to the airports; civilian agencies of military government and of the German local governments then handled procurement, storage, financing, and movement to the airfields of civilian supplies. But the Army still performed important logistical activities in order to keep the airlift going.

The EUCOM Transportation Division set up and maintained traffic control points at the the two air bases in the U.S. zone, Rhein-Main and Wiesbaden. The post transportation officer in Berlin set up a Transportation Corps airhead at Tempelhof to exercise traffic control there. By the end of 1948 six heavy truck companies of the Transportation Corps were assigned to Operation VITTLES. Army engineers went to work to expand the airfield facilities at Berlin, to improve those at Rhein-Main and Wiesbaden, and to construct quarters for the additional aircrews being brought into the Frankfurt area. Expansion of airfield facilities at Berlin included two new runways at Tempelhof and the contruction of the Tegel Air Base. These projects themselves required air shipments (by December 1948) of 5,562 tons of asphalt, 3,300 tons of pierced plank, 671 tons of heavy construction equipment, and 505 tons of general engineer supplies and spare parts. Ordnance support for the airlift involved special programs of vehicle maintenance both in Berlin and in the U.S. zone. As of November 1948 the 1,182 ordnance ve-

hicles being used for Operation VITTLES were requiring 118 rebuilt vehicles, 732 rebuilt tires, and 659 tons of spare parts and supplies per month above what had been normal. Signal Corps units had to expand communications facilities and maintain the Signal Corps equipment used by the Air Force. Quartermaster units provided subsistence and individual clothing and equipment for men assigned to the airlift, and gasoline and oil for the airplanes and trucks. In April 1949 aviation gasoline requirements reached a peak of 15,604,800 gallons for the month. It took three ocean-going tankers and 1,500 rail tank cars a month to get the gasoline to the air bases.

Through the winter the Berlin airlift continued to carry food, clothing, coal, raw materials, and medicines to the 2,500,000 people of the Western sectors of Berlin. By the spring of 1949 shipments by the American and British Allies had reached an average daily air delivery rate of 8,000 tons. On the record day (16 April 1949) nearly 13,000 tons were delivered—more than was being brought into Berlin by rail and water before the imposition of the blockade. The results suggested that the air supply operation might go on indefinitely, and American leaders seemed determined to do just that if necessary. At last, on 4 May 1949, the Western Allies arrived at an agreement with the Russians for lifting the blockade, and on 12 May all transport, trade, and communication services between the Eastern and Western Zones of Germany were restored. Nevertheless the airlift continued in order to build up a reserve against a possible renewal of restrictions. It gradually reduced in scope until the last load was flown from Rhein-Main to Tempelhof on 30 September 1949.

THE BERLIN AIRLIFT. *Unloading supplies from C–47's at Tempelhof Airfield.*

European Lines of Communication

Forces stationed in Europe, whatever their size and purpose, had to have assured supply lines to provide them with the food, clothing, and equipment necessary for their existence and for the performance of their mission. That mission in the beginning, of course, was conceived to be one of occupation and military government in Germany. In those circumstances setting up a line of communications was principally a problem of administration to be worked out in the most economical and efficient way. Little thought, supposedly, had to be given to such tactical considerations as disposition of troops and the facilities for a supply line to serve them. But as soon as the military problem in Europe was seen as one of meeting threats of new aggression from the East more than one of controlling Germany, it became necessary to revise the thinking on matters of delivering supplies and to give consideration to the continuation of effective supply in the event of a resumption of war in Europe.

To provide port facilities for civil and military needs in the United States Occupation Zone of Germany after the conclusion of World War II, the United States arranged for an enclave including the port cities of Bremen and Bremerhaven to be set aside under U.S. control, and for goods to move from those ports southward across the British Zone to Hesse. Bremerhaven became the military port serving American occupation forces. The line of communication connecting Bremerhaven with U.S. installations in southwest Germany ran through Bremen-Hanover-Kassel to Frankfurt. From Frankfurt one line branched southwestward to Wurzburg and Nuremberg, while another continued southward through Mannheim to Karlsruhe and then turned southwest to Stuttgart, Augsburg, and Munich. Running generally north and south as it did, this line of communication paralleled the Soviet Zone boundary, and thus lay athwart the route of advance of any major attack from East Germany. At Kassel the line of communication was within twenty miles of Soviet-occupied Thuringia. No defensible barrier protected it against possible attack from the east.

For purposes of the occupation the arrangement seemed logical and satisfactory. The United States did not have to depend upon the port and transportation facilities of any other country, and the costs involved were borne by German mark funds provided under the occupation statutes. Then the Russian blockade of Berlin in 1948 opened the eyes of everyone concerned to the reality of the danger of a Communist attack. In June 1950 the attack of North Korean forces across the 38th parallel emphasized that danger. Unloading schedules for 1951 called for an average of 79,000 long tons a month, and a peak of 100,000 long tons a month at the Bremerhaven Port of Embarkation. If complete dependence on the Bremerhaven line of

communication continued, commanders had visions of the whole American Army in Germany being imperiled by a sudden thrust of Communist forces across their supply route. Consequently, security had to supersede economy and convenience in logistical thinking, and friends had to be called upon to make other facilities available.

Under the stimulus of the Berlin blockade, the Logistics Division of the European Command in 1948 and early in 1949 set about investigating the possible establishment of a line of communication across France. In November 1949 the Joint Chiefs of Staff approved the move, and straightway the European Command appointed a team to survey the proposed route and to meet with French military representatives to determine what installations, facilities, and services would be required.

The matter of concluding an agreement with the French Government introduced a situation almost without precedent in recent international military affairs: negotiations for the army of one nation to set up a complete line of communication across the territory of another fully sovereign, friendly state in peacetime. It was to be expected that the strong Communist elements in France would fully exploit the novelty to show that the United States was establishing military bases in France in preparation for war and in violation of French sovereignty. For this reason it was essential that the negotiations proceed most carefully and diplomatically. Both French and American negotiators were anxious to avoid political repercussions in France, to limit the inflationary pressures resulting from large-scale local spending which might dislocate elements of the French economy, and to discourage situations that might lead to ill-feeling and clashes between the local civilian populations and the U.S. troops who would be stationed among them. The U.S. Army was also anxious that France assume a major share of the costs of the line of communication.

Eleven months after the first military discussions on the subject and five months after the opening of diplomatic negotiations, Ambassador David Bruce of the United States and Alexandre Parodi, Secretary-General of the French Ministry of Foreign Affairs, on 6 November 1950, signed the agreement on the line of communication. The basic agreement provided very simply that a line of communication would be established from the La Pallice–Bordeaux area to the German frontier over which the principal means of movement would be by railways. Procedures for its establishment and operation were to be worked out by the military authorities of the two countries. The agreement was to remain in effect for five years, and would be renewed automatically unless terminated by six months' advance notice by one of the parties.

In line with the thinking which underlay the establishment of communications across France, it was necessary to reorient logistic support facilities in Germany. Since tactical considerations had superseded the occupation mission in Germany, and since dependence upon the Bremerhaven line of communication was being minimized, it seemed prudent to move all these installations west of the Rhine where they could be disposed to receive supplies being shipped across France, and where they might find a measure of protection against attack from the east. But all German territory west of the Rhine was in the French Zone of Occupation (except the North Rhineland in the British Zone). At the same time Allied planners thought that it would be well to assign to the French responsibility for defending a portion of the battle line if and when an attack should come. This led to the consideration of an exchange of territory by redrawing the boundaries of the occupation zones, but French Foreign Minister Robert Schuman suggested that the objective might be achieved more simply by agreeing to exchange certain facilities and to permit troops to be located without regard to zonal boundaries, while retaining those boundaries for the purpose of administrative responsibilities. Schuman's proposal was agreeable to both the British and the Americans. Specific arrangements depended upon further agreements to be worked out to cover questions of jurisdiction of forces, revision of budgetary procedures so that one nation could account for the costs of its forces in more than one zone, acquisition of real estate in various zones, procedures for hiring local labor, local procurement for the forces of one nation in the zone of another, improvement of uniform transportation regulations, and responsibilities for occupation damages. American and French high commissioners and military commanders on 2 March 1951 signed an agreement on an exchange of facilities and a transfer of troops between the two zones of occupation. The relocation program called for the phase-out of engineer, medical, and signal, most ordnance, and a major part of quartermaster depot activities over the next two years.

The peace treaty with Italy, which became effective 15 September 1947, provided that all occupation forces should be withdrawn from that country within ninety days. The last ship carrying American troops sailed from Leghorn on 14 December. In Italy, therefore, no American troops remained who could accept logistic missions for forces now being disposed to meet the threat of attack. As in France, new agreements had to be made so that troops could return, and installations had to be set up to carry out the decision to establish a line of communication which in Italy would be for the purpose of supplying current needs for U.S. Forces, Austria, and building up emergency stockpiles for the support of war for that force as well as Trieste United States Troops (TRUST). The operation came under the control of U.S. Forces, Austria. The line of communication would extend from the port of Leghorn on the Ligurian Sea northeastward some 300 miles through Verona to the Austrian border, and thence to the Camp Drum Storage Depot at Innsbruck in the French Zone of Austria.

The program in Italy was but a fraction of the size of the one undertaken to establish the line of communication across France, but the diplomatic negotiations were even more drawn out. Communist agitators were more active in Italy than in France, and the Italian Government had to move slowly in accepting new foreign commitments. The American Embassy in Rome began negotiations with the Italian Government 25 September 1950; arrangements were concluded nine months later, on 29 June 1951. A leak to the press (perhaps a trial balloon to test political opposition to the agreement) late in June created some last-minute problems and further delays when members of the Italian Parliament demanded a full discussion of the negotiations, but at last an acceptable arrangement was concluded in the form of an exchange of notes between Italy's foreign minister, Count Carlo Sforza, and United States Ambassador James C. Dunn.

Aid to Western Europe and NATO

As an integrated program of military aid, mutual defense assistance developed mainly from an alarming necessity to do something about building the defenses of Western Europe. There had been earlier assistance programs for the Philippines, for Greece and Turkey, and for China. But as a co-ordinated, long-term proposition, the Mutual Defense Assistance Program had as its first objective the matériel support to European Allies that would make the North Atlantic Treaty really effective.

The forerunner of the North Atlantic Treaty Organization (NATO) was the Western Union Defense Organization, which developed under the Treaty of Economic, Social and Cultural Collaboration and Collective Self-Defence, signed at Brussels on 17 March 1948 by Belgium, France, Luxembourg, the Netherlands, and the United Kingdom, thereafter referred to collectively as the "Five Powers." Like the Treaty of Alliance and Mutual Assistance which the French and British had signed at Dunkerque a year earlier, the Brussels Pact was intended to remain in force for fifty years. To carry out the aims of the treaty, the Five Powers established elaborate machinery for consultation and co-ordination.

Given the strength to back up the determination expressed by the nations of Western Europe in the Brussels treaty of 1948, a drive toward unity of purpose was the immediate consequence of the peril of Communist expansion toward the west. It was possible that future generations would be grateful for the Soviet threat that stimulated unity in Europe and resulted in better living for all concerned; for the moment, however, prospects seemed hopeless without early and effective logistical support from the United States. Even when large-scale programs of American assistance became certain, possibilities of violent Soviet counteraction as well as the recognized military advantage the Soviet then held in Europe left only the most stout-hearted free from pessimism.

In contrast with that of the United States, demobilization of Soviet armed forces proceeded gradually after World War II. Soviet Army strength dropped to about 2.5 million early in 1947, and stabilized there, at least for the next six years. In addition to Regular Army troops, Russia maintained some 400,000 security police. Also to be counted on the side of Soviet strength were some sixty-eight divisions in the satellite countries of Eastern Europe, and twenty-four regiments of East German "police" forces. Not to be discounted were the Communist fifth columns to be found in the countries of Western Europe, where they infiltrated the armed forces, interfered with logistical operations of ports and lines of communication, and hampered industrial production. It was not unlikely that their effect would be considerable in wartime.

In the post-World War II period Soviet forces with their stockpiles of equipment had the advantage of jumping-off places in the satellite countries and East Germany, where relatively dense rail and highway networks were available to them. Up to a certain point, military operations would be easier to support from this area than from Russian territory itself, while deep in the rear, out of reach of the battle area, the large-scale Soviet industry would be replenishing the stockpiles. In the event of war in Europe the Soviet Achilles' heel of limited transportation facilities would probably not be exposed very early in the conflict.

While determined to fight aggression with whatever they had, the leaders of the Brussels Treaty Powers recognized that they had to depend on the United States for a great part of the support that would permit more than token resistance. In answer to a question put by the Defense Committee, the Permanent Military Committee stated (12 May 1948) firmly and frankly that in the event of an attack by the USSR, however soon it might come, the Five Powers were determined to fight as far east in Germany as possible. If the Soviet Union overran Western Europe, irreparable harm would be done before the countries could be recaptured because of the Soviet policy of deportation and pillage. Preparations by the Five Powers, therefore, would aim at holding the Russians on the best position in Germany covering the territory of the Five Powers in such a way that sufficient time would be gained for American military power to intervene decisively.

A summary of Inventories of Military Forces and Resources submitted to the Western Union Military Committee in August 1948 revealed pathetic weaknesses. All the ground forces these once mighty powers could raise among themselves for 1949 were ten divisions and thirteen brigades "in being," and a hope that another twelve divisions and nine brigades could be mobilized within three months' time. Americans were used to practically abolishing their ground forces in time of peace; not so the French who had boasted the greatest army in the world in the 1930's. Worst of all was the equipment situation. Lists showed serious deficiencies in tanks, antiaircraft artillery, engineer equipment, and most types of guns; little or no equipment was available for additional forces in the event of mobilization. Much of the World War II equipment was not serviceable, and it could not be quickly rehabilitated because of shortages of spare parts and technicians.   Most of the difficulties of complete mobilization of trained reserves could be boiled down to the shortage of matériel.

The North Atlantic Treaty, signed on 4 April 1949 and coming into effect on 24 August 1949, brought the United States into active participation with the Western European nations in developing plans and programs for defense.   In addition to the Five Powers of the Brussels Pact, Norway, Denmark, Iceland, Portugal, and Italy associated themselves with activities under the North Atlantic Treaty.   Most significantly, the United States, together with those European states and Canada, committed itself not only to come to the assistance of any member attacked in the North Atlantic area, but to contribute to a program of mutual matériel assistance.   "For the first time," said the Secretary of Defense in his annual report, "we have to face the security problems of our allies, in peace time, and to accept responsibility in quarters where in the past we gave only advice." [2]

The treaty provided for consultation among the parties, but it did not envisage an active military organization.   Probably it took the Communist *coup d'etat* in Czechoslovakia and the Berlin blockade to bring the North Atlantic Treaty Organization into being.   Two other events changed its character—the announcement in September 1949 of an atomic explosion in the Soviet Union and the Communist attack in Korea on 25 June 1950.   The immediate fear of Europeans was that they might be next. France inquired in August 1950 if the

---

[2] *Second Report of the Secretary of Defense for the Fiscal Year 1949* (Washington, 1950), p 24

United States was prepared to contribute ground forces for the defense of Western Europe and whether forces of the Allies should be integrated under a supreme commander.   The reply of the United States was an unprecedented affirmative on both counts.

In Europe the Joint American Military Advisory Group (JAMAG) had prepared a study which recommended the organization of the European area as a single combined theater, with certain subordinate commands, and the immediate appointment of a theater commander designate.   At the meeting of the North Atlantic Council in September 1950 (before the Inchon landing in Korea had restored confidence in the Korean situation) Secretary of State Dean Acheson presented the American proposal for an integrated command in Europe under a supreme commander.   After a recess for consultation with their home governments on this and related matters, the representatives approved the plan on 26 September.   General Eisenhower, then president of Columbia University, learned in October that he might be recalled to active duty to take over the Allied command in Europe. Meeting again in Brussels in December, the North Atlantic Council approved a recommendation of the Defense Committee for the establishment of Supreme Headquarters, Allied Powers, Europe, and to ask General Eisenhower to take the Supreme Command.   In February 1951—as the United States Senate debated the President's plans for sending four additional divisions to Europe—SHAPE was established physically in temporary facilities at the Astoria Hotel in Paris.   On 2 April the new command became operational.   On 27 May the 4th Division arrived in Germany.

Clearly one of the most significant consequences of the war in Korea was the reinforcement of Europe. What would have been the condition of European defenses without the stimulus of a Korean War was difficult to say. It did seem clear that if the Communists contemplated forceful expansion in Western Europe, they had made it infinitely more difficult for themselves by their attempts at expansion in far-off Korea; Premier Stalin had his answer to the question on which the Kaiser and Hitler had been kept guessing. Even if two wars too late, the United States and the powers of Western Europe together had made their position clear. How effective would be these steps for revitalized mutual defense depended very largely on the matériel that could be found for the forces concerned.

By unanimous invitation the North Atlantic Treaty Organization was open for admission to other European states. The first extension of membership was to Greece and Turkey, effective 18 February 1952. For some, admission of these nations strained the designation "North Atlantic," but British and French leaders long had regarded the Eastern Mediterranean as a critical area for their own security, and Greece and Turkey had been the first recipients of the kind of aid from the United States that developed into the Mutual Defense Assistance Program. The forces of Greece and Turkey, being built up with the assistance of American matériel and advisers, were welcome additions to the strength of the Western European Powers.

An inevitable weakness in the international military structure existed in the provisions for logistic support. Initial emphasis on the creation of combat units resulted in serious shortages of service troops and of certain critical equipment necessary for the support of combat units. Each nation retained responsibility for the logistical support of its own forces, and the result was a lack of flexibility in the supply system. In October 1952 SHAPE offered recommendations for an improved over-all supply organization, but no organization could overcome the current lack of operational reserve stocks. Truly a co-ordinated international military command structure in peacetime was in itself no mean achievement. With the appointment of a Supreme Commander for Europe, the Allies had already accomplished, even before the outbreak of a possible European war, what had taken three and one-half years to bring about in World War I, and, so far as the United States was concerned, had taken two years (although an embryonic headquarters had been established eight months earlier) to accomplish in World War II.

To a great extent the success of the North Atlantic Treaty Organization depended on effective and immediate matériel assistance from the United States. The need to furnish arms to the nations of Western Europe had been considered by the United States concurrently with its consideration of entering into a North Atlantic pact, with Marshall Plan economic assistance serving as an example for development of military assistance supply requirements. A co-ordinated defense plan prepared by the Western Powers, employing presently available means, was to be supplemented by a determination of how measures undertaken by the Five Powers and mutual assistance among themselves (including co-ordinated production and supply and standardization of equipment) could improve their collective military potential. The United States would then provide supplemental assistance where needed and in return expect reciprocal assistance to the extent practicable.

Lists of minimum deficiencies, prepared by country, service, and dollar value for each priority, were reviewed by the U.S. delegation of observers to Western European Union in its role as forerunner of the Joint American Military Advisory Group.

The Fiscal Year 1950 program included $1.159 billion for the Western European countries, of which $859.7 million was for Army equipment. By far the largest beneficiary was France, for whom well over half of the total was programed. Over 80 percent of the total Army funds were to be committed for long lead-time equipment, including tanks, other combat vehicles, heavy trucks, field artillery and antiaircraft guns, radar, and heavy engineer equipment.

Before the North Atlantic Treaty Organization had begun to assume form the five Brussels Treaty powers had begun an integrated program of military construction which they referred to generally as "infrastructure." The original program called for completion of thirty-five airfields by the end of 1951 at a cost of approximately $92.7 million. With the development of the North Atlantic Treaty Organization, the infrastructure program was expanded to include the participation of the broader membership and the requirements of the combined European command. Thereafter the original program was referred to as the "first slice," and projects approved for subsequent years became parts of second, third, and fourth slices. Types of facilities programed as common infrastructure included air bases, communications facilities, gasoline and oil storage facilities and pipelines, headquarters, radar warning installations, navigational aids, naval bases, and training facilities. All of these were in addition to facilities which member nations provided individually, such as the American lines of communication across France and across Italy.

The basis for logistic planning and for building up and equipping NATO forces had to be the strategic plans. International strategic plans for the defense of Western Europe had to be based upon logistical feasibility in the same way as joint war plans for the United States. A function comparable to that of the Munitions Board for testing the industrial feasibility of strategic plans in the United States had to be carried out. For this purpose the North Atlantic Council at its September 1951 meeting in Ottawa established the Temporary Council Committee. The full committee actually included representatives from all twelve NATO powers, but its detailed work was charged to an Executive Bureau of three leaders, W. Averell Harriman of the United States (chairman of the committee), Jean Monnet of France, and Richard A. Butler (or his deputy, Sir Edwin Plowden) of Great Britain—a group which came to be known as the "Three Wise Men." The committee's job was to study the economic and political capabilities of the NATO countries to determine how much of the military requirements could be met, and what portion each state could bear. In setting up the committee the council "noted the danger of inflation, the burdens which increased defense efforts place on the balance of payments, and the obstacles to an adequate defense arising from price and allocations pressures on raw material supplies." [3]

These men and their staff studied economic statistics, analyzed production poten-

---

[3] Communiqué, Seventh Session North Atlantic Council, 20 September 1951, *NATO Handbook* (1952), p. 61.

tial, and listened to the testimony of defense officials and economic experts of the various countries. On the basis of the gross national product of each of the NATO countries they determined what they considered to be the maximum defense effort each country could make without overburdening its economy. In December 1951 the Temporary Council Committee submitted its report for study by member governments in preparation for the meeting of the council scheduled to be held in Lisbon in February 1952. The report indicated what should and could be done to give effect to the requirements study which the council also would be considering at the Lisbon meeting. The committee recommended specific actions for effective arrangements for operational logistical support, improved machinery for supply and production planning, and NATO machinery for determining priorities in training, equipment, and military construction for forces under NATO commands, as well as specific actions on standards of readiness of forces, better training and organization, and improved command arrangements.

At Lisbon the North Atlantic Treaty powers adopted, with certain modifications, the Temporary Council Committee recommendations. Of particular significance were the force goals accepted. Going far beyond the scope of previous commitments, the NATO powers agreed upon a program of fifty divisions (exclusive of Greek and Turkish units) for 1952. These fifty divisions, the "firm force goals," were to include twenty-five active divisions that could become operational immediately in an emergency, and twenty-five reserve divisions. Some of the reserve divisions were to be ready within twenty-four hours, some within seventy-two hours, some within ten

days, and all were to be capable of mobilization within thirty days after a future D-day. Previous force goals for Western European Union as well as for NATO had listed reserve divisions capable of mobilization within ninety days. Shortening that time to thirty days in the 1952 goals was hardly less significant than the increase in the total number accepted as provisional goals for 1953, and planning goals for long lead-time matériel. Whether or not the goals set at Lisbon were too ambitious to be reached was another matter. A press dispatch of 27 February said that "sources at General Eisenhower's headquarters" had made it clear that talk of a combat-ready fifty-division Atlantic pact army by the end of 1952 "smacks more of fancy than fact," and indicated that the publication of such a figure was "both misleading and unfortunate." [4]

Actually the Lisbon goals were in large part met in numbers of aircraft, naval vessels, and army divisions by the end of 1952, though the combat effectiveness of the units fell considerably short of the planned achievement. The goal of twenty-five active divisions was reached by early 1953, but it took a few months more for all twenty-five reserve divisions (those to be available within thirty days after D-day) to be organized. Units themselves had been strengthened, and additional items of major equipment had been provided, but serious deficiencies continued in service units, in logistical establishments, and in stocks of ammunition and other supplies. The next task was to overcome those deficiencies and to improve the combat effectiveness of existing units rather than to create additional units. As commander of SHAPE, General Ridgway

---

[4] The Washington *Post*, February 27, 1952, p. 3.

was not satisfied to have twenty-five reserve divisions only on paper. By personal inspection and evaluation he listed separately units which, for reasons of shortages of equipment or an incomplete or unsatisfactory training program, could not in fact be considered available for combat on thirty days' notice or less.

The war in Korea made more difficult the problems of logistic support for U.S. forces in all other parts of the world. Interpreting the threat of communism to be world-wide, the President and his military advisers were anxious to build up U.S. strength in other strategic areas while increasing combat strength in Korea. In 1951 the garrison in Alaska was strengthened, ground forces were dispatched to Iceland, construction of new air bases was rushed in Greenland and North Africa, and four additional divisions were sent to Europe. In the world-wide game of chess, the king had to be covered as the knights were advanced to meet attacks on other parts of the board.

In actuality the Far East was the primary theater during the 1950–53 period, for that was where active combat operations were going on. But potentially Europe was the decisive theater, and as such it had to be an area of major concern even while active operations were being supported on the other side of the globe. With a population of over 230,000,000 and an industrial plant second only to that of the United States, Western Europe was critical for the security of the United States. With Western Europe's industry the free world could outproduce the Soviet bloc by nearly four to one. Joined to that of the Soviet bloc, Western European production might offset completely that industrial advantage of the free world over the Communist countries.

Should Soviet forces overrun Europe, the United States would find itself in the awful dilemma of having to resort to the pitiless bombing of friendly nations or of seeing the great industrial resources of those countries combined against it.

Yugoslavia and Spain

Other European countries, though less remotely situated than some of the NATO members, presented more perplexing problems for military co-ordination. In particular Yugoslavia and Spain fell into this category. Yugoslavia was frankly Communist, but Tito's break with the Kremlin in 1948 opened the way for collaboration against further Soviet aspirations in the Balkans. Prudence required the exploitation of every sign of weakness in the Communist bloc.

With an army of some thirty-two divisions, and a total strength given variously at from 300,000 to 500,000 men, Yugoslavia offered an attractive area for the extension of military assistance. In 1949 and 1950 the Export-Import Bank extended three loans amounting to a total of $55 million to Yugoslavia, but the United States made no direct grant assistance available until the latter half of 1950. This took the form of economic assistance to relieve the stress arising from a serious drought that year, mounting Yugoslav indebtedness, and economic pressures being applied by the Soviet bloc. Then followed an allocation of $29 million in MDAP funds for raw materials for the needs of the armed forces. At the same time the governments of the United States, the United Kingdom, and France agreed upon a tripartite program of economic assistance in which the American contribution amounted to 65 percent. In May and June 1951 an American military mission held informal exploratory discussions with Yugoslav military leaders to determine the nature and extent of military assistance which would be needed to keep the Yugoslav armed forces effective during the next several years. Under a bilateral agreement signed 14 November 1951, Yugoslavia became a recipient of regular mutual defense assistance. The mission established in Belgrade to supervise the program was known as the U.S. Military Assistance Staff, Yugoslavia, though its functions were similar to those of military assistance advisory groups in other countries.

Anxious to temper the misgivings of European Allies, the U.S. administration moved slowly in the direction of military assistance to Spain. Less sensitive to the attitudes of allies, Congress took matters into its own hands to appropriate funds for Spanish assistance. The first step, in the fall of 1950, was the authorization of loans of up to $62.5 million for economic assistance. Slightly more than $52.8 million of this amount was approved for loans by the Economic Cooperation Administration (and the Mutual Security Agency), and loan agreements covering $35 million had been signed up to April 1952. Then in the Mutual Security Appropriations Act, approved in October 1951, Congress provided: "for economic, technical and military assistance, in the discretion of the President under the general objectives set forth in the declaration of policy contained in the titles of the Economic Cooperation Act of 1948 and the Mutual Security Act of 1951, for Spain, $100,000,000." But conditions were not yet ripe for military assistance to Spain, and the President allocated none of these funds for expenditure. In July 1951 Admiral Forrest P. Sherman entered into exploratory discussions with Spain's General Francisco Franco in order to determine a possible basis for mutual defense assistance. A month later a joint military survey team headed by Maj. Gen. James W. Spry, USAF, arrived in Spain to continue the discussions. Congress carried over the unspent $100 million in Mutual Security appropriations to the next fiscal year (1953), and authorized an additional $25 million for that fiscal year. By June 1952 the U.S. Government was contemplating a program to include the use of the $125 million already authorized for grants of miiltary equipment and for consumer goods and for developing Spanish industry, and the expenditure, over a three-year period, of $390 million for the construction of air and naval bases and of $15 million for the rehabilitation of railroads. Also in June 1952 the Joint Chiefs of Staff reconsidered an earlier action designating the Army as executive agency for the Joint U.S. Military Group, Spain, and redesignated the chief of staff of the Air Force as executive agent in the negotiations for mutual aid and base rights then being conducted. The negotiations dragged on for months. Spain's estimates on the needs of its Air Force and Navy did not vary greatly from the planned assistance, but its requests for modernization of its Army went far beyond anything American planners had in mind. Franco, it appeared, was willing to grant base rights, but at a price that was as yet completely out of the question. The Director for Mutual Security, on the recommendation of the State Department, withheld approval of the program for Spain pending conclusion of three agreements: (1) base rights, (2) military assistance, (3) economic aid. The proposed Army program was $37 million.

The Federal Republic of Germany

Even more puzzling than the questions of Yugoslavia and Spain in the build-up of defenses for Western Europe was the position and contribution of Germany. The solution lay beyond the scope of U.S. initiative in a bilateral arrangement: the whole North Atlantic alliance was concerned. The problem was how to bring German economic and military potential into the defense of Western Europe while satisfying Western European neighbors that it would not threaten their security.

At the same time that he proposed the organization of a supreme headquarters for Allied forces in Europe (the meeting of the North Atlantic Council in September 1950) Secretary of State Acheson presented a proposal for seeking units from the Federal Republic of Germany for NATO forces. The immediate French reaction was one of reluctance to see Germany rearmed in any way before France could rebuild its own strength. At a meeting of the North Atlantic Defense Committee in Washington in October, Jules Moch, the French Defense Minister, proposed a far-reaching innovation. The French could entertain no suggestions for reconstituting German divisions or a German general staff, but, said Moch, why not bring the Germans in as part of a unified European Army? After a year's preliminary work, the six nations developed a comprehensive plan for a European Defense Force, within the framework of the European Defense Community, under which forces would be integrated for the common defense of Western Europe. Once formed, this force would come under SHAPE in the same way as the allocated forces of the United States, Canada, and the United Kingdom. The effect would be to make Germany an "associate member" of NATO. All of the North Atlantic Treaty powers approved the European Defense Community plan at the Lisbon meeting of the North Atlantic Council in February 1952, but early promise of success began to give way to doubts as delays developed on ratification of the pact.

Having proposed it, France proceeded to kill the project when the French parliament refused to ratify the agreement. Although Secretary of State John Foster Dulles warned that there was no alternative, Foreign Minister Anthony Eden of Great Britain immediately set out to find one, and did find it in the revitalization of Western European Union to which both Germany and Italy were admitted. It was not until 1955 that the Federal Republic of Germany became a member of NATO, and German units were added to the NATO forces, paving the way for U.S. military assistance to a former enemy.

Military Aid in the Far East

Military assistance to the Far East presented appreciably different, and in some ways considerably more complex, problems than those encountered in Europe and the Near East.

Because conditions varied greatly from one country to another, individual programs were worked out for each of the Far Eastern countries, and no unified effort in the postwar period to 1954 either among the recipient nations or in execution by the United States fostered a NATO-type structure, although proposals for a Pacific pact were offered from time to time. Far East aid programs were linked mainly by the threat of Communist aggression or subversion that ran like a red thread through all the military aid programs, and also by the circumstances that the countries served occupied the same quarter of the globe and received mutual defense assistance under the same title of the Mutual Defense Assistance and Mutual Security Acts.

The United States did enter into a mutual defense treaty with the Philippine Republic on 1 September 1951, thus formalizing a relationship previously based on executive agreements, and on the same date a pact with Australia and New Zealand, commonly referred to as the ANZUS pact was signed. In each case the parties agreed that an armed attack on any of the parties would be deemed an attack on the metropolitan territory of all the parties, or the island territories under their jurisdiction in the Pacific, or on their armed forces, public vessels, or aircraft in the Pacific.

But the United States' policy so far was opposed to establishing formal machinery for defense co-operation as had been done for the North Atlantic area. Furthermore, no mutual defense assistance program was involved for Australia or New Zealand.

While sympathetic to suggestions for co-ordinating the aid programs in the Asiatic and Pacific areas, Maj. Gen. George H. Olmsted, who had been director of the Office of Military Assistance in the Department of Defense, cautioned against a policy that would seem to assign inferior status to Far Eastern participants in any co-ordinated effort. He told the House Foreign Affairs Committee in March 1953:

From the military standpoint the problem in Asia is one problem and the several little shooting wars are just parts of that one problem.

If we would view the area as an area, rather than a number of isolated and independent countries, we have potentially there a balanced economy that could well nigh be self-sufficient.

There has been some stirring and some talk, as you know, on the political side about integration of the area. Nothing could be more fatal to our standing in the area than to popularize the expression of "Asians fight Asians."

These people, for an understandable reason, do not like that concept and that really is not the problem. It is the free world and communism that is the issue, not Asians or Europeans or North Americans.[5]

The competition for resources between United States forces in Europe and in the Far East also was manifest in the military aid programs. Doctrines of "Asia first" and "Europe first," often with little relevancy to their strategic and logistic merits, became embroiled in U.S. domestic politics. European fears of a "pull to the Pacific" in military aid had some justification in the U.S. support of South Korea and in the increasing U.S. interest in Southeast Asia following the outbreak of the Korean War. But U.S. policy in those areas was related to a global pattern, based on the premise that if the free world were to be held safe from communism, overt Communist aggression in Korea had to be stopped. Whether later programs for arming a large South Korean army could be justified on the same basis was another question. The focal point of interest in Southeast Asia was Indochina where military aid to the French and Indochinese forces could have important results for the defense of Europe by easing the strain on the French in that remote area. In the spring of 1953 the new Secretary of State, John Foster Dulles, indicated that there might be a substantial shift in U.S. aid from Europe to the Far East.

---

[5] Statement of Maj Gen George H. Olmsted, former Director OMA, OSD, 11 Mar 53, *Mutual Security Act Extension, Hearings before House Committee on Foreign Affairs,* 83d Cong., 1st sess., p 7.

China was the principal recipient of U.S. assistance in the Far East, and the Philippines and Korea as well as China received special consideration as beneficiaries of military aid programs developed some time before the Mutual Defense Assistance Program. In this sense the Far East had a clear priority over Europe in military assistance (though not in economic aid) until 1949. By the time the Mutual Defense Assistance Program began, the Communists had overrun continental China and thereafter military assistance to China, including Formosa, was suspended until after the Korean War. Earlier transfers of surplus property to the Republic of Korea had been completed, but Mutual Defense Assistance, just beginning when the war started, was suspended for that country too, and replaced by larger programs of direct assistance out of Department of Defense funds.

Indochina replaced China as the principal Far Eastern recipient (exclusive of support for the Korean War) of U.S. military assistance. The increasing Communist threat to Indochina brought Thailand into the assistance program in October 1950. A mutual security survey team was refused access to Burma, but that country did receive ten Coast Guard patrol vessels under MDAP. Indonesia, too, had serious misgivings about accepting U.S. assistance. The Indonesian Government did sign an agreement to receive aid, but it led to the downfall of the premier. That country received small quantities of small arms, trucks, and radios under the original MDAP for its National Police Mobile Brigade as a means of promoting internal security. Shipments under the original program continued, but there were no programs for Indonesia for fiscal years 1952 and 1953. The military assistance advisory group sent to

Indonesia in 1950 was withdrawn in January 1953, and the Indonesian Government converted what remained of the previously approved mutual defense assistance program to a reimbursable basis. Beginning slowly in 1950, the Mutual Defense Assistance Program was building up to significant proportions in the Far East by 1952 and 1953.

Destroy them, disarm them; rebuild them, rearm them—that was the pattern of conquest and containment as U.S. policy adjusted itself to the shift from world war to cold war. After pursuing a policy in the mid-1940's aimed frankly at complete demilitarization of an aggressive Japan, in the 1950's the United States perforce turned to a policy of rearming a reluctant Japan. Much to the disappointment of Americans who saw in "total victory" and "unconditional surrender" the solution of all international problems, the removal of one threatening power only paved the way for the rise of another, no less troublesome and no less threatening. Such an extreme disturbance to the balance of power in the Far East as the defeat of Japan entailed required extreme concern for the security of U.S. interests in that area, for the inevitable result was the extension of Soviet influences into the power-vacuum thus created. Indeed, it was the attempt by the USSR to fill that vacuum that gave to the Korean War its special strategic significance. Apart from its importance as a symbol of United Nations collective action and as an indication of determination on the part of the United States to fight if necessary to contain communism, the Korean War was for the United States a primary step in maintaining the security of Japan. It had become clear that, failing the build-up of Nationalist China to the status of a Great Power in the

Far East, the only alternative to complete Soviet domination was the rebuilding of Japanese strength. Just as, in the view of American policy makers, a possible hostile combination of Soviet and German strength in Europe was the most serious eventuality against U.S. security in Europe, so Soviet control of Japan, and with it control of East Asia's greatest industrial plant, would be the most serious development against the United States in the Pacific.

In 1948 a Japanese police force, armed with American pistols and other light equipment, was organized for local protection. But the Korean War impelled formation of postwar Japanese military forces, when the deployment of U.S. divisions to Korea practically denuded Japan of effective defense forces. Concerned about the situation, General MacArthur in July 1950 took action to activate four Japanese divisions, with a total of 75,000 men, and cabled the Joint Chiefs of Staff for confirming authority. With equipment furnished by the United States, this force would be organized as the equivalent of "light divisions," of the U.S. Army. In American planning the force was referred to as "Special FECOM Reserve;" locally, it was given euphemistic designations, first as the "Japanese National Rural Police Reserves," later as the "Japanese National Police Reserve," and still later as the "National Safety Force." In December 1950 the U.S. Army added requirements for heavy equipment for the Japanese force, and already U.S. plans anticipated its ultimate expansion to ten divisions with a total strength of 250,000 men.

At the time of the signing of the Japanese Peace Treaty at San Francisco, 8 September 1951, the United States also concluded a security treaty with Japan. Noting the threat of possible aggression against Japan, together with Japan's inability at that time to provide adequately for its own defense, the security treaty formed the legal basis for stationing United States troops in Japan as a security measure after occupation terminated when the peace treaty became effective 28 April 1952. The security treaty also assumed that Japan would "increasingly assume responsibility for its own defense."

Concerned about a Japanese tendency to procrastinate in building up defense forces, Secretary of State Dulles, during a visit to the Far East in August 1953 obtained a personal interview with Japanese Premier Shigeru Yoshida. Indicating U.S. interest in Japanese rearmament, Dulles pointed out that Japan was spending only about 2½ percent of its national income on defense, while Italy—in a less exposed position—was spending 7 percent. Premier Yoshida insisted, however, that Japan for the time being could not go beyond the four divisions then being maintained in the National Safety Force. Dulles reportedly answered that it was strange that South Korea, with a population less than a quarter as great as Japan's, had raised seventeen divisions and was trying to increase this number to twenty.

Yoshida was responding to the political climate in Japan. Rearmament had become a prime domestic issue and, as in Germany, a large segment of the population in this once militaristic state openly opposed rearmament. This anti-military attitude had had the full encouragement of the United States only a few years before, when, with American blessing, the Japanese had included in their new constitution (promulgated 3 November 1946, effective 3 May 1947) a chapter on the renunciation of war which remained in force in 1953. The

Liberal Party of Premier Yoshida was opposed to a constitutional amendment to permit rearming. About as far as Yoshida was willing to go in making concessions to the rival Progressive Party on this point was to join with the leader of that party (Mamoru Shigemitsu) in September 1953 in proposing to change the name of the National Safety Force to National Defense Force and to authorize it to oppose any foreign invasion of Japan.

This announcement seemed to be aimed at justifying grants of U.S. military aid under the Mutual Defense Assistance Program. Negotiations on a bilateral agreement as required under the Mutual Security Act had been dragging on for months. There already was a U.S. military advisory group in Japan. This Security Advisory Group, organized under the Far East Command to train the Japanese in the use of American equipment, became the Military Assistance Advisory Group (MAAG) as soon as the bilateral agreement became effective, and from that time military aid to Japan became a regular MDAP project. Negotiations had begun in July 1953; the bilateral agreement was signed in March 1954, and became effective on 1 May 1954. Thereafter, too, funds for military aid to Japan were provided in the Mutual Security Program budget rather than included in regular Army appropriations. Thus the United States brought to full tide a policy of collaboration with another erstwhile enemy in order to curb the aggressive designs of a former ally.

Mutual Defense Assistance Program

In general the Mutual Defense Assistance Program got off to a slow start. Most foreign aid actually delivered during Fiscal Year 1950 had already been scheduled under previous programs. It was obvious from the beginning that a large part of the funds appropriated for Fiscal Year 1951 could not be committed for specific programs before the end of that fiscal year. The original act itself was not approved until 6 October 1949, the appropriation act was approved three weeks later, and the required bilateral agreements were not completed with the European countries until 27 January 1950. Fiscal year 1950 was half gone, and supply action had not even begun. Foreign requirements reported by preliminary survey teams could not be reprogrammed until the State and Defense Departments agreed upon criteria. The military assistance advisory groups could contribute little to reprogramming for fiscal year 1950 in the time left to them after their arrival in foreign countries. Procedures still had to be worked out for meeting all the administrative problems involved in such a complex undertaking.

Actually the General Appropriations Act passed in September 1950 contained $1.223 billion for MDAP (for all services), and already, a month after the commitment of ground forces to action in Korea, President Truman had asked Congress for additional funds for military aid. Here was clear testimony of the stimulus to foreign aid which the Korean War provided. The Supplemental Appropriations Act, passed less than three weeks after the General Appropriations Act, included an additional $4 billion for the Mutual Defense Assistance Program—nearly a billion more than it provided for expansion of the Army itself and for its conduct of operations in Korea. In addition nearly $300,000,000 (for all services) remained unobligated from the 1950 appropriation. At the end of June 1950 the

Army had obligated $470 million, and spent only $25.6 million of the $524.8 million in MDAP funds allocated to it.

The Mutual Defense Assistance Act of 1951 carried the proviso that economic recovery was to have priority over programs of military assistance. By 1951 the economic recovery of European nations, with the benefit of the Marshall Plan, had progressed notably, but external threats to security seemed as dangerous as ever. The Marshall Plan ended officially with the enactment of the Mutual Security Act, approved 10 October 1951, which brought economic and technical assistance as well as military assistance programs under the general supervision of a single Director for Mutual Security. From that time military assistance received the emphasis. Even the economic programs frequently had to be justified as contributing toward the effective military defense of the countries concerned. Military aid under the Mutual Security Program continued to be known as the Mutual Defense Assistance Program. The new act continued the general title designations of countries with some modifications: Title I provided for economic, technical assistance, and military aid programs for Europe, Title II for the Near East and Africa, Title III for Asia and the Pacific, and Title IV for the Western Hemisphere. The program was to end 30 June 1954. The Mutual Security Act of 1952, approved 20 June, made a number of additions and amendments to the original law, but retained its principal provisions. The President signed the appropriation bill on 15 July 1952. Carrying a total of $4.22 billion for foreign military aid, the appropriation act represented a reduction of nearly 8 percent from the amount Congress had authorized just a month before, and a cut of 22 percent from the amount the President had requested. The total appropriation, for economic and technical assistance as well as for military aid, was $5.995 billion.

United States' assistance groups sent to the countries designated to receive aid were a distinctive feature of the Mutual Defense Assistance Program. In general the military assistance advisory groups consisted of Army, Navy, and Air Force sections, each one headed by the senior officer of the respective service except that the chief of the MAAG might designate the next senior member of his section as section chief. The senior officer, whatever his service, was chief of the MAAG. His responsibility on general policy matters was to the U.S. ambassador or minister in the country where located, but on questions of military programming, supply, and related questions, he reported in Europe to the Joint U.S. Military Advisory Group in London (later the Military Assistance Division, U.S. European Command) and in other areas directly to the Department of the Army as executive agency for the Joint Chiefs of Staff. Section chiefs were authorized direct communication with the ambassador, with their respective military departments in Washington, and with corresponding components of the recipient country's armed forces on questions affecting their service. The strength of MAAG sections was determined by agreement between the Departments of State and Defense. Individual assignments were as directed by the service concerned.

The Military Assistance Advisory Group together with the economic or technical assistance mission, under the Ambassador or Minister, formed the Country Team. The chief of diplomatic mission was charged with over-all co-ordination within the country of the activities of U.S. representatives providing all types of assistance under the Mutual Security Program. In countries receiving aid under the Act for International Development (popularly known as the "Point Four Program" by reason of its origin as the fourth major foreign policy recommendation in President Truman's inaugural address of 1949), a State Department Technical Cooperation Administration mission from the Mutual Security Agency (formerly Economic Cooperation Administration) participated. If a country was receiving both economic and military assistance, as a general rule a single mission from the agency having the major interest would perform the functions of both. In any case, military assistance programs were not to be isolated from other forms of assistance intended to contribute to the strength, stability, and well-being of the countries concerned.

By early 1953 it was clear that fulfillment of mutual defense assistance programs was running at least eighteen months behind—about the lead time required for initial procurement of items most difficult to manufacture.

The Mutual Defense Assistance Program was not adapted to furnish military equipment to allies under wartime conditions. War would not wait for the months of programming, reprogramming, revision, co-ordination, and multilateral approval. It was ironic that when the Korean War started, the far-reaching program of foreign military aid which was just beginning to become effective could offer no help in supplying allies willing to participate in the collective action. Plans and programs aimed solely at building strength for war left void an area meriting serious consideration: the action to be taken should the war break out for which all these preparations were being made. A year after the start of the Korean War had pointed so forcibly to the need for such plans, none had yet been drawn up. In March 1954 G–4 stated: "up-to-date guidance for war-time aid to allies is required at earliest practicable date by G4 and Technical Services." In October 1951 the Joint Chiefs of Staff approved guidance prepared by the Joint Logistics Plans Committee and the Joint Strategic Plans Committee to govern wartime aid. With this guidance the Strategic Logistics Branch of G–4 Plans Office developed a study, based on the Joint Mobilization Plan and Joint Chiefs of Staff criteria, to show Army mobilization requirements for aid to allies after a future D-day. The study was submitted to the Munitions Board in early 1952, but when its foreign military aid requirements were added to those already established for U.S. forces, the total mobilization requirement was found to be not feasible industrially. Clearly, additional guidance based upon revisions in strategic assumptions and capabilities would have to be provided in the new mid-range plan then being prepared. In April 1953 G–4 completed the preparation of draft directives, in co-ordination with U.S. European Command and Far East Command, calling for studies to develop a tentative scale of Army wartime aid to bring mobilization requirements within capabilities.

CHAPTER XXXIV

The Korean War

The full implications of the early morning attack of North Korean forces across the 38th parallel in Korea on 25 June 1950 were not immediately clear. Border raids over the parallel had been frequent for some time but there had been little indication of a major attack. However, when word came from John J. Muccio, U.S. Ambassador to Korea, that this was indeed an all-out attack, officials in Washington and Tokyo moved swiftly to do something about it. Their immediate reaction was limited to sponsoring United Nations resolutions, bringing American civilians out of Korea, and sending supplies to the already hard-pressed Republic of Korea Army. It took but one day for the urgency of the situation to be impressed upon President Truman sufficiently for him to order sea and air forces to the aid of South Korea. The Republic of Korea (ROK) Government fled to Taejon on 27 June, and the capital city of Seoul fell on the next day. On 30 June the President announced that U.S. Army forces were to be committed to ground combat in Korea.

On 1 July, less than twelve hours after the Far East Command (FEC) [1] received authority to commit troops to ground combat, airplanes carrying advance elements of

an understrength infantry battalion of the 24th Division landed near Pusan on the southeastern tip of Korea. Moving northward by railway train and by truck, these men first met the enemy north of Osan, about twenty miles south of Seoul, on 5 July.

In certain ways the steps toward military intervention in Korea on the part of the United States amounted to something of a repeat performance, compressed within a few days and to a limited area, of the steps taken in the months of 1940 and 1941 that had led to involvement in World War II. They were a recapitulation too, in some respects, of the early months of U.S. participation in World War I. In each case the hope had been, in the beginning, that the U.S. contribution could be limited to logistic support—to the provision of matériel. Then it had become necessary to provide naval and air escort to insure the arrival of the goods being furnished. Finally it had become clear that American ground forces would have to join the battle if the aggressor were to be turned back.

Comparative Logistic Positions

It was inescapable that logistic capabilities would determine to a major extent the amount of force the United States could bring to bear in Korea. Warfare 5,000 miles from the shores of continental United States hardly could fail to impose critical

---

[1] Commanders of Far East Command during the Korean War were, in turn: General MacArthur, General Ridgway, and General Clark.

problems of logistics support, but they were by no means one-sided.

In Korea itself the North Koreans held the advantage of controlling the greater part of local industrial facilities. Plants producing perhaps 75 percent of the industrial output of Korea, including nearly all of the heavy industry, lay north of the 38th parallel. Transportation facilities, on the other hand, probably were as good in the south as in the north. The Japanese-built railways had been maintained in fairly good condition in both sections of the country. The main line was double-tracked, standard gauge, winding through rugged hills from Pusan to Seoul (a distance of about 250 miles) and then on through North Korea. By 1949 railway repair shops were functioning efficiently in South Korea, and 7,000 of a total of 9,000 freight cars were in operation. North Korea had no shops equipped to build locomotives, and the principal repair shops at Ch'ongjin were reported to have been destroyed in 1945.

Large stockpiles of weapons and equipment that the Japanese had left in Manchuria, as well as quantities of American-made equipment that Chinese Communists had captured from the Chinese Nationalists would be available—particularly if Chinese Communist forces should intervene—to reinforce the weapons and equipment the Soviet Union had furnished to the North Korean Army. On the other side, large stocks of American surplus World War II equipment remained on the Pacific islands where it might be made available to South Korean and United Nations forces.

Important productive, repair, and storage facilities in Manchuria, China, and eastern Siberia would be available to the Communists, but munitions production in that area would not be enough to support sustained military operations. Communist China, including Manchuria, was producing artillery ammunition in 1950 at a rate probably close to 90,000 rounds a year—enough to last three to five months in the kind of military operations then developing in Korea. Annual production of small arms ammunition was, roughly, enough to provide 250,000 men with five cartridges a day for each man. China did not produce enough steel for its own use. There was some important local production of steel in Manchuria—the Showa Steel Works at Anshan had a theoretical capacity of 1,330,000 tons in 1945—but the large-scale removal of machinery by the Soviet Union after V–J Day undoubtedly had impaired Manchurian industrial capabilities to a point from which it had not yet recovered. Other industrial facilities in adjacent areas of Soviet Siberia, particularly the great steel mill at the rapidly growing city of Komsomolsk (about 500 miles north of Vladivostok), would have to be taken into account. But the extent to which these facilities in the Far East could add to Communist war-making capabilities in Korea would depend to a considerable degree on how much of their products could be moved to Korea over the relatively meager transportation facilities available. Three railway lines, all single track, connected Manchuria with North Korea. Manchuria itself had a little more than 6,000 miles of railroads, and all the rest of China had another 6,000 miles.

More than offsetting all this were the productive, repair, and storage facilities in Japan, the Philippines, and intervening islands, which would be available to the United Nations Command in supporting the South Koreans. With its steel production back up to 330,000 tons in December 1949, and reaching an annual rate of over 5,000,000 tons for 1950, Japan had reassumed its position as the leading industrial power of the Far East. Japanese industry turned out 29,000 motor vehicles in 1949. Railway mileage in Japan was over 2½ times as great as that of all China combined, and enough freight cars were available to move some 10,000,000 tons of goods a month. In addition the Japanese had 75,-000 motor trucks on hand, and a fairly good highway system.

Finally, backing up the stockpiles and the local production available to Communist forces in Korea were the vast resources of the Soviet Union itself. During and since World War II the Russians had added significantly to the industrial facilities of Siberia, but still the major centers of heavy industry upon which the Far Eastern area depended for needs beyond its local capacity were in the Kuznetsk Basin, nearly 4,000 miles from the Korean battle area, and the Urals, another thousand miles farther away. Again transportation capabilities were the key to the logistic support that could be provided from the industrial centers of the Soviet Union. In 1946 it took twelve days for an express train to run the 5,800 miles over the Trans-Siberian Railway from Moscow to Vladivostok, though plans were being announced for returning to the prewar schedule of nine days for certain trains. Freight trains, of course, could be expected to take considerably longer. Yet the Soviet Union had been able to save so much of its rolling stock from World War II, and had been able to recover from that conflict to such an extent that by 1950 the Trans-Siberian Railway

could carry perhaps as much as 14,000 tons of military supplies a day to the Far East in a sustained effort. A more severe restriction on the amount of goods that could be delivered to Korea from the Soviet Union was the capacity of the Chinese Eastern Railway across Manchuria. This was a single-track line, and its standard gauge made transshipment necessary at the Manchurian border. But by routing about half of the freight over the line branching from the Trans-Siberian at Chita to enter Manchuria from the west, and carrying the remainder farther on the Trans-Siberian to go around Manchuria to the north and then enter from the east at Suifenho, possibly 13,000 tons a day, or 390,000 tons a month could be shipped into Manchuria. Necessary local traffic would reduce this amount, but even so, as much as 339,000 tons of military goods per month could be shipped into Manchuria.

The United States could, of course, offset the Communist capacity with the domestic production and ocean shipping facilities at its command. And the distance of the United States from the battle area was not appreciably greater than that of the Soviet industrial centers. The economic distance, that is to say the distance reckoned in terms of the cost of transporting a given quantity of goods, even from Chicago to Korea probably was much less than from Stalinsk in the Kuznetsk. The ocean connection between the United States and Korea permitted relatively cheap water transportation for most of the distance, whereas the Soviet Union was restricted almost wholly to a land connection for moving matériel to the Far East. So long as U.S. sea and air power controlled the Pacific Ocean, it would be a connecting link in logistic support, not a barrier.

Attack and Response

All aspects of logistical activity had to receive prompt attention in July 1950 as the North Korean forces raced southward to complete their conquest of South Korea before sizable and effective combat units and matériel resources could be built up to oppose them. The immediate problem facing the United Nations Command was to get men and supplies to Korea quickly and in numbers sufficient to stabilize the situation and hold on long enough to permit a build-up. This involved dipping into reserve stocks of U.S. World War II equipment, expanding transportation facilities, setting in motion programs to obtain additional supplies and equipment from new production, taking steps to obtain additional funds by supplementary appropriations, and expanding and reopening necessary installations to handle the mobilization of men and matériel needed to meet the emergency.

Unfortunately, a large part of the ROK military equipment was lost in the first few days of the operations. Indeed, a great deal of it was put to use by the enemy. It became necessary to re-equip the ROK forces, and at the same time supply U.N. forces so that they could take their places in the battle lines.

Lights burned late in the Pentagon in the weeks after 25 June 1950 as staff officers and civilian assistants worked long hours and through weekends to get troops and critical supplies moving for support of the developing combat operations. During the weekend from noon Friday, 7 July, to noon Monday, 10 July, Supply Division, G–4, disposed of twenty-four actions:

(1) Referring to a letter of Secretary of the Air Force Thomas K. Finletter to Secretary of the Army Frank Pace, Jr., offering airlift if needed, G–4 prepared a disposition form for Lt. Gen. Matthew B. Ridgway, Deputy Chief of Staff for Administration, listing 100 tons of high priority air cargo assigned to 3.5-inch rockets and 4.2-inch mortar ammunition, and estimating a need for further shipments of rockets and 4.2-inch mortar ammunition. (2) Conferred with the director and staff of the Division of Korea Program of the Economic Cooperation Administration (ECA) on maintaining liaison between the Army and ECA relative to shipments of civilian supplies to Korea. (3) Submitted a report, at the request of G–3, showing the equipment status of certain infantry, airborne, and armored units in the United States. (4) Co-ordinated with G–3 in preparing warning movement orders for the 2d Infantry Division and other units in first priority alerted for the Far East Command. (5) Furnished information informally for the Deputy Chief of Staff for Administration to answer an inquiry from the Office of the Secretary of Defense on the availability of bridging equipment in the Far East Command; this information was to the effect that there were no shortages in organizational bridging equipment, but how much was stockpiled in Japan was uncertain. (6) In a teleconference with Far East Command asked the status of bridging equipment. (7) Informed General Ridgway that, even with the diversion of equipment being procured for the Mutual Defense Assistance Program, approval of General MacArthur's request for four divisions with full combat and service support probably would exhaust certain categories of supplies in the Special Reserves, and further warned the Deputy Chief of Staff that immediate emphasis would have to be put on expediting overhaul and rebuild programs, renovation of ammunition, and

essential new procurement, and that any delay in these efforts would put additional serious drains on reserves and depot stocks in the United States. (8) Prepared a report on the availability of troop and aerial cargo delivery parachutes. (9) Forwarded a message prepared in the Office of the Chief of Ordnance to the Far East Command inquiring of the supply of 4.2-inch mortar ammunition with M–2 and M–3 fuses; FEC answered with a report on the availability of shells with M–8 and M–9 fuses; again queried FEC on ammunition with M–2 and M–3 fuses. (10) Prepared a disposition form to the Assistant Chief of Staff, G–4, stating that for planning purposes fifteen days should be allowed for the movement of tanks from inland points of departure to western ports of embarkation, and that all types of tanks shipped by the Military Sea Transportation Service could reach Yokohama from San Francisco in fifteen days, and Pusan in sixteen days. (11) Prepared a disposition form for Assistant Chief of Staff, G–4, reporting the arrival at Fairfield, California, of an instruction team with 3.5-inch rockets and launchers en route by air to the Far East. (12) Received confirmation of the airlift of 159 recoilless rifles from Aberdeen Proving Ground to Fairfield en route to the Far East. (13) Queried Far East Command by telecon on the advisability of shipping certain discretionary and Class IV items. (14) Queried G–3 to find out whether troops moving to the Far East should carry gas masks; the decision was yes. (15) Participated in a conference with representatives from the Engineer Corps, Medical Department, Ordnance Corps, Quartermaster Corps, and Signal Corps where it was decided to assign technical service expediters at Fort Lewis, Washington, to route requisitions for alerted units directly to supply sources by telephone when possible and let the post catch up with the necessary paper work later. (16) Sent radio messages to the commands and agencies concerned giving instructions for filling equipment shortages for the 2d Division and other alerted units. (17) Notified G–3 that use of certain ammunition for 37-mm. antiaircraft guns was being suspended because of the danger of premature explosions. (18) Submitted a report to the Office of Military Assistance, Department of Defense, on the supply status of the Mutual Defense Assistance Program for Korea as of 25 June for use in congressional hearings. (19) Assembled information for the Control Office, G–4, on all equipment furnished Korea by the Department of the Army. (20) Received a report from the Chief of Ordnance on the current status of ammunition supplies. (21) Prepared a study on the distribution of sniperscopes in the continental United States. (22) Prepared a study on the status of tanks in the 66th, 70th, 72d, and 73d Tank Battalions. (23) Authorized the technical services to spend appropriated monies from any fund necessary to meet expenses for supplies, depot operations, and repair of equipment for units alerted for movement to the Far East. (24) Received notice from G–3 that the 2d Infantry Division would move overseas under reduction table strength; informed the technical services.[2]

The 2d Infantry Division was preparing for a field maneuver to make up some of its training deficiencies when, on 8 July, it received word that it was being alerted for early movement overseas. The division had

---

[2] Daily Diary, Supply Div G–4, 1200, 7 Jul to 1200, 10 Jul 50. Copy in Hist Records, Supply Planning Br G–4.

to be brought up to strength, shortages of equipment filled, tonnage and space requirements figured, ships ordered, loading plans made, and eleven cargo ships and ten troop transports loaded in twenty-nine days.

On 8 August the 9th Regimental Combat Team (less the 3d Battalion) attacked the North Koreans. Just a month had passed since the first word that these units would be moving overseas. The last tactical elements came into port in Korea on the 20th. Probably the quickest preparation and movement of an entire infantry division from home station to overseas battlefield to that time in the Army's history had been completed.

After about twelve weeks when the race between North Korean advances and American build-up was touch and go, the whole complexion of the war changed almost overnight. On 15 September General MacArthur, with characteristic boldness, sent X Corps into an amphibious assault at Inch'on, far up the west coast of the Korean peninsula opposite the capital city of Seoul. The logistical build-up made this amphibious envelopment possible more than three months ahead of the schedule assumed in G–4 planning. The audacity and the surprise of the landing paid rich dividends. The next day the Eighth Army [3] struck out from its Pusan beachhead and, after some difficult fighting, broke through enemy defenses. By the last week in October United Nations forces had taken the North Korean capital, P'yongyang, and, by further amphibious landings on the east coast and by advances inland, they were moving rapidly northward toward the Yalu

River on the Manchurian border. Thus within six weeks of the Inch'on landing U.N. forces had broken out from their precarious beachhead, and had driven to the line that earlier plans had anticipated reaching about a year later. The end of the war appeared to be in sight.

In the first months of the Korean War a large share of the Army's total resources of men and matériel and most of its reserve stocks of ammunition and other supplies went into the emergency effort to stop aggression in Korea. But that effort was effective. Within three months the Army deployed more than 100,000 men and nearly 2,000,000 tons of supplies and equipment to the Korean peninsula. More than that, the first big steps were taken to make certain that there would be more supplies where those had come from.

Chinese Intervention and U.S. Build-up

Even as General MacArthur, on 15 October 1950, was reassuring President Truman at their Wake Island conference that Chinese Communist intervention in Korea was unlikely, or if it did come would not amount to more than about 60,000 troops, twice that number were pouring across the Yalu River. By mid-November the Red Chinese had moved 30 divisions, totaling approximately 300,000 men into North Korea without detection by the United Nations Command. On 24 November General MacArthur announced the launching of a "win the war" offensive inspiring hopes of "getting the boys home by Christmas." Then a Communist counterattack against the ROK II Corps gained some six miles through the center of United Nations lines. Communist attacks gained

---

[3] Commanders of the Eighth Army during the Korean War were, in turn: General Walker, General Ridgway, General Van Fleet, and General Taylor.

momentum on 26 November, and by the 27th it was evident that a full-scale Chinese Communist offensive was underway with apparently no less an objective than driving all the United Nations forces into the sea. The collapse of the ROK II Corps in the center of the U.N. line imperiled the whole situation. The optimism of rapid advances gave way to the despair of retreat before continuing Chinese assaults through a frozen country swept by winds of northern winter. Casualties, lost equipment, and confusion prevailed in the opening sequences of what General MacArthur termed a "new war." The lightning indeed had struck twice in Korea, and the second bolt was, if anything, worse than the first.

Emergency Supply Shipments

On receiving the grim news of the Chinese Communist successes and U.N. matériel losses, officers in Washington sought effective ways to ease the logistics situation, but found it difficult to establish a sound basis for action. The Chief of Staff, General J. Lawton Collins, had left by air for Tokyo to obtain firsthand the requirements needed but it would be several days before he could report the results of his visit. To await an accurate assessment of specific losses and the preparation and processing of requisitions might cause a delay in delivery of matériel that would be disastrous. General Larkin and Maj. Gen. William O. Reeder, Deputy Assistant Chief of Staff, G-4, developed a plan of action. If whole units were losing their equipment, why not take the table of organization and equipment of an infantry division as the measure of items and quantities to be shipped and send at once all the equipment needed to outfit a whole infantry division? This was an example *par excellence* of the principle, "the impetus of supply is from the rear." There would be no waiting for requisitions, no query to the theater on its needs, no waiting for status of equipment reports. Equipment for an infantry division would be assembled and shipped in the shortest possible time, and the theater simply would be informed that the shipment was on the way. The supplies went out in record time, but the ships were redirected from Korea to Japan, since officers in Japan were already making emergency shipments to re-equip units in Korea.

Expansion of U.S. Military Effort

As soon as he had learned the extent of the difficulties of the 2d Infantry Division in Korea, Secretary of the Army Pace had directed the Army Staff to "pull out all the stops" in the procurement program. The program on which the Army had been operating for an ordered build-up of military strength by 1954 had become wholly inadequate after the Chinese counteroffensive in Korea. Secretary Pace regarded the Chinese intervention, as he had the original attack in June, as much more than a threat to the tactical situation in Korea. He considered it another impressive indication of the danger to the security of the world at large. And in the bigger and faster build-up which the Chinese attack touched off, the defense of Western Europe continued to hold high priority.

The stimulus that the Chinese Communist attack gave to the expansion of military strength carried with it certain dangers. One was the possibility that deep apprehension over the turn of events in Korea would lead to such a large-scale military effort on the part of the United States there as to leave unguarded what was, in the view of the high command, the more important strategic area of Western Europe. A second danger, in the view of high Army officials, was that people would become so concerned about the danger to national security that they would demand immediate full mobilization, which might have the effect of retarding rather than promoting military preparedness. When General Ridgway reported to the Army Policy Council on 6 December that the General Staff had arrived at a tentative plan for increasing the strength of the Army from 16 divisions and 1,263,000 men to 21 divisions and 1,530,000, Secretary Pace agreed to the use of those figures for planning purposes, but he cautioned that the immediate problem was to build up supplies of matériel. Agreeing with this view, Assistant Secretary of the Army Karl R. Bendetsen observed, "The faster you mobilize personnel in units, the more you slow down production capacity." [4] Too rapid mobilization of additional troops would have the effect of adding to the demands for equipment and facilities for training purposes, while at the same time taking away manpower and skills from the industries attempting to produce that equipment.

A little over a week later, 14 December, Secretary Pace told the Army Policy Council, "We do not intend to be stampeded into a vast personnel program, since the real controlling factor in expanding our forces is that of procurement." The next day the Army announced that two more National Guard divisions were being ordered to active duty which would bring the total in federal service to six. The same day Pace emphasized procurement of matériel before personnel, New York's governor, Thomas E. Dewey, said that there should be total mobil-

ization, swift creation of a 100-division Army, and a call-up of all National Guard divisions "tomorrow morning." [5]

Undoubtedly reserve stocks of World War II equipment had saved the supply situation in the beginning, but by early 1951 deliveries from new procurement would be reaching significant proportions. As it had on policy in general, active Communist aggression in Korea had a primary and a secondary effect on procurement. The first was the necessity to determine requirements for the operation being undertaken in Korea to meet that aggression—to replace reserve supplies being used immediately, to anticipate the needs for winter clothing and equipment, and to get the equipment necessary for such special operations as amphibious and airborne operations. The secondary effect was the need to determine requirements for a general build-up of armed strength to meet the increased worldwide threat suggested by the Korean attack. The impact of the Chinese invasion resulted in (1) speeding up the armament program; (2) expanding procurement objectives, and (3) broadening the industrial base to make possible further rapid expansion if necessary in the future.

The major significance of the conflict in Korea would be much more in political and logistical terms than in tactical. First of all the American action had indicated a willingness to fight if necessary to deny further Communist expansion by force of arms. That was as significant for Greece and Turkey and for Berlin as it was for Korea. Beyond that the attack in Korea, and more important the Chinese Com-

[4] Min, 51st Mtg, Armed Forces Policy Council (AFPC) 6 Dec 50.

[5] Min, 52d Mtg AFPC, 14 Dec 50. Text of Address, 14 Dec 50, The New York Times (late city edition), December 15, 1950, p. 2.

munist intervention, had awakened the United States to the threat to its security, and this had resulted in undertaking an enlarged program of rearmament and industrial preparedness. The longer the war in Korea dragged on, the more certain would it become that one result would be to put the United States in the best long-term preparedness position in its history. Responsible civilian and military leaders alike shared the view that the preparedness program had to be based on an assumption of a long period of tension, and that the build-up should seek to escape the crisis-to-crisis approach in favor of a plateau of preparedness which would furnish a more satisfactory continuity of strength with which to meet not only current threats but also those that would be sure to arise in the future. In carrying out this policy the President, the Secretaries, and the Joint Chiefs of Staff were determined to hold the nation steadfastly to a course midway between the Scylla of hysteria and the Charybdis of complacency.

Special Problems

The Army was furnishing supply support for the Air Force, Navy, and Marine Corps, for the Army of the Republic of Korea and for United Nations participants, for various civilian groups, and for Japanese reserve police forces activated to maintain local security when U.S. occupation troops moved out to Korea.

Levels of supply and troop strengths were more or less constant; at least they could be planned for in relatively precise terms. More elusive was the determination of requirements for Class IV supplies to support the operations contemplated in the theater. The approved procedure resembled that developed during World War II—the theater,

on the basis of its planned operations, prepared a list of projects that then served as a guide for planning Class IV supply. Approval of the projects by Department of the Army then gave the theater commander the authority to requisition and store Class IV supplies as provided for in bills of materials submitted with the projects. Late in the war a five-quarters (fifteen months) Class IV supply forecast system was adopted. This was intended to assure a more uniform flow of materials by providing a constant review of requirements and revisions of current status of supply for the benefit of each supply agency concerned.

A serious drag on the logistical effort for operations in Korea was the overoptimism of high-level officials who insisted on assigning dates no more than six to twelve months in advance by which hostilities were supposed to end.

That an early end to hostilities in Korea should be assumed after the collapse of the North Korean Army in October 1950 was understandable, though a more accurate appraisal of Chinese Communist capabilities might even then have counseled caution. Less understandable was the continuation of such assumptions in the midst of all-out Chinese counterattacks. Throughout the first half of 1951—even when General MacArthur was doubting the ability of the United Nations to keep a foothold in Korea—the official Department of Defense assumption remained that hostilities would end by 30 June 1951, which meant that no supplies could be purchased for a conflict in Korea continuing after that date. Since order and shipping time to Korea was 120 days, in March supplies being shipped for support of operations after 30 June had to be obtained by further depletion of depot stocks and by diversion of production that had been intended for other world-wide commitments. At the end of December 1952 the Department of Defense again—and with more reason, as it turned out—directed the preparation of budget estimates on the assumption that there would be no combat operations in Korea in Fiscal Year 1954. In other words, the conflict would now end by 30 June 1953.

In spite of the heavy tonnage handled, a number of items persisted on lists of critical shortages. Ordnance equipment and supplies still listed as "critical" in mid-1951 included ammunition, spare parts, helicopters, tank bulldozers, tractors, heavy trucks, water trailers, and hot tire patches. Critical engineer items included motorized cranes, pumps, generators, entrenching tools, rock crushers, pneumatic floats and assault boats, and spare parts. Shortages continued in such quartermaster items as combat boots, typewriters, forklifts, parachutes, bath units, laundry units, and spare parts. Signal equipment listed as critical included field wire and very high frequency (VHF) relay and terminal equipment. Of course shortages were expressed in terms of authorized allowances; if those allowances provided for more than actually was needed of given items, then the "real" shortages were not so great as such compilations might suggest. There was no indication that supply shortages actually had interfered seriously with combat effectiveness during that first critical year.

More serious was the condition of the Army's supply reserves in the United States. By July 1952 the drain on Army supply resources as a result of the conflict in Korea was becoming pronounced. The Army's supply position was coming to what might be referred to as the second stage logistical crisis in the early phases of a war effort. The first stage would be the immediate crisis of moving sufficient supplies and equipment

to sustain the forces in meeting the initial attack and denying to the enemy a quick victory. That crisis had been met. Now, the second-stage was that point where stocks were being depleted and new production was not yet able to equal requirements. In World Wars I and II the resistance of allies during the early phases had given to the United States the time it needed to meet this second-stage crisis. In Korea it was World War II surplus, and the fact that the war was a localized conflict, which gave hope that this crisis could be met again.

Priorities for Supplies

High officials and officers of the Department of the Army were anxious to keep in view the concept that for the United States Western Europe potentially was the most important strategic area. Consolidation of a European defense system continued to be the main objective. Secretary of the Army Pace considered the most important lesson to come out of the Korean situation to be this: a really effective U.S. land force participation was needed as a deterrent to aggression in sensitive areas, of which Western Europe was the most important.

Here was the beginning of a repetition of the tug of war that during World War II had developed between the Pacific and European theaters for favor in logistical support. A great dread of the Army high command in the early 1950's was that overemphasis on requirements for the Far East would lead to the neglect of European defense. And in the Army's view the defense of Western Europe, with all its industrial resources, its manpower, and its strategic bases, was absolutely essential to the security of the United States. The leaders holding this view saw Korea not as an isolated problem but as only one step in a world-wide Communist move for domination. But at the moment the contest for equipment was between a potential war in Europe and a going conflict in Korea. Tactical reverses in Korea magnified the need for equipment there. In September 1951, then, a revision of the priority groups put the Far East Command at the top for the equipment of troops, though Europe was not forgotten.

Another priorities problem arose in connection with the foreign assistance programs. From the beginning the assumption was that current commitments for the Mutual Defense Assistance Program and the North Atlantic Treaty Organization would be met, though priority would be on shipments to support the Korean operations. Shipments of property earmarked for the Fiscal Year 1950 Mutual Defense Assistance Program were not to be interrupted for any reason except to meet demands of the Far East Command which could not be met from Army stocks or procurement. For 1951 MDAP requirements, matériel could be transferred from stocks held for a claimant in a higher priority if new procurement could replace it by the time the higher claimant needed it.

New Weapons and Vehicles

Weapons

The U.S. Army fought in Korea with virtually the same weapons and vehicles it had used in World War II, although there were a few significant changes. The World War II bazooka, the 2.36-inch rocket launcher, gave way to a new 3.5-inch model early in the conflict. Depots in the United States shipped to the Far East over 14,800 of the new bazookas between July 1950

and July 1951, and 5,400 more in the following year. At first rushed to Korea by special airlift to help stop the North Korean drive in the summer of 1950, the new bazookas, ironically, may have damaged more American than enemy tanks, for the Communists soon stopped using tanks but in the fall and winter counteroffensives they captured a number of bazookas and turned them on the Americans.

Undoubtedly the greatest innovation in infantry weapons since World War II was the recoilless rifle—the infantry's own artillery. Both the 57-mm. and 75-mm. recoilless guns had been combat tested in World War II, but they had had little actual use until Korea. These weapons had the firepower of light field artillery without the weight and complications of recoil mechanisms and heavy mounts. In a way they had taken the place of the 37-mm. gun the infantry had used in World War I, but they were far more effective against pillboxes, caves, and emplacements as well as against groups of personnel and unarmored vehicles.

Some new items did not win the favor expected of them. In 1950 and early 1951 ordnance officers in the United States were looking to every possible source for sniperscopes and snooperscopes—devices using infrared light for aiming rifles at night—to meet urgent and heavy demands for the Far East Command. Then when the equipment reached the troops it remained largely unused—supply officers could not persuade units to requisition the scopes.

Tanks

When the Korean War broke out, neither light nor medium tanks were in production in the United States, and most tooling for

World War II models had been disassembled or reconverted to civilian production. But the Army was in the midst of a program for converting 800 Pershing tanks, a 46-ton type developed near the end of World War II, to M46 Pattons. As it became clear that the emergency would require more tanks than could be supplied from those on hand or due in—if any were to be kept in reserve or transferred to military assistance programs—the question of which models should be put into production arose. Of a new series of tanks being developed, none had been fully tested and standardized. World War II models, on the other hand, had been thoroughly tested and industry knew how to build them, but they lacked the firepower, maneuverability, and heavy armor of the new tank designs. In either case it would be necessary to retool and set up production facilities. The Chief of Staff and the Secretary of the Army decided to gamble on producing the new models without full testing.

The decision was not so difficult for the new light tank, the T41 (later called the Walker Bulldog in honor of Lt. Gen. Walton H. Walker, of the Eighth Army, who was killed in an accident in Korea), because the prototype had been tested. Designed to replace the M24 Chaffee as the standard light tank, the Walker Bulldog weighed twenty-five tons, carried a high-velocity 76-mm. gun, and could reach a speed of 35 to 40 miles an hour.

Thought to be a more difficult problem, though it actually turned out more satisfactorily, was that of the medium tank. While the M26 Pershings were being converted to M46 Pattons, a completely new medium tank, the T42, was on the drawing boards. Design work on the turret of the new tank had been completed at the time of the Korean attack, but drawings for the complete vehicle were not expected to be finished before November 1950. In the interest of speed, the Army chiefs decided to wed the new turret, with an improved 90-mm. gun and a new fire control system, to what was basically the M46 (and M26) hull. The resulting hybrid became the M47. Bypassing the usual mock-up pilot model and engineering and service board tests, on 17 July 1950 the Army ordered the M47 into production. Ten months later the new models began to come off the assembly lines. Another eleven months passed, however, before the inevitable "bugs" could be eliminated. The Army announced acceptance for delivery to troops in April 1952. At $240,000, the new tank cost just three times as much as the World War II Pershing.

At the same time development continued on other models. One of these, the Patton 48 (T48), the first completely new tank developed since World War II, promised to become the standard tank for the mid-1950's. It went into production in the summer of 1952. Wider tracked than older models, the 49-ton T48 had a one-piece cast hull. It was powered by an improved version of the Continental air-cooled engine of the earlier M46 and M47 with Allison cross-drive transmission and power steering. Its one-piece cast turret mounted an improved 90-mm. gun and a new-type rangefinder.

Completing the family of new tanks was the first heavy tank to go into production for the U.S. Army—the T43. In 1952 a heavy tank was defined as one weighing between fifty-six and eighty-five tons. The T43, a heavily armored monster, mounted a 120-mm. gun. It went into production late in 1952 at the Newark, Delaware, plant of the Chrysler Corporation, but its production was not pushed until demands for the new mediums could be satisfied.

Actually no new model tanks reached Korea in time to effect the fighting. A tank is a long-lead-time item. The design and manufacture of the thousands of parts and the assembly of a tank meeting the strict Army specifications is not something that can be done overnight. In the circumstances of the "creeping mobilization" of 1950–53, more than the ordinary delays could be expected—delays similar to those that hampered other areas of defense production as well. These included shortages of machine tools, conflicts between civilian business and defense work in the allocation of scarce facilities and materials, and lack of enough skilled engineers, supervisors, and inspectors to cover both continuing defense production and continuing civilian production.

Trucks

In the type of fighting that developed in Korea the supply of ordinary cargo trucks probably was more significant than the supply of tanks. The Ordnance Corps had been developing new models, and after testing some 300 of a new type in Korea with favorable results, shipments began in the summer of 1952 with a view to replacing all World War II models then in use. As replaced, the old trucks went to rebuild shops in Japan, and then were issued to the Republic of Korea Army, Japanese security forces, and to other countries under the Mutual Security Program. In general the new trucks were slightly bigger, somewhat better, and much more expensive. The new 2½-ton general cargo truck, though still

rated a 2½-ton, was designed to carry that load cross-country; on the highway its pay load was five tons.[6] The new model had six wheels (but usually without the dual wheels of the older models) mounting much bigger tires; it had a more powerful engine (145 or 146 horsepower), and the General Motors model had hydramatic transmission. The initial price of the Reo model of the new truck was over $7,000, though in February 1953 the price was listed at $6,759 for the Reo and $6,165 for the General Motors, whereas the "old reliable" of World War II had cost about $2,500. The new jeep, slightly larger than the old, with a more powerful engine and bigger, if less reliable, battery, was priced at $2,162, or more than twice the cost of the World War II model. These vehicles went directly from the manufacturer to the port of embarkation, saving time and the considerable expense of handling at ordnance depots and transshipment. But this direct shipment had the disadvantages of an uneven flow of vehicles to port and the added costs resulting from interruption to shipping schedules.

Army Aviation

Another development which gained significance for logistic support in Korea was the expansion of Army aviation. After separation of the Air Force from the Army in 1947, the only aviation left to the Army was the organic light liaison plane used mainly for artillery spotting and tactical

---

[6] Originally the 2½-ton capacity rated for the World War II type of general cargo truck was intended as its pay load on the highways, with half that capacity cross-country, but in May 1944 the War Department announced that the 2½-ton 6x6 truck could carry a 100 percent overload on smooth, hard roads.

observation. While the Military Air Transport Service, operated by the Air Force, carried Army cargo from the United States to the Far East, and the Far East Air Forces had that responsibility within the theater, the Army still needed aircraft for local transportation. The Marine Corps had its own aviation, including tactical combat planes as well as transport aircraft, besides the support of the Navy's air arm. The Army, on the other hand, was completely dependent upon the Air Force. It had even to obtain Air Force consent to get some planes of its own. Doubtless the example of Marine Corps units fighting side by side with the Army units in Korea did much to encourage the development of transport aviation in the Army.

Aside from the difficulties of expanding production, the chief deterrent to development of Army aviation was the insistence of the Air Force (with Defense Department concurrence) that Army aviation should be bound by strict limitations. At last in November 1952 the Air Force acceded to a "Memorandum of Understanding" that removed weight limitations on helicopters but defined the uses to which the Army could put them; weight limitations were retained for other types of aircraft. According to the memorandum, Army aviation could be used for observation, command and control of forces, liaison, aerial wire laying within the combat zone, transportation of supplies and personnel within the combat zone, artillery and topographic survey, and medical evacuation within the combat zone. All these were permissible so long as a conventional plane weighing not more than 5,000 pounds (or a helicopter) were used. Such artificial limitations, not necessarily related to the Army's missions, tended to

hamper the program for aviation support. It was much the same as if the Transportation Corps, for example, had objected to the use of trucks larger than 1½-ton capacity by the Quartermaster Corps, with the difference that the Quartermaster Corps could have gone ahead using bigger trucks anyway. Still, the agreement on helicopters was a notable achievement for the Army, and the Chief of Staff looked forward to building up a force of 2,200 light planes and helicopters.

The helicopter came of age as the favorite vehicle for local air transportation in Korea. Before World War II the Army had taken an interest in the development of rotary-wing aircraft, but it was not until the Korean War that it came into common use for combat support. Able to hover like a hummingbird and needing no specially built runways, the helicopter was ideal for delivering supplies to small isolated units and for evacuating casualties from areas inaccessible to surface motor transportation. The demand for helicopters in Korea became so great that they were a critical supply problem throughout the war.

Helicopters in use during this period were generally of two categories. The Bell H–13 and the Hiller H–23 were the standard utility models, while most of the cargo helicopters being built were the Sikorsky H–19 and, later, the Piasecki H–21. The H–19 carried a pay load of 1,800 pounds; it could carry ten passengers or eight litter cases. The boomerang-shaped H–21, with an engine at each end, was double the size of the H–19 and could carry twice as many passengers and more than twice as heavy a cargo. Improved liaison fixed-wing planes, including one light twin-engine model, also were in production by 1952.

A Helicopter With Outside Litter Carriers *approaching a small clearing in Korea to take out casualties.*

Petroleum Products

As motor transportation played an ever greater role in the movement and support of armies, motor fuels and lubricants (POL) assumed increasing importance as elements of supply. This was true particularly of the U.S. Army, which had come to put such complete reliance upon motor transportation that any extended interruption of the fuel supply could strangle the whole combat effort. Approximately 65 percent of the tonnage of all supplies shipped into the Far East Command was petroleum products. The more than 170,-000 tons a month of gasoline and oil going into Korea in April and May 1951 were 4.25 times as much as the tonnage of food supplies, and over 3.54 times the tonnage of ammunition going in during the same period. Petroleum products comprised the one class of supply furnished by the U.S. Army for all United Nations forces—ground, sea, and air—in Korea. The Air Force had responsibility for arranging the financing and the consignment to the Far East Command of high grade aviation gasoline, jet fuel, and aviation lubricants, but the Army had that responsibility for all other petroleum products, and within the theater the Army was responsible for all distribution, including aviation fuel, gasoline, and oils.

Handling POL cut across service lines in a pecular way. POL was owned by the respective military services, the tankers to move it were controlled by the Navy's Military Sea Transportation Service, the requirements were computed by the military services and the theaters, and the Armed Services Petroleum Purchasing Agency acted as purchasing agent for all the armed forces. Within the Army, the Quartermaster Corps had over-all responsibility for petroleum supply, but the construction, maintenance, and operation of pipelines and of terminal facilities were functions of the Corps of Engineers, and the operation of tank cars and trucks and the arrangement of air transportation and local water transportation were functions of the Transportation Corps.

The "Ammunition Shortage"

Probably no single item of supply received more attention in the support of operations in Korea than ammunition. To a public convinced that the American "miracle of production" had won World War II, it was almost inconceivable that in mid-1952, after more than two years of operations, reports of ammunition shortages still should be coming from Korea; yet such was the case. Local shortages that developed from time to time could be attributed generally to difficulties of local distribution under adverse tactical and climatic conditions, over rugged terrain, with poor transportation facilities. Other limitations resulted in a situation where, for a number of important

weapons, total stocks in the Far East Command frequently fell below the full authorized level of supply (90 days), and at times dropped well below the defined "safety" level (60 days). Factors contributing to this situation were: (1) the unusually high rate of fire deemed necessary to offset the enemy's large numbers in particular situations; (2) the fact that no ammunition production lines of any consequence were in operation in the United States; and (3) the fact that it took about a year and a half to establish production lines and get volume production. Maintaining the right levels of ammunition supply in all units in such diverse conditions as prevailed on the Korean battlefields was no easy matter, but it was most important. Shortages of ammunition could result in tactical reverses and loss of life; overages would waste resources.

The Army's ammunition supply system was based on a "continuous refill system" according to which each unit carried a prescribed "basic load of ammunition" set by the theater commander, which was replenished as used. The basic load was supposed to be an amount that the unit could carry on its own transportation, and it was the responsibility of each unit commander to maintain it. Ordinarily the ammunition supply point filled orders consisting only of a statement on a transportation order that certain ammunition was necessary to replenish the basic load. Successive commanders, from theater commander down to lower units, controlled the consumption of ammunition by prescribing "available supply rates of ammunition." These rates, expressed in rounds per weapon per day in the tactical units, represented the consumption that could be sustained with available supplies. In addition, commanders made up estimates of the number of rounds per weapon per day needed to sustain operations of a designated force without restriction for a specific period. This estimate, referred to as the "required supply rate of ammunition" formed the basis for ammunition supply planning in connection with given operations.

On the basis either of combat necessity or of tonnage, no category of supply held a more important place in the combat zone than ammunition. Ammunition made up over half of the tonnage of supplies reaching division areas.

Shortly after the outbreak of hostilities in Korea, Far East Command requested and obtained a temporary increase in the approved ammunition day of supply for four common types of mortar and artillery ammunition amounting to an increase of three to six times over the previous day of supply. The immediate effect, of course, was to reduce by that same ratio the quantities of those types of ammunition on hand as expressed in days of supply. For example, the 3,240 rounds of 105-mm. howitzer ammunition in a depot in the Far East, which previously had represented six days of supply for the field artillery of an infantry division, suddenly fell to a single day of supply without the expenditure of a single round. Planners who could take comfort in assuming that sixty days of this ammunition was available at a certain place became uneasy when they found that the level had been reduced to ten days. Here, in effect, was the making of a psychological shortage without any valid combat experience upon which to base it. In October 1950 Far East Command agreed to a return to the smaller ammunition day of supply for mortars and howitzers.

When the Chinese struck in the spring of 1951, General Van Fleet, now commander of the Eighth Army, determined to smother the offensive in artillery fire. He said, "I want so many artillery holes that a man can step from one to another." He authorized a rate of fire five times as great as the approved ammunition day of supply. Under this "Van Fleet day of fire," artillery expenditures skyrocketed.[7]

Expenditures of artillery ammunition during the Battle of Soyang reached almost unheard-of proportions. In the seven days from 17 to 23 May 1951, the twenty-one battalions (including four Marine and two Republic of Korea battalions) supporting X Corps fired 309,958 rounds, or more than 8,730 tons. The magnitude of this effort becomes even more striking when compared to the 94,230 rounds that thirty-five battalions fired in support of the Third Army's attack toward Bastogne during the ten days from 22 to 31 December 1944. During the assault on Metz in 1944 the XX Corps expended 10,000 tons of artillery ammunition in ten days. At Soyang, daily expenditures were 50,102 rounds, representing 1,378 tons, on 20 May, and 49,586 rounds, representing 1,456 tons, on 22 May. On 17 May the 38th Field Artillery Battalion alone fired 11,981 rounds—an average of almost one round per gun every two minutes for the whole twenty-four hour period. Total expenditures for the period 10 May–7 June amounted to over 644,000 rounds, or some 18,000 tons of artillery ammunition. The tonnage of ammunition used by the X Corps during this period was nearly double the tonnage of all other supplies consumed. Between 15 and 22 May the daily expenditures of ammunition averaged 73 percent of

---

[7] Command Report, Eighth U.S. Army, May 1951, sec. I, p. 88.

the tonnage of all supplies expended, and it reached as high as 82.6 percent.[8]

Artillery ammunition expenditures attained even higher rates in a series of attacks against hill positions near Inje between 18 August and 5 September 1951. In fifteen days of hard fighting five battalions of 105-mm. howitzers supporting the 2d Division each fired an average of 10,000 rounds a day, and three 155-mm. howitzer battalions fired an average of 7,500 rounds a day apiece, for a total of 1,087,500 rounds. Figured at $26 and $40 per round for the two calibers, the total cost of artillery ammunition expended in the support of one division in a series of rugged battles covering fifteen days thus amounted to about $33,000,000. Whether such high expenditures of ammunition were justified was open to serious question. Doubts on this point arose at X Corps headquarters, and on 2 September the corps commander advised the 2d Division, "We have the distinct impression that two of your battalions are trying to compete for the world's record. We don't want you to cut down on this expenditure where it is really needed. We feel that there is some wasteful firing."[9]

A great deal of public discussion centered on reports of ammunition shortages and the imposition of rationing in Korea. The extent of those shortages and the nature of any rationing depended pretty much on the point of view. At no time were there shortages in Korea in the sense that all theater stocks of critical items were exhausted. Sometimes units locally ran out of ammunition when they did not receive resupplies quickly enough, but the pipelines never were empty. Though theater stock levels varied a great deal, the matter was largely relative. Actually, the build-up of ammunition levels in the Far East Command to 90 days for ground forces in Korea, approved by the Department of the Army in the fall of 1952, amounted to nearly 180 days, if figured on the basis of actual experience in Korea instead of on the basis of the exaggerated ammunition day of supply then in force.

It was also true that theater stocks of ammunition remained considerably below maximum authorized levels (though above the minimum safety level for nearly all items) at the end of 1952. Far more serious, however, than any immediate threat of acute ammunition shortages in Korea was the Army's over-all ammunition position. Expenditures in Korea had nearly exhausted Army stocks of World War II ammunition, and the great danger was that a new incident in some other part of the world might create immediate demands for ammunition that simply could not be met. The critical nature of this logistical phase, when reserves were becoming exhausted and new production had not yet caught up with demand, doubtless applied more emphatically to ammunition than to any other kind of supply. By the end of 1952 new production was reaching the point where it could support demands for the Far East, but it still took some time before reserves in the United States could be restored.

---

[8] Statistics may be found in: After Action Report, Third U.S. Army (1944–1945), I, 188; (XX Corps at Metz) Randolph Leigh, *American Enterprise in Europe: The Role of the SOS in the Defeat of Germany* (Paris: *Imprimateur par* Bellenand, 1945), p. 124; (battle of the Soyang River) Report, Battle of the Soyang River, An analysis of Artillery Support, 1–29 May 1951, an. to Incl 4. OCMH files.

[9] Mark S. Watson, "Ammunition Expenditure in Korea," *Ordnance* (September–October 1952), p. 254; Cost figures in Ammunition Br, Industrial Div, OCofOrd; X Corps commander quoted in "Bloody Ridge," August–September 1951, prepared by Capt. Edward C. Williamson and others, pp. 27–28. MS in OCMH.

Undeniably the production of ammunition in the States after the North Korean attack was painfully slow in reaching significant proportions. Total expenditures for Army ammunition deliveries from 1 July 1950 through 30 June 1951 came to only $62,300,000—less than double the $33,-000,000 worth of ammunition the five artillery battalions supporting the 2d Division near Inje expended in fifteen days. In the second year of the Korean War, 1 July 1951–30 June 1952, deliveries of Army ammunition of all types amounted to $892,-900,000. This production was low whether compared with consumption in Korea, or with ammunition delivered in World War II in the first two years after Pearl Harbor, or with orders placed. The picture began to brighten by the end of 1952. Indeed Maj. Gen. Elbert L. Ford, Chief of Ordnance, reported that the over-all production of artillery ammunition in the last half of 1952 represented a thirtyfold increase over the one million rounds produced in the last six months of 1950.[10]

Much of the delay was unavoidable under the circumstances. From one to two years were required to start up ammunition production lines under the best of conditions, and a number of other factors contributed to further delays. One factor still related to finance. Not until the second supplemental appropriation, approved in January 1951, could ordnance procurement officers begin to place contracts for significant amounts. The lead time for major new production, consequently, had to be measured from January 1951 rather than from July 1950. Contracts placed between January and June 1951 would show as part of the obligations for the fiscal year, but deliveries under those orders could not be made effective until much later. The unrealistic planning assumption that the war would end within a few months made some shortages a certainty; moreover, the whole concept of creeping mobilization—an ordered build-up of armaments production with the least possible disturbance to the civilian economy—carried with it elements of delay that would have been less conspicuous under conditions of full mobilization. Shortages of machine tools and special-purpose equipment needed for the manufacture of ammunition components added to the delays of returning ammunition plants to production. The fact that no deliveries of 60-mm. mortar ammunition came from new production for two years after the beginning of the Korean conflict is partly attributable to design changes. In this case development problems became so great that it was necessary to go back to the World War II type of ammunition until the difficulties could be overcome. Another cause of delay was shortages in materials; in particular a shortage of aluminum (required for fuses) seriously hampered production of both 60-mm. and 81-mm. mortar ammunition. Finally, a crippling steel strike in the summer of 1952 caused production losses estimated as high as 37 percent for some types of ammunition. On 23 July 1952 the Chevrolet Shell Plant at St. Louis, principal producer of 105-mm.

[10] Rpt, ORDGC–BP, data as of 30 March 1953, Status of Ordnance Corps Ammunition Program Army and All Customers, Funds FY 1951, 1952, 1953, pp. 215–17 (see also: Your Army Dollars, as of 30 June 1951, Office, Chief of Finance, p. 77, and DA Financial Statement, June 1952, Army Progress Report 16–A, p. 56); (1942 and 1943) Army Services Forces, Statistical Review, World War II, pp. 75–76; (total ammunition production, 1952) DOD, OPI, Release 93–53, 8 February 1953; (monthly cumulative figures) Production Forecast Sheets, Ammunition Br, Industrial Div, OCofORD.

ammunition, had to shut down because of lack of steel.

Actually, then, it was early 1953 before artillery ammunition, made of new components, began to come from the production lines in quantity. Loading plants, on the other hand, began significant production from available components something over a year earlier.

Supply Distribution From the United States

The principal source of supplies for United Nations forces in Korea was, of course, the United States. Hardly less significant, particularly in the early months of the conflict, was the extensive program of rebuilding World War II equipment collected in Japan. A third major source of supply, important in filling gaps between demand and supply, was procurement from local merchants and manufacturers in Japan and Korea.

Although supply to the Far East during the Korean War never was put on the completely automatic basis that generally would have been the case for a new theater initiating military operations, the Department of the Army did approve automatic resupply for units moving to the Far East from the United States. This continued until October 1950, when Far East Command requested termination of automatic resupply except for sixty days resupply of ammunition and parts for equipment then not being used in the command. Far East Command could submit requisitions during the early weeks of the conflict without regard to levels of supply or formal justification. It was only necessary for the command to establish priorities for movement of the supplies it requested. As in World War II, each port of

embarkation had specific responsibility for the supply of forces in a particular area of the world. For support of operations in Korea, the ports of embarkation at New York, New Orleans, and Seattle, as well as commercial ports on the west coast and on the Gulf of Mexico, served as outports of San Francisco. (*Map 25*)

Emergency demands of forces in Korea triggered a far swifter reaction than had been possible in the weeks following the Pearl Harbor attack in 1941. The Oversea Supply Division, even though at greatly reduced strength in June 1950, was an effective, going organization capable of rapid expansion. In 1948, the Oversea Supply Division had been brought directly under the Assistant Chief of Staff, G–4 (then the Director of Logistics). This meant a certain division of responsibility at the ports, for the ports of embarkation remained under the command of the Chief of Transportation. On the other hand, the Oversea Supply Division, by the very nature of its function, had to deal with all the technical services in getting supplies; this seemed more logically a function of G–4 than of an agency of one of the technical services. The closest co-operation between the chief of the Oversea Supply Division and the port commander was, of course, essential, since the Oversea Supply Division continued to be involved in cargo planning and in expediting cargo through the port.

Once sufficient shipping had been put into service early in the conflict, overseas movement of supplies and troops proceeded relatively smoothly under the supervision of the Navy's Military Sea Transportation Service. When the need for certain items was especially urgent (as rockets and launchers), the items were shipped by air when practicable. High priority cargo be-

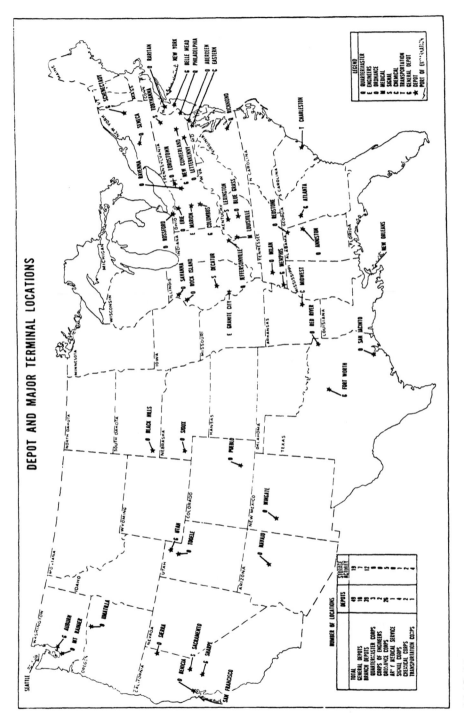

DEPOT AND MAJOR TERMINAL LOCATIONS

MAP 25

yond the capacity of available airlift went by MARINEX (Marine Express), top-loaded, when possible, on fast vessels sailing directly to the oversea destination.

A giant step forward in transportation of military matériel was taken with the initiation of Container Express (CONEX) service. Developed by the Transportation Corps, the system unitized small packages into uniform loads in reusable steel containers. The containers, called cargo transporters, could be tiered three high, could be loaded on the deck of a ship or squared to the hatch, and handled by ordinary ship's gear. They could also be transported on the standard Army 6x6 truck, on commercial or military flat-bed or open-top semitrailers, and on flat or gondola railway cars. After a test period from June to December 1951, Far Eastern Command reported enthusiastically on the system and recommended that it be expanded in the theater. The test shipments had been made from Japan to Korea by sea, and within Korea by rail. In November 1952 CONEX service began on a trial basis from the United States to the Far East when, to relieve the critical shortage of engineer spare parts, thirty transporters were put into service from the Columbus General Depot in Ohio to the Yokohama Engineer Depot in Japan. Operating on a fixed schedule, a group of three transporters left Columbus by commercial truck each week for San Francisco from where it was shipped via MARINEX to Yokohama. Government vehicles delivered the transporters to the consignee point where they were emptied immediately and returned to port for movement to the depot in the continental United States. The average time of delivery was twenty-seven days, and that of the round trip was fifty-five days—an estimated 25–30

days' saving in depot-to-depot transportation time. Reports indicated that handling was facilitated, damage and pilferage minimized, and overpacking requirements reduced. With the success of this trial run, use of the CONEX system for shipments to Yokohama increased to nine weekly by May 1953.[11]

Support of United Nations Forces

Allied forces in Korea other than those of the United States and the Republic of Korea never reached as much as 10 percent of the total troop strength. The United States provided one-half or more of the logistic support for these forces, but this amounted to a relatively small fraction of the total supplies and services furnished United States and Korean forces. Yet the significance of United Nations participation in the Korean operations, and of American logistical support therefor, can not be measured alone in the numbers of troops involved. The problems of co-ordination, negotiation, and accounting were as great as though the troop contributions had been several times as large. It took about as much paper work to record the disposition of ten vehicles as of a hundred. Negotiations for concluding satisfactory agreements on financial arrangements were hardly less involved for the settlement of accounts amounting to a million dollars than for accounts of a hundred million dollars. Aside from the demonstration of solidarity for United Nations principles which the military contributions of twenty other nations indicated, probably the most important result of those contributions was the ex-

---

[11] Office, Chief of Transportation, TC in the Current National Emergency: The Post-Korean Experience, CONEX A Milestone in Unitization, pp. 3–5. Copy in OCMH.

perience in international logistic co-operation, which would be of value in future collective police actions and coalition wars.

National differences in customs, tastes, and religions led to many complications in supplying United Nations forces. Moslems could not eat pork, and the Hindus of the Indian Ambulance Company could not eat beef because of religious restrictions; the Indians had to have curry powder and rice; Thais and Filipinos too wanted rice, strong spices, and strong brands of tea and coffee. The Dutch missed their milk and cheese; the French missed their wine; and nearly all the European troops wanted a great deal more bread than the American ration provided. The Storage Division of the Yokohama Quartermaster Depot, beginning in February 1951, prepared "spice packs" to accompany shipments of B rations to Korea so that individual units could season the food to their taste. One type of packet contained soda and baking powder; another contained eleven different spicing elements. A special hot sauce supplement was provided for Thailand and Ethiopian troops who apparently would eat most any ration if it had enough hot sauce on it. Types of provisions furnished to particular countries changed from time to time; in May 1952 only three countries—Canada, Norway, and Sweden—were accepting the complete American ration with nothing added and nothing subtracted.

The financial arrangements entailed in paying for logistical support in the Korean War were complicated. The United States of course paid for all that went to its forces.

The eighteen members of the United Nations (other than the United States) who gave some kind of assistance in Korea incurred financial indebtedness to the United States for U.S. matériel they used in the course of operations. The other forty-two members (twenty-nine of whom supported the General Assembly resolution on the unification of Korea in October 1950, and twenty-six of whom voted in favor of the General Assembly resolution of 1 February 1951 declaring Communist China an aggressor) incurred no financial obligation.

The Army had to keep account of its costs, and this included the support of other United Nations forces. Congress needed to know, in approving programs and appropriations, what the cost of providing support were. Foreign governments were anxious to have accounts kept straight so they would know the amount of indebtedness they were incurring and would have an indication of their participation as equal partners. Some officials in the Department of the Army were fearful lest support granted without provision for repayment might leave the United States open to unfriendly foreign propaganda which might suggest that the United States was following a policy of hiring mercenaries to do its fighting. The Army prepared no separate budget to cover the support of United Nations forces. This support came out of the regular funds of the technical services, though separate records had to be kept.

Expansion of the Republic of Korea Army

As the Korean conflict settled into a stalemate apparently without end, an alternative to the indefinite commitment of American forces seemed to be to build a Republic of Korea Army that could relieve American divisions in the defense of that country, or that could make a major contribution toward breaking the stalemate. With peace talks giving no promise of an early armistice, pressure toward that end began to increase on both sides of the Pacific in the spring of 1952. It was to become a theme for much of the discussion in the presidential campaign of that year.

General Clark, in response to a request from the Chief of Staff, had submitted a plan to expand the Republic of Korea Army to twenty divisions within a period of eighteen months, but he did so with grave misgivings about the over-all logistical implications of such a build-up within such a short period of time.

Even if the suggested expansion of ROK forces were successful in permitting the withdrawal of American forces, it was to be questioned whether such a course would have been wise from the point of view of international politics. What had begun as a common United Nations effort would then be completely lost, and the Korean War would be reduced to a civil war. At the same time, it was doubtful whether the South Koreans themselves would have been enthusiastic about the complete withdrawal of American combat divisions. Perhaps a more serious concern for the United States was the loss of matériel that would be involved. Weapons and equipment then in the hands of American and other United Nations forces in Korea could still be considered a matériel reserve for use elsewhere in the Far East, or in other parts of the world if necessary, but if they were handed over to the Republic of Korea they could not be counted on for use anywhere else in the world. A further fact that could not be ignored was the danger that some matériel, if given to the ROK Army, might fall into the hands of the Communists. Doubtless the Chinese Communists would have the capability of overrunning even a 20-division South Korean Army if there were no other

forces to deter them, and as had happened in the case of some of the Chinese Nationalist forces, equipment delivered for the defense of Korea might actually be turned against it. Moreover, there was no getting away from the fact that such a large-scale turnover of equipment to the Republic of Korea could not help but delay by another year or more the fulfillment of the North Atlantic Treaty Organization programs, would delay further the arming of Japanese security forces, would make necessary the continuation of the 50 percent ceiling on critical items for training units in the United States, and would continue the gamble of getting along without reconstituting the matériel reserves in the United States. Early in February 1953 President Eisenhower authorized General Clark to add two divisions to the Republic of Korea Army immediately to make a force of fourteen divisions plus six separate regiments with an over-all ceiling (including marines) of 507,880. A few days later the Joint Chiefs of Staff recommended to the Secretary of Defense that the program for expanding the Republic of Korea Army to twenty divisions be implemented immediately.

Far East Command

Organization for Logistics

The logistical mission of Far East Command encompassed broad responsibilities for support of: (1) United Nations forces in Korea, (2) the defense of the Far East Command; (3) forces of the Republic of Korea Army, Navy, and Air Force beyond the capabilities of the Korean Government to support; (4) Korean augmentation to U.S. Army (Korean soldiers integrated into American units), and the Korean Service

Corps; (5) prisoners of war and civilian internees in Korea, (6) the U.S. Military Advisory Group to the Republic of Korea (KMAG), (7) civil assistance in Korea as necessary to support military operations; (9) a program of civil relief and economic aid until those responsibilities were assumed by United Nations civil agencies; (9) a planned program for moving and processing refugees in Korea; (10) a planned movement of exchanged prisoners of war and civilian internees in the event of an armistice; (11) a program to develop and equip armed forces of the Republic of Korea to assume increasing responsibility in the defense of the Republic; (12) Japanese security forces; and (13) the Ryukyuan Central Police Force.

The Japan Logistical Command, under Maj. Gen. Walter L. Weible, was the agency to which the Eighth Army in Korea submitted its requisitions for supplies, and it was, in turn, the requisitioning agency of the Far East Command for supplies from the United States. Within Japan it operated ports, depots, and other installations for logistic support. It carried out its administrative responsibilities through three area commands. In order to save troop spaces in its own service units, the Japan Logistical Command used table of distribution rather than table of organization units wherever the substitution would effect a saving. Often it was possible to fill the supervisory spaces with military personnel, and then to fill out the unit with local labor.

The first use in combat operations of a logistical command organized under an approved table of organization was in Korea. And in Korea it was used in a way considered "exceptional" in the statements of doctrine which had accompanied the development of this type of organization—it was

being used in the combat zone, as a subordinate element of an army. In September 1950 the 2d Logistical Command, organized as a Type C table of organization logistical command, replaced the Pusan Logistical Command. The primary mission of the 2d Logistical Command was to receive, store, and forward supplies for the Eighth Army in Korea. It also forwarded most of the Eighth Army's requisitions to the Japan Logistical Command. Eighth Army headquarters retained direct control of requisitioning ammunition, petroleum products, and perishable foods because of the difficulty of determining a satisfactory basis for requisitioning those items under the 60-day requisitioning policy then in effect. After the Inchon landing the 3d Logistical Command, a Type B organization, went in to that area to perform the same kind of support functions for X Corps that the 2d Logistical Command was performing for Eighth Army.

After some experience in Korea, the consensus of those concerned seemed to be that the table-of-organization logistical command was sound in concept and realistic in proposed missions. Its great advantage was in that it represented an approved voucher against which a commander could draw service troops when he was called upon to set up a logistical support organization. Something might have been gained by additional flexibility.

The most critical problems commanders faced in Korea were little different from those commanders met in World War II—service personnel and labor. The labor problem could always be expected in any similar logistical organization; yet no labor organization as such had been developed in the logistical command. Actually the 2d Logistical Command eventually employed over 100,000 Koreans, either directly or indirectly, as well as others who worked on local procurement contracts. This put many soldiers of all ranks in the positions of supervisors, and it had the effect of making the 2d Logistical Command a much larger organization than anticipated. Finding the right number of men with the needed military occupational speciality numbers, and supervising scores of small specialists units created major administrative problems.

When Lt. General Walton H. Walker assumed command of all U.S. ground troops in Korea on 12 July 1950, the total strength of his Eighth Army, in Korea and in Japan, was 2,602 officers, 237 warrant officers, and 40,307 enlisted men. In the course of the next several months U.S. elements in that army expanded sixfold. On 16 July 1950 all ground forces of the Republic of Korea Army came under the command of the Eighth Army; a year later they outnumbered all the U.S. elements assigned to that army. What had begun as the advance headquarters of an understrength army was soon tantamount to the headquarters of an army group plus the advance section of a communications zone. The Eighth Army's logistical mission included logistical support for all United Nations forces in Korea with the exception of ammunition and technical supplies for air units, equipment peculiar to the Marine Corps, and items furnished other United Nations forces by their own governments, plus support of the Korean Civil Assistance Program.

In July 1952 General Clark issued instructions to be effective 21 August, establishing the Korean Communications Zone (KCOMZ) to relieve the Commanding General, Eighth Army, of responsibility for logistical and territorial operations not immediately related to the conduct of combat operations in Korea, and to relieve him of responsibility for political relations with the Government of the Republic of Korea.[12] This permitted the 2d Logistical Command to fall into place as earlier Army doctrine had envisaged the logistical commands: under the new set-up it became the operating agency for the Korean Base Section. As of November 1952 the Korean Communications Zone co-ordinated the work of four subordinate commands: (1) the Korean Base Section, operated by 2d Logistical Command, (2) the 3d Military Railway Service, (3) the U.N. Prisoner of War Command, and (4) the U.N. Civil Assistance Command. Theoretically the Korean Base Section was only one of four operational commands for which KCOMZ headquarters was the co-ordinating agency. However, in practice, this arrangement amounted to a layering of headquarters to some extent. Here was a communications zone having only one section, a section that had territorial boundaries co-extensive with those of KCOMZ itself. Although KCOMZ was conceived as a planning and policy-making headquarters, with Korean Base Section as the operational command for supply activities, it was not possible to maintain sharp lines of distinction.

Another major organizational change became effective 1 October 1952 when Headquarters, U.S. Army Forces, Far East (USAFFE), absorbed Japan Logistical Command and became the Army's principal administrative headquarters in Japan. This still left the administrative organization somewhat different from that outlined in field service regulations. Actually Army

---

[12] For his part, General Ridgway preferred the arrangement under which he had operated as Eighth Army commander, with the logistics structure part of his own command.

Forces, Far East, with responsibility for fifth echelon maintenance and for logistical support of Korean Base Section, was functioning as the base section of a theater communications zone, as well as theater communications zone headquarters and theater army forces headquarters. The position of Korean Communications Zone in that framework was analogous to an advance section of a communications zone, with one important difference—under the "normal" organization KCOMZ would have been subordinate to an over-all communications zone—Army Forces, Far East—actually, until 1 January 1953, KCOMZ had equal status with Army Forces, Far East, as a major subordinate command of the Far East Command. Nevertheless, co-ordination between the two logistical headquarters—with frequent visits of staff officers and commanders, exchanges of personnel, and direct communication—probably was as close as though one command had been subordinate to the other.

Supply

Supply from the United States became effective quickly, but not nearly enough arrived to meet all requirements during the early months of the conflict. Fortunately for the United Nations effort, large quantities of World War II equipment were still in Japan and on the Pacific islands, and Japanese labor and facilities were at hand to recondition that equipment.

In the first four months of the war the ordnance rebuild program, begun in Japan that spring, turned out 489,000 small arms, 1,418 artillery pieces, 34,316 pieces of fire control equipment, 743 combat vehicles, and 15,000 general purpose vehicles. The program not only saved the tactical situation

in all probability, but dollars as well—and the resources and time which those dollars represented. During the next two years dollar savings resulting from all the rebuild operations of the various services in Japan were estimated as high as $9.5 million.

Another fortunate circumstance for the United States was Korea's proximity to Japan, the leading industrial power of the Orient, whose industrial resources were at the command of U.S. forces. Had a war occurred in an area such as the Middle East the possible result is fearful to contemplate. When the accelerated rebuild program, which in itself depended upon Japanese industry, was not enough to close the gap between immediate requirements for Korea and shipments arriving from the United States, it was possible to make up much of the difference by purchases from Japanese merchants and manufacturers. From the beginning of the Korean conflict, when the Eighth Army obtained such emergency items as landing net clips, manila rope, lumber, crushed rock, pallets, sandbags, carbon tetrachloride, and life preservers from Japanese sources, local procurement was an essential feature of supply operations.

Attempts to set up automatic resupply shipments directly from the United States to Korea during the early weeks of the conflict were not particularly effective. The shipping time was too long, and the tactical situation was changing too rapidly. Automatic resupply shipments from Japan to Korea, however, were the rule for the first several months. During that period of uncertainty, when United Nations forces were withdrawing, defending, and attacking in rapid succession up and down the length of the Korean Peninsula, it was nearly impossible to find a firm basis for preparing requisitions. Since at first practically everything was needed, availability of both supplies and carriers governed supply shipments to Korea. The inevitable results were evidenced in the uneconomical use of shipping, loss of time in unloading when ships jammed Korean ports, delivery of noncritical supplies while critical items awaited unloading, and added shipping costs.

The depot system in Korea was much more simple than that found, for example, in World War I or World War II in France, where intermediate and advance depots shared the burdens of depot operations in getting supplies forward, but the result was a greater complexity of problems. Finding that the doctrine, "the impetus of supply is from the rear" had lost its relevance in some respects, unit supply officers in Korea resorted to various expedients to pull supplies forward. The long supply lines could be likened to a long-range electrical transmission line over which electrical energy loses its force unless booster stations are used. In Korea the "booster stations", that is, the intermediate depots, were missing, an omission especially significant for Class II and IV supplies which did not fall within the daily distribution pattern. The long distance separating depots from combat divisions seemed to dull the sense of urgency of the men operating the depots. Some divisions found it useful to station expediters near the depots to see that badly needed supplies moved forward. (*Map 26*)

Pusan, the primary depot area as well as the primary port in Korea throughout the war, was probably the most lucrative target for enemy bombing in all Korea. Destruction of the port and storage facilities in the Pusan area would have almost paralyzed the United Nations' operations. Certainly no lesson is to be learned from the fact that the enemy did not take advantage

of the circumstances. On the contrary, everyone seemed to recognize the danger, but because of the shortage of service personnel and the lack of suitable facilities and necessary transportation lines elsewhere—together with a certain amount of inertia—little was done to correct the situation.

Transportation

Probably the greatest limitation on port capacity in Korea, other than the lack of skilled stevedores, was the lack of transportation facilities for moving cargo out of the port areas. The practice of establishing depots in the transportation facilities at the port seriously aggravated the situation. Pusan, with a potential capacity of 45,000 measurement tons a day, had an actual average daily discharge rate of only about 14,000 tons in Fiscal Year 1951. Other ports had similar transport limitations. As a result, ships sometimes had to stand by in the outer harbors as long as twenty-five days—once, 36 vessels were at the port of Inchon, and they had an average in-port time of twenty-two days.

Geography severely limited transportation within Korea. An almost uninterrupted chain of mountains extending from northern Korea all along the east coast and through the middle of the peninsula channeled communications through intervening valleys and corridors and along the lowlands of the west coast.

The logistical effort in the country depended above all upon the successful operation of the railroads. The Military Railway Service supervised operations, and local employees of the National Railway actually ran the trains and did most of the repair work under a contract arrangement that subsequently resulted in a credit to the

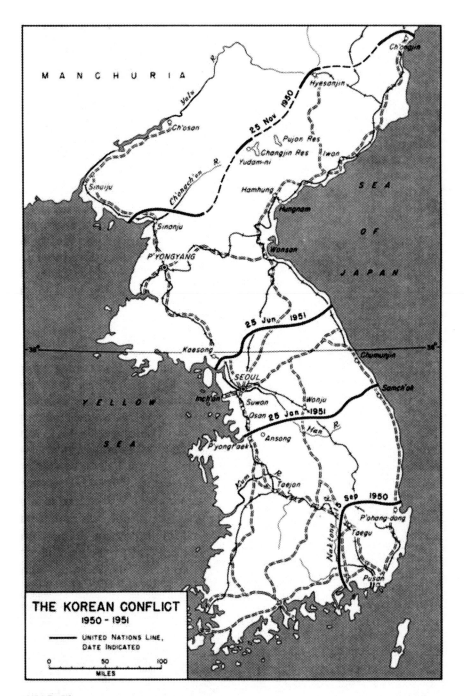

THE KOREAN CONFLICT
1950 - 1951

—— UNITED NATIONS LINE,
DATE INDICATED

0   50   100
MILES

MAP 26

South Korean Government approximating $1,000,000 a month plus $3,500,000 a month for operating supplies and maintenance. On an average day in 1951 over thirty trains were dispatched—about 25 carrying supplies to forward railheads, 3 or more carrying troops, 2 or more taking casualties to the rear, and the remainder transporting goods to supply points or other rear area destinations. Each train, with 20 to 40 cars, carried about 500 tons of freight or 1,000 passengers for average distances of 100 miles.

The most difficult part of the whole transportation system was the delivery of supplies to front-line units. Driving conditions were bad enough in rear areas over the narrow, rough mountain roads where guerrilla bands often menaced motor convoys. In forward areas, road maintenance and the road net were inadequate, and when trucks could not get through men had to carry the supplies. All the cross-country mobility of the 2½-ton trucks and the jeeps was of no avail over the mountainous positions the United Nations forces held on much of the Korean front. In an attack road improvement and cargo vehicles could not keep up with the infantry advancing over mountainous terrain. The answer to these difficulties was found in the organization of companies of Korean hand carriers. Improvised cable lifts performed further valuable service in delivering supplies and bringing out casualties from almost inaccessible battle positions.

Although helicopters were slow in comparison to other aircraft, they could be used to build up supplies very rapidly in a local situation, and the supplies could be delivered precisely at the designated spot. In a matter of minutes helicopters could deliver a day's supplies to a front-line company over terrain that would take hours to traverse on land. With supplies in cargo nets, a helicopter had to remain no longer than thirty seconds at the landing area for unloading; if casualties were to be evacuated on the return trip, it took only three or four minutes to unload the supplies and load the casualties. As a means of getting a seriously wounded patient to an aid station the helicopter was unequaled. Although influenced by the weather, helicopters could still fly in weather that grounded other types of aircraft. Although slow, and so presumably a good target for ground fire, the helicopter could hover close to the ground and fly up valleys out of sight of the enemy until close to its destination, thus losses to enemy fire were very low.

Maintenance

Difficulties of maintaining equipment in Korea appeared almost from the outset. The added strain on vehicles from intensive use over poor roads and mountainous terrain, mechanical weaknesses in some tanks, and periods of intensive artillery fire all contributed, but much of the trouble in the early months seemed to have been more the result of a shortage of well-trained men to handle organizational and field maintenance than defects in the design or materials of the equipment itself, most types of which had held up well under strenuous combat conditions in World War II. Shortages (or misuse) of tank repair men in infantry regiments was especially noticeable. For the first year and a half an especially acute problem was the shortage of spare parts for the great variety of highly specialized engineer equipment that had to be kept in operation. CONEX shipments, begun in November

PORT OF PUSAN

1952, proved to be the solution to most of this problem.

Quartermaster Service Centers

The perfection of Quartermaster service centers was one of the outstanding developments of Quartermaster troop services in Korea. That the various Quartermaster service units supporting a corps, previously operating independently of each other, should be brought together in a single location under central control seems to have been accepted originally in the U.S. Fifth Army in Italy during the latter phases of World War II. The idea did not receive general application, however, until the Korean War, when a center, made up of many Quartermaster units, was organized to support each U.S. corps. The first center, Quartermaster Service Center Number 3, went into operation for X Corps on 1 May 1951. The practice was to lay out the service center along a stream, with shower and clothing exchange point upstream from the laundry, and repair and maintenance facilities adjacent to the laundry. Centralized messing facilities and billets for the troops were located apart from the working areas. At the shower point men entered, turned in their dirty clothes, drew soap, towels, and shaving equipment, had a hot shower in a tent that could accommodate forty men at a time, and then drew a clean set of clothing.

Service Troops

Although the proportion of service troops to combat troops in the U.S. Army was subject to frequent criticism, actually the theater division slice was considerably smaller—35,000 in Korea and 6,000 in Japan—than had been anticipated. But this was only an illusory streamlining resulting from a shortage of service troops. Local civilian employees had to take the place of considerable numbers of service troops. In the Japan Logistical Command about one military space was being saved for every two civilians employed. As of March 1951, approximately 145,000 civilians in Japan could be considered as working in support of operations in Korea. During the same period another 100,000 or more civilians (excluding members of the Korean Service Corps) were working for Army service units in Korea. All these people had to be supplied in one way or another.

Battlefield Evacuation

A significant medical fact of World War II was that about 24 percent of men who died from wounds (men who survived long enough to reach a medical installation) died before they reached installations equipped for major surgery. The practice in World War II of assigning platoons of field hospitals, reinforced by surgical teams, to support division clearing stations made surgery available closer to the front lines than it had been before, and apparently this was an important factor in reducing the mortality rate from that experienced in World War I.

Still, a relatively small percentage (21 percent according to two surveys) of patients reached surgical treatment during what surgeons have termed the "golden period" of the first six hours after receiving the wounds. Undoubtedly the reduction in mortality among men wounded in action in Korea was due in large part to reductions in lapsed time before surgical treatment for those seriously wounded. Evacuation of critically wounded men by helicopter to mobile surgical hospitals was one major factor affecting this result. A second was the expansion of the idea of providing surgical teams by the establishment of mobile army surgical hospitals.

Developed on paper in 1947 on the basis of the portable surgical hospitals, and the larger surgical hospitals of World War II, the standard mobile army surgical hospital was a 60-bed hospital unit designed to be located with or near division clearing stations in order to provide surgical treatment for casualties too badly injured to be evacuated further to the rear without first receiving such attention.

Talk and Fight

Accustomed to associating armistice overtures with peace, the peoples of the world welcomed with enthusiasm the announcement in June 1951 that Communist leaders had agreed to open truce negotiations. But hope soon gave way to disappointment as conversations dragged on month after month, first at Kaesong and then at Panmunjom. Armistice negotiations began in July 1951, were broken off by enemy delegates in August, and were resumed in October. The delegates reached an impasse in May 1952; the conferences were suspended completely in October 1952 and did not resume until April 1953. The armistice was signed 27 July 1953.

While negotiations went on so did the fighting, but with a difference—the fact that the negotiations were underway influenced the character of ensuing operations. Some of the most difficult fighting of the entire conflict took place in the autumn of 1951, but offensives tended to be limited in scope. Following the agreement upon a preliminary line of demarcation in November 1951, the warfare became more nearly stabilized while negotiations on other points continued sporadically for more than two years.

The logistical implications were important. First of all, the military services were alert to the likelihood of an armistice, and there was no question of being caught by a surprise armistice with no plans for adjusting to the new situation. Indeed, staff officers had been making plans for halting supplies and withdrawing troops from Korea ever since the successful landing at Inchon in September 1950. Cut-backs had actually been ordered in procurement and shipment of some supplies shortly before the Chinese intervention became a certainty in late November 1950. At the conference with President Truman on Wake Island in October 1950, General MacArthur and General Bradley had discussed plans for redeploying units from Korea to Europe and the United States. The Army staff had drawn plans for posthostilities logistical support.

Even while demobilization and redeployment plans had to be held in abeyance as truce negotiations and combat proceeded, the relatively stabilized warfare permitted a more orderly logistical support for the troops still engaged. Regularized procedures could replace improvisation, and new procedures could be perfected free of the stresses of rapidly changing battle positions. As stalemate developed at the conference table, its effects appeared on the battlefield.

At the end of 1952, when Communist authorities had given no indication of a willingness to resume armistice negotiations, and when many Americans were becoming impatient with the continuation of the stalemate, suggestions were offered for a new United Nations offensive. Some suggested amphibious assaults on one or both coasts of North Korea, and possibly an airborne attack over the Communist defensive works as well, which would have no less an objective than a return to the Manchurian border. Even if such a plan were successful, there would be no reason to suppose that the Chinese Communists would demobilize their forces as a result. It seemed more likely that they would continue the fight at the Yalu, and since an approach to this region had been enough to incite them to intervention in 1950, it was not unlikely that again they would attempt to build up for a major offensive. At best, the results of this proposal would be to exchange a stalemate on the relatively short front near the 38th parallel for another stalemate on a front three or four times as long, located close to enemy sources of supply but much further removed from U.N. supply bases.

Others suggested settling for a line north of P'yongyang in the vicinity of Korea's narrow "waist." This supposedly would have gained much-needed prestige for the United Nations without incurring the risk or the logistical strain involved in a drive to the Yalu. This suggestion, too, would have lengthened United Nations lines of communication while shortening those of the Communists.

Lengthened lines of communication

would mean additional miles of roads to be built and maintained, railroads to be repaired and operated, communication wire to be strung, and radio stations to be set up. With the longer turn-around times that greater distances would mean for trucks and railway cars, it was questionable whether there would have been enough cars and trucks—there were hardly enough to maintain large-scale operations in the positions then occupied—to sustain major operations for any length of time. On the other hand, to the extent that the ports of Chinnamp'o (on the west coast) and Wonsan (on the east coast), and over-the-beach operations elsewhere could have relieved dependence on railway and highway transportation, the effect would have been to shorten rather than to lengthen the lines of communication by an advance north to the waist. The port of Wonsan had an estimated military unloading capacity of 7,400 tons a day and Chinnamp'o had an estimated capacity of about 3,000 tons a day. Hungnam, some distance north of Wonsan, had an estimated capacity of 8,300 tons a day. It also should be noted that Ch'ongjin, much farther north on the east coast, had an estimated capacity of 19,700 tons a day, including berthing for twelve Liberty-size vessels, and that Najin (Rashin), still closer to the Siberian border, had an estimated capacity of 9,000 tons per day including berthing for eleven Liberty-size vessels; with a combined capacity nearly as great as that of Pusan, these ports could have been useful in shortening the lines of communication for the support of forces along the northern border of Korea. Whether or not enemy aircraft and submarines would have permitted full use of the northern ports was, of course, another question.

In short, the effect of lengthened lines of communication had to be calculated in terms of requirements for trucks, cars, railway and highway equipment and materials and the availability of alternative water transportation, before a valid conclusion could be offered as to whether any particular proposed tactical operation could be recommended from the standpoint of its effect upon those communications. The other element to be considered was the additional quantities of supplies, particularly ammunition, that would have to be moved over those lines to support the contemplated operation.

When an armistice agreement began to appear imminent in the spring of 1953, the immediate result was an increase rather than a reduction in a number of supply activities. Anxious not to be caught with shortages that would be frozen by armistice stipulations against any build-up of combat material, commanders urged rapid replenishment of such supplies in order to reach authorized levels.

This increased activity applied particularly to ammunition. Heavy expenditures of ammunition had reduced the supply on hand appreciably, and extraordinary steps were required to restore authorized levels. Special ammunition ships dispatched from Japan and others sent directly to Korea with cargoes from the United States brought additional supplies of ammunition to the Korean ports. The arrival of the ammunition called for extra effort on the part of units and dock workers of the Korean Base Section to discharge the additional vessels and keep the ports and beaches cleared. Safety precautions for handling and storing ammunition were relaxed as the port companies undertook to discharge 7,000 long tons a day.

Summary

Many Americans were disappointed when the Korean conflict ended on terms of less than total victory. But something even more important than total victory may have been gained in this demonstration of restraint in the conduct of limited war for limited objectives. In an age when total victory was associated with total destruction, perhaps it was more urgent than ever that total war be avoided as long as the national safety and essential freedoms were not sacrificed. This, indeed, presumably was the objective of the whole United Nations effort in Korea. If the United States was engaged in a limited war in Korea in order to forestall a third world war, then so far it was successful. If the United States was engaged in a limited war in Korea in order to prevent the extension of Communist domination to South Korea, then in that too it was successful.

The Korean Experience

It is difficult to draw generalizations from the Korean experience that would have application at other times and places. There never could be "another Korea." Even resumption of hostilities in Korea itself would be under very different conditions from those prevailing in June 1950, when only by drawing heavily on World War II equipment in the Far East and in the United States and on the resources of Japan it was possible to meet the logistical requirements.

Before June 1950, neither the Far East Command nor the Department of the Army appeared to have any prepared plan for support of military operations in Korea. The decision to go into Korea with ground forces was an almost instantaneous one supported by a spontaneous recommendation from the Far East Command without detailed reference to logistical plans and analyses. To general questions raised in the Department of the Army about the logistical feasibility of a campaign in Korea, affirmative responses were given based more upon faith than upon studied inquiry. At that moment the question was not one of what could be done, but of what must be done. In meeting the first critical demands, Army leaders in Washington, Tokyo, and Pusan had to play it by ear. Detailed planning did begin once the war was a reality, but it might have been done more quickly and more effectively had more thorough planning preceded it.

There could have been no Korean War without a World War II preceding it. Stocks being maintained in the various matériel reserves were made up almost entirely of World War II supplies, for there had been virtually no new procurement of most items since the end of World War II. In addition, great quantities of World War II equipment remaining on the Pacific islands fed the rebuild plants in Japan to make up serious shortages. The importance of World War II in the logistical support of the Korean War went beyond the matter of essential matériel reserves. The very procedures by which the ports of embarkation and the technical services were able to fill requisitions and build up shipments quickly were the result largely of practices developed during World War II.

The total tonnage of supplies of all classes shipped from the United States to the Far East during the three years and one month of the Korean War—(approximately 31,500,000 measurement tons) was more than twice the tonnage shipped from the United States in support of the American

Expeditionary Force in World War I during the nineteen months from June 1917 through December 1918. It was 82 percent greater than the total shipment of supplies (17,239,000 measurement tons)[13] for the support of Army ground and air forces in the Southwest Pacific Area in World War II in the thirty-seven months from August 1942 to August 1945.

The dollar cost to the United States of military operations in Korea for goods and services can only be approximated very roughly. On the basis of data prepared in the Statistical Analysis Section, Supply Planning Branch of G–4, the Office of the Comptroller of the Army estimated the total cost to the Army of operations in Korea for the period 27 June 1950–30 June 1953 to be about $17,200,672,000. This sum includes $11,756,134,000 for supplies shipped to the Far East (excluding equipment which accompanied troops), $1,522,925,000 for contractual services for movement of troops and supplies, and $1,729,152,000 for the cost of activities of installations both in the United States and the Far East directly supporting the Korean operations. The pay of soldiers in table of organization and equipment units amounted to about $2,192,461,000 for the period.[14]

The Big Picture

The war in Korea was but a part of a sequence of climactic events characterizing the cold war. The international tensions between Communist states and the Free World set Korea apart from earlier punitive expeditions of the United States. On many occasions the United States had supported armed intervention—from Tripoli to Mexico, and from Nicaragua to China—but seldom had those actions carried such overtones of high policy as were found in the Korean War. In Korea the whole worldwide tension between the United States and the Soviet Union was thrown into sharp relief.

Probably the most important result of the Korean War for the United States was that it served to alert Americans to the general danger of Communist aggression at a time when they were looking hopefully toward trimming their defense expenditures and commitments for logistic support for allied nations. The Korean conflict consequently set in motion a long-term rearmament program through which the United States would be more nearly prepared to meet future emergencies, and particularly to accept total mobilization should that become necessary.

Actually it was the Chinese Communist attack in November and December 1950, rather than the original North Korean attack of the preceding June, that provided the more important stimulus to the rearmament program. After the Chinese intervention, the United Nations faced, as General MacArthur said, an entirely "new war." Only after intervention by the Chinese Communists did the President proclaim a national emergency—largely for the benefit of logistical expansion. Only then were supplementary budgets prepared on a scale commensurate with the total situation.

A series of top-level decisions that followed had far-reaching consequences for the military position of the United States, all of them relating to the entire world situation rather than to Korea alone. The first of these was that Korea must be regarded

---

[13] Army Service Forces, *Statistical Review, World War II*, app. G, p. 132. Copy in OCMH.

[14] Estimate of Cost of Korean Operations, Period 27 June 1950–30 June 1953, Accounting and Financial Policy Div, OCA.

in a worldwide setting as the most emphatic warning of the threat of communism in the world at large, and that Europe, the potentially decisive area in an all-out war, must not be neglected. Accordingly, in the bigger and faster build-up that the Chinese Communists touched off the defense of Western Europe continued to hold a high priority. Indeed, because of the war in Korea, reinforcements were sent to Europe.

A second major decision of the Army high command was that matériel mobilization should take precedence over personnel mobilization. Secretary of the Army Pace regarded matériel procurement as the controlling factor in the expansion of forces, and he resisted pressure to embark on a vast personnel mobilization program that might in fact retard matériel procurement and so military preparedness. This was the first American war where matériel mobilization actually received the first emphasis.

Another basic decision—actually a matter of national policy—was that for "creeping mobilization." That is to say, industrial mobilization would be partial rather than total, and it would be accomplished with the least possible dislocation of the domestic economy. Secretary of Defense George C. Marshall and his successor Robert A. Lovett, as well as Army officials shared the thoughts that prompted the decision: Since it seemed that world tensions would continue for an indefinite time, too rapid industrial mobilization would invite the risks of matériel obsolescence and would compound the difficulties of maintaining satisfactory long-term preparedness. The policy attempted to get away from the American proclivity for living from crisis to crisis with build-up and let-down, and establish a plateau of preparedness that would furnish a more satisfactory continuity of strength

with which to meet current and future threats.

Closely related to that policy was the decision to develop a broad industrial production base. This put primary emphasis on rebuilding military strength upon long-term industrial mobilization aimed at developing capacity to produce in great quantities rather than on immediate quantity production at the expense of greater capacity later. This was based upon the assumption that rapid industrial mobilization was the key to meeting emergency threats to the national security. Under this policy orders for arms and equipment to support operations in Korea, and to build up stockpiles in Europe and the United States, were placed so as to best serve long-range industrial preparedness. Thus smaller orders with several companies were favored over large orders with a single producer. Three production lines running on single shifts were preferred to a single production line running on three shifts because of the obvious advantage in expanding output quickly. The program required greater effort on the part of the people administering it, and sometimes perhaps it was a little more costly, but Secretary Lovett and military officials working with him held to the firm conviction that such a policy was essential for the military preparedness of the United States. Creeping mobilization and the broad production base probably were the fundamental logistical concepts of the Korean conflict. They shaped the whole war effort by treating war in Korea as a limited war while preparing for a total effort should that become necessary.

Another decision, this one emanating from the Office of the Secretary of Defense over the opposition of the Department of the Army, had less fortunate consequences.

That was the decision to base military budget guide lines on the assumption of an early termination of the conflict. The Army, therefore, could not budget for operations support in Korea for a projected period; it could only replace ammunition and other supplies already used and it could not buy supplies for future use. After-the-fact supplementary appropriations had to cover expenditures for operations in Korea. Not until 1953–54, as hostilities ended, did the budget catch up with the war. Perhaps in the circumstances this was a tribute to political realism, but it seems that budget projections would have both benefited the industrial mobilization program and have been more in keeping with the theory of long-term industrial preparedness.

The Korean War had worldwide logistical ramifications. While it is true that the war stimulated the movement of additional troops and supplies to Europe, it must be recognized that beyond a certain point Korea loomed as a competitor with Europe and other areas for available material resources. It was a repetition, in a way, of the World War II contest for resources between the European and the Pacific theaters, but in 1950–53 the going war in Korea had some advantages over a potential war in Europe. The Truman Administration consistently regarded Europe as the vital area in the world picture. Then what was essentially a question of high military strategy became ensnarled in domestic politics and outstanding spokesmen appeared to support each cause.

The Eisenhower Administration never denied the vital importance of Western Europe in the world strategy against Communist expansion, but it was inclined to put somewhat greater emphasis on Asia than had been the case earlier. One of the most outstanding examples of this new emphasis was the decision to accept the full program of arming and equipping twenty divisions for the Republic of Korea Army. This decision, too, had worldwide implications. With no plan for a corresponding increase in the procurement program, the decision to expand the ROK Army to twenty divisions amounted to denying equipment for further building up European forces or for replenishing American reserve stocks. It meant that most equipment was likely to be tied down in Korea permanently and probably would not be available for use in emergencies in other parts of the world. If peace were maintained during the mid-1950's, the full implications of that decision for Europe and other areas probably would pass unnoticed. If hostilities should break out again in Korea, it might appear as a most fortunate decision (unless the new outbreak turned out to be the result of an attack by the strengthened South Koreans). But the possibility of emergencies elsewhere could not be ignored. This decision, like so many military decisions by their very nature, belonged in the realm of calculated risks—though leaders were likely to disagree on what calculations should be taken into account.

Logistical support of the Korean War had far-reaching consequences for the U.S. position in the Far East, and it also had far-reaching consequences in the worldwide struggle against the spread of communism. For the United States the Korean War was the second greatest of its wars from the standpoint of its logistical contributions. The best measure of success in that effort would be the extent to which it might help avoid a future conflict that might become the greatest war.[15]

---

[15] For sources upon which Part V is based see Bibliography, pages 729–35

PART SIX

THE USES OF LOGISTICAL EXPERIENCE

CHAPTER XXXV

Some Principles of Logistics

Is it possible, on the basis of 175 years of experience, to draw any principles of logistics having general applicability? By habitual use, or by results becoming evident in ignoring them, certain prescriptions may be said to have come to light which, with necessary reservations and qualifications, may be offered as tentative principles, not as unalterable laws or maxims, but simply as general guides. No relative order of importance can be assigned to these or other principles except the first, and the primary purpose of all logistics always must be identified with the objective of the battle or campaign, or the object of the war, which in turn derives from the national purpose.

These principles might include the following:

First with the Most
Equivalence
Matériel Precedence
Economy
Dispersion
Flexibility
Feasibility
Civilian Responsibility
Continuity
Timing
Unity of Command
Forward Impetus
Information
Relativity

As characteristic patterns of logistical conduct, they are conceived as having many facets and being of broad applicability. While it is not practical here to review all the aspects to which they have some application, nor to develop all the qualifications in any such generalizations, certain points of extension and of caution may be suggested in the interest of making the logistics experience more meaningful.

The First With the Most

The primary purpose of logistics is to deliver adequate potential or actual fire power or shock to the critical places at the critical times for achievement of tactical and strategic objectives. It is, in short, as Nathan Bedford Forrest is reported to have put it, "to get there first with the most." All else is subordinate to this primary purpose.

Rapid changes in weapons and equipment in the more recent periods make it necessary to modify somewhat this statement. Although "to get there first with the most" probably is a fair expression of the primary concern of Army logistics over the years, it is not enough to be first with inferior weapons and equipment. Although quantity frequently has made up for lack of quality, and sometimes vice versa, the ideal has been to have both, so that now this primary aim of logistics might better be stated, "to get there first with the most and the best." Nor is this all: It is not to be supposed that victory goes automatically to the side with the superior means, and many battles have turned on other, less measurable factors. Still, it is difficult to find instances in modern war where a decidedly stronger economic power ultimately has succumbed to a weaker.

Basic to all logistic planning is the art of asking the right questions. In suggesting that the primary aim of logistics is "to get there first with the most" (and the best), the question may be asked: Where is "there?" The answer probably would be: The critical point. And where is the critical point? Very likely it will relate to logistics—a major river, a railway center, a road junction, an industrial area. It simply is a case of mingling logistic with strategic and tactical considerations in the basic decisions of war—choosing objectives, deciding where and when to do battle, assessing the costs of continuing battle. Even the decision whether to attack or to defend depends essentially on the relative logistic positions, on which side can bring the superior force to bear at the critical point. Indeed, intelligence doctrine in the U.S. Army has been based upon relative logistic positions, for the first concern of intelligence has been not to attempt to guess what the enemy *will do,* but to determine what he *can do,* that is, to analyze enemy capabilities, and capabilities depend fundamentally on relative logistic positions. Again, it is not to be suggested that the issue of battle necessarily turns on this calculation; if that were so, the whole process could be left to calculating machines. But knowing the enemy's capabilities certainly provides major elements for the application of the leadership necessary to control any situation.

Equivalence

Strategy and tactics and logistics are different aspects of the same thing. If com-

pletely separated they become meaningless. Subject to the primary purpose, no distinction in importance can be made between combat functions and service or logistical functions. No distinction should be drawn on this basis in establishing priorities for the assignment of officers, enlisted men, or equipment.

Strategy, tactics, and logistics stand at the points of a triangle, or perhaps it would be more accurate to say that they comprise three arcs of a circle, without beginning or ending, each arc influencing, and influenced by, each of the others.

All this is to re-emphasize the *equivalence* of strategy, tactics, and logistics. Yet with all the emphasis given in recent times to the importance of logistics, it still remains secondary in much popular and professional thinking. The very language of emphasis given to logistics betrays a downgrading in its discussion. Statements to the effect that "logistics is an indispensable ingredient in modern war" by their very forcefulness suggest a secondary role, for who would say, "strategy is an indispensable ingredient in war?"

Matériel Precedence

Matériel mobilization should precede manpower mobilization, and mobilization of troops for logistical support should precede the mobilization of troops for combat training. The key to rapid mobilization is the availability of weapons and equipment, and it is more important to have matériel "in being" than to have unequipped forces in being.

Throughout most of their history Americans have put manpower mobilization ahead of matériel mobilization, both in time and in emphasis, and in doing so they have put the cart before the horse. Far more men were mobilized than could be equipped or effectively used in the War of 1812. Taylor was embarrassed by more men than he could supply in Mexico. McClellan was "troop poor" in the early phases of the Civil War, when all the states rushed men to the Army more rapidly than they could be cared for. Overmobilization of manpower was notorious in the Spanish-American War. The Dodge Commission, after that war, and Secretary of War Root recognized the primacy of matériel readiness, but their views had little visible effect on policy. In World War I the first emphasis again was placed on manpower, until draft calls had to be delayed while the cantonments and basic clothing and equipment were made ready. On the eve of World War II men called into service trained with sticks for guns when they might better have remained in shops and factories for another year or two to help produce the weapons and equipment they would need. None of the National Guardsmen or draftees called into federal service in 1940 saw combat action before two years, and the bulk of the men brought into the Army in 1940, 1941, 1942, and 1943 did not see action before 1944. What caused the delay? Certainly not lack of training time. Nobody claimed that it took more than a year to build and train a completely new division—replacements with only thirteen to seventeen weeks of training performed quite satisfactorily. No. Lack of equipment caused the delay—equipment with which to complete training, and equipment with which to fight. To get major items into production required one to two years, but in American habits of thought, early manpower mobilization probably was necessary to give visible evidence that some-

thing was being done, and to provide visible requirements for equipment.

Mobilization planning, never refined until after World War I, had indeed given attention to matériel requirements in the 1920's and 1930's. The General Staff had based its plans on the M-day concept, and had calculated what matériel reserves would be needed to equip the planned forces until new production could become effective. An important aspect of the plan was the designation of plants to enter into the production of stated items, and to obtain and set aside the industrial tools that would permit them to do so. Then when the emergency came, mobilization was more gradual than had been expected and the whole plan was largely passed over.

After World War II the stockpiling of matériel reserves and industrial equipment reserves received greater attention than ever before, though the reserves depended upon World War II leftovers, and the prospect of keeping them current by continuous turnover was not bright until the foreign military aid programs provided a way for replacing old equipment with new.

What was needed was implementation of a "matériel in being" concept, where adequate mobilization equipment would be kept on hand and up to date. This probably was more important to the national defense by permitting rapid mobilization than all of the programs for the organization and training of reserve forces. General Reeder, former Deputy Assistant Chief of Staff, G-4, has remarked that the Army throughout its history seldom if ever has had any divisions except in wartime or for mobilization in a national emergency that were really combat ready; although sometimes certain units have been so designated, even the most advanced of them could not compare in readiness even with a mediocre wartime division. "The men may have their wills drawn, their allotments made, and their immunizations completed, but they have not had their matériel. Even though they may show their assets in good position by showing those not physically present to be 'on requisition' or 'due in' the depot may not even be working on it yet for lack of funds." [1]

At the end of the Korean War the concious encouragement of a broad production base to promote industrial preparedness was frustrated to an extent by Secretary of Defense Charles E. Wilson's policy of "more bang for a buck." This suggested a preference for immediate return over long-range preparedness, and for concentration in fewer plants in order to effect an immediate saving in costs.

A problem closely related to procurement has been finance. During the Revolution and the War of 1812 it dominated most other aspects of military support. For the remainder of the history it has been a story of feast or famine—strict limitations in peacetime, with almost never enough appropriations even to build up the most modest reserves; then huge appropriations in wartime with a mandate to spend them wisely and quickly. During most of its history the United States has not needed a large Military Establishment, and Congress, reflecting the attitude of the country, was unwilling to provide for one. Though the attitude was probably a justifiable one, some advantage would have been gained by greater attention to matériel readiness. However, the Army itself, devoting much

of its effort to appeals for larger forces when there was no evident need, failed to provide the leadership for maintaining greater degrees of matériel preparedness in the interwar periods.

Economy

Logistic resources are almost always limited, and it is necessary to concentrate them in the best way to achieve the primary mission. In all cases the cost of an operation or activity must be considered, and the least expensive means consistent with the primary purpose should be chosen. The ratio of secondary requirements to primary requirements should be kept low. Productibility of a given item may be as important as battlefield performance. Oversupply should be avoided.

Logistics requirements may be divided into primary requirements (those for direct support of tactical units) and secondary requirements (those necessary for support of the means used to meet the primary requirements). The most efficient military transportation system, other things being equal, is the one in which the ratio of secondary requirements to primary results is lowest. This was a matter of concern to Sherman during the Civil War when he suggested that an army could not be supplied by horses and wagons at a greater distance than 100 miles from its base, for in that distance the horses would consume the entire contents of their wagons. It was a matter of concern in the operation of the Red Ball Express during World War II when trucks were rushing gasoline forwarded to the fast-moving columns of the First and Third Armies, although a 2½-ton truck then carrying gasoline in 5-gallon containers could travel over 3,300 miles before con-

---

[1] Interview with Maj Gen William O. Reeder, June 1962

suming its load. In air transportation, up to 1953, the ratio of secondary requirements to pay load was by far the greatest of all. In fact, the logistical problems in terms of tonnage which air transportation created were greater than those it solved. For each five tons of cargo a C–54 carried across the Pacific from San Francisco to Japan, that airplane consumed about eighteen tons of gasoline. Two Victory ships, transporting 15,000 tons of cargo from San Francisco to Yokohama, consumed approximately 7,000 barrels of fuel oil, or 14,000 barrels for the round trip. Aircraft of the C–54 type carrying the same tonnage over the same route consumed about 1,140,000 barrels of high-grade aviation gasoline for the flights in both directions. Victory ships carried enough fuel to make two such round trips. Aircraft had to refuel frequently at bases served by tankers. Thus to move a given 15,000 tons of cargo to Japan by sea required two ships. To move it by air required 3,000 air flights plus eight ships to carry the gasoline. And all this made no allowance for the greater number of man-hours required for operating and servicing the aircraft, nor for the highly trained crews, nor for the extra refinery capacity needed to supply the aviation gasoline.

Yet this was not the whole picture of the secondary logistical factors that had to be taken into account in arriving at the economic cost of air transportation. The cost of maintaining large quantities of supplies in the long supply pipelines, and of maintaining large quantities of reserve stocks at various points—with the costs of warehousing, stock control, maintenance, local transportation, and multiple handling entailed—had to be weighed against the costs of air flights which might permit curtailment of the other costs. The use of jet transports capable of making many more trips with much greater capacity than the C–54's, and using low-grade fuel instead of aviation gasoline besides, brightened prospects for increasingly economical use of air transportation.

The generation of secondary logistical problems in dealing with primary problems applies to the whole chain of requirements determination. The process of satisfying requirements in turn creates new requirements. In connection with transportation, as noted above, requirements for forage or fuel for the means of transportation have to be taken into account as well as the requirements for the supported unit. Other secondary considerations which must also be taken into account include the supply of vehicles, aircraft, or vessels, and their accessories and maintenance, and the provision of drivers or crews and their sustenance.

This same kind of consideration applies on a broader scale to the whole range of troops and facilities, whether in Army service commands, communications zones, bases, or zone of the interior, whose function it is to provide supplies and services for other troops. In all support activities there seems to be a tendency for what Rear Admiral Henry E. Eccles has called the "logistical snowball" to develop [2]—where an increasing share of the logistical activity of a base goes to the support of the base itself. The ultimate would seem to have been reached in those cases where a base consumed more supplies than it shipped out over an extended period, and so became a net drain on the logistics system.

Still another operation of secondary requirements is found in the production of

[2] Henry E. Eccles, *Logistics in the National Defense* (Harrisburg, Pa.: The Stackpole Co., 1959), pp. 102–14.

weapons and equipment. Certainly this has been an important consideration in accepting or rejecting new weapons, adopting model changes, and standardization. Ease of production with available raw materials and facilities may be as important for a given item as battlefield performance. Modification in design probably has been as often the result of needs to step up production or to substitute for scarce materials as of improvement in the operation or utility of the equipment.

Other secondary factors have to be taken into account in a decision to adopt a new weapon. It will mean a delay in production for retooling, assembling materials, and adapting available labor. It will bring with it new problems of repair and supply of spare parts, and it may require the production of new types of ammunition which will further complicate the problems of production and supply distribution. At any given time such secondary requirements have to be weighed against the anticipated advantages of the new weapon and undoubtedly they account for much of the resistance in the Army at various times to the adoption of new weapons or equipment which in themselves may have appeared quite desirable and acceptable. Conversely, such considerations have led to the adoption of models considered inferior to others already accepted and in production, as in the adoption of the Enfield rifle in World War I in preference to the Springfield. These considerations are related to the whole question of whether it is likely to be more economical to store a given article, or to dispose of it and buy a new one later—or indeed, to buy the same one back.

At the same time it always has been necessary in applying the principle of economy to guard against deceptive appearances and to recognize that outside factors frequently mitigate against strict application of the principle. This can be seen in connection with placing procurement contracts.

Various types of contracts have proved to be useful under various conditions. The lump-sum contract has appeared most desirable when feasible, though a disposition to make allowances for every possible contingency has tended to inflate its costs. The cost-plus-a-percentage-of-cost contract was open to such abuse that it was outlawed, although actual performance under this kind of agreement in World War I was probably better than was generally assumed. The revised version, cost-plus-a-fixed-fee, is open to the same abuses but also may have advantages in actually reducing costs under close supervision. It is almost necessary when some new item of equipment is being developed or is going into initial production. Acceptance of renegotiation and price redetermination in World War II provided powerful leverage for close-pricing, and incentive-type contracts where savings were shared had further effects in this direction. Open advertising and competitive bids generally have been regarded as the normal method of contracting, though contracting by direct negotiation became more and more prominent in the more recent war emergencies, and in connection with the development of new weapons and equipment.

Although Congress long has laid down the policy that military procurement should be guided by getting acceptable quality for the lowest price, outside pressures have been repeatedly at work to influence Army procurement for other purposes. Economic benefits of government contracts were recognized in the Civil War. Isolationist sentiment operated against procurement for preparedness in 1916 and again in 1940 and 1941 by objections to obtaining such items as landing craft and "overseas caps." At times the Army has had to make allowance in its procurement for assisting dairy farmers at the expense of margarine processors, aiding small business, aiding areas of unemployment distress, and preferring American to foreign products. It has been difficult to allow military considerations alone to govern the opening or closing of an installation, the choice of a new weapon system, or the curtailment of a program, for representatives of the areas, the companies, the workers, the raw-materials producers, the political parties, the military services, and other interests directly or indirectly affected inevitably have brought pressure to bear on the decision. In the years ahead this may be one of the greatest of all logistical—or indeed the greatest of all national security—problems.

Dispersion

Within reasonable bounds storage and other logistical activities should be dispersed, and multiple lines of communication should be used when possible in order to minimize losses from enemy action, ease congestion of activities and transportation facilities, and draw upon multiple sources of supply. Multiple sources of procurement should be used in order to develop a broad production base which will facilitate rapid expansion and lessen the impact of mobilization in a particular area.

The idea of dispersal and drawing upon multiple sources of supply may run counter to the principle of concentration, but it always has had some relevance for logistics, and with the introduction of weapons of mass destruction it has become an impera-

tive. Actually the very force of a great concentration has gained from the divergence of resources, so that tactical concentration has gone hand in hand with logistical divergence. A shift in bases, as McClellan's on the Peninsula, or Grant's at Vicksburg, or Sherman's from Atlanta to Savannah, often has added to the strength of the force. The only real justification for the invasion of southern France in 1944 was the opening of a new line of communication through the major port of Marseille. The greatest battles of the Pacific were fought by concentrations of forces coming from widely scattered areas, and supplied from bases thousands of miles apart.

In economic mobilization the question arises as to the weight to be given to considerations of economy and to the advantages of dispersion. In conditions of total mobilization, this question is less urgent, for all possible sources are used. But when mobilization is only partial, as in the Korean War or in the years of cold war, it may be as important to develop a broad production base capable of rapid expansion as it is to maintain a certain level of current production. Then dispersion may be more costly in terms of current output, but will contribute a great deal more in terms of long-range preparedness.

On the basis of experience in the supply build-up in the United Kingdom in World War II and in the roll-up of equipment in the Pacific for the support of operations in Korea, there is something to be said for the suggestion that the United States in cooperation with its allies, should stockpile all kinds of military supplies at strategic points near areas of potential danger in various parts of the world. This suggestion proposed that cadres of logistical commands could receive, store, and protect the supplies; then, if an emergency developed, service troops could be flown to the bases nearest the threatened area to begin full-scale supply operations. It would be a problem to maintain significant quantities of matériel in remote places, but such distribution would make possible lower depot levels in the United States, and its usefulness was demonstrated in Korea where equipment that had been left unattended for years on Pacific islands played an essential part in the success of operations. An implicit disadvantage of inflexibility in this kind of dispersion of matériel reserves is not necessarily true in present-day world conditions when a threat in one quarter of the globe has had to be met by preparations and alertness in all quarters, lest an even bigger fire break out on another continent while a small conflagration draws all attention to itself. It is normally beyond the capabilities of available aircraft to fly divisions with all their heavy equipment across the oceans, but it is entirely feasible to fly the men, at least an emergency force of limited size, if the equipment can be picked up on the other side.

Flexibility

Since often it is not possible to count on prior strategic plans, it is necessary to be prepared to support any of a number of different plans or decisions, and to support changes in plans or decisions indicated by the fortunes of war. To support flexibility in plans there should be flexibility in forces—a versatility in troops and organization as well as in storage and other facilities to meet changing needs.

For operations short of total war the proper sequence of high-level planning would seem to be: strategy→manpower→ production. For total war it may be as well to assume an initial sequence of production→manpower→strategy. In any case no generalization can be made that logistical planning depends on strategic planning, because production lead times often are so great that production plans must be put into effect long before detailed strategic plans can be drawn. About the best that can be done is to prepare for the widest possible range of strategic possibilities in order to keep open the opportunity of choice to meet a situation as it develops. Once a decision has been taken for a specific operation—a decision which itself must be governed by logistical feasibility—then of course logistical calculations must be made and troops and equipment and transportation assembled for its support. In the long range, logistics comes before strategy in a sense; for the shorter range, logistics depends upon strategy, but in turn it limits tactics and in turn is dependent upon them.

Planning had not anticipated the Korean emergency, and for the first months it was necessary to improvise. Perhaps this experience suggests that something might be gained by developing detailed plans for supporting various types of possible operations in potential areas of conflict in all parts of the world. It is patently impossible to have concrete plans to meet all eventualities, yet there is an advantage to be won in the very process of planning—even if the plans themselves have to be discarded when the emergency arrives. In the planning process certain data must be gathered and evaluated, procedures considered, limitations studied, assets analyzed, all of which makes actual support when the necessity arises simpler and quicker and more efficient. Even if all proposed lines of action have to be rejected in favor of something entirely new, at least the search for workable plans will not be delayed by blind alley approaches which already have been discovered. Moreover, new data can be put to use more quickly and effectively if the basic questions have been sought out in advance.

Feasibility

Not only are strategic and tactical plans limited by the feasibility of logistic support, but logistic plans themselves are subject to capabilities of the national economy, the availability of other resources, and the limitations of secondary requirements.

Logistics, like politics, might be defined as "the art of the possible." Indeed it might well be regarded as the factors of possibility in military operations. But the definition of the possible changes, and it has been a part of the function of logistics to extend the possible. Sometimes, as has been suggested, a single logistical factor is clearly the limiting one. Then all kinds of complicated calculations might be avoided by a precise definition of this one limitation. Still, all assumptions of rigid limitation are dangerous. Although the feasibility dispute, turning on the question of what the economy could bear in military mobilization, was one of the great controversies of World War II, President Roosevelt's approach seems characteristic of the American approach—not how much *can* be done, but what *must* be done in order to defeat the enemy. Nevertheless it was no use engaging in dreamworld strategy divorced from logistical feasibility. Disregard of logistical limitations has led to the disappointing collapse of defensive efforts when the forces engaged might have held out much longer if their ammunition and rations had not run out.

It has led to failures in making victory decisive by vigorous follow-up. It has led to the halting of great offensives when armies have outrun their supplies. It has led to prolonged conflicts when mobilization did not match requirements.

Civilian Responsibility

Procurement activity must be co-ordinated with the needs of the civilian economy, and the chief reliance for the production of military goods remains on private industry.

One of the factors lying beneath the intensity of the feasibility dispute of World War II was the question of control of the economy—whether the Army was attempting to take over. On the other hand, the tradition for civilian control has been so well established as at times (for example, the artificial limitations on the size of the General Staff in Washington) to hamstring military activities.

There always has been a question as to whether the procurement of supplies for the Army is in itself essentially a military function. Generally, though not always, it has been treated so in the United States, but always there have been suggestions for a different approach, and at least since World War I there has been special arrangement for civilian supervision. In recent times the Army has prided itself on adopting the most modern business methods. But then other questions arise: How does a career in the Army especially qualify a person in the methods of business? Would it not be better to turn the whole procurement function over to experienced, professional business men? This might be done either by creating a separate civilian department of supply, as the British did, or by contracting with large private corporations to do the military buying. The argument usually has been that the user ought to control the procurement. But an ordnance procurement officer can hardly be regarded as representing the user any more than might some civilian agent, for an infantry or armored or artillery unit is the user of a weapon. If the Army can be regarded as the user, so might the Department of Defense, or even the government.

Actually, of course, a civilian agency of the government, the Treasury Department, did do military procurement for a time. At various times, particularly during the Revolution and the War of 1812, the contracting system was used by which an individual or a company contracted to provide certain supplies for a certain period of time, and did all the necessary purchasing. In the American experience these arrangements were not altogether satisfactory. The contract system of the Revolution, under the direction of Robert Morris (himself the head of the Treasury) showed a measure of success, because it was almost bound to be a vast improvement over a supply system which had broken down completely, but Morris's regime came at a time when private credit often was better than the public credit. Undoubtedly different systems can be made to work almost equally well, and a secret to successful procurement seems to have been an arrangement wherein the interest of the purchaser could be identified immediately with the interest of the Army. At the same time, the Army always has depended upon private industry to a great degree, and its programs have had to be keyed to the civilian economy. The assignment of special responsibilities for supervising procurement to the Assistant or Under Secretary of War during and since World War I has assured special attention to ultimate civilian control.

A closely related question has been the extent to which the Army should depend upon private industry or should operate its own manufacturing plants. A considerable feeling during the early years was that government facilities should produce all essentially military goods—that private businessmen could not be expected to produce goods solely for war purposes. It was a feeling recurring later, particularly in the 1930's, that such government production was necessary for taking the profits out of war. But Alexander Hamilton's policy of developing government arsenals for a certain share of needed production and letting long-term contracts to encourage the development of a private arms industry led to a compromise which probably has served all needs best. Government arsenals have set production standards, given reliable cost data, and quickly adapted to changing needs, while private manufacturers also have contributed improved designs and production methods, and provided a basis for expansion. The Army could not have begun to meet its requirements for modern total war without the wholesale conversion of private industry to war production. But reliance on private industries also permitted pressures to be brought to bear that attempted to influence military procurement in favor of local economic interests, and the operation of these pressures in the selection of weapon systems and the manufacture of components promises to be one of the major problems of national security.

Continuity

The perfection of logistical organization and the development of production models of essential equipment should be a continuous process in peacetime for war. Organization should be such that no fundamental change is necessary to meet an emergency. For an effective army, war cannot be regarded as a temporary condition foreign to its purpose.

Not until the assumed necessity for a constant plateau of preparedness in the years of cold war following the Korean War did the Army really begin to apply a policy of continuity to its structure and activities for peace and war. The peace of the postwar world turned out to be something different from periods of peace in the past, so that even the distinction between peace and war tended to be blurred. In these circumstances, the continuity which always would have been desirable came to be seen as a necessity. The Army's recent unprecedented emphasis on research and development for new weapons and equipment, and its search for better organization reflects this concern.

Timing

Timing must be relative to the objective, whether in high-level procurement or tactical supply. Requirements must be anticipated. In standardizing production careful timing is necessary to avoid either an abundance of obsolete equipment or too small quantities of better models. In field operations, opportunity for decisive action should not be lost while awaiting additional supplies which may be needed only because of the delay. Timing often is the key to all logistics.

The timing of expeditionary forces, of troop movements, of standardization of items of equipment, and of procurement is likely to be as important to the results of an action as the action itself. Since it is patently impossible to plan sufficiently ahead

in detail for logistics to be tied to specific strategic plans, the only thing to do is to develop resources in a way that will permit the greatest possible flexibility in strategic and tactical decisions. Greater emphasis on the mobility of advance bases and on the versatility of troops for service as well as for combat functions might add a good deal to military flexibility in general.

Unity of Command

Logistics is a function of command. Control of logistics is essential to control of strategy and tactics. In a given area, or for a given mission, a single authority, identical with the command authority, should be responsible for logistics. Rationing or other logistical restrictions should be passed only as far as the next lower command without any effort to define how they should be applied specifically in lower units. In logistical activities, control of single functions such as railways, long-distance trucking, or pipelines should be centralized.

Nearly everyone has agreed that there should be unity of command for logistics, but there has been no general agreement about what that means. In the first place, how far should a commander's control extend to the rear? In World War I the extension of direct War Department control over the Services of Supply could have been justified in the name of unity of command; so could the retention of SOS under the overseas commander. Either arrangement probably could have been made to work, but in either case the necessity of relying on requisitions from the theater for supplies might be questioned.

A second aspect of unity of command has had to do with interservice control. During World War II some aspects of Army-Navy unity were fairly developed, especially in the Central Pacific, but there was not the complete integration of structure and resources which might have been expected for that kind of warfare. In Korea the Army furnished common items for Air Force and Marine units, and there was, at the end, a joint staff organization. In the U.S. European Command General Ridgway insisted that if his unified command were to be effective it must include control, and not just general co-ordination, over logistics.

A frequent debilitating influence on logistics has been that trait of human nature expressing itself as "localitis" or "parochialism." Too often individual or special interests have taken precedence over the general interest, and local pride and loyalty have operated against over-all achievement. On many occasions competition among the bureaus or technical services for limited materials or transportation—each anxious to accomplish its own mission, but with little concern for the others—has militated against the total war effort. Competition, as among theaters or armies in a single World War II theater, has been a constant threat to orderly planning and has been evident to some degree in every war. Often the allocation of resources has appeared to be as much the result of the force of the personality of the commander as of relative requirements and strategic plans. "Moonlight requisitions," commandeering convoys consigned to another organization, unauthorized cannibalization of vehicles, all are expedients resorted to by units large and small anxious to look after their own missions without concern for others. Interservice rivalry has grown with the increasing co-operation among the armed forces and with unification. Where is one to get advice which is both informed and un-

biased? It is difficult indeed to find an officer who will support a proposal likely to weaken the position of his own service or his own command. Localism is not at all peculiar to military affairs, and to understand it may be to forgive it, but it does not make it any the less objectionable. How to overcome it, how to broaden the perspective of responsible leaders at all levels, remains an especially serious problem for logistics.

Forward Impetus

It has become well-established doctrine in the U.S. Army since the Civil War that the impetus of supply is from the rear, and a system of continuous replenishment from the rear has become standard. Forward commanders should be relieved of all possible details without impairing their control of their own logistics. Automatic supply should be developed whenever possible to further that aim.

Probably no principle of modern logistics has been better established than this one, yet certain implications of the axiom were still being questioned during World War II. Automatic supply, for instance, in World War II was found to be rather less satisfactory than in World War I, and frequently resulted in seriously unbalanced stocks, accumulation of unnecessary reserves, and waste. In Korea, automatic supply operated quite effectively. The development of electronic computers and automatic data processing appeared to open the way for putting almost all supplies on requisition with good prospect for quick action. On the other hand, the use of such equipment should make it possible for supply centers in the zone of the interior to have better information on the supply situation of a theater than the theater commander himself, in which case requisitioning might be a formality to be dispensed with in favor of even more fully automatic supply.

Information

Accurate, up-to-date information is vital to effective logistical planning and to supply distribution. Ideally, information processes should engender a minimum of paper work and transmit all of, and only, the best and most relevant details.

Effective logistics operations, from supply distribution to long-range planning, require all the best possible information that affects requirements: strategic and tactical plans, resources (their limitation and possibilities), location and availability of types and kinds of equipment. Moreover, unless the information is accurate, relevant, and current it serves no purpose.

Supplies shipped or stored without adequate documentation at various times have been lost to the use of the command concerned. It is as important to know where supplies are located as to have them physically present. At headquarters the need for precise information has produced an ever-increasing load of paper work. The accumulation of paper work and enlarging a staff to meet its demands, thus engendering more paper work, has always been a problem and one that has grown by leaps and bounds, particularly in this country since the Civil War, until it was stated in a 1961 management study that the Army had "gone overboard in substituting paper for action," and that it often spent more on paper work to keep track of an item than the item was worth.[3]

[3] Analysis of U.S. Army Logistics, USALMC Project 1–61, 20 April 1962.

An expanded staff also adds to the number of concurrences required for full staff co-ordination, and thereby creates a concomitant problem. Because a chief of a major General Staff office cannot possibly review all the decision papers in his organization, the practice is to pass up for his resolution only those matters on which concurrence cannot be obtained. This practice has the built-in possibility that, in efforts to resolve nonconcurrences, information may become obscured. Concurrence procedures tend to follow a well-established system of precedence; it is often frustrating, always time-consuming, and inevitably contributes to the workload. On the other hand, the result more often than not is that the official who is to make the decision can do so with the assurance that he has the essential information pertinent to the problem.

Relativity

All logistics is relative to time, to place, to circumstance. Preparedness never can be absolute, but only relative to the time and place of possible conflict and to potential enemies. Moreover, logistical activities cannot be isolated. One area or command must be related to another to meet requirements for the whole.

Since all logistical resources are limited, every decision for build-up or cutback or priority or a new project has implications for other areas or other activities or projects. Logistical factors always have to be regarded as relative. The decision to invade North Africa meant postponement of the invasion of western Europe; division of resources for the Pacific between the Pacific Ocean Area and the Southwest Pacific virtually determined the strategy of the two-pronged offensive against the Japanese. The decision to arm and equip twenty divisions of the Republic of Korea Army meant that a certain accumulation of equipment would be available for the defense of South Korea, but it also meant a loss of flexibility in making that equipment available for use in other areas. Since World War II the spread of foreign military assistance around the world has posed questions about an effective concentration of friendly forces anywhere, and the whole question of preparedness to resist aggression at various points throughout the world, or of preparedness in general, has had to be related to the capabilities of a potential enemy.

CHAPTER XXXVI

Some General Conclusions

Which has been the most important aspect of logistics for the U.S. Army? One might as well ask which is more important, the gun or the ammunition; or which is more important for a truck, the motor, the drive shaft, or the fuel. By the very nature of logistics one or more elements of supply, transportation, or services almost always must be limiting factors in any given situation. If Korea, for instance, had been a country covered with rail lines and express highways, and all the rolling stock, vehicles, and fuel desired had been available then something else—possibly the supply of ammunition—would have been the limiting factor. Then if all the ammunition in the world had been available, yet another factor—perhaps the supply of artillery tubes—would have set the logistic limitation. Almost never can all logistic requirements be satisfied in an exact balance, and as long as that is true, and as long as military operations are governed by the finite, some phase of logistics is bound to be a limiting factor. It therefore would serve no useful purpose to isolate one element of logistics and show that it limited the scope of given military operations, unless it also could be shown that all the other logistical requirements could have been met to support the operations in question.

The critical link in the chain of factors making up military logistics may vary a great deal from one situation to another. For one country at a given time and place, the limiting factor in logistics may be manufacturing capacity. That is to say, all the equipment that can be turned out from accessible industrial plants can be delivered to the military forces, but the productive capacity itself sets the limits as to what can be done. For another country or under other circumstances the availability of raw materials may set the limit for logistics.

Transportation

Probably the most common limiting factor in U.S. Army logistics has been transportation. Whenever shortages of supplies or equipment have appeared at the battle fronts, from the Revolutionary War to the Korean War, more often than not it has been the result of some shortage in transportation somewhere along the line.

While transportation might be the most general limiting factor on logistics as a whole, the limitations of transportation itself might be determined by a small segment of the total transportation system—shipping, port facilities, roads, railroads, vehicles, or other facilities. To pursue the problem a step further, limitations of highway transportation, for instance, might be due to poor roads, to lack of motor vehicles or animals, to shortages of fuel or forage; limitations of railway transportation might be set by the track, the restoration of damaged bridges, availability of rolling stock, fuel, operating personnel, or other factors. Generally most transportation difficulties for U.S. Army forces, once support activities have been stepped up after the initial impact of war, have been found within the theaters of operations rather than in the long supply lines from the zone of the interior, but again a qualification may be necessary. In the support of oversea operations, shipping was the factor most prominent in logistic calculations and strategic planning, and this being so, it is likely that steps to overcome that kind of shortage would be taken before a major expedition would be launched, so that almost inevitably, the transportation shortages would be shifted to the far end of the line.

Probably nothing influenced the changing character of war more than the revolution in transportation, though old ways retained a certain relevance in some conditions, and it was easy to anticipate or exaggerate the real significance of new or spectacular ways at given times and places.

Hand-carrying of supplies never has disappeared. On many occasions it was the only way to get food and ammunition up to the front lines in both World Wars, and in the mountains of Korea it took on renewed significance with the organization of Korean Service Corps carrying parties.

Animals had almost disappeared from the Army by World War II, but they had to be brought back for carrying supplies over the difficult country of Sicily, the Italian mainland, and Burma. The very quaintness for men of the U.S. Army in using mules and dealing with the problems of forage and other supplies for them is an indication of the completeness of motorization only two decades after horses and mules had been essential for the supply of all American combat divisions. For the German Army in World War II, requisitions for forage, horse-shoes and harness were not at all strange; horses still were drawing artillery and pulling supply carts for the infantry companies in the German forces in the west. It came as something of a surprise to German generals in 1944 when they saw how rapidly a fully motorized army could advance across France so long as fuel could be brought up.

Railroads made their first great impact on American warfare in the Civil War, though it must not be forgotten that in that war steamboats were as important as railroads. Since then the role of railroads in logistics has continued to grow, but the motor truck carried a large share of supplies in the theaters of operations in World War II.

The use of air transportation in World War II and in the Korean War, both for transoceanic hauls and forward delivery—including the use of the helicopter in frontline supply and evacuation in Korea—indicated air transport as the area of spectacular achievement in the future. But sometimes recognition of the potential of aviation indicated by isolated examples led to serious exaggeration of its real significance for logistical support up through 1953.

The importance of air transportation in delivering relatively small quantities of highly important items of supply or relatively small numbers of men in time to influence immediate situations cannot be minimized. But in view of the limited tonnage capabilities and high cost, there still was serious question as to the role air transportation should play in the general military transportation system of the early 1950's. Even speed, when the cargo involved more than a few tons, was better served by sea transportation.

In May 1950 the Military Air Transport Service was carrying about 70 tons of cargo a month to Japan. By the end of August 1950 that rate had reached 100 tons a day. But that was the equivalent of only about 3,000 tons a month—less than three-fourths of 1 percent of the total cargo moved to the Far East during that month. The Army's share of air cargo was only about 3,700 tons for the whole first year of the Korean War. This included most of the 3.5-inch rockets and launchers used in Korea up to mid-September 1950, as well as recoilless rifles and ammunition, whole blood, airdrop equipment, and other high-priority items. In such deliveries as these the airlift was most valuable. Bazookas and rockets could be sent quickly to the battle areas where they were needed at once, in any numbers that could be obtained, as they came from the assembly lines. Had it been a question of delivering all those same items within thirty days, and the circumstances such that none would be needed until all arrived, then it would have been just as well to send them by ship.

If a situation had come up in which, say, 15,000 tons of high-priority cargo were needed within thirty days in order to prepare for an amphibious landing (such as the one at Inchon), two Victory ships could have delivered the whole amount within the month, including loading time, sailing time, and unloading time. The available airlift could not have delivered that quantity of supplies in less than five months. On long flights across the Pacific, a C–54 type of aircraft could carry about five tons of cargo. At peak operations during the Korean War, no more than about 200 such aircraft could be counted upon for sustained use, each one averaging about three round trips to the Far East from the west coast a month. Actual capabilities of the Pacific airlift in 1952 averaged about 2,225 tons a month for the whole Pacific area. Total tonnage of all kinds flown to the Far East in 1951 amounted to about 23,000 tons, and in 1952 to about 30,000 tons.

The Air Force budgeted for the Army's air transportation requirements, and no reimbursement was necessary (as it was for sea transportation); nevertheless the relative costs had to be taken into account in broad military plannnig. The contract rate for a C–54 type of aircraft making one round trip between the west coast and the Far East was $25,000. With a capacity of five tons, this meant a cost of $5,000 a ton for air cargo (or $2,500 if the plane carried a full load both ways). The cargo rate by sea transportation was $17 a measurement ton, or equivalent to about $38 a short ton.

By the end of the Korean War the air age really had not yet arrived insofar as normal transportation was concerned, and examples intended to emphasize how the world had shrunk in point of time-distance were sometimes exaggerated. It might be suggested, for example, that Tokyo was closer in time to San Francisco than Philadelphia was to New York during the Revolution because an airplane in 1953 could span the Pacific more quickly than a horse-drawn coach could go from New York to Philadelphia in 1780. But this comparison is not altogether a fair one, for it compares a very special method of travel with a common method. An army might march from New York to Philadelphia in a matter of six or seven days (Washington's army in 1781, with some delays, covered the distance in about twelve days). In 1953 no army could reach Tokyo from San Francisco in that time. It took nine days after the first warning for first elements of the 2d Division to begin moving from Tacoma, Washington, in July 1950, and twenty-nine days for the entire division to complete preparations and sail; thirty-four days elapsed from the time that the first ship sailed from Tacoma until the last tactical unit arrived at Pusan.

A special kind of revolution in the Army's transportation after World War II had to do with control. Except for Navy operation of Army ships during World War I, and to a limited extent in World War II, the Army always had insisted on controlling its own transportation. The organization of the consolidated Military Air Transport Service under the operational control of the Air Force and the transfer of the Army Transport Service to the Navy Military Sea Transportation Service, left the Army with control over neither air nor sea transportation for its own support. The experience of two world wars and the Korean conflict indicated that the new transportation services would be no less dependable and probably more efficient in the total effort.

One great weakness of logistics has been a failure of transportation for the support of the exploitation and pursuit phases of an action. This weakness cannot always be blamed for failures to follow up victories. McClellan had no want of transportation for supplies at Antietam, and Meade had more than enough on hand to pursue Lee after Gettysburg. This was not true for Hodges and Patton in 1944. Then the spirit was there but the flesh was not. Plans had not been drawn to take advantage of Hodges' and Patton's unexpectedly rapid advance. The necessary hundreds of big trucks that would have had to be ordered a year earlier were not there. The hundreds of transport aircraft and of units and equipment to prepare landing fields, which might have helped ease the situation, were not available.

Like the G–2, the G–4 must be a pessimist. He must stock reserves against unexpected loss; he may build up stockpiles for an attack or for a prolonged defense, but the one contingency for which it is most difficult for him to prepare is the breakthrough. Nothing could be more embarrassing to the logistician than success. Possibly a major contribution of future development of air transportation would be in providing the means for adapting to breakthrough and rapid forward thrust. Indeed, with more of the combat functions of aviation going to rocket-propelled missiles, the main future use of manned aircraft may be for transportation. And perhaps the rapid delivery of small quantities of items will also be a future function of rockets, though again the matter of relative cost should warn against exaggeration of the early significance of another new and spectacular mode of transportation.

Oversea Warfare and Mobility

Two of the greatest contributions of the United States to the art of war have been the support of large-scale ground operations across the oceans and amphibious assault of defended beaches. After its first oversea expedition and amphibious operations against Mexico in 1846, the Army did little in that direction until the War with Spain when it landed forces in the Caribbean and in the Philippines. With the co-operation of British and other allies in World War I and II and the Korean War in controlling the seas, the United States was able to take advantage of the vast ocean communications to build up and maintain forces in all quarters of the globe. Sea communications has been one of the major logistical advantages of the United States, but it has taken special organization, procedures, and facilities to make full use of it.

Many of the amphibious operations in the Pacific were mainly Marine Corps actions, though Army forces participated in a number of them, and the biggest amphibious assaults of all time—North Africa, Sicily, Normandy, Leyte, Luzon, and Okinawa—were essentially Army operations. Congestion of shipping and getting supplies ashore and in orderly storage as needed were continuing problems. Unloading capacities at the ports and local transportation beyond the ports probably were the greatest logistical problems of World War II. In this connection a plan considered for the Pacific but not carried out because it had not been adopted soon enough to obtain the necessary equipment may deserve consideration in future planning. This was to send trains of commodity-loaded, ocean-going barges to serve as floating storage off the invasion beaches. Warnings and orders against the use of ships for storage had become so ingrained in the Army's thinking that apparently little thought had been given to planning it that way deliberately. Commodity-loaded ships were dispatched to support the Normandy and Pacific landings, but the assumption always was that they would be unloaded and released as soon as practicable. On the Pacific islands it was necessary to construct hasty shelters for supplies, unload the supplies to make room for other ships to dock, and, when the war had passed on, to try to pick up the remaining supplies or let them go to waste. With a system of floating depots, giving to the Army something equivalent to the Navy's fleet replenishment at sea, it might have been possible to overcome most of the problems. Shelter in the form of specially designed barges

would have been at hand. They could have been moved to various sections of the coast as needed; they could move out to receive new supplies from arriving ships which would then not have to wait for space at a pier; and as combat operations moved on to other islands, the depot barges could have been moved out—without further handling of the supplies—to support the new operations.

This idea might have some relevance for land operations as well—perhaps there is also a place for deliberately planning to keep forward reserves on wheels, moving them up to units on call. This had actually been done from the Civil War to the Korean War, but always over the strong protests of transportation officers who, with reason, insisted that such use of railway cars seriously crippled transportation for resupply from the rear areas, and often led to serious congestion. But possibly with requirements for railroad cars and truck semitrailers calculated on the basis of such use, and with traffic planned on the same basis, an additional element of mobility and so of flexibility might be gained. In spite of the speed of modern vehicles, logistics has not kept pace sufficiently to permit modern armies to move much more rapidly over great distances on land than they did in earlier times. Washington's and Rochambeau's armies took fifteen days to march 200 miles from the Hudson to the Chesapeake en route to Yorktown. Sherman's army covered 300 miles from Atlanta to the sea in thirty-nine days, and 425 miles from Savannah to Goldsboro in fifty days. In 1944 in the race across France, Patton's Third Army went from Saint-Hilaire, near the base of the Brittany Peninsula, 400 miles to Nancy in thirty-eight days. The Eighth Army in Korea, in its pursuit in 1950 from the

Naktong to the Ch'ongchon, nearly 400 miles, made it in thirty-four days.

Service Troops

A continuously recurring problem throughout all the wars of the United States has been the matter of finding men to perform the various service tasks necessary for logistical support. It has raised questions of the number of men needed; of whether civilians or soldiers should be used, and if civilians are to be used how they should be supervised; the extent to which local labor should be used in foreign countries; and if soldiers are used whether they should be from specialized units or be taken from units on the line; of classification and training of personnel; and of morale and efficiency.

It has become common to make the ratio of combat troops to service troops a measure of efficiency in the Army. By itself this ratio means nothing. What counts is the total amount of effective fire power that can be brought to bear against the enemy. If the greatest total of effective power can be delivered with one combat man for each service man then this is the desired ratio, but if 1,000 service troops for one combat man are needed to achieve that maximum, then that is the desired ratio. If it impairs combat effectiveness to maintain a small ratio of service to combat troops then such a ratio is to be avoided rather than sought. The concept of the division slice, that is, the average strength of a combat division plus proportionate shares of supporting troops, is useful in estimating troop and supply requirements for preliminary planning, but it cannot be taken as any kind of standard for a particular situation. It is impossible even to suggest a desirable ratio of service to com-

bat troops. Obviously many more service troops will be needed in one situation than in another, and the number will vary according to whether good transportation facilities are available, whether roads and railroads must be built, the length of the supply lines, the availability of local labor, the type of operations being supported, and other factors which cannot be anticipated. Furthermore, the implication which some may read into the division slice that the proportion of overhead troops to combat troops remains constant even in a given situation is unwarranted. In 1818 Secretary of War Calhoun had pointed out that the size of the peacetime Army at any time should have very little to do with the size of the staff needed to prepare for mobilization and war. During World War II the average size of the division slice in the theaters turned out to be 40,000 men—17,000 men in the division, 5,500 men in supporting combat units in corps and army, and 17,500 service troops in army and communication zone. Taking into account troops in the United States, the average division slice world-wide, was 60,000 men. In the theaters service troops equaled 43 percent of the division slice (not counting service troops in division organic units).[1] During the Korean War the situation in the Far East was such that whatever the ratio happened to be, it would not necessarily be reasonable for other areas. In Japan, American forces had the services of an effective labor force which could not be counted upon in all possible theaters of operations. Japan Logistical Command estimated that if all the supply and service functions of the command had been carried out without the use of Japanese workers,

---

[1] FM 101–10, pp. 101–02, 492.

an additional 200,000 to 250,000 service troops would have been required. The use of local labor in Korea was much less efficient, though hardly less significant, than in Japan. By the fall of 1951, U.S. forces in Korea were employing over 77,000 native workers in the rear areas in addition to the 50,700 members of the Korean Service Corps and 30,000 other laborers within the corps areas.

During colonial times civilian contractors not only furnished supplies, but they cleared roads, built boats, drove wagons, and operated storehouses for military forces. This practice continued, in declining degree, in the Army of the Republic. When civilians could not be found as drivers, soldiers were sometimes used, but reluctantly, since it weakened combat strength. Schuyler used soldiers for construction work at Ticonderoga but he advised against it, for he felt that it "not only ruins soldiers, but is more expensive." On the other hand the amphibian troops with Washington manned boats when needed, and also excelled in combat. During the War of 1812 workers for the Ordnance Department were given a new military status, though still not as soldiers. In the Seminole War (1836–42) soldiers had to do practically all their own work from building roads to bringing up supplies for their own support. In the Mexican War, Mexican labor was used to unload ships and operate river boats, but the lack of service troops was a major problem. In vain Quartermaster officers urged the formation of a corps of quartermaster troops and, in the interest of discipline and dependability, the use of enlisted wagon drivers instead of hired teamsters.

With the increased magnitude of operations in the Civil War, the problem became more pronounced. There were more Engineer troops, who gave a good account of themselves, and a few Ordnance and Signal Corps men, and some officers and noncommissioned officers assigned to the other services; however, teamsters, laborers, and specialists of various kinds still were generally civilians hired for the purpose or line soldiers temporarily detached from their regiments. An increasing number of freed Negro "contrabands" performed valuable services as the war progressed. Hermann Haupt expressed a preference for trained civilians in his railway construction work, but he accomplished some of his greatest triumphs of bridge building with untrained soldiers.

As Secretary of War (1904–08) William Howard Taft recommended the formation of a general service corps to replace civilian employees and soldiers released from line units for duty as wagon masters, teamsters, engineers, firemen, carpenters, blacksmiths, overseers, clerks, and laborers. He failed to win approval for his recommendation, but by the time of World War I it had become generally accepted that enlisted service troops of various kinds should perform most of those duties. Men who had never seen a ship were organized into stevedore battalions, men unfamiliar with motor vehicles were assigned to truck companies, men who had never been near an Army depot were assigned to run them, and all learned to do their jobs well in Pershing's SOS. But Pershing never did have the service troops he needed. His staff calculated that the SOS should comprise 26 percent of the total strength of the AEF, but it never reached that figure. When, after several months of almost exclusive priority to infantry troops to satisfy British and French demands, Pershing faced a critical shortage of men to support his newly formed First Army, he ordered that five infantry divisions be broken up for assignment to logistical tasks and for use as replacements.

Foreign civilian labor on a large scale—and prisoners of war where feasible—supplemented soldier labor in World Wars I and II and in the Korean War, and in each case organization and policies had to be improvised. The use of local labor, especially in Japan and Korea in the 1950's, undoubtedly reduced the number of service troops required, though not necessarily in the equivalent of the number of local workers employed. On the other hand, Army service units had a much greater responsibility than otherwise would have been the case by reason of the logistic support furnished to the other United Nations troops and the Republic of Korea Army, as well as to U.S. Marine and Air Force units. Curiously enough, the number of service troops actually on duty in the Far East in 1951 turned out to be very close to the 43 percent of theater forces established in the Army's planning data on the basis of World War II experience.

Finding enough skilled technicians for logistical support activities is a problem that has grown with each technological advance in warfare. A shortage of trained specialists in the Army had become so acute by June 1950, even before the attack in Korea, that the Department of the Army published a directive providing for qualified men to be sent to specialists schools involuntarily if enough qualified volunteers were not available. Someone had to do those service jobs if the Army was to carry out its missions at all.

The morale of men assigned to communications zone duties has suffered from long and irregular hours of work, as well as from the awareness of a certain resentment

against "rear echelon" troops on the part of combat men and others who intimate that a man is doing something less than his full share unless he is firing a gun at the enemy. On the other hand, the morale of infantrymen suffers from continued exposure to danger over extended periods of time when the only relief seems to be in becoming a casualty and the only reward for success in battle is an opportunity to attack another, perhaps more difficult, objective the next day.

Apparently moved by an underlying compulsion to fairness—that all men ought to be placed in jeopardy of life and limb in combat to about the same extent—G-3 offered a proposal in 1951 that all men be given the same basic training, and that individuals be interchanged between combat and noncombat units. The suggestion deserved more serious consideration than the summary dismissal G-4 gave it on the basis of an ingrained assumption that special branch training was essential and that an interchange of soldiers between combat and logistical duties would reduce the effectiveness of both. More to the point might have been a proposal for rotating divisions between combat and logistical assignments. How better to achieve the flexibility needed to meet varying requirements for service troops as conditions change? How better to meet the competing demands for quality personnel between front and rear? How better to improve the morale of all concerned?

Although many examples of the rotation of men between service chores and combat functions can be found in the Army's history, it has always been done as an expedient to meet a necessity of the moment and never as a deliberate policy with the prior planning and training necessary to make it most effective. The implication in planned rotation of this kind is that every soldier would have at least two military occupation specialty numbers, one for combat (for example, rifleman or tank driver) and one for service support (laborer or crane operator). There would be no difficulty in having the engineers, quartermasters, ordnance men, or signalmen of the division's organic units adapt themselves to corresponding duties in rear areas. There is, similarly, no reason why a rifleman should not be able to serve as a hospital corpsman, or why an artillery gunner should not also handle ammunition at communications zone depots. A tank driver able to perform third-echelon maintenance or a truck driver able to overhaul the engine might be able to perform his primary duty better for having the secondary capability. Men serving in volunteer fire departments in many communities throughout the country are trained to operate modern fire-fighting equipment, but they also continue their duties as clerks, grocerymen, teachers, garagemen, or whatever their occupation may be. The same is true of soldiers of the National Guard and organized reserves—a soldier in war need not be less versatile. Undoubtedly, a large share of the tasks connected with Army logistical activities could be done with relatively little specialized training. Combat engineers pride themselves on their combat role. Why should not the same be true of all service troops, and if engineers can be trained to fight as infantrymen, why cannot infantrymen be trained to work as engineers, or quartermasters, or transportation men? In rotation, men could gain the satisfaction of full participation in the military effort, and have some hope of relief now and then from the oppression of the battlefield. Moreover,

civilian occupation specialties would become relevant in the assignment of all men, and not at the expense of combat units.

Logistical headquarters and installations could have permanent staffs of officers, warrant officers, and specialists to command, supervise, and perform highly skilled tasks; but for the major part of their personnel they would depend on the assignment of infantry or other divisions prepared for all-purpose duty. Divisions would be assigned as needed to corps for combat or to logistical commands or other headquarters for service functions. If there should be a breakthrough and rapid pursuit on some part of the front, some divisions, instead of being rushed to the front to add to the supply problems, might be rushed to the rear to help overcome the supply problems of a rapidly extending line of communication. In their training periods, too, divisions might rotate between combat training and supply activities. At one time a division would be assigned to a camp for field training; at another it would be assigned as station complement to operate one or more posts; at another it might be assigned to depots to handle supplies; at another to load ships at a port of embarkation; and at still another time it would be attached to a corps for combat maneuvers. Such an arrangement might permit a degree of flexibility never previously attained, but for which a great need has appeared in every war in which the United States has participated.

The way to become "lean" and "streamlined" and "highly mobile" is not, as has so often been assumed, to reduce the division slice, that is, to reduce the proportion of service troops. The more likely way to develop a fast-moving, hard-hitting force is to give it enough service support.

Coalition Warfare

One of the most important developments for the U.S. Army in the twentieth century has been its participation in coalition warfare and programs of mutual assistance. After the early alliance with France in the Revolutionary War, the United States had no further experience with coalition efforts until the China Relief Expedition in 1900. Much more significant was World War I, when the United States, as an "associate" of the Allied Powers, geared its military production through 1918 to a division of labor with England and France, and participated on various interallied economic councils and committees, on the Supreme War Council, and on the Military Board of Allied Supply. In World War II the U.S.-British alliance, although never formalized by treaty, probably was the closest international military collaboration in history. Through the instrument of lend-lease the United States made major contributions to virtually all United Nations participants. Though relations at times were strained, major efforts went into both the procurement and the delivery of supplies and equipment to the Soviet Union and to China. American assistance provided almost the entire means for the resurrection of French military strength.

After World War II the Army found itself in a new, significant role as the principal agent for the execution of the Mutual Defense Assistance Program and the organization of military assistance advisory groups for co-ordinating supply in allied countries around the world. Perhaps the experience with the French alliance during the Revolution when the United States was the beneficiary of foreign assistance was still of consequence. France at that time had made no

effort at strict screening of requirements and close supervision of supply activities, but treated the United States in all respects as an equal.

Support of United Nations forces in Korea brought new complications and new experience in the logistics of coalition warfare. In the long run it is possible that the experience gained in supporting the other United Nations forces will provide the most valuable lessons of the Korean War. While the relative number of troops furnished by other members of the United Nations was small, and the supplies and services furnished them was an almost insignificant fraction of the total, the real significance of United Nations participation is not to be measured in these terms alone.

While it was unlikely that any future allied military effort would adopt completely the same policies as those applied in Korea, the fact that experience had been gained would provide some standards for planning whereas heretofore there had been practically none. Above all, it might be expected that in the future serious consideration would be given to flexible methods of providing and financing military equipment for allies in wartime. In 1950 a program of military assistance—the Mutual Defense Assistance Program—already was in operation, its purpose presumably to build up allied strength for more effective participation in a coalition war; yet procedures had not been worked out for continuing that assistance under conditions of war for which preparations were being made. As a result the Korean emergency had to be met with stopgap measures, an experience that, hopefully, would result in the development of procedures for a continuation in wartime of matériel assistance that would be even more essential in some future emergency.

CHAPTER XXXVII

The Continuity of Change

The evolution of U.S. Army logistics has followed the experience of war—to an extent—and the revolutions in warfare accompanying the industrial revolution of the whole period of the nation's existence. Increasingly frequent references to the "growing complexities of modern warfare" are above all logistical allusions, for they usually refer to the production, repair, and operation of new types of weapons, vehicles, and other equipment. These revolutions have proceeded at an ever-quickening pace. A soldier under Washington somehow transposed to the army with Scott in Mexico probably would have less feeling of unfamiliarity than, say, a soldier under Pershing transposed to the armies of Eisenhower or MacArthur in World War II. Still, the growing rapidity of change did not alter the bonds of continuity nor render invalid the experience of the old for adaptation to the new.

The age of change saw manufacturing move from the home or the small shop to the big factory, and invention move from the shop to the laboratory. The introduction of interchangeable parts paved the way for mass production and automation which moved ahead as first steam, then electricity replaced direct water power, and oil and gas surpassed wood and coal in many plants as direct fuel. It was the age when sail and animal power gave way to steam and the internal combustion engine; when the speed of communication leaped above the speed of transportation to almost instantaneous electrical transmission. All these advances became evident in the manufacture of military weapons and equipment and in the transportation of troops and supplies.

The telegraph and the steamboat modernized the Mexican War to some degree, and then, with the added facilities of the railroads, made of the Civil War in a sense "the first modern war." In the twentieth century the revolution in warfare already evident in the Civil War rushed toward completion, but it would not be accomplished in the first twenty years of the century despite the magnitude of World War I. New weapons changed the character of war markedly, but the real revolution in warfare did not come until the revolution in transportation had spread through military operations completely. The revolution is not in the introduction of the railroad, the motor truck, and the airplane, but in their widespread use. Industrialization without motorization and mechanization, or with rudimentary motorization and mechanization, characterized the War with Spain and World War I, respectively, and in the latter, mobility on the battlefields of the Western Front was lost. Aside from its great magnitude, what was the chief characteristic of war in the first fifth of the twentieth century? Was it not this very lack of mobility? Greatly increased tonnages of supplies and equipment could be produced, and could be moved overseas. They could be moved by railroad to the vicinity of the battlefield. But motor transportation had not been developed to the point where it could with equal speed move those vast quantities of supplies to the battlefield, and across the battlefield; therefore dependence for this last stage of transport continued to be on horses and mules, which themselves required transportation and provisions. The horse virtually disappeared from the battle lines in World War I, but not from the supply lines. This was the period of transition—a period of stabilized warfare between the mobility of the Civil War and the mobility of World War II when American motor vehicles compounded the mobility that German panzer divisions had restored· to the battlefield, and once more logisticians faced the nightmare of armies outrunning their supplies.

The armies of World War I were more closely tied to the railroads than ever before, and their range of operations beyond the railheads was less, not more, than in the Civil War. Every improvement in equipment and every expansion in industrial capacity simply added to the matériel requirements and to the burden on transportation, but did not relieve any of the burden on the soldier's back. The requirement of about four and one-half pounds of supplies per man per day for the Civil War soldier multiplied to thirty pounds per man per day as an "absolutely essential" minimum, and sometimes figured at forty and even fifty pounds for the American Expeditionary Forces in France. Caesar's men carried as much as seventeen days' rations in their packs; Napoleon's soldiers carried bread and flour for fifteen days; the Civil War soldier ordinarily carried three days' rations,

and not infrequently had to carry an extra five days' hard bread and coffee; the soldier of World War I, while carrying an even heavier load, seldom carried more than two days' rations.

Increases in military production tended merely to increase the demand and, as war became more industrialized, competition between the fighting forces and the factories for the manpower needed for a maximum war effort also increased. At the turn of the century it was calculated that for each man in the armed forces the product of one man in war industries and services was required.

Industrialization introduced a whole new dimension into logistics. "Here for the supply officer will be yet further difficulties; for time and space calculations, instead of being based on the standard performance of man and beast, which within small limits has not changed, will depend on the skill of the engineer and the output of the factory." [1]

War contributed greatly to the quickening pace of the industrial revolution, which in turn was to have such an impact on modern war. Eli Whitney introduced the principle of interchangeable parts into the arms industry. Improved steel and the growth of mass production grew out of immediate demands of war. The Civil War revealed to industry in the United States potential and opportunities never before recognized, and industrial expansion in the succeeding decades brought new capacity and new requirements to the wars of the twentieth century. Again, the enforced co-ordination and rationalization of industry during World War I paved the way for the great expansion of

[1] G. C. Shaw, *Supply in Modern War* (London: Faber and Faber, 1938), p. 165.

the 1920's, and carried the process of multiplication of supply requirements forward to World War II. The impact of industrialization on war was not always recognized at the time of its greatest growth— or it was misinterpreted. Jean de Bloch, a noted student of modern war, was so impressed with the phenomenon that in 1899 he published an impressive study, *The Future of War in Its Technical, Economic and Political Relations.* In this study (which the World Peace Foundation, with a rare sense of timing, reissued in 1914) de Bloch assembled weighty statistical evidence to prove that the dimensions of modern armaments and the organization of society had rendered the prosecution of war an economic impossibility.

For the position of the United States in world affairs, 1890 was a highly significant date. That year the United States surpassed Great Britain in the production of pig iron and steel. Already ahead of France, Germany, and Russia in output of pig iron by 1870, and in output of steel by 1875, American industrial production showed remarkable increases during the whole period between the Civil War and World War I.

Even so, the United States entered World War I with a sense of military inferiority, for the production of military goods not only had failed to keep pace with U.S. industrial expansion, but it had not kept up with the other major powers of the world. Nevertheless the potential existed, and even though soldiers of the AEF had to depend on France and Great Britain for most of their finished weapons, that potential was clearly demonstrated in the war production program.

In World War II the American potential, by force of necessity, had to be developed to the greatest achievement of military production in history. No longer the chief recipient, but instead the chief provider of weapons and equipment, the United States had become in fact the "arsenal of democracy"—and would continue to be after that war, with military assistance programs around the world and as the leader of a coalition in limited war in Korea.

Administration

In this increasingly complex modern war logistical activities demanded more and more attention. The whole field of administration and logistics was one in which the Army had been forced to excel. For the Army in mid-twentieth century, fighting was becoming secondary to administration. Already noticeable in World War I, and more so in World War II, the trend accelerated in the Korean conflict.[2] Much to their consternation, a great many old soldiers who longed for the smell of gunpowder and the chatter of machine guns faced the more likely prospect of having to settle for the smell of mimeograph ink and the chatter of typewriters. Officers and men who felt they were contributing nothing to a war effort if they were not on the firing line had to develop a broader view of war's requirements. Back in the 1930's the *U.S. Army Recruiting News* carried a brief feature in each issue entitled, "Things the Army Does Besides Fight." A report of what the Army did besides fight in the 1950's would have practically filled the paper—as in fact to a lesser degree it would have in the 1930's if viewed more broadly. Actually most of the Army did not fight—

---

[2] For a penetrating discussion of this trend see Kent Roberts Greenfield, *The Historian and the Army* (New Brunswick, N.J.; Rutgers University Press, 1954), pp. 73–75, 90–93.

an infantryman on leave from a combat area, accustomed to being surrounded by infantrymen like himself and to think of the Army as made up mainly of the same kind of soldiers, was much surprised at how relatively few infantrymen he might see in the cities of the rear areas. He represented a military minority. Most of the Army was not in the combat arms—the infantry, armor, and artillery. Most of it was in the technical services—the engineers, quartermasters, medics, and chemical, signal, and transportation units—and in the administrative services and the headquarters which guided and supervised the tactical and service units from the combat zone to the Pentagon. In the late fifties the Army lost altogether its status as a distinctive combat force and its mission became to raise, organize, equip, and train components for assignments to unified commands. Actually this was not a great change, for the Army General Staff never had controlled operations in the theaters.

The Army's administrative and supply and service functions were not confined to the support of its own units; it also had broad responsibilities for supporting the other services—especially the Air Force, and in Korea the Marine Corps—and for executing the military aspects (and sometimes the civilian aspects, too) of the government's foreign assistance programs. The Army was the executive agency for the Joint Chiefs of Staff for the Far East Command, a unified command; Army Forces, Far East, was executive agency for the commander in chief, Far East Command, in matters of logistics affecting more than one service. At the same time the Army was the executive agency for the Joint Chiefs of Staff for the European Command, and it was executive agency for the Department of Defense

for the Mutual Defense Assistance Program, and the agency for providing necessary logistical support for other members of the United Nations in Korea. Again in the late fifties, even those direct lines of participation were weakened as new procedures provided that service commanders take their orders directly from the Joint Chiefs of Staff acting for the President and the Secretary of Defense without any one service acting as "executive agent."

Whether because of de-emphasis resulting from lack of apparent need, or overemphasis on economy in the country when it came to military affairs, the Army, at least until after World War II, never was able to achieve an organization and structure in peacetime that could serve it well logistically in war. It must be granted that the bureau system did hold up fairly well, with relatively minor modifications, in the Mexican War and, after a slow start, in the Civil War. But major overhauls were necessary in top organization for the War of 1812, for the War with Spain (even if it was *ex post facto*), for World War I, and for World War II.

Though Secretaries of War Calhoun and Root saw clearly the Army's function in peacetime as being one of preparation for war, they never were able to shake the attitude of the Army—or the country—that peacetime was "normal," and that extraordinary measures naturally would be necessary whenever a war emergency interrupted the peacetime routine. The assumption seems to have been that without the prospect of war there was no real reason for the Army's existence, but the prospect of war (and wartime organization) has not been greatly in evidence in the Army's peacetime organization. Each time war has come the Army has had to reorganize.

The Army has always had a certain

penchant for reorganization. The Topographical Engineers went back and forth, combined with or separated from the Corps of Engineers; Ordnance and Artillery were married and divorced; Subsistence was combined with Quartermaster, and Transportation separated from Quartermaster; but on the whole the bureaus intrenched themselves over the years so that even the creation of the General Staff was little more than superstructure added to structure—a frosting of apparent co-ordination and control over the cake of the old-line bureaus. Then the reorganization during World War I jarred the structure with the Purchase, Traffic, and Storage Division under General Goethals, exercising real control in many areas simply because control had to rest somewhere.

Army Service Forces in World War II went a step further toward centralized control. At the end of the war a great deal of debate went on over the question of continuing the ASF in peacetime (again the assumption that the peacetime structure should be different). The ASF was promptly abolished, but the substance of its central direction and control was carried over to the new General Staff organization by 1948. The new service, the Supply and Procurement Division of the General Staff (later redesignated the Logistics Division, then the Office of the Assistant Chief of Staff, G–4, and still later the Office of the Deputy Chief of Staff for Logistics) was more akin to Army Service Forces (less the latter's personnel functions) and to its World War I counterpart, Purchase, Traffic, and Storage Division, than to the World War II G–4.

The logistical organization of the Department of the Army proved to be equal to the shock of the Korean emergency with some expansion of personnel, and only relatively minor readjustments in organizational structure. In some ways the Army's service and supply organization still was bound up in too much red tape, encouraged too much duplication of effort, and was too ponderous for speedy operation. Some officers and civil officials thought a thoroughgoing reorganization would promote greater efficiency. Others felt that an all-out mobilization would require a return to something like the Army Service Forces of World War II. But many were satisfied that the organization of G–4 and the technical services that had been effective in peacetime and for the Korean War would serve as well for any future emergency. The relatively smooth transition from peace to war of which it was capable recommended the current organization when it seemed likely that one emergency would follow another for a long time to come.

Most suggestions for further reorganization were more concerned with recasting the technical services than the general staff structure. Several of these suggestions went back to something like that which General Somervell had proposed during World War II for functional reorganization. One would have taken advantage of the lesson General Somervell had learned in his first failure and applied in 1945: to alter the substance without tampering with the historical designations, so that all procurement might be assigned to the Ordnance Corps, and all storage and distribution to the Quartermaster Corps, while the other technical services would perform the services of their specializations without supply functions. Others thought this arrangement awkward, and proposed that a whole new matériel command with functional divisions be set up. These discussions foreshadowed events that transpired during the next decade: establishment of the Defense Supply Agency; reorganization of Headquarters, Department of the Army; abolition of the offices of most of the technical service chiefs; and establishment of the Army Matériel Command.

Organization for logistical support in the theaters of operations never has been completely clear and satisfactory. Washington's position as Commander in Chief and as commander of the main army in the Revolution left some anomolies in his relations with the government and with the other armies. It was not always clear, for instance, whether the quartermaster with the Northern Army was responsible to the commander of the Northern Army, to Washington, to the quartermaster in Philadelphia, or to the Board of War and the Continental Congress. Scott, while commander of the army in Central Mexico was also General in Chief of the U.S. Army, but he had sharp differences with the War Department on matters of supply. Pershing's organization in France was rather well developed, but relationships, particularly of the G–4 and the special staff of General Headquarters with Services of Supply, were not well defined, nor was GHQ control of the Advance Section in keeping with the SOS organization. There also was conflict between territorial and functional organizations—the base sections and the military railroad, for instance. Many of these difficulties reappeared in the communications zone organization in Europe in World War II, when responsibilities again were not clear between theater and communications zone headquarters. There was besides the added complication of Supreme Headquarters, Allied Expeditionary Force, with its own G–4 staff section. In the island warfare of the Pacific the prefer-ence was for an Army service command organization attached to the field armies, and the communications zone did not ordinarily provide close support.

During the Korean War the administrative organization of the Far East Command retained certain discrepancies until the beginning of 1953 by which time it had developed a theater structure closely paralleling that outlined in established doctrine. The principal modifying factor on the higher level was the United Nations Command Headquarters—principally the main divisions of Far East Command Headquarters with the addition of combined staff sections including members from other co-operating nations. But the actual direction and execution of logistical activities continued to be on a national basis, and the logistical organization developed by 1953 generally "followed the book," with certain local adaptations. The principal deviations were in the designation of the Korean Communications Zone and in the organization of a single section headquarters under it. Actually Army Forces, Far East, served as the theater communications zone headquarters, while Korean Communications Zone was a base or intermediate section, yet the resulting anomaly, if such it was, probably was traceable to the book itself. In a unified command where an Army officer was commander in chief, it was to be expected that he would command military operations directly through the field army commander (or army group commander if there was one). With no tactical functions, the theater army headquarters, in this case Army Forces, Far East, was concerned almost wholly with administration and logistics. In these circumstances a separate theater communications zone headquarters would have been superfluous.

Perhaps more serious than the approved anomaly of the theater logistical structure was the "layering" of logistical headquarters in Korea resulting from the establishment of a single section headquarters (Korean Base Section) under Korean Communications Zone Headquarters. It is true that the supervisory functions of KCOMZ were broader—they included control of the 3d Military Railway Service and responsibilities for area administration, prisoners of war, and civil affairs—yet in supply functions duplication of effort often appeared in practice between KCOMZ and Korean Base Section. The attempt of the higher headquarters (KCOMZ) to restrict its activities to planning, policy making, and supervising proved to be impractical. On the other hand Korean Base Section, which was supposed to be the operational headquarters for supply, found itself at a disadvantage in having the railroad under a separate headquarters. A single headquarters, with complete operational control of all facilities, seemed to be more desirable for a communications zone not requiring two or more sections. Several months after the end of hostilities, the two headquarters were combined and subordinate area commands were set up.

Requirements

Requirements for supplies and equipment needed for the conduct of war, in quantities as well as in kinds, changed with the changing character of war. Military operations naturally reflected the development of new weapons, new vehicles, new food preparations, and new devices of all kinds. Requirements for trucks and gasoline and rubber tires replaced requirements for wagons and horses and forage. But many new items, such as telephones and radios and gas masks and barbed wire and medium tanks and airplanes, were not replacements for older equipment and weapons at all, but additions to the lengthening list of items considered essential for the modern army.

The emphasis placed on research and development since World War II added to the burden of keeping requirements accurate and logistical planning current, but it also made possible the rapid expansion of military power, the one danger being that innovation would become such a fetish that change would be sought for its own sake and many useful items of equipment would thus be prematurely discarded. Such psychological obsolescence of matériel would have the effect of reducing serviceable reserves and adding unduly to procurement objectives. The old dilemma of highest quality and greatest quantity would continue with even greater force than before.

In terms of total tonnage, requirements for the support of Army units in combat seemed to grow interminably. This has been due in part to the constant addition of new items of equipment, to the use of heavier artillery weapons and more automatic weapons with higher rates of ammunition consumption, and to the increasing use of heavier tanks and trucks on which modern mobile warfare depended. It also has been the result of a tendency to carry to the battlefield the nation's rising standard of living—to make necessities of items which in other armies or in earlier times would have been considered the greatest luxuries. Secretary of War Calhoun as early as 1818 remarked on the disparity between what an American soldier required and what would satisfy a "Turk." In North Africa in 1942–43 it was taking .7 of a measurement ton a month on the average to supply a British soldier, while it was taking 1.3 measurement tons to supply an American.[3]

The change in the nature of requirements pretty much relegated to mythology the prospect of an Army's living off the country. Although Grant and Sherman and Wilson at various times during the Civil War had been able to cut their supply lines and live off the country, in those situations almost continuous movement to new forage was possible, and relatively little expenditure of ammunition was necessary. Gasoline, though much more efficient than hay and oats for moving supplies, was not to be found stored in barns or growing in the countryside, and neither was the ammunition which comprised a constantly growing element of the average supply requirement. By the time of World War II, fuel and ammunition accounted for about two-thirds of the tonnage of average daily supply for ground and air forces. In an attack against a hastily organized defensive position, an infantry division on the average fired 386 tons of ammunition a day, and the armored division used 361 tons a day. An armored division—extending out to a length of forty-six miles if moving in a single close column—consumed 146,000 gallons of gasoline in one hundred miles; and nearly twice that if moving across country under battle conditions. An infantry division needed 68,500 gallons of gasoline to move its vehicles one hundred miles.[4]

Possibly U.S. Army units were too closely tied to their vehicles, too road-bound. The

heavy losses in Korea when enemy road-blocks cut lines of withdrawal would suggest this. At any rate it made a strange case to plead disadvantage in encountering an enemy not relying so heavily on motor transportation.

Research and Development

A great change of recent times has been in the Army's attitude from one of almost total rejection of any new idea for weapons and equipment, as evidenced to some extent by General Scott during the Mexican War and General Ripley during the Civil War, to an attitude of active encouragement of research and development. The Army of the nineteenth century made little if any attempt to ferret out new ideas, and when one was proposed the burden of proof for the worth of the device was entirely on the inventor. The Army of the twentieth century, especially since the stimulus of the mobilization of science and technology during World War II, has encouraged research and development both to meet future requirements and to improve present matériel. Developments in the decade following the Korean War have strengthened some of the tentative principles and general conclusions drawn from earlier experience, and have raised doubts about others. In any event, sweeping revolutions in weapons and equipment, transportation, communications, and organization were bound to have an impact that would change the patterns of Army logistics.

The increasing emphasis on research and development after the Korean War began to pay off in whole new families of weapons and vehicles. The most spectacular developments were the rockets and missiles. Before the end of the Korean War a 280-mm.

---

[3] C. B. A. Behrens, *Merchant Shipping and the Demands of War*, "History of the Second World War—United Kingdom Civil Series" (London: Her Majesty's Stationery Office and Longmans, Green & Co., 1955), p. 370; FM 101–10, August 1949, p. 303.

[4] FM 101–10, August 1949, pp. 244–47, 269.

gun designed to fire an atomic projectile had been produced, and important strides had been taken toward the development of rocket-propelled delivery systems for tactical nuclear projectiles as well as for conventional high explosives. The Honest John was a free rocket carrying a 1,500-pound warhead for a distance of up to about fifteen miles, and the Little John was being developed as a smaller weapon able to do about the same thing. In the guided missile category, the Corporal was the most important for short-range tactical use, with a range of about 75 miles, but it would be replaced by the more powerful Sergeant. For longer ranges, the Redstone, a liquid-fuel missile, six feet in diameter and sixty-nine feet long, was one of the first effective models, while the Pershing was being developed as a solid-fuel replacement for it. The Jupiter C, using liquid fuel, had a range of some 3,300 miles. Nike Ajax was the first in a family of surface-to-air guided missiles, and it was to be replaced by Nike Hercules. Most controversial was the Nike Zeus which the Army was developing as an antimissile missile. In addition, there were the Hawk for low altitude antiaircraft missions, and Talos, inherited from the Navy.

In more conventional weapons, too, rapid changes were taking place. A new rifle, the M14, designed to fire a standardized 7.62-mm. NATO cartridge, was adopted to replace the M1 rifle, the carbine, and the Browning automatic rifle, though it was being made obsolete even before it came into full use. A new M60 machine gun, using the NATO cartridge loaded in a link belt, and firing at a rate of 600 rounds a minute, replaced all the old .30-caliber machine guns, and was assigned to all rifle companies instead of to separate heavy weapons companies. The 81-mm. mortar replaced the 60-mm. in the rifle companies.

The Patton 48 medium tank and the M103 heavy tank came into full use, but a new medium tank, the M60, carrying a 105-mm. gun and powered by a 750-horsepower diesel engine, was being developed to replace both.

Probably the greatest innovation for the infantry was the introduction of the armored personnel carrier, a cross-country vehicle operated by a crew of two, and capable of carrying ten passengers. A newer aluminum model of this vehicle was being developed, weighing only half as much as the earlier model. Experiments with "aerial jeeps," "flying platforms," and other contrivances intended to increase battlefield fire power and mobility promised further logistical modifications.

With the wholesale introduction of new types of weapons, and completely new categories of increasing complexity, the greatest immediate logistical problem was in the supply of parts to keep them operational. The most difficult aspect of this problem was in estimating requirements without the benefit of meaningful experience factors.

Transportation

Long-range jet transports pointed the way to great changes in the transportation picture, as greater speed, greater capacity, and the use of lower grade fuel promised some reduction in the expensive secondary requirements of air transportation. This might in turn change the whole pattern of the distribution system in the interest of saving the costs of stockpiling reserves along lengthy supply lines. Still it seemed that in the foreseeable future the greatest use of air transportation would be in the movement of personnel to areas where equipment had been prepositioned. It seemed unlikely that for some years to come ocean carriers would be superseded as the principal means of transporting matériel, for developments promised a tremendous speed-up in ocean transportation and automation made its great impact on loading and unloading, which always had been the bottlenecks in ocean shipping. By the 1960's a ten-man gang using new equipment could load a ship at San Francisco in just two shifts, where a few years before the same job took a fourteen-man gang twelve shifts to complete; six longshoremen could unload the cargo from a Liberty ship in nine days whereas earlier it would have taken eighteen men fourteen days. To speed up the unloading of vessels the Army developed a continuous circuit tramway system, and for moving cargo inland from beaches it developed an overland conveyor system. Equally revolutionary for cross-country transportation off the beaches was the logistical cargo carrier, a car with a capacity of fifteen tons, equipped with huge tires for cross-country movement, which could be linked with other cars to form a tractor-drawn overland train needing neither tracks nor roads.

Communication

Perhaps the most spectacular revolution of all was in communication. The introduction of automatic data processing promised to have a greater impact on logistics than either the telegraph or the radio. It provided the basis for unprecedented centralization of control over supply, and for procedures to speed up the whole supply operation. Depots could be linked together and requisitions handled quickly at national inventory control points. With the use of data processing and new procedures, processing time at the source of supply soon was reduced by more than one-half. Standard requisitioning and inventory control procedures (referred to as MILSTRIP) and standard transportation and movement procedures (MILSTAMP) soon were being extended to all services, and the Department of Defense itself was becoming the principal co-ordinator of military supply.

The Organization Revolution

Recurring proposals for functionalizing the Army logistical organization and modifying or eliminating the technical services or bureaus as separate entities finally came to fruition in 1962, accomplishing what many had assumed never could be done. Of the technical service chiefs, only the Chief of Engineers and the Chief of Transportation, but with only service functions, remained under the supervision of the Deputy Chief of Staff for Logistics, while a new Chief of Support Services acquired most of the service functions of The Quartermaster General. The Surgeon General, also with only service functions, was placed under the Deputy Chief of Staff for Personnel; the Chief Signal Officer continued his service functions under the Deputy Chief of Staff for Operations. The supply operations previously performed by the technical services were assigned to a new organization, the Army Matériel Command, while responsibilities for research and development and testing, and for battlefield logistics doctrine, were assigned to the Combat Developments Command. The Quartermaster, Ordnance, and other corps remained as designa-

A LARGE-SCALE COMPUTER AND CREW *in a data processing area of the Pentagon.*

tions for service troops, but with the limited exceptions noted above, there no longer would be a bureau or a chief at the top.

The Department of Defense itself entered the logistical organization revolution with the establishment of the Defense Supply Agency (DSA). In effect, the Defense Supply Agency is a "fourth service of supply"—it is a joint agency under military direction responsible, not to the Joint Chiefs of Staff, but directly to the Secretary of Defense, its control extending over all federally catalogued supplies for all services. By mid-1963 it was handling more than one-third of all military supplies, and soon thereafter it was handling at least half of all the supplies. The Defense Supply Agency, geared for war as well as peace, is developing a harmonized system of supply among the services so that requisitions can be funneled into central points and referred automatically to depots and field agencies, with the probability that the whole system of oversea supply divisions in filling requisitions from oversea theaters can be bypassed. In the future the history of Army logistics would be an integral part of Navy and Air Force logistics history and that of the Department of Defense.

Experience for the Future

No one aspect of the Army's logistical experience can be singled out as most valuable in providing guidelines for the future, for the future is, as always, uncertain. One thing can be forecast with assurance—the continuation of change. But it may also be assumed that, however far-reaching the changes, there must always be links with the past. Any general conclusions drawn from history as a whole must include the principle of change and the principle of continuity. No situation can ever be exactly the same as a previous one, nor can any situation be absolutely unique, having no connections with the past. Through experience, whether it is derived from actual participation in events or vicariously as through the study of history, one becomes aware of the swiftness and magnitude of change. Moreover, in experience is the raw material for the imagination necessary to cope with change and to influence its course.

In searching the experience of World War II it seems probable that the war in the Pacific will have the greatest relevance for the kind of logistical activity that may be required from the Army in the immediate future. This appears to be so for two quite different reasons. First, in case of a general war, or anything approaching total war, the very existence of nuclear weapons is likely to require a dispersal of troops and resources over wide areas so that co-ordinating movements and bringing troops and resources together as needed may raise problems akin to those of supporting operations in the Pacific, wherever the locale of a new war might be. Secondly, the more immediate prospects of guerrilla warfare and "brush-fire" wars and crises at widely separated points, from Lebanon to Formosa, or Cuba to Vietnam, raise the problems of supporting relatively small forces over vast distances. For the same reasons an increasing relevance might be found, too, in the experience of the War with Spain, and even earlier in the support of Army operations on the Great Plains and in the mountains of the west between 1865 and 1890.

Whatever the future may hold, study of the experiences of all of the past will be needed. For military affairs this study must include a continuing concern with the experience of logistics.

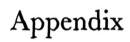

HEADQUARTERS
UNITED STATES ARMY LOGISTICS MANAGEMENT CENTER
FORT LEE, VIRGINIA 23801

LOGISTICS · MANAGEMENT · INFORMATION

May 1965

> This issue is devoted entirely to an elementary treatment of the logistics element of the Army. Logistics personnel are encouraged to pass it on to others who may benefit from its use. In effect, it is a "Logistics Primer."

U.S. ARMY LOGISTICS

The dedicated men and women engaged in United States Army logistics activities can take pride in their roles in national defense. Their work reflects the realization that successful accomplishment of the deterrence and combat missions depends greatly upon effective logistics.

Logistics performance in the Army traditionally has been outstanding. The mobilization and support of a huge fighting team in World War II with supply lines extending around the globe attest to U.S. Army logistics capabilities.

But the Army cannot rest on past laurels in logistics. The complexity of modern weapons is multiplying, the geographical areas of possible conflict are expanding, and the need for economy in the national defense continues. Recognizing that the United States is at the apex of defense of the free world, and acknowledging the success of potential enemies in improving their own military capabilities, the challenges to Army logistics today are even greater than the challenges of the past.

THE ORIGIN OF LOGISTICS

The word "logistics" is derived from the Greek adjective "logistikos" meaning "skilled in calculating." The first administrative use of the word was in Roman and Byzantine times when there was a military ad-ministrative official with the title "Logista." At that time the word apparently implied a skill in the science of mathematical computations. Research indicates that the first use of the word with reference to an organized military administrative science was by the French writer, Jomini, who, in 1838, devised a theory of war upon the trinity of strategy, ground tactics, and logistics. The French still use the words "logistique" and "loger" with the meaning "to quarter."

The military activity known as logistics probably is as old as war itself. In the early history of man when the first wars were fought, each man had to find his own food, stones, and knotted clubs. Each warrior was his own logistician. Not until later when fighters joined as groups and fighting groups became larger was there any basis for designating certain men to specialize in providing food and weapons to the combatants. These men who provided support to the fighters constituted the first logistics organization.

In today's usage, logistics is the function of providing all of the materiel and services that a military force needs in peace or war. It is the bridge between our combat troops and the industry and natural resources of our nation. An objective of the Army is to widen this bridge and shorten its span.

In official Department of Defense language, logistics is "the science of planning and carrying out the movement and maintenance of forces. In its most comprehensive sense, those aspects of military operations which deal with: (a) design and development, acquisition, storage, movement, distribution, maintenance, evacuation, and disposition of materiel; (b) movement, evacuation, and hospitalization of personnel; (c) acquisition or construction, maintenance, operation and disposition of facilities; and (d) acquisition or furnishing of services."

Logistics is not an exact science. There is no mathematical formula or set of tables which tell us precisely what supplies or services will be needed, where and when they will be needed, or the best way to provide them. The responsible officials must make judgments on these matters, using both intuition and scientific weighing of alternatives as the situation requires and permits. Their judgments must be based not only upon professional knowledge of the numerous aspects of logistics itself but also upon an understanding of the interplay of closely related military considerations, such as strategy, tactics, intelligence, training, personnel, and finance.

ITS MAGNITUDE

No single industry in the U. S. economy equals Army logistics activities in scope and magnitude. Army logistics activities cover the complete spectrum of a business activity from construction of a manufacturing plant to supplying a pencil. Logistics activities are performed worldwide, but depend primarily on national resources found within the U.S.

Because the Army logistics system is so big, it must be as efficient as possible as a matter of economy. However, economy must not take precedence over responsiveness and effectiveness because in war the first "runner-up" is the loser.

To illustrate the magnitude of U.S. Army logistics, even in the "Cold War era," the following figures pertaining to Fiscal Year 1963 are cited:

The Army had an active-duty strength of over 975,000 people. Nearly 400,000 of them were outside the Continental United States. Another 1,358,000 dependents were a part of the military family.

The Army employed over 484,000 civilians. Nearly 166,000 were outside the CONUS, including over 146,000 foreign nationals.

The Army received 11.8 billion dollars in new obligational authorities. Over 2.5 billion dollars were for major items of equipment, over 1.3 billion dollars were for research and development activities, and over 3.6 billion dollars were for pay of active duty military personnel.

The value of all procurement actions was over 6.3 million dollars.

Approximately 1.7 billion dollars was expended for maintenance of materiel. Approximately 620 million dollars was spent for maintenance of facilities.

New construction completed during the year cost 193 million dollars.

The inventory of real property owned by the Army was valued at over 10.7 billion dollars in acquisition cost. Over 882 million dollars of this inventory was in foreign countries. The total real property inventory consisted of over 12 million acres. In addition, the Army disposed of over 37 thousand acres and reported to General Services Administration another 58 thousand acres as excess.

The inventory of the Army's personal property was valued at over 24.8 billion dollars. This included over 83 million dollars worth of inventory in transit at the end of the year.

The Army owned and controlled over 337 thousand units of family housing.

The Army operated 207 computers at 116 locations. In addition, there were 300 punched-card activities.

Medical services consisted of over 450 thousand hospital admissions, and over 17 million out-patient visits.

The Military Assistance Program support to about 80 nations and international organizations through grant aid and sales amounted to 805 million dollars and 459 million dollars, respectively.

Through the Agency for International Development (AID), the Army provided materiel valued at about 25 million dollars to approximately 20 countries.

The Army stored approximately 400 million pounds of household goods in 2,400 warehouses in the United States. It also contracted for 70 million square feet of storage space for us in the event of mobilization.

The Army had over 118 million square feet of covered storage space in the Continental United States.

The Army operated 3,255 messes, 143 clothing sales stores, and 73 laundries. Its 173 commissary stores registered sales totaling 330 million dollars.

The number of different items carried by even our large mail order companies is dwarfed by the variety of items which the Army must have available for war and for keeping units and men ready for war. Our inventories include nearly everything from turnbuckles to tanks and from beans to bazookas. The items range in cost from less than a cent apiece to over a million dollars each. The number of different kinds of repair parts for the most complicated Army weapons runs into the hundreds of thousands.

Due to the magnitude of US Army logistics and the snowballing effect of any inadvertencies or misjudgments in the system, the margin of permissible human error is necessarily very small. Logistics support is so critical to successful operations that perfection must be the goal. The Army is proud of its overall logistics support record.

ITS PECULIARITIES

In addition to size, there are many other things which make Army logistics different from a commercial enterprise. In some respects, these differences might be called handicaps; but the Army prefers to regard them simply as challenges which make its work more interesting and important.

Army logistics has more stockholders to whom it is answerable than any American business enterprise. Each taxpayer shares in the ownership of Army property and each person eligible to vote can influence the management of this Government property.

Many of these "stockholders" have had military service and attained enough first-hand knowledge of Army logistics to give them a personal interest in it. In that respect, the Army undoubtedly gets more suggestions and questions from its stockholders than does any corporation.

A private enterprise normally can plan operations several years in advance and the management gets guidance from stockholders only for the launching of new programs or when changing the role and direction of the firm; the Army also plans several years in advance but must justify its operations annually as a part of the appropriation process.

While large business enterprises manufacturing or selling more than one line of products can absorb losses in some of their products by doing better in others, Army logistics support must be effective in all aspects. Even a temporary lack of certain items of supply or services, such as gasoline or radio communications, can result in the loss of a battle.

Both industry and the Army play for high stakes; however, the penalty for failure differs. A business failure causes financial distress, but a lost war can mean national destruction.

Because the stakes are so high and the consequence of failure so grave, the Army must use the relative tranquility of peace to prepare itself for war—a war it neither relishes nor encourages. For generations the American public found it difficult to correlate a love of peace with military preparedness. However, history and the international environment have taught

the citizens of the United States that military preparedness is the cornerstone of sovereign, peaceful survival.

The training challenge to Army logistics is much greater than to any single United States industry. This is so not only because of the great number of people to be trained and the complexity of the tasks for which they are to be trained, but also because of the high rate of personnel turnover and the need for cross-training in the military. The military must accept the probable loss of personnel by enemy action and train its people to assume other jobs with little warning.

Although logistics is the furnishing of the wherewithal for combat, Army logistics units must be prepared to fight as combat troops in defense of their resources and assigned areas. The whole logistics system must balance responsiveness with dispersal and must be able to continue its support mission during and after the infliction of enemy damage.

THE TRUE MEASURE OF ITS EFFECTIVENESS

The effectiveness of the Army's logistics support system is measured by its ability to support the fighting units in sustained combat.

The Army's logistics is pointed toward victory.

LOGISTICS ORGANIZATION FOR DEFENSE

The Department of Defense is supervised by the Secretary of Defense. He is a civilian who is appointed by the President and serves as a member of his Cabinet. The Secretary of Defense is assisted by a civilian staff and by the Joint Chiefs of Staff who serve as the principal military advisers to the Secretary of Defense and to the President.

The Assistant Secretary of Defense (Installations and Logistics) advises and assists the Secretary of Defense in the formulation of general policies for logistics activities. He also is a member of the Defense Supply Council which advises and assists the Secretary of Defense in the direction and control of the Defense Supply Agency. The Director of Research and Engineering assists the Secretary in research and development of new items.

The Defense Supply Agency is responsible for wholesale procurement and distribution of certain items common to the three Military Departments.

These include subsistence, clothing, petroleum, medical supplies, construction materials, industrial supplies, general supplies, and electronic supplies.

The three Military Departments have development and retail support responsibility for the above common items and complete support responsibility for the much greater number of items used only by them.

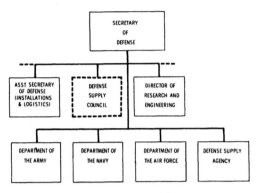

DOD ORGANIZATION FOR LOGISTICS

LOGISTICS ORGANIZATION OF THE ARMY

The mission of U.S. Army logistics is to provide materiel and service support to the Army, and to other U.S. Military Departments and allies under special arrangements.

Overall responsibility for all Army matters, including Army logistics, is vested in the Secretary of the Army. He has a staff that includes the Assistant Secretary of the Army for Installations and Logistics and the Assistant Secretary of the Army for Research and Development. The Chief of Staff of the Army is the senior military officer in the Army, and his Deputy Chief of Staff for Logistics (DCSLOG) and Chief of Research and Development are his principal logistics advisors.

The Army Materiel Command is responsible for operation of the Army wholesale supply system. The Combat Developments Command is responsible for development of logistics doctrine for Army-in-the-Field units. The Continental Army Command (comprising the six continental Armies and reserve units), the Army element of the Strike Command, the Army Air Defense Command, Army components of oversea commands, and allies under the Mutual Assistance Program, are all "customers" of Army logistics. They

have logistics units doing their portion of Army retail logistics tasks.

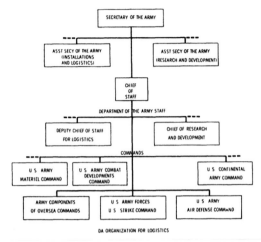

DA ORGANIZATION FOR LOGISTICS

THE ARMY MATERIEL COMMAND

This new command has the mission of providing logistics support which will enable the Army to be ready constantly for immediate deployment for any type of combat under any geographical or climatic condition.

It directs the activities of the vast complex of depots, laboratories, arsenals, proving grounds, test ranges, procurement offices, and transportation terminals throughout the United States.

The Commanding General, Army Materiel Command, directs these activities through five "commodity commands," a Supply and Maintenance Command, and a Test and Evaluation Command.

Each of the five "commodity commands" is charged with development and production of related equipment and supplies. This general grouping of items provides for effective and efficient Army logistics management. It also fosters mutual development of understanding and common goals between industry and the commodity commands, both working as professionals in a joint effort to enhance the security of the United States.

The Supply and Maintenance Command performs those functions which pertain to all commodities and relate directly to customer satisfaction, such as depot activities (receiving, storage, maintenance, and issue),

4

stock control, and shipping. This grouping of common functions is necessary in order to achieve optimum uniformity and economy, avoid duplication of effort by the commodity commands, and to allow the commodity commands to concentrate their efforts toward progressive development and production of materiel for a modern Army.

The Test and Evaluation Command works with the commodity commands in the research and development phases of new equipment production and provides for maximum integration of engineering and service testing. It commands the proving grounds and arranges for troop tests in the field.

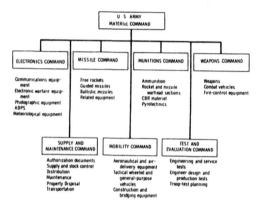

AMC ORGANIZATION FOR LOGISTICS

ELEMENTS OF LOGISTICS

As in any other huge undertaking, it is necessary to divide Army logistics into manageable elements. This is done by the Army in many ways for different purposes. One common way, which is generally applicable at all levels, is to divide Army logistics into the two arbitrary and extremely broad activities of "materiel" and "services."

These two logistics activities are usually distinguishable because "materiel" refers to the providing of items whereas "service" is generally non-material in nature. However, maintenance of materiel is sometimes considered as a "service" as are other services (such as transporting supplies or constructing facilities) which are often essential in effectively providing the materiel. Still other logistics services (such as hospitalization and evacuation, food service, laundry

and bath, and movement of people) are provided to individuals but use materiel in the process.

In a generic sense, all of logistics is a "service" to the combat and training missions of the Army. On the other hand, all of logistics can be considered as a materiel function in the sense of providing goods and services to the combat forces.

Undoubtedly, there is more understanding of the logistics "service" functions, (such as transportation, hospitalization, construction, and non-tactical communications) than of the function of providing the materiel. This is so because these services have civilian counterparts, responsibility for them can be assigned in rather neat packages, and they are relatively few in number. There is less understanding about the many facets of "supply of materiel"—the approximately one million items that the Army uses, or must have ready for use, in the event of war.

THE SUPPLY OF MATERIEL

There are many different levels of installations and units and many different phases of the Army supply system. In a support function so vital to combat, there cannot be a sharp break among the various parts of the supply system. However, two large segments of the Army supply system are discernible. They are the "wholesale logistics" element and the "Army in the Field" element. These are imperfect terms; however, they are useful in delineating, in a general manner, between two broad areas of logistics operations.

The Army Dictionary defines "Army Wholesale Logistics" as: "The Army Logistics System less army in the field logistics; includes complete logistic support of the Army Wholesale Logistics complex itself, and of special Army activities retained under direct control of Headquarters, Department of the Army."

The same source identifies "Army-in-the-Field Logistics" as: "That portion of the Army Logistics System which pertains to functions internal to theaters of operations, units and organizations deployed in oversea theaters, and army in the field units in the continental United States."

The entire responsibility for the operation of the wholesale system is vested in a single commander, the Commanding General of the Army Materiel Command. This assignment provides a clear-cut channel for business contacts with the Army, presents a single source of wholesale Army supply support to users, and encourages uniformity and economy.

Responsibility for "retail supply" is assigned to supported commanders, *i.e.*, the using units. For example, the retail element of supply in Europe is under the Commander in Chief, U.S. Army Europe, and the retail supply at administrative posts in the United States is under the Commanding Generals of the continental Armies, who report to the Commanding General, U.S. Continental Army Command. This arrangement makes Army supply immediately responsive to the needs of the supported Commander—an important precept in Army logistics philosophy.

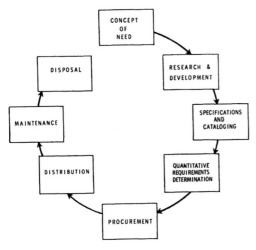

THE LIFE CYCLE OF AN ITEM OF ARMY MATERIEL

CONCEPT OF NEED

The life of a hypothetical item of Army materiel begins as a gleam in someone's eye.

The idea for a new item not in the Army supply system and not available commercially can be conceived in several ways:

A soldier might conceive an idea on the battlefield in an oversea theater as he is confronted by the enemy, the elements, and a particular situation.

An engineer in an industrial enterprise might conceive a new substance for military application.

A technician in one of the Army's many laboratories under the Army Materiel Command might think of a special military use for a newly developed material.

An Army planner in the Combat Developments Command might see the need for a special new weapon or piece of equipment to cope with a probable enemy capability of the future.

This concept of the need for an item is reviewed within the Army to validate battlefield requirements for the item and estimate the technological capability of producing it. A Research and Development Project for the item is then established.

RESEARCH AND DEVELOPMENT

The mission of the research and development phase is to bring into being a new item fully ready to be produced in quantity and to take its place in the hands of soldiers stationed at critical points around the world.

This is a crucial phase of the logistics effort. The competition with the enemy is both acute and chronic in the race to develop and produce superior weapons. Realizing that the U. S. might well face numerically superior forces, we must insure that our soldiers have superior arms.

The logical sequence in this phase is to conduct basic and applied research, design the item, develop a prototype, conduct engineering tests, conduct service tests, and evaluate the item as it is used in the field by troops.

Research and development requires a great amount of planning and a multitude of decisions. The Army uses laboratories, proving grounds, and test facilities of its own, plus the nation's industry and civilian institutions, as well as considerable foreign research, in the critical effort to keep the United States and its allies in the foreground of weaponry and other equipment.

SPECIFICATIONS AND CATALOGING

Once an item has been developed, tested, and accepted for inclusion in the Army system, specifications must be drawn. Adequate specifications are necessary so that quality control can be maintained in purchasing the item either in quantity for stockage, or on a special-order or as-needed basis.

The Army must also insure that the new item is classified and listed in the Federal Supply Catalog for purposes of identification.

6

QUANTITATIVE REQUIREMENTS DETERMINATION

The requirements function applies to items developed to meet peculiar military specifications and to items available commercially.

Requirements determination is essentially determining how many of an item are needed and when. This must be done for the approximately one million items used by the Army. Inextricably involved is the planning which must be done to obtain money for these items.

There are a multitude of factors affecting requirements, such as estimates of potential enemy intentions and capabilities, location of probable operations as to climate and other elements of the environment, lead time on delivery, wear-out and obsolescence aspects, support to be furnished non-Army activities, availability of new items and funds, and the necessity of standardizing.

The most difficult task in requirements planning is to determine the amount of reserve stocks needed for mobilization purposes. This requires estimates of whether the war will be general or limited, when and where it will occur, and whether we must rely on stocks in existence at the outbreak of war.

PROCUREMENT

The buying job begins after the establishment of firm qualitative and quantitative requirements. It is then necessary to obtain the item according to specifications and at lowest cost to the Government. It is necessary to obtain the highest degree of competition, and to insure that contracts are spread, where practical, to provide a broad mobilization base for emergency production. In some cases, it is also necessary to assist small businesses and economically distressed areas.

The Army constantly strives to bring the maximum amount of competition into play in all of its procurement, regardless of the method used. "Formal advertising" is the preferred method. It is used wherever the circumstances of the case allow. But even in those cases where there cannot be formal advertising, maximum competition is sought. Formal advertising is sometimes not feasible because of secrecy; an inability to describe highly complex, often entirely new items in firm and sufficiently detailed contract language; or the need for deliberate development of additional producers. Contracting by negotiation, therefore, does not mean contracting without competition.

By use of incentive-type contracting wherever practical, the Army is rewarding contractors for speed and quality of development and production.

DISTRIBUTION

The distribution function involves a vast array of considerations. We must consider reducing time and transportation requirements by putting stock close to using units, dispersing stocks to minimize vulnerability to attack and pilferage, reducing variety for the sake of simplicity, and streamlining all supply activities for economy and mobility.

Inherent in the mission of the Army is the necessity to defeat enemy land forces and to seize, occupy, and defend land area. To do this, the Army must stay on the ground and "up front." Unlike Air Force planes, the tanks and armored personnel carriers of the Army cannot return great distances for replenishment of fuel, rations, and other supplies. Unlike Navy ships, the combat vehicles of the Army are not capable of carrying the necessary supplies for sustained operations. The Army cannot leave an area undefended while it goes back and resupplies its combat vehicles because the enemy will surely fill the gap. Therefore, it is necessary to operate under a concept of continuous supply from the rear forward.

Ammunition, rations, and vehicle fuel are generally most vital to battle and constitute the most weight and bulk. However, repair parts constitute a much greater number of different items. Any repair part can be of crucial importance, but it would be completely impractical to have each vehicle carry a spare for each part it might need. Therefore, the most frequently needed items are kept closest to the probable place of need.

On the one extreme, a spare sparkplug for a truck in a forward tactical unit in a theater of operations would be kept on hand by the unit motor sergeant. At the other extreme, a complete engine might not be available any closer than a depot in the rear of the theater of operations. In between these extremes, a spare carburetor might be kept on hand by the mobile direct-support unit that provides field maintenance support while a replacement transmission might be kept in field army depots.

In order to know how close to the front to locate each item, the supply planner must consider such factors as the frequency of need for the item based on past consumption records; the tactical operations, terrain, and weather; the effect if the item were not furnished quickly; the transportation time and distance;

the chance of loss to the enemy if the item is stocked too close to the front; the number of persons required to handle or guard the stock; the skilled people available to install the repair parts; etc.

Deciding where to put the purchased items, moving them there, and protecting them after movement pending issue to the user, are very critical phases of the supply system. They determine whether the combat troops are going to get sufficient items where and when needed. A continuous flow of supplies to landbased soldiers is all important. Supplies must be transported to combat troops so that they can sustain their advances in the offensive and hold ground on the defensive.

MAINTENANCE

Logistics does not end with the development, procurement, and distribution of an item to the user. The Army's equipment must always be serviceable; the logistics system helps with the eternal maintenance task.

The best-trained Army in the world is helpless without serviceable equipment. A broken hydraulic line or a missing oil seal can stop a tank as effectively as an enemy mine or bazooka shell. Maintenance consists of those things done to keep the equipment in operating condition.

Maintenance in the Army today is performed at many levels, or "echelons" as they are called. The amount of work that may be done at each echelon depends upon the time, tools, and skills usually available there. Thus, at first echelon, the driver or operator may do little more than clean, oil, and make minor adjustments. At the other end, a fifth-echelon or depot shop may completely disassemble and rebuild the item. Actually, maintenance begins in the research and development stage where "ease of maintenance" is considered in the design.

The increasingly complex equipment in the modern Army has complicated the maintenance task. Maintenance of a World War II tank was simple compared to maintenance of modern Army missiles and electronic gear. The skills, time, and numbers of repair parts required have increased dramatically.

The Army is giving the care and maintenance of equipment a high priority of command attention at all levels. This emphasis is necessary because the equipment in a military man's hands today is the equipment which he might fight with tomorrow.

SURPLUS DISPOSAL

This is the last step in the Army life of items. The major decision involved is when to get rid of items in order to avoid burdensome obsolescence and excessive inventory costs. At this point, the primary aims are to get a maximum return to the taxpayer on investment and to give all buyers equal opportunity to buy surpluses. At the same time we must avoid upsetting local civilian markets and we must prevent usable war materiel from getting into enemy hands.

One of the peculiar aspects of the disposal function is the necessity of selling at "scrap" prices the obsolete military items that have no practical use in a civilian activity. For example, a tank in excellent condition, but significantly inferior to newer model Soviet tanks, simply cannot be sold like a "used car."

MANAGEMENT CONTROLS

Throughout all of the steps in the life of an item, there is deliberate application of management control techniques. The Army has adopted, and in many cases pioneered, the most sophisticated concepts of management for the direction of its multi-billion dollar operation. The goal is to establish a logistics management system which meets the requirements of higher authority and the Army itself in peacetime but which, with pre-planned alterations, will also provide effective and efficient logistics support in war.

The great danger is that the bookkeeping and administration can become false economy and interfere with the effectiveness of logistics support. In World War II, General Brehon Somervell, Commanding General, Army Service Forces, said, "I am just not going to have the issue of necessary supplies and equipment delayed because some fellow somewhere has not signed some piece of paper. We must get these supplies in the hands of the troops when they are wanted."

The challenge to the Army is clear. It must use the most modern applicable management techniques which can be developed in managing its logistics support requirements in order to assist the commanders in accomplishing their training and operational tasks. Toward this objective, the Army, industry, and educational institutions throughout the nation are engaging in a dynamic exchange of ideas and information in order to develop management systems appropriate to the environment of the future.

8

PROJECT MANAGEMENT

The Army controls the logistics functions relating to selected items or systems that are of extreme complexity and importance—such as the CHINOOK aircraft, the Nike missile, and the Main Battle Tank—by the designation of Project Managers. Each Project Manager has full authority over planning, directing, and controlling tasks and resources. His job is to develop, produce, and deliver the item or system to the using units.

Project Managers use the most modern management techniques and tools, such as PERT (Program Evaluation and Review Technique), in coordinating tasks and reviewing progress. The objective is to reduce the delivery time to troops and achieve the optimum efficiency in developing and producing new weapons and equipment.

LOGISTICS PERSONNEL

Because of the dependence of operations upon logistics support, a significant portion of the attention of commanders at all levels is taken up by logistics matters.

Each field commander has a staff or operating element concerned primarily with logistics. This extends from the Company or Battery Supply Sergeant on up through Battalion and Regiment S4; Division, Corps, and Field Army G4; and Deputy Chiefs of Staff for Logistics at Theater of Operations level. In addition, there are whole units, such as Division Support Commands and Logistical Commands, whose missions are to provide logistics support.

The Army has a Logistics Officer Program in which there are designated over 1000 outstanding officers who normally fill the key officer logistics positions. In view of the special skills and technical training which these officers must possess, they are thoroughly screened before selection and their careers are carefully managed in order to develop them for increasingly difficult assignments. These officers remain identified with the combat arms or technical and administrative branches and generally alternate between assignments with their own branches and broader logistics assignments.

There is also a Logistics Career Program for reserve officers not on active duty. Of an authorized 1000 such reservists, about 600 have been selected to augment the regular Logistics Officer Program participants when necessary.

In addition to the especially designated Logistics Officers, there are thousands of officers of all branches of the Army who are performing in logistics positions or specialist positions as a part of the overall Army Logistics System.

Assisting these officers are many enlisted personnel with years of training and experience in the various phases of supply and services. The Noncommissioned Officer Logistics Program for management of careers of senior logistics enlisted personnel is receiving new impetus.

Continuity and special managerial skills are provided by civilian employees, ranging from the men who physically handle supplies through the technical experts to the senior civilian logisticians of the Army—the Assistant Secretary for Installations and Logistics and the Assistant Secretary for Research and Development.

These are the people who constitute the logistics team dedicated to the tremendous challenges of today and the future.

LOGISTICS TRAINING

Training of personnel in all phases of logistics is of particular importance to combat readiness.

Army logistics personnel must know the combat support requirements of soldiers and units in the field and the capabilities of industry to meet these needs. In addition they must know the best method of getting this support where it is needed, when it is needed, and at minimum cost in manpower, materiel, and money.

General logistics subjects are integrated into the Army school training programs. The branch service schools provide specialized training in their functional areas, particularly for enlisted personnel and junior officers. The Army War College and the Command and General Staff College cover the interplay of logistics and strategy/tactics. The U.S. Army Logistics Management Center provides logistics management training at the national and wholesale level for both military and civilian personnel. The U.S. Army Management School and the U.S. Army Management Engineering Training Agency assist in the training of logistics personnel by teaching management theory and management techniques, respectively.

Logistics is emphasized in maneuvers and field exercises. The largest logistics training exercise, known as LOGEX, is held annually at Fort Lee, Virginia, and provides simulated experience in war-time logistics at various headquarters and operating levels in one or more Theaters of Operation.

As a matter of achieving and maintaining the highest possible state of training, the Army must insure that military personnel, during their tours of duty in the Continental United States, perform those duties which will train them best for the type of assignments which they are likely to have during oversea assignments.

THE INTEGRITY OF LOGISTICS

There have been intermittent attempts to scatter the logistics functions and to split the supervision of them, but the parts keep coming back together because of their inherent interrelationships. Even the semantics of logistics is lacking in unanimity, but, as was so well pointed out in Admiral Eccles book, *Logistics in the National Defense*, the name is not the important thing. The word "logistics" could disappear from our vocabulary entirely without affecting the integrity of these inherently related activities.

One of the continuing facts that survives the advancement of technology, tactics, and organization is this basic integrity of the logistics functions. Through it all, the groupment of all functions of logistics, as defined in AR 320-5, is still sound from a management and control standpoint and is necessary to insure efficiency of operation, both in the field and at high management levels. All logistics activities are dependent upon each other; their performance results in competition for the use of the available service troops and transportation resources. The fact that all elements of logistics have the common objective of providing total support for combat forces is a unifying influence. At the various levels, the commander must depend upon a single, professional logistician to integrate and coordinate the overall logistics effort to assure effective and efficient support.

General Brehon Somervell, who commanded the Services of Supply during World War II, said:

"It is obvious that, when operations must be carried on at sea, in the air, and on the ground, logistics planning must be organized to provide the correlated requirements for the three combat forces and to integrate the means for getting them to the scene of action. These activities must be so controlled that each force is provided with what it needs without waste or shortage, in a word, with the utmost efficiency. A single head can guide and direct such planning more efficiently than any kind of committee action."

Felix J. Gerace

FELIX J. GERACE
Colonel, GS
Commandant

Bibliography of Sources Consulted

PART ONE

The Formative Period

Manuscript Sources

Ephraim Blaine Papers. Library of Congress, Washington, D.C.
John Campbell. Memo to Brig. Gen. Edward Hand, 12 April 1777. Morristown, Head-quarters Collection, Morristown, New Jersey.
Joseph and Charles Hoff Letterbook. Morristown Headquarters Collection, Morristown, New Jersey.
Joseph Lewis Letters. Morristown Headquarters Collection, Morristown New Jersey.
Robert Morris Papers. Diary in the Office of Finance. Library of Congress, Washington, D.C.
Orderly Book of Burgoyne's Army, July 16, 1777 to October 6, 1777. Fort Ticonderoga Museum, Ticonderoga, New York.
Washington Headquarters Collection. Morristown, New Jersey.
Washington Papers. Library of Congress, Washington, D.C.
Ely Whitney Papers. Yale University, New Haven, Connecticut.

Printed Primary Sources and Documents

"American State Papers." Class I: *Indian Affairs.* Class V: *Military Affairs.* Washington: Gales and Seaton, 1832.
The Annual Register. London, 1777.
Barriger, John B. *Legislative History of the Subsistence Department of the United States Army from June 16, 1775 to August 15, 1876.* Washington: General Publications . . . Subsistence Deptartment, 1876.
Bassett, John S., ed. *Correspondence of Andrew Jackson.* Washington: Carnegie Institution of Washington, 1926–35. 7 vols.
Burgoyne, John. *A State of the Expedition from Canada, As Laid before the House of Commons.* London, 1780.
Burnette, Edmund C., ed. *Letters of Members of the Continental Congress.* Washington: Carnegie Institution of Washington, 1921–36. 8 vols.
Doniol, Henri. *Histoire de la Participation de la France à l' Établissement des États-Unis d'Amérique, Correspondence Diplomatique et Documents.* Paris: Imprimerie Nationale, 1884–89. 5 vols.
Fitzpatrick, John C., ed. *Writings of George Washington from the Original Manuscript Sources, 1745–1799.* Washington: Government Printing Office, 1931–44. 39 vols.
Foner, Philip S., ed. *Basic Writings of Thomas Jefferson.* Garden City, N.Y.: Halcyon House, 1950.
Force, Peter, ed. *American Archives . . . A Documentary History of . . . The North American Colonies.* Washington: St. Clair Clarke & Peter Force, 1837–53. 4th and 5th series, 9 vols.
Ford, Worthington C., and others, eds. *Journals of the Continental Congress.* Washington: GPO, 1904–37. 34 vols.

Hetzel, A. R., ed. *Military Laws of the United States.* 3d ed. Washington, 1846.

Historical Papers Relating to the Corps of Engineers and to Engineer Troops in the United States Army. Washington Barracks, 1904.

Histories of Administrative Bureaux of the War Department. Washington: GPO, 1901.

"Journal of the Late Principal Proceedings of the Army," *The London Magazine.* August 1777. 436–39.

Journal of the Votes and Proceedings of the Colony of New York 1766-1776. Albany, N.Y.: J. Buel, 1820.

Lodge, Henry Cabot, ed. *The Works of Alexander Hamilton.* New York: G. P. Putnam's Sons, 1904. 12 vols.

Meng, John J. *Despatches and Instructions of Conrad Alexandre Gerard, 1778–1780.* Baltimore: The Johns Hopkins Press, 1939.

New York Division of Archives and History. *The American Revolution in New York: Its Political, Social, and Economic Significance.* Albany, N.Y.: The University of the State of New York, 1926.

The North American Colonies. "Regulations for the Order and Discipline of Troops of U.S. Army, 1779." Washington, 1837–53. 5th series, III.

Organization of the Military Peace Establishment of the United States. Washington, 1815.

Pargellis, Stanley M., ed. *Military Affairs in North America; 1748–1765: Selected Documents from the Cumberland Papers in Windsor Castle.* New York, 1936.

Proceedings of a General Court Martial . . . for the Trial of Maj. Gen. Schuyler, 1 Oct 1778. Published in *Collections of the New York Historical Society for 1879.* New York, 1880.

Proceedings of a General Court Martial . . . for the Trial of Maj. Gen. St. Clair, August 25, 1778. Philadelphia, 1778.

Roberts, James A., ed. *New York in the Revolution As Colony and State.* 2d ed. Albany: Brandow Printing Co., 1898.

Smith, William Henry, ed. *The St. Clair Papers.* Cincinnati: Robert Clarke & Co., 1882. 2 vols.

Thacher, James. *A Military Journal During the American Revolutionary War from 1775 to 1783.* 2d ed. Boston: Cottons & Barnard, 1827.

Thian, Raphael P. *Legislative History of the General Staff of the Army of the United States, 1775 to 1901.* Washington: GPO, 1901.

Weedon, George. *Valley Forge Orderly Book.* New York: Dodd, Mead and Company, 1902.

Wharton, Francis, ed. *The Revolutionary Diplomatic Correspondence of the United States.* Washington: GPO, 1889. 6 vols.

Secondary Sources

Adams, Henry. *History of the United States of America During the First Administration of James Madison.* New York: C. Scribner's Sons, 1921. 2 vols.

Adams, James Truslow. *Atlas of American History.* New York: Charles Scribner's Sons, 1943.

Alden, John Richard. *The American Revolution, 1775–1783.* The New American Nation Series. New York: Harper & Brothers, 1954.

Andrews, Charles M. *The Colonial Period of American History.* New Haven, Conn.: Yale University Press, 1934–38. 4 vols.

Bassett, John S. *Life of Andrew Jackson.* New York: The Macmillan Company, 1911. 2 vols.

Beers, George L. *British Colonial Policy, 1754–1765.* New York: P. Smith, 1933.

Beirne, Francis F. *The War of 1812.* New York: E. P. Dutton & Co., Inc., 1949.

Bemis, Samuel Flagg. *The Diplomacy of the American Revolution.* New York: D. Appleton-Century, 1935.

Bernardo, C. Joseph and Eugene H. Bacon. *American Military Policy: Its Development Since 1775.* Harrisburg, Pa.: Military Service Publishing Co., 1955.

Bill, Alfred Hoyt. *The Campaign of Princeton, 1776–1777.* Princeton: Princeton University Press, 1948.

————. *Valley Forge: The Making of an Army.* New York: Harper and Brothers, 1952.

Birkhimer, William E. *Historical Sketches of the Organization, Administration, Materiel and Tactics of the Artillery, United States Army.* Washington: James J. Chapman, 1884.

Bishop, James L. *History of American Manufacture.* Philadelphia: E. Young & Co., 1864. 2 vols.

Blake, William P. "Sketch of the Life of Eli Whitney, the Inventor of the Cotton Gin," *New Haven Historical Papers,* V. Abstract of paper read before the New Haven Historical Society, November 28, 1887.

Bolles, Albert S. *The Financial History of the United States from 1774 to 1789.* New York: D. Appleton and Company, 1879.

Bolton, Charles K. *The Private Soldier Under Washington.* New York: Charles Scribner's Sons, 1902.

Bonsal, Stephen. *When the French Were Here . . . the French Forces in America and Their Contribution to the Yorktown Campaign.* New York: Doubleday, Doran & Co., 1945.

Bowman, Allen. *The Morale of the American Revolutionary Army.* Washington: American Council on Public Affairs, 1943.

Boyd, Thomas A. *Mad Anthony Wayne.* New York: Charles Scribner's Sons, 1929.

Brackenridge, H. M. *History of the Late War Between the United States and Great Britain.* Philadelphia: James Kay, Jr., and Brother, 1839.

Brandow, John Henry. *The Story of Old Saratoga.* 2d ed. Albany, N.Y.: The Brandon Printing Co., 1919.

Brown, Harvey E. *Medical Department of the Army from 1775 to 1873.* Washington: Surgeon General's Office, 1873.

Burnett, Edmund C. *The Continental Congress.* New York: The Macmillan Company, 1941.

Carrington, Henry B. *Battles of the American Revolution, 1775–1781.* New York: A. S. Barnes & Co., 1876.

Channing, Edward. *A History of the United States.* New York: The Macmillan Company, 1905–25. 6 vols.

Cleaves, Freeman. *Old Tippecanoe: William Henry Harrison and His Time.* New York: Charles Scribner's Sons, 1939.

Clendening, Logan. *Behind the Doctor.* New York: A. A. Knopf, 1933.

Corwin, Edward S. *French Policy and the American Alliance of 1778.* Princeton, N.J.: Princeton University Press, 1916.

Cronau, Rudolf. *The Army of the American Revolution and Its Organizer.* New York: Published by the author, 1923.

Darling, Arthur Burr. *Our Rising Empire, 1763–1803.* New Haven: Yale University Press, 1940.

De Fonblanque, Edward B. *Political and Military Episodes in the Latter Half of the Eighteenth Century Derived from the Life and Correspondence of the Right Hon. John Burgoyne, General, Statesman, Dramatist.* London: Macmillan and Co., 1876.

Deyrup, Felicia J. *Arms Makers of the Connecticut Valley: A Regional Study of the Economic Development of the Small Arms Industry 1798–1870.* Northampton, Mass.: Smith College, Department of History, 1938.

Dillin, J. G. W. *The Kentucky Rifle.* Washington: National Rifle Association of America, 1924.

Dunbar, Seymour. *A History of Travel in America.* Indianapolis: Bobbs-Merrill Company, 1915. 4 vols.

Duncan, Louis C. *Medical Men in the American Revolution, 1775–1783.* Carlisle Barracks, Pa.: Medical Field Service School, 1931.

Durfee, W. F. "The History and Modern Development of the Art of Interchangeable Construction in Mechanism," *Transactions of American Society of Mechanical Engineers* (New York, 1893), 1225.

East, Robert A. *Business Enterprise in the American Revolutionary Era.* New York: Columbia University Press, 1938.

Falk, Stanley Lawrence. "Soldier-Technologist: Major Alfred Mordecai and the Beginnings of Science in the United States Army." Unpublished Ph.D. dissertation, Georgetown University, 1959.

Fortescue, Sir John W. *The Royal Army Service Corps: A History of Supply and Transport in the British Army.* Cambridge: The University Press, 1930–31. 2 vols.

———. *A History of the British Army.* London: Macmillan and Co., Limited, 1899–1930. 3 vols.

Freeman, Douglas S. "The Freeman Letters on George Washington," *American Heritage,* VII (February, 1956).

———. *George Washington, A Biography.* New York: Charles Scribner's Sons, 1948–54. 6 vols.

French, Allen. *The First Year of the American Revolution.* Boston: Houghton Mifflin Company, 1934.

Frothingham, Thomas G. *Washington, Commander-in-Chief.* Boston: Houghton Mifflin Company, 1930.

Fuller, Claud E. *The Whitney Firearms.* Huntington, W. Va.: Standard Publications, Inc., 1946.

———. *The Breech-Loader in the Service.* Topeka, Kans.: The Arms Reference Club of America, 1933.

Furse, George Armand. *Military Expeditions Beyond the Seas.* London: William Clowes & Sons, 1897. 2 vols.

Garrison, Fielding H. *An Introduction to the History of Medicine.* 4th ed. Philadelphia: W. B. Saunders Co., 1929.

Goebel, Dorothy B. *William Henry Harrison.* Richmond, Va.: William B. Burford, 1941.

Gottschalk, Louis R. *Lafayette and the Close of the American Revolution.* Chicago: University of Chicago Press, 1942.

———. *Lafayette Joins the American Army.* Chicago: University of Chicago Press, 1937.

Greene, Everts B. *The Revolutionary Generation, 1763–1790.* New York: Macmillan Company, 1943.

Greene, Francis V. *The Revolutionary War and the Military Policy of the United States.* New York: Charles Scribner's Sons, 1911.

Greene, George W. *Life of Major General Nathanael Greene.* New York: Hurd and Houghton, 1867–71. 3 vols.

Haggard, Howard W. *The Doctor in History.* New Haven, Conn.: Yale University Press, 1934.

Haiman, Miecislaus. *Kosciuszko in the American Revolution.* New York: Polish Institute of Arts and Sciences in America. 1943.

Hamilton, Holman. *Zachary Taylor, Soldier of the Republic.* Indianaplois: The Bobbs-Merrill Company, 1941.

Harrington, Virginia D. *The New York Merchant on the Eve of the Revolution.* New York: Columbia University Press, 1935.

Harte, Charles Rufus. "Connecticut's Iron & Copper," *Annual Report [of the] Connecticut Society of Civil Engineers.* New Haven, Conn., 1944, 131–66.

Haskin, William L. *The History of the First Artillery from Its Organization in 1821 to January 1, 1876.* Portland, Maine: B. Thurston & Co., 1879.

Hatch, Louis C. *The Administration of the American Revolutionary Army.* New York: Longman's, 1904.

Haven, Charles T., and Frank A. Belden. *A History of the Colt Revolver.* New York: William Morrow & Co., 1940.

Hicks, James E. *Notes on United States Ordnance.* Mount Vernon, N.Y.: Published by the author, 1940.

Hill, Forest G. *Roads, Rails and Waterways: The Army Engineers and Early Transportation.* Norman, Okla.: University of Oklahoma Press, 1957.

Hittle, James D. *The Military Staff: Its History and Development.* Harrisburg, Pa.: Military Service Publishing Co., 1949.

Holland, Josiah G. *History of Western Massachusetts.* Springfield, Mass.: S. Bowles, 1885. 2 vols.

Huidekoper, Frederic L. *The Military Unpreparedness of the United States.* New York: Macmillan Company, 1916.

Hume, Edgar Erskine. *Victories of Army Medicine.* Philadelphia: J. B. Lippincott Co., 1943.

Ingersoll, L. D. *A History of the War Department of the United States.* Washington: Francis B. Mohun, 1879.

Jacobs, James Ripley. *The Beginning of the United States Army, 1783–1812.* Princeton, N.J.: Princeton University Press, 1947.

Jameson, J. Franklin. "St. Eustatius in the American Revolution," *The American Historical Review,* VIII (July, 1903), 683–708.

Jessup, Philip C., and Francis Deák. *Neutrality, Its History, Economics and Law.* Vol. I: The Origins. New York: Columbia University Press, 1935.

Johnson, Melvin M., Jr., and Charles T. Haven. *Ammunition: Its History, Development and Use, 1600 to 1943.* New York: W. Morrow & Co., 1943.

————. *For Permanent Victory.* New York: William Morrow and Co., 1942.

Johnson, Victor L. *The Administration of the American Commissariat During the Revolutionary War.* Philadelphia: University of Pennsylvania Press, 1941.

Kremers, Edward and George Urdang. *History of Pharmacy.* Philadelphia: J. B. Lippincott Co., 1951.

Landers, Edward E. L. *Virginia Campaign and Blockade and Seige of Yorktown.* Washington: GPO, 1931.

Lefferts, Charles M. *Uniforms of the American, British, French, and German Armies . . . in the American Revolution, 1775–1783.* New York: J. J. Little and Ives Co., 1926.

Lenz, Ellis C. *Muzzle Flashes.* Huntington, W. Va.: Standard Publications, 1944.

Lewis, Berkeley R. *Small Arms and Ammunition in the United States Service.* Smithsonian Miscellaneous Collections, Vol. 129. Washington, 1956.

Loescher, Burt G. *The History of Rogers Rangers.* San Francisco: Printed by the author, 1946.

Logan, Hershel L. *Cartridges.* Huntington, W. Va.: Standard Publications, 1948.

Lossing, Benson T. *The American Revolution.* New York: New York Book Company, 1875. 2 vols.

Lundin, Leonard. *Cockpit of the Revolution: The War for Independence in New Jersey.* Princeton: Princeton University Press, 1940.

MacMunn, Sir George F. *The American War of Independence in Perspective.* London: G. Bell and Sons, Ltd., 1939.

Maryland Historical Magazine. "Provisioning the Continental Army," IX (September, 1914).

McAfee, Robert B. *History of the Late War in the Western Country . . . .* Lexington, Ky.: Worsley & Smith, 1816.

McMaster, John B. *A History of the People of the United States from the Revolution to the Civil War.* New York: Appleton and Company, 1833–1913. 8 vols.

Miller, John C. *Triumph of Freedom, 1775–1790.* Boston: Little, Brown and Co., 1945.

Mirsky, Jeannette and Allan Nevins. *The World of Eli Whitney.* New York: Macmillan Company, 1952.

Monaghan, Frank. *John Jay.* Indianapolis: Bobbs-Merrill Co., 1935.

Montross, Lynn. *Rag, Tag, and Bobtail: The Story of the Continental Army, 1775–1783.* New York: Harper and Brothers, 1952.

Morales, Padron Francisco. *Spanish Help in American Independence.* Madrid: Publicaciones Españolas, 1952.

Nevins, Allan. *The American States During and After the Revolution, 1775–1789.* New York: The Macmillan Company, 1927.

Nickerson, Hoffman. *The Turning Point of the Revolution.* Boston: Houghton Mifflin, 1928.

North, Simon D., and Ralph H. North. *Simeon North, First Official Pistol Maker of the United States.* Concord, N.H.: Rumford, 1913.

Norton, Charles B. *American Inventions and Improvements in Breech-Loading Small Arms . . . and Other Munitions of War.* Springfield, Mass.: Chapin & Gould, 1810.

Osgood, Herbert L. *The American Colonies in the 17th Century.* New York: Macmillan Company, 1904. 3 vols.

———. *The American Colonies in the 18th Century.* New York: Columbia University Press, 1924. 4 vols.

Palmer, John M. *General von Steuben.* New Haven, Conn.: Yale University Press, 1937.

Parkman, Francis. *Montcalm and Wolfe.* Boston: Little, Brown & Co., 1903. 2 vols.

Pargellis, Stanley M. *Lord Loudon in North America.* New Haven, Conn.: Yale University Press, 1933.

Patterson, Samuel White. *Horatio Gates, Defender of American Liberties.* New York: Columbia Unversity Press, 1941.

Pollard, H. B. C. *A History of Firearms.* London: Geoffery Bles, 1926.

Pratt, Julius W. *Expansionists of 1812.* New York: Macmillan Company, 1925.

Preston, John H. *A Gentleman Rebel: The Exploits of Anthony Wayne.* New York: Farrar and Rinehart, Inc., 1930.

Risch, Erna. *Quartermaster Support of the Army: A History of the Corps, 1775–1939.* Washington: GPO, 1962.

Rodenbough, T. F. *From Everglade to Canon with the Second Dragoons.* New York: D. Van Nostrand, 1875.

Roe, Jospeh W. and Richard S. Kirby. *Eli Whitney and Interchangeable Manufacture.* New Haven, Conn., 1938.

Roosevelt, Theodore. *The Winning of the West.* New York: G. P. Putnam Sons, 1889–1906. 6 vols.

Rossman, Kenneth R. *Thomas Mifflin and the Politics of the American Revolution.* Chapel Hill, N.C.: University of North Carolina Press, 1952.

Sawyer, Charles W. *Firearms in American History.* Various publishers, 1910–20. 3 volumes.

Schlesinger, Authur Meier. *The Colonial Merchants and the American Revolution, 1763–1776.* New York: Facsimile Library, Inc., 1948.

Scott, James Brown. *DeGrasse à Yorktown.* Baltimore: The Johns Hopkins Press for *Institut français de* Washington, 1931.

Sharpe, Philip B. *The Rifle in America.* New York: Funk & Wagnalls Co., 1938.

Silver, James W. *Edmund Pendleton Gaines, Frontier General.* Baton Rouge, La.: Louisiana State University Press, 1949.

Smith, Walter H. B. *Rifles.* Harrisburg, Pa.: Military Service Publishing Co., 1948.

Smith, Zachary F. *The Battle of New Orleans.* Louisville: J. P. Moston & Co., 1904.

Snell, Charles W. *Saratoga.* National Park Service Historical Handbook Series No. 4. Washington, 1950.

Snell, S. H. P. *Fort Ticonderoga: A Short History.* Reprinted for the Fort Ticonderoga Museum, 1954.

Spears, John R. *Anthony Wayne.* New York: D. Appleton & Co., 1903.

Sprague, John T. *The Origin, Progress, and Conclusion of the Florida War.* New York: D. Appleton & Co., 1848.

Stephenson, Orlando. "The Supply of Gunpowder in 1776," *The American Historical Review,* XXX (January, 1925), 281.

Stevenson, David. *Sketch of the Civil Engineering of North America.* London: John Weale Architectural Library, 1838.

Stone, William L. *The Campaign of Lieutenant General John Burgoyne.* Albany, N.Y.: Joel Munsell, 1877.

Stourzh, Gerald. *Benjamin Franklin and American Foreign Policy.* Chicago: University of Chicago Press, 1954.

Sumner, William Graham. *The Financier and the Finances of the American Revolution.* New York: Dodd, Mead and Company, 1892. Vols. I and II.

Swank, James Moore. *History of the Manufacture of Iron in All Ages and Particularly in the United States from Colonial Times to 1891.* 2d ed. Philadelphia: Published by the author, 1892.

Upton, Emory. *The Military Policy of the United States.* 4th impression. Washington: GPO, 1917.

Van Doren, Carl C. *Mutiny in January . . . Crisis in the Continental Army.* New York: Viking Press, 1943.

Van Tyne, Claude H. *The American Revolution, 1776–1783.* The American Nation Series. New York: Harper & Brothers, 1907.

———. "French Aid Before the Alliance of 1778," *American Historical Review,* XXX (October, 1925), 20–40.

Wallace, Willard M. *Appeal to Arms, A Military History of the American Revolution.* New York: Harper and Brothers, 1950.

Ward, Christopher. *The War of the Revolution.* Edited by John Alden. New York: Macmillan Co., 1952. 2 vols.

Wasson, R. Gordon. *The Hall Carbine Affair: A Study in Contemporary Folklore.* New York: Pandick Press, Inc., 1948.

Weeden, William B. *Economic and Social History of New England.* Boston: Houghton Mifflin Company, 1891. Vols. I and II.

Weig, Melvin J. *Morristown, A Military Capital of the Revolution.* Washington: National Park Service, 1950.

Wildes, Harry Emerson. *Anthony Wayne.* New York: Harcourt, Brace & Company, 1941.

Williamson, Harold T. *Winchester, The Gun That Won the West.* Washington: Combat Forces Press, 1952.

Wilson, Mitchell. *American Science and Invention.* New York: Simon and Schuster, 1954.

Winsor, Justin, ed. *The American Revolution (Narrative and Critical History of America).* Boston: Houghton Mifflin Company, 1884–89. 8 vols.

Wright, John W. "Some Notes on the Continental Army," *William and Mary College Quarterly Historical Magazine,* XI (April, July, 1931), 81–105, 185–209.

PART TWO

Emergence of Modern Warfare

Manuscript Sources

Henry, Robert S. "Railroads in Two Wars." Address before the 69th meeting of the Ohio Valley Transportation Advisory Board, Indianapolis, Ind., June 23, 1943. Typescript.

Historical Papers Relating to the Corps of Engineers. Occasional Papers. The Engineer School, 1904.

Woodward, John Henry (Bvt. Major, Army of the Potomac). A Narrative of the Family and Civil War Experience and Events of His Life. Manuscript in possession of Lt. Col. Frederick Woodward Hopkins, Santa Rosa, Calif.

Printed Primary Sources and Documents

Congressional Globe. 38th Congress, 1st Session.

Hetzel, A. R., ed. *Military Laws of the United States.* 3d ed. Washington City: Department of War, 1846.

Letterman, Jonathan. *Medical Recollections of the Army of the Potomac.* New York: D. Appleton & Co., 1866.

Medical and Surgical History of the War of the Rebellion (1861–65). (Prepared in accordance with Acts of Congress under Direction of Surgeon General Barnes, U.S. Army. II, part 3. Washington, 1875–88.)

Scott, Lt. Col. Robert N. *The War of the Rebellion: A Compilation of the Official Records of the Union and Confederate Armies.* Washington: GPO, 1880–1902. 129 volumes, including 1 volume of index and 3 volumes of atlases.

Secretary of War.
  Report, 5 December 1846.
  Report, 2 December 1847. (Reports of the Secretary of War subsequent to 1847 and up to 1921 include the reports of bureau chiefs and departmental and field commanders.)
  Report, 8 November 1865.
  Report, 22 November 1865.
  Report, for the Year 1876.

Thian, Raphael P. *Legislative History of the General Staff of the Army of the United States, 1775 to 1901.* Washington: GPO, 1901.

U.S. Army.
  General Orders of the Army of the Potomac. National Archives. Regulations (Revised) 1857 and 1861.
  Report of Brig. Gen. Nelson A. Miles, Commanding, Division of the Pacific, in Report of Major General Commanding the Army to the Secretary of War for the Year 1889.
  Report of the Surgeon General, the Major General Commanding the Army, and Maj. Gen. Nelson A. Miles, Commanding, Department of the Missouri, in Report of the Secretary of War, 1891.

U.S. House of Representatives:
  Document No. 4, 29th Congress, 2d Session. Reports of the Bureau Chiefs.
  Document No. 10, 29th Congress, 2d Session. Account of Government Receipts and Expenditures.
  Document No. 46, 29th Congress, 2d Session. Ordnance Reports.
  Document No. 119, 29th Congress, 2d Session. Correspondence and Army Orders.
  Document No. 2, 30th Congress, 1st Session. Estimates of Appropriations.
  Document No. 7, 30th Congress, 1st Session. Government Receipts and Expenditures.
  Document No. 8, 30th Congress, 1st Session. Reports of Bureau Chiefs.
  Document No. 10, 30th Congress, 1st Session. Correspondence and Army Orders.
  Document No. 60, 30th Congress, 1st Session. Correspondence and Army Orders.
  Document No. 74, 30th Congress, 1st Session. Correspondence and Army Orders.
  Document No. 1, 35th Congress, 1st Session. Estimates of Appropriations.
  Document No. 1, 36th Congress, 1st Session. Estimates of Appropriations.
  Document No. 67, 37th Congress, 2d Session. Interest of Members of Congress in Government Contracts.

———. Notes [by Frémont] on the Subject of Contracting for Small Arms.

Document No. 2, 38th Congress, 1st Session.   Estimates of Additional Appropriations.

Document No. 1, 39th Congress, 2d Session.   Message of the President of the United States.

House Report No. 2, 37th Congress, 2d Session.   Report and Testimony of Select House Committee Appointed to Inquire into Government Contracts.

U.S. Senate

Reports, 38th Congress, 2d Session, Vol. III, Part 2.   Conduct of the [Civil] War.

Document No. 178, 47th Congress, 1st Session.   Report of the Board on Heavy Ordnance and Projectiles, 18 May 1882.

Secondary Sources

Adams, George Worthington.   *Doctors in Blue: The Medical History of the Union Army in the Civil War.*   New York: H. Schuman, 1952.

Alcarez, Ramon.   *The Other Side: Notes for the History of the War Between Mexico and the United States.*   Translated and edited by Albert C. Ramsey.   New York: John Wiley, 1850.

Anderson, Robert.   *An Artillery Officer in the Mexican War, 1846–1847.*   New York: G. P. Putnam's Sons, 1911.

Ashburn, P. M.   *A History of the Medical Department of the United States Army.*   Boston: Houghton Mifflin Company, 1929.

Athearn, Robert G.   *William Tecumseh Sherman and the Settlement of the West.*   Norman, Okla.: University of Oklahoma Press, 1956.

Badeau, Adam.   *Military History of Ulysses S. Grant.*   New York: D. Appleton & Co., 1868–88.   2 vols.

Bailey, Edward W.   "Echoes from Custer's Last Fight," *Military Affairs,* XVII (Winter, 1953).

Barriger, John W.   *Legislative History of the Subsistence Department of the U.S. Army from June 16, 1775 to August 15, 1876.*   Washington: General Publications, 1876.

Bates, David H.   *Lincoln in the Telegraph Office: Recollections of the United States Military Telegraph Corps During the Civil War.*   New York: Century Co., 1907.

Billings, John D.   *Hardtack and Coffee.*   Boston: George M. Smith & Co., 1887.

Birkhimer, William E.   *Historical Sketch of the Organization, Materiel and Tactics of the Artillery, United States Army.*   Washington: James J. Chapman, 1884.

Bishop, James L.   *History of American Manufacture.*   Philadelphia: E. Young & Co., 1864.   2 vols.

Black, C. F.   *The Railroads of the Confederacy.*   Chapel Hill, N.C.: University of North Carolina Press, 1952.

Bolles, Albert S.   *Industrial History of the United States from the Earliest Settlements to the Present Time.*   Norwich, Conn.: Henry Bill Publishing Co., 1881.

Brown, Harvey E., comp.   *Medical Department of the Army from 1775 to 1873.*   Washington: Surgeon General's Office, 1873.

Bruce, Robert Van.   *Lincoln and the Tools of War.*   Indianapolis: Bobbs-Merrill Co., 1955.

Buckeridge, J. O.   *Lincoln's Choice.*   Harrisburg, Pa.: The Stackpole Co., 1956.

Bucklin, Sophronia E.   *In Hospital and Camp.*   Philadelphia: John E. Potter & Co., 1869.

Catton, Bruce.   *Glory Road.*   Garden City, N.Y.: Doubleday, 1954.

———.   *Mr. Lincoln's Army.*   Garden City, N.Y.: Doubleday, 1951.

———.   *A Stillness at Appomattox.*   Garden City, N.Y.: Doubleday, 1954.

Chanal, Francois Victor Adolphe de.   *The American Army in the War of Secession.*   Leavenworth, Kan.: G. A. Spooner, 1894.

Chinn, George M.   *The Machine Gun: History, Evolution, and Development of Manual, Automatic, and Airborne Repeating Weapons.*   Washington: GPO, 1951.

Clark, Victor S. "Manufacturing Development During the Civil War," *Military Historian and Economist*, III, No. 2 (April, 1918).

Cleveland, H. W. S. "The Use of the Rifle," *Atlantic Monthly*, IX, (March, 1862).

Cole, Arthur Charles. *The Irrepressible Conflict, 1850–1865.* Vol. 7 of *A History of American Life.* New York: Macmillan Company, 1938.

Crook, George. *General George Crook, His Autobiography.* Edited by Martin F. Schmitt. Norman, Okla.: University of Oklahoma Press, 1946.

Custer, George Armstrong. *My Life on the Plains.* New York: Sheldon & Co., 1874.

David, Robert Beebe. *Finn Burnett, Frontiersman.* Glendale, Calif.: Arthur H. Clark Co., 1937.

DeVoto, Bernard. *The Year of Decision.* 1st ed. Boston: Little, Brown & Company, 1943.

Dewey, Davis Rich. *Financial History of the United States.* New York: Longmans, Green & Co., 1918.

Deyrup, Felicia J. *Arms Makers of the Connecticut Valley: A Regional Study of the Economic Development of the Small Arms Industry, 1798–1870.* Northampton, Mass.: Smith College, Department of History, 1938.

Dillin, John Grace Wolfe. *The Kentucky Rifle.* Washington: National Rifle Association of America, 1924.

Dunbar, Seymour. *A History of Travel in America.* Indianapolis, Bobbs-Merrill Company, 1915. 4 vols.

Duncan, Louis C. "Evolution of the Ambulance Corps and Field Hospitals," *Military Surgeon*, XXXII (March, 1913).

Dunn, Jacob Piatt. *Massacres of the Mountains: A History of the Indian Wars of the Far West.* New York: Harper & Bros., 1886.

Dyer, Brainerd. *Zachary Taylor.* Baton Rouge, La.: Louisiana State University Press, 1946.

Dyer, Frederick H. *A Compendium of the War of the Rebellion.* Des Moines, Iowa: The Dyer Publishing Co., 1908.

Dyer, George C. *Naval Logistics.* Annapolis: United States Naval Institute, 1960.

Elliott, Charles Winslow. *Winfield Scott: The Soldier and the Man.* New York: The Macmillan Company, 1937.

Emmitt, Robert. *The Last War Trail: The Utes and the Settlement of Colorado.* Norman, Okla.: University of Oklahoma Press, 1954.

Falk, Stanley Lawrence. Soldier-Technologist: Major Alfred Mordecai and the Beginnings of Science in the U.S. Army. Unpublished Ph.D. dissertation, Georgetown University, 1959.

Fite, Emerson David. *Social and Industrial Conditions in the North During the Civil War.* New York: Macmillan Company, 1910.

Fougera, Katherine Gibson. *With Custer's Cavalry.* Caldwell, Idaho: The Caxton Printers, Ltd., 1940.

Freeman, Douglas Southall. *R. E. Lee, A Biography.* New York: Scribner's 1934–35. 4 vols.

Fuller, Claud E. *The Breech-Loader in the Service.* Topeka, Kans.: The Arms Reference Club of America, 1933.

———. and Richard D. Steuart. *Firearms of the Confederacy.* Huntington, W. Va.: Standard Publications, 1944.

Furber, George C. *The Twelve Months Volunteer . . . Journal of a Private . . . in Mexico, 1846–1847.* Cincinnati: J. A. & U. P. James, 1848.

Furse, George Armand. *The Organization and Administration of the Lines of Communication in in War.* London: William Clowes & Sons, 1894.

———. *Provisioning Armies in the Field.* London: William Clowes & Sons, 1899.

Ganoe, William A. *History of the United States Army.* New York: D. Appleton-Century Co., 1942.

Gosnell, H. Allen. *Guns on the Western Waters.* Baton Rouge, La.: Louisiana State University Press, 1949.

Graham, W. A. *The Custer Myth: A Source Book of Custeriana.* Harrisburg, Pa.: The Stackpole Co., 1953.

Grant, Ulysses S. *Personal Memoirs of U. S. Grant.* New York: C. L. Webster, 1885–86. 2 vols.

Gras, Norman Scott Brian, and Henrietta M. Larson. *Casebook in American Business History.* New York: F. S. Crofts & Co., 1939.

Hafen, Leroy R., and Carl Coke Rister. *Western America.* New York: Prentice-Hall, 1941.

Haines, Francis. *The Nez Perces.* Norman, Okla.: University of Oklahoma Press, 1955.

Hamilton, Holman. *Zachary Taylor, Soldier of the Republic.* Indianapolis: Bobbs-Merrill Co., 1941.

Hancock, Cornelia. *South After Gettysburg: Letters from the Army of the Potomac, 1863–1865.* Edited by Henrietta S. Jaquette. Philadelphia: University of Pennsylvania Press, 1937.

Hanson, Joseph Mills. *The Conquest of the Missouri.* New York: Murray Hill Books, Inc., 1946.

Hart, Albert Bushnell. *Salmon Portland Chase.* Boston and New York: Houghton Mifflin Company, 1899.

Haskin, William L. *The History of the First Regiment of Artillery from Its Organization in 1821 to January 1, 1876.* Portland, Maine: B. Thurston & Co., 1879.

Hassler, Warren W., Jr. *General George B. McClellan: Shield of the Union.* Baton Rouge, La.: Louisiana State University Press, 1957.

Haupt, Hermann. *Military Bridges.* New York: D. Van Nostrand, 1864.

———. *Reminiscenses of General Hermann Haupt.* Milwaukee: Wright & Joyce Co., 1901.

Haven, Charles T., and Frank A. Belden. *A History of the Colt Revolver and Other Arms Made By Colt's Patent Fire Arms Manufacturing Company from 1836 to 1940.* Foreword by Stephen V. Grancsay. New York: William Morrow & Co., 1940.

Haydon, F. Stansbury. *Aeronautics in the Union and Confederate Armies.* Baltimore: Johns Hopkins Press, 1941.

Hendrick, Burton J. *Lincoln's War Cabinet.* Boston: Little, Brown & Co., 1946.

Henry, Robert S. *The Story of the Mexican War.* Indianapolis: The Bobbs-Merrill Co., Inc., 1950.

Henry, William S. *Campaign Sketches of the War with Mexico.* New York: Harper & Brothers, 1847.

Herbert, Walter H. *Fighting Joe Hooker.* Indianapolis: Bobbs-Merrill Co., 1944.

Hesseltine, William B. *Lincoln and the War Governors.* New York: Alfred A. Knopf, 1948.

Hicks, James E. *Notes on United States Ordnance.* Mount Vernon, N.Y.: Published by the author, 1940. 3 vols.

Hines, Walker D. *War History of American Railroads.* New Haven, Conn.: Yale University Press, 1928.

Hitchcock, Henry. *Marching with Sherman.* Edited by M. A. DeWolfe Howe. New Haven, Conn.: Yale University Press, 1927.

Hittle, James D. *The Military Staff, Its History and Development.* Harrisburg, Pa.: Military Service Publishing Co., 1949.

Holley, Alexander L. *A Treatise on Ordnance and Armor.* New York: D. Van Nostrand, 1865.

Horsford, E. N. *The Army Ration.* New York: D. Van Nostrand, 1864.

Hosmer, James Kendall. *The Appeal to Arms, 1861–1863.* New York: Harper & Brothers, 1907.

———. *Outcome of the Civil War, 1863–1865.* Vol. XXI of *The American Nation* Series. New York: Harper & Brothers, 1907.

Hughes, John T. *Doniphan's Expedition.* Cincinnati: J. A. & U. P. James, 1848.

Hunter, Louis C. *Steamboats on the Western Rivers.* Cambridge, Mass.: Harvard University Press, 1949.

Ingersoll, L. D. *A History of the War Department of the United States.* Washington: Francis B. Mohun, 1879.

Johnson, Melvin M., and Charles T. Haven. *Ammunition: Its History, Development and Use, 1600 to 1943.* New York: W. Morrow & Co., 1943.

———. *For Permanent Victory.* New York: William Morrow and Co., 1942.

Johnson, Virginia Weisel. *The Unregimented General: A Biography of Nelson A. Miles.* Boston: Houghton Mifflin Company, 1962.

Joinville, Francois Ferdinand Philippe Louis Marie d'Orleans, Prince de. *Army of the Potomac: Organization, Commander, and Campaign.* New York: A. D. F. Randolph, 1862.

Kamm, Samuel Richey. *The Civil War Career of Thomas A. Scott.* Philadelphia: University of Pennsylvania Press, 1940.

Kearney, Thomas. *General Philip Kearney, Battle Soldier of Five Wars.* New York: G. P. Putnam's Sons, 1937.

Kenley, John R. *Memoirs of a Maryland Volunteer in the War with Mexico.* Philadelphia: J. B. Lippincott & Co., 1873.

Kreidberg, Marvin A., and Merton G. Henry. *History of Military Mobilization in the United States Army, 1775–1945.* Department of the Army Pamphlet 20–212. Washington: GPO, 1955.

Leech, Margaret. *Reveille in Washington, 1861–1865.* New York: Harper & Bros., 1941.

Lenz, Elis C. *Muzzle Flashes.* Huntington, W. Va.: Standard Publications, 1944.

Lewis, Berkeley R. *Small Arms and Ammunition in the United States Service.* Smithsonian Miscellaneous Collections, Vol. 129. Washington, 1956.

Lewis, Lloyd. *Captain Sam Grant.* Boston: Little, Brown & Co., 1950

Liddel Hart, B. H. *Sherman: Soldier, Realist, American.* New York: Dodd, Mead & Co., 1930.

Lyman, Theodore. *Meade's Headquarters, 1863–1865: Letters of Colonel Theodore Lyman from the Wilderness to Appomattox.* Edited by George R. Agassiz. Boston: The Atlantic Monthly Press, 1922.

Macartney, Clarence E. N. *Grant and His Generals.* New York: McBride, 1953.

Manucy, Albert. *Artillery Through the Ages.* National Park Service Interpretive Series, History No. 3. Washington: GPO, 1955.

Mattison, Ray H. *The Army Post on the Northern Plains, 1865–1885.* Gering, Nebr.: Courier Press, 1960, 1962.

Maurice, Sir Frederick B. *Statesmen and Soldiers of the Civil War: A Study of the Conduct of the War.* Boston: Little, Brown & Co., 1926.

Maxwell, William Quentin. *Lincoln's Fifth Wheel: The Political History of the United States Sanitary Commission.* New York: Longman's Green & Co., 1956.

McClellan, George Brinton. *McClellan's Own Story; the War for the Union, the Soldiers Who Fought It, the Civilians Who Directed It and His Relations to It and to Them.* New York: C. L. Webster & Company, 1887.

———. *Mexican War Diary.* Edited by William Starr Myers. Princeton, N.J.: Princeton University Press, 1917.

McCormac, Eugene Irving. *James K. Polk: A Political Biography.* Berkeley, Calif.: University of California Press, 1922.

Meigs, Montgomery C. "General M. C. Meigs on the Conduct of the Civil War," *American Historical Review,* XXVI (January, 1921), 285–303.

Meneely, A. Howard. *The War Department, 1861, A Study in Mobilization and Administration.* New York: Columbia University Press, 1928.

Miers, Earl Schenck. *The Web of Victory: Grant at Vicksburg.* New York: Alfred A. Knopf, 1955.

Miller, F. T. *Photographic History of the Civil War.* New York: The Review of Reviews Co., 1911. 10 vols.

Montross, Lynn. *War Through the Ages.* New York: Harper & Brothers, 1946.

National Park Service. *Soldier and Brave.* Vol. XII of *The National Survey of Historic Sites and Buildings.* New York, 1963.

Nevins, Allan. *Frémont, The West's Greatest Adventurer.* New York: Harper & Bros., 1928.

Newberry, J. S. *The United States Sanitary Commission in the Valley of the Mississippi During the War of the Rebellion, 1861–1866.* Cleveland: Fairbanks, Benedict & Co., 1871.

Paris, Louis Philippe Albert, comte de. *History of the Civil War in America.* Philadelphia: Porter & Coates, 1875–88, 4 vols.

Parsons, Lewis Baldwin. *Rail and River Army Transportation in the Civil War.* St. Louis: Press of Perrin and Smith, 1899.

Perkins, J. R. *Trails, Rails and War: The Life of General G. M. Dodge.* Indianapolis: Bobbs-Merrill, 1929.

Plum, William R. *The Military Telegraph During the Civil War in the United States.* Chicago: Jansen, McClurg & Co., 1882. 2 vols.

Pratt, Edwin A. *The Rise of Rail Power in War and Conquest, 1833–1914.* London: P. S. King & Son, Ltd., 1915.

Pratt, Fletcher. *Stanton, Lincoln's Secretary of War.* New York: W. W. Norton & Co., 1953.

Randall, J. G. *The Civil War and Reconstruction.* Boston: Heath, 1937.

———. *Confiscation of Property During the Civil War.* Indianapolis: Mutual Printing and Lithographing Co., 1913.

———. *Lincoln the President.* New York: Dodd, Mead Co., 1945. 2 vols.

Ripley, Roswell S. *The War with Mexico.* New York: Harper & Brothers, 1849. 2 vols.

Risch, Erna. *Quartermaster Support of the Army: A History of the Corps, 1775–1939.* Washington: GPO, 1962.

Rister, Carl Coke. *The Southwestern Frontier, 1865–1881.* Cleveland: The Arthur H. Clark Co., 1928.

Rives, George Lockhart. *The United States and Mexico, 1821–1848.* New York: C. Scribner's Sons, 1913.

Rodenbough, T. F. *From Everglade to Canon with the Second Dragoons.* New York: D. Van Nostrand, 1875.

Sandburg, Carl. *Abraham Lincoln: The War Years.* New York: Harcourt, Brace & Co., 1939.

Schouler, James. *History of the United States of America Under the Constitution.* Washington: W. H. Morrison, 1886–1913.

Scott, Winfield. *Memoirs of Lieutenant General Scott.* New York: Sheldon & Co., 1864, 2 vols.

Semmes, Raphael. *Service Afloat and Ashore During the Mexican War.* Cincinnati: William H. Moore & Co., 1851.

Semple, E. C. *American History and Its Geographic Conditions.* Boston: Houghton Mifflin Co., 1903.

Shannon, Fred A. *The Organization and Administration of the Union Army, 1861–1865.* Cleveland: The Arthur H. Clark Co., 1928.

Sharpe, Henry G. "The Art of Supplying Armies in the Field As Exemplified During the Civil War," *Journal of the Military Service Institution* (January, 1896).

———. *The Provisioning of the Modern Army in the Field.* Kansas City, Mo.: Franklin Hudson Publishing Co., 1905.

Sharpe, Philip B. *The Rifle in America.* New York: Funk & Wagnalls Co., 1938.

Sheridan, Philip H. *Personal Memoirs of P. H. Sheridan.* New York: C. L. Webster & Co., 1888. 2 vols.

Sherman, William Tecumseh. "The Grand Strategy of the War of the Rebellion," *Century Magazine* (February, 1888), 582–98.

———. *Memoirs of General William T. Sherman.* 4th ed. New York: Webster and Co., 1891.

Shryock, Richard H. *The Development of Modern Medicine.* Philadelphia: University of Pennsylvania Press, 1936.

Smith, Justin H. *The War with Mexico.* New York: Macmillan Co., 1919.

Spaulding, Oliver L. *The United States Army in War and Peace.* New York: G. P. Putnam's Sons, 1937.

Stille, Charles J. *History of the United States Sanitary Commission.* Philadelphia: J. B. Lippincott & Co., 1866.

Summers, Festus Paul. *The Baltimore and Ohio in the Civil War.* New York: G. P. Putnam's Sons, 1939.

Symonds, Henry Clay. *The Report of a Commissary of Subsistence.* Sing Sing, N.Y.: H. C. Symonds, 1888.

Thian, Raphael P. *Notes Illustrating the Military Geography of the United States, 1813–1880.* Washington, Department of War, 1881.

Thomas, Benjamin P., and Harold M. Hyman. *Stanton: The Life and Times of Lincoln's Secretary of War.* New York: Alfred A. Knopf, 1962.

Thomas, George R. "Civil War Signals," *Military Affairs,* XVIII, No. 4 (Winter, 1954), 188.

Thompson, Gilbert. "The Engineer Battalion in the Civil War," *Source Book of the Peninsula Campaign.* Fort Leavenworth, 1921.

Turner, George E. *Victory Rode the Rails: The Strategic Place of the Railroads in the Civil War.* Indianapolis: Bobbs-Merrill Co., 1953.

Twitchel, Ralph E. *The History of the Military Occupation of the Territory of New Mexico from 1846 to 1851.* Denver, Colo.: Smith Brooks, Co., 1909.

Upham, Cyrus B. "Arms and Equipment for Iowa Troops in the Civil War," *The Iowa Journal of History and Politics,* XVI (January, 1918), 3–52.

Upton, Emery. *The Military Policy of the United States.* 4th impression. Washington: GPO, 1917.

Van Horne, Thomas B. *History of the Army of the Cumberland.* Cincinnati: R. Clarke & Co., 1875.

Walker, Francis A. *History of . . . Second Corps in . . . Army of the Potomac.* New York: C. Scribner's Sons, 1886.

Wallace, Edward S. *General William Jenkins North, Monterrey's Forgotten Hero.* Dallas: Southern Methodist University Press, 1953.

Wasson, R. Gordon. *The Hall Carbine Affair: A Study in Contemporary Folklore.* New York: Pandick Press, Inc., 1948.

Weber, Thomas. *The Northern Railroads in the Civil War, 1861–1865.* New York: King's Crown Press, 1925.

Weeden, William B. *War Government, Federal and State, in Massachusetts, New York, Pennsylvania and Indiana, 1861–1865.* Boston: Houghton Mifflin Co., 1906.

Weigley, Russell F. *Quartermaster of the Union Army: A Biography of M. C. Meigs.* New York: Columbia University Press, 1959.

Wilcox, Cadmers M. *History of the Mexican War.* Washington: The Church News Publishing Co., 1892.

Wiley, Bell I. *The Life of Billy Yank, the Common Soldier of the Union.* Indianapolis: Bobbs-Merrill Co., 1952.

Williams, Kenneth P. *Lincoln Finds a General, A Military Study of the Civil War.* New York: The Macmillan Co., 1952, 1957. 4 vols.

Williams, Thomas H. *Lincoln and His Generals.* New York: Alfred A. Knopf, Inc., 1952.

Wilson, Mitchell. "Abraham Lincoln and the Repeating Rifle," *Scientific American,* CXXV-A (December, 1903).

————. *American Science and Invention.* New York: Simon and Schuster, 1954.

PART THREE

Warfare Overseas

Manuscript Sources

National Archives Record Groups.   Automatic Weapons: 00 WD 472.5/11; 100 WD 472.583
    misc.; 00 WD 472.5/142; 472.5/171; 00 WD 472.5/167; 00 WD 472.5/347; 00 WD
    472.5/278; 00 WD 472.5/629; 00 WD 472.5/396; 00 WD 472.5/610; 00 WD 472.5/671.
———.   Machine Guns.   00 WD 422.5/826; 00 WD 472.5/831; 00 WD 472.5/1120.
U.S. Army, Office of the Chief of Military History.   Selected Documents on Railway Artillery
    and the Methods of Its Use in 1918.

Printed Primary Sources and Documents

Congressional Record, 26 June 1916.
The Dodge Commission.   Report of the Commission Appointed by the President to Inves-
    tigate the Conduct of the War with Spain.   Washington, 1900.   8 vols.
Martin, Franklin H.   *Digest of the Proceedings of the Council of National Defense During the World*
    War.   Washington: GPO, 1934.
Military Board of Allied Supply.   Report of the Military Board of Allied Supply.   Washing-
    ton, 1924.   3 vols.
National Archives.   Handbook of Federal War Agencies and Their Records, 1917–1921.
    Washington: GPO, 1943.
Secretary of War.   Reports [for the years] 1898, 1899, 1907, 1908, 1909, 1911, 1912, 1913,
    1914, 1916, 1919.
Secretary of the Treasury.   Annual Reports of the Secretary of the Treasury on the State of
    Finances for Fiscal Years Ending 30 June 1915, 30 June 1916, 30 June 1917, 30 June
    1918, 30 June 1919.
U.S. Government.   40 U.S. Statutes.
U.S. House of Representatives.
    House Report 74, 42d Congress, 3d Session.   Report of House Committee on Military
        Affairs on House Bill 495, Army Staff Organization.
U.S. Senate.
    Document No. 664, 64th Congress, 2d Session.   Government Manufacture of Arms,
        Munitions, and Equipment.
    Document No. 119, 68th Congress, 1st Session.   Maj. Gen. William H. Carter, Creation
        of the American General Staff.   Personal narrative of the General Staff system of the
        American Army, 22 January 1924.
    Document No. 193, 72d Congress, 2d Session.   Franklin H. Martin, Digest of the Pro-
        ceedings of the Council of National Defense During the World War.
    Hearings Before the Committee on Military Affairs, 65th Congress, 2d Session.   Investi-
        gation of the War Department.   Washington, 1918.
U.S. State Department.
    Papers Relating to the Foreign Relations of the United States, 1917.   Supplements 1 and
        2 *The World War,* 2 vols. in each supplement.   Washington, 1932, 1933.
U.S. War Department.
    Annual Reports [for the years] 1917, 1918, 1919.
    Decisions of the War Department Board of Contract Adjustment and Decisions of the
        Appeal Section, War Department Claims Board.   Washington: GPO, 1920–21.
        8 vols.

U.S. War Department—Continued
    Document No. 532, Office of the Chief of Staff, 1916.   Army War College Study.   Strategic Location of Military Depots, Arsenals, and Manufacturing Plants.
    The Genesis of the American First Army.   Washington: GPO, 1938.
    The United States Army in World War I, 1917–1918 (Documentary History).   Washington, GPO, 1948.

Secondary Sources

Alger, Russell Alexander.   *The Spanish-American War.*   New York: Harper & Bros., 1901.
American Battle Monuments Commission.   *American Armies and Battlefields in Europe.*   Washington, GPO, 1938.
Anderson, Troyer S.   History of the Office of the Under Secretary of the Army, 1914–1941.   Prepared for the Office of the Under Secretary of War, 1947.   Office, Chief of Military History.   Manuscript.
Ashburn, P. M.   *A History of the Medical Department of the United States Army.*   Boston: Houghton Mifflin Company, 1929.
Ayres, Leonard P.   *The War with Germany, a Statistical Summary.*   Washington, GPO, 1919.
Bach, Christian, and Henry N. Hall.   *Fourth Division in the World War.*   Issued by the Division, 1920.
Baker, Charles Whiting.   *Government Control and Operation of Industry in Great Britain and the United States During The World War.*   New York: Oxford University Press, 1921.
Baker, Chauncey B.   *Transportation of Troops and Material.*   Kansas City, Mo: Franklin Hudson Pub. Co., 1905.
Baker, Ray Stannard.   *Woodrow Wilson Life and Letters.*   Garden City, N.Y.: Doubleday, Doran & Co.   Vol. V: *Neutrality,* 1914–15 (1935).   Vol. VI: *Facing War, 1915–17* (1937).   Vol. VII: *War Leader* (1939).   Vol. VIII: *Armistice* (1939).
Baruch, Bernard M.   *American Industry in the War.*   Washington: GPO, 1921.
Beamish, Richard J., and Francis A. March.   *America's Part in the World War.*   Philadelphia: John C. Winston Co., 1919.
Bernardo, C. Joseph, and Eugene H. Bacon.   *American Military Policy: Its Development Since 1775.*   Harrisburg, Pa.: Military Service Publishing Co., 1957.
Bigelow, John, Jr.   *Reminiscences of the Santiago Campaign.*   New York: Harpers, 1899.
Bliss, Gen. Tasker H.   "The Evolution of the Unified Command," *Foreign Affairs* (December 15, 1922).
Blount, James Henderson.   *The American Occupation of the Philippines, 1898–1912.*   New York: G. P. Putnam's Sons, 1912.
Bond, Col. Paul S.   Use of Inland Waterways in World War I.   Historical Section, Army War College, 1942.   Office, Chief of Military History.   Manuscript.
Bonsal, Stephen.   *The Fight for Santiago.*   New York: Doubleday & McClure Co., 1899.
Breckinridge, Henry.   *Preparedness.*   New York: Sun Printing and Publishing Assn., 1916.
Bullard, Arthur.   *Mobilizing America.*   New York: Macmillan Co., 1917.
Carter, William Harding.   *The Life of Lieutenant General Chaffee.*   Chicago: University of Chicago Press, 1917.
Cater, Harold Dean.   Evolution of the American General Staff.   Office, Chief of Military History.   Manuscript.
Chadwick, French Ensor.   *Relations of the United States and Spain: The Spanish-American War.*   New York: Scribner's, 1909.   2 vols.
Chambrun, Jacques Aldebert de Pineton, comte de.   *The American Army in the European Conflict.*   New York: The Macmillan Company, 1919.
Chinn, George M.   *The Machine Gun, History, Evolution, and Development of Manual, Automatic, and Airborne Repeating Weapons.*   Washington: GPO, 1951.
Churchill, Winston S.   *The World Crisis.* 1916–1918.   New York: Scribner's, 1927.   4 vols.

Clarkson, Grosvenor B. *Industrial America in the World War.* Boston and New York: Houghton Mifflin Co., 1923.

Clementel, Etienne. *La Guerre et le commerce, la France et la politique interalliée.* New Haven, Conn: Yale University Press, 1931.

Crowell, Benedict, and Robert Forrest Wilson. *How America Went to War.* New Haven, Conn.: Yale University Press, 1921. 6 vols.

Crowell, J. Franklin. *Government War Contracts.* New York: Oxford University Press, 1920.

Crozier, William. *Ordnance and the World War.* New York: Scribner's, 1920.

Daggett, Aaron S. *America in the China Relief Expedition.* Kansas City: Hudson-Kimberly Publishing Company, 1903.

Daniels, Josephus. *The Wilson Era, Years of Peace.* Chapel Hill, N.C.: University of North Carolina Press, 1944.

Davis, R. H. *Cuban and Porto Rican Campaigns.* New York: C. Scribner's Sons, 1899.

Dawes, Brig. Gen. Charles G. *A Journal of the Great War.* Boston: Houghton Mifflin Company, 1921. 2 vols.

Dickson, Capt. T. C. "The U.S. Magazine Rifle, Model of 1903," *Journal of the U.S. Infantry Association,* I (July, 1904), 33–50.

Dixon, Frank Haight. *Railroads and Government.* New York: C. Scribner's Sons, 1922.

Dixon, Frank Haight, and Julius Parmalee. *War Administration of the Railways in the United States and Great Britain.* New York: Oxford University Press, 1918.

Elliott, Charles Burke. *The Philippines: To the End of the Commission Government.* Indianapolis: Bobbs-Merrill, 1917. 2 vols.

Evolution of Supply in the United States During World War I. Office, Chief of Military History. Manuscript.

Fredericks, Pierce G. *The Great Adventure.* New York: Dutton, 1960.

Friedel, Frank. *The Splendid Little War.* Boston: Little, Brown & Co., 1958.

Funston, Frederick. *Memories of Two Wars.* New York Scribner's, 1911.

George, David Lloyd. *War Memoirs.* London: Ivor Nicholson & Watson, 1933–36. 6 vols.

Gillespie, Lt. Col. James B. Renting, Requisition and Claims Service. Historical Section, Army War College, 1942. Office, Chief of Military History. Manuscript.

———. Résumé of Salvage Operations in the AEF, World War I. Historical Section, Army War College, 1942. Office, Chief of Military History. Manuscript.

Goddard, C. H., Lt. Col. Transportation Problem, AEF, World War I. Historical Section, Army War College, 1942.

Goltz, Baron Colmar von der. *The Nation in Arms.* Translated by Philip A. Ashworth. London: Hodder and Stoughton, 1914.

Graves, William S. *America's Siberian Adventure, 1918–1920.* New York: Peter Smith, 1931.

Hackworth, Green H. *Digest of International Law.* Washington, GPO, 1940–44.

Hagedorn, Herman. *Leonard Wood, A Biography.* New York and London: Harper & Bros., 1931. 2 vols.

Hagood, Johnson. *The Services of Supply: A Memoir of the Great War.* Boston and New York: Houghton Mifflin Company, 1927.

Halstead, Murat. *Full Official History of the War with Spain.* Chicago: J. S. Ziegler & Co., 1899.

Harbord, James G. *The American Army in France 1917–1919.* Boston: Little, Brown & Company, 1936.

———. "A Chief of Staff in the Theater of Operations." Address at the Army War College, 6 April 1939.

———. *Leaves from a War Diary.* New York: Dodd, Mead & Company, 1925.

Haseltine, Col. W. E. Turnarounds of Transports of the American Expeditionary Forces in France, 1917–1919. Historical Section, Army War College, 1942. Office, Chief of Military History. Manuscript.

Hendrick, Barton J. *The Life and Letters of Walter H. Page.* Garden City, N.Y.: Doubleday, Page & Co., 1922–25. 3 vols.

Hicks, James E. *Notes on United States Ordnance.* Mount Vernon, N.Y.: Published by the author, 1940.

Hines, Walker D. *War History of American Railroads.* New Haven, Conn.: Yale University Press, 1928.

History of the Third Division, United States Army, in the World War. Issued by the Division, 1920.

Hittle, James D. *The Military Staff: Its History and Development.* Harrisburg, Pa.: Military Service Publishing Co., 1944.

Holme, John G. *The Life of Leonard Wood.* Garden City, N.Y.. Doubleday, Page & Co., 1920.

Hoover, Herbert. *The Memoirs of Herbert Hoover.* New York: The Macmillan Company, 1951.

Houston, David F. *Eight Years with Wilson's Cabinet.* Garden City, N.Y.: Doubleday, Page & Co., 1926. 2 vols.

Huidekoper, Frederic L. *The Military Unpreparedness of the United States.* New York: Macmillan Company, 1916.

Hurley, Edward Nash. *The Bridge to France.* Philadelphia: J. B. Lippincott Co., 1927.

James, Marquis. *Alfred I. DuPont, The Family Rebel.* Indianapolis: Bobbs-Merrill, 1941.

Jessup, Philip C. *Elihu Root.* New York: Dodd, Mead & Co., 1938. 2 vols.

Johnson, Melvin M., Jr., and Charles T. Haven. *Ammunition: Its History, Development and Use, 1600 to 1943.* New York: W. Morrow & Co., 1943.

Johnson, Virginia Weisel. *The Unregimented General: A Biography of Nelson A. Miles.* Boston: Houghton Mifflin Company, 1962.

Kenamore, Clair. *From Vauquois Hill to Exermont.* St. Louis: Guard Publishing Co., 1919.

Kennan, George. *Campaigning in Cuba.* New York: The Century Co., 1899.

Kennan, George F. *Soviet-American Relations, 1917–1920.* Vol. II. *The Decision to Intervene.* Princeton, N.J.: Princeton University Press, 1958.

Knappen, Theodore MacFarlane. *Wings of War.* New York: G. P. Putnam's Sons, 1920.

Kreidberg, Marvin A., and Merton G. Henry. *History of Military Mobilization in the United States Army, 1775–1945.* Department of the Army Pamphlet 20–212. Washington, GPO, 1955.

Kutz, C. R. *War on Wheels: The Evolution of an Idea.* Harrisburg, Pa.. Military Service Publishing Co., 1940.

Larned, Maj. Paul. Information on the Requirements, Storage, Supply, and Transportation of Petroleum Products. Historical Section, Army War College, 1942. Office, Chief of Military History. Manuscript.

———. Résumé on the Ports of Embarkation and Ports of Debarkation, World War I. Historical Section, Army War College, 1942.

Leland, Waldo G., and Newton D. Mereness, comps. *Introduction to the American Official Sources for the Economic and Social History of the World War.* New Haven, Conn.: Yale University Press, 1926.

LeRoy, James A. *The Americans in the Philippines.* Boston: Houghton Mifflin, 1914. 2 vols.

Liddell Hart, B. H. *A History of the World War, 1914–1918.* Boston: Little, Brown and Co., 1935.

Lvddon, Col. W. G. *British War Missions to the United States, 1914–1918.* London and New York: Oxford University Press, 1938.

March, General Peyton C. *The Nation at War.* Garden City, N.Y.: Doubleday, Doran & Co., 1932.

Marcosson, Isaac. *S.O.S., America's Miracle in France.* New York: John Lane Co., 1918.

McAdoo, William Gibbs. *Crowded Years.* Boston and New York: Houghton Mifflin Company, 1931.

McCleary, Maj. Oliver S. The Shortage of Essential War Materials in the Lumber Industry and the Handling of the Labor Problem by the Army During World War I. Historical Section, Army War College, 1942. Office, Chief of Military History. Manuscript.

McEntee, Girard Lindsley. *Military History of the World War.* New York: Scribner's, 1937.

Miles, Nelson A. *Serving the Republic.* New York: Harper & Bros., 1911.

Miley, John D. *In Cuba with Shafter.* New York: Scribner's, 1899.

Millett, Francis David. *The Expedition to the Philippines.* New York: Harper and Brothers, 1899.

Millis, Walter. *Arms and Men: A Study in American Military History.* New York: Putnam, 1956.

———. *The Martial Spirit: A Study of Our War with Spain.* Boston and New York: Houghton Mifflin Co., 1921.

Mock, James R., and Evangeline Thurber. *Report on Demobilization.* Norman, Okla.: University of Oklahoma Press, 1944.

Morton, Maj. C. G. "Machine Guns in Our Army," *Journal of the U.S. Infantry Association,* I (July, 1904).

Nelson, Otto. *National Security and the General Staff.* Washington: Infantry Journal Press, 1946.

Oberholtzer, Ellis Paxson. *A History of the United States Since the Civil War.* New York: The Macmillan Co., 1937.

O'Brien, Col. James A. Regulating Stations, AEF, World War I. Historical Section, Army War College, 1942. Office, Chief of Military History. Manuscript.

Palmer, Frederick. *Bliss, Peacemaker.* New York: Dodd, Mead, 1934.

———. *John J. Pershing, General of the Armies.* Harrisburg, Pa.: The Military Service Publishing Co., 1948.

———. *Newton D. Baker.* New York: Dodd, Mead & Co., 1931.

———. *Our Greatest Battle.* New York: Dodd, Mead & Co., 1919.

Palmer, John M. *Washington—Lincoln—Wilson, Three War Statesmen.* New York: Doubleday, Doran & Co., 1930.

Parsons, William Barclay. *The American Engineers in France.* New York: D. Appleton and Co., 1920.

Paxson, Federic L. *America at War, 1917–1918.* Boston: Houghton Mifflin Co., 1939. 2 vols.

———. *American Democracy and the World War, Pre-War Years 1913–17.* Boston: Houghton Mifflin Co., 1936.

———. *American Democracy and the World War, Postwar Years, Normalcy, 1918–23.* Los Angeles: University of California Press, 1948.

Pershing, John J. *Final Report, American Expeditionary Forces.* Washington: GPO, 1920.

———. *My Experiences in the World War.* New York: Federick A. Stokes Co., 1931. 2 vols.

Pridham, C. H. B. *The Superiority of Fire, A Short History of Rifles and Machine Guns.* London: Hutchinson's Scientific and Technical Publications, 1945.

Pringle, Henry F. *The Life and Times of William Howard Taft.* New York: Farrar & Rinehart, Inc., 1939. 2 vols.

———. *Theodore Roosevelt.* New York: Harcourt, Brace & Co., 1931.

Pusey, Merlo J. *Charles Evans Hughes.* New York: The Macmillan Company, 1951. 2 vols.

Requin, Edouard Jean. *America's Race to Victory.* New York: Fred A. Stokes, 1919.

Richardson, James D. *A Compilation of the Messages and Papers of the Presidents 1789–1917.* Washington: GPO, 1896–99. 20 vols.

Risch, Erna. *Quartermaster Support of the Army: A History of the Corps, 1775–1939.* Washington: GPO, 1962.

Roosevelt, Theodore. "The Rough Riders," *Scribner's Magazine,* XXV (January, 1899).

Root, Elihu. *Military and Colonial Policy of the United States.* Cambridge, Mass.: Harvard University Press, 1916.

Salter, J. A. *Allied Shipping Control, an Experiment in International Administration.* Oxford: Clarendon Press, 1921.

Sawyer, Robert K. "Viva Villa," *Military Review* (August, 1961), 60–75.

Schwan, Maj. Theodore. *Report on the Organization of the German Army.* Washington: GPO, 1894.

Seymour, Charles. *American Diplomacy During the World War.* Baltimore: Johns Hopkins Press, 1942.

——. *The Intimate Papers of Colonel House.* Boston and New York: Houghton Mifflin Co., 1928. 3 vols.

——. *Woodrow Wilson and the World War.* New Haven, Conn.: Yale University Press, 1921.

Shanks, Maj. Gen. David C. *As They Passed Through the Port.* Washington: The Cary Publishing Co., 1927.

Sharpe, Henry G. *The Quartermaster Corps in the Year 1917 in the World War.* New York: The Century Co., 1921.

Shaw, George C. *Supply in Modern War.* Preface by J. F. C. Fuller. London: Faber and Faber, 1938.

Sherwood, Elmer W. *The Diary of a Rainbow Veteran.* Terre Haute, Ind.: Moore-Laugen Co., 1939.

Simonds, Frank H. *History of the World War.* Garden City, N.Y.: Doubleday, Page & Co., 1920. 5 vols.

Sims, William Snowden, and Burton J. Hendrick. *Victory at Sea.* New York: Doubleday, Page & Co., 1920.

Spaulding, Oliver L. *The United States Army in War and Peace.* New York: G. P. Putnam Sons, 1937.

—— and John W. Wright. *The Second Division American Expeditionary Force in France, 1917–1919.* New York: The Historical Committee, 2d Division Association, 1937.

Splawn, Walter Marshall William. *Government Ownership and Operation of Railroads.* New York: Macmillan Company, 1928.

Stimson, Henry L, and McGeorge Bundy. *On Active Service in Peace and War.* New York: Harpers, 1948.

Tansill, Charles C. *America Goes to War.* Boston: Little, Brown & Co., 1938.

Taylor, A. J. P. *The Struggle for Mastery in Europe, 1848–1918.* Oxford: The Clarendon Press, 1954.

Temperley, H. W. V. *A History of the Peace Conference in Paris.* London: Oxford University Press and Hodder & Stoughton, 1920–24. 6 vols.

Titherington, Richard H. *A History of the Spanish-American War of 1898.* New York: D. Appleton and Co., 1900.

United States Army in World War II:
  Smith, R. Elbertson. *The Army and Economic Mobilization.* Washington: GPO, 1959.
  Vigneras, Marcel. *Rearming the French.* Washington: GPO, 1957.

War Department. *Order of Battle of the U.S. Land Forces in the World War.* Vol. I: *American Expeditionary Forces.* Vol. II: *American Expeditionary Forces.* Vol. 3, Part 1: *Zone of the Interior.* Vol. 3, Part 2: *Zone of the Interior.* Washington: GPO, 1937, 1931, 1949, 1949.

Wheeler, Joseph. *The Santiago Campaign.* New York: D. Biddle, 1898.
Wilgus, William J. *Transporting the A.E.F. in Western Europe.* New York: Columbia University Press, 1931.
Willoughby, William Franklin. *Government Organization in War Time and After.* New York: D. Appleton and Co., 1919.
Wood, William, and Ralph Henry Gabriel. *The Pageant of America: In Defense of Liberty.* New Haven, Conn.: Yale University Press, 1928.
Woytinsky, W. S., and E. S. Woytinsky. *World Population and Production Trends and Outlook.* New York: Twentieth Century Fund, 1953.

PART FOUR

Logistics of Global Warfare

Manuscript Sources

Eccles, Rear Adm. Henry E. (USN Ret). Memorandum for the author, 9 July 1963.
U.S. Army. OAC GSUSA Staff Study, Organization of the Department of the Army, 15 July 1948.
————. The Organizational History of the Munitions Board, 24 August 1948. Office of the Chief of Military History.

Printed Primary Sources and Documents

Department of the Army (War Department).
   War Department Circular 256, Reorganization of Corps Headquarters and Organic Troops, 16 October, 1943.
   Department of Army Field Manual 100–10, Field Service Regulations, September, 1949.
   War Department Technical Manual 38–42, Disposition of Excess and Surplus Property in Oversea Commands, February 1946.
Department of State. Office of the Foreign Liquidation Commissioner. Report to Congress on Foreign Surplus Disposal, January 1947.
Eisenhower, General of the Army Dwight D. *Report of the Supreme Commander to the Combined Chiefs of Staff on the Operations in Europe of the Allied Expeditionary Forces 6 June 1944 to 8 May 1945.* Washington, n.d.
Lutes, LeRoy, Lt. Gen. *Logistics in World War II: Final Report of Army Service Forces.* November, 1948.
Office of Contract Settlement. War Contract Terminations and Settlements. Washington, 1944–1947. 10 vols.
————. Report by the Director of Control Settlement to the Congress, 5th Report, October 1945.
Reeder, Maj. Gen. W. O., Assistant Chief of Staff, G–4. "Supply Management," Lecture, 1 April 1952, at the Industrial College of the Armed Forces. ICAF No. L52–135.
U.S. Army
   Annual Report of the Army Service Forces, 1945.
   Army Service Forces Manual 419, Disposition of Excess and Surplus Army Service Forces Military Property in the United States.
   Biennial Reports of the Chief of Staff of the United States Army, 1 July 1943 to 20 June 1945, to the Secretary of the Army.
   Continental Advance Section, ETO, History of CONAD. Heidelberg, 1945.
   Final Report of the Chief of Staff, U.S. Army, to the Secretary of the Army, 7 February 1948.

U.S. Army—Continued
  First U.S. Army.   Report of Operations, 20 August 1943 to 1 August 1944.   G–4 Division,
    NATOUSA–MTOUSA.   Logistical History of NATOUSA–MTOUSA, 11 August
    1942–30 November 1945.   Naples, 1946.
  G–4, GSUSA, File 400.703.   Disposal of Surplus.
  Logistics Reports: G–4, GSUSA Monthly Progress Reports.   G–4 Reviews of the Month.
    Logistical Operations Summaries.   (These are the same report under different titles).
  Omaha Beach Provisional Engineer Special Brigade Group.   Operations Report, Neptune.
  Report of the Chief of Transportation, Army Service Forces, in World War II.
Secretary of the Army.
  Annual Report, 1948.
  Annual Report, Fiscal Year 1949.   Included with the Second Report of the Secretary of
    Defense, 1949.
Secretary of Defense.   First Report, 1948.
United States Government.
  50 U.S. Code Annotated, Section 1.
  Public Law 11, 77th Congress, 55 U.S. Statutes at Large 32.
  Public Law 457, 78th Congress, 2d Session.   Surplus Property Act.
U.S. House of Representatives.
  Document No. 432, 79th Congress, 2d Session.   Appendix V, British Master Agreement,
    23 February 1942, of 21st Report to Congress on Lend-Lease Operations.
  Document No. 663, 79th Congress, 2d Session.   22d Report to Congress on Lend-Lease
    Administration.
  Reports No. 1767, 1873, 2081, 2148, 2246, 77th Congress, 2d Session.   Interim Reports
    of Special Committee No. 3 on Materiel, Procurement and Personnel, House Com-
    mittee on Military Affairs.
  Report No. 2729, 79th Congress, 2d Session.   Special Committee on Postwar Economic
    Policy and Planning.   Final Report, Reconversion Experience and Current Economic
    Problems.
U.S. Senate.
  Hearings Before Special Senate Committee Investigating the National Defense Program.
    79th Congress, 1st Session.
  Report No. 10, Part 5, 78th Congress, 1st Session. Additional Report of the Special
    Committee Investigating the National Defense Program.   Renegotiation of War
    Contracts.
  Report No. 10, Part 13, 78th Congress, 1st Session.   Additional Report. . . . Trans-
    portation.
  Report No. 110, Part 5, 79th Congress, 2d Session.   Additional Report. . . . Investi-
    gations Overseas–Surplus Property Abroad.

Secondary Sources

Army Service Forces, International Division.   Lend-Lease as of September 10, 1945.   Office,
  Chief of Military History.   14 typescript volumes.
Automobile Manufacturers Association.   *Freedom's Arsenal.* Detroit: Published by the
  Association, 1950.
Ballantine, Duncan S.   *U.S. Naval Logistics in the Second World War.* Princeton, N.J.:
  Princeton University Press, 1949.
Baxter, James P., 3d.   *Scientists Against Time.* Boston: Little, Brown and Co., 1946.
Blum, Albert A.   "Birth and Death of the M-Day Plan," in Harold Stein, ed., *American
  Civil-Military Decisions.*   A Book of Case Studies.   A Twentieth Century Fund Study
  published in cooperation with the Inter-University Case Program by University of
  Alabama Press. 1963.

Bradley, Omar N. *A Soldier's Story.* Henry Holt and Company, 1951.

Brigante, John E. *The Feasibility Dispute.* Washington, 1950.

Brookings Institution. *Major Problems in United States Foreign Policy, 1947.* Washington: The Brookings Institution, 1947.

Bryant, Arthur. *The Turn of the Tide.* New York: Doubleday & Co., Inc., 1957.

Butcher, Harry C. *My Three Years With Eisenhower.* New York: Simon and Schuster, 1946.

Campbell, Levin H. *The Industry-Ordnance Team.* New York: McGraw-Hill Book Co., Inc., 1946.

Catton, Bruce. *The War Lords of Washington.* New York: Harcourt, Brace, 1948.

Chandler, Lester V., and Donald H. Wallace. *Economic Mobilization and Stabilization.* New York: Henry Holt and Co., 1951.

Chief Historian, EUCOM. Disposal of Surplus Property, 1 July 1946–30 June 1947. Office, Chief of Military History. Manuscript.

Churchill, Winston S. *The Second World War.* Vol V: *Closing the Ring.* Vol VI: *Triumph and Tragedy.* Boston: Houghton Mifflin, 1951, 1953.

Civilian Production Administration. *Industrial Mobilization for War: History of the War Production Board and Predecessor Agencies, 1940–1945.* Vol I: *Program and Administration.* Washington, 1947.

Clark, Mark W. *Calculated Risk.* New York: Harper and Brothers, 1950.

Clay, Lucius D. "The Army Supply Program," *Fortune,* XXVII (February, 1943).

Connery, Robert H. *The Navy and Industrial Mobilization in World War II.* Princeton, N.J.: Princeton University Press, 1951.

Craf, John R. *A Survey of the American Economy, 1940–1946.* New York: North River Press, 1947.

Craven, Wesley F., and James L. Cate, eds. *The Army Air Forces in World War II.* Vol VI: *Men and Planes.* Chicago: University of Chicago Press, 1954.

Crowell, Benedict, and Robert Forrest Wilson. *How America Went to War.* New Haven, Conn.: Yale University Press. 6 vols.

Dawson, Raymond H. *The Decision to Aid Russia, 1941.* Chapel Hill, N.C.: University of North Carolina Press, 1959.

Eccles, Rear Adm. Henry E. (USN Ret). *Operational Naval Logistics.* Harrisburg, Pa.: The Stackpole Co., 1950.

————. *Logistics in the National Defense.* Harrisburg, Pa.: The Stackpole Co., 1959.

Eisenhower, Dwight D. *Crusade in Europe.* New York: Doubleday, 1948.

Greenfield, Kent Roberts, ed. *Command Decisions.* New York: Harcourt, Brace and Company, 1959.

————. *The Historian and the Army.* New Brunswick, N.J.: Rutgers University Press, 1954.

Groves, Leslie R. *Now It Can Be Told: The Story of the Manhattan Project.* New York: Harper's, 1962.

Hagood, Johnson. *The Services of Supply.* Boston and New York: Houghton Mifflin Company, 1927.

Hamilton, Capt. James W. "Operation Reverse," *Army Transportation Journal,* II (September, 1946).

Haydon, Frederick S. "War Department Organization, August 1941–March 1942," *Military Affairs,* XVI (Spring and Fall, 1952).

Heiss, Brig. Gen. Gerson K. "Operation Roll-up," *Ordnance,* XXXVI (September-October, 1951).

Hewlett, Richard G, and Oscar E. Anderson, Jr. *The New World, 1939/1946.* Vol I: *A History of the United States Atomic Energy Commission.* University Park, Pa.. Pennsylvania State University Press, 1962.

Hunt, Pearson, J., and others. *Problems of Accelerating Aircraft Production During World War II.* Boston. 1946.

Huston, James A. *Biography of a Battalion*. Gering, Nebr.: Courier Press, 1950.

———. "The Red Ball Rolls Again," *U.S. Army Combat Forces Journal* (August, 1955), 38–44.

———. Airborne Operations. Office, Chief of Military History. Manuscript.

Industrial College of the Armed Forces. *Economics of National Security*, XI.

Ingersoll, Ralph. *Top Secret*. New York: Harcourt, Brace & Co., 1946.

Janeway, Eliot. *The Struggle for Survival*. In *The Chronicles of America* Series. New Haven, Conn.: Yale University Press, 1951.

Kearns, Col. E. B., Jr. "Quartermaster Corps in the Far East," *The Quartermaster Review*, XXVIII (May–June, 1949).

Kennedy, Sir John. *The Business of War*. New York: Morrow, 1958.

Kreidberg, Marvin A., and Merton G. Henry. *History of Military Mobilization in the United States Army, 1775–1945*. Department of the Army Pamphlet 20–212. Washington: GPO, 1955.

Lane, Frederic C., and others. *Ships for Victory*. Baltimore: Johns Hopkins Press, 1951.

Larkin, Thomas B. "Maintaining the American Soldier," *The Military Engineer*, XL (January, 1948).

Legere, Lawrence J., Jr. Unification of the Armed Forces. Unpublished Ph.D. dissertation, Harvard University, 1950. Copy in Office, Chief of Military History.

Leigh, Randoph. *48 Million Tons to Eisenhower*. Washington: *The Infantry Journal* Press, 1945.

———. *American Enterprise in Europe; The Role of the SOS in the Defeat of Germany*. Paris: Imprimateur par Bellenand, etc., 1945.

Leighton, Richard M. "Overlord Revisited: An Interpretation of American Strategy in the European War, 1942–1944," *The American Historical Review*, LXVII (July, 1963).

Lodge, O. R. *The Recapture of Guam*. *The Marine Corps Monograph* Series. Washington: GPO, 1954.

March, Peyton C. *The Nations at War*. Garden City, N.Y.: Doubleday, Doran & Co., 1932.

Marp. Lt. Donald. "Pilgrims of 1946," *Army Transportation Journal*, II (May, 1946).

Marshall, S. L. A. *The Soldier's Load and the Mobility of a Nation*. Washington: Combat Forces Press, 1950.

Miller, John Perry. *Pricing of Military Procurements*. New Haven, Conn.: Yale University Press, 1949.

Millis, Walter. *Arms and Men: A Study in American Military History*. New York: Putnam, 1956.

Montgomery, Bernard L. Field Marshal the Viscount of Alamein. *Memoirs of Field Marshall Montgomery of Alamein, K.G.* Cleveland: World Publishing Co., 1958.

———. *Normandy to the Baltic*. Boston: Houghton Mifflin Co., 1948.

Morgan, Lt. Gen. Sir Frederick. *Overture to Overlord*. New York: Doubleday, 1950.

Morison, Samuel E. *Strategy and Compromise*. Boston: Little, Brown and Co., 1958.

———. *The Two-Ocean War: A Short History of the United States Navy in the Second World War*. 1st ed. Boston: Little, Brown & Co., 1963.

Nelson, Donald M. *Arsenal of Democracy*. New York: Harcourt, Brace & Co., 1946.

Nelson, Otto L. *National Security and the General Staff*. Washington, Infantry Journal Press, 1946.

Nicholas, Jack D., George B. Peckett, and William O. Spears, Jr. *The Joint and Combined Staff Officer's Manual*. Harrisburg, Pa.: The Stackpole Co, 1959.

New York University Conference of Problems of Termination and Reconversion. Chicago, 1944.

Novick, David Melvin Ashen, and W. C. Truppner. *Wartime Production Controls*. New York, Columbia University Press, 1949.

O'Brien, John Lord, and Manly Fleishman. "The War Production Board Administrative Policies and Procedures," *George Washington Law Review*, XIII (Decenber, 1944).

Office of the Chief Engineer, General Headquarters, Army Forces Pacific. *Engineers of the Southwest Pacific: 1941–1945.* Vol. VIII: *Critique.* Washington, GPO, n.d. 8 vols.

Ogorkiewics, Richard M. *Armor, A History of Mechanized Forces.* New York: Praeger, 1960.

Patton, George S. *War As I Knew It.* Boston: Houghton Mifflin Co., 1947.

Rochford, Maj. Charles E. "The Overseas Supply Division at Ports of Embarkation," *Military Review,* XXVIII (June, 1948).

Rossen, S. McKee. *The Combined Boards of the Second World War.* New York, 1951.

Schon, Hebert L. "The Return of Our War Dead," *The Quartermaster Review,* XXVI (July–August, 1946).

Sherwood, Robert E. *Roosevelt and Hopkins: An Intimate History.* New York: Harper & Brothers, 1948.

Smith, Walter Bedell. *Eisenhower's Six Great Decisions.* New York: Longmans, Greene, 1956.

Smyth, Henry DeWolf. *Atomic Energy for Military Purposes: The Official Report on the Development of the Atomic Bomb Under the Auspices of the United States Government, 1940–1945.* Princeton, N.J.: Princeton University Press, 1945.

Smithies, Arthur. *The Budgetary Process in the United States.* New York: McGraw-Hill, 1955.

Sparrow, Maj. John C. *History of Personnel Demobilization in the United States Army.* Department of the Army Pamphlet 20–210. Washington: GPO, 1951.

Staley, Eugene. "The Myth of the Continents," *Foreign Affairs,* XIX (April, 1944).

Stettinius, Edward R., Jr. *Lend-Lease: Weapons for Victory.* New York: The Macmillan Co., 1944.

Stimson, Henry L., and McGeorge Bundy. *On Active Service in Peace and War.* New York: Harper & Bros., 1947.

Stout, Wesley W. *Secret.* Detroit: Chrysler Corp., 1947.

Strum, Lt. Col. W. C. "Disposition of Surplus Property," *The Quartermaster Review,* XXVI (May–June, 1947)

Sykes, Col. J. F. Jr. "Logistics and World War II Army Strategy," *Military Review,* XXXV (February, 1956)

United Kingdom Civil Series: History of the Second World War: [London: Her Majesty's Stationery Office and Longmans, Green & Co.]

    Behrens, C. B. A. *Merchant Shipping and the Demands of War.* 1955.

    Hall, Duncan H. *North American Supply.* 1956.

    Hall, Duncan H., and C. C. Wrigley. *Studies of Overseas Supply.* 1956.

    Hancock, W. K., and M. M. Gowing. *British War Economy.* 1949.

    Hargreaves, E. L., and M. M. Gowing. *Civil Industry and Trade.* 1952.

UNITED STATES ARMY IN WORLD WAR II [Printed by Government Printing Office]:

    Greenfield, Kent Roberts, Robert R. Palmer, and Bell I. Wiley. *The Organization of Ground Combat Troops.* 1947.

    Harrison, Gordon A. *Cross Channel Attack.* 1951.

    Holley, I. B., jr. *Buying Aircraft: Procurement of Air Matériel in World War II.* 1964.

    Howe, George F. *Northwest Africa: Seizing the Initative in the West.* 1957.

    Leighton, Richard M., and Robert W. Coakley. *Global Logistics and Strategy, 1940–1943.* 1955.

    MacDonald, Charles B. *The Siegfried Line Campaign.* 1963.

    Matloff, Maurice. *Strategic Planning for Coalition Warfare, 1943–1944.* 1959.

    Matloff, Maurice, and Edwin M. Snell. *Strategic Planning for Coalition Warfare, 1941–1942.* 1953.

    Miller, John, jr. CARTWHEEL: *The Reduction of Rabaul.* 1959.

    ———. *Guadalcanal: The First Offensive.* 1949.

    Millet, John D. *The Organization and Role of the Army Service Forces.* 1954.

    Milner, Samuel. *Victory in Papua.* 1957.

UNITED STATES ARMY IN WORLD WAR II—Continued

Morton, Louis. *The Fall of the Philippines.* 1953.

———. *Strategy and Command: The First Two Years.* 1962.

Motter, T. H. Vail. *The Persian Corridor and Aid to Russia.* 1952.

Palmer, Robert R., Bell I. Wiley, and William R. Keast. *The Procurement and Training of Ground Combat Troops.* 1948.

Pictorial Record: The War Against Japan. 1952.

Pictorial Record: The War Against Germany: Europe and Adjacent Areas. 1951.

Pogue, Forrest C. *The Supreme Command.* 1954.

Risch, Erna. *The Quartermaster Corps: Organization, Supply and Services.* 1953. 2 vols.

Romanus, Charles F., and Riley Sunderland. *Stilwell's Command Problems.* 1955.

———. *Stilwell's Mission to China.* 1953.

———. *Time Runs Out in CBI.* 1959.

Ruppenthal, Roland G. *Logistical Support of the Armies.* 1953, 1959. 2 vols.

Smith, Clarence McKittrick. *The Medical Department: Hospitalization and Evacuation, Zone of Interior.* 1956.

Smith, R. Elberton. *The Army and Economic Mobilization.* 1959.

Smith, Robert Ross. *The Approach to the Philippines.* 1953.

Stauffer, Alvin P. *The Quartermaster Corps: Operations in the War Against Japan.* 1956.

Terrett, Dulany. *The Signal Corps: The Emergency (To December 1941).* 1956.

Thompson, George Raynor, and others. *The Signal Corps: The Test (December 1941 to July 1943).* 1957.

Thompson, Harry C., and Lida Mayo. *The Ordnance Department: Procurement and Supply.* 1960.

Treadwell, Mattie E. *The Women's Army Corps.* 1954.

Vigneras, Marcel. *Rearming the French.* 1957.

Wardlow, Chester. *The Transportation Corps: Movements, Training, and Supply.* 1956.

———. *The Transportation Corps: Responsibilities, Organization, and Operations.* 1951.

Watson, Mark Skinner. *Chief of Staff: Prewar Plans and Preparations.* 1950.

United States Naval Operations in World War II:

Morison, Samuel Eliot. Vol. II: *Operations in North African Waters, October 1942–June 1943.* Boston: Little, Brown & Co., 1947.

———. Vol. VI: *Breaking the Bismarcks Barrier, 22 July 1942–1 May 1944.* Boston: Little, Brown & Co., 1950.

———. Vol. VIII: *New Guinea and the Marianas, March 1944–August 1944.* Boston: Little, Brown & Co., 1953.

———. Vol. XI: *The Invasion of France and Germany.* Boston: Little, Brown & Co., 1957.

———. Vol. XIII: *The Liberation of the Philippines: Luzon, Mindanao, the Visayas, 1944–1945.* Boston: Little Brown, & Co., 1959.

U.S. Bureau of the Budget. *The United States at War: Development and Administration of the War Program by the Federal Government.* Washington: GPO, 1946.

U.S. War Production Board, Steel Division. *Steel Expansion for War.* Reprint. Cleveland: Steel, 1945.

Vagts, Alfred. *Landing Operations.* Harrisburg, Pa.: Military Service Publishing Co., 1946.

———. *Loading Operations.* Harrisburg, Pa.: Military Service Publishing Co., 1946.

Walton, Francis. *Miracle of World War II.* New York: Macmillan, 1956.

Willoughby, Charles A., and John Chamberlin. *MacArthur, 1941–1951.* New York: McGraw-Hill, 1954.

Wilmot, Chester. *The Struggle for Europe.* New York: Harpers, 1952.

Yoshpe, Harry B. "Economic Mobilization Between Wars," *Military Affairs,* XV, No. 4 (Winter, 1951) and XVI, No. 2 (Summer, 1952).

PART FIVE

The Shadow of Conflict

Manuscript Sources

Interview. Author with Hon. Archibald S. Alexander, Under Secretary of the Army, 17 April 1952.
————. Author with Col. D. L. Coates, Executive Office, Supply Division, G–4, 27 November 1952.
————. Author with Colonel Dean E. Coonley, 3 September 1952.
————. Author with William M. Gray, G–4, Distribution Division, Issues Section, 20 November 1952.
————. Author with Lt. Gen. Thomas B. Larkin, Assistant Chief of Staff, G–4, April 1952.
————. Author with Lt. Col. E. Carroll McHenry, Supply Division, G–4, 27 November 1952.
————. Author with Lt. Col. Victor H. Moore, Deputy Executive, Office, Armed Services Petroleum Purchasing Agency, 5 February 1953.
————. Author with Maj. Gen. William O. Reeder, Deputy Assistant Chief of Staff, G–4, December 1952.
————. Author with Brig. Gen. Paul F. Young, 15 December 1952.
Second Logistical Command (Pusan), Monthly Activities Reports.
United States Army.
   Chief of Transportation. Disposition Form to Chief of Military History, subject: Data on Monthly Cargo Shipments from POE's. 25 February 1952.
   Comptroller. Report on Measures and Recommendations of Major Importance to the Improvement of the Army, 1 July 1950–30 December 1952.
   Corps of Engineers. Corps of Engineers Historical Summary, 25 June 1950–8 September 1951. 30 October 1951.
   General Staff. G–4 Historical Summary, 1951–1952.
United States Department of Defense. Staff Study, Department of Defense Operations under MDAP, June 1952.

Printed Primary Sources and Documents

Commission on Organization of the Executive Branch of the Government. Task Force Report on National Security Organization, January 1949, and National Security Organization, February 1949.
Department of the Army.
   Field Manual 100–10, "Field Service Regulations Administration," September 1949.
   Field Manual 110–10, "Joint Logistics Policy and Guidance," June 1952.
   Regulations 145–20, "Reserve Officers' Training Corps Supply and Equipment," 11 October 1948.
   Special Regulations 140–420–1, "Organized Reserve Corps, Supply and Accounting Procedures," 18 May 1949.
   Special Regulations 145–420–10, "Reserve Officers Training Corps, Requisitioning and Distribution of Quartermaster Items for ROTC Instruction," 13 May 1949.
   Special Regulations 145–425–5, "Reserve Officers Training Corps, Droppage Allowance for Items of Nonexpendable Property Issued to Reserve Officers Training Corps," 20 July 1950.
   Special Regulations 725–10–2, "Issue of Supplies and Equipment, Processing Requisitions," 8 June 1949.
   Special Regulations 730–5–1, "Oversea Supply, Distribution," 15 July 1949.

Department of Defense.
    Directive 5128–7, Charter of the Research and Development Board, 5 May 1952.
Department of State.
    Aid to Greece and Turkey: A Collection of State Papers Supplement to the Department of State Bulletin,
        XVI, No. 409A, 4 May 1947.
    Department of State Bulletin, XXII, 26 June 1950.
    Foreign Service Dispatch No. 8. American Embassy, Rome, to Department of State,
        subject: Arrangement for Lines of Communication in Italy, concluded 29 June 1951.
        2 July 1951.
    Third Report to Congress on Assistance to Greece and Turkey.   Department of State Publication
        No. 3278.
    Fifth Report to Congress on Assistance to Greece and Turkey, period ending 30 September 1948.
        Department of State Publication No. 3371.
    Sixth Report to Congress on Assistance to Greece and Turkey, period ending 31 December 1948.
        Department of State Publication No. 3467.
    Seventh Report to Congress on Assistance to Greece and Turkey, period ending 31 March 1949.
        Department of State Publication No. 3594.
    The Story in Documents.   Department of State Publication No. 3556.   March 1950.
    Eighth Report to Congress on Assistance to Greece and Turkey, period ending 30 June 1949.
        Department of State Publication No. 3674.
    United States Policy in the Korean Conflict, July 1950–February 1951.   Department of State
        Publication 4263, September 1951.
    *Third Semiannual Report to Congress on the Mutual Defense Assistance Program, October 6, 1950 to
        March 31, 1951.*   Department of State Publication No. 4291.   July 1951.
    North Atlantic Treaty—Accession of Greece and Turkey.   Department of State Publication
        No. 4541.
Executive Order No. 10338.   "Mutual Security Act of 1951."   4 April 1952.
Munitions Board Committee on Facilities and Services.   Report to the Secretary of Defense
    on Elimination of Duplication and Overlapping of Facilities and Services, FY 1949.
Munitions Board Order 51–34, "Munitions Board Organization and Functions," 10 April
    1954.   Copy in Office of the Chief of Military History.
Readiness for Mobilization: A Report on the Role and Activities of the National Security
    Resources Board, 1947–1952.   12 January 1953.   Copy in Office of the Chief of
    Military History.
Secretary of the Army.   Annual Reports of the Secretary of the Army for the years 1948 and
    1949.
Secretary of Defense.
    Amendment to Directive, subject: Munitions Board Charter, 13 September 1950.   Copy
        in Office of the Chief of Military History.
    Memorandum for Secretaries of the Army, Navy and Air Force; the Joint Chiefs of Staff;
        Chairman, Munitions Board; Chairman, Research and Development Board.   Subject:
        Department of Defense Supply System, 17 November 1949.
    First Report of the Secretary of Defense, 1948, with Appendices.
    Second Report of the Secretary of Defense, 1949.
    Semiannual Report of the Secretary of Defense, 1 January–30 June 1951.
Strategic Bombing Survey.   *The Effects of Strategic Bombing on the German War Economy.*   Wash-
    ington, 1945.
———.   *Summary Report: The War Against Japan.*   Washington, 1945.
Supreme Allied Commander, Europe.   First Annual Report, 2 April 1952.
———.   Second Annual Report, 30 May 1953.
United States Army.
    Command and General Staff College, Sub-course 60–27, Logistics (Army)—Theater of
        Operations.

United Stated Army—Continued
   Directory and Station List of the United States Army, 1 November 1951.
   Eighth United States Army, War Diary and Command Reports, 1950–1953.
   U.S. Army General Staff. G–4 Historical Summary, 1951–1952.
   ———. G–4 Review of the Month, December 1947–January 1948. 29 February 1948.
   ———. G–4 Review of the Month. 31 December 1948.
   ———. G–4 Review of the Month, 1 January 1949–1 July 1949.
   ———. Logistical Operations Summary, 1 July 1950.
   U.S. Army Group, Greece, Brief History of USAGG, Procurement, 24 May 1947–31 August 1949.
   U.S. Army Logistics Support Panel, Report, 15 October 1951.
   Office of The Adjutant General, Statistical and Accounting Branch. Weekly Estimate of Army Command Strength as of 26 June 1950. 3 July 1960.
   Office of the Chief of Finance. Monthly Financial Reports.
   Office of the Comptroller, Management Division. Staff Study, subject: Organization of Department of the Army. 15 July 1948.
   U.S. Army Troop Program, 1 February 1949.
U.S. European Command. EUCOM Annual Narrative Reports, 1950, 1951.
United States Government.
   Public Law 253, 80th Congress, National Security Act of 1947.
   Public Law 267 (61 U.S. Stat.), 80th Congress, Military Appropriation Act, 1948.
   Public Law 216, 81st Congress, Amendments to National Security Act of 1947.
   Public Law 581, 81st Congress, Army Organization Act of 1950.
United States House of Representatives.
   Document No. 534, 80th Congress, 2d Session, 16 February 1948. Assistance to Greece and Turkey, 2d Report, covering period to 31 December 1947.
   Hearings before the House Committee on Armed Services, 6–21 October 1949. The National Defense Program, Unification and Strategy. 81st Congress, 1st Session.
   Hearings before House Committee on Foreign Affairs. Mutual Security Act Extension. 82d Congress, 2d Session.
   Hearings before House Committee on Foreign Affairs. Mutual Security Act Extension. 83d Congress, 1st Session.
   Hughes, Gen. E. S., before House Subcommittee on Appropriations, 14 March 1947. 80th Congress, 1st Session.
   McLain, Lt. Gen. R. S., Comptroller of the Army. Statement before the Subcommittee on Procurement of the House Armed Services Committee, 15 February 1952. 82d Congress, 2d Session.
   Report 187, Hearings before a Subcommittee of the House Committee on Armed Services, 1–20 March 1950. 81st Congress, 2d Session.
   Ring, Rear Adm. Morton L. Testimony before the House Subcommittee of the House Committee on Armed Services Inquiring into Military Supply Policies and Practices, 12 February 1952. 82d Congress, 2d Session.
United States Military Advisory Group to the Republic of Korea. Semiannual Reports.
United States Military Government of Germany. Monthly Report of the Military Governor, U.S. Zone, No. 5, 20 December 1945.
   ———. Monthly Report of the Military Governor, U.S. Zone, No. 19, 1–31 January 1947.
United States President (Truman). Reports to Congress on the Mutual Security Program, Third Report for Six Months Ending 31 December 1952.
United States Senate.
   Hearings before Senate Subcommittee on Appropriations on the Department of Defense Appropriations for 1953. 82d Congress, 2d Session.
   Hearings before Subcommittee No. 2 of the Senate Committee on Armed Services, April 1953. Ammunition Shortages in the Armed Services. 83d Congress, 1st Session.

United States Senate—Continued
   Hearings before the Senate Committee on Armed Services and the Committee on Foreign
      Relations. Military Situation in the Far East (The "MacArthur Hearings"). 82d
      Congress, 1st Session.
   Hearings before Senate Committee on Foreign Relations. Mutual Security Act of 1952.
      82d Congress, 2d Session.
   Marshall, George C., Secretary of Defense. Testimony before the Senate Committee on
      Armed Services and Foreign Relations, 8 May 1951. 82d Congress, 2d Session.
   Report from the Senate Committee on Armed Services. Army Organization Act of
      1950, 2 June 1950. Report 1776. 81st Congress, 2d Session.

Secondary Sources

Alexander, Lt. Col. R.P., and Capt. Avery E. Kolg. "A New Concept in Military Railroad
      Service," *National Defense Transportation Journal* (March–April, 1951), 55.
Armstrong, Maj. Gen. George E. "Military Medicine in Korea," *The Military Surgeon*, CX
      (January, 1952), 10–11.
The Army Almanac: A Book of Facts Concerning the United States Army. Harrisburg, Pa.: Mili-
      tary Service Publishing Co., 1950.
Army Transportation Journal, I (January, 1946), 10. "Bringing 'Em Back."
Automobile Manufacturers Association. *Freedom's Arsenal.* Detroit: Automobile Manu-
      facturers Association, 1950.
Balzak, S. S., V. F. Vasyutin, and Ya. G. Feigin. *Economic Geography of the USSR.* New
      York: Macmillan, 1949.
Baya, Lt. Col. G. Emery. "Army Organization Act of 1950," *Army Information Digest*, IV
      (August, 1950).
————. An Explanation of the Army Organization Act of 1950. Prepared in the Man-
      agement Division, Office of the Comptroller of the Army. Copy in Office, Chief of
      Military History.
Beebe, Gilbert W., and Michael F. DeBakey. *Battle Casualties: Incidence, Mortality, and
      Logistic Considerations.* Springfield, Ill.: Thomas, 1952.
Boleyn, Lt. Col. Paul T. "Logistical Organization for an Overseas Theater," *Military Review*,
      XXXI (May, 1951) 36–40.
Booth, Brig, Gen. Donald P. "The Role of the JCS in the Generation of Materiel Require-
      ments," Industrial College of the Armed Forces, 13 October 1948. ICAF No.
      L49–29.
Bower, R. H. "Helicopters for the Army," *Aeroplane*, Vol. 83, No. 2141 (1 August 1952),
      156–57.
Brodie, Bernard. "Strategic Implications of the North Atlantic Pact," *Yale Review*, XXXIX
      (Winter, 1950), 193–208.
Brookings Institution. *Major Problems of United States Foreign Policy, 1949–1950.* Prepared by
      the International Studies Group. Washington: The Brookings Institution, 1949.
Brown, Wm. Adams, and Redvers Opie. *American Foreign Assistance.* Washington: Brook-
      ings Institution, 1953.
Buerger, Lt. (j.g.) Paul T. "Medical Support for Mountain Fighting in Korea," The
      Military Surgeon, CIX (December, 1951), 698–99.
Burleson, Maj. D. L., "Ration-Run, Korean Style," *Canadian Army Journal*, (April, 1951), 21.
Cameron, Meribeth E., Thomas H. D. Mahoney, and George E. McReynolds. *China, Japan
      and the Powers.* New Haven, Conn.: Yale University Press, 1948.
Campbell, John C. *The U.S. in World Affairs, 1945–1947.* Published for the Council on
      Foreign Relations. Harper & Bros., 1947.
————. *The U.S. in World Affairs, 1948–1949.* Published for the Council on Foreign Rela-
      tions. Harper & Bros., 1949.

Chinese Ministry of Information. *China Handbook.* New York: Macmillan, 1950.

Clay, Lucius D. *Decision in Germany.* New York: Doubleday, 1950.

Coats, James G. "The Supply Distribution Cycle," *Military Review,* XXXII, No. 1 (April, 1952). 44–52.

Combat Forces Journal, III (April, 1953). "Report on the Eighth Army."

Cressey, George B. *Asia's Lands and Peoples.* 2d ed. New York: McGraw-Hill, 1951.

Dallin, David J. *Soviet Russia and the Far East.* New Haven, Conn.: Yale University Press, 1948.

Denniston, Col. Alfred B. "Some Accomplishments of Unification in the Field of Logistics," *Military Review,* (April, 1951).

Dobb, Maurice. *Soviet Economic Development Since 1917.* London, Routledge & Paul, 1948.

Ely, Louis B. *The Red Army Today.* Harrisburg, Pa.: Military Services Publishing Co., 1951.

Feldman, Maj. Gen. Herman. "Logistic Support for the Unified Command and Overseas Theater," *Military Review,* XXXI (July, 1951), 3–10.

Fox, Lt. Ted. "Division Combat Medical Service," *The Military Surgeon* (May, 1951), 427–29.

Fudge, Lt. Col. Russel O. "Turks' Friends and Advisors," *U.S. Army Ground Combat Forces Journal,* II (June, 1952), 30–32.

Hargrave, Thomas J. "Agency of Preparedness," *The Quartermaster Review,* XXVII (March–April 1948).

———. "Security Through Planning," *Ordnance,* XXXII (January–February, 1948), 238–39.

Henry, Lt. Col. Charles W. "The Ammunition Supply System," *Combat Forces Journal,* II (January, 1952), 28–32.

Holmes, Brig. Gen Noel G. "The Ordnance Ammunition Center," *Ordnance,* XXXVII (September–October, 1952), 264–69.

Howard, Col. R. A., Jr. "The Munitions Board," *The Quartermaster Review,* XXX (March–April, 1951).

Jacques, Philippe G. "The Joint Chiefs of Staff," *The Quartermaster Review,* XXIV (January–February, 1950).

Johnston, Col. Kilbourne. "Department of the Army Reorganized," *Army Information Digest* (December, 1948).

Joint U.S. Military Advisory and Planning Group. Brief History of JUSMAPG, 1 January 1948–31 August 1949. Reports and Records Center.

Lauterback, Richard E. *Through Russia's Back Door.* New York: Harper & Bros., 1946.

Legere, Lawrence J., Jr. Unification of the Armed Forces. Unpublished Ph.D. dissertation, Harvard University, 1950. Copy in Office, Chief of Military History.

Leigh, Randolph. *48 Million Tons to Eisenhower.* Washington: *The Infantry Journal Press,* 1945.

Lutes, Lt. Gen. LeRoy. "The Munitions Board." Lecture at the Industrial College of the Armed Forces, 27 October 1948. ICAF No. L49–33.

Marston, Col. Anson D. "Doctrine and Reserve Components," *The Quartermaster Review,* XXX (March–April, 1950), 21–23

Maynard, Lemuel. "Mobilizing Munitions," *The Quartermaster Review,* XXX (May–June, 1951).

McCune, George M., and Arthur L. Grey, Jr. *Korea Today.* Cambridge: Harvard University Press, 1950.

Mikhailov, Nicholas. *Soviet Russia, The Land and Its People.* New York: Sheridan House, 1948.

Millis, Walter, ed. *The Forrestal Diaries.* New York: The Viking Press, 1951.

Munroe, Lt. Clark C. *The Second United States Infantry in Korea 1950–1951.* Tokyo, 1952.

Nation's Business, XXXVI (July, 1948).

NATO: *Facts About the North Atlantic Treaty Organization.* Paris: NATO Information Service, 1962.

Nelson, Otto L. *National Security and the General Staff.* Washington: Infantry Journal Press, 1946.

Newsweek, 17 August 1953, "Fallen Hopes Engulf the Land of the Rising Sun," 34–36.

———, 19 November 1951, "NATO Problems: Aims Too High, Tensions Grow." 25–27.

Norman, Col. R. G. "Unique Operations–Tokyo QM Depot," *The Quartermaster Review* (January–February, 1952), 24, 110.

Occupation Forces in Europe:

Lay, Elizabeth S. Berlin Air Lift, 1 January–30 September 1949. Historical Division, Headquarters, European Command.

Moenk, Jean R. Establishment of Communications Through France, 1950–1951. Historical Division, U.S. Army Europe, 1952. 2 vols. Mimeographed. Copy in Office, Chief of Military History.

O'Donnell, James P. "We're All Fouled Up in France," *The Saturday Evening Post*, (April 11, 1953), 40–41.

Paone, Rocco M. History of Foreign Military Aid. Office, Chief of Military History. Manuscript.

The Quartermaster Review (July–August, 1951), "News From Overseas," 6–7, 150–52.

Reeder, Maj. Gen. W. O. "Supply Management." Lecture at the Industrial College of the Armed Forces, 1 April 1952. ICAF No. L52–135.

Reinhardt, Col. George C. "How Do We Get the Word," *Military Review*, XXXII (August, 1952), 33–36.

———. "The Logistical Command," *Military Review*, XXX (January, 1951), 25–30.

Richards, George. "Procurement of Defense Materiel," *The Quartermaster Review*, XXIV (January–February, 1950).

Rigg, Lt. Col. Robert B. *Red China's Fighting Hordes.* Harrisburg, Pa.: Military Services Publishing Co., 1951.

Royal Institute of International Affairs. *Defense in the Cold War: The Task for the Free World.* London, 1950.

Scholin, Allen R. "Science: Key to Defense Progress," *The Quartermaster Review*, XXIV (January–February, 1950).

Schwartz, Harry. *Russia's Soviet Economy.* New York: Prentice-Hall, 1950.

Scott, Stanley L. "The Military Aid Program," *Annals of the American Academy of Polictial and Social Science*, (November, 1951), 47–55.

Shabad, Theodore. *Geography of the USSR; A Regional Survey.* New York: Columbia University Press, 1951.

Somers, Herman Miles. "Civil-Military Relations in Mutual Security," *Annals of the American Academy of Political and Social Science*, Vol. 288 (July, 1953), 27–35.

Spector, Ivar. *Soviet Strength and Strategy in Asia.* Seattle: University of Washington Press, 1950.

UNITED STATES ARMY IN THE KOREAN WAR:

Appleman, Roy E. *South to the Naktong, North to the Yalu.* Washington: GPO, 1961.

Miller, John, jr., Maj. Owen J. Carroll, and Margaret E. Tackley. *Korea 1951–1953.* Washington: GPO, 1956.

Office, Chief of Military History. *Korea 1950.* Washington: GPO, 1956. Photographs and maps.

Sawyer, Robert K. *Military Advisors in Korea: KMAG in Peace and War.* Washington: GPO, 1962.

Schnabel, Lt. Col. James F. Policy and Direction: The First Year. Manuscript.

Westover, Capt. John G. *Combat Support in Korea.* Washington: Armed Forces Press, 1955.

U.S. Far East Command, Headquarters, Military History Division. Logistical Problems and Their Solution (EUSAK). Copy in Office, Chief of Military History. Manuscript.

Wallace, Henry A. *Soviet Asia Mission.* New York: Reynal & Hitchcock, 1946.

Watson, Mark S. "Ammunition Expenditure in Korea," *Ordnance* (September–October, 1952), 251–54.

White, Col. V. R. "Mission and Operation of Overseas Supply Division, San Francisco Port of Embarkation." Presentation before the National Quartermaster's Conference, Washington, 30 October 1951. Copy in Office, Chief of Military History. Manuscript.

Williamson, Capt. Edward C., and others. Bloody Ridge, August–September 1951. Military History Section, Eighth Army. Copy in Office, Chief of Military History. Manuscript.

Wilmot, Chester. "If NATO Had to Fight," *Foreign Affairs*, XXXI (January, 1953), 200–14.

Yount, Brig. Gen. Mason J. "Our New European Supply Line," *Army Information Digest*, VI (October, 1951), 56.

Glossary

A–4	Logistics staff, Army Air Forces
AAF	Army Air Forces
ACofS	Assistant Chief of Staff
AEF	Allied Expeditionary Force (World War II)
AEF	American Expeditionary Forces (World War I)
AGF	Army Ground Forces
AKA	Cargo ship, attack
A.R.A.	American Railway Association
APA	Attack transport
APD	Converted destroyer transport
ASF	Army Service Forces
Bolero	Code name for build-up of troops and supplies in the United Kingdom in preparation for a cross-Channel attack
CBI	China-Burma-India theater
CCS	Combined Chiefs of Staff
Class I	Supplies consumed at an approximately uniform daily rate under all conditions, and that are automatically issued
Class II	Supplies for which allowances are fixed by tables of allowances and tables of basic allowances
Class III	Fuels and lubricants other than aviation
Class III–A	Aviation fuels and lubricants
Class IV	Supplies and equipment for which allowances are not prescribed, or which require special control measures and are not otherwise classified
Class V	Ammunition, explosives, and chemical agents
CMP	Controlled Materials Plan
CONEX	Container Express (Worldwide cargo transporter service)
DCofS	Deputy Chief of Staff
DSA	Defense Supply Agency
Dukw	2½-ton amphibious truck
EPF	Emergency Plant Facilities
ETO	European Theater of Operations
FM	Field manual
G–1	Administration section of division or higher staff (World War I, AEF); personnel section of division or higher staff (from 1921)
G–2	Intelligence section of division or higher staff (World War I, AEF); intelligence section of division or higher staff (from 1921)

G–3	Operations section of division or higher staff (World War I, AEF); operations and training section of division or higher staff (from 1921)
G–4	Supply section of division or higher staff
G–5	Training section of division or higher staff (World War I, AEF); Civil Affairs Division of SHAEF or AFHQ (World War II)
GHQ	General headquarters
GSUSA	General Staff, United States Army
J–1	Joint Staff plans section
J–2	Joint Staff intelligence section
J–3	Joint Staff operations section
J–4	Joint Staff logistics section
J–5	Joint Staff general administration section
JAAF	Joint Action Armed Forces
JAMAG	Joint American Military Advisory Group
JCS	Joint Chiefs of Staff
JUSMAPG	Joint United States Military Advisory and Planning Group
KATUSA	Korean Augmentation to the United States Army
KCOMZ	Korean Communications Zone
KMAG	U.S. Military Advisory Group to the Republic of Korea
LCI	Landing craft, infantry
LCM	Landing craft, mechanized
LCT	Landing craft, tank
LCVP	Landing craft, vehicle, personnel
LSD	Landing ship, dock
LSM	Landing ship, medium
LST	Landing ship, tank
M-day	General mobilization day
MAB	Munitions Assignments Board
MARINEX	Marine express (cargo stowed and shipped for fastest water movement in lieu of air shipment)
MDAP	Mutual Defense Assistance Program
MULBERRY	Artificial harbor on Normandy beachhead
NATO	North Atlantic Treaty Organization
NOTS	Naval Overseas Transport Service
OEM	Office of Emergency Management
OFLC	Office of the Foreign Liquidation Commissioner
OMAHA	Code name for Normandy beachhead
OPA	Office of Price Administration
OPM	Office of Production Management
ORANGE	Code name for one of the pre-World War II "color" basic war plans
OVERLORD	Code name for plan for the invasion of northwest Europe, spring 1944
POA	Pacific Ocean Area
POM	Preparation for overseas movement

QMC	Quartermaster Corps
RAINBOW	Series of pre-World War II war plans, which superseded the "color" plans
ROK	Republic of Korea
ROUNDUP	Various 1941–43 plans for a cross-Channel attack
SEAC	Southeast Asia Command
SHAEF	Supreme Headquarters, Allied Expeditionary Force
SHAPE	Supreme Headquarters, Allied Powers, Europe
SLEDGEHAMMER	Plan for limited-objective attack across the Channel in 1942
SOS	Services of Supply
SPAB	Supply Priorities and Allocations Board
SS & P	Service, Supply, and Procurement
SWPA	Southwest Pacific Area
T. A.	*Type américain* (World War I troop train in France made up according to U.S. specifications)
TRUST	Trieste United States Troops
T. U.	*Type unique* (French standard troop train, World War I)
USAFFE	U.S. Army Forces, Far East
USAGG	U.S. Army Group, Greece
USCINCEUR	U.S. Commander in Chief, Europe
USFET	U.S. Forces, European Theater
VITTLES	Berlin airlift
WPB	War Production Board
WPD	War Plans Division
V–E Day	Victory in Europe
V–J Day	Victory in Japan
XYZ	Motor transport operation plan, World War II

Index

INDEX

INDEX

Printed in the United States
123559LV00004B/170/A

9 781410 213686